S0-AWH-302

WHO'S WHO IN
ROCK & ROLL

WHO'S WHO IN
ROCK & ROLL
Edited by John Tobler

CRESCENT BOOKS
NEW YORK

Half title:
November 1976. The Band's last farewell concert in San Francisco, immortalized in 'The Last Waltz' by Martin Scorsese. l to r: Dr John, Joni Mitchell, Neil Young, Rick Danko, Van Morrison, Bob Dylan and 'Robbie' Robertson

Title page:
17th December 1983, Madison Square Garden - The 'ARMS' concert in aid of multiple sclerosis research. Three great ex-Yardbirds guitarists on the same stage. l to r: Jimmy Page, Ray Cooper, Ronnie Lane, Eric Clapton, Charlie Watts, Ronnie Wood, Jeff Beck

The publishers would like to thank John Tobler for acting as consultant editor and for his contribution in writing certain parts of the text. They would also like to thank the following contributors:

Alan Clayson, B.J.Cole, Andrew Doe, Roger Dopson, Mike Evans, Tom Ferguson, Hugh Fielder, Bob Fisher, Michael Heatley, Mike Howard, Dave Laing, Barry Lazell, Dave McAleer, John Platt, Mark Prendergast and Harry Shapiro.

First published in 1991 by
The Hamlyn Publishing Group Ltd
part of Reed International Books
Michelin House, 81 Fulham Road
London SW3 6RB

Copyright © Reed International Books Ltd 1991

All rights reserved. No part of this publication may be reproduced, stored in a retrieval system, or transmitted in any form or by any means, electronic, mechanical, photocopying, recording or otherwise, without the permission of the copyright holders.

This 1991 edition published by Crescent Books, distributed by Outlet Book Company, Inc., a Random House Company, 225 Park Avenue South, New York, New York 10003

Printed and bound in Hong Kong

ISBN 0-517-056879

87654321

CONTENTS

INTRODUCTION

The appearance of "Who's Who In Rock'n'Roll" has coincided with a boom in the reissue on Compact Disc of great rock albums of the past. With so much timeless rock music again available and sounding better than ever, one aim of this book has been to attempt comprehensive listings of each performer's important albums and to put them into some kind of historical context.

It is impossible in a detailed work of this kind to include everyone's favorite artist, but hopefully there are no important omissions. To allow sufficient space to do each act's achievements, history and personnel changes justice the number of entries has been limited to around 500. We don't think we missed anyone crucial, but if we did, we apologize.

The qualification for an act to receive a detailed entry in "Who's Who In Rock'n'Roll" is not easy to describe - many different shades of rock music are represented, from rockabilly to reggae and from soul to stadium rock, and inclusion here has as much to do with quality of output as with commercial success, so some of the entries feature lists of dozens of hits, while others highlight significant releases. Longevity as regards artistic credibility is more important than pure chart success, although each act's Number One hits are listed - thus novelty acts and five-minute wonders have mainly been omitted. The vast majority of entries include a 'Greatest Hits' listing, with US & UK chart-toppers and often fascinating comparisons of relative success on opposite sides of the Atlantic, but this is not a chart book. Rather, it's a guide to major stars and also to artists whose underrated masterpieces are receiving a second chance (with technological help) to achieve their just deserts.

This book is unashamedly aimed at those who have lived through a decade or more of great and sometimes inspiring popular music, and those who want to know more about the immortals who spearheaded rock 'n'roll, Merseybeat, Psychedelia, Folk/Rock, Country/Rock, punk/New Wave, etc. It is not a pop annual, but a user-friendly text book, written by experts

Sting considers whether to throw in the towel or shoot the piano player (Phil Collins) during rehearsals for the 1985 Live Aid show at Wembley

and enthusiasts, opinionated at times, but not spiteful.

"Who's Who In Rock'n'Roll" is designed to stimulate interest in the half-forgotten albums gathering dust in everyone's record collection. No individual will own every record mentioned in this book, and anyone who is not intrigued enough to investigate some album they missed cannot really be a believer in what John Sebastian called 'the magic of rock'n'roll'. We believe that many of the entries in "Who's Who In Rock'n'Roll" contain more detailed and accurate information than any previous publication of this type. Comparatively well-known facts - Stephen Stills auditioning for The Monkees, the early careers of the individual Eagles - rub shoulders with rarely documented real names and dates of birth (and death) in a readable chronology designed to fascinate and occasionally raise eyebrows.

Whatever your taste and whatever the depth of your knowledge, there is much for you to appreciate and learn within these pages.

ABBA

Anni-Frid Lyngstad (vocals)
Agnetha Faltskog (vocals)
Bjorn Ulvaeus (guitar, vocals)
Benny Andersson (keyboards, vocals)

Abba, an acronym of the first names of the quartet's members, was the first act from a non-English-speaking country to achieve worldwide superstardom, and their eight years of fame produced nine No. 1 singles and eight chart-topping albums in the UK, although US success was less spectacular. However, when in pre-*Glasnost* days the quantity of albums imported into Russia was subject to government control, in one year Abba's were the only Western albums imported by the USSR.

Prior to forming Abba, each member of the group had been a domestic star in Sweden – Faltskog (born Jonkopping, Sweden, 1950) and Lyngstad (born Narvik, Norway, 1945) were solo artists, while Ulvaeus (born Gothenberg, Sweden, 1945) and Andersson (born Stockholm, Sweden, 1946) had respectively worked with The Hootenanny Singers and The Hep Stars ('the Swedish Beatles'). In 1971 Ulvaeus and Faltskog married, and simultaneously Ulvaeus and Andersson began work as producers and songwriters for Polar Music, a prominent Swedish music company.

In 1972, the four members-to-be of Abba cut a single, 'People Need Love', which was released under the name of Bjorn & Benny with Svenska Flicka, and bubbled under the US Top 100. Benny and Anni-Frid became engaged, and in 1973, the quartet attempted to represent Sweden in that year's Eurovision Song Contest with 'Ring Ring', a song they wrote and performed under the unwieldy name of Bjorn, Benny, Anna & Frida. Although another song was chosen to represent Sweden in the contest, 'Ring Ring' was released throughout Europe and became a hit in many countries, after which the quartet adopted the name of Abba.

In 1974, they again tried the Eurovision route, this time with more success. 'Waterloo', the song written by Ulvaeus and Andersson which they performed as Abba, was the runaway winner of Eurovision 1974, and became their first UK No. 1 as well as reaching the US Top 10, while an album also entitled 'Waterloo' briefly charted in numerous countries. The group's next three UK singles were less successful, but in late 1975, 'S.O.S.' returned them to the UK Top 10 and was the first of 18 consecutive UK Top 10 hits which continued until the end of 1981.

Basing their image on that of The Mamas & Papas, and with a string of highly commercial songs written by Bjorn and Benny, they became the most consistently successful act in the world during this period. The only country where they were never able to become permanent chart residents was the US, where they achieved 20 hits, although most were minor. Their biggest worldwide hit (and only US No. 1) was 'Dancing Queen' (1976), written for and performed at the wedding of the King and Queen of Sweden. In 1978 a feature film, *Abba – The Movie*, was a predictable success, and a move towards disco music on the 'Voulez-Vous' album (1979) coincided with a greater lyrical depth resulting from the pressures of success on the two couples (Benny and Anni-Frid had also married). Ultimately, both couples divorced, at which point the group fell apart.

Both Anni-Frid and Agnetha returned to solo careers, but despite working with such noted producers as Phil Collins and Mike Chapman, the Abba magic was inevitably missing. Benny and Bjorn meanwhile collaborated with Tim Rice on an acclaimed musical, *Chess*, but all four erstwhile Abba members seemed to have gone into retirement at the start of the 1990s.

The quartet's early work inevitably brought criticism from rock fans – the Eurovision Song Contest produces little rock credibility – but by the end of their reign in the world's charts, Abba were accurately viewed as among the most notable pop stars of their era. With the paucity of talent appearing at the start of the 1990s, a reunion album (at least) would be an almost guaranteed success along the lines of the Second Coming.

(l to r) Bjorn, Anni-Frid, Agnetha and Benny – Swedish supertroupers ABBA

Greatest Hits

Singles	Title	US	UK
1974	Waterloo	6	1
1975	Mamma Mia	32	1
1976	Fernando	13	1
1976	Dancing Queen	1	1
1977	Knowing Me Knowing You	14	1
1977	The Name Of The Game	12	1
1978	Take A Chance On Me	3	1
1980	The Winner Takes It All	8	1
1980	Super Trouper	45	1
Albums			
1976	Greatest Hits	48	1
1976	Arrival	20	1
1978	The Album	14	1
1979	Greatest Hits Vol. 2	46	1
1979	Voulez-Vous	19	1
1980	Super Trouper	17	1
1981	The Visitors	29	1
1982	The Singles – The First Ten Years	62	1

Paula ABDUL

Paula Abdul was born in Los Angeles in 1963 of Brazilian and Syrian parents. This pop/dance artist first scored as a choreographer, winning many awards including the 1986 MTV Choreographer of the Year award for work on Janet Jackson's 'Nasty' video. She also choreographed videos and shows for Luther Vandross, Duran Duran, ZZ Top and The Jacksons, who originally discovered her when she was a cheerleader.

Her debut album, 'Forever Your Girl', was released on Virgin in 1988, the year she hit the Black Top 10 with the L.A. and Babyface production, 'Knocked Out', and '(It's Just) The Way You Love Me'. Her next single, 'Straight Up', was a US No. 1 as were the next two, 'Forever Your Girl', and 'Cold Hearted', (which had been the 'B' side of 'Straight Up'). A re-issue of '(It's Just) The Way You Love Me' also made the US Top 3. When 'Opposites Attract' became her fourth gold single and hit the top she became the first act to have four US chart-toppers from a debut LP.

Her album, 'Forever Your Girl', hit No. 1 in the US in its 64th chart week and went on to sell over seven million. It was not only the first album by a female to spend 50 weeks in the US Top 10 but it also spent more weeks in the Top 10 than any other artist's debut album.

In 1989 Paula won five MTV awards including Best Female Video for 'Straight Up' and Best Choreography for 'Cold Hearted'. In 1990 an album of remixes of her tracks entitled 'Shut Up And Dance' became the highest ever charted re-mix LP in the US and went platinum. She also spent a record 68 consecutive weeks in the US singles Top 40.

In 1991 Paula worked on the choreography for Jim Morrison's bio-pic, appeared in 'LA Gear' ads and released her much awaited second album.

Greatest Hits

Singles	Title	US	UK
1989	Straight Up	1	3
1989	Forever Your Girl	1	24
1989	Cold Hearted	1	46
1990	Opposites Attract	1	2
Albums			
1988	Forever Your Girl	1	5
1989	Shut Up And Dance	7	40

AC/DC

Bon Scott (vocals)
Angus Young (guitar)
Malcolm Young (guitar)
Mark Evans (bass)
Phil Rudd (drums)

Definitely not to be taken to have any bisexual implications, AC/DC, largely composed of children of immigrants, came out of Sydney, Australia, in the mid-'70s where they had developed a strong following, aided by the rasping, raucous vocals of Bon Scott (born 1946, Scotland) and guitarist Angus Young (born 1959, Scotland) who had a predilection for dressing up as a schoolboy in short trousers and cap and nodding his head manically during breakneck guitar solos while sweating profusely. The group's career was guided by Angus's elder brother George Young and Harry Vanda, who had briefly tasted fame in The Easybeats with their 1966 international million-seller, 'Friday On My Mind'. Vanda and Young produced AC/DC's first two albums in Australia on Albert Records – 'High Voltage' in 1974 and 'TNT' in 1975 – before the band was signed by Atlantic Records.

They toured Britain and the US to promote their 'Dirty Deeds Done Cheap' album in 1976 and soon found a core audience to appreciate their heavy rock anthem 'Problem Child' and the lascivious 'Big Balls'. They broke through the following year with 'Let There Be Rock' which had the power and aggression to compete with the punk onslaught, helped by their refusal to adopt the overblown macho HM clichés of their elders. Bassist Mark Evans returned to Australia soon after to be replaced by Cliff Williams (from English group Home) for 'Powerage' in 1978 and the live 'If You Want Blood – You've Got It' the same year.

Their switch to producer 'Mutt' Lange for 1979's 'Highway to Hell' album secured their American breakthrough when it reached the US Top 20, but on February 19, 1980, singer Bon Scott choked to death in the back of a car in South London after a drinking binge. After a short break, the band regrouped with a new singer, Brian Johnson (born Newcastle-upon-Tyne in England) from pop band Geordie, who quickly imposed his similar but authentic style on the respectively titled 'Back in Black' album released at the end of that year. It sold 12 million copies worldwide and catapulted the band into the big league.

Through the first half of the 1980s, AC/DC pursued the tried and trusted album/world tour formula, grossing bigger numbers each time with their albums 'For Those About To Rock', 'Flick Of The Switch' and

Cheerleader to chartleader – Paula Abdul

AC/DC – over-the-top Aussies led HM reply to the punk revolution

'Fly On The Wall', which came out at two year intervals. When drummer Phil Rudd quit in 1983 for 'personal reasons', Manchester-born drummer Simon Wright was recruited from the little-known Tytan without producing any discernible difference in the group's sound.

After 'Who Made Who', from the soundtrack of the *Maximum Overdrive* movie in 1986, AC/DC slowed up, but 'Blow Up Your Video' in 1988 still brought them hits with 'Heatseeker' and 'That's The Way I Wanna Rock'n'Roll'. They returned in 1990 with a new drummer, Chris Slade from The Firm, an album, 'The Razor's Edge', and a hit single, 'Thunderstruck'.

Greatest Hits

Albums	Title	US	UK
1980	*Back In Black*	4	1
1981	*Dirty Deeds Done Cheap*	3	–
1981	*For Those About To Rock We Salute You*	1	3
1988	*Blow Up Your Video*	12	2

Adam **ANT**

Stuart Leslie Goddard (born 1954) was a North London art student in the late 1970s when punk struck. He was already cutting his rock teeth in Bazooka Joe and The B-Sides but he was lured by the fashionable end of the New Wave, particularly by Malcolm McLaren and Vivien Westwood's notorious 'Sex' shop in London's Kings Road. He struck up connections in the art-punk crowd and performed a couple of tracks in Julian Temple's *Jubilee* movie, which was the springboard for the formation of Adam And The Ants with Lester Square and Andy Warren from the B-Sides. His first album on the independent Do It label, 'Dirk Wears White Socks', explored a fascinating array of pyscho-sexual fantasies but created little musical impact.

Soon afterwards, Malcolm McLaren 'stole' Adam's Ants to form the nucleus of Bow Wow Wow with singer Annabel Lwin. Adam was unperturbed by this theft and when the new Ants he'd formed with guitarist Marco Pirroni (who also became a valuable songwriting collaborator) failed to ignite with the 'Car Trouble' single, he turned to McLaren for advice. The result was a deal with CBS, an Afro-percussive beat, a stylish pirate's outfit and a video-enhanced swashbuckling, sexy image to accompany his 'Kings Of The Wild Frontier' album in 1980. Teenage bedlam swept swiftly across the UK as 'Dog Eat Dog', 'Antmusic' and 'Kings Of The Wild Frontier' made the UK Top 5. An earlier song, 'Young Parisians', rode in to the UK Top 10 on the strength of his sudden fame and even 'Car Trouble' finally managed

to force its way into the UK Top 40.

In May 1981, Adam hit No. 1 for five consecutive weeks with 'Stand And Deliver' and repeated the feat four months later with 'Prince Charming', the title track of his new album. He could deliver the goods live, but was also well aware of the vagaries of the teenybop market and after 'Ant Rap' peaked at No. 3 at the end of 1981, Adam disbanded his Ants, taking care to keep Marco Pirroni, and went solo. The switch was justified when 'Goody Two Shoes' made No. 1 in June 1982 and gave him a US breakthrough later that year. But that was the peak – although 'Friend Or Foe' made the UK Top 10 his audience was growing up and away, and neither the Phil Collins-produced 'Puss in Boots' (guess the image) in 1983, 'Apollo Nine' in 1984 nor 'Vive Le Rock' in 1985 could halt the slide, at which point he turned his attention to film. However, in 1990 he was back with 'Manners And Physique'.

Greatest Hits

Singles	Title	US	UK
1981	*Stand And Deliver*	–	1
1981	*Prince Charming*	–	1
1982	*Goody Two Shoes*	12	1
Albums			
1980	*Kings Of The Wild Frontier*	44	1
1981	*Prince Charming*	94	2
1982	*Friend Or Foe*	16	5

Bryan **ADAMS**

A singer/songwriter/guitarist from Vancouver, Adams (born 1959) notched up considerable kudos in his home country at the start of the 1980s with hits – most written with fellow composer Jim Vallance – for Canadian Ian Lloyd and US band Prism; he built on this success by forming his own five-piece band, who broke into the American market via a support tour with Foreigner and two US Top 20 entries. 'Cuts Like A Knife' and 'Straight From The Heart'. The album of 'Cuts Like A Knife' went on to make the US album chart in 1983, as did the album 'Reckless' at the end of 1984.

Adams's first UK hit came early in 1985 with 'Run To You' which was also his first US Top 10 hit. The latter half of the decade saw him consolidate with a series of hits on both sides of the Atlantic, including the millionselling album 'Into The Fire' (1987), while featuring strongly in 'charity' type concert events that included Live Aid, an Olympics benefit album and the Nelson Mandela 70th Birthday concert. 1990 saw the re-release of the 'Reckless' album, and its re-entry into the charts.

With guitarist Keith Stott almost as big a pull at concert dates, Adams has remained an active 'street-level' player; his collaborative

Adams – live circuit all-rounder

work (he penned 'Tears Are Not Enough' for the Canadian Live Aid effort), sessions and live appearances being as important a part of his output as what appears on vinyl.

Greatest Hits

Singles	Title	US	UK
1985	*Run To You*	6	11
1985	*Heaven*	1	38
1985	*Summer Of 69*	5	42
1987	*Heat Of The Night*	6	54
Albums			
1983	*Cuts Like A Knife*	8	21
1984	*Reckless*	6	7
1987	*Into The Fire*	7	10

AEROSMITH

Steven Tyler (vocals)
Joe Perry (guitar)
Brad Whitford (guitar)
Tom Hamilton (bass)
Joey Kramer (drums)

Just as The Rolling Stones were starting to look a little old for the new generation of rock fans in the mid-'70s, along came Aerosmith. Formed in 1970, singer Steven Tyler (born 1948) revelled in his facial similarities to Mick Jagger, while guitarist Joe Perry (born 1950) cloned Keith Richards's riffs to his own ends. They built their reputation by working the New England bar and college circuit incessantly, playing free gigs outside Boston University when no paid work was forthcoming, until in 1973, CBS signed them and released their eponymous debut album.

By the time 'Get Your Wings' produced by Jack Douglas, came out in 1974, they had spread their cult status across America via more intensive touring and chalked up a minor hit with 'Dream On'. The reward came with their third album, 'Toys In the Attic', which spent nearly two years in the US chart and 31 weeks in the Top 40. 'Dream On' returned to become a Top 10 hit early in 1976 and 'Walk This Way' did the same a year later.

They kept up the pace with the 'Rocks' album, which reached the Top 3 in 1976, 'Draw The Line', which made the Top 20 in 1978 and 'Live Bootleg', which did the same later that year. They also appeared in the *Sgt Pepper's Lonely Hearts Club Band* movie singing 'Come Together', but the excesses of their rock'n'roll lifestyle were starting to catch up with them. Soon after the 'Night In The Ruts' album in late 1979, Joe Perry quit to form The Joe Perry Project, releasing 'Let The Music Do The Talking' in 1980 and 'I've Got The Rock'n'Rolls Again' in 1982, but neither achieved notable success.

Meanwhile, Aerosmith were having a hard time trying to get it together without him – drummer Brad Whitford bailed out, and when 'Rock In A Hard Place' finally emerged in 1982 with replacements Jim Crespo (guitar) and Rick Dufay (drums), it seemed the band's bolt was shot. In 1985, the original line-up re-formed, cleaned up, signed to Geffen and started the climb back with 'Done With Mirrors'.

They were given an unexpected boost in 1986 when Run DMC roped in Tyler and Perry for their cover of 'Walk This Way', which was a major hit. The next year, Aerosmith were back in the charts on their own account with 'Dude, (Looks Like A Lady)' and a cover of The Beatles song, 'I'm

Down', included on the 'Permanent Vacation' album. The hits have continued, most recently with 'Love In An Elevator' from the 'Pump' album in 1989.

Greatest Hits

Singles	Title	US	UK
1976	*Dream On*	6	–
Albums			
1976	*Rocks*	3	–

The **ALARM**

Mike Peters (*vocals, guitar, bass, harmonica*)
Dave Sharp (*guitar, vocals*)
Eddie Macdonald (*bass, vocals*)
Nigel Twist (*drums, vocals*)

Formed in 1981 in their native North Wales, The Alarm mixed the punkish rabble-rousing approach of the early Clash with the musical refinement of U2, with whom they toured extensively during the 1980s as opening act. All were born in 1959, and were previously in less successful bands. In late 1981, the group released a debut single, 'Unsafe Building', on their own Red Cross label, and in 1982, signed to Miles Copeland's Illegal label. After a move to the IRS label in 1983, the group's first UK Top 20 hit was the bizarre '68 Guns', while an eponymous 12″ EP provided their US album chart debut in the same year, but was not released in the UK.

Some of the tracks on the EP were included on their 1984 UK debut album, 'Declaration', which also spawned two lesser UK hit singles and reached the Top 50 of the US album chart and the Top 10 in Britain. 1985 saw the release of a follow-up album, 'Strength', which reached the Top 20 in

Britain at the end of that year after three further UK Top 50 hit singles. As early as 1984, the group had displayed folk inclinations, both with onstage use of acoustic guitars and by releasing a version of 'Bells of Rhymney' on the flip-side of 'The Chant Has Just Begun', but when they released the nostalgic 'Spirit of '76' as a single in 1986, the public found the new direction less appealing, and it peaked outside the UK Top 20.

After a break of nearly two years, during which they moved strongly towards their Celtic roots they returned in late 1987 with 'Eye Of The Hurricane', another UK Top 30 album which included three UK hit singles, the biggest of them 'Rain In The Summertime', a Top 20 item. In 1988, they toured the US opening for Bob Dylan, after which came a live album, 'Electric Folklore', produced by Gary Katz (of Steely Dan fame) with extended versions of several hits. In 1989 came 'Change', an album produced by Tony Visconti, where the band openly displayed their Celtic roots. A special version of the album featured Peters singing in Welsh, and one track, 'New South Wales', featured a Welsh male voice choir.

Although every album by The Alarm has been certified gold, they have somehow failed to achieve the major stardom widely predicted initially. The release in 1990 of 'Standards, A Best Of' package, may yet redress the balance for a potentially huge group, whose ludicrous haircuts may remarkably have affected their appeal.

Greatest Hits

Singles	Title	US	UK
1983	*68 Guns*	–	17
1985	*Strength*	61	40
1986	*Spirit of '76*	–	22
Albums			
1984	*Declaration*	50	6
1985	*Strength*	–	18

Hair-tearing time for Aerosmith's Tyler

Welsh wizards the Alarm, waking up to their Celtic heritage

ALBION BAND

The Albion Band is the brainchild of Ashley Hutchings, born in London in 1945. A bass player, his first band of note was Fairport Convention (see separate entry), of which he was a founder member and played on their first four albums. In late 1969, he left to form Steeleye Span (see separate entry), like Fairport a folk/rock band, whom he led for three albums before leaving to launch The Albion Country Band in 1972 with Simon Nicol and Dave Mattacks, who had both left Fairport at that time, but, would rejoin. This group did not make an album, but appeared on 'No Roses' by Shirley Collins (whom Hutchings later married) and 'Morris On', a Fairport-related album of traditional English morris dance tunes. In 1973, The Albion Country Band cut its sole album, 'Battle Of The Field', which was not released until 1976, before folding, after which Hutchings cut two documentary albums, 'The Compleat Dancing Master' (released 1974) and 'Rattlebone & Ploughjack' (released 1976).

In early 1974 Hutchings and Shirley Collins launched The Etchingham Steam Band, a low-key outfit which folded in 1975 without releasing an album, after which Hutchings formed The Albion Dance Band with Nicol, Mattacks, Collins, and John Tams (vocals), Graeme Taylor (guitar), Mike Gregory (drums) and others, later including Ric Sanders (violin, ex-Soft Machine, later in Fairport Convention). Most of this line-up cut 'The Prospect Before Us' for EMI's Harvest label and followed it in 1978 with 'Rise Up Like The Sun', by which time the group name had been abbreviated to The Albion Band. Meanwhile, Hutchings continued to record solo projects, including 'Son Of Morris On' (1976) and 'Kicking Up The Sawdust' (1977) as well as producing albums during the 1970s for Shirley Collins and Martin Carthy (another ex-member of Steeleye Span).

At the end of the 1970s, The Albion Band became involved with the National Theatre in London, making live music for such productions as 'Lark Rise To Candleford' (which was released as an album by the band with Keith Dewhurst in 1979) and others. 1982 brought a new Albion Band album, 'Light Shining', by which time the band had left Hutchings en masse to form Home Service, a group whose commercial success never matched with immense critical acclaim. This new Albion Band included Cathy LeSurf (vocals, ex-Fiddler's Dram, who had a UK Top 3 hit in 1979 with 'Day Trip To Bangor'), multi-instrumentalist Phil Beer and Trevor Foster (drums). In 1983 Hutchings resurrected The Albion Dance Band name for 'Shuffle Off', and in 1984 The Albion Band proper released 'Under The Rose', followed in 1985 by 'The Christmas Album'.

In 1986, Hutchings not only toured with The Albion Band, but also made a solo album, 'An Hour With Cecil Sharp And Ashley Hutchings', a tribute to the UK's most celebrated collector of folk songs, and in 1987 released his first real solo album, 'By Gloucester Docks I Sat Down And Wept', a brilliant conceptual work featuring actors as well as musicians like Clive Gregson, Christine Collister and Polly Bolton (vocals); Phil Beer, Graeme Taylor and Dave Mattacks. Also in 1987 came 'Stella Maris' by The Albion Band, followed in 1988 by 'The Wild Side Of Town', featuring music from a natural history TV series, on which the band collaborated with broadcaster Chris Baines. The same year also saw the release of a new Albion Dance Band album, 'I Got New Shoes'.

Still in 1988, Hutchings formed a short-term group, The Ashley Hutchings All Stars, featuring Clive Gregson, Polly Bolton, Dave Mattacks, John Shepherd (keyboards, and by that time also an Albion Band Member) and Pete Zorn (guitar, sax). A live album by this band 'As You Like It', was released in 1989, at which point The Albion Band were renamed Albion Band '89. With a line-up of Hutchings (bass, vocals), Beer (vocals, numerous instruments), Shepherd (keyboards), Foster (drums) and Simon Care (melodeon, concertina), they recorded 'Give Me A Saddle, I'll Trade You A Car'.

In 1990, the group released the appropriately titled '1990'. While none of the numerous albums by Hutchings or any variation on The Albion Band root has bothered the chart compilers, Ashley Hutchings has continually made interesting and often vital music with roots in both rock and traditional folk. There is little need for a *Greatest Hits* listing – any of the above albums will reward the discerning listener.

ALLMAN BROTHERS BAND

Duane Allman (guitar)
Gregg Allman (keyboards, vocals, guitar)
Berry Oakley (bass)
Richard 'Dickey' Betts (guitar, vocals)
Jai Johanny Johanson aka Jaimoe (born John Lee Johnson) (drums)
Butch Trucks (drums)

The Allman Brothers Band is known not only for its often brilliant R&B music, but also due to the tragic deaths of two founder members within a little over a year. Duane and Gregg Allman were born in Nashville in 1946 and 1947 respectively, and formed their first bands in Florida during the 1960s, where they had moved with their widowed mother a few years before. The first one of note was The Allman Joys, who briefly recorded without success before moving to Los Angeles, where they formed Hourglass, a band which cut two unsuccessful albums for Liberty Records in 1967/8.

After demos for a third were rejected, the brothers returned to Florida, where they cut an album's worth of tracks released some years later as 'Duane & Gregg Allman', but Gregg was contractually obliged to return to California to make a solo album. Duane meanwhile established himself in Florida as a promising blues guitarist with a distinctive 'bottleneck' style, jamming with a local band, The 31st Of February, whose members included Florida native Dickey Betts (born 1943) and Berry Oakley (born 1948, Chicago).

Around that time, Duane was invited to play guitar on albums by Wilson Pickett (see separate entry), and the late King Curtis, and impressed Atlantic Records so much that he was called to New York to play on 'Soul 69' by Aretha Franklin (see separate entry). He tried to assemble a trio with Jaimoe (born 1944, Mississippi), who had worked with Otis Redding (see separate entry) and Berry Oakley, but when Betts and Butch Trucks (born Florida) also joined, the results were exciting. Soon Gregg Allman had returned to fill the role of lead singer, and the band was complete.

During these early days, Duane Allman's session work with Boz Scaggs (see separate entry), Arthur Conley, etc., helped to keep the band solvent until their debut album, 'The Allman Brothers Band', was released in early 1970. It briefly appeared in the US album chart, while a follow-up album, 'Idlewild South', released later that year, made the Top 40 of that chart. Soon after it was completed, Duane recorded with Eric Clapton (see separate entry) in Derek & The Dominos, and those sessions produced 'Layla', one of Clapton's biggest hits.

In March 1971, the Allman Brothers Band recorded a live double album in New York, 'At Fillmore East', which reached the Top 20 of the US album chart. During the recording of their fourth album, 'Eat A Peach', in October 1971, Duane Allman was killed in a motorcycle accident. The remaining quintet completed the album, which reached the Top 5 of the US album chart. Almost exactly one year later, during sessions for the follow-up album, 'Brothers & Sisters', Berry Oakley also died in a motorcycle crash, but once again the album was eventually completed, with Lamar Williams on bass. Before it was released, the first two albums were reissued as 'Beginnings' which remained in the US chart for a year. Additionally, two recommended double albums by Duane Allman, 'Anthology' (1972) and 'Anthology Volume II' (1974), were released and featured much of his session work with a variety of artists as well as with Hourglass and The Allman Brothers Band.

During the chart residency of 'Beginnings', it was overtaken by 'Brothers & Sisters', which topped the US album chart for five weeks and included a US Top 3 single, 'Ramblin' Man', featuring Betts and fellow guitarist Les Dudek. Still in 1973, Gregg Allman's solo album, 'Laid Back', also reached the US Top 20, and included a US

Top 20 hit single, 'Midnight Rider', and in 1974, a live double album, 'The Gregg Allman Tour', was also a chart item. Meanwhile Betts had also released a solo album, 'Highway Call', which reached the US Top 20. The Allman Brothers Band was still extant, and had recruited keyboard player Chuck Leavell, who played on their 1975 album, 'Win, Lose or Draw', which was a US Top 5 hit.

At this point, Gregg Allman had become involved both with Cher (see separate entry) to whom he was later briefly married, and a lawsuit over drugs, as a result of which he testified against an employee of the band in return for his own case being dropped. Betts left the band in protest, while Leavell, Williams and Johnson formed Sea Level, and The Allman Brothers Band folded. Gregg Allman cut an album with Cher as Allman & Woman, 'Two The Hard Way', and made another solo album, 'Playin' Up A Storm' (released in 1977), while Betts made 'Dickey Betts & Great Southern' (1977, US Top 40) and 'Atlanta's Burning Down' (1978). Two compilation double albums by The Allman Brothers, 'The Road Goes On Forever' (1975) and the live 'Wipe The Windows – Check The Oil – Dollar Gas' (1976) had kept the group name before the public. In 1978 Allman, Betts, Trucks and Jaimoe, plus Dan Toler (guitar) and David Goldflies (bass), cut a new album, 'Enlightened Rogues', which reached the US top 10. Two subseqeunt albums, 'Reach For The Sky' (1980) and 'Brothers Of The Road', were less successful, and the band split up in 1982.

The mid-1980s were a quiet time for its ex-members, although finally Gregg Allman formed a new Gregg Allman Band with Dan Toler and David Toler (drums), and made two albums for Epic, 'I'm No Angel' (1987) and 'Just Before The Bullets Fly' (1988), while Betts coincidentally also made an album for Epic, 'Pattern Disruptive', on which Butch Trucks played. None of these albums was very successful, although a boxed set covering the history of the group and its main members, 'Dreams', was a major critical success in 1989, and in 1990 The Allman Brothers Band reformed with Allman, Betts, Jaimoe, Trucks and new members Warren Haynes (guitar), Johny Neal (keyboards) and Allen Woody (bass) for a new album, 'Seven Turns', while a 20-year-old album recorded with the original line-up (including Duane), 'Live At Ludlow Garage', was also released in 1990.

Greatest Hits

Singles	Title	US	UK
1973	*Ramblin' Man*	2	–
Albums			
1972	*Eat A Peach*	4	–
1973	*Brothers & Sisters*	1	42
1975	*Win, Lose Or Draw*	5	–
1979	*Enlightened Rogues*	9	–

All things to Allmen, Duane blesses the Brothers in the Band

AMERICA

Gerry Beckley (guitar, vocals)
Dan Peek (guitar, vocals)
Dewey Bunnell (guitar, vocals)

An unlikely name for a folk-rock outfit formed in England, but each of the trio was the son of US servicemen who had been posted to England during the 1960s. Gerry Beckley and Dan Peek were born in the US, (Beckley, Texas, 1952 and Peek, Florida, 1950). They attended school in London where they began playing and composing their own songs along with Dewey Bunnell (born 1952 in Yorkshire, England).

Producer Ian Samwell (an original member of Cliff Richard's backing band when they were still The Drifters, writer of Cliff's debut hit, 'Move It' and later producer-promoter of singer Linda Lewis) and London hippy-scene DJ Jeff Dexter signed the group in 1971 to make a debut LP, 'America', for Warner Bros. Two singles from the album sold over a million, 'A Horse With No Name' and 'I Need You'.

Their sound personified soft rock, a smoother version of the folk nuaunces of Crosby, Stills & Nash. All three sang, played guitar and wrote songs. They continued with a series of easy-on-the-ear albums, several produced by George Martin, and their success in the US was consolidated with hit singles released to prelude each album, including 'Tin Man' (from 'Holiday', 1974) and 'Sister Golden Hair' taken from 1975's 'Hearts'.

Peek left in in 1977 when he became a born-again Christian, launching a solo recording career on a religious label. The remaining

America – transatlantic triumphs for soft rock trio

duo continued, switching to the Capitol label in 1980, and the single 'You Can Do Magic' made the American Top 10 in 1982. Their brief comeback continued with an album produced by former member of Argent, Russ Ballard 'View From The Ground'. Two more minor hits in 1983 brought America's late resurgence to an end.

Arriving with a highly fashionable sound in the early 1970s, America surprised many with over ten years of considerable and consistent success, finding a niche with a burgeoning AOR audience seeking an antidote to pubescent punk in the latter half of the decade. Of some interest to collectors may be that the titles of the vast majority of their albums start with the letter 'H' – even their 'Greatest Hits' compilation was titled 'History'!

Greatest Hits

Singles	Title	US	UK
1972	Horse With No Name	1	2
1974	Tin Man	4	–
1975	Lonely People	5	–
1975	Sister Golden Hair	1	–
Albums			
1972	America	1	–
1974	Holiday	3	–
1975	Hearts	4	–
1975	History	3	–

The **ANIMALS** (and Eric **BURDON**)

Eric Burdon (vocals)
Alan Price (keyboards)
Hilton Valentine (guitar)
Chas Chandler (bass)
John Steel (drums)

The Animals were originally The Alan Price Combo, formed in 1961 in Newcastle-upon-Tyne, UK, by Price (born 1941), who recruited Chandler (born 1938), Steel (born 1941) and Valentine (born 1943). Aspiring blues singer Burdon (born 1941) joined from The Pagans in 1962, and they honed their R&B repertoire during a residency at Newcastle's Downbeat Club, changing their name to The Animals after local tough guy 'hero' Animal Hog. A move in 1963 to the larger Club A-Go-Go swelled their Newcastle audience tremendously, and a locally recorded demo EP made for sale to the fans attracted attention from London, culminating in a BBC radio debut on *Saturday Club* in December, and a recording offer from producer Mickie Most. Most placed the group with EMI early in 1964, and a single, 'Baby Let Me Take You Home', was released to coincide with their first UK tour, supporting Chuck Berry. It reached the UK Top 20, and was followed in June by 'House Of The Rising Sun', which shot to UK No. 1 within

Burdon, with bowler, and the Animals

two weeks of issue, also hitting the top in the US two months later.

A run of major hits followed, as 'I'm Crying', 'Don't Let Me Be Misunderstood', 'Bring It On Home To Me', 'We Gotta Get Out Of This Place' and 'It's My Life' all went Top 20. Price, however, left the group in May 1965, failing to see eye-to-eye with Burdon over the musical direction of the group, and also haunted by a fear of flying which was turning overseas tours into nightmares for him. He would move on to a lengthy and very successful solo career in the UK, while Dave Rowberry (born 1943) took over his keyboards slot.

At the end of 1965, The Animals also split from Most and EMI, as Burdon sought a freer hand with the group's material. He found it with Decca and producer Tom Wilson, and more major hits followed with 'Inside Looking Out' and 'Don't Bring Me Down', though Steel quit midway between the two, and was replaced by former Nashville Teens drummer Barry Jenkins (born 1944). Then, in September 1966, the group suddenly called it a day, with only Burdon wanting to continue. He recorded briefly with session men, then relocated in LA at the end of the year to form Eric Burdon & The Animals, which retained Jenkins on drums and brought in Londoners John Weider (born 1947) and Vic Briggs (born 1945) on guitars and Henry McCulloch (born 1945) on bass.

The new group's sound shifted radically from the R&B style of the original The Animals, and instead reflected Burdon's ever-growing preoccupation with psychedelia and the US West Coast counter-culture. Clearly right for the times, it produced acid-tinged experimental albums like 'Winds Of Change' and 'The Twain Shall Meet', which in turn yielded a new run of hit singles, including 'When I Was Young', 'San Franciscan Nights', 'Monterey' and 'Sky Pilot'. In mid-1968, another wholesale change of personnel saw Zoot Money (keyboards) and Andy Summers (guitar, later with Police) replacing

Briggs and McCulloch. Renamed Eric Burdon & The New Animals, the group toured extensively in the US and Japan, before Burdon decided to lay it to rest after a Christmas concert back at home in Newcastle.

Burdon planned a film career in Hollywood, but instead began working in 1970 with black funk band Night Shift, who changed their name to War as the collaboration commenced. The liaison produced two albums, 'Eric Burdon Declares War' and 'The Black Man's Burdon', and a million-selling US Top 3 single in 'Spill The Wine'. It ended early in 1971 when Burdon quit during a European tour suffering from exhaustion, and left War to carry on alone (which they did with some success).

Burdon remained active, if barely commercially successful, through the 70s, recording solo, with bluesman Jimmy Witherspoon, and as leader of the Eric Burdon Band. In 1976, however, the original Animals regrouped to play for fun at Chandler's house, and gelled so well that they cut a whole LP in a hired mobile studio. Chandler issued the set, wryly titled 'Before We Were So Rudely Interrupted . . .' on his own Barn label the following year, and while not a huge seller, the project sparked the idea of further non-permanent reunions by the original Animals to record and tour. This they followed through in 1983, cutting the LP 'Ark' for IRS Records, and following it with lucrative US and world tours. Though Burdon, Price and Chandler in particular have since pursued further individual projects (the former has a warts-and-all autobiography, *I Used To Be An Animal . . . But I'm Alright Now*, published in 1986), the door still remains open for further Animals regroupings.

Greatest Hits

Singles	Title	US	UK
1964	House Of The Rising Sun	1	1
1970	Spill The Wine (Burdon & War)	3	–
Albums			
1964	The Animals	7	6
1966	Most (Best) Of The Animals	6	4

Paul **ANKA**

Canadian export Anka (born 1941) was almost unique among late 1950s pop idols in being an accomplished singer-songwriter from the word go, an astute businessman, and a teenager whose style only tangentially relied on rock'n'roll.

The son of Lebanese immigrant parents living in Ottawa, Anka first tried breaking into the music biz at 14 when he cut a one-off single on vacation in LA. For his second shot, at Easter 1957, he went to New York armed with a song he had written about his unrequited crush on the Ankas' 18-year-old babysitter, Diana Ayoub. ABC Records' Don Costa signed him on the strength of 'Diana', and was justified when it became an immediate worldwide smash, topping both US and UK charts, and globally selling over nine million as Anka toured the UK, Europe and Australia.

Writing prolifically, he kept up a run of hits, mostly in the semi-melodramatic beat-ballad pattern established by 'Diana' until the early 1960s. 'Lonely Boy' (featured in his first movie *Girls' Town*, in which he co-starred with Mamie Van Doren) was another chart-topper, while 'You Are My Destiny', 'Put Your Head On My Shoulder', 'It's Time To Cry' and 'Puppy Love' were additional million-sellers and a further dozen singles made the US or UK Top 20. In October 1958 he played his composition 'It Doesn't Matter Anymore' to Buddy Holly, and gave the song to the enthused Holly to record at what would be one of his final sessions.

Anka's mature business attitude saw him pushing his career out of the restraints of teen idoldom early on: he debuted in Las Vegas in mid-1959, and in June 1960, became the youngest-ever performer at New York's Copacabana. In the 1960s he married, had four daughters, wrote film music (for *The Longest Day*, in which he also appeared as an actor), moved to Vegas, and had a song-writing coup to rival 'Diana' when his English rewrite of 'Comme D'Habitude' as 'My Way' was adopted by Frank Sinatra.

During the early 1970s, he was responsible, with Kris Kristofferson, for the 'discovery' of both Steve Goodman and John Prine, and an unexpected return to major record sales occurred in the mid-1970s, when '(You're) Having My Baby', a duet with Odia Coates about pregnancy which briefly put him at odds with women's organizations, began a new run of US Top 20 hits.

After more than 30 years of virtually drowning beneath songwriting royalties ($30,000 a year from Johny Carson's *Tonight* show theme alone), Anka continues to write and perform apace.

Greatest Hits

Singles	Title	US	UK
1957	*Diana*	1	1
1959	*Lonely Boy*	1	3
1974	*(You're) Having My Baby*	1	5
Albums			
1960	*Paul Anka Sings His Big 15*	4	–
1974	*Anka*	9	–

Joan **ARMATRADING**

A black singer/songwriter whose work displays considerable emotion and often intense lyrical depth, Armatrading was born on the Caribbean island of St Kitts in 1950,

Critic's choice – Joan Armatrading

but spent her formative years in Birmingham, England, where she moved with her parents as a child. Around 1971, she teamed up with Pam Nestor, another black singer/songwriter, when both were in a touring cast of the musical *Hair*, and they began to write songs together. These came to the attention of David Platz of Essex Music, who commissioned an album, 'Whatever's For Us', produced by Gus Dudgeon and with Nestor lending vocal support, which was released on Platz's Cube label in the UK and by A&M, with whom Armatrading has remained ever since, in the US.

The partnership with Nestor was short-lived, and it wasn't until her eponymous third album in 1976, produced by Glyn Johns, that Armatrading made the commercial break-through long predicted by critics. It featured her only UK Top 10 hit to date, 'Love & Affection', and the partnership with Johns lasted for three further albums, 'Show Some Emotion' (1977), 'To The Limit' (1978), and ended after the 1979 live album, 'Steppin' Out'. In 1980, 'Me Myself I', produced by Richard Gottehrer, became Armatrading's first US Top 40 album and her second to reach the UK Top 10, after which came two albums produced by Steve Lillywhite, 'Walk Under Ladders' (1981) and 'The Key' (1983), the latter also making the US Top 40. At the end of 1983 came 'Track Record', a compilation album which reached the Top 20 in the UK, and in 1985, Mike Howlett produced her 'Secret Secrets' album, which also reached the UK Top 20.

Subsequently, Armatrading has produced her own albums: 'Sleight Of Hand' (1986), 'The Shouting Stage' (1988, with Mark Knopfler of Dire Straits guesting) and 'Hearts & Flowers' (1990). After nearly 20 years as a recording artist, Joan Armatrading has a devoted following, although her absolute refusal to talk about her personal life has kept

her a mysterious and somewhat untouchable figure, whose talents has never been in question, but whose desire for privacy may have inhibited her commercial appeal.

Greatest Hits

Singles	Title	US	UK
1976	*Love and Affection*	–	10
1983	*Drop The Pilot*	78	11
Albums			
1977	*Show Some Emotion*	52	6
1980	*Me Myself I*	28	5
1981	*Walk Under Ladders*	88	6
1983	*The Key*	32	10

ASIA

John Wetton (bass/vocals)
Steve Howe (guitar)
Geoff Downes (keyboards)
Carl Palmer (drums)

An archetype of the supergroup syndrome spawned by 1970s progressive rock – but a decade too late. After Emerson, Lake & Palmer and his short-lived PM, Carl Palmer (born 1951) joined forces with Howe (born 1947) (ex-Yes) and Downes (ex Buggles and Yes), and John Wetton (born 1949) who had worked with such bands as Family, Roxy Music and Uriah Heep.

Their debut album, 'Asia', with its glossy full-page trade ads reminiscent of a movie blockbuster, seemed an anachronism in post-punk 1982, and was panned by the street-cred conscious British music press. However, its sophisticated sound and smooth vocal delivery worked well on American AOR radio, and the LP was No. 1 in the US for over two months. Two tracks from the album went into the singles chart, 'Heat Of The Moment' and 'Only Time Will Tell'.

Although their Canadian-recorded follow-up album , 'Alpha' attacked the US Top 10, a promo tour had to be cancelled midway through lack of support. Palmer's ex-colleague from ELP, Greg Lake, replaced John Wetton in late 1983 to appear in a marathon pan-US/Japan live TV gig before standing down for Wetton to return. The band continued sporadically through the 1980s making forays into the AOR album market (their third, 'Astra' appeared in 1985) and the American stadium circuit.

Greatest Hits

Singles	Title	US	UK
1982	*Heat Of The Moment*	4	46
1982	*Only Time Will Tell*	17	54
1983	*Don't Cry*	10	33
Albums			
1982	*Asia*	1	14
1983	*Alpha*	6	5

Wheelin' and dealin' Roy Benson (far right), twenty years in the driving seat

ASLEEP AT THE WHEEL

Ray Benson (born Ray Benson Seifert)
(bandleader, vocals, guitar)
Leroy Preston *(drums, guitar)*
Lucky Oceans (born Reuben Gosfield) *(steel guitar)*
Danny Levin *(piano)*

Ray Benson is the sole ever-present member of this unique group dedicated to keeping alive Western Swing music, and his intense dedication to this ideal is presumably a reason why the group has had over fifty different members since its launch in 1970.

The band's 12 albums have come through seven separate recording contracts, the only lasting relationship being with Capitol, for whom AATW made five albums between 1975 and 1979. Their general lack of commercial success has made it hard for the band to survive, but critical acclaim, including three Grammy Awards, may be sufficient compensation for the constant touring which is necessary for survival. Oceans supposedly conceived the group name in the outhouse of a ranch in West Virginia rented by Benson in which the band rehearsed. After that, it took three years, during which time they relocated in Los Angeles at the suggestion of a college friend of Benson's who was road manager for Commander Cody & His Lost Planet Airmen, before their combination of Western Swing, R&B, country and rockabilly attracted recording interest.

After 'Comin' Right At Ya' for United Artists and 'Asleep At The Wheel' for Epic, both of which also featured Chris O'Connell (vocals), Floyd Domino (born Jim Haber, piano) and guest spots from legendary country fiddler Johny Gimble, neither of which charted, the group again relocated, this time to Austin, Texas, which remains their base. The first three Capitol albums crept into the Top 200 of the US LP chart, as did

their first for MCA, 'Framed', in 1980. By then, Preston and Domino had left the band, and a five-year hiatus ensued until the release of 'Pasture Prime' on the group's own label in 1985, since when the line-up has hardly changed, and still includes, beside Benson, Larry Franklin (fiddle, guitar, vocals), Tim Alexander (piano, vocals), John Ely (steel guitar), Jon Mitchell (bass), David Sanger (drums) and Mike Francis (sax).

During the second half of the 1980s, the group also made two further albums for Epic, who re-signed the band many years after dropping them. Both '10' and particularly 'Western Standard Time' were critical successes, if not hugely commercial, and their first album for Arista in 1990 was 'Keepin' Me Up Nights'.

Greatest Hits

Albums	Title	US	UK
1975	*Texas Gold*	136	–
1977	*The Wheel*	162	–

The ASSOCIATION

Terry Kirkman *(vocals, keyboards)*
Jim Yester *(vocals, guitar)*
Gary (Jules) Alexander *(vocals, guitar)*
Russ Giguere *(vocals, guitar)*
Brian Cole *(vocals, bass)*
Ted Bluechel Jr. *(vocals, drums)*

The Association were the epitome of semi-hip West Coast close vocal harmony during the latter half of the 1960s, steering a unique commercial course between MOR and the rock underground.

Kirkman recruited the others in Southern California in mid-1965, and they debuted live in Pasadena in November, also cutting an

oblivion-bound one-off single for the Jubilee label. Successful club and college dates in early 1966 led to a firmer deal with LA's Valiant Records, and their second single for the label, 'Along Comes Mary', reached the US Top 10 in May, despite some interpretations of its lyric as a drug celebration. Kirkman's soft ballad 'Cherish' was a huge follow-up, topping the US chart in August and also pulling their debut album into the Top 10.

After this success, however, the group confounded all advice and expectations by releasing the offbeat, experimental 'Pandora's Golden Heebie Jeebies', written by Alexander. It was only a moderate success, and Alexander promptly split the ranks in April 1967, to be replaced by Larry Ramos. Valiant was then purchased by Warner Bros, and the group transferred to the major label, to hit the peak of their success soon afterwards via consecutive million sellers in the lightly grooving 'Windy' and the gentle 'Never My Love' – both songs acquired from outside writers. US radio voted them 1967's Group of the Year on the back of these two hits and the Top 10 album 'Insight Out'.

1968 opened with another US Top 10 hit, 'Everything That Touches You', but the group's chart star waned fairly quickly thereafter, as subsequent singles lost the commercial punch of earlier hits. 'Time For Livin'' stalled at US No. 39, but because the group chose to visit the UK to promote it, ironically became their only British hit, just missing the Top 20. At the end of the year, Alexander rejoined the line up, and early 1969 saw the compilation LP 'Greatest Hits' deliver a US Top 5 swansong. The group then contributed a batch of songs for the Ali McGraw/Richard Benjamin film *Goodbye Columbus*, but it failed to give them the boost which Simon & Garfunkel had received from 1968's similar *The Graduate*, and yielded no significant single or soundtrack album hits.

They continued to have moderately selling albums into the early 1970s, but could not regain commercial impetus. Giguere left to go solo in mid-1970, and was replaced by Richard Thompson (not the erstwhile Fairport Convention member), but a harsher blow came two years later when Cole died of an apparent drug overdose. A period in lower-profile cabaret work was followed by an inevitable split, though the 1980s did see a couple of well-received reunions for live work, and a surprise minor US hit single with 'Dreamer' in 1981.

Greatest Hits

Singles	Title	US	UK
1966	*Cherish*	1	–
1967	*Windy*	1	–
Albums			
1966	*And Then . . . Along Comes The Association*	5	–
1968	*Greatest Hits*	4	–

Frankie AVALON

Avalon (born Francis Avallone, 1939) was a teenage trumpet player from Philadelphia who sang at first only reluctantly, but who became one of America's biggest teen idols for a couple of years during the void left by Elvis Presley's absence in the Army.

He first came to notice in 1957 as a member of Rocco & The Saints, a local teen band in which he played trumpet. Signed by Philly entrepreneur Bob Marcucci to his fledgeling Chancellor label, the group appeared briefly in the movie *Disc Jockey Jamboree*, alongside Jerry Lee Lewis and others, but Marcucci saw more potential in Avalon than the others, and recorded him as a solist despite the youngster's initial reluctance to put down his trumpet and move out of the ranks.

After a couple of flops, Avalon took off, aided by boyish good looks, the proximity in Philadelphia of Dick Clark's *American Bandstand*, and some frequently crass but usually commercial teen-appeal material. He had million-selling No. 1 US hits with 'Venus' in 1959 and 'Why' in 1960, and also made the US Top 10 with schlock-rockers 'Dede Dinah' and 'Gingerbread', and teen romances 'Bobby Sox To Stockings', 'A Boy Without A Girl', and 'Just Ask Your Heart'. His record sales began to fall off rapidly by the end of 1960, but by then Avalon had already had a straight acting role in *The Alamo*, and he directed his energies at Hollywood, appearing in productions like *Voyage to the Bottom of the Sea* and then American International's string of beach party movies in which he co-starred with Annette Funicello, and which were a drive-in staple for much of the 60s.

Avalon had a chart reprise in 1976 with a disco-style remake of 'Venus' and two years later parodied his own younger image when he played the rock star in the 'Beauty School Dropout' sequence of the blockbuster film version of *Grease*.

Philly heart throb Frankie

Greatest Hits

Singles	Title	US	UK
1959	*Venus*	1	16
1960	*Why*	1	20
Albums			
1959	*Swingin' On A Rainbow*	9	–

AVERAGE WHITE BAND

Hamish Stuart *(guitar, vocals)*
Alan Gorrie *(bass, vocals)*
Onnie McIntyre *(guitar)*
Roger Ball *(alto, baritone sax)*
Malcolm 'Molly' Duncan *(tenor, soprano sax)*
Robbie McIntosh *(drums)*

Out of the soul-band mould of the mid 1960s, The Average White Band was formed in 1972 by six dues-paid Scotsmen from the Dundee and Glasgow music circuit. They first attracted attention as the support act for Eric Clapton in January, 1973, at the Rainbow Theatre, and this was soon followed by an impressive debut album on MCA, 'Show Your Hand'.

The AWB broke into the US with their eponymous second LP, which topped the US chart. Produced for Atlantic Records by Arif Mardin, who had produced Aretha Franklin among others, it included what became the band's best known track, the instrumental 'Pick Up The Pieces', which made the UK Top 10 and topped the US chart.

The band's sound reflected the black disco-soul movement of the time, and they spent most of 1974–5 living in and touring America. Robbie McIntosh died there in September 1974 of a heroin overdose, and although the band were stunned – they were old friends as well as musical colleagues – they were quickly back on the road with pick-up drummers before recruiting black drummer Steve Ferrone, like McIntosh a veteran of Brian Auger's Oblivion Express. The band settled on the West Coast of the US as their third album, 'Cut The Cake' (1975) went gold. Its title track was a vocal remake of 'Pick Up The Pieces', which, like the original, made the US Top 10.

The AWB toured with ex-Drifter Ben E. King, cutting 'Benny And Us' in 1977, which failed to emulate their earlier successes. 'Shine', their 1980 album, put them back on the map briefly, with a hit single 'Let's Go Round Again', but the band's image and sound seemed at odds with dance floor music emerging in the early 1980s. New York ex-punk Richie Stotts (ex-Plasmatics) guested on guitar on 'Cupid's In Fashion' in 1982, but the band was finished as such, its most representative sound occasionally surfacing in a session capacity as the Dundee Horns.

Greatest Hits

Singles	Title	US	UK
1974	*Pick Up The Pieces*	1	5
1975	*Cut The Cake*	10	37
1980	*Let's Go Round Again*	–	12
Albums			
1974	*Average White Band*	1	6
1975	*Cut The Cake*	4	28
1976	*Soul Searching*	8	60

Well above average, 'Seventies Scots soul stylists AWB

B-52s

Cindy Wilson (guitar, vocals)
Kate Pierson (organ, vocals)
Ricky Wilson (guitar)
Fred Schneider III (keyboard, vocals)
Julian Keith Strickland (drums)

This eccentric party-music group were formed in 1976 in Athens, Georgia and named themselves after the hairstyle worn by Pierson (born 1948) and Cindy Wilson (born 1957). Apart from Pierson, a New Jersey native, the other members – Cindy, her brother Ricky (born 1953), Schneider (born 1951) and Strickland (born 1953) – are from Georgia. The group moved to New York in 1977 and appeared regularly at the New Wave music haunt, Max's Kansas City. Word soon spread about this wacky visual group and they quickly became transatlantic cult favourites.

Their first US success came in 1979 with their eponymous debut album, which by 1986 had earned them a platinum disc. 1979 also saw their debut UK Top 40 single, 'Rock Lobster', a song originally released on an independent label before their signing with Island Records. In the early 1980s, the band scored four more transatlantic chart albums; the gold LP, 'Wild Planet' (1980), 'The Party Mix Album' (1981), 'Mesopotamia' (1982, produced by David Byrne of Talking Heads) and 'Whammy!' (1983). In 1986 their 'Rock Lobster' re-charted in Britain reaching the Top 20 of the singles charts.

After Ricky Wilson's untimely death (rumoured Aids-related) in 1985, Strickland switched to guitar and in 1986, a new album, 'Bouncing Off The Satellites', found little success. In 1989, this quirky group changed labels to Reprise and had their biggest successes with the double platinum album, 'Cosmic Thing', produced by Don Was and Nile Rodgers. The album also included two US Top 3 singles, 'Love Shack' (a double MTV award winner), and 'Roam', which featured Schneider's distinctive vocals.

The renewed interest in the group meant that in 1990 they returned to touring after a five-year hiatus, prior to recording a new album.

Greatest Hits

Singles	Title	US	UK
1990	Love Shack	3	2
1990	Roam	3	17
Albums			
1980	Wild Planet	18	18
1989	Cosmic Thing	4	8

BAD COMPANY

Paul Rodgers (vocals)
Mick Ralphs (guitar)
Boz Burrell (bass)
Simon Kirke (drums)

From the moment they formed in 1973, Bad Company were a supergroup primed for success. Rodgers (born 1949) and Kirke (born 1949) came from the already legendary Free, Ralphs (born 1944) was a founder member of Mott The Hoople and Burrell

(born 1946) had played with King Crimson. Signing to Led Zeppelin manager Peter Grant's Swansong label gilded their chances and their debut US tour early in 1974 was extended from six weeks to three months, even before their eponymous debut album hit the streets! When it did, in August 1974, it shot to the top and stayed four months in the US Top 40, yielding a Top 5 single with 'Can't Get Enough'. In the UK, their success was always less spectacular.

They stuck to their one-dimensional style, embellished by sturdy riffs from Ralphs and hoarse vocals by Rodgers, for the follow-up albums: 'Straight Shooter' (which made the US Top 3, and its attendant Top 10 single, 'Feel Like Makin' Love') in 1975, 'Run With The Pack' in 1976, 'Burnin' Sky' in 1977 and 'Desolation Angels', which reached the US Top 3 in 1979, each accompanied by a mammoth arena tour. However, by then they seemed uninspired and increasingly short of motivation. After the obligatory tour, they couldn't be bothered to continue, nor even to disband. Burrell and Kirke played low-key gigs for fun and Rodgers finally re-emerged in 1982, joining The Firm with Jimmy Page, but despite two albums and US tours, this provided few sparks. Ralphs meanwhile toured with Dave Gilmour's solo band and eventually reformed the band in 1986 without Rodgers. Former Ted Nugent vocalist Brian Howe joined for the 'Fame and Fortune' album and in 1990 they released another album, 'Holy Water'.

Greatest Hits

Singles	Title	US	UK
1974	Can't Get Enough	5	15
1975	Feel Like Makin' Love	10	20
Albums			
1974	Bad Company	1	3
1975	Straight Shooter	3	3
1979	Desolation Angels	3	10

Joan **BAEZ**

The queen of the American folk revival in the mid-1960s, Baez has had mixed fortunes as a recording artist, but has retained a loyal international following as a live performer.

Born in 1941 in New York, she learned guitar and traditional folk songs as a teenager in Boston. Her flawless soprano took the 1959 Newport Folk Festival by storm, and she was quickly signed to Vanguard Records, which released her eponymous debut album in 1960. At this time her repertoire was strictly traditional, featuring Appalachian ballads, folk blues and civil rights anthems like 'We Shall Overcome'.

Already a major figure on the folk scene, in 1963 Baez took the then little-known Bob

Paul Rodgers and Mick Ralphs, frontline good guys finding themselves in Bad Company

Folk femme and freedom fighter Joan Baez

Dylan on tour with her, exposing him to her own large folk following. Dylan's influence led to Baez's recording contemporary songs, one of which, 'There But For Fortune', by Phil Ochs, was a UK hit in 1965.

Also in 1965, Baez founded her Institute For Non-Violence in California – her pacifist beliefs have led to numerous clashes with the US government. Musically, she was drawn towards country music, first recording in Nashville in 1968. With producer Norbert Putnam, she made 'Any Day Now' (a double-LP of Dylan songs), 'One Day At A Time' (1970, with songs by Kris Kristofferson and Mickey Newbury) and 'Blessed Are . . .' (1971). The latter provided her biggest hit single, a version of The Band's 'The Night They Drove Old Dixie Down'.

From 1972 to 1977, Baez was signed to A&M, where she used more orthodox soft-rock backings and gave prominence to her own compositions. The most notable of these was 'Diamonds And Rust' (1975), about her relationship with Dylan, whom she joined on the *Rolling Thunder Revue* tour in 1976. 'Come From The Shadows' contained the equally successful 'Love Song To A Stranger', while A&M also released 'From Every Stage' (1976), perhaps the best of her numerous live recordings.

Despite the aid of producers David Kershenbaum ('Blowin' Away', 1977) and Barry Beckett ('Honest Lullaby', 1979), her albums for the Californian label, Portrait, were unimpressive. Dropped by the label in 1980, she continued to tour all over the world with her international repertoire of songs in Spanish, French and Russian as well as English.

In the mid-1980s, rock manager Danny Goldberg set up the Gold Castle label as a home for folk-based performers, including Baez. Her albums for Gold Castle have inclu-

ded 'Recently' (1987), 'Diamonds And Rust in The Bullring' (1989, recorded in concert in Spain) and 'Speaking of Dreams' (1990).

John Baez has published two volumes of autobiography, *Daybreak* (1968) and *And A Voice To Sing With* (1988). She was also one of the few performers to sing both at Woodstock in 1969 and Live Aid in 1985.

Greatest Hits

Singles	Title	US	UK
1965	*There But For Fortune*	50	8
1971	*The Night They Drove Old Dixie Down*	3	6
Albums			
1964	*Joan Baez In Concert Part 2*	7	8
1975	*Diamonds And Rust*	11	–

BANANARAMA

Sarah Dallin (*vocals*)
Keren Woodward (*vocals*)
Siobhan Fahey (*vocals*)

A product of punk's 'anything goes' ethos as far as ability being any kind of yardstick to performance, the trio started working the London pub and club scene as an accapella act in 1981. Then-fashionable DJ Garry Crowley, who had worked with Fahey at Decca Records, helped them put together some demos which led to a single for Demon Records, 'Ai A Mwana', produced by Paul Cook formerly of the Sex Pistols. It entered the UK independent charts, and was

reissued by London Records, which signed the group later that year.

Fun Boy Three used the trio as named backing vocalists on 'It Aint What You Do, It's The Way That You Do It', a UK Top 5 hit single in 1982. Bananarama were now well known and (again with Fun Boy Three) revived The Velvettes hit, 'Really Sayin' Something', which became their first UK Top 5 hit. More UK single hits followed, and in 1983, they cracked the US market with single and LP chart debuts with 'Shy Boy' and 'Deep Sea Skiving' respectively.

Their first UK Top 3 hit came in 1984 with 'Robert De Niro's Waiting'. Minor hits occurred regularly on either side of the Atlantic through 1984, and despite their profile being raised somewhat by their appearance in the Band Aid chorus at the end of the year, a bout of inactivity in 1985 – only one single all year – led to rumours of their imminent break up.

Their fortunes changed radically in 1986, when they worked with the production team of Stock, Aitken and Waterman. A revival of the 1970 Shocking Blue hit, 'Venus', made the UK Top 10, and topped the US singles chart, while their first SAW-produced album, 'True Confessions', also did better in the US, hitting the Top 20. They managed to attract television exposure, their image often seeming more familiar than their records. A BBC TV documentary, *In At The Deep End*, showing the making of a pop promo video featured them, as did Stock/Aitken/Waterman's production of 'Let It Be' for the Zeebrugge Ferry Disaster Fund. The single featuring many other contemporary pop stars, topped the UK chart in 1987.

Getting into the swing, Bananarama balanced their bets between punk and pop

More hits followed in 1987, including 'I Heard a Rumour', (US Top 5, UK Top 20), and 'Love In The First Degree' (UK Top 3), before Siobhan Fahey married The Eurythmics' Dave Stewart, when she left the group to settle in California.

Her replacement, Jacqui Sullivan, conformed to the group's image of satinized sexuality perfectly, and the hits continued with another UK Top 10 'I Want You Back' and a 'Greatest Hits' album.

Bananarama managed to retain some of their hip credibility by continued association with the 'alternative' show-biz mafia, most noticeably in their 1987 Comic Relief single of 'Help', on which they collaborated with the high-profile comedy duo French and Saunders.

As a 'girlie' vocal group in an era when rock was male-dominated, Bananarama have always seemed enigmatic, starting as part of an 'alternative' post-punk attitude, but soon finding that their femininity was more exploitable.

Greatest Hits

Singles	Title	US	UK
1982	It Ain't What You Do It's The Way That You Do It	–	4
1982	Really Sayin' Something	–	5
1984	Robert De Niro's Waiting	95	3
1986	Venus	1	8
1987	I Heard A Rumour	4	14
1987	Love In The First Degree	–	3
1988	I Want You Back	–	5
Albums			
1983	Deep Sea Skiving	63	7
1984	Bananarama	30	16
1988	The Greatest Hits Collection	15	3

The **BAND**

Jaime 'Robbie' Robertson (guitar, vocals)
Richard Manuel (piano, vocals)
Garth Hudson (organ)
Rick Danko (bass, vocals)
Levon Helm (drums, vocals)

The Band first came to wide prominence as Bob Dylan's backing group on his transitional (folk to rock) world tour of 1965, then as the musicians who helped Dylan recreate his musical persona in 1967's reclusive 'Basement Tapes' sessions. It was from this latter collaboration that their own commercial success developed.

The group's origins predated the Dylan association – Helm (born 1935) was the American drummer in Canadian rocker Ronnie Hawkins's group, The Hawks, during the latter's brief US hitmaking period in 1959. Hudson (born 1937), Danko (born 1943), Robertson (born 1944) and Manuel (born 1945) were all Canadians, and gradually

Dr. John, Joni Mitchell, Neil Young, Van Morrison and Bob Dylan at The Band's Last Waltz

replaced earlier members of the Hawks when Hawkins became less of an international star in the early 1960s. Heard on Roulette recordings like 1963's 'Who Do You Love', they left Hawkins in 1964 to perform as Levon & The Hawks. Dylan heard them playing in East Coast US clubs, and the invitation to tour followed, but their only record with him at this time was the cut-live-in-Liverpool B-side, 'Just Like Tom Thumb's Blues'.

When Dylan retired to Woodstock, NY, in mid-1967 after injuring himself on his motorbike, he invited the former Hawks to join him. As well as basement collaborations at Great White (Dylan's house), they also worked on their own original songs, and it was a mixture of this material which they assembled as their debut Capitol album. Entitled 'Music From Big Pink' (after their own Woodstock house), it was initially credited to the individual members; dubbing themselves The Band was their minimalist gesture towards a collective identity.

Released in 1968 and critically acclaimed, the album showed The Band's individual style fully-honed: impassioned (often traded) vocals on songs with a built-in maturity removed from the familiar preoccupations of pop/rock, and an instinctive grounding in American (predominantly rural) working-class idioms, which made them neo-traditional without being overtly folky. The next album, 'The Band', offered more the same, and sold more than the debut, reaching the US Top 10. Popular singles like 'The Weight', 'Up On Cripple Creek' and 'Rag Mama Rag' came from these two albums, yet The Band never earned a Top 10 single, a surrogate success being Joan Baez's cover of 'The Night They Drove Old Dixie Down', a 1971 million seller.

1970's 'Stage Fright' was not a live album, but justified its title by building a more

autobiographical element into the ongoing dramas in their original songs, the pressures of touring as a top recording act now being much apparent (they also played live with Dylan again at two major events: the 1969 Isle of Wight Festival, and 1971's Concert For Bangladesh in New York). The group's touch lightened again on 'Cahoots' in 1971; this too lived up to its title by including guest collaborators Allen Toussaint and Van Morrison, while the group committed their stage act to vinyl on the 1972 double set, 'Rock Of Ages'.

When Dylan left CBS and signed briefly to Geffen Records, The Band backed him for 1974's 'Planet Waves' album, counterpointing it with their own album of 1950s nostalgia, 'Moondog Matinee'. A US tour with Dylan was recorded, and the subsequent live double album, 'Before The Flood', spotlighted them as both accompanists and in their own right.

The Band collectively ran out of steam in 1976. Tired of touring, aware of the absent sparkle on albums like 1975's 'Northern Lights – Southern Cross' and 1977's 'Islands', and with former driving force Robertson devoting much energy to outside production, they announced a split. It was to be the grandest exit in rock history, as a farewell concert in San Francisco became a star-studded event featuring Dylan, Van Morrison, Neil Diamond, Eric Clapton and many other erstwhile collaborators and friends. Filmed by Martin Scorsese, the event was immortalized as the 1978 movie (and triple LP), *The Last Waltz*.

After the split, Hudson and Manuel kept a low profile, as did Danko after one solo album. Helm was considerably more active, first forming the RCO All-Stars with an array of top session players, and then popping up as an actor in the Loretta Lynn biopic, *Coal Miner's Daughter*. Robertson also acted, in

Carney with Gary Busey and Jodie Foster, and became Martin Scorsese's regular musical associate.

In the mid-1980's, The Band somewhat unexpectedly reunited as a touring unit, but could not persuade Robertson, busy with production and film scores, to rejoin them. His role was filled by guitarist James Wieder, but the spirit left the whole enterprise when an apparently heavily depressed Manuel committed suicide in March 1986.

Robertson finally made his debut as a fully fledged solo artist in 1988, his critically rated eponymous album and a single, 'Somewhere Down The Crazy River', both becoming major sellers.

Greatest Hits

Singles	Title	US	UK
1968	*The Weight*	63	21
1969	*Up On Cripple Creek*	25	–
1970	*Rag Mama Rag*	57	16
Albums			
1969	*The Band*	9	25
1970	*Stage Fright*	5	15
1972	*Rock Of Ages*	6	–

The BANGLES

Susanna Hoffs (guitar, vocals)
Vicki Peterson (guitar, vocals)
Annette Zilinskas (bass, vocals)
Debbie Peterson (drums, vocals)

Known for intricate harmonies and a mix of styles ranging from folk-rock to mainstream pop, the roots of The Bangles started in 1980 when Hoffs joined the Peterson sisters, who had played in The Fans, to form LA group The Colours. In 1981, they were joined by bassist Annette Zilinskas, became The Bangs, formed Down Kiddie records and released the single, 'Getting Out Of Hand'. They appeared on a Posh Boy compilation album and in 1982 were renamed The Bangles, to avoid confusion with an East Coast group also called The Bangs, and record a mini LP, 'The Bangles', for Faulty Products.

In 1983, with new bassist Michael Steele (ex-Runaways), they joined CBS and their 1984 album, 'All Over The Place', made the US and UK Top 100s. Their first single success came in 1986 with a song written for them by Prince, 'Manic Monday' a Top 3 hit on both sides of the Atlantic. Their second album, 'Different Light', took 50 weeks to make the US Top 10, but went double platinum thanks to 'Walk Like An Egyptian', which topped the US chart and was the Top US Single of 1987, when their version of Simon & Garfunkel's 'A Hazy Shade of Winter', from the film *Less Than Zero*, was another US Top 3 hit.

Their biggest single came in 1989 with 'Eternal Flame', co-written by Hoffs. It became not only the first US No. 1 by a white female group since 1964, but also topped the UK chart for four weeks – a record for a female group. 'Everything', the album on which it featured, also went platinum and in 1990 their 'Greatest Hits' album reached the UK Top 5.

The most successful female vocal/instrumental act of all time was put on ice in 1989 and a solo album from Hoffs was due for release in 1991.

Greatest Hits

Singles	Title	US	UK
1986	*Walk Like An Egyptian*	1	3
1989	*Eternal Flame*	1	1
Albums			
1986	*Different Light*	2	3
1989	*Everything*	15	5

The BEACH BOYS

Brian Wilson (bass, vocals)
Carl Wilson (guitar, vocals)
Dennis Wilson (drums, vocals)
Alan Jardine (guitar, vocals)
Mike Love (vocals)

Formed in 1961, The Beach Boys are arguably the most influential American band of all time, and unquestionably one of the longest lived, although their creative heyday lies some twenty years in the past. All except Jardine (born 1941 in Lima, Ohio) are natives of Los Angeles.

Dennis (born 1944) was the only true surfer in the band, and it was at his instigation that brother Brian (born 1942) and cousin Mike (born 1941) wrote and recorded 'Surfin', a regional hit on a local independent label, which enabled the Wilsons' father Murry to hassle a deal with Capitol Records (after having been turned down by almost every other label in town). At this point, the band were almost complete musical novices: Brian was self-taught on piano and Carl (born 1946) had learned guitar from John Maus (later of The Walker Brothers). Before the Capitol contract was signed, Jardine left to pursue dentistry studies and was replaced by neighbour David Marks (born 1948). Their debut album, 'Surfin' Safari' (1962), included their first US Top 40 hit with the title track. 'Surfin' USA', the first of three albums released in 1963, made the US Top 3, with the title track a Top 3 US single, thus establishing them as the top US band. The first two Beach Boys albums were nominally produced by Capitol A&R man Nik Venet, but in reality by Brian Wilson, a situation Capitol was forced to acknowledge by the release of 'Surfer Girl', which ended the group's overt surf cycle after both album and single made the US Top 10.

The switch to cars and hot rods served only to increase the band's following, with both 'Little Deuce Coupe' and 'Shut Down Volume 2' going high in the US album charts and also generating US Top 10 singles in 'Be True To Your School' and 'Fun, Fun, Fun' respectively. Mid-1964 saw the next logical thematic shift, to general (if firmly California-oriented) good-time, as exemplified by the 'All Summer Long' album, from which came the group's first US No.1 and first UK Top 10 hit, 'I Get Around'. Prior to recording this album, Jardine had returned to the fold, displacing Marks). 'All Summer Long' also showcased Brian's increasingly complex productions and hinted at his growing introspection. The year closed with two important events: 'Beach Boys Concert' became their first US chart topping LP and at the same time, Brian underwent the first of several nervous breakdowns, and withdrew from regular touring for some twelve years.

'Today', the first fruit of this new arrangement, foreshadowed future directions – one side of up-tempo Beach Boy-style songs, one side of personal Brian Wilson tunes. On the road, Brian was replaced initially by session guitarist Glenn Campbell (not yet the dream of the everyday housewife) and later more permanently by Bruce Johnston (born 1942), another Los Angeleno who had been a part of the LA recording scene since the late 50s. A re-recorded 'Help Me Rhonda' became the group's second US No. 1 single, a feat which 'California Girls' almost equalled. 'Summer Days (And Summer Nights!!)', the group's last consciously good-time album, included both tracks, and reached the US Top 3.

Free from the rigours of touring, Brian began to take more time over his composing and recording, an attitude which obliquely resulted in 'Beach Boys Party!', a Top 3 album in the UK. While preparing for the 'Pet Sounds' album, Capitol's demands for a new LP became ever more pressing, so the band took three days of studio time and a few friends, the result being a US Top 10 album and a US/UK Top 3 single in 'Barbara Ann' (released without the band's knowledge or approval).

'Pet Sounds' (1966) is generally regarded as Brian's, and The Beach Boys', finest moment but, although a critical success, and despite setting new production, performing and engineering standards, and containing four Top 40 hits ('Sloop John B', 'God Only Knows', 'Wouldn't it be Nice?' and 'Caroline, No', the last released as a Brian Wilson record), the album wasn't the almost obligatory huge hit, only just reaching the US Top 10. Undaunted, Brian pressed on with The Beach Boys most famous song – 'Good Vibrations'. Costing a reputed $50,000 and recorded at three studios over four months, the single became a pre-Christmas chart-topper on both sides of the Atlantic, and also

Surf smoothies heading for hippy hedonism, the Beach Boys spanned the sixties and beyond

signalled months of silence from The Beach Boys' camp as Brian, assisted by Van Dyke Parks and the cream of LA's session mafia, worked on the tracks for the legendary, much bootlegged 'Smile' album, a project abandoned in mid-1967 amid the virtual disintegration of The Beach Boys, the increasing unreliability and eccentricity of Brian, and the emerging rock counter-culture that The Beach Boys had once pioneered, but which now regarded them as an anachronism.

The tattered remnants of 'Smile', in the form of the 'Smiley Smile' album and the US Top 20 single, 'Heroes & Villains' did nothing to stem the band's decline in the late 1960s. Each successive album – 'Wild Honey' (1967), 'Friends' (1968) and '20/20' (1969) – sold fewer and fewer copies, the single hits dried up (1968's 'Do It Again' was their last US Top 20 single for eight years) and the concert crowds thinned. Brian became essentially a part-time Beach Boy, Carl generally taking up the slack, and without the band's immense popularity everywhere *except* the USA, The Beach Boys' saga may have ended with the expiration of their Capitol contract.

Though Warner-Reprise offered the group their own label, Brother Records, in 1970, the association hit the rocks straight away when their 'Sunflower' album was a critical success but a commercial disaster. A change of management coupled with a forced adoption of the prevailing eco-political awareness ensured that 1971's 'Surf's Up' garnered both favourable reviews and reasonable sales, but, this momentum was rapidly dissipated by the departure from the group of Bruce Johnston, an injury to Dennis Wilson's hand which prevented him from drumming for several years, the introduction of Blondie Chaplin and Ricky Fataar, both non-white South Africans, and a weak album in 'Carl & The Passions – So Tough' (1972). Drastic mea-

sures were called for, hence the group shipped their entire operation – including a most unwilling Brian – to Holland for the summer of 1972. The resulting album, 'Holland', was a mild success, and was also the group's last album of original material for three years.

In 1974, Capitol decided to revive the group's back catalogue. A modest proposal produced immodest results as 'Endless Summer' – an album assembled at such speed that the incorrect versions of some songs were used – raced to the top of the US chart, where it remained for over a year. In 1975, the similarly conceived 'Spirit of America' made the US Top 10 with equal facility, leaving Warners – and the band – wondering how to sell new material as fast as Capitol was shipping the oldies.

The answer, apparently, was the return to both studio and stage of Brian Wilson, who had rarely been involved since the 'Smile' debacle, and around this debatable premise was constructed the 'Brian's Back!' campaign of 1976. The results were mixed: '15 Big Ones' was a US Top 10 album, and a version of Chuck Berry's 'Rock & Roll Music' made the US Top 5, but the album could be charitably described as uneven, Brian was far from being 'back', and a winter bout of in-group dissension dissipated the chart momentum. 1977's 'The Beach Boys Love You' was essentially a Brian Wilson solo album in everything but name, released against the background of a disintegrating relationship with Warners, and was to some extent overshadowed by the first true solo Beach Boys album, Dennis Wilson's 'Pacific Ocean Blue', a critical favourite which only just dented the Top 100 of the US chart.

1978 saw The Beach Boys in the embarrassing position of having signed to James Guercio's Caribou label while still owing

Warners an album, a situation remedied by the release of a rag-bag of out-takes and second-rate new recordings called 'MIU'. However, earlier that year, Mike Love (with help from Alan Jardine and Brian) had scored a surprise US Top 30 hit with 'Almost Summer', a movie theme song performed by Celebration, a pick-up band composition mainly of Beach Boys sidemen. The association with Caribou ultimately proved unsatisfactory, producing just three new studio albums in five years. Neither 'L.A. (Light Album)' (1979) – for which Bruce Johnston returned to the fold – 'Keepin' The Summer Alive' (1980) nor the imaginatively titled 'The Beach Boys' (1985) caused much chart fuss (although 'Getcha Back' from the 1985 album charted respectably high).

Since 1985, the band has concentrated on one-off single deals, usually with a movie tie-in, with little success . . . until 1988, when 'Kokomo', from the Tom Cruise film *Cocktail*, slept outside the chart for some months, then commenced a slow-but-steady rise to top of the US chart – 22 years after their last No. 1 single, 'Good Vibrations'. Also in 1988, Brian Wilson at last delivered his long-awaited, eponymous solo album, to critical acclaim but modest sales. Previous solo sets from Carl ('Carl Wilson' in 1981 and 'Young Blood' in 1983) and Mike Love ('Looking Back With Love', 1981) sank almost without trace.

As the band approaches its 30th anniversary, it could be said with some justification that their greatest recent achievement has been to stay more or less intact, especially after Dennis Wilson drowned in December 1983. As a touring attraction, the band are as popular as ever, yet creatively all but moribund. Brian Wilson these days is only nominally a Beach Boy, a strange state of affairs for the man who single-handedly not only 'invented' California, but also irrevocably changed the course of rock and pop in the mid-1960s. His second solo album, due in 1991, is seen as pivotal in establishing him firmly in his solo career: if not, it's probably back to the band and play those oldies one more time. Whatever, his place, and that of The Beach Boys, in musical history is assured – as long as there's a summer, there will be Brian Wilson/Beach Boys music on the airwaves.

Greatest Hits

Singles	Title	US	UK
1964	*I Get Around*	1	7
1965	*Help Me Rhonda*	1	27
1966	*Good Vibrations*	1	1
1968	*Do It Again*	20	1
1988	*Kokomo*	1	25
Albums			
1964	*Beach Boys Concert!*	1	–
1974	*Endless Summer*	1	–
1976	*20 Golden Greats*	–	1
1983	*Very Best Of The Beach Boys*	–	1

The **BEAT/GENERAL PUBLIC**

Ranking Roger (vocals)
Dave Wakeling (vocals)
Everett Morton (drums)
David Steele (bass)
Andy Cox (guitar)
Saxa (saxophone)

Brightest of the ska revival bands of the 1970s 2-Tone explosion, The Beat were formed in Birmingham in 1978 and picked up 'toaster' Ranking Roger (born 1961) en route. Wakeling (born 1956), Cox (born 1956) and Steele (born 1960) had met on the Isle of Wight, returning to the former pair's home town to pick up drummer Morton (born 1951), an ex-Joan Armatrading sideman. Jamaican-born Saxa (born 1931) who arrived later, was a local legend who had played with Prince Buster, cementing a link between old and new.

After a one-off UK Top 10 single for 2-Tone in 1979, covering the Miracles' 'Tears Of A Clown', they toured with The Specials before forming their own label Go Feet. Their first album, 'I Just Can't Stop It', was a classic dance album: chattering guitars, elastic bass and a twin vocal attack doing justice to topical lyrics dealing with race, unemployment, romance and teenage problems without drawing breath. The ironic 'Hand Off – She's Mine', became their second UK Top 10 hit, while 'Mirror In The Bathroom' and 'Best Friend/Stand Down Margaret' (an attack on Thatcher, with royalties to CND) also made the UK Top 10.

They attempted to crack the US by constant touring (they were known in the USA as The English Beat due to a coincidence of names). 1981's album 'Wha'appen' saw a slowing down of tempo, a more thoughtful approach and a lack of singles success, 'Doors To Your Heart' made the UK Top 40, but by 'Special Beat Service', in 1982, the pace of life on the road had hit home. With a final irony they returned to the Top 40 in 1983 after a near two-year absence with a remixed track from their first album, 'Can't Get Used To Losing You': a naïve ska cover of the Andy Williams standard, it symbolically returned them to 1979.

Wesley Magoogan (born 1951) had replaced the ailing Saxa, but the group needed more than new blood and it was no surprise when they announced their retirement. Steele and Cox formed Fine Young Cannibals (see separate entry) while Wakeling and Roger took on the US market once more as General Public. Their debut album, 'All The Rage', recorded with ex-Dexys and Specials members, proved uninspired, and 1989 saw Roger cut a solo album for RSD General Public apparently no more after a further album 'Hand To Mouth', had flopped.

The Beat were, with Madness, the brightest and best prospects to emerge from 2-Tone. Had they conserved their energies and

explored new avenues instead of touring incessantly, their success could have been longer-lived.

Greatest Hits

Singles	Title	US	UK
1980	*Mirror In The Bathroom*	–	4
1981	*Can't Get Used To Losing You*	–	3
1985	*Tenderness (General Public)*	27	–
Albums			
1980	*Just Can't Stop It*	142	3
1981	*Wha'appen*	126	3
1982	*Special Beat Service*	39	21

The **BEATLES**

John Lennon (guitar, vocals)
Paul McCartney (bass, vocals)
George Harrison (guitar, vocals)
Pete Best (drums)
Stuart Sutcliffe (bass)

The Beatles were the catalyst not only for much of pop music's development over the last 30 years, but also, due to the magnitude of their global success, probably the biggest single influence on the shaping of worldwide popular culture after the advent of rock'n'roll itself.

Fortunate always in their ability to become a whole greater than the sum of their parts, and to have a naturally gifted songwriting team whose personal strengths and weaknesses often provided a perfect whole, the group were never technical virtuosi, yet became the yardstick of virtuosity and vision against which all subsequent music has been instinctively tested.

Their origins, inevitably, were totally derivative, but they had the luck and instinctive good judgement to absorb just the right influences and nurture them at just the right time. Formed in Liverpool in 1957 after a casual meeting between schoolboys John Lennon (born 1940) and Paul McCartney (born 1942), the group, which George Harrison (born 1943) joined a year later, were originally known as the Quarrymen. By 1960, they had regrouped with drummer Pete Best (born 1941) and guitarist Stuart Sutcliffe (born 1940) as The Beatles, and were honing their act first in Liverpool clubs and then in a lengthy club sojurn in Hamburg, W. Germany, where the combination of Presley, Chuck Berry, Everly Brothers and Buddy Holly influences and their own original guitar/harmony material was shaped via endless gruelling sets before demanding audiences.

At the end of 1961 Sutcliffe left the group (he was to die tragically just four months later), and Liverpool businessman Brian Epstein became their manager. Epstein recognized that the group's musical approach,

while not untypical of the scene in Liverpool itself, was notably fresh compared to the post rock'n'roll, teen idol-cum-novelty mainstream of 1962 British pop, where most guitar groups twanged instrumentals or backed a Cliff Richard/Elvis Presley-clone vocalist. This very factor proved an initial barrier to Epstein's attempts to gain the group a recording contract, but eventually EMI's George Martin also heard some potential. Epstein made some strategic changes, like sharpening up their casual dress (into a hair-suit image destined to overturn the male fashion world), and more notably on a musical level, replacing Best with new drummer/occasional vocalist Ringo Starr (born 1940).

'Love Me Do', a Lennon/McCartney original, was the debut single, becoming a Top 20 UK hit, and creating enough of a buzz about the group to accelerate the follow-up, 'Please Please Me', to the top of the UK chart early in 1963. From this point, the Merseybeat boom, quickly followed by a general beat group explosion, swept over staid British pop, filling the charts with young performers using the new ground rules established by The Beatles. The traditional regime would never reassert itself.

The group, as the leaders of the revolution, rapidly moved from being fresh newcomers to a true cultural phenomenon, with record sales accelerating as they went. 'From Me To You' topped the UK chart, 'Twist and Shout' was a huge-selling EP, the group's first two albums monopolized the UK No. 1 album slot from April 1963 until May the following year, 'She Loves You' topped a million UK sales, hit No. 1 twice and remained Britain's biggest-selling single until 1977, and 'I Want To Hold Your Hand' almost went one better by selling over a million virtually on the day of release. 1963 in Britain was the year of Beatlemania – a phrase coined by a press which, along with the general establishment, reversed the stance it had generally taken over Presley and 1950s rock, and cheered right along with the general hysteria.

On a quieter but more musically pertinent note, Lennon and McCartney also instituted a songwriting revolution. Their songs began to be covered early in 1963, at first by other Epstein-managed acts like Billy J Kramer, who found them a useful ticket to the charts. By the end of the year, virtually every performer in Britain was clamouring to cover The Beatles' songs, and more importantly, the concept of a self-contained group providing its own original material became the norm, rather than the exception. Also, since The Beatles highlighted their own favourite influences via cover versions, singer/songwriter rockers like Berry, Holly and Carl Perkins, and the commercial R&B sounds of Tamla Motown and the US girl group, were swung into prominence – The Beatles were certainly the original spark of the R&B boom in Britain, even though it is often regarded as eclipsing Merseybeat.

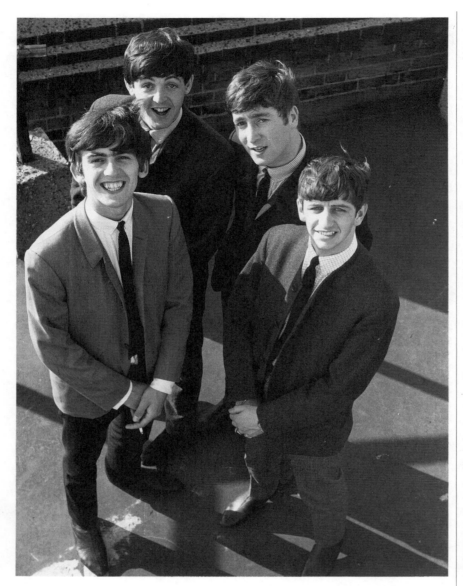

George, Paul, John and Ringo, the fab four Mersey Moptops who changed the face of pop

1964 saw the whole phenomenon repeated in America and on a global scale. The previous almost total one-way traffic of pop from the US to Britain was unprecedentedly reversed when 'I Want To Hold Your Hand' topped the US chart, and was swiftly followed by reissued earlier Beatles hit singles. Soon the whole 'British Invasion' – The Dave Clark Five, The Searchers, The Rolling Stones, and scores more – followed. Ever since, the transatlantic hit route has been two-way. April 1964 saw The Beatles in the top five positions in the US chart, a never-repeated domination. 'Can't Buy Me Love' became another million seller and in the summer the group's first feature film, the low-budget *A Hard Day's Night*, was a global box-office smash. Its title track and 'I Feel Fine' racked up millions more singles sales, the soundtrack album did the same and the group toured widely to huge, hysterical audiences.

Though Beatlemania had dissipated by 1965 (except where the group happened to be on tour – a chore they abandoned in mid-1966), The Beatles remained dominant players in the fast-evolving scenario of 1960s pop music. Still willing, as they had been from the start, to consider new influences, they absorbed and reflected new developments (Bob Dylan, psychedelia) from a position of pre-eminence in which they were ultimate innovators, thereby invariably creating trends followed by others. Putting stage work behind them, their songwriting matured rapidly, and they acquired sophistication in the recording studio, encouraged by producer George Martin.

The mid-1960s are littered with Beatle landmarks which seem as much part of our shared cultural heritage as that of the group: the success of a second film, *Help!*, and the much-criticized slightness of its made-for-TV

follow-up, *Magical Mystery Tour* in 1967, the MBE awards in 1965, the Lennon/Jesus controversy in the US in 1966, the *Our World* global telecast in 1967, and, of course, the hit songs, ('Yesterday', 'Strawberry Fields Forever', 'Eleanor Rigby', 'All You Need Is Love') and albums ('Rubber Soul', 'Revolver', and particularly the epochal 'Sergeant Pepper's Lonely Hearts Club Band') which stand as benchmarks in musical history.

There were few negative developments in the group's career before 1967, but in that year, Epstein suddenly died and his managerial direction was lost, while public flirtations with drugs and the meditation guru, Maharishi Mahesh Yogi, tested public credibility. The group set up Apple, designed as an umbrella for their collective and individual activities, but although this was to have some success as a record label over the next couple of years, with Beatle-inspired talents like Mary Hopkin, Billy Preston and Badfinger, it also became the archetypal disorganized freeloader's paradise, and a financial black hole for its owners.

The music of The Beatles continued to innovate ahead of the field, but by 1968 it was no longer being made in the same way. Lennon and McCartney had been writing separately for some time, generally applying each other's finishing touches in the studio, while 'Sergeant Pepper' included some largely solo pieces. By the time 1968's double album, 'The Beatles', was released, solo work was the rule rather than the exception; many of its tracks only had two Beatles (Ringo plus the songwriter) playing on them. This was partly a reflection of new, individually motivated lifestyles freed from the bonds which had virtually forced them to live together during the group's earlier years, but also signalled more frequent musical and personal disagreements: Lennon's liaison with Yoko Ono from May 1968, to which he clearly attached more importance than previous musical comradeship, was a case in point, but it little affected the quality and success of their work – the double album and 1968/69 singles 'Hey Jude' and 'Get Back' were among their biggest ever.

The early 1969-shot film, *Let It Be*, designed as a documentary about The Beatles making an album, also showed the fraught conditions under which they group related to each other in the studio. Particularly with Lennon's tangential work with his Plastic Ono Band, McCartney and Harrison dabbling in film music, and Ringo actually starring in movies, distintegration seemed imminent. In the event, the group reconvened in mid-1969 to cut 'Abbey Road', an album which seemed more collaborative than 'The Beatles', and which also demonstrated Harrison's full maturity as a songwriter on 'Something' and 'Here Comes The Sun' (both later covered as much as most Lennon/McCartney songs).

Business disagreements were the final straw. Both Apple's and the group's financial nightmares had to be sorted out, and irreconcilable disagreements occurred between three members, who wanted the notoriously tough Allen Klein (manager of The Rolling Stones) brought in, and McCartney, who didn't. Ultimately, he instigated in late 1970 the legal moves which dissolved The Beatles' partnership. The year had already seen more solo than collective Beatle activity (including McCartney's first solo LP and more Plastic Ono Band hits by Lennon), plus the final group album, 'Let It Be', recorded before 'Abbey Road', which was essentially a soundtrack album of the movie project and caused controversy due to its post-production by Phil Spector. Nevertheless, it provided The Beatles with two classic swan song singles via its title track and 'The Long And Winding Road' – both of which McCartney was still performing two decades later.

All four ex-Beatles had massive solo successes in the 1970s and beyond (see separate entries) and the commercial resilience of their recorded work has proved matchless, with latter-day compilations and reissues equalling the sales of many original releases, notable examples being 'Love Me Do''s 20th anniversary reissue, which saw it in the UK Top 5, 'Twist And Shout' making the US Top 30 in 1986 after movie soundtrack use, and the huge sales of the entire LP catalogue at the end of the 80s when it became available on CD. Speculation about the group's reuniting was always rife during the 1970s, though no moves towards it were ever made by the ex-Beatles themselves, and Lennon's death in 1980 settled the matter with utter finality.

Greatest Hits

Singles	Title	US	UK
1962	Love Me Do	1	4
1963	Please Please Me	3	1
1963	From Me To You	41	1
1963	She Loves You	1	1
1963	I Want To Hold Your Hand	1	1
1964	Can't Buy Me Love	1	i
1964	A Hard Day's Night	1	1
1964	I Feel Fine	1	1
1965	Eight Days A Week	1	–
1965	Ticket To Ride	1	1
1965	Help!	1	1
1965	Yesterday	1	8
1965	We Can Work It Out/		
	Day Tripper	1	1
1966	Paperback Writer	1	1
1966	Yellow Submarine/		
	Eleanor Rigby	2	1
1967	Penny Lane/		
	Strawberry Fields Forever	1	2
1967	All You Need Is Love	1	1
1967	Hello Goodbye	1	1
1968	Lady Madonna	4	1
1968	Hey Jude	1	1
1969	Get Back	1	1
1969	The Ballad Of John and Yoko	8	1
1969	Come Together	1	4
1970	Let It Be	1	2
1970	The Long And Winding Road	1	–

Albums			
1963	Please Please Me		
	(US: Introducing The Beatles)	2	1
1963	With The Beatles	–	1
1964	Meet The Beatles	1	–
1964	The Beatles' Second Album	1	–
1964	A Hard Day's Night	1	1
1964	Beatles For Sale	–	1
1965	Beatles '65	1	–
1965	Beatles VI	1	–
1965	Help!	1	1
1965	Rubber Soul	1	1
1966	Yesterday . . . And Today	1	–
1966	Revolver	1	1
1967	Sergeant Pepper's Lonely		
	Hearts Club Band	1	1
1967	Magical Mystery Tour	1	31
1968	The Beatles (White Album)	1	1
1969	Abbey Road	1	1
1970	Let It Be	1	1
1973	The Beatles: 1967–1970	1	2
1977	The Beatles At		
	The Hollywood Bowl	2	1

Jeff **BECK**

Jeff Beck (born 1944) remains potentially the greatest British rock guitarist of all time, although he has never achieved the consistency his many admirers would welcome. Impressed as a teenager by rock'n'rollers like Cliff Gallup (of Gene Vincent's Blue Caps), he experimented with the guitar before meeting Jimmy Page when both were at art college. The first groups in which he played, neither of which recorded, were The Deltones and The Tridents (both early 1960s) and his earliest recordings appear to be on the compilation albums, 'Anthology Of British Blues', which also feature Page, Eric Clapton, Albert Lee, Mick Fleetwood, etc.

He first attracted wider attention by replacing Clapton in The Yardbirds (see separate entry) in early 1965, playing on hits like 'Heart Full of Soul', 'Evil Hearted You' and 'Shapes of Things', as well as appearing with them in the celebrated Antonioni movie, *Blow Up*. By then, Page had also joined the group, and the potential for such explosive players working together was immense, but the alliance was brief. Beck then went solo with Mickie Most producing him, resulting in three UK hit singles in 1967/68, including 'Hi-Ho Silver Lining' (on which he also sang) and an instrumental version of 'Love Is Blue'. Beck had assembled a group of Rod Stewart (vocals), Ron Wood (bass) and Mickey Waller (drums), but Most would not allow Stewart to sing on the hits, feeling that Beck was the star – in fact, Stewart was hardly known at the time. However, the group was allowed to play on their two albums, 'Truth' (1968), which also featured Page, Keith Moon of The Who, Nicky Hopkins (piano) and

Beck – potentially the greatest

John Paul Jones (later in Led Zeppelin), and 'Beck-Ola' (1969), by which time Waller had been replaced by Tony Newman. This group has been cited by Beck as the inspiration for Led Zeppelin, which Page and Jones formed shortly after 'Truth' was released.

When Stewart and Wood joined The Faces, Beck was left without a band. After a fruitless attempt to work with Elton John, he recruited a new band of Bobby Tench (vocals, guitar), Max Middleton (keyboards), Clive Chaman (bass) and Cozy Powell (drums), and this line-up cut 'Rough And Ready' (1971) and 'The Jeff Beck Group' (1972), after which Beck teamed up with Tim Bogert (bass, vocals) and Carmine Appice (drums), both ex-Vanilla Fudge, for a shortlived supergroup known as BB&A. After an eponymous 1973 studio album, which included 'Superstition' written for Beck by Stevie Wonder, whose own version was a hit, plus a live album only released in Japan after the group had fallen apart, Beck decided to make purely instrumental albums.

Beck guested on Wonder's 'Talking Book' album and on several albums by jazz/rock star Stanley Clarke, and was tipped as replacement for Mick Taylor in The Rolling Stones, but preferred to remain his own boss. In 1975 'Blow By Blow', a totally instrumental album produced by George Martin, on which Beck was backed by Middleton, Phil Chen (bass) and Richard Bailey (drums), became his biggest ever US album, and like his 1976 followup, 'Wired', went gold. The latter featured Middleton and Bailey, plus Jan Hammer and Narada Michael Walden from The Mahavishnu Orchestra and Wilbur Bascomb (bass), Beck then joined Hammer's group for a year long world tour, from which came an album with the catchy title of 'Jeff Beck With The

Jan Hammer Group Live in 1977'. A three-year hiatus ended in 1980 with the release of 'There And Back', with Hammer, Tony Hymas (keyboards), Mo Foster (bass) and Simon Phillips (drums), before another long gap, during which Beck toured with contemporaries like Page, Clapton, Steve Winwood, Joe Cocker, Bill Wyman and Charlie Watts to raise money for multiple sclerosis research, as Ronnie Lane (ex-Small Faces) was suffering from the disease.

In 1985, he briefly reunited with Rod Stewart for a US tour, which produced a superb cover of Curtis Mayfield's 'People Get Ready', which was included on Beck's next album, 'Flash' (1985), on which production duties were shared by Nile Rodgers (of Chic) and Arthur Baker, and the supporting musicians included Hammer and Hymas. Beck was featured on the first two solo albums by Mick Jagger, 'She's The Boss' (1985) and 'Primitive Cool' (1987), and in 1986 released as a single a version of 'Wild Thing', The Troggs hit. Another long gap ended in 1989, when he appeared on 'Waltz Darling', an album by Malcolm McLaren, which also featured 'Bootsy' Collins, and also released another totally instrumental album on his own account, 'Jeff Beck's Guitar Shop', with backing by Hymas and drummer Terry Bozzio (ex-Frank Zappa).

Clearly, Jeff Beck is neither prodigious nor consistent, yet his unique ability has made him legendary – if the adage about leaving an audience wanting more is correct, Beck should be much more commercially successful. Perhaps one day his achievements will equal his potential . . .

Greatest Hits

Singles	Title	US	UK
1967	Hi-Ho Silver Lining	–	14
1985	People Get Ready		
	(with Rod Stewart)	48	–
Albums			
1968	Truth	15	–
1969	Beck-Ola	15	39
1975	Blow By Blow	4	38

The **BEE GEES**

Robin Gibb (vocals)
Barry Gibb (vocals, guitar)
Maurice Gibb (vocals, guitar)
Vince Melouney (guitar)
Colin Peterson (drums)

One of a very small number of vocal groups to achieve major commercial success in three successive decades (and the only such to have also written all its own hits), the name The Bee Gees is an acronym of 'Brothers Gibb'. The original group was formed as The Gibbs, (then the BG's) in 1962 in Brisbane, Australia, by teenagers Barry (born 1947) and twins Robin and Maurice (born 1949), some years after they had emigrated to Australia with their parents from their native UK.

The group recorded with moderate success in Australia, but it was not until early 1967, when they had already decided to return to Britain to develop their career, that they ironically topped the Australian chart with 'Spicks And Specks'. Arriving in the UK, they signed for management with Australian entrepreneur Robert Stigwood, who boosted the group to a quintet by adding Australian musicians Vince Melouney (born 1945) and former child actor Colin Peterson (born 1946), and negotiated a record deal with Polydor in the UK and Atlantic in the US. The group's first UK-originated single was an enigmatic Beatles-influenced ballad, 'New York Mining Disaster 1941', which highlighted the key ingredients of their early style: plaintive vocals, strong melody, and trademark sibling harmonies.

It was a Top 20 hit on both sides of the Atlantic, and their debut album made both the US and UK Top 10s. Further ballads like the much-covered 'To Love Somebody', 'Holiday', 'Words' (also recorded by Elvis Presley) and 'I Started A Joke' maintained the hit streak, while both 'Massachusetts' (1967) and 'I've Gotta Get A Message To You' (1968) topped the UK singles chart. Maurice Gibb also made the headlines in Britain by marrying Scottish singer Lulu. The group personnel, however, proved unstable. Melouney quit in late 1968 due to musical differences and was not replaced, after which the Gibbs began to have musical disagreements, and Robin – lead vocalist on most singles up to then – also departed, to work solo. As he enjoyed a massive UK solo hit in late 1969 with the very Bee Gee-ish 'Saved By The Bell', the group seemed suicide-bent, as the other two Gibbs dispensed with drummer Peterson. Nevertheless, as a duo they equalled Robin's chart status with the country-styled 'Don't Forget To Remember Me', and also made the quickly forgotten film, Cucumber Castle. As 1969 ended, Barry Gibb announced he was also leaving, and briefly The Bee Gees ceased to exist.

Stigwood pulled things back together during 1970, persuading Barry to stay on and Robin to rejoin. The reunion was clearly heartfelt, as although there were many subsequent solo Bee Gees projects, none ever again affected the continuity of the Gibb triumvirate as The Bee Gees. The 1969 quarrels, however, had affected their UK following, and a hit revival came first in the US, where 'Lonely Days' and 'How Can You Mend A Broken Heart' both sold a million in 1971.

After coasting on the back of several smaller hits, the brothers hit a musical crisis in 1974 when a new album was rejected by Stigwood's own RSO label to which they were signed. Identifying the expiry date of their original style, the Gibbs abandoned it, teaming up with a new creative producer, Arif Mardin, who gave their music a sharp soulful edge, as exemplified by the million selling album, 'Main Course', and the 1975 chart-topping single 'Jive Talkin' ', which also restored them to the UK Top 10. By the second half of the 1970s, the trio's music, as guided by Mardin,

Barry, Robin and Maurice – the Brothers Gibb relaxing by the family saloon

was synonymous with the fast-growing disco style, and the ensuing momentum gave them further hits in this vein, notably 'Nights On Broadway' and the 1976 US chart-topper 'You Should Be Dancing'. This development made them the obvious choice as music providers when Robert Stigwood decided in 1977 to make a feature film based around the disco dancing phenomenon, *Saturday Night Fever*. Starring John Travolta, it was a box-office smash which yielded the biggest-selling soundtrack album of all time, almost all written and performed by The Bee Gees.

Now producing themselves in collaboration with Karl Richardson and Albhy Galuten, the brothers topped the US chart with three consecutive singles from the film: 'How Deep Is Your Love', 'Stayin' Alive' and 'Night Fever'. Bee Gees music totally dominated the US chart of late 1977/early 1978, with hits which they wrote for Samantha Sang ('Emotion'), Yvonne Elliman ('If I Can't Have You') and their younger soloing brother, Andy Gibb ('I Just Want To Be Your Everything', '(Love Is) Thicker Than Water' and 'Shadow Dancing') filling the gaps between their own triumphs. This hit streak kept them buoyant until the end of the decade – 'Too Much Heaven', 'Tragedy' and 'Love You Inside Out' were also million-sellers, and Barry Gibb wrote and produced Frankie Valli's theme song to another smash movie musical, *Grease*. Even appearing themselves in a flop film, Stigwood's *Sergeant Pepper's Lonely Hearts Club Band*, did not dent the Gibb credibility too much.

As the disco boom faded, the group's chart momentum decelerated sharply in the 1980s. *Stayin' Alive*, the 1983 sequel to *Saturday Night Fever*, to which they similarly contributed, was a much lesser success, as were various solo recording projects which the brothers attempted. Their major successes during the 1980s were as writers/producers of hits for Barbra Streisand, Kenny Rogers, Dionne Warwick and Diana Ross.

A second hit comeback finally occurred in 1987, when 'You Win Again' topped the UK chart, the group received an Ivor Novello award for two decades of outstanding contribution to British music, and renewed worldwide exposure came on the 1988 Nelson Mandela Birthday concert. This renewed success was muted only by the sudden death in March 1988 of the trio's younger brother Andy, whose five-year US hit career they had virtually launched.

Greatest Hits

Singles	Title	US	UK
1967	Massachusetts	11	1
1968	I've Gotta Get A Message To You	8	1
1971	How Can You Mend A Broken Heart	1	–
1975	Jive Talkin'	1	5
1976	You Should Be Dancing	1	5
1977	How Deep Is Your Love	1	3
1978	Stayin' Alive	1	4
1978	Night Fever	1	1
1978	Too Much Heaven	1	3
1979	Tragedy	1	1
1979	Love You Inside Out	1	13
1987	You Win Again	75	1
Albums			
1968	Idea	–	4
1977	Saturday Night Fever (soundtrack)	1	1
1979	Spirits Having Flown	1	1
1979	Bee Gees Greatest	1	6

Pat BENATAR

Born in Long Island, New York, in 1953, Patricia Andrzejewski sang opera at college and was paying her way towards a future in health education as a singing waitress when a musical career began to seem more attractive. She was specializing in ballads until she won a talent contest in New York club and met manager Rick Newman, who steered her rock-wards after she changed her name and fronted a band featuring guitarist/songwriter Neil Geraldo, whom she later married.

In 1978 Benatar signed to Chrysalis Records, who placed her with producer Michael Chapman, hot after major hits with Blondie and The Knack. Her first album, 'In The Heat Of The Night' (1979), reached the US Top 20 and yielded two US Top 30 singles, 'Heartbreaker' and 'We Live For Love'. Her next album, 'Crimes Of Passion', produced by Keith Olsen, consolidated her position, peaking in the US Top 3 and providing a US Top 10 single, 'Hit Me With Your Best Shot', which crossed her over from rock to pop.

Benatar's frail persona contrasted with the standard raunchy hard rock female image and her powerful but pristine voice was given a fuller and more melodic range for her third album, 'Precious Time', which topped the US charts in the summer of 1981, and included two more US Top 20 singles, 'Fire And Ice' and 'Shadows Of The Night'. 'Get Nervous', her fourth album, reached the US Top 5 in late 1982 and was followed by 'Live From Earth'. One of the two songs on the album recorded in a studio, 'Love Is A Battlefield', became her first US Top 5 single and a major international hit, helped by an innovative video which added narrative to the song.

In late 1984 'We Belong' was another international hit, taken from her 'Tropico' album, and the theme song from *Legend of Billie Jean*, 'Invincible', reached No. 10 a year later, but she was becoming tired of touring and soon afterwards, took a break to start a family. Although she returned in 1988 with the 'Wide Awake In Dreamland' album, she resisted going back on the road to promote it.

Greatest Hits

Singles	Title	US	UK
1983	Love Is A Battlefield	5	49
1984	We Belong	5	22
Albums			
1980	Crimes Of Passion	2	–
1981	Precious Time	1	30

George BENSON

The ultimate cross-over artist, who managed to retain the credibility he enjoyed with jazz audiences despite a move from contemporary jazz guitar to easy listening-oriented vocals, Benson (born 1943) began playing professionally in his native Pittsburgh at the age of eight with local R&B bands, in which he sang, but showed greatest promise on the guitar. In 1954 he cut a single for RCA's Groove R&B label, 'It Shoulda' Been Me'.

A move to New York in 1963 saw him join organist Brother Jack McDuff, a star of the jazz-soul movement of the early 1960s. Two albums with McDuff brought him into contact with his prime instrumental influence, jazz guitar virtuoso Wes Montgomery. Benson signed with Columbia in 1966 to make albums under his own name, including 'It's Uptown' and 'Benson Burner'. He kept prestigious jazz company; his 'Giblet Gravy' album (1967) featured a quartet that also included pianist Herbie Hancock, and he was offered a job with Miles Davis, which he turned down, although he recorded with Davis in 1968.

After Wes Mongomery, who himself had a jazz guitar album in the US Top 20, 'A Day In The Life', died in 1969, his producer, Creed Taylor, signed Benson. Four albums

Benson – crossing over with quality

later, in 1971, Taylor set up a new jazz label, CTI, on which Benson made 'Beyond The Blue Horizon'. Although it didn't chart, a single from it, 'White Rabbit', received a lot of pop radio airplay. His CTI work hinted at things to come. While his guitar playing was high on quality but modest in sales, his vocal efforts were starting to bite through commercially. 'Bad Benson' was his best selling album for the label, reaching the US Top 100 in 1974. By this time he was an established part of the contemporary jazz mainstream, but with his sights set on more lucrative goals.

Signing with Warner Brothers in 1976 brought Benson the success he'd wanted. 'Breezin'' topped the US album chart, while a single from it, Leon Russell's 'This Masquerade', made the US Top 10. The album sold over a million, won three Grammy awards and established a change of emphasis from guitar to vocals. Previous labels A&M and CTI cashed in on his success. CTI re-released 'Good King Bad', while A&M reissued both 'The Other Side Of Abbey Road', a jazz guitar version of the entire Beatles album, and Benson's collaboration with jazz flautist Joe Farrell which made the US Top 100.

His second collection for Warners, 'In Flight' reached the US Top 10 and the UK Top 20, and at the same time covers of the old Nat Cole/Bobby Darin hits 'Nature The Night' and 'Turn Your Love Around' did well as singles. Benson continued to command the respect of fellow musicians and singers, regardless of critical reaction and clearly the wider public agreed. The title track from 'In

Your Eyes' was a UK Top 10 hit in 1983, and a TV-advertised 'Love Songs' collection topped the UK album charts two years later. Over ten years Benson chalked up more than a dozen US Top Ten hits as well as phenomenal album sales.

He dismisses criticism of 'selling out', insisting that if he wants wider success, it can be achieved by being 'fashionable' – anyway his performances, particularly live, possess a quality and taste that are second nature to him. Benson has never completely neglected the less commercial field in which he began. He still collaborates with jazz players like guitarist Earl Klugh, whom he partnered in the late 1960s.

Greatest Hits

Singles	Title	US	UK
1980	*Give Me The Night*	4	7
Albums			
1976	*Breezin'*	1	–
1980	*Give Me The Night*	3	3
1985	*Love Songs*	–	1

Chuck **BERRY**

Charles Edward Berry (born 1926) has an almost unique importance in rock music, both as one of its most individual early singer-player-songwriters, and as a huge influence upon the second generation of

major rock performers (notably including The Beatles and The Rolling Stones). This influence continues widely today, despite Berry's own eclipse as an innovator. Having acquired, during reputedly delinquent adolescent years in St Louis, musical influences ranging from the blues and Louis Jordan to Nat 'King' Cole and guitarist Les Paul, Berry led his own trio as a singer/guitarist in the city at the beginning of the 1950s, while training at the same time for a 'proper' job as a hairdresser and beautician.

The salon took a permanent back seat in 1955, when Muddy Waters saw Berry playing in Chicago, and recommended him to approach Chess Records. Signed on the strength of demos of self-penned material, he cut his debut single, 'Maybellene', which displayed most of the elements basic to his style: a jumpy blues/country rockabilly stew driven by a constant guitar riff, and a lyrical preoccupation with 1950s teenage materialism – cars and romance. With heavy support from pioneer rock'n'roll DJ Alan Freed (who took co-writing credit), it was a Top 5 smash in the US, bringing Berry *Billboard's* 'Most Promising R&B Artist' award for 1955, and elevating him to name status on the rock package tours organized by Freed and others. A cameo role in the movie *Rock Rock Rock* followed in 1956, and Berry also scored a second major hit with 'Roll Over Beethoven'.

His most consistent run of success began with 1957's keenly observed adolescent anthem, 'School Days', which was a million seller and his first UK success. 'Rock And Roll Music' followed, then 'Sweet Little Sixteen' (another million seller) and Berry's most-covered original, 'Johny B Goode'. He had a second film role, in Alan Freed's *Mr. Rock And Roll*, and in mid-1958, even appeared at the Newport Jazz Festival (filmed as *Jazz On A Summer's Day*). Berry's musical triumphs, however, were frequently offset by severe blows to his private life, particularly those of a legal nature. In mid-1959, he was charged with violating the Mann Act, by transporting a minor across a state line for immoral purposes. The case revolved around a Texan Indian girl employed in his St Louis nightclub, who later confessed to working as a child prostitute. The case against Berry was technical, and initially put aside amid suspicions of racism, but the system finally caught up with him, and he served time in a Federal Prison in 1962/63. His record sales had dwindled with the advent of the teen idol era, but in 1961 he had already inaugurated his major long-term business project, Berry Park, a 30-acre amusement area in his home state of Missouri.

While Berry was incarcerated, his back-catalogue's seminal influence on rock's young guns – Beach Boy Brian Wilson borrowed rhythms and adapted songs ('Sweet Little Sixteen' mutated into 'Surfin' USA'), and The Beatles, Stones and scores of other British groups covered and re-publicized their

Chuck Berry's guitar licks and teen-life lyrics encapsulated 'Fifties rock'n'roll

favourites – Chuck's own oldies were re-marketed in the UK as part of the 1963 R&B fad, and 'Memphis Tennessee' (issued to counter UK vocalist Dave Berry's cover) belatedly became his first UK Top 10 hit.

In 1964, free to tour and record again, Berry came back at full strength just as demand for him was peaking, and a new run of hits ensued: 'Nadine', 'No Particular Place To Go' (Top 10 on both sides of the Atlantic), 'You Never Can Tell' and 'Promised Land'. Their success prompted a new recording offer from Mercury Records as his Chess contract expired, and the $50,000 advance was too much for Berry's financially acquisitive instincts (he liked to be paid in cash, in advance) to resist. Commercially, the move was a disaster, producing a few records that were only interesting for their experimentation (like a bluesy set with The Steve Miller Band) but a totally hitless late 1960s. Eventually, an appearance at the Toronto Rock Festival in 1969, alongside John Lennon's Plastic Ono Band and several other major names, lifted Berry's public profile once again, and in 1970, he similarly boosted his musical credibility by re-signing to Chess Records and adding 'Tulane' to his *oeuvre* of classic songs.

1972 witnessed Berry's belated and unexpected commercial peak, as the *double-entendre* singalong, 'My Ding-A-Ling', an audience participation exercise recorded live in the UK, topped both British and American charts, becoming his all-time biggest seller (and its parent album, 'The Chuck Berry London Sessions', his biggest-selling LP). The remainder of the decade saw him fall back increasingly on rehashing past glories on stage, with little to offer on record. He portrayed his younger self effectively in the Alan Freed biopic *American Hot Wax*, but within a month of playing for President Carter at the White House, fell foul of the law again and was sentenced to four months in jail for tax evasion.

Berry's 60th birthday in 1986 was marked by a star-backed concert in St Louis, organized by Rolling Stone Keith Richards. This was filmed, and later appeared as the movie *Hail! Hail! Rock'n'Roll*, alongside the publication of Berry's autobiography. Promotional interviews for the latter hinted at upcoming retirement, and indeed the only subsequent Berry news has been bad news, with a further arrest in 1990 relating to alleged pornographic activities.

Greatest Hits

Singles	Title	US	UK
1958	Sweet Little Sixteen	2	16
1972	My Ding-A-Ling	1	1
Albums			
1963	Chuck Berry On Stage	29	6
1972	The London		
	Chuck Berry Sessions	8	–
1964	No Particular Place To Go	10	3

BLACK SABBATH

Tony Iommi (*guitar*)
Terry 'Geezer' Butler (*bass*)
John 'Ozzy' Osbourne (*vocals*)
Bill Ward (*drums*)

Straight out of the Midlands mafia of Birmingham beat in the late 1960s, Black Sabbath was formed by four musicians who had known each other since schooldays. Osbourne (born 1948) had worked with Rare Breed, Ward (born 1948) and Iommi (born 1948) with Mythology. After recruiting bass player Butler (born 1949), they played jazz-oriented blues under the name of Earth, then caught the post-Cream/Zeppelin bug of what was to become heavy metal. Jazz, and blues were sublimated to repetitive, volume-dominated riffs and a histrionic vocal approach; the name change in 1969 said it all – this was apocalyptic rock of the seminal variety.

Their eponymous debut album encouraged a press image of black magic and quasi-occultism with appropriate sound effects and lyrics that dwelt on death, doom and destruction. The album charted on both sides of the Atlantic. 'Paranoid' followed in 1971, the title track dealing with the topic of mental illness, even more taboo than drugs, despair and teen angst. The single of 'Paranoid' was their biggest hit, while the album topped the UK LP chart and stayed in its US equivalent for over a year.

Their albums continued to sell heavily with a loyal fan following in the UK, although the band was spending more and more time in the US, where their theatrics and basic approach appealed to teenagers as a rejection of progressive rock, that heralded pomp rock to come.

Iommi's wailing guitar and Osbourne's increasingly hysterical vocals were dominant, the two focal points of the band. For musical effect, but without disturbing the now established image of the band, a keyboard player (Gerald Woodruffe) operated from the wings in concerts, while Rick Wakeman performed the chore on 'Sabbath Bloody Sabbath' (1973).

The band's frantic schedule came to a temporary halt in 1974 with the collapse of their management company, but by 1976 they were back in the studios for 'Technical Ecstasy'. The time off had seen Iommi and Osbourne on musically divergent paths, and the former's insistence on a horn section for the album led to the latter's dissatisfaction and eventual departure in 1979. Although musically the changes were probably positive, Osbourne's stage presence was what fans identified with, and his own career now became the focus of attention for many of them, along with the attendant publicity which he was eager to court.

He was replaced by an American, Ronnie James Dio (born 1949), while Carmine Appice's brother, Vinnie, took over on drums from Bill Ward who was having health problems. Three big-selling albums followed – 'Heaven and Hell', 'Mob Rules' and 'Live Evil' – between 1980 and 1983, before the band split once again. A short stint with Ian Gillan on vocals produced 'Born Again' in 1983, before the band's final demise.

The 'Sabbath sound, by the mid-1980s regarded as pioneering in the by-then rampant heavy metal genre, lived on in Ozzy's solo activity, in which he featured ex-Sabbath material and perpetuated much of the outrage and shock appeal that characterized the original group.

The original line-up got together again for Live Aid in 1985, while Iommi put together a new band which released the album 'Seventh Star' in 1986 under the name 'Black Sabbath with Tony Iommi'. The album made the UK Top 30, but failed to precipitate a Sabbath revival on anything like the scale of their previous following.

Greatest Hits

Singles	Title	US	UK
1970	Paranoid	61	4
Albums			
1970	Black Sabbath	23	8
1970	Paranoid	12	1
1971	Master Of Reality	8	5
1973	Sabbath Bloody Sabbath	11	4
1981	Mob Rules	29	12
1983	Born Again	39	4

Satanic majesties – 'Sabbath success signalled demonic dabblings in the disc world

BLIND FAITH

Eric Clapton (guitar, vocals)
Steve Winwood (vocals, keyboards)
Ric Grech (bass)
Ginger Baker (drums)

The first band to be dubbed a 'super-group', Blind Faith emerged in mid-1969 from the ashes of Cream and Traffic, both of which had broken up towards the end of 1968. The band was completed by bass player Ric Grech (born Bordeaux, November 1946) drafted in from Family, whom he had left prior to their US tour.

Somewhat naïvely, Clapton and Winwood hoped they would be able to play together and escape the hullabaloo that had surrounded their previous bands. It became all too clear too soon that the rock'n'roll circus would be performing in overdrive to promote Blind Faith. The band's debut concert in London's Hyde Park in front of 100,000 people disappointed a crowd expecting Cream Mark 2. From there, the band went on the inevitable US tour playing the largest venues for the shortest time to earn the most money and there were ugly scenes as fans in huge arenas fought to get closer to the front. The tour effectively ended the band with Clapton quitting.

They left one album, 'Blind Faith', as their legacy. The cover, depicting a half naked girl of around eleven caused a stir, but despite a cool response from the critics, it topped the charts on both sides of the Atlantic. In retrospect, it was a quality product with some excellent playing and promise for the future – had the band stayed together. Winwood's influence dominated, but the stand-out track was Clapton's stately 'Presence of the Lord'.

After it was all over, Clapton took a breather behind Delaney and Bonnie, Winwood reformed Traffic, while Ric Grech followed Baker into the drummer's chaotic Airforce. During the early 1970s, Grech played on a number of sessions from Gram Parsons

to The Bee Gees, but later faded from view. Alcohol took its toll and sadly he died in March 1990 of medical complications arising from a haemorrhage.

Greatest Hits

Albums	Title	US	UK
1969	*Blind Faith*	1	1

BLONDIE (and Deborah HARRY)

Deborah Harry (vocals)
Chris Stein (guitar)
Fred Smith (bass)
Billy O'Connor (drums)

A unique synthesis of New Wave rock credibility with traditional showbiz glamour, courtesy of an eye-catching vocalist, Blondie were the major success story of America's mid-1970s punk movement. Formed in New York in 1974 from the remnants of The Stilettos, a local outfit with three female singers plus backing musicians, Blondie only retained Harry (born 1945) as vocalist, and a backing trio led by Stein (born 1950). Initially sticking to a 1960s-styled girl group repertoire, they played regularly at CBGB'S club, where the New York punk movement was busily fermenting, and soaked up influences from fellow regulars like Tom Verlaine's Television.

1975 saw personnel changes – O'Connor left for law school and was replaced by Clem Burke (born 1955), Smith joined Television and made way for Gary Valentine, and Jimmy Destri (keyboards) expanded the group into a quintet. This line-up cut the LP 'Blondie' (1976) with producer Richard Gottehrer; issued on Private Stock, in early 1977 it helped the group secure a national US tour with Iggy Pop, and a UK visit supporting Television, after which Valentine left, and

Frank Infante replaced him for the recording of a second LP with Gottehrer. By then, Blondie's contract had been purchased by Chrysalis, who released the album, 'Plastic Letters'. While Blondie were shuffling personnel again (Infante moved to guitar and British bass player Nigel Harrison joined), their revival of the hit by Randy & The Rainbows, 'Denise' (retitled 'Denis'), which was extracted from 'Plastic Letters', became a UK Top 3 hit in 1978. The album also reached the UK Top 10, but only made the US Top 75.

Blondie's US and worldwide breakthrough came via their next album, 'Parallel Lines', produced by former glitterpop specialist Mike Chapman, who refined their spiky sound. The key single was the disco-flavoured 'Heart of Glass', which topped the UK chart in 1979 and repeated the feat in the US, just ahead of a second UK No. 1, 'Sunday Girl'. At this time, Debbie Harry was a pop music icon, who completely transcended the image of the group as a whole, and this charisma, plus a flair for acting, helped her to a dramatic role in the film *Union City*, for which Chris Stein wrote the music, while in Europe Blondie remained among the most consistent hitmakers.

Their 'Eat To The Beat' album (late 1979) spun off further hits in 'Atomic' and 'Union City Blue' (written for, but not used in, the movie), while another transatlantic No. 1 single early in 1980 was 'Call Me', featured on the soundtrack of the Richard Gere movie *American Gigolo*, a one-off production by German disco wizard Giorgio Moroder, who had written the instrumental track to which Harry added a lyric. She also had another 1980 movie role, opposite singer Meat Loaf in *Roadie*.

At the end of 1980, the album 'Auto-american' produced two more million-selling singles, the reggae-styled 'The Tide Is High' (written by John Holt and originally cut by Jamaican group The Paragons) and the surreal rap-rocker 'Rapture' but at this point the Blondie bubble burst, strained by internal dissent – Infante even sued the others, claiming exclusion from group decisions. Harry cut a solo album with Chic producers Nile Rodgers and Bernard Edwards, the artistically and commercially lacklustre 'Koo Koo', which was followed by the final Blondie LP, 'The Hunter'. Despite Chapman's continued production presence, it used weaker material and seemed to lack conviction, and few were surprised when the group broke up in October 1982.

As their former colleagues moved off into other work (Destri made a solo album, 'Heart On A Wall' in 1981, while Burke later joined The Eurythmics), Harry and Stein stayed together as a couple (as they had been for some years), and co-wrote a book about the group, but otherwise followed solo projects. Harry starred opposite James Woods in the controversial film *Videodrome*, while Stein

Winwood, Grech, Baker and Clapton rehearsing short-lived supergroup Blind Faith

'The Monroe of the 'Seventies' Deborah Harry became the sex symbol of punk with Blondie

launched his own label, Animal Records, but when he was struck down by a debilitating disease, Harry retired from all performing to devote herself to nursing him back to health.

In the late 1980s, Harry returned, as an actress (in the John Waters film *Hairspray*), and – with vocal style and image little changed – as a singer. Her 1987 album 'Rockbird' spun off a strong comeback single, 'French Kissin' (In The USA)', and 1989's gently self-mocking 'Def, Dumb and Blonde' did similarly with 'I Want That Man'. In 1990, Harry joined a host of acts (including U2 and Neneh Cherry) in contributing to the AIDS-benefit album of Cole Porter tunes, 'Red Hot and Blue'.

Greatest Hits

Singles	Title	US	UK
1979	*Heart Of Glass*	I	I
1979	*Sunday Girl*	–	I
1980	*Atomic*	39	I
1980	*Call Me*	I	I
1980	*The Tide Is High*	I	I
1981	*Rapture*	I	5
Albums			
1978	*Parallel Lines*	6	I
1979	*Eat To The Beat*	17	I

BLOOD, SWEAT and TEARS

Al Kooper (keyboards, vocals)
Steve Katz (guitar, vocals)
Fred Lipsius (saxophone, piano)
Dick Halligan (trombone, flute, keyboards)
Randy Brecker (trumpet)
Jerry Weiss (trumpet)
Jim Fielder (bass)
Bobby Colomby (drums)

Formed by former Bob Dylan session player Al Kooper (born 1944), after the disbandment of Blues Project, Blood, Sweat and Tears were, in their time, more influential than their short-lived success would suggest.

Born in New York City, Kooper had a solid background in rock dating back to 1958 when he was a member of the Royal Teens, who had a US Top 10 hit with 'Short Shorts'. As an apprentice recording engineer, he gained a reputation as a session guitarist, before teaming up with songwriters Irvine Levine and Bob Brass, with whom he wrote a US No. 1 hit, 'This Diamond Ring', for Gary Lewis And The Playboys in 1965. After playing organ on Bob Dylan's classic 'Like A Rolling Stone', he formed The Blues Project with Steve Katz (born 1945) in 1966.

They made three albums before disbanding in 1968, when Kooper and Katz formed the original rock quartet version of BS&T, with Fielder (born 1947) and Colomby (born 1944). The line-up was almost immediately augmented by a four-piece horn section involving Brecker (born 1945), Weiss (born 1946), Halligan (born 1943) and Lipsius (born 1943) and set the so-called 'jazz rock' style that became the band's trademark in their debut album 'Child Is Father To The Man' (1968). The LP made the US and UK Top 50 with its mix of Kooper originals and covers, but the band seemed doomed when in early 1969 Kooper, Weiss and Brecker left.

Against all odds the replacements – British-Canadian vocalist David Clayton-Thomas (born 1941) and a new trumpet section of Lew Soloff (born 1944) and Chuck Winfield (born 1943) took the band to new heights. Their debut album, 'Blood, Sweat and Tears', topped the US chart for seven weeks. The big voice of Clayton-Thomas against 'sophisticated' horn arrangements

Blood, Sweat and Tears – smooth arrangements represented the 'acceptable' face of rock

appealed to the fledgling AOR market, who put three singles from the LP into the US Top 3 slot, each selling over a million copies: 'You've Made Me So Very Happy', 'Spinning Wheel' and Laura Nyro's 'And When I Die'. By the end of 1969 the album had sold two million copies and won a Grammy Award as Album of the Year.

The 'respectable' appeal of this crossover fusion, which santized both the rock and jazz content, led to the band's being promoted by the US Information Agency to its overseas officials as an example of 'cultural developments in the homeland'. This led directly to a 1970 State Department tour of Romania, Poland and Yogoslavia. Their third album, 'Blood, Sweat and Tears 3' topped the US chart for two weeks in 1970 and made the UK Top 20, while a single, 'Hi-De-Ho', was a US Top 20 hit. Despite the next album, 'BS&T4' making the US Top 10, frequent changes of personnel culminated in Clayton-Thomas leaving for a solo career in 1972.

Lesser releases followed, and Clayton-Thomas returned in 1974. The only remaining original member, drummer Colomby, left in 1976, after which a new line-up acquired a new deal with ABC Records, but only modest sales resulted. The band effectively folded in the 1980s, but Clayton-Thomas surfaces from time to time – most recently in 1988 – to play live dates under the BS&T banner – the name sold 35 million records at its peak when it was synonymous with the 'acceptable' face of rock during the early 1970s.

Greatest Hits

Singles	Title	US	UK
1969	*You've Made Me So Very Happy*	2	35
1969	*Spinning Wheel*	2	–
1969	*And When I Die*	2	–
Albums			
1969	*Blood Sweat and Tears*	1	15
1970	*Blood Sweat and Tears 3*	1	14

BLUE OYSTER CULT

Eric Bloom (guitar, vocals)
Allen Lanier (keyboards, synthesizers)
Albert Bouchard (drums, vocals)
Joe Bouchard (bass, vocals)
Donald 'Buck Dharma' Roeser (guitar, vocals)

The favourite heavy-metal band of rock critics, Blue Oyster Cult were formed in 1970 in New York under the auspices of *Crawdaddy* writer Sandy Pearlman, who fancied himself as a lyricist, and fellow scribe Richard Meltzer, who fancied himself as a part-time vocalist. After a couple of false starts under names like The Stalk Forrest Group and Soft White Underbelly and an album for Elektra that has never been released, they signed with CBS in 1971, by which time Pearlman had become their manager/producer.

Their self-titled debut album that year blended subtlety with savage and spellbinding guitar outbursts from Roeser, who laid down the group's quintessential style with 'Cities On Fire With Rock'n'Roll'. The band's much heralded mystical qualities – aided and abetted by near inaudible lyrics – were further enhanced by a logo supposedly belonging to offspring-eating Greek God Chronos.

It was two years before their next album, but they didn't miss another year during the rest of the 1970s. 'Tyranny And Mutation' (1973), 'Secret Treaties' (1974) and the live double album, 'On Your Feet Or On Your Knees' (1976), furthered the group's reputation by occasionally diving off the deep end and leaving behind a haunting impression, but 'Agents Of Fortune' also in 1976, brought them commercial success with Roeser's Byrds-influenced '(Don't Fear) The Reaper', which reached the Top 20 of the singles charts on both sides of the Atlantic, spending over three months in both charts and becoming one of the all-time classic rock tracks. The album also featured a guest vocal appearance (and a couple of songs) by Lanier's girlfriend Patti Smith, who had previously supplied a track for 'Secret Treaties'.

They retreated to their inner sanctum for 'Spectres' (1977) and another live album, 'Some Enchanted Evening' (1978), after which they opted for a more traditional heavy-metal approach. 'Mirrors' (1979) and 'Cultosaurus Erectus' found the group running low on ideas, although they raised a minor US hit with 'Burnin' For You' in 1981 from their roller-coaster concept album, 'Fire Of Unknown Origin'.

Soon afterwards, drummer Albert Bouchard, one of the main songwriters in the

More myth than magic, Blue Oyster Cult

band, left. The suspicion that the tensions that the band had hitherto thrived on were starting to hold them back grew when Roeser started releasing a series of Buck Dharma solo albums containing stronger material than the band were producing. Nevertheless, they ploughed their way through the 1980s, briefly linking up with British sci-fi writer Michael Moorcock along the way, and they continue to lead a charmed, if not charming life.

Greatest Hits

Singles	Title	US	UK
1976	*(Don't Fear) The Reaper*	12	15
Albums			
1975	*On Your Feet Or On Your Knees*	22	–
1981	*Fire Of Unknown Origin*	24	–

The **BLUES BROTHERS**

Joliet Jake Blues (John Belushi) (vocals)
Elwood Blues (Dan Aykroyd) (harmonica, vocals)

Steve Cropper (guitar)
Matt Murphy (guitar)
Paul Shaffer (keyboards)
Donald 'Duck' Dunn (bass)
Steve Jordan (drums)
Lou Marini (saxophone)
Tom Scott (saxophone)
Alan Rubin (trumpet)
Tom Malone (horns)

Originally a comedy concept for US comedians Belushi (born 1949) and Aykroyd, The Blues Brothers, backed by authentic R&B stars like Cropper and Dunn (both ex-Booker T & The MGs), were for a short time highly successful, both on film and as recording stars.

In 1978 the band cut 'Briefcase Full Of Blues', which topped the US album chart and included a US Top 20 single, 'Soul Man'. A project launched as a novelty had become a smash hit, and then became a feature film, which also involved soul greats like Ray Charles, James Brown and Aretha Franklin, who all appeared on the soundtrack album. The backing band was similar, but with Murphy Dunne replacing Shaffer and Willie Hall instead of Jordan, and the album, which made the US Top 20 in 1980, included a US Top 20 single, 'Gimme Some Lovin' '.

However, it was never likely that what had started as an affectionate joke could be sustained for long, and after the less successful 'Made In America' album (also 1980), the idea was rested in favour of other comedy concepts. When *The Blues Brothers* was released on video, it instantly became a hit, as had the movie ten years earlier. The Blues Brothers could easily have been revived during the 1980s, had not Belushi died of a drug overdose in 1982 – while he had moved

Aykroyd and Belushi (the ones wearing the shades) front the allstar Blues Brothers band

into the music industry with great success, he ironically also died a classic rock-star death. An album titled 'Best Of The Blues Brothers' was a minor US hit shortly before he died.

In 1990, the band, with different vocalists, toured the world with great success under The Blues Brothers banner.

Greatest Hits

Albums	Title	US	UK
1978	*Briefcase Full Of Blues*	1	–
1980	*The Blues Brothers –*		
	Original Soundtrack	13	–

Marc **BOLAN** and **T. REX**

When he died in a road accident in 1977, Marc Bolan was emerging from one of several nadirs suffered since his pop career waned earlier in the decade. On the evidence of steady posthumous album sales and an undiminishing following rabid for any recording on which he's even breathed, there was every chance that Bolan would have made a chart comeback – albeit less sustainable than when he rose from the underground to glam-rock superstardom in 1971.

A former child actor, London Mod Mark Feld (born 1947) modelled clothes before becoming folk-singer 'Toby Tyler' when the hunt was on for a British 'answer' to Bob Dylan (see separate entry). When the job went to Donovan (see separate entry), Feld Tyler spent several months in Paris from which he returned with his familiar stage name, and an interest in magic and mythology. All aspects of this new image were discernible on Bolan's first single, 1965's 'The Wizard'.

After an inauspicious television debut (on *Ready Steady Go*) with his third single, 'Hippy Gumbo', Bolan's manager, Simon Napier

Bell, persuaded him to join John's Children, an early psychedelic group, but soon after they'd scored a minor hit with the risqué 'Desdemona' – a Bolan composition – he left to form Tyrannosaurus Rex.

Though originally conceived as an amplified quintet, the new outfit made its name as a duo with Bolan cross-legged on a prayer mat, warbling to his acoustic guitar. He was accompanied by hand-percussionist Steve Peregrine-Took (died 1980) who was replaced in 1969 by Micky Finn, another denizen of the hippy community centred round London's Ladbroke Grove. From humble beginnings as buskers, Tyrannosaurus Rex became regular

fixtures at the 'happenings' that filled the alternative culture's social calendar in flower-power England. Championed by hip Radio One disc jockeys – notably John Peel – Bolan and his partner's albums (mostly bearing long and fanciful titles) hovered just inside the Top 20 of the UK album chart, demonstrating that attendant singles in the lower reaches of the Top 50 were but a surface manifestation of a deeper groundswell of support.

On all his records, Bolan's often indecipherable vibrato was a constant factor but, after employing 'cello, organ and electric bass on Tyrannosaurus Rex's fourth album, there was an increasing emphasis on electric instrumentation and a fuller production. With its cover photograph of Bolan gripping a solid-body Stratocaster, 1971's 'T. Rex' album was the link between Tyrannosaurus Rex and the 'T. Rexstasy' – akin to Beatlemania – that, while alienating Bolan's older audience, would peak in 1973 at Wembley's Empire Pool when a scream-rent performance was documented in *Born to Boogie*, Ringo Starr's first essay as a film director. As well as T. Rex's grip on the Top 5 in many territories (with the US a conspicuous exception) for two fat years, Bolan's income was supplemented by *The Warlock of Love* – a best-selling volume of his poems – and chart-busting re-issues of Tyrannosaurus Rex product.

While the pixified scenarios of Bolan's lyrics remained, these were now underlined by chugging hard rock – frequently augmented by strings, horns and vocal chorale – instead of the pattering bongos and lone acoustic of yore. Though 1972's 'Children of the Revolution' was a marked change of pace, 'T. Rex's overall adherence to the formula established

The 'bopping elf' becomes Electric Warrior as post-hippy Bolan spearheads glam rock

by its first two chart-toppers was partly to blame for Bolan's sudden chart decline in late 1973. Through a combination of an acquired teen-idol arrogance and his excessive thrift, he also lost his wife and assistant manager, June Child – and, crucially, the services of producer Tony Visconti who also worked with David Bowie (see separate entry).

There was always a competitive edge to Bolan and Bowie's friendship, and, to Marc's chagrin, David was chief among those out-flanking him in the glam-rock stakes. A year-long tax exile in the US in 1975 compounded Bolan's standing as a has-been whose vinyl output now included cover versions, thinly disguised plagiarisms and further desperate strategies to regain his lost glory.

Onstage, however, it was business as usual as demonstrated by a sold-out UK tour in 1976, supported by The Damned – for whom Bolan was something of an icon. Indeed, he was one of the few older pop stars generally palatable to punk devotees and practitioners. This acceptance was reciprocated when New Wave acts were invited to appear after Bolan gladly agreed to host a TV children's pop series a few months before his death. Each week, he was allocated time to give the cheering boys and girls selections from his backlog of hits – a most fitting valediction.

Greatest Hits

Singles	Title	US	UK
1971	Hot Love	–	1
1971	Get It On (retitled		
	Bang a Gong in US)	10	1
1972	Telegram Sam	–	1
Albums			
1971	Electric Warrior	32	1
1972	My People Were Fair And Had Stars In Their Hair But Now They're Content To Wear Stars On Their Brow Prophets/Seers And Sages And The Angels Of The Ages (double album re-issue)	–	1
1972	Bolan Boogie	–	1

BON JOVI

John Bon Jovi (vocals)
Richie Sambora (guitar)
David Bryan (keyboards)
Alec Such (bass)
Tico Torres (drums)

Few bands played more gigs than Bon Jovi in the latter half of the 1980s and their reward was to start the 1990s as the top-selling hard rock band on the planet.

John Bongiovi, as he was born in 1962, paid his dues on the New Jersey bar circuit and worked briefly as an assistant at the legendary New York Power Station studio.

Sheer hard work put New Jersey's Jovi in the pantheon of power-pop megastars

Encouraged by a demo recording of 'Runaway' that became a turntable hit in Detroit, Denver, New York and Minneapolis, he assembled a group, which he named Bon Jovi, for what was supposed to be a brief club tour, but they enjoyed the experience so much that the other members left their previous bands and after touring America with ZZ Top, Bon Jovi signed to Mercury in July 1983.

'Runaway', featured on their self-titled debut album released in 1984, was a minor hit. Their second album, '7800 Degrees Fahrenheit', briefly reached the US Top 40 the following year, but spent most of the autumn bubbling under. It contained no hit singles, but the group's reputation was growing on both sides of the Atlantic via constant tours – they were introduced to Europe on a Kiss tour – and soon after the release in September 1986, of their third album, 'Slippery When Wet', produced by Bruce Fairbairn, they exploded with two US chart-topping singles: 'You Give Love a Bad Name' and 'Livin On A Prayer'. A third single, 'Wanted, Dead Or Alive', proved their staying power, and the album spent two months at No. 1 and over a year in the charts, selling 14 million copies worldwide.

By the spring of 1987, their first two albums had both gone platinum, and their US tour that year set records for gross receipts, speed of ticket sales and band merchandise, as they played to two million people over 135 gigs. During the tour, members of Journey, Van Halen, Kiss, Cheap Trick, Def Leppard, and Motley Crue all jostled in the wings to appear on the band's encore jams.

The band had no difficulty writing while on the road and supplied Cher's comeback hit, 'We All Sleep Alone', and songs for Ted Nugent, Cinderella and Loverboy, as well as contributing a track titled 'Back Door Santa' to the Special Olympics benefit LP at the end of 1987. Even so, they still had to whittle 30 songs down to 11 for their next more personal

album, 'New Jersey', released in September 1988, which was recorded in Vancouver again with Bruce Fairbairn producing. While 'New Jersey' failed to match the phenomenal sales of 'Slippery When Wet', it still sold nine million copies and produced two more hit singles, 'Bad Medicine' and 'Born To Be My Baby', as the band toured the world yet again, including a headline appearance at the Moscow Peace Festival in 1989. 'New Jersey' was also the first American rock album to be released in the USSR on the state-owned Melodiya label.

When the band finally took a break, Jon Bon Jovi embarked on a movie soundtrack album, released in the summer of 1990, which featured contributions from Jeff Beck, Elton John and Little Richard. Jon's backing band featured Waddy Wachtel and Aldo Nova on guitar, Journey's Randy Jackson (bass), John Cougar Mellencamp's Kenny Aronoff (drums) and Benmont Tench, of Tom Petty & The Heartbreakers (keyboards).

Greatest Hits

Singles	Title	US	UK
1986	You Give Love A Bad Name	1	14
1987	Livin' On A Prayer	1	4
Albums			
1986	Slippery When Wet	1	6
1988	New Jersey	1	1

Gary U.S. **BONDS**

Bonds (born Gary Anderson, 1939) is a rare example of the rock artist who managed two quite separate peaks of popularity, with the best part of two decades in between.

In 1959 Gary Anderson was living in Norfolk, Virginia, where he fronted local rock band The Turks. Record shop owner Frank

Guida signed them to record in the primitive studio behind his store, and they cut 'New Orleans', written by Guida as a C&W number, but stomped into a rocker by the band and given a weird 'outdoor' feel by the studio's odd acoustics. Guida released it on his own LeGrand label, and the singer, expecting it to be credited to Gary Anderson & The Turks, was shocked to hear a local DJ announce the disc as 'U.S. Bonds'. Guida apparently couldn't resist the lure of 'buy U.S. Bonds' as a PR campaign.

'New Orleans' reached the US Top 10 at the end of 1960, and began an 18-month run of similarly styled hits, the biggest being the immediate follow-up 'Quarter To Three', which topped the US chart in June 1961 and sold over a million, despite being recorded when all concerned were more than a little drunk. Others included 'School Is Out', its sequel 'School Is In', and two cash-ins on the 1962 dance craze: 'Dear Lady Twist' and 'Twist Twist Senora'. The later hits were credited to Gary U.S. Bonds, after the pertinent US authority had decided that enough was enough.

Bonds continued to play live dates and to write songs through the 1960s and 70s, but a chance meeting with long-time fan Bruce Springsteen (who had long performed 'Quarter To Three' on stage) at a New Jersey club in 1978 led to his rediscovery by the mainstream. Springsteen and Miami Steve van Zandt produced the album 'Dedication' in 1980 and its follow-up 'On the Line' in 1982, both being released by EMI and restoring Bonds to the charts. A second run of chartmaking singles was also extracted from these LPs, the biggest being the Springsteen-penned 'This Little Girl' and 'Out Of Work'. In the mid-1980s, Bonds put together a new band called The American Men, and moved on to produce his own records. Although his chart flame dimmed again, the Springsteen-associated comeback has continued to keep his profile high as a live attraction.

'Quarter To Three' a quarter-century smash

Greatest Hits

Singles	Title	US	UK
1960	*New Orleans*	6	16
1961	*Quarter To Three*	1	7
Albums			
1961	*Dance 'Til Quarter To Three*	6	–

BONZO DOG DOO-DAH BAND

Vivian Stanshall (vocals)
Neil Innes (vocals, piano)
Rodney Slater (sax, trumpet)
Roger Ruskin Spear (sax, kazoo, robots)
Vernon Dudley Bowhay-Nowell (guitar, banjo)
Sam Spoons (percussion)
'Legs' Larry Smith (drums)

Formed in 1965 out of a very British tradition of musical pastiche and surrealism, the original Bonzo Dog Doo Dah Band continued the rock tradition established by The Alberts and The Temperance Seven in the traditional jazz movement of the early 1960s. Based at an art college in London, they mixed 1920s jazz, blues, musical parody and theatrical anarchy as the Bonzo Dog *Dada* Band.

Their line-up fluctuated wildly, with up to thirty participants on stage at times, though they reduced to a septet for work on the London pub scene. Roger Spear (born 1943) made a kinetic contribution – gadgets and robots that frequently ran amok on stage. Due to its increasing complexity, the band moved to the club and college cabaret circuit, cutting a 1966 single, 'My Brother Makes The Noises For The Talkies', without success. A follow-up did no better, but a change of label in 1967 resulted in the 'Gorilla' album, which despite mediocre sales became an instant cult item and pointed to the increasingly rock-oriented direction of their musical humour.

A cameo appearance in The Beatles movie, *Magical Mystery Tour*, established their hip credibility, and a residency on TV's satirical *Do Not Adjust Your Set* series confirmed them as a part of the humorous style adopted by the Monty Python team, some of whom also worked on *Do Not Adjust Your Set*. 1968 saw the departure of Spoons and Bowhay-Nowell, and the recruitment of a bass player Dennis Cowan (born 1947), in its move towards rock. Paul McCartney (under the pseudonym Apollo C. Vermouth) produced 'I'm The Urban Spaceman', a UK Top 5 hit single, and their 1969 album, 'The Doughnut In Granny's Green House', also charted, as did 'Tadpoles' in the same year.

A US tour supporting Sly And The Family Stone (!) did nothing to help their morale, and after the album 'Keynsham' they disbanded. Smith (born 1944) and Slater (born 1944) followed Bowhay-Nowell and Spoons

The Bonzos – art school anarchy rampant in rock and robots revue

to Bob Kerr's Whoopee Band, an outfit like The Temperance Seven and similar to the original art school Bonzos. Ruskin Spear took his robots onto the college and art centre circuit as his Giant Kinetic Wardrobe, while Stanshall (born 1943) and Innes (born 1944) joined a satire/poetry revue also involving ex-members of The Scaffold and Liverpool Scene, under the title of Grimms.

Stanshall introduced his 'Sir Henry At Rawlinson End' on a 1972 reunion LP, 'Let's Make Up And Be Friendly', developing the character in the early 1980s for a book and feature film. He also acted as narrator in sections of Mike Oldfield's 'Tubular Bells' in 1973. While 'Legs' Larry cropped up as a polka-dot suited compete on US tours by Elton John and Eric Clapton, Innes – after forming a group he called The World – develop his association with Monty Python member Eric Idle in the *Rutland Weekend Television* series. This in turn spawned the Rutles, the definitive Beatles send-up, which began as a TV film (with George Harrison appearing in it) followed by an album. Each musical period of the 'Pre-Fab Four' was affectionately parodied, Innes doing most of the arranging, playing and singing himself.

A 1976 album, 'Rutland Times', perpetuated the RWTV myth, and Innes continued to tour, either with Python packages or his own occasional band Fatso. A double album, 'History of the Bonzos' appeared in 1974. Viv Stanshall emerged again in 1985 with a Christmas musical *Stinkfoot*, while Innes continues to work in TV shows, commercials, and on a variety of related projects.

Greatest Hits

Singles	Title	US	UK
1968	I'm The Urban Spaceman	–	5
Albums			
1969	The Doughnut In Granny's Greenhouse	–	40
1969	Tadpoles	–	36

BOOKER T & The MG'S

Booker T Jones (organ)
Steve Cropper (guitar)
Lewis Steinberg (base)
Al Jackson Jr (drums)

Booker T (born 1944) & The MG's (an acronym for 'Memphis Group') were the studio house band of Memphis's Stax label during the 1960s and early 1970s, playing on record behind (and backing on stage) acts like Otis Redding, Sam & Dave and Eddie Floyd. They also found major success as one of the USA's most readily identifiable instrumental groups.

The original quartet had been Stax house musicians for some time, and Cropper (born

The ultimate studio house band (left to right) Jones, Steinberg, Jackson and Cropper

1941) had played in the Mar-Keys (whose 'Last Night' was a 1961 million-seller), when in 1962 they cut two of their own instrumentals in spare studio time at the end of a session with singer Billy Lee Riley. Stax released them as a single, and 'Green Onions' sold a million (having started life as the B-side, before its bluesy organ/guitar interplay proved irresistible). Though mainly confined to the studio and thus rarely playing live in the early years, the group followed their smash with a few smaller hits and some successful albums, whose contents tended to re-hash hits by other using The MG's signature sound (like The Ventures). In 1964, the unpunctual Steinberg was replaced by Donald 'Duck' Dunn (born 1941), another ex-Mar-Key, to complete The MGs' classic line up.

In 1967 the group toured Europe with Otis Redding, and also backed him at the Monterey Pop Festival, while three years later they supported Creedence Clearwater Revival at London's Royal Albert Hall. This heightened profile boosted record sales, and later hits included covers of the Young Rascals hit, 'Groovin'', the movie theme 'Hang 'Em High', the Caribbean-tinged 'Soul Limbo' (later BBC-TV's cricket coverage theme), and 'Time Is Tight', their second biggest seller and a Top 10 US and UK hit, included in Jones's score for Jules Dassin's film *Uptight*.

Following an idiosyncratic cover of the entire Beatles 'Abbey Road' LP, titled 'McLemore Avenue' (the Stax studio address), and the musically mature 'Melting Pot', the group collapsed when Jones, tired of studio constraint, left in May, 1971, and was soon followed by Cropper. The quartet worked apart during the first half of the 1970s – Dunn and Jackson as sessionmen, (making an unsuccessful MG's album with Bobby Manuel and Carson Whitsett in the vacant roles), Cropper as a freelance producer/occasional soloist, and Jones, who moved to LA with his new wife, Priscilla Coolidge (sister of Rita), as a producer and recording vocalist.

In October 1975 Jackson was killed by an intruder in his home, and a group reunion

seemed impossible, but surprisingly they occasionally reformed after 1977, either as Booker T & The MGs (for a poor LP on Asylum) or playing in bands like Levon Helm's RCO All-Stars and the Blues Brothers Band. Cropper and Dunn were mainstays of this combo who backed comedians John Belushi and Dan Aykroyd, and appeared in the eponymous movie. In 1979, 'Green Onions' at last became a major UK hit after its inclusion as a 'mod anthem' in The Who-inspired 1960s nostalgia film, *Quadrophenia*.

Jones and Cropper recorded solo albums during the 1980s, but at the start of the 1990s, Booker T & The MGs reunited once again at the MIDEM festival on a bill of classic 1960s soul performers.

Greatest Hits

Singles	Title	US	UK
1962	Green Onions	3	7
			(in 1979)
1969	Time Is Tight	6	4
Albums			
1962	Green Onions	33	11
1971	Melting Pot	43	–

BOOMTOWN RATS

Bob Geldof (vocals)
Johnny Fingers (keyboards/vocals)
Gerry Cott (guitar)
Pete Briquette (bass/vocals)
Garry Roberts (guitar/vocals)
Simon Crowe (drums/vocals)

Alongside The Sex Pistols, The Jam and The Clash, arguably the most talented and vital group to emerge from the late 1970s' UK Punk/New Wave trip, The Boomtown Rats were formed in 1975 in Dun Laoghaire, Eire, by Dubliner Geldof (born 1954). Known initially as The Nightlife Thugs, and briefly as Bound For Glory, they eventually took their name from that of the gang in a Woody Guthrie book. Although at first a heads-down R&B band, they changed under the influence of ex-rock journalist Geldof, their most articulate and belligerent member, who found himself increasingly obliged not only to write lyrics but also to sing them and, although it was not his intention to front the band, he eventually became a fine vocalist.

The group made an instant impact on a jaded Irish Rock scene, establishing a massive local reputation, and quickly attracting sundry UK A&R scouts, before eventually signing with Ensign, a relatively new independent label, and moving to London in 1976, where they began working the clubs and the burgeoning punk circuit. Geldof's angst-ridden material sat easily on the back of the New Wave (although he went to some lengths to deny that they were a Punk band), and after supporting Tom Petty & The Heartbreakers on a UK tour, their eponymous debut album emerged in 1977. It registered immediately, making the UK Top 20 and spawning two UK hit singles, 'Looking After No. 1' and 'Mary Of The Fourth Form.' Their second album, 'Tonic For The Troops', established them as a bona fide first division group, remaining in the UK album charts for almost a year and providing further hit singles in 'She's So Modern', 'Like Clockwork' and 'Rat Trap', their first UK No. 1.

Inevitably, comparisons were drawn with the early Rolling Stones – Geldof's onstage posturings and Jaggerisms were too obvious to be ignored, and with his flair for self-publicity, he welcomed the chance to be spokesman for a generation. Verbose, eloquent, and with a sharp wit, his endearing Irish brogue rapidly established him as a mainstream media figure.

In 1979, the group undertook a successful international tour, consolidating their status with their biggest-selling single, the controversial 'I Don't Like Mondays' (inspired by Geldof's reaction to an incident in California when a bored 16-year-old girl randomly shot and wounded eight of her schoolchums and killed her headmaster and janitor, explaining her actions thus: 'I don't like Mondays – this livens up the day'). Although it topped the UK charts for a month (propelled by a powerful video) and was their only US hit single, its progress in the US was impaired by an unofficial radio embargo, as the girl's parents fought to get the record banned.

The resultant album, 'The Fine Art Of Surfacing', included two further hits, 'Diamond Smiles' and 'Someone's Looking At You', but in truth, they had peaked and although 'Mondo Bongo' (1981) achieved their highest UK album chart placing (and yielded their last big single, 'Banana Republic'), it vanished quickly as they became unfashionable virtually overnight. 1982's 'V Deep' peaked well outside the UK Top 50, and was their last chart album. Geldof's street credi-

bility, already impaired by frequent TV appearances, had taken a further dive following his appearance in the movie version of Pink Floyd's The Wall, but in 1984, with his career at a seriously low ebb, he threw himself tirelessly and selflessly into the Band Aid project, co-writing 'Do They Know It's Christmas?' with Ultravox's Midge Ure and bullying the UK record industry and many of his fellow artists to create what rapidly became the UK's biggest-selling single of all time, with all the proceeds going to famine-racked Ethiopia.

This in turn led to the huge Live Aid event in 1985, which Geldof again tirelessly masterminded and organised, and which subsequently earned him a well-deserved knighthood. The Boomtown Rats disintegrated at around this juncture, and Geldof has since pursued an erratic solo career, earning guarded praise for his two solo albums, 'Deep In The Heart Of Nowhere' (1986) and 1990's 'The Vegetarians Of Love', which each spun off a UK hit single, 'This Is The World Calling' and 'The Great Song Of Indifference' respectively. He remains something of a mainstream media personality (he has probably earned more from his autobiography. Is That It?, and an appearance in a TV commercial for milk than he ever did as a Boomtown Rat), yet he cannot yet be totally written off musically.

Greatest Hits

Singles	Title	US	UK
1978	Rat Trap	–	1
1979	I Don't Like Mondays	73	1
1980	Someone's Looking At You	–	4
1980	Banana Republic	–	3
1990	The Great Song Of Indifference (Bob Geldof solo)	–	15
Albums			
1978	Tonic For The Troops	112	8
1979	The Fine Art Of Surfacing	103	7
1981	Mondo Bongo	116	6

Pat BOONE

Pat Boone (born 1934), a descendent of Western pioneer Daniel Boone) was the second biggest record-seller of the 1950s, after Elvis Presley. Though he initially considered himself a rock'n'roller, he represented the antithesis of what many perceived as the undesirable aspects of rock. Boone was smart, polite, well-educated, religious, a do-gooder by nature and even married, so he became both a teen idol and a 'parents-preferred' performer. Most of his rock records were bleached covers of R&B hits, and few have stood the test of time, but having ascertained that his true forte was for romantic material, Boone cut some of the most enduring ballads of the 1950s.

After making country singles as a teenager (he married country star Red Foley's daughter Shirley), Boone's major break came in 1954 when he won the Ted Mack and Arthur Godfrey TV talent shows, which led to a deal with Dot Records, a young label specializing in white-orientated rehashes of black hits. His first run of hits, cut as he also embarked on an English degree at Columbia University, fell amost entirely into this genre, exemplified by his first million-seller, 'Ain't That A Shame' (an R&B chart-topper but a smaller pop hit for Fats Domino), his Little Richard covers, 'Long Tall Sally' and 'Tutti Frutti', and his second gold disc, 'I'll Be Home', an evocative ballad 'borrowed' from The Moonglows. The success of the last, (it topped the UK chart for six weeks in 1956, and was a consistent 'forces favourite' for years after), was a turning point, as it showed Boone as a consummate balladeer, yet still sold to teenagers. The next chart-topper/million-seller, 'I Almost Lost My Mind', covered an Ivory Joe Hunter song, but by this time Boone was such a hot property that strong original material was being offered him, much of it in a ballad vein – like the theme from the Gary Cooper film, Friendly Persuasion, which ended 1956 as a further million seller.

1957 was Boone's biggest year, with five more gold discs, including his all-time top seller, 'Love Letters In the Sand', which topped 3½ million. It was included in his starring movie debut, Bernardine, a summer box-office success, while at the end of the year the chart-topping (and Oscar-nominated) 'April Love' was the title song from a second successful movie. He also began a weekly US TV series which ran until 1960 and cemented him as a major, if youthful, family entertainer who had transcended rock'n'roll. At the end of the 1950s, with Presley in the US Army, Boone's sales also declined as younger idols arrived on the scene, but he gained further gold discs for 'A Wonderful Time Up There' and 'Sugar Moon', received his degree from Columbia, wrote a best-selling book of advice for teenagers entitled Twixt Twelve And Twenty, and starred in more hit movies like Mardi Gras and Journey To The Centre Of The Earth.

Boone was still a chart force to be reckoned with in the early 1960s, when the jaunty death disc, 'Moody River', and a novelty rocker, 'Speedy Gonzales', were both million sellers, but his hit streak all but ended with the advent of The Beatles and the 'British Invasion,' though he was still a popular movie property through the first half of the decade. The late 1960s and 1970s saw him, as an established entertainer, able to fill international concert halls with ease, but recording was generally restricted to country or religious material. Daughter Debby Boone had a gigantic solo hit in 1977 with 'You Light Up My Life', the Oscar-winning title theme from a movie, which spent a barely precedented 10 weeks atop the US chart, and sold over two million.

Boone himself remained active as a live and TV performer during the 1980s (making an unexpected cameo appearance in TV's *Moonlighting*, for instance), but most recent recordings have been for gospel labels.

Greatest Hits

Singles	Title	US	UK
1955	Ain't That A Shame	1	7
1956	I'll Be Home	4	1
1956	I Almost Lost My Mind	1	14
1957	Don't Forbid Me	1	2
1957	Love Letters In The Sand	1	2
1957	April Love	1	7
1961	Moody River	1	18
1962	Speedy Gonzales	2	6
1977	You Light Up My Life		
	(Debby Boone)	1	48
Albums			
1957	Pat's Great Hits	3	–
1958	Star Dust	2	10

BOSTON

Tom Scholz (guitar, vocals)
Brad Delp (guitar, vocals)
Barry Goudreau (guitar)
Fran Scheehan (bass)
Sib Hashian (drums)

Boston, named after the Massachusetts city, was formed by Tom Scholz (born 1947), a high-powered designer working there for the Polaroid corporation, who made highly polished demos of his own compositions in his spare time, on which he played and sang everything. In 1976, he signed to Epic Records, and with local musicians Delp

and Goudreau (both born 1951) and Sheehan and Hashian (both born 1949), he re-recorded the original demos to produce an eponymous album. With a sleeve featuring a guitar-shaped spaceship, 'Boston' became an instant hit album, peaking in the US Top 3 and the UK Top 20 and selling several million copies, strongly assisted by its inclusion of three US hit singles, the biggest 'More Than A Feeling', a hard rock classic.

In 1977, the group followed up this multi-platinum debut with 'Don't Look Back', which topped the US album chart and reached the UK Top 10, while the title track became a US Top 5 single and a minor UK hit. After a long tour, Scholz put the group on ice, only re-emerging in 1986 with a new album, 'Third Stage', which topped the US chart and reached the UK Top 40. By this time, Scholz and Delp were the only remaining originals, and were assisted on the album by drummer Jim Masdea and guitarist Gary Pihl. Two excerpted singles, the chart-topping 'Amanda' and 'We're Ready', reached the US Top 10, but there was little UK interest in the group's new work.

With three huge-selling albums, there is no need for Scholz, who also designed the successful 'Rockman' guitar amplifier, to ever work again – the group's many fans will no doubt hope that they do, even if critics, who tend to deride the band's anonymity, will not be concerned if they don't.

Greatest Hits

Singles	Title	US	UK
1976	More Than A Feeling	5	22
1976	Don't Look Back	4	43
1986	Amanda	1	–
Albums			
1976	Boston	3	11
1977	Don't Look Back	1	9
1986	Third Stage	1	37

Smooth, polished and anonymous – Boston's success confounded the critics but not the fans

David **BOWIE**

Bowie (born David Jones, 1947) is one of the few rock artists not only to have had success over four decades, but also to have had the varied stages of his own career cited as major influences on succeeding generations of musical style, from glam-rock to punk/new wave and the early Gothic and techno/romantic bands. Yet his own commercial success, particularly in the US and in terms of record sales, has been inconsistent.

His early professional career, from 1964 when he formed R&B band The King Bees shortly after leaving school, was a series of earnest almost-theres which never quite happened – frustrating in a highly creative period when hit careers were being launched almost daily. The R&B and psychedelic eras, via groups like The Manish Boys and The Lower Third, then his Tony Newley/English whimsy solo period, left Bowie's work by the chart wayside. Before 1969 he was driven to other artistic outlets, like mime and fringe theatre with Lindsay Kemp, and his 'performance club' the Beckenham Arts Lab. UK chart success finally came when 'Space Oddity' reached the UK Top 5 in 1969, helped by the space-craze climate generated by the US moon landing. The song earned him an Ivor Novello award for its originality, but Bowie found it impossible to follow up what the public regarded as a novelty. Subsequent singles and two albums, 'David Bowie' and 'The Man Who Sold The World', aroused esoteric interest – e.g. the dress he wore on the sleeve of the latter.

Bowie married Angie Barnett in 1970 and had a son, Zowie, the following year, but was going nowhere commercially until Peter Noone (ex-Herman of The Hermits) successfully covered his song 'Oh You Pretty Thing', and he found a major record deal on the strength of self-penned demos which became his next album, 'Hunky Dory'. This sold slowly, and it took the hard graft of a long UK tour with the band he dubbed The Spiders From Mars (Mick Ronson on guitar, Trevor Bolder on bass, and Mick Woodmansey on drums) to score an album breakthrough with the conceptual follow-up, 'Ziggy Stardust & The Spiders From Mars' and its single, 'Starman', both of which made the UK Top 10. Bowie built his stage persona around the Ziggy character for 18 months, and even when he publicly retired it, the image provided a visual role model for much of the mid-1970s UK glam-rock brigade.

A solid commercial run followed for Bowie in the UK into the mid-1970s. The 'Hunky Dory' album charted after its successor, and the two earlier albums were reissued to chart success. Follow-up albums 'Aladdin Sane', the 60s covers collection 'Pin-Ups', the conceptual 'Diamond Dogs' and the inevitable 'David Live' found UK Top 10 action, as did singles like 'The Jean Genie', 'Life On Mars', 'Rebel Rebel', 'Knock On Wood', and even a reissue of his 1967 comic novelty, 'The Laughing Gnome'. He also found time to produce records for others, notably Mott The Hoople's 'All The Young Dudes' (a Bowie song) and Lou Reed's 'Walk On The Wild Side'.

US success in this period was patchier: Bowie would always be troubled by inconsistent sales, and only two of the above albums made the US Top 10, and only a 1973 reissue of 'Space Oddity' gave him a US Top 20 single, while in 1984 an inspired cover of his 'The Man Who Sold The World' gave Lulu her first hit in five years. In 1975 when Bowie made his major movie acting debut in *The Man Who Fell To Earth*, he also assumed a funky soul style on 'Young Americans' and 'Station To Station' albums, and found his biggest success to date in the US, where both albums made the Top 10 (as they did in the UK), and the single 'Fame', co-written with John Lennon, was his first US chart topper/million seller. (Oddly, and almost simultaneously, a reissue of 'Space Oddity' topped the UK chart.)

1977–9 saw a further change of musical style, as Bowie became strongly European-oriented (even living in Berlin for a time, where he made the film *Just A Gigolo*) and introduced a sometimes de-humanizing synthesized Euro-sound to his music, on the albums 'Low', 'Heroes' and 'Lodger', all co-produced with avant-garde hero Brian Eno. 'Sound and Vision', 'Heroes' and 'Boys Keep Swinging' were UK Top 10 singles from these albums, but meant little in the US, where Bowie's departure from the mainstream led to minimal airplay. The 1980s opened with Bowie divorcing his wife, and throwing himself into a non-musical stage project in the US, taking the title role in *The Elephant Man*. A more straightforward rock/pop album, 'Scary Monsters And Super Creeps', topped the UK chart in 1980, as did the single, 'Ashes To Ashes', an oblique lyrical sequel to 'Space Oddity'. He returned to the top in a 1981 duet with Queen on their joint composition, 'Under Pressure'.

Bowie's recording contract expired in 1982, and the hiatus brought more acting ventures: the BBC TV play, *Baal*, and the movies *The Hunger* (with Catherine Deneuve) and *Merry Christmas Mr Lawrence* (with Tom Conti). In 1983 a new record deal began with Nile Rodgers (ex-Chic) producing the album, 'Let's Dance', which largely did use a dance-music framework. The title track, his first million seller since 'Fame', was also Bowie's first single to top both the UK and US charts, while the album was also a transatlantic smash. It launched the worldwide Serious Moonlight tour, and also spun off two further Top 10 singles, 'China Girl' and 'Modern Love'. The following year's similarly styled album, 'Tonight', was less successful, particularly with the critics, although it briefly topped the UK chart, and yielded another UK/US Top 10 single, 'Blue Jean'.

In 1985 Bowie performed at Live Aid, and he and Mick Jagger cut a duet revival of the Martha & The Vandellas classic, 'Dancing In The Street', as a Live Aid fund-raising project; it topped the UK chart for a month and made the US Top 10, becoming his last major US hit to date. In 1986, most of his activity was film-oriented, with roles in a musical, *Absolute Beginners*, and a fantasy, *Labyrinth*. Neither was a box-office winner, but Bowie's theme songs for each gave him more UK hit singles, with *Absolute Beginners* making the Top 3.

1987's album, 'Never Let Me Down', was a poorer seller than its immediate predecessors, but Bowie regenerated his on-stage appeal via the 'Glass Spider' tour, another round-the-world trek. With Peter Frampton (who had been involved in the 1960s Arts Lab) on guitar, this tour was more rock-oriented and less theatrical than Serious Moonlight, and to some extent anticipated Bowie's next musical project, the group Tin Machine, a hard rock quartet in which he served, without special billing, as vocalist. The band made a 1989 album which had qualified commercial success, but more column inches were directed at Bowie's 1989 tour with a difference: its repertoire consisted entirely of his back-catalogue songs, the selection tailored to demand from each territory visited. The object, Bowie explained, was to give the old material a final airing in front of his fans, after which he said he would put the entire repertoire behind him forever. Ever a style chameleon, the likely nature of his next musical direction as a soloist in the 1990s is open to conjecture.

Greatest Hits

Singles	Title	US	UK
1973	*Space Oddity*	15	1
1975	*Fame*	1	17
1980	*Ashes To Ashes*	–	1
1981	*Under Pressure* (with Queen)	29	1
1983	*Let's Dance*	1	1
1985	*Dancing In The Street* (with Mick Jagger)	7	1
Albums			
1973	*Aladdin Sane*	17	1
1973	*Pin-Ups*	23	1
1974	*Diamond Dogs*	5	1
1980	*Scary Monsters And Super Creeps*	12	1
1983	*Let's Dance*	4	1
1984	*Tonight*	11	1

David Bowie as his most celebrated alter ego, Ziggy Stardust

David **BOWIE** ◀ ◀ ◀

The **BOX TOPS**/Alex **CHILTON**

Alex Chilton (vocals, guitar)
Gary Talley (lead guitar)
John Evans (organ)
Bill Cunningham (bass)
Danny Smythe(drums)

Innovative and eccentric, Chilton (born 1950) enjoyed his only commercial success to date with Memphis white soul outfit The Box Tops, who scored a worldwide hit with 'The Letter' in 1967. Like most of their output, it featured the cream of Memphis sessioneers and the production skills of Dan Penn and Spooner Oldham. Smythe and Evans were replaced by Tom Boggs and Rick Allen respectively, and although 'Cry Like A Baby' was another global smash, Chilton left in 1969 to pursue (unsuccessfully) a solo career in New York.

He returned to Memphis in 1970, and after an abortive attempt at recording a solo album, formed Big Star in 1971 with Chris Bell (guitar, vocal), Andy Hummel (bass, piano, vocal), and Jody Stephens (drum, vocal). An album ('No. 1 Record') was released in 1972 and showed a band swimming against the tide of 'Progressive' rock with a collection of British-style melodic pop-rock songs. In late 1972, disagreements between Bell and Chilton led to the former's departure. Several years later, Bell released his only solo single, 'I Am The Cosmos'. He died in a car crash in Memphis in December 1979.

Big Star carried on as a trio and released 'Radio City' (1974), again melodic, but now with a rawer edge, which included Chilton's classic 'September Gurls'. Like 'No. 1', however, 'Radio City' suffered from poor distribution and despite critical praise sank without trace. Hummel quit, leaving Chilton and Stephens to record a third album in autumn 1974, but it remained unreleased until 1978 due to lack of record company

Two-hit wonders The Box Tops

interest. When 'Third' appeared, it proved to be a major departure from its predecessors – stylistically owing more to post-Floyd Syd Barrett than to The Beatles.

Chilton went solo but released only one EP and a single during the period 1975–9, finally issuing his first album, the patchy 'Like Flies On Sherbert' in 1980. Subsequent albums ('Live In London', 'Feudalist Tarts', 'High Priest' and 'Black List') have seen him carve his own niche with a deranged brand of R&B influenced guitar pop. Chilton has also been active as a producer, most notably with The Cramps and Tav Falco's Panther Burns, for whom he occasionally plays guitar.

Greatest Hits

Singles	Title	US	UK
1967	The Letter	1	5
1968	Cry Like A Baby	2	15

Paul **BRADY**

Northern Irish singer/songwriter Paul Brady (born 1947) has yet to achieve the adulation as a recording artist he receives as a songwriter. Initially working in small-time rocks bands in Dublin, his first taste of fame was as singer/guitarist with Irish MOR folk group The Johnstons in the early 1970s. Credibility came when he replaced Christy Moore in Planxty in 1974, when he was regarded as a pillar of traditional Irish folk music, playing tin whistle and mandolin. In 1976, he made an eponymous duo album with Andy Irvine of Planxty, and in 1977, a highly regarded solo album, 'Welcome Here Kind Stranger'. In 1980, he re-emerged with 'Hard Station', a contemporary folk/rock album, including originals like 'Crazy Dreams', 'Busted Loose' and 'Nothing But The Same Old Story', whose barely suppressed anger over his country's tribulations provided inspiration. Among those who covered Brady's songs from 'Hard Station' and 1983's 'True For You' were Tina Turner, Dave Edmunds and Santana, but Brady's own sales were limited.

By 1984, after replacing his spectacles with contact lenses, he worked with Mark Knopfler of Dire Straits on the soundtrack to the David Puttnam movie, *Cal*, and recorded 'Full Moon', a live album of material from his previous two albums, at the Half Moon in Putney, South London, with a hot band. In 1986 came 'Back To The Centre', his debut for Phonogram (who later reissued 'Hard Station' and 'True For You'). Eric Clapton, Loudon Wainwright III and Larry Mullen Jr. of U2 guested on the album, and even with great songs like 'Walk The White Line' and 'The Island', it failed to chart. So did 1987's 'Primitive Dance', which included Brady's own version of 'Paradise Is Here' (written for

Tina Turner), the title song to an Irish feature film, *Eat the Peach*, a cover of Ike & Tina Turner's 'It's Gonna Work Out Fine', and guest stars like Mark Knopfler and Maire Brennan of Clannad, plus a plug from Bob Dylan.

Brady's next album, 'Trick Or Treat' (1991), was recorded in the US with ex-Steely Dan producer Gary Katz – its title track is a duet with Bonnie Raitt. As yet, Paul Brady has no chart history, but any Brady album from the 1980s onwards will repay those with good taste.

BREAD

David Gates (vocals, guitar, keyboards)
James Griffin (vocals, guitar)
Robb Royer (vocals, keyboards)

Among the most popular soft rock acts of the 1970s was Bread. Gates (born 1940), from Oklahoma (where he worked with Leon Russell) met Memphis-born Griffin when he was producing Pleasure Fayre, a group which included Royer. Signed to Elektra, the trio's eponymous debut album, with drummer Jim Gordon, was a minor hit, and for 1970's 'On The Waters', with Mike Botts as permanent drummer, softer material by Gates predominated, and a single, 'Make It With You', topped the US chart. Griffin and Royer, using the pseudonyms of Arthur James and Robb Wilson, had co-written 'For All We Know', the theme song to the feature film *Lovers And Other Strangers*, which was a million seller for The Carpenters and won an Oscar for Best Film Song of 1970, but Bread's next single was another Gates song, 'It Don't Matter To Me', which made the US Top 10, as 'On The Waters' went gold.

1971's elaborately packaged 'Manna' album also went gold, and included two more Gates-penned hits. 'If', a US Top 5 hit for Bread, was covered in 1975 by *Kojak* actor Telly Savalas as a chart-topping monologue in the UK. By 1972 Royer had been replaced by multi-instrumentalist Larry Knechtel (the pianist on Simon & Garfunkel's 'Bridge Over Troubled Water'). Bread's US Top 3 album, 'Baby I'm-A Want You', included four US Top 40 Gates-penned hits, the title track and 'Everything I Own' both going into the Top 5. A 1974 cover of the latter song by reggae star Ken Boothe topped the UK chart. At the end of 1972 'Guitar Man' was a US Top 20 album and the title track a US Top 20 single, as were 'Sweet Surrender' and 'Aubrey' (also from the album), but dissent between Gates and Griffin over the choice of singles led to Bread's demise in early 1973.

Later that year, 'The Best of Bread' made the Top 3 of the US album chart, and in 1974, a second 'Best Of' album also went gold, as Gates and Griffin discovered solo

Guitar man Gates (left) with Bread-heads Royer, Botts and Griffin

success was difficult. In 1977 they reunited with Botts and Knechtel for 'Lost Without Your Love', another gold album whose title track was also a hit single, but had disbanded again before a TV advertised compilation, 'The Sound Of Bread', topped the UK album chart and went double platinum. In 1987 Boy George reached the top of the UK chart with a cover of 'Everything I Own', but Bread has yet to reunite.

Greatest Hits

Singles	Title	US	UK
1970	Make It With You	1	5
1971	If	4	–
1971	Baby I'm-A Want You	3	14
1972	Everything I Own	5	32
Albums			
1972	Baby I'm-A Want You	3	9
1973	The Best Of Bread	2	7
1977	The Sound Of Bread	–	1

Elkie BROOKS

Born in 1945, vocalist Elkie Brooks (real name Elaine Bookbinder) has yet to achieve US popularity to match her UK fame. Dubbed 'Manchester's Brenda Lee' at age 15, she worked with jazz bandleaders Eric Delaney and Humphrey Lyttleton, before releasing unsuccessful R&B singles. In 1968, she formed 12-piece jazz/rock band Dada with her guitarist husband Pete Gage and co-vocalist Robert Palmer, but its eponymous 1970 album was too ambitious, and in 1972

the group slimmed down to R&B sextet Vinegar Joe. Sales of its three albums (1972's 'Vinegar Joe' and 'Rock'n'Roll Gypsies' and 1973's 'Six Star General') did not equal its live popularity, and it folded in 1974. Brooks signed to A&M as a solo artist, but her 1975 debut album, 'Rich Man's Woman', was a flop, after which 'Two Days Away' (1977), produced by veteran hitmakers Jerry Leiber & Mike Stoller, reached the UK Top 20 and included two UK Top 10 hits, 'Pearl's A Singer' and 'Sunshine After the Rain'.

1978's 'Shooting Star' album (produced by David Kershenbaum) reached the UK Top 20 without a big single, and for 1979's 'Live and Learn', she returned to Leiber & Stoller, but with less success. In 1981 a semi-compilation,

Elkie – like Pearl, a singer

'Pearls', was a UK Top 3 album, and in 1982, Pearls II (produced by Gus Dudgeon) reached the UK Top 5. Neither 'Minutes' nor 'Screen Gems' were too successful in the mid-1980s, and Brooks left A&M. In 1986 'No More The Fool' (released on a new label) restored her to the Top 5 of the UK album chart and spawned three hit singles, while the TV-advertised compilation album, 'The Very Best of Elkie Brooks', also reached the Top 10 in 1986.

In 1988 'Bookbinder's Kid' was less successful, and after another change of label in 1989 (to a TV marketing company), her 'Inspiration' album restored her to the UK chart. A Great British vocalist, Brooks has never earned a US hit, although she remains strongly in contention in the UK.

Greatest Hits

Singles	Title	US	UK
1986	No More The Fool	–	5
Albums			
1981	Pearls	–	2
1982	Pearls II	–	5
1986	No More The Fool	–	5

James BROWN

James Brown (born 1928), known variously as The Godfather Of Soul, Mr Please Please Please and Mr Dynamite, spent his late teenage years in a juvenile corrective institution in his native South Carolina. Ironically, after a career spanning nearly forty years – during which he initiated more changes in Black American music (and repeated himself more often) than almost anyone else – Brown again found himself behind bars in 1989.

Having sung with gospel groups and learnt to play drums and organ, Brown formed The Famous Flames in 1954. Based in Georgia, they toured the area playing a fusion of gospel and raucous R&B, heavily inspired by Louis Jordan. In 1956, their first single, 'Please Please Please', entered the US R&B chart and would eventually sell over a million copies in the US.

The group's extensive touring schedule and Brown's explosive live performances pushed 'Try Me' (1958) into the US Top 50, and in 1959, Brown signed a management deal with Ben Bart of the Universal Attractions booking agency, who encouraged him to develop his stage act into a tour de force which was to break all R&B box office records. In 1960, 'Think' gave Brown his first US Top 40 single.

Brown's style had developed into a hysterical brand of melodramatic soul/blues that was to pave the way for many major soul names of the 1960s.

In the early 1960s, Brown continued with

James Brown, self-styled Godfather of Soul

hits like the US Top 75 single, 'The Bells' (1960), and the US Top 50 entry 'I Don't Mind' (1961) and 'Lost Someone' (1961). In 1962 his stage act was recorded for the now-legendary 'Live At The Apollo' album, which gave him his first US chart album, reaching the Top 3 in 1963. In 1964, Brown surpassed himself with the 'Out Of Sight' single which took R&B into uncharted territory with re-petitive riffs, topped by his screaming vocals, providing the basis for modern funk.

'Papa's Got A Brand New Bag' (1965) was a development of this process, and gave Brown his first US Top 10 single as well as a UK Top 30 debut. 'I Got You (I Feel Good)' hit the US Top 5 and UK Top 30 in the same year in the same 'new dance' vein, while the ballad, 'It's A Man's Man's Man's World' (1966) reached the US pop Top 10 and was a R&B No. 1, also giving Brown his biggest 1960s UK hit.

In 1967, Alfred 'Peewee' Ellis replaced Nat Jones as Brown's main musical collaborator, and with him followed through his develop-ing funk style. 'Cold Sweat' that year was the first sample of their work together, a US Top 10 and R&B No. 1 single, which set a new pace for dance music – fast and furious funk that was physically demanding on dancers as well as performers, although prevailing fashion in white music led to his audience becoming far less universal.

'Licking Stick, Licking Stick' (1968), was probably the epitome of Brown's feverish funk, but the same year he also established himself as a social voice; he publicly con-demned the riots after the assassination of Martin Luther King, and released 'America Is My Home' and the US Top 10 single, 'Say It Loud, I'm Black And I'm Proud'. The latter was a million seller, and an anthem of the black consciousness movement in the late 1960s.

'Funk' culture was developing through 1969, when Brown initiated The Popcorn, a dance of his own invention. The single, 'Mother Popcorn', reached the US Top 20 while an instrumental, 'The Popcorn', made the US Top 30. Offspins of Popcornmania included the album, 'James Brown Plays and Directs The Popcorn', before 1969's 'Ain't It Funky Now' and 1970's 'Funky Drummer' heralded major changes in Brown's musical set up.

The Famous Flames disbanded and Brown brought in The JBs, who included William 'Bootsy' Collins on bass, his brother Phelps on guitar and trombonist band leader Fred Wesley. They released 'Get Up (I Feel Like Being A) Sex Machine' (1970) which was to become a worldwide dancefloor classic. More multi-layered than some of Brown's releases with The Famous Flames, the record benefit-ted from the all-round talent of each member of the new band.

The JBs style of complex funk carried them through the early 1970s with US Top 20 hits such as 'Super Bad' (1970), 'Hot Pants' (1971) and 'Get On The Good Foot' (1972).

In 1973, Brown and Wesley scored two movies, *Black Caesar* and *Slaughter's Big Rip Off*, while the 1960 hit, 'Think' was revived in different versions twice in three months. The mid-1970s for James Brown included a plethora of re-recordings of past hits, notable exceptions being 'The Payback' (1974) and 'Get Up Offa' That Thing' (1976).

He made a cameo appearance in the *Blues Brothers* movie in 1980, and in the UK, scored Top 50 singles with 'Rapp Payback' (1981) 'Bring It On . . . Bring It On' (1983) and his 1984 collaboration with Afrika Bam-baata 'Unity (The 3rd Coming)'.

During 1985, vintage James Brown mate-rial was big news on the UK club scene, which led to a quest for rare and deleted cuts and heavily influenced sampling on rap re-cords. Brown is one of the most frequently sampled artists to date, and has been the main inspiration for rap breakbeats in the last five years. His last major hit, apart from re-releases and remixes, was the UK and US Top 5 hit, 'Living For America', the 1986 theme tune from the movie *Rocky IV*, re-corded at the request of Sylvester Stallone.

Brown was jailed in 1989 for alleged bank-robbery and firearms offences, though his prison regime did allow for him to be seen and heard in more than one television inter-view.

Greatest Hits

Singles	Title	US	UK
1965	*Papa's Got A Brand New Bag*	8	25
1965	*I Got You*	3	29
1966	*It's A Man's Man's Man's World*	8	13
1968	*I Got The Feelin'*	6	–
1986	*Living In America*	4	5
Albums			
1962	*Live At The Apollo*	2	–
1964	*Pure Dynamite!*		
	Live At The Royal	10	–
1988	*Best Of James Brown –*		
	Godfather Of Soul	–	17

Jackson **BROWNE**

Singer/songwriter Clyde Jackson Browne (born 1948 in West Germany, where his father served in the US Army) is highly regarded both for his poetic early work and his later politically motivated songs.

Starting as a teenage folk/rock performer in Los Angeles, he briefly joined The Nitty Gritty Dirt Band, contributing two songs to their 1966 debut album before signing to Nina Music, the publishing company attached to Elektra Records, and working in New York with Velvet Underground chanteuse Nico, who cut three of his songs on her *Chelsea Girl* album in 1968. Other artists like Tom Rush began to cover his songs, and by 1971 he had signed to Asylum Records (which ironically later merged with Elektra, for whom he had started to make an album which was eventually abandoned).

With help from David Crosby and guitarists Clarence White and Albert Lee, 'Jackson Browne' (also known as 'Saturate Before Using') was released in 1972, almost reaching the Top 50 of the US album chart, while a single from it, 'Doctor My Eyes' was a US Top 10 hit – surprisingly, the song was a 1973 UK Top 10 hit for The Jackson Five! Browne was very friendly with label-mates The Eagles, writing 'Nightingale' for their debut album, which also included 'Take It Easy', their first US Top 20 hit single, which he co-wrote with Glenn Frey. He cut the latter song himself on 'For Everyman' (1973), which also featured 'Redneck Friend', on which one 'Rockaday Johnnie' (aka Elton John) played piano and others helping out included Bonnie Raitt, Joni Mitchell, Frey, Crosby and Don Henley, plus multi-instrumentalist David Lindley, who worked with Browne for some years thereafter. The album made the US Top 50, and also included one of Browne's most-covered songs, 'These Days'.

Also in 1973 he appeared on the sleeve of 'Desperado' by The Eagles, for which he co-wrote 'Doolin-Dalton' with Frey, Henley and J.D. Souther. This same team also wrote 'James Dean' for 'On The Border', the 1974 Eagles album, and the end of that year saw the release of Browne's own third album, the

Songwriter with a social conscience Jackson Browne

exquisite 'Late For The Sky', his first to reach the US Top 20. His personal life then became tragic, as his wife committed suicide in March 1976, and his late 1976 album, 'The Pretender', reflected his grief, also becoming his first million seller as well as his first UK chart album. He also produced his friend and label-mate Warren Zevon's eponymous 1976 album, and co-produced Zevon's 'Excitable Boy' (1978).

In 1978 Browne released 'Running On Empty', an album recorded while touring (in hotels, at soundchecks, etc.), which became his second million seller and spawned a UK hit single in his excellent cover of 'Stay', a 1960s hit for Maurice Williams & The Zodiacs. Browne also became heavily involved in MUSE (Musicians United For Safe Energy), both helping to organize and participating in the 'No Nukes' concert at New York's Madison Square Garden. A live triple album of this event featuring Browne, Bruce Springsteen, Bonnie Raitt, Tom Petty, etc. reached the Top 10 of the US album chart in 1980. Later that year, Browne's sixth album, 'Hold Out', topped the US album chart, although many found it inaccessible.

In 1982 he scored a Top 10 US hit single with 'Somebody's Baby', which was featured in the movie *Fast Times At Ridgmount High*, and in 1983 returned with a US Top 10 album, 'Lawyers In Love' which included three US Top 40 hit singles. In 1986, Browne duetted with Clarence Clemons (from Springsteen's E Street Band) on 'You're A Friend Of Mine', a US Top 20 single. Having involved himself primarily in political causes for most of the 1980s, Browne released 'Lives In The Balance', an outspoken album which nevertheless reached the Top 30 of the US album chart in 1986. He was also one of the

star attractions at the 1988 London concert staged for Nelson Mandela's 70th birthday. In 1989, he released another political album, 'World In Motion'. While no-one can doubt his sincerity, perhaps many would prefer him to use his exceptional songwriting talents on romantic topics, at which he proved himself a superstar in the early 1970s.

Greatest Hits

Singles	Title	US	UK
1972	Doctor My Eyes	5	–
1978	Stay	20	12
1982	Somebody's Baby	7	–
Albums			
1976	The Pretender	5	26
1978	Running On Empty	3	28
1980	Hold On	1	44

Tim BUCKLEY

A prodigiously talented singer-songwriter who emerged originally from the mid-1960s folk/rock scene, Buckley (born in Washington DC, 1947) was highly rated, but his potential always outweighed his success. After working with bassist Jim Fielder (later of Buffalo Springfield and Blood, Sweat & Tears) around the LA clubs, he went solo. His striking voice and idiosyncratic style attracted the attention of Frank Zappa's manager, Herb Cohen, who secured him a deal with Elektra Records. His eponymous debut album (1966) was critically acclaimed, having reputedly been recorded in three days, and he was tipped for stardom.

In 1967 he moved to New York where he worked occasionally with Nico (ex-Velvet Underground), while George Harrison, a big fan, tried to get Brian Epstein interested. Buckley's second album, 'Goodbye And Hello', attracted excellent reviews and made slight US chart headway. Often considered to be his best (it included 'Morning Glory', co-written with poet Larry Beckett and later covered by Blood Sweat & Tears), it showcased his expressive voice with more sophisticated and adventurous music than before.

He continued to impress as a powerful live performer and in 1969 released his most successful album, the introspective, jazzy 'Happy Sad'. He switched to Zappa's Straight label for his next album, the John Coltrane-influenced 'Blue Afternoon' (1969) before completing his obligations to Elektra with the free-form, avant-garde 'Lorca' in 1970. It sold poorly, as did the same year's 'Starsailor', which found him even deeper in experimental territory. Disillusioned by his lack of commercial success, he concentrated on film music, returning in 1972 with 'Greetings From LA'. Surprisingly accessible, funky, danceable R&B, it didn't sell, despite good reviews. However, he persevered in this vein,

and after moving to Zappa & Cohen's DiscReet label, cut 'Sefronia' (1973) and 'Look At The Fool' (1974). Both received excellent reviews, yet neither sold. He died in 1975, apparently after mistaking a lethal dose of heroin and morphine for cocaine. Buckley's work can genuinely be described as timeless, as demonstrated by the release in 1990 of 'Live In London', a double CD of a 1968 concert, which captures him at his best and created as much interest as his earlier albums.

Greatest Hits

Albums	Title	US	UK
1969	Happy Sad	81	–

BUFFALO SPRINGFIELD

Stephen Stills (vocals, guitar)
Neil Young (vocals, guitar, piano)
Richie Furay (vocals, guitar)
Bruce Palmer (bass)
Dewey Martin (drums)

Formed in Los Angeles in 1966 by Texan Stills (born 1945) and Furay (born 1945, Ohio) when they moved to California after an album with a New York-based 10-piece folk group, The Au Go Go Singers, Buffalo Springfield (named after a steamroller!) were one of the most influential folk/rock acts of the 1960s, despite existing for only two years.

Stills had encountered Toronto-raised Neil Young (born 1945) on the folk club circuit and tried to contact him, while Young had actually arrived in LA with fellow Canadian Palmer, but couldn't find Stills until the latter saw Young's hearse in a traffic jam on Sunset Boulevard. With the addition of Martin (ex-Dillards), the group made an eponymous debut album for Atlantic's Atco subsidiary featuring six songs each by Stills and Young. As it was released, the group cut a Stills-penned song about the celebrated Sunset Strip riots, 'For What It's Worth', which became a US Top 10 hit. This track replaced 'Baby Don't Scold Me', written by Young, although early UK copies of the album contain the latter song and omit the hit.

Palmer was deported on more than one occasion for minor drug offences and visa/work permit infringements, and several temporary bass players filled in, including Jim Fielder (ex-Mothers Of Invention and later with Blood, Sweat & Tears), who helped out on 'Buffalo Springfield Again', the group's first US Top 50 album, which included three minor US hit singles among four songs by Stills and three each by Young and Furay. An album entitled 'Stampede' was actually completed in early 1967 and shelved – it later appeared as a bootleg – and was replaced by 'Again', and this seemed to add to the problems caused by Palmer's brushes with authority, and by Young, who left and rejoined the group several times (due, he claimed, to 'nerves – I was going crazy'), and was absent for their appearance at the Monterey Pop Festival.

In late 1967 the group began a third album, during which Palmer again left, his place being taken by Jim Messina, who was engineering the album, but was ultimately credited as producer when it was released as 'Last Time Around' in 1968, three months after the band had finally folded. Messina and Furay then formed Poco, Stills joined David Crosby and Graham Nash, and Young made two solo albums before expanding CSN into CSN&Y.

Palmer made an obscure solo album, 'The Cycle Is Complete', and Martin the equally obscure 'Dewey Martin & Medicine Ball' during the 1970s. After their demise, Buffalo Springfield's work was compiled as 'Retrospective – The Best Of Buffalo Springfield' (1969) and 'Buffalo Springfield', a 1976 double album with a previously unreleased nine minute version of 'Bluebird', from 'Again'. Both compilations made the US album chart, and ultimately, the public were aware of the significance of a group which was the nursery for many later milestones of popular music.

Greatest Hits

Singles	Title	US	UK
1967	For What It's Worth	7	–
Albums			
1967	Buffalo Springfield Again	44	–
1968	Last Time Around	42	–
1969	Retrospective	42	–

Solomon **BURKE**

Solomon Burke (born 1936), one of many great 1960s soul singers on Atlantic Records, was also important to the music's development, bringing a gospelly intensity to the cooler rhythms of 1950s R&B.

Appropriately, Burke's life and music were linked with the church even at the height of his secular success. A preacher since boyhood at the House of God for All People Church in Philadelphia, and a Gospel broadcaster via his show *Solomon's Temple*, he recorded in the mid-1950s for the Gospel label, Apollo, but had no success until 1961, when, after a spell at college, he signed to Atlantic. The odd combination of a country ballad, 'Just Out Of Reach', and his pleading vocals produced a

US Top 30 soul classic. A four-year run of hits followed, varying from country crossovers like 'He'll Have To Go', through intense chuggers like 'Cry To Me' (much covered by British R&B groups), 'Got To Get You Off My Mind', and 'If You Need Me' (also a hit for Wilson Pickett), to pure gospel rave-ups like 'Everybody Needs Somebody To Love' (covered by The Rolling Stones, and later re-sanctified and used in Burke's church as a fund-raising anthem). Tagged 'The King of Rock & Soul', Burke's stage act was heavy with the showmanship of the consummate preacher, often ending with the singer enthroned in crown and ermine. However his sales fell when stablemates and competitors like Pickett, Otis Redding, Joe Tex, and especially James Brown (whom Burke strongly disliked), found major success.

After 1968 the consistency of his material plummeted, and the early 1970s saw much label-hopping and few hits. Late in the decade, he reduced his secular activities to concentrate on religious work as the Bishop of his church, and through the 1980s preaching was his main preoccupation, with recordings wholly inspirational in content, yet retaining the fiery earthiness which had made him a soul star. Burke's main secular work in recent years has been an occasional 'Soul Clan' reunion concert with his Atlantic stablemates of the 60s.

Greatest Hits

Singles	Title	US	UK
1961	Just Out Of Reach	24	–
1965	Got To Get You Off My Mind	22	–

Johnny **BURNETTE**

A Memphis schoolfriend of Elvis Presley, Burnette (born 1934) was an outstanding 1950s rockabilly singer whose quality was only recognized in retrospect after he became a pop star in the early 1960s.

Burnette's Rock & Roll Trio, comprising himself on vocals and guitar, his older brother Dorsey (stand-up bass), and Memphis neighbour Paul Burlison (lead guitar), formed in 1952, became a regular attraction at the city's Hideaway Club. After Presley's local success, the trio auditioned for Sam Phillips at Sun, only to be rejected for sounding too much like Elvis. A move to New York in 1956 paid off with TV success on *Ted Mack's Amateur Hour* and a record deal with Coral Records, but hot rockabilly singles like 'Tear It Up' didn't sell, although the trio did appear in the Alan Freed movie, *Rock Rock Rock*, performing 'Lonesome Train (On A Lonesome Track)'.

By late 1957 the disillusioned trio had split and the Burnettes moved to LA, where they concentrated initially on songwriting – suc-

Stephen Stills' seminal steamroller Buffalo Springfield

Burnette – retrospective rockabilly recognition

cess came via several titles cut by Ricky Nelson, including 'Waiting In School', 'Believe What You Say' and 'Just A Little Too Much'. Johnny recorded with Dorsey for Imperial Records, and as a soloist for Freedom, but with little success, until he signed to Liberty in 1960.

Working with producer Snuff Garrett, he forged a new string-backed beat-ballad style which clicked with the Top 10 hit 'Dreamin'' and its even bigger follow-up 'You're Sixteen', a million seller. Briefly, Burnette rivalled Liberty's top seller Bobby Vee, but lacked Vee's staying power and the hits dried up in 1962 after a US Top 20 hit with the cornily patriotic 'God, Country And My Baby'. Label changes to Chancellor, Capitol, and others did not produce strong material or a comeback, and the 1964 'British Invasion' swept away the US teen style.

Johnny Burnette would almost certainly have moved into country music (as brother Dorsey did), but after forming his own label for new projects, he died in a boating accident in August 1964. In a pleasing coda, Burnette's son Rocky scored a big hit with the neo-rockabilly 'Tired Of Toein' The Line' in 1980, while Dorsey's son, Billy, joined Fleetwood Mac in 1989.

Greatest Hits

Singles	Title	US	UK
1960	Dreamin'	11	5
1960	You're Sixteen	8	3

Kate **BUSH**

Few artists have perfected the art of maintaining a successful rock career while keeping the music business at arm's length like Kate Bush. Born in 1958 in South London, she was signed to EMI Records as soon as she left school at the age of 16 on the strength of a demo tape financed by Dave Gilmour of Pink Floyd, who had been introduced to her by a friend.

Far from hustling her into a studio, EMI allowed her to develop her talents in her own time. She studied dance and mime with Lindsey Kemp, augmenting her own musical abilities, and finally recorded her first album in 1977. She insisted that EMI release 'Wuthering Heights', a haunting but eccentric and abrasive song in which her voice soared across four octaves, as the first single. EMI was reluctant, but acquiesced after tests showed that British DJs were prepared to play it. Released in early 1978, the single scaled the UK charts rapidly and spent four weeks at No. 1, helped by a video that emphasized her strikingly sensual looks. It subsequently charted in 18 other territories and topped the charts in five of them. Only the USA remained relatively immune from its bizzare charms.

Her debut album, 'The Kick Inside', reached the UK Top 3 on the back of the single and topped the charts in five other countries. The second single from the album, the more mature sounding 'Man With The Child In His Eyes', reached the UK Top 10 in the summer of 1978. Thus established on her own terms, Bush recorded the follow-up album, 'Lionheart', released at the end of that year. It yielded a UK Top 20 single with the vocally dexterous 'Wow'. Now with two albums' worth of material, she set about preparing a live show which drew on the mime and ballet styles she'd learnt with Lindsey Kemp and proved every bit as innovative as the music she was pioneering. A live EP from her UK tour, 'Kate Bush On Stage', reached the UK Top 20 in 1979, but she became disillusioned at her inability to reach the high standards of perfection on

stage that she'd set herself in the studio, and to date has never toured again. Instead, she concentrated her efforts on producing albums and promoting them with equally creative videos. Her third album, 'Never For Ever' (1980), included 'Babooshka', which reached the UK Top 5 (the closest she has come so far to emulating 'Wuthering Heights') and the Top 20 hit, 'Breathing',as well as 'Delius', a tribute to one of her favourite classical composers.

By this time, she was in total control of her music and visual image and worked almost exclusively with a close-knit circle of family and friends, including Peter Gabriel, with whom she duetted on 'Don't Give Up' on his 'So' album. 'The Dreaming' in 1983 and 'Hounds Of Love' in 1985 each confirmed the progress she was making within her self-contained world and the latter finally gave her an American breakthrough with a Top 30 single, 'Running Up That Hill', which also helped the album into the charts. She has becoming increasingly interested in folk styles and included a 25-minute Celtic suite on the album.

The compilation album, 'The Whole Story' (1988), reassured EMI that, at her best, she was a still a commercial commodity but she stuck to her folk guns for 'The Sensual World' (1989), which featured the Bulgarian singing combo, Trio Bulgarka. Kate Bush will doubtless continue to make albums in her own fashion, as and when she deems fit.

Greatest Hits

Singles	Title	US	UK
1978	Wuthering Heights	–	1
1980	Babooshka	–	5
Albums			
1978	The Kick Inside	–	3

'Kathy come home' proved a crucial chorus for Kate

Jerry **BUTLER**

A distinctive soul vocalist whose cool, controlled stage act and vocal style earned him the title 'The Ice Man', Butler (born 1939) achieved both consistent critical and commercial success in a much-changing genre from the late 1950s through to the 1970s.

His first break came in Chicago in 1957, when after several years in church choirs and doo-wop groups, Butler and Curtis Mayfield (see separate entry) joined R&B group The Roosters, revamping it as The Impressions. Their debut single, the intense 'For Your Precious Love', made the US Top 20, but their label, with an eye more on the vocalist than the group, insisted that the billing on this and follow-ups must be 'Jerry Butler & The Impressions', causing antagonism among his colleagues which prompted Butler to leave. He was then re-signed as a soloist, and the group temporarily disbanded, with Butler continuing to work in the studio with Mayfield, their co-composition 'He Will Break Your Heart' providing his first solo hit in late 1960.

A year later, Butler broadened his audience appeal beyond straight R&B confines with Henry Mancini's 'Moon River', which shared US chart honours with the composer's original, and began a run of sophisticated ballad hits such as the first version of Bacharach/David's 'Make It Easy On Yourself', Mayfield's 'Need To Belong', Butler's own 'I Stand Accused', and the standard 'Let It Be Me', duetted with label-mate Betty Everett.

Vee Jay, the Chicago-based label for which Butler recorded, closed in 1966, and he moved to Mercury Records. His 'Ice Man' approach (a tag bestowed by Philadelphia DJ George Woods) was at odds with the funkier Stax/Atlantic and Motown soul sounds then charting, but after a brief hiatus, he returned to the US Top 40 with 'Mr. Dream Merchant' in late 1967, and hit a completely new stride when he met Kenny Gamble and Leon Huff in Philadelphia in 1968. The trio's songwriting and production liaison yielded two critically acclaimed albums, 'The Ice Man Cometh' and 'Ice On Ice', and further hit singles like 'Never Give You Up', 'Hey Western Union Man', 'Moody Woman', and his biggest ever hit 'Only The Strong Survive', a 1969 million-seller.

In 1970 Butler left the increasingly busy Gamble & Huff, establishing his own Songwriters Workshop in Chicago to encourage and collaborate with young writers and performers. This spawned a 1972 million-seller, Butler's duet on 'Ain't Understanding Mellow' with young protégée Brenda Lee Eager. During the 1970s, he opened publishing and record label offshoots of the Workshop, but also took a non-musical direction via a multinational drinks distributorship. New record deals with Motown and Philadelphia International in the late 1970s produced only minor

commercial success, and Butler focussed on live performance, TV commercials (for McDonald's, among others) and his business and local political interests.

In the 1980s, he ran for and gained political office in Chicago, and largely retired from recording, but maintained his performing profile, reuniting with The Impressions for a 1983 tour, 25 years after 'For Your Precious Love'.

Greatest Hits

Singles	Title	US	UK
1964	*Let It Be Me*		
	(with Betty Everett)	5	–
1969	*Only The Strong Survive*	4	–
Albums			
1969	*The Ice Man Cometh*	29	–
1969	*Ice On Ice*	41	–

Paul **BUTTERFIELD**

Butterfield, a brilliant R&B harmonica player, vocalist and band leader, was born in Chicago in 1942. Where John Mayall and Alexis Korner could claim to have fathered white R&B in Britain during the 1960s, Butterfield was the major R&B figurehead in the US at that time.

Playing around Chicago clubs, Butterfield recruited a rhythm section of Jerome Arnold (bass) and Sam Lay (drums), both ex-members of Howlin' Wolf's band, plus guitarist Elvin Bishop and a little later, second guitarist Mike Bloomfield (born 1943, Chicago). Bloomfield had already been signed to CBS Records by legendary A&R man John Hammond (Senior), so special permission was required for him to record with Butterfield, who signed to Elektra. First attempts at an album were supposedly unsatisfactory, although tracks which probably came from that session appeared on a now famous compilation album, 'What's

Shakin'', which also showcased The Lovin' Spoonful, Tom Rush, Al Kooper and a pick-up group known as Eric Clapton & The Powerhouse featuring Steve Winwood, Jack Bruce (of Cream) and Paul Jones (from the Manfred Mann group).

The eponymous debut album by The Paul Butterfield Blues Band, augmented by keyboard player Mark Naftalin, was released in 1965 and made the US chart for over two months, attracting critical praise. When the band, plus both Kooper and Barry Goldberg on keyboards, backed Bob Dylan at the Newport Folk Festival, the folk establishment were critical of Dylan for going electric, although Bloomfield went on to play on several Dylan albums. Butterfield's 1986 album, 'East West' (with Billy Davenport replacing Lay), was more successful, spending over six months in the US chart, after which Bloomfield left to launch The Electric Flag.

In early 1967, Butterfield cut an EP in London with John Mayall, and on his return replaced Arnold (with Bugsy Maugh) and Davenport (with Phil Wilson). Rather than hiring another guitarist, he used a brass section of Gene Dinwiddie and David Sanborn (saxes) and Keith Johnson (trumpet) on 1968's 'The Resurrection Of Pigboy Crabshaw' (a nickname used by Bishop), which achieved Butterfield's highest ever US album chart position just outside the Top 50, although it lacked the charisma of the albums featuring Bloomfield. That year's 'In My Own Dream' featured the same line-up plus Al Kooper guesting on keyboards, but was less successful, and 1969's 'Keep On Moving', with Buzzy Feiten, Rod Hicks and Ted Harris respectively replacing Bishop, Maugh and Naftalin, even less so, although all three albums briefly reached the US chart.

In 1971, after introducing Ralph Wash (guitar) and George Davidson (drums), 'The Butterfield Blues Band Live', a double album produced by Todd Rundgren, returned the band to the US Top 100, but that year's 'Sometimes I Just Feel Like Smilin'', with Dennis Whitted (drums) and four horn players,

Blues blower Butterfield, a catalyst for white American R&B

was the smallest hit thus far, and Butterfield moved to Bearsville Records.

Before the release of the first album with his new band, Better Days, 'Golden Butter', a double album compilation of Elektra material, was a minor US hit in 1972. Better Days featured Geoff Muldaur and Amos Garrett (guitar), Ronnie Barron (keyboards), Billy Rich (bass) and Christopher Parker (drums). While only two of its nine tracks used a horn section, the band's eponymous album only made the US Top 150, although it fared better than the same year's 'It All Comes Back', Butterfield's final chart album.

After 'Put It In Your Ear' (1976), Butterfield worked separately with both Levon Helm and Rick Danko (of The Band), but underwent major surgery before he could complete his 'North South' album in 1981 (the year in which Mike Bloomfield died). After an unsuccessful 1986 comeback album, 'Paul Butterfield Rides Again', this largely unsung hero also died in May 1987.

Greatest Hits

Albums	Title	US	UK
1966	East West	65	–
1968	The Resurrection Of Pigboy Crabshaw	52	–

The BYRDS

Jim McGuinn (vocals, guitar)
Gene Clark (vocals, guitar)
David Crosby (vocals, guitar)
Chris Hillman (vocals, bass)
Michael Clarke (drums)

Although The Byrds were only hugely successful for a period of three years, the influence of this Los Angeles folk/country/ rock group has been a major factor in the history of popular music ever since.

Prior to the group's formation, McGuinn (born 1942 in Chicago) had worked with early 1960s folk acts like The Limeliters and The Chad Mitchell Trio (which also spawned John Denver) and recorded with Judy Collins, among others. Gene Clark (born 1941, Missouri) had spent a year as a member of The New Christy Minstrels (which also featured Barry McGuire) and David Crosby (born 1941, Los Angeles) had worked with Les Baxter's Balladeers, and this trio recorded a few obscure tracks as The Jet Set and a single as The Beefeaters.

With the addition of drummer Michael Clarke (born 1944, New York, real name Michael Dick), and Crosby on bass, the group rehearsed, but found that Crosby was an unwilling bass player, so Chris Hillman (born 1942, San Diego) was recruited. Hillman, a guitar and mandolin player who had recorded with bluegrass group The Scottsville Squirrel

Barkers and also with The Golden State Boys (who were renamed The Hillmen for their sole 1962 album), quickly learned bass as well, and in 1964, the group (still as The Jet Set) cut an album's worth of tracks which were released many years later as 'Preflyte' and reissued in the late 1980s as 'In The Beginning', on both occasions credited to The Byrds.

In late 1964 the group signed with Columbia (CBS) Records and changed their name to The Byrds (with unorthodox spelling à la The Beatles). Their first single, 'Mr. Tambourine Man', written by Bob Dylan, was an international smash hit, with 12 string guitar and excellent vocal harmonies providing a highly distinctive sound, although it later transpired that session players were responsible for virtually all the instrumental work. A second single, 'All I Really Want To Do', also written by Dylan, was a lesser US hit, although it reached the Top 5 of the UK singles chart, but the group's debut album, also titled 'Mr. Tambourine Man', reached the Top 10 on both sides of the Atlantic. 'Turn! Turn! Turn!', a musical adaptation by folk singer Pete Seeger of a passage from the biblical Book of Ecclesiastes, was their third single and second US chart-topper, and also the title track of their second album, which reached the US Top 20.

A fourth single, 'Set You Free This Time', was only a minor hit, and in March 1966, after recording a group original, 'Eight Miles High' (which was a US Top 20 hit, and might have gone higher had there not been suspicion that it was about drugs), Gene Clark left the group, who then completed a third album, 'Fifth Dimension', which peaked outside the US Top 20. As well as 'Eight Miles High', this included two more hit singles, '5D (Fifth Dimension)' and 'Mr. Spaceman' – within 18 months, the group had scored seven hit singles (including two US chart-toppers) and three hit albums, making them among the hottest acts in the world, with hit singles in Europe as well as the US.

A fourth album, 'Younger Than Yesterday', which many feel is their finest hour (although its chart performance disagrees) was released in early 1967. The album contained two US Top 40 hits, 'So You Want To Be A Rock-'n'Roll Star' (written about supposedly manufactured groups like The Monkees) and another Dylan song, 'My Back Pages'. McGuinn incidentally changed his name from Jim to Roger around this time. Later that year, Crosby grew apart from his colleagues, and after the release of 'Greatest Hits' (which predictably reached the Top 10 of the US LP chart), and 'Lady Friend', a single which he composed, whose B-side was

Dylan disciples The Byrds helped define folk rock – with the aid of session musicians

appropriately 'Don't Make Waves', the theme song to a Tony Curtis B-movie about a swimming pool salesman (!), he left to form Crosby, Stills & Nash with Stephen Stills (ex-Buffalo Springfield) and Graham Nash of The Hollies.

Gene Clark briefly rejoined, but was as unhappy as before, and the trio of McGuinn, Hillman and Michael Clarke recorded 'The Notorious Byrd Brothers' (1968) with session musicians. Also highly rated, the album struggled into the US Top 50, and only included one small hit single. Its sleeve showed the three looking through doors of a stable, with a horse (which has been said to be how the other members regarded Crosby!) gazing through a fourth. As well as several albums with combinations of CS&N (and Neil Young), Crosby also released a solo album, 'If I Could Only Remember My Name', in 1971, which reached the US Top 20.

At the end of 1967 McGuinn and Hillman recruited Kevin Kelley (drums) and Gram Parsons (born 1946, Florida, real name Cecil Connor) on vocals and guitar. Parsons had been leader of The International Submarine Band ('Safe At Home', their one album, is often cited as the first country/rock record), and was to have an immense influence on the group, despite being a Byrd for less than a year. Hillman especially was open to country music influences, and McGuinn also approved of Parsons's idea of country music played by a rock group, so 'Sweetheart Of The Rodeo' was recorded in Nashville, the country music capital of the US. Although it is regarded today as a pioneering and seminal work, it was the least successful album released by The Byrds up to that point. Due to contractual problems, Parsons hardly appeared on the album, although he was heavily involved in its recording.

At the end of 1968, he left the band, refusing to go on a tour of South Africa (not, according to Hillman, because of apartheid, but because of Parsons's preference for hanging out in Los Angeles with his new friends, The Rolling Stones). He was temporarily replaced by the group's tour manager, Carlos Bernal, but after the tour, Hillman also left, ironically to join Parsons in The Flying Burrito Brothers, and McGuinn was forced to rebuild the group.

The brilliant country and rock guitarist, Clarence White (born 1944), who had worked as a session musician on two previous Byrds albums, was invited to join the group, and White suggested his colleague in the group Nashville West, Gene Parsons, as replacement drummer when Kelley also left. John York played bass on 'Dr Byrds & Mr Hyde' (1969), the first Byrds album which failed to reach the US Top 100, and on the far more acclaimed 'Ballad Of Easy Rider', the group's highest charting album since 'Greatest Hits', but was replaced in late 1968 by Skip Battin, previously half of Skip & Flip, who scored the US Top 20 hits in 1959.

The line-up of McGuinn, White, Gene Parsons and Battin remained together for almost three years, cutting three albums: 'Untitled' (1970), an acclaimed double album of which half was recorded live, and which included the group's first UK Top 20 hit single since 1965, 'Chestnut Mare', 'Byrdmaniax' (1971) and 'Farther Along' (also 1971), each of which was less successful than its predecessor, although many feel this was the most consistently excellent live line-up of the group.

Parsons was replaced by John Guerin in late 1972, who was himself replaced by Dennis Dragon in early 1973, soon after which Battin also left, and in February 1973 when White left to rejoin his brothers, Roland and Eric, in The Kentucky Colonels, a bluegrass group, McGuinn laid the old group to rest. Gene Parsons later joined the reformed Flying Burrito Brothers, Battin went on to work with other groups in California, including The New Riders Of The Purple Sage and yet another line-up of The Flying Burrito Brothers, while White was tragically killed by a drunken driver in 1974.

At the end of 1972, McGuinn and the other four original Byrds reunited to record a new album, simply titled 'Byrds', for David Geffen's Asylum label, and it reached the US Top 20, although few regard it as one of the group's best efforts. Before returning for the reunion, Gene Clark had cut several critically regarded solo albums, including 'Echoes', 'White Light' and 'Roadmaster', without chart success, and also worked for 18 months with banjo virtuoso Doug Dillard as Dillard & Clark (which also included for a few months Bernie Leadon, later of The Eagles, and Clark's erstwhile Byrd colleague, Michael Clarke).

Neither 'The Fantastic Expedition Of Dillard & Clark' (1968) nor 'Through The Morning, Through The Night' (1969) troubled the chart compilers, although Crosby had become very successful with Stills and Nash, while Hillman had been joined in The Flying Burrito Brothers by Clarke (and Leadon). None of the original Byrds particularly wished to pursue the reunion after the album was completed, so Crosby stayed with CS&N, Michael Clarke eventually joined Firefall, Hillman became involved in numerous projects (see separate entry) and McGuinn started a solo career while Gene Clark continued with his.

Clark's 'No Other' (1974) was his most commercially successful solo album, but his 1977 album, 'Two Sides To Every Story', failed to chart. McGuinn experienced minor US chart success with his first three solo albums, 'Roger McGuinn' (1973), 'Peace On You' (1974) and 'Roger McGuinn & Band' (1975), but was less successful with 'Cardiff Rose' (1976) and 'Thunderbyrd' (1977). After a European tour in 1977 when McGuinn, Clark and Hillman each fronted their own

bands, but sometimes encored as a partially reunited Byrds, the trio signed with Capitol Records, releasing an eponymous album in 1979 which reached the US Top 40. This was followed by the considerably less successful 'City' in 1980, before Clark departed, just as he had in The Byrds. McGuinn and Hillman then cut an album scintillatingly titled 'McGuinn/Hillman', also in 1980, which was still less successful.

No new albums bearing McGuinn's name were released during the 1980s, although he occasionally guested on albums by such diverse acts as The Beach Boys and Elvis Costello, as well as touring Europe as opening act on a bill with Tom Petty & The Heartbreakers and Bob Dylan. In 1990 he signed to Arista Records, and his first album for a decade is expected at the time of writing.

Clark released 'Firebyrd' in 1984 without attracting much attention, and more recently worked with Carla Olson on a duet album, 'So Rebellious A Lover', but has rarely recorded in ten years. In 1988, Crosby, who had been imprisoned for drug offences, made his second solo album, 'Oh Yes I Can', whose release coincided with the publication of his autobiography, *Long Time Gone*, which he co-wrote with Carl Gottlieb.

In the late 1980s, a group led by Michael Clarke, with no other original group members, toured as The Byrds to the consternation of McGuinn, Hillman and Crosby, who instituted a lawsuit to stop Clarke. However, Clarke initially won the case, although the issue was further clouded when McGuinn and Hillman guested on an award-winning album by The Nitty Gritty Dirt Band, 'Will The Circle Be Unbroken II', on which they reprised their version of Bob Dylan's 'You Ain't Going Nowhere' (previously on 'Sweetheart Of The Rodeo'), which became a US country hit.

McGuinn, Hillman and Crosby reunited to record a few tracks for inclusion on a 90 track CD retrospective boxed set, which is eagerly awaited by Byrds fans everywhere, and is the latest of many compilations of the group's catalogue. Neither Gene Clark nor Michael Clarke were involved in the new recordings, and at the time of writing, it is uncertain whether the reunion will result in a complete new Byrds album in 1991. However, The Byrds will undoubtedly remain legendary.

Greatest Hits

Singles	Title	US	UK
1965	Mr Tambourine Man	1	1
1965	All I Really Want To Do	40	4
1965	Turn! Turn! Turn!	1	26
1966	Eight Miles High	14	24
1971	Chestnut Mare	–	19
Albums			
1965	Mr Tambourine Man	6	7
1966	Turn! Turn! Turn!	17	11
1967	Greatest Hits	6	–
1973	Byrds	20	31

J.J. CALE

His limited commercial success belies the fact that J.J. Cale inspired 1980s AOR virtually single-handedly – his bluesy, laid-back licks and whispered vocal style laid the groundwork for the Coffee-Table Rock of Eric Clapton and Dire Straits.

Born John Cale in Oklahoma City in 1938, he played guitar from the age of 10. After high-school bands (often with schoolfriend Leon Russell), he formed J.J. Cale & The Valentines, and in 1959, moved to Nashville to work as a country singer and/or songwriter and played in the Grand Ole Opry's road band. In 1964 he and Russell moved to Los Angeles, where they worked the bars and clubs with local musicians like Delaney & Bonnie, and gained studio experience, which led to an obscure pyschedelic album, 'A Trip Down Sunset Strip' (1967). Credited to The Leather Coated Mind, it was in fact Cale and Russell and friends – Cale wrote several tracks and co-produced. He also cut some unsuccessful singles for Liberty, including his original version of 'After Midnight'.

He returned to Tulsa in 1968 and built a small studio – Carl Radle (another Oklahoman who worked with Russell, Delaney & Bonnie and Clapton) sent Cale's demos to Denny Cordell, who was launching Shelter Records with Leon Russell, and signed Cale. After Clapton's 1970 US Top 20 hit with 'After Midnight', Cale's debut album, 'Naturally', appeared in 1971, not quite making the US Top 50, but including two US Top 50 singles, 'Crazy Mama' and a re-recorded 'After Midnight', plus 'Magnolia', which was covered by Poco and Jose Feliciano. Cale then

J.J. – gone fishin', naturally

opened Crazy Mama's, a studio in Nashville where he cut much of his subsequent work. His second album, 'Really' (1973), sold poorly, despite excellent reviews.

Cale spurned publicity, but continued to release albums: 'Okie' (1974), 'Troubadour' (1976), which included 'Cocaine', a US Top 30 hit in a Clapton cover, the imaginatively entitled '5' (1979), 'Shades' (1981), 'Grasshopper' (1982) and '8' (1983), most of which charted higher in the UK than the US. After a long silence, when he supposedly worked on movie soundtracks, he re-emerged in 1989 with 'Travel-Log' (released on Silvertone), a collection of tracks recorded between 1984 and 1989 with musicians like James Burton, Jim Keltner, and Spooner Oldham. The album was ecstatically reviewed, and charted in many countries, but Cale's reaction was typical: 'The trouble with success is that you don't get time to go fishing'.

Greatest Hits

Singles	Title	US	UK
1974	*Crazy Mama*	22	–
Albums			
1972	*Naturally*	51	–
1976	*Troubadour*	84	53
1989	*Travel-Log*	13	–

John CALE

Classically trained multi-instrumentalist Cale (born Wales 1940) studied at Goldsmith's College, London from 1960 to 1963 where he became involved with experimental electronic and classical music. Under a Leonard Bernstein scholarship, Cale made his way to Lennox, Massachusetts in 1963 to study Modern Composition, but left when it was decided that his music was 'too destructive'. Moving to New York, Cale became involved with avant-garde composer La Monte Young, and later with the young Lou Reed, leading to the formation of The Velvet Underground (see separate entries).

Following his acrimonious departure from the Velvets in 1968, Cale pursued a varied career before releasing his first solo album, playing on and arranging fellow ex-Velvet Nico's 'Marble Index' (1969), producing The Stooges (see separate entry) and The Modern Lovers (see separate entry) and playing on albums by Nick Drake and Mike Heron. Cale's debut, 'Vintage Violence' (1971) was a far cry from his previous more avant-garde work, being eleven deftly arranged melodic songs, but his next two outings were totally dissimilar. 'Church of Anthrax' (1971) was an improvised collaboration with experimentalist Terry Riley, while 'The Academy In Peril' (1972) contained only one song, the other tracks being piano pieces or orchestral works with the Royal Philharmonic Orchestra.

'Paris 1919' (1973) saw a return to and refinement of the style of his first album, blending Cale's classical background with his rock'n'roll approach on a strong selection of material. However its rich textures were largely discarded for 1974's 'Fear', whose stark black and white cover perfectly matched its contents. 'Fear' marked Cale's first collaboration with ex-Roxy Music keyboardist Brian Eno, and an appearance on 'June 1st 1974', a live album with Eno, Nico and Kevin Ayers followed.

'Slow Dazzle' (1975) saw Cale adopting a rockier sound, although the album also contained some calmer moments, including a sparse treatment of Elvis Presley's 'Heartbreak Hotel'. Cale toured to promote 'Slow Dazzle', but unfortunately his contract with Island Records required a swift follow-up and the resultant 'Helen Of Troy' was disappointing. Later in 1975 Cale produced the debut album from New York poetess Patti Smith, and the majority of his appearances over the next four years were as producer (Squeeze, Sham 69, Menace) or as guest musician (Ian Hunter, Julie Covington, Kate & Anna McGarrigle), with only one new vinyl release, 1977's 'Animal Justice' EP.

In 1978 Cale formed his own short-lived label, Spy, and in 1979 released a fine live album of new material, 'Sabotage', while 1981 saw a new studio set 'Honi Soit' on A & M, which failed to sell in large quantities despite a more commercial sound. The same fate befell 1982's 'Music For A New Society', Cale's most critically acclaimed work but ironically his worst-selling album. Sadly the next album, 'Carribean Sunset' (1984), was a scrappy affair, and when it was followed by a perfunctory live album ('Comes Alive', 1984), it seemed that Cale's inspiration had reach an all-time low. 1985's 'Artificial Intelligence' did nothing to dispel that view.

More production work followed, including the debut by The Happy Mondays, before Cale returned to the fray with the more successful 'Words For The Dying', based around orchestral settings of Dylan Thomas poetry, in some ways a return to the 'Academy In Peril' period. Following the death of the Velvet's mentor Andy Warhol, Cale was re-united with Lou Reed for 'Songs For Drella' (1990), a musical tribute to Warhol which was jointly credited, although the album is largely Reed's work. Also in 1990, Cale and Eno joined forces once more for the impressive 'Wrong Way Up' project, a partial return to form. Although Cale has never enjoyed even the limited commercial success of Reed, he remains an influential figure, and the best of his work is of a remarkably high standard.

Greatest Hits

Albums	Title	US	UK
1981	*Honi Soit*	154	–
1990	*Songs For Drella*	–	–

Kingsize codpiece is crowning climax at Cameo concerts

CAMEO

Larry Blackmon *(vocals, drums)*
Thomas Jenkins *(vocals)*
Gregory Johnson *(keyboards)*
Wayne Cooper *(vocals)*

Formed in New York in 1974 by Larry Blackmon (born 1956) and Gregory Johnson as The New York City Players, the above core was augmented by back-up musicians once they expanded into a solid R&B/funk band which played 200 shows a year. The original name caused confusion with the already successful Ohio Players, and was changed to Cameo for their 1977 debut album, 'Cardiac Arrest', produced by Blackmon by default because nobody else wanted the job. Though their sound was harder than the prevailing disco boom, Cameo found solid success through the later 1970s and into the 1980s, bolstered by the dance-friendly musical climate. Their hit singles were confined to the US R&B chart, but several albums provided moderate crossovers, and the sixth, 1980's 'Cameosis', earned a gold disc, and made the US Top 30.

In 1981 the group trimmed its line-up to a quartet. Two years later, they began recording for Blackmon's own Atlanta Artists label, and in 1984 achieved a pop crossover hit single on both sides of the Atlantic with 'She's Strange'. 1985's 'Single Life' was their first UK Top 20 hit, and Britain became a focus of the group's continued commercial success through the remainder of the 1980s.

In 1986 Cooper was replaced by Nathan Leftenant, and Blackmon as producer hired additional musicians for sessions or tours. The group had its biggest hits with the transatlantic Top 10 album, 'Word Up', and its pumping, staccato title track. Concerts of this era were highly visual, as Blackmon performed wearing a king-size, brightly coloured codpiece.

Cameo's light dimmed somewhat when Blackmon spent much of his energy on the production and promotion of other Atlanta Artists acts like the Reddings (sons of Otis). However, his acceptance by the wider musical community was evidenced by a guest vocal appearance on Ry Cooder's 1987 LP, 'Get Rhythm'.

Greatest Hits

Singles	Title	US	UK
1986	*Word Up*	6	3
Albums			
1986	*Word Up*	8	7

Glen **CAMPBELL**

A veteran of popular music with over 30 years of varied experience, Glen Campbell (born 1936 in Arkansas) epitomizes the frequent dilemma of the middle-aged pop star who finds that constant changes of fashion have made them irrelevant. Like many of his contemporaries, he has returned – with some success – to his country music roots.

After paying his dues on the road during the 1950s, at which time he became an above-average guitarist, he worked as a session musician in Los Angeles for the first half of the 1960s. He also briefly joined The Champs (of 'Tequila' fame), and worked with The Beach Boys (replacing Brian Wilson, who gave up touring with the band) before Bruce Johnston became a permanent Beach Boy. In 1985, Wilson produced an unsuccessful single for Campbell, 'Guess I'm Dumb'.

Campbell's purple period came from 1967 to 1971 when he scored 13 US Top 40 hits after changing his emphasis to singing rather than playing, plus two more duetting with Bobbie Gentry, although few reached the Top 10. His recordings of both 'Gentle On My Mind' (written by John Hartford) and 'By The Time I Get To Phoenix' (written by Jimmy Webb) won Grammy Awards in 1967/8, while subsequent successes with songs by Webb included 'Wichita Lineman' and 'Galveston'. Tuneful country-tinged ballads became Campbell's trademark, and frequent TV appearances propelled him into the lucrative but unhip 'family-entertainer' bracket which ironically had been the aim of many early rock'n'rollers who expected brief fame as chart stars.

In 1975 Campbell topped the US singles chart with 'Rhinestone Cowboy' (a description which seemed appropriate) and in 1977, repeated the feat with 'Southern Nights', while a 1976 TV advertised compilation topped the UK album chart. By 1980 he was firmly entrenched in country-inclined middle-of-the-road music, and rated by the end of the decade among the all-time most successful country artists, with over 70 US country chart hits to his credit, including duets with Gentry, Rita Coolidge, Anne Murray and Tanya Tucker. He also featured in several cowboy movies, notably *True Grit* (starring John Wayne), and on occasion has worked with The Highwaymen (Willie Nelson, Johnny Cash, Waylon Jennings and Kris Kristofferson) when one of the others is absent. Campbell is no longer a pop star, but an elder statesman of country music.

Greatest Hits

Singles	Title	US	UK
1975	*Rhinestone Cowboy*	1	4
1977	*Southern Nights*	1	28
Albums			
1968	*Wichita Lineman*	1	–
1969	*Galveston*	2	–
1971	*Greatest Hits*	39	8
1976	*20 Golden Greats*	–	1

Glen Campbell – paid his dues

CANNED HEAT

Bob Hite *(vocals)*
Alan Wilson *(vocals, guitar, harmonica)*
Henry Vestine *(guitar)*
Larry Taylor *(bass)*
Frank Cook *(drums)*

The most inspired and competent electric blues group to emerge from North America in the late 1960s, Canned Heat's reverential approach to its repertoire was balanced by an underlying humour that once extended to a Christmas single with The Chipmunks – though more typical collaborations were those with Memphis Slim, John Lee Hooker and other blues veterans who had captured the adolescent imaginations of Wilson and Hite who formed the band in 1966.

Wilson (born 1943) played slide trombone in campus jazz combos while studying music at Boston University. Enriched with warmly enthusiastic detail, a thesis on blues was instrumental in earning him a master's degree. Moving to Los Angeles in 1965, he met Hite (born 1943), a supermarket shelf-filler who was the life-and-soul of impromptu sessions in local blues venues. Like Wilson, Hite was a keen record collector and learned authority on a wide spectrum of blues forms ranging from slave field hollers to modern rock'n'roll. At Hite's instigation, much archive material was later either reissued or made available for the first time – notably on Liberty's 'Legendary Masters' series.

Cook, ex-Mother of Invention, Vestine (born 1944) and Taylor (born 1942) – whose professional career began in the employ of Jerry Lee Lewis (see separate entry) – were recruited by Hite and Wilson from among those jamming in the clubs. As demonstrated by the selections on their eponymous debut album, the new group delved back as far as the 1920s for some of their material; their very name was taken from a song recorded in 1928 by Mississippi bluesman Tommy Johnson.

Before the quintet's appearance at the celebrated Monterey festival in 1967, Cook had been replaced by Adolpho 'Fito' de la Parra (born 1946). 'Fito' played on 'Boogie With Canned Heat', the album that defined a style based on loose, simple structures often extrapolated into alien realms, evidenced by psychedelic passages in the lengthy 'Fried Hockey Boogie', built round the droning rhythm that became synonymous with Canned Heat after 'On The Road Again' – composed and sung by Wilson – was a huge international hit the following year.

Wilson's counter tenor was also to the fore in the follow-up, 'Goin' Up The Country' but, onstange, it was the hirsute, portly Hite who carried the show via a strain of jocular and sometimes indelicate continuity – a quality particularly appreciated when the band played the Woodstock Festival in 1969. Hite's was

the lead vocal on Wilbert Harrison's 'Let's Work Together', the million-seller from 'Future Blues', an album that also contained Wilson's 'My Time Ain't Long' – too apt a title in view of the partially sighted, depressive Bostonian's suicide in 1970.

Without Wilson, Canned Heat endured a period of confusing personnel changes, characterized mainly by the comings and goings of Taylor and Vestine – the latter vacancy filled by the jazzier Harvey Mandel who next joined the outfit led by Hite's friend, John Mayall. Others passing through the ranks included Stan Webb from Chicken Shack and Hite's guitarist brother Richard.

Throughout the 1970s, the outfit's stylistic determination remained rooted in good-time blues – though they updated themselves by adapting just enough of prevailing trends not to alienate an older following. Still a reliable draw at open-air gatherings, their albums – many of them 'live' – sold steadily if unremarkably with singles a mere sideshow to their earnings on the road. Hite's fatal heart attack in 1981 was seen by the group's management as regrettable but by no means disastrous. Therefore, with Ricky Kellogg at the central microphone, de la Parra as token 'original member' and the ritual placing of the

late Wilson's guitar on the boards at each performance, it was business as usual in the short term. However, as shown by a 1988 album of nothing but all the old favourites taped at some outdoor festival in Australia, Canned Heat survive in name largely as peddlars of second-hand nostalgia, although a later version of the band also featured the return of Vestine and Taylor.

Greatest Hits

Singles	Title	US	UK
1968	On The Road Again	16	8
1969	Goin' Up The Country	11	19
1970	Let's Work Together	26	2
Albums			
1968	Boogie With Canned Heat	16	5

Freddy **CANNON**

Cannon (born Freddy Picariello, 1939) holds the distinction of being one of the very few rock singers of his generation to top the UK album chart, a feat he never equalled in his native US, or with any single.

Alan Wilson (at back, centre) and Bob Hite (front, centre), deceased founders of Canned Heat

He performed in the mid-1950s as Freddy Carmen, before New York production duo Frank Slay and Bob Crewe toughened up his surname and recorded him on the self-penned rocker, 'Tallahassie Lassie'. Promoted on the *American Bandstand* TV show, it made the US Top 10 in 1959, also reaching the UK Top 20 despite an equally big local cover version from Tommy Steele. The follow-up, a raucous belt through the 1915 oldie, 'Way Down Yonder In New Orleans', was Cannon's biggest-selling single, a Top 3 hit on both sides of the Atlantic at the start of 1960. The sales prompted his producers to cut an album – by no means normal with a rock act at the time – built around a concept of place-name song titles. 'The Explosive Freddy Cannon' topped the UK chart, but made no headway whatever in the US LP lists. 1960/61 saw a steady run of medium-sized international hits like 'The Urge', 'Transistor Sister' and 'Muskrat Ramble', and Cannon toured frequently abroad.

In 1962 he cut a second million seller, 'Palisades Park' (written by *The Gong Show* host Chuck Barris), a Top 20 UK hit, and his UK chart swansong. As Beatlemania struck America, Cannon moved to a larger label, and unlike most of his US rock contemporaries, was not immediately buried, chartwise, by the avalanche of British hits, making the US Top 20 in 1964 and 1965 with 'Abigail Beecher' and 'Action', in the same style he had always used. If the late 1960s were bleaker, the 1970s advent of rock revival shows and tours embraced Cannon as a nostalgia act, and he has played the oldies circuit ever since, making a surprise US chart comeback in 1981 (paired with Dion's old group, The Belmonts) with the appropriately titled 'Let's Put The Fun Back In Rock'n'Roll'.

Greatest Hits

Singles	Title	US	UK
1959	Way Down Yonder		
	In New Orleans	3	3
1962	Palisades Park	3	20
Albums			
1960	The Explosive Freddy Cannon	–	1

CAPTAIN BEEFHEART

Just about as far off the wall as you can get, Don Van Vliet (born 1942, in Glendale, California) was never likely to make much commercial headway. With his chaotic, oft-improvised mix of 12-bar blues/avant-garde jazz/neo-Classics, and his unique, gruff, 7½ octave range (arguably the greatest white blues voice of all time) he certainly leaves a distinct impression. A child prodigy with a remarkable talent for sculpture and a high school contemporary of the equally bizarre Frank Zappa, Van Vliet was a self-taught

Bizarre bluesman Beefheart – British success threatened his avant garde credibility

musician, quickly mastering harmonica and sax. After playing in local R&B groups, he and Zappa tried unsuccessfully to form The Soots, after which Zappa moved to LA to form The Mothers; adopting his Captain Beefheart identity from the ill-fated project, Van Vliet in 1964 assembled the first Magic Band, a loose ensemble which would change constantly over the ensuing years.

He cut two singles for A&M in 1964 (reissued as a 12″ EP by Demon), which sold well enough locally for an album to be recorded which A&M rejected. In a move which presaged his *modus operandi* for the next 15 years, he broke up the band, changed labels (to Buddah), and re-recorded virtually the same album, which emerged in 1967 as 'Safe As Milk'. With a young Ry Cooder on slide guitar, it received phenomenal reviews, notably in the UK and Europe, which have always enjoyed Beefheart's work.

Although recorded in 1968, 'Mirror Man' was delayed by Buddah for two years, so Beefheart cut 'Strictly Personal' for Blue Thumb, although after it had been remixed without his approval, he disowned it. In 1969, he signed to Zappa's Straight Records and was allowed total artistic freedom for 'Trout Mask Replica', a double album acknowledged as a classic. Despite being totally uncommercial – the avant-garde meeting the Blues in a head-on collision, melodically erratic, and lyrically surreal – it almost reached the UK Top 20, but failed to chart in the US.

'Lick My Decals Off Baby' (1971), a baroque blues album, did make the UK Top 20 after more critical support. By this time, Beefheart had struck a purple patch: the finally released 'Mirror Man' even charted in the UK (much to Beefheart's chagrin) and he was also a major contributor to Zappa's 'Hot Rats' project. However, his relationship with Zappa soured, and he moved to Reprise for two 1972 albums, the surprisingly accessible 'The Spotlight Kid', which reached the UK Top 50 and was his US chart debut, and 'Clear Spot'. While these were his biggest albums, at that

point he elected for a two-year hiatus, to paint.

Although 1974's magnificent 'Unconditionally Guaranteed' saw a return to form, it was not a commercial success, and by the end of the decade, after a brief stint as lead singer with Zappa's Mothers, and several more unsuccessful albums, he had all but quit the music scene completely, spending increasingly more time working as an artist at his mobile home in the Mojave Desert. In 1986, an exhibition of his work took place in London. Captain Beefheart is an acquired taste, to say the least – any of the above albums should indicate his unique qualities.

Greatest Hits

Albums	Title	US	UK
1969	Trout Mask Replica	–	21
1971	Lick My Decals Off Baby	–	20

Belinda **CARLISLE**

Belinda Carlisle was born in Hollywood in 1958. In 1978 she became a founder member and lead singer of the first really successful all-girl rock group, The Go-Go's. The group hit gold with their 'Vacation' album and double platinum with their US chart topper 'Beauty And The Beat', and scored a string of hit singles, including 'We Got The Beat'.

The group split in 1985, and Carlisle worked on her solo LP, 'Belinda' for IRS records, with help from another former Go-Go's member Charlotte Caffey. The album went gold and hit the US Top 20, and a single from it, 'Mad About You', reached the US Top 3. British success came with her first MCA album, 'Heaven On Earth' (1988) and a track from the album, 'Heaven Is A Place On Earth', which featured Thomas Dolby on keyboards and backing vocals by Michelle

Former Go-Go girl Belinda

Phillips, topped the charts on both sides of the Atlantic. The album went double platinum in the UK, selling over three million world-wide, and gave her big transatlantic hit singles with 'I Get Weak', written by Diane Warren, and 'Circle in The Sand' from the pen of her producer, Rick Nowels, who co-wrote her No. 1 hit. No doubt sales were helped by excellent videos directed by film star Diane Keaton.

Carlisle's next album, 'Runaway Horses' (1989) went gold, and a single taken from it, 'Leave a Light On', featuring a guitar solo by George Harrison, also hit the US and UK Top 20. In 1990 The Go-Go's re-united, supposedly only for a few US appearances. Belinda, who is without doubt a star of the video age, is an avid animal rights campaigner and is involved in many environmental and 'green' projects. She is married to Morgan Mason, (son of the late film star James Mason), and lives in a home once owned by Clark Gable.

Greatest Hits

Singles	Title	US	UK
1988	Heaven Is A Place On Earth	1	1
1988	Circle In The Sand	7	4
Albums			
1988	Heaven On Earth	4	4
1989	Runaway Horses	37	4

Kim CARNES

When Californian singer/songwriter Kim Carnes (born 1946) achieved her biggest success in 1981, it was ironically with a song which she did not write.

Involved in music from her teenage years, Carnes learnt her trade as a ballad singer in night clubs before joining The New Christy Minstrels, a notable incubator for talent which at various times produced Barry McGuire, Kenny Rogers, Gene Clark (of The Byrds), John Denver, etc. After marrying another Minstrel, Dave Ellingson, the couple worked as songwriters, and during the 1970s, Carnes recorded with only minor success, her biggest success coming in 1978 with a US Top 40 duet with country singer Gene Cotton, 'You're A Part Of Me', before she became the first artist signed to the EMI-America label in 1979. In 1980 she and Ellingson wrote the songs for Kenny Rogers's 'Gideon' album which reached the US Top 20 and included a Top 5 duet between Rogers and Carnes, 'Don't Fall In Love With A Dreamer', and also made the US Top 10 on her own account with a cover of Smokey Robinson's 'More Love'.

This chart activity set the scene for her 1981 triumph with 'Bette Davis Eyes', a song originally recorded in 1974 by Jackie de Shannon, who co-wrote it with Donna Weiss. The Carnes version topped the US chart for nine weeks, and won Grammy Awards as both Record of the Year and Song of the Year. The album on which it was included, 'Mistaken Identity', also topped the US chart, and Carnes was finally in demand after nearly 20 years of dues-paying – she and Tina Turner were the guest stars on a Rod Stewart concert televised live to an estimated audience of 35 million.

Subsequent hits have been minor, although Carnes set a strange record in 1985 when she became the first artist to simultaneously appear in the US chart with a solo single ('Invitation To Dance'), a duet ('Make No Mistake, He's Mine', with Barbra Streisand) and as a member of a trio ('What About Me?' with Kenny

Kim – Mistaken Identity with Bette Davis Eyes

Rogers and James Ingram, a Top 20 hit). She was also one of the US stars who sang on USA For Africa's 'We Are The World'.

In the late 1980s, Carnes signed a long-term deal with MCA, debuting with the impressive 'View From The House' album in 1988. Never a 'flavour of the month' artist, Carnes may yet return to the top of the chart.

Greatest Hits

Singles	Title	US	UK
1980	Don't Fall In Love With A Dreamer (with Kenny Rogers)	4	–
1981	Bette Davis Eyes	1	10
Albums			
1981	Mistaken Identity	1	26

The CARPENTERS

Brother and sister team Richard (born 1946) and Karen (born 1950) were among the very few acts whose music appeals to both young and old and to pop and rock fans. The enduring qualities of their timeless music were underlined when a compilation album of their hits topped the UK album chart seven years after Karen's tragic death.

Born in Connecticut, the siblings moved with their parents to the Los Angeles suburb of Downey during the 1960s, where Richard, a talented pianist and arranger, formed a jazz trio which also featured Karen on drums, plus college friend Wes Jacobs on bass. After winning a talent contest, they cut a few unreleased tracks, but after Jacobs left to study music, they formed a folk/rock band. Spectrum, which also included John Bettis, who began to write lyrics to Richard's melodies.

Spectrum's life was brief, and Richard and Bettis worked as a duo at Disneyland (which inspired a later hit single, 'Mr Guder'), after which Richard and Karen, who had been encouraged to sing as well as play drums, recorded demos with noted session musician Joe Osborn, on which their brilliantly layered harmony vocals were showcased. The demos reached Herb Alpert, who signed them to his A&M label in 1969. Their debut album, 'Offering', was not a hit (although it later charted under the title 'Ticket To Ride' when it was reissued in 1971), and their debut single, a cover of the aforementioned Beatle hit, was only a minor US chart success in 1970.

Later that year, at the suggestion of Burt Bacharach & Hal David, who wrote the song, they covered '(They Long To Be) Close To You', previously recorded by Dionne Warwick in 1963, and it became the first of 24 US hits during the 1970s. After initially covering songs written by others ('We've Only Just Begun' – originally a TV commercial for a bank – and 'Rainy Days And Mondays' by

Richard and Karen Carpenter – pop perfectionists par excellence

interest in The Carpenters occurred as a result of a TV movie, *The Karen Carpenter Story* – when this and a TV compilation of video clips were screened in the UK in late 1989, several Carpenters albums reappeared in the UK chart, and when 'Only Yesterday', a 'greatest hits' compilation, was released in the UK, it sold a million within a year, some indication of how much the music of The Carpenters has remained of interest. Richard meanwhile released a solo album with such guest vocalists as Dusty Springfield, and continues to improve and remix old recordings featuring Karen, who is more revered now than during her tragic lifetime. Her technically perfect but expressive voice remains unique, and no pretenders have threatened her vacant throne.

Greatest Hits

Singles	Title	US	UK
1970	*(They Long To Be) Close To You*	1	6
1970	*We've Only Just Begun*	2	28
1971	*For All We Know*	3	18
1971	*Rainy Days And Mondays*	2	–
1971	*Superstar*	2	18
1972	*Hurting Each Other*	2	–
1973	*Sing*	3	–
1973	*Yesterday Once More*	2	2
1973	*Top Of The World*	1	5
1974	*Please Mr. Postman*	1	2
Albums			
1970	*Close To You*	2	23
1971	*Carpenters*	2	12
1972	*A Song For You*	4	13
1973	*Now And Then*	2	2
1973	*The Singles 1969–1973*	1	1
1975	*Horizon*	13	1
1976	*A Kind Of Hush*	33	3
1981	*The Singles 1974–78*	–	2
1990	*Only Yesterday*	–	1

Roger Nichols and Paul Williams, 'Superstar' by Bonnie Bramlett and Leon Russell, 'For All We Know' from the movie *Lovers And Other Strangers*), the first hit single written by Richard and Bettis was 'Goodbye To Love' in 1972, which featured a superb guitar solo by Tony Peluso. The Carpenter–Bettis team then wrote 'Yesterday Once More' as the centrepiece of the fifth Carpenters album, 'Now And Then', which included a well-performed medley of oldies, followed by their first chart-topper, 'Top Of The World', in 1973, by which time they had won three Grammy Awards.

The duo's first No. 1 album, a hits compilation, came in the same year, and was swiftly followed by a second No. 1 single in 1974 with a cover of 'Please Mr. Postman', a 1961 US chart-topper for The Marvelettes which also appeared on the first album by The Beatles, but by the end of 1975, Karen was starting to suffer from anorexia nervosa, the potentially fatal 'slimmer's disease'. Coin-

cidentally, the fortunes of The Carpenters in the US took a downturn, although for no obvious reason, their popularity in the UK increased, and their subsequent singles reached higher UK chart positions.

The quality of the duo's output had remained excellent, but rock critics in the late 1970s seemed to feel that The Carpenters were somehow lacking in street cred with the onset of New Wave/punk music. In 1979, while Richard was hospitalized for several months, Karen embarked on a solo album with producer Phil Ramone, but this was never released, and in 1981, she and Richard cut a new album, 'Made In America', which fared less well in the US than any original album since their debut. With a brief and disastrous marriage behind her, Karen showed signs of recovery from her disease, but in February, 1983, she died at her parents' home in Downey of a heart attack caused by the anorexia.

By the end of the 1980s, a rebirth of

Mary Chapin **CARPENTER**

At the start of the 1980s, new talented singer/songwriters were often ignored, as the music industry grew more impatient to find the next Beatles and ignored the art of great troubadours in favour of identikit dance and Heavy Metal. However, a few smart females, like Nanci Griffith, were marketed as country rather than folk, and entered the mainstream that way. A similar route was adopted by Mary Chapin Carpenter (like Mary Jane or Mary Anne, but less orthodox), who was born in New Jersey, but moved around the US and Japan (her father worked for *Life* Magazine) until she settled in Washington DC and started working the folk clubs during the second half of the 1970s.

After winning five local awards in 1986, Carpenter and her guitarist/producer John Jennings planned her debut album, 'Hometown Girl', as an independent release – until the tapes were heard by a big wheel at CBS, who

Mary Chapin – chart eludes hometown girl

signed her up immediately. With nine original songs plus a good cover of the Tom Waits song, 'Downtown Train', 'Hometown Girl' was more than a promising debut, it heralded the arrival of a new star. Rosanne Cash heard Carpenter's version of John Stewart's 'Runaway Train' (which had been left off the 'Hometown Girl' album) and topped the US country charts with her own version.

Two years later, Carpenter's second album, 'State Of The Heart', featured a more mature look and ten more originals plus the highly contagious 'Quittin' Time', co-written by a founder member of Bread, Robb Royer. The album excited interest both among country and folk aficionados, and a first European trip in 1990, when her third album, 'Shooting Straight In The Dark', confirmed her long term potential, augured well for a future in the pop chart as well as in country.

At the time of writing, Mary Chapin Carpenter has yet to reach the pop chart – by the time this is read, that should no longer be true, and any of the albums mentioned above will illustrate that point. Anyone who calls their music publishing company Getarealjob Music deserves our support.

The CARS

Ric Ocasek (vocals, guitar)
Ben Orr (vocals, bass)
Elliott Easton (guitar)
David Robinson (drums)
Greg Hawkes (keyboards)

One of the few 70s bands who combined New Wave awareness with a sharp pop sensibility, The Cars formed in Boston, Mass., in 1976. Each member was already a veteran of the local scene: Ocasek (born Richard Otcasek in Maryland, 1941), Orr (born Benjamin Orzechowski) and Hawkes had worked on folk combo Milkwood's eponymous 1972 album for Paramount Records, while Robinson was an original Modern Lover with Jonathan Richman and Jerry Harrison (later of Talking Heads) and played on their first album. Robinson gave The Cars their name and Ocasek wrote the songs which they recorded themselves and serviced to local radio stations and music papers, while building a strong following at Boston's Rat Club, and eventually signing to Elektra and recording their debut album in London with producer Roy Thomas Baker who had overseen Queen's success.

'The Cars' (1978), a US chart resident for many months, included two US Top 40 hits, 'Just What I Needed' and 'My Best Friend's Girl', the latter also reaching the UK Top 3. Over the next three years, the group released million selling albums: 'Candy-O' (1979), 'Panorama' (1980) and 'Shake It Up' (1981), each produced by Baker and each providing at least one guaranteed radio-friendly single to give the album maximum exposure. Although it may sound calculated, then at least the music didn't.

After 'Shake It Up', the band took a break to develop individual projects, mainly producing other artists. Ocasek produced Suicide and Iggy Pop, as well as making a solo album, 'Beatitude' (1983), which made the US Top 30. When the group reconvened, the results were even stronger than before – 1984's 'Heartbeat City' album, produced by the group with Robert John 'Mutt' Lange, included four US Top 20 singles including 'Drive', which reached the US Top 3, subsequently becoming the theme song for Live Aid in 1985.

At the end of 1985 their 'Greatest Hits' compilation was predictably big, and its one previously unreleased track, 'Tonight She Comes', was a US Top 10 hit single, fortuitously coinciding with the breakthrough of MTV in America as a significant pop medium. Ocasek released another solo album, 'This Side Of Paradise', in 1986 which made the US Top 40 and gave him a US Top 20 hit with 'Emotion In Motion'; Orr released a solo album, 'The Lace', but the next year the band was back together for a new album, 'Door To Door'.

Greatest Hits

Singles	Title	US	UK
1978	My Best Friend's Girl	35	3
1981	Shake It Up	4	–
1984	Drive	3	4
Albums			
1979	Candy-O	3	30
1984	Heartbeat City	3	25

Guitarist Ric Ocasek (centre) was the driving force behind Boston new wavers The Cars

Million dollar hits for Cash

Johnny **CASH**

'**H**ello, I'm Johnny Cash' is probably the best-known introduction in country music. Cash is country music's most famous living star, and his momentous and remarkable career of over 35 years is a testimony to both his undoubted talent and his strength of character. As a figurehead for country music, Johnny Cash has been an ambassador whose work may never be bettered. Born in 1932 in Arkansas, he was one of six children of an under-privileged family, and did not record until 1955, after four years in the USAF. Newly married to his first wife, Vivian Liberto, he moved to Memphis, Tennessee, to become a salesman, and in the evenings played country music, as singer/guitarist with backing provided by two friends, Luther Perkins (guitar) and Marshall Grant (bass).

Known as Johnny Cash & The Tennessee Two, the trio performed on a local radio station, which led to a successful audition before Sam Phillips of Sun Records in Memphis. This was during the era when Phillips signed Elvis Presley, Carl Perkins, Jerry Lee Lewis and Roy Orbison – certainly the most incredible string of country-oriented acts ever attached to a single label. Cash, Lewis, Perkins and Presley once recorded together informally after Presley had left Sun Records, the results being released many years later as 'The Million Dollar Quartet', although this gospel-oriented collection is far from the highlight of Cash's recording career, while the more recent 'Class of '55' album, which marked a reunion with Perkins, Lewis and Orbison, was also disappointing.

Many feel, with some justification, that the pinnacle of Cash's recorded output came during his time with Sun, although this represents but a fraction of his alleged hundreds of albums (including reissues and compilations). Like many entertainers, Cash's popularity and success have escalated with longevity, but like Presley, Lewis and Perkins, his earliest records are regarded as his best – many popular singers lose the hunger which first brought them to fame when success ensures that eating is no longer a problem. Cash's three years with Sun produced a dozen hit singles, and while only 'I Walk The Line' (a million-seller), 'Ballad Of A Teenage Queen' and 'Guess Things Happen That Way' made the US Top 20, each of the three topped the US country chart. Several other Sun sides, like 'Folsom Prison Blues', 'Big River' and 'Home Of The Blues', are as popular as the chart hits, and this period also included another half dozen country hits.

The period with CBS, to whom he was signed for 28 years from 1958, was not initially a success comparable to Presley's achievements at RCA. While Cash's Sun releases had been very popular, he only achieved minor success in his first four years with the new label, although that era did include his self-penned 'Tennessee Flat-Top Box', a small hit for Cash in 1961/62, but a country chart-topper for his daughter, Rosanne, in 1988. The fallow period ended in mid-1963 when 'Ring Of Fire' became his second million seller and first US Top 20 pop hit in five years.

Many of his singles were poor when judged by the high standards of his earlier work – 'Everybody Loves A Nut' is not the type of song that anyone who wants to be taken seriously should cut, although his brilliant version of 'Orange Blossom Special' from 1965 also came from this period, which is regarded as Cash's darkest hour.

As a huge live attraction, he might play 300 gigs per year, which involved considerable mileage, and as a result, began to use 'uppers', amphetamines, which are designed to reduce the desire for sleep, but can lead to abnormal behaviour and addiction. In 1965 Cash was convicted of drug abuse and received a suspended jail sentence and a fine, but not a cure – in 1966, while under the influence of drugs, he was arrested for picking flowers from the garden of a private house. The turning point came when he married June Carter, the co-writer of 'Ring Of Fire', and a country star in her own right whose mother, Maybelle, had been an original member of The Carter Family.

With June's help, Cash entered the most successful period of his career. Between early 1968, when a live version of 'Folsom Prison Blues' actually recorded in the jail gave him his first country No. 1 for five years, and the end of 1972, he had scored 12 Top 5 country hits, including 'A Boy Named Sue' (his best-known hit in the UK, and a US Top 3 pop chart hit), 'Sunday Morning Coming Down' (written by Kris Kristofferson, Cash's latter-day colleague in The Highwaymen), and 'A Thing Called Love'. His albums were also selling to a wider audience – 'Greatest Hits' sold a million in 1967, while 'At Folsom Prison' (1968) and 'At San Quentin' (1969) did the same.

By 1970 it had become clear that Cash's humanitarian qualities, as exemplified by playing concerts in prisons, were motivated by his strong Christian beliefs – in fact, his grandfather had been a Baptist minister, so he was following in a family tradition when he appeared onstage with the celebrated evangelist Billy Graham, whose approval of Cash no doubt brought the latter an even bigger audience. This was further increased by the publication in 1975 of his autobiography, *Man In Black* (a reference to his ever-present onstage costume), which has sold a million copies worldwide – a considerably more impressive achievement than selling a million records. More recently, he also wrote an impressive biography of St. Paul, *Man In White*, which had nothing to do with country music, but seemed to parallel Cash's own experiences in leading a Christian life after his unhappy involvement with drugs.

As the 1970s progressed, Cash's purple period died away, although he was still capable of topping the chart, as he proved in 1976 with the clever novelty song, 'One Piece At A Time' – the hybrid automobile described in the song was actually constructed when a film was made to accompany the song. By the end of the decade, many members of the Cash family were involved in recording and performing – June and her sisters worked as The Carter Family within The Johnny Cash Show, which also featured their son, John Carter Cash. Both his daughter, Rosanne, who had been brought up by her mother in California, and June's daughter, Carlene, had recording careers, and were married to singers – Rosanne, now a star in her own right, to country hero Rodney Crowell, and Carlene (briefly) to English artist/producer Nick Lowe.

As well as his solo hits, Johnny Cash has charted with eight partners, most frequently as a duo; his duets with June Carter between 1964 and 1970 included a US Top 40 hit with 'If I Were A Carpenter', and more recent work in collaboration with Waylon Jennings, Willie Nelson, Kris Kristofferson and sometimes Glen Campbell as The Highwaymen brought more million sellers. He has also recorded with such rock giants as Bob Dylan and Paul McCartney. In 1986, Cash signed with Mercury Records, and has continued to sell albums in reasonable quantities, although his vast back catalogue inevitably tends to overshadow new albums like 'Classic Cash', in which, perhaps unwisely, he re-recorded a number of his past hits. In 1989, he was back on the road only a short time after recovering from heart surgery.

Johnny Cash's contribution to the international acceptance and popularity of country music cannot be exaggerated – he is the biggest country star ever, and with nearly 50 crossover US pop chart hits, remains light years ahead of the competition. His reasons for continuing to work may have more to do with his enjoyment of live performance than financial reasons.

Greatest Hits

Singles	Title	US	UK
1969	A Boy Named Sue	2	4
1972	A Thing Called Love	–	4
Albums			
1969	Johnny Cash At San Quentin	1	2
1970	Hello, I'm Johnny Cash	6	6

Rosanne CASH

To be the offspring of a superstar is not an easy option, and the history of popular music is littered with kids who relied on reflected parental glory rather than talent. One who has made her own mark as a singer and songwriter is Rosanne Cash (born 1955), daughter of Johnny Cash.

She spent her early teenage years in California with her mother after her parents divorced, working in her father's show from 1973, although not initially as a performer. In 1979 she married singer/songwriter Rodney Crowell, and he produced demos which led to her signing with CBS, to whom her father was signed. Her first US country hit came in 1979 with 'No Memories Hangin' Round', a duet with Bobby Bare, from her 'Right Or Wrong' album (1980), since when she has combined a recording career with motherhood. Her 1981 album, 'Seven Year Ache', reached the US Top 30 and included three

Rosanne, keeping Cash in the family business

US Country chart-topping singles in the title track, 'My Baby Thinks He's A Train' and 'Blue Moon With Heartache', two of which she wrote herself, while the album, like most of her output, was produced by Crowell. 1982's 'Somewhere In The Stars' album was less successful, with fewer self-penned songs, but 'Rhythm & Romance' (1985) included four US Country Top 5 hits, two of which, 'I Don't Know Why You Don't Want Me' (which also won a Grammy Award) and 'Never Be You', topped the US Country chart.

She returned in 1987 with 'King's Record Shop', which included four US Country chart-toppers: John Hiatt's 'The Way We Make A Broken Heart', 'Tennessee Flat Top Box' (previously a 1962 Country No. 1 for its writer, her father), 'If You Change Your Mind' (which she co-wrote) and John Stewart's 'Runaway Train'. During this period, a duet between Rosanne and Crowell, 'It's Such A Small World' (from Crowell's 'Ashes & Diamonds' album), also topped the US Country chart, giving her five US Country No. 1 hits in under 18 months!

As her success outside the US was considerably less, her 1989 compilation album was titled 'Hits 1979–1989' in the US and 'Retrospective 1979–1989' elsewhere. Her first original album for three years, 'Interiors' (1990), was as introspective as its title suggests, bravely reflecting her interest in female emancipation, a cause not traditionally popular in country music circles, although it happily signals her wish to continue recording.

Greatest Hits

Singles	Title	US	UK
1981	Seven Year Ache	22	–
Albums			
1981	Seven Year Ache	26	–
1989	Hits 1979–1989	–	–

Harry CHAPIN

A remarkable writer of story-telling songs, Chapin (born 1942) was one of the most fascinating US singer/songwriters of the 1970s, and was returning to success when he was killed in an accident.

The son of a big-band drummer. Chapin and his brothers Steve and Tom formed a band after singing in a Brooklyn choir, after which Harry worked as a film-maker, one of his documentaries being nominated for an Oscar in 1969. The idea of forming a group with the three Chapins and Carly and Lucy Simon (to be called Brothers & Sisters) was dropped when his brothers returned to college to avoid the draft, and Harry formed a group with three friends, one of them a cello player, to perform his songs.

His first album, 'Heads and Tales' (1972),

was a sizeable hit, spending six months in the US chart, and included a US Top 30 single, 'Taxi'. Elektra founder Jac Holzman, who signed Chapin and produced the album, gave 'Circle' from Chapin's follow-up, 'Sniper And Other Love Songs', to the New Seekers, who scored a UK Top 5 hit with their sanitized version of the song. A prolific writer, Chapin released an album each year up to 1981 (with two in 1976), reaching the US album chart with each one. 1973's 'Short Stories' included a second US Top 40 hit, 'W.O.L.D.', the story of a disc jockey's decline, which was his only UK hit, while 'Verities And Balderdash' (1974) was his only US Top 5 album, going gold and including 'Cat's In The Cradle', a song which topped the US singles chart concerning parents neglecting their children.

Later albums reflected his accelerating political sensibilities, often with less commercial success, but his solid body of fans ensured brief US chart entries, especially for his 1976 double album, 'Greatest Stories – Live', which went gold. Leaving Elektra after another live double, 'Legends Of The Lost & Found' (1980), Chapin signed to the newly formed Boardwalk label and in 1981 released 'Sequel', whose title track continued the story of his first hit, 'Taxi', and becoming his first US Top 30 hit for six years and the album his biggest for four. However, he was killed in a traffic accident in 1981, ironically while on the way to a benefit concert for one of the many charities he supported by raising literally millions of dollars.

In 1988 'The Last Protest Singer', an unfinished album on which he was working at the time of his death, was released, but is probably of less interest than most of the albums released in his lifetime.

Greatest Hits

Singles	Title	US	UK
1972	Taxi	24	–
1974	W.O.L.D.	36	34
1974	Cat's In The Cradle	1	–
1980	Sequel	23	–
Albums			
1974	Verities And Balderdash	4	–
1976	Greatest Stories – Live	48	–

Tracy CHAPMAN

Proof that rock music could still come up with an overnight sensation in 1988 – black singer/songwriter Tracy Chapman was born in Cleveland in 1964. Her parents split up when she was four and she was an introverted child, reading books and listening to Bob Dylan, Joni Mitchell, Aretha Franklin and Al Green. After attending a private school in Connecticut, she went to university in Massachussetts with its coffee-house environment, where she honed her folk-music skills in the early 1980s.

Tracy – Mandela date her launching pad

Signed to SBK Publishing after the president's son saw her and called his father, she made her first album with David Kershenbaum, who had produced Joan Baez, Richie Havens and Joe Jackson. In rapid succession, she signed to Elektra Records and to manager Elliot Roberts (manager of Neil Young and others), despite the concept of a black solo folk singer being ultimately unfashionable. However, the combination of her songs and her shy yet intense onstage persona captivated every music-biz mogul she met.

On the release of her eponymous debut album in 1988, Roberts decided to launch her first in the UK. The organizers of that year's Nelson Mandela Birthday Tribute Concert in London fell under the spell and booked her for a three-song set on a side stage during an interval between major acts. Her performance was impressive, but when Stevie Wonder suddenly pulled out of his 'surprise' appearance when a computer disc was mislaid, Tracy was asked to fill the gap and played two more songs. In minutes, she mesmerized a world-wide TV audience as well as the 75,000 crowd, and only days later, her album shot to the UK Top 3, closely followed by a Top 10 single with 'Fast Car'. The same thing happened around the world.

Later that year, as she joined Bruce Springsteen, Sting and Peter Gabriel on a six-week global tour in aid of Amnesty International, sales of her album topped two million. Her 1989 follow-up album, 'Crossroads', could never match public expectation, and for a while it seemed she might disappear as fast as she had arrived, but she has wisely gone to ground in order to develop at her own pace.

Greatest Hits

Singles	Title	US	UK
1988	*Fast Car*	6	5
Albums			
1988	*Tracy Chapman*	1	1
1989	*Crossroads*	9	1

Ray **CHARLES**

The musical innovations of Ray Charles (born 1930) were arguably the biggest single factor in the evolution of modern soul music. Artists from Sam Cooke to James Brown, Otis Redding and Aretha Franklin all bore witness that their greatest influence was Charles.

Yet Ray Charles Robinson, who'd grown up in Florida, and contracted glaucoma at the age of six, which left him blind, began his playing career as a carbon copy of his hero, Nat King Cole.

He'd learned piano at Blind School from a local musician, Wylie Pittman, and his initial influences were Schubert, Bud Powell, Art Tatum and Cole. He began working around Florida with gigging bands before moving to Seattle, Washington as R.C. Robinson and The Maxim Trio. Based on the sound of the Nat Cole Trio, they signed to a local label in 1949, and recorded a debut single 'Confession Blues' (a US R&B Top 3 hit), as Ray Charles, dropping his surname to avoid confusion with the boxing champ who also sang, Sugar Ray Robinson.

A series of records followed, gradually moving towards a bluesier style under the influence of US West Coast vocalist Charles Brown, and Charles's own experience touring with R&B star, Lowell Fulson. He also scored an early success as arranger and pianist on the 1954 US R&B No. 1 hit, 'Things That I Used To Do' by Guitar Slim.

The first major change came as the fledgling Atlantic Records bought his contract, and label founder Ahmet Ertegun supervised his move towards a more up-tempo style, with the boogie-based 'Mess Around'. The novelty single, 'It Should've Been Me' hit the US R&B Top 10 in 1954, and Charles once again led a small band of his own.

It was with 'I've Got A Woman', recorded in 1955, that Charles introduced the fusion of blues and gospel music which was to revolutionise R&B and popular music generally. Utilizing gospel chord sequences, his blues-drenched piano and a 'preaching' vocal delivery, songs like 'Hallelujah I Love Her So' and 'A Fool For You' forged a style that dominated the US R&B charts in the mid 1950s.

Singers began covering Charles's numbers and his live concerts took on the character of

'The Preacher', 'High Priest of Soul' and 'Genius' – all used to describe the unique Ray Charles

secular prayer meetings. With the female backing quartet, The Raeletts, the call-and-response rapport between preacher and congregation was emulated by Charles and ecstatic audiences. Captured on two seminal live albums – 'At Newport' (1958) and the US Top 20 entry 'In Person' (1960) – his concerts revealed him as a consummate jazz pianist who also occasionally played alto saxophone, fronting a highly competent band.

Simultaneous with acclaim as an R&B artist came recognition from the jazz fraternity, fans and musicians. He made 'The Great Ray Charles' in 1957, an album of instrumentals, the same year he had his first US Top 10 hit with 'Swanee River Rock'; he spearheaded the 'soul jazz' movement with two albums, 'Soul Brothers' (1959), and 1962's 'Soul Meeting' with MJQ vibraphone star Milt Jackson. His publicity dubbed him 'The Genius', and in 1959 'The Genius of Ray Charles' on which he was backed by a big band of Basie and Ellington alumni, arranged by Charles, Quincy Jones and others, was a US Top 20 album.

1959 also saw the release of his first million seller, 'What'd I Say', which made the US Top 10, and was possibly the most influential R&B single ever released. A six-minute evocation of his technique at its most raw and sensual, it captured the imagination of a generation of fans – not least budding musicians in England such as Stevie Winwood, Eric Burdon and Joe Cocker.

A 1960 label change saw his debut single under the new contract, 'Sticks And Stones', in the solid small band idiom of his up-tempo classics, making the US Top 40, while the US Top 10 album, 'Genius Hits The Road' included a mesmerizing reworking of Hoagy Carmichael's 'Georgia On My Mind' which was his debut in the UK Top 30 and topped the US chart.

This period saw Charles at his artistic and commercial peak, continually spreading his wings in both repertoire and style. 'Genius + Soul = Jazz' (1961), a US Top 5 album, included the US Top 10 instrumental single, 'One Mint Julep' and arrangements by Quincy Jones. In October 1961 Percy Mayfield's 'Hit The Road Jack' was Charles's third million-selling single, topping the US chart and making the UK Top 10, while a contrasting album of cool jazz duets with Betty Carter confirmed his constant ability to match popularity with style.

Up-tempo singles continued to chart with 'Unchain My Heart' and 'Hide Nor Hair', both making the US Top 20 in early 1962, followed by yet another dip into new waters which would confound critics and fans alike, yet prove his most commercially successful move yet.

The 'Modern Sounds In Country And Western Music' album (1962) used the 'Georgia' formula of lush strings and choral arrangements on a collection of country standards. It topped the US chart, and the single from it, 'I Can't Stop Loving You' went on to reach No. 1 in the US and UK, the album also going Top 10 in the UK.

A second volume of the country album followed in 1963, delivering more singles hits including 'Take These Chains From My Heart', a UK Top 5 and US Top 10 entry, and 'You Are My Sunshine'. The million-selling 'Busted', which reached the US Top 5, came from 1963's US Top 3 album, 'Ingredients In A Recipe For Soul'.

As soul music per se took hold via Motown and Memphis, Charles's eclectic approach to material became more and more mainstream. A long-term heroin problem came to a head with his arrest in 1966, after which a cured Ray Charles again appeared in the UK and US Top 50 with two covers of Beatles songs, 'Yesterday' (1967) and 'Eleanor Rigby' (1968).

Despite modest showings in the charts, Charles's albums over the years, like his live appearances, have continued to mix small band funk, string-laden ballads and even disco-synthesized modern R&B that at their best – as in the 1975 'Renaissance' and 'True To Life' two years later – confirm Charles's position in the Hall of Fame of R&B and soul.

Greatest Hits

Singles	Title	US	UK
1959	*What'd I Say*	6	–
1960	*Georgia On My Mind*	1	24
1961	*Hit The Road Jack*	1	6
1962	*I Can't Stop Loving You*	1	1
Albums			
1962	*Modern Sounds In Country And Western Music*	1	6
1962	*Ray Charles Greatest Hits*	5	16
1962	*Modern Sounds in Country and Western Music Vol. 2*	2	15
1963	*Ingredients In A Recipe For Soul*	2	–

CHEAP TRICK

Robin Zander (vocals, guitar)
Rick Nielsen (guitar)
Tom Petersson (bass)
Bun E Carlos (drums)

One of the more unlikely pop/metal combos to emerge in the late 70s, Cheap Trick never quite looked what they seemed. Neilson (born 1946) and Tom Petersson (born 1950) had been in Grim Reaper in the 1960s and released a 1969 album under the name of Fuse. Cheap Trick formed in 1972 in Illinois, when Petersson and songwriter Neilson (with his ever-present baseball cap) linked up with blond singer/guitarist Zander (born 1952) and chain-smoking drummer Bun E Carlos (born Brad Carlson), but it was five years before their eponymous debut album was released on Epic. Produced by Jack Douglas, who had worked with Aerosmith, it failed to convey the unique quality of Neilson's quirky songs that relied on a blend of power pop guitar and hard rock.

They switched to Tom Werman as producer for 'In Colour' (1977), which made the Top 100 of the US album charts, and 'Heaven Tonight' (1978), which made the Top 50, bringing out the band's wacky flair on songs like 'Surrender', which dealt with the unlikely topic of parents making out on the sofa to their son's Kiss albums (!). Their 1979 album, 'Live At The Budokan', broke them in the US – initially only available in Japan, it sold so well as an import that it was domestically released and reached the US Top 5, spawning a US Top 10 hit, 'I Want You To Want Me'.

Later in 1979 came a third studio album, 'Dream Police', again produced by Werman, which made the US Top 10. They switched to Beatles producer George Martin for 1980's

Cheap Trick, with (left to right) Neilson, Zander, Carlos and Petersson

'All Shook Up' album, which highlighted their pop sensibilities still further and made the US Top 30. Petersson quit soon after the record came out and was replaced by Jon Brant and they changed producers again, bringing in Roy Thomas Baker for 'One On One' (1982) which reached the US Top 40, although 1983's 'Next Position Please' was less successful. In 1985 they returned to the US Top 40 with 'Standing On The Edge', and in 1988 after Petersson had rejoined, topped the US singles chart with 'The Flame', taken from the US Top 20 album, 'Lap Of Luxury', their biggest album in years, and in the same year reached the US Top 10 with a cover of the Elvis Presley hit, 'Don't Be Cruel'. In 1990 they were back in the Top 20 of the US singles chart with 'Can't Stop Falling Into Love', from their US Top 50 album, 'Busted'.

Greatest Hits

Singles	Title	US	UK
1979	I Want You To Want Me	7	29
1988	The Flame	1	–
Albums			
1979	Cheap Trick At Budokan	4	29
1979	Dream Police	6	41

Chubby **CHECKER**

Checker (born Ernest Evans, 1941) occupied a pivotal role in pop music at the start of the 1960s as the most successful exponent of the teen-dance movement which dominated the US charts until the advent of The Beatles – particularly that dancefloor/cultural phenomenon, the Twist.

Given his stage name by DJ Dick Clark's wife, who noted his likeness to a young Fats Domino, Checker was originally signed to record for his ability to copy vocal styles of stars – his 1959 debut single, 'The Class', found him imitating Presley, Domino and others. He found his forte in 1960, when, at Dick Clark's suggestion, he covered Hank Ballard's dance song, 'The Twist' – Checker's version topped the US chart with a million-plus sales.

Checker rapidly became the Doyen of Dance Crazes, as the formula proved reworkable in umpteen variations: 'The Hucklebuck', 'Dance The Mess Around' and 'The Fly' were all big US hits in 1960/61, and 1961's 'Pony Time' was a second million-seller. A year after the first smash, he came up with another US Top 10 hit in 'Let's Twist Again', noting that the original craze was outlasting its gimmicky follow-ups, and the Twist as a dance step was spreading to adult clubs, and catching overseas attention.

At the end of 1961 the Twist became the social rage of New York, and a bandwagon on which everybody from Sam Cooke to Frank Sinatra would jump into the US charts, but Checker kept ahead of the pack: 'The Twist' was reissued and topped the US chart for a second time – an achievement only shared by Bing Crosby's 'White Christmas'.

As the dance became an international rage in 1962, Checker's hits spread overseas, with 'Let's Twist Again' giving him a UK Top 3 hit, but he moved on again to other dances by year's end, via 'Slow Twistin'' (a US Top 3 duet with Dee Dee Sharp), and the double-sided US Top 3 hit, 'Limbo Rock'/'Popeye The Hitch-Hiker' (another million seller), and kept it up through 1963 with hits like 'Birdland', the throwback 'Twist It Up' and 'Loddy Lo'.

Checker's nemesis was his almost total identification with dance crazes; the arrival of British beat groups in 1964 being enough to sink his chart ambitions. The later 1960s were low-key years, and not until the 1970s boom in nostalgia tours did his Twist King status become an asset rather than an albatross. In 1975 'Let's Twist Again' was a UK Top 10 hit again, as the dance enjoyed a teen revival.

Checker's nostalgia value remains bankable, as was amply demonstrated in 1988 when he guested with hot rap trio The Fat Boys on a rap remake of 'The Twist', which was a Top 20 hit on both sides of the Atlantic, and saw Checker performing with them to a world-wide TV audience at the Nelson Mandela Birthday Concert.

Greatest Hits

Singles	Title	US	UK
1960	The Twist	1	44
1961	Pony Time	1	27
1961	Let's Twist Again	8	2
1962	The Twist (reissue)	1	14
Albums			
1960	Twist With Chubby Checker	3	13
1961	Your Twist Party	2	–

CHIC

Bernard Edwards (bass)
Nile Rodgers (guitar)
Tony Thompson (drums)

Formed in 1977 Chic were the most creative and innovative of the successful artists of the 'Disco Era'. Edwards (born 1952) and Rodgers (born 1952) had worked together in The Apollo Theater orchestra, moving with

Lots of twists and turns have marked Chubby's chequered career

Thompson into The Big Apple Band, who eventually backed short-lived vocal group, New York City. Around the mid-1970s, the three musicians began to offer demo tapes around New York consisting of a stripped-down soul rhythm which incorporated elements of Motown's pop sensibility and the rawness of James Brown, mixed into the all-pervading disco beat.

Their first single 'Dance Dance Dance (Yowsah Yowsah Yowsah)' (1977) was a Top 10 hit on both sides of the Atlantic, after which Norma Jean Wright, Alfa Anderson and later Luci Martin (replacing Wright), on vocals joined the nucleus of Chic. It was 1978's 'Le Freak' that propelled the group into the forefront of popular music and firmly established a Chic sound.

Unusually for a dance act, Chic enjoyed enormous album sales – their eponymous debut album was a modest hit but the follow-up 'C'est Chic', was quickly certified platinum helped by sales of 5 million for the 'Le Freak' single. A modified version of the album including earlier hits reached the UK Top 3.

Alongside Chic, Edwards and Rodgers began producing other artists, beginning with Norma Jean Wright, who left the Chic fold and enjoyed modest success with 'Saturday'. Her success prompted Chic's record label to assign their declining girl group, Sister Sledge, to the duo, who provided them with instant hits during 1979, notably 'He's The Greatest Dancer' and 'We Are Family', both total Chic soundalikes. Also in 1979, Chic's second US chart-topper, 'Good Times', consolidated Edwards and Rodgers reputation as innovators. Its influence, particularly Edwards' bass lines, appeared in countless records over the next few months, including Queen's 'Another One Bites The Dust', and was 'borrowed' wholesale by The Sugarhill Gang for 'Rappers Delight', which launched the direction of black music up to the 1990s.

The third album, 'Risqué', also went platinum, and was a perfectly realized piece of work – highly unusual for artists working in the disco genre – which proved to be their commercial peak. The results of their production contract with Diana Ross propelled her back into the forefront, after many years of lacklustre work. 'Upside Down' topped singles charts all over the world in 1980, but it became apparent that Ross had interfered with their production – while retaining the overall feel of a Chic recording, it was not the record Edwards/Rodgers produced, and subsequently they demanded – and got – full control. A project with Aretha Franklin the same year threw up similar problems, and the duo did not complete it.

By the early 1980s, Chic's albums and singles were not selling as well and their productions (Blondie, Sheila B. Devotion and the soundtrack, 'Soup For One') were disappointing. Rodgers and Edwards separated as producers, both with a desire to be accepted in the rock mainstream, an ambition

they both achieved. Their individual solo albums were poorly received, but their production work remained solid. Edwards produced the Duran Duran spin-off, Power Station, but Rodgers achieved greater fame in 1983 when he revitalized David Bowie's career with the 'Let's Dance' album, which featured Thompson on drums (as had Power Station). He also produced Mick Jagger's solo album, 'She's The Boss', Madonna's 'Like A Virgin', 'The Honey Drippers' (Robert Plant) as well as Duran Duran, The Thompson Twins and the late blues guitarist, Stevie Ray Vaughan, who ironically was first brought to the world's attention by Rodgers, who used him on Bowie's 'Let's Dance'.

A Chic reunion is rumoured for the early 1990s, but even if does not take place, the group's influence on the popular music of the 1980s is immeasurable.

Greatest Hits

Singles	Title	US	UK
1977	Dance Dance Dance		
	(Yowsah Yowsah Yowsah)	6	6
1978	Le Freak	1	7
1979	I Want Your Love	7	4
1979	Good Times	1	5
Albums			
1978	C'est Chic	4	2
1979	Risqué	5	29

CHICAGO

Peter Cetera (bass, vocals)
Robert Lamm (keyboards, vocals)
Terry Kath (guitar)
James Pankow (trombone)
Lee Loughnane (trumpet)
Walter Parazaider (saxophone)
Danny Seraphine (drums)

Four music students at Chicago's De Paul University, Pankow (born 1947), Seraphine (born 1948), Parazaider (born 1945, aka Walt Perry) and Loughnane (born 1946) formed The Missing Links in 1966 with cabaret pianist Lamm (born 1944), and soon after Cetera (born 1944), with Kath (born 1946) completing the group in 1967. After a name change to The Big Thing, they worked the Chicago club circuit, and at the suggestion of another De Paul alumnus, record producer James Guercio (born 1945), changed the name again to Chicago Transit Authority after he began managing them.

Guercio's influence helped them to sign with CBS (for whom he produced the musically similar Blood, Sweat & Tears), and their eponymous debut album was a double which made the US Top 20 (during a chart residency of three years) and the UK Top 10. The group's mix of jazzy horn arrangements, a rock rhythm section and accessible material

appealed to the maturing post-hippie generation, while retaining hip credibility by including protest chants recorded at the 1968 Chicago Democratic Convention.

Legal threats over the group's use of the name by the actual Chicago Transit Authority persuaded them to abbreviate it to simply Chicago, by which name they appeared at the ultra-trendy Toronto Peace Festival, where John Lennon's Plastic Ono Band made their live debut. Their first UK Top 10 single came in 1970 with a cover version of 'I'm A Man' (a 1967 hit for The Spencer Davis Group), while their debut US Top 10 single was 'Make Me Smile' also in 1970, after which the oddly-titled '25 Or 6 To 4' made both the US and UK Top 10s. A second double album, provocatively titled 'Chicago II' in the US, and simply 'Chicago' in the UK, made the US Top 5 and the UK Top 10, while a third consecutive double album, 'Chicago III' (1971), made the US Top 3, but was a comparative stiff in the UK, where the group's popularity plummeted, perhaps due to their apparent inability to be concise. This was highlighted by the same year's 'Chicago At Carnegie Hall', a four-LP boxed set which reached the US Top 3, but failed to chart in Britain.

1972's 'Chicago V', their first single album, topped the US chart and briefly charted in the UK, and included a US Top 3 single, 'Saturday In The Park', while the following year's 'Chicago VI' again topped the US chart and included two US Top 10 singles, but was unlisted in the UK. The same pattern occurred for 'Chicago VII', a US chart-topper with two Top 10 singles and a UK flop, although it did contain a minor US hit single, 'Wishing You Were Here', which featured backing vocals by three members of The Beach Boys, for whom Guercio was playing bass at the time.

A personnel change came before the next album, with the recruitment of Brazilian percussionist Laudir de Oliveira, but this failed to signal a new direction, and 'Chicago VIII' and 'Chicago IX – Chicago's Greatest Hits' (both 1975) continued the familiar pattern, topping the US chart and failing in the UK. However, 1976's 'Chicago X' was the group's biggest album in the UK for six years, and included 'If You Leave Me Now', a single which topped the charts in both Britain and America. In 1978 Kath accidentally killed himself with a gun he thought was empty, and that year's album broke the sequence by having the non-numerical title of 'Hot Streets', and was their first album not to reach the US Top 10 since their debut. Donnie Dacus was recruited to replace Kath, while Guercio's involvement with the band as manager/producer also ended.

In 1982, Bill Champlin (keyboards, vocals) joined the group from The Sons of Champlin, and the group's first album for the strongly artist-oriented Full Moon label was 'Chicago 16' (the Roman numerals had finally bitten

Chicago – playing by numbers, and not just on the cover

the dust), which was their first US Top 10 hit in five years, and their first UK chart album for six. It included 'Hard To Say I'm Sorry', a single which featured in the movie *Summer Lovers* and topped the US chart and made the UK Top 10. 1984's 'Chicago 17' included two more major singles, 'Hard Habit To Break' and 'You're The Inspiration', and the album also charted respectably, but in 1985, Cetera left for a highly successful solo career which produced two US No. 1 hits in 1986, 'Glory Of Love' and a duet with Amy Grant, 'The Next Time I Fall'.

Cetera was replaced by Jason Scheff (son of noted session musician Jerry Scheff), and the formula continued with another change of label (to Warner/Reprise), which produced a US chart-topping single, 'Look Away', in 1988, and a UK Top 20 album, 'The Heart Of Chicago', in 1989. While one cannot but admire the group's resilience in surviving for over 20 years as a major act, their initial novelty value soon became as routine and predictable as their album titles, although clearly they can still be inspired enough to produce occasional big singles.

Greatest Hits

Singles	Title	US	UK
1976	If You Leave Me Now	I	I
1982	Hard To Say I'm Sorry	I	4
1988	Look Away	I	–
Albums			
1972	Chicago V	I	24
1973	Chicago VI	I	–
1974	Chicago VII	I	–
1975	Chicago VIII	I	–
1975	Chicago IX –	I	–

Lou **CHRISTIE**

Born Lugee Sacco in 1943, Christie's distinctive falsetto made 'The Gypsy Cried' (1962) the first of a series of hit singles.

Growing up in Pittsburgh, Sacco soon became part of the local pop scene, recording with vocal groups The Classics and Lugee And The Lions before going solo as Lou Christie. Co-written with Twyla Herbert, 'The Gypsy Cried' sold a million after it was nationally released in the US. Although Christie was branded by some critics as a Del Shannon/Four Seasons soundalike, he used the same high-pitched vocal trademark on another Top 10 hit, 'Two Faces Have I' (1963), but his career was interrupted by army service, and on his return his manager, Bob Marcucci (who had also masterminded the careers of Frankie Avalon and Fabian), acquired a new record deal.

Linking up again with Herbert (described in press releases as a 'mystic twenty years his senior'), against his label's advice, Christie released his best single, 'Lightnin' Strikes' (1966), whose slick changes of pace made it a US No. 1 and his first UK success. The similar-sounding follow-up, 'Rhapsody In The Rain', sold less well mainly because it was banned by many radio stations for being 'suggestive'.

After later singles failed, Christie returned to the world's charts in 1969 with 'I'm Gonna Make You Mine'. 'Are You Getting Any Sunshine' made less impact and in the 1970s, he moved to the UK. In later years, he recorded infrequently, scoring a minor US hit in 1974 with the oldie 'Beyond The Blue Horizon' and duetting with both Lesley Gore and Pia Zadora. He briefly reverted to the

name Sacco for an album, but was more typically found re-creating his 1960s glory at rock revival concerts.

Greatest Hits

Singles	Title	US	UK
1963	The Gypsy Cried	24	–
1963	Two Faces Have I	6	–
1966	Lightnin' Strikes	I	II
1969	I'm Gonna Make You Mine	10	2

CLANNAD

Maire Brennan (harp, vocals)
Paul Brennan (flute, guitar, keyboards)
Ciaran Brennan (bass, synthesizer)
Patrick Duggan (mandola, guitar)
Noel Duggan (guitar, keyboards, vocals)

Irish folk group founded in 1976 by the Brennan family (their name often rendered in Gaelic – Ni Bhraonain – on album sleeves), whose father Leo was a noted Irish band leader. Clannad is literally the Gaelic for Family. Originally a four-piece with Paul Brennan on lead vocals, Maire (born 1952) was added for her skill as a harpist as much as for her singing ability.

Perfecting their craft at local folk festivals and at the Brennans' bar, Leo's Tavern, at Gweedore on Ireland's west coast, they recorded numerous albums on labels, like 1978's 'Clannad in Concert' on Ogham, 1980's 'Crann Ull' on Tara, but with little more than regional success. 1982's 'Fuaim' saw a more keyboard-based sound emerging, courtesy of Eithne Brennan, a temporary addition to the ranks.

Clannad moved into the lucrative rock market after the success of the atmospheric TV signature tune 'Theme From Harry's Game' in 1982. A Top 5 UK hit, it won an Ivor Novello Award in 1983. Its New Age-meets-folk blueprint was followed by Eithne leaving the group, renaming herself Enya, and working with one-time Clannad producer Nicky Ryan to produce the music for the BBC series *The Celts* (released as 'Enya' in 1987) and 1988's UK chart-topper 'Orinoco Flow' and a Top 5 album 'Watermark'.

Chief songwriter Paul Brennan had written 'Harry's Game', the lead track on 1983's 'Magical Ring' which mixed atmospheric mood pieces with recognizable outside songs like 'I See Red' and went gold. 1984's 'Legend' album was inspired by TV's *Robin of Sherwood* and was the group's second TV spin-off success: they wrote and performed music for all 26 episodes. Previously nominated for 'Harry's Game', 'Legend' won a British Academy Award in 1985. The same year's 'Macalla', their most assured musical outing to date and the most effective merging of folk

The Brennans meet the Duggans in a Gaelic get-together with Clannad

From cult hero to world superstar, Clapton's guitar supremacy has spanned three decades of rock

and rock influences, saw U2's Bono guesting on the hit single 'In A Lifetime'.

The album proved a relative commercial disappointment, compared with its predecessors, so Greg Ladanyi/Russ Kunkel (the team behind Jackson Browne) were brought in to produce 1987's Sirius', which lacked much of their early charm, due to relentless drums by co-producer Kunkel and extra keyboards (by Bruce Hornsby and others). Although it peaked lower than 'Macalla', Clannad achieved sell-out status on the UK concert circuit.

The compilation 'Pastpresent' (1989) sold 250,000 to become their best-selling album, while the same year's 'Atlantic Realm' was another TV link-up by Paul and Ciaran (though strangely using the group name) for a wildlife series.

Paul left the group before 1990's 'Anam', produced and arranged by Ciaran alone, which marked a return to a more traditional folk base. Paradoxically, their profile in rock terms is still enviably high: U2 still use 'Harry's Game' as the closer to their live performances.

Greatest Hits

Singles	Title	US	UK
1982	*Theme From Harry's Game*	–	5
1986	*In A Lifetime*	–	20
Albums			
1984	*Legend*	–	15
1989	*Pastpresent*	–	5

Eric CLAPTON

Eric Clapton (born 1945) is undoubtedly one of rock's most popular and successful guitarists. He dropped out of art school in 1963 to join The Roosters (with Tom McGuinness, later of Manfred Mann) playing unsuccessful R&B. McGuinness and Clapton moved up another blind alley with Casey Jones And The Engineers, before Clapton was recruited into The Yardbirds in October 1963 to replace Tony Topham. Clapton became the star of their show, earning the ironic nickname 'Slowhand'. He featured on the first two Yardbird singles, 'I Wish You Would' and 'Good Morning Little Schoolgirl', but although The Yardbirds recorded a live album with Sonny Boy Williamson, Clapton left in March 1965 after their first big hit, 'For Your Love', because he felt The Yardbirds were becoming too commercial.

Clapton was a blues purist, his idols being the Chicago blues men – Muddy Waters, Buddy Guy, Otis Rush etc. The only band playing this type of music in Britain at that time was John Mayall's Bluesbreakers, which Clapton joined in April 1965. Here he consolidated his reputation as Britain's premier blues guitarist. Apart from a bizarre episode when he went AWOL attempting to play his way around the world with a bunch of friends which ended six weeks later in Greece, Clapton stayed with Mayall until July 1966 and the formation of Cream.

By then Clapton was a fully fledged guitar hero, confirmed by the graffiti which allegedly appeared all around London declaring 'CLAPTON IS GOD'. More tangible evidence was the release in August 1966 of the album he cut with John Mayall, 'Bluesbreakers' (aka the 'Beano album' – the reason obvious to anyone who has it) – still *the* classic British blues album. All his major influences and the breadth of his skill as a blues player were showcased on outstanding tracks like 'Steppin' Out', 'Hideaway', 'All Your Lovin', 'Have You Heard' and his solo vocal debut on 'Ramblin' On My Mind'. To this, one would add his guitar solo on 'Stormy Monday', which appeared on Mayall's 'Primal Solos' album (1977) from a date at the Flamingo club in April 1966, around the time the 'Bluesbreakers' album was recorded, on which some say that Clapton has never played better.

Clapton was a restless spirit and when the chance came to play with the best rhythm section in Europe, Ginger Baker and Jack Bruce, he took it and they formed Cream (see separate entry). The unwelcome deification of Clapton continued and after a slowish start in the UK, Cream went to America in 1967 and again in 1968 to rapturous receptions and large gate receipts. Eventually, Clapton tired of playing the same songs every night and even claimed that sometimes he would stop playing without either of the other two noticing. By the end of 1968, Cream had run its course. Meanwhile Clapton's attention was caught by The Band's 'Music From Big Pink', and his ears were opened to a more melodic, less frantic style of playing. The abortive Blind Faith (see separate entry) was a stepping stone from the heavy power blues thrash of Cream to the infinitely more laid-back style of Delaney and Bonnie, a southern white soul outfit with whom Clapton briefly worked in 1970. It was partly Delaney Bramlett's influence that led Clapton to release his eponymous solo debut albums in 1970, but as with the Blind Faith album, Clapton fans were disappointed at the lack of soloing. However songs like 'After Midnight', which brought the reclusive J.J. Cale to prominence, and 'Let It Rain' were signs of things to come.

Despite the solo album and several stage and studio guest appearances most notably with The Beatles ('The Beatles' White Album, 1968), Aretha Franklin ('Live At The Fillmore', 1968), and John Lennon ('Live Peace' in Toronto, 1969), Clapton still sought anonymity. With Delaney and Bonnie's musicians, he formed Derek And The Dominos and in 1970 the band cut the double album 'Layla And Other Assorted Love Songs' featuring Duane Allman, but it

was a critical and commercial flop in both the US and UK.

Through 1971 and early 1972, Clapton's personal life began to fall apart. He lost his friends Jimi Hendrix (in 1970), Duane Allman (killed in a motorcycle accident in October 1971) and his grandfather who had brought him up. The album into which he had poured so much was scorned and he was rejected by 'Layla', George Harrison's wife, Patti Boyd. Ironically, when 'Layla' was a smash hit single in 1972, Clapton had become addicted to heroin and all but retired from music. From 1971 to 1974, he made only three public appearances; George Harrison's Bangladesh concert; a Leon Russell gig (both 1971) and in 1973, a London 'comeback' concert organized by Pete Townshend with Stevie Winwood, Ric Grech and Ron Wood among others.

It wasn't until mid-1974, that Clapton recorded what became '461 Ocean Boulevard'. The release of the album finally scotched any notion that Clapton would return to the blitzkrieg guitar work-outs of the 1960s and was a further consolidation of his approach on the first solo album. Starved of Clapton product, fans took the album to No. 1 in America and No. 3 in the UK, and the cover of Bob Marley's 'I Shot The Sherriff' into the UK Top 10. The tour that followed was patchy, primarily caused by Clapton's drinking which had replaced the heroin, and the albums for 1975–6,, 'There's One In Every Crowd' and 'No Reason To Cry', were among his worst. Fortunately 'EC Was Here' (1975), a live blues album did much to remind us that Clapton was still a guitar force.

All subsequent albums have followed a similar pattern, a mixture of ballads, blues and AOR, no album entirely successful, but each containing some timeless tracks including 'Cocaine' and 'Wonderful Tonight' from 'Slowhand' (1977); 'Tulsa Time' from 'Backless' (1978); and 'I Can't Stand It' from 'Another Ticket' (1981). The double live 'Just One Night' (1980) showed the strengths of Clapton's concert performances and did well in the charts.

Clapton played at Ronnie Lane's ARMS concert for multiple sclerosis in 1982, released the rather ordinary 'Money And Cigarettes' album in 1983 (the first on his own 'Duck' label) and joined the world for Live Aid in 1985. This appearance was a turning point for Clapton; since then, he has become a leading light in the rock establishment and more internationally popular than ever before. 'Behind The Sun' (1985) featured the stunning 'Same Old Blues', but 1986's 'August' was probably the best for ages – produced by Phil Collins, the album included 'It's In The Way That You Want It', 'Tearing Us Apart' (with Tina Turner) and Robert Cray's 'Bad Influence'.

Not surprisingly, Clapton has always used the finest musicians over the years, including Carl Radle, Jamie Oldaker, Duck Dunn, Roger

Hawkins and Albert Lee. Recent bands have featured Steve Ferrone (drums) and Nathan East (bass) with live guest appearances by Phil Collins, the ubiquitous percussionist Ray Cooper and Mark Knopfler. Interestingly, Clapton's most haunting guitar in recent years came in his incidental film music; the TV play, *Edge of Darkness* and the John Hurt/Terence Stamp movie *The Hit*.

Everything Clapton does now is on the grand scale; a boxed set of his music 'Crossroads'; 18 nights at the Royal Albert Hall in 1990 following his 1989 release 'Journeyman' (with Robert Cray guesting) and back to the RAH for another 24 nights in 1991. Over the years, critics have carped while ever-increasing numbers of fans have purchased the product by the truckload. As a songwriter and performer, the latter-day Clapton has played it relatively safe and eschewed the role of technically innovative guitarist. Nevertheless, listening to many of the mile-a-minute HM guitar players is a sharp reminder that it takes a master like Clapton to really make a guitar gently weep.

Greatest Hits

Singles	Title	US	UK
1974	*I Shot The Sheriff*	I	9
1978	*Lay Down Sally*	3	39
Albums			
1974	*461 Ocean Boulevard*	I	3
1977	*Slowhand*	2	23
1980	*Just One Night*	2	3
1986	*August*	37	3
1989	*Journeyman*	I6	2

The Dave **CLARK FIVE**

Stan Saxon (lead vocals, saxophone)
Mick Ryan (lead guitar)
Rick Huxley (rhythm guitar)
Chris Walls (bass)
Dave Clark (drums)

The Dave Clark Five began as an undistinguished North London outfit with a bias towards sax-dominated instrumentals, but within three years, they became a reliable draw on the Home Counties ballroom circuit, and were developing the pounding, quasi-military beat that would be the bedrock of the rowdy chartbusters for which they'll always be remembered.

By the time their debut single, 'Chaquita', was released in 1962, Huxley (born 1942) had transferred to bass, and Walls and Ryan had been replaced by guitarist Lenny Davidson (born 1942) – and Mike Smith (born 1943) who, as well as playing keyboards, took over lead vocals when Saxon also left. The outfit finally stabilized with the arrival of saxophonist/multi-instrumentalist Denis West Payton (born 1943) from a jazz combo that

Where's the drummer? Despite derogatory digs, Dave (centre) laughed all the way to the bank

was managed by Dave Clark (born 1942).

In their leader, the Five had a man with an instinct for the manoeuvres necessary to make headway in the pop jungle. Controlling virtually every aspect of the enterprise, Clark did not turn his group fully professional until after three UK Top 10 hits.

Their fifth single, a version of 'Do You Love Me', a hit by The Contours, reached the UK Top 30 in 1963. Aided by some crass publicity, 'Glad All Over' and 'Bits And Pieces' – both written by Smith and Clark – established the Five as one of the country's foremost pop acts. This breakthrough was repeated overseas – particularly in the US – where they were one of the few 'British Invasion' groups to sustain chart success after 1964. Their concentration on this market and comparative neglect of their home following was best exemplified when 'Over And Over', a US chart-topper, barely touched the UK Top 50. Nevertheless, Clark and Davidson's 'Catch Us If You Can' from the group's only major feature film (directed by John Boorman) was a Top 5 hit on both sides of the Atlantic.

1968's schmaltzy 'Everybody Knows' (sung by Davidson) was their last sizeable US hit, but before disbanding in 1971, they regained some lost popularity in Britain via much bandwagon-jumping and covers of US hits. Their biggest latter-day chart strike was 'Good Old Rock'n'Roll', a medley of showstoppers that had got them through rough

nights in provincial dance halls during their days in the circuit ten years earlier.

Payton and Davidson withdrew from the music business but Huxley, proprietor of a music equipment shop, trod the boards briefly with The Barron Knights. Using session players, Clark and Smith soldiered on as 'Dave Clark And Friends' until 1973 when Smith teamed up with Michael d'Abo, formerly of Manfred Mann. When this duo floundered, Smith found employment mainly as producer of advertising jingles.

Clark ploughed his creative resources and vast earnings into many lucrative ventures – including the exploitation of the *Ready Steady Go* TV archives and *Time*, a West End musical praised mostly for its spectacular visual effects. He also negotiated the issue of the Five's 'Twenty-Five Thumping Great Hits' in 1978 – a repackaging that demonstrated that, within the limits of mainstream pop's epic vulgarity, The Dave Clark Five were craftsmen of the highest order.

Greatest Hits

Singles	Title	US	UK
1964	Glad All Over	6	1
1965	Over And Over	1	45
Albums			
1964	Glad All Over	3	–
1964	A Session With The Dave Clark Five	–	3
1978	25 Thumping Great Hits	–	7

Guy CLARK

Texas has produced many great musicians, but perhaps of most note are the Lone Star State's singer/songwriters. One of the best is Guy Clark (born 1941), whose superb songs often paint verbal pictures.

Clark became a full-time songwriter in the early 1970s, his most famous songs including 'Desperados Waiting For A Train' (covered by numerous artists), 'Texas 1947' and 'L.A. Freeway' (about his ill-disguised hate of that city where he worked as a contracted songwriter). By 1975, he had a recording contract, and cut the classic 'Old No. 1', which included apart from those mentioned several other much covered originals. Despite critical acclaim and guest spots by Emmylou Harris, Rodney Crowell and Steve Earle, the album was not a big seller, which also applied to its equally excellent 1976 follow-up, 'Texas Cookin'', with help this time from Waylon Jennings, Hoyt Axton, Jerry Jeff Walker and others, plus songs like 'The Last Gunfighter Ballad' and 'Virginia's Real'.

In 1978 Clark changed labels for a third (eponymous) album featuring Don Everly, Albert Lee and K.T. Oslin but with four cover versions alongside his own songs, while 1981's 'South Coast Of Texas' included two songs co-written by Clark and Crowell, and guests Rosanne Cash and Ricky Skaggs. Crowell also produced 1983's 'Better Days', a partial return to form after two rather unsatisfactory albums. This included fine songs like 'The Randall Knife' (written about Clark's father), 'The Carpenter', and his friend Townes Van Zandt's 'No Deal'.

As he was making little commercial progress, Clark then retired from recording to concentrate on songwriting, sometimes collaborating with his wife, Susanna, whose 'Easy From Now On' (co-written with Carlene Carter) was memorably covered by Emmylou Harris. After the rock group U2 expressed enthusiasm for his work, Clark's 1989 comeback album, 'Old Friends', was released in the UK on U2's label. It was no more successful than its predecessors, but Clark remains a consummate artist held in great esteem both by his peers and by critics. The comparative lack of interest of the rest of the world is hard to explain – 'Texas No. 1' is essential.

The CLASH

Joe Strummer (vocals, guitar)
Mick Jones (guitar, vocals)
Keith Levine (guitar)
Paul Simonon (bass)
Terry Chimes (drums)

The most overtly political of UK punk bands, The Clash epitomized the aggression and anger of Britain's blank generation,

Punk Strummer in policy clash leads to group's demise

directing their venom at the boring old farts of the music industry. That they finally fell victim to many of the ills they railed against in no way detracts from their importance, and they fought for their principles longer and harder than most. It was ironic that Joe Strummer (born John Mellors in 1952) had been privately educated, although his stance was genuine enough. His first band, The 101'ers, a pub/rock combo, cut a single 'Key to Your Heart', but as it was released, he met Mick Jones (born 1956), who lived on the 18th floor of a London tower block and had been rehearsing in a band called London SS.

Jones told Strummer to ditch The 101'ers and join forces with him and Paul Simonon (born 1956), plus Levine, who was a group member for a short time, before joining John Lydon's Public Image Ltd. They wrote a series of fierce, agit-punk anthems – 'White Riot', London's Burning' and 'Career Opportunities' – while looking for a drummer, finally recruiting Terry Chimes. On stage, their playing was at best rudimentary but their commitment more than compensated, and they soon achieved maximum street credibility. In 1976 they signed to CBS, releasing a debut single, 'White Riot', in early 1977, which made the UK Top 40.

Their eponymous debut album, recorded in three weekends and produced by their sound engineer, Mickey Foote, featured their often reggae-tinged punk anthems and a version of Junior Marvin's 'Police And Thieves', but CBS's parent company refused to release it in the US because of its poor sound quality. However, it made the UK chart, and reportedly became one of the most imported albums ever in the US – and was finally released in America two years later. By this time, Nick 'Topper' Headon had replaced Terry Chimes (who was billed on the album

as Tory Crimes), and repeated harassment from officialdom only enhanced their status among their fans.

They agreed to use a recognized producer for the second album, 'Give 'Em Enough Rope', and Sandy Pearlman (of Blue Oyster Cult fame) gave it a supercharged sound. Released in 1978, it included two UK hit singles, 'Tommy Gun' and 'English Civil War', and previewed their first US dates, providing the first taste of UK punk for a curious audience, in much the same way as The Rolling Stones had taken British R&B to the USA a decade earlier.

Their third LP, 'London Calling', released in 1979 and produced by Guy Stevens, was a double album but all four sides were used to expound their manifesto and a lengthy US tour helped it into the US Top 30 and gave them their first US hit single with 'Train In Vain (Stand By Me)', a track on 'London Calling' which was not mentioned on either the label or sleeve of the album. Back in the UK, their single chart presence continued with 'The Cost Of Living' EP (featuring a version of the Bobby Fuller Four's 'I Fought The Law', the title track of 'London Calling' and 'Bankrobber'). They also starred in their own feature movie documentary, *Rude Boy*.

They finally overreached themselves with 'Sandanista!' in 1980, a 3-LP set which would have been a fair double album and a better single album, although such was their growing popularity in the US, where they toured repeatedly, that it fared better in the charts than its predecessor. The group's insistence that it should retail for the price of a double album did not improve their relationship with CBS. There were more ominous signs when veteran producer Glyn Johns (Rolling Stones, Eagles, Steve Miller, etc.) completed their unfinished 'Combat Rock' album, but it was a

much tighter affair (and a single album to boot!) which sold a million copies, reached the US Top 10, and included a US Top 10 single, 'Rock The Casbah'.

They were now more popular in the US than their native UK, but were also regarded as the type of 'stadium' act they had derided in their early days and cracks began to show. First Topper Headon bailed out, a victim of drug abuse, and was replaced by Peter Howard, then Jones was fired by Strummer and Simonon, which sent their UK credibility reeling. When they finally reappeared in 1985 with 'Cut The Crap', Strummer, Simonon and Howard had been joined by two unknown young musicians, but nothing could disguise the uninspiring quality of their music. The negative reaction hastened the band's dissolution in early 1986, but in reality they had died as soon as Jones was expelled.

Jones formed Big Audio Dynamite with reggae musician/film-maker Don Letts and embarked on a career that was seldom dull – particularly when Jones nearly died of pneumonia in 1988 – if never hugely successful. Strummer undertook a series of solo projects that included movie soundtracks (*Sid And Nancy* and *Walker*), acting (*Straight to Hell*) and more political rock with Latino Rockabilly War Band. He even co-produced Big Audio Dynamite's 'No 10 Upping Street' album (a reference to the British Prime Minister's address of 10, Downing Street), but so far Strummer and Jones have resisted all offers to reform Clash even though a re-released single hit No. 1 in the UK in 1991.

Greatest Hits

Singles	Title	US	UK
1979	*London Calling*	–	11
1982	*Rock The Casbah*	8	30
1991	*Should I Stay Or Should I Go*	–	1
Albums			
1978	*Give 'Em Enough Rope*	–	2
1979	*London Calling*	27	9
1982	*Combat Rock*	7	2

Jimmy **CLIFF**

With his 'Wild World' smash composed by white singer-songwriter Cat Stevens (see separate entry), Cliff's name springs readily to mind when considering those who popularized Jamaican music in the early 1970s. Since then, the multi-talented Cliff has lost commercial momentum but, as the course of this patchy career has already proved, a relaunch cannot be ruled out.

In 1962 James Chambers (born 1948) began working as an entertainer after auditioning for Leslie Kong, a noted Chinese-Jamaican record producer and proprietor of a Kingston studio. As 'Jimmy Cliff', Chamber's debut single, 'Hurricane Hattie', and its rapid succession of follow-ups, sold well enough to establish him – despite his youth – as a power in the fledgling West Indian record industry. It was, indeed, on Cliff's recommendation that Kong signed Bob Marley (see separate entry) that same year.

After providing a 'native' example of ska singing for Jamaica in 1964's World's Fair in New York, Cliff was invited to London by Island Records mogul Chris Blackwell, then on the crest of a wave with 'My Boy Lollipop,' a worldwide chartbuster for Millie, another Caribbean vocalist.

During a four-year wait for similar recognition, Cliff ticked over as a writer of hits for others – among them The Pioneers' 'Long Shot Kick The Bucket' which entered the UK charts in the same month in 1969 as Cliff's own 'Wonderful World Beautiful People'. Cliff was thus well-placed to broaden his style to suit both mainstream pop and the post-Woodstock album market.

His next single, 'Vietnam', was only a minor hit and – though he bounced back with 'Wild World' – the failure of 1971's 'Another Cycle', an album recorded at trendy Muscle Shoals, brought about Cliff's return to his musical roots with his memorable contributions to the movie soundtrack of 1972's *The Harder They Come* (directed by fellow Jamaican Perry Henzell) in which he also landed a much-praised starring rôle. That his violent, subtitled film was patronized universally by white collegians demonstrated now far West Indian culture had travelled since Cliff made 'Hurricane Hattie' twenty years earlier.

Greatest Hits

Singles	Title	US	UK
1969	Wonderful World Beautiful People	25	6
1970	Wild World	–	8

Pioneer reggae songwriter Jimmy Cliff

Patsy CLINE

The best work of many stars who die prematurely has usually been achieved, and only rarely is it justifiably felt that better was to come. A case in point was Patsy Cline, who was still on the way up when she died in 1963. Born Virginia Hensley in 1932, Cline was a superb country singer for whom the now much-used term 'crossover' (when an artist moves from a specialist field into the mainstream pop/rock area) could have been coined. Strongly independent, Cline was not prepared to compromise to achieve success. After piano lessons as a child, she began singing in her teens and won a trip to Nashville in a competition in 1948, but only got a record deal in 1954 after an apprenticeship in honky tonks.

After appearing at the Grand Ole Opry in 1955, she was heading for stardom, but Nashville's establishment disapproved of her progressive attitudes, and would have consigned her to obscurity had not producer Owen Bradley cut an obvious hit with her in 'Walkin' After Midnight', which not only cruised to the Top 3 of the US Country chart but also the Top 20 of the US pop chart in 1957, after a national TV slot on the influential show hosted by Arthur Godfrey.

The next three years, when she toured with both country and rock'n'roll shows, produced no more hits, but in 1961, when she was finally given songs appropriate to her talent, she began a run of country hits which crossed over to the pop chart and which continued until the end of her life, including 'I Fall To Pieces' (1961, US Top 20), 'Crazy' (1961, US Top 10) and 'She Got You' (1962, US Top 20) plus six more within two years. She was returning from playing a benefit concert when she was killed in a plane crash along with country stars Hawkshaw Hawkins and Cowboy Copas, and her next single, 'Sweet Dreams (Of You)', reached the US Top 50 posthumously.

As country music lost direction, Cline's old hits became popular again, and in 1973, she became the first female solo performer elected to the Country Music Hall of Fame. In 1985 a bio-pic, *Sweet Dreams*, starred Jessica Lange as Cline, and a soundtrack album with Cline's vocals was a substantial seller. In the late 1980s, country star k. d. lang whose backing band is called the Reclines, featured several songs associated with Cline in concert and on record, and like Cline, refused to compromise.

Greatest Hits

Singles	Title	US	UK
1957	Walkin' After Midnight	12	–
1961	I Fall To Pieces	12	–
1961	Crazy	9	–
Albums			
1962	Patsy Cline Showcase	73	–
1963	The Patsy Cline Story	74	–

The COASTERS

Carl Gardner *(lead tenor vocals)*
Leon Hughes *(tenor vocals)*
Billy Guy *(baritone vocals)*
Bobby Nunn *(bass vocals)*

The Coasters formed out of The Robins, a Los Angeles group which made the US R&B chart in 1954/55 with 'Riot In Cell Block #9' and 'Smokey Joe's Café', in collaboration with young writer/producers, Jerry Leiber & Mike Stoller. When this duo signed a 1955 production deal with Atlantic Records, Robins members Gardner (born 1928) and Nunn (born 1925) went with them, and recruited Hughes and Guy to form The Coasters. Their first single, 'Down In Mexico', was a US R&B chart hit, and cemented the style already established by Leiber & Stoller with The Robins, which became The Coasters' stock-in-trade: musical playlets strong on humour and ironic comment on black urban low-life, with vocalists adopting character voices.

This mixture came to the commercial boil in 1957 (when Hughes had been replaced by Young Jessie from The Flairs) with the double-sided million-seller 'Searchin'' / 'Young Blood', both sides of which made the US Top 10. In 1958 both producers and group moved to New York, but Nunn and Jessie, who were reluctant to uproot, were replaced by Cornell Gunter and Will 'Dub' Jones. Sax sessioneer King Curtis also became a virtual group member and his playing was quickly heard to effect on the US No. 1 hit, 'Yakety Yak'. More classic ghetto soap operas followed, as 'Charlie Brown', 'Along Came Jones' and 'Poison Ivy' were consecutive US Top 10 hits in 1959, but the group's commercial success slumped the following year, in spite of one of their most critically rated singles, 'Shoppin' For Clothes'. Significantly, Leiber & Stoller's workload had widened to include other burgeoning acts like The Drifters, and The Coasters no longer had first call upon them. 1961's much-revived belly dancer opus, 'Little Egypt', was the last sizeable Coasters hit. Gunter left the line-up and was replaced by Earl Carroll (ex-Cadillacs), but the group notably failed to join the 1960s commercial R&B boom which elevated The Drifters and others to new heights.

By the 1970s, when the group had a surprise chart coda with a revival of The Clovers hit, 'Love Potion No. 9', they had experienced several personnel changes, and former members were working with their own versions of The Coasters in opposition to the original group, keen for action on the new rock/nostalgia revival market. Bogus groups toured overseas to initially unaware audiences until lawsuits finally sorted out the confusion. The Coasters never recovered their commercial success, but the legacy of their early hits remained undimmed as decades passed and the songs were still played and

Soul satirists of rock'n'roll, the Coasters

covered. Fittingly, Gardner, Guy, Jones and Gunter came together as The Coasters at Atlantic's 40th birthday concert in May 1988.

Greatest Hits

Singles	Title	US	UK
1958	Yakety Yak	1	12
1959	Charlie Brown	2	6

Eddie **COCHRAN**

Cochran (born 1938), with Chuck Berry and Buddy Holly, was one of rock music's first great singer/songwriter/guitarists, with a genius for studio production and experimentation well ahead of its time, all cut short by a tragic early death.

A proficient guitarist in his early teens, Cochran worked with Hank Cochran (unrelated) as hillbilly rockers The Cochran Brothers during 1954/55. Going solo the following year after seeing Elvis Presley perform, he worked in LA as a session guitarist, at which time he began to collaborate with songwriter Jerry Capehart, and cut a one-off single, 'Skinny Jim'. His major break came via a one-song cameo, 'Twenty Flight Rock', in the first great rock'n'roll movie, The Girl Can't Help It.

In 1957 he charted with 'Sitting In The Balcony', and in 1958 made the US Top 10 hit, 'Summertime Blues', a rock classic of the 1950s, still familiar (and widely covered) over three decades later. It encapsulated his Berry-like grasp of instinctive and effective teenage idiom allied to snappy, guitar-driven production, a blend which was reprised on further anthems like 'C'mon Everybody' (a UK Top 10 hit in 1959), 'Somethin' Else' and 'Weekend'. Cochran was devastated by the death of his friend, Buddy Holly (whom he

would have joined on the fateful tour but for work on the movie, Go Johnny Go), and tried to avoid flying thereafter. However, at the end of 1959, he was invited, along with another close colleague, Gene Vincent, to the UK for a three-month tour.

He was an instant, huge success in Britain, with adulation outweighing anything he had experienced in the US, and noted TV and radio performances on Boy Meets Girls and Saturday Club. As the tour drew to a close, he was offered another, which he accepted on the proviso that he make an interim two-week return to the US for recording. On the way to London Airport from the final UK gig, the taxi hired by Vincent, Cochran and his fiancée, Sharon Sheeley, burst a tyre and crashed. All the occupants were badly hurt; Cochran, with multiple head injuries, died within hours.

The US forgot him relatively quickly, but he became a legendary posthumous rock figure in Britain, where 'Three Steps To Heaven' topped the chart within months of his death, and singles and albums charted for years afterwards, with newly discovered material from his lengthy studio experiments still finding a ready UK and European market into the 1980s. His repertoire has been consistently covered for 30 years by major acts from The Who to The Sex Pistols, and 'C'mon Everybody' made the UK Top 20 again in 1988 after its use in a Sharon Sheeley-inspired TV ad for Levis.

Greatest Hits

Singles	Title	US	UK
1958	Summertime Blues	6	18
1959	C'mon Everybody	35	6
1960	Three Steps To Heaven	–	1
Albums			
1960	Eddie Cochran Memorial Album	–	9

Cochran on camera in 'The Girl Can't Help It', the pick of the rocksploitation pics

Bruce COCKBURN

Bruce Cockburn (born in Ottawa, 1945) is essentially from the same mould as Canada's other premier singer/songwriters, like Joni Mitchell, Neil Young, The Band, Gordon Lightfoot, and notably Bryan Adams, with whom comparisons are more readily obvious. After busking in Europe as a teenager and three years at Boston's Berklee School of Music, he paid his musical dues as organist in a Top 40 covers band and as harp player in a blues band. Having built up a considerable repertoire of self-penned material, he began working solo, his eponymous debut album appearing in 1970. His early albums (on Canadian label True North) attracted scant attention, but the fourth, 'Night Vision' (1973 – released only in Canada, as were his next three albums) was the first in a run of hit albums which led to superstardom as he swept up Juno (Canadian Grammy) awards.

His international fortunes improved when he finally broke into the US Top 40 with 'Wondering Where The Lions Are', a single from his eleventh album, 'Dancing In The Dragon's Jaw', which made the US Top 100. In the 1980s he frequently worked in Europe, where he developed a loyal cult following, especially in Germany – his 'If I Had A Rocket Launcher' from the superb 1984 album, 'Stealing Fire', attracted substantial UK airplay.

An excellent, inventive guitarist and one of the few singer/songwriters to operate successfully within mainstream rock, his songs have made massive strides from his initial folk roots, touching on jazz, reggae and rock, and lyrically taking in everything from naïve folkie optimism through fierce political statement to serious religious commitment.

While Cockburn is Canada's biggest indigenous rock star, with 15 hit albums, only time will show whether he can escape the shackles of his somewhat parochial status and achieve parallel worldwide success. The UK release of 'Bruce Cockburn Live' (1990), with versions of many of his best known songs, may help him to reach a wider market.

Greatest Hits

Singles	Title	US	UK
1980	*Wondering Where The Lions Are*	21	–
Albums			
1980	*Dancing In The Dragon's Jaws*	45	–

Joe COCKER

Perhaps the fact that John Robert Cocker (born 1944) comes from England's industrial heartland and was once a gas fitter makes his soulful voice even more authentic – despite his white skin, Cocker has lived the

Despite setbacks, Joe's got by – with a little help from his friends

blues. After unsuccessfully recording as Vance Arnold in 1964, he formed The Grease Band with friends from his home town of Sheffield. 'Marjorine', Cocker's debut single, was a minor hit in 1968, and later that year, his soulful version of 'With A Little Help From My Friends', a song from the 'Sergeant Pepper' album by The Beatles, topped the UK chart. An album titled after the hit reached the US Top 40, after which Cocker and the band were surprise stars of the celebrated Woodstock festival and the subsequent feature film.

His second album, 'Joe Cocker!', made the US Top 20 and a single from it, Leon Russell's 'Delta Lady', was a UK Top 10 hit, but The Grease Band then folded after a projected US tour was cancelled. In early 1970, Cocker was warned that if he failed to fulfil contracted US dates, he would be blacklisted, and Russell recruited a 20-piece band composed mainly of American musicians. Under the banner of Mad Dogs And Englishmen, the party played 65 concerts in two months, resulting in a feature movie and a live double album which made the US Top 3.

Various stop-gap compilations were released over the next few years, as Cocker suffered from poor health, eventually relocating in Los Angeles in 1974. He then released his first properly conceived album for some years, 'I Can Stand A Little Rain', which made the US Top 20 and included a US Top 5 single, 'You Are So Beautiful'. 1975 produced 'Jamaica Say You Will', and 1976 'Stingray', both of which briefly reached the Top 100 of the US album chart, as did 1978's

'Luxury You Can Afford', which was produced by Allen Toussaint. After a guest performance with The Crusaders which produced a hit single, 'I'm So Glad I'm Standing Here Today', Cocker was in the commercial wilderness until 1982, when he released the excellent 'Sheffield Steel' album, recorded at Compass Point in The Bahamas with Island boss Chris Blackwell producing and the celebrated rhythm section of Sly Dunbar and Robbie Shakespeare.

That year saw him back at the top of the US charts with 'Up Where We Belong', a duet with Jennifer Warnes which was featured in the popular movie, *An Officer and a Gentleman*. In 1984 Cocker signed his first long-term contract since the early 1970s, and while his standing in the US and UK has hardly altered, he is now a million-selling artist in Germany. Albums like 'One Night of Sin' (1989) and 'Live' (1990) confirm that Cocker's powers have not diminished – as an interpreter (of great songs by Randy Newman and Jimmy Webb especially), he remains unmatched.

Greatest Hits

Singles	Title	US	UK
1968	*With A Little Help From My Friends*	68	1
1975	*You Are So Beautiful*	5	–
1982	*Up Where We Belong* (with Jennifer Warnes)	1	7
Albums			
1970	*Mad Dogs And Englishmen*	2	16
1974	*I Can Stand A Little Rain*	11	–

Cohen relaxes between slapstick stage routines

Leonard **COHEN**

A lugubrious Canadian singer/songwriter, Leonard Cohen (born Montreal, 1934), proved that, like Bob Dylan, poets with an unconventional voice can succeed in rock-'n'roll. He was a poet in the 1950s and a novelist in the 1960s (most notably with *Beautiful Losers*), before his growing interest in folk music encouraged him to set his poems to music. Judy Collins cut the record 'Suzanne' in 1966 and after appearing at the 1967 Newport Folk Festival, Cohen signed to CBS.

His debut album, 'Songs Of Leonard Cohen' (1968), pitted his haunting, mournful voice against a simple but atmospheric backing, and his powerful if gloomy lyrics – a blend of eroticism and existentialism – quickly provided cult status. 1969's 'Songs From A Room' included 'Bird On A Wire' (later covered by artists from Joe Cocker to Jennifer Warnes to The Neville Brothers), but the adulation and intensity of his fans when he toured unnerved him, and 1971's 'Songs Of Love And Hate' betrayed his confusion.

Since then, his career has been increasingly sporadic, if seldom without interest. His next studio album ended a four-year hiatus, although CBS filled the gap with 'Live Songs' (1973), taken from a 1971 tour. 'New Skin For The Old Ceremony' (1974) trod familiar ground, and 'Greatest Hits' (1975), while hardly an accurate title, included his much covered compositions like 'Suzanne', 'Sisters Of Mercy' and 'Hey, That's No Way To Say Goodbye'.

'Death Of A Ladies Man' (1977) was produced by Phil Spector and veered towards rock'n'roll, not to mention unreconstituted chauvinism. It failed to damage his reputation among the ladies, however, and 1979's 'Recent Songs' featured a number of duets with Jennifer Warnes, who later recorded her own album of Cohen songs, 'Famous Blue Raincoat'. 'Various Positions' in 1985 and 'I'm Your Man' in 1988 returned to the simpler

style which has always suited him best and he has mellowed in middle age, even touring occasionally. However, he may forever be humorously referred to as 'Laughing Lennie', an inappropriate epithet for a mainly melancholic and downbeat songwriter.

Greatest Hits

Albums	Title	US	UK
1968	*Songs of Leonard Cohen*	83	13
1969	*Songs From A Room*	63	2
1971	*Songs Of Love And Hate*	145	4

Lloyd **COLE** and The **COMMOTIONS**

Lloyd Cole (vocals, guitar)
Stephen Irvine (drums)
Neil Clark (guitar)
Lawrence Donegan (bass)
Blair Cowan (keyboards)

S cots singer/songwriter Cole (born 1961) was catapulted from obscurity to chart and critical fame in 1984 by 'Perfect Skin', a catchy commercial tune that melded Byrds-like guitar, off-hand Velvet Underground vocals and enough literary allusions to satisfy the most learned music press scribes. He looked set for a long stay at the top, although it failed to reach the UK Top 20, but was an impressive sampler for an impressive debut LP, 'Rattlesnakes': a must for every student's bedsit and a Top 20 fixture for months.

While other Scots hopes had flattered to deceive, Cole cranked out consistently catchy guitar pop with a commercial edge: 'Forest Fire' was near miss, while 'Lost Weekend' and 'Brand New Friend' both from 1985's 'Easy Pieces' album, went Top 20 in Britain. Then the momentum faded and 1987's 'Mainstream' saw the formula go stale surprisingly rapidly, posibly due to the song-writing being group-credited rather than to Cole and one (varied) collaborator.

Cole then ditched The Commotions (except for Cowan) and moved to New York, where he grew stubble, modelled for liquor advertisements, recruited Lou Reed sideman Robert Quine on guitar and producer Fred Maher on drums and cut the solo album, 'Lloyd Cole', in 1989: the lead cut, 'Don't Look Back', suggested bridges had been burned. The crossed-out portrait on the cover might have indicated that he had belatedly realized it was his music, not his image, that had attracted fans, and his solo disc evinced less interest than the compilation '1984–1989'.

A talented songwriter whose band was in retrospect underestimated, Cole made the mistake of taking himself too seriously, to be at one with his influences (almost all American) rather than feeding off them. Yet with many of his role models still in business, he has plenty of time to come back – a process he began late in 1990 with 'Downtown', a single recorded for the film *Bad Influence*.

Greatest Hits

Singles	Title	US	UK
1985	*Brand New Friend*	–	19
1985	*Lost Weekend*	–	17
Albums			
1985	*Easy Pieces*	–	5
1987	*Mainstream*	–	9

Cole causes a commotion before going solo

Have guitar, will travel – bluesman Collins

Albert COLLINS

An under-rated Texan blues guitarist, singer and songwriter, Albert Collins (born 1932) was regarded as something of a prodigy. He was influenced by T-Bone Walker, John Lee Hooker and his cousin, Lightnin' Hopkins, who taught him the D Minor tuning and high-register guitar technique which became his trademark. At the age of 15 he toured locally with Clarence 'Gatemouth' Brown, and formed his own band, The Rockets, around 1949, becoming a 'guitar for hire' with Little Richard (replacing Jimi Hendrix) and The Drifters, among others.

His recording career began in 1958 with 'The Freeze' and the 'cold' motif continued on local labels with 'Frosty' and 'Snow Cone'. His early singles were compiled on 'The Cool Sound of Albert Collins' (1962). Introduced to a national label in 1968 by Canned Heat's Bob Hite, Collins released three albums including 'Love Can Be Found Anywhere Even In A Guitar' (1968) and 'Trash Talkin'' (1969). Hite's patronage meant appearances at prestigious venues like the Fillmore West (captured on his 'Alive and Cool' album), but fame was short-lived: after recording 'There's Gotta Be A Change' (1971) on producer Bill Szymczyk's doomed Tumbleweed label, Collins spent most of the 1970s with no label or regular band, although he was never short of work. When he played in the North Western States, he often hired the Seattle band led by Robert Cray to back him, giving Cray some much needed exposure. In 1978 Collins signed for the independent blues label, Alligator Records. Subsequent albums have included 'Icepickin'' (1978); 'Frostbite' (1980); 'Frozen Alive' (1981); 'Don't Lose Your Cool' (1983); 'Live in Japan' (1984) and 'Cold Snap' (1986) plus a 'reunion' album 'Showdown' (1985) with fellow Texan Johnny Copeland and Robert Cray – all shot through with Collins' distinctive biting Telecaster sound. Some recognition of his talent came with

Grammy nominations, a guest appearance at Live Aid in Philadelphia, courtesy of George Thorogood, and in 1990 five honours in the Handy Blues Awards – something at least to show for over forty years on the road. Even if his 'Greatest Hits' list is non-existent, all his albums make rewarding listening.

Phil COLLINS

After a varied career as a child actor, knitwear model and member of the little known Flaming Youth, Phil Collins (born 1951) became drummer for Genesis in 1970 and when Peter Gabriel quit the band in 1975, Collins also became vocalist. While few believed he could follow the mercurial Gabriel, he succeeded by sounding similar and replacing the theatrics with a common, down-to-earth touch, which expanded the band's cult status in the US into mainstream chart activity, especially after Collins wrote their first Top 20 hit, 'Misunderstanding', in 1980.

Always a workaholic, Collins guested on albums by Brian Eno, John Cale and Robert Fripp among others, and in 1976, co-founded a part-time jazz/rock group, Brand X, which released several albums between 1976 and 1982, the most sucessful being 'Moroccan Roll' (1977).

In the late 1970s, Collins's marriage collapsed and his songwriting became more personal, as his first solo album, 'Face Value' (1981), revealed. It featured Eric Clapton on 'If Leaving Me Is Easy', while Collins produced it, designed the sleeve and wrote the sleeve notes by hand, which became a trademark. It peaked higher in the US than any Genesis album, and included two US and three UK Top 20 singles.

Phil contemplates Albert's hairdo (above)

After the next period of work with Genesis and after producing a UK Top 50 hit for Frida from Abba, 'I Know There's Something Going On', Collins wrote his second album, 'Hello, I Must Be Going', in five weeks, adding a cover of The Supremes hit, 'You Can't Hurry Love', which topped the UK singles chart and made the US Top 10 in early 1983, when the album reached the Top 10. As Genesis reached the big league, Collins found time to produce and/or play on albums by Eric Clapton, Robert Plant, Peter Gabriel, John Martyn, Howard Jones and Adam Ant. When he wrote the movie them for *Against All Odds*, the result was his first US chart-topper, 'Take A Look At Me Now' (1984), which also won a Grammy for Best Male Pop Vocal Performance, and started a run of seven US Top 10 hits in two years, including four No. 1s. 'No Jacket Required', his third solo album, also produced four US Top 10 hits and won a Grammy Award as 1985's Album of the Year.

Collins was prominent on the Band Aid single, 'Do They Know It's Christmas', in 1984, and at the Live Aid concert in 1985 managed to appear in London and Philadelphia on the same day by using Concorde. He also became interested in acting, and after a cameo role in *Miami Vice*, starred in *Buster* – the story of England's Great Train Robbery – alongside Julie Walters. Inevitably, his song from the film, a cover of 'Groovy Kind of Love', a 1960s hit by The Mindbenders, topped the US and UK charts in 1988, and if that wasn't enough, 'Two Hearts' earned him another Grammy in 1988.

As Genesis had also reached a new commercial peak during 1986–7, 'But Seriously . . . ', the next Collins solo album emerged in late 1989, displaying more of Collins's own social conscience than before, with songs about homelessness ('Another Day In Paradise'), South Africa ('Colours') and war ('That's Just The Way It Is'). Once more, the hits piled up and the album sold 10 million copies, an astonishing eight million of them in Europe. In late 1990, the commercial fire was stoked still further with 'Serious Hits – Live', a banker for speedy platinum status.

Greatest Hits

Singles	Title	US	UK
1982	*You Can't Hurry Love*	10	1
1984	*Against All Odds (Take A Look At Me Now)*	1	2
1985	*One More Night*	1	4
1985	*Sussudio*	1	12
1985	*Separate Lives (with Marilyn Martin)*	1	4
1988	*A Groovy Kind of Love*	1	1
1988	*Two Hearts*	1	6
1990	*Another Day In Paradise*	1	2
Albums			
1981	*Face Value*	7	1
1985	*No Jacket Required*	1	1
1989	*But Seriously . . .*	1	1

Judy **COLLINS**

Best known for her 1971 version of 'Amazing Grace' which re-entered the UK singles chart eight times in the early 1970s, Collins was one of the most poignant singers of the 1960s folk revival, later turning to show tunes and standards and having one of her greatest successes with Stephen Sondheim's 'Send In The Clowns'.

The daughter of a Denver radio announcer, Collins (born 1939) made her Chicago debut as a folksinger in 1960 and was signed by Jac Holzman to his Elektra label. 'A Maid Of Constant Sorrow' (1961) won her comparisons with Joan Baez but by the time of 1964's 'Judy Collins No. 3' her US album chart debut, she was attempting more adventurous material like Tim Hardin's anti-war song 'Come Away Melinda'. Her most innovative album was 'In My Life' (1966). Using an orchestral backing and produced by ragtime expert Joshua Rifkin, it included the first recordings of songs by the then unknown Leonard Cohen. On 'Wildflowers' (1967) Collins did the same for the work of Randy Newman and Joni Mitchell, whose 'Both Sides Now' was a US Top 10 hit for Collins.

The elegiac 'My Father' on arguably her finest album, 1969's 'Who Knows Where The Time Goes?' was the first of Judy Collins' own compositions to make an impact, while the title track was written by Fairport Convention vocalist, Sandy Denny. She was the subject of the Crosby, Stills & Nash classic, 'Suite: Judy Blue Eyes', and her own songwriting was at its best on 'True Stories And Other Dreams' (1973).

After the success of 'Send In The Clowns' in 1975, Collins recorded less frequently, dividing her time with acting, film-making and politics. Among her later albums were 'Running For My Life' (1980) and 'Times Of Our Lives' (1982), on which she sang Andrew Lloyd Webber's 'Memory'.

After 'Home Again' (1984) Collins ended her long association with Elektra Records. 'Trust Your Heart' (1987) included a new version of 'Amazing Grace' which became the title of Judy Collins's autobiography.

Greatest Hits

Singles	Title	US	UK
1968	Both Sides Now	8	14
1971	Amazing Grace	15	5
1975	Send In The Clowns	36	6
Albums			
1968	Wildflowers	5	–
1975	Judith	17	7

COMMANDER CODY and the LOST PLANET AIRMEN

George 'Commander Cody' Frayne *(piano, vocals)*
John Tichy *(guitar, vocals)*
Steve Davis *(pedal steel)*
Billy C. Farlow *(harmonica, guitar, vocals)*
Bill Kirchen *(guitar)*
Andy Stein *(violin, saxophone)*
Bruce Barlow *(bass)*
Lance Dickerson *(drums)*

The brew served by the good Commander was always potent: operating in an area largely of their own making, they did more to drag country into rock's mainstream than almost anyone, their high-octane, anarchic fusion of C&W, western swing, rockabilly and boogie woogie defying all convention. Frayne first formed groups at Michigan University, including The Amblers, Fantastic Surfing Beavers, and The Lorenzo Lightfoot Athletic Club & Blues Band. He formed the first Lost Planet Airmen in 1967, but

although they quickly built up a small, loyal following, they realized that their prospects as a C&W group in Detroit (local competition included Mitch Ryder and Ted Nugent) were limited and ground to a halt.

Kirchen and Farlow moved to San Francisco to form The Ozones, and found far more receptive audiences: Cody and the rest swiftly joined them and, thus reconstituted, they swallowed The Ozones, reverted to their old name, and established a reputation as the hottest band in town. Their 1971 debut album, Lost In The Ozone, made the US Top 100: combining original material with oldies, including a remake of Johnny Bond's 'Hot Rod Lincoln' which was a US Top 10 hit. Their second album 'Hot Licks, Cold Steel And Truckers' Favourites' (US Top 100, 1972) was the killer: recorded for $5,000, it captured their live presence perfectly and included another small hit, 'Beat Me Daddy Eight To The Bar'. The third album, 'Country Casanova' (1973), included a minor hit, 'Smoke, Smoke, Smoke That Cigarette', plus the controversial 'Everybody's Doing It' (which rhymed 'trucking' with 'fucking' and caused EMI to omit it from the album's UK release!)

By the mid-1970s, the group's personnel had changed, and despite regular albums, they found it hard to maintain previous high standards. Their eponymous 1975 debut album for Warner Bros saw a brief return to form and it reached the US Top 100, but within two years the band had split up. Frayne continues to work as Cody: he enjoyed an off-the-wall European hit in the early 1980s with 'Two Triple Cheese (Side Order Fries)', and in 1986 cut 'Let's Rock' with sundry Lost Planet Airmen (including Kirchen and Barlow), an album very much in the style of their earlier work.

Greatest Hits

Singles	Title	US	UK
1972	Hot Rod Lincoln	9	–
Albums			
1975	Commander Cody & His Lost Planet Airmen	58	–

The COMMODORES / Lionel RICHIE

Lionel Richie *(vocals, keyboards)*
Thomas McClary *(guitar)*
Ronald La Praed *(bass, trumpet)*
William King *(trumpet)*
Milan Williams *(various)*
Walter 'Clyde' Orange *(vocals, drums)*

Funk/soul act The Commodores were formed in 1967, from two Alabama groups, The Jays and The Mighty Mystics, the latter including Lionel Richie (born 1949). After their first recording, 'Keep On

Goodtime music that went against the grain of progressive rock, the Airmen in full flight

Dancin' ' (1969), they supported The Jackson Five on tour in 1971, and that year signed to Motown. Their third Motown single, the instrumental 'Machine Gun', in 1974 was a UK Top 20 hit and a year later they had a US R&B No.1 with 'Slippery When Wet' and US Top 40 LPs with 'Caught In The Act' and 'Movin' On'.

'Sweet Love' in 1976 was the first of ten US Top 10 hits which included 'Easy' (a UK hit again in 1988), the disco classic 'Brick House' (1977), 'Sail On' (1979) and 'Oh No' (1981). The group were also among the top black album artists, having four US Top 5 albums – 'Commodores' and 'Commodores Live!' (1977), their first UK Top 10 album, 'Natural High' (1978), and 'Midnight Magic' (1979). A duet with Diana Ross, 'Endless Love', (1981) gave Richie his first taste of solo success. He left the group later that year after finishing their album 'In The Pocket', and the following year, a compilation album, 'Love Songs', gave them their biggest UK hit. Richie's replacement as lead singer, McClary, went solo in 1983 and was, in turn, replaced by Englishman J.D. Nicholas (ex-Heatwave). The single and album 'Nightshift' (1985) took the group into the Top 20 but despite a label change their sales slumped.

Before going solo Richie had produced and written hits for Kenny Rogers, including 'Lady' and 'I Don't Need You', and his own eponymous debut album in 1982 was a transatlantic Top 10 hit, selling over four million copies in the US, where three tracks from it made the Top 5 including the Grammywinning 'Truly'. 'Can't Slow Down' (1983) was his biggest album to date, and went on to become Motown's most successful LP selling over 10 million in the US and 1.7 million in the UK, five singles from it becoming transatlantic Top 20 hits. In 1984 he signed a $8.5 million sponsorship deal with Pepsi. Later that year 2.6 billion people watched him perform 'All Night Long' at the closing ceremony of the Los Angeles Olympics.

In 1985 he wrote and sang on the biggest selling single of the 1980s, the quadruple platinum 'We Are The World' by USA For Africa, and when his Oscar-winning song 'Say You, Say Me' topped the US chart in 1986, it made him the first writer to have penned No. 1 hits in nine successive years. His 1986 album, 'Dancing On The Ceiling', sold four million and again contained a string of hits, the biggest being the title track. His 12th solo single, 'Ballerina Girl', gave him his twelfth US Top 10 hit in 1987.

Greatest Hits

Singles	Title	US	UK
Commodores			
1978	Three Times A Lady	1	1
1979	Still	1	4
Lionel Richie			
1981	Endless Love (with Diana Ross)	1	7
1982	Truly	1	6
1983	All Night Long (All Night)	1	2
1984	Hello	1	1
1985	Say You, Say Me	1	8
Albums			
Commodores			
1978	Natural High	3	8
Lionel Richie			
1983	Can't Slow Down	1	1
1986	Dancing On The Ceiling	1	2

Ry **COODER**

Acclaimed among critics and discerning punters for his excellent taste and resurrection of bygone styles, Ryland P. Cooder (born 1947) has never achieved huge commercial success, but is regarded with the utmost respect by his infinitely more commercially successful peers.

Born into a Los Angeles family who were fond of music, he began playing guitar as an infant (when he also accidentally blinded himself in one eye), and became involved with the local folk and blues scene as a teenager, working behind singer/songwriter Jackie De Shannon in 1963. By then Cooder was also familiar with protest songs (via his parents), bluegrass (which he hardly pursued in later life) and country blues – he paid legendary bluesmen like the Rev. Gary Davis to teach him their guitar techniques, and remains an expert of the genre. He was a member of The Rising Sons, with Taj Mahal, appearing on the latter's 1967 debut album, and also on Captain Beefheart's celebrated 'Safe As Milk' album the same year. By this time Cooder was also playing sessions for the likes of The Everly Brothers, Randy Newman, Gordon Lightfoot, etc, and via Jack Nitzsche, worked with The Rolling Stones, whom he was tipped to join as replacement for Brian Jones. He is credited on their 'Let It Bleed' album, and also on the soundtrack album to the Mick Jagger movie, *Performance*.

In 1970 his eponymous debut solo album established the pattern of his later career – critical applause and disinterest from the general public. He also worked on Little Feat's eponymous debut album before his own second album, 'Into The Purple Valley' (1971), his brief US album chart debut. Later albums like 'Boomer's Story' (1972), 'Paradise And Lunch' (1974), 'Chicken Skin Music' (1976, on which Cooder explored both the Hawaiian guitar music of Gabby Pahinui and the ethnic music of the Texas/Mexico border) and 'Showtime' (1977, a live album featuring the Tex/Mex band from its predecessor) continued the pattern of great reviews and small sales, but after 1978's somewhat misconceived 'Jazz' album, Cooder's most commercial era began with 'Bop Till You Drop' (1979), his first album to make the US Top 100 and UK Top 40. His 1980 follow-up, 'Borderline', was preceded by 'The Long

Ry – from Purple Valley to Blue City

Riders', an album of Cooder's score to the celebrated Walter Hill movie about Jesse James. In 1982 'The Slide Area' became his last non-soundtrack album for five years – while it was his only UK Top 20 album, it was a comparative failure in the US, and subsequently, the majority of Cooder's released work has been on film soundtracks, including 'The Border' (1982), 'Paris, Texas' (1985), 'Alamo Bay' (1985), 'Blue City' and 'Crossroads' (both 1987), although in 1987 he returned to 'real' albums (and touring, which he had previously abandoned out of economic necessity) with 'Get Rhythm' an album which proved to the discerning faithful that their hero retained an interest in more than just film music.

As with several other artists in this book, chart positions are of little use in a list of items recommended for first-time listening. Most of the non-soundtrack albums are worthy of note, after which 'The Long Riders' should be the first soundtrack investigated. Among Cooder's associates on his albums are John Hiatt, David Lindley, Van Dyke Parks, Bobby King and Terry Evans, Flaco Jiminez and actor Harry Dean Stanton.

Greatest Hits

Albums	Title	US	UK
1979	Bop Till You Drop	62	36
1981	Borderline	43	35
1982	The Slide Area	105	18

Sam **COOKE**

Sam Cooke (born 1935) moved into pop in the mid-1950s from gospel music, and his smooth, restrained vocal style, infused with the spiritual uplift of gospel, was com-

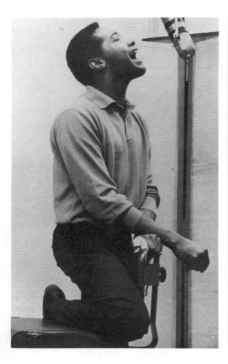

Soul stirrer Sam, a church voice in the charts

mercially successful, widely imitated and a major influence on the development of 1960s soul music from R&B.

The son of a Baptist preacher, Cooke sang in gospel choirs as a child, and by 1955 was lead tenor with The Soul Stirrers, a leading US gospel group. He first recorded secular material at the suggestion of A&R man Bumps Blackwell, but the results were disliked by the label to which the group was signed. When Blackwell moved to a new label in 1957, Cooke went with him as a soloist. By the end of that year, he was topping the US chart with the breezy 'You Send Me', a showcase for his light, subtly gymnastic voice. A string of hits followed, as Cooke immersed himself in the pop mainstream, spending up to eight months each year on tour. The songs varied from ballads ('I Love You For Sentimental Reasons'), through dance novelties ('Everybody Loves To Cha Cha Cha') to commercial pop ('Only Sixteen', 'Wonderful World'), but the trademark was a restrained backing track emphasizing an immaculate vocal.

After signing to a major label in 1960, Cooke's recording horizons began to widen with his first million-seller, the gospelly, muscular 'Chain Gang'. Other commercial winners in the early 1960s were the much-covered 'Cupid', 'Another Saturday Night', the bluesy 'Little Red Rooster', and his biggest dance success, 'Twistin' The Night Away', while the pleading intensity of his vocal roots was also allowed to reassert itself on ballads like 1962's 'Bring It On Home To Me' and 1965's posthumously-released social awareness anthem, 'A Change Is Gonna Come'.

Cooke matched his commercial and artistic successes with business acumen, making several Caribbean tours (to become a seminal influence on the region's musical development), launching his own label in 1961 to promote protégé talent, and taking a soulful nightclub act into New York's Copacabana and other major venues to expand his audience, but it all ended in December 1964, when he was shot dead in an LA motel in a bizarre incident involving two women.

Twenty-two years later, he was inducted into the Rock'n'Roll Hall of Fame (and 'Wonderful World' made the UK Top 3 after use on a Levis TV ad), but Cooke's influence had already helped mould soul music – and the careers of scores of black performers who owed him a stylistic or inspirational debt – before he died. Ironically, his tragic demise occurred on the very eve of soul's emergence as an internationally popular genre.

Greatest Hits

Singles	Title	US	UK
1957	*You Send Me*	1	29
1960	*Chain Gang*	2	9
Albums			
1958	*You Send Me*	16	–
1986	*The Man And His Music*	–	8

Alice **COOPER**

Widely credited as the man who pioneered hard-rock theatrics and acclaimed as one of the great showmen of rock, Alice Cooper (born Vincent Furnier, a preacher's son in 1945), formed his first band, The Earwigs, in Phoenix, Arizona in 1966, with Glen Buxton (guitar), Michael Bruce (guitar, keyboards), Neal Smith (drums) and Dennis Dunaway (bass), who followed him all the way to stardom. As that group name suggests, they were strongly influenced by the British beat boom. After changing it to The Spiders and again to The Nazz (not the Todd Rundgren band), they finally fixed on Alice Cooper – allegedly via a Ouija board – and moved to Los Angeles where their reputation on the freak scene soon attracted the attention of manager Shep Gordon, who got them a deal with Frank Zappa's Straight Records. Their early albums, 'Pretties For You' (1969) and 'Easy Action' (1970), failed to raise their profile above cult level and their outrageous shows cost more to stage than they recouped.

Over $100,000 in debt, they moved to Detroit where they built up a harder reputation, while producer Bob Erzin made their music raunchier. 'Love It To Death', their 1971

Warner's props and make-up department put Alice well on the way to Wonderland

debut album for Warner Brothers, set the new standard for their high-energy hard rock and included 'I'm Eighteen', a US Top 30 single which became an anthem for that generation. The group released three more albums in the next two years: 'Killer' (1971), 'School's Out' (US Top 3 in 1972), and 'Billion Dollar Babies' (US No. 1 in 1973), plus a shoal of hit singles including 'School's Out' (UK No. 1), 'Elected' (UK Top 5), 'Hello Hurray' and 'No More Mr Nice Guy', Furnier/Cooper's increasingly outrageous stage show with his pet boa constrictor, electric chairs, gallows, chickens, dolls he destroyed and raw meat by the bucketful, caused mayhem across the US, but ensured that 1974's Billion Dollar Babies tour broke records.

Unfortunately the lunacy began to affect the band, who often found their violent theatrics mirrored in reality. As Alice Cooper degenerated into self-parody, Furnier sacked the band (who made an unsuccessful album as Billion Dollar Babies), went solo as Alice – the name had theoretically covered the whole group – and returned to Hollywood for 'Welcome To My Nightmare', an album he made with former Lou Reed sidemen. Apart from 'Only Women Bleed' (a US Top 20 hit) most of the spark had gone, and Alice Cooper, the erstwhile guru of rebellious teenagers was transformed into a chat show guest. While still capable of a few late 1970s hits, like 'I Never Cry', 'You And Me' and 'How You Gonna See Me Now', he was doing it one-handed: the other hand continually clutched a beer can.

The early 1980s are best forgotten – and probably are by Alice! In 1985 he signed to MCA and his 'Constrictor' album included the theme of the cult horror movie *Friday The 13th Part 6: Jason Lives*. In the UK, Cooper's reputation remained, and he gained popularity with 1989's 'Trash' album and its hit single, 'Poison'. If the menace is now somewhat contrived live, it possesses more conviction than a decade earlier.

Greatest Hits

Singles	Title	US	UK
1972	School's Out	7	1
1972	Elected	26	4
1977	You and Me	9	–
Albums			
1972	School's Out	2	4
1973	Billion Dollar Babies	1	1
1989	Trash	20	2

Elvis **COSTELLO**

Brought up in Liverpool, Declan McManus (born 1954) cut his teeth as a London pub-rocker with the group Flip City before reinventing himself as DP Costello and playing folk clubs. Costello was a family name:

Costello caught between Presley and Holly in rock schizophrenia shock

Elvis was a more obvious steal and showed an iconoclastic streak that blighted his US success when he slammed Ray Charles in 1978.

Hawking his songs to record companies by personal audition, Costello shocked A&R executives into unanimous rejection. Stiff, the independent label so influential in the new wave with The Damned, Ian Dury, etc, took him on and linked him with Nick Lowe, house producer and previously singer with Costello's heroes, Brinsley Schwarz. Stiff co-founder Jake Riviera (Andrew Jakeman) was to play Colonel Parker.

Costello's appearance as bespectacled angry young man with his debut single, 'Less Than Zero', in 1977, broke the ground for such as Joe Jackson. His first album, 'My Aim Is True', saw him backed by US country-rockers Clover masquerading as The Shamrocks. 'Red Shoes', a UK hit single,

helped the album into the UK Top 20, while the outstanding ballad 'Alison' was one of three Costello compositions later covered by Linda Ronstadt: Costello complained but took the money. 'Watching The Detectives', probably his most effective single track, was backed by members of Graham Parker's band, The Rumour: reggae style emphasized common ground with The Clash, etc.

Linking with a permanent band, The Attractions – Bruce Thomas, Pete Thomas (no relation) and Steve Nieve (real surname Mason), 1978's 'This Year's Model' album saw him at the peak of Angry Young Mandom, and in peak songwriting form, with tracks like '(I Don't Want To Go To) Chelsea' satisfying critics with cinematic references in the lyrics and the public with a hard-edged yet melodic song. The album made the UK Top 5.

'Armed Forces' in 1979 took him into the pop market, a sound based on Nieve's bubbling synths and included 'Oliver's Army', his biggest single with lyrics concerning mercenaries but a catchy chorus. It was his first and only US Top 10 album. 'Get Happy!!' saw him investigating soul – 20 tracks of Stax-style black-influenced material including the hit cover of Sam & Dave's 'I Can't Stand Up For Falling Down' taken at three times the original's pace. Like its predecessor, it made the UK Top 3 to equal Costello's commercial peak.

Released in 1980 'Trust' was underestimated but classic pop: his most personal album. Sales disappointed, so he took another style – country – and cut 'Almost Blue' in Nashville with producer Billy Sherrill and Clover's John McFee on pedal steel an added Attraction. A sticker on the album sleeve pointed out the C&W contents 'may produce radical reaction in narrow minded people', but it made the UK Top 10, while a single, 'Good Year For The Roses' hit MOR market.

1982's 'Imperial Bedroom' album took his pop to an over-produced apogee but only marginally increased his commercial potential. 1983's 'Punch the Clock' seemed to owe much to the Langer/Winstanley production team (Madness, etc.) and contained a classic pop single in 'Everyday I Write The Book' which reached the UK Top 30 and US Top 40. Costello twice packaged B-sides, outtakes, non-LP singles etc, firstly as 'Taking Liberties' (entitled '10 Bloody Marys and 10 Hows Your Fathers' in the UK) and later in the decade, 'Out Of His Idiot'.

'Goodbye Cruel World' (1984) repeated the 'Punch The Clock' formula to lesser effect: a pair of solo tours featuring radical reinterpretation of songs suggested dissatisfaction. A hits compilation made the UK Top 10 in 1985, after which his first Attraction-less album since his debut was 1986's 'King Of America', featuring US musicians like James Burton and Glen D. Hardin who had been associated with country/rock hero Gram Parsons as well as with the 'other' Elvis. The following year saw 'Blood and Chocolate', an unfocussed album and the last to feature the band that gave him his musical muscle.

The Attractions (who cut their own album without Costello, 'Mad About The Wrong Boy' in 1980) then split, Bruce Thomas later recounting his experiences in the semi-fictional book *The Big Wheel* (1990). Nieve made two solo instrumental albums and directed TV host Jonathan Ross's house band.

Costello produced The Pogues (whose erstwhile bass player Cait O'Riordan he was later to marry) and kept a low profile until 1989's 'Spike', which included songs co-written with Paul McCartney (others appeared on McCartney's 'Flowers In The Dirt'): although patchy, it saw a return to the Top 10 of the UK album chart and included the hit 'Veronica'. He now has the record

company and clout to conquer the US (10 Top 30 LPs there to 1986) but probably doesn't feel the need.

A director of Demon Records, who now hold his back catalogue and will inherit his future recordings, he has total control over his career. His clever wordplay has inspired Roddy Frame, Prefab Sprout's Paddy McAloon etc., and has managed to prosper despite his eclecticism: every musical style he had adopted so far has brought him hits – though tellingly not always with his own songs. Costello compositions have been covered by Dusty Springfield, Dave Edmunds, Robert Wyatt ('Shipbuilding', an anti-Falklands War anthem), while he covered his own songs as The Imposter (two hits, 'Pills And Soap' and 'Peace In Our Time').

Greatest Hits

Singles	Title	US	UK
1979	Oliver's Army	–	2
1980	I Can't Stand Up For		
	Falling Down	–	4
Albums			
1979	Armed Forces	10	2
1980	Get Happy!!	11	2
1983	Punch The Clock	24	3

COUNTRY JOE & The FISH/
Country Joe McDONALD

Country Joe McDonald (vocals, guitar)
Barry Melton (guitar)
David Cohen (keyboards)
Bruce Barthol (bass)
Gary 'Chicken' Hirsch (drums)

Viewed 20 years on, Country Joe & The Fish seem to epitomize the entire late

1960's hippie-dippy/politico-druggie/peace and love (man)/flower power/anti-establishment mayhem (aka the Woodstock generation) more than any other West Coast band.

McDonald (born in California in 1942) was virtually born to be a political activist, having been named after Joe Stalin! After a spell in the US Navy, he settled in Berkeley, California, where he wrote protest songs and worked as a folk singer. He recorded 'The Goodbye Blues' in 1964 with Blair Hardman before joining The Instant Action Jug Band, whose guitarist was Melton, with whom he formed the first incarnation of Country Joe & The Fish in 1965 and recorded EPs for *Rag Baby*, a local politico-folk magazine: these included an early version of the infamous 'Fish Cheer' later amended to spell another four-letter word beginning with the letter 'F' (gimme an 'F', gimme a 'U', etc).

Ringleaders of the burgeoning San Francisco scene, The Fish combined politics, poetry, anarchy, blues, and country with eclectic enthusiasm – as was evident in the psychedelic 'Electric Music For The Mind And Body' (1967) on folk-blues label Vanguard. A strong debut, including protest, social satire, drugs, and love songs, it presented a far tighter and more melodic sound than that of their contemporaries. Fuelled by their appearance at the Monterey Pop Festival, the album reached the US Top 40.

A second album, 'I Feel Like I'm Fixin' To Die' (1968), was also a hit, McDonald's irritatingly catchy title track being adopted by the anti-Vietnam brigade. The same year's 'Together' was their highest-charting album, but the title proved inaccurate: the band split, leaving McDonald and Melton the only original Fish. Unable to maintain a settled line-up, their albums fluctuated with their personnel, but the excellent 'Here We Go Again' set plus their memorable appearance at Woodstock, recalled former glories. McDonald

Country Joe and The Fish – politico cheer-leaders for the peace'n'love generation

began making solo albums, including 'Thinking Of Woody Guthrie' (1969), 'Tonight I'm Singing Just For You' (1970) and the lyrically explicit soundtrack album to the *Quiet Days In Clichy* movie, initially pursuing a solo career alongside The Fish. By 1970, after an obscenity bust (for inciting the audience to join in The Cheer), the group folded, their last album, 'CJ Fish' a rather sad finale. Melton continued as a solo performer, recording five albums during the 1970s.

McDonald's subsequent recorded output has been prodigious – around 20 albums, of which only three made the US chart: 'War, War, War' (1971), 'Incredible! Live!' (1972) and 'Paradise With An Ocean View' (1975). He also worked with Jane Fonda and Donald Sutherland in their *FTA* (Fuck The Army) revue which toured Army bases, withdrawing after a row with Fonda, although he has continued to promote the cause of Vietnam veterans. In 1973 he reunited with Melton and briefly relocated to Paris, and in 1976 reformed The Fish for an unsuccessful album, 'Reunion'.

Increasingly concerned with ecological issues, he continues to be one of the world's busiest troubadours, lending his weight and reputation to any cause which he believes worthy, occasionally working with Melton (often billed as Country Joe & The Fish), and still regularly cranking out albums.

Greatest Hits

Albums	Title	US	UK
1967	Electric Music For The Mind And Body	39	–
1968	Together	23	–

Robert **CRAY**

One of the most innovative blues artists of the 1980s, Robert Cray (born 1953) squeezed new life out of what was regarded as a stagnant style and introduced it to a new generation. His careful blend of southern soul and traditional blues has taken over where the Stax sound stopped and he has expanded his following, guesting with Tina Turner and Eric Clapton. The son of a serviceman, Cray was raised on a musical diet of Ray Charles, Sam Cooke, Bobby Bland, Soul Stirrers, Five Blind Boys Of Mississippi, Jimi Hendrix and The Beatles, as his family moved around the US and Germany before settling in Tacoma, Washington. After persuading his high school to book his hero, Albert Collins, for his graduation party, Cray formed his own band in 1974 with bassman Richard Cousins. They built up a local reputation and in 1978 signed to a small independent label. They recorded a blues-based album, 'Who's Been Talkin'', which sat on the shelf for two years as the label went out of business.

Cray moved to another independent label for his first released album, 'Bad Influence' (1983), which earned good reviews, and Cray further enhanced his reputation with 'Showdown', an album where he shared the billing with Albert Collins and Johnny Copeland. His own band line-up stabilized with Peter Boe on keyboards and David Olson on drums and when 1985's 'False Accusation' album gained greater acclaim, the major labels moved in. Mercury won the chase, but wisely left Cray with producers Bruce Bromberg and Dennis Walker for 'Strong Persuader' (1986), with The Memphis Horns guesting. Its superior quality improved his commercial profile and won a Grammy Award. He also appeared in Chuck Berry's tribute film, *Hail! Hail! Rock'n'Roll*, alongside Keith Richards and Eric Clapton (who had covered 'Bad Influence') and in a Tina Turner worldwide TV special.

Cray promoted his 1988 album 'Don't Be Afraid Of The Dark', with a major world tour which included a bill-topping appearance in the USSR in front of 150,000 people. He also co-wrote 'Old Friend' with Eric Clapton for the latter's 'Journeyman' album and performed on John Lee Hooker's award-winning comeback album, 'The Healer'. For 1990's 'Midnight Stroll' album, Cray adjusted his band line-up, adding Jimmy Pugh (keyboards), Tim Kaihatsu (guitar) and Kevin Hayes (drums) and retaining Cousins and The Memphis Horns. He has continually increased his popularity since his debut, and he now ranks as a superstar of modern R&B.

Greatest Hits

Albums	Title	US	UK
1986	Strong Persuader	13	34
1988	Don't Be Afraid Of The Dark	32	13

CREAM

In April 1966 drummer Ginger Baker saw Eric Clapton playing with John Mayall's Bluesbreakers. Baker suggested to Clapton that they collaborate. Clapton agreed, on condition that Jack Bruce would be the bass player, and the result was Cream.

Peter 'Ginger' Baker (born 1939 in London) had worked with many trad and mainstream jazz bands before 'crossing over' into R&B with Alexis Korner's Blues Incorporated in 1962, where he played with bassist Jack Bruce (born John Symon Asher Bruce, 1943, in Scotland). Korner's organist was the legendary Graham Bond who left with Bruce and Baker to form The Graham Bond Organisation in 1963 with John McLaughlin and saxophonist Dick Heckstall-Smith. Bruce later joined John Mayall and then Manfred Mann. Baker also left Bond after the meeting with Clapton.

Managed by Robert Stigwood, Cream made its debut at the August 1966 Windsor Festival to great acclaim before the usual round of dues paying gigs around the London club scene. Clapton's ideas that Cream would be a Chicago-style blues band were demolished by their first single, the pop-oriented 'Wrapping Paper', co-written by Bruce and poet/lyricist Pete Brown in a vain attempt to get a hit. Its follow up, 'I Feel Free', a UK Top 20 single, was more representative with Bruce's distinctive wailing vocal sound and Clapton's famous 'woman tone' guitar effect. The debut album, 'Fresh Cream', which made the US Top 40 and UK Top 10, was an equal split between original material and interpretations of blues classics like Willie Dixon's 'Spoonful', Robert Johnson's 'Four Until Late' and 'Rollin' and 'Tumblin'' by Muddy Waters.

Baker, Clapton and Bruce in the early days of the world's first supergroup, Cream

Cream teamed up with producer-musician Felix Pappalardi for their 1967 album, 'Disraeli Gears', a very different album from 'Fresh Cream' starting with the pink dayglo cover. Peter Brown resumed his writing partnership with Bruce to produce the classic 'Sunshine Of Your Love' while Clapton co-wrote both the engimatic 'Tales Of Brave Ulysses' and the re-working of Albert King's 'Crosscut Saw', 'Strange Brew'. Only one straight blues cover, 'Outside Woman Blues', was included; the standard of production and quality of the original material were improved, and it made the Top 5 in both the US and UK.

By then, the subsequent history of Cream had been set. When they played San Francisco's Fillmore West, the audience screamed for them to extend each song – henceforth, they used the songs as starting points for long improvisations, which became the hallmark of Cream's live performances – Clapton's searing blues guitar racing ahead of the merciless rhythmic drive of Bruce and Baker.

Cream all but deserted the UK in 1968. The half-studio, half-live double album, 'Wheels Of Fire' laid bare the essential duality of the band. The live album showcased 'Spoonful', the devasting 'Crossroads', 'Traintime' and Baker's wonderfully indulgent solo 'Toad'. The studio sides ranged from the sophisticated rock of 'White Room', 'Deserted Cities of the Heart' and 'Those Were The Days' and a spine-chilling version of Howlin Wolf's 'Sittin' On Top Of The World' to the psychedelic pop banality of 'Pressed Rat and Warthog' and the austere classicism of 'As You Said'. 'Wheels of Fire' was certified platinum, but all was not well with the band – personal squabbles and the tedium of endless concerts playing the same songs took their toll. They called it a day at the end of 1968 with farewell concerts in USA and UK and the album 'Goodbye', became their only chart-topping UK album.

After taking Baker into Blind Faith, Clapton pursued a solo career (see separate entry) as did Baker with his own bands Airforce, Baker Gurvitz Army, Salt and Energy plus short-lived stints with Atomic Rooster and Hawkwind. He also opened a studio in Nigeria where Wings recorded their 'Band On The Run' album. Abortive business ventures included polo ponies and olive groves, but Baker has made recent impressive albums with Bill Laswell ('Horses and Trees' and 'The Middle Passage') heavily influenced by the percussion sound of North Africa. Bruce's subsequent career has been patchy – forgettable associations with Leslie West (West, Bruce and Laing) and Robin Trower, but more than compensated for by a string of excellent albums notably 'Songs For A Tailor' (1969), 'Out of the Storm' (1974), and 'How's Tricks?' (1977).

Over the years Clapton has played informally with Bruce while Bruce and Baker joined Courtney Pine at the Nice Jazz Festi-

val, but a reunion is highly unlikely. From the standpoint of their combined musical talent, Cream were arguably the finest rock band of all time and it is best that their memory remains locked in the music they left.

Greatest Hits

Singles	Title	US	UK
1968	*Sunshine Of Your Love*	5	25
1968	*White Room*	6	28
Albums			
1966	*Fresh Cream*	39	6
1967	*Disraeli Gears*	4	5
1968	*Wheels of Fire*	1	3
1969	*Goodbye*	2	1
1969	*Best Of Cream*	3	6

CREEDENCE CLEARWATER REVIVAL

John Fogerty (vocals, guitar)
Tom Fogerty (guitar)
Stu Cook (bass)
Doug 'Cosmo' Clifford (drums)

Creedence were America's biggest-selling rock group during 1969/70, via a muscular rockabilly based style which bucked the trend on their native West Coast towards post-psychedelic musical complexity, and displayed clear roots infusions from country, blues and New Orleans R&B. That they spearheaded their success with taut, exciting singles also helped reverse a trend to anti-singles snobbery by much of the late 1960s rock vanguard.

John Fogerty (born 1945), Cook (born 1945) and Clifford (born 1945) were schoolmates in El Cerrito, California, who began to play together in their mid-teens, eventually being joined by Fogerty's older brother Tom (born 1941).

By 1963 they were playing around San Francisco as Tommy Fogerty & The Blue Velvets, and a year later signed to the local Fantasy label as The Golliwogs, unsuccessfully apeing the British Invasion sound. Half the group were drafted early in 1966, and it was upon his discharge in mid-1967 that John Fogerty took up the reins (as writer, lead singer, lead guitarist and producer) using a style more reflective of his own musical influences. The name change to Creedence Clearwater Revival was a new start, and in 1968, their revival of the Dale Hawkins rocker, 'Suzie Q', made the US Top 20. Early in 1969 Fogerty's song, 'Proud Mary', a rocking paean to a Mississippi steamboat, was the group's first million seller, defining both their sound and Fogerty's long-distance obsession with Southern culture which fuelled much of his best material. 'Bad Moon Rising', 'Green River' and 'Down On The Corner' all succeeded it in the US Top 3 as the year progressed, and the first of these was their only UK chart-topper. There were also two million-selling albums, 'Bayou Country' and 'Green River' mixing Fogerty originals with carefully chosen revivals. The group also played Woodstock and a host of other major festivals, and the response from progressively inclined rock fans was as fervent as that from the AM pop radio audience.

1970 saw Fogerty's songwriting and commercial acumen undimmed as the albums

Festival following retains Creedence credibility alongside platinum platters

'Willy & The Poorboys' and 'Cosmo's Factory' became million sellers and spawned more singles of similar status: 'Travelin' Band', 'Up Around The Bend' and the country-ish 'Lookin' Out My Back Door'. A triumphant UK concert at the Royal Albert Hall in May was recorded (though tapes were jumbled and a US show erroneously appeared as the album 'The Royal Albert Hall Concert').

In January 1971 Tom Fogerty, likely tired of forever being in his brother's shadow, quit for a solo career. This precipitated the end of the golden Creedence period, as the other two members of the remaining trio began to push John Fogerty for more creative input into the group's music. 'Have You Ever Seen The Rain' and 'Sweet Hitch-Hiker' were typical Fogerty flourishes and comfortable Top 10 singles, but the 'Pendulum' album, cut just before Tom's departure, showed signs of weariness which reflected internal group pressures. For the follow-up, 'Mardi Gras', democracy rampaged through songs, vocals and production, and the group's magic evaporated as John Fogerty lost his grip on proceedings. Reviews and sales were poor, and the group announced its disbandment in October 1972.

John Fogerty immediately cut a rocking country album under the thin pseudonym of The Blue Ridge Rangers, which included two US Top 40 singles, 'Jambalaya' and 'Hearts Of Stone'. He then fell out with Fantasy, which was getting Creedence mileage with big-selling compilations, and in 1975 signed a solo deal with Asylum Records, releasing the 'John Fogerty' album, on which he played every instrument. The album's main hit single was 'Rockin' All Over The World', subsequently covered and virtually appropriated by Britain's Status Quo, although another minor hit from the album, 'Almost Saturday Night', was covered by Dave Edmunds and others and regarded as a classic.

A 1976 follow-up Fogerty solo album, 'Hoodoo', was withdrawn just before its planned release, and heavily disillusioned with the record industry, he retired from music to a rural life for the best part of a decade, only reappearing for two one-off Creedence reunions, at their old high school and Tom Fogerty's re-marriage.

Cook, Clifford and the older Fogerty all continued working in their post-Creedence days, the former two together in bands with Don Harrison and Doug Sahm, and the latter as a soloist and briefly with the group Ruby, but all to little commercial note. After some years out of the music business, Tom Fogerty died in 1990.

John Fogerty, however, eventually made a comeback, topping the US chart in 1985 with the million-selling 'Centerfield' album. Along with matured songwriting, this displayed much of the old trademark Creedence sound, notably on its extracted hit single 'The Old Man Down The Road'. 'Eye Of The Zombie' a year later was more sombre and less com-

mercial, though it made the US Top 30. Since then, Fogerty has not recorded, although occasional live performances happily suggest that he has not completely retired.

Greatest Hits

Singles	Title	US	UK
1969	*Proud Mary*	2	8
1969	*Bad Moon Rising*	2	1
Albums			
1969	*Green River*	1	20
1970	*Cosmo's Factory*	1	1
1985	*Centerfield* (John Fogerty solo)	1	42

KID CREOLE & The COCONUTS

This exotic neo-Caribbean disco group was formed in the late 1970s by August Darnell (born 1951), after he left a similar (but less commercial) combo known as Dr Buzzard's Original Savannah Band, in which he played bass, and 'Sugar Coated' Andy Hernandez (aka Coatimundi, born 1950) played vibraphone under, the leadership of Darnell's brother, 'Stoney' Browder. The jazzy Savannah Band made three albums between 1976 and 1980, the most successful being their eponymous 1976 US Top 30 debut, which went gold during almost a full year in the chart and spawned two US hit singles, including a US Top 30 item, 'Cherchez La Femme'. Characterized by ultra-sophisticated music and production, the band fell apart as its 1980 album was being released, and Darnell and Hernandez launched the some-

what more accessible Kid Creole group. With The Coconuts, a glamorous female vocal trio including Darnell's wife, Adriana Kaegi, and an exotic and expert band in costume, the group's musical soap operas were a remarkable spectacle.

Signed to Mothercare babywear heir Michael Zilkha's Ze label, they released an excellent album in each of the first four years of the 1980s, attracting immense critical acclaim, but only achieving significant success with 1982's 'Tropical Gangsters' (US title: 'Wise Guys'), which made the UK Top 3, although 1983's 'Doppelganger' and 1984's 'Best Of' ('Cre-ole') almost reached the UK Top 20. After a 1981 UK chart debut with 'Me No Pop I', a single featuring the short, rotund Coatimundi (a contrast with the sharp-suited Darnell), the group scored three UK Top 10 singles in six months of 1982, 'I'm A Wonderful Thing Baby' making the Top 5 and 'Annie I'm Not Your Daddy' the Top 3, although this success was hardly approached in the US.

The 'Doppelganger' album was made into a 1984 UK TV Special, *There's Something Wrong In Paradise*, but the group then began to crumble, as Coatimundi and The Coconuts embarked on unsuccessful solo careers. Darnell soldiered on, as group members joined and left and hard-won UK fame evaporated. A cameo in the movie *Against All Odds*, a guest spot on Barry Manilow's 1988 *Swing Street* album, a Montreux Jazz Festival booking, but little record success accrued for Darnell, until Prince wrote a song for the Creole character, 'The Sex Of It', which strongly relaunched the band in 1990 with a new label and new album, 'Private Waters In

Flanked by a couple of Coconuts, Kid Creole stays cool despite the heat

The Great Divide', which suggested that the Kid Creole sound is happily unchanged in ten years. Hopefully the public will act upon the critical raves this time.

Greatest Hits

Singles	Title	US	UK
1982	Annie I'm Not Your Daddy	–	2
Albums			
1982	Tropical Gangsters	–	3

Jim CROCE

Gritty singer/songwriter/guitarist whose material came out of a rural country, rather than urban folk, tradition. Playing accordian from the age of six, Croce (born 1943) worked folk clubs and bars from the early 1960s as a duo with his wife Ingrid (born 1947), also a songwriter. Their 1969 debut album 'Jim and Ingrid Croce' stiffed, and Croce was soon back playing the bars and driving a truck.

In 1970 he began a collaboration with Maury Muehleisen (born 1949), playing on the latter's 'Gingerbread', before being signed himself by producers Terry Cashman and Tommy West. His first solo album, 1972s 'You Don't Mess Around With Jim', topped the US chart and was a colourful evocation of the bars and car washes of small-town America. The title track was a US Top 10 single, and 'Operator' also made the US Top 20.

With Muehleisen on lead guitar, more big-

Jim Croce – posthumous hits

selling albums and singles hit the charts. 'Life and Times' was a US Top 10 album in 1973, spawning his biggest-selling single 'Bad Bad Leroy Brown', a US chart-topper.

Croce and Muehleisen died in a plane crash in September 1973, not long after completing 'I Got A Name', which topped the US album chart a month later. Posthumous hits followed, including another US No. 1, 'Time In A Bottle' and in 1974 'I'll Have To Say I Love You In A Song', a US Top 10 single. His albums continue to be reissued, repackaged and recompiled; the music – a straightforward crossover between country folk and pop – remains fresh nearly two decades later, although he was never more than a cult figure in the UK.

Greatest Hits

Singles	Title	US	UK
1972	You Don't Mess Around With Jim	8	–
1973	Bad Bad Leroy Brown	1	–
1974	Time In A Bottle	1	–
Albums			
1972	You Don't Mess Around With Jim	1	–
1973	I Got A Name	2	–
1974	Photographs And Memories/ Greatest Hits	2	–

CROSBY STILLS NASH & YOUNG

With their ethereal harmonies, gritty guitar solos and on-stage rivalries, CSN & Y were one of the greatest rock supergroups of the early 1970s. With the exception of Canadian Neil Young (born 1945) and, possibly, Stills' first two albums, no individual member produced solo work to match the group's two great albums, and later reunions were for the most part disappointing.

They began as a trio who had risen to fame with top 1960s groups. Texan Stills (born 1945) had been guitarist and songwriter with Buffalo Springfield, Englishman Nash (born 1942) was still leading the keening harmonies of The Hollies and Californian Crosby (born David van Cortland, 1941) was a founder member of The Byrds.

The three met in 1968 and began jamming and writing together in a hazy, acoustic style. After deciding to record together, they signed with the label to which Stills was contracted with Buffalo Springfield, negotiating Nash and Crosby out of their contracts elsewhere. After rehearsals in London and New York, they went into a California studio to make 'Crosby Stills & Nash', an album which sold over three million and provided hit singles with Nash's airy hippie anthem, 'Marrakesh Express', and Stills's 'Suite: Judy Blue Eyes', dedicated to Judy Collins.

For their first major international tour, the

trio added Stills's ex-Buffalo Springfield colleague, Young, as lead guitarist, at the suggestion of Atlantic Records boss, Ahmet Ertegun. Their second gig was in August 1969, at the Woodstock Festival. The event inspired Joni Mitchell to write the celebratory 'Woodstock', which was recorded by the new quartet of Crosby, Stills, Nash & Young as their first single.

It was soon followed by 'Déjâ Vu' (1970), one of the era's quintessential albums. Perhaps heralding the splits to come, each member contributed his own songs, but as a whole the set provided a mirror image of a moment when the hippie idyll was about to collapse. Among the highlights were Nash's hit single, 'Teach Your Children', and Crosby's edgy 'Almost Cut My Hair'.

In August 1970 the National Guard killed four anti-war protestors at Kent State University. Young reacted by composing the angry, passionate 'Ohio', which was released eight days later and reached the US Top 20. By then, the long-standing love/hate relationship between Young and Stills, compounded by other pressures, had led to a group breakdown. 'Ohio' was the last studio recording by the quartet for 18 years.

However, recordings of CSN & Y on tour were edited by Graham Nash and released in 1971 as the appropriately named double-album 'Four-Way Street', another multi-million seller, which topped the US chart.

By now, each member of the group had set out on a solo career. Stills began most promisingly, as 'Love The One You're With', from his debut album, was a transatlantic success. He followed up by forming the country-rock flavoured Manassas with ex-Byrd Chris Hillman, which cut two acclaimed albums in 1972/3 before Stills returned to solo work and a series of less inspired albums.

Both Crosby and Nash reached the Top 20 in the UK and US with their respective 1971 solo albums, 'If I Could Only Remember My Name' and 'Songs For Beginners'. The following year, they released an equally popular duet LP and in 1973 joined Neil Young on some dates during his US tour, which led eventually to a wildly successful reunion tour when CSN & Y played to capacity crowds. However, personal animosities were once again aroused, which led to the abandonment of a planned studio album. Instead, the quartet's fans had to be satisfied with 'So Far', a 'greatest hits' album compiled by Nash, which topped the US chart at the end of 1974.

The rest of the decade saw various duets and trios combining and splitting, touring and recording. A Stills/Young Band album, 'Long May You Run' (1976), sold 500,000 while Crosby and Nash made two albums together before re-forming the original trio with Stills in 1977.

With the success of a full-scale US tour, the 'CSN' album was a million-seller and included the Top 10 single, 'Just A Song

CSN&Y summed up the virtues and vices of laid-back late 'Sixties stadium rock

Before I Go'. The trio played at a 1979 New York anti-nuclear gig, filmed and recorded as 'No Nukes', and recorded 'Daylight Again'. With most of the material composed by Stills, this album underlined the trio's popularity, going platinum in the US, but making little impact in Europe.

The 1983 release of a live album, 'Allies', coincided with Crosby's arrest on drug and firearms charges. For the next three years, a series of treatment programmes and further misdemeanours kept him away from music, apart from a Live Aid appearance with Stills, Nash and Young. In the meantime, both Stills and Nash released lacklustre and poorselling solo efforts.

Yet another reunion, in 1988 for the Atlantic Records' 40th Birthday celebrations, led to the release of only the second studio album by the quartet. 'The American Dream' was respectfully reviewed but soon afterwards, the four individuals again went their separate ways. While Young's reputation as a solo artist reached new heights during the late 1980s, the other three were in danger of seeming 1960s curios even to a younger generation which warmed to such contemporaries as The Grateful Dead and Bob Dylan.

Greatest Hits

Singles	Title	US	UK
1970	Woodstock	11	–
1970	Ohio	14	–
1977	*Just A Song Before I Go	7	–
1982	*Wasted On The Way	9	–
Albums			
1970	Déjà Vu	1	5
1971	Four-Way Street	1	5
1977	*CSN	2	23
1982	*Daylight Again	8	–
(*Crosby Stills & Nash only)			

Rodney CROWELL

After achieving international exposure as a founder member of Emmylou Harris's Hot Band, Texan singer/songwriter Rodney Crowell turned his attention to straighter country music in Nashville after three solo country/rock albums. His Nashville success should be a stepping stone to mainstream rock acceptance.

Fronting his own band, The Arbitrators, in 1965, Crowell (born 1950) moved to Nashville in 1972 after signing to Presley hit writer Jerry Reed as a songwriter. When Emmylou Harris needed a duet singer for her mainly star-packed Hot Band in 1975, Crowell was chosen effectively as replacement for the late Gram Parsons, with whom Emmylou had duetted until Parsons died (see separate entries). After working live with The Hot Band for three years and appearing on several of the classic Harris albums, he attempted a solo career with 1978's under-appreciated 'Ain't Living Long Like This', an album which included such Crowell classics as 'Leaving Louisiana In The Broad Daylight', 'Viola!', 'An American Dream', 'Song For The Life' and the title track, and featured the entire Hot Band plus Ry Cooder, Willie Nelson and Dr John. Remarkably, it failed to chart, and Crowell married Rosanne Cash, daughter of Johnny, before 1980's 'But What Will The Neighbors Think', again with a stellar cast, which was a minor US hit. 1982's eponymous album, with the classic "Til I Gain Control Again', did little better, and Crowell retreated to concentrate on songwriting for several years. He returned to recording in 1986 with 'Street Language', which included three minor country hit singles, after which 1988's 'Diamonds & Dirt' included three No. 1 country singles, 'It's Such A Small World' (a duet with his wife), 'I Couldn't

Leave You If I Tried' and 'She's Crazy For Leavin' ', which he co-wrote with Guy Clark. After being nominated for several CMA Awards but winning none, Crowell's 1989 album, 'Keys To The Highway', was less acclaimed, although its impact may have been lessened by the competing compilation, 'The Rodney Crowell Collection', which included his early classics.

Rodney Crowell's musical tastes incline as much to rock as to country, which may prevent him reaching the mainstream audience his talents (both as performer and songwriter) so clearly deserve. His pop chart track record gives no indication of his best work – 'The Rodney Crowell Collection' is a fine example of his early country/rock, 'Diamonds And Dirt' being one of his recent hits.

Greatest Hits

Singles	Title	US	UK
1980	Ashes By Now	37	–

The CRUSADERS

Wilton Felder (tenor, sax, bass)
Nesbit 'Stix' Hooper (percussion)
Joseph Sample (keyboards)
Wayne Henderson (trombone)

Originally a spin-off trio from a Houston, Texas, high-school marching band, the group was formed in 1956 by Hooper (born 1938), Felder (born 1940) and Sample (born 1939) who played a broad-based blend of jazz, blues and R&B. Under the names Chitterling Circuit, The Nite Hawks and The Swingsters, they evolved their own brand of 'Gulf Coast jazz' before all entering Texas Southern University. There they were joined by Wayne Henderson (born 1939) to form the nucleus of The Modern Jazz Sextet.

In 1958, the original quartet moved to Los Angeles and concentrated on danceorientated R&B as The Nighthawks, before reverting to a jazz approach once more as The Jazz Crusaders in 1961. A Californian answer to Art Blakey's Jazz Messengers, they aroused critical interest at a time when 'soul' (blues-based jazz) was very much in vogue, long before any notions of jazz-rock, crossover or fusion were in currency.

Their debut album attracted praise, and their subsequent five albums over the next four years sold very well by jazz standards, and in 1966 they scored a US Top 100 single with a cover of Stevie Wonder's 'Uptight (Everything's Alright)'. They continued to release popular-style jazz albums, while being much in demand collectively and individually on the LA session scene. During the late 1960s, their albums began to appear in the lower reaches of the US Top 100, as did 'Old

Socks, New Shoes' in 1970. By 1971, they were garnering a wide following with their funk-slanted sound, and dropped the 'Jazz' in their name to become simply The Crusaders, an eponymous double album making the US Top 100 during a six-month chart residency.

Their albums were gradually making a bigger impact, and 1973's double album, 'The 2nd Crusade' made the US Top 50 while topping the jazz chart. Another jazz chart-topper, 1974's 'Southern Comfort', made the Top 40 of the US Pop Chart, and earned them their first gold disc. An unheard of breakthrough for an instrumental group came in 1975, when The Rolling Stones invited them to open on their UK tour dates – the subsequent album, 'Chain Reaction' was their best-selling yet, hitting the US Top 30. It was the first album to involve guitarist Larry Carlton who played on seven of their collections on a freelance basis.

Wayne Henderson left for a solo career in 1976, and the group continued as the original trio, hiring extra players and vocalists as required. Their albums continually topped the jazz chart, although purists claimed their music had moved far enough away to disqualify them from the category, and made the US Top 40, the second half of 1976 being marked by a sell-out US stadium tour followed by equally successful dates in Europe.

A new label marked another shift in direction in 1979 with the album 'Street Life', which featured lead vocals by Randy Crawford. The single, 'Street Life', made the US Top 40 and the UK Top 5, and the album went Top 20 in the US and Top 10 in the UK, topping the US jazz chart for a record 20 weeks, as they also toured with Crawford. The same formula was adopted on 1980's 'Rhapsody and Blues', which featured soul stylist Bill Withers on, 'Soul Shadows', while 1981's 'Standing Tall' album had Joe Cocker on 'I'm So Glad I'm Standing Here Today'.

One of their most ambitious collaborations took place at London's Royal Festival Hall in 1981, where they played with blues guitar supremo B.B. King and the Royal Philharmonic Orchestra, resulting in a double album, 'Royal Jam'. Despite the departure of 'Stix' Hooper in 1983, by 1984 they were back in the charts on both sides of the Atlantic with the disco-oriented 'Ghetto Blaster' with new drummer Leon 'Ndugu' Chancler (ex-Santana). Remaining founders Sample and Felder both made the charts with solo projects, the Felder album, 'Secrets', featuring Bobby Womack, making the US Top 100, while Sample's 'Oasis' album made the Top 10 of the jazz chart.

Celebrating the group's 30th Anniversary, Sample and Felder put together 'The Good and Bad Times' in 1986, featuring top jazz session players and vocalist Nancy Wilson, but 'Life In The Modern World' (1988) saw The Crusaders as an occasional unit, with the nucleus players spending more time on their own solo projects or other people's sessions.

Classic girlie group The Crystals, ultimate example of the Spector sound

In their heyday, their career mirrored the popular acceptance of an aspect of jazz through deliberate attempts at soul and funk fusions, from the 'soul' jazz movement of the late 50s, through collaborations with contemporary jazz-inclined artists like Withers, instrumentalists Bobby Hutcherson, Roy Ayers and many more.

Greatest Hits

Singles	Title	US	UK
1979	*Street Life*	36	5
Albums			
1974	*Southern Comfort*	31	–
1975	*Chain Reaction*	26	–
1978	*Images*	34	–
1979	*Street Life*	18	10
1980	*Rhapsody And Blues*	29	40

The **CRYSTALS**

Barbara Alston (vocals)
Mary Thomas (vocals)
Dee Dee Kennibrew (vocals)
Lala Brooks (vocals)
Pat Wright (vocals)

The Crystals, a bunch of Brooklyn high-school girls who sang together for fun, took up the invitation of songwriter Leroy Bates (whose daughter Crystal gave them their name) to record demos for him at publisher Hill & Range Music in 1961, and it was at his office that they met Phil Spector, who signed them as the first act on his new Philles label.

The debut single, 'Oh Yeah, Maybe Baby', meant nothing until DJs picked up on its B-side, a ballad titled 'There's No Other (Like My Baby)'. When this made the US Top 20, Spector used punchier, more dramatic production on 'Uptown' – the beginnings of his signature 'Wall Of Sound' and a second Top 20 hit. After a controversial 1962 release, 'He Hit Me (And It Felt Like A Kiss)', which was widely shunned due to its apparent lyrical masochism, The Crystals had their biggest hit with the ultra-commercial 'He's A Rebel', which topped the US chart and reached the UK Top 20. Lead vocal on this was by non-group member Darlene Love, since Spector needed to record the song quickly in LA to beat a rival version, and The Crystals were busy in New York. Love also sang on the US Top 20 follow-up, 'He's Sure The Boy I Love'.

1963 saw the Spector Sound and Philles at their commercial peak, with The Crystals a major part of the success via two giant international hits. 'Da Doo Ron Ron' and 'Then He Kissed Me', but soon afterwards, Spector threw all his efforts behind new protégees The Ronettes, and The Crystals were effectively sidelined. After two under-promoted minor hits in 1964, they left Philles, but unsympathetic material and production from a new label proved the change to be a waste of time, and the group split in mid-decade. Like many of their contemporaries, they re-grouped in the 1970s to take advantage of the oldies/nostalgia boom, and with changing membership have played the oldies circuit ever since.

Greatest Hits

Singles	Title	US	UK
1962	*He's A Rebel*	1	19
1963	*Da Doo Ron Ron*	3	5
1963	*Then He Kissed Me*	6	2

The CULT

Ian Astbury (vocals)
Billy Duffy (lead guitar)
Jamie Stewart (rhythm guitar)
Kid Chaos (bass)
Les Warner (drums)

Frontman Astbury (born 1962) under the name Ian Lindsay, originally formed Southern Death Cult in Bradford, UK, after seeing the phrase in a newspaper headline. The group enjoyed some UK indie-chart success in 1983 with the No. 1 'Fat Man'. The band, which consisted of three others musicians who were known only as Buzz (guitar), Barry (bass) and Acky (drums), broke up after a tour supporting Bauhaus on which they attracted frantic media hype.

Astbury reformed the group as Death Cult with Duffy (born 1961) from Theatre of Hate, Stewart and drummer Ray Mondo both from Ritual. Meanwhile a compilation of studio, demo, stage and radio sessions, 'Southern Death Cult', made the Top 50 of the UK album charts in 1983. The new line-up released an EP and two singles, none of which made any impact and a change of drummer in late 1983 preluded the final name amendment to The Cult in 1984, when the single, 'Spiritwalker', topped the UK independent chart.

After their US debut tour in 1984, the band's 'Dreamtime' album reached the UK Top 30, and by the end of the year, 'Resurrection Joe' was a minor UK hit single. Mark Brzezicki of Big Country took over on drums in 1985 as two singles, 'She Sells Sanctuary' and 'Rain', made the UK Top 20 and 'Love' the Top 5 of the UK album chart. A UK Top 30 single, 'Revolution', was taken from the LP as the band began a long tour of North America and Europe, with Les Warner now the permanent drummer. Recordings made in the UK were remixed in New York at Def Jam studios by producer Rick Rubin, who decided to recut the whole album; the result was 'Love Removal Machine', a UK Top 20 single, followed by 'Electric', a Top 5 album. Kid Chaos was added on bass, Stewart switching to rhythm guitar, and a single from 'Electric', 'Li'l Devil', almost reached the UK Top 10.

The band's career faltered in 1988 after they moved to Los Angeles, split with their manager and fired Warner, but they returned in 1989 with a UK Top 3 album, 'Sonic Temple'. With a popular live following and loyal record-buying public, The Cult managed to evolve an unlikely amalgam of punk and late 1960s metal, the Zeppelin-led music that was originally anathema to 1970s New Wavers.

Greatest Hits

Singles	Title	US	UK
1985	She Sells Sanctuary	–	15
1987	Li'l Devil	–	11
Albums			
1985	Love	–	4
1987	Electric	38	4
1989	Sonic Temple	10	3

CULTURE CLUB

Boy George (vocals)
Jon Moss (drums)
Roy Hay (guitars, keyboards)
Mikey Craig (bass)

When it seemed that rock had lost its capacity to shock in the early 1980s, Boy George popped up to shake America's sexual psyche once again. The UK was always more tolerant of male transvestites but the US had problems handling Boy George's gender-bending. However, parental outrage could not prevent his remarkable score of six Top 10 singles in just over a year.

Born George O'Dowd in London in 1961, he rebelled against his suburban background early in his teens by dressing outrageously. He became a leading light on the fashionable night-club scene, earning money by designing clothes. His first foray into the music business came in 1979 when he auditioned for Bow Wow Wow, Malcolm McLaren's post-Sex Pistols project. He spent three months as Annabel Lwin's co-vocalist, before forming Culture Club with Moss (born 1957), Craig (born 1960) and Hay (born 1961).

Having watched friends fumble their way ineptly around the record business they acquired a strong manager, Tony Gordon, and a deal with Virgin that guaranteed artistic freedom. Boy George now had the vehicle to indulge his androgynous fantasies to the hilt. The first two singles flopped but the warm reggae-styled 'Do You Really Want To Hurt Me' topped the UK charts in late 1982, and made the US Top 3 in early 1983. Like the rest of the songs on the 'Kissing To Be Clever' album, it was a group original, and another UK Top 3 hit, 'I'll Tumble 4 Ya', came from the album, although a third Top 3 hit, 'Time (Clock Of The Heart)' was omitted from it, but included on the US version.

Boy George was a pop phenomenon on both sides of the Atlantic, selling nearly as many posters as records and handing out beauty tips to adolescent boys – and girls. In late 1983 the second Culture Club album, 'Colour By Numbers', reached the Top 3 and spawned four hit singles including the chart-topping 'Karma Chameleon'.

The bubble burst almost as quickly as it had inflated. Their third album, 'Waking Up With The House On Fire' (1984), was an artistic mistake, although it went platinum in the US. For 1986's 'From Luxury To Heartache' album, the producer was Arif Mardin and a Top 20 US hit, 'Move Away', resulted. By then Boy George was being hounded by the media, who knew he was a heroin addict and harried him into a confession during the summer of 1986. The band never recovered but George did briefly and topped the UK chart with his first solo single, a

Culture Club represented crossover of a different kind with George's camp Karma

seamless cover of Ken Boothe's reggae version of Bread's 'Everything I Own'. Later tracks from his 'Sold' album and his anti-gay discrimination anthem, 'No Clause 28', got nowhere. By 1990, he was back on the club scene, making house records as Jesus Loves You and hanging out with the Hare Krishna sect.

Greatest Hits

Singles	Title	US	UK
1983	Do You Really Want		
	To Hurt Me	2	1
1983	Karma Chameleon	1	1
1987	Everything I Own		
	(Boy George solo)	–	1
Albums			
1983	Colour By Numbers	2	1

The **CURE**

Robert Smith (guitar, vocals)
Michael Dempsey (bass)
Laurence Tolhurst (drums)

F ormed in 1976, during the genesis of punk, the group from Sussex, UK, was launched by Robert Smith (born 1957) as The Easy Cure. After playing locally through 1977, they came to the notice of a small independent London label after shortening

their name to The Cure and a debut single, 'Killing An Arab', came from the one-off deal. It attracted the attention of Chris Parry of Fiction Records, who signed the group to a recording and management deal. In 1978 their debut album, 'Three Imaginary Boys', reached the UK Top 50.

A 1979 tour as support to Siouxsie & The Banshees was appropriate as both bands were developing a similar style of Gothic punk; when Banshees guitarist John McKay left Siouxsie, Smith deputized, beginning a long on-off relationship with The Banshees. Two singles, 'Jumping Someone Else's Train' and 'I'm A Cult Hero' (under the pseudonym Cult Heroes), made little impression, and Dempsey left the band in 1980, to be replaced by Simon Gallup, while Mathieu Hartley was added on keyboards.

The band's fortunes began to change with the album, '17 Seconds', which made the UK Top 20, and a single, 'A Forest', which almost reached the UK Top 30, after which Hartley left the group, who reverted to a trio format.

Further single releases were minor UK Top 50 hits but albums paved the way for a breakthrough; 1981's 'Faith' made the UK Top 20 and a 1982's 'Pornography' the UK Top 10. As the single, 'The Hanging Garden', hit the UK Top 40, wrangles broke out which resulted in Gallup's departure – Steve Goulding replaced him and 'Lol' Tolhurst switched to keyboards.

From late 1982 Smith alternated Cure commitments with playing for The Banshees until the end of 1983, the year which saw singles 'The Walk' and 'The Love Cats' hit the UK Top 20 and Top 10. The late 1980s brought the US success that had long eluded them, with a US Top 40 entry for the single, 'Just Like Heaven' (1988). Robert Smith's angst-strewn songs were perhaps summed up in 1989's 'Disintegration' LP, which he wrote on his 30th birthday, to be followed in 1990 by the most surprising development yet, 'Mixed Up', a collection of dance floor remixes of some of The Cure's cult classics.

Greatest Hits

Singles	Title	US	UK
1983	The Love Cats	–	7
1984	The Caterpillar	–	14
1988	Just Like Heaven	40	28
Albums			
1986	Standing On A Beach –		
	The Singles	48	4
1989	Disintegration	12	3

The **DAMNED**

Dave Vanian (vocals)
Brian James (guitar)
Captain Sensible (bass)
Rat Scabies (drums)

T he first UK punk band to release a single, The Damned were also the first punk band to appear on TV, to release an album, to tour the US, to disband and to reform. Inspired by the new movement, Brian James (born Brian Robertson) and Rat Scabies (born Chris Miller, 1957) were among numerous young hopefuls involved in London SS, the ultimate rehearsal band of British punk/rock, with, among others, Mick Jones, who went on to form The Clash. In 1975 they linked up with former gravedigger Dave Vanian (born David Letts) and Captain Sensible (born Ray Burns, 1955) who each added a bizarre sartorial touch. After gigging around London clubs, The Damned signed to the fledgling New Wave label Stiff Records in 1976.

Their debut single, 'New Rose' was a perfect punk anthem, backed by a breakneck version of the Lennon/McCartney Beatle classic, 'Help'. A minor UK hit in late 1976, it brought valuable exposure to both band and label. The group's on-stage theatrics contrasted with the grim anger of the hardcore punks, but their debut album, 'Damned Damned Damned' (1977), was a blur of speed

Pre-Gothic punk poseurs – an early picture of later manic-looking Cure

(l to r) James, Sensible, Vanian'n'Scabies – Damned but not forgotten

and energy that summed up punk's musical essence, reaching the UK Top 40 during a two-month chart stay.

Also in 1977 they spearheaded the UK punk invasion of the US with gigs in New York and Los Angeles, and supported Marc Bolan on his last UK tour, but surprisingly blew their credibility when Pink Floyd drummer Nick Mason produced their second album of the year, 'Music For Pleasure', which featured a second guitarist, Lu (real name Robert Edmunds). The album sold poorly, and suggested a lack of material, and the group seemed to have been left behind by the New Wave. Main writer Brian James soon quit, and Stiff dropped the band, who soon split up.

1979 saw the first of many reunions, with Sensible moving to guitar and Algy Ward replacing him on bass for a third album, 'Machine Gun Etiquette', which surprised the doubters, leaning towards pop-punk and including three UK Top 50 UK hits with 'Love Song' making the Top 20. Throughout the 1980s, they continued to record, releasing six albums on three different labels, but maintaining a fan base that just kept them viable and scoring a 1986 UK Top 3 hit with a cover version of Barry Ryan's 1968 classic, 'Eloise'.

Captain Sensible, meanwhile, had topped the chart as a solo artist with a novelty version of Rodgers & Hammerstein's 'Happy Talk' in 1982, after which he left the band, although he has appeared at every 'farewell' performance by The Damned.

Greatest Hits

Singles	Title	US	UK
1982	*Happy Talk* (Captain Sensible solo)	–	1
1984	*Glad It's All Over/Damned On 45* (Sensible solo)	–	6
1986	*Eloise*	–	3
Albums			
1985	*Phantasmagoria*	–	11

Terence Trent **D'ARBY**

Terence Trent D'Arby was born in New York in 1962 and lived in Chicago and Florida before joining the army in 1980. While stationed in Germany (in Elvis Presley's old regiment) he fronted local band The Touch, which included Frank Itt, and recorded several tracks which Polydor released in 1989.

He moved to London in 1984, spent two years working on songs for his first album and signed with CBS in 1986. His blend of funk and rock combined with his unmistakable image was instantly successful and he hit the UK Top 10 with his first single, 'If You Let Me Stay'. His much anticipated album, 'Introducing The Hardline According To Terence Trent D'Arby' (co-produced by Heaven 17's Martin Ware), entered the UK chart at No. 1, something no American act had previously achieved with their debut album, and sold nearly 1.5 million in the UK. His next single, 'Wishing Well', also made the UK Top 5. 'Sign Your Name' reached the UK Top 3 in 1988, when he won 'The Best International Newcomer' award at the BRITS awards.

Also in 1988 he topped the US chart with 'Wishing Well' and shortly afterwards made the US Top 5 with both 'Sign Your Name' and with his debut album, which went double platinum. Following this success proved difficult and his next album, 'Neither Fish Nor Flesh' (1989), not only missed the US Top 40 and spent only a brief period in the UK Top 20, but did not include any hit singles. In late 1989 he also released an unsuccessful single under the pseudonym Incredible E.G. O'Reilly.

This unpredictable and often outspoken singer is a superb performer and a strong writer and as such should have little trouble hitting again in the 1990's.

Greatest Hits

Singles	Title	US	UK
1987	*Wishing Well*	1	4
1988	*Sign Your Name*	4	2
Albums			
1987	*Introducing The Hardline According To Terence Trent D'Arby*	4	1
1989	*Neither Fish Nor Flesh*	61	12

British breakthrough makes D'Arby's day

Bobby Darin – finger clickin' good

Bobby **DARIN**

Darin (born Walden Robert Cassotto, 1936) began his recording career as a rock'n'roll singer, but proved to be a musical chameleon who could equally well score major hits with big band swing and introspective folk music. After dropping out of college in 1955 determined to make it in showbiz, Darin recorded a cover of Lonnie Donegan's 'Rock Island Line' and other singles with no success, but broke through in 1958 with the self-penned novelty rocker, 'Splish Splash', which sold a million. Similar singles like 'Queen Of The Hop' and 'Plain Jane' consolidated this success, and the classic uptempo teen ballad, 'Dream Lover', was a second million seller in 1959, topping the UK chart and reaching the US Top 3.

The follow-up was a startling contrast, as Darin delivered a Sinatra-esque swing reading of Brecht/Weill's 'Mack The Knife', from *The Threepenny Opera*. This topped the US chart for two months, as well as hitting No. 1 in the UK, and along with the similarly styled 'That's All' album, firmly established Darin as an adult, as well as a teenage, entertainer. It also won him a pair of Grammy awards – a rare accolade in those days for anyone with rock'n'roll credentials.

1960 saw him in Las Vegas and around the nightclub/cabaret circuit, and his singles continued to swing the standards, producing major hits with 'Beyond The Sea', 'Clementine', 'Bill Bailey' and 'Lazy River'. Hollywood also

beckoned: he married film starlet Sandra Dee and launched a prolific movie career of his own, which would encompass films as varied as *Pepe, Come September* (with this wife), *State Fair* (a musical with Pat Boone and Ann-Margret), *Too Late Blues*, the tough war drama *Hell Is For Heroes* (with Steve McQueen), and *Captain Newman MD*, which brought him an Oscar nomination as Best Supporting Actor.

His records became more varied again in 1961/62, and included a rock treatment of 'You Must Have Been A Beautiful Baby', the R&B-styled 'Multiplication' and self-explanatory album, 'Bobby Darin Sings Ray Charles', plus the country-ish self-penned 'Things', another million seller. Late in 1962 he switched labels, hit big in a continued country vein with 'You're The Reason I'm Living' and '18 Yellow Roses' during 1963, and saw his record sales plummet when the 1964 British invasion arrived.

By 1966 Darin had found a new commercial direction via folk music, which gave him his last Top 10 hit on both sides of the Atlantic with a cover of Tim Hardin's 'If I Were A Carpenter'. He leaned heavily on material by Hardin and John Sebastian for a while, before launching his own label in 1968, and adopting the complete singer/songwriter stance on the album 'Born Walden Robert Cassotto'. Somewhat ironically, he also wrote Tim Hardin's only US chart single, 'Simple Song Of Freedom'.

In 1971 he had surgery to insert artificial heart valves, and his health was suspect

thereafter, but he signed a new recording deal with Motown, went back to his swing style in cabaret, and in 1973 launched his own TV series and made the movie, *Happy Mother's Day*. His weak heart caught up with him, however, and finally failed in December 1973, during an operation in a California hospital.

Greatest Hits

Singles	Title	US	UK
1959	*Dream Lover*	2	1
1959	*Mack The Knife*	1	1
Albums			
1959	*That's All*	7	15
1960	*This Is Darin*	6	4

Spencer **DAVIS GROUP**

Steve Winwood (vocals, keyboards)
Spencer Davis (guitar)
Mervyn 'Muff' Winwood (bass)
Pete York (drums)

First known as The Rhythm & Blues Quartet, the Birmingham-based group formed in 1963, when teacher and part-time folk/blues singer/guitarist Davis (born 1942) met York (born 1942) and Winwood brothers Steve (born 1948) and Muff (born 1943), who were playing in The Muff-Woody (traditional) Jazz Band. After a year building up a live

Spencer Davis – got those Birmingham blues

reputation with US R&B chart covers, they were signed by Chris Blackwell's fledgeling Island Records, which licensed their material to a bigger label to gain mainstream promotion. The debut single, a revival of John Lee Hooker's 'Dimples', flopped, but covers of 'I Can't Stand It' (originally by The Soul Sisters) and Brenda Holloway's 'Every Little Bit Hurts', highlighting Winwood's impressive (for a 16-year-old) Ray Charles-ish vocals, broke into the UK Top 50, and brought critical recognition.

The major breakthrough occurred at the beginning of 1966, when a powerfully driven version of 'Keep On Running', written by Jamaican singer Jackie Edwards (a Blackwell protégée), topped the UK chart, deposing 'We Can Work It Out' by The Beatles. Its momentum spurred both the group's first two albums into the UK Top 5, and the follow-up single, 'Somebody Help Me' (another Edwards song), was a second chart-topper.

Major US success came with Winwood's own composition, 'Gimme Some Lovin'', which hit the UK Top 3 in late 1966, and the US Top 10 early in 1967, by which time both Winwood brothers had already given Davis notice of their intention to quit the group. The original line-up's swansong was 'I'm A Man', co-written by Steve Winwood with producer Jimmy Miller, another Top 10 hit on both sides of the Atlantic.

The Winwoods left for separate careers, Steve to form Traffic, join Blind Faith and Ginger Baker's Airforce and eventually follow a solo career (see separate entries), and Muff to become a producer and later a label executive. Their replacements were vocalist/organist Eddie Hardin and guitarist Phil Sawyer, and this line-up had a UK Top 30 hit with the psychedelically-styled 'Time Seller', and appeared in the film *Here We Go Round The Mulberry Bush*, but it was clear that the distinctive elements of the group's style had departed with Steve Winwood, and a struggle for musical identity followed.

When the hits stopped after 1968's 'Mr Second Class', Hardin and York split to work as a duo, and Davis replaced them with bassist Dee Murray and drummer Nigel Olsson, who lasted a year before also moving on, to play with Elton John. Davis then made no further attempts to reform the band, but moved to California, where he had a low-key solo career (with occasional highlights, like teaming with Dusty Springfield) for several years before eventually following Muff Winwood into A&R work.

Greatest Hits

Singles	Title	US	UK
1965	*Keep On Running*	76	I
1966	*Somebody Help Me*	47	I
Albums			
1966	*The Second LP*	–	3
1966	*Autumn '66*	–	4

Chris De Burgh – Into The Light with Flying Colours

Chris **DE BURGH**

Argentina-born singer/songwriter (born 1948) of a diplomatic family, real name Christopher Davison, he studied in Eire and made that country his home. Emerging just too late for the King/Taylor/Cat Stevens singer/songwriter heyday, his first album, 'Far Beyond These Castle Walls' (1975), was less than successful in most areas but spawned a No. 1 single in Brazil! He performed for some years as a support act, seemingly without the universal appeal to break out of a dedicated fan following. Live crowd-pleasers like that bawdy 'Patricia The Stripper' alternated with delicate, sensitive ballads. 'A Spaceman Came Travelling', a Yuletide allegory betraying his religious beliefs, was nearly a hit several Christmases running. Both these were from 'Spanish Train and Other Stories' (1975).

He became famous for story songs like 'Don't Pay The Ferryman' (a surprise US hit, though he'd always been big in Canada) and found most success with producer Rupert Hine, and it was their first collaboration. 'The Getaway', that opened De Burgh's chart account in 1982. Two years later, 'Man On

The Line' made the Top 20 and featured guest vocals from Tina Turner.

De Burgh's style of songwriting had always veered dangerously close to maudlin, and it was when he allowed sentimentality full reign that he had his biggest hit, 'Lady In Red', from 1986's 'Into the Light'. Two years later, 'Flying Colours' was his first chart-topper, thanks to the hit single, 'Missing You'.

His keening, high-pitched tenor is not to all tastes, but De Burgh's fans – still loyal, now greater in number – back him to the hilt, as demonstrated by 'High On Emotion', the 1990 live album cut appropriately in Dublin, which served to reprise his best-known songs and reached the UK Top 20. No fewer than three hits collections exist, two of which went Top 10, presumably bought by those with many years' catching up to do!

Greatest Hits

Singles	Title	US	UK
1986	*Lady In Red*	3	I
1988	*Missing You*	–	3
Albums			
1986	*Into The Light*	–	2
1988	*Flying Colours*	–	I

DEEP PURPLE

Rod Evans (vocals)
Ritchie Blackmore (guitar)
Jon Lord (keyboards)
Nick Simper (bass)
Ian Paice (drums)

Prime exponents of British heavy metal, Deep Purple took a few albums and line-up changes before becoming international superstars during the 1970s. Blackmore (born 1945) had played in 1960s pop groups like The Outlaws and worked with producer Joe Meek before he joined Lord (born 1941), who had been classically trained before joining R&B combo The Artwoods and psychedelic

pop group The Flowerpot Men, which also included Nick Simper. Recruiting Evans and Paice from The Maze, they signed to EMI, debuting with 'Shades Of Deep Purple' in 1968. The album made little impact in the UK but their version of Joe South's 'Hush' was a Top 5 US single, which pushed the album into the US Top 30. Two more albums then emerged within a year, 'Book Of Taliesyn' and 'Deep Purple', before Evans and Simper left.

New singer Ian Gillan (born 1945) and bassist Roger Glover (born 1945) had both been in pop group Episode Six and added a dynamic chemistry to the band. After 1970's over-ambitious classical/rock fusion album, 'Concerto For Group And Orchestra' written

by Lord and recorded live with the Royal Philharmonic Orchestra at London's Royal Albert Hall, they delivered 'Deep Purple In Rock' later that year. The album remains a landmark in heavy rock, with Gillan's screeching vocals pitted against Blackmore's fierce guitar bursts, Lord's grandiose keyboards and Paice and Glover's solid rhythms. Many tracks became classics, in particular 'Black Night', a UK Top 3 single which dramatically broadened their following, 'Speed King', 'Strange Kind Of Woman' (also UK Top 10) and the extended epic, 'Child In Time'. The album made the UK Top 5 during a long residency, but failed to ignite in the US. However, they had found their niche and 'Fireball' (1971) not only reached the US Top 40 but became their first UK chart-topping album, while the title track was a UK Top 20 single. In 1972 'Machine Head' was their first US Top 10 album, again topping the UK chart and spawning a US Top 5 single, 'Smoke On The Water'. With several archetypal heavy metal tracks under their belt, Purple now had a monstrous live set which they toured relentlessly around the US, where they ranked second only to Led Zeppelin.

They also achieved massive success in Japan and their excellently recorded live double album, 'Made In Japan', sold huge quantities as an import before US domestic release took it into the US Top 10 and UK Top 20. By this time, personality clashes within the band were eating away the group's cohesive strengths, and the aptly titled 'Who Do We Think We Are!' album (1973) lacked spirit, despite reaching the US Top 20 and UK Top 5. Before long, Gillan and Glover quit after falling out with Blackmore, Gillan to form his own band (see separate entry) and Glover to work producing other bands. Their replacements were little known vocalist David Coverdale (born 1951) and bassist Glenn Hughes (ex-Trapeze).

The new line-up's debut album, a Top 10 US and UK hit, was the bluesier and more melodic 'Burn' (1974), but after the same year's 'Stormbringer', Blackmore rebelled against the funkier sound and left. The band recruited Tommy Bolin, a noted US guitarist, and returned to their heavier roots for 'Come Taste The Band', but Bolin's taste for drugs and his erratic style hindered the band's live shows and Coverdale stormed out after a 1976 gig in Liverpool, whereupon the group disbanded, leaving numerous live tapes that were steadily issued in various formats over the next few years. Bolin died of a heroin overdose in 1977.

Blackmore meanwhile formed Rainbow with singer Ronnie James Dio and drummer Cozy Powell, and this band enjoyed some success during the late 1970s, but Blackmore's unpredictability led to its line-up constantly changing. Dio was replaced after 1978's 'Long Live Rock'n'Roll' album by Graham Bonnet, and Roger Glover joined the band

In at the deep end, Purple pioneered early 'Seventies mainstream metal

after producing them. Despite UK hit singles like 'Since You've Been Gone' and 'All Night Long', the band failed to take off in the US even after Bonnet's replacement by Joe Lynn Turner gave the band a more mid-Atlantic flavour.

By 1984 nobody's solo career had approached the Deep Purple legend, which still seemed bankable, and the Gillan/Blackmore/Lord/Glover/Paice line-up decided to sink their differences and re-unite. 'Perfect Strangers' reached the US Top 20 and UK Top 10 and set up a successful world tour. The reunion continued through two more albums but by 1990 the financial painkillers could no longer soothe the old enmities and Gillan quit again. 1990 found Joe Lynn Turner as Deep Purple's latest vocalist on the 'Slaves And Masters' album.

Ironically, Coverdale was the most successful of them all. Whitesnake, which he formed in 1978, at one time also included Lord and Paice after a project known as Paice, (Tony) Ashton & Lord was a disastrous failure. Whitesnake had scored nine UK hit albums by 1989, largely by using the Purple blueprint.

Greatest Hits

Singles	Title	US	UK
1968	Hush	4	–
1970	Black Night	–	2
1972	Some On The Water	4	–
1980	Since You've Been Gone (Rainbow)	57	6
Albums			
1971	Fireball	32	1
1972	Machine Head	7	1
1980	Deepest Purple	–	1
1981	Difficult To Cure (Rainbow)	50	3
1981	Come And Get It (Whitesnake)	–	2

DEF LEPPARD

Joe Elliott (vocals)
Pete Willis (guitar)
Rick Savage (bass)
Steve Clark (guitar)
Rick Allen (drums)

Heavy metal group formed in 1977 in their hometown Sheffield by Elliott (born 1959) and Willis who had both been in Atomic Mass together with Savage (born 1960) and Clark (born 1960).

In 1979 they formed Bludgeon Riffola label and using a temporary drummer, released a three-track EP, 'Getcha Rocks Off', before signing with Vertigo and charting with their debut single 'Wasted'. Rick Allen joined as permanent drummer in 1980, when the group were regarded by the media as front runners of the 'New Wave Of British Heavy Metal'. Their debut LP, 'On Through The Night', made the UK Top 20 and the US Top 100,

Def Leppard – Hysteria rampant as album rocks records worldwide

eventually selling a million copies. Their second album, 'High 'n' Dry' (1981), was a transatlantic Top 40 hit and in time also passed the million mark, but not before Wilson had been replaced by Phil Collen, who previously worked in Girl.

'Pyromania', released in 1983, sold seven million in the US and was only kept off the top spot by Michael Jackson's 'Thriller'. With help from MTV, they also scored three US Top 40 singles from the album – the biggest, 'Photograph', just missing the Top 10. Their next album, 'Hysteria', took three years to record and in the middle of recording, Allen lost an arm in a car crash, yet with a specially adapted drum kit, continued with the group. The album was released in 1987 and became the biggest selling album by a UK band, selling over 12 million worldwide, including

nine million in the US where it reached No. 1 after 49 weeks in the chart. It entered the UK chart at No. 1 and six singles from it made the Top 40. In the US, it became the first million selling CD by a metal act and included four Top 10 singles.

In January 1991 guitarist Steve Clark was found dead at his London home leading to speculation about the band's future – but it seems they will continue.

Greatest Hits

Singles	Title	US	UK
1987	Pour Some Sugar On Me	2	18
1988	Love Bites	1	11
Albums			
1983	Pyromania	2	18
1987	Hysteria	1	1

DELANEY and BONNIE

Vocalists Delaney Bramlett (born 1939) and Bonnie Lynn (born 1944) met and married in Los Angeles in 1967. Delaney worked with The Champs and then The Shindogs, house band for the TV rock show *Shindig*. Bonnie had sung behind Fontella Bass, Albert King and was Ike and Tina Turner's first white Ikette.

The duo's debut album, 'Home' (1968), backed by Booker T And The MGs, was not released at the time and they formed a loose association of musicians including Leon Russell (keyboards) JJ Cale, Duane Allman and Dave Mason (guitars) and Carl Radle (bass), before signing a new deal, as Delaney and Bonnie & Friends, using Bobby Whitlock (keyboards), Jim Keltner (drums) and horn players Bobby Keys and Jim Price. The album, 'Accept No Substitute' (1969), was a compelling fusion of white soul, country and gospel. They attracted the attention of Eric Clapton who invited them on to Blind Faith's US tour; Clapton set up a UK/European tour which he joined, hoping for a sideman role after Blind Faith split. 1970's excellent 'On Tour' featuring Clapton was their best-selling album, and Delaney produced and arranged Clapton's first solo album and co-wrote most of the tracks. Delaney and Bonnie toured briefly with The Plastic Ono Band, but then everything fell apart when a headlining tour of the US was cancelled, Clapton left, and they lost most of their band to Leon Russell and thus to Joe Cocker's Mad Dogs & Englishmen touring party.

'To Bonnie From Delaney' (1970) and 'Motel Shot' (1971) both contained some well-crafted country blues and they also boasted US Top 20 single success with 'Never Ending Song Of Love' (1971) and 'Only You Know And I Know' (1971). Ironically, their last album prior to divorce was 'Together' (1973). Each has released four solo albums with little success. Bonnie Bramlett made news in 1979 by punching out Elvis Costello for calling Ray Charles 'a blind ignorant nigger'. Subsequently she became a born-again Christian and released a powerful but ignored gospel album.

Greatest Hits

Singles	Title	US	UK
1969	*Coming Home*	–	16
1971	*Never Ending Song Of Love*	13	–
1971	*Only You Know And I Know*	20	–
Albums			
1970	*On Tour*	29	39

John DENVER

A 1970's singer-songwriter in an all-American mould who made distinctive though innocuous records in a folk-country idiom, which sold huge amounts in what became known as the AOR market, John Henry Deutschendorf (born 1943) was the son of a New Mexico-based airforce pilot with three aviation records. Renaming himself Denver, he moved round the US, studying architecture in Texas, where he became involved in the folk scene, and ended up in LA where he auditioned successfully at the prestigious Ledbetter's venue.

He briefly played with John Stewart, after the latter had left The Kingston Trio, out of which came two classic 1960s songs, Stewart's 'Daydream Believer' (a 1967 hit for the Monkees), and Denver's 'Leaving On A Jet Plane' which went gold for Peter, Paul & Mary. Denver spent four years with the Chad Mitchell trio, making his solo album debut in 1969 (the year of his 'Jet Plane' success), with 'Rhymes and Reasons'.

Albums were replacing singles as the prime unit of a vastly changing rock industry, and Denver's first chart album was 'Poems Prayers and Promises', which made the US Top 20 in 1971. It included a US Top 3 single 'Take Me Home Country Roads' (also a hit for Olivia Newton-John).

For the next few years, Denver could do no wrong for the emergent audience for MOR music, and a subsequent 34 singles in the US best-sellers included four chart-toppers in 1974/75 – 'Sunshine On My Shoulders', 'Annie's Song' (also a UK chart topper), 'Thank God I'm A Country Boy' and 'I'm Sorry'.

His across-the-board appeal meant huge-selling albums, although some which failed to reach the US Top 20 nevertheless went gold or platinum by sheer longevity in the US Top 100. Others, like 1974's 'Back Home Again' and 1975's 'Windfall' topped the US chart; and 1972's 'Rocky Mountain High' and 1975's 'An Evening With . . . ' were also huge sellers.

His MOR status also resulted in some unlikely collaborations, not least of which was the 'World Game' album with The Wailers, duets with Placido Domingo (the single 'Perhaps Love') and Sylvie Vartan ('Love Again') and a 'Christmas Together' album with The Muppets!

Denver's image had become something of a cliché by the late 1970s, his blonde mop-top, granny glasses and clean-cut affability the apogee of MOR folk-rock. His desire to be a passenger on the first commercial flight to the moon was widely applauded by his detractors.

Greatest Hits

Singles	Title	US	UK
1971	*Take Me Home Country Roads*	2	–
1974	*Sunshine On My Shoulders*	1	–
1974	*Annie's Song*	1	1
1975	*Thank God I'm A Country Boy*	1	–
1975	*I'm Sorry*	1	–
Albums			
1973	*Greatest Hits*	1	–
1974	*Back Home Again*	1	3
1975	*Windsong*	1	14
1975	*An Evening With John Denver*	2	31
1976	*Live In London*	–	2

DEPECHE MODE

David Gahan (vocals)
Martin Gore (synthesizer)
Andy Fletcher (bass synthesizer)
Vince Clarke (synthesizer)

Ultra-successful electro pop/rock band formed in the late 1970s in Basildon, Essex. Fronted by Gahan (born 1965) they first recorded on a Some Bizzare compilation

Post-modern Music For The Masses met by massive Modemania

in 1980. In 1981 their first album, 'Speak And Spell', and two singles, 'New Life' and 'Just Can't Get Enough', made Top 20. Clarke (born 1961), their main composer, left in 1981 to form Yazoo and was replaced by ex-Hitman Alan Wilder. Gore (born 1961) then became their main writer.

They were one of the UK's most successful acts in the 1980s, scoring an enviable 16 Top 20 singles and eight Top 10 albums. Among their biggest singles were 'See You' (1982), 'Everything Counts' (1983), 'People Are People' and 'Master And Servant' (1984) and on the album front, 'Some Great Reward' (1984), 'Black Celebration' (1986) and '101' (1989) were their biggest hits.

They first appeared in the US in 1982 but did not make the Top 100 until late 1984. However, their profile in the US has steadily increased to the point where they are one of the most popular touring acts. In 1988 they concluded their nine-month world tour playing to 70,000 people in California. In the 1980s they scored four US gold albums and their most successful album to date came in 1990 with the plantinum-selling 'Violator'. Their first successive US Top 40 singles came in 1990 with 'Personal Jesus', which went gold, and 'Enjoy The Silence', their first US Top 10 single.

Very few acts are still on the way up after a decade at the top, but this synthesizer-led quartet, who specialize in brooding yet danceable and hook-filled songs, still have a big future ahead of them.

Greatest Hits

Singles	Title	US	UK
1984	*People Are People*	13	4
1990	*Enjoy The Silence*	8	6
Albums			
1987	*Music For The Masses*	35	10
1990	*Violator*	7	2

Neil **DIAMOND**

O riginally a songwriter rather than performer, Neil Diamond (born Noah Kaminsky, 1941) grew up on the mean streets of Brooklyn. After seeing Pete Seeger perform, he bought his first guitar in his mid-teens, and immediately wrote his first song, 'Hear Them Bells'. He hawked his songs around the Brill Building song factory in its early 1960s heyday, where he was eventually taken up by Jeff Barry and Ellie Greenwich. He wrote his first hit song, 'Sunday and Me' for Jay And The Americans (1965, US Top 20), signing at the same time to Bert Berns's newly established Bang label.

Diamond's own first single, 'Solitary Man', was a minor success, but he was writing major hits for other artists, notably The Monkees with 'I'm A Believer' and 'A Little

Neil Diamond came up trumps with a winning run of chart aces

Bit Me, A Little Bit You'. 1966 brought his first US Top 10 hit, 'Cherry Cherry', and his compositions were also scoring for Deep Purple ('Kentucky Woman'), Cliff Richard ('I'll Come Running') and Lulu ('The Boat That I Row').

His songs up to this point were straight production-line pop, until 1968 and a move to UNI Records produced the semi-autobiographical 'Brooklyn Roads'. His work gained momentum, gravitating between a calculated commercialism that created his first US No. 1, 'Cracklin' Rosie', and the experimental 'African Trilogy' sequence from the same album, 'Tap Root Manuscript'.

More hits followed, including another chart topper, 'Song Sung Blue', in 1972, amid increasing critical accusations of pretentiousness which focussed on his 1973 soundtrack album, 'Jonathan Livingstone Seagull'. 'Seagull' was Diamond's debut LP under a new million-dollar deal, and was balanced by more straight-to-the-heart balladry that established him firmly at the top of the MOR market. These self-penned standards, including 'Sweet Caroline' and 'He Ain't Heavy, He's My Brother', were encapsulated on live concert albums that likewise enjoyed huge sales.

Various forays away from the straight and narrow of concert superstar included collaborations with Barbra Streisand that included a No.1 in 1978, 'You Don't Bring Me Flowers', the much maligned *Jazz Singer* movie of 1980 and an unlikely appearance in The Band's *The Last Waltz* after having his 1976 album, 'Beautiful Noise', produced by Robbie Robertson.

'Best Of . . . ' and 'Greatest Hits' collections peppered the charts through the 1980s, interspersed with infrequent new releases, like 1984's 'Primitive' (a UK Top 5 hit), still attract a loyal following worldwide.

Greatest Hits

Singles	Title	US	UK
1969	*Sweet Caroline*	4	8
1970	*Cracklin' Rosie*	1	3
1972	*Song Sung Blue*	1	14
1978	*You Don't Bring Me Flowers* (with Barbra Streisand)	1	5
Albums			
1972	*Moods*	5	7
1973	*Jonathan Livingstone Seagull*	3	35
1974	*Serenade*	3	11
1981	*The Jazz Singer*	3	14

Bo **DIDDLEY**

R&B singer/guitarist Diddley (born Ellas Bates, 1928) is one of the rare breed of artists who had little commercial success in their own right, but proved so influential on later musicians – in his case via the ubiquitous 'shave-and-a-haircut, two bits' rhythm pattern patented on his first single – that he occupies a legendary space in the rock pantheon.

Born in Mississippi, he grew up in Chicago as Ellas McDaniel, after being adopted by his mother's cousin. As a teenage Golden Gloves boxer, he gained the nickname Bo Diddley, which stuck when he began to regularly play blues and R&B in South Chicago clubs in 1951.

Spotted by local label Chess Records in 1955, he had an immediate national R&B chart hit with his first single, 'Bo Diddley' – subsequently one of the all-time most covered (and adapted) rock songs, although at the time it did not cross over to the pop charts. Tours and live work across the US followed as R&B artists joined the rock'n'roll explosion; Diddley toured with a group which included his sister 'The Duchess' on back-up guitar and vocals, pianist Otis Spann, and bassist/percussionist Jerome Green.

Diddley followed his debut with other singles later to be widely covered by admirers – 'Who Do You Love', 'Pretty Thing', etc. – but they did not follow label-mate Chuck Berry into the 1950s pop charts. His records, most of which were variations on that signature rhythm pattern of 'Bo Diddley', or its heavy slow blues B-side, 'I'm A Man', instead tended to influence other musicians – Buddy Holly, for example, on 'Not Fade Away'.

Diddley finally cracked the US pop chart in 1959, when the novelty, 'Say Man', which had Diddley and Jerome Green trading insults over a pounding 'Bo Diddley' beat, reached the US Top 20. 'Road Runner' and 'You Can't Judge A Book By The Cover' followed it to middling pop success.

In 1963 when the UK R&B boom broke, Diddley found himself its twin focus, along with Chuck Berry. Several belatedly issued albums made the UK charts, and 'Pretty Thing', 'Mona' and 'Hey Good Lookin'' reached the singles lists, as hundreds of British groups from The Rolling Stones downwards covered his songs on stage and record.

Chart success abated in the late 1960s, but Diddley had become acknowledged as a seminal influence and remained a regular player on the international live rock circuit. He was a natural for major nostalgic events like 1969's 'Toronto Rock'n'Roll Revival Concert', where he played with John Lennon and others. The rock nostalgia tours of the 1970s continued this trend.

Diddley has continued to be a regular live attraction ever since, his seminal style weathering every sea change in rock music; in 1979, he even played as opening act for The Clash on their first US tour. Recordings during recent times have been more sporadic, 1973's 'London Bo Diddley Sessions' (with UK name musicians in support) and 1976's '20th Anniversary Of Rock'n'Roll' albums probably being the highlights.

Greatest Hits

Singles	Title	US	UK
1959	*Say Man*	20	–
Albums			
1962	*Bo Diddley*	117	11

DION and the **BELMONTS**

Dion DiMucci (born 1939) is one of the great survivors of rock'n'roll; a performer whose work has spanned five decades, and whose fortunes swayed between chart action and comparative obscurity, but whose vocals have always retained a tough, yearning quality which makes him unique. The first phase of his career was as lead singer with New York doo-wop group Dion & The Belmonts, a streetcorner quartet formed in 1957 by Dion and fellow Bronx teenagers Fred Milano (born 1940), Carlo Mastrangelo (born 1939), and Angelo D'Aleo (born 1941). After some failed recordings as Dion & The Timberlanes, they rechristened themselves in 1958 after Belmont Avenue in the Bronx, and in short order, both the uptempo 'I Wonder Why' and the ballad, 'Don't Pity Me', made the US Top 30, and the group received national exposure, including touring on the 1958/59 winter trek through the American North West, during which Buddy Holly was killed.

In 1959 the group had their first million-seller with 'A Teenager In Love', only to lose D'Aleo, who was drafted into the US Navy. They continued as a trio and concentrated on ballads, the biggest of which was their second million seller, a 1960 revival of Rodgers & Hart's 'Where Or When'. Later that year, the group split, Dion finally yielding to advice that suggested he had a bigger future as a soloist. His first major solo success was 'Lonely Teenager', a mid-tempo teen-ballad which reached the US Top 20 at the end of the year, but in 1961 his releases sold comparatively badly, and ironically it was the Dion-less Belmonts who returned to the US Top 20 with 'Tell Me Why'.

Dion changed direction, and in collaboration with songwriter Ernie Maresca, came up with 'Runaround Sue', a hard-edged hand-clapping rocker with prominent vocal group support (from The Del Satins). It was a US chart-topper, his first solo million-seller, and launched a run of similar street-tough smashes through 1962, including 'Lovers Who Wander', 'Little Diane', 'Love Came To Me', and another million-seller, 'The Wanderer'. Dion could be seen singing some of these in cameo roles in two movies, *Teenage Millionaire* and *Twist Around The Clock*. The Belmonts also had a US Top 30 hit, 'Come On Little Angel', which was their last big seller prior to a slide from favour.

In 1963 Dion began cabaret dates and signed a new recording deal. Neither of these moves diluted his recording punch: 'This Little Girl', 'Donna The Prima Donna', and revivals of The Drifters oldies, 'Ruby Baby' and 'Drip Drop', were all worthy successors to the sweaty macho swank of 'The Wanderer', and all major hits, with 'Ruby Baby' selling a million. However, he was having personal problems, notably with drugs, and began to become an erratic performer and a difficult artist just when the 'British Invasion' blitzed the US chart, and strong commercial fightbacks were needed. Dion began to insist on experimenting with blues and folk material, and singles like 'Hoochie Coochie Man' and 'Spoonful' failed to reach the charts. One of his better moves was a one-off 1967 reunion with all three Belmonts, which produced the album 'Together Again', exploring the quartet's various early black music influences.

In 1968 after finally kicking his heroin habit, Dion was without a record deal when his old label from the 1950s offered him Dick Holler's poignant song of martyrdom 'Abraham, Martin And John'. His rendition gave him another million-seller, and its reflective, folky style set the mould for subsequent 1970s albums like 'Sit Down Old Friend', 'You're Not Alone' and 'Suite For Late Summer', which showed him as the sensitive singer/songwriter. Exceptions to the pattern were another reunion with The Belmonts for a Madison Square Garden concert, which produced an oldies-filled live album, and an unlikely alliance with Phil Spector in 1975, resulting in the 'Born To Be With You' album, which was not released in the US.

At the end of the 1970s, Dion committed himself to Christianity, and while he continued to perform a secular act, most of his recordings over the next few years were inspirational albums for Christian labels. Not until 1989, after he had raised his live profile by performing some of his gutsy early 1960s repertoire with Bruce Springsteen, did he again cut a contemporary rock album. The resulting 'Yo Frankie', produced by Dave Edmunds, was his most streetwise effort since 1963, drawing on both roots and contemporary rock, and garnering both airplay and critical acclaim for quintessential Dion anthems like the (autobiographical?) 'King Of The New York Streets'.

Greatest Hits

Singles	Title	US	UK
1959	*A Teenager in Love*	5	28
1961	*Runaround Sue*	1	11
1962	*The Wanderer*	2	10
Albums			
1961	*Runaround Sue*	11	–
1962	*Lovers Who Wander*	12	–

DIRE STRAITS

Mark Knopfler (vocals, guitar)
John Illsley (bass)
David Knopfler (guitar)
Pick Withers (drums)

As punk and New Wave music raged around them, Dire Straits clung to their musical aspirations in London clubs, emerging to huge acclaim that led to their virtually defining the genre of adult rock (AOR) by scoring one of the biggest selling albums – more specifically CDs – of the 1980s, 'Brothers in Arms'. University graduate/teacher Mark Knopfler (born 1949), formed the band in 1977 in South London with brother David (born 1951) and a rhythm section. A demo of 'Sultans Of Swing' was played on R&B aficionado Charlie Gillett's radio show (and released via his Oval label on the 'Honky Tonk Demos' compilation). It brought them a record contract with Phonogram but when 'Sultans Of Swing' was released as a single in 1978, it spent just one week in the UK Top 30. The album provoked moderate interest when it emerged – enough to convince noted R&B producers Jerry Wexler (an exec at Warner Bros, their US label) and Barry Beckett to produce their next album.

During its recording in the Bahamas, the debut album took off and made the US Top 3 in 1979, while 'Sultans Of Swing' was a US Top 5 single. Interest grew everywhere except (ironically) for the UK, although 'Sultans Of Swing' did go Top 10; 'Communique', their second album, did not emulate its predecessor's success, but made the US Top 20 helped by a mammoth tour. They continued to make Top 20 albums with 'Making Movies' (1981) and 'Love Over Gold' (1982), although losing David Knopfler (replaced by keyboard player Hal Lindes) and Pick Withers (replaced by

Terry Williams) along the way. They also clocked up several UK hit singles, the biggest 'Romeo And Juliet' (1981, UK Top 10) and 'Private Investigations' (1982, UK Top 3).

A 1983 world tour produced the double live 'Alchemy' album, which allowed Mark Knopfler to spend two years working on a follow-up. 'Brothers In Arms', a 1985 multi-platinum monster around the world and a nine-week US chart-topper. 'Money For Nothing' was a US chart-topping single, and 'Walk Of Life' made the Us Top 10 and the UK Top 3, helped by another world tour.

Rather than trying to top 'Brothers', Knopfler retreated from the mega-hype, which had made him increasingly uncomfortable to a low-key solo career, recording soundtrack albums for *Local Hero* and *The Princess Bride*, producing Bob Dylan's 'Infidels' album, plus albums by Randy Newman, Aztec Camera and Willy De Ville, and periodically turning out with Eric Clapton. In 1988, the band were induced to reform and headline the Nelson Mandela Birthday Tribute concert at London's Wembley Stadium televised live around the world, for which they were joined by Clapton. 1988 also saw the UK chart-topping hits album, 'Money For Nothing', on the title track of which Sting guested as vocalist.

Knopfler was then nearly ready for another Dire Straits album, after one more extra-curricular fling in 1989 as one of The Notting Hillbillies, with pre-Straits chums Brendan Croker and Steve Phillips. The new decade found him recording with Dire Straits (now including Guy Fletcher on keyboards) and during 1990 he previewed new material at the Knebworth Festival with Elton John and Eric Clapton. The next album/world tour are among 1991's biggest potential highlights.

Greatest Hits

Singles	Title	US	UK
1982	*Private Investigations*	–	2
1985	*Money For Nothing*	I	4
1986	*Walk Of Life*	7	2
Albums			
1978	*Dire Straits*	2	5
1982	*Love Over Gold*	19	I
1985	*Brothers In Arms*	I	I
1988	*Money For Nothing*	62	I

Fats DOMINO

The epitome of New Orleans rock'n'roll, Antoine Domino (born 1928) had acquire the nickname 'Fats' by his early teens when he was already playing the club circuit in his native city. His debut single in 1949, 'The Fat Man' sold a million, and set the style for R&B coming out of the Crescent City, reflecting a rich musical heritage that was a melting pot for French, Spanish, Cajun and Caribbean influences. Domino was no one-off, sharing his background and style with Amos Milburn, James Booker and his own mentor, Professor Longhair.

The early 1950s saw Domino, working closely with trumpeter and arranger Dave Bartholemew whose band he had joined in the mid-1940s, produce a string of R&B hits which included the 1952 R&B No. 1 'Goin' Home', before 'Ain't That A Shame' (1955) launched Domino into the new rock'n'roll-oriented national pop charts. The record made the US Top 10 and the UK Top 30 eighteen months later. It heralded a string of huge sellers which would eventually put Domino's global record sales only behind those of Elvis Presley in the latter half of the 1950s.

Alongside the Domino/Bartholemew originals – 'I'm In Love Again' (1956), 'Blue Monday' (1957), and 'I'm Walkin' (1957), all US Top 5 singles, were covers of older standards like 'When My Dreamboat Comes Home' (1956) and 'My Blue Heaven' (1956), both US Top 20 hits, well suited to Domino's vocal approach and the well-rounded sax breaks of Herbie Hardesty and Lee Allen. The biggest smash of all was a recycled oldie, 'Blueberry Hill' (1956) which reached the US Top 3 and the UK Top 10, sales of which topped three and a half million worldwide.

By 1958, Fats Domino had sold over thirty million records in six years, most of them in the three years after 1955. As the decade came to a close, rock'n'roll sales were giving way to smoother material, but Fats still had US Top 10 hits with 'Whole Lotta Loving' (1958) and 'I Wanna Walk You Home' (1959), the latter also a UK Top 20 single. 'Walkin' To New Orleans' (1960) with Domino's piano triplets over soaring strings was one of his biggest US Top 10 hits, also reaching the UK Top 20.

Domino's early 1960s output actually pro-

Knopfler's Love Over Gold in Dire Straits as Brothers In Arms produce Money For Nothing

The Fats Domino effect knocked spots off 'Fifties chart opposition

duced some of his finest tracks such as 'Natural Born Lover' (1960), backed with 'My Girl Josephine', the haunting 'What A Price' (1961), and the irresistible shuffle beat of 'Let The Four Winds Blow' (1961), which were as good as anything he had ever done.

Domino at his 1950s commercial peak appeared in a number of rock'n'roll movies, most of them teen exploitation fodder, although he did appear in the best of the bunch, *The Girl Can't Help It*, singing a truncated version of 'Blue Monday'.

In 1963 he changed labels, but his days as a chart regular were all but over, and he had switched again by 1965. His sound did not gel with the styles of the 1960s – though ironically his last US Top 100 entry was a 1968 version of The Beatles' Domino-flavoured 'Lady Madonna'.

From the 1968 album, 'Fats Is Back', it was evident that his sound hadn't really changed at all over the years, and indeed most of the New Orleans regulars still go on the road with him including Hardesty and Allen, in what amounts to a faultless celebration of the essence of New Orleans rock'n'roll at its most commercially successful.

Greatest Hits

Singles	Title	US	UK
1956	*I'm In Love Again*	3	12
1956	*Blueberry Hill*	2	6
1957	*Blue Monday*	5	23
1957	*I'm Walkin'*	4	19
Albums			
1957	*Rock and Rollin'*		
	With Fats Domino	17	–
1970	*Very Best of Fats Domino*	–	56

Lonnie **DONEGAN**

Far more important/influential than he is ever given credit for, Donegan (born Anthony James Donegan, 1931) was a key figure in popularizing US roots music in the UK in the 1950s, his engaging hybrid of folk-blues (via the Leadbelly/Woody Guthrie songbook) and English music hall yielding a string of UK hits.

After playing as a drummer with The Wolverines Jazz Band while in the Army, he switched to banjo and formed his own jazz combo in 1951, adopting the 'Lonnie' prefix in 1952 after defying a Musicians Union ban to back his idol Lonnie Johnson at London's Royal Festival Hall. He later joined Ken Colyer's Jazz Band (Colyer was probably the man most responsible for introducing skiffle into the UK), before trombonist Chris Barber launched his own band using Colyer's entire backing group, including Donegan. Skiffle, an anathema to many purist traditional jazz buffs, was accepted by UK pop fans as US negro folk music, and Donegan, who fronted a skiffle spot in Barber's shows, soon became its leading exponent.

In 1954 Barber's band recorded an album which included a raucous version of Lead-belly's 'Rock Island Line'. Over the next 12 months, continual requests and airplay led to its release as a single, credited to The Lonnie Donegan Skiffle Group, and in 1956, it made the UK Top 10 during a 22-week run, and repeated the feat in the US, seeing off a cover by Bobby Darin and taking worldwide sales to well over a million. Donegan promptly went solo, switching labels: 'Lost John'/'Stewball' immediately made the UK Top 3 and was a minor US hit. On a 4-week US tour (where despite his Cockney accent, he was billed as 'The Irish Hillbilly', although he came from Glasgow!) he made his American TV debut on *The Perry Como Show:* unable to take his own band or back himself on guitar due to MU restrictions, his US touring group included Dorsey Burnette on bass.

He continued to enjoy UK chart success throughout 1956, consolidating his break-through with another UK Top 10 hit, 'Bring A Little Water Sylvie'/'Dead Or Alive', also denting the singles charts with an EP, 'Skiffle Session', and, remarkably, an album, 'Lonnie Donegan Showcase'. For the next few years, he barely put a foot wrong – during a run of 26 hit singles, he scored three UK chart-toppers: 'Cumberland Gap', 'Gamblin' Man'/'Putting On The Style' (both 1957) and 'My Old Man's A Dustman' (1960), the latter being the first record by a British artist to enter the UK charts at No. 1, and one of the first records to sell a million copies in the UK alone.

Other major hits included 'Don't You Rock Me Daddy-O' (UK Top 5, 1957), 'Grand Coolie Dam' (UK Top 10, 1958), 'Tom Dooley' (UK Top 3, 1958 – a spirited cover of The Kingston Trio's US chart-topper), 'Does Your Chewing Gum Lose Its Flavour' (UK Top 3, 1959 – based on a 1920s Boy Scouts song, which also became a belated US Top 5 hit in 1961, and gave Donegan a third million-seller), 'Battle Of New Orleans' (UK Top 3, 1959 – a cover of Johnny Horton's US chart-topper), 'I Wanna Go Home' (UK Top 5, 1960 – a version of the traditional 'Wreck Of The John B', later revived by The Beach Boys as 'Sloop John B'), 'Have A Drink On Me' (UK Top 10, 1961), 'Michael Row The Boat' (UK Top 10, 1961 – a cover of The Highwaymen's US chart-topper), 'The Party's

Over' (UK Top 10, 1962), and finally Lead-belly's 'Pick A Bale Of Cotton' (UK Top 20, 1962).

Although the hits dried up, his career continued to thrive – ever popular on the UK club/cabaret circuit, he became a regular on TV variety shows and continued to tour the US. His songs have been recorded by many other artists – in 1967, Tom Jones covered his 'I'll Never Fall In Love Again' (UK Top 3/US Top 10), and he is a hugely successful music publisher whose Tyler Music company owns the copyright to much of the Leadbelly and Guthrie material he 'adapted' in the 1950s, plus some 1960s Moody Blues material, including 'Nights In White Satin'.

Following a heart attack, he relocated in 1976 to Lake Tahoe, on the Nevada/California border. Two years later he cut a new album, 'Putting On The Style', updating several of his 1950s hits, which briefly made the UK chart. Produced by Adam Faith, it featured a host of contemporary stars including Albert Lee, Rory Gallager, Brian May, Elton John, Ringo Starr, Ron Wood, Leo Sayer, ad infinitum, all of which were only too delighted to pay homage to the man who provided their earliest inspiration.

Greatest Hits

Singles	Title	US	UK
1956	Rock Island Line	8	8
1957	Cumberland Gap	–	1
1957	Gamblin' Man/Putting		
	On The Style	–	1
1959	Does Your Chewing Gum		
	Lose Its Flavour	5	3
1960	My Old Man's A Dustman	–	1
Albums			
1962	Golden Age Of Donegan	–	3

DONOVAN

A 1960s singer/songwriter, Donovan (born 1946) moved effortlessly from protest folk to flower power rock, precisely mirroring the era's trivial elements as much as the significant.

Donovan Leitch's family moved from Glasgow to London when he was ten. He first emerged on television's *Ready Steady Go* as a sub-Dylan protest-folkie, complete with denim cap and 'This Guitar Kills' emblazoned on his guitar, a nod in the direction of Woody Guthrie's 'This Machine Kills Fascists'. His first two singles, 'Catch The Wind' and 'Colours', were both UK Top 5 self-penned hits in 1965. His own compositions tended to be poetic rather than political in content, although he often performed noted protest anthems like Buffy St Marie's 'Universal Soldier' for added credibility.

He was treated as a British Bob Dylan, appearing in the 1965 documentary *Don't Look Back*, with his role model, but flower power provided a more natural setting for his psychedelic nursery-rhymes, and with hit producer Mickie Most producing, both 'Sunshine Superman' (1966) and 'Mellow Yellow' (1967), were quintessential anthems of the era – and big transatlantic hits. More childlike ditties led to a pastoral double album, 'A Gift From A Flower To A Garden' (1968) which included a UK Top 5 single, 'Jennifer Juniper', written about Jenny Boyd, sister-in-law to Beatle George Harrison and later married to Mick Fleetwood of Fleetwood Mac.

By the end of the decade he was more successful in the US than the UK, though he remained in the UK chart with singles like 1968's 'Hurdy Gurdy Man', and 1969's 'Goo Goo Barabajagal' (which featured Jeff Beck). By 1970, record sales reflected his fall from commercial grace.

1970's 'Open Road' album was his US Top 20 swansong, although a return to Mickie Most for 1971's 'Cosmic Wheels', which led to a temporary resurgence in popularity. After moving to rural Ireland in the mid-1970s, he devoted himself to writing music for film and theatrical projects like *The Pied Piper of Hamlin* (1972) in which he also starred, and *Brother Sun, Sister Moon* in 1973.

After a lengthy retirement, he re-emerged in 1990 with a new album, 'Rising', in the wake of several mentions of his influence by bankable UK acts like Happy Mondays and Brise Smith of The Adult Net.

Greatest Hits

Singles	Title	US	UK
1966	Sunshine Superman	1	2
1967	Mellow Yellow	2	8
1968	Hurdy Gurdy Man	5	4
Albums			
1965	What's Bin Did And		
	What's Bin Hid	–	3
1966	Sunshine Superman	11	25
1967	Mellow Yellow	14	5
1969	Donovan's Greatest Hits	4	–
1970	Open Road	16	30

The **DOOBIE BROTHERS**

Tom Johnston (guitar, vocals)
John Hartman (drums)
Patrick Simmons (guitar, vocals)
Dave Shogren (bass)

F ormed in 1970 when second guitarist Simmons (born 1950) joined San Jose-based Pud, The Doobie Brothers (reputedly named after local slang for a marijuana cigarette) were to enjoy two careers: the first as a hard-rocking biker band, the second as an AOR supergroup.

Their eponymous debut album (1971) showed few signs of greatness, though by 1972's 'Toulouse Street', the sound had been expanded significantly by second drummer Mike Hossack (born 1950) and the introduction of melodic bass player Tiran Porter. The anthemic, phased 'Creedence updated' sound of 'Listen To The Music' brought them a US Top 20 single, while 1973's 'The Captain And Me' made the US Top 10 and confirmed them as rising rock stars alongside the likes of the Allman Brothers with its hit singles, 'Long Train Runnin' ' and 'China Grove'.

Live shows were spectacular with flash-bombs and voicebox guitar from Simmons, one half of a potent front line made even stronger by the introduction of ex-Steely Dan axeman Jeff 'Skunk' Baxter in 1974. They had already followed up with 'What Were Once Vices Are Now Habits' (on which Keith Knudsen replaced Hossack) which, though a weaker album than its predecessor, made the US Top 5 and included a US chart-topping single with the untypically Cajun-sounding 'Black Water', originally the flip side of the less successful 'Another Park Another Sunday'. 'Stampede' (1975) equalled its predecessors' success and confirmed The Doobies as hard-rocking heroes with a penchant for soul illustrated by a US Top 20 single cover of the Isley Brothers' 'Take Me In Your Arms (Rock Me)'.

Denim-clad Dylan clone, Donovan

95

Founder member Johnston dropped out with health problems, later recording two listenable solo albums. His replacement was not another guitarist but Baxter's Steely Dan colleague, Michael McDonald. His keyboards and mellifluous vocals signalled an inexorable switch into AOR, which the briefly returning Johnston was unable to prevent.

Nor should he have tried, on commercial grounds at least – the new, super-smooth Doobies cut two transitional albums, 'Takin' It To The Streets' (1976) and 'Livin' On The Fault Line' (1977), both US Top 10 before a 'Best Of' closed the chapter.

1978's 'Minute By Minute' revealed a new Doobies, producing Californian pop rather than gritty guitar rock. It hit the top in the US, as did the single 'What A Fool Believes', with classic white soul vocals from McDonald. The die was cast: 'One Step Closer', another successful US Top 3 album, perfected the formula.

The Doobies finally stopped rolling when the band, weakened through the departures of Hartman (to be a vet), Baxter (back to the studio) and Porter (quit the music business), ground to a halt in 1982 with a live double souvenir – amazingly their first live LP –

following in 1983. McDonald opted for a solo career (see separate entry) as did Simmons with conspicuously less success: his 1983 'Parade' yielded a US Top 30 hit in 'So Wrong'. Knudsen and latest recruit guitarist John McFee formed country-rockers Southern Pacific. Other short-lived new boys Cornelius Bumpus (sax), Willie Weeks (bass) and Chet McCracken (drums) returned to session work.

The 'Toulouse Street' line-up reformed in 1988 to cut 'Cycles', an album which cloned their first familiar and critically despised sound. Extra percussion was provided by Bobby LaKind, a fixture in the touring line-up (thought not on album) since the mid 1970s. 'The Doctor', a clone of 'China Grove', shot into the US Top 10 as if they'd never been away.

Greatest Hits

Singles	Title	US	UK
1975	*Black Water*	I	–
1979	*What A Fool Believes*	I	3I
Albums			
1975	*Stampede*	4	I4
1979	*Minute By Minute*	I	–
1980	*One Step Closer*	3	53

'Minute By Minute' a switch to fast-food approach for McDonald's Doobie output?

The **DOORS**

Jim Morrison *(vocals)*
Ray Manzarek *(keyboards)*
Robbie Krieger *(guitar)*
John Densmore *(drums)*

Although the life of The Doors as a group was around six years, their huge influence on much of the music of the 1980s has resulted in their albums selling steadily for the two decades since they were active.

The group formed in 1965 in Los Angeles, when Morrison (born Florida, 1943) was attending the University of California, Los Angeles (UCLA) met fellow-student Manzarek (born Chicago, 1935), and impressed the later with his poems/lyrics. After deciding to form a band, they recruited Densmore (born Los Angeles, 1945), from The Psychedelic Rangers, and recorded demos with Manzerek's two brothers and a female bass player. The latter trio seemed unable to relate to Morrison's songs, and the group reverted to a trio until Densmore suggested another Psychedelic Ranger, Robbie Krieger (born 1946, Los Angeles). With Manzarek playing bass-lines on a second keyboard, The Doors (named after Aldous Huxley's novel, *The Doors Of Perception*) were complete, although it took most of 1966 (which included an abortive period signed to Columbia/CBS, during which nothing of note was recorded) before they were spotted by Jac Holzman, founder of Elektra Records, during a stint supporting Love at LA's Whiskey-Au-GoGo.

After signing with Elektra, the group recorded their classic eponymous debut album with producer Paul Rothchild. When it was released in early 1967, it swiftly became a local, then national, then international sensation, fuelled by the US chart-topping success of an abbreviated version of a track from the album, 'Light My Fire', as a single. Before the end of the year, a follow-up album, 'Strange Days', had been released and became their second million selling US Top 3 album, but by then Morrison had been charged with a breach of the peace after a Connecticut concert. It would be the first instalment in a continuing series of battles with authority which lasted until the end of his life.

Demand for the group was such that their third album, 'Waiting For The Sun', did not appear until late 1968, in the wake of two US Top 40 singles, 'The Unknown Soldier' (for which the group made a promotional film clip in which Morrison appeared to be shot – this was many years before promos became obligatory) and their second US No. 1 single, 'Hello I Love You'. The album again sold a million and this time topped the US album chart, but before the release of their fourth album, 'The Soft Parade', Morrison had been arrested several more times. A charge of 'lewd and lascivious behaviour' resulted from a concert in Miami in early 1969, and this became authority's chance for revenge on this

The Doors – '91 biopic marked 20th anniversary of Morrison's death

rabble-rousing rock star who their children worshipped because of his anti-establishment stance.

'Touch Me', the first single from 'The Soft Parade', became their third million-selling single, but three other excerpted singles were only minor successes, perhaps due to the threat to Morrison's liberty, but perhaps equally because the album seemed to display less spontaneity than its predecessors. Within nine months, another album, 'Morrison Hotel', was released and marked a decided swing back towards the R&B which had formed the basis of the group's music at the start. A single taken from the album, 'Road-house Blues', was only a minor hit at the time, but would become a feature of Status Quo's concerts in later years.

Less than six months after 'Morrison Hotel', a double album, 'Absolutely Live', recorded at concerts at the beginning of the year, became their sixth US Top 10 album in three years, and only a few months later came a 'Best Of' compilation, '13'. By then, Morrison had been found guilty of the charge relating to the Miami incident, and sentenced to a prison term, against which he had appealed.

After completing another new album, 'L.A. Woman', in early 1971, Morrison moved to Paris with his common-law wife, Pamela Courson, theoretically to concentrate on writing poetry. The album was released while Morrison was still in Europe, and reached the US Top 10, but on July 3, 1971, he died of a heart attack while in a bath. Two singles from the album, 'Love Her Madly' and 'Riders On The Storm', reached the US Top 20.

The decision of the surviving group members to continue as a trio seemed odd, in view of Morrison's immense importance to the group, but their two albums in that form augmented by session musicians, 'Other Voices' (1971) and 'Full Circle' (1972), both reached the US album chart, although lower down and for shorter periods than any of the albums featuring Morrison, to which another compilation, 'Weird Scenes Inside The Gold-mine', was added in 1972. By the end of that year, Manzarek had left for a solo career, while Krieger and Densmore had formed The Butts Band with three UK-based musicians.

Albums by various ex-Doors have failed to capture the public's interest, but whenever interest seems to be waning, an unheard album featuring Morrison will emerge – in 1973 came 'Best Of The Doors', in 1978 'An American Prayer' (Morrison reading his poetry with posthumous musical backing from the surviving trio), in 1980 'Greatest Hits' (following the use of Doors music in Coppola's acclaimed movie, *Apocalypse Now*), in 1983 'Alive She Cried' and in 1987 'Live At The Hollywood Bowl'. A book on Morrison, *No-One Here Gets Out Alive*, by Danny Sugerman and Jerry Hopkins, has been a strong seller for ten years, and a feature film on his life, directed by Oliver Stone, was released in early 1991.

Some doubt that Morrison is really dead, since no-one who saw his corpse remains alive, Courson having died in 1974 from a suspected heroin overdose, but dead or alive, his popularity has, if anything, increased both because of the regular supply of new albums and as a result of numerous latterday rock personalities displaying (and admitting to) his influence. The introduction of the compact disc also strongly helped The Doors to retain their popularity, which shows no sign of diminishing.

Greatest Hits

Singles	Title	US	UK
1967	*Light My Fire*	1	49
1968	*Hello I Love You*	1	15
1969	*Touch Me*	3	–
1971	*Riders On The Storm*	14	22
Albums			
1967	*The Doors*	2	–
1967	*Strange Days*	3	–
1968	*Waiting For The Sun*	1	16
1970	*Morrison Hotel*	4	12

Lee DORSEY

A slight, good humoured, unaffected char-acter with a joyfully large personality, Lee Dorsey (born 1926) was the principal vocal interpreter, the public persona, of much of writer/producer Allen Toussaint's best work of the 1960s and 1970s. Toussaint said of the singer, 'If a smile had a sound it would be the sound of Lee Dorsey's voice. No wonder he inspired so many of my favourite songs, songs that, if not for him, I would never have written.'

From New Orleans, Dorsey grew up in Portland, Oregon. After some success as a lightweight prize fighter, 'Kid Chocolate', and an overseas stint in the US Navy he settled back in New Orleans, where he established a modest auto repair business that he maintained until his death from emphysema on December 1, 1986. His concurrent singing career was almost a hobby, 'I never knew whether I was a better body-and-fender man or vocalist,' he said of himself with typical tongue in cheek.

He first recorded in the late 1950s, scoring a regional hit with a perky, self-composed R&B romp, 'Lottie Moe'. Headhunted by Marshall Sehorn, then southern promo man cum talent scout for New York-based Fury Records, Dorsey hit the national charts in 1961 with an infectious two and a half minutes of splendid nonsense, 'Ya Ya' (successfully covered in Europe by 'Our Pet', Petula Clark), which was followed by several variations of nursery-like simplicity, all magically endowed with Dorsey's irresistible personality and sterling New Orleans accompaniment, generally supervised by and featuring on piano the then uncredited Toussaint.

When Sehorn and Toussaint formed their

own production company in 1965, they tempted Dorsey back out of his garage to become their premier attraction, the consummation of a triumvirate that resulted in many of the best New Orleans recordings over the following decade.

Dorsey's Toussaint-conceived hits such as 'Ride Your Pony' (1965), 'Get Out Of My Life Woman', 'Working In The Coal Mine' and 'Holy Cow' (all 1966), exemplify the 1960s New Orleans soul sound. He was equally stimulating and convincing during the next phase, on recordings such as 'Everything I Do Gohn Be Funky' (1969) and, in particular, his 'Yes We Can' album (1970), fronting the syncopated team who recorded in their own right as The Meters. The Pointer Sisters, Robert Palmer and a number of others have paid musical tribute to Dorsey's original recordings.

With Toussaint as ever, Dorsey was still making fine recordings (1977's 'Night People' album) when changing musical and commercial values had put him on the back burner. He didn't mind, he was just as happy fixing fenders.

Despite his delightfully off-the-cuff attitude about all things show-busy, Lee Dorsey was an immediately recognisable singer and always a crowd-pleasing performer. Whether supporting James Brown, Jerry Lee Lewis or headlining over Pink Floyd in the 1960s, or rampaging around with The Clash at the end of the 1970s, he always won over his audience. It would have been churlish to have poopooed such a naturally talented and engaging entertainer.

Greatest Hits

Singles	Title	US	UK
1961	Ya Ya	7	–
1966	Get Out Of My Life Woman	44	22
1966	Working In The Coal Mine	8	8
1966	Holy Cow	23	6
Albums			
1966	The New Lee Dorsey	129	34

DR HOOK

Ray Sawyer (vocals, guitar)
Dennis Locorriere (vocals, guitar, bass)
George Cummings (lead guitar, steel guitar)
Bill Francis (keyboards, vocals)
Jay David (drums)

Originally known as Dr Hook & The Medicine Show (named as Sawyer wore an eye-patch à la Captain Hook in *Peter Pan*), this pop/rock/country combo enjoyed considerable success during the 1970s, largely through their use of left-field songs written by cartoonist/free thinker Shel Silverstein. Fronted originally by Sawyer (born 1937), whose place as main vocalist was eventually

taken over by the more distinctive Locorriere (born 1949), the group were a bar band until Ron Haffkine, who was looking for such a band to perform Silverstein's songs in the 1970 movie, *Who Is Harry Kellerman And Why Is He Saying All Those Terrible Things About Me?*, signed them for management and got them their own record deal. Their 1972 debut album, 'Dr Hook', included the song which will always be associated with them, 'Sylvia's Mother', a UK Top 3/US Top 5 hit, and took the album into the US Top 50.

Before the follow-up album, 'Sloppy Seconds', also released in 1972, the group had expanded with the addition of a rhythm guitarist, Rik Elswit (born 1945), to support Cummings (born 1938), and a dedicated bass player, Jance Garfat (born 1944), joining Sawyer, Locorriere, Francis (born 1942) and David (born 1942). The album, which again made the US Top 50, was completely written by Silverstein and included two US hit singles, notably 'The Cover Of "Rolling Stone"', a Top 10 hit, which led to the group actually being featured on the periodical's front cover. 1973's 'Belly Up' album was less successful, although it featured several bizarre Silverstein songs like 'Penicillin Penny', 'Roland The Roadie And Gertrude The Groupie' and 'Acapulco Goldie', all of which probably upset the establishment.

1974's 'Fried Face' featured new drummer John Wolters, who replaced Jay David, but the album was virtually suppressed when the group declared itself bankrupt, which was the title of their first album after signing a new record deal. While 'Bankrupt' was not a huge hit album, it nevertheless included the group's biggest single in four years, their cover version of Sam Cooke's 'Only Sixteen', and after Cummings left the group, 1976's 'A Little Bit More' restored them to the Top 100 of the US album chart, and included a hit single in the title track which made the US Top 20 and UK Top 3. Before their 1977 album, 'Making Love And Music', Bob Henke (guitar) had joined, but the album failed to chart.

In 1978, by which time the group were relying far less on Silverstein's odd compositions, and more on Locorriere's lead vocals, their 'Pleasure & Pain' album went gold, featuring two US Top 10 hits, 'Sharing The Night Together' and 'When You're In Love With A Beautiful Woman', the latter topping the UK singles chart, while 1979's 'Sometimes You Win' included two big US and UK singles, 'Better Love Next Time' and 'Sexy Eyes'.

The group continued to record through most of the 1980s, but apart from a UK Top 3 album with 'Greatest Hits', were rarely as successful as they had been in the previous decade, and are rarely mentioned today. Sawyer embarked on a parallel solo career which brought little fruit, while Locorriere has recently surfaced as a Nashville-based songwriter. The whereabouts of the others are unknown.

Greatest Hits

Singles	Title	US	UK
1972	Sylvia's Mother	5	2
1976	A Little Bit More	11	2
1979	When You're In Love With		
	A Beautiful Woman	6	1
Albums			
1972	Sloppy Seconds	41	–
1976	A Little Bit More	62	5
1980	Greatest Hits	142	2

DR JOHN

A seminal figure in modern New Orleans rhythm & blues, Dr John (real name Malcolm 'Mac' Rebennack, born 1941) worked as a local session guitarist from the late 1950s. He heard country music and blues in his father's record store in New Orleans, and by 1958 was on recording dates with the many independent R&B labels in the city, such as Ace, Rex, Ebb and Specialty, with artists like Joe Tex, Huey 'Piano' Smith and noted New Orleans pianist Roy Byrd (aka Professor Longhair).

He wrote and arranged the legendary local hit 'Light's Out', by Jerry Byrne who had played in Rebennack's high-school group, The Spades. Further influential singles followed, including Art Neville's 'What's Going On' and 'Losing Battle' by Johnny Adams.

In 1959 Rebennack put out a single under his own name on Ace, an atmospheric instrumental with a blistering baritone sax solo from Alvin Tyler, 'Storm Warning'. He also toured, backing New Orleans-based rock stars Byrne and Frankie Ford.

In 1961 he was shot in the hand, ending his guitar playing. He played bass in a dixieland band before taking up organ and piano, playing sessions for producer/arranger Harold Baptiste. He led his own groups under various names – Drits & Dravy, Morgus & The Ghouls – before moving to Los Angeles in the mid-1960s with Baptiste, who was producing Sonny & Cher for Atlantic. Rebennack produced Jesse Hill, playing with the latter's Zu Zu Band, before Baptiste and he created Dr John Creaux the Night Tripper, his nom-de-plume from 1968. Signed to Atlantic, his debut album, 'Gris Gris', featured a hypnotic mix of voodoo chants, swamp blues and general mumbo-jumbo and included 'Walk On Gilded Splinters' which was subsequently covered by, among others, Humble Pie.

A similar feel permeated 'Babylon' (1969), though 1970's 'Remedies' began to anticipate his return to basic New Orleans R&B. By the early 1970s, top names considered it an honour to play on his albums. 'The Sun, Moon and Herbs' (1971) included Clapton and Jagger, and in 1972 'Gumbo' confirmed his status as a Louisiana legend. He collaborated with Allen Toussaint and The Meters for 'In The Right Place', which made the US album charts in 1973, with a US Top 10 single, 'Right Place, Wrong Time'. After a disappointing 'super session' album with Mike Bloomfield and John Hammond Jr., his last chart album was 'Desitively Bonaroo' in 1974.

Rebennack continued to appear on a galaxy of star albums, by artists like Van Morrison and Eric Clapton, and The Band's 'Lazt Waltz', while recording and touring regularly as Dr John. Late 1990 saw him guesting on Ringo Starr's all-star album.

Greatest Hits

Singles	Title	US	UK
1973	Right Place, Wrong Time	9	–
Albums			
1973	In The Right Place	24	–

The DRIFTERS

Throughout their existence, The Drifters were perceived to be an original group who, through the decades, hired and fired so many members that later incarnations are considered to be merely a group of singers arbitrarily using a name which is now almost public domain. The truth of the matter is that the very original 1953 Drifters were a hand-picked group who had not worked together before making records. They were put together by and for vocalist Clyde McPhatter (born 1933) the son of a Baptist preacher. Having moved to New Jersey, the teenage McPhatter honed his tenor voice in the choirs of his father's church and subsequently in his own high school group, The Mount Lebanon Singers.

After an appearance at Harlem's Apollo Theater he came to the attention of Billy Ward, a vocal coach who was in the process of forming a group called The Dominoes. Ward hired McPhatter as co-lead singer and his hand-picked group went on to become the top US vocal group of the era having 22 US R&B hits. In 1953, McPhatter was fired by Ward, but obtained a major label deal immediately, with a new vocal group to be formed around him. McPhatter enrolled some of his friends from The Mount Lebanon Singers for his first sessions where, legend has it, the name Drifters was coined, but co-producers Ahmet Ertegun and Jerry Wexler were unhappy with the group. Another group of friends in the Gospel field, The Thrasher Wonders provided the first Drifters line-up with Bubba and Gerhart Thrasher and Willie Ferbee. Ferbee soon left, replaced by another Gospel veteran, Bill Pickney, and this line-up recorded such US R&B hits as 'Money Honey', 'Honey Love', 'Bip Bam', 'Such A Night', and an interpretation of 'White Christmas' which gave them a Top 100 US pop chart entry.

Up On The Roof, Under The Boardwalk or At The Club, they just carry on Driftin'

George Treadwell, a trumpet player and husband of Dinah Washington, was brought in as manager, buying the name from McPhatter in 1954 when the latter was drafted into the US Army. McPhatter would later pursue a successful solo career but died in 1972 following a lengthy spell of drink and drug problems. Treadwell managed the group in a manner inspired by the strict regime of Billy Ward: McPhatter was replaced by Johnny Moore (born 1934), in turn replaced by Bobby Hendricks and the group carried on, but with little commercial success. By 1958, the group were becoming disenchanted with their manager and record label but instead of negotiating Treadwell simply fired them all and hired a little known New York group, The Crowns, to become the new Drifters in order to fulfil recording and concert obligations. The Crowns were: Ben E. King (born 1938), Doc Green, Charles Thomas and Elsberry Hobbs. However, Pinckney and The Thrashers continued to work as The Drifters amid a flurry of lawsuits.

King's distinctive baritone, with the skills of producers Leiber and Stoller gave the group their first major US pop hit, 'There Goes My Baby' (1959), the first R&B record to use a string section. Under the aegis of Leiber & Stoller, The Drifters went from strength to strength. Utilizing leading New York-based pop writers, US Top 20 hits 'Dance With Me', and 'This Magic Moment' preceded their first international hit, 'Save The Last Dance For Me', which made No. 1 in the US and went Top 3 in the UK. After the success of 'Save The Last Dance For Me', King went solo, enjoying such US hits as 'Spanish Harlem' (US Top 10, 1960), 'Don't Play That Song' (US Top 20, 1962) and 'Stand By Me', which made the US Top 10 in 1961 and gave him a UK No. 1 in 1987. King was replaced by Rudy Lewis, who sang lead on US Top 10 hits 'Up On The Roof' and 'On Broadway'. Lewis was another Gospel alumnus, having been a member of The Clara Ward Singers. Despite being owned by Treadwell (and after his death by his second wife Fay), and having little creative input, the group were hugely influential, spawning a constant flow of vocal groups emulating their latinesque style. After Lewis's untimely death during the session which produced the US Top 5 and UK Top 50 single, 'Under The Boardwalk' (1964), lead vocals were taken over by Johnny Moore who had rejoined the group in 1964. Moore's is the distinctive voice heard on hits like 'Saturday Night At The Movies' (1964) 'At The Club' (1965) and 'Come On Over To My Place' (1965).

By 1965 the Top 40 pop hits were over and they struggled through the rest of the decade. At the start of the 1970s, there were upwards of 20 groups, each with at least one bona fide former member in tow, working the club circuit in America as The Drifters.

In 1972, without a record deal, Fay Treadwell and Johnny Moore took The Drifters to Europe where their 1960s recordings had been climbing into the UK Top 10. The group signed a UK record deal, sticking to the Leiber/Stoller formula of using top pop writers, like Tony Macaulay, Cook-Greenaway and Barry Mason to custom-make records for the group.

All their 1970s UK hits were virtual remakes of their 1960s hits in strict, formula fashion, the group scoring Top 5 hits with 'Kissing In The Back Row' (1974), 'There Goes My First Love' (1975) and 'You're More Than A Number In My Little Red Book' (1976) along with six other UK Top 40 entries in the period 1973–6.

Since the late 1970s The Drifters, whoever may be in the group, have become a staple of the European cabaret scene, repackages of their hits regularly appearing as TV-marketed albums and as recently as 1988, Ben E. King rejoined Moore for a major tour. The situation regarding ownership of the name has stabilized with Johnny Moore's group having the rights for the world outside the US, while Charlie Thomas's Drifters have the US and Bill Pickney still operates as The Original Drifters, each incarnation with its own sound by virtue of their distinctive lead singers. An undeniable influence over the development of soul music, The Drifters will probably be around forever.

Greatest Hits

Singles	Title	US	UK
1959	There Goes My Baby	2	–
1960	Save The Last Dance For Me	1	2
1962	Up On The Roof	3	–
1964	Under The Boardwalk	4	–
1972	At The Club	–	3
1974	Kissing In The Back Row Of The Movies	–	2
1975	There Goes My First Love	–	3
1976	Hello Happiness	–	12
1976	You're More Than A Number In My Little Red Book	–	5
Albums			
1975	24 Original Hits	–	2

DURAN DURAN

Simon Le Bon (vocals)
Andy Taylor (guitar)
Nick Rhodes (keyboards)
John Taylor (bass)
Roger Taylor (drums)

Photogenic pop/rock group formed in Birmingham, UK, in 1978 by Rhodes (real name Bates, born 1962) and John Taylor (born 1960). The quintet, named after a character in the Jane Fonda film, *Barbarella*, had various personal changes before settling in 1980 on Andy Taylor, (born 1961), Roger Taylor (born 1960) and Le Bon (born 1958).

Their 1981 debut single, 'Planet Earth' was a UK hit and they became front-runners of the 'New Romantic' movement. Their eponymous debut album was one of five in the UK and four in the US to reach the Top 10. Among their five platinum albums in the US are 'Rio' (1982) and 'Big Thing' (1988).

They were a top transatlantic teen appeal act in the 1980s, scoring 16 UK and 10 US Top 20 singles including 'Hungry Like The Wolf', 'Union Of The Snake' and 'The Wild Boys'. Known for their outstanding videos, in 1984 they became the first UK act to earn a gold video. Le Bon sang on the Band Aid hit and the group appeared on Live Aid in 1985. Also during 1985, Andy and John Taylor (who are not related) formed Power Station, a part-time group featuring vocalist Robert Palmer, which hit both the US and UK single and album Top 20s. Also in 1985 Le Bon, Rhodes and Roger Taylor formed the short-lived Arcadia, whose first single, 'Election Day', was their only Top 10 hit.

In 1986 Roger and Andy Taylor left and the remaining trio released the 'Notorious' album and scored two more US Top 5 singles with 'Notorious' (1987) and 'I Don't Want Your Love' (1988). In 1989, they returned to the UK Top 10 singles chart as Duranduran with 'All She Wants Is'. In 1990, with new members Warren Cuccurullo (guitar, ex-Missing Persons), and Sterling Campbell (drums, ex-Cameo and Cyndi Lauper's band), they returned briefly to the UK Top 10 with their 'Liberty' album.

Greatest Hits

Singles	Title	US	UK
1983	Is There Something I Should Know	4	1
1984	The Reflex	1	1
1985	A View To A Kill	1	2
Albums			
1983	Seven And The Ragged Tiger	8	1
1984	Arena	4	6

Video virtuosi Duran Duran, with (second left) mainman Simon Le Bon

Bob DYLAN

Once messianic and still an enigma, Dylan's original genius remains greater than his talent. For all his artistic faux pas – like a shambling performance on Live Aid in 1985 – and his mesmerically ugly voice, each new Dylan release is always a special event.

Robert Allen Zimmerman (born 1941) was raised in middle-class comfort in Hibbing, a Minnesota mining town. At high school, he sang with a rock'n'roll outfit but at university in Minneapolis, his yardstick of 'cool' had become folk hero Woody Guthrie rather than Elvis Presley. Working the folk clubs in the city's bohemian quarter, Zimmerman adopted his familiar stage name (after Welsh writer Dylan Thomas).

In 1959 he abandoned his studies to move to New York's Greenwich Village, where the civil rights movement fused with folk music as 'protest' by 1962 when Dylan was signed by producer John Hammond, who had also discovered noted jazz singers Billie Holiday and Bessie Smith. Hammond's superiors expressed little enthusiasm for the new signing's downhome intonation, untutored phrasing and eccentric breath control, but Dylan had an idiosyncratic harmonica technique, was a fair acoustic guitarist and there were few complaints about the intrinsic content of his eponymous debut album, the subsequent 'Freewheelin'' and 1964's 'The Times They Are A-Changin''. These collectively embraced semi-traditional material as well as impromptu 'talking blues' and more earnest Dylan originals such as 'Blowing In The Wind' (a 1963 hit for Peter, Paul & Mary), 'Masters Of War', 'A Pawn In Their Game' and like comments on topical and socio-political issues that were outlined less skilfully by Phil Ochs, Tom Paxton and fellow mainstream folk intellectuals.

Dylan had been hailed at 1963's Newport Folk Festival, but many fans were disturbed by the lyrics of 'My Back Pages' and other items on 1964's 'Another Side Of Bob Dylan', which seemed to reject earlier profundities as strained and naïve, and included more personal statements such as 'Ballad In Plain D' and the protracted 'Restless Farewell'. Those who heard his rare rockabilly single, 'Mixed Up Confusion', were even more resentful, although his 'Freewheelin'' version of the 1920s blues, 'Corrina Corrina', had also been underpinned by amplified backing. He was thought to have 'sold out' altogether on the transitional 'Bringing It All Back Home', with its opening 'Subterranean Homesick Blues', (partially lifted from Chuck Berry's 'Too Much Monkey Business').

Discernible too was Dylan's captivation with British beat groups and their US imitators who had reciprocated by covering his songs, like The Animals with 'Baby Let Me Follow You Down' (retitled 'Baby Let Me Take You Home') and 'House Of The Rising Sun' (also from the 'Bob Dylan' album),

Acoustic Dylan considers going electric, just like a Rolling Stone

Them ('It's All Over Now Baby Blue') and The Byrds ('Mr Tambourine Man' and many others). He was also courted for unreleased compositions such as 'If You Gotta Go, Go Now', a UK hit for Manfred Mann (who, Dylan felt, most effectively interpreted his songs). The job of a British Dylan went initially to Donovan who, with harmonica harness and nasal inflection, began as a more beatific edition of the master.

Outraged purists heckled when Dylan, playing a solid-body Stratocaster, took the stage at Newport with The Paul Butterfield Blues Band, and undertook a 1965 tour of Britain (documented in Don Pennebaker's *Don't Look Back* movie) with The Hawks (aka The Band) who used to back Canadian rock-'n'roller Ronnie Hawkins. Undaunted, he used Band members, Nashville session players and organist Al Kooper on 'Highway 61 Revisited' and 1966's 'Blonde On Blonde',

both vital to serious analysis of his music. From these albums, songs like 'Desolation Row', 'Like A Rolling Stone', 'Just Like A Woman' (another smash for Manfred Mann) and the singalong rock-Dada hybrid, 'Rainy Day Women Nos. 12 and 35', were jolting pop's under-used brain into reluctant action with their rapid-fire literariness, incongruous connections (e.g. 'Ma Rainey and Beethoven once unwrapped a bed-roll' from 'Tombstone Blues') and streams of consciousness. Betraying an absorption with Dylan through constant replay of his albums were The Beatles (e.g. 'I'm A Loser') and The Rolling Stones ('Get Off Of My Cloud'), while The Kinks, Yardbirds and others were incorporating Dylan numbers into their live shows. Also, countless Dylan songs were (and still are) covered by artists as diverse as Cher, Elvis Presley, Duke Ellington and The Four Seasons. Though it meant hard work for lyricists, Tin Pan Alley songsmiths began writing Dylan-type songs from Benny Hill's 'What A World' spoof to P.F. Sloan's all-purpose 'Eve of Destruction' for Barry McGuire, a 1965 US chart-topper.

With poker face and barbed-wire hair, Dylan traded sillier answers for silly questions by journalists before, in self-defence, he banned press interviews completely and stonewalled his more intense admirers. Being such a discourteous riddle grew tiresome, and cynics doubted that the motorcycle accident that ended this phase in June 1966 had actually happened, but he woke from a week's concussed oblivion with a broken neck, mild paralysis and amnesia, with no hope of full recovery for at least a year.

During his enforced sabbatical, this minstrel-to-a-generation was a popular subject for bootlegging. Defying every known copyright law, such records came to prominence with an illicit Dylan double-album, 'Great White Wonder', sold enough to qualify for a gold disc. As Dylan became as unreachable as Presley, a more sinister development was the obsessed 'Dylanologist' (one of many) who advertised in a New York underground newspaper for a Dylan urine sample.

Incommunicado to nearly all but his immediate family and the few who were his equals in the pop hierarchy, Dylan's professional relationship with The Band continued as they recorded the celebrated 'Basement Tapes' with him in their 'Big Pink' house, near Bob's own rural home in Bearsville, upstate New York. Unissued officially until 1975, these recordings circulated widely, eliciting a plethora of lucrative late 1960s covers by Julie Driscoll & Brian Auger ('This Wheel's On Fire'), Fairport Convention and Manfred Mann ('The Mighty Quinn').

A re-emergence on stage at a Woody Guthrie Memorial Concert in 1968 preceded 'John Wesley Harding', an austere, understated album that steered pop away from the psychedelic contrivance that masked many essentially banal perceptions. Even more of a departure from 'Blonde On Blonde' etc, was 1969's 'Nashville Skyline' which featured a duet with Johnny Cash and, in songs from 'I Threw It All Away' to the lighter 'Peggy Day', broader C&W lyrics, though 'Country Pie' lent itself to an adventurous 'pomp-rock' treatment by The Nice.

Dylan's first major live show since his accident was with The Band at 1969's Isle of Wight Pop Festival, where he delivered an adequate one-hour show – for most onlookers, it was sufficient that he'd simply been there. Recordings from this 'comeback' era turned up on the mistitled 'Self-Portrait', a controversial double album that confounded expectation with playful tries at recent hits by Paul Simon and Gordon Lightfoot, The Everly Brothers hit 'Let It Be Me' and the traditional 'Days Of '49'.

These stumblings were dismissed as a writer's block, but 1970's 'New Morning' was unexciting, even if it threw up royalty-earners like 'If Not For You' (as covered by Olivia Newton John and Dylan's friend and sometime songwriting partner, George Harrison).

Much in the same vein as his free association sleeve notes, 1971's *Tarantula* was Dylan's only published novel. A more characteristic vocational tangent was at George Harrison's Bangladesh spectacular at Madison Square Gardens, and his economic ability as a film actor was first realized in 1973 with the apt role of 'Alias' in Sam Peckinpah's *Pat Garrett And Billy The Kid*, for which Dylan wrote a score containing the evocative 'Knockin' On Heaven's Door'.

This episode concluded with a brief defection away from the label for which he has otherwise always recorded for 'Planet Waves', a return to form that he (and The Band) promoted on his first US tour of the 1970s. Edited highlights were heard on 'Before The Flood', the double live album that precipitated his return to CBS/Columbia Records.

In his absence, they had unleashed 'Dylan', a vinyl rag-bag that sounded like 'Self-Portrait' out-takes, but this dubious album was forgotten in the wake of 1975's million-selling 'Blood On The Tracks', generally cited as a Dylan masterpiece. Riven with fragmented intrigue and narrative twists, the words of 'Tangled Up In Blue', the melancholy 'Idiot Wind', 'Simple Twist Of Fate' and others in this consistently strong collection were enhanced by lean arrangements and Dylan's imaginative melodies. Radical re-inventions of 'Blood On The Tracks' items and older artefacts in Dylan's canon were aired on the Rolling Thunder Tour, a series of mostly unpublicized gigs by Dylan and a pot-pourri of guest stars like Joan Baez and ex-Byrd Roger McGuinn. Included on an itinerary that stretched into 1976 were benefit nights for the jailed boxer Ruben Carter (whose plight was detailed on 'Hurricane', a single taken from the powerful 'Desire', an album made with his Rolling Thunder band). This trek also produced *Hard Rain* (a TV special with attendant soundtrack album) and sequences for Dylan's lengthy, self-financed (and self-indulgently obtuse) *Renaldo And Clara* movie.

During 1978's extensive world tour, 1960s classics were refashioned for electric rock group and female chorus – spanning every renowned avenue of his recording career, he'd also taken note of Jimi Hendrix's 1968 overhaul of 'All Along The Watchtower' (from 'John Wesley Harding') and Bryan Ferry's 'A Hard Rain's Gonna Fall' (off 'Freewheelin'') from 1973. En route came a new studio album, the attractive if complex 'Street Legal', from which 'Baby Stop Crying' was a UK Top 20 hit.

Dylan's next strategy was as outrageous in its way as his 'going electric' had been. Mystified and then furious audiences were treated to recitals in which he stuck solely to his Grammy-winning single, 'Gotta Serve Somebody' and other selections from 1979's 'born again' 'Slow Train Coming' album and its equally preachy successor, 'Saved'. Evangelism was less prevalent on 1981's patchy 'Shot Of Love', which included a tribute to the late Lenny Bruce.

A brake was applied to public activity until 1983's secular 'Infidels' which, though dull in retrospect and politically suspect, convinced many that, musically, it and 1984's cluttered 'Empire Burlesque' (with Tom Petty & The Heartbreakers) were approximations of vintage Dylan. Older fans were excited by the release in 1986 of 'Biograph', a 53-song boxed set featuring 18 unreleased tracks, which helped to restore their battered faith after the disappointment of more recent recordings. 1985 found him in London exploring ideas for an instrumental album with Dave Stewart (of The Eurythmics) before a tour with the Petty combo. A trait of this and later tours was the inclusion of an ad-libbed cache of iconoclastic covers like 'Here Comes The Sun', and Kyu Sakamoto's 'Sukiyaki'(!).

In, 1986 the tour party repaired to the studio for the 'Knocked Out Loaded' album, 'modern' enough to seem dated in 1990. Commensurate with poor sales for this and a dubious 'live' album with The Grateful Dead were audience figures for Dylan's next film, *Hearts Of Fire*, in which some reckoned he was typecast as an ageing pop star. His detractors also pounced on 'Down In The Groove', an album with only four new compositions (two written with The Grateful Dead's Robert Hunter) scattered among standards like 'Shenandoah' and Wilbert Harrison's 'Let's Work Together'. Dylan's membership of The Traveling Wilburys was said to be responsible for the 'renaissance' that was the endearingly murky 'Oh Mercy' (produced in New Orleans by Daniel Lenois), but 1990's 'Under The Red Sky' was supposedly another trough, despite an all-star cast.

Rose-tinted memories of 'Highway 61 Revisited' and even 'Blood On the Tracks' have blinded older critics to many Bob Dylan records of the 1980s that are far less objectionable than the increasingly bland offerings of some of his now more commercially fêted contemporaries.

Greatest Hits

Singles	Title	US	UK
1965	*Like A Rolling Stone*	2	4
1965	*Positively Fourth Street*	7	8
1966	*Rainy Day Women # 12 & 35*	2	7
1969	*Lay Lady Lay*	7	5
Albums			
1963	*The Freewheelin' Bob Dylan*	22	1
1965	*Bringing It All Back Home*	6	1
1968	*John Wesley Harding*	2	1
1969	*Nashville Skyline*	3	1
1970	*Self-Portrait*	4	1
1970	*New Morning*	7	1
1974	*Planet Waves*	1	7
1975	*Blood On The Tracks*	1	4
1976	*Desire*	1	3

The **EAGLES**

Glenn Frey (guitar, vocals)
Bernie Leadon (guitar, vocals)
Randy Meisner (bass, vocals)
Don Henley (drums, vocals)

Formed in 1971 by members of Linda Ronstadt's backing band, The Eagles were the most successful country/rock band of the 1970s, and rumours suggest a reformation in the 1990s. Frey (born 1948), from Detroit, worked with Bob Seger during the 1960s before forming Longbranch Pennywhistle with singer/songwriter John David Souther in California. Leadon (born 1947), from Minnesota, had worked in The Flying Burrito Brothers in California before joining Ronstadt, while Meisner (born 1946), a Nebraskan, was a founder member of Poco and also in Rick Nelson's Stone Canyon Band. Henley (born 1947), a Texan, had cut an album with a group called Shiloh.

David Geffen launched Asylum Records at the same time as the formation of The Eagles, who became one of the label's first signings. In 1972 their debut album, Eagles, was produced in London by Glyn Johns, who had produced The Rolling Stones, The Steve Miller Band, etc. It included three US hits: 'Take It Easy' (written by Frey and Asylum labelmate Jackson Browne), 'Witchy Woman' and 'Peaceful Easy Feeling', and reached the Top 30 of the US album chart. The 1973 follow up, 'Desperado', a concept album, included smaller hits in 'Tequila Sunrise' and 'Outlaw Man', after which the group used a guest guitarist, Don Felder, on part of their third album, 'On The Border'. Released in 1974 this was initially produced by Glyn Johns, but after Johns fell out with some members of the group, was completed by Bill Szymczyk. Containing three US hit singles, 'Already Gone', 'James Dean' and their first million-selling single (and first US No. 1), 'The Best Of My Love', 'On The Border' achieved gold status and was the Eagles first UK hit album.

In 1975 a fourth LP, 'One Of These Nights', topped the US album chart for five weeks. By then, Felder, a native Californian, had joined the group, and Leadon's participation became less as Henley and Frey assumed main songwriting duties. The album included three US Top 5 singles – the million-selling title track, 'Lyin' Eyes', which won a Grammy Award, and 'Take It To The Limit', co-written by Frey and Henley with Meisner – and by the end of 1975 Leadon had left the group. 'Journey Of The Sorcerer' (included on the 'One Of These Nights' album), was later used as the theme music to the cult TV

The Eagles – 'Seventies supremos of country rock

series, *A Hitch-Hiker's Guide To The Galaxy*. Leadon re-emerged in 1977 collaborating on an album with Michael Georgiades, and briefly joined The Nitty Gritty Dirt Band at the end of the 1980s, as well as working as a session musician.

His replacement in The Eagles, Joe Walsh, was introduced by Bill Szymczyk, now their permanent producer. Walsh's recording career began in the late 1960s when he fronted The James Gang (produced by Szymczyk), before an acclaimed solo career. As he joined The Eagles, a compilation album, 'Their Greatest Hits 1971–1975', topped the US chart, was certified platinum, reached the Top 3 in the UK and was voted Album of the Year for 1976 by the US National Association of Record Merchandisers. The next original Eagles album (and the first to feature Walsh), 'Hotel California', took almost a year to complete, but after its 1976 release, topped the US album chart and was certified platinum. The first single taken from it, 'New Kid In Town', was a million-selling US chart-topper and both the album and the single won Grammy Awards. The new album spawned two more hit singles in the million-selling title track and 'Life In The Fast Lane' (co-written by Walsh, Frey and Henley), but Meisner left the group before the end of the year, later embarking on a solo career, and in 1989, rejoined Poco for 'Legacy', a reunion album featuring the original members of that group. In early 1978 'Hotel California' and 'New Kid In Town' won their Grammy Awards and the million-selling soundtrack album to the feature film *FM* featured tracks by The Eagles and by Walsh and Meisner as solo acts. Ironically, Meisner's replacement in The Eagles was Timothy B. Schmidt, another Californian, who had originally replaced Meisner in Poco.

The next original album by The Eagles,

'The Long Run', took even longer to complete, and before it emerged, the band released a 1978 Christmas single, a cover version of 'Please Come Home For Christmas', a blues classic written by Charles Brown, which did not appear on the album. In 1979 'Heartache Tonight', the first single from 'The Long Run', was a million-selling US No. 1 and won a Grammy Award, and the album itself topped the US LP chart. Both its title track and 'I Can't Tell You Why' also reached the US Top 10. By the end of 1980, following the platinum-certified 'Eagles Live' double album, the group decided to split up, although 'Seven Bridges Road', a final single from the live album, was a small US hit in early 1981. During the rest of the 1980s, group members embarked upon solo projects – Felder, Schmidt and Walsh enjoyed little commercial acclaim, but Henley and Frey achieved international success.

The Eagles were the most significant and successful American group of the second half of the 1970s, and are evidently still missed – 'The Best Of The Eagles' spent six months in the UK album chart in 1988. The group personified Californian music, and should they reunite, their immense success could occur all over again.

Greatest Hits

Singles	Title	US	UK
1974	*Best Of My Love*	1	–
1975	*One Of These Nights*	1	23
1976	*New Kid In Town*	1	20
1977	*Hotel California*	1	8
1979	*Heartache Tonight*	1	40
Albums			
1975	*One Of These Nights*	1	8
1976	*Their Greatest Hits 1971–1975*	1	2
1977	*Hotel California*	1	2
1979	*The Long Run*	1	4

Steve **EARLE**

Earle is one of the most successful of the 'New Country' acts to have emerged during the 1980s, although his greatest success came through taking an extremely 'rockist' route. Earle (born 1955) moved to Nashville in 1974 after a period playing folk music in clubs in his home state of Texas, but struggled in the country music capital and eventually returned to Texas. He assembled a band, The Dukes, and began touring with a set which attempted to merge the 'Outlaw' style of Willie Nelson and Waylon Jennings (who covered an early song by Earle, 'The Devil's Right Hand') with a traditional rock'n'roll approach. Touring and demos brought a recording deal in 1983, but the results were unsatisfactory, although an album of this material was later released as 'Early Tracks' following the success of 'Guitar Town', his first major label album in 1986. This album was an engaging mixture of country and rock'n'roll, with echoes of Duane Eddy, Buddy Holly and Bruce Springsteen, ably performed by The Dukes, whose line-up at that time included Richard Bennett (guitar), Bucky Baxter (pedal steel), Ken Moore (keyboards), Emory Gordy Jr. (bass/ mandolin) and Harry Stinson (drums).

1987's 'Exit O' was more of the same, but with a grittier feel and fewer of the soft edges of Earle's debut. 'Copperhead Road' in 1988 gave Earle his breakthrough; a fully fledged rock album, it brought Earle a far larger audience than his contemporaries, although alienating many of his country fans. Backing on one track was by The Pogues – apparently the result of a late-night drinking session with the London/Irish band, and the song, 'Johnny Come Lately', came close to giving Earle his first chart entry.

Also in 1988 Earle produced the second album from Cambridge band The Bible, and spent much of the next 18 months touring, playing lengthy sets and sounding increasingly 'Springsteenesque' – even performing songs by the latter on stage. He became heavily involved in promoting the career of Belfast band Energy Orchard, and in 1990 released 'The Hard Way', virtually 'Copperhead Road Pt.2', which emulated its predecessor's success.

With an image reminiscent of an earlier generation of country rock'n'rollers like Jerry Lee Lewis and Johnny Cash (he's been married four times and he's had the occasional brush with the law), Earle seems set on following in Springsteen's footsteps, although some of his material lacks depth, and a more accurate comparison may well end up being with faded 1970s rocker, Bob Seger. Time alone will tell.

Greatest Hits

Albums	Title	US	UK
1988	Copperhead Road	–	44
1990	The Hard Way	100	22

EARTH, WIND and FIRE

Maurice White (vocals, drums, percussion)
Verdine White (bass)
Philip Bailey (vocals, percussion)
Andrew Woolfolk (sax, flute)

Maurice White (born 1944) played drums with Booker T. Jones (of The MGs) in the late 50s and played on many early 1960s Chess records. He was a member of the successful Ramsey Lewis Trio between 1966 and 1969, then formed The Salty Peppers who became Earth, Wind & Fire in 1970, but had limited success. With only the White brothers from the original line-up, the group, now including Bailey from The Stoval Sisters Band, moved labels in 1972 and a year later Woolfolk joined.

In 1973, this innovative act, who fused soul, jazz and rock, released the first of their 12 US Top 40 albums, 'Head To The Sky', one of their four gold and eight platinum LPs. They became one of America's top live acts (with a mystical and very elaborate stage show) and made the US Top 10 with albums such as 'Spirit' (1976), the Grammy-winning 'All 'n All' (1977), 'I Am' (1979), 'Faces' (1980) and 'Raise' (1981). They had eight gold singles including 'Sing a Song' (1975), 'Getaway' (1976), 'Got To Get You Into My Life' (1978) and, after finally charting in the UK, had three transatlantic Top 10s: 'September' (1978), the Grammy-winning 'Boogie Wonderland' (1979, combined with The Emotions) and 'Let's Groove' (1981).

Maurice disbanded the group in 1984 and he and Bailey went solo, with the latter having a transatlantic hit duet with Phil Collins, 'Easy Lover', in 1985. The group reunited in 1987 as a quintet with the addition of ex-Commodore Sheldon Reynolds and their 'Touch The World' album returned them to the US Top 40 and singles from it were major black/dance hits in the US. In 1990 their eighteenth album, 'Heritage', which included guests M.C. Hammer, The Boys and Sly Stone was a Top 10 black music hit, but failed to return this influential black group to their earlier heights.

Greatest Hits

Singles	Title	US	UK
1975	Shining Star	1	–
1979	After The Love Has Gone	2	4
1981	Let's Groove	3	3
Albums			
1975	That's The Way Of The World	1	–
1975	Gratitude	1	–
1979	I Am	3	5

Sheena **EASTON**

Glasgow-born ex-drama student Easton (born 1959) briefly made the UK chart with her debut single, 'Modern Girl', in 1980. Then a TV documentary *Big Time*, tracing the marketing of a pop star, made her an overnight celebrity, and her next single '9 To 5', reached the UK Top 3. The debut single then reached the UK Top 10. To avoid confusion with the identically titled Dolly Parton/Lily Tomlin movie, '9 To 5' was released in the US as 'Morning Train', and topped the US chart. Other UK Top 20 singles included 'One Man One Woman',

Earth Wind and Fire, a funky fusion of musical elements

'Big Time' debut full of Easton promise

'When He Shines' and the James Bond movie theme 'For Your Eyes Only', before she moved to the States to promote her debut album 'Sheena Easton' (UK title 'Take My Time') which made the US Top 30 and UK Top 20.

Shrewd management strategy aimed at the US paid off, with a 1983 duet with Kenny Rogers, a version of Bob Seger's 'We Got Tonight', making the US Top 10. A raunchier change of direction under the guidance of Prince resulted in another US Top 10 hit in 1984, 'Strut', and a Prince composition, 'Sugar Walls', making the US Top 10 in 1985. Easton became the first-ever singer to have singles in the *Billboard* Top 10 black music, disco, pop, MOR and country charts.

Since the mid-1980s she has been virtually ignored in the UK and a minor superstar in the US. Her 1985 album, 'Do You', with producer Nile Rodgers, followed in 1988 by another gold album, 'The Lover In Me', confirmed a move to a Madonna-style image of post-modern torch singer.

Greatest Hits

Singles	Title	US	UK
1981	Morning Train (9 to 5)	1	3
1981	For Your Eyes Only	4	8
1983	We've Got Tonight		
	(with Kenny Rogers)	6	28
1988	The Lover In Me	2	–
Albums			
1981	Sheena Easton		
	(UK title: Take My Time)	24	17
1984	A Private Heaven	15	–

The EASYBEATS

Stevie Wright (vocals)
Harry Vanda (guitar)
George Young (guitar)
Dick Diamonde (bass)
Gordon Fleet (drums)

Though they only scored two UK Top 20 hits while a functioning unit, The Easybeats were among the more insidious colonial infiltrators of British pop – after first making it in Australia.

No Easybeat was actually a native Australian. Vanda (born 1947) was a veteran of The Starfighters, a top Dutch instrumental unit, and met fellow Dutchman Diamonde (born 1947) in a hostel near Sydney which catered for recent migrants. In 1964 the two formed The Starlighters with Britons Young (born 1947) and Wright (born 1948) whose dedication to his art was such that he shed real tears during agonized ballads with the aid of an onion-smeared handkerchief. When Fleet (born 1945) – an ex-Mojo – was recruited, he advised modelling their sound and look upon that of the Merseybeat groups he'd known back in England and also coined the name Easybeats, after a popular British radio series.

Becoming immensely popular in New South Wales, national recognition for The Easybeats came with their second single, 'She's So Fine' – in the style of the early Kinks – topping all regional charts. After three more No. 1s in less than a year, the group chanced a US tour in 1966 but their Australian hits flopped there and the group's quest for global fame took them to London.

Via heavy pirate radio exposure, the group's first UK-recorded single, 'Friday On My Mind' (produced by Shel Talmy), became their biggest international smash. This memorable expression of escape from the working week was revived by David Bowie in 1975, and remains a much played 1960s classic. After their debut UK album, 'Good Friday', Tony Cahill replaced the homesick Fleet as the outfit waited until 1968 for another hit – with the atypically doom-laden 'Hello How Are You' – and that, as far as Britain was concerned, was that for The Easybeats. This mood was reflected in the attendant album, 'Vigil', a ragbag of mismatched covers and originals of psychedelic persuasion. By sickening coincidence, another single, 'St. Louis' had just entered the US Top 100 when the group disbanded after a farewell tour of Australia in 1969. 'Friends', the final album attributed to The Easybeats, consisted largely of demos taped by Vanda and Young, the quintet's main songwriters. The pair assisted with Wright's solo return to the Australasian Top 40, and the greater success of AC/DC (see separate entry). Containing two of Young's younger brothers, AC/DC had evolved from a plan to relaunch an Easybeats fronted by yet another Young

sibling, Alex (alias George Alexander, formerly of Grapefruit).

Vanda and Young have also been responsible for many pseudonymous studio-only creations such as Paintbox, Band Of Hope and Whichwhat, but only Flash And The Pan enjoyed any commercial acclaim, beginning with a minor UK chart entry in 1978, and in 1983 reaching the UK Top 10 with 'Waiting For A Train' – on their own Easybeat label.

Greatest Hits

Singles	Title	US	UK
1966	Friday On My Mind	16	6
1983	Waiting For A Train		
	(as Flash And The Pan)	–	7

ECHO and the BUNNYMEN

Ian McCulloch (vocals)
Will Sargeant (guitar)
Les Pattinson (bass)

While Liverpool missed the initial punk explosion, the city was at the forefront of the second wave of bands at the end of the 1970s. McCulloch (born 1959), Sargeant (born 1958) and Pattinson (born 1958) had played in sundry Liverpool bands before they united in 1978 to debut at Eric's Club – close to the demolished Cavern Club – with a drum machine they called Echo.

They built up a cult following, signing to the local independent Zoo label and releasing their first single, 'Pictures On My Wall', in 1979. At the end of that year, having replaced Echo with Pete De Freitas (born 1961), they signed to another independent, Korova (this time associated with WEA). 'Rescue' grazed the UK singles chart in 1980 and the debut album, 'Crocodiles', made the UK Top 20 with its strong lyrical imagery and stark sound drawn from 1960s influences like The Doors and Leonard Cohen.

They developed steadily with a strong image, scoring minor hit singles with 'Crocodiles' and 'A Promise', gaining cult status with the 'Shine So Hard' video and live EP, before finally cracking the UK Top 20 with 'The Back Of Love' (1982) and the Top 10 with 'The Cutter' from their UK Top 3 album, 'Porcupine'. Despite another UK Top 10 single with 'The Killing Moon' and a second UK Top 5 album, 'Ocean Rain', in 1984, they achieved little in the US, while in the UK, they were overtaken by bands who had once supported them like U2.

1985's 'Best Of' album, 'Songs To Learn And Sing', went Top 10 in the UK, but De Freitas left to form the Sex Gods as the band lost impetus, though he had returned by the 1987 release of a new album, 'Echo And The Bunnymen', whose title and brief chart life betrayed its lack of inspiration. Their final hit

The twang was the thang on Duane Eddy's echo-laden epics

in 1988 was a cover of 'People Are Strange' (The Doors), produced by original Door Ray Manzarek. After De Freitas died in a 1988 motor cycle accident, McCulloch left the group and his first solo album, 'Candleman', (1989) briefly made the UK Top 20, while Pattinson and Sargeant released a new Bunnymen album, 'Reverberations', in 1990.

Greatest Hits

Singles	Title	US	UK
1983	The Cutter	–	8
Albums			
1983	Porcupine	–	2
1984	Ocean Rain	87	4
1987	Echo And The Bunnymen	–	4

Duane EDDY

Highly regarded by younger fretboard icons like George Harrison, Jeff Beck and Dave Edmunds (see separate entries), New Yorker Eddy (born 1938) refined the 'twangy guitar' approach by booming the melodies of his instrumentals solely on the bottom strings of his Gretsch through a customized amplifier and echo chamber.

An admirer of Chet Atkins, Eddy had become a fair country guitarist when his family moved to Phoenix in 1951. Four years later, he was discovered by Tucson disc-jockey Lee Hazlewood who wrote and produced Eddy's debut single, 'Soda Fountain Girl', a vocal duet with Jimmy Delbridge from a local C&W outfit. On leaving high school, Eddy broadened his style through lessons with jazz guitarist Jim Wyberle, and undertook his first professional engagements with Al Casey's Arizona Hayriders who accompanied him on 'Movin' 'n' Groovin' ', another Hazlewood creation. The blueprint of this twelve-bar instrumental's overall sound was Bill Justis's jogalong 'Raunchy', but, issued on a Philadelphia label, 'Movin' 'n' Groovin' ', made the US Top 100 in 1958.

The million-selling 'Rebel Rouser', the team's second single, set the main pattern – a repeated guitar riff anchoring a sax obligato – for the next few years as hit followed contrived hit. Some were based on folk tunes, but others included Al Casey's 'Ramrod', Henry Mancini's 'Peter Gunn' and Eddy and Hazlewood's own 'Forty Miles Of Bad Road'. Pertinent to these triumphs were Eddy's immobile, enigmatic persona when fronting his backing band, The Rebels, and a flair for acting that landed him mainly bit-parts in cinema and television films – for which he

often twanged on soundtracks that embraced further smashes like 1960's 'Because They're Young' – a musical departure in its use of strings – and 'Ballad of Paladin' (after the hero of TV western Have Gun – Will Travel).

After parting briefly with Hazlewood in 1960, Eddy's self-produced singles struggled, but he managed a brief comeback when, reunited with his mentor, he scored his last big hit for many years with 1962's 'Dance With The Guitar Man'. Purists felt that Eddy's style on this single had been adulterated by the female chorus framing the expected low-down picking. Less lucrative deviations came as Eddy absorbed passing trends exemplified in albums such as 'Twistin' and Twangin' ' and 'Duane Does Dylan'.

Even without record success, Eddy was still guaranteed plenty of work – he was voted Pop Personality of the Year in a 1960 UK poll. A surprise UK Top 10 hit in 1975, with Tony Macauley's 'Play Me Like You Play Your Guitar', put him in a favourable position to negotiate higher booking fees even if he had to wait until the next decade for another hit when a mood of renewed veneration for pop's Methuselahs led to a link-up with The Art Of Noise for a 1986 remake of 'Peter Gunn' – and, under the supervision of George Harrison and Jeff Lynn among others, an eponymous new album which, for those who hadn't heard much of Duane for many years, was much as they might have expected him to sound in the 1980s.

A footnote to this project was the selection of 'The Trembler', an opus by Indian sitarist Ravi Shankar to which Eddy had added a bridge passage – thus producing the composing credit 'R. Shankar-D. Eddy' – one of the strangest ever to be printed on a record label.

Greatest Hits

Singles	Title	US	UK
1958	Rebel Rouser	6	19
1960	Because They're Young	4	2
1961	Pepe	18	2
1962	(Dance With) The Guitar Man	12	4
1975	Play Me Like You Play Your Guitar	–	9
Albums			
1959	Have 'Twangy' Guitar Will Travel	5	6
1960	The Twang's The Thang	18	2

Dave EDMUNDS

Undoubtedly the outstanding Welsh rock'n'roll star, Edmunds has enjoyed success (if not always hits) in four decades of production and performance. A singer/guitarist, Edmunds (born 1944) worked in minor Cardiff bands before making his recording debut as a member of The Human

Beans in 1967. With John Williams (later known as John David) on bass and new drummer Bob 'Congo' Jones, The Beans renamed themselves Love Sculpture and in 1968, made the UK Top 10 with a breakneck version of Khachaturian's popular classical piece, 'Sabre Dance', which had been recorded live for a radio session. Overnight, Edmunds was a hero, although on the grounds of speed rather than good taste, but the group's two albums, 'Blues Helping' (1968) and 'Forms And Feelings' (1970), were much closer to R&B than to rocking up classics. After a disastrous US tour, the group folded, and Edmunds began to spend his time at the fast-expanding Rockfield Studio, as he had production ambitions.

In late 1970 his self-produced revival of the Smiley Lewis R&B hit, 'I Hear You Knocking', on which he played and sang everything, topped the UK chart and made the US Top 5. After an under-appreciated album, 'Rockpile', in 1971, he spent much of 1972 as musical director for the David Essex movie, *Stardust* (in which he also performed) before signing with Rockfield's own label in 1972. He scored two UK Top 10 hit singles in the first six months of 1973 with cover versions of girl group hits of the 1960s, 'Baby I Love You' and 'Born To Be With You', produced in a style clearly copied from Phil Spector, but achieved by multiple overdubbing.

A 1975 album, 'Subtle As A Flying Mallet', was less successful, and Edmunds became friendly with Nick Lowe, eventually forming a group called Rockpile which they jointly led, but which could not record as Edmunds and Lowe were signed to rival labels as solo artists. This did not prevent them playing on each other's albums, and Edmunds made a series of dynamic albums: 'Get It' (1977), 'Tracks On Wax 4' (1978) and 1979's 'Repeat When Necessary', a UK Top 40 hit. By 1980 Rockpile – completed by Billy Bremner (guitar, vocals) and Terry Williams (drums) – could finally record under the group name, but their sole album, 1980's 'Seconds Of Pleasure', was hugely disappointing and precipitated their falling apart. Edmunds had by then scored six UK hit singles (notably 1979's 'Girls Talk'), and returned to his solo career with another UK Top 40 album, 'Twangin'', plus acclaim for his highly successful production of the debut album by US punkabilly trio, The Stray Cats.

In 1982, with a new band including erstwhile Love Sculpture bass player Williams/David, Dave Charles (drums, ex-Help Yourself) and often Geraint Watkins (keyboards), Edmunds released his seventh original solo album, 'DE7', in 1982 and entrusted production of his 1983 album, 'Information', to ELO mastermind Jeff Lynne. While Lynne became highly regarded as a late 1980s producer, this was his first 'outside' production, and was a virtual flop.

Edmunds and Lynne co-produced 1984's 'Riff Raff' album, which was also unsuccessful, and after an excellent, but commercially ignored 1987 live album, 'I Hear You Rockin'', Edmunds retreated to production, where he had built a good reputation for his work with The Everly Brothers, k.d. lang, Status Quo, Shakin' Stevens and The Fabulous Thunderbirds.

In 1989/90, Edmunds returned to the live fray, leading an All-Star revue which also comprised the legendary Dion, whose 1989 comeback album, 'Yo Frankie', was produced by Edmunds, ex-Fabulous. ThunderBirds vocalist Kim Wilson, legendary R&B guitar hero Steve Cropper and singer/songwriter Graham Parker. Alongside the tour came the first Edmunds studio album since 1984, 'Closer To The Flame', an uncertain but promising return. Edmunds remains a potential superstar, but has yet to regain the artistic consistency and commercial appeal he has lacked since the late 1970s.

Greatest Hits

Singles	Title	US	UK
1968	Sabre Dance (Love Sculpture)	–	5
1970	I Hear You Knocking	4	1
1973	Baby I Love You	–	8
1973	Born To Be With You	–	5
1979	Girls Talk	65	4
Albums			
1981	Twangin'	48	39
1982	DE 7th	46	60

ELECTRIC LIGHT ORCHESTRA

Roy Wood (guitar, vocals)
Jeff Lynne (guitar, vocals)
Bev Bevan (drums)
Rick Price (bass)

Taking over where The Beatles left off after 'Magical Mystery Tour', Electric Light Orchestra scored an impressive ten hit albums and 20 hit singles by 1980, using string players as part of a rock group.

ELO's driving force was Jeff Lynne (born 1947), who played in Birmingham band The Idle Race before joining the final incarnation of innovative pop band The Move in 1971, for whom he wrote their final classic, 'Do Ya'. Led by the mercurial Roy Wood, The Move had chalked up a string of psychedelic-tinged hits, but Wood had grander ideas which appealed to Lynne. Together with Move drummer Bev Bevan (born 1945), they assembled ELO during the death throes of The Move, experimenting with a mixture of rock and classical sounds.

They made a good start when '10538 Overture' made the UK Top 10 in 1972 as a prelude to their eponymous debut album (US title 'No Answer'), but Wood and Price left to form Wizzard and ELO looked doomed.

However, Lynne and Bevan persevered, recruiting Richard Tandy (keyboards, born 1948) and Michael de Albuquerque (bass) plus a fresh string section for 1973's 'ELO II', which included a US/UK hit single, a version of 'Roll Over Beethoven' mixing Chuck Berry with Beethoven's Fifth Symphony. Lynne continued his symphonic ideas in the same year's 'On The Third Day', which failed to chart in the UK. Their US breakthrough came with 1974's 'Eldorado' album, which reached the US Top 20, and included a US Top 10 hit, 'Can't Get It Out Of My Head' (which ironically failed to make the UK charts).

With De Albuquerque's replacement Kelly Groucutt (born 1945, bass) plus Mik Kaminski (born 1951, violin) Melvyn Gale (born 1952, cello) and Hugh McDowall (born 1953, cello) in addition to Lynne, Bevan and Tandy, six US tours in the next three years maintained momentum. A live album recorded in California, 'The Night The Lights Went Out In Long Beach', was released only in Germany, after which Lynne continued to produce inspired albums: 'Face The Music' (1975, US Top 10, including a US/UK Top 10 single, 'Evil Woman'), 'A New World Record' (1976, US/UK Top 10, with a US/UK Top 10 single, 'Telephone Line'), 'Ole Elo' (1976, a compilation from the first five albums released in the US, where it made the Top 40) and a double album, 'Out Of The Blue' (1977, US/UK Top 5, with several hit singles), which many regard as the pinnacle of their career, as their futuristic stage show during this era was genuinely astounding.

The departure of all but Lynne, Bevan, Groucutt and Tandy in 1977 failed to disturb the band's momentum as Lynne began to use keyboards as well as guitar, and 1979's 'Discovery' repeated the formula, topping the UK chart, reaching the US Top 5 and yielding two more US/UK Top 10 singles, 'Shine A Little Love' and 'Don't Bring Me Down', plus two more UK Top 10 hits, 'The Diary Of Horace Wimp' and the double-sided hit, 'Confusion'/'Last Train To London'. A 1979 'Greatest Hits' album predictably made the UK Top 10/US Top 40, and the group survived the dubious *Xanadu* movie starring Olivia Newton-John, with whom they combined for the Lynne-written title track which topped the UK singles chart in 1980 and made the US Top 10, while the soundtrack album reached the US Top 5 and UK Top 3.

1981 brought 'Time', which topped the UK chart and made the US Top 20 and included their final Top 10 single, 'Hold On Tight', but Lynne had grown tired of touring and after 1983's 'Secret Messages', with its UK Top 20 single, 'Rock'n'Roll Is King', he put ELO on ice, turning to production for others, starting with Dave Edmunds's 1983 album, 'Information'.

ELO briefly regrouped as a trio of Lynne, Bevan and Tandy for 1986's 'Balance Of Power' and its US Top 20 swansong, 'Calling

ELO fantasies peaked with a gigantic flying saucer descending over astonished audiences

America', but by this point, Lynne was living largely in Los Angeles and was not interested in more touring. In 1987, he produced the stunning comeback album by George Harrison, 'Cloud Nine', as well as working on Roy Orbison's final album, 'Mystery Girl', and 'Full Moon Fever' by Tom Petty & The Heartbreakers, plus Randy Newman's 'Land Of Dreams' album and Beach Boy boss Brian Wilson's eponymous debut album. He also became one of an ad-hoc recording band of superstar buddies, The Traveling Wilburys (see separate entry), which featured Bob Dylan, George Harrison, Roy Orbison and Tom Petty. Their eponymous debut album was a world-wide-hit, tinged only by the sad death of Orbison soon afterwards, but the rest of the group reunited in 1990 for a second album, disturbingly titled 'Volume 3'.

Also in 1990, Lynne shook off all remaining ELO shackles and released his first solo album, 'Armchair Theatre', with help from Harrison, Del Shannon, Richard Tandy and many others. He is rated at the start of the 1990s as one of the world's most respected songwriters, producers and performers.

Greatest Hits

Singles	Title	US	UK
1976	Livin' Thing	13	4
1977	Telephone Line	7	6
1979	Don't Bring Me Down	4	3
1980	Xanadu (with		
	Olivia Newton John)	8	1
1981	Hold On Tight	10	4

Albums			
1976	A New World Record	5	6
1977	Out Of The Blue	4	4
1979	Discovery	5	1
1980	Xanadu (with		
	Olivia Newton John)	4	2
1981	Time	16	1

Joe **ELY**

A Texan singer/songwriter/guitarist who emerged during the late 1970s and has continued to improve despite occasional dead-end detours, Joe Ely (born 1947) has achieved the most unique distinction of re-signing to a major label who dropped him five years before.

A master of both R&B and country/rock, Ely travelled the world as a teenager, working in a circus among other non-musical jobs. In 1972 he based himself in Lubbock (home of Buddy Holly), and with other local musicians including a musical saw player (!), formed The Flatlanders with two other notable singer/songwriters, Jimmie Dale Gilmore and George 'Butch' Hancock. The group cut an album's worth of material for a subsidiary of the celebrated Sun label, but it was unreleased until 1980. In 1977, with his road-polished band featuring guitarist Jesse Taylor, Ely signed with MCA (ironically Holly's label), and between 1977 and 1981, made four studio albums, the most successful in chart

terms being 1981's 'Musta Notta Gotta Lotta' (which featured an expanded band).

Many feel that his eponymous debut album and especially 1978's 'Honky Tonk Masquerade' (named in *Rolling Stone* as one of the finest albums of the 1970s) were better than 1979's 'Down On The Drag' and 'Musta Notta', as the earlier albums included superior songs (by Ely and 'Butch' Hancock), and later work (influenced by UK punks The Clash, whose Joe Strummer guested on Ely's 1981 'Live Shots' album, a minor US chart item) was somewhat less distinguished.

1984's 'Hi-Res' was an experimental electronic album, after which MCA rejected a 1985 album, 'Dig For Love', and Ely regrouped with a new band (featuring another stunning guitarist, David Grissom) and made two superb independently-released albums, 'Lord Of The Highway' (1987) and 'Dig All Night' (1988). Another London-based independent label, Sunstorm, also released two compilation albums of material from the early MCA albums – 'Milkshakes And Malts' showcased the Ely recordings of songs written by Hancock and 'Whatever Happened To Maria?' did the same for Ely's self-penned material.

In 1990 Ely cut a superb live album, 'Live At Liberty Lunch', which was intended for independent release, but was picked up by MCA, launching Ely towards another well-deserved peak. Recommending albums on the basis of chart positions is inappropriate – the long unavailable early albums will certainly re-appear, and everything since 1986 is very worthwhile.

EMERSON, LAKE and PALMER

Keith Emerson (keyboards)
Greg Lake (bass, vocals)
Carl Palmer (drums)

F oremost among the British progressive rock bands of the early 1970s, ELP was conceived when Keith Emerson (born 1944) of The Nice met Greg Lake (born 1948) of King Crimson, in late 1969. A plan to team up with Jimi Hendrix and Mitch Mitchell was rapidly aborted when Mitchell turned up with two bodyguards, so they turned to ex-Arthur Brown/Atomic Rooster man Carl Palmer (born 1951).

The new 'supergroup' made their debut at the 1970 Isle Of Wight Festival, performing Emerson's version of Mousourgsky's 'Pictures At An Exhibition'. Their musical skills – they monopolized magazine polls for most of the 1970s – were matched only by their flamboyance on stage as they fused rock and classical influences with all the subtlety of a blow torch. Their eponymous debut album released in 1970 made the UK Top 5 and US Top 20, and its 1971 follow-up, 'Tarkus', topped the UK charts and went Top 10 in the US, while their live 'Pictures At An Exhibition' album made the UK Top 3 and US Top 10. In 1972, their fourth album in less than two years, 'Trilogy' cracked the US Top 5 and included a US hit single, 'From The Beginning'.

Their stage shows became wildly self-indulgent and the music followed suit. 1974's 'Brain Salad Surgery' matched 'Trilogy's' UK Top 3 peak and went gold in the US, and the live triple album, 'Welcome Back My Friends To The Show That Never Ends', captured the musical excesses of their monumental 1973/74 US tour and made both the US and UK Top 5, but they then dispersed to indulge in ego-massaging solo projects, Emerson scoring a UK solo hit with 'Honky Tonk Train Blues' in 1976 and Lake with an unlikely Yuletide hit, 'I Believe In Father Christmas', in 1975, which re-charted in 1982 and 1983.

ELP re-emerged with the double album, 'Work Volume 1', in 1977, three sides of which featured solo outings by the individuals and only one side the trio, but it made the UK Top 10 and US Top 20, and spawned a UK Top 3 hit single in Aaron Copland's 'Fanfare For The Common Man'. Also in 1977, 'Works Volume 2', a compilation of singles and unreleased material, briefly made the UK Top 20 and US Top 40 and a vast tour with a full symphony orchestra proved hideously uneconomic. After 1978's disappointing 'Love Beach', their lowest-charting album, the brief temperamental truce ended and they broke up. Palmer formed PM, whose sole album was largely ignored, as was ELP's posthumously released 'In Concert' album. Emerson retreated to film scores, Lake made an eponymous solo album and after PM folded, Palmer joined Asia with ex-Yes guitarist Steve Howe, keyboard player Geoff Downes and bassist/singer John Wetton. For a mega-gig in Japan, televised worldwide, Wetton was replaced by . . . Greg Lake!

Emerson and Lake finally settled their differences in 1986 but Palmer was not interested in a reunion of ELP, so the obvious choice (he had the right initial!) was seasoned UK drum star Cozy Powell. 'Emerson Lake & Powell' found Emerson again indulging his classical penchants with a version of Holst's 'Mars' from 'The Planets Suite'. The album reached the US Top 30 and UK Top 10, but the group split after a few live dates and Powell moved on. Emerson and Lake tried again with a now convinced Palmer in 1988, but this formation was still-born, so Emerson and Palmer recruited Richard Berry and under the name of 3, released a 1988 album, 'To The Power Of Three', which attracted little interest.

Greatest Hits

Singles	Title	US	UK
1975	I Believe In Father Christmas (Greg Lake)	–	2
1977	Fanfare For The Common Man	–	2
Albums			
1971	Tarkus	9	1
1972	Trilogy	5	2
1974	Brain Salad Surgery	11	2
1975	Welcome Back My Friends . . .	4	5

ERASURE

Vince Clarke (keyboards)
Andy Bell (vocals)

Formed in 1985 by synthesizer player Vince Clarke and singer Andy Bell, Erasure quickly found a large following with its brand of dance rhythms crossed with Bell's camp, glitzy stage persona.

Clarke (born 1961) had played guitar in folk-gospel bands before becoming a founder-member of Depeche Mode. He left the group in 1981 to form the highly successful Yazoo with singer Alison Moyet. When Moyet opted for a solo career two years later, Clarke recorded as The Assembly with Feargal Sharkey, former vocalist with Irish punk band The Undertones. The duo had a Top 10 hit with 'Never Never' (1983) before Sharkey too struck out on his own.

Clarke and his producer Eric Radcliffe next planned to make an album using ten different lead singers but instead decided to advertise for a new, permanent, partner. They chose Bell, (born 1956) a former choir-boy and lead singer with Peterborough band The Void. Provoking unflattering comparisons between Bell and Moyet, the duo's first singles and album 'Wonderland' made little impact in Britain and it was only after 'Sometimes' (1986) had become a hit throughout Europe that it reached the UK Top 10.

By 1987 Erasure had found its own style. 'The Circus' reached the UK Top 10 and its accompanying tour consolidated the group's popularity in Europe. Bell and Clarke toured America with Duran Duran, and 'Victim Of Love' topped the US dance chart. 'Two Ring Circus', an album of re-mixes and re-recordings, confirmed their hold on the club scene, but it was the release of 'The Innocents' (1988) which brought Erasure's breakthrough to the mainstream US audience. Both 'Chains' and 'A Little Respect' were US hits, selling even better in Europe.

The EP, 'Crackers International', was the duo's eighth successive Top 20 hit in the UK and the follow-up, 'Drama', was equally successful. Bell and Clarke's popularity continued as 'Wild!' (1989) topped the UK chart.

Greatest Hits

Singles	Title	US	UK
1986	Sometimes	–	2
1988	A Little Respect	14	4
1989	Crackers International (EP)	–	2
Albums			
1988	The Innocents	49	1
1989	Wild!	57	1

Gloria ESTEFAN & the MIAMI SOUND MACHINE

The band started in 1973 as The Miami Latin Boys, a trio led by keyboard player Emilio Estefan (Gloria's future husband and manager). Cuban-born (in 1957), Gloria first sang with them a year later. In 1975 they became Miami Sound Machine and recorded their first single, 'Renecer', on a local label.

The group's 1979 debut album was picked up for the Latin market by CBS International.

Erasure – cracked it internationally with 'The Innocents'

After much Latin success, their first English language recording, 'Dr Beat', was a UK Top 10 in 1984 and a year later 'Conga' was their first US hit, with 'Bad Boy' soon becoming their first transatlantic Top 20 record. Their 1986 debut English language album, 'Primitive Love', sold a million copies in the US, reaching the US Top 40, and they became the year's Top Singles Act in the US.

After becoming Gloria Estefan & The Miami Sound Machine in 1987, their 'Let It Loose' album made the US Top 10, selling over two million copies. After a two-year absence, and with the group name not featured, Gloria returned to the UK charts in 1988 with her US chart-topping single, 'Anything For You'. A resurgence of interest started in the UK, with earlier US hits charting, and 'Let It Loose', now re-titled 'Anything For You', topping the UK album chart and selling over a million in the UK alone.

Gloria's 1989 solo album, 'Cuts Both Ways', entered the UK chart at No. 1, going multi-platinum, and a self-composed track from it, 'Don't Wanna Lose You', topped the US singles chart.

The much-toured act were honoured by having a Miami street named 'Miami Sound Machine Boulevard'. Gloria was named BMI Songwriter of the Year in 1989 and was presented with a Golden Globe in 1990 to commemorate the sale of over five million records outside the US.

A bad road accident in 1990 tragically put back the recording and release of a new album.

Greatest Hits

Singles	Title	US	UK
1988	Anything For You	1	10
1989	Don't Wanna Lose You	1	6
Albums			
1987	Let It Loose (UK title: Anything For You)	6	1
1989	Cuts Both Ways	8	1

Melissa **ETHERIDGE**

A passionate singer/songwriter who has achieved success by hard road work, Melissa Etheridge (born 1961) is a singer/songwriter of the old school, whose songs on the tribulations of romance seem to strike a chord in many. Originally from the state of Kansas, Etheridge was inspired to write songs as a pre-teen, and after picking up the rudiments of both guitar and piano, she played in cover bands before attending Berklee School Of Music for a year, after which she worked the Boston club circuit, playing many styles of music, including pop, rock, country and her own – mainly R&B – songs. Next came a move to Los Angeles for five years of

the same, before Island Records founder Chris Blackwell spotted her in a small club, and signed her in 1986. Her first recorded songs were written for the movie, *Weeds*, and by the end of that first year, she had recruited a band to back her, but early recordings proved that her songs were swamped by a large ensemble, and she started again simply backed by jazz/rock bass player Kevin McCormick and drummer Craig Krampf, singing and accompanying herself on acoustic guitar. Her 1988 eponymous debut album, recorded live in the studio, was produced by the musicians with engineer Niko Bolas, and went gold in the US, platinum in many other countries, and earned a Grammy nomination.

1989's follow up album, 'Brave And Crazy', was largely the mixture as before – again produced by McCornick, Etheridge and Bolas, it featured a new drummer, Mauricio Fritz Lewak, and also included lead guitarist Bernie Larsen, with guest spots from such notables as Waddy Wachtel and Scott Thurston (who had appeared on the earlier album) and U2's Bono.

With both her first two albums making the US Top 30, Melissa Etheridge is clearly on course to become one of the old-style superstars of the 1990s, although her lack of single success to date may hamper her in achieving the across the board popularity her talent so obviously deserves.

Greatest Hits

Singles	Title	US	UK
1989	The Angels	97	–
Albums			
1988	Melissa Etheridge	22	–
1989	Brave & Crazy	22	–

EURYTHMICS

Annie Lennox (vocals, flute)
Dave Stewart (guitar, keyboard)

In Annie Lennox, Eurythmics possessed the most admired and the most striking British rock singer of the 1980s. Their live shows were memorable for Lennox's dramatic and spellbinding performances and the manic energy of writer/producer Dave Stewart, who supplied a series of notable hit songs.

Stewart (born 1952, Sunderland) had previously been a member of Longdancer, a folk-rock band signed to Elton John's Rocket label. With Peet Coombes and Lennox (born 1954), he formed The Catch in 1977, changing its name to The Tourists in 1979. The band had UK hits with a revival of Dusty Springfield's 1965 hit, 'I Only Want To Be With You', and 'So Good To Be Back Home Again' (1980) before splitting up.

Lennox and Stewart renamed themselves Eurythmics (taking the name from a type of dance and mime education) and in 1982 recorded 'In The Garden' with German producer Conny Plank. This was the prelude to a series of massive international hits beginning with the haunting 'Sweet Dreams (Are Made Of This)' – a US No. 1 – 'Love Is A Stranger' and 'Who's That Girl?'. From the beginning, Eurythmics singles were accompanied by imaginative videos scripted by the duo themselves and the film of 'Who's That Girl?' featured Bananarama, whose Siobhan Fahey would later marry Stewart.

As the group set off on a major world tour in 1984, a new album, 'Touch', containing the insistent 'Here Comes The Rain Again', was released. Eurythmics also recorded music for

Annie Lennox and Dave Stewart, a potent partnership as Eurythmics

the film version of George Orwell's *1984*, including 'Sexcrime' which reached the UK Top 10 but flopped in the US. From 1985 the partners pursued solo activities in parallel with regular Eurythmics recording and touring. With Stevie Wonder on harmonica, 'There Must Be An Angel' from 'Be Yourself Tonight' was the group's first UK No. 1, while Lennox combined with Aretha Franklin to create the powerful anthem, 'Sisters Are Doing It For Themselves' (1985), and appeared in Hugh Hudson's film, *Revolution*.

1986's 'Revenge' album was the group's biggest seller to date, containing such songs as 'When Tomorrow Comes'. Stewart had also gained a reputation as one of rock's foremost producers, working with Bob Dylan, Mick Jagger, Bob Geldof and Daryl Hall, He also launched his own label, Anxious.

While Lennox and Stewart were named UK Songwriters of the Year in 1987, 'Savage', with its minor hit, 'I Need A Man', sold less well than its predecessors. In 1988 Stewart returned to the studio while Lennox revived Jackie De Shannon's 'Put A Little Love In Your Heart' with Al Green. However, 'We Too Are One' (1989), on which Stewart shared the production credits with veteran American Jimmy Iovine, saw a return to form and the album topped the UK charts. It included the hit singles 'Revival' and 'The King And Queen Of America'.

Greatest Hits

Singles	Title	US	UK
1983	Sweet Dreams		
	(Are Made Of This)	1	2
1985	There Must Be An Angel		
	(Playing With My Heart)	22	1
Albums			
1983	Sweet Dreams		
	(Are Made of This)	15	3
1984	Touch	7	1
1985	Be Yourself Tonight	9	3
1986	Revenge	12	3
1989	We Too Are One	34	1

Betty EVERETT

Apart from a slack period in the mid-1960s, Everett has consistently appeared in the US soul charts since 1963, crossing occasionally into the pop chart. Overseas, the story has been much the same: turntable hits which sometimes crack the Top 40.

From Mississippi, Everett (born 1939) migrated to Chicago, starting her recording career with a succession of independent labels before enjoying an immediate smash with Clint Ballard Jnr.'s 'You're No Good'. A 1964 cover by The Swinging Blue Jeans diminished UK and European sales considerably, although pirate radio and the more discerning discotheques favoured the Everett original.

Though a minor UK hit, 1964's 'It's In His Kiss (The Shoop-Shoop Song)' was her furthest inroad as a soloist into the US pop chart. However, its successor, 'Getting Mighty Crowded' – her UK Top 30 debut – was only a minor US pop hit, although her romantic duet with Jerry Butler of 'Let It Be Me' was a US Top 5 hit and a follow-up duet of 'Our Day Will Come' reached the US Top 50.

After changing labels, Everett's mainstream status improved marginally in 1968 with 'There'll Come A Time' and lesser hits for UNI such as 'Sugar', a disco favourite. Since the early 1970s, she has recorded under the supervision of Johnny 'Guitar' Watson, but, despite vinyl tributes like Linda Ronstadt's 1975 revival of 'You're No Good' and a 1980s retread of 'Getting Mighty Crowded' by Elvis Costello, Betty Everett's prolific output remains mostly the property of specialists.

Greatest Hits

Singles	Title	US	UK
1964	It's In His Kiss		
	(The Shoop-Shoop Song)	6	34
1964	Let It Be Me (with Jerry Butler)	5	–
1965	Getting Mighty Crowded	65	29

EVERLY BROTHERS

Purveyors of the purest harmonies in the history of rock'n'roll, Isaac Donald Everly (born 1937) and younger brother Phillip Everly (born 1939), the sons of midwestern C&W radio performers, Ike and Margaret Everly, were virtually born to rock. After touring and broadcasting regularly with their parents from the mid-1940s, they were veteran performers by their early teens, and could not have envisaged any other life. Supreme stylists and genuine innovators, the Everly Brothers were the point where country music met rock'n'roll, and with their soaring, crystal-clear harmonies and crisp acoustic guitars, they redefined the public perception of rock'n'roll in the 1950s with their interpretations of Felice & Boudleaux Bryant's poignant yet rocking songs and their tuneful, sensitive covers of much harder rock material, bringing a hitherto unconceived finesse to rock'n'roll.

Nevertheless, they were far from overnight successes, and struggled to find a foothold during their formative years. Encouraged initially by Chet Atkins, Don successfully pitched several songs at Nashville ('Thou Shalt Not Steal' by Kitty Wells made the Top 20 of the US country chart in 1954), where they eventually relocated in 1955. Their first single, Don's 'The Sun Keeps Shining'/'Keep A-Loving Me', did nothing, and they were quickly dropped. A year's hardship and obscurity followed, and they were about to move to Chicago when Wesley Rose (of

noted music publishers Acuff-Rose) took over as their manager: he persuaded Cadence Records boss Archie Bleyer (who had turned The Everly Brothers down six months earlier) to take another listen, and this time Rose signed them to a three-year deal.

Their association with Acuff-Rose allowed them free access to the superb material written by the Bryant husband and wife team, although ironically, 'Bye Bye Love' had been rejected by numerous acts before the Everlys first cut it for Cadence. Transformed with a brisk new acoustic intro from Don, plus their unique harmonies, it stormed to the top of the country chart in 1957 and crossed over to both the US pop chart, where it reached the Top 3 and remarkably, made the Top 5 of the US R&B chart, selling over a million copies. Within weeks, it had also reached the UK Top 10.

Overnight, they became huge stars. As well as their obvious talents, their dark, brooding yet clean-cut good looks ensured massive media attention and teen appeal, and they immediately found themselves in great demand: regulars on the Grand Ole Opry, one-nighter package tours, network TV spots for Ed Sullivan, Perry Como (which exposed them to UK audiences), Alan Freed, etc. During the next three years, they barely had time to draw breath as hit followed hit – 14 US Top 40 hits (including seven gold discs) during this period alone, records of extraordinary quality including 'Wake Up Little Susie', 'All I Have To Do Is Dream'/'Claudette', 'Bird Dog'/'Devoted To You', 'Problems', '('Til) I Kissed You', 'Let It Be Me'. Backed by the cream of Nashville's sessionmen – most notably Chet Atkins & Hank Garland (guitar), Floyd Cramer (piano), Floyd 'Lightnin'' Chance (bass) and Buddy Harman (drums) – all were classic, timeless vignettes, epitomizing their era.

In 1960, they left Cadence to become the first signing to the new Warner Bros. label, signing a 10-year contract reputedly worth over $1,000,000, an unheard-of sum at that time. Their first release, 'Cathy's Clown' (UK catalogue number WB 1) became their biggest-ever single, topping both the US and UK charts (for five and eight weeks respectively), and also topping the US R&B charts. The change of label paid dividends initially as they continued to rack up big hits – 'So Sad'/'Lucille', 'Walk Right Back'/'Ebony Eyes', 'Temptation' – interspersed with a couple of previously-unissued Cadence tracks, 'When Will I Be Loved' and 'Like Strangers'. Additionally, they began making a serious impact on the albums market, with UK/US Top 10 items like 'It's Everly Time' and 'A Date With The Everly Brothers'. However, management disagreements over the decision to release their version of Bing Crosby's 'Temptation' as a single (although it topped the UK chart, it only made the US Top 30) led to a split with Rose, which in turn cost them access to the Bryant song catalogue.

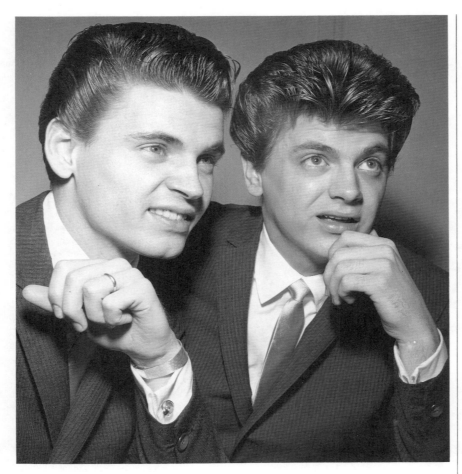

Don and Phil Everly, an essential evocation of the late 'Fifties and early 'Sixties

By 1962, they seemed to be losing direction: conscripted into the US Marine Corps Reserves, they were unable to play concerts, and after scoring with 'Crying In The Rain' (US/UK Top 10) and 'That's Old Fashioned', (US Top 10), the hits began to dry up. A disastrous UK tour in late 1962, when Don collapsed and had to return to the US, leaving Phil to complete the tour alone, did little to boost their stock, and despite 1963's more successful UK trip (headlining a bill opened by the then almost unknown Rolling Stones), their records were peaking ever lower in the chart.

By 1965, they had reunited with Wesley Rose, but although they remained a major live draw, the Beat Boom had eroded their fan base in the US, and while they scored occasional UK hits like 'The Price Of Love' (Top 3) and 'Love Is Strange' on the back of a successful tour, neither charted in the US. Nevertheless they recorded several excellent albums during the mid-1960's, including 'Rock & Soul', 'Beat & Soul' and 'Two Yanks In England', the last cut in London using UK sessionmen, including Jimmy Page, John Paul Jones and members of The Hollies, who wrote several of the tracks.

The late 1960s saw a gradual return to their musical roots, including the critically acclaimed 'Roots' album in 1969. Moving to a fresh label in the early 1970s, they cut two countryish albums, the second of which, 'Pass The Chicken And Listen', saw them back in Nashville with Chet Atkins. But despite huge critical acclaim, neither album sold, and in July 1973, ten years of frustration and disillusionment finally surfaced in a spectacular manner during a gig, when Phil smashed his guitar onto the stage, and stalked off.

They saw out the 1970s pursuing patchy solo careers which generated scant commercial success, although they included several interesting releases: in 1973, Phil cut a superb version of Albert Hammond's 'The Air That I Breathe', which The Hollies promptly copied and converted to a massive worldwide hit, while Don enjoyed several minor US country hits. However, two UK TV-advertised albums repackaging the best of their back catalogue were successful during this period, 'Walk Right Back With The Everly Brothers', which made the Top 10, and 'Living Legends'. During the early 1980s, Phil scored two US country hits before making a remarkable UK chart comeback with a Top 50 single, 'Louise' and an eponymous album, followed immediately by the Top 10 hit, 'She Means Nothing To Me', an unlikely liaison with Cliff Richard and Mark Knopfler, which was in turn followed by a big US

country hit, 'Who's Gonna Keep Me Warm'.

A few months later, in September 1983, Don & Phil mounted their emotionally charged and hugely successful comeback at London's Royal Albert Hall: the live double album, 'Reunion Concert', restored them to the lower regions of both the US and UK album charts, and led to a new recording contract. 'EB '84' (UK title: 'The Everly Brothers'), their first 'new' album for 11 years, made both the US and UK Top 40, and their version of Paul McCartney's 'On The Wings Of A Nightingale' was also a transatlantic hit single. Subsequent albums have tended to promise more than they deliver, but there is a magic in the sibling harmonies of The Everly Brothers which cannot be over-rated.

Greatest Hits

Singles	Title	US	UK
1957	Bye Bye Love	2	6
1957	Wake Up Little Susie	1	2
1958	All I Have To Do Is Dream	1	1
1958	Bird Dog	1	2
1959	Problems	2	6
1959	('Til) I Kissed You	4	2
1960	Cathy's Clown	1	1
1961	Walk Right Back/Ebony Eyes	7	1
1961	Temptation	27	1
1962	Crying In The Rain	6	6
1965	The Price Of Love	–	2
Albums			
1960	It's Everly Time	9	2
1960	The Fabulous Style Of The Everly Brothers	23	4
1960	A Date With The Everly Brothers	9	3
1975	Walk Right Back With The Everly Brothers	–	10
1984	EB '84 (UK title: The Everly Brothers)	38	36

FABIAN

After the demise of classic rock'n'roll, Fabian was among the more bearable products of the late 1950s, when the US charts were full of insipid boys-next-door – all doe eyes, hair spray and bashful smiles – groomed for transient stardom who sang any piffle put before them. The storm centre of this turnover of puppets was Philadelphia, where two local talent scouts, Peter De Angelis and Bob Marucci, discovered Fabian Forte Bonaparte (born 1943) in Frankie Avalon's Teen And Twenty youth club in 1957. Impressed by his Latinate good looks, the two swept aside obstacles like his vocal short-

Fabian – fails to foil Feds

comings, truncated his name and signed him to Chancellor Records where he was promoted as a tamed Elvis.

Backed by The Four Dates, Fabian's first two singles were only regional hits, but appearances on Dick Clark's nationally transmitted *American Bandstand* TV show and a heavily publicized coast-to-coast tour had the required effect on teenage girls, and Fabian found himself suddenly in the US Top 40 with 'I'm A Man', an opus by top New York songwriters Pomus and Shuman who also came up with even more lucrative smashes in the blues-tinged 'Turn Me Loose' and 'Hound Dog Man', title theme to Fabian's movie debut.

More substantial film roles came after his record career peaked with 1959's rocking million-selling 'Tiger' and its associated album, 'Hold That Tiger'. As well as the expected teenpics with their lip-synched musical interludes and vacuous plots, he managed not to make a fool of himself with Bing Crosby and Tuesday Weld in 1960's *High Time*, and as John Wayne's sidekick in *North To Alaska*.

Fabian's fall was as fast as his rise after Congress singled him out as an example of one of the exploited ciphers in the payola scandal. Interviewed at the time, Fabian goofed by revealing the technological strategies needed to boost his gruff voice in the recording studio. His first serious flop was 1960's 'About This Thing Called Love' and the continued downward spiral was only punctuated by minor hits.

Well into the 1960s, the sharp-eyed could still spot Fabian in cinematic bit-parts, notably in the 1962 war epic *The Longest Day*, though he was in greater evidence in 1965's *Ride The Wild Surf*, *Fireball 500* (a 1968 hot-rod potboiler with old friend Avalon) and similar celluloid ventures more commensurate with his talent.

Greatest Hits

Singles	Title	US	UK
1959	*Turn Me Loose*	9	–
1959	*Tiger*	3	–
1959	*Hound Dog Man*	9	46
Albums			
1959	*Hold That Tiger!*	5	–
1959	*Fabulous Fabian*	3	–

The FABULOUS THUNDERBIRDS

Kim Wilson (*vocals, harmonica*)
Keith Ferguson (*bass*)
Jimmie Vaughan (*guitar*)
Mike Buck (*drums*)

Formed in 1975, they played bars and honed their craft, performing downhome Texas R&B with a smattering of Chicago blues and Memphis soul thrown in. The group, Wilson (born 1951), Vaughan (born 1951, older brother of Stevie Ray), Ferguson (born 1946) and Fran Christina (born 1951, who replaced original drummer Mike Buck), paid their dues singularly and collectively: Wilson was ex-Lowell Fulsom band, Vaughan a pupil of Freddie King, while the T-Birds were employed as backing band to Muddy Waters for a time.

Signed to Chrysalis in 1979 via Denny Bruce's Takoma label, releasing their eponymous debut LP that year, they were immediate hits in the UK, where they supported a similarly eclectic four-piece, Rockpile, on tour. Bassist Nick Lowe contributed material to 1981's 'Butt Rockin'', and produced 'T-Bird Rhythm', but Dave Edmunds was to prove the more fruitful collaborator in the long run. Their straightforward, no-nonsense live stance extended to the studio; 1980's LP 'What's The Word' was recorded in just five days. They mixed their own material with a varied set of covers, from 'Slim Harpo' to the standard 'Cherry Pink And Apple Blossom White'.

Producer Edmunds added a long-awaited commercial sheen for 1986's 'Tuff Enuff', their first US Top 10 single and taster for the 800,000-selling LP of the same name which was a big US hit with the corporate muscle of their new label, CBS behind it. Its less successful successor, 'Hot Number' emerged in 1987, when 'Portfolio' also reprised the Chrysalis era with no little style.

Jimmie Vaughan left in 1990 after 15 years' service, putting the group's future in doubt: sadly, plans to team up live with brother Stevie Ray that led to an album, 'Family Business', were cut short with the latter's death in August 1990. He and his former colleagues had worked hard for what commercial success they had enjoyed.

Greatest Hits

Albums	Title	US	UK
1986	*Tuff Enuff*	13	–

Archetypal toughnut Texas rockers, as fast and flash as their namesake auto

The Faces, 'Seventies supergroup with grassroots cred as goodtime concert band

The **FACES**

Rod Stewart (vocals)
Ron Wood (guitar)
Ian McLagan (keyboards)
Ronnie Lane (bass, vocals)
Kenny Jones (drums)

After a sluggish start, The Faces surfaced as one of the most popular concert attractions of the early 1970s. With Stewart as Jack-the-Lad front man, their infectious, boozy flair on the boards did not translate too well to vinyl – although, on the strength of their image and reputation, their later studio albums were best sellers.

When Steve Marriott left The Small Faces (see separate entry) in January 1969, the remaining personnel – Jones (born 1948), McLagan (born 1946) and Lane (see separate entry) – were at a loss for several weeks before recruiting Wood (born 1946) and then Stewart (see separate entry), both unhappy in the Jeff Beck Group. After some chaotic engagements as Quiet Melon, the new quintet's investors persuaded them to revert to an abbreviation of their previous – and more negotiable – name, even to tour the US as the 'Small Faces' to wring what they could from the old group's belated US chart breakthrough.

Hard graft on the club and college circuit bore fruit in 1971 with their third album, 'A Nod's As Good As A Wink . . . To A Blind Horse', and 'Stay With Me', its attendant single, high in their respective UK charts. These products also made a big impression in the US although the group as a chart act went off the boil within a year.

After the next album, 'Ooh-la-la', The Faces were to issue little more fresh material, bar a one-off UK Top 20 single, 'You Can Make Me Dance, Sing Or Anything' in 1974 – the same year as a high-spirited but musically inadequate 'live' album. Among reasons for this seeming indolence was the greater success of Stewart's more disciplined solo records, even though these were carefully scheduled not to clash with Faces releases.

At first, the singer's separate chart strikes were regarded as an enhancement of the group's corporate career. Repertoires overlapped in concert, and Stewart made a point of regularly employing The Faces as accompanists on his solo tracks. They were visible backing him on television when his 'Maggie May' spent several weeks topping both the US and UK charts.

By 1974 The Faces weren't much of a band any more. As he had with the Marriott outfit, Lane took a share of lead vocals, and he was most disgruntled when billing began to read 'Rod Stewart *and* The Faces'. The last straw was Stewart's untimely public criticism of 'Ooh-la-la' – which he later denied, despite taped evidence.

With Lane's resignation, The Faces rallied by enticing the dexterous Tetsu Yamauchi from Free (see separate entry) but another crack appeared when Wood recorded 'I've Got My Own Album To Do', a venture that was remarkable for its sleeve credits which included Keith Richards of The Rolling Stones (see separate entry). Through Richards, Wood became a temporary Stone in 1975 while holding down his post as a Face when the band embarked on what was to be its final US tour.

Though this trek embraced the expected ramshackle joviality onstage, rehearsals in Miami had been marred by serious disagreements such as Stewart's outvoted wish to augment the group with an extra guitarist and a string section to enhance selections from his latest solo offering. Furthermore, as well as increased contractual complications of his recording with The Faces, it was necessary for Stewart to quit Britain for a year to lessen his obligations to the tax office.

Now a full-time Rolling Stone, Wood still records the occasional solo album but, more recently, his extra-mural activities as a painter have taken precedence. His first exhibition opened in 1988.

After The Faces disbanded, a reformation of the Small version with Marriott and, briefly, Lane was a natural regression for McLagan and Jones after a re-issued 'Itchycoo Park' made the UK Top 10 in 1975. Two 'comeback' albums were recorded but all fans of the reconstituted Small Faces wanted to hear were the sounds of yesteryear.

Rather than continuing to milk nostalgia, McLagan became an auxiliary Rolling Stone for a 1982 world tour, while Jones – after a flop solo single – served The Who for a while as replacement for the late Keith Moon. Exemplified by McLagan's later – and highly-waged – stint backing Bob Dylan (see separate entry), continued demand for McLagan and Jones as jobbing musicians, affirms the respect held in the highest circles of pop for former Faces, Small or otherwise.

Greatest Hits

Singles	Title	US	UK
1971	Stay With Me	17	6
1973	Cindy Incidentally	–	2
Albums			
1971	A Nod's As Good As A Wink . . .		
	To A Blind Horse	6	2
1973	Ooh-La-La	21	1

FAIRPORT CONVENTION

Judy Dyble (autoharp, vocals)
Ian Matthews (vocals, guitar)
Simon Nicol (guitar, vocals)
Richard Thompson (guitar, vocals)
Ashley Hutchings (bass)
Martin Lamble (drums)

Prime instigators of the UK folk/rock movement, the perennially innovative Fairports were the first group to successfully integrate traditional English folk material into mainstream rock, thus taking folk to an entirely new audience. With the group's constantly fluctuating personnel (well over 20 different members and numerous line-ups), their influence on British electric folk-rock has been phenomenal, as virtually every ma-

Despite innumerable personnel changes, The Fairports have always represented the essence of British folk-rock

jor band who has worked in this field is a Fairport spin-off somewhere along the line.

Taking their name from Simon Nicol's parents' house, they formed in North London in 1967, originally as a quartet: Nicol (born 1950) and Hutchings (born 1945), who had both been members of a small-time acoustic blues outfit, The Ethnic Shuffle Orchestra, plus the precociously-talented Thompson (born 1949) and drummer Shawn Frater, who barely made it through rehearsals before being replaced by Martin Lamble (born 1949). After a few local gigs they realized the need for a frontline vocalist, to which end they recruited two: Dyble (born 1949), followed by Matthews (born Ian Macdonald, 1946), who joined from British surf band Pyramid.

At this stage they were developing into a reasonable facsimile of a US West Coast close-harmony rock group, and as such slotted comfortably into London's burgeoning underground scene. American manager-producer Joe Boyd secured residencies for them at clubs like UFO and Middle Earth, and arranged deals for a single, 'If I Were A Ribbon Bow' (1967) and their eponymous debut album (1968). Dyble left after the album's release (briefly joining Giles, Giles & Fripp, who later became King Crimson, before teaming up with ex-Them member Jackie McAuley as Trader Horne) and unwittingly reshaped Fairport's destiny in the process: replacement Sandy Denny (born Alexandra Denny, 1947) had been both a solo folksinger and briefly in The Strawbs, and her influence on the band would be both profound and immeasurable, introducing traditional English folk songs into their repertoire and encouraging her new colleagues to write similarly slanted material. The extent of her influence was readily evident on their second album (and first for a new label). 'What We Did On Our Holidays' (1969) confirmed Thompson to be a potent creative force and included two Fairport classics, 'Meet On The Ledge' and 'Fotheringay'. During the recording of their next album, Matthews quit the band, striking gold in 1970 with Matthews Southern Comfort and 'Woodstock', a UK No. 1 single.

Fairport completed the third album as a quintet, but immediately prior to its release suffered the tragic loss of drummer Lamble (killed when their van crashed after a gig). The 'Unhalfbricking' album made the UK Top 20 in 1969, while 'Si Tu Dois Partir' (a French translation of Bob Dylan's 'If You Gotta Go, Go Now'), made the Top 30 of the UK singles chart. Following serious consideration, they decided to continue (adding drummer Dave Mattacks), restoring their ranks to a sextet with the addition of violinist Dave Swarbrick, a highly-regarded veteran of the traditional folk scene who had been a vital contributor to their last album, notably to the remarkable 'A Sailor's Life'.

With Swarbrick aboard, their transformation was completed and although it only lasted three months, this remains their most crucial line-up, staying together just long enough to produce THE seminal British folk/rock album, 'Liege & Lief', by far their most acclaimed work. Released in late 1969, it reached the UK Top 20, although its influence and legacy far outweigh any commercial benchmarks. Five of its eight tracks were traditional tunes adapted to contemporary rock, 'Tam Lin' and 'Matty Groves' making the transition with exhilarating success.

Having achieved an artistic peak to which few bands could ever hope to aspire, a split was inevitable. There was too much talent for one group, too many clashes of direction. Hutchings left to start Steeleye Span (see separate entry) and Denny also left, initially forming Fotheringay with her then boyfriend, Australian-born Trevor Lucas (ex-Eclection), after which she pursued a sporadically successful solo career. The Fairports took on experienced R&B bassist Dave Pegg (born 1947, ex-Birmingham band The Uglies) and cut their fifth album without a recognized lead singer.

Released in 1970, 'Full House', which included the infectious 'Walk Awhile', was their third consecutive UK Top 20 album. This line-up remained stable for over a year and built a cult following in the US, where they cut 'Live At The LA Troubadour', an album which remained unissued for seven years. Thompson left in early 1971 for a highly acclaimed solo career (see separate entry) and this time Fairport carried on as a four-piece with Nicol switching to lead guitar. 'Angel Delight' (1971, their only UK Top 10 album to date) continued where 'Full House' had left off, further demonstrating Swarbrick's influence, as did 'Babbacombe Lee', a concept album, released only months later, based on the true story of a condemned murderer in Victorian times who cheated the hangman.

Last remaining founder-member Nicol left at the end of 1971 (to form the Albion Country Band with Hutchings) after which Fairport's personnel fluctuated wildly – Mattacks also joined The Albion Country Band,

Roger Hill (guitar) and Tom Farnall (drums) briefly replaced Nicol and Mattacks, and Hill was himself replaced by David Rea (guitar), and an album recorded with Rea was never issued. Stability was resumed after nine months of uncertainty in late 1972 when Mattacks returned, and both Trevor Lucas (guitar/vocals) & US-born Jerry Donahue (guitar) joined from the now-defunct Fotheringay, adding country music influences to the Fairport repertoire. This line-up stayed intact for 18 months and recorded two fine albums, 'Rosie' and 'Nine' (both 1973). In a highly unlikely move, Sandy Denny (who later married Lucas) rejoined them midway through the World Tour which yielded 'Live Convention' (1974). Mattacks left again and was replaced by ex-Grease Band drummer Bruce Rowland (after Paul Warren had temporarily joined for a European tour), and Rowland appeared on 'Rising For The Moon' (1975), their last UK chart album for more than a decade.

They fell into disarray again in 1976, when Denny (who tragically died two years later), Lucas and Donahue gave way to Roger Burridge (mandolin/violin), Dan Ars Bras (guitar), and Bob Brady (piano, ex-Wizzard), who stayed with Fairport (as they were by now billed) just long enough to appear on 'Gottle O'Geer' and undertake a European tour, after which all three left. Simon Nicol returned towards the end of 1976, by which time they were about to change labels after a dozen mainly excellent albums for Island (UK), which finally released the 1970 'Live At The LA Troubadour' set in early 1977, just prior to their first album for another label, 'A Bonny Bunch Of Roses' (1977). Both this album and 1978's 'Tippler's Tales' were critically well-received but sold poorly, so the group announced its forthcoming retirement, splitting in 1979 after a farewell tour — following which they issued 'Farewell Farewell', a limited-edition collectors' album. Within a couple of years the last line-up (Swarbrick, Nicol, Pegg, Rowland) had re-formed and gone back on the road. Personnel changes during the 1980s have seen Mattacks return in place of Rowland (who now lives in Scandinavia), and Swarbrick (who left to launch Whippersnapper) replaced by Ric Sanders (violin, ex-Soft Machine, etc.) and Martin Allcock (guitar). Allcock and Pegg are also concurrently members of Jethro Tull.

A major reunion festival takes place each summer at Cropredy in Oxfordshire, at which many former Fairports perform with the current band — virtually every ex-member has contributed.

Several low-key albums turned up on Pegg's Woodworm label during the 1980s, including 'Gladys' Leap' (1985), the excellent instrumental album 'Expletive Delighted' (1986, with Richard Thompson and Jerry Donahue guesting), while in 1987 Joe Boyd's Hannibal label released 'Heyday', a superb collection of BBC radio sessions from the late

1960s with a line-up of Denny, Matthews, Thompson, etc. Various group members, including Pegg, Nicol, Sanders and Allcock have also released solo albums. At the end of the 1980s, the group signed to the New Routes label, for whom they have recorded two further albums: 'Red & Gold' (1989, their first UK chart album since 1975) and 'The Five Seasons' (1991).

Later Fairport line-ups have tended to feature instrumental virtuosity as opposed to the notable past vocalists, but this quintessentially British band has earned a significant position in the pantheon of popular music which shows no sign of diminishing as their 25th anniversary approaches. The majority of albums mentioned above repay investigation.

Greatest Hits

Singles	Title	US	UK
1969	*Si Tu Dois Partir*	–	21
Albums			
1969	*Unhalfbricking*	–	12
1970	*Liege and Lief*	–	17
1970	*Full House*	–	13
1971	*Angel Delight*	200	8

Marianne **FAITHFULL**

Much changed from the convent girl who logged a smattering of lightweight hit singles in the 1960s, Faithfull (born 1947) enjoyed a remarkable comeback in the late 1970s with a voice grippingly shorn of former soprano purity.

From Austrian aristocratic stock, the Reading schoolgirl was attending a party where Rolling Stones manager Andrew

Drugs bust mars Marianne's image

Oldham suggested that her cultured beauty might lead to a future as a pop star. An amateur folk singer, she had no qualms about the scheme and, proving Oldham's judgement correct, took 'As Tears Go By' – written for her by Stones Mick Jagger and Keith Richards – into the UK and US charts in 1964. Apart from odd miscalculations like versions of Dylan's 'Blowing in the Wind' and 'Yesterday' by The Beatles, Marianne's winning streak ran through 1965 with songs of like persuasion, including Jackie De Shannon's 'Come And Stay With Me' and 'This Little Bird', a John D. Loudermilk opus that beat a rival treatment by The Nashville Teens.

Two Faithfull albums were released in 1965, the poppier 'Marianne Faithfull' and 'Come My Way', which drew from her folk repertoire. In 1966 Marianne was less easily hoisting her records into the charts, but was making headway as an actress – attempting Shakespeare and Chekhov on the stage and with leading roles in feature films such as 1968's *Girl on a Motorcycle* and *I'll Never Forget Whatshisname*.

With Jagger – who had replaced husband John Dunbar in her affections – she was scheduled to star in 1969's *Ned Kelly* movie, but a suicide attempt precluded her participation. The highly strung Faithfull's innocent schoolgirl image had already been tarnished indelibly by her frank and public opinions on free love, and her involvement in the Stones' drug busts. She also claimed to have had a hand in composing the group's 'Sister Morphine', which was also the B-side of her final 1960s single, Goffin and King's 'Something Better'.

In a customized – and revealing – nun's habit, she duetted with David Bowie (see separate entry) during the latter's 1973 US television spectacular, but her emergence from a wretched heroin odyssey accelerated three years later when, reunited with producer Oldham, she recorded the Waylon Jennings song, 'Dreaming My Dreams', a water-testing single that was a hit in Eire if nowhere else. Then came a new album, 'Faithless', in a country vein and containing a few originals. Her singing was rougher and deeper, but no less enchanting for that.

1979's 'Broken English' confirmed her return – even eliciting her first UK hit single in twelve years with a spin-off single, 'The Ballad Of Lucy Jordan'. Faithfull's rise from the pit continued with 1981's 'Dangerous Acquaintances', but a subsequent six-year vinyl silence was broken only by contributions to an album of Kurt Weill covers and the movie soundtrack to *Trouble In Mind*.

As well as tackling compositions by Dr John and Tom Waits (see separate entries) and a re-make of 'As Tears Go By', 'Strange Weather' found Faithfull in the realms of Billie Holiday and Dinah Washington. However, every avenue of her musical career was visited on 'Blazing Away', a 1990 concert album from a New York cathedral in which the audience lapped up her husky passion as the prerogative of a tattered glamour.

Greatest Hits

Singles	Title	US	UK
1964	As Tears Go By	22	9
1965	Come And Stay With Me	26	4
1965	This Little Bird	32	6
1965	Summer Nights	24	10
Albums			
1965	Marianne Faithfull	12	15

Georgie FAME

Lancashire schoolboy Clive Powell (born 1943), a self-taught pianist and vocalist, so favoured the music of Fats Domino (see separate entry) that he named his first group The Dominoes. In 1958 he moved south to London and was re-christened Georgie Fame by Larry Parnes, a famous impresario of the time, who saw him initially as a rock'n'roller and potential all-round entertainer in the Tommy Steele mould. But on the fabled pop Svengali's package tours, Fame more often led backing bands for stars like Billy Fury, whom he served for two years.

1962 found Fame managed by the proprietors of Soho's Flamingo Club where he worked as front man of The Blue Flames, a band whose ever-changing personnel included guitarist John McLaughlin, drummer Jon Hiseman and others of lesser renown. No more the rocker he never quite was, Fame had ditched piano for organ, and gave the Flamingo's 'Mod' customers a fusion of the pop end of jazz, the latest developments in soul and R&B, and innovative shades of ska and bluebeat.

After two independent singles in 1963, Fame cut an atmospheric live album which anticipated 'jazz-rock' by five years. Three flop singles later, he topped the UK chart with Jon Hendricks' 'Yeh Yeh', which precipitated a sarcastically titled album, 'Fame At Last', and an erratic Top 40 performance spread over several years. It took until 1966 for Fame to equal his 'Yeh Yeh' triumph with the self-penned 'Get Away'. His third album with the Blue Flames, 'Sweet Things', lingered in the chart, but the band was dismissed so that Fame and arranger Harry South could record the daring 'Sound Venture' with noted jazz veterans like Stan Tracey and Tubby Hayes. Light years from the Flamingo now, he was the only white vocalist in a touring Motown revue and in 1967 sang with the Count Basie Orchestra at the Royal Albert Hall.

Fame acquitted himself admirably on these prestigious occasions, although his income still hinged on record sales. Losing his grip on the album chart by 1967, he managed five

consecutive UK Top 40 singles, culminating with a Christmas chart-topper in the gimmicky 'Ballad of Bonnie and Clyde', his only major US hit.

The most lucrative product of the lean period that followed was 1971's 'Rosetta' single, one of his duets with ex-Animal Alan Price. Parallel to this middle-of-the-road alliance, Fame released curate's egg albums like 'Seventh Son' (produced by Price) and 1973's 'Georgie Does His Thing With Strings'. In 1974 he hit the road with a Blue Flames of top session players, but this trek and its attendant album quickly fizzled out. By the mid-1970s, Fame no longer depended on chart honours, thanks partly to his appearance in TV commercials, etc., although he made an unlikely but successful return at the end of the 1980s as leader of Van Morrison's backing band.

Greatest Hits

Singles	Title	US	UK
1964	Yeh Yeh	21	1
1966	Get Away	–	1
1967	The Ballad Of Bonnie And Clyde	7	1
Albums			
1966	Sweet Thing	–	6

Georgie Fame with the Blue Flames, a leading light in British rhythm and blues

FAMILY

Roger Chapman (vocals)
Charlie Whitney (guitar)
Jim King (saxophone)
Rick Grech (bass and violin)
Rob Townshend (drums)

An amalgamation of two Leicester bands, Jim King & The Farinas and The Roaring Sixties, Family formed in 1966. Led by the songwriting partnership of Chapman (born 1944) and Whitney (born 1944), after a one-off single they established their own repertoire before their debut album, 'Music In A Doll's House' (1968, produced by Dave Mason of Traffic), which made good use of the band's diverse instrumental talents. Their songs were characterized by Chapman's manic, braying vocals and his demented on-stage persona and the band were quickly adopted by the London underground scene – their thinly disguised exploits were portrayed in Jenny Fabian's novel, *Groupie*.

Their second album, 'Family Entertainment' (1969), maintained the band's promise reaching the UK Top 10, while the band supported The Rolling Stones at their Hyde Park concert that summer, but Jim King left and was replaced by John 'Poli' Palmer. 1970's 'A Song For Me' did even better, making the UK Top 5, but their brittle brilliance did not survive their first US tour; Rick Grech quit to join Blind Faith and the band fell out with promoter Bill Graham (which damaged their US career prospects). The band recovered with John Weider (bass, violin) replacing Grech, making the UK Top 10 with the half live/half studio album, 'Anyway', and their two biggest hit singles, the 'Strange Band' EP (featuring 'The Weaver's Answer', a 1969 UK Top 20 hit) and 'In My Own Time' (UK Top 5, 1970).

Despite the continued excellence of albums like 'Fearless' (1971) and 'Bandstand' (1972), the band could not even achieve a major breakthrough after another UK Top 20 hit, 'Burlesque', in 1972. The US remained a lost cause and after Palmer and Weider left, the band survived one more album, 'It's Only A Movie', before breaking up in 1974. Chapman and Whitney formed 'Streetwalkers', who released five albums in the next four years, most notably 'Red Card'. At the end of the 1970s, Chapman embarked on a solo career, also guesting on an album by Mike Oldfield.

Greatest Hits

Singles	Title	US	UK
1971	In My Own Time	–	4
Albums			
1970	A Song For Me	–	4

Bryan FERRY / ROXY MUSIC

Bryan Ferry (vocals)
Graham Simpson (bass)
Andy Mackay (saxophone, woodwinds)
Brian Eno (keyboards, vocals)
Phil Manzanera (guitar)
Paul Thompson (drums)

As the thinking man's glam-rockers, Roxy Music had in Bryan Ferry (born 1945) one of the most charismatic and insidiously outrageous British rock figures of the 1970s. Both with the group and as a soloist, Ferry's fusion of often outmoded pop conventions with the avant-garde – later moderated – centred on his literate compositions, idiosyncratic keyboard style and a detached vocal delivery where an intrinsically limited range was warped to his own devices.

From Washington, a northern English mining town, Ferry graduated to the University of Newcastle in 1964. A fine-art student by day, he sang at night with The Banshees and then The Gas Board. After a spell at the Royal College of Art, he taught ceramics in a London girls school while failing an audition for King Crimson and founding Roxy Music

with ex-Gas Board bass guitarist Graham Simpson.

A music press advertisement produced Andy Mackay, player of woodwinds and owner of a synthesizer, who recommended the erudite Brian Eno as sound engineer – though this electronics boffin swiftly found himself operating his gadgets and supplying backing harmonies onstage. After an orchestral timpanist proved impractical, rock drummer Paul Thompson was recruited. Auditions concluded with Phil Manzanera from Quiet Sun ousting former Nice guitarist David O'List.

Via private functions and the support of *Melody Maker* scribe Richard Williams, Roxy Music's leap to pop stardom began at 1972's Lincoln Festival after signing with EG Management, who leased the band's recordings to other labels (initially Island). 1972's debut album 'Roxy Music', the mannered 'Virginia Plain' single and their flashy stage costumes divided critics but appealed to Lou Reed,

Alice Cooper, David Bowie and artists of similar eye-shadowed persuasion. Though no US breakthrough matched the sextet's invasion of the UK charts, they were much favoured by Andy Warhol's New York set.

Simpson's exit necessitated the use of a succession of bass players, but momentum was sustained with 'Pyjamarama' in the UK Top 5, and the 'For Your Pleasure' album, which featured a sharp polarization between its experimental second side and more straightforward ironies like the maddeningly catchy opener, 'Do The Strand' and spooky 'In Every Dream Home A Heartache'. Numbers of this hue and Ferry's performances in formal evening dress elicited whispers that here was The Ultimate in Camp. These became louder after 'These Foolish Things', his solo album of non-originals such as Bob Dylan's earnest 'A Hard Rain's A-Gonna Fall' and, with no lyrical revision, Lesley Gore's 'It's My Party'.

Ferry (in formals) fusing radical rock with raunchy revivalism

When replaced by Curved Air's Edwin Jobson (keyboards and violin) in 1973, Eno extended his own career beyond Roxy Music to intriguing solo albums, his accurately named Obscure record label and collaborations with acts as diverse as the Portsmouth Sinfonia and David Bowie. The subsequent reduction of Roxy Music to merely Ferry's accompanists was not perceptible on 'Stranded' with its co-writing credits for other personnel such as Mackay on 'A Song For Europe' (on which Ferry ventured into Gallic *chanson* territory). Although it contained a smash in the deliberately trite 'All I Want Is You', 1974's 'Country Life' marked time artistically, regurgitating previous melodies and gimmicks.

As well as two hit singles, Ferry's next solo album, 'Another Time Another Place', included a self-penned title track. If 'You Go To My Head' was a comparative miss, his forays into the Top 10 continued with 'Let's Stick Together' and an EP, while less commercially successful were projects by Mackay (with the quirky 'In Search Of Eddie Riff' album), and Manzanera with 1975's 'Diamond Head' as well as a one-off reformation of Quiet Sun, a part in Stomu Yamash'ta's 'Go' extravaganza and a live album with 801 (an amalgam that included Eno). Such tangents were symptomatic of Roxy Music's impending 'devolution' in 1977 after 'Siren', its singles (of which 'Love Is The Drug' became their biggest ever US single) and the 'Viva!' concert album.

This furlough brought two more Manzanera albums ('Listen Now' and 'K Scope') as well as Mackay's lucrative hand in TV's *Rock Follies* series (with its spin-off UK chart-topping album) and, after a trip to China, his poorly received 'Resolving Contradictions' concept album. Ferry met trouble too after his 'In Your Mind' album with its 'This Is Tomorrow' and 'Tokyo Joe' singles sold well. While his old records span on punk turntables, Ferry's unacceptable jet-set image prejudiced certain reviewers against 1978's 'The Bride Stripped Bare', a pot-pourri ranging from the traditional 'Carrickfergus' to 'When She Walks In The Room' (concerning his loss of fiancée Jerry Hall to Mick Jagger) to Lou Reed's 'What Goes On', all recorded in Switzerland.

A flop single, 'Trash', initiated Roxy Music's regrouping (with hired help) in 1978 but lost ground was regained with the elegant 'Dance Away' and 'Angel Eyes', both UK Top 5 hits from the 'Manifesto' album. Minus Thompson, 1980's 'Flesh And Blood' was a slicker affair but its revivals of 'In The Midnight Hour' and The Byrds classic, 'Eight Miles High', intimated that Ferry was short of ideas. Soon reinforcing this opinion was a reverential chart-topping cover of the recently murdered John Lennon's 'Jealous Guy' in 1981, and two instrumentals that consumed time on 1982's 'Avalon'. It was almost the overall ethereal mood that counted more than individual items, exemplified by 'Avalon' itself and the wistful 'More Than This'.

In 1984 Mackay, Manzanera and vocalist James Wraith (as The Explorers) cut the first of several releases developing the 'Avalon' sound – apart from a 'live' mini-album and big-selling compilations, 'Avalon' was Roxy Music's finale. When not indulging themselves with personal whims such as Manzanera's 'Primitive Guitars' in 1982, the guitarist and Mackay remain in demand for session work, TV themes and incidental music. The title song of Ferry's post-Roxy album, 'Boys And Girls', was beset with technical problems when he sang it on 1985's Live Aid. As well as more feathery emanations, the album was also notable for 'Slave To Love' and other strong dance numbers. An even greater emphasis on rhythm was apparent on 'Limbo' and 'The Right Stuff', singles from 1987's 'Bête Noire' album, with its star-studded cast and associated video, shot before an audience of ecstatic Ferry fans somewhere in the South of France.

Greatest Hits

Singles	Title	US	UK
1975	*Love Is The Drug* (Roxy Music)	30	2
1981	*Jealous Guy* (Roxy Music)	–	1
Albums			
1973	*Stranded* (Roxy Music)	–	1
1979	*Manifesto* (Roxy Music)	23	7
1980	*Flesh And Blood* (Roxy Music)	35	1
1982	*Avalon* (Roxy Music)	–	1
1985	*Boys And Girls* (Bryan Ferry)	–	1
1986	*Street Life – 20 Greatest Hits* (Ferry & Roxy Music)	–	1

The FIFTH DIMENSION

Florence LaRue
Marilyn McCoo
Billy Davis
Lamont Mclemore
Ron Townson (*vocal group*)

This black vocal harmony group's major hits displayed little of the soulful edge most vocal groups purveyed at the time. Discovered by manager Marc Gordon while touring with Ray Charles, the former took the folkish/close harmony style reintroduced by groups like The Mamas & Papas and dressed it up with songs from writers like Jimmy Webb and Laura Nyro under the production talents of Bones Howe. Gordon signed the group to a major pop music label on the US West Coast.

Their first hit came with a cover of The Mamas & Papas hit, 'Go where You Wanna Go', but the main thrust of their long career came from the alliance with Webb, who provided the material for 1968's hugely innovative 'Magic Garden' album.

As an act, they were highly polished giving them a natural introduction to the world of cabaret and the stages of Las Vegas. Despite the quality of songs provided by the likes of Webb and Laura Nyro ('Wedding Bell Blues', 'Stoned Soul Picnic') and Bacharach/David ('One Less Bell To Answer'), the group became veered increasingly towards MOR, and failed to move with the dramatic changes taking place in the early 1970s in black music.

They broke up in 1975 when McCoo (born 1943) and Davis (born 1940), by now married, departed for a solo (duo) career. A new group signed with the same label as the McCoo/Davis duo, who hit straight away with a US chart-topper 'You Don't Have To Be A Star'. The reformed group attracted a little notoriety in 1976 by covering 'Love Hangover' by Diana Ross before the Ross version was issued as a single, but Ross eventually won the race. In 1978, the group actually signed to Motown, while McCoo/Davis moved into network television with their own variety show. Reunion rumours are very regular and would probably now achieve much success.

Greatest Hits

Singles	Title	US	UK
1967	*Up Up And Away*	7	–
1968	*Stoned Soul Picnic*	3	–
1969	*Aquarius/Let The Sunshine In*	1	11
1969	*Wedding Bell Blues*	1	16
1970	*One Less Bell To Answer*	2	–
Albums			
1967	*Up Up And Away*	8	–
1969	*The Age Of Aquarius*	2	–
1970	*Greatest Hits*	5	–
Marilyn McCoo & Billy Davis			
1976	*You Don't Have To Be A Star*	1	–

FINE YOUNG CANNIBALS

Roland Gift (*vocals*)
Andy Cox (*guitar*)
David Steele (*bass, keyboards*)

Cox (born 1956) and Steele (born 1960) worked together in 1978 in Birmingham-based group The Beat (aka The English Beat in the US). After four hit LPs and 13 hit singles in the UK, they folded in 1983, when the duo were joined by distinctive singer Gift (born 1962), from ska group Akrylix, to form Fine Young Cannibals.

The distinctive pop/rock trio's debut single, 'Johnny Come Home', hit the UK Top 10, and their eponymous debut album just missed the UK Top 10 and the US Top 40. Their next two UK Top 10 singles came with revivals – in 1986, with the Elvis Presley song, 'Suspicious Minds', and in 1987 with a version of The Buzzcocks' 'Ever Fallen In Love'.

In 1988, Steele and Cox had a UK Top 20 single, 'I'm Tired Of Getting Pushed

Cannibals – recipe for record success or just a flash in the pan?

Around', under the name Two Men A Drum Machine And A Trumpet, while Gift made his film acting debut in *Sammy And Rosie Get Laid*. In 1989 they broke through in the US with 'The Raw And The Cooked': the album entered the UK chart at No. 1, and topped the US chart in its 49th week of release, going double platinum on the way. The album included two US No. 1 singles, the million-selling 'She Drives Me Crazy', and 'Good Thing', from the film *Scandal*, in which Gift also appeared.

In 1990 the group picked up the BRITS award for Top British Group which they returned, saying that the awards show had turned into a promotion vehicle for Margaret Thatcher. They are involved in various 'green' events and in projects helping young homeless people. An album of remixes of previous material, 'Raw And Remixed', came out in late 1990.

Greatest Hits

Singles	Title	US	UK
1989	She Drives Me Crazy	1	5
1989	Good Thing	1	7
Albums			
1989	The Raw And The Cooked	1	1

Roberta FLACK

A pianist singer/songwriter, Roberta Flack (born 1939) was discovered by keyboard player Les McCann playing in Washington nightclubs. McCann got her a recording contract in 1969, and her debut album, 'First Take', was a phenomenon topping the pop album charts for five weeks in 1970. The first single hit from the album was a version of Carole King's 'You've Got A Friend', a duet with former college classmate Donny Hathaway, who she in turn recommended to her label. Her second album, 'Chapter Two', consolidated her fame as an important artist at a time when black music was making serious inroads into the introspective album market via Curtis Mayfield, Stevie Wonder and Marvin Gaye.

By the release of 1972's 'Quiet Fire', Clint Eastwood had released his directorial movie debut, *'Play Misty For Me'*. A jazz R&B fan of long standing, Eastwood used Flack's version of folksinger Ewan MacColl's 'The First Time Ever I Saw Your Face' in the film. Unable to resist the demand for the song, her label pulled it from 'First Take' as a single, whereupon it promptly shot to No. 1 for a period of six weeks in the US and peaked in the UK Top 20.

Her second chart-topper came with 1973's 'Killing Me Softly With His Song' a lyric inspired by a Don McLean concert performance. A third came in 1974 with the much covered 'Feel Like Makin' Love'.

Throughout the rest of the 1970s, Flack recorded little and concentrated much of her time on social work for underprivileged children. Her friend Donny Hathaway, now a major star, was becoming a problem for his family due to encroaching mental disorders and in 1978 she recorded with him again in the hope of stabilizing his life. The result, 'The Closer I Get To You', was a major US Top 3 hit, but sadly, in 1979 Hathaway committed suicide and in 1980 Flack enjoyed her biggest UK hit with 'Back Together Again', a radically remixed old recording with Hathaway.

During the early 1980s, Flack recorded several duets with Peabo Bryson, culminating

Flack – faultless performer, killing us softly with her song

in the 1983 UK Top 3 hit, 'Tonight I Celebrate My Love'. More recently, she has enjoyed little major commercial success, but is a consummate artist who can eventually transcend the vagaries of chart music.

Greatest Hits

Singles	Title	US	UK
1972	*First Time Ever I Saw Your Face*	1	14
1973	*Killing Me Softly With His Song*	1	6
1974	*Feel Like Making Love*	1	34
1978	*The Closer I Get To You*		
	(with Donny Hathaway)	2	42
1980	*Back Together Again*	–	3
1983	*Tonight I Celebrate My Love*		
	(with Peabo Bryson)	16	2
Albums			
1970	*First Take*	1	47
1972	*And Donny Hathaway*	3	31
1973	*Killing Me Softly*	3	40
1978	*Blue Lights In The Basement*	8	–

The FLAMIN' GROOVIES

Cyril Jordan (guitar, vocals)
Roy A. Loney (vocals, rhythm guitar)
George Alexander (bass)
Tim Lynch (guitar)
Danny Mihm (drums)

Never a part of the 'peace and love'/psychedelic scene of the late 1960s, the commitment of San Francisco's Flamin' Groovies to the three-minute pop/rock song marked them out from their contemporaries and sustained them over two decades. Led by guitarist Jordan (born 1948), the band began life as The Chosen Few in 1966, changing their name to Lost And Found before eventually settling on The Flamin' Groovies. In 1968 they released a self-financed mini-album, 'Sneakers', which, coupled with a reputation for high-octane live shows, brought them a major label deal for 1969's 'Supersnazz' album, a mixture of band originals and rock'n'roll standards – a formula The Groovies would return to on future releases. A label change preceded the next two albums, 'Flamingo' (1970) and 'Teenage Head' (1971), both produced by US rock critic Richard Robinson, a constant fan of the band, which, despite critical acclaim (particularly for 'Head'), failed to sell.

1971 saw Lynch (born 1946, later arrested for drug offences and draft evasion) replaced by James Farrell, and Chris Wilson recruited to replace Loney (born 1946), who would later launch his own career with The Phantom Movers, their fine first album with the new set-up 'Out After Dark' (1979) featuring Mihm on drums. This line-up moved to Europe, where they were held in high esteem, recording four singles with Dave Edmunds producing, including the bona fide rock'n'roll

classic, 'Slow Death'. The band returned to the US in 1973, where Mihm was replaced (later joining Lynch in Hot Knives), initially by Terry Rae then by David Wright, but the staggered release of the Edmunds singles maintained interest in Europe, and they returned to the UK to record the classic 'Shake Some Action' album (1976), again with Edmunds in the producer's chair, which saw a move away from the R&B slant of their earlier albums towards a mid-1960s pop/rock sound. The radio-friendly title track nearly gave them a UK hit, and a tour with The Ramones reinforced their (pre-)Punk credentials. Mike Wilhelm (formerly with 1960s San Francisco punk band The Charlatans) joined in place of Farrell for 'Now' (1978), which included covers of classic Beatles, Stones and Byrds songs. Further touring in the US and Europe preceded the release of 'Jumpin' In The Night' (1979), co-produced by Jordan, which contained no fewer than seven covers, indicating that Jordan's Beatles/Byrds fixation was in danger of reducing the band to the status of mere 1960s copyists. The band fragmented shortly after its release, with singer Wilson joining London garage/psychedelic outfit, The Barracudas.

Sightings of the band during the 1980s were rare, although they apparently continued to gig, and it was not until 1987 that the latest chapter of the group's story appeared, in the shape of an excellent live album, 'One Night Stand', recorded in Australia the previous year, with Jordan and Alexander (born 1946) the only originals in a line-up completed by Jack Johnson (guitar, vocals) and Paul Zahl (drums). European dates followed, but no more has been heard from the band since, and their current status remains uncertain. Each of their 1970s albums is most worthy of reappraisal – if and when this occurs, hopefully Cyril Jordan will be available to receive long-delayed but well-deserved acclaim.

FLEETWOOD MAC

Peter Green (guitar, vocals)
Jeremy Spencer (guitar, vocals)
Mick Fleetwood (drums)
John McVie (bass)

The story of Fleetwood Mac is the greatest rock'n'roll soap opera ever told, and twenty four years later, the plot remains quite unpredictable.

The group formed in 1967 around Green (born 1946), who had successfully replaced Eric Clapton in John Mayall's Bluesbreakers. Green took another Bluesbreaker, Fleetwood (born 1942) with him, a third, McVie (born 1945) followed after a handful of gigs when bass player Bob Brunning (now a London headmaster) deputized, and Green recruited

Spencer (born 1948), who was obsessed by slide guitarist Elmore James.

With a large student following for their authentic blues/R&B, their 1968 eponymous debut album spent several months in the UK Top 10, and 'Black Magic Woman' (later a US Top 5 hit for Santana) and 'Need Your Love So Bad' were minor UK hit singles. Six months later, a second UK Top 10 album, 'Mr Wonderful' (US title: 'English Rose'), featured guest appearances from various friends, including pianist Christine Perfect (soon to be Mrs John McVie). Green then recruited a third guitarist, Danny Kirwan (born 1950), mainly to compensate for Spencer's increasing reluctance to play anything but slide guitar. At the end of 1968, an ethereal instrumental, 'Albatross', rocketed to the top of the UK charts, but the group members were ill-equipped for their new pop star status, and the follow-up single was a stark, mournful but exquisite ballad, 'Man Of The World', which made the UK Top 3. However, Green had become paranoid and 1969's 'Then Play On' seemed directionless, but still made the Top 10 of the UK album chart.

The hit singles continued with the uninhibited 'Oh Well' (UK Top 3, 1969), but Green, who had taken to playing in a white robe, announced his 1970 retirement, which was marked with a UK Top 10 hit, 'The Green Manalishi'. The rest of the band recorded the 'Kiln House' album, on which Kirwan's songwriting flourished, but this was not the Fleetwood Mac the UK public expected, although it was their first album to reach the US Top 100. Prior to the album's release, Christine McVie (keyboards, vocals) joined the band, whose members resolved to concentrate on the US market. Spencer disappeared hours before a 1970 show in Los Angeles, lured away by a religious sect, and in desperation the band contacted Peter Green, who helped them complete the US tour, but would not rejoin permanently.

The rest of the band elected to soldier on, recruiting American guitarist/songwriter Bob Welch (born 1946) and started again from scratch. 1971's 'Future Games' album owed less to the band's blues roots than to post-acid West Coast rock, and was better appreciated in the US than the UK. By the end of 1971 Kirwan's health was deteriorating, and although he contributed five tracks to the disjointed 'Bare Trees' album, he was gone by the time of its 1972 release. He was replaced by two more British musicians, singer Dave Walker and guitarist Bob Weston, and the band plodded steadily onwards in the US with 1973's 'Penguin' album, which featured more songs by Christine McVie. In the UK they were forgotten until the 1973 reissue of 'Albatross' reached the Top 3 of the singles chart, leaving the group with an identity crisis as they toured the UK after a lengthy absence to be greeted by requests for a hit song they had excised from their repertoire.

When the Mac was not as big (l to r) Fleetwood, McVie, Green and (front) Spencer

Dave Walker's tenure with the band ended after the next album, 1973's largely anonymous 'Mystery To Me', Bob Weston's affair with someone else's wife wreaked still more havoc, and the band ground to a halt halfway through a US tour. As if these problems weren't enough, their sometime manager formed a new Fleetwood Mac including none of the group's past or present members and sent them on a US tour. It took the genuine band many months and dollars to sort out, and the album that emerged at the end, 'Heroes Are Hard To Find', seemed scarcely worth the effort, although it became their first to reach the US Top 40. Although Welch contributed seven songs, he was exhausted, his marriage was under pressure and at the end of 1974, he left the band for an eventual solo career.

Recovering from catastrophes was now a way of life and Fleetwood and the McVies automatically began to prepare for their next album. Assessing a studio, Fleetwood met singer/writer/guitarist Lindsey Buckingham (born 1947) and his singer/songwriter girl-friend, Stevie Nicks (born 1948), who were recording their second album (under the name Buckingham Nicks) but were induced to join Fleetwood Mac in 1974. The new line-up recorded its first album, simply titled (like their 1968 debut album) 'Fleetwood Mac', in ten days, rejuvenated by the vitality that Buckingham and Nicks brought to their song-writing. The chemistry gelled still further when they embarked on a lengthy tour, but it took over a year before radio began to appreciate the album's airplay potential. When the Christine McVie-penned single,

'Over My Head', made the US Top 20, the album began to sell faster than it could be pressed, topping the US chart, where it remained listed for 16 months, and spawning two US Top 20 singles, 'Rhiannon' and 'Say You Love Me', in 1976. However, the traumas were accumulating faster than the royalties. The McVies divorced, the Buckingham/Nicks relationship and Fleet-wood's marriage both broke up, yet somehow they managed to record the flawless 'Rumours' album, released in 1977, which surpassed 'Fleetwood Mac', selling 25 million copies worldwide. Four singles from the album made the US Top 10: the chart-topping 'Dreams', 'Go Your Own Way', 'You Make Loving Fun' and 'Don't Stop'. The group, which had been together for longer than any previous line-up, toured extensively and Mick Fleetwood was reconciled with his wife, Jenny (about whom Donovan had writ-ten 'Jennifer Juniper' in the 1960s). Back in the UK, Peter Green was hospitalized after attacking his accountant, who was trying to give him a massive royalty cheque.

Fleetwood Mac's 1979 album, 'Tusk', was a double which took two years and $1 million to complete (in marked contrast to previous albums). It topped the UK album charts and reached the Top 5 in the US, where two excerpted singles, 'Sara' and the title track, were Top 10 hits. A 1980 double live album was a holding operation as the band's work rate diminished, but a new studio album, 'Mirage', emerged in 1982, staying five weeks at the top of the US chart and yielding a Top 5 single, 'Hold Me'.

Successful at it was, it was becoming increasingly difficult to hold the band together, as solo projects became an increas-ingly simpler alternative to walking the band's emotional tightrope. Nicks had taken the plunge with spectacular success in 1981, when her solo debut, 'Bella Donna', topped the US album chart, helped by US Top 10 single duets with Tom Petty ('Stop Draggin' My Heart Around') and Eagle Don Henley ('Leather And Lace'). Her 1983 follow-up, 'The Wild Heart', produced another US Top 5 single, 'Stand Back', and 1985's 'Rock A Little' did the same with 'Talk To Me'. Lindsey Buckingham's 1981 solo album, 'Law And Order', included a US Top 10 single, 'Trouble', while Christine McVie also had a US Top 10 hit with 'Get A Hold On Me', a single from her eponymous 1984 solo album. By contrast, Mick Fleetwood's 1980 solo album, 'The Visitor', was an expensive flop, and he filed for bankruptcy in 1984 after losses in the property market and a second marital collapse.

In 1987 the group re-assembled for the first Fleetwood Mac album in five years. 'Tango In The Night' was not an immediate success, but a sudden spurt of hit singles – 'Little Lies', 'Big Love' and 'Everywhere' – sent the album to the top of the US and UK charts. The prospect of touring was too much for Lindsey Buckingham, who had been planning a solo career for some time. His era with the band was encapsulated on the 1988 'Greatest Hits' compilation, which made the UK Top 3. He was replaced by two singer/guitarists, Rick Vito and Billy Burnette, who joined for the 'Tango In The Night' world tour and stayed for the band's 1990 album, 'Behind The Mask'.

At the end of 1990, the soap opera scriptwriters had still not finished with Fleetwood Mac. After publication of Mick Fleetwood's autobiography, Stevie Nicks and Christine McVie were said to have decided not to take part in future band activities. Confused? You probably will be . . .

Greatest Hits

Singles	Title	US	UK
1968	Albatross	–	1
1969	Man Of The World	–	2
1969	Oh Well	–	2
1973	Albatross (reissue)	–	2
1977	Dreams	1	24
1977	Don't Stop	3	32
1982	Hold Me	4	–
1987	Big Love	5	9
1987	Little Lies	5	5
1988	Everywhere	4	14
Stevie Nicks			
1981	Stop Draggin' My Heart Around (with Tom Petty)	3	50
1981	Leather & Lace (with Don Henley)	6	–
1985	Talk To Me	4	–
Albums			
1968	Fleetwood Mac	–	4
1975	Fleetwood Mac	1	23
1977	Rumours	1	1
1982	Mirage	1	5
1987	Tango In The Night	7	1
1988	Greatest Hits	14	3
Stevie Nicks			
1981	Bella Donna	1	11

Eddie FLOYD

Known principally as the originator of the much-covered soul standard, 'Knock On Wood', Floyd (born 1935) was a record producer of some note and, in collaboration with Steve Cropper of Booker T's MG's, composer of hit songs for such as Solomon Burke, Otis Redding and Wilson Pickett (who was among his successors as lead vocalist in The Falcons). This gospel outfit included the adolescent Floyd, who joined after his family moved from Montgomery, Alabama, to Detroit. His chief reason for leaving The Falcons in 1962 was his frequent attendance at the local Flame Show Bar to watch Johnnie Ray, Dinah Washington, Brook Benton and others who had transmuted gospel fervour for secular purposes.

Floyd's first solo outings were for Lu Pine, to whom he was obligated as a Falcon. Other obscure singles appeared on Atlantic and his own Safice Records. Since fellow Falcon Joe Stubbs was the brother of Four Top Levi Stubbs, and that The Primettes – later The Supremes – sang on a few Floyd sessions, it is odd that he was not signed to Tamla Motown rather than the Memphis-based Stax/Volt for 'Knock On Wood' in 1966.

After topping the US R&B chart, the single crossed into the worldwide pop charts. Though artists as diverse as Count Basie and Toots & The Maytals tried 'Knock On Wood', the most commercially successful variations on the Floyd blueprint were by David Bowie in 1974 and by disco star Amii Stewart in 1979. Like 'Louie Louie', 'Gloria' and similar standards, it also figured in the repertoires of countless pop groups the world over. None made as insidious an impact, but Floyd continued to enjoy steady sellers, like his own 'Things Get Better', which followed 1967's 'Raise Your Hand' into the UK Top 50 – and retreads of Sam Cooke's 'Bring It On Home To Me' and The Temptations' 'My Girl'. Now a resident of Washington, Floyd's output on disc is irregular, though he remains active as a cabaret entertainer.

Greatest Hits

Singles	Title	US	UK
1966	Knock On Wood	28	19
1968	Bring It On Home To Me	17	–

FLYING BURRITO BROTHERS

Gram Parsons (vocals, guitar, piano)
Chris Hillman (vocals, guitar)
Chris Ethridge (bass)
Sneeky Pete Kleinow (pedal steel guitar)

Formed in 1968 by Parsons and Hillman after both had left The Byrds (see separate entry), The Flying Burrito Brothers were among the first and best exponents of country/rock, a genre which Parsons probably invented. Parsons (born Cecil Connor, 1946) had formed The International Submarine Band, who made a few pioneering recordings for minor labels, after which he joined The Byrds in 1968 for their 'Sweetheart Of The Rodeo' album, recorded in Nashville. After refusing to go with the group on a South African tour (he preferred to stay in London with friends from The Rolling Stones), he made his peace with Hillman, and they decided to jointly lead The Flying Burrito Brothers (a name coined by Ian Dunlop of The Submarine Band).

After recruiting Kleinow (born 1935) and Ethridge, the group's classic debut album, 'The Gilded Palace Of Sin', used several different drummers, and was a bigger success

critically than commercially. It was followed in 1970 by 'Burrito De Luxe', by which time Ethridge had left the band, Hillman had moved to bass, Bernie Leadon had joined on guitar and banjo and a permanent drummer, another ex-Byrd, Michael Clarke, had been recruited. This real-life musical chairs would continue throughout the group's career. Possibly because 'Burrito De Luxe' failed to make the US chart, Parsons then left the band for a solo career which was hugely acclaimed (but only after his 1973 death), and was replaced by singer/guitarist Rick Roberts. The group's 1971 eponymous album was still only a minor success, and that led to Kleinow and Leadon leaving, the latter to form The Eagles (see separate entry) in 1972. With Al Perkins (pedal steel guitar) and Kenny Wertz (guitar, banjo), the only surviving members, the group soldiered on, adding bluegrass musicians Byron Berline (violin) and Roger Bush (double bass) from Country Gazette as auxiliary members for what was essentially a live 'Best Of' album, 'Last Of The Red Hot Burritos', in 1972.

At that point, the group effectively folded as Hillman and Perkins joined Manassas, the group led by Stephen Stills, but Roberts, Wertz, Bush and Berline recruited additional musicians for a European tour, resulting in 1973's 'Live In Amsterdam' double album. In 1974, a double album compilation with many unreleased tracks, 'Close Up The Honky Tonks', peaked higher in the US chart than any of the group's previous albums, but Roberts, perhaps the most likely ex-Burrito to keep the group alive, had already embarked on a solo career which produced two albums, 1972's 'Windfalls' and 1973's 'She Is A Song', before he rejoined Michael Clarke in Firefall.

The Burritos – hot band with seminal reputation

In 1974 a reformed group with originals Kleinow and Ethridge plus cajun fiddle player Floyd 'Gib' Guilbeau, ex-Byrd Gene Parsons (drums) and singer/guitarist Joel Scott Hill, tried again, but while their 1975 debut album, 'Flying Again', again peaked higher in the US chart than any of the previous Burritos albums, Ethridge again left after one album and was replaced by Clyde 'Skip' Battin, who had worked with Gene Parsons as the rhythm section of The Byrds. This line-up's 1976 album, 'Airborne', was overshadowed by the release of 'Sleepless Nights', another compilation featuring Gram Parsons, which was a minor US chart hit.

Subsequently, Kleinow and Guilbeau kept the group's name alive, much to the disgust of several ex-members. Although albums have been released by those whose connections with The Flying Burrito Brothers were tenuous (to say the least), various combinations of Kleinow, Guilbeau and singer/guitarists John Beland and Greg Harris enjoyed a number of US country chart hits in the early 1980s. There is almost certainly a group billed as The Flying Burrito Brothers gigging somewhere in the world at the present time.

Although none of their albums was a commercial success, the group's influence on numerous later acts is genuinely immeasurable. A 'Greatest Hits' listing would be meaningless, and many would agree that the essential work of this seminal group can be found on their first four albums.

Dan **FOGELBERG**

US singer/songwriter (born 1951) who dropped out of a degree in painting to record his own music after being spotted by Eagles' manager Irving Azoff. Recording his first album in Nashville (1973's 'Home Free') pigeonholed him as country, although soft rock would have been more accurate. Fogelberg was given a harder edge on 1974's 'Souvenirs' by ex-James Gang guitarist Joe Walsh who produced it. 'Part Of The Man' was Fogelberg's US Top 40 debut single.

Initially enjoying life on the West Coast, he sessioned for Roger McGuinn, Jackson Browne, Randy Newman, etc., then rejected the lifestyle in favour of rocky mountain Colorado. From employing a backing group, Fool's Gold (who recorded their own album), he subsequently restricted his live work in favour of recording.

A commercial breakthrough came with 'Twin Sons Of Different Mothers', a 1978 collaboration with jazz flute-player Tim Weisberg, which went platinum, and spawned the US Top 30 hit, 'The Power Of Gold'. 1979's 'Phoenix' sold over two million copies, yet differed little from the four post-debut albums that had preceded it. Now

Gentle man Dan, doyen of the soft-rock scene

producing himself, the radio-friendly Fogelberg began a run of US hit singles: 'Longer' (US Top 3) from 'Phoenix' preceded three in 1981, 'Same Old Lang Syne', 'Hard To Say' and 'Leader Of The Band', all US Top 10 successes.

The 1980s saw him enjoy the security of success by diversifying: 'The Innocent Age' (1981), was a double album 16-part song cycle based on his childhood, featuring Emmylou Harris on guest vocals, that stayed three months in the US Top 10. 'High Country Snows' (1984) was a bluegrass album with many featured musicians from the world of country music, while 'Exiles' (1987) was a step into AOR. Another three-year gap preceded 1990's 'Wild Places' Never likely to mean much in Britain, Fogelberg has carved a niche as one of America's biggest selling soft-rockers.

Greatest Hits

Singles	Title	US	UK
1980	Longer	2	59
1981	Hard to Say	7	–
Albums			
1979	Phoenix	3	42
1981	Innocent Age	6	–

FOREIGNER

Mick Jones (guitar, vocals)
Ian McDonald (flute, keyboards, guitar)
Al Greenwood (keyboards)
Lou Gramm (vocals)
Ed Gagliardi (bass)
Dennis Elliott (drums)

Formed by New York-based Spooky Tooth veteran Jones (born 1944) in 1976 to cash in on the US adult-oriented rock boom that had made a chart-topper of his former colleague Gary Wright. McDonald (born 1946) and Elliott (born 1950), ex-King

Crimson and If respectively, were also British, hence the name.

Gravel-voiced Gramm (born 1950) was a vocalist in the Paul Rodgers (Bad Company/Free) mould, and the music played to his strengths: their first three singles, 'Feels Like The First Time', 'Cold As Ice' and 'Long Long Way From Home' were all clichéd yet competent radio-friendly rockers and all US hits. An eponymous 1977 debut album was followed by 'Double Vision', with a hit single in the title track, but the UK remained comparatively immune to their charms.

'Head Games' (1979) continued the formula with one-time Peter Frampton sideman Rick Wills replacing Gagliardi (born 1952): by the following year's imaginatively titled '4', he, Gramm, Jones and Elliott were the sole personnel. Aside from a raucous US Top 5 single, 'Urgent', with guest star Junior Walker, this album notably introduced a balladic feel with 'Waiting For A Girl Like You', Gramm's voice floating above synths from guest Thomas Dolby. The formula reached its peak with 'I Want To Know What Love Is', a transatlantic No. 1 in 1984 from the UK chart-topping album 'Agent Provocateur', which also yielded a US Top 20 hit, 'That Was Yesterday'.

This peak looked to be a farewell, as Gramm cut the solo 'Ready Or Not' (released in 1987, with US Top 5 single, 'Midnight Blue') and Jones moved into production (Van Halen, Billy Joel and others). Reformed for 1987's 'Inside Information' album, the group scored US Top 10 hits with 'I Don't Want To Live Without You' and 'Say You Will'.

Another Gramm album, 'Long Hard Look', preceded Jones's first solo effort but the signs are that with the group continuing to mine a rich seam of somewhat featureless music, sporadic reformations are likely in the years ahead. Along with Journey, Foreigner represent corporate rock on which the larger US record labels are built.

Greatest Hits

Singles	Title	US	UK
1978	Double Vision	2	–
1981	Waiting For A Girl Like You	2	8
1984	I Want To Know What Love Is	1	1
Albums			
1981	4	1	5
1984	Agent Provocateur	4	1

The **FOUR SEASONS**

Frankie Valli (lead vocals)
Tommy DeVito (guitar, vocals)
Nick DeVito (vocals)
Hank Majewski (bass, vocals)

Valli (born Francis Castelluccio, 1937), Tommy DeVito (born 1936), Majewski,

The 1960s and 1970s saw several successful Seasons for Valli (second left) and the boys

1965	Let's Hang On	3	4
1967	Can't Take My Eyes Off You		
	(Frankie Valli)	2	–
1974	My Eyes Adored You		
	(Frankie Valli)	1	5
1975	Who Loves You	3	6
1976	December 63 (Oh What A Night)	1	1
1976	Silver Star	38	3
1978	Grease (Frankie Valli)	1	3
Albums			
1963	Sherry and 11 Others	6	20
1964	Rag Doll	7	–
1975	Who Loves You	38	12
1976	Greatest Hits	–	4

The **FOUR TOPS**

Levi Stubbles Jnr. (lead vocals)
Renaldo Benson (backing vocals)
Abdul Fakir (backing vocals)
Lawrence Payton (backing vocals)

The most consistently successful male group signed to Motown, The Four Tops began as Detroit teenagers harmonizing for their own amusement in Mills Brothers/Inkspots fashion. Becoming popular at local talent shows, the quartet embarked upon their career as The Four Aims, changing to their more familiar name (and Stubbles shortening his surname to Stubbs) for their 1956 debut single, 'Kiss Me Baby'. Further flop singles in a variety of styles on several labels emerged during their long years on the road throughout North America before Motown boss Berry Gordy Jnr. spotted them on a bill with Billy Eckstine. After recording for Gordy's short-lived jazz subsidiary, Workshop, they transferred to the main label in 1964.

Their immediate US hit, 'Baby I Need Your Loving', was checkmated in the UK by a cover version by The Fourmost, but their fourth Motown single, the million-selling 'I Can't Help Myself', established them internationally – a breakthrough consolidated later that year with 'It's The Same Old Song', and in 1966 with 'Reach Out I'll Be There', a song generally considered to be their classic with its impassioned chorale and adventurous instrumentation. In the wake of 'Bernadette', 'Seven Rooms Of Gloom' and other smashes, even a pre-Motown reissue made the US chart. By 1968 the group had resorted to soulful covers of such songs as The Left Banke's 'Walk Away Renee', Tim Hardin's 'If I Were A Carpenter' and The Moody Blues's hit, 'A Simple Game'. A pairing-up on record with The Supremes also sustained momentum following Motown's loss of its main hitmaking team, Lamont Dozier, Brian Holland and Eddie Holland, who had written and produced the hottest hits of both acts.

After a worrying period of misses, the group left Motown in 1972 to gain a fresh lease of chart life with 'Keeper Of The Castle'

and Nick DeVito formed in New Jersey, in the mid-1950s. As The Four Lovers they had a minor US hit 'You're The Apple Of My Eye' in 1956. In 1960 Valli, Nick Massi (born 1935) and Tommy DeVito worked as session musicians for Bob Crewe of Swan Records. Crewe began writing songs with Bob Gaudio (ex-Royal Teens and composer of their 1958 novelty hit, 'Short Shorts') designed to exploit Valli's extraordinary three-octave voice. With a line-up of Valli, Tommy DeVito, Massi and Gaudio, success came in 1962 with their first single, 'Sherry' for the largely black Vee Jay label, as The Four Seasons, named after a restaurant. Like The Righteous Brothers later on, they were regarded as black until a TV appearance on *American Bandstand* revealed their obvious Italian-American origins. Dominated by Valli's amazing falsetto, they enjoyed massive success over the next four years: their US chart-toppers included 'Big Girls Don't Cry' and 'Rag Doll', while 'Let's Hang On' was a US Top 3 hit. Popular on both sides of the Atlantic (eight UK Top 40 entries by 1966) they maintained that status during the 'British Invasion', led by The Beatles.

Their basic sound was anachronistic, based heavily on 1950s vocal group styles (particularly black) and their early albums mixed new originals with covers of 1950s hits. Adherence to their formula caught up with them by the late 1960s. An attempt at change (1968's progressive album, 'Genuine Imitation Life Gazette') proved a dismal failure and led to their breaking with Crewe. By 1970 both Massi and DeVito had left and the group worked mainly in cabaret, with little notable

record success. However, Valli enjoyed a concurrent solo career aimed at the MOR market and scored four late 1960s solo hits, including the future singles-bar staple, 'Can't Take My Eyes Off You'. A gap followed, but the mid-1970s saw him return to the charts with more big hits including a US chart-topper. The group struggled on, but even an association with the Motown off-shoot, MoWest, in the early 1970s failed to re-launch them significantly.

In 1975 a reformed band fronted by Valli successfully cashed in on the disco boom and suddenly not only their music, but also their satin shirts with huge collars, were all the rage again. For two years they were in the charts until once more they became outdated. Valli's title song to the 1978 movie, *Grease*, topped the US chart, but subsequently, the pattern of break-ups and reformations has continued (e.g. 'Reunited Live '81'). Valli & The Four Seasons now seem irretrievably part of the nostalgia circuit. Always shrewd businessmen, they usually formed their own publishing companies and became a profit-sharing partnership, while almost every time they left a label they retrieved their masters, thus assuring a more than healthy income from reissues, such as the late 1980s triple CD boxed set, '25th Anniversary Collection'.

Greatest Hits

Singles	Title	US	UK
1962	Sherry	1	8
1962	Big Girls Don't Cry	1	13
1963	Walk Like A Man	1	12
1964	Rag Doll	1	2

Motown magic, the pop of the Tops

and 1973's 'Ain't No Woman', each composed and produced by Brian Potter and Dennis Lambert. A more personal triumph was the well-received 'Main Street People', which included some group originals, mainly by Benson.

The group then suffered another lean period, even maintaining a vinyl silence – apart from repackagings – from 1978 until 1981 when they proved their resilience again with three hit singles from their disco-oriented Casablanca album, 'Tonight', including their first UK Top 3 hit in ten years and their first US Top 20 hit for eight, 'When She Was My Girl'. 1982's 'One More Mountain' was much less fruitful but an appearance in the *Grease II* movie brought a minor 1982 hit in 'Back To School Again'.

During the group's busy world-wide concert schedule, the loudest ovations are reserved for their meticulously choreographed chartbusters for Motown – actually responsible for a mere third of their vinyl output. However, the group returned briefly to the fold in 1986 with the rather non-commital 'Hot Nights' album before moving away again. In early 1988, they bounced back into prominence with a US Top 40 single, 'Indestructible' (used as NBC-TV's signature tune for that year's Olympic Games coverage), and at the end of that year, scored their first UK Top 10 hit in seven years with 'Loco In Acapulco', from the soundtrack to the movie, *Buster*.

Greatest Hits

Singles	Title	US	UK
1965	I Can't Help Myself	1	23
1966	Reach Out I'll Be There	1	1
1966	Standing In The		
	Shadows Of Love	6	6
Albums			
1967	Four Tops Greatest Hits	4	1

Peter **FRAMPTON**

Singer/guitarist Frampton (born 1950), was a founder member of The Herd in 1966. They scored three UK Top 20 singles and Frampton was dubbed 'The Face of '68', but he became disenchanted with the pop straitjacket. In 1969, he joined ex-Small Face Steve Marriott in Humble Pie, which he left in 1972 to pursue a solo career. After session work with George Harrison and Harry Nilsson, he was able to call on heavyweight back-up (including Ringo Starr, Billy Preston and Klaus Voorman) for his debut solo album, the critically acclaimed 'Winds Of Change' (1972).

Frampton then formed his own band, Frampton's Camel, with ex-Spooky Tooth drummer Mike Kellie (replaced by John Siomos); Mickey Gallagher (keyboards) and Rick Wills (bass), touring the US extensively and recording an eponymous album in 1973. The band folded in 1974 but Frampton kept on touring with old Herd colleague Andy Brown and Siomos. With 'Frampton' (1975) the guitarist began to make some commercial impact as a solo artist, but superstardom quickly followed with the double live album, 'Frampton Comes Alive' (1976). Many regard it as strange that it should have been so successful, but the figures speak for themselves: 15 million plus sales, in the charts for two years and at the time the biggest selling live album ever. Three hit singles came from the album and by the end of 1976 Frampton had reputedly grossed over $70 million in royalties and concert fees.

The title track of the follow-up album, 'I'm In You' (1977), went Top 3 in the US, but from there it was slowly downhill, starting with his movie debut in the disastrous *Sgt. Pepper's Lonely Hearts Club Band* (1978). Problems mounted – depression, drinking

and a car crash in the Bahamas. Subsequent albums have been undistinguished; 'Where Should I Be' (1979); 'Breaking All The Rules' (1981); 'The Art Of Control' (1982) and 'Premonition' (1986).

Greatest Hits

Singles	Title	US	UK
1976	Show Me The Way	6	10
1977	I'm In You	2	41
Albums			
1976	Frampton Comes Alive	1	6
1977	I'm In You	2	19

Connie **FRANCIS**

Though she was the most successful female recording artist of the late 1950s, Connie Francis is not a name that springs readily to mind when discussing classic rock. While she cut polite versions of 'I Hear You Knocking', 'Heartbreak Hotel', etc., her following embraced both teenagers and their parents after her initial impact with a perky revival of a 1920s opus, 'Who's Sorry Now', which made the US Top 5 and topped the UK singles chart.

A prodigious child of musical forebears, Concetta Franconero (born 1938) had mastered the piano accordion at four to become a mainstay of talent and radio shows around New Jersey before entering Newark Arts High School where she studied music theory and orchestration. George Scheck, a local TV personality, became her manager in 1949 and told her to concentrate on singing, anglicize her name and lose some weight, after which he found her regular spots on national TV variety revues.

By 1955 her voice had matured to a throaty contralto, and her chart debut, 'The Majesty of Love', a duet with country star Marvin Rainwater in which she was the junior partner, allegedly sold a million (although its single week in the US chart at No. 93 makes this unlikely!) As a teenage starlet, she sang duets with Paul Carr in the 1957 movie, *Jamboree*, in which she also acted in a vacuous plot with musical excerpts by other artists. 'Who's Sorry Now' came a year later.

In an era when saccharine sounds were popular, among further Francis million sellers were 'My Happiness', 'Lipstick On Your Collar' (her second UK No. 1), 'Among My Souvenirs' and other retreads of old songs. 1960 brought four more million sellers: 'Mama' (an Italian song with new English lyrics), 'Everybody's Somebody's Fool' (a 1960 US chart-topper), 'My Heart Has A Mind Of Its Own' (another US No. 1, spoofed by Tom Petty in 1989 as 'My Mind Has A Heart Of Its Own') and 'Many Years Ago', and she also procured a rich crop of smashes from jobbing New York tunesmiths

Connie's Cupid arrows British best-sellers bullseye

FRANKIE GOES TO HOLLYWOOD

William 'Holly' Johnson *(vocals)*
Paul Rutherford *(vocals)*
Gerard O'Toole *(guitar)*
Peter Gill *(drums)*
Mark O'Toole *(bass)*

Johnson (born 1960) began his musical career in Liverpool cult band, Big In Japan, and had recorded as a solo artist for a local independent label before joining up with ex-Opium Eaters and Spitfire Boys members Rutherford (born 1959), Mark O'Toole (born 1964), Gerald O'Toole – quickly replaced by Brian Nash (born 1963) – and Gill (born 1964) to form this pop/dance group in 1982.

Taking their name from a headline referring to either UK singer Frankie Vaughan or Frank Sinatra, the group were initially rejected by two major labels before signing the deal which led to their first single, 'Relax', a UK No. 1 despite an airplay ban by the BBC. The follow-up, 'Two Tribes', another original composition entered the UK singles chart at No. 1 and stayed there for nine weeks. The combined sales of their first two singles (with their numerous remixes) topped 3.4 million – a UK record for an act's first two releases.

Their debut album 'Welcome To The Pleasure Dome' (1984), broke the UK record for advance orders and their third single, 'The Power Of Love', also made No. 1. US success was on a smaller scale, although 'Relax' reached the Top 10 when re-issued in 1985 and their debut album went gold. They broke another record when the album's title track and 'Rage Hard' (1986) made them the first act to have their first five singles reach the UK Top 5. Their 'Liverpool' album in 1986 and its singles were less successful and the band split in 1987, both Johnson and Rutherford pursuing solo careers.

A court case with the band's record label revealed that only Johnson had actually appeared on the band's first two hits, which were constructed by producer Trevor Horn and session musicians. In 1989 Johnson's 'Blast' album reached No. 1 in the UK and spawned three UK Top 20 singles, 'Love Train', 'Americanos' and 'Atomic City'.

like Paul Anka and, especially, the Howard Greenfield-Neil Sekada team whose efforts included 'Stupid Cupid' and the main title theme of Connie's 1961 movie with George Hamilton, *Where The Boys Are*. Her final US chart-topper, 'Don't Break The Heart That Loves You', came in 1962.

Typecast as an older friend in whom you can always confide, Connie's film roles continued even when her records were no longer automatic hits. This trend was exemplified by 1964's *Looking For Love* and *When The Boys Meet The Girls* (with Herman's Hermits, Liberace and Sam The Sham), which were mostly period comedies spiced with lip-synched ephemera.

Never at ease as a teen idol, Connie's vinyl output from 1961 had relied increasingly on sentimental ballads, recordings in foreign tongues and themed albums such as the best-selling 'Italian Favourites'. She also displayed a fondness for Country & Western music, from the 1957 duet with Marvin Rainwater to a more recent duet of 'Bye Bye Love' with Hank Williams Jnr.

The trauma of her 1974 rape in a New York hotel caused a lengthy withdrawal from public life but, as demonstrated by the British chart performance of a 1977 hits compilation, Connie Francis survives as an international star for the many who still remember her 56 US Top 100 singles in 13 years.

Frankie – Holly would go too, as group eventually split up

Greatest Hits

Singles	Title	US	UK
1984	*Relax*	10	1
1984	*Two Tribes*	43	1
1984	*The Power Of Love*	–	1
Albums			
1984	*Welcome To The Pleasure Dome*	33	1
1986	*Liverpool*	88	5
1989	*Blast* (Holly Johnson solo)	–	1

Aretha **FRANKLIN**

The daughter of Rev. C.L. Franklin, a famous US gospel preacher and singer in the 1950s, Aretha Franklin (born 1942) cut her first recordings of hymns at her father's Detroit church at the age of 14. By 18, she had been spotted by John Hammond, and had moved to New York, acquiring a manager, Joe King, where she made her first secular album, 'The Great Aretha Franklin' (1960) which took in R&B and jazz classics. The debut single, 'Today I Sing The Blues', reached the US R&B Top 10, and the following year she entered the US Top 100 with 'Won't Be Long', recorded with the Ray Bryant Trio, while a version of 'Rock-a-bye Your Baby With A Dixie Melody' hit the US Top 40.

In 1962 came a second album, 'The Electrifying Aretha Franklin', and marriage to her then manager Ted White. In the same year, the singles 'Don't Cry Baby' and 'Try A Little Tenderness' reached the US Top 100 and the album, 'The Tender, The Moving, The Swinging Aretha Franklin' made the US Top 75. The following three years saw a lull in her

fortunes, although her output of material included five further albums, before Atlantic made a successul bid for her contract in 1966. She was put under the production auspices of Jerry Wexler, who believed that Franklin's strong vocal style needed to be redefined in the black music market.

In 1967, Franklin's first work with Wexler, the raw soul single 'I Never Loved A Man (The Way I Loved You)' topped the US R&B chart and made the US Top 10. It was followed by the classic 'Respect', a US No. 1, 'Baby I Love You', which reached the US Top 5, and 'You Make Me Feel (Like A Natural Woman)', a US Top 10 single. The album, 'Aretha Arrives' made the US Top 5 in the same year, and she was named Billboard's Top Female Vocalist for 1967.

In 1968 Franklin won her first Grammy Award for 'Respect', and the same year saw a string of hits including 'Chain Of Fools', a US Top 3 single, and 'Think', a US Top 10 and UK Top 30 entry, her first self-penned millionseller. The 1968 albums 'Lady Soul' and 'Aretha' both made the US Top 5 (UK Top 30 and Top 10 respectively), and 'Aretha In Paris' reached the US Top 20. The single, 'I Say A Little Prayer', gave her a UK Top 5 single, also reaching the US Top 10. Within two years Aretha had become a formidable chart success after nearly a decade of misplacement in the soul market.

1969 saw another Grammy Award, for 'Chain of Fools', and US Top 20 positions for the singles 'Eleanor Rigby', 'The Weight' and 'Share Your Love With Me'. The albums 'Soul 69' and 'Gold' both made the US Top 20, but Aretha's failing marriage to Ted White caused problems in the same year, and the two were later to divorce.

Another Grammy came her way for 'Share

Aretha Franklin – for nearly thirty years the undisputed First Lady of Soul

Your Love With Me'. This success was to carry on through the 1970s highlighted by US Top 10 singles 'Bridge Over Troubled Water' and 'Rocksteady', the US Top 3 hit 'Spanish Harlem' in 1971, and the US Top 10 albums 'Live At The Fillmore West' (1971) and the gospel set 'Amazing Grace' in 1972. 'Until You Come Back To Me' (1973) gave her another US Top 5 hit, while her 10th Grammy Award came in 1975 for 'Ain't Nothing Like The Real Thing'. In 1976, she co-produced the soundtrack for the movie, *Sparkle* from which the US Top 40 single, 'Something He Can Feel', was taken. In 1978 she married the actor, Glynn Turman.

The 1980s opened with Aretha appearing as a waitress in *The Blues Brothers* movie singing 'Think', and the decade also marked a label change. Her first album under the new deal, 'Aretha', made the US and UK charts.

Numerous collaborations into the 1980s have added to Franklin's worldwide chart success, including 'Love All The Hurt Away' with George Benson (1981), the 'Jump To It' album (1982) produced by Luther Vandross, 'Sisters Are Doin' It For Themselves' with The Eurythmics in 1985, and 1987's 'I Knew You Were Waiting (For Me)' with George Michael. 'Who's Zoomin' Who' and 'Freeway Of Love' both brought her more solo success in 1985. In 1987, Franklin's father died after two years in a coma after being shot during a civil rights demonstration. In 1988, she paid tribute to him by recording the double album 'One Lord, One Faith', back in the church in Detroit where she debuted as a child.

More collaboration occurred in the 1990

album 'Through The Storm', which included tracks featuring Elton John and Whitney Houston.

Greatest Hits

Singles	Title	US	UK
1967	Respect	1	10
1967	Chain of Fools	2	43
1971	Spanish Harlem	2	14
1973	Until You Come Back To Me (That's What I'm Gonna Do)	3	26
1985	Freeway Of Love	3	51
1987	I Knew You Were Waiting (For Me) (with George Michael)	1	1
Albums			
1967	I Never Loved A Man The Way I Love You	2	36
1968	Aretha: Lady Soul	2	25
1968	Aretha Now	3	6

FREE

Paul Rodgers (vocals)
Paul Kossoff (guitar)
Andy Fraser (bass)
Simon Kirke (drums)

With their 1970 'All Right Now' anthem, Free personified the British hard-rock style that swept across Europe and the US over the next decade, but sadly were never stable for long enough to take advantage of it.

Kossoff (born 1950) and Fraser (born 1952) were already playing together in London in 1968 when they spotted Paul Rodgers (born 1949) singing in a blues band. With Kirke (born 1949) they modelled themselves on Cream and were given their name by Britain's R&B Godfather, Alexis Korner. Despite building a strong following on the college circuit, neither of their first two albums, 'Tons Of Sobs' (1968) and 'Free' (1969), made a major chart impact. 'All Right Now', written by Rodgers and Fraser, was a UK Top 3/US Top 5 single in 1970, and the 'Fire And Water' album, with an extended version of the hit, built strongly on its success. The band looked set for stardom, but the follow-up, 'Stealer', flopped to the band's dismay. They broke up in 1971, only to score posthumous UK Top 5 hits with 'My Brother Jake' and the album, 'Free Live'.

Rodgers and Fraser formed their own bands, Peace and Toby, while Kossoff and Kirke joined Texan keyboard player John 'Rabbit' Bundrick and Japanese bassman Tetsu Yamauchi for the 'Kossoff, Kirke, Tetsu & Rabbit' album in 1971. In 1972 the original Free line-up regrouped, but although 'Free At Last' (1972) and 'Heartbreaker' (1973) made the UK Top 10 and 'Wishing Well' was a Top 10 single, they were largely going through the motions. Kossoff's drug problems made him increasingly unreliable and he made no contribution to 'Heartbreaker', leaving at the end of 1972. Fraser also bailed out and Tetsu and Rabbit were drafted in before the band disintegrated. To rub salt in the wound, 'The Free Story', a 1974 hits compilation, made the UK Top 3. Rodgers and Kirke launched the mega-successful Bad Company, Kossoff formed Back Street Crawler but died of drug abuse in 1976, Bundrick later played with The Who, and Tetsu joined The Faces.

Greatest Hits

Singles	Title	US	UK
1970	All Right Now	4	2
Albums			
1970	Fire And Water	17	2
1971	Free Live	–	4
1974	The Free Story	–	2

Alan **FREED**

A disc-jockey who played a considerable part in bringing rock'n'roll to the general public, Freed (born 1922) began broadcasting on local radio whilst an engineering student (and amateur trombonist) at Ohio State College. His course was interrupted by World War II service in the Signals Corps before his 1942 discharge due to hearing problems.

Three years as an announcer led to his own record show in Akron until a move to a Cleveland station where, encouraged by re-

Free – 'All Right Now' saw 1991 revival via TV ad for chewing gum

cord shop owner Lee Mintz, he began airing 'sepia music' (i.e. R&B). Though racist factions labelled him a 'nigger lover' and provided legal harassment, his *Moondog Rock and Roll Party* (named after its theme tune, 'Blues For Moon Dog' by Todd Rhodes) became popular with a white adolescent audience through Freed's adventurous programming, manic presentation style and jive talk – which included the catch-phrase 'rock'n'roll', a traditional blues metaphor for sexual union. Freed's integrity was such that he refused to spin sanitized white covers of black originals.

In 1952 his first attempt at promoting a rock'n'roll stage show turned into a riot as nearly 30,000 teenagers arrived at a 10,000-capacity stadium. Confining such activities to theatres with tiered seating, Freed's reputation grew, despite a long airwaves absence after sustaining injuries in a road accident.

A major New York station soon afforded Freed national recognition as The King of Rock and Roll – as he was often erroneously billed when compering at Brooklyn's Paramount Theatre and in cameos in *Rock Around The Clock, Don't Knock The Rock* and further films of the genre. One of the other stars in 1958's *Go Johnny Go*, Chuck Berry (see separate entry), had allowed Freed a songwriting credit for 'Maybelline', a 1955 million-seller, to ensure airplay. Less questionable was Freed's creative role in the composition of items by The Moonglows and other black vocal groups. Freed was also persuaded to cut a few records with his own Rock'n'roll Orchestra.

On principle, Freed did not sign an affadavit denying involvement in commercial bribery. Consequently, he became a scapegoat as the payola storm clouds gathered in 1960, particularly when, despite promises of im-

munity, he would not testify in court. The only disc-jockey to be subpoenaed, he was fined and given a short suspended sentence in 1962 on two counts of bribery. His continued decline was punctuated by an ill-judged migration to Los Angeles, heavy drinking and in 1964, accusations of tax evasion. Freed was unable to stand trial as he was suffering from uraemia – a disease that killed him a year later.

The wretchedness of his fall did not change lay opinion about Freed's catalytic importance as a harbinger of youth culture. In 1973 The Band (see separate entry) paid respects with their 'Moondog Matinee' album, and in 1978 Freed was the subject of *American Hot Wax*, a movie which, like the man himself, caught the spirit of early rock-'n'roll.

Peter **GABRIEL**

When Peter Gabriel quit Genesis in 1974, the band was just starting to build a reputation in America although they were firmly established in Britain and Europe. Gabriel (born 1950) co-founded the English public school progressive rock band in 1967, but felt increasingly restricted by the group format during the recording of 'The Lamb Lies Down On Broadway'. In a conscious move away from familiar territory, Gabriel's debut solo album was recorded in Toronto in 1976 with US session heavies, including keyboard player Larry Fast and bassist Tony Levin, and produced by Bob Ezrin, noted for his Alice Cooper and Lou Reed albums. Released in 1977, 'Peter Gabriel' (the title he gave to each of his first four solo albums), reached the UK Top 10 and included a UK Top single, 'Solsbury Hill', but made little impact in the US.

1978's second 'Peter Gabriel' album, produced by King Crimson guitarist Robert Fripp, was more experimental and although it made the UK Top 10, included no obvious single, and when his US label could hear no hits on his third 'Peter Gabriel' album in 1980, it was released by a rival major company, after which it became his biggest US success thus far, reaching the Top 30. More significantly it included 'Biko', a contemporary protest song which became an anti-apartheid anthem for the growing protest movement in South Africa. In the UK the album topped the charts and the eccentric 'Games Without Frontiers' single (possibly inspired by a bizarre pan-European populist TV competition series, *Jeux Sans Frontières*), reached the Top 5, but it was his back-catalogue royalties from

Genesis, by then starting to break big, that paid most of the bills, particularly after he put his own money behind the ambitious but financially disastrous WOMAD world music festival in 1982. He took part in a Genesis reunion to cover his losses.

Gabriel's passion for world music, his flair with synthesized sounds and the interest in human psychology that permeated his lyrics finally began to pay dividends on his fourth 'Peter Gabriel' album, also released in 1982 and re-titled 'Security' for the US market for which he had signed to a third label. 'Shock The Monkey', aided by an arresting video, was a modest hit on both sides of the Atlantic, but any attempt at a career move was doomed: the double album, 'Peter Gabriel/Plays Live', failed to attract new punters and he did himself more good with the soundtrack to *Birdy* (1985), which he co-produced with Daniel Lanois and consisted of evocative instrumental reworkings of earlier songs.

When 'So', again made with Lanois, was released in 1986 it was his first 'new' album for four years. Propelled by the sublime 'Sledgehammer' single (a Top 5 single in the US and UK that owed more to Motown than world music and for which a multiple-award-winning video was made at great expense) and 'Big Time', 'So' went platinum, peaking in the US Top 3, and entering at the top of the UK chart in its first week of release. In addition to his own world tour, Gabriel also took part in a charity tour for Amnesty International including the Conspiracy Of Hope tour in the US, and a world-wide Human Rights Now! tour with Bruce Springsteen and Sting, as well as Nelson Mandela's Birthday Tribute in London in 1988. He also launched his own world music label and space-age studio, Real World, and recorded another film score, for Martin Scorsese's controversial *Last Temptation Of Christ*. By the end of 1990, there was no sign of a new album and 'Shaking The Tree', a 'Best Of', was released instead, although a new release has been promised.

Greatest Hits

Singles	Title	US	UK
1980	*Games Without Frontiers*	–	4
1986	*Sledgehammer*	1	4
Albums			
1980	*Peter Gabriel* (Third Album)	22	1
1982	*Peter Gabriel/Security*	28	1
1986	*So*	2	1

Rory **GALLAGHER / TASTE**

Part of the late 1960s blues boom, guitarist Gallagher (born 1949) grew up in Cork in Eire. After a typical Irish dancehall outfit, The Fontana Showband, he formed a blues

Multi-faceted World Music enthusiast Peter Gabriel

trio, Taste, with like minds Norman Damery and Eric Kittrington. They played the British and European club circuit and released an eponymous debut album in 1969, with Gallagher (guitar, vocals) joined by Richard McCracken (born 1948) on bass and John Wilson (born 1947) on drums. A more produced follow-up in 1970 'On The Boards', made the UK Top 20, and Gallagher, a consummate player and blues stylist of little pretension and ferocious technique with a leaning towards bottleneck playing, was one of the guitar heroes of the era's open-air festivals.

After two live albums, 'Live Taste' and the posthumously released 'Taste Live At The Isle of Wight', Gallagher began to operate under his own name in 1971. Backed by Wilgar Campbell (drums) and Gerry McAvoy (bass), he released an eponymous solo album in 1971, which briefly made the UK Top 40 and heralded his biggest commercial successes 'Live In Europe', (a 1972, UK Top 10), and 'Blueprint' (1973, UK Top 20). He continued with various trio line-ups, and several 1970s albums were minor chart hits in the UK and US, and popular among loyal groups of fans all over Europe including 1973's 'Tattoo', 1979's 'Top Priority' and 1980's 'Stage Struck'.

Respected within the music fraternity, he played on the 'London Session' albums of both Muddy Waters (1972) and Jerry Lee Lewis (1973), as well as the Lonnie Donegan tribute album, 1977's 'Puttin' On The Style'. Gallagher continues to tour Europe and further afield, despite an aversion to flying, and his 1990 comeback album (after several years when he abandoned recording) 'Fresh Evidence', showed no sign of the old fire being dampened.

Greatest Hits

Albums	Title		US	UK
1970	On The Boards	(Taste)	–	18
1972	Live In Europe		101	9
1973	Blue Print		147	12

Art GARFUNKEL

While Paul Simon took most of the creative initiative during his hitmaking partnership with New Yorker Garfunkel (born 1941), the latter has since given a good if sporadic account of himself in the charts. Prior to the duo's 1970 split, Garfunkel had started a parallel career as a film actor. However, despite a role in 1969's *Catch 22* and co-starring with Jack Nicholson in *Carnal Knowledge*, he has not fulfilled this early promise. Musically, the reverse was the case. After some unhappy solo performances that relied heavily on Simon & Garfunkel material, his breathy, gentle tenor came into its own in the recording studio where it floated effort-

Art's 'Angel' signalled Breakaway from Simon and Garfunkel songbook

lessly over orchestrated accompaniment in 1973's 'Angel Clare'.

Moderately successful, this album heralded 1975's 'Breakaway' with its production, by Richard Perry, of well-crafted songs from professional composers like Gallagher & Lyle – and Paul Simon – but a smooth UK chart-topping revival of the 1959 arrangement by The Flamingos of 'I Only Have Eyes For You' was the album's principal single. Of much the same formula was 1978's 'Watermark' album which spawned a US hit single, a version of Sam Cooke's 'Wonderful World'.

1979 was a good year for Garfunkel with his UK best-seller, 'Fate For Breakfast' and attendant singles, that began with 'Bright Eyes', Mike Batt's theme to the *Watership Down* cartoon feature film. A US miss, this anthem of the animal rights movement was followed by the lesser UK Top 40 entry, 'Since I Don't Have You'. The comparative failure of 1981's 'Scissors Cut' album may

have prompted Garfunkel's reunion with Simon for a New York show, the subsequent 'Concert In Central Park' album and a world tour. Though this episode was not all smiles, one imagines that Garfunkel's bank manager was pleased.

The artist next broke cover in 1988 with 'Moment Of Truth' which was in the same easy-listening vein as its five predecessors, and included a retread of Percy Sledge's 'When A Man Loves A Woman'.

Greatest Hits

Singles	Title	US	UK
1973	All I Know	9	–
1975	I Only Have Eyes For You	18	1
1979	Bright Eyes	–	1
Albums			
1973	Angel Clare	5	14
1975	Breakaway	7	7
1979	Fate For Breakfast	67	2

Latterday troubles darkened the life of Marvin Gaye, musical backbone of the Motown sound

Marvin **GAYE**

fter an honourable discharge from military service, Marvin Gaye (born 1939) began his musical career with various Washington doo-wop groups before joining The Marquees in 1957. After some unsuccessful recordings under the wing of Bo Diddley, The Marquees were recruited by Harvey Fuqua, who was reforming his doo-wop outfit, The Moonglows, and had previously met Gaye while judging a talent contest which Gaye won. As Harvey & The Moonglows they moved to Chicago where they recorded tracks including 'Almost Grown' in 1958.

In 1960, Fuqua and Gaye left the group, moving to Detroit, with Fuqua signing a solo deal, and Gaye finding work as a session drummer for Berry Gordy's fledgling Motown organisation, playing on early hits for The Miracles and singing back-up for The Marvelettes. The following year, he married Gordy's sister Anna, and signed with Motown as a solo artist at the same time.

His first two Motown releases, the single 'Let Your Conscience Be Your Guide' (1961) and the album 'The Soulful Moods Of Marvin Gaye' (1961), both failed to chart but after touring with the Motown Revue, Gaye scored his first US Top 50 single, 'Stubborn Kind Of Fellow' (1962).

In 1963, came three US Top 30 singles, 'Hitch Hike', 'Pride & Joy', and 'Can I Get A Witness', while his UK breakthrough came in 1964 with the Top 50 single, 'Once Upon A Time', a duet with Mary Wells, which was a US Top 20 hit, as was a second duet with Wells, 'What's The Matter With You Baby?'. 'How Sweet It Is To Be Loved By You' was Gaye's first solo Top 50 hit in the UK, also reaching the US Top 10, in 1965.

Two duets with Kim Weston, including the UK and US Top 20 single 'It Takes Two' (1967), and a pair of solo US Top 10 singles preceded his lengthiest series of collaborations with a female singer: his duet with Tammi Terrell on 'Ain't No Mountain High Enough' (1967) was a US Top 20 hit. Together they scored four US Top 10 singles, 'Your Precious Love' (1967), 'If I Could Build My Whole World Around You' (1967), 'Ain't Nothing Like The Real Thing' (1968) and 'You're All I Need To Get By', but tragedy struck in October 1968 when Terrell collapsed with a brain tumour in Gaye's arms onstage. A further four US Top 50 singles by the duo were subsequently released, including the UK Top 10 hit, 'The Onion Song' (1969). 'I Heard It Through The Grapevine', which became the biggest-selling single for Motown to date and has since been regarded a pop classic, was released in 1968, becoming Gaye's anthem, reaching No. 1 in the US and UK. Throughout the 1960s, soul standards, dance tracks, ballads and pure pop were all included in Gaye's repertoire, the only common feature being the sheer quality of the vocals.

In the 1970s Gaye developed a highly individual style, with very personal self-penned lyrics given a more 'heartfelt' delivery, backed by mellow R&B based tunes rather than the previous soul/pop. Tammi Terrell died from a brain tumour in 1970 after a long battle, and for a time Gaye maintained a low profile. He returned in 1971 with the US Top 5 singles 'What's Going On', a comment on the Vietnam war, and 'Mercy Mercy Me', both from the US Top 10 album 'What's Going On'.

In 1973 he wrote and performed the soundtrack to the film, *Trouble Man*, and later in the same year the seductive 'Let's Get It On', album reached the US Top 3 and the title track gave him his second US No. 1 single, reaching the UK Top 40. A collaboration with Diana Ross brought similar success for Motown; 'Diana & Marvin' was a UK Top 10 album, the single 'You're A Special Part Of Me' climbed into the US Top 20 and 'You Are My Everything' was a UK Top 5 hit.

Other memorable releases in the 1970s included the US Top 5 album 'I Want You' (1976) the dance track 'Got To Give It Up' which topped the US singles chart in 1977 and 'Here My Dear' (1979) – a double album bemoaning his unhappy relationship with Anna Gordy, who had previously divorced him and added to his financial problems.

Financial pressure led to his exiling himself in Hawaii where cocaine addiction added to his problems, resulting in a suicide attempt. His remaining years were plagued by drug related difficulties; a monotony only to be broken after a label change by the success of 'Sexual Healing' in 1982, and the album, 'Midnight Love', which was awarded a Grammy for Best Vocal Performance of the Year. It was his final accolade.

Increasingly disturbed through drug addiction, Gaye frequently threatened to take his own life; in a violent argument on April 1, 1984, Marvin Gaye was shot dead by his church minister father.

Greatest Hits

The **J. GEILS BAND**

J. Geils (guitar)
Peter Wolf (vocals)
Magic Dick (harmonica)
Danny Klein (bass)
Stephen Jo Bladd (drums)

Formed in Boston in 1967, via the amalgamation of The J Geils Blues Band, an acoustic trio comprising Geils (born Jerome Geils, 1946), Klein (born 1946) and Magic Dick (born Dick Salwitz, 1945) and The Hallucinations, a 1950s-oriented R&B/doo wop outfit, which included Wolf (born Peter Blankfield, 1946) and Bladd (born 1942). Five dedicated R&B/rock'n'roll buffs, they developed a set which drew heavily upon their collective influences, eventually adding Seth Justman (born 1951) on keyboards, and emerging at the end of the 1960s as a tight, hard-nosed R&B band, unfashionable but intensely powerful live, as their reputation around Boston attested.

Their eponymous 1971 debut album drew heavily on covers of classic blues riffs. While it barely made the US Top 200, it earned them much critical acclaim – eg Most Promising New Band in *Rolling Stone*. Working in similar musical areas to those pioneered by Paul Butterfield and Canned Heat, although with a harder rock edge, they rapidly became established as the ultimate support band of the early 1970s. Album sales increased accordingly: two 1972 albums, 'The Morning After' and 'Full House' (a live album) made the US Top 100, and their fourth album, 'Bloodshot' provided them with a mainstream commercial breakthrough in 1973, going gold and making the US Top 10, and including a US Top 30 single, 'Give It To Me', an unlikely slice of white reggae.

They successfully began to broaden their musical direction and continued to make inroads into the US album charts: 'Ladies Invited' (1973) almost made the US Top 50, 'Nightmares . . . And Other Tales From The Vinyl Jungle' (1974) made the US Top 30 and 1975's 'Hotline' the US Top 40, before 'Must Of Got Lost' brought them a US Top 20 single in 1975. They remained with Atlantic,

for whom they ultimately made nine albums, the last two being 'Live – Blow Your Face Out' (1976) and 'Monkey Island' (1977), before moving to fresh pastures in 1979, when their career immediately took a major upswing, which proved to be temporary. Their first album under the new deal, 'Sanctuary' went gold, spawning two minor US hit singles, while its follow-up, 'Love Stinks' (1980), became their first US Top 20 album in seven years.

After a longer gap than previously, their twelfth original album, 'Freeze-Frame' topped the US album chart for a month in 1982 and was their first to go platinum, also becoming their only album to reach the UK Top 20 and including three hit singles: 'Centrefold' (US No. 1, UK Top 3), 'Freeze Frame' (US Top 5, UK Top 30) and 'Angel In Blue'.

However, Wolf, who was married for several years to movie star Faye Dunaway, left the band in 1983 following the release of 'Showtime', another gold album, which left them without a charismatic frontman. Wolf's first two solo albums charted strongly in the US – 1984's 'Lights Out' made the US Top 30, and its title track became a US Top 20 single, while 'Come As You Are' also charted much higher than his erstwhile former colleagues could manage with 1984's 'You're Getting Even While I'm Getting Odd'. Whether or not the band, with or without Wolf, can ever recapture their early 1980s success is difficult to predict.

Greatest Hits

GENESIS

Peter Gabriel (vocals)
Tony Banks (keyboards)
Mike Rutherford (bass)
Anthony Phillips (guitar)
Chris Stewart (drums)

The British public-school system produces more politicians than rock groups, but the sounds of the 1960s motivated the pupils of Charterhouse school and in 1967, Peter Gabriel (born 1950), Tony Banks (born 1950), Mike Rutherford (born 1950) and Anthony Phillips (born 1951) formed a band.

They gave a demo tape to Charterhouse old boy Jonathan King, a pop star by virtue of his 'Everyone's Gone To The Moon' hit, who gave them their name and acquired a record-

ing contract for them, but their debut concept album, 'From Genesis To Revelation' (1969), was naïve, ambitious and ignored. Shaken but undeterred, they spent five months on a new set of songs, resulting in a new record deal, and 'Trespass' was released in 1970, but touring proved too much for main songwriter Phillips, who left along with their third drummer John Mayhew (who had replaced John Silver, who had replaced Chris Stewart).

After a short crisis, the remaining trio decided to carry on, recruiting guitarist Steve Hackett (born 1950) and drummer Phil Collins (born 1951). The band soon acquired an identity, developing their dramatic, grandiose style on 'Nursery Cryme' (1971) and 'Foxtrot', their 1972 UK Top 20 album chart debut, building a following in the UK and Europe. Gabriel also provided a stronger visual focus by shaving his head and wearing strange costumes. The budget-priced 'Genesis Live' (1973) made the UK Top 10, and in 1974, their first UK hit single was 'I Know What I Like (In Your Wardrobe)' from their UK Top 3 album, 'Selling England By The Pound'. The US began to take notice in 1974 when the conceptual double album, 'The Lamb Lies Down On Broadway' reached the Top 50 (and Top 10 in the UK), and the accompanying tour broke new ground in rock presentation.

When Gabriel left to go solo after the tour, it was widely considered a terminal blow for the band. Drummer Phil Collins eventually also became lead vocalist, sounding uncannily like Gabriel. The 1976 album, 'A Trick Of The Tail', made the UK Top 3 and the US Top 40, and the group toured with former Yes and King Crimson drummer Bill Bruford added to the line-up. 1977's 'Wind And Wuthering' album made the US Top 30, but slipped slightly in only making the UK Top 10. Bruford was replaced by Chester Thompson (ex-Weather Report and Frank Zappa) for the inevitable tour – while the same year's double live album, 'Seconds Out', reached the UK Top 5, it only made the US Top 50.

Hackett, who felt that his material was being increasingly ignored, then left the band, having already released a 1975 solo album, 'Voyage Of The Acolyte'. He went on to a reasonably successful career with half a dozen solo albums, before moving on to other projects, including GTR with former Yes guitarist Steve Howe. Genesis now became a core trio, with Thompson and US guitarist Daryl Stuermer as touring additions. What was needed was a US hit single, which came with the Top 30 item, 'Follow You Follow Me', which also went Top 10 in the UK. Their more commercial sound helped both 'And Then There Were Three' (1978) and their first UK chart-topping album, 'Duke' (1980), into the Top 20 of the US album chart, and additionally the band scored their first US Top 20 single with 'Misunderstanding', a song written by Phil Collins, who

Collins' (second left) singing a revelation after Gabriel's early exodus from Genesis

followed its success with his first solo album (see separate entry). The UK favoured the more strident 'Turn It On Again', which went Top 10.

1982's 'Abacab' again topped the UK charts and made the US Top 10, producing hit singles with 'No Reply At All' and the title track, which went Top 10 in the UK. The US was finally ready for 'Three Sides Live' (the fourth side of the double album featuring studio tracks), which went Top 10 in 1983. 1984's 'Genesis' album did the same, and included a US Top 10 single, 'That's All', and won a 'Best Instrumental' Grammy for 'Second Home By The Sea'. Collins's simultaneous solo career had taken off by then and Banks and Rutherford also had chart success with solo projects. Rutherford's most successful extramural activity came in the second half of the 1980s, when he formed Mike And The Mechanics with former Ace vocalist/keyboard player Paul Carrack. They scored US Top 10 hits in 1986 with a movie theme, 'Silent Running (On Dangerous Ground)' and 'All I Need Is A Miracle', and a US Top 3 album, 'The Living Years'.

Genesis reunited in the same year for the 'Invisible Touch' album, which topped the UK charts and made the US Top 3, spawning five US Top 5 singles: 'Invisible Touch' (their first US No. 1), 'Throwing It All Away', 'Land Of Confusion', 'Tonight Tonight Tonight' and 'In Too Deep' (which was also the theme to the movie, *Mona Lisa*). After a mammoth world stadium tour, the trio dispersed for further solo projects. They are expected to start work on another Genesis album in 1991.

Greatest Hits

Singles	Title	US	UK
1983	Mama	73	4
1986	Invisible Touch	1	15
1986	Throwing It All Away	4	22
1986	In Too Deep	3	19
1987	Land Of Confusion	4	14
1987	Tonight Tonight Tonight	1	18
Albums			
1973	Selling England By The Pound	70	3
1976	A Trick Of The Tail	31	3
1980	Duke	11	1
1981	Abacab	7	1
1983	Genesis	9	1
1986	Invisible Touch	3	1

GERRY and The PACEMAKERS

Gerry Marsden (guitar, vocals)
Leslie Maguire (piano, sax, guitar)
Les Chadwick (bass)
Freddie Marsden (drums)

As prime exponents of Merseybeat, Gerry and The Pacemakers topped the UK chart with each of their first three singles – a record only equalled by Frankie Goes To Hollywood (see separate entry) twenty years later. A veteran of Liverpool country & western specialists The Red Mountain Boys, Gerry (born 1942) formed The Mars-Bars in 1958 with brother Freddie (born 1940). Enlisting Chadwick (born 1943), they became the Marsden Trio and then Gerry And The Pacemakers. As a late addition to a bill

headed by Gene Vincent (see separate entry) at Liverpool Boxing Stadium in 1960, they became local stars.

After turning professional, they were augmented by the gifted Maguire (born 1941) for residencies in Hamburg and a full booking schedule at home. Teaming up with manager Brian Epstein at first made little difference to the group, as he was preoccupied with launching The Beatles, but early 1963 yielded a recording contract, and the spearheading of the Liverpool chart invasion with Gerry's arrangement of Mitch Murray's catchy 'How Do You Do It'.

While his Pacemakers laboured behind him, Gerry's effervescent geniality and instinctive crowd control carried the stage act single-handedly. After a second UK chart-topper with another Mitch Murray song, 'I Like It', his aspirations to be an 'all round entertainer' became apparent on the 'How Do You Like It' album, in which the expected Merseybeat was mixed with orchestrated standards like Rodgers and Hammerstein's 'You'll Never Walk Alone', the third UK No. 1, which penetrated folklore as the Liverpool Football Club anthem. A showbiz natural, Gerry steered his boys into pantomime, cabaret and ventures far removed from their artistic origins on Merseyside's depressed Dingle suburb.

1964 began with Gerry's own composition, 'I'm The One' in the UK Top 3, but danger signs were perceptible when the next single, 'Don't Let The Sun Catch You Crying' stalled outside the Top 5, although it was their debut US hit, which was consolidated by reissues of earlier UK smashes. Starring roles in the period film *Ferry Across the Mersey* with its evocative title song (revived in 1983 by Frankie Goes To Hollywood) were an attempt to broaden their appeal, but Gerry's first serious flop was 'It's Gonna Be All Right', which missed the UK Top 20 in late 1964, and the downward spiral continued with covers of Bobby Darin's 'I'll Be There' and 1965's tearjerking 'Walk Hand In Hand'. Although the game was up in the UK, 'Girl On A Swing' sold well in Europe, North America and Australia. However, with their very name a millstone round their neck by 1967, Gerry and The Pacemakers threw in the towel.

After fruitless bids for solo hits, Gerry indeed emerged as an all-round entertainer, initially on children's TV, before gladly taking the male lead in the London West End musical *Charlie Girl*. Backed by an off-the-peg Pacemakers, he remains a mainstay of English nostalgia and variety revues such as 1990's *Gerry's Christmas Cracker* season in Birmingham. Lately, his career has been buoyed by windfalls such as the use of 'Ferry Across The Mersey' for a chart-topping single with other well-known Merseyside artists (including Paul McCartney and Holly Johnson) in aid of the Hillsborough Disaster Fund in 1989. Four years earlier Marsden had also led another all-star group, The Crowd, to No. 1 with a fund-raising re-make of 'You'll Never Walk Alone' for victims of a similar soccer stadium tragedy in Brussels.

Greatest Hits

Singles	Title	US	UK
1963	*How Do You Do It*	9	1
1963	*I Like It*	17	1
1963	*You'll Never Walk Alone*	–	1
1985	*You'll Never Walk Alone*		
	(with The Crowd)	–	1
1989	*Ferry Across The Mersey*	–	1
Albums			
1963	*How Do You Like It?*	–	2
1965	*Ferry Across The Mersey*	13	19

Ian **GILLAN**

One of the quintessential hard rock singers, Gillan (born 1945) first came to international fame as vocalist with Deep Purple, a group for whom he co-wrote many memorable songs, before solo success and another spell with the group in the 1980s.

After playing in local bands, including The Moonshiners, The Javelins and Wainwright's Gentlemen, during his late teens, in 1965 Gillan was asked to join Episode Six, a long-running London band (1963–70) whose members at various times included bass player Roger Glover and drummer Mick Underwood. In mid-1969 both Gillan and Glover joined Deep Purple, a band whose three albums to that point had fared better in the US than the UK. With the two recruits, Deep Purple became international superstars with two albums, 'Fireball' and 'Machine Head', topping the UK chart, but Gillan and guitarist Ritchie Blackmore, who was the group's dominant instrumentalist, clashed, and both Gillan and Glover left the band after four highly successful years. During this period, Gillan also sang the title role in the hugely successful double album of the Tim Rice/Andrew Lloyd-Webber musical, *Jesus Christ Superstar*, which was an immense seller and topped the US album chart in 1971.

After leaving Deep Purple, he pursued non-performing business ventures for a year before re-emerging in late 1975 with The Ian Gillan Band, whose first album, 1976's 'Child In Time', briefly made the UK chart. Two 1977 albums, 'Clear Air Turbulence' and 'Scarabus', were less successful, while two live albums recorded in Japan, 'Live At Budokan Vols 1 & 2', were only released in Japan at the time. In 1978 the band, which was without a UK record deal, fell apart, and Gillan took keyboard player Colin Towns from the old band and recruited bass player John McCoy and other musicians (eventually including Mick Underwood from Episode Six and several guitarists, notably Bernie Torme) to form a

Gerry (front) with The Pacemakers (clockwise) brother Freddie, Les Maguire and Les Chadwick

band simply known as Gillan. Between 1979 and 1982 this group scored five UK Top 20 chart albums: 'Mr. Universe' (1979), 'Glory Road' (1980), 'Future Shock' and 'Double Trouble' (1981) and 'Magic' (1982), owing their success to almost constant touring, the hard rock credentials of Gillan himself, and the punkish attitudes of McCoy and Torme.

During the late 1970s and early 1980s, there had been regular suggestions that the classic line-up of Deep Purple (Gillan, Glover, Blackmore, Jon Lord and Ian Paice) should reform, and after The Ian Gillan Band folded, many felt that the long-awaited Purple reunion was on the cards. Instead, Gillan spent a year as vocalist with Black Sabbath, cutting a UK Top 5 album, 'Born Again', with them, after which he finally agreed to rejoin Deep Purple in late 1984, cutting three successful albums with the group before rivalries with Blackmore again forced him to leave. During this

period, he also released a solo album, 'What I Did On My Vacation' (1986), and an album also featuring Roger Glover, 'Accidentally On Purpose' (1988).

In 1990 he returned with a new band composed of contemporaries of a similar vintage, and cut his first solo album in several years, 'Naked Hunter', as well as fronting an all-star group for Life-Aid Armenia, which used one of his most famous songs, 'Smoke On The Water' (originally recorded by Deep Purple), as the spearhead release.

Greatest Hits

Singles	Title	US	UK
1980	*Trouble*	–	14
1981	*New Orleans*	–	17
Albums			
1980	*Glory Road*	183	3
1981	*Future Shock*	–	2

GO-GO'S

Belinda Carlisle (vocals)
Charlotte Caffey (guitar)
Jane Wiedlin (guitar)
Margot Olaverra (bass)
Elissa Bello (drums)

Formed in LA in 1978 by Carlisle (born 1958, formerly of Black Randy & The Metro Squad) and Wiedlin (born 1958) who brought in Caffey (born 1953, ex-Eyes and Manual & The Gardeners) and Olaverra and Bello, they were originally called The Misfits and thought of initially as a punk novelty act, but went on to become the first really successful self-contained all-girl group.

They steered away from punk and towards New Wave pop/rock when Bello was replaced by Gina Schock (formerly in Edie Massey And Her Eggs). In 1980 they toured Britain with The Specials and recorded 'We Got The

Beat' on Stiff. Also in 1980 Olaverra was replaced by ex-Girlschool and Textones member Kathy Valentine. In 1981, their first album, 'Beauty And The Beat', was produced by veteran Richard Gottehrer who had worked with Blondie. The album topped the US chart for six weeks and went double platinum. Two singles from it, 'We Got The Beat' (written by Caffey), which earned them a gold record, and 'Our Lips Are Sealed' (co-written by Wiedlin), also hit the US Top 20.

In 1982 they returned to the US Top 10 with their gold album, 'Vacation', and the title track as a single. In 1984, their album, 'Talk Show', and single, 'Head Over Heels', made the US Top 20. In the UK, they had no big hits, although the song 'Our Lips Are Sealed' went Top 10 for its co-writer Terry Hall and his group, Fun Boy Three, in 1983.

In 1985, the group went their separate ways and both Carlisle and Wiedlin have since had big solo transatlantic hits. The

group reunited for a benefit show for the Californian Environmental Protection Initiative in 1990.

Greatest Hits

Singles	Title	US	UK
1982	We Got The Beat	2	–
1982	Vacation	8	–
Albums			
1981	Beauty And The Beat	1	–
1982	Vacation	8	75

Steve **GOODMAN**

An engaging singer/songwriter from Chicago, Goodman (born 1948) was a critical favourite whose own records rarely achieved the success widely predicted for them, but whose songs were covered by major stars who made them into hits.

After an appearance on a local sampler album, 'Gathering At The Earl Of Old Town' (later nationally available), Goodman was 'discovered' by the unlikely duo of Paul Anka and Kris Kristofferson. After impressing Kristofferson when he opened for him, the actor/singer introduced Goodman to Anka, who was singing Kristofferson's 'Help Me Make It Through The Night' in his act. Anka recommended Goodman to the label for whom he recorded, and Goodman went on to make two excellent albums, 'Steve Goodman' (1972), which included his three biggest songs, 'You Never Even Call Me By My Name', which was David Allan Coe's breakthrough country hit in 1975, 'City Of New Orleans' (a US Top 20 hit for Arlo Guthrie in 1972), which was covered by literally dozens of artists, and 'Somebody Else's Troubles' (1973). Goodman also recommended his friend, John Prine, to Anka and Kristofferson, and Prine likewise was signed by a major label. Unfortunately for Goodman, Prine's career took off and Goodman remained a cult figure.

Although his albums had failed to chart, Goodman swiftly got a new deal on a label which specialized in notable singer/songwriters. While his next two albums, 'Jessie's Jig And Other Favourites' (1975) and 'Words We Can Dance To' (1976), were minor US hits, 1977's 'Say It In Private', 1979's 'High And Outside' and 1980's 'Hot Spot' failed to chart. At this point, Goodman, who had suffered from leukemia since the early 1970s, was in poor health, but by 1983 he had launched his own record label, Red Pajamas, with the help of his (and Prine's) manager, Al Bunetta. The first album to be released on the label was a live album by Goodman, 'Artistic Hair', whose sleeve showed an almost bald Goodman, perhaps the result of treatment aimed at curing his ailment. Soon afterwards came 'Affordable Art', part

'Beauty and the Beat' girls The Go-Gos, fronted by Belinda Carlisle

of which was also live recordings, and then 'Santa Ana Winds', on which Emmylou Harris and Kris Kristofferson guested, but on September 20, 1984, Steve Goodman died from kidney and liver failure after a bone marrow transplant operation.

Goodman didn't appear on the fourth album on his label, released after his death, a double titled 'Tribute To Steve Goodman', on which many paid their musical respects to a man they adored and admired. The contributions included Prine, whose career he helped to launch, Bonnie Raitt, Arlo Guthrie, John Hartford, David Bromberg and The Nitty Gritty Dirt Band. New listeners are advised to follow Goodman's career from the start – a list of non-existent hits would be missing the point.

Lesley GORE

The 19 US hits in five years earned by Gore (born 1946) and her professional survival today were earned mainly by well-presented, consistently strong material with an impassioned delivery that was evident when this daughter of a well-heeled New Jersey swimwear manufacturer sang 'It's My Party' at a friend's soiree in 1962, and it was suggested that she send a demo of it to Mercury Records. Produced by Quincy Jones (later producer of Michael Jackson), the million-selling 'It's My Party', 'It's Judy's Turn To Cry' sequel and attendant album, 'I'll Cry If I Want To', established Lesley as a pedlar of adolescent love triangle sagas. Notable among further smashes were 'You Don't Own Me' (covered by Gore's then British equivalent, Dusty Springfield) and 'Maybe I Know', one of two items featured by the artist in 1964's celebrated pop movie, *The TAMI Show* in which she held her own against the likes of James Brown, The Supremes and The Rolling Stones (see separate entries). The following year, she appeared in another film, *Ski Party*, miming to 'Sunshine, Lollipops And Rainbows', co-written by pianist Marvin Hamlisch, a future Oscar-winning tunesmith.

By 1967's 'California Nights' album, Gore was trying more mature songs – though she was not above a 1970 duet of The Fleetwoods hit, 'Come Softly To Me' with *Hair* star Oliver Tobias. One of the few white vocalists to record for Motown, her 'Someplace Else Now' album consisted entirely of her own compositions, but the nearest she came to a 1970s hit was with the single, 'Immortality' in 1975 – though her presence was felt by proxy in a 1973 version of 'It's My Party' by Bryan Ferry and a more radical arrangement of the song by Dave Stewart and Barbara Gaskin which topped the UK chart in 1981.

She was featured on two items in the soundtrack to the *Fame* movie (for which her brother Michael had penned Irene Cara's title

hit), and was last heard on vinyl in 1987, singing a medley of 'Since I Don't Have You' and 'It's Only Make Believe' with Lou Christie, a performer of the same early 1960s vintage.

Greatest Hits

Singles	Title	US	UK
1963	*It's My Party*	I	9
1964	*You Don't Own Me*	2	–
Albums			
1963	*I'll Cry If I Want To*	24	–

Eddy GRANT

In 1960, Edmond Montague Grant (born 1948) emigrated with his family from British Guiana to North London. At school he became known as a multi-instrumentalist but elected to concentrate on lead guitar when he formed The Equals with drummer John Hall, rhythm guitarists Pat Lloyd and Lincoln Gordon, and Gordon's twin brother Dervin on vocals. Operating without the almost obligatory bass player, the outfit turned professional in 1965 when offered gigs in Europe. In 1966 the group signed a record deal on the strength of a demo of Grant's 'Baby Come Back'. Re-made and released as a single, it topped charts in Europe, but was a B-side in the UK; however, after 'I Get So Excited' made the UK Top 50 in 1968, 'Baby Come Back' came into its own in both the UK and US, as did its associated album, 'Unequalled'. Sales of the follow-up album, 'Explosion', reflected the modest chart positions of the three Equals singles that preceded a UK Top 10 comeback with 'Viva Bobby Joe', another opus by Grant, who also wrote for other acts like The Pyramids, whose sole hit was his 'Train Tour To Rainbow City'.

Ex-Equal Eddie

With Grant's hair dyed bright orange for TV, 1970's 'Black Skin Blue-Eyed Boys' was an apt chart farewell by the racially mixed Equals, who he left to fend for themselves a few months later. The group then vanished into a cabaret nether-world. For all their mainstream pop unoriginality, Grant's songs for The Equals earned considerable royalties which he invested wisely in a production company, his own Ice record label and a Barbados recording complex (with The Rolling Stones among its clients). In 1979, a dreadlocked Grant resurfaced as a recording artist with the angry 'Living On The Front Line', which reached the UK Top 20. Less volatile lyrics prevailed for three lesser hits, including the title track of 1981's 'Can't Get Enough' album and 1982's catchy 'I Don't Wanna Dance', which trailed Grant's biggest selling album, 'Killer On The Rampage' (on which no other musician played). Its second single, 'Electric Avenue', took Grant into the US Top 10, his first such excursion since The Equals.

A refinement of princicpal elements in Grant's musical past, 1988's 'File Under Rock' ranged from Third World militancy to a tribute to Chuck Berry. Its main single was the rousing anti-apartheid anthem, 'Gimme Hope Jo'anna' (addressed to the Soul African capital of Johannesburg). In his fusion of industry and imagination, Grant may still be making well-received records in old age at a pace that could involve further long periods of vanishing from the public eye.

Greatest Hits

Singles	Title	US	UK
1968	*Baby Come Back* (The Equals)	32	I
1982	*I Don't Wanna Dance*	53	I
1983	*Electric Avenue*	2	2
Albums			
1967	*Unequalled Equals* (The Equals)	–	10
1982	*Killer On The Rampage*	10	7

The GRATEFUL DEAD

Jerry Garcia *(guitar, vocals)*
Bob Weir *(guitar, vocals)*
Ron 'Pig Pen' McKernan *(keyboards)*
Bill Kreutzmann *(drums)*
Phil Lesh *(bass, vocals)*

The 'Dead have their origins in numerous folk bands from south of San Francisco in the early 1960s. By 1965 one such band, Mother McCree's Uptown Jug Champions, had become an electric R&B band, The Warlocks with a line-up of Garcia (born 1942), Weir (born Robert Hall, 1947) McKernan (born 1945), Kreutzmann (born 1946) and Lesh (born Philip Chapman, 1940). Living close was writer turned L.S.D. guru Ken Kesey, who had gathered around

The Grateful Dead – once renowned as the loudest band around with 23 tons of equipment

him a group of like-minded experimenters known as The Merry Pranksters. During the autumn of 1965 the Pranksters began holding wild parties known as the 'Acid Tests', at which The Warlocks, swiftly renamed The Grateful Dead, became the house-band, and linked up with lyricist Robert Hunter and artist Rick Griffin. The free-form nature of these events had a direct influence on the band's lifestyle and possible directions for their music – neither they nor it would be the same again. Hunter was to become Garcia's song-writing partner, while Griffin would regularly contribute cover art. The Dead became local heroes, living in the Haight-Ashbury district. Signing to a major label, much was expected of their eponymous first album (1967), but most people were disappointed by its muddy and unadventurous R&B sound.

Musically the band improved vastly during 1967, as they incorporated more original material into their act and individual numbers began to stretch out. Their second album, 'Anthem Of The Sun' (1968) reflected these changes, and featured two new members, Mickey Hart and Tom Constanten, Hart being added as second drummer and percussion expert, and Constanten (an avant-garde musician) as a new keyboard player, leaving Pig Pen to front the band during their remaining R&B workouts. Despite some

memorable passages, the album's rather messy production and uneasy blending of live and studio material made for disruptive listening. The follow-up 'Aoxomoxoa' (1969), an all-studio effort, was musically dense and lyrically obscure, again making it hard to listen to. With worse sales than their first two albums, it left the band heavily in debt to their record company. To alleviate the situation and in an attempt to release a true representation of the band's sound, they released a double album, 'Live Dead' (1970), culled from live performances earlier that year.

By the time of its release, the Haight-Ashbury scene had fallen apart, its ideas diffused and diluted. Consciously or otherwise The Dead reacted by simplifying their music. Their two 1970 studio albums, 'Workingman's Dead' and 'American Beauty', both US Top 40 albums, are much lower-key affairs, almost acoustic in places, and 1970 saw the departure of Constanten and Hart, the former to resume his previous career, the latter, allegedly because his father, who had been managing the band, had absconded with some of their funds. Mickey Hart rejoined in 1975. This period also witnessed the gradual demise of the gregarious Pig Pen, whose alcoholic intake had begun to affect his health, and he is missing from much of the second live album, 'Grateful Dead' (1971), which again made the US Top 30.

Pig Pen's ill-health led to the recruitment of a new keyboard player, Keith Godchaux, in 1971, joined by his wife Donna (on backing vocals). Pig Pen rejoined in December 1971, in a diminished capacity, staying until 1972, when he left permanently, sadly dying in 1973. Prior to his last performance, he had been part of the band's first tour of Europe, which resulted in the US Top 30 album 'Europe '72', a triple. By this time the band were well outside the rock mainstream, but had gradually built a huge army of dedicated fans, 'The Deadheads'. The band also became increasingly involved in outside activities. Garcia, Lesh and Hart had been in the original New Riders Of The Purple Sage and Weir temporarily joined another local outfit, Kingfish. Both he and Garcia also formed their own bands (Garcia's has continued to function through the years in various forms) and virtually all the band released solo albums. The most musically successful were the debuts recorded by Weir and Garcia ('Ace', and 'Garcia', both 1972). The early 1970s also saw The Dead administration ('The Family') involved in all manner of activities – their own record labels, travel agency, recording studios, etc.

The band's own albums of the period were, by their own standards, mixed. The studio albums 'Wake Of The Flood' (1973) and 'From The Mars Hotel' (1974), both US Top 20, the latter also Top 50 in the UK, have their moments, but 'Steal Your Face', another live album (recorded 1974 but not released until 1976) was disappointing. A period of retirement and reflection (and the rejoining of Mickey Hart) led to the infinitely superior 'Blues For Allah' (1976) which saw a return to a more experimental approach. Subsequent albums continued to be patchy. 'Terrapin Station' (1977) has an interesting if overproduced suite and is generally listenable, whereas 'Shakedown Street' (1978) and 'Go To Heaven' (1980) were widely regarded as low points. Nonetheless, from the late 1970s on, the band became the subject of critical reassessment, if only because it was realized that even if their albums didn't sell, they were one of the biggest grossing live acts in the US and a genuine institituion. Two live double albums released in 1981 the largely acoustic 'Reckoning' and the electric 'Dead Set' sparked some genuine interest in the general rock world. Both of them featured new keyboard player, Brent Mydland, who had replaced both of the Godchauxs in 1979 (Keith Godchaux died in a car accident shortly afterwards).

The increasing attention that the band was receiving in no way prepared anyone, least of all the band, for their hit album 'In The Dark' and hit single 'Touch Of Grey', both of which reached the US Top 10 in 1987. A 1989 album, 'Built To Last', preceded another world tour, which generated yet another live album, 'Without A Net' (1990). Never without their problems, however, the 1990s started on a sad note with the death of Brent Mydland, from a suspected drug overdose. On their European tour in late 1990, his place was taken by Bruce Hornsby (a temporary guest star) and Vince Welnick, the latter joining the band on a permanent basis.

Greatest Hits

Singles	Title	US	UK
1987	Touch Of Grey	9	–
Albums			
1970	Workingman's Dead	27	69
1976	Blues For Allah	12	45
1987	In The Dark	6	57
1989	Built To Last	27	–

Al GREEN

A soul singer in the classic tradition, Green (born 1946) was actually expelled by his father from the family gospel group, The Green Brothers, when he was caught listening to the "profane" music of Jackie Wilson. The family moved from Green's Arkansas birthplace to Grand Rapids, Michigan, where he fronted Al Greene & The Soul Mates, getting a debut US Top 50 hit on their own Hot Line Records with 'Back Up Train' in 1968.

Susequently signed by a trumpet plyer friend, turned producer and vice-president at Hi Records of Memphis, Willie Mitchell, Green had a stab at various ideas before getting a hit. He tried soul ('One Woman'), a cover of The Beatles' hit, 'I Wanna Hold Your Hand', and so on, until a moody version of The Temptations' hit, 'I Can't Get Next To You' made the US Top 100 early in 1971. At the end of the year he cracked the chart in a big way with 'Tired Of Being Alone', his own composition, making the US Top 20 and UK Top 5.

More hits followed with the successful recipe of Mitchell's tight, controlled rhythmic backdrop to Green's understated, deliberately restrained delivery, including the 1971 US chart topper, 'Let's Stay Together', 'I'm Still In Love With You' in 1972, 'Here I Am' (1973) and 1974's 'Sha La La (Make Me Happy)'. His singing, with its Otis Redding texture combined with the soulful dexterity of Sam Cooke, always had a spiritual quality, an introspection, a hidden angst, that was just hinted at but always there.

Around the time 'Sha La La' was climbing into the US Top 10, Green was confronted in his Memphis home by an ex-girlfriend who poured boiling hot grits over him, occasioning second degree burns, before shooting herself. It was the culmination of various personal problems for Green, who after the incident moved closer to religion until, early in 1976, he became the minister of his own

Post punk, neo-hippy, new psychedelic West Coast revivalists, Green On Red

Full Gospel Tabernacle Church, a year after receiving a twelfth gold disc awarded for his 'Al Green Explores Your Mind' album.

Following his church ordination, Green began recording and performing religious material, particularily after a near-fatal fall off stage in 1979. In 1980, 'The Cream of Al Green. The Lord Will Make A Way' was the first of a series of gospel-only albums, followed by 1982's 'Higher Plane' and a short run on Broadway in a gospel musical, *Your Arm's Too Short To Box With God*.

The late 1980s saw a move back to secular circles. Green appeared at the Nelson Mandela Birthday concert in June 1988, and released a duet single with Annie Lennox of Eurythmics, 'Put A Little Love In Your Heart'. And the old Green magic still had them in its spell – a compilation 'Best Of' album made the UK Top 20, while 'Let's Stay Together' was reissued – after being used on a British TV commercial for aftershave!

Greatest Hits

Singles	Title	US	UK
1971	Tired Of Being Alone	11	4
1971	Let's Stay Together	1	7
1972	I'm Still In Love With You	3	35
1972	You Ought To Be With Me	3	–
1988	Put A Little Love In Your Heart	9	28
Albums			
1972	Let's Stay Together	8	–
1972	I'm Still In Love With You	4	–
1973	Call Me	10	–
1975	Greatest Hits	17	18

GREEN ON RED

Dan Stuart (vocals, guitar)
Chris Cacavas (keyboards, vocals)
Jack Waterson (bass, vocals)
Alex McNicol (drums)

On their night, a great live band, but frustratingly inconsistent, Green On Red first came to attention in 1983–4 as part of the so-called 'Paisley Underground', a loose grouping of 60s-influenced bands from the Los Angeles and San Francisco areas, which turned out to be largely the invention of a US rock press desperate to create a new California scene. Originally formed as The Serfers in 1979, the band became Green On Red in 1981, recording their first, eponymous mini-album in 1982. A derivative bunch of songs, it showed a band heavily influenced by The Velvet Underground, as did the subsequent scrappy 'Gravity Talks' (1983).

1985 saw the band's line-up change with the arrival of guitar player, Chuck Prophet IV, who brought a new sound, reminiscent of early Neil Young & Crazy Horse, first show-cased on the excellent 'Gas, Food, Lodging', which garnered critical acclaim on both sides of the Atlantic. Shortly after this, Stuart collaborated on an album of bar band/country material, 'The Lost Weekend' with Dream Syndicate vocalist Steve Wynn as Danny & Dusty.

In 1985 the band released the fine 'No Free Lunch' album, after which drummer McNicol left, replaced by Keith Mitchell. The following year the 'Killer Inside Me' set appeared, but was a major disappointment, featuring only a handful of good songs, and despite some fine live shows, the band split from their label and each other. Keyboard player Cacavas went on (via session work) to produce his own solo album and band, both named 'Junkyard Love' (1989), featuring Mitchell on drums, while the same year Waterson released his own 'Whose Dog Is It Anyway' album.

Stuart and Prophet carried on as Green On Red, recording 'Here Comes The Snakes', hailed as their finest album, in 1988 with a floating line-up. Distribution problems delayed its UK release until 1989, when the band undertook a chaotic European tour, which yielded a surprisingly good live album 'At The Town And Country Club'. Both 'Snakes' and its studio follow-up 'This Time Around' (1989) showed an increasing debt to The Rolling Stones, the latter being produced by veteran hitmaker Glyn Johns (Who, Stones, etc).

Prophet took time off to record his own album, 'Brother Aldo' in 1990, which showed a fondness for a more country sound than might have been expected, subsequently re-uniting with Stuart for a new Green On Red album released in March 1991.

The GUESS WHO

Chad Allan (vocals)
Randy Bachman (guitar, vocals)
Bob Ashley (bass)
Gary Peterson (drums)

From Canada, The Guess Who was a 'garage' band formed in the wake of the British Beat boom in North America. Originally known as Chad Allan & The Silvertones, then The Reflections, then Chad Allan & The Expressions, they finally settled on The Guess Who in 1965.

A US Top 40 cover of Johnny Kidd's 'Shakin' All Over' opened their chart score in 1965 before Allan and Ashley were replaced by Burton Cummings (keyboards, vocals) and first Bruce Decker then Jim Kale (bass). A run of million-sellers began in 1969, mainly written by Bachman (born 1943), with 'These Eyes', 'Laughing' and 'No Time' (plus the platinum album 'Wheatfield Soul') before he too left in the summer of 1970, just as his 'American Woman' topped the US singles chart, to rejoin Allan in Brave Belt.

The name Guess Who became more and more appropriate as various changes of personnel followed, despite Top 40 hits into the mid-1970s that included 'Hand Me Down World', 'Share The Land' and 'Clap for The Wolfman' (with assistance from noted disc jockey, Wolfman Jack). As a solo singer-songwriter, Cummings (born 1947) made the US Top 40 with 'Stand Tall' in 1976 and 'You

Saved My Soul' in 1981. Bachman had planned to work with ex-Nice keyboard player Keith Emerson after leaving Guess Who, but illness prevented the alliance and he brought out a solo album, 'Axe', in 1970, then went on to form Brave Belt with Allan, brother Robbie Bachman (born 1953) on drums, and C.F. Turner (born 1943) on bass. Two albums later, another Bachman brother Tim replaced Allan, and a hard-driving trucker image was encouraged with the name Bachman-Turner Overdrive, (known to unkind critics as Bachman-Turner Overweight, as the group were far from sylph-like).

Their eponymous debut album charted in 1973, and the 'Let It Ride' single made the US Top 30 in 1974. Tim Bachman moved to production, making way for Blair Thornton (born 1950) and subsequent major hits included the 1974 US chart-topper, 'You Ain't Seen Nothin' Yet', a UK Top 5 hit. Subsequent albums included the platinum 'Four Wheel Drive' in 1975, 'Head On' in the same year, and 'Freeway' in 1977.

The roadster imagery couldn't trundle on forever, and Randy Bachman's departure in 1977 heralded the band's demise as BTO. The early 1980s saw Ironhorse as Randy Bachman's new venture, but the change to locomotive power didn't stay on the rails for long; after a US Top 40 album, 'Sweet Lui-Louise', (1979) and a lesser follow-up in 1980, it was full circle to do revival gigs with a reformed Guess Who, followed by a 1984 reunion of Bachman-Turner Overdrive.

Greatest Hits

Singles	Title	US	UK
Guess Who			
1969	*These Eyes*	6	–
1970	*No Time*	5	–
1970	*American Woman*	1	19
Bachman-Turner Overdrive			
1974	*You Ain't Seen Nothing Yet*	1	2
Albums			
Guess Who			
1970	*American Woman*	9	–
Bachman-Turner Overdrive			
1974	*Bachman-Turner Overdrive II*	4	–
1974	*Not Fragile*	1	12
1975	*Four Wheel Drive*	5	–

GUNS N' ROSES

W. Axl Rose (vocals)
Tracii Guns (guitar)
Izzy Stradlin (guitar)
Michael 'Duff' McKagan (bass)
Rob Gardner (drums)

Indiana residents Rose (born William Bailey, 1962) and Stradlin (born Jeff Isabelle, 1967) linked with guitarist Guns (who supplied the other half of the name) and drummer Gardner in LA in 1985. Michael 'Duff' McKagan (born 1965) completed the line-up: he was previously in the unsigned Road Crew, whose British-born guitarist Slash (Saul Hudson, born 1965) and drummer Steven Adler (born 1965) joined when Gardner and Guns declined to tour outside Los Angeles.

Word of mouth gathered a rabid following in 1986, and Geffen Records beat the pack to sign LA's loudest, proudest and dirtiest band. Linking with producer Mike Clink, (engineer for Heart and UFO), their first album, 'Appetite For Destruction', was released in 1987. They showed their anarchic streak by releasing a private pressing 'Live?!*@ Like A Suicide', on their own Uzi Suicide label, combining two original songs and a couple of covers, including Aerosmith's 'Mama Kin'.

The official album courted controversy with a robot rape scene on the cover (which ended up on the inner sleeve): shops banned it, but it sold well, boosted by tours supporting Motley Crue and Iron Maiden. The third single, 'Sweet Child O'Mine' (written for Rose's future wife, Erin Everly), hit the top of the US charts as Rose lost his voice, but the album following suit after nearly a year in the chart.

Thrash shock tactics rendered Guns N'Roses image more apparent than their music

They toured the US with mentors Aerosmith and played at the 1988 Castle Donington Monsters of Rock Festival (marred by two deaths in the crowd). Heavy touring prevented their recording a follow-up, so the original EP was repackaged with bonus tracks and issued as 'G N'R Lies'. This shot to the US Top 5 to join the six million-selling 'Appetite', making the band the first in the 1980s to have two albums in the US Top 5 simultaneously. Even when not on tour, their behaviour courted publicity: Stradlin urinated in an aeroplane and fought Motley Crue's Vince Neil at the 1989 MTV awards. Adler's alleged drug problems saw him replaced by The Cult's Matt Sorum, but late 1990 saw the world still waiting for the second album proper as their cover of Bob Dylan's 'Knockin' On Heaven's Door' appeared on the *Days Of Thunder* soundtrack. They had come a long way on the strength of so few recorded tracks, fast and furious heavy metal and a decidedly punk-influenced attitude.

Greatest Hits

Singles	Title	US	UK
1988	*Sweet Child O' Mine*	1	6
1989	*Patience*	4	10
Albums			
1987	*Appetite For Destruction*	1	5
1988	*G N'R Lies*	2	22

Merle **HAGGARD**

One of the giants of US country music, Merle Haggard (born 1937) is one of a handful of 20th-century performers deserving the accolade, 'living legend'. Unlike many of his contemporaries he has indeed lived most of his songs. In true mythical American style, he was born into a family of Dustbowl farmers who migrated to California where Merle was born in a converted boxcar.

A wild teenager, he was imprisoned in 1957 for armed robbery and served 3 years in San Quentin. During his term, Johnny Cash performed for the inmates and Haggard decided on a career in country music. On his return to his Bakersfield home, he was be-friended by Buck Owens and his wife Bonnie (whom Haggard would eventually marry), making his first recordings in 1962 and enjoying several country chart hits before signing to a major label in 1965.

Between 1965 and 1976, Haggard recorded many bona fide country classics including 24 US country No. 1 hits. His group, The Strangers, are named after his first US Country Top 10 hit, '(My Friends Are Gonna Be) Strangers'. Unlike many country performers Haggard had no pretensions to be an 'all round entertainer', taking his stylistic influences from country music's greatest innovators such as Hank Williams, Lefty Frizzell, Jimmie Rodgers, Buck Owens and folk pioneer Woody Guthrie. Because of this eclectic mix, Haggard was a great influence on the emerging country/rock movement in American music during the late 1960s.

His popularity with college students took an unfortunate turn when his 1969 tongue-in-cheek hit, 'Okie From Muskogee', satirizing left-wing politics and hippies, was taken seriously by right-wing elements. He has remained aloof from social commentary to this day. He changed labels in 1977 and again in 1981.

Haggard's songwriting, so evocative of blue-collar America, and his vocal style, rooted in the true greats of both pre- and post-war country music, have ensured his stature outside the confines of the C&W genre. Although modern country music is steeped in showbusiness glitz and his later recordings have largely consisted of duets with contemporaries such as George Jones and Willie Nelson, he is still a major contender.

Greatest Hits

Singles	Title	US	UK
1969	*Okie From Muskogee*	41	–
1974	*If We Make It Through December*	28	–
Albums			
1970	*Okie From Muskogee*	46	–
1970	*A Tribute To The Best Damn Fiddle Player In The World (Or, My Salute To Bob Wills)*	58	–
1983	*Poncho and Lefty (with Willie Nelson)*	37	–

Bill **HALEY**

Bill Haley was the first real star of the rock'n'roll era, although it may seem odd that a chubby 30-year-old with a ludicrous kiss curl should be the world's signpost to nirvana.

William John Clifton Haley (born 1925), a singer who could yodel and who also played rhythm guitar, was first consumed by country music – an early group he led was known as The Saddlemen. He started recording in 1948, and by 1953 had renamed his group The Comets (intended as a play on Haley's Comet) and turned his back on country music, after which he began to achieve greater success. In 1954 he and The Comets recorded 'Rock Around The Clock', which was a complete failure when first released. The follow-up, 'Shake Rattle & Roll', a cover version of the original by black R&B shouter Joe Turner, was his first big hit, and he had three more small hits before 'Rock Around The Clock' was chosen to be played over the

Introducing black R&B to white teenagers, Haley was as influential as the more youthful Elvis Presley

opening credits of a 'teenage rebellion' movie, *Blackboard Jungle*, starring Glenn Ford as a teacher whose pupils give him a rough ride.

The record's strident back beat, coupled with the reaction to the movie, enabled it to sell several million copies. Seeing kids like themselves rebelling against authority, young Americans were excited by music which their parents apparently loathed. Earlier movies like *The Wild One*, with Marlon Brando as a surly and inarticulate rebel, and James Dean in *Rebel Without A Cause*, his second consecutive role as a moody dreamboat who rejected the values of an older generation, had laid the ground as the Western world finally approached the end of post-war austerity.

Sadly for Haley, he did not resemble Brando or Dean, or even the schoolkids in *Blackboard Jungle*. He had lucked upon something which others were also discovering, but when 'Rock Around The Clock' reached the top of the chart in 1955 (largely due to its being featured in the controversial movie) he was The King. When the film was shown in Britain, over-excited youths smashed up cinemas and the record topped the UK chart as well. Haley and the group capitalized on this popularity by releasing new singles every few weeks, and in 1955 scored nine separate US hits.

The band were hardly teen-fodder either – screaming saxophonist Rudy Pompilli wore studious black-rimmed spectacles, and double bass player Al Rex balanced on top of his instrument or held and played it like a guitar. Guitarist Frannie Beecher was a superb player, but no-one noticed until some years later, and few remember drummer Ralph Jones. Compared to the 20-year-old Elvis Presley, Haley & Co. seemed like a novelty act, which is exactly what they were. Bill Haley was plainly uncomfortable as the spokesman for a younger generation, and the ridiculous haste with which *Don't Knock the Rock*, one of the earliest and least substantial rock'n'roll movies, followed the pioneering *Rock Around The Clock*, the first film of the genre, suggested that Haley was not convinced that this new music was here to stay, and wanted to milk it for as much as possible before the golden goose became egg-bound.

Haley was dethroned by Elvis Presley in early 1956, and overtaken in influence by several others, including the first black rock-'n'roll stars, Chuck Berry and Little Richard. Haley's limited vision involved different priorities – he was an experienced musician, not an upstart who was no different from his audience, and he kept trying. 'See You Later Alligator' was another classic, and even if a rock'n'roll version of 'When The Saints Go Marching In' doesn't sound too appealing, 'Saint's Rock'n'Roll' was memorable in 1956. Haley also cut the first live rock album, 'Rock'n'Roll Stage Show', plus hits like 'Rip It Up', 'Rudy's Rock' and 'Rockin' Through The Rye', but by 1957, when he became the first US rocker to tour Britain, he was halfway to

comparative oblivion.

The rest of his life was spent trying to recapture his crown, but his age and lack of adaptability were against him. When he died in 1981 of a heart attack at the age of 56, he had sold over 50 million records, making him one of the biggest stars of rock music, besides being its first icon, and its earliest pioneer.

Greatest Hits

Singles	Title	US	UK
1955	*Rock Around The Clock*	1	1
1956	*See You Later Alligator*	7	6
1956	*Rockin' Through The Rye*	78	3
Albums			
1956	*Rock Around The Clock*	12	34
1956	*Rock'n'Roll Stage Show*	18	–

Daryl **HALL** and John **OATES**

US white soul/AOR duo formed in 1972 after Hall (born 1949) and Oates (born 1949) linked up in unsuccessful folk-rock Gulliver: a fellow member was singer/

songwriter Tim Moore. Both had histories with minor groups, Philadelphian Hall with the Temptations-inspired Temptones, and New Yorker Oates with The Masters.

After a first album, 1972's 'Whole Oats', they decided to explore a mutual love of soul music, resulting in the classic 'Abandoned Luncheonette' (1973), produced by Arif Mardin and containing the single, 'She's Gone'. A US Top 10 hit as a 1976 reissue, it topped the US R&B chart in 1974 when covered by black vocal group Tavares – a compliment indeed. The combination of Hall's falsetto and Oates' chocolate-brown voice proved a winning blend. 1974's 'War Babies' dissipated the momentum, with producer Todd Rundgren making the album sound like one of his own – however, its theme of urban paranoia was entertaining.

Switching record labels from Atlantic to RCA, they linked with producer Chris Bond to churn out a string of formula white-soul albums, reverting to 'Luncheonette' style. Somewhat cynically/clinically, they used top sessioneers in the studio rather than their road band, and hit the jackpot with a clutch of singles successes including the US Top 10 single, 'Sara Smile', and their first US No. 1,

Hall (left) and Oates – white-eyed soul that crossed over American AOR and R&B audiences

'Rich Girl'.

Albums were less rewarding, and a decision to split from Bond found them overindulgent on albums like 'Beauty On A Backstreet'. 1980's 'Voices' gave them a passport back to the top with a cover of The Righteous Brothers' 'You've Lost That Lovin' Feelin'' – in many ways, they were the Brothers' contemporary counterparts. Paul Young's cover of the album's 'Every Time You Go Away' was a UK Top 5 hit, but Hall & Oates themselves found British hits hard to come by. With more US chart-toppers in 'Kiss On My List' and their finest hour, 'I Can't Go For That (No Can Do)' they could afford not to worry. All the hits appeared on 1984's 'Rock'n'Soul Part 1' compilation.

Impatient to escape the hackneyed hit framework, Hall recorded an adventurous solo album, 'Sacred Songs', in 1976, abetted by King Crimson's Robert Fripp, but RCA delayed its release for four years because it was non-commercial; his second solo album, 'Three Hearts In The Happy Ending Machine' (1986), displayed markedly less radicalism and more guest stars (producer Dave Stewart from The Eurythmics, Joni Mitchell, Bob Geldof, etc.).

1981's 'Private Eyes' saw the recording debut of a souped-up road band featuring Tom 'T-Bone' Wolk and ex-Scratch Band guitarist G.E. Smith, later to tour with Dylan. 'Maneater' was a rare UK Top 10 hit in 1982. A split announced after 1985's 'Big Bam Boom' proved less than permanent, though Hall sang with Elvis Costello on a single, produced Diana Ross and cut his previously mentioned second solo LP.

On their reunion, the duo switched labels for 1988's 'Ooh Yeah', an album that, despite the US hit 'Everything Your Heart Desires', suggested time apart was needed. They reunited for 1990's 'So Close' which added a hard-rock edge (courtesy of producer Jon Bon Jovi) to the soul sheen. Hall and Oates' biggest feat was their acceptance by US blacks, who often put their singles at the top of the R&B chart. 'Live At The Apollo' in 1985 saw them on stage with Eddie Kendricks and David Ruffin of The Temptations – a role reversal unthinkable when Hall had been a Temptone. The two groups' music may compare in sales but hardly in influence.

Greatest Hits

Singles	Title	US	UK
1976	Rich Girl	I	–
1980	Kiss On My List	I	33
1981	Private Eyes	I	32
1981	I Can't Go For That (No Can Do)	I	8
1982	Maneater	I	6
1984	Out Of Touch	I	48
Albums			
1981	Private Eyes	5	8
1982	H_2O	3	24
1984	Big Bam Boom	5	28

Tim HARDIN

Compared to less worthy contemporaries, singer/songwriter/guitarist Hardin (born 1940) enjoyed little personal commercial success but became renowned for other artists' interpretations of his compositions. A descendant of 19th-century bandit John Wesley Hardin, Tim's immediate forebears were musical. Schooled in Oregon, he settled in Massachusetts on discharge from the US Marines in 1961. With a strong reputation in Boston folk clubs, he cut an album the following year which was not released until 1967 when it surprised many later fans by revealing unsuspected roots in jazz and R&B, although Hardin had always tended towards jazzy vocal phrasing in concert.

His style had fully matured in 1966 when, after an acclaimed appearance at the Newport Folk Festival, he was signed to the discriminating Verve label, for whom he cut 'Tim Hardin I' and 'Tim Hardin II', the albums that were the corner-stone of his work. Containing his most covered songs, including 'Lady Came From Baltimore' and 'Black Sheep Boy' (both recorded by Scott Walker), 'Misty Roses' (fetchingly reworked by Colin Blunstone, late of The Zombies), and 'Reason To Believe' which was the flip-side to Rod Stewart's 1971 international chart-topper, 'Maggie May'. However, the best-remembered Hardin opus is 'If I Were A Carpenter', which provided hits for Bobby Darin and The Four Tops (whose version Hardin loathed). This classic was also covered by performers as diverse as The Swinging Blue Jeans, Bob Seger, Leon Russell and Mr & Mrs Johnny Cash, and even provoked an 'answer' disc, 'If You Were A Carpenter'.

Sadly, Hardin never improved upon these two albums, but when he lived in Woodstock and was friendly with Bob Dylan and The Band (see separate entries), he scored his only significant US chart entries, ironically with a Top 50 single of Bobby Darin's 'Simple Song Of Freedom', and the thematic album, 'Suite For Susan Moore and Damion' (his wife and son), subtitled 'We Are One, One, All In One'. He boasted that it was to folk what 'Sergeant Pepper' was to pop, but its content betrayed its packaging, and it suffered unkind reviews for its sections of declaimed poetry.

In the 1970s Hardin moved to Britain to escape business difficulties and try to cure his drug abuse. Accordingly, his output suffered, even if some enjoyed 1971's album of non-originals, 'Bird On A Wire'. 'Painted Head' in 1973 was patchy, but 1974's follow-up album, 'Nine', was a significant improvement, and 'The Homecoming Concert', a live album from an Oregon auditorium, indicated a return to form, but it was also Hardin's epitaph, just preceding his 1980 death in Los Angeles.

Emmylou HARRIS

Since the death of Gram Parsons, who was largely responsible for inventing the country/rock musical genre, Emmylou Harris (born 1947) has released a body of work which is unequallled.

From Birmingham, Alabama, Harris was initially a folk singer, who was known in Greenwich Village circles. In 1970 she cut her debut album, 'Gliding Bird', for a small label, and it included covers of songs by Bob Dylan, Hank Williams and Fred Neil, as well as her own originals and the title track, written by her first husband, Tom Slocum. The album

Emmylou Harris has trawled an American musical heritage much wider than the usual Nashville material

stiffed and her marriage failed, so she moved to Washington DC, where Rick Roberts of The Flying Burrito Brothers heard her sing and recommended her to Parsons, who was looking for a female duet partner. In 1973, she joined Gram Parsons and is featured on the two Parsons studio albums, 'GP' (1973) and 'Grievous Angel' (1974), the latter released after Parsons died in late 1973. With the help of Eddie Tickner, who had managed Parsons and saw huge promise in Harris, she cut 1975's 'Pieces Of The Sky', a superb album on which she was backed by fine session players, who had worked on the Parsons albums (and many of whom were simultaneously in Elvis Presley's backing band). It made the Top 50 of the US album chart and included a minor US hit single, a cover of The Louvin Brothers song, 'If I Could Only Win Your Love'. Her 1976 follow-up album, 'Elite Hotel', made the US Top 30 and went gold, by which time Tickner and Harris had assembled a stellar backing group, The Hot Band, who both toured and recorded with her, and featured guitarist James Burton, ex-Cricket Glen D. Hardin and the previously unknown Rodney Crowell. 1977's 'Luxury Liner' album was a similar success, and in that year she also married Brian Ahern, who had produced the three hit albums.

1978's 'Quarter Moon In A Ten Cent Town' was her third consecutive US Top 30 album, although the same year's 'Profile', a compilation album, was less successful. In 1979 'Blue Kentucky Girl' was closer to country than country/rock, but made the US Top 50, and 'Roses In The Snow' (1980) returned her to the US Top 30, although 'Light Of The Stable', a 1980 Christmas album on which Neil Young, Willie Nelson, Dolly Parton and Linda Ronstadt guested, just failed to reach the US Top 100. Her two 1981 albums, 'Evangeline' and 'Cimarron', were respectively US Top 30 and Top 50 hits, but 1982's live album with a considerably changed Hot Band, 'Last Date', was her least successful regular album since 'Pieces Of The Sky'. 1983's 'White Shoes' was her final album produced by Ahern – their marriage ended around this time.

Remarkably, she became professionally, then romantically, involved with English songwriter Paul Kennerley, whom she met when guesting on the latter's under-appreciated concept album, 'The Legend Of Jesse James'. They wrote and produced 1985's excellent album, 'The Ballad Of Sally Rose' and 1986's similarly impressive 'Thirteen', but in 1987, Harris moved completely towards traditional country music both with the Award-winning double platinum 'Trio' album, on which she shared the billing with Ronstadt and Parton, and the 'live in the studio' bluegrass album, 'Angel Band' (whose title came from that of the band she was leading before meeting Parsons 15 years earlier).

In 1989 'Bluebird' proved that her exquisi-

te musical taste had not deserted her, and 1990 brought two albums: 'Duets', a compilation of older recordings on which she was joined by an array of major names, including The Band (with whom she appeared on their 'Last Waltz' farewell album), Roy Orbison, Willie Nelson, Neil Young, George Jones, Southern Pacific (who had recorded a song entitled 'A Girl Like Emmylou') and many more (but not Bob Dylan, although she did guest on his 1976 album, 'Desire'), and 'Brand New Dance', a new album which was again up to her usual enviably high standards. In 1990 Emmylou Harris occupies a unique position, where she is equally admired by fans of country music of country/rock, with a catalogue of excellence behind her which very few can match.

Greatest Hits

Albums	Title		US	UK
1976	Elite Hotel		25	17
1977	Luxury Liner		21	17
1978	Quarter Moon In A			
	Ten Cent Town		29	40
1980	Roses In The Snow		26	–
1981	Evangeline		22	53
1987	Trio (with Dolly Parton			
	and Linda Ronstadt)		6	60

George **HARRISON**

The record-buying public first became aware of Harrison (born 1943) as one of The Beatles, in which he was very much junior partner to John Lennon and Paul McCartney. Nonetheless, his growth as a songwriter was foremost among pressures that caused the group's disbandment – especially when his 'Something' emerged as one of the most covered songs of all time.

Long before The Beatles officially dissolved, Harrison's solo career had started with an imaginative fusion of psychedelia and Indian music in his 1968 soundtrack to the cult movie, *Wonderwall*. Less well received was 'Electronic Sounds' – little more than exploratory twiddles on a nascent synthesizer.

A more emphatic twitch in the group's death throes was George's inviting Eric Clapton to the session for 'While My Guitar Gently Weeps' from 'The Beatles' (double white) album. In return, Clapton elicited Harrison's help in writing 'Badge' for Cream. When Clapton teamed up with Los Angeles-based Delaney and Bonnie and Friends in 1969, George joined their European tour, where he gained confidence as a slide guitarist. To his abandoned sitar studies, George attributed an intangible quality in his distinctive bottleneck style.

Harrison's two songs on 'Abbey Road' by The Beatles were subjected to wider syndication than those of McCartney and Lennon,

he was well-placed to strike out on his own. 'All Things Must Pass', his 1970 triple album, sold five million world-wide, despite its high retail price and one record in the package being devoted to meandering jams by George and his backing band – which included most of the ubiquitous Friends. Much of 'All Things Must Pass' articulated George's spiritual beliefs, as epitomized by 'My Sweet Lord', its first single. As well as reaching No.1 in many territories, it was regarded as a bona-fide gospel song, although many noted its melodic similarity to the pointedly secular 'He's So Fine', a 1963 hit for the Chiffons.

'All Things Must Pass' was the principal source for George's two New York concerts in August, 1971 to raise funds for the war-torn innocents of Bangladesh. Fronting a big band and introducing many illustrious guest stars, George had his finest hour, even though turgid bureaucracy decimated the cash generated by the Concerts for Bangladesh and the greater amounts accrued by a live album, a film and other by-products, such as George's Material World Charitable Foundation.

Also donated to the Foundation were royalties from the next Harrison album, the self-produced 'Living In The Material World', which was bereft of the gratuitous musical frills that Phil Spector had lent its predecessor. However, it provoked much criticism for its preachy overtones.

These were less pronounced on Harrison's third post-Beatles offering, 'Dark Horse', which chronicled much of his emotional and vocational turbulence. This album was promoted during a troubled 1974 tour of North America. Despite many press organs trashing the shows, concert recordings that have surfaced demonstrate that it was a courageous venture artistically, embracing as it did an Indian orchestra and radical reworkings of Beatles hits and Harrison's solo output.

Out of his depth with mid-1970s stadium rock, George retired to his Henley-on-Thames studio – the most sophisticated private recording complex in the world – to cut 'Extra Texture', a new album that was dismissed by reviewers for its lyrical self-obsession and long, dull melodies. As well as the poor chart showing of most of the acts signed to his new Dark Horse record label, Harrison's reputation as a composer was sullied in 1976 when a New York court found him guilty of 'subconscious plagiarism' over the 'He's So Fine' – 'My Sweet Lord' matter. Fortunately, George was able to home in on humourous aspects of his humiliating episode in 'This Song', the first single from 'Thirty-Three And A Third' – which, if a surface improvement on 'Extra Texture', masked a creative bankruptcy as Harrison rummaged through his stockpile of songs rather than write new material. More telling was 'True Love', the first Harrison cover version to be issued as a single – and a flop into the bargain.

Though he submitted himself to an exten-

George Harrison with occasional musical sparring partners Eric Clapton and Jeff Lynne

Greatest Hits

Singles	Title	US	UK
1970	*My Sweet Lord*	1	1
1973	*Give Me Love (Give Me Peace On Earth)*	1	8
1987	*Get My Mind Set On You*	1	2
Albums			
1970	*All Things Must Pass*	1	4
1973	*Living In The Material World*	1	2

Isaac HAYES

First coming to prominence in the mid-1960s as a songwriter, when he and David Porter penned hits like 'Hold On I'm Coming' for Sam & Dave, Isaac Hayes (born 1942) was to be one of the pivotal soul artists of the early 1970s, blending funky rhythms, symphonic arrangements and sexy monologues into a style which launched a whole black music genre, and was the first inspiration for Barry White, among others. Born in rural Tennessee, Hayes became an amateur musician in Memphis during his teens, and graduated to session work in 1964, moving into writing and production with Porter a year later. His 1968 debut solo album was undistinguished, but the 1969 follow-up was his first seriously considered solo effort, when his label gained a major new distribution deal and wanted to promote it with a mass release of albums. 'Hot Buttered Soul' introduced a formula of extending familiar songs into richly arranged mini-symphonies or settings for lengthy monologues, or 'raps', as Hayes dubbed them.

Its originality proved commercial, sending the album into the US Top 10, where 'The Isaac Hayes Movement' and 'To Be Continued' followed it in 1970. Hayes was invited to score the black detective movie *Shaft*, and in 1971, this brought him his greatest success. The 'Theme From *Shaft*' single was a million-selling chart-topper which won a Grammy Award and an Oscar, while the largely instrumental double soundtrack album also topped the US chart. After this, his music went into decline as he tried to reconcile the larger-than-life image he had attained (part chain-draped sex object and part black Messiah) with developing his style and avoiding self-parody. Albums after '*Shaft*' increasingly failed to tread this fine line, and while 'Black Moses' (1972) and 1973's live set, 'At The Sahara Tahoe', were big sellers, commercial success then began to dwindle. Further demands were also made on Hayes by film and TV producers for more

sive media blitz for 'Thirty-Three And A Third', such a junket was less intense for his eponymous 1979 LP composed largely at his home-from-home on Maui. 'Faster' resulted from George's resumption of a long-dormant interest in motor racing but restrained items such as 'Soft Touch' and 'Dark Sweet Lady' were more typical fare on 'George Harrison'.

Music became less a concern as Harrison became more involved in film work. His procuring the budget needed for the Monty Python team's *Life of Brian* led to 1980's formation by George and business manager Denis O'Brien of Handmade Films, today a pillar of British cinema. Though the sharp-eyed would spot executive producer Harrison in occasional minor tableaux, more pertinent to his calling were soundtrack contributions like 'Only A Dream Away' for *Time Bandits*.

Concerned by increasingly lower sales figures for Harrison albums, Warner Brothers insisted that four tracks on his 'Somewhere In England' be replaced by more up-tempo product. George responded to this brief with tracks that included the cantering hit single 'All Those Years Ago', an encapsulation of thoughts about John Lennon's assassination in 1980. That same year, Lennon had been irked by passages in *I Me Mine*, George's autobiography, written with help from Handmade publicist Derek Taylor.

In 1982 George released what he thought

would be his final album. Apart from an amusing arrangement of The Stereos oldie, 'I Really Love You' – a Merseybeat favourite – 'Gone Troppo' was a refinement of the serene, vaguely Polynesian seam mined on 'George Harrison'.

Seldom seen for most of the 1980s, Harrison found a full life beyond tilting for hit records. Among his diverse occupations were Handmade, gardening and an admirable concern for pressing environmental issues. In 1985 he joined other guest performers on a televised concert starring his old idol Carl Perkins, and via Dave Edmunds, its musical director, he met Jeff Lynne who would co-produce 1987's 'Cloud Nine', George's 'comeback' album which spawned two hit singles, including a US chart-topper.

It was an attempt to tape a European B-side for one of these that brought about The Travelling Wilburys 'supergroup', consisting of Harrison, Lynne, Bob Dylan, Tom Petty and the late Roy Orbison. The four surviving Wilburys reconvened in 1990 to cut the single 'Nobody's Child' – which The Beatles had recorded with Tony Sheridan 19 years earlier – after George's wife, Olivia, requested her husband's aid in the Romanian Angel Appeal, an orphans' charity.

With the Wilburys' debut album, George completed his recording commitments to Warner Brothers, and he may elect to finance

145

Medallion man of funk, Isaac Hayes

Shaft-style soundtrack music, but the theme from *The Men* and the music from *Tough Guys* and *Truck Turner* failed to recapture the magic or the sales.

In the mid-1970s Hayes switched labels and moved towards developing disco styles, but his only huge seller from this period was 'Disco Connection', a UK Top 10 single. By 1977 he was officially declared bankrupt. Returning from the brink, Hayes changed labels again and teamed with Millie Jackson for an album, and regained the upper US chart reaches with the single and album, 'Don't Let Go'. The 1980s found him concentrating more on acting (*Escape From New York* and several TV movies), much of his musical activity being in production work. Another new deal in 1986 indicated a return to active recording, but it has not revived Hayes's commercial profile.

Greatest Hits

Singles	Title	US	UK
1971	*Theme From Shaft*	1	4
Albums			
1969	*Hot Buttered Soul*	8	–
1971	*Shaft*	1	17

HEART

Nancy Wilson *(guitar, vocals)*
Ann Wilson *(vocals)*
Roger Fisher *(guitar)*
Howard Leese *(keyboards, guitar)*
Steve Fossen *(bass)*
Michael Derosier *(drums)*

Among the earliest hard rock bands fronted by females, Heart have retained their popularity throughout two decades of recording and touring.

Strongly influenced by Led Zeppelin, the group was formed in Seattle in 1972 as White Heart by Ann Wilson (born 1951), Fisher and Fossen. Two years later, ex-folk singer Nancy (born 1954) joined the group. Moving north to Vancouver, they signed as Heart to a local label. In 1976, following the US Top 40 single 'Crazy On You', 'Magic Man' reached the US Top 10, and 'Dreamboat Annie', a US Top 10 album, went on to sell 2 million copies.

The group changed labels, recording further US Top 20 albums, 'Little Queen' (1977), 'Magazine' and 'Dog And Butterfly' (both 1978), and 'Bebe Le Strange' (1980), which provided a US Top 10 single with a version of 'Tell It Like It Is', originally a hit for Aaron Neville. Fisher left in 1980, Nancy Wilson and Howard Leese taking over the lead guitar chores. In 1982, Nancy Wilson made her acting debut in the film *Fast Times At Ridgemount High* while personnel changes brought in ex-Spirit bassist Mark Andes and drummer Denny Carmassi from heavy rock band Montrose.

This line-up recorded the US Top 30 album 'Private Audition' (1982) and the less successful 'Passionworks' (1983), and the following year, Ann Wilson had a US Top 10 single when she duetted with Mike Reno (lead singer of Loverboy) on 'Almost Paradise', the love theme from the movie *Footloose*.

Changing labels, Heart entered the most dynamic phase of their career. Both 'Heart', a US No. 1, which also reached the UK Top 20 (1985), and 'Bad Animals' (1987), which reached the Top 5 in the US and Top 10 in the UK, were multi-million sellers and each included a crop of hit singles. The most notable of these was 'Alone', written by Billy Steinberg and Tom Kelly, authors of Madonna's 'Like A Virgin'. It reached No. 1 in the US singles chart and was Heart's first Top 10 hit in Britain.

Another Ann Wilson soundtrack duet, 'Surrender To Me', recorded with Robin Zander of Cheap Trick, preceded 'Brigade' (1990). Produced by Richie Zito, this album included a return to Nancy Wilson's folk roots, with some tracks featuring dobro and harmonica and included another hugely successful single, 'All I Wanna Do (Is Make Love To You)'.

Greatest Hits

Singles	Title	US	UK
1985	*Never*	4	–
1986	*These Dreams*	1	8
1987	*Alone*	1	3
1987	*Who Will You Run To*	7	30
1990	*All I Wanna Do (Is Make Love To You)*	2	8
Albums			
1976	*Dreamboat Annie*	7	36
1977	*Little Queen*	9	34
1985	*Heart*	1	50
1987	*Bad Animals*	5	7
1990	*Brigade*	3	3

Jimi **HENDRIX**

Jimi Hendrix (born Johnny Allen in 1942, renamed James Marshall in 1946) first took up guitar around 1958 and, self-taught, he quickly became one of the most accomplished guitarists in the Seattle area playing chart covers with The Rocking Kings and The Tomcats.

In 1961 he joined the US Army and trained as a parachutist, but unhappy with Army discipline, faked an injury and was discharged in 1962. For the next four years, he was a 'guitar for hire', playing mainly on the R&B/soul package circuit behind the likes of Jackie Wilson and Curtis Mayfield and later with The Isley Brothers and Little Richard. In 1965 he moved to New York, playing with King Curtis, Curtis Knight, Joey Dee & The Starliters and Carl Holmes & The Commanders. In 1966 he formed his own band, The Blue Flames, playing gigs in Greenwich Village which earned the respect and admiration of many fine guitarists, including Mike Bloomfield and John Hammond.

Hendrix was also watched by visiting British musicians, including Chas Chandler of The Animals, who planned to go into production once The Animals finished their farewell US tour in August 1966. Chandler wanted to record the Tim Rose arrangement of a Billy Roberts song, 'Hey Joe'. Together with Animals manager Mike Jeffrey, he persuaded Jimi to come to England.

Once in London, Jimi took the club scene by storm. His good looks and charm captivated the women, his scintillating guitar playing stunned and frightened all the best guitarists – Clapton, Beck and Townshend – and the wild stage act, which he had been developing since he left the Army, thrilled everybody. Following auditions, Jimi teamed up with guitarist Noel Redding, who switched to bass, and ex-Georgie Fame drummer Mitch Mitchell to form The Jimi Hendrix Experience. Chart success was immediate with 'Hey Joe', 'Purple Haze' and 'The Wind Cries Mary' all crashing the UK Top 10 in 1967. The band toured Europe and the UK before headlining the Monterey Pop Festival, and released two UK Top 5 albums 'Are You Experienced' and 'Axis: Bold As Love'. Hendrix's synthesis of citified blues, urban R&B, Dylanesque lyricism and futuristic electronic experimentation with his Fender Stratocaster, make these albums milestones in the history of rock.

Like Cream, the Experience spent much of 1968 in the US where most of the next double album, 'Electric Ladyland', was recorded – another monumental achievement with classic tracks like 'All Along The Watchtower', 'Voodoo Chile' and the gorgeous sound painting of '1983 (A Merman I Should Turn To Be)'. While the album was being recorded, 'Smash Hits' was released to satisfy the demand for Hendrix product.

Were they experienced? Looking back through the purple haze of history, probably not

Behind the scenes, internal wrangling, commercial pressure and Jimi's desire to progress away from autodestruction and guitar pyrotechnics saw the band fold in mid-1969. Only Mitchell remained to play the Woodstock Festival, after which Jimi semi-retired to take stock of his situation. Drugs began to impinge, but after a failed experiment with drummer Buddy Miles and bassist Billy Cox which produced the 'Band of Gypsys' live album, and an abortive attempt by the management to revive The Experience, Hendrix settled with Cox and Mitchell to record some excellent new material in his own New York studio, Electric Lady. Much of this can be heard on the 'Cry of Love' and 'Rainbow Bridge' albums and showed that Hendrix in 1970 was anything but a spent force. During that summer, Hendrix came to Europe for the Isle of Wight Festival and European dates, and it was in London on September 18 that he accidentally took an overdose of barbiturates and died.

Since his death, Hendrix's influence has been all-embracing from Yngwie Malmsteen to Prince, from Patti Smith to Living Colour. Along with Louis Armstrong and Charlie Parker, he must rate as one of the most inspired and accomplished musicians of 20th-century popular music. Sadly, few of his posthumously released albums have lived up to expectations.

Greatest Hits

Singles	Title	US	UK
1967	Hey Joe	–	6
1967	Purple Haze	65	3
1967	The Wind Cries Mary	–	6
1968	All Along The Watchtower	20	5
1970	Voodoo Chile	–	1
Albums			
1967	Are You Experienced	5	2
1968	Axis: Bold As Love	3	5
1968	Smash Hits	6	4
1968	Electric Ladyland	1	6
1970	Band of Gypsys	5	6
1971	Cry of Love	3	2

HERMAN'S HERMITS

Peter 'Herman' Noone (vocals, piano, guitar)
Karl Green (guitar, harmonica)
Keith Hopwood (guitar)
Derek Leckenby (guitar)
Barry Whitwam (drums)

When he met up with The Hermits early in 1964, Peter Noone (born 1947) was a bit-part actor, best known for a role in TV's *Coronation Street*; they were a struggling group called The Heartbeats. The combination clicked, and within months they moved to London from their native Manchester to record with Mickie Most. His choice of Gerry Goffin and Carole King's plaintive 'I'm Into Something Good' was inspired: it shot to the top of the UK charts, sending the toothy Noone on to TV screens for a second time.

The Hermits – Whitwam (born 1946), Hopwood (born 1946), Leckenby (born 1945) and Green (born 1946) – were credited on record, even though session musicians like Jimmy Page and Big Jim Sullivan were employed to back Noone in the studio. The Hermits guitarists co-wrote some of the material, but most came from Tin Pan Alley's professional tunesmiths. Early UK Top 10 hits included 'Silhouettes', Sam Cooke's 'Wonderful World', 'No Milk Today' and 'There's A Kind Of Hush'.

In 1965 they outsold every group in the US bar The Beatles, with six Top 10 hits and sales of nearly 10 million. Americans enjoyed music-hall songs like 'Mrs Brown You've Got A Lovely Daughter' and 'I'm Henry VIII, I Am' both US chart toppers: other cover versions were by quintessentially British songwriters like The Kinks' Ray Davies ('Dandy') and Donovan ('Museum').

The group continued to score UK Top 10 hits – 'Something's Happening' and 'Sunshine Girl' in 1968, 'My Sentimental Friend' in 1969, 'Years May Come Years May Go' in 1970 – becoming Peter Noone and Herman's Hermits thereafter. Noone's solo career started in 1971 with a cover version of David Bowie's 'Oh You Pretty Thing', his only UK Top 20 hit in his own right. It was a daring but unsuccessful attempt to change the innocent image that had brought him such success. He attempted a comeback fronting American popsters The Tremblers in 1980 before taking a role in *The Pirates of Penzance*. Leckenby and Whitwam continued giggling with others as The Hermits.

Greatest Hits

Singles	Title	US	UK
1964	I'm Into Something Good	13	1
1965	Mrs Brown You've Got A Lovely Daughter	1	–
1965	I'm Henry VIII, I Am	1	–
Albums			
1965	Introducing Herman's Hermits	2	–
1965	Herman's Hermits On Tour	2	–

John HIATT

A respected songwriter and performer, Hiatt's compositions have been recorded by artists as diverse as Iggy Pop, The Neville Brothers and Doctor Feelgood. Born in Indianapolis (1952), he played in local rock and R&B band White Duck before moving to Nashville in the early 1970s. There he signed a major label deal, recording the critically acclaimed albums 'Hangin' Around The Observatory' (1974) and 'Overcoats' (1975), produced by top sessionman Glen Spreen.

In the late 1970s, Hiatt played in folk clubs before changing labels for 'Slug Line' (1979) and 'Two Bit Monsters' (1980). Both were produced by Denny Bruce, best known for his work with virtuoso guitarist Leo Kottke. At this point, Hiatt also played in Ry Cooder's band as rhythm guitarist and backing vocalist, appearing on the albums 'Borderline' (1980), 'Slide Area' (1982) and 'The Border' soundtrack (1982). A further label change saw British-based producer Tony Visconti brought in to handle 'All Of A Sudden' (1982). Like Hiatt's previous efforts, this was an artistic success but a commercial failure and on 'Riding With The King' (1983), Ron Nagle and British singer/producer Nick Lowe took producer credits, producing one side each.

After recording 'Warming Up To The Ice Age' (1985) Hiatt changed labels again, releasing the impeccable 'Bring The Family' album (1987) on which he was backed by Cooder, Lowe and top session drummer Jim Keltner. By now Hiatt was enjoying considerable success with cover versions of his material, as Dylan recorded 'The Usual' for the film *Hearts of Fire* and Roseanne Cash had a major country hit with the tearful 'The Way We Make A Broken Heart'. A new partnership with producer Glyn Johns saw 'Slow Turning' (1988), recorded with his own band, The Goners, and the same team worked on 'Stolen Moments' (1990). Hiatt also guested on The Nitty Gritty Dirt Band's 1989 album 'Will The Circle Be Unbroken Volume 2'.

Chris **HILLMAN**

An artist whose career has spanned four decades, Chris Hillman (born 1942) has often remained a lieutenant (rather than a general) until his current highly successful venture leading The Desert Rose Band.

A child prodigy, Hillman's brilliance as a teenage mandolin player led to obscure albums with bluegrass groups The Scottsville Squirrel Barkers and The Golden State Boys, who were renamed The Hillmen after their young star for the 1962 album he made with them. In 1964 he was invited to join The Jet Set, who became The Byrds (see separate entry) as bass player in 1965, and remained with them for their first six original albums (which included most of the group's best-known hits). After the ground-breaking 'Sweetheart Of The Rodeo' album (recorded in Nashville, the home of country music), Hillman and fellow-Byrd Gram Parsons formed the pioneering Flying Burrito Brothers (see separate entry) in 1969. Hillman was co-leader of the first line-up with

Parsons before the latter's death, and continued until the original band folded around 1972, when he was invited to join Manassas, the group launched by Stephen Stills (see separate entry). After two excellent albums, Manassas split up, whereupon Hillman participated in the eponymous reunion album by The Byrds in 1973.

He then joined the manufactured Souther Hillman Furay Band with singer/songwriter J.D. Souther and ex-Poco founder Richie Furay. Unfortunately, the two albums by this combo, 1974's eponymous debut and 1975's 'Trouble In Paradise', promised more than they delivered, apparently because its principals had too little in common for the concept to work, and Hillman then produced two disappointing solo albums, 1976's 'Slippin' Away' and 1977's 'Clear Sailing', before teaming up with fellow original Byrds, Roger McGuinn and Gene Clark, for two albums, 1979's 'McGuinn, Clark & Hillman' and 1980's 'City'. At this point, Clark left the trio, and McGuinn & Hillman cut what appeared to be an eponymous 'contractual obligation' album in 1980. Unable to interest major labels in signing him, Hillman returned to his bluegrass roots, recording for a well-regarded specialist label for whom he made two superb albums, 1982's 'Morning Sky' and 1984's 'Desert Rose', helped by friends like erstwhile Eagle Bernie Leadon, session stars James Burton and Glen D. Hardin and harmony vocalist supreme Herb Pedersen (ex-Dillards) plus SHF band colleague/pedal steel player Al Perkins and bass player Bill Bryson (ex-Bluegrass Cardinals).

By 1987 Hillman had launched The Desert Rose Band, singing and playing guitar and mandolin himself, with Pedersen (vocals,

guitar, banjo), bass player Bryson, the remarkable John Jorgensen (lead guitar, vocals), plus country music pedal steel star J.D. Maness and noted country drummer Steve Duncan. The group's 1987 eponymous debut, 1988's 'Running' and 1990's 'Pages Of Life' were all highly successful albums in terms of the US country chart, each spawning several country hit singles, and 1991 will see the release of a 'Greatest Hits' album by the band. In late 1990, Hillman, Roger McGuinn and David Crosby again recorded together as The Byrds, both for a Roy Orbison tribute and also to cut four new tracks for inclusion in a 4-CD boxed set of Byrds material. After many adventures and dozens of albums (many of them highly successful), Hillman must be termed one of the great survivors of the 1960s, who is equally successful (albeit in a slightly different musical field) in the 1990s. Hillman at his best should be heard on Byrds, Flying Burrito Brothers, Manassas, later solo and Desert Rose Band albums.

The **HOLLIES**

Allan Clarke (lead vocals)
Graham Nash (vocals, guitar)
Victor Jones (guitar)
Eric Haydock (bass)
Don Rathbone (drums)

Second to The Beatles, The Hollies survived Merseybeat's collapse as the most distinguished Lancashire group, but despite their lingering hip sensibility, it was a combination of nostalgia and a British TV ad for

The Hollies (l to r) Nash, Elliott, Clarke, Hicks and Haydock

an American light beer that sent their 20-year-old hit, 'He Ain't Heavy (He's My Brother)', up the UK charts in 1988.

Nash and Clarke (both born 1942) first sang together at primary school functions, and in 1959, won a Manchester talent contest. Seduced by the dynamic versatility of larger outfits, they formed The Deltas in 1961 with Haydock, Rathbone and Jones, but at Christmas 1962, they were jokingly introduced as The Hollies. Shortly after Jones had been replaced by Tony Hicks (born 1943) from another Lancashire instrumental quartet, The Dolphins, The Hollies (dubbed 'Manchester's Beatles' in *Merseybeat*) were spotted by EMI talent scout Ron Richards, who produced their first single, 1963's 'Just Like Me', a UK Top 30 hit. Rathbone's resignation necessitated the hiring of another Dolphin, Bobby Elliott (born 1942) for the next single, 'Searchin'', a second Coasters cover in the repertoire of myriad other groups, which almost made the UK Top 10. The group's third single, a cover of 'Stay' by Maurice Williams & The Zodiacs, achieved that status.

When their 1964 arrangement of Doris Troy's 'Just One Look' went even higher, The Hollies' sound was established. Enhanced by the guitar work of the under-rated Hicks, this hinged on severe vocal harmonies ranging from Hicks's baritone to Nash's soaring counter tenor with Clarke's edgy drawl usually carrying the melody. These idiosyncracies were applied to many more chartbusters including 1965's chart-topping 'I'm Alive' and, a year later, the breathtaking 'I Can't Let Go', which served to obscure memories of a much-criticized cover of George Harrison's 'If I Needed Someone' (which George himself didn't like), and a personnel change when Bernard Calvert (yet another Dolphin) supplanted Haydock, who briefly led the ill-fated Haydock's Rockhouse.

The group's US breakthrough came when 'Look Through Any Window' was a 1965 Top 40 hit, but they would always be guaranteed a fair hearing in the US after their 1966 Top 5 hit, 'Bus Stop'. Under the pseudonym 'L. Ransford', Clarke, Hicks and Nash's own 'Stop Stop Stop', plus the accolade of their songs being recorded by The Everly Brothers provoked Nash's insistence that all future Hollies A-sides would be originals. The artistic extremes of the new policy were contrasted in the adventurous 'King Midas In Reverse' and its bigger selling follow-up, the twee 'Jennifer Eccles'.

This attitude also pervaded the album lists where challenging efforts like 'For Certain Because' and 1967's 'Evolution' could not match sales of earlier Merseybeat-styled collections. 'Greatest Hits' packages, and 1969's 'Hollies Sing Dylan', were among the factors which caused Nash's exit to the Crosby, Stills & Nash 'supergroup' and his replacement by Terry Sylvester from The Swinging Blue Jeans.

Although obliged once more to look to outside writers for hit records, the group were able to continue delivering hits, if less frequently. The quality of their own originals became erratic, although Clarke's unexpected and pulsating 'Long Cool Woman In A Black Dress' was a deserved 1972 hit, signalling the end of his unhappy sojourn as a solo artist. When the group's recording contract expired the previous year, he had seized the opportunity to make a solo album, 'My Real Name Is 'Arold'. Elliott and Hicks particularly disapproved, and he was fired when they invited Mikael Rickfors from Sweden's Bamboo to front the group for a minor hit single, 'The Baby', and 1972's 'Romany', an album on which songs by Hicks and his Oxfordshire neighbour, Kenny Lynch, were unveiled. With 'Romany' eliciting as lukewarm a public reaction as Clarke's second solo venture, 'Headroom', the prodigal returned, although there would be further Clarke solo releases, including 1981's 'Best Of Allan Clarke' collection and a more recent album released exclusively in Germany.

During the mid-1970s, the group returned to the UK Top 3 and US Top 10 with a fine version of Albert Hammond's 'The Air That I Breathe', after which they took the recommendation of Clarke, who had recorded a few Bruce Springsteen items, and scraped into the US Top 100 with Springsteen's 'Sandy'. In the early 1980s, they charted in the UK with Mike Batt's blood-and-thunder 'Soldier's Song' and made the Top 30 with the hits medley, 'Holliedaze', for which Nash joined Clarke, Hicks and Elliott for the required TV promotion.

Nash stayed on to record a 1983 US Top 30 revival of The Supremes hit, 'Stop In The Name Of Love', and the 'What Goes Round' album with his old group. The 'He Ain't Heavy' windfall would be mimed on TV by Hicks, Elliott and Clarke plus the four jobbing musicians they'd engaged for 1988's sold-out world tour. While currently resting on past laurels, the presence in their ranks of proficient songwriters suggests that The Hollies may be capable of more unexpected strokes.

Greatest Hits

Singles	Title	US	UK
1965	*I'm Alive*	–	1
1966	*Stop Stop Stop*	7	2
1969	*He Ain't Heavy, He's My Brother*	7	3
1972	*Long Cool Woman In A Black Dress*	2	32
1988	*He Ain't Heavy, He's My Brother* (reissue)	–	1
Albums			
1964	*Stay With The Hollies*	–	2
1968	*Greatest Hits*	11	1
1969	*Hollies Sing Dylan*	–	3
1978	*20 Golden Greats*	–	2

Buddy HOLLY and The CRICKETS

Buddy Holly (born Charles Hardin Holley, 1936) was ahead of his time. From west Texas, his early influences were Country and Western (his earliest recordings were as a C&W duo with high school friend Bob Montgomery) but he was profoundly influenced by seeing an early Elvis Presley gig. As well as playing with Montgomery, Holly also

Tougher (and louder!) live than the college-kid image suggested, Buddy Holly and The Crickets

worked in a duo with drummer Jerry Allison – and the interplay between Holly's guitar and the drums later became a distinctive part of Holly's sound, even when other instruments were added.

As a result of exposure created by working with Montgomery, Holly cut several unsuccessful sides in Nashville in 1956, including an early version of the classic, 'That'll Be The Day'. Backing him on some of the sessions were Allison, guitarist Sonny Curtis and bassist Don Guess, known at the time as The Three Tunes.

Returning to Texas, Allison and Holly – along with bassist Larry Welborn – became The Crickets. Holly's major breakthrough came after the band started recording at Norman Petty's studio in Clovis, New Mexico in 1957. The trio cut a new version of 'That'll Be The Day', which reached the US Top 3, and, topped the UK chart. By the end of 1957, the group had notched up two more massive hits, 'Oh Boy' (b/w 'Not Fade Away') and 'Peggy Sue' (b/w 'Every Day'). The latter, despite being the same musicians, was the first under Holly's name rather than the group's. Although these were 'group' records, the major talent was obviously Holly's – the distinctive vocal (with the much imitated catch), the intelligent lyrics and the memorable tunes – but a vital contribution was made by Petty, who pioneered techniques with Holly like double-tracking vocals and overdubbing. He also worked as Holly's manager and took co-writing credit on several songs.

1958 was Holly's big year, when the band toured Europe and Australia and had further hits, including 'Rave On'. By the end of that year, in terms of record sales, he was far more popular in the UK than the US. Also in 1958, Holly moved to New York, causing a split with The Crickets. The move changed his outlook and was reflected in a desire to broaden his music and – arguably – to try completely new ideas. The results included a move towards recording ballads like 'It Doesn't Matter Anymore' (a Paul Anka song) with a large orchestra. What he would have done subsequently is speculation, since Holly died in the infamous plane crash in Iowa on February 3, 1959, which also claimed the lives of Ritchie Valens and The Big Bopper.

What he might have done is irrelevant; what is incontestable is that Holly left a body of work as fine as any other from that era and his influence on other musicians (especially English ones – The Beatles, The Hollies *et al.*) has been remarkable, and a list of cover versions of Holly's songs would fill a small book. If nothing else, Holly proved that you could wear glasses and *still* be a rocker.

Having already split from Holly, The Crickets (by that time Allison plus bassist Joe Mauldin) missed the fatal air-crash. Back in Texas they had regrouped with Sonny Curtis on guitar and continued to record with little success. In pre-Beatle era, they charted in the UK with Goffin and King's 'Please Don't

Ever Change', and also toured and recorded with Bobby Vee, before breaking up in the mid-1960s. A re-formation in the early 1970s succeeded thanks to a combination of nostalgia and the rise of 'country-rock'. Since then, further break-ups and line-up changes have taken place (at one point in the early 1970s, famed English musicians Ric Grech and Albert Lee were in the band) and a late 1980s album, 'T Shirt', proved a testament to their longevity and popularity, which has been assisted by the efforts of Paul McCartney, who purchased the rights to Holly's catalogue of classic songs.

Greatest Hits

Singles	Title	US	UK
1957	That'll Be The Day (Crickets)	3	1
1957	Oh Boy (Crickets)	10	3
1957	Peggy Sue (Buddy Holly)	3	6
1958	Rave On (Buddy Holly)	37	5
1959	It Doesn't Matter Anymore		
	(Buddy Holly)	13	1
Albums			
1959	The Buddy Holly Story	11	2
1962	Bobby Vee Meets The Crickets	42	2
1978	20 Golden Greats	55	1

John Lee **HOOKER**

The venerable Hooker (born 1917) continues to mature as a working musician and add to a recorded output that has been growing since 1948 when his career took off with the million-selling 'Boogie Chillun'. His

credentials as a bluesman are impeccable: an upbringing in Clarksville, Mississippi (rural birthplace of the legendary Robert Johnson), adolescence in Memphis, migration north, purchase of an electric guitar and discovery by a record company talent scout during a club residency in a Detroit suburb.

After the unadorned 'Boogie Chillun' topped the 'sepia' charts, Hooker made his US TV debut in 1949 as further specialist hits such as 'Driftin' ', 'Hobo Blues' and a re-make of his first single, 'I'm In The Mood', as well as a lengthy stint as a disc-jockey and a host of pseudonymous recordings established him as a major blues exponent. As such, he was recognized by British bandleader Chris Barber who underwrote UK tours by Hooker and other black bluesmen who found favour with white bohemia. During his UK visits in the early 1960s, he was often backed by one of myriad native R&B outfits he had inspired. Among these was The Spencer Davis Group, whose 1963 single, Hooker's leering 'Dimples', was eclipsed when the original was issued (as a taster for a compilation album) and made the UK Top 30. In versions of 'Boom Boom', 'I'm Mad Again' and other examples of Hooker's gutbucket hollering and eccentric rhythmic shifts, The Animals, Yardbirds, Them and other groups also paid their respects.

In the late 1960s Hooker's music sounded even more urbanized with horn sections and female choruses. In 1971 a double album collaboration with a reverential Canned Heat, 'Hooker'n'Heat', reprised 'Boogie Chillun' etc. specifically for the white rock market and reached the US Top 100. This red-letter year also saw arrangements of Hooker's composi-

John Lee Hooker – hero to hundreds of blues players

tions by The Doors ('Crawling King Snake'), Sam the Sham ('Goin' Upstairs') and the J. Geils Band ('Serves You Right To Suffer').

Though advancing years diminished his activities, Hooker was remembered during the next two decades with covers by The Allman Brothers Band (1974's 'Dimples') and George Thorogood & The Destroyers (1986's 'One Bourbon, One Scotch, One Beer'). In 1989 Hooker enjoyed critical acclaim and made the UK chart with 'The Healer', an album on which the accompanying cast included Robert Cray, George Thorogood and, for a Grammy-winning duet of 'I'm In The Mood', Bonnie Raitt. More recently, he has been seen both on stage and in the studio with Van Morrison, another famous lifelong fan.

Greatest Hits

Singles	Title	US	UK
1962	Boom Boom	60	–
1964	Dimples	–	23
Albums			
1971	Hooker'n'Heat (with Canned Heat)	73	–
1989	The Healer	62	63

Bruce HORNSBY

A keyboard-playing singer/songwriter from Virginia, Bruce Hornsby (born 1954) attended the Berklee School of Music before working as a contract songwriter for a Hollywood song factory, where he achieved minimal success. He then decided to try his luck on his own, performing original songs he had written with his brother John, a lawyer. After some time working in Sheena Easton's backing group, in 1984 he formed a band, The Range, which included David Mansfield (ex-Bob Dylan, etc), George Marinelli (guitar), Joe Puerta (bass) and John Molo (drums), and signed with a major label. His debut album, 'The Way It Is', was partly produced by Huey Lewis, who in 1987 topped the US chart with a Hornsby song, 'Jacob's Ladder', although by then, Hornsby was already famous on his own account, as 'The Way It Is' sold over two million copies. The title track topped the US singles chart, another single, 'Mandolin Rain', made the US Top 5, and the group won a Grammy as Best New Artists of 1986, although interestingly, the single first took off in the UK, where Hornsby's jazz-influenced piano style made an instant impression – he claims to have been strongly influenced by Keith Jarrett.

After extensive international touring, 1988 saw the release of a second album, 'Scenes From The Southside', which included Hornsby's own version of 'Jacob's Ladder', but the lyrical accessibility of the debut album seemed curiously absent, although it included

Hornsby – home in the Range?

a US Top 5 single, 'The Valley Road', while Mansfield had been replaced by Peter Harris. Nevertheless, Hornsby was one of numerous guest stars on 'Will The Circle Be Unbroken Volume Two', the Grammy Award winning 1989 album by The Nitty Gritty Dirt Band, who backed Hornsby on a new version of 'The Valley Road'. By 1990's 'A Night On The Town' album, The Range had become a quartet after Harris departed, and at the end of that year, Hornsby toured as guest keyboard player with The Grateful Dead after the death of the latter's Brent Mydland.

Hornsby is one of the more intriguing new talents of the 1980s, and it is strongly to be hoped that he is able to recapture the early brilliance of his superior songwriting.

Greatest Hits

Singles	Title	US	UK
1986	The Way It Is	1	15
1987	Mandolin Rain	4	70
1988	The Valley Road	5	44
Albums			
1986	The Way It Is	3	16

Whitney HOUSTON

From New Jersey, Whitney Houston (born 1963) is the daughter of soul/gospel singer Emily 'Cissy' Houston and cousin of Dionne Warwick. Singing in a gospel choir as a child, when she sometimes toured with her mother (who often worked with Elvis Presley and Aretha Franklin), Whitney was a successful fashion model and sang backing vocals for acts like Lou Rawls and Chaka Khan before recording duets with Teddy Pendergrass (their single 'Hold Me' just missed the US Top 40) and Jermaine Jackson. In 1985 her debut solo single, 'You Give Good Love', was a US Top 3 hit (its 'B' side, 'Greatest Love Of All' later topped the US chart) and she then had seven consecutive US chart-toppers, breaking the record held jointly by The Beatles and The Bee Gees. Her eponymous debut album topped the US album chart for 14 weeks and has sold over 13.5 million

Whitney Houston, one of the most successful female artists of the 'Eighties

world-wide, making it the biggest selling album ever by a female and the top-selling debut album ever.

In 1987 her 'Whitney' album was a transatlantic No. 1 in its first week – the first time a female had accomplished this in the US, where it topped the chart for 11 weeks and sold over 12 million. In the UK, she became the first female to sell a million with her first two albums and the first black woman to top the album chart.

This soulful pop superstar won Grammy Awards for 'Saving All My Love For You' and 'I Wanna Dance With Somebody' and was chosen to sing America's Olympic anthem, 'One Moment In Time', in 1988. In 1990 her third album, 'I'm Your Baby Tonight', continued her phenomenal success on both sides of the Atlantic.

Greatest Hits

Singles	Title	US	UK
1985	*Saving All My Love For You*	I	I
1986	*How Will I Know*	I	5
1986	*The Greatest Love Of All*	I	8
1987	*I Wanna Dance With Somebody*	I	I
1987	*Didn't We Almost Have It All*	I	4
1988	*So Emotional*	I	5
1988	*Where Do Broken Hearts Go*	I	14
1988	*One Moment In Time*	5	I
Albums			
1985	*Whitney Houston*	I	2
1987	*Whitney*	I	I

HOWLIN' WOLF

With his earthy lyrics and guttural bass-baritone, Wolf (real name, Chester Burnett 1910–76) was a major icon during the 1960s resurgence of interest in the blues. His principal influence during a Mississippi delta boyhood was his brother-in-law, Sonny Boy Williamson II, who taught Wolf to play harmonica, and singer-guitarist Charlie Patton. Apart from a term in the US army, Wolf worked on a cotton farm, performing only at weekends, but became a full-time musician on moving to Arkansas in 1948, backed by one of the first electric blues bands in the Deep South, whose personnel included guitarist Willie Johnson and Junior Parker on harmonica. In the early 1950s, Wolf worked as a disc-jockey in Memphis, and was spotted by Ike Turner, then a freelance talent scout, at a club booking with his group. This led to his first record deal, but the tracks he cut at Sam Phillips's Sun studio were more crucial, as they were then sold to Chess in Chicago where Wolf migrated in 1952.

Though the Windy City left an indelible mark on his style, Wolf did not abandon his rural roots as he entered the most commercially fruitful part of his career. Composed either by himself (under his real name) or bass

player Willie Dixon and lacquered with Hubert Sumlin's terse lead guitar, many of the singles he released up to 1964 would surface as set works for white artists as varied as The Rolling Stones (who took his 'Little Red Rooster' to the top of the UK singles chart), The Doors (who covered 'Back Door Man'), Love Sculpture ('Wang Dang Doodle') and Electric Flag ('Killing Floor').

After visiting England in the early 1960s as part of an American Folk-Blues Festival package, he was fêted by middle-class R&B fans for a stage act of sweaty intensity and sexual braggadocio. A re-issue of his 1956 single, 'Smokestack Lightning' even made the lower reaches of the UK chart in 1964, and also penetrated the repertoires of The Yardbirds and Manfred Mann, while 'Sitting On Top Of The World', 'I Ain't Superstitious' and other Wolf items were interpreted by UK acts like The Jeff Beck Group, Cream, Led Zeppelin, Ten Years After and Savoy Brown.

Like other celebrated elderly bluesmen, Wolf was advised to aim more directly at the rock market by working with some of the eminent white players he had inspired, but was disappointed with the first venture in this vein, 1969's 'The Howlin' Wolf Album', although 1971's 'London Sessions', with the likes of Bill Wyman, Steve Winwood, Charlie Watts and Eric Clapton, which was issued on The Rolling Stones' own label, was more than satisfactory as Wolf growled reprises of many classics his helpmates had popularized. Numerous compilation albums of his work are available, but potential emptors are advised to caveat before purchase.

INXS

Michael Hutchence *(vocals)*
Tim Farriss *(guitar)*
Andy Farriss *(keyboards)*
Jon Farriss *(drums, vocals)*
Gary Beers *(bass, vocals)*
Kirk Pengilly *(guitar, sax, vocals)*

Formed in 1977 in Sydney, Australia, as the Farriss Brothers, this top rock act's personnel has remained unchanged.

In 1980 they released their first single 'Simple Simon', and their first local hit was 'Just Keep Walking' from their eponymous debut LP. Their second album, 'Underneath The Colours', went gold in Australia in 1981, and in 1983 their debut US Top 40 single was 'The One Thing', and their 'Shabooh Shoobah' album was also a hit. Their 1984 album, 'The Swing', and its first single,

'Original Sin', in which Nile Rodgers and Dave Stewart were involved, kept them in the US charts. Their excellent stage show was seen world-wide in Live Aid which helped their 'Listen Like Thieves' album and 'What You Need' single into the UK charts and the US Top 20, with the former going platinum.

After a successful world tour in 1987, their 1988 album, 'Kick', was a transatlantic Top 10 hit selling four million in the US and a million in the UK. Four US Top 10 singles came from the album, including 'New Sensation' and 'Never Tear Us Apart' and the US chart-topping 'Need You Tonight', which reached the UK Top 3.

Charismatic Hutchence, who as a child recorded 'Jingle Bells' for a 'talking doll' company, was voted the hunkiest pop star in the US, which no doubt helped INXS win five MTV awards in 1988. In 1989 members of the group worked on outside projects with Hutchence recording as half of Max Q. In 1990, their seventh album, 'X', gave them another major transatlantic hit.

Greatest Hits

Singles	Title	US	UK
1988	*Need You Tonight*	I	2
1988	*Devil Inside*	2	47
Albums			
1987	*Kick*	3	9
1990	*X*	5	2

IRON MAIDEN

Dave Murray *(guitar)*
Paul Di'Anno *(vocals)*
Steve Harris *(bass)*
Doug Sampson *(drums)*

A heavy-metal band who have become almost a parody of the genre, Iron Maiden were formed in London in 1976 by bass player Harris (born 1957). In the face of punk, and the fact that established HM bands were already on the stadium circuit, Iron Maiden led the so-called 'New Wave of British Heavy Metal', a move to fill the gap at street level.

Guitarist Murray (born 1958) came from South London band Urchin, and with Harris, Di'Anno (born 1959) and Sampson completing the line-up, the band built a solid grass-roots following. An indie EP consisting of demos sold heavily at gigs and indie shops, while a mail order EP and tracks on a compilation album preceded a major label deal. A change of drummer to Clive Burr (born 1957), ex-Samson, and the addition of guitarist Dennis Stratton (born 1954) heralded the album 'Iron Maiden' (1980), which included the anthemic title track. The album's artwork, if not its music, set them apart, introducing 'Eddie' the band's homi-

Maiden – their '91 'Send Your Daughter' single caused uproar over title, video, lyrics – the lot

Rudolph Isley
Ronald Isley
O'Kelly Isley
Original line-up 1969–85 as above plus
Ernie Isley
Marvin Isley
Chris Jasper and Everett Collins *(vocal group)*

One of the most important and influential black recording acts of all time, variations of The Isleys' line-ups are still scoring hits into the 1990s having enjoyed major hits in every decade since the 1950s.

Formed as a family gospel act in their hometown of Cincinnati, they turned to secular music at the encouragement of their mother, moving to New York in 1957. After initially recording for small New York-based companies in a neo-doowop style they were signed to a major label, releasing 'Shout Parts 1 and 2', structured on their live performance improvisation of Jackie Wilson's hit 'Lonely Teardrops'. It sold a million copies without making much impression on the charts, and despite originating another future rock classic, 'Respectable', the Brothers changed labels.

They were produced, without success, by Leiber & Stoller, and another label change, in 1961, saw them under the production guidance of Bert Berns, who recycled a song originally recorded by The Topnotes, 'Twist And Shout'. Despite its modest chart performance, the song was again recycled a year later (1962) by The Beatles, thereby elevating The Isleys overnight to almost legendary status (other British beat groups interpreted songs like 'Respectable' and 'Shout' *ad infinitum*).

Although their reputation as live performers was well-established, recording success was more erratic. They changed labels twice more and appeared as guests on several Motown revue shows before Berry Gordy signed them to Motown in 1965. There, the Holland/Dozier/Holland team produced their first big hits, including 'This Old Heart Of Mine', 'I Guess I'll Always Love You' and 'Behind A Painted Smile'.

Bothered by the constrictions of the Motown 'production line', they left the label in 1969, recruiting younger brothers Marvin and Ernie, a guitarist hugely influenced by Jimi Hendrix (who had, for a time, been a member of The Isleys's band), along with cousin Chris Jasper, to become The Isley Brothers – 3+3, and began an almost 20-year run of hit records on their own label, T-Neck. Tasking their own unrestrained vocals, Ernie's rock guitar and the sparse rhythm tracks introduced by James Brown, the Brothers neatly defined black rock, and enjoyed a string of huge dance hits between 1969 and 1971.

Noting the emergence of singer/songwriters and the easy access found by certain soul stars to the album charts, The

cidal zombie mascot, who would appear on all future covers. A tour support spot with Judas Priest helped the album into the UK Top 5. Another ex-Urchin, Adrian Smith, replaced Stratton late in 1980, and the band released a half-live, half-studio set, 'Killers'. Soon after this they made their first US tour, again opening for Judas Priest.

The most successful period yet for the band saw ex-Samson vocalist Bruce Dickinson (born 1958) replacing Di'Anno in 1981, the single 'Run For The Hills' making the UK Top 10, with the album 'Number of the Beast' topping the LP chart. It also went gold in America. Burr left in 1983, replaced by ex-Streetwalkers drummer 'Nicko' McBain (born 1954), and the band scored UK chart singles with 'Flight of Icarus' and 'The Trooper', while the album 'Piece of Mind' made the UK Top 5, and went platinum in the US.

More successful albums followed as the band's image moved from punk-HM to archetypal sword-and-sorcery – enhanced by a huge 'Eddie' lurching about the concert stage. The next three albums, 'Powerslave' (1984), 'Live After Death' (1985), and 'Somewhere In Time' (1986), all made the UK Top 3, while in the US they reached the Top 20.

Their biggest UK seller came in 1988 with the No. 1 album 'Seventh Son Of A Seventh Son', which again went Top 20 in the US, and the single 'Can I Play With Madness' (UK Top 5) reinforced their supremacy in the UK heavy metal stakes.

In 1990, Smith left to concentrate on a solo career with his band 'Adrian Smith And Project (ASAP)', replaced by Janick Gers (ex-White Spirit), who had played with Dickinson on his own successful solo album, 'Tattooed Millionaire', also in 1990.

Greatest Hits

Singles	Title	US	UK
1982	Run To The Hills	–	7
1988	Can I Play With Madness	–	3
1988	The Evil That Men Do	–	5
1991	Send Your Daughter To The Slaughter	–	1
Albums			
1982	The Number of the Beast	33	1
1984	Powerslave	21	2
1985	Live After Death	19	2
1986	Somewhere In Time	11	3
1988	Seventh Son of a Seventh Son	12	1

Isleys recorded 'Giving It Back' (1971), a typically ironic title for an album which parodied white rock's habitual practice of purloining R&B standards for its own consumption and contained covers of many contemporary rock hits from Stephen Stills's 'Love The One You're With' to Bob Dylan's 'Lay Lady Lay'.

Dissatisfied with sales, and anxious to crack the more lucrative rock album market, they switched distribution of 'T-Neck' in 1973, leading to an unprecedented explosion of international success, fuelled by the hit singles, 'Who's That Lady' and 'Summer Breeze' (written by Seals and Croft). Subsequent albums were wholly self-composed and produced, displaying a remarkable talent for mixing ethereal ballads with hard rock and funk workouts, many with less than subtle racial overtones.

Every album went gold or platinum until the mid-1980s, when irritation at their distributor's inability to break them into the white market led to the group's splitting into two separate units. The youngsters remained, as Isley Jasper Isley, while The Isley Brothers changed labels yet again.

The last five years have been inconsistent for both groups. Isley Jasper Isley made a dismal debut but returned quickly with a major hit, 'Caravan Of Love' (successfully covered in the UK by The Housemartins). Sadly, they could not consolidate this success and broke up soon after, Ernie Isley and Chris Jasper pursuing solo careers. The Isley Brothers' 1985 album, 'Masterpiece' (1985), did not go gold and was the last recording to feature O'Kelly, who died in 1986. Their follow-up 'Smooth Sailin'' (1989), featured the vocals of Ronald, who by 1989's 'Spend The Night' had effectively emerged as a solo act, the album being credited to 'The Isley Brothers featuring Ronald Isley'. Ronald was also producing Angela Winbush, who reciprocated for The Isleys and during 1990 they toured the US together, further fuelling rumours that as a group the Isley Brothers were effectively defunct.

Greatest Hits

Singles	Title	US	UK
1966	*This Old Heart Of Mine*	12	3
1966	*I Guess I'll Always Love You*	–	11
1969	*Behind a Painted Smile*	–	5
1969	*It's Your Thing*	2	30
1973	*That Lady*	6	14
1975	*Fight The Power*	4	–
1976	*Harvest For The World*	–	10
Isley Jasper Isley			
1985	*Caravan Of Love*	51	52
Albums			
1966	*This Old Heart Of Mine*	140	23
1973	*3+3*	8	–
1975	*The Heat Is On*	1	–
1976	*Harvest For The World*	9	50
1977	*Go For Your Guns*	6	46
1978	*Showdown*	4	50
1980	*Go All The Way*	8	–

Twistin' and shoutin', the Isleys' influence was felt years ahead of their own chart success

IT'S A BEAUTIFUL DAY

David LaFlamme (violin, vocals)
Linda LaFlamme (keyboards)
Pattie Santos (vocals, percussion)
Bill Gregory (guitar)
Tom Fowler (bass)
Val Fuentes (drums)

Formed by virtuoso/classically-trained violinist LaFlamme in San Francisco in 1967, It's A Beautiful Day (the name emanating from the meteorological conditions on the day they formed) were at the forefront of the second wave of US West Coast groups. Despite making a strong initial impact, they were unable to consolidate. As the group existed only as a vehicle for LaFlamme's pyrotechnics and was racked by a bewildering array of personnel changes, continuity was always a recurring problem.

LaFlamme (born 1941) was playing violin at the age of five and later appeared as soloist with the Utah Symphony Orchestra. After US Army service, he moved to California, experiencing several musical styles: Country & Western, folk, R&B, jazz (with The John Handy Concert Ensemble) and embryonic rock (jamming with future members of Big Brother & The Holding Company and in an early version of Dan Hicks & His Hot Licks). By the time he formed IABD, LaFlamme was something of a seasoned veteran, playing a specially adapted solid-body five-string violin.

The group caused an immediate stir, LaFlamme's distinctive soloing making them a major local draw. Their eponymous debut album (featuring the classic 'White Bird', which became a favourite of FM Radio) was cut for a local label, but licensed by a major, making the US Top 50, by which time wife Linda had departed to form Titus' Mother. Boosted by a European tour, it also made the UK charts. Following further staffing adjustments, 'Marrying Maiden' was an even bigger success (US Top 30, UK Top 50), but it was the group's commercial peak. As members came and went, the spiralling fortunes of their live performances matched that of their album sales, and a constant stream of mutating styles merely exacerbated their decline. 'Choice Quality Stuff'/'Anytime', 'Live At Carnegie Hall' and 'It's A Beautiful Day . . . Today' all struggled to chart between 1972 and 1973, and they finally folded in 1974 after the failure of their sixth album, '1001 Nights'.

LaFlamme re-emerged briefly in 1977 with a solo album, 'White Bird', a minor chart entry, while the updated title track just made the US Top 100, but the follow-up, 'Inside Out' did nothing, since when he has rarely been mentioned in dispatches.

Greatest Hits

Albums	Title	US	UK
1969	*It's A Beautiful Day*	47	58
1970	*Marrying Maiden*	28	45

The JACKSON 5

Jackie
Tito
Marlon
Jermaine
Michael Jackson *(vocal group)*

Throughout the 1970s, The Jackson 5 were among the most popular pop vocal groups throughout the world, their career going into decline only when the youngest, Michael (born 1958), began his rise to super-stardom.

Their father Joe Jackson had been a guitar-ist with Wilson Pickett's early group, The Falcons. Settling in Gary, Indiana, he coached his five eldest sons as a vocal group from the mid-1960s. After recording 'Big Boy' for a local label, The Jackson 5 was signed by Berry Gordy to his Motown label in 1969. With intense, falsetto lead singing from Michael, the family's first four Motown singles reached No. 1 in America. The songs were written by a consortium of Motown staffers, and the carefully choreographed Jackson 5 stage act made them teeny-bop stars and even inspired a TV cartoon series.

After the US Top 3 singles, 'Mama's Pearl' and 'Never Can Say Goodbye' (later a 1975 disco hit for Gloria Gaynor) in 1971, the quintet's hits were less spectacular. However, there were US Top 10 successes with 'Sugar Daddy' (1971), 'Dancing Machine' (1974) and, in Britain, a Top 10 version of Jackson Browne's 'Doctor My Eyes' (1972). Amid legal wrangles, four of the group changed labels in 1975, and in 1977 the single, 'Enjoy Yourself' reached the US Top 10. Later that year, 'Show You The Way To Go' was a UK No. 1, reaching the Top 30 in the US. By now they had been renamed The Jacksons and Randy (born 1961) had replaced Jermaine, who stayed with Motown and set out on a solo career that continued through the 1980s. His most successful singles included 'Let's Get Serious', Top 10 in the UK and US (1980), 'Do What You Do', Top 10 UK and Top 20 US (1985), and 'I Think It's Love', which reached the US Top 20 in 1986, while in 1980, the 'Let's Get Serious' album reached the US Top 10 and the UK Top 30.

Although by now Michael was concentrat-ing on solo work, he worked with the remain-ing brothers on the 'Destiny' (1979), 'Triumph' (1980) and 'Victory' (1984) albums, all Top 40 in both the UK and US, but they had only occasional singles success with such songs as 'Shake Your Body' (1979) and 'State Of Shock' (1984) on which Mick Jagger joined Michael on vocals. Still led by Jackie, The Jacksons returned to the album charts in 1989 with '2300 Jackson Street'.

Greatest Hits

Singles	Title	US	UK
1969	*I Want You Back*	1	2
1970	*ABC*	1	8
1970	*The Love You Save*	1	7
1970	*I'll Be There*	1	4
1971	*Mama's Pearl*	2	25
1971	*Never Can Say Goodbye*	2	33
1974	*Dancing Machine*	2	–
1977	*Show You The Way To Go*	28	1
1979	*Shake Your Body*	7	4
1984	*State Of Shock*	3	14
Albums			
1970	*The Jackson 5 Christmas Album*	1	–
1983	*18 Greatest Hits*	–	1
1984	*Victory*	4	3

Janet JACKSON

The youngest member of the Jacksons, the world's most successful recording family, Janet Jackson (born 1966 in Gary, Indiana) first appeared with The Jackson Five in 1973/4 (doing impressions of Mae West and Cher!). As a pre-teen, she was in the US TV sitcom, *Good Times*, which was followed by appearances in top TV shows *Different Strokes* and *Fame*.

'Seventies superkids The Jackson 5, their records grew up with them, from teenysoul tunes to disco dancetracks

Janet with more Jackson jive

In 1982 Jackson reached the US Top 100 with her eponymous album and two singles from it. Her 1984 album, 'Dream Street' (which included a duet with Cliff Richard), was not successful and neither was her marriage that year to James DeBarge of the Debarge family singing group. For a while it seemed she would only achieve limited success (like her older sister Latoya), but in 1986 the turning point of her career came with the 'Control' album, produced by Jam & Lewis. Its first single, 'What Have You Done For Me Lately?', was a transatlantic Top 5 hit and others followed, like 'Nasty', 'Control' and 'Let's Wait Awhile', resulting in an amazing five Top 5 hits from the album. 'Control' went platinum in the UK and topped the US chart, going quintuple platinum, and making her America's top-selling artist of 1986.

Known for energetic and streetwise dance-oriented videos, she has twice won awards for Best Choreographed Video of the Year in the MTV awards, firstly for 'Nasty' (choreographed by Paula Abdul) and later for 'Rhythm Nation'.

In 1989 she released her fourth album, 'Rhythm Nation 1814', in which she took a bigger share in the writing and production with Jam & Lewis. This dance-oriented album with a social conscience topped the US chart for a month, went quadruple platinum and produced six Top 5 singles including 'Alright', 'Come Back To Me' and 'Black Cat', equalling the record set by her brother Michael.

Greatest Hits

Singles	Title	US	UK
1986	When I Think Of You	1	10
1989	Miss You Much	1	22
1990	Escapade	1	17
1990	Black Cat	1	15
Albums			
1986	Control	1	8
1989	Janet Jackson's Rhythm Nation 1814	1	4

Joe **JACKSON**

After a series of New Wave hits in the late 1970s, Joe Jackson (born 1954) pursued a varied musical career through the 1980s, frequently drawing on jazz and R&B styles. After winning a piano scholarship to London's Royal College of Music and playing saxophone in the National Youth Orchestra, he surprisingly spent the mid-1970s in pub bands, backing cabaret act Coffee And Cream on a TV talent show and becoming musical director at a suburban outpost of the Playboy Club, as well as recording (with little success) as a member of a group, Arms & Legs, with Mark Andrews (vocals).

He moved back to London in 1978 and recorded a series of demos which led to a major label recording contract. His first single, 'Is She Really Going Out With Him?', attracted attention, but it was his debut album, 'Look Sharp', that charted first, reaching the US Top 20 and UK Top 40 early in 1979. The single became a UK hit that summer, shortly before his second album. 'I'm The Man', went Top 20 in the UK and Top 30 in the US, and gave him a UK Top 5 single with 'It's Different For Girls'. However, Jackson was tiring of his beat group style and after 1980's 'Beat Crazy' album stalled outside the US and UK Top 40, he made an abrupt musical switch to 1981's 'Jumpin' Jive' album, which romped through the pre-rock'n'roll bop and jive catalogue. It put him back in the UK Top 20 and narrowly missed the US Top 40.

He moved to live in New York in 1982 and soaked up local influences for that year's 'Night And Day' album, which broke into the US and UK Top 5, helped by the transatlantic Top 10 single, 'Steppin' Out'. He followed it in 1983 with a lacklustre film soundtrack for *Mikes's Murder*, but recovered with 'Body

Joe - 'I'm The Man'

And Soul' in 1984, which put him back in the Top 20 of the US & UK album charts and included a US Top 20 single, 'You Can't Get What You Want (Till You Know What You Want)'. Since then, he has maintained a restless career: 1986's 'Big World' album went back to basics and made the US Top 40, but 1987's mainly instrumental orchestral/jazz album, 'Will Power', paid no chart dividends. 1988's double 'Live 1980–1986' featured four different band line-ups and 1989's 'Blaze Of Glory', a collection of new songs, was likewise only mildly successful. He parted company with his record label in 1990 after 12 years.

Greatest Hits

Singles	Title	US	UK
1980	It's Different For Girls	–	5
1982	Steppin' Out	6	6
1984	You Can't Get What You Want (Till You Know What You Want)	15	–
Albums			
1979	I'm The Man	22	12
1982	Night And Day	4	3

Michael **JACKSON**

Michael Jackson (born 1958) joined family group The Jackson Five in 1964 and sang lead on their four US chart-toppers before recording solo in 1971. His debut album, 'Got To Be There' (1972) included the transatlantic Top 5 singles 'Rockin' Robin' and the title track. His second LP that year, 'Ben', made the US Top 5 and its title track was his first US solo No. 1.

His next two albums, 'Music And Me' in 1973 and 'Forever, Michael' in 1975, both missed the Top 40 and with The Jackson Five he left Motown, where they had been so successful. He starred in the movie, *The Wiz*, in 1977, when he first met Quincy Jones, who produced him from then on. In 1979 his single, 'You Can't Win', was a minor hit, but his album, 'Off The Wall', became a transatlantic Top 10 item, and the Grammy-winning single 'Don't Stop 'Til You Get Enough' topped the US chart. The album sold over 10 million and also spawned the US Top 10 hits 'Off The Wall', 'She's Out Of My Life' and another chart-topper, 'Rock With You'. He rejoined The Jacksons for their 'Triumph' tour in 1980 and in 1981, his 1975 Motown recording 'One Day In Your Life', became his first UK No. 1. In 1982, his Top 3 duet with Paul McCartney, 'The Girl Is Mine', previewed the 'Thriller' album, which topped the US chart for 37 weeks and has sold a record 40 million plus copies worldwide. This pop/soul/dance masterpiece won a record eight Grammys and contained seven US Top 10 singles – with its expensive and well choreographed videos, it is said to have

Michael Jackson – all tied up for the immediate future

The JAM / STYLE COUNCIL

Paul Weller (vocals, guitar)
Bruce Foxton (bass)
Rick Buckler (drums)

One of the most uncompromising UK New Wave bands, The Jam's initial energy came from 1960s R&B more than 1970s punk. Although their style was never accepted in the US, they scored over a dozen UK Top 10 hits in five years. Formed by schoolmates Paul Weller (born 1958) and Rick Buckler (born 1955), who recruited Bruce Foxton (born 1955), The Jam worked the London club circuit in 1976, establishing their own 'mod' identity within the burgeoning punk scene and provoking comparisons with The Who. Their 1977 debut single, 'In The City', was a speedy, riff-driven New Wave anthem that made the UK Top 40, and their identically titled album reached the UK Top 20 as the band toured around Britain. Their second single, 'All Around The World', made the UK Top 20, and six months after their debut album, a second, 'This Is The Modern World', appeared, but seemed to demonstrate little progress either musically or commercially.

Weller's songwriting and sharp lyrics had moved up a gear for 1978's 'All Mod Cons', which reached the UK Top 10. More Top 20 singles followed, like 'Down In The Tube Station At Midnight' and 'Strange Town', as well as a fine cover of a Kinks oldie, 'David Watts'. The group's next album, 'Setting Sons', was a sombre affair which reached the UK Top 5 and included a UK Top 3 single, 'Eton Rifles'. In 1980, the band had two chart-topping singles, the double A-sided 'Going Underground'/'Dreams Of Children' and 'Start', before the more danceable 'Sound Effects' album made the UK Top 3. After two more UK Top 5 singles in 1981, 'Funeral Pyre' and 'Absolute Beginners', The Jam

changed the face of 80s music.

His second duet with McCartney, 'Say Say Say', in 1983 gave him another US chart topper and he also signed a deal with Pepsi Cola that year which earned him $20 million. His 1984 video 'The Making of Michael Jackson's Thriller' was the first music video to go platinum and at the end of that year he joined The Jacksons 'Victory' tour giving his $5 million earnings from it to children's charities.

In 1985 he co-wrote and sang on the Ethiopian Relief fund-raising single 'We Are The World' by USA for Africa, which sold 4.5 million, and he also bought The Beatles song catalogue for $47.5 million.

His album 'Bad' in 1987 became the first LP to enter both the US and UK charts at No. 1. In the US it sold six million, including two million in the week of release. In the UK,

it sold nearly three million giving him two of the UK's three biggest sellers ever. To promote 'Bad', he made the most expensive videos ever and went on a year-long, record-shattering world tour. The first single from 'Bad', 'I Just Can't Stop Loving You' (a duet with Siedah Garrett), was a US No. 1, as were a record-breaking four others.

In 1988 his video, 'The Legend Continues', became the UK's biggest-ever seller, the Michael Jackson autobiography *Moonwalk* was published, and an identically titled film was premiered.

In 1990 this reclusive superstar, who was the first entertainer to earn over $100 million in a year, was presented with a special award for selling over 110 million records in the 1980s and started the 1990s off on a good foot by signing a deal with a clothing company worth over $10 million.

Paul Weller (centre) post-punk Jam sessions ended in Style

peaked in 1982 with two chart-topping singles, 'A Town Called Malice' and 'Beat Surrender', plus a No. 1 album, 'The Gift', but Weller had outgrown The Jam, which disbanded after a farewell tour and live album, 'Dig The New Breed'.

While Foxton's solo career was short-lived like Buckler's group, Time UK, Weller formed The Style Council with keyboard player Mick Talbot, who had worked in mod bands The Merton Parkas and Dexy's Midnight Runners. They reversed into soul music from a jazzier direction, starting with two 1973 UK Top 5 singles, 'Speak Like A Child' and 'Long Hot Summer', and their 1974 debut album, 'Cafe Bleu', made the UK Top 3. Weller finally sneaked into the US Top 30 with 'My Ever Changing Mood', another UK Top 5 hit, but he was taking an increasingly political stance and the band played many benefit gigs as well as Live Aid in 1985. Their next album, 'My Favourite Shop', topped the UK chart in 1985, containing some biting social commentary as well as a hit single, 'Walls Come Tumbling Down', but 1986's 'Home And Abroad' album was far less successful.

Although their 1987 album, 'The Cost Of Loving', made the UK Top 3, the band seemed to lose impetus, and after the 1988 album, 'Confessions Of A Pop Group', stalled outside the UK Top 10, things went suspiciously quiet. By the end of 1990 they were missing, presumed dead, and Weller was getting a new band together.

Greatest Hits

Singles	Title	US	UK
1979	Eton Rifles	–	3
1980	Going Underground/Dreams Of Children	–	1
1980	Start!	–	1
1982	A Town Called Malice/Precious	–	1
1982	The Bitterest Pill (I Ever Had To Swallow)	–	2
1982	Beat Surrender	–	1
Albums			
1980	Sound Effects	–	2
1982	The Gift	–	1
1982	Dig The New Breed	–	2
1983	Snap	–	2
The Style Council			
Singles			
1983	Speak Like A Child	–	4
1983	Long Hot Summer	–	3
1984	My Ever Changing Moods	29	5
Albums			
1984	Cafe Bleu	–	2
1985	Our Favourite Shop	–	1
1987	The Cost Of Loving	–	2

JAN & DEAN

Though tragic circumstances prevented them from transcending their origins, a sun-drenched moment of pop's most optimistic and innocent era will always belong to Jan & Dean.

While Dean Torrence (born 1940) was studying design and Jan Berry (born 1941) medicine at the Los Angeles University High School, both were members of The Barons, a vocal sextet who recorded demos with the assistance of drummer Sandy Nelson and pianist/future Beach Boy Bruce Johnston. The outfit fragmented but Berry, Torrence and Arnold Ginsberg persuaded a small LA label to issue 'Jennie Lee', an opus concerning a local strip-teaser. As Torrence had just been conscripted, this 1958 hit was attributed to 'Jan & Arnie', as were the flops and minor hits that followed before Ginsberg's departure and Torrence's demobbing.

Lou Adler, an army acquaintance of Torrence who had had chart success with Sam Cooke, supervised 'Baby Talk', 'Clementine' and other releases preceding Jan & Dean's signing with a bigger label in 1962 and their intertwining with Brian Wilson's Beach Boys. For example, Torrence sang lead on the 1966 Beach Boys hit, 'Barbara Ann', while Wilson co-wrote and added his falsetto to 1963's Utopian 'Surf City', Jan & Dean's biggest single.

The surf music influence was also felt on 'Dead Man's Curve', 'The Little Old Lady (From Pasadena)', 'Ride The Wild Surf' and other hits concerning Californian teen culture. Contributing more creative input to the duo's music, Berry branched out into production of singles by their Matadors backing group and his actress girlfriend Shelley Fabares (later, Mrs Lou Adler), as well as 'Jan & Dean's Pop Hits Symphony', an orchestral album conducted by George Tipton (who would likewise minister to Nilsson in 1971). As dubious were Jan & Dean's stab at folk-rock (1965's 'Folk'n'Roll' album), and the 'Jan & Dean Meet Batman' album.

Apart from hosting the celebrated pop movie, *Gather No Moss* (aka *Teenage Command Performance* aka *The TAMI Show*), the pair's sole major film was 1966's *Easy Come Easy Go*, which was notable for an off-set accident resulting in Berry's broken leg (still in plaster on the 'Filet Of Soul' album cover). This mishap was trifling compared to the tragic car crash that left Berry severely paralysed that same year.

During his partner's slow recovery, Torrence's musical ventures included solo recordings and membership of the Legendary Masked Surfers (with Bruce Johnston and Terry Melcher) but the failure of these led him to concentrate on his Kittyhawk Graphics art studios, and the co-ordination of Jan & Dean compilation albums.

The climax of 1978's *Dead Man's Curve*, a bio-pic about Jan & Dean, was a mock-up of their troubled 'comeback' show in 1973 at the Hollywood Palladium but, with Berry in ruder health, their occasional appearances in subsequent nostalgia revues have been better received, with the result that their 1985 album of new material has been doing brisk business in the foyers.

Greatest Hits

JEFFERSON AIRPLANE/JEFFERSON STARSHIP/STARSHIP

Marty Balin (vocals)
Signe Tole Anderson (vocals)
Paul Kantner (guitar, vocals)
Jorma Kaukonen (guitar, vocals)
Jack Casady (bass)
Alexander 'Skip' Spence (drums)

Formed in San Francisco, 1965, by Balin (born Martyn Buchwald, 1942) who had previously cut a couple of singles and had worked with LA folk group, The Town Criers. He had become co-owner of a local club, The Drinking Gourd, and having changed its name to The Matrix, he needed a house band – to which end he recruited Kantner (born 1942), Kaukonen (born 1940), Anderson, drummer Jerry Peloquin and stand-up bassist Bob Harvey. Jefferson Airplane built a massive local reputation and were ranked alongside The Grateful Dead and Quicksilver Messenger Service as one of the city's premier bands. The Matrix soon became established as *the* San Francisco gig, serving as a shop window for new bands and subsequently attracting record labels. RCA duly signed Airplane in October 1965, after Peloquin had been replaced by Spence and Harvey had given away to Casady (born 1944).

'Jefferson Airplane Takes Off' appeared in 1966 and spent three months in the US album chart, although it failed to reach the Top 100. Spence quit to form Moby Grape and was replaced by jazz drummer Spencer Dryden (born 1943), and when Anderson left to have a baby, Grace Slick (born Grace Wing, 1939) joined from local rivals The Great Society to complete the seminal Airplane line-up. Slick was a considerably more powerful and creative presence than Anderson, and the Airplane moved from laid-back, bluesy folk/rock to inventive psychedelia. Their second album, 'Surrealistic Pillow' was a monster, selling nearly a million copies in 1967, making the US Top 3 and establishing them as a major band. It included two US Top 10 singles, 'Somebody To Love' and the controversial 'White Rabbit', both million-sellers and both previously from Great Society's repertoire.

'After Bathing At Baxters' (US Top 20) and 'Crown Of Creation' (US Top 10) albums followed in quick succession in 1968, the former provoking a rift with RCA over the label's deletion of a word from the album's lyric sheet (!) By now, Balin and Slick had developed into an awesome front line and were at something of a performing peak, standing eye to eye, trying to out-howl one another. 1969's live album, 'Bless It's Pointed Little Head' (US Top 20, UK Top 40) managed to capture some of that power. During that year, the group appeared at both the Woodstock and Altamont Festivals, and also released the 'Volunteers' album, (US Top 20, UK Top 40) after which Dryden defected to the New Riders Of The Purple Sage. Replacement Joey Covington had been drumming with satellite group Hot Tuna (formed a couple of years earlier by Casady & Kaukonen in parallel with Airplane).

An enforced lay-off (due to Slick's pregnancy) led to members undertaking various spinoff projects, making the early 1970s a confusing era for fans. Hot Tuna released an eponymous live album which made the US Top 30, a low-key semi-acoustic set featuring Casady, Kaukonen, and Will Scarlett (harmonica), while Kanter & Slick released a science-

Slick tricks from Grace and Paul kept Airplane in orbit as Starship

fiction concept epic, 'Blows Against The Empire', which made the US Top 20 credited to Paul Kantner & Jefferson Starship. Meanwhile, RCA had issued 'The Worst Of Jefferson Airplane' in 1971 (US Top 20), and Balin, who had been increasingly frozen out, quit the band, disillusioned; after a few gigs with Hot Tuna, he produced a local group, Grootna, and formed Bodacious DF.

At this stage, it became even more confusing as product flooded the market, credited to just about everyone: Hot Tuna, whose personnel now included veteran black violinist Papa John Creach (born 1917) released a second album, 1971's 'First Pull Up, Then Pull Down', which made the US Top 50, Jefferson Airplane reconvened (with peripatetic members of Hot Tuna) to launch their Grunt label with the 'Bark' album (US Top 20, UK Top 50), 1971's 'Sunfighter' album, which made the US Top 100, was credited to Slick & Kantner, Creach released two 'solo' albums featuring sundry Airplane/Tuna members, some of whom guested on David Crosby's 'If Only I Could Remember My Name' album, Hot Tuna's third album, 'Burgers', made the US Top 100 in 1972, and Airplane released their last studio album for nearly two decades, 'Long John Silver', which made the US Top 20 and UK Top 30.

With new drummer John Barbata (ex-Turtles) and ex-Quicksilver Messenger Service bassist/singer David Freiberg – Casady, Kaukonen and Covington were all absent – they played a free gig in New York in 1972 and broke up. Hot Tuna finalised the split by becoming permanent and '30 Seconds Over Winterland', a live album from Airplane's last US tour, failed to reach the US Top 50 in 1973, the year Slick, Kantner & Freiberg released the oddly-titled 'Baron Von Tollbooth & The Chrome Nun' album, which peaked outside the US Top 50. Slick's first solo album, 'Manhole', appeared early in 1974 and failed to make the US Top 100, as did Hot Tuna's 'The Phosphorescent Rat'.

Also in 1974, Kantner, Slick, Freiberg, Creach, Barbata, Craig Chaquico (guitar) and Peter Kangaroo (born Peter Kaukonen, bass) toured as Jefferson Starship (after which sessionman Pete Sears took over on bass) and as Jefferson Starship, cut the 'Dragonfly' album (US Top 20, 1974) which restored them to gold status. Balin rejoined in time for 1975's 'Red Octopus' album, which effectively launched them on a fresh career, as it topped the US chart for a month, selling 2.5 million units (their first multi-platinum album) and including a million-selling US Top 3 single, 'Miracles'. Its huge success set them up for the rest of the 1970s, and they evolved into a mainstream AOR band, working to a watertight formula which virtually guaranteed platinum records: 1976's 'Spitfire' made the US Top 3 and UK Top 30, and included a US Top 20 single, 'With Your Love', 1978's 'Earth' made the US Top 5, and yielded two hit singles, 'Count on Me' (US Top 10) and

'Runaway' (US Top 20), and 1979's 'Freedom At Point Zero' (US Top 10 and UK Top 30), which included 'Jane' (US Top 20, UK Top 30). These were punctuated with the release of two compilation albums: 'Flight Log (1966–1976)' (US Top 40, 1977), a double album anthologising Airplane, Tuna, Starship, etc., and 'Gold' (US Top 20, 1979), drawn solely from the more recent Starship material.

The later period saw their personnel fluctuate drastically, but seemingly without any adverse effect: Slick and Balin both quit during 1978, being replaced by Mickey Thomas (ex-Elvin Bishop); drummer Barbata gave way to Aynsley Dunbar (ex-Journey), who was in turn replaced by Don Baldwin (ex-Elvin Bishop); Slick returned; and, following a stroke, nobody seemed too sure about Kantner. Yet their success continued unabated with three US Top 30 albums: 1981's 'Modern Times', 1982's 'Winds Of Change' and 1984's 'Nuclear Future'.

Spinoff projects were only marginally less successful: Balin's 1981 solo album, 'Balin', reached the US Top 40 and included a US Top 10 single, 'Hearts', and a US Top 30 single, 'Atlanta Lady' (although his next album, 'Lucky', failed to make the US Top 100); Slick released two solo albums, 1981's 'Dreams' (US Top 40, UK Top 30), and 'Welcome To The Wrecking Ball' (US Top 50, 1982), before returning to the fold; and Kantner released 'The Planet Earth Rock & Roll Orchestra' in 1983.

Kantner's uncertain status was resolved in 1985 when he left the band, followed immediately by Freiberg. This led to another major overhaul, which in turn precipitated their Third Coming: obliged to drop the 'Jefferson' prefix as part of the termination agreement with Kantner, they restructured themselves simply as 'Starship', with a streamlined personnel comprising Slick, Thomas, Sears, Chaquico and Baldwin. Aiming directly at the MTV/AOR market, incredibly they struck multi-platinum immediately: 1985's 'Knee Deep In The Hoopla' (US Top 10) spawned two US chart-topping singles, 'We Built This City' (their first ever US No. 1 single, and a Top 20 breakthrough in the UK, after nearly 20 years), and 1987's 'Sara'. 1987's 'No Protection' (US Top 20, UK Top 30) did very nearly as well, spinning off the US & UK chart-topper, 'Nothing's Gonna Stop Us Now' and 'It's Not Over' (US Top 10).

Kantner reunited with former colleagues Balin and Casady to form the KBC Band, which gradually became permanent, and Slick (effectively the last near-original member) left Starship in 1988 (as had Sears). In 1989, a reformed Jefferson Airplane of Slick, Kantner, Balin, Casady and Kaukonen (no doubt inspired by the astonishing success of similarly elderly acts) released an eponymous album, probably setting a new record for taking nearly 25 years to be so imaginative.

Greatest Hits

Singles	Title	US	UK
1967	*Somebody To Love* (Jefferson Airplane)	5	–
1975	*Miracles* (Jefferson Starship)	3	–
1981	*Hearts* (Marty Balin)	8	–
1985	*We Built This City* (Starship)	1	12
1985	*Sara* (Starship)	1	–
1987	*Nothing's Gonna Stop Us Now* (Starship)	1	1

Albums			
1967	*Surrealistic Pillow* (Jefferson Airplane)	3	–
1975	*Red Octopus* (Jefferson Starship)	1	–
1976	*Spitfire* (Jefferson Starship)	3	30
1978	*Earth* (Jefferson Starship)	5	–
1985	*Knee Deep In The Hoopla* (Starship)	7	–

JETHRO TULL

Ian Anderson (vocals, flute)
Mick Abrahams (guitar)
Glenn Cornick (bass)
Clive Bunker (drums)

Led by the dictatorial Ian Anderson (born 1947), Jethro Tull have enjoyed a highly successful 20+-year career. Anderson's flamboyant character and often innovative music were strong enough to withstand the vagaries of rock fashions and during the 1970s, the band released seven US Top 10 albums.

In 1968 Anderson was part of northern English blues septet, The John Evan Band, which broke up after an abortive attempt to crack the London scene. Anderson and Glenn Cornick (born 1947) stayed in the south of England, meeting up with Mick Abrahams (born 1943) and Clive Bunker (born 1946) to form Jethro Tull (named after an 18th-century agricultural inventor). With his long, unruly hair, wild eyes, tatty overcoat and one-legged flute-playing, Andreson was a charismatic front man, and Tull's music was an equally quirky mix of blues, jazz and folk. After an abortive single, 'Sunshine Day', on which they were mistakenly billed as Jethro Toe, the band's debut album, 'This Was', made the UK Top 10 in late 1968, but Abrahams soon left over musical differences and formed Blodwyn Pig.

Anderson replaced him with Martin Barre (born 1946) who contributed to the matchless single, 'Living In The Past', which reached the UK Top 3 in 1969 (and the US Top 20 in 1972). The 'Stand Up' album, released later that year on the new Chrysalis label launched by the group's managers, Terry Ellis and Chris Wright, demonstrated Anderson's melodic and lyrical flair and topped the UK charts as well a making the US Top 20, where Anderson's antics made a strong impact.

UK Top 10 singles 'Sweet Dream' and

Uncharacteristically agile acrobatics for a mere flute player, Tull's Ian Anderson never let you forget he was a Rock Star too

'The Witch's Promise' were followed by the 'Benefit' album, which reached the UK Top 3 and US Top 20. By now, former members of The John Evan Band were returning as members of Jethro Tull, starting with keyboard player John Evan himself (born 1948) and continuing with bassist Jeffrey Hammond-Hammond (born 1946) replacing Cornick.

'Aqualung', a grandiose 1971 concept album that caused controversy with its views on religion, took them into the US Top 10 for the first time. When Bunker quit, Anderson – now the only original member – recruited John Evan Band drummer Barriemore Barlow. After a UK hit with 'Life Is A Long Song', the group released 1972's concept album, 'Thick As A Brick', which topped the US charts and paved the way for the 'Living In The Past' compilation which made the US Top 3 later that year.

Anderson pursued his concept formula to more extravagant lengths: 1973's 'A Passion Play' topped the US charts, 1974's 'War Child' made the US Top 3, and they had a US Top 20 hit single with 'Bungle In The Jungle', although critics decried their 'pretentious' approach. 'Minstrel In The Gallery', which went Top 10 in 1975, returned to the song format and 'MU – The Best Of Jethro Tull' made the US Top 20, but sales fell for Anderson's next concept, 'Too Old To Rock-'n'Roll, Too Young To Die', in 1976, before reviving with 1977's folk-influenced 'Songs From The Wood'.

The group's line-up continued to evolve with keyboard player/arranger David Palmer and bassist John Glascock joining as Anderson continued with folk influences for two more albums, 'Heavy Horses' (1978) and 'Stormwatch' (1979). Glascock's death following heart surgery in 1979 nearly forced Anderson to go solo on 'A', which featured Fairport Convention bassist Dave Pegg (who later also played concurrently with Tull) and keyboard player Eddie Jobson, but it emerged in 1980 as another Tull album, their least successful since 'This Was' 12 years before.

In 1983 Anderson finally released a solo album (ironically with keyboard player Peter Vettese), 'Walk Into Light'. After surviving innumerable changes of musical fashion, the group's career prospered during the 1980s as their albums continued to chart, including 'Broadsword And The Beast' (1982), 'Under Wraps' (1984), 'Crest Of A Knave' (1987, which earned a Grammy for Best Heavy Metal Album!) and 1989's critically acclaimed 'Rock Island'. There seems little reason why Anderson and his band of employees should not continue indefinitely.

Greatest Hits

Singles	Title	US	UK
1969	*Living In The Past*	11	3
1970	*The Witch's Promise*	–	4
Albums			
1969	*Stand Up*	20	1
1970	*Benefit*	11	3
1972	*Thick As A Brick*	1	5
1972	*Living In The Past*	3	8
1973	*A Passion Play*	1	13
1974	*War Child*	2	14

Billy JOEL

Joel once said that he saw himself primarily as a composer, and certainly he became a master songwriter, equally adept with mainstream ballads ('Just The Way You Are'), catchy rockers ('Uptown Girl') and social commentaries ('We Didn't Start The Fire'). Although he was to become one of the most highly paid performers of the 1980s, he had little success in his early years as a musician. Born in 1949, Joel grew up in Long Island, studied classical piano and spent three years boxing before joining his first rock group, The Echoes, in 1964. Joel played sessions as a pianist for producer George 'Shadow' Morton, including work on the Shangri-Las' 'Leader Of The Pack'.

The band became The Lost Souls and The Emerald Lords before Joel joined The Hassles, a psychedelic rock band which recorded two albums in 1967–8. With drummer Jon Small he released one hard rock album, as Atilla, in 1969. After recovering from a nervous breakdown, Joel made his solo debut album, 'Cold

---

Billy Joel – rock with a social cutting edge

Spring Harbor' (1971), and, after a label change, scored his first US Top 30 hit with the album and single 'Piano Man' (1974), a mournful ballad based on his experience as a lounge bar pianist. In 1975 the 'Streetlife Serenade' album reached the US Top 40. At this stage, his record company saw Joel as an American equivalent to Elton John and even hired members of John's former band, Nigel Olsson and Dee Murray, to play on 'Turnstiles' (1976).

However, his career did not really take off until the 1977 release of 'The Stranger'. Its four hit singles included 'Just The Way You Are', among whose 20-plus cover versions were those by Frank Sinatra and Barry White, whose grunting style brought him a million-seller. This was the start of a ten-year run of hit records. While 'Allentown' (from the 1982 album 'The Nylon Curtain') was a stark commentary on unemployment and the same album's 'Goodnight Saigon' was a graphic musical portrait of the Vietnam war, many of his songs were tributes to the rock greats. They included 'It's Still Rock'n'Roll To Me' (1980), the Phil Spector-styled 'Say Goodbye To Hollywood' (1981) and the Four Seasons-inspired 'Uptown Girl' (1983). That song came from 'An Innocent Man', all of whose tracks were rooted in classic rock and pop styles.

In 1985 Joel married top model Christie Brinkley, and his place in the US rock hierarchy was underlined by his participation in the famine relief record 'We Are The World' – though his Brooklyn scepticism led him to comment on how similar the song was to composer Lionel Ritchie's Pepsi ads. That year also saw a highly successful 'Greatest Hits' double album. 'The Bridge' (1986) featured a guest appearance by one of Joel's all-time heroes, Ray Charles, and the following year Joel made a short tour of Russia, from which came the live album 'Kohyept' (1988), recorded in Leningrad.

The 1980s ended on a high note for Joel as 'Storm Front' (1989), co-produced with Mick Jones of Foreigner, became his ninth Top 10 album in the US, and the US No. 1, 'We Didn't Start The Fire', took his tally of US Top 20 singles to 21. It was also one of his most powerful songs, recalling the political events to which his 'baby boomer' generation had been witness.

Greatest Hits

Singles	Title	US	UK
1980	*You May Be Right*	7	–
1980	*It's Still Rock'n'Roll To Me*	1	14
1983	*Tell Her All About It*	1	4
1983	*Uptown Girl*	3	1
1989	*We Didn't Start The Fire*	1	7
Albums			
1977	*The Stranger*	2	25
1979	*52nd Street*	1	10
1980	*Glass Houses*	1	9
1983	*An Innocent Man*	4	2
1985	*Greatest Hits Vols 1 & 2*	6	7
1989	*Storm Front*	1	5

Elton **JOHN**

In partnership with lyricist Bernie Taupin, John has composed many of the best-loved rock ballads of the 1970s and 1980s; as a dynamic and outrageous showman, he has also become one of the top live performers of the rock era.

Born Reg Dwight (1947), his father was a trumpeter who played in the 1950s with dance band Bob Miller and the Millermen. The young Dwight soon showed a precocious talent for piano playing, and, with Trinidadian honky-tonk pianist Winifred Atwell as an early influence, he began lessons at the age of four. In 1958 he won a scholarship to study part-time at the Royal College of Music.

After some sessions as a pub pianist, he formed Bluesology with Stu Brown, influenced by the emerging British R&B movement. When the band won a talent contest in 1965, Dwight turned professional and Bluesology began to back black American artists such as Wilson Pickett, Patti Labelle and the Blue Belles, Billy Stewart and The Drifters on their UK and European tours. They also made their first record: 'Come Back Baby', written and sung by Dwight.

In 1966, the group took another direction when they joined forces with R&B singer Long John Baldry, becoming a 9-piece soul revue, but it soon swung towards the cabaret circuit when Baldry topped the UK chart with the ballad 'Let The Heartaches Begin'.

For avid soul fan Dwight this was the final straw. He changed his name to one inspired by two group members (sax player Elton Dean and John Baldry himself) and began to look for a new direction and a solo career.

As Elton John he attended an audition for singers and composers which he failed but which put him in touch with young lyricist Bernie Taupin. John and Taupin recorded demo discs at studios owned by Dick James Music, and were subsequently signed to a publishing and recording contract by erstwhile Beatles publisher and 1950s vocalist Dick James. The first Elton John single was 'I've Been Loving You' (1968), and during this period he appeared on records by The Hollies and Tom Jones as well as numerous 'sound-alike' hits albums as a session musician.

1969 was a transitional year for Elton John as both songwriter and recording artist. The ballad, 'I Can't Go On Living Without You' was an unsuccessful finalist for the UK entry in the Eurovision Song Contest, while both a single, 'Lady Samantha', and an album, 'Empty Sky', won good reviews though sales were low.

'Elton John' (1970) was produced by Gus Dudgeon (who had produced the David Bowie hit 'Space Oddity') and the sparse arrangements of 'Empty Sky' were replaced by orchestral backings. John formed his own band, with Caleb Quaye on guitar, bassist Dee Murray (ex-Spencer Davis and Mirage) and drummer Nigel Olsson (ex-Plastic Penny).

John made his US debut in 1970, and shortly after began the first of numerous US tours as the 'Elton John' album began to climb the US chart, reaching the Top 5 and the UK Top 20.

Over the next six years, John toured world-wide and recorded virtually non-stop. Under the deal with James there were two albums to be delivered each year. 'Tumbleweed Connection' (1970), a singer-songwriter collection, was a UK and US Top 10 album, and was followed by the live '17.11.70' and the soundtrack album, 'Friends'. Another album of singer-songwriter material, 'Madman Across The Water', reached the US Top 10 later that year, but John hit his stride with 1972's 'Honky Chateau', the first of seven consecutive US No. 1 albums.

The album had a different feeling from his earlier collections; John, Taupin and the touring band of Olsson, Murray and guitarist Davey Johnstone had ensconced themselves in the famed Chateau d'Herouville near Paris and Dudgeon was able to achieve a sound and mood close to that of the live show.

The next two albums, 'Don't Shoot Me, I'm Only The Piano Player' (1973) and 'Goodbye Yellow Brick Road' (1973), were also made in France and both were UK No. 1s; but in 1974 John cut 'Caribou' at the Colorado studio of James William Guercio, famous for his work with Chicago and the Beach Boys. This was followed by the autobiographical 'Captain Fantastic & The Brown Dirt Cowboy' (1975), which told the story of

Taupin and John's early career, and the undistinguished 'Rock Of The Westies', which reached the UK Top 5 in 1975. That year, John also appeared in Ken Russell's film *Tommy*, from which 'Pinball Wizard' gave him a UK Top 10 hit.

As well as being the last full-scale Taupin-John collaboration for seven years, the 1976 album 'Blue Moves' was the first Elton John record on Rocket, a label formed by the singer with Taupin, Dudgeon and his manager John Reid. Among other artists signed to Rocket were Neil Sedaka and Kiki Dee, whose duet with Elton, 'Don't Go Breaking My Heart' was a transatlantic No. 1 single.

The first half of the 1970s was the period of some of Taupin/John's most enduring compositions. The roll-call includes 'Your Song', 'Rocket Man', 'Daniel', 'Goodbye Yellow Brick Road' and, perhaps above all, Bernie Taupin's tribute to Marilyn Monroe, 'Candle In The Wind'. However, his punishing schedule took its toll on the superstar. On two occasions concerts were cancelled after he collapsed, and in 1977 at Wembley he announced his "retirement" from live performance. In fact, the lay-off lasted little more than a year, and in the meantime John recorded 'A Single Man' (1978) with a new lyricist, Gary Osborne. One track featured backing vocals by members of the Watford soccer team, whose chairman John had become in 1976.

In 1979 he had his first instrumental hit, the piano solo 'Song For Guy'; but he also made an undistinguished excursion into disco with the 'Victim Of Love' album, produced by Pete Bellotte in Munich. More significantly, John broke new ground as the first Western rock star to appear in Israel and in the USSR. His concerts in Leningrad and Moscow were featured in the film *To Russia With Elton*.

'21 At 33' (1980) found John working with new collaborators Judie Tzuke and Tom Robinson as well as Osborne and Taupin. But its sales were disappointing, and Pretenders producer Chris Thomas was brought in to help out on the albums 'The Fox' (1981) and 'Jump Up!' (1982), which included 'Empty Garden', the heartfelt tribute to the late John Lennon, who had joined John on stage in New York in the mid-1970s. A studio recording of The Beatles' 'Lucy In The Sky With Diamonds', with Lennon on rhythm guitar, was a US No. 1 in 1974.

1983 turned out to be Elton's most successful year in the UK since his 1970s heyday. Reunited with Bernie Taupin, he created two UK Top 10 hit singles in 'That's Why They Call it The Blues' (US Top 5) and 'I'm Still Standing' (US Top 20). Although the albums 'Too Low For Zero' (1983) and 'Breaking Hearts' (1984) reached the UK Top 10, they fared less well in the US, as did 1985's UK Top 5 album 'Ice On Fire'. For the 1985 UK and US Top 10 hit, 'Nikita', John received vocal support from George Michael, with whom he sang at Live Aid.

Even in one of his more conservative outfits, Elton never loses his flair for snappy dressing

Despite a lengthy lawsuit involving Dick James, concluded in 1985, Elton John ended the 1980s as he had entered the 1970s – as one of the most popular artists in the world. 'Live In Australia', recorded on his 1986 world tour, and 'Reg Strikes Back' (1988) were highly successful. And in 1990 he achieved his first solo No. 1 single in his home country when 'Sacrifice' (from 'Sleeping With The Past') topped the UK chart.

Greatest Hits

Singles	Title	US	UK
1972	Crocodile Rock	1	5
1973	Daniel	2	4
1973	Goodbye Yellow Brick Road	2	6
1974	Bennie And The Jets	1	–
1974	Lucy In The Sky With Diamonds (with John Lennon)	1	10
1975	Philadelphia Freedom	1	12
1975	Island Girl	1	11
1976	Don't Go Breaking My Heart (with Kiki Dee)	1	1
1990	Sacrifice/Healing Hands	18	1
Albums			
1972	Honky Chateau	1	2
1973	Don't Shoot Me, I'm Only The Piano Player	1	1
1973	Goodbye Yellow Brick Road	1	1
1974	Caribou	1	1
1974	Elton John's Greatest Hits	1	1
1975	Captain Fantastic & The Brown Dirt Cowboy	1	2
1975	Rock Of The Westies	1	5
1989	Sleeping With The Past	23	1

Janis **JOPLIN/BIG BROTHER** & The **HOLDING COMPANY**

Bessie Smith's most famous – and ultimately tragic – fan, Joplin was the finest white blues singer of her era, and possibly of all time. Although as infamous during her lifetime for her drink, drug, and sexual excesses (used to cover her loneliness and insecurity) as for her magnificent, raunchy voice, she has deservedly achieved legendary status in the 20 years since her untimely death, as her two platinum posthumous albums tesfity.

Joplin (born 1943) came from a middle-class Texan family, and was a loner as a child, growing up on a diet of Bessie Smith, Leadbelly and bluegrass. She left home in 1960 to sing in the bars of Houston and Austin, later moving to the West Coast, where she worked as a folksinger and first got the taste for illicit substances. After returning to Texas in 1966 to clean up and to front a country group, she was invited back to California to join Big Brother & The Holding Company, house band at San Francisco's Avalon Ballroom. Formed six months earlier, the group had made little impact without a lead singer; its initial line-up comprised Sam Andrew (guitar) Peter Albin (bass, guitar, vocals), James Gurley (guitar) and David Getz (drums, piano, vocals).

Joplin's style soon changed radically: having joined the group essentially as a folksinger, their raucous approach and loose, bluesy intensity drew increasingly powerful performances from the new singer. The group became a sensation in the Bay Area and within a few months were the outstanding group on the West Coast. Their 1967 eponymous debut album for an independent label made the US Top 100, but the turning point came with their show-stopping performance at the Monterey Pop Festival that year, which led to their being signed by Bob Dylan's manager, Albert Grossman, who secured them a deal with a major label. Their next album, 'Cheap Thrills' (whose sleeve, by artist Robert Crumb, remains a classic artefact of the era) topped the US album charts for eight weeks in 1968, selling a million copies and elevating Joplin to superstar status. 'Piece Of My Heart' was a US Top 20 single from the album, and the group's previous label cashed in with a couple of US Top 100 singles of earlier material.

By this time, Joplin had outgrown the rest of the group, which she left at the end of 1968, taking Andrew with her to form the Kozmic Blues Band, whose initial line-up also included Brad Campbell (bass), Terry Clements (saxophone) and Marcus Doubleday (trumpet), although its personnel would later fluctuate. After a brief hiatus, Big Brother decided to carry on, with Nick Graventies as vocalist and David Shallock on bass. Their next album, 'Be A Brother', featured Joplin, uncredited, on a couple of tracks and made a small impression on the US Top 200.

Having achieved near-superstardom, Joplin developed into an outrageous, full-blown media personality and tried to live up to her hell-raising/blues mama image. Having spent much of 1969 on the road, the soulful 'I Got Dem Ol' Kozmic Blues Again, Mama!' album was released at the end of the year and reached the US Top 5, going gold. The soul-based Kozmic Blues Band were dismantled and eventually superseded by The Full Tilt Boogie Band, comprising Campbell, John Till (guitar), Richard Bell (piano), Ken Pearson (keyboards) and Clark Pierson (drums), with whom she toured heavily. Increasingly dependent on drugs and alcohol, her behaviour was becoming erratic: arrested for bad mouthing a policeman in late 1969, she was busted a few months later for using profane language onstage. At the same time, she was making marvellous music; and although destined to remain unfinished, the sessions for her next album found her at her spine-tingling best. Then, in October 1970, she was found dead of an accidental heroin overdose in a Hollywood hotel.

'Pearl', the posthumously released album which is her finest work, topped the US charts for nine weeks in 1971, spinning off a US No. 1 single, her definitive version of Kris Kristofferson's 'Me & Bobby McGee', thus underscoring and guaranteeing her legendary status. Predictably, the market was flooded with other releases, notably the live double album, 'In Concert' (partly recorded with Big Brother and partly with The Full Tilt Boogie Band), which reached the US Top 5 in 1972, 'Greatest Hits' (1973, US Top 40, which later went platinum) and the double album soundtrack to the film documentary, *Janis*, which almost reached the US Top 50 in 1974. As late as 1982, 'Farewell Song', a collection of oddments featuring Big Brother, The Butterfield Blues Band, The Kozmic Blues Band and The Full Tilt Boogie Band, just failed to reach the Top 100 of the US album chart. Sadly, in death Joplin was considerably more commercially successful than in life.

Greatest Hits

Singles	Title	US	UK
1968	Piece of My Heart		
	(Big Brother)	12	–
1971	Me & Bobby McGee	1	–
Albums			
1968	Cheap Thrills (Big Brother)	1	–
1969	I Got Dem Ol' Kozmic Blues		
	Again, Mama!	5	–
1971	Pearl	1	50
1972	In Concert	4	30

JOURNEY

Neil Schon (guitar, vocals)
George Tickner (guitar)
Ross Valory (keyboards)
Prairie Prince (drums)

Built on a formidable touring schedule and near-flawless musical format of polished, harmonious, melodic guitar-based hard rock, Journey epitomized 1980s AOR, and with a string of platinum albums under their belts, they certainly got something right, despite the savaging they received from rock critics during the early 1980s.

Formed originally in San Francisco in 1973

Janis Joplin, 'Sixties incarnation of the hard-bitten booze-swilling blues shouter

From the day of Departure, they sought new Frontiers, venturing where no man . . .

as a Santana spin-off by ex-Santana guitarist Schon (born 1955), who recruited the highly experienced Valory (born 1950, ex-Frumious Bandersnatch, Steve Miller Band, etc.), Prince (born 1950, from the Tubes) and Tickner (a highly regarded sessionman), they were joined shortly afterwards by Gregg Rolie (born 1948, vocals/keyboards/guitar), a founder member of Santana. Initially called The Golden Gate Rhythm Section, the name Journey was adopted as the result of a competition held by a San Francisco radio station. Prince rejoined The Tubes after only a couple of gigs, and was replaced by the very experienced Aynsley Dunbar (born 1946), veteran of the UK blues boom and a pedigree which included spells with John Mayall, Frank Zappa, Jeff Beck, David Bowie, etc., plus his own group, Retaliation.

After their eponymous 1975 debut album, Tickner pulled out. Recorded without a recognized frontline vocalist (although Rolie, who took most of the vocals, had done the same with Santana), the album relied heavily upon instrumentals, but nevertheless made the US Top 200, a performance improved upon by 1976's 'Look Into The Future' and 1977's 'Next', both of which broke into the US Top 100. They were faced with the absolute need for an accomplished lead singer if they were to progress further. Robert Fleischmann joined briefly, lasting one tour

before being replaced by Steve Perry (born 1949, formerly with Tim Bogert's Alien Project). Perry proved to be the required catalyst, as their fourth album, 1978's 'Infinity', finally broke them: although peaking outside the US Top 20, it stayed in the US Top 100 for two years, going platinum, and yielding three US Top 100 singles. Musically it presented a radical departure from their earlier, less structured work, peddling clinically commercial AOR riffs with huge success.

Dunbar left shortly afterwards, later joining Jefferson Starship amid the usual shouts of 'musical incompatibility'. Clearly unhappy with their revised musical direction, he was replaced by Steve Smith, previously Dunbar's roadie and one-time member of Montrose.

Released after a brief UK tour (to complete indifference), 'Evolution' made the US Top 20 in 1979, and included their first US Top 20 single, 'Lovin', Touchin', Squeezin'', plus two further US Top 100 hits. A compilation album of material from the first three albums, 'In The Beginning', briefly made the US chart in 1980 and was swiftly followed by their first US Top 10 album, 'Departure', and 1981's double live 'Captured', which also made the US Top 10. As it was released, Rolie, exhausted after seven years on the road, was replaced by Jonathan Cain (born 1950), ex-keyboard player with The Babys. 1981's multi-platinum 'Escape' topped the US chart

and was their biggest album to date, spending a year in the US Top 20, and even becoming their first UK chart album in 1982. It included four US hit singles, especially 'Who's Crying Now' (Top 5), and 'Open Arms', which spent six weeks in the US Top 3 behind Joan Jett's 'I Love Rock'n'Roll' and became their first million-selling single. 1983's 'Frontiers' spent nine weeks as the challenger to Michael Jackson's chart-topping 'Thriller' album and became their only UK Top 10 album to date, including a US Top 10 single, 'Separate Ways (Worlds Apart)', and three other US Top 30 hits.

At this juncture, various group members became involved in outside projects – Schon had collaborated with Jan Hammer on a couple of albums, 'Untold Passion' (1981) and 'Here To Stay' (1983), and cut a live album, 'Through The Fire', with Sammy Hagar, Kenny Aaronson, and Santana's Mike Shrieve which just missed the US Top 40. Perry scored a US Top 20 hit single duetting with Kenny Loggins on 'Don't Fight It' (1982), while his solo album, 'Street Talk' (1984), reached the US Top 20 and featured four US Top 40 singles, including 'Oh Sherrie' (Top 3), and he also contributed to USA For Africa's chart-topping charity single, 'We Are The World'.

In 1985, Journey made the US Top 10 with 'Only The Young', from the movie soundtrack to *Vision Quest* – their first release for two years. In 1986, they reconvened as a trio of Schon, Perry and Cain for a new album, 'Raised On Radio', which restored them to platinum status and spawned the by now obligatory four US Top 20 singles, including 'Be Good To Yourself' (Top 10), following which they undertook another sabbatical.

While Journey exemplified the bizarre syndrome of the 1980s where individual musicians were largely anonymous in comparison with the identity and sound of the group to which they belonged (other examples include Foreigner, REO Speedwagon, Toto), their extended success and mammoth record sales make them more than a footnote to rock history. If and when they decide to embark on another voyage, their instant US popularity is virtually assured. Journey was also the first group to market a video game based on one of its albums ('Escape').

Greatest Hits

Singles	Title	US	UK
1981	*Who's Crying Now*	4	46
1982	*Open Arms*	2	–
1983	*Separate Ways (Worlds Apart)*	8	–
1984	*Oh Sherrie* (Steve Perry solo)	3	–
Albums			
1980	*Departure*	8	–
1981	*Captured*	9	–
1981	*Escape*	1	32
1983	*Frontiers*	2	6
1984	*Street Talk* (Steve Perry solo)	12	59
1986	*Raised On Radio*	4	22

JOY DIVISION/NEW ORDER

Ian Curtis *(vocals)*
Bernard Sumner *(guitar, vocals)*
Peter Hook *(bass)*
Stephen Morris *drums)*

Formerly known as Stiff Kittens and Warsaw, Manchester band Joy Division were signed to Factory Records in 1979 by label owner Tony Wilson, who personally financed their debut album 'Unknown Pleasures'. Curtis (born 1951) sang in a detached, eerie fashion which was combined with trance-like rhythms in a post-punk style heavily influenced by David Bowie and The Velvet Underground. By the time the single 'Transmission', was released later that year, they had attracted a huge cult following. 'Love Will Tear Us Apart' reached the UK independent song chart in 1980 and the band found their live workload increasing, which, along with the rush to complete a new album put pressure on the fragile Curtis, who suffered from epilepsy. Curtis hanged himself in the early hours of May 18 1980, and his greatest success was to be posthumous.

Two months later, 'Love Will Tear Us Apart' reached the UK Top 20, later to be covered by The Swans, Paul Young and P.J. Proby, and the second album 'Closer' entered the UK Top 10. Even after Joy Division had ceased to exist, their popularity and success increased. 'Still' (1981), a double album compilation of live and studio material, reached the UK Top 5, their early John Peel Radio Show sessions were released in 1986, another posthumous single 'Atmosphere' became an independent chart-topper in 1988 and double compilation album, 'Substance' reached the UK Top 10.

The three remaining members of the band – Sumner (aka Albrecht, born 1956), Hook (born 1956) and Morris (born 1957) – joined forces with Gillian Gilbert (born 1961) in 1981, to form New Order – a name which attracted much hostile press because of alleged Nazi connotations. The four played their first gig together as Manchester's Squat Club, with Gilbert on keyboards and occasional guitar, and their first single, 'Ceremony', reached the UK Top 40.

The debut album, 'Movement' reached the UK Top 30 and they toured Europe throughout 1981 and 1982. The single 'Temptation' entered the UK charts in 1982 in the same month the Hacienda opened – a Manchester nightclub in which New Order have a financial interest. By the end of that year, they had achieved worldwide recognition.

In 1983 the group recorded in New York with dance producer Arthur Baker and released the '12-inch only' single, 'Blue Monday'. With its hypnotic dance beat it reached the UK Top 20, and the same year, the self-produced album, 'Power, Corruption And Lies', reached the UK Top 5.

The Baker collaboration brought the band

more success towards the end of 1983 with 'Blue Monday' entering the US dance and rock charts and the Baker-produced 'Confusion' similarly a dance hit on both sides of the Atlantic. 'Blue Monday' stayed in The UK Top 100 for the best part of a year and has since become the UK's best-selling 12-inch single of all time.

In 1984 another Baker production, 'Thieves Like Us', hit the UK singles chart, followed by 'The Perfect Kiss', which was the group's first release on Quincy Jones' Qwest label in the US.

By now, New Order had attracted an extraordinary cross section of both independent rock and dance bands. Their 'Low Life' album was a success on both sides of the Atlantic, and in 1986 'Shellshock' was featured on the soundtrack of the teen movie, *Pretty In Pink* confirming their transformation from independent cult status to pop chart regulars.

In 1987 'True Faith' made the UK Top 5, and later won the BPI Best Music Video Award; their double album 'Substance', which consisted of 12-inch single remixes, was one of the first rock LPs to be released in DAT format. 'Fine Time', released as a trailer to the 1989 album 'Technique' charted, and in 1990 New Order peaked with a UK No. 1 in 'World In Motion', recorded with the English World Cup soccer team, with lyrics by comedian Keith Allen.

Greatest Hits

Singles	Title	US	UK
New Order			
1987	*True Faith*	32	4
1988	*Blue Monday*	–	3
1990	*World In Motion*	–	1
Albums			
Joy Division			
1980	*Closer*	–	6
1981	*Still*	–	5
1988	*1977–1980 Substance*	146	7
New Order			
1987	*Substance*	36	3
1989	*Technique*	32	1

JUDAS PRIEST

Rob Halford *(vocals)*
Glenn Tipton *(guitar)*
K.K. Downing *(guitar)*
Ian Hill *(bass)*
John Hinch *(drums)*

UK heavy metal exponents Judas Priest first emerged recognizably when Hill and Downing recruited vocalist Rob Halford (born 1951) in 1971. Their indie label 1974 debut album, 'Rocka Rolla', drew the interest of a grass-roots following, but neither this attempt nor the 1975 follow-up, 'Sad Wings Of Destiny', with newly joined drummer

Alan Moore, sold in any significant quantity.

A move to a major label hitched their fortunes up a notch, and led to a support spot on Led Zeppelin's 1977 US tour. Another drummer, Les Binks, had taken over by this time (the drumstool having also been briefly occupied by sessionman Simon Phillips) and the 'Stained Class' and 'Killing Machine' albums in 1978 (the latter re-titled 'Hell Bent For Leather' in the US) established them in the front line, 'Machine' including the UK Top 20 single 'Take On The World'. Their first American hit was the 1979 live in Japan album 'Unleashed In The East', after which the drummer was again replaced, this time by Dave Holland (ex-Trapeze). 'British Steel', in 1980, was their biggest UK album, making the Top 5, with two UK Top 20 singles, 'Living After Midnight' and 'Breaking The Law', and in 1982 'Screaming for Vengeance' became their first gold album in the US.

Through the 1980s Priest moved to a more thoughtful working of the HM genre, recording unlikely cover versions which have included Fleetwood Mac's 'Green Manalishi' and Chuck Berry's 'Johnny B. Goode'. Despite a concentrated workmanship, typified in 1986 by 'Turbo', a US Top 20 album, by the close of the decade their releases were not making the impact of their earlier product, 1988's 'Ram It Down' just missing the UK Top 20 album list. In 1990 a protracted US legal case saw the band cleared of accusations of recording 'satanic' messages backwards on their albums and allegedly causing the suicide of two fans thereby.

Greatest Hits

Singles	Title	US	UK
1980	*Living After Midnight*	–	12
1980	*Breaking The Law*	–	12
Albums			
1980	*British Steel*	34	4
1982	*Screaming For Vengeance*	17	11

B.B. **KING**

Perhaps the most respected of all present-day blues exponents, King (born 1925) has defined what are now clichés of the idiom. Recognized principally for his clean, jazz-tinged style with its note-bending trademark, he is also a singer whose extemporizations and easy falsetto came from his time in gospel quartets during his Mississippi boyhood. As a 14-year-old plantation labourer, Riley B. King was given a guitar as part of his wages. While there is evidence that he listened to players as diverse as T-Bone Walker and Django Reinhardt, the most immediate influ-

Riley 'B.B.' King, the guitarists' guitarist

ence was his cousin, Bukka White. Moving to Memphis in 1945, King received tuition from Robert Lockwood, stepson of the remarkable Robert Johnson, before working with the city's first negro-manned radio station as a musician and disc-jockey, earning the nom de turntable 'Beale Street Blues Boy' (soon truncated to just 'B.B.').

After an obscure single in 1949, King's signing to a Californian label in 1950 marked the real start of his recording career. After 'Three O'Clock Blues' topped the US 'sepia' chart, King would always be lionized by a black urban public. Notable among later specialist hits were 1955's million-selling 'Everyday I Have The Blues' (previously recorded by Memphis Slim, Lowell Fulson and Joe Turner), 'Woke Up This Morning' and 1960's 'Sweet Sixteen'. Mostly characterized by brassy big band arrangements, these also embraced rapid single-note guitar flurries developed – like the tubby King's disarmingly self-deprecative stage manner – during a relentless touring schedule throughout North America.

A label change in 1961 made no sudden difference to King's workload as recordings like 1965's riveting Chicago concert album, 'Live At The Regal', continued to sell steadily, but when Mike Bloomfield, Eric Clapton and other well-known white guitarists were sincerely loud in praising him, it made commercial sense for King to aim his music at a wider market. After 1969's half-live, half-studio 'Live And Well' album, the same year's studio album, 'Completely Well' spawned the Grammy-winning 'The Thrill Is Gone', King's only US Top 20 single. Renowned guest artists on later projects included Carole King (on 1970's 'Indianola Mississippi Seeds') and for 'In London', Steve Marriott, Ringo Starr and Alexis Korner. King then played more gigs in mainstream pop venues, and recorded unlikely items such as The Lovin' Spoonful's 'Summer In The City' (on 1973's patchy 'Guess Who').

One of the few surviving links between post-war blues and contemporary rock, King has been awarded an honorary university doctorate and, in tuxedo and bow-tie, has worked with orchestras and also with Ray Charles, Miles Davis, The Crusaders, and has long been capable of filling both Caesar's Palace in Las Vegas and the Royal Albert Hall in London. Symptomatic of this continued veneration was the inclusion of King's version of 'In The Midnight Hour' in 1985's *Into The Night* movie soundtrack, his 1987 Grammy Award for Lifetime Achievement and his cameo on a U2 single in 1989. The vast majority of his scores of albums clearly demonstrate that his position as the ultimate bluesman is richly deserved.

Greatest Hits

Singles	Title	US	UK
1969	The Thrill is Gone	15	–
Albums			
1969	The Thrill Is Gone	38	–
1970	Indianola Mississippi Seeds	26	–
1971	Live At Cook County Jail	25	–

Ben E. KING

At a time when every fourth record in the UK chart was either a revival or a reissue of an old song, snippet coverage of his 'Stand By Me' in a 1987 TV commercial facilitated King's return to the UK singles chart after a long absence. To a lesser degree, the use of the song in a film of the same name repeated the trick in the US.

Benjamin Earl Nelson (born 1938) adopted the surname of an uncle on migrating from his native North Carolina to New York as a professional singer. From grumbling bass singer with The Crowns, he was promoted to lead vocalist when the group replaced the entire personnel of The Drifters in 1959. With a string section often assuming the part usually allocated to saxophone or guitar, King emoted 'There Goes My Baby', 'Dance With Me', 'Save The Last Dance For Me' and other smashes of the group's high summer and he was well-placed to begin a solo career in 1960.

Following a US hit with the evocative 'Spanish Harlem', the partly self-penned 'Stand By Me', was initially only a moderate seller, although it inspired many covers. The most successful of them by Kenny Lynch, Cassius Clay (aka Muhammad Ali) (!) and John Lennon. Likewise, King's 1963 Italian translation, 'I (Who Have Nothing)' was recorded to lucrative effect by Welsh balladeers Shirley Bassey and, in 1970, Tom Jones.

This type of material and his versions of 'I Could Have Danced All Night', 'Perfidia' and other showbiz standards compounded King's tilting at mainstream cabaret but, as in 1964's

'Around The Corner' – about a black youth's affair with a white girl – he also took on quite tough items. He was no slouch as a straight soul shouter either, as demonstrated by 'Don't Play That Song You Lied', and 'Seven Letters', as well as his membership of the ad hoc Soul Clan with Don Covay, Joe Tex and others for the 'Soul Meeting' single and an eponymous album. In 1970, he stretched out further with the 'progressive' 'Rough Edges' collection, in which Bob Dylan's 'Lay Lady Lay' nestled uneasily with a retread of Wilson Pickett's 'In The Midnight Hour'.

In the early 1970s King rested on his laurels with repackagings and a 1972 concert reunion with the Drifters. However, a one-shot disco outing in 1975, 'Supernatural Thing', precipated a US comeback and encouraging sales for 1975's 'Supernatural' album. By the close of the decade he had attempted to reach a hipper audience with arrangements of Van Morrison's 'Into The Mystic' and, on 'Benny And Us' – an album collaboration with The Average White Band – as well as John Lennon's 'Imagine'.

The 1980s saw less effective stabs at disco, with albums 'Music Trance' and 1981's 'Street Tough', before King frontèd The Drifters again for a global tour. After cutting Arthur Alexander's 'You Better Move On' with his old group, a dearth of new recordings prefaced 1988's 'Spin Myself Around'. That this single flopped did not prevent King filling London's Palladium theatre when visiting the UK in the wake of the 'Stand By Me' windfall.

Greatest Hits

Singles	Title	US	UK
1961	Spanish Harlem	10	–
1961	Stand By Me	4	27
1975	Supernatural Thing (Part 1)	5	–
1986	Stand By Me (reissue)	9	1
Albums			
1961	Spanish Harlem	57	30
1977	Benny & Us (with Average White Band)	33	–
1987	Stand By Me (The Ultimate Collection)	–	14

167

Carole KING

Born Carole Klein, in 1942, Carole King wrote songs with Paul Simon while at college, later pursuing her talent at Don Kirshner's legendary Brill Building 'song factory' in New York. In 1959 she was the subject of fellow Brill Building writer Neil Sedaka's hit, 'Oh Carole', but her answer record, 'Oh Neil', was a flop.

Teaming up with Gerry Goffin (who later became her first husband), she wrote dozens of classic teen angst and romance hits between 1960 and 1967, including 'Will You Love Me

Carole King, feelin' like a Natural Woman

Tomorrow' (The Shirelles, 1960), 'Take Good Care Of My Baby' (Bobby Vee, 1961), 'Halfway To Paradise' and 'I'll Never Find Another You' (Tony Orlando, both covered in the UK by Billy Fury, 1961), 'The Loco-motion' (Little Eva, 1961 – Eva Boyd was King's babysitter), 'One Fine Day' (The Chiffons, 1963), 'I'm Into Something Good' (Herman's Hermits, 1964). These were well-crafted songs, with simple lyrics and memorable tunes, but by the mid-1960s, her lyrics were maturing, as demonstrated by 'Goin' Back', a 1966 UK hit for Dusty Springfield (which was covered by The Byrds, who also recorded 'Wasn't Born To Follow'), 'Pleasant Valley Sunday' (The Monkees) and particularly 'Natural Woman' (Aretha Franklin).

King's own recording career had started slowly. Between 1960 and 1962 she recorded flops for several labels, but in 1962 scored an international hit with 'It Might As Well Rain Until September', which proved to be a one-off. In 1965 she helped form the short-lived Tomorrow label, whose roster included New York rock band The Myddle Class, whose bassist, Charles Larkey, became King's second husband and writing partner. In 1968, along with guitarist Danny Kortchmar, the couple formed City, who cut one album which was essentially a vehicle for King's songs. After the album failed, she became a genuine solo artist.

Her first album under her own name, 'Writer' (1970), was a moderate success, but the follow-up, 'Tapestry' (1971) eventually sold ten million copies world-wide and thrust her into the vanguard of the new generation of singer/songwriters. Containing classics like the US chart-topping single, 'It's Too Late', 'You've Got A Friend' (covered by James Taylor), 'Smackwater Jack' and an emotional reading of 'Will You Love Me Tomorrow', it was obvious that she was streets ahead of her youthful rivals.

Her follow-up albums, 'Music' (1971) and 'Rhymes And Reasons' (1972), confirmed her status, but were largely retreads of 'Tapestry'.

With 1973's 'Fantasy', she attempted to broaden her subject matter to include social issues as well as romantic ones, but with mixed results. 'Wrap Around Joy' (1974) which followed it, at least provided her with her first big single hit, 'Jazzman', since 'It's Too Late'.

She has continued to make albums quite regularly, the most interesting being 'Pearls' (1980), a collection of remakes of Goffin and King classics. The fact that few have approached the excellence or success of 'Tapestry' does not diminish her stature as either a songwriter or a performer.

Greatest Hits

Singles	Title	US	UK
1962	It Might As Well Rain		
	Until September	22	3
1971	It's Too Late	1	6
1974	Jazzman	2	–
Albums			
1971	Tapestry	1	4
1971	Music	1	18
1972	Rhymes And Reasons	2	40
1974	Wrap Around Joy	1	–
1976	Thoroughbred	3	–

The **KINKS**

Ray Davies (vocals, guitar, harmonica)
Dave Davies (vocals, guitar)
Pete Quaife (bass)
Mick Avory (drums)

Even without leading The Kinks, Ray Davies (born 1944) would have been recognized as an outstanding composer. However, after the first flush of hits with the group, he dared to follow a path so un-fashionable that lesser talents overtook The Kinks in commercial terms. Yet while many of their 1960s rivals work today's nostalgia circuit, The Kinks remain vague contenders with their new output.

The group was started by backing singer Robert Wace who, with connections in high places, found bookings at society gatherings. After one particularly embarrassing date in 1962, Wace retreated to the less public role of group manager, a task he shared (not always harmoniously) with stockbroker Grenville Collins and music-biz veteran Larry Page. Sales of the quartet's first two singles – London hybrids of Merseybeat – were not encouraging but the exhilarating if primitive 'You Really Got Me' (later cited as nascent heavy metal) shot to the top of the UK chart in 1964. To maximize cash flow, the group were obliged to rush out their eponymous debut album, largely a mixture of Ray Davies originals and R&B covers, but its raw drive ensured a long spell in the UK album chart.

Hit followed hit for three years. Though

they mainly pursued the riff-based 'You Really Got Me' format, The Kinks weren't afraid of commercial risks, such as 1965's 'See My Friend', which anticipated the injection of both Indian sounds and bisexuality into pop. Later that year, deliberate guitar feedback preluded the B-side, 'I Need You'.

The rowdy style of their bigger hits was reflected in disorderly behaviour on the road. An onstage brawl resulted in hospital treat-ment for Dave Davies (born 1947) and rumours of the group's disbandment. They were further beset by a lengthy American Federation of Musicians' ban for 'unprofes-sional conduct'.

Courted by artists as diverse as The Pretty Things and Peggy Lee for songs he felt were unusable by The Kinks, the prolific Ray Davies found songwriting a more viable proposition than riots on tour with the group. On *Ready Steady Go* in 1965, The Kinks previewed 'A Well Respected Man', the first of Davies's intrinsically English songs, in which literate lyrics were set to idiosyncratic music. The scenarios and characters created in albums like 1966's 'Face To Face' and, especially, 1968's 'Village Green Preservation Society' could be updated parlour poetry. Ray Davies's laconic singing was better suited to this phase of The Kinks' saga, and his natural skill as an actor came into its own when he took the lead in a BBC TV drama in 1966, the first of many extramural ventures that included 1985's *Return To Waterloo*, a TV play he wrote. His younger brother was thrust briefly into the spotlight in 1967 when 'Death Of A Clown', one of his two lead vocals on the 'Something Else' album, was issued as a single. Its Top 5 placing was sufficiently heartening to allow Dave three more shots in his own right, but only 'Suzannah's Still Alive' made further chart impact. In the 1980s he resumed his sporadic solo career with three albums.

In 1966 Quaife (born 1943) left The Kinks briefly to front Maple Oak, who recorded a solitary flop single. John Dalton (born 1943) from Mark Four (later The Creation) filled in, and was the obvious replacement when Quaife left again in 1969. His exit involved problems with the group's record label, which ignored objections that budget-priced repack-aging of old Kinks material would adversely affect the group's new albums. Viewing The Kinks as short-term hit-makers, they allowed the group to sign elsewhere when their con-tract expired in 1971. From a knockabout spontaneity, their stage act was now aimed at a more adult audience. Wishing to perform the more complex sounds of hits like 'Dead End Street', 'Waterloo Sunset' and 'Autumn Almanac', they hired sidemen for concerts that now resembled an old-fashioned music hall.

After a period of ebbing record success, 'Lola' restored The Kinks to the UK Top 10, doing likewise in the US, where their cult following was enough for 'Some Mother's

From raunchy R&B to swinging London lyricism, the Kinks often fell between two stylistic stools

Son' from 1969's 'Arthur Or The Decline And Fall Of The British Empire' to be sung by protestors outside the White House during the Viertnam moratorium.

A concept album, 'Arthur' was a reliable pointer towards more grandiloquent projects in which The Kinks merely backed Ray Davies for increasingly theatrical presentations promoting 'Lola Versus Powerman And The Money-Go-Round' (with sharp lyrical digs at Wace, Collins and Page), 'Muswell Hillbillies', 'Everybody's In Showbiz Everybody's A Star' (with 'live' tracks and the turntable hit, 'Celluloid Heroes'), 'Preservation Acts One and Two', 1975's 'Soap Opera' and 'Schoolboys In Disgrace', nearly all projecting a specific and recurrent mood. Generally, these were unconvincing, but individual songs, like 'One Of The Survivors' and 'The Hard Way', were undeserved failures as singles. Ray Davies announced in 1973 that the group – then augmented with John Gosling (keyboards) – was finished, which represented a personal and financial nadir epitomized by a messy divorce and the winding-down of Konk, the group's own label, which had signed Claire Hamill and Tom Robinson's Cafe Society.

Slowly the tide turned, and, with an unexpectedly high position for 1979's 'Low Budget' in the US album chart, the group moved up the Adult-Orientated Rock hierarchy. Their music, too, acquired a harder edge, tailored as it was for headlining in stadiums rather than theatres. They returned to the singles Top 20 in 1983 with 'Come Dancing' (from 'State Of Confusion'), but their presence there had been felt by proxy over the previous decade via cover versions by David Bowie, The Jam, Van Halen and The Pretenders (whose Chrissie Hynde had a lengthy love affair with Ray Davies). In the

1980s the group's early work was kept before the public with hit covers by The Stranglers, The Fall and Kirsty MacColl. Later offerings by the group – now with Jim Rodford (bass) and drummer Robert Henrit (ex-Argent) as full-time personnel – such as 'Think Visual' and 1989's 'UK Jive' have been patchy, although 'Quiet Life', Ray Davies's solo contribution to the movie soundtrack of *Absolute Beginners*, was the equal of many of his best-known Kinks songs.

Greatest Hits

Singles	Title	US	UK
1964	*You Really Got Me*	7	1
1965	*Tired Of Waiting For You*	6	1
1966	*Sunny Afternoon*	14	1
Albums			
1964	*Kinks*	–	3
1965	*Kinda Kinks*	–	3
1966	*Greatest Hits*	–	9

KISS

Paul Stanley (guitar, vocals)
Peter Criss (guitar, vocals)
Gene Simmons (bass, vocals)
Ace Frehley (drums)

With their grotesque make-up, Gothic, over-the-top stage show and monolithic riffing, Kiss seemed to lampoon Heavy Metal, caricaturing themselves. Nonetheless, their gross cross-fertilization of Bowie, Glam Rock, sundry cartoon characters, and bone-crunching hard rock struck the right chord, alienating parents and rock critics alike, and earning unquestioning support from a pre-

dominantly teenage market who idolized them, rewarding them with numerous platinum and gold albums.

Formed in New York in 1972 by Stanley (born Paul Stanley Eisen) and Simmons (born Gene Klein), who met Criss (born Peter Crisscoula, 1947) via an ad in *Rolling Stone*, and Frehley (born Paul Frehley) from an ad in *Village Voice*, the quartet rehearsed and experimented with make-up and costumes for several months, emerging to play in New York clubs. Signed to Casablanca Records (predominantly a disco label), their somewhat pedestrian early albums, 'Kiss' and 'Hotter Than Hell' (both 1974), disappointed but nevertheless made brief US Top 100 chart showings, as did a single, 'Kissin' Time'. Heavy touring boosted 1975's 'Dressed To Kill' album, which made the US Top 40 and became their first gold album, and from which a stage favourite, 'Rock & Roll All Nite', was another US Top 100 single.

By this stage, Kiss had a massive grass roots following, and it took a live album to finally break them: their second 1975 album, 'Alive!', made the US Top 10, and included a second (live) version of 'Rock & Roll All Nite', which made the Top 20 of the US singles chart. This established a pattern which would sustain throughout their career: while rarely registering heavily with singles (they only ever had one US Top 10 hit), their success was built upon their phenomenal crowd-pulling power, which converted into album sales. 1976's 'Destroyer' was their first platinum album, making the US Top 20 and including their classic US Top 10 single, 'Beth', which was a major change of direction, presenting a softer, melodic and more commercial style. The album was their UK chart debut, also belatedly reactivating 'Alive!' (No. 49) and prompting a brief UK tour, which was only partially successful due to the band's insistence on conducting interviews wearing full make-up. It took several years before Kiss made any impact in the UK. 1976's 'The Originals' was an opportunistic exercise in marketing: a triple album set repackaging their first three releases, including a comic book history of the band, which was surprisingly successful, making the US Top 40. Marvel Comics later took the comic concept to its logical conclusion, publishing several Kiss titles.

Kiss continued to release platinum albums more or less annually: 'Rock & Roll Over' (US Top 20, platinum, 1976), 'Love Gun' (US Top 5, platinum 1977), 'Alive II' (US Top 10, platinum, 1977), 'Double Platinum' (a double album 'Best Of', US Top 30, 1978), 'Dynasty' (US Top 10, platinum, 1979). In a wholly unprecedented – but quite logical – move, all four group members released eponymous solo albums simultaneously in 1978, which all made the US chart – Simmons and Frehley both made the Top 30, Stanley the Top 40 and Criss the Top 50. Frehley's album included a US Top 20 single, 'New York Groove'.

Tongue in cheek? Just letting it all hang out was Gene Simmons' usual reply

1980's 'Kiss Unmasked' barely made the US Top 40 (despite the fact that it eventually went gold), and Criss left to go solo just prior to its release. Although Eric Carr proved a worthy successor, his joining the band coincided with a downturn of fortunes for Kiss, as the excellent concept album, 'Music From The Elder' (featuring songs co-written by Lou Reed) peaked well outside the US Top 50. Frehley also left in 1982, prompting several temporary 'replacements': Bob Kulick, Vinnie Vincent, and Mark St John took it in turns to deputise, Kulick eventually settling in. 1982's 'Creatures Of The Night' album, which was more successful in the UK than the US, marked a return to their earlier gross style, and rekindled interest – in the UK, a compilation album, 'Killers' also made the Top 50.

Kiss revealed themselves without stage make-up for first time in 1983, as did the album sleeve to that year's 'Lick It Up', which made the UK Top 10 and US Top 30, and 1984's 'Animalize' (US Top 20, UK Top 10)

restored them to platinum status. They remain one of world's foremost Heavy Metal bands and although considerably less prolific in the 1980s, continued to sell enormous quantities of albums, such as 1985's 'Asylum' (US & UK Top 20) and 1987's 'Crazy Nights' (US Top 20, UK Top 5), while the latter's title track provided them with their first UK Top 30 single, peaking in the Top 10. Simmons has continued to pursue extra-curricular activities during the 1980's, most notably as an actor.

Greatest Hits

Singles	Title	US	UK
1976	Beth	7	–
1987	Crazy Crazy Nights	71	7
Albums			
1975	Alive!	5	49
1977	Love Gun	4	–
1977	Alive II	7	60
1983	Lick It Up	24	7
1987	Crazy Nights	18	4

Gladys **KNIGHT** and the **PIPS**

Gladys Knight
Merald 'Bubba' Knight
Brenda Knight
William Guest
Eleanor Guest (vocal group)

From Atlanta, Georgia, Gladys Knight (born 1944) was a child singer with the Morris Brown and Wings Over Jordan gospel choirs before forming a vocal group in 1952 with her elder brother Merald (born 1942), her sister Brenda and cousins William (born 1941) and Eleanor Guest. They performed at social and church functions singing a mixture of gospel songs and ballads, before turning professional in 1957 at the instigation of another cousin, James 'Pip' Woods, who became their manager and dubbed the group with his nickname.

Their record debut came the same year with 'Whistle My Love', a single which sold disappointingly despite opening spots on tours by Jackie Wilson and Sam Cooke. Brenda and Eleanor both left the group a year or so later to get married, and were replaced by Edward Patten (born 1939) another cousin, and Langston George.

They were back in the studio in 1960, recording an old Johnny Otis song, 'Every Beat Of My Heart', for a local Atlanta label. After a cool start, a lease deal with a bigger label helped break the record nationally in 1961, by which time the group had re-recorded the song for the Fury label in New York, the net result being that the Fury version reached the US Top 50 while the original topped the US R&B chart and made the US pop Top 10.

Another hit on Fury followed early in 1962, 'Letter Full Of Tears', which reached the US Top 20. A third single on the label, 'Operator', only just made the US Top 100, after which George left the line-up. Gladys herself was to leave later in the year to marry and have a baby, the Pips sticking together as session singers until 1964.

Her return in 1964 saw a new contract with an independent label which resulted in a US Top 40 hit, 'Giving Up', produced by Van McCoy. A subsequent lesser US hit, 'Lovers Always Forgive', pre-dated the label's demise, and the group was once again in limbo until a guest spot on a Motown package led to their signing with Berry Gordy in 1966.

Their debut on a Motown subsidiary label, 'Just Walk In My Shoes', failed to chart, but the Norman Whitfield-produced 'Take Me In Your Arms And Love Me' went Top 20 in the UK. Later in 1967, they topped the US R&B charts with 'I Heard It Through The Grapevine', which also made the US pop chart Top 3 and UK Top 50, pre-dating Marvin Gaye's version.

More Motown hits followed, including 1968's 'The End Of Our Road' and 'The Nitty Gritty' and 'Friendship Train' (both

Knight Train to Georgia tops pops for Pips

1969), all making the US Top 20. Whitfield was dropped as producer before the group's second million seller, 'If I Were Your Woman' (1971), the start of a ballad-oriented phase that included the US Top 20 single 'I Don't Want To Do Wrong' and a cover of Kris Kristofferson's 'Help Me Make It Through The Night', which made the US Top 40 and UK Top 2.

A move away from Motown after 1973's US Top 3 hit 'Neither One Of Us (Wants To Be The First To Say Goodbye)' marked the start of their most successful string of hits. Five million-sellers in a row: 'Where Peaceful Waters Flow' and the US chart-topper 'Midnight Train To Georgia' in 1973; 'Best Thing That Ever Happened To Me', 'I've Got To Use My Imagination' and the film-featured 'On And On' in 1974 firmly established the group in the superstar category. A US Top 10 album, 'Imagination' confirmed this status.

Since their UK Top 5 hits, 'The Way We Were' in 1975 and 1977's 'Baby Don't Change Your Mind', Knight's best sales have been in the album market, reflecting a working life that has moved more and more to the cabaret/supper-club circuit in latter years, though the group can still fill concert venues worldwide.

As well as numerous compilations, among their hottest later albums were 1980's 'About Love', which reached the US Top 50 under a then-new record deal, and the gold 'Visions', which made the US Top 40 three years later.

Never to be dismissed from the pop stakes, the group reappeared on the US Top 20 having topped the US R&B chart with 'Love Overboard' in 1988.

Greatest Hits

Singles	Title	US	UK
1967	I Heard It Through The Grapevine	2	47
1973	Neither One Of Us (Wants To Be The First To Say Goodbye)	2	31
1973	Midnight Train To Georgia	1	10
1974	Best Thing That Ever Happened To Me	3	31
Albums			
1973	Neither One Of Us	9	–
1973	Imagination	9	–
1976	The Best Of	36	6
1977	30 Greatest	–	3

Billy J. KRAMER

The third of Brian Epstein's Merseyside clients to reach the UK Top 10, Kramer's achievements have guaranteed him a footnote in pop history, even if he was never able to recapture the success he enjoyed in 1963–4. As rhythm guitarist with Billy Forde & The Phantoms, William Ashton (born 1943) adopted the stage name Billy Kramer on transferring to The Coasters, primarily an instrumental unit. When his guitar was stolen, Kramer agreed to become the group's singer. Though only amateurs, the Coasters and Kramer rose to third place in *Merseybeat's* 1963 popularity poll, their individuality lying in Kramer's boyish good looks and pleasant croon, which, if required, became a polite growl.

While Kramer impressed Epstein, The

Coasters were replaced by The Dakotas, a more accomplished outfit from Manchester. Under George Martin's supervision, the pairing's debut single was an arrangement of a track from the first Beatles album, 'Do You Want To Know A Secret'. At John Lennon's suggestion, Kramer's name on the record label was split with a non-signifying 'J'. Lennon also supplied 'Bad To Me', the second hit for Kramer & The Dakotas. Seeing out 1963 in fine fashion was another Beatles-penned smash, 'I'll Keep You Satisfied', as well as an instrumental UK Top 20 hit, 'The Cruel Sea', by The Dakotas alone.

Kramer's fourth single, 'Little Children', was his biggest US hit, but momentum was lost with the emergence of fresher British acts like The Animals and The Kinks. Not helping either was Chad & Jeremy's US-only cover of Kramer's next single, Paul McCartney's 'From A Window'. Kramer's desire to update his image was thwarted by commitments to pantomine and variety, and 1965 began with a serious miss in 'It's Gonna Last Forever' and the related departure of most of the original Dakotas. Finishing eight places below composer Burt Bacharach's own version, 'Trains And Boats And Planes' was Kramer's final hit.

After his recording contract was not renewed in 1967, Kramer recorded in many different styles for a plethora of other labels, major and minor, who continue to issue Kramer output to the present day, though records soon became incidental to a livelihood earned mainly in cabaret and nostalgia revues. Among highlights of his later recordings were an orchestrated version of the Bee Gees song 'Town Of Tuxley Toymaker', which received much UK airplay, and the more adventurous '1941', an undeserved flop. Another heroic failure was 1983's poignant 'You Can't Live On Memories', but a revival at this late date seems unlikely.

Greatest Hits

Singles	Title	US	UK
1963	Do You Want To Know A Secret	–	2
1963	Bad To Me	9	1
1964	Little Children	7	1
Albums			
1963	Listen To Billy J. Kramer	–	11
1964	Little Children	48	–

Kris KRISTOFFERSON

A singer/songwriter and film star, Texan Kris Kristofferson (born 1937) has rarely achieved the artistic success his musical genius has deserved, although his solid body of albums include a plethora of notable songs. Born Kristoffer Kristofferson, son of a US Air Force major general, he grew up in California. After obtaining a degree at Pomona

Kris Kristofferson – songwriter, actor, singer . . . in that order?

Isle of Wight Festival for a bill topped by The Doors, Sly & The Family Stone, Miles Davis, Jimi Hendrix and many other contemporary superstars. Among the members of his band was Billy Swan and Dennis Linde (see below). His 1971 album 'The Silver Tongued Devil And I', featured the hauntingly beautiful 'Epitaph (Black And Blue)', written for and sung by Kristofferson at the funeral wake of Janis Joplin, one of his old flames. Five months later, Joplin posthumously scored her biggest ever hit with her version of Kristofferson's 'Me & Bobby McGee', which topped the US chart.

In 1972 Kristofferson not only released two albums, 'Border Lord' and 'Jesus Was A Capricorn', but also starred in his first movie, *Cisco Pike*, which was followed in 1973 by his fine lead performance in Sam Peckinpah's last film, *Pat Garrett and Billy the Kid*, which also starred Bob Dylan. Also in 1973 he married singer Rita Coolidge, with whom he released duet albums in 1973 ('Full Moon') and 1974 ('Breakaway'), the latter including the song 'Lover Please', written by Kristofferson's long-time friend and fellow musician, Billy Swan, who had a No. 1 hit in 1974 with the self-penned 'I Can Help'. Among other notable musicians who appeared on Kristofferson albums over the years were Fred Tackett (Little Feat), Glen Clark (Delbert & Glen) and Dennis Linde (writer of 'Burning Love', one of the best latter-day Elvis Presley hits). Also in 1974 came Kristofferson's fifth solo album, 'Spooky Lady's Sideshow', which like all its precedessors reached the US Top 100, and he also starred in the feature films *Bring Me the Head of Alfredo Garcia* and *Alice Doesn't Live Here Any More*, the latter directed by Martin Scorsese, and in 1976, 'Who's To Bless . . . And Who's To Blame' was his least successful album since the start.

1976 also brought his biggest leap to cinematic celebrity when he starred opposite Barbra Streisand in the second remake of the 1937 movie, *A Star Is Born*, in which he played the part of a rock star on the downhill slide while his singer girlfriend (played by Streisand) is on the way up. A highly successful soundtrack album topped the US album chart for six weeks, although virtually all the musical credit went to Streisand for the soulful 'Love Theme (Evergreen)', on which Kristofferson vocally assisted her, which topped the US singles chart. In the same year, his 'Surreal Thing' album, perhaps influenced by the music in *A Star Is Born*, had a much heavier rock feel than many of his previous efforts, and included 'The Golden Idol', a song apparently written some years previously, which lyrically appears to allude, like many of his songs, to his friendship with Janis Joplin. The album was an even smaller hit than its predecessor.

Films and songwriting seemed to vie with for his attention during this period, as he completed another two films in 1976, *The Sailor Who Fell From Grace with the Sea* and

College and through winning short story contests, he was awarded a Rhodes Scholarship in 1958 to study English literature at Oxford University, England, after which he followed his family's wishes by joining the US Army, spending five years as a helicopter pilot in West Germany.

Due next to teach English literature at West Point Military Academy, Captain Kristofferson decided instead to leave the service and pursue a career as a songwriter in Nashville, where he worked as a cleaner at Columbia recording studios while Bob Dylan was recording his legendary 'Blonde on Blonde' double album. He also earned a crust as a janitor in a local bar, the Tally Ho Tavern, frequented by musicians and songwriters. Broke and hungry, he pushed his songs to

anyone who would listen until finally Roger Miller cut a Kristofferson song, 'Me & Bobby McGee', later also covered by artists as diverse as Janis Joplin, Gordon Lightfoot and Jerry Lee Lewis. In fact almost everyone had a hit with it – except Kristofferson. More cover versions of Kristofferson songs followed by artists such as Johnny Cash ('Sunday Morning Coming Down') and both Sammi Smith and Gladys Knight & The Pips ('Help Me Make It Through The Night').

After signing a record deal in 1969, these songs were among the classics on his debut album, 'Kristofferson' (later re-issued as 'Me And Bobby McGee'), which is still regarded by many as his finest work. In 1970 'Kristofferson' (as he was bizarrely billed in some papers) was the unknown opening act at the

Vigilante Force, neither having any musical content. 1978 brought his biggest original album since 1974, 'Easter Island', the title track of which concerns the mysterious monolithic heads on that island, plus two more films, *Semi Tough*, with Burt Reynolds, and the trucking movie, *Convoy*, based on a song by country singer C.W. McCall. In 1980 Kristofferson appeared in the epic financial disaster, *Heaven's Gate*, directed by Michael Cimino, which reputedly made the largest ever loss in the world of the cinema, with box office takings of $1.5 million against a total cost of $57 million!

It seemed that songwriting was being pushed further into the background, but in 1979 Kristofferson released both a third duet album with Coolidge, 'Natural Act', and a new solo album, 'Shake Hands With The Devil', while his final solo album before moving labels was 1981's 'To The Bone'. His marriage to Rita Coolidge had ended in divorce and the songs on the album reflect the bitterness and disillusionment of a failed relationship, illustrated by 'Nobody Loves Anybody Anymore'. In 1982 he teamed up with Willie Nelson, Dolly Parton and Brenda Lee for a double concept album, 'Winning Hand', and in 1984 starred with Willie Nelson in the feature film *Songwriter*, for which he also contributed to the soundtrack album, which made the US chart. In 1985 with Nelson, Waylon Jennings and Johnny Cash, Kristofferson was involved in the million-selling 'Highwayman' album, but otherwise appeared to have chosen in favour of films. Then in 1986 he came back with a new wife and the first album of a new deal, 'Repossessed'. 1990 brought another solo album, 'Third World Warrior', plus 'Highwayman 2', again with Cash, Nelson and Jennings. While he has had little recent commercial success, Kristofferson is certainly one of the most skilful and inspired songwriters of the rock'n'roll era, and he could easily return to contention at any time.

Greatest Hits

Singles	Title	US	UK
1971	*Loving Her Was Easier*	26	–
1973	*Why Me*	16	–
Albums			
1971	*The Silver-Tongued Devil And I*	21	–
1973	*Full Moon* (with Rita Coolidge)	26	–

Major LANCE

Part of what is now considered to be the 'old school' of sweet soul singers, ex-boxer Lance (born 1942) worked around his native Chicago and, along with his contemporary, Curtis Mayfield, helped establish a Chicago soul sound.

Lance had already recorded unsuccessfully on Mercury when he moved to the CBS-distributed Okeh label, where the formula of Mayfield songs, arrangements by veteran Johnny Pates and production by Carl Davis resulted in a string of hits between 1963 and 1965. 'The Monkey Time' was the first, a US Top 10 hit, followed by 'Hey Little Girl' and the even more successful 'Um Um Um Um Um Um', which was covered chartwise in the UK by Wayne Fontana & The Mindbenders. 'The Matador' in 1964 completed a run of US Top 20 entries, while 'Rhythm' and 'Come See' were among strong US R&B hits that did moderately well in the US pop charts.

Lance's records drew comparison with The Impressions, Mayfield's group, largely because the latter often provided backing vocals. In 1968, he changed labels, along with Carl Davis, to Dakar, and made a showing in the R&B list with 'Follow The Leader'. A 1970 US R&B hit, 'Stay Away From Me (I Love You Too Much)', was on Mayfield's Curtom label and was Lance's final US pop hit, after which, in 1972, he recorded for the Volt and Playboy labels. He toured the UK where he had become something of a cult figure on the Northern Soul club scene (despite having only one minor UK hit), though he never again produced the hits he had enjoyed in his heyday.

Greatest Hits

Singles	Title	US	UK
1963	*The Monkey Time*	8	–
1963	*Hey Little Girl*	13	–
1964	*Um Um Um Um Um Um*	5	40
Albums			
1964	*Um Um Um Um Um Um/ The Best of Major Lance*	100	–

Ronnie LANE

Lane (born 1946) was the bass player with The Small Faces (see separate entry) and later The Faces (see Rod Stewart), whom he left in 1973 to concentrate on a solo career. In The Faces, Lane had always sung some of his own songs, which were generally more countrified than the band's patented inebriated R&B material. His first venture after leaving The Faces was The Passing Show, a short-lived travelling revue in a circus tent which featured performances by Lane alongside traditional sideshow entertainment, from which grew Lane's own outfit, Slim Chance.

In 1974 he scored two UK hit singles, 'How Come' and 'The Poacher' and an album, 'Anymore For Anymore', featuring a Slim Chance line-up of Steve Bingham (bass), Kevin Westlake (guitar), Bruce Rowland (percussion), Billy Livsey (keyboards), Jimmy Jewel (saxophone) plus Scottish multi-instrumental duo Benny Gallagher and Graham Lyle. After the album, Gallagher & Lyle left to pursue their own career, and Lane changed labels and formed a completely new band for his second album, 'Ronnie Lane's Slim Chance', with Ruan O'Lochlainn (saxophone), Glen Le Fleur (drums), Steve Simpson (guitar, mandolin, violin), Charlie Hart (keyboards) and Brian Belshaw (bass). This line-up toured, but O'Lochlainn left before the next album, 1976's peerless 'One For The Road', as did drummer Le Fleur, replaced by Colin Davey. 'Mahoney's Last Stand', a soundtrack album with fellow ex-Face Ron Wood followed, but none of the albums sold in large numbers, and little was heard of Lane until late 1977 when he recorded an album with Pete Townshend (see separate entry), 'Rough Mix', containing a 50/50 split of Townshend and Lane items. Townshend and Lane were both followers of the guru Meher Baba, and had collaborated on Townshend's 1972 solo set, 'Who Came First'.

Two years elapsed before Lane's next album, 'See Me', with a supporting cast of players which included Eric Clapton, during which time rumours of Lane's failing health had circulated. He was diagnosed as suffering from multiple sclerosis, and since then has virtually retired from music, making only one UK appearance, at the 1983 ARMS (Action for Research into Multiple Sclerosis) charity concert at London's Royal Albert Hall, when he upstaged the assembled rock superstars (Clapton, Beck, Page, Winwood etc.) by closing the show with an immensely moving version of Leadbelly's 'Goodnight Irene'. Currently, Lane lives in Texas, where he is receiving treatment for his condition, and apparently still plays the occasional gig.

Greatest Hits

Singles	Title	US	UK
1974	*How Come*	–	11
1974	*The Poacher*	–	36
Albums			
1974	*Anymore For Anymore*	–	48
1977	*Rough Mix*	45	44

k.d. lang

One of the most exciting new artists to have emerged in the country-music-related area in many years is k.d. lang, a Canadian female of androgynous appearance, who spells her name without capital letters, like the popular poet e.e. cummings.

kathy dawn lang (born 1962) spent her childhood in Alberta, starting to play piano at age seven and guitar at 10, and by her teenage years was both a musician and a performance artist. By 1983 she had formed a band to back her, dubbing them the reclines (in memory of her musical heroine, the late Patsy Cline, whose superb vocal style and irreverently controversial personal approach she has adopted).

Her debut album with the reclines, 'A Truly Western Experience', was released on a Canadian independent label but reached the ears of Seymour Stein, founder of a celebrated New York label, who signed her and the band. In 1984 a more widely distributed album, 'Angel With A Lariat' (produced by Dave Edmunds), was her major label debut, but neither artist nor producer was particularly happy with the results, although the album was the first on which Ben Mink (violin, mandolin, etc.), Gordie Matthews (lead guitar) and Michel Pouliot (drums) had played together as members of the reclines. The group were not involved in 1988's 'Shadowland', lang's breakthrough album, which was produced by Owen Bradley (erstwhile producer of Patsy Cline) and included guest vocals by three other noted Nashville stars, Brenda Lee, Loretta Lynn and Kitty Wells. Although it sold extremely well, and was a long-time resident of the US country album charts, US country radio would not play the album on air, apparently because lang did not fit the required image of a female country singer – she looks more like George Jones than Tammy Wynette. Nevertheless, less-biased observers praised the album, and *Rolling Stone* magazine voted her female singer of the year.

1989's 'Absolute Torch And Twang' reunited lang with the reclines, who now included Matthews, Mink, Pouliot, John Dymond (bass) and Michael Creber (piano), and featured mainly songs co-written by lang and Mink. Once again, the album was a major seller among those with open minds, but acceptance in country music's mainstream looks no nearer – perhaps k.d. should aim at the rock audience, where acceptance may be both easier to achieve and ultimately more rewarding; after which she could return to country music, where her remarkable vocal talent properly belongs, as a big star. Both 'Shadowland' and 'Absolute Torch And Twang' are classic albums, but have yet to achieve the significant pop chart positions they so richly deserve in the US and UK.

174

Cyndi **LAUPER**

The witty 'Girls Just Want To Have Fun' made the talented Lauper (born 1953) one of the most promising female singers of the mid-1980s. However, her later career found her slow to capitalise on that success.

A New Yorker, she spent a year studying art before joining NY bands Doc West and Flyer in 1974, and founded Blue Angel with John Turi in 1978. The group soon attracted attention from record companies and in 1979 released a self-titled album, but the record was a commercial failure and the group split up amid a series of legal actions which left Lauper bankrupt in 1982.

She returned to part-time singing in bars and found a new manager in David Wolff, who negotiated a record deal which resulted in a debut album, 'She's So Unusual' (1983), recorded with Philadelphia rock group The Hooters. The 'Girls Just Want To Have Fun' single (1983) was a Top 3 hit in the US and UK, and the ballad 'Time After Time', (memorably covered by Miles Davis three years later) reached No. 1 in the US, and was her second UK Top 3 entry. Two further singles, 'She Bop' and 'All Through The Night' also made the US Top 5 in 1984.

In 1985 Lauper was a member of USA For Africa, the superstar group which made the charity record 'We Are The World'. She also sang the theme from the movie *The Goonies*. Lauper's second solo album, 'True Colors', appeared the following year, but provided only two hits in America, both of which flopped in the UK.

Reportedly having become a born-again Christian, Cyndi Lauper now took a break from recording, returning in 1989 with 'A Night To Remember', which contained the UK and US Top 10 single 'I Drove All Night', like 'True Colors' composed by top songwriting team Billy Steinberg and Tom Kelly.

Greatest Hits

Singles	Title	US	UK
1984	*Girls Just Want To Have Fun*	2	2
1984	*Time After Time*	1	3
1984	*She Bop*	3	46
1986	*True Colors*	1	12
1987	*Change Of Heart*	3	67
Albums			
1984	*She's So Unusual*	4	16
1986	*True Colors*	4	25

LED ZEPPELIN

Robert Plant (vocals)
Jimmy Page (guitar)
John Paul Jones (bass)
John Bonham (drums)

The ultimate heavy metal band, Led Zeppelin released just nine albums during their 11-year existence, but each one was a huge success and they remain a cornerstone of rock history, as the 1990 success of their first-ever compilation, 'Remasters', proved. They largely ignored singles and TV opportunities, while their best known song, 'Stairway To Heaven', has never appeared as a single.

Jimmy Page (born 1944) was a leading session guitarist in the 1960s, playing on numerous hits from The Who's 'Can't Explain' and Them's 'Baby Please Don't Go' to 'It's Not Unusual' by Tom Jones and Joe Cocker's 'With A Little Help From My Friends'. He had already turned down one offer from The Yardbirds in 1964 after Clapton quit, but joined them two years later on bass after Paul Samwell-Smith left. The band were making fewer hits but were still a popular live attraction, particularly in the US. When Jeff Beck fell ill, Page moved to lead guitar and when Beck returned, they briefly adopted a twin guitar formation before Beck left for good in 1968. The band disintegrated and Page was left with the name and a contracted tour of Scandinavia.

He linked up with John Paul Jones (born John Baldwin, 1946), a session bass player with whom he had worked on numerous sessions by Lulu, Donovan, Dusty Springfield, etc. With Peter Grant as manager, they looked for musicians to relaunch The Yardbirds and were recommended to Robert Plant (born 1948), a vocalist who had worked in Band Of Joy with drummer John Bonham (born 1948), before several unsuccessful 1967 solo singles. Plant them suggested Bonham's name, and the quartet toured Scandanavia as The New Yardbirds.

After cutting their first album in 30 hours in 1968, they played their first gigs as Led Zeppelin, a name allegedly suggested by Who drummer Keith Moon. Peter Grant secured a US record deal and the eponymous debut album was released in early 1969 to coincide with a US tour. 'Led Zeppelin' was an astonishing display of musical prowess that combined heavy blues (e.g. Willie Dixon's 'You Shook Me') with their own R&B-influenced epics like 'Dazed And Confused'. Live, the band more than matched their vinyl assault and they quickly started headlining their own shows and selling out in New York and Los Angeles as the album reached both the US and UK Top 10s.

'Led Zeppelin II', written and recorded on the hoof in America, built solidly on the success of their debut and was an instant No. 1 on both sides of the Atlantic with 400,000 US advance orders before its late 1969 release, as the band toured the US for the fourth time in a year. By the end of 1969 Led Zeppelin had sold $5 million worth of albums in the US and 'Led Zeppelin II', which topped the US charts for seven weeks, went on to spend over two and a half years in the US Top 40. They also scored their only US Top 10 single with 'Whole Lotta Love', which became the band's anthem.

The first hiatus in the band's phenomenal rise came early in 1970 when a member of the aristocratic von Zeppelin family threatened legal action over the abuse of the family name, causing the group to play a Danish concert as the Nobs, but soon afterwards they grossed $800,000 for a 27-date US tour before retiring to a Welsh country cottage,

Bron-y-Aur, to rehearse their next album. In the summer of 1970, they headlined the Bath Festival before 200,000 people and also toured Europe and the US again before releasing 'Led Zeppelin III' in late 1970. Although the hard rock element was still to the fore (notably in 'Immigrant Song', a US Top 20 hit), the band placed more emphasis on acoustic, folk-based material – despite critical reservations, it topped the album charts in the US and UK.

Their next live appearances were in 1971 on a 'back to the roots' UK tour where the band returned to small UK venues where they played for their original fee while the punters paid original ticket prices. This was far more successful than a subsequent European tour, which was marred by riots. Led Zeppelin's fourth album, released in 1971, had no title nor band name, but symbols on the inner sleeve were said to represent each group member.

It just failed to make No. 1 in the US (although it topped the UK charts), but became their most consistent seller, thanks to 'Stairway To Heaven', a track which the band refused to release as a single despite much pressure. In 1972 they undertook their eighth US tour, playing 3-hour sets, before their biggest ever UK tour. They finally agreed to give their fifth album a title, 'Houses Of The Holy', although it did not appear on the sleeve.

Despite criticisms over its confused direction, the album topped the US charts in 1973, as the band toured yet again, breaking the record for the biggest ever gross take for a gig (previously held by The Beatles at Shea Stadium) in Florida, and being robbed of the fee for their New York gigs from their hotel deposit box. These were the last Led Zeppelin gigs for 18 months as the band worked on a film/live album, formed their own record label, Swansong, and worked on a new studio album.

1975 saw the release of a double album, 'Physical Graffiti', which again topped the charts, spending six weeks as US No. 1. After three lengthy London shows, the band retreated into tax exile, but Plant and his wife were badly injured in a car crash in Greece and a planned world tour was cancelled. Plant could not walk unaided until the following year, when 'Presence' again topped the album charts. The long-awaited movie and double soundtrack album, *The Song Remains The Same*, finally emerged in late 1976 and inevitably topped the charts, which the band celebrated with their US TV debut on *Don Kirschner's Rock Concert*.

In 1977 a 51-date US tour ended in disaster and tragedy when a security man was badly beaten up and three days later, Plant's son died from a sudden stomach infection. The tour was abandoned and Zeppelin never played America again. Nothing more was heard from the band for a year and rumours, fuelled by Page's fascination with the occult and the

Zeppelin – they Led heavy onslaught (l to r) Plant, Bonham, Page and Jones

works of Aleister Crowley, began to spread that the band was jinxed, which were increased when John Bonham broke two ribs in a car crash.

In late 1978 the band cut a new album at Abba's studios in Sweden, and in the summer of 1979, made their live return with two shows at Knebworth in the UK before 180,000 people, shortly before the new album, 'In Through The Out Door', proved their continuing popularity by entering the US chart at No. 1. A 1980 European tour was planned as a warm-up to a US tour, but during rehearsals in September, drummer John Bonham was found dead in bed at Jimmy Page's house, having choked on his own vomit after a mammoth drinking session. Soon after the band announced their retirement.

Plant was the first to re-emerge, gigging with his part-time band, The Honeydrippers, in 1981. his first solo album, 'Pictures At Eleven' (1982), made the Top 5 in both the US and UK, while an album of unissued Zeppelin material, 'Coda', also made the US and UK Top 10s in 1982, soon after Page had released a solo album, the soundtrack to the movie *Death Wish II*. Plant's second album, 'The Principle Of Moments', went Top 10 in the US and UK in 1983 and in 1984, he did even better with 'The Honeydrippers Volume 1' on his own Es Paranza label, The 10-inch album made the US Top 5 and featured Page,

Jeff Beck and Nile Rodgers, while a single from it, 'Sea Of Love', made the US Top 3. Page had by now formed The Firm with Bad Company's Paul Rodgers and their eponymous debut album went Top 20 in the US and UK. In 1985 Zeppelin reformed (with Phil Collins on drums) for a brief set at the Philadelphia Live Aid concert.

Plans to reform the group for a new album with Tony Thompson of Chic on drums were scuppered after rehearsals, and Page rejoined The Firm for 1986's 'All The Kings Men' album, while Plant resumed his solo career with 1988's 'Now And Zen', another Top 10 US and UK album. Zeppelin again reformed for a one-off gig in New York, with John Bonham's son, Jason, on drums, to celebrate the 40th Anniversary of Atlantic Records, for which they had recorded exclusively. Plant guested on Page's solo album, 'Outrider', and continued his own solo career with 1990's 'Manic Nirvana'.

Greatest Hits

Singles	Title	US	UK
1969	*Whole Lotta Love*	4	–
1983	*Big Log* (Robert Plant)	20	11
1984	*Sea Of Love* (Honeydrippers)	3	56
Albums			
1969	*Led Zeppelin II*	1	1
1970	*Led Zeppelin III*	1	1
1971	(untitled fourth album)	2	1

1973	*Houses Of The Holy*	I	I
1975	*Physical Graffiti*	I	I
1976	*Presence*	I	I
1976	*The Song Remains The Same*	I	I
1979	*In Through The Out Door*	I	I
1982	*Pictures At Eleven* (Robert Plant)	5	2
1984	*Volume One* (Honeydrippers)	4	56
1985	*The Firm* (The Firm)	17	15
1988	*Outrider* (Jimmy Page)	26	27
1988	*Now And Zen* (Robert Plant)	6	10

Brenda **LEE**

Though a mere slip of a girl, Lee (born 1944) scored over 50 US pop hits in 13 years. Her mature voice slid from raucous lust through lazy insinuation to intimate anguish even during the harmless bounce of 'Sweet Nothin's', 'Let's Jump The Broomstick' and other ditties that were pop hits from 1957 to the early 1960s.

Via local radio and, by 1956, wider exposure on Red Foley's *Ozark Jubilee* show, Brenda Mae Tarpley – known as 'Little Brenda Lee' – was guaranteed enough airplay for her debut single, a version of Hank Williams's 'Jambalaya', to hit the US country charts before her first pop hit, 1957's 'One Step At A Time'. The novelty aspect of her extreme youth facilitated greater triumphs for 'Little Miss Dynamite', with the million-selling 'Rockin' Around The Christmas Tree' and further jaunty rockers, before the 1960s brought a larger proportion of heartbreak ballads like 'I'm Sorry', 'Emotions' and 'Break It To Me Gently'. 1963 was a vintage year in Britain with the title track of her 'All Alone Am I' album, 'Losing You' (a French translation) and 'I Wonder' all cracking the Top 20, while 'As Usual' made the UK Top 5 at the start of 1964. That year also ended well with the turbulent 'Is It True', and 'Christmas Will Be Just Another Lonely Day', but was followed by a rapid chart decline. Though she might have weathered prevailing trends, family commitments led Lee to cease touring and record only sporadically after 1966's 'Bye Bye Blues' album.

Lee resurfaced in 1971 with a major country hit in Kris Kristofferson's 'Nobody Wins' and later offerings that enabled her to rise anew as a US country music star. When country found favour with a younger audience in the mid-1980s, veneration for its veterans found her guesting with Kitty Wells and Loretta Lynn on 'new traditionalist' k.d. lang's 1988 album, 'Shadowland', produced by Owen Bradley (who had produced many early Lee records). In Europe Brenda Lee remains mainly a memory, albeit a pleasant one – as shown by a UK Top 20 album placing for her 'Little Miss Dynamite' hits compilation in 1980, and Coast To Coast's hit revival of 'Let's Jump The Broomstick'.

Greatest Hits

Singles	Title	US	UK
1959	*Sweet Nothin's*	4	4
1960	*I'm Sorry*	I	12
1960	*I Want To Be Wanted*	I	31
1962	*Speak To Me Pretty*	–	3
1962	*All Alone Am I*	3	7
1964	*As Usual*	12	5
Albums			
1960	*Brenda Lee*	5	–
1960	*This Is . . . Brenda*	4	–
1963	*All Alone Am I*	25	8

John **LENNON**

Though his two best-selling volumes of verse, stories and cartoons, and a bit-part in Richard Lester's *How I Won The War* movie (1967) were mere sideshows to his pivotal role in The Beatles, the late Lennon (born 1940) was well into a career as a non-Beatle long before the quartet was officially dissolved in 1971.

In 1966, he'd met Yoko Ono, a Japanese-American experimental artist. After she replaced Paul McCartney as his creative partner (as she had Lennon's first wife in his affections), he and Ono made a trilogy of albums filled with sounds not usually thought of as musical. Their initial effort, 'Two Virgins', was remarkable for its cover – a full frontal shot of the two naked leaving no doubt as to whether Lennon had been circumcized – while its successor, 'Life With The Lions', was concerned mainly with Ono's miscarriage. Most self-centred of all was 1969's

Lennon – spikey Scouse rock'n'roller resold as saint

boxed 'Wedding Album' (with a photo of a piece of wedding cake), an espousal also detailed in 'The Ballad Of John And Yoko', the final Beatles UK No. 1. To say things most people didn't want to hear, the Lennons made their headline-hogging lives an open and ludicrous book with press conferences from inside kingsize white sacks, the letter that accompanied John's renouncement of his MBE and other bewildering pranks. Taped at one of their 'Bed-Ins' was Lennon's peace anthem, 'Give Peace A Chance', attributed to the ad hoc 'Plastic Ono Band', which was his first hit record without The Beatles.

With hastily rehearsed accompanists, including Eric Clapton, the Lennons next performed at a Canadian pop festival. Released as 'Live Peace In Toronto 1969', their set consisted principally of 1950s classic rock, Yoko's screech-singing and an early arrangement of 'Cold Turkey', a later version of which was a hit – recorded, like 1970's 'Instant Karma', as Lennon put it, 'as an escape valve from The Beatles'. A lengthy and cacophonous 'Cold Turkey' was a feature of his last UK stage appearance in a 'Plastic Ono Supergroup' (with George Harrison and Keith Moon, among others) at a London ballroom in December 1969.

After The Beatles disbanded, Lennon's eponymous solo debut album was the cathartic result of a course of Primal Scream therapy under American psychologist Dr Arthur Janov. The album featured personal exorcisms (e.g. 'Mother, Isolation') as well as stark rejections of former heroes and ideals (notably 'God') and a self-projection as 'Working Class Hero'. Similar confessions appeared in interviews too, as did the almost audible snigger whenever Lennon sniped at McCartney. His old colleague was pilloried further in 'How Do You Sleep' from 1971's 'Imagine' album, which also contained love songs (such as 'Oh Yoko' and the apologetic 'Jealous Guy') and a utopian title track that became Lennon's most memorable post-Beatle song.

On leaving England forever in 1972, Lennon's attempts to settle in the US were hindered by official harassment, perhaps resulting from anti-government sentiments expressed on an earlier hit single, 'Power To The People', and on his and Ono's slogan-ridden 'Some Time In New York City', a double-album on which they were backed by Elephant's Memory. It also included excerpts from both the Lyceum show and a jam session with Frank Zappa's Mothers of Invention, but apart from rare inspired moments, the kindest critics agreed that it was documentary rather than recreational. Lennon left Ono in 1973 for a 15 month 'lost weekend' in California where he fell in with Harry Nilsson, Keith Moon and other hard livers, and his problems during this period were reflected in 'Mind Games' and 'Walls And Bridges', which included hit singles in 'Whatever Gets You Through The Night' (with Elton John) and 'No. 9 Dream' but neither of these albums nor 1975's 'Rock'n'Roll' – favourite covers – set the world on fire.

Reunited with Yoko (who presented him with a son in 1975) and finally granted US residential status, Lennon spent five years as a househusband in New York's exclusive Dakota apartments. After 'Cookin'', an apt donation to 1976's 'Ringo's Rotogravure' album, not a song was heard commercially from Lennon as the myth of him as retired grew. His songwriting well was not as arid as many imagined and in 1980, he and Ono recorded two albums worth of new material. The first, 'Double Fantasy', was released that autumn, a few weeks before Lennon was shot dead outside the Dakota on December 8.

The tragedy gave 'Double Fantasy' and its follow-up, 'Milk And Honey', an undeserved piquancy, although Lennon's 'Watching The Wheels' and 'Woman' followed the first single '(Just Like) Starting Over' into the world's charts. Overall, both albums seemed artistically slight items from a duo too detached from the everyday, but a wave of international grief reversed the fall of 'Double Fantasy' and '(Just Like) Starting Over' from their respective listings. Numerous – and notorious – Lennon biographies helped million-selling repromotions and a rash of tribute discs invaded the charts within a month of the cremation.

Greatest Hits

Singles	Title	US	UK
1971	Imagine	1	–
1974	Whatever Gets You Through The Night	1	36
1975	Imagine	–	1
1980	(Just Like) Starting Over	1	1
1980	Woman	2	1
Albums			
1971	Imagine	1	1
1974	Walls And Bridges	1	6
1980	Double Fantasy	1	1
1982	The John Lennon Collection	–	1

Gary LEWIS and The PLAYBOYS

Gary Lewis (vocals, drums)
Al Ramsey (guitar)
John West (guitar)
David Costell (bass)
David Walker (keyboards)

Gary Lewis (born 1946) was the son of movie comic Jerry Lewis, and for a few months in 1965, he and The Playboys were the US's biggest-selling rock band. Originally formed to play at neighbourhood parties in Hollywood, they were hired for a summer season at Disneyland in 1964, and spotted by A&R man Snuff Garrett, who put them in the studio with arranger Leon Russell.

Al Kooper's song, 'This Diamond Ring', originally intended for Bobby Vee, was their debut single, which topped the US chart and sold a million copies. TV appearances cemented the fresh-faced group's appeal to the younger teen set, who brought the follow-ups in almost as heavy numbers: 'Count Me In' and the corny sing-a-long, 'Save Your Heart For Me', both reached the US Top 3, 'Everybody Loves A Clown' made the US Top 5, and the Lewis/Russell/Garrett composition, 'She's Just My Style', rounded off 1965 by making the US Top 3.

More major hits followed in 1966, notably 'Sure Gonna Miss Her' and the exuberant 'Green Grass', by British writers Cook and Greenaway. The bubble was forcibly burst, however, when Lewis was drafted into the Army at the start of 1967. Given the chance to join an entertainment unit, he refused, not a little upset by the unwanted interruption of

Gary Lewis and The Playboys – Disneyland discoveries in 'Diamond Ring' disc debut triumph

his hitmaking career, and instead worked out his draft as a military clerk in Korea. Singles by the group were still released during this period, but without Lewis around to promote them, they were not hitting the earlier heights.

By mid-1968 Lewis was a civilian again, and regrouped The Playboys with new personnel. A revival of Brian Hyland's 'Sealed With A Kiss' put him back in the US Top 20, but a stab at The Cascades' 'Rhythm Of The Rain' was less successful, and he did not chart again in the US. Lewis disbanded the group, and in the early 1970s tried an unsuccessful singer-songwriter approach before eventually finding a comfortable live nostalgia circuit niche (with yet more Playboys), concentrating on his early hits. Around this time, in early 1975, he also belatedly had a surprise UK hit, when his 1966 US Top 20 hit, 'My Heart's Symphony', hugely popular as an obscure dance-floor classic, was reissued and reached the Top 40.

Sports coverage to the Fore good news for Huey

Greatest Hits

Singles	Title	US	UK
1965	*This Diamond Ring*	1	–
1965	*Count Me In*	2	–
1965	*Save Your Heart For Me*	2	–
Albums			
1966	*Golden Greats*	10	–

Huey **LEWIS** and the **NEWS**

Huey Lewis (vocals)
Chris Hayes (guitar)
Sean Hopper (keyboards)
Johnny Colla (guitar, saxophone)
Mario Cipollina (bass)
Bill Gibson (drums)

The nucleus of Huey Lewis (born Hugh Cregg, 1950) and The News started out in the late 1970s as country rock band Clover, who gigged around their native California before leaving home and trying their luck in the UK. Despite two albums in 1976 and 1977, the band were swamped by the rising tide of punk and after backing Elvis Costello on his debut album, they returned to Marin County where they continued to jam together in clubs and bars.

After a strictly one-off tilt at the disco market with 'Exodisco' in 1980, Lewis and the band reverted to their R&B roots. Their eponymous debut album caused few ripples but they eventually scored a US Top 10 hit with 'Do You Believe In Love' from their second album, 'Picture This', which made the US Top 20 in 1982. For their third album, 'Sports', in 1983, the band selected a cunning blend of pop and R&B which struck paydirt, topping the US chart and selling over 7 million copies, yielding four US Top 10

singles: 'Heart And Soul', 'I Want A New Drug' (which Ray Parker Junior surreptitiously lifted for the theme song for the *Ghostbusters* movie and eventually settled with Lewis out of court), 'The Heart Of Rock & Roll' and 'If This Is It'.

Lewis made his movie debut with a cameo role in *Back To The Future* in 1985, but more importantly wrote the theme song, 'The Power Of Love', which topped the US charts and made the UK Top 20. 1986's 'Fore' album again topped the US chart (and made the UK Top 10) with two more US chart-topping singles, 'Stuck With You' and 'Jacob's Ladder' (written by the then unknown Bruce Hornsby), as well as major hits with 'Hip To Be Square', 'I Know What I Like' and 'Doing It All For My Baby', but 1988's follow-up album, 'Small World', failed to maintain the group's momentum, although 'Perfect World' was a US Top 3 hit.

Greatest Hits

Singles	Title	US	UK
1985	*The Power Of Love*	1	9
1986	*Stuck With You*	1	12
1986	*Hip To Be Square*	3	41
1986	*Jacob's Ladder*	1	–
1988	*Perfect World*	3	48
Albums			
1983	*Sports*	1	23
1986	*Fore*	1	8

Jerry Lee **LEWIS**

As self-obsessed as a genius can be, singing piano-player Lewis (born 1935) still makes younger rock'n'rollers seem tame with an electrifying stage presence that displays

taste, unpredictability and a forgivable arrogance in compatible amounts. Though he helped in writing a couple of his many hits, examples like 1966's 'Lincoln Limousine', a MacGonagallesque requiem to President Kennedy, prove that the self-styled 'Killer' is less a composer than an inspired interpreter of songs written by others. Whether performing 'Hound Dog', Sam and Dave's 'Hold On I'm Coming', or 'Over The Rainbow' (a 1979 country hit), Lewis remains in control, though his repeated insistence on referring to himself in the third person in a version of 'White Christmas' necessitated the editing out of his spot in a Johnny Cash TV special.

Such an incident was mild compared to others in the Killer's turbulent years, riven as they are with high living, destitution, stimulant abuse, police arrests, several marriages, last-minute tour cancellations, his shooting of a bass guitarist and the accidental deaths of two sons and a wife. There are also the bouts of loud piety that have recurred from a poor upbringing dominated by the local Assembly Of God Church.

Cousin of disgraced TV evangelist Jimmy Lee Swaggart, Lewis was apparently expelled in 1950 from Bible College in Texas for pounding out hymns in the manner he had absorbed from the Southern melting pot of Country & Western, blues and gospel. These musical styles coupled with hard-won experience gained in tough Louisiana bars and on a weekly radio show enabled Lewis to present a fully developed style when he successfully auditioned for Sun Records in Memphis in 1955.

On the same label as Elvis Presley and Carl Perkins, he held his own with a reworking of Ray Price's 'Crazy Arms' but his career was launched nationally when a frantic appearance on national TV put his second single high in 1957's US pop chart as well as the country and R&B lists. First cut by Big Maybelle five years earlier, 'Whole Lotta Shakin' Goin' On' encapsulated the Killer's nonchalant vocal lust and punishment of the ivories with trademark glissando sweeps and gratuitous obligato. A similarly exciting formula was applied to 'Great Balls Of Fire', 'Breathless' and 1958's movie title opus, 'High School Confidential', but his chart decline resulted from the media storm during a 1958 UK tour, when it transpired that Myra Lewis, a 14-year-old in his entourage, was not only his cousin but also his third wife (although her age was not regarded as scandalous in the US's Deep South). As the world's press fuelled public self-righteousness, the tour collapsed, airplay for his records ceased, and he was obliged to work for peanuts.

Oddly, it was the UK which brought Lewis in from the cold, receiving him with affection in 1962 after an arrangement of Ray Charles's 'What'd I Say' returned him to the UK Top 10. Further 1960s hits were few, but his shows were sell-outs again and the Myra incident was forgotten. In the US, he was critically praised for his portrayal of Iago in *Catch My Soul*, Jack Good's rock'n'roll version of *Othello*.

While 'Whole Lotta Shakin'' was always a highlight of his live shows, a sustained chart comeback was only tenable after his 1968 US country hit, 'Another Time Another Place'.

Lewis then concentrated on this genre, with 'What Made Milwaukee Famous', a 1971 race through 'Me And Bobbie McGee' and a crossover to the pop chart cover of The Big Bopper's 'Chantilly Lace'. Notable later were a re-make of 'Drinkin' Wine Spo-Dee-O-Dee' (from his star-studded double album 'The Session' recorded in London), 1977's more painfully apt 'Middle Age Crazy' and 'Let My Fingers Do The Talking', a 1986 UK turntable hit.

Recovery from a near-fatal stomach operation in 1981 halted his usually erratic concert schedule and caused him to refuse an invitation to play on the 1983 Rolling Stones album, 'Undercover'. Other UK stars paid their respects during a troubled London performance by the Killer in 1990, but for all the maturity inherent in his later recordings, little seemed to have changed for Lewis since 'Whole Lotta Shakin''.

Greatest Hits

Singles	Title	US	UK
1957	Whole Lotta Shakin' Goin' On	3	8
1957	Great Balls Of Fire	2	1
Albums			
1962	Jerry Lee Lewis Vol. 2	–	14
1964	The Greatest Live		
	Show On Earth	71	–
1973	The Session	37	–

Hellraiser Jerry Lee – a lurid life of bars, bandrooms, bible-bashing and boogie

LITTLE FEAT

Lowell George (guitar, vocals)
Bill Payne (keyboards)
Roy Estrada (bass)
Richie Hayward (drums)

In their 1970s heyday, Little Feat created a rich brew of blues, country and jazz topped off with Lowell George's evocative songwriting and guitar-playing. George (born 1945) had played with Hayward in Factory before joining The Mothers Of Invention, while Hayward played with Fraternity Of Man, the group that sang 'Don't Bogart That Joint' in the film *Easy Rider*. George had met Estrada in The Mothers, while Payne (born 1949) was a classically trained pianist.

The first, eponymous album (1971), produced by Russ Titelman, contained two of George's most memorable songs, 'Truck Stop Man' and the much-covered eulogy to truck-driving, 'Willin''. After 'Sailin' Shoes' (1972), Estrada joined Captain Beefheart's Magic Band and Little Feat added ex-Lead Enema guitarist Paul Barrere, plus Kenny Gradney (bass) and congas-player Sam Clayton, both of whom had previously played with Delaney & Bonnie. 'Dixie Chicken' (1973) was highly praised but soon after its release the group split up. After record company pressure, Little Feat re-formed in 1974 to make the US Top 40 album, 'Feats Don't Fail Me Now'. The next year's European tour helped 'The Last Record Album' into the UK Top 40, and in 1976 the band played a series of UK stadium gigs with The Who. By now George was heavily involved in drugs, and he wrote only one song for the UK Top 10 album 'Times Loves A Hero' (1977), which again went Top 40 in the US. He produced the Grateful Dead's 'Shakedown Street' album, and rejoined Little Feat for a tour in support of the live-double 'Waiting For Columbus' (1978), which reached the US Top 20 and the UK Top 50; but the reunion was short-lived as Payne and Barrere joined Nicolette Larsen's band.

With Little Feat now officially disbanded, George made a solo album, 'Thanks, I'll Eat It Here', and set out on tour with a new band. But on June 19, 1979, he died of a heart attack caused by drug abuse. The rest of Little Feat performed at a benefit for George's family and later issued 'Down On The Farm', containing tracks recorded before the 1978 split. 'Hoy Hoy!' (1981) was a further selection of unreleased Little Feat material. Barrere cut a solo album in 1983, while the other members concentrated on sessions and tours as backing musicians. Then, nearly a decade after the group had separated, Barrere, Payne, Clayton and Hayward regrouped with Fred Tackett (guitar) and singer Craig Fuller, formerly of Pure Prairie League. Both 'Let It Roll' (1988) and 'Representing The Mambo' (1990) sold well in the US.

Greatest Hits

Albums	Title	US	UK
1977	Time Loves A Hero	34	8
1978	Waiting For Columbus	18	43

LITTLE RICHARD

Since shedding most of his artistic load by the late 1950s, the career of Little Richard (born 1935) has been built on an image of a self-styled 'King Of Rock'n'Roll' in billowing drapes, pencil moustache and precarious pompadour, hollering, for example, 'Long Tall Sally' in 1957's *Don't Knock The Rock* while punishing a grand piano with parts of his anatomy other than his fingers. Among those who borrowed from this mercurial black entertainer's act were James Brown, Wilson Pickett and his former sideman, Billy Preston, and he was clearly a major influence on one element of Paul McCartney's vocal style.

Richard Wayne Penniman first performed in public at the Seventh Day Adventist Church in Macon, Georgia. On winning a 1950 talent contest, Penniman began recording largely undistinguished jump blues. Down on his luck, he was working in a bus depot canteen when, on Lloyd Price's advice, he sent a demo of a gospel opus, 'He's My Star', to the Hollywood-based Specialty label, who put him under the supervision of New Orleans bandleader Robert 'Bumps' Blackwell. A 1955 session spawned 'Tutti Frutti', sexual doggerel as joyous gibberish palatable to a white public. Despite an embarrassed cover by Pat Boone, 'Tutti Frutti' swept the outrageous Penniman into the pop charts where he remained for the next three years with double A-sides containing such rock-'n'roll classics as 'Rip It Up', 'Lucille', 'Good Golly Miss Molly' and the 1957 film song, 'The Girl Can't Help It'. Though 'Send Me Some Lovin'' was a slowish ballad, most of Penniman's other hits were frantic 12-bars, usually with a brash sax solo but dominated by pounding keyboards and a bombastic vocal.

This memorable chapter closed with a dearth of new ideas, epitomized by revivals of ancient standards like 'Baby Face', and Penniman's sudden renunciation of showbusiness and enrolment in a theological college. He recorded little but sacred material until 1964's 'Bama Lama Bama Loo', which was similar to his earlier hits, but only a moderate seller. Other than odd exhilarations like 'I Need Love' or 1966's 'Get Down With It' (later adapted by Slade), the decade passed with desperate re-makes of his 1950s classics and stabs at soul with versions of 'Dancing In The Street' and 'The Way You Do The Things You Do'. More credible were 'Freedom Blues' and 1970's 'The Rill Thing' album as well as his cameo in the Canned Heat tribute single, 'Rocking With The King', a 1972 US hit.

Little Richard's predictable boarding of the nostalgia bandwagon was successful, though it started badly when his onstage narcissism was booed during a 1972 rock'n'roll spectacular in London. In the later 1970s he embraced religion once more, releasing only gospel items and becoming friends with the likewise 'born again' Bob Dylan. Cast as a street-corner evangelist, Penniman was seen on television in a 1986 episode of *Miami Vice* but was more recognizable as the invisible voice from the past bellowing 'Good Golly Miss Molly' on the soundtrack of 1985's *Mask* movie.

Richard's 'Tutti Frutti' – perhaps the perfect single definition of rock'n'roll

Greatest Hits

Singles	Title	US	UK
1957	Long Tall Sally	6	3
1958	Baby Face	41	2
Albums			
1957	Here's Little Richard	13	–

LITTLE STEVEN

Steve Van Zandt (born 1950) cut his teeth in the same New Jersey neighbourhood as Bruce Springsteen, singing in local groups Shadows and The Source in the mid-1960s. Heavily influenced by Mowton and black R&B, he produced, wrote songs for and played lead guitar with the first line-up of Southside Johnny & The Asbury Jukes. His first original song to be recorded, 'I Don't Wanna Go Home', was the title track of the Jukes' 1976 debut album. At this point, he was known as 'Miami Steve', dropped when he tired of Springsteen associations.

He became Springsteen's on-stage right-hand man in the mid-1970s, retaining the position of lead guitarist and on-stage foil, later filled by Nils Lofgren. His project, The Disciples Of Soul had already taken off, with 1983's debut album, 'Men Without Women', attracting attention as much for his Springsteen connections as for the music it contained. Produced concurrently with Springsteen's 'Born In The USA' and Gary US Bonds' 'Dedication', it was his catalyst to leave Springsteen's employ. Van Zandt also produced Lee Dorsey, Ronnie Spector, The Drifters, The Coasters and others.

The Disciples of Soul lined up in late 1983 as drummer Dino Danelli (ex-Rascals), bassist Jean Beauvoir, percussionist Monti Ellison, keyboard players Pee Wee Weber and Zoe Yanakis (replacing Rusty Cloud). This line-up was notable for the absence of the horn section which featured permanently on the first album cut, 'Solidarity', a reggae-inflected track later covered by Black Uhuru. 'Voice of America' was coolly received, but Van Zandt shot back into the spotlight with a protest record in 1985, his own composition 'Sun City'. Credited to Artists United Against Apartheid it went Top 40 on both sides of the Atlantic. Featuring 49 artists who disapproved of the South African government and the practice of Western groups of playing at the Sun City resort controlled by it, all proceeds went to political prisoners in South Africa. A subsequent album also made the US Top 40.

A comeback of sorts in 1987 with 'Freedom No Compromise' and single 'Bitter Fruit' failed to excite, and his bandana-bedecked visage was less frequently seen. But with Springsteen now bandless, there is always the possibility . . .

Greatest Hits

Singles	Title	US	UK
1985	Sun City (as Artists United		
	Against Apartheid)	38	21
1987	Bitter Fruit	–	66
Albums			
1982	Men Without Women	–	73
1987	Freedom No Compromise	–	52

Nils LOFGREN

S inger/songwriter/guitarist Lofgren (born 1951) took up accordion before picking up the guitar in imitation of his elder brother Tom (a future band member). At 17 he ran away from his Detroit home to New York's Greenwich Village where he jammed with Eric Burdon & The Animals. He then passed through many bands in the Washington area, cutting two singles with Paul Dowell & The Dolphins in 1969, until he founded Grin with drummer Bob Berberich and, eventually, bassist Bob Gordon.

Neil's 'Goldrush' pays off for Nils

He was given a shortcut to fame by Neil Young, playing piano and some acoustic guitar with Crazy Horse on Young's 1970 'After The Goldrush'. He played on Crazy Horse's own debut, but declined to join the band full-time, cutting four albums with Grin before deciding to go it alone. Released in early 1975, his eponymous solo debut album was full of 'tunes two or three minutes long . . . they end before you get tired of them', including 'Keith Don't Go' a rock'n'roll tribute to his hero Keith Richards. Half of 1976's follow-up 'Cry Tough' was produced by ex-Blues Project keyboard player Al Kooper.

By 1977's 'I Came To Dance', his song-writing muse had dried up, while the live double 'Night After Night', released the same year was disappointing. After a break, he pulled out his best album since his solo debut in 1979's Nils, bolstered by a songwriting collaboration with Lou Reed.

After two commercially unsuccessful albums, he returned to Neil Young's side for 1983's 'Trans' album and tour. Solo again, he signed in Britain with an independent label for 'Flip' (named after his habit of taking a trampoline on stage) in 1985 and the double 'Code Of The Road', recorded live in London, a year later. He got to know the road only too well with Bruce Springsteen, taking Steve Van Zandt's place from 1984 until the E Street Band's 1990 dissolution. As well as resurrecting his solo career, in 1990 he appeared as part of Ringo Starr's band alongside Rick Danko, Levon Helm, Joe Walsh, etc. Destined to be a sideman, the weakness of Lofgren's self-penned material was the only factor holding him back from solo stardom.

Greatest Hits

Singles	Title	US	UK
1985	Secrets In The Street	–	53
Albums			
1976	Cry Tough	32	8
1977	I Came To Dance	36	30

LOGGINS and MESSINA

T hrough the middle 1960s Jim Messina (born 1947) led the California band Jim Messina & The Jesters, who made two surf-oriented albums before folding, Messina moving on to studio work as engineer and guitarist. After working on some of their sessions as engineer, he joined Buffalo Springfield in 1967 in place of Bruce Palmer, before forming Poco in 1968 with Richard Furay. Meanwhile Kenny Loggins (born 1948), having majored in music in California, left college to join first Gator Creek, then Second Helping, neither enjoying much success. After a one-tour stint with West Coast psychedelic band The Electric Prunes in 1969, he became a professional songwriter with a music publishing company.

Towards the end of 1970 Messina left Poco to go into full-time production work, and in 1971 Loggins had his first songwriting hit in the US with 'The House At Pooh Corner' by The Nitty Gritty Dirt Band, also writing three other tracks on their album, 'Uncle Charlie And His Dog Teddy'. Loggins was subsequently signed as a solo singer/songwriter and introduced to Messina with a view to him producing the debut Loggins album. The collaboration was more involved than either had anticipated, and the album came out as 'Kenny Loggins With Jim Messina Sittin' In' later in 1971. The album went Top 75 in the US and the duo made their live debut fronting The Kenny Loggins Band With Jim Messina.

By 1973 they had found a niche in the soft-rock market, with their second album 'Loggins And Messina' (1972) making the US Top 20 and including their only US Top 5 single, 'Your Mama Don't Dance', which was also covered by Elvis Presley. The end of 1973 saw 'Full Sail' hit the US album Top 10, and six months later the live double album 'On Stage' reached the Top 5. Another US Top 10 album, 'Mother Lode' (1974), was followed by 1975's 'So Fine', which featured revivals of 1950s classics and made the album Top 30. 'Native Sons' album (1976), which reached the US Top 20, proved to be their last as a partnership. After a final concert in Hawaii, they formally split, followed early in 1977 by the compilation 'Best Of Friends' and a year later by the live 'Finale', neither of which sold in any quantity.

1977 saw Loggins's solo career established with the release of the 'Celebrate Me Home' album, which went platinum in the US, reaching the Top 30, followed by a support tour slot with Fleetwood Mac. The next year 'Nightwatch', also a platinum-earner, went Top 10 in the US and included the US Top 5 single duet with Fleetwood Mac's Stevie Nicks, 'Whenever I Call You Friend'. 'Keep The Fire' reached the Top 20 of the US album chart in 1979, and other hit albums followed, including the double 'Kenny Loggins Alive' (1980) and Loggins' first move into film work with the soundtrack album 'Caddyshack' in 1980, which generated another Top 10 US single in 'I'm Alright'.

While Jim Messina made the US Top 100 with both his first and second solo albums, 'Oasis' (1979) and Messina (1981), it was Loggins who enjoyed more US Top 20 placings with the album 'High Adventure' and the singles 'Don't Forget It' and 'Heart to Heart', all in 1982.

Loggins' move to film work was consolidated with 'Footloose', the movie theme which was a 1984 million seller and his first UK smash, reaching No. 1 in the US and the Top 10 in the UK singles chart, while the soundtrack album also reached No. 1 in the US. The Tom Cruise film *Top Gun* provided a 1986 vehicle for Loggins' craftsmanship, the 'Danger Zone' theme making the US Top 5 and the soundtrack album topping the US chart, while, perhaps predictably, his 1988 album 'Back To Avalon', Top 75 in the US, included a US Top 10 single, 'Nobody's Fool', the theme from the film *Caddyshack 2*.

Greatest Hits

Singles	Title	US	UK
1972	*Your Mama Won't Dance*	4	–
Albums			
1974	*On Stage*	5	–
1974	*Motherlode*	8	–
KENNY LOGGINS			
Singles			
1978	*Whenever I Call You Friend*	5	–
1984	*Footloose*	1	6
1986	*Danger Zone*	2	45
Albums			
1978	*Nightwatch*	7	–

LOS LOBOS

David Hidalgo (vocals, guitar, violin, accordion)
Louie Perez (drums, guitar)
Conrad Lozano (bass, guitarron)
Cesar Rosas (guitar, bajo sexto)

Formed as a teenage band in East LA in 1974, Los Lobos began playing 'mainstream' rock, but in 1978 switched to playing acoustic renditions of Mexican folk music until the need to make some money meant dusting down the amplifiers. They released a small number of a self-financed albums before signing an independent deal for their first full

Tex-Mexers Los Lobos, breaking big with Valens vehicle 'La Bamba'

release, the EP 'And A Time To Dance' (1983), which contained the Grammy-winning song 'Anselma', featuring sax player Steve Berlin of the Blasters, who subsequently joined Los Lobos. They toured worldwide in 1985 to promote their first album, 'How Will The Wolf Survive', produced by T-Bone Burnett.

Individual band members have been much in demand; Cesar Rosas and David Hildago appeared on Ry Cooder's 1985 soundtrack 'Alamo Bay'; Rosas recorded with Bob Dylan; Hidalgo guested on Elvis Costello's 'King Of America' (1986) and the whole band backed Paul Simon on 'All Around The World' for 'Graceland' (1987). Their own 1987 album, 'By The Light Of The Moon', was also produced by Burnett. However, their biggest success came that year with their involvement in the Ritchie Valens biopic, *La Bamba*; they scored the soundtrack and had a worldwide hit with the title track, Hidalgo dubbing the singing voice of Ritchie Valens throughout the film. As if to exorcise the ghost of *La Bamba*, they then issued an acoustic album of Mexican folk songs, 'La Pistola Y El Coranzon' (1988), sung in Spanish and utilizing uniquely Mexican instruments.

In 1989 they backed John Lee Hooker for one track on his album 'The Healer'. Possibly an attempt to break free of the Tex-Mex label, 1990's mainstream 'The Neighbourhood' was perhaps too much like corporate California.

Greatest Hits

Singles	Title	US	UK
1985	*Don't Worry Baby*	–	57
1987	*La Bamba*	1	1
1987	*Come On Let's Go*	21	18

Albums			
1985	*How Will The Wolf Survive*	–	77
1987	*By The Light Of The Moon*	–	77
1987	*La Bamba* (soundtrack)	–	24

LOVE

Arthur Lee (vocals, guitar)
Bryan Maclean (vocals, guitar)
John Echols (guitar)
Ken Forssi (bass)
Alban 'Snoopy' Pfisterer (drums)

Fronted by the charismatic Lee (born in Memphis, 1944), Love emerged from Los Angeles in 1965 with a folk/rock style strongly influenced by The Byrds, but which later expanded drastically to take in elements of R&B, jazz and rock. A seminal 1960s US West Coast band, their influence and reputation far outstripped any commercial successes – in chart terms they were only ever a fringe band – yet their recorded legacy includes at least two absolutely vital albums.

Lee's first recording band was The LAGs (short for Los Angeles Group, in polite homage to Booker T & The MGs), after which he and Echols formed Love with Don Conka (drums) and others. Known initially as The Grass Roots, a name Lee conceded to another LA band which recorded before his group, Love regrouped with a revised line-up, including Maclean, who had worked as a roadie for The Byrds, and established a strong underground reptutation in Los Angeles, eventually becoming the first rock band signed by the previously ethnic Elektra label, and headliners on the night Elektra boss Jac Holzman first saw The Doors, who were opening for Love. Released in 1966, their eponymous debut album almost reached the US Top 50 and included a single, a cover of Bacharach & David's 'My Little Red Book', which also approached the US Top 50. If their debut had been firmly rooted in folk/rock, the follow-up, 'Da Capo', broke entirely new ground. Although it peaked lower in the US Top 100, it is regarded as something of a milestone album, with Lee previewing the idea of heavy metal with the powerful '7 And 7 Is', a US Top 40 single. Meanwhile, 'Revelation', the single track on the second side of the album, was pioneering in its self-indulgent refusal to recognize the point at which a good idea outstays its welcome, and was a foretaste of the progressive rock to come later that decade.

Erratic live performances and frequently changing personnel – drummer Don Conka was replaced by Pfisterer for the first album, while he was himself replaced by Michael Stuart for 'Da Capo', as Pfisterer moved to keyboards and saxophonist Tjay Cantrelli was added – held them back, and they became the perennial Underground band, as evidenced by the commercial failure of their finest recorded work, 'Forever Changes'. Released in 1968 to tumultous critical acclaim, it remains Arthur Lee's 'Sergeant Pepper', surreal lyrics, orchestral passages, strings and horns all lending it a strong psychedelic feeling unequalled in the US at that time. Yet it failed to reach the Top 150 of the US album chart, although it did make the UK Top 30.

Maclean, who had written the classic single 'Alone Again Or' from the third album, attempted a solo career without success, while Lee recruited an entirely new line-up, including George Suranovich (drums), Frank Fayad (bass) and either Jay Donellan (aka Jay Lewis) or Gary Rowles (guitar), but the

Lee – late 'Sixties Love affair

resulting albums, 'Four Sail' and 'Out Here', did little business.

Following further personnel changes, Love toured the UK in 1970, where Lee recorded a still unreleased album with Jimi Hendrix, only one track of which has ever appeared, 'The Everlasting First', which was included on 1971's 'False Start' album, the failure of which caused Lee to disband Love. His 1973 solo album, 'Vindicator', was no more successful, and the following year, with another new line-up, he cut a new Love album, 'Black Beauty', which also remains unreleased due to the collapse of the label to which Lee was signed. Disheartened, Lee resurrected Love again in 1974 with a younger line-up augmented by session players for 'Reel To Real', laying them to rest again just as quickly upon the album's inevitable failure.

In 1981, Lee released an eponymous solo album (with an updated version of '7 and 7 Is'), while 'Love Live', which also featured Bryan Maclean, was also released that year, although it had been recorded several years before. Lee continued to base himself in Los Angeles, although several subsequent attempts to reform Love all failed. Maclean helped to launch the career of his half-sister, Maria McKee. At least two of the other early members of the group were reportedly in San Quentin prison during the 1970s after being convicted of armed robbery.

Greatest Hits

Singles	Title	US	UK
1966	My Little Red Book	52	–
1966	7 and 7 Is	33	–
1970	Alone Again Or	99	–
Albums			
1966	Love	57	–
1967	Da Capo	80	–
1968	Forever Changes	154	24

Lyle **LOVETT**

One of the more adventurous latterday singer/songwriters from Texas, Lyle Lovett (born 1957) has enjoyed greater critical acclaim than commercial success. At a time when the mundane is more acceptable than the extraordinary, his tendency towards experimentation has not always endeared him to the accountants who control the contemporary music industry. From a German farming community near Houston, Lovett gained a degree in journalism, during his studies also starting to write songs, which he performed in folk clubs, backing himself on guitar. After a guest vocal (and visual) appearance on Nanci Griffith's 'Last Of The True Believers' album, Lovett made his own demo tape, which eventually resulted in a contract with a major label. His 1986 eponymous debut album featured a sleeve dedication from the

doyen of Texas singer/songwriters, Guy Clark, and attracted great critical praise, although, as it was initially targetted at a country music audience which found it too off-beat, success was limited.

However, Lovett was warmly welcomed in Europe, where a member of Britain's Royal Family declared herself a fan, and 1987's 'Pontiac' album, which veered towards jazz, was probably more successful in the Old World than the New. For his 1989 album, 'Lyle Lovett & His Large Band', he worked with a bigger combo (as the name suggests), the result often veering towards R&B-slanted jazz, with a horn section and backing vocalists.

The writer of numerous fine songs (e.g. the first album's 'If I Were The Man You Wanted', covered by Griffith, and 'This Old Porch', co-written with and also recorded by Robert Earl Keen, Jr., and the second album's bizarre 'If I Had A Boat'), he is not averse to unlikely cover versions like the third album's 'Stand By Your Man' (an irreverent nod to the country mainstream). Lyle Lovett's main requirement at this point is an audience which is in sympathy with his special talents, both as a songwriter and also as a performer. In the latter capacity he can be seen to advantage when working with cellist John Hagen as a unique duo.

The **LOVIN' SPOONFUL** / John **SEBASTIAN**

John Sebastian (vocals/autoharp/guitar)
Zal Yanovsky (guitar)
Steve Boone (bass)
Joe Butler (drums)

The Lovin' Spoonful were the definitive New York folk/rock good-time band. Sebastian (born 1944) was a fixture on the Greenwich Village folk scene in the early 1960s, Yanovsky (born 1944) was another folkie who worked with Sebastian in the short-lived Mugwumps (a primitive combo that also featured Denny Doherty and Cass Elliott, both later in the Mamas & Papas), while Boone (born 1943) and Butler (born 1944) were local rock'n'roll musicians.

Founded in 1964, partly inspired by and partly as a response to the 'British Invasion', The Spoonful combined blues, folk and country with a pop sensibility. Sebastian had a talent for writing memorable songs which dealt with the perils and joys of late adolescent relationships. After a brief false start, the band signed a recording deal in 1965 and that year made the US Top 10 with their debut single, 'Do You Believe In Magic'.

While most of the newer bands aped English Mod styles, The Spoonful were quintessentially American, and for two years every single was a US smash. In April 1966, they

Sebastian (right) – a daydreamin' Summer In The City for 'Spoonful

had their first UK success when their third single, 'Daydream', went Top 3, which it also did in the US. The effervescent 'Summer In The City' (1966) was a US No. 1 (UK Top 10), and the country-flavoured 'Nashville Cats' (1966) reached the US Top 10 and the UK Top 30, although the Top 3 US single, 'Did You Ever Have To Make Up Your Mind?', failed to chart in the UK. The albums 'Do You Believe In Magic' (1965) and 'Daydream' (1966) – a UK and US Top 10 entry – mixed Sebastian originals with traditional folk, blues and jug band material which, although well-played and fun, usually paled next to the originals. The third album, 'Hums' (1966), was better balanced. Despite another Top 20 US single, the heavily orchestrated 'Darlin' Be Home Soon' (1967), the first sign of disharmony came when Yanovsky left in 1967 after a drugs arrest in San Francisco and subsequent allegations of collaboration with the police. Replaced by Jerry Yester, the band came up with more US Top 30 singles in 'Six O'clock' and 'She's Still A Mystery' but most subsequent singles were disappointing. Sebastian stayed long enough to cut one last album, 'Everything Playing' (1967), but the others hung on and produced a last-gasp effort, the disappointing 'Revelation Revolution '69' (1968).

After lying low for a while Sebastian's solo career took a sudden upswing following his tie-dyed acoustic appearance at Woodstock in August 1969 (and its subsequent inclusion in the film). In the era of 'soft-rock', his first album 'John B. Sebastian' (1970) reached the US Top 20, and songs like 'She's A Lady' boded well for the future. Unfortunately, it rapidly became obvious that his songs had lost their edge, and in particular his self-mocking wit seemed to have deserted him. These flaws are all too apparent on his subsequent albums 'The Real Live John

Sebastian' (1971), which reached the US Top 75, 'The Four Of Us' (1971), and 'Tarzana Kid' (1974), on the last two of which he is surrounded by star sidemen who still seemed unable to lift the material. Sebastian's last album (to date) at least had one surprise – the title song, 'Welcome Back' (the theme music for a TV comedy show) was a US No. 1 single in 1976. The record's success brought him back into the public eye, but he was unable to follow it up and has subsequently all but disappeared. He is still believed to harbour ambitions to write a hit musical.

Greatest Hits

LOVIN' SPOONFUL

Singles	Title	US	UK
1966	Daydream	2	2
1966	Did You Ever Have To Make Up Your Mind?	2	–
1966	Summer In The City	1	8
Albums			
1966	Daydream	10	–
1967	Best Of	3	–

JOHN SEBASTIAN

Singles			
1976	Welcome Back	1	–
Albums			
1970	John B. Sebastian	20	–

Loretta **LYNN**

The undisputed queen of country music and the genre's most prolific hitmaker of the 60s and 70s, either solo or duetting with Conway Twitty. Although Lynn has never had a pop hit she possesses an enviable string of US country chart Top 10 hits, including several No. 1s. She was the subject of a highly

praised movie, *Coal Miner's Daughter* which won Sissy Spacek an Oscar for her portrayal of Lynn, the subsequent soundtrack album with vocals by Spaceck, making the US Top 40 in 1980. The older sister of country star Crystal Gayle, Lynn (born 1935) was brought up in the poverty of the Kentucky coalmining communities, married at the age of 13 and gave birth to four children in quick succession (she was a grandmother at 32!). Lynn spent her leisure time writing and singing, greatly influenced by Patsy Cline.

After her private recording, 'I'm A Honky Tonk Girl', financed by her husband, became a hit on an independent label, Cline's producer, Owen Bradley, signed her to a major label. Her early hits were influenced by other major country female stars, but she eventually developed a style of her own and in her ever-maturing writing spoke eloquently to the 'working women' of America.

Her major hits included such forthright statements as 'Don't Come Home A-Drinkin', With Lovin' On Your Mind', 'You Ain't Woman Enough (To Take My Man)', 'Coal Miner's Daughter', 'The Pill' and 'One's On The Way'.

Despite the success of her autobiography and the subsequent film, Lynn failed to break the pop or international charts, although many of her biggest selling albums breached the lower parts of *Billboard's* pop album charts on their sales alone.

Greatest Hits

Albums	Title	US	UK
1967	Don't Come Home A-Drinkin'	80	–
1971	Coal Miner's Daughter	81	–
1971	We Only Make Believe (with Conway Twitty)	78	–
1972	Lead Me On (with Conway Twitty)	106	–

Phil **LYNOTT**

At the late Lynott's wedding reception, his father-in-law, British TV comedian Leslie Crowther, joked about the social disadvantages of being both black and Irish, but these characteristics did not hinder Lynott's rise to stardom as both leader of Thin Lizzy and as a solo artist.

After stints with Dublin's Black Eagle and Skid Row, singer/bass player Lynott (born 1950) enjoyed a local hit, doing a version of Tim Rose's 'Morning Dew', with Orphanage before he and the group's drummer, Brian Downey, formed Thin Lizzy with guitarist Eric Bell in 1970. Hinged mainly on Lynott's then rather introspective 'progressive' compositions, their eponymous debut album and 1972's 'Shades Of A Blue Orphanage' were at odds with the hard rock that had generated so much interest in Ireland that it became more convenient for the trio to base themselves in London.

A profitable overhaul of the traditional 'Whisky In The Jar' ensured the third album, 'Vagabonds Of The Western World', enough airplay for its principal single (and stage favourite) 'The Rocker', to sell well without making the UK chart. During this period, Bell was replaced by Gary Moore (ex-Skid Row) before the recruitment of two lead guitarists, Scotsman Brian Robertson and Scott Gorham, an American.

'Nightlife' and 1975's 'Fighting' set the scene for 'Jailbreak', a major breakthrough in the album charts that was sustained with 'Johnny The Fox'. Aided by a hit single, 'The Boys Are Back In Town', 'Jailbreak' also took off in the US, but further headway there was thwarted by Lynott's contraction of hepatitis plus personnel arguments leading to the departure of Robertson and an unsettled spell with a succession of guitarists that included Moore again and Snowy White, although Robertson returned briefly for 'Bad Reputation' with its 1977 smash, 'Dancing In The Moonlight'.

In Europe, Thin Lizzy peaked commercially with the atmospheric 'Live And Dangerous' concert album and 1979's Celtic 'Black Rose' before repetition of earlier ideas on 'Chinatown' and 'Renegade' precipitated the group's decline. Lynott's solo career had started in 1980 with respectable sales for 'Solo In Soho' which embraced three UK Top 40 singles, including 'King's Call' (a tribute to Elvis Presley) and 'Yellow Pearl', co-written by Midge Ure, but two years later, 'The Phil Lynott Album' yielded far less. More tangential had been Lynott's hand in albums by Johnny Thunders and Gary Moore, and a chance to play the title role in a mooted Jimi Hendrix film biography. He was also involved in a Christ-mas single by The Greedies (with ex-members of Thin Lizzy and The Sex Pistols), and a similar venture in 1983 with Roy Wood and Chas Hodges as The Rockers. A few months prior to his sudden 1985 death, Lynott made the UK Top 10 with 'Out In The Fields', a duet with Moore, whose 1987 album, 'Wild Frontiers', contained a Thin Lizzy-style requiem to his old colleague.

Greatest Hits

Singles	Title	US	UK
1973	Whisky In The Jar	–	6
1976	The Boys Are Back In Town	12	8
1981	Yellow Pearl (Phil Lynott solo)	–	14
Albums			
1976	Jailbreak	18	10
1977	Bad Reputation	39	4
1978	Live And Dangerous	84	2
1979	Black Rose (A Rock Legend)	81	2
1983	Thunder And Lightning (Phil Lynott solo)	159	4

LYNYRD SKYNYRD

Ronnie Van Zant (vocals)
Allen Collins (guitar)
Gary Rossington (guitar)
Bob Burns (drums)
Leon Wilkerson (bass)
Billy Powell (keyboards)

Next to The Allman Brothers Band, Lynyrd Skynyrd were the most re-nowned 'Southern boogie band' of the 1970s. Their career was tragically cut short by a plane crash in 1977, although the group later re-formed.

The nucleus of the band were high-school buddies Van Zant (born 1949), Collins and Rossington, who formed a group called My Backyard in 1965. The change of name to Lynyrd Skynyrd was inspired by a school gym teacher, Leonard Skinner. They were dis-covered playing in an Atlanta bar in 1972 by ex-Blood, Sweat And Tears keyboard player Al Kooper. Kooper produced the first album, 'Pronounced Leh-Nerd Skin-nerd', which reached the US Top 30, and was notable for its attempt to outdo the Allmans by using three lead guitarists (including new member Ed King) and for a US Top 20 hit single 'Freebird', a tribute to the late Duane Allman, which became the band's best-known piece. After touring with The Who, the group recorded 'Second Helping' (1974), which entered the US Top 20 and went Top 50 in the UK. The album included the US Top 10 single, 'Sweet Home Alabama', a defence of 'redneck' virtues written as a reply to Neil Young's scathing 'Southern Man'.

In 1975 King and Burns left the group, with Artimus Pyle joining on drums. The same year the group released the US Top 10

The Boys Are Back In Town – Phil Lynott (standing) with Thin Lizzy

Ronnie Van Zant (right) lead singer with Lynyrd Skynyrd, killed in the band's 1977 plane crash

album, 'Nuthin' Fancy', which entered the UK Top 50, and they made their first UK appearances. Former Allman Brothers/Derek & The Dominos producer Tom Dowd was brought in for 'Gimme Back My Bullets' (1976), a US Top 20 and UK Top 40 album. With the addition of a further guitarist, Steven Gaines, Lynyrd Skynyrd were now reaching the peak of their popularity and a double live album, 'One More For The Road', reached the US Top 10 and sold over a million copies in the US. In 1977 the group began a 50-date tour which ended when a small plane carrying the band crashed in Mississippi. Van Zant, Gaines, his sister Casie (a backing singer) and the group's manager were killed. The just-released 'Street Survivors' climbed into the US Top 5 and gave the band a UK Top 20 album. The following year, 'Skynyrd's First And Last', containing unreleased material, was a US Top 20 hit, also making the UK Top 50.

With female vocalist Dale Krantz, Derek Hess (drums) and guitarist Barry Harwood, the remaining members formed the Rossington-Collins Band in 1979 and released 'Anytime, Anyplace, Anywhere' (1980) and 'This Is The Way' (1981), both of which were US Top 20 albums, before splitting up two years later. During the 1980s, Pyle formed his own group and Powell joined Christian rock band Vision, but in 1987 the two joined Rossington in a reunion tour. Other members of the group were Leon Wilkerson, Ed King, Dale Krantz (now married to Rossington) and guitarist Randall Hall. The lead vocalist was Ronnie's brother Donnie Van Zant, who had previously fronted 38 Special. 'For The Glory Of The South' a live double from the tour, was released in 1988.

Greatest Hits

Singles	Title	US	UK
1974	Sweet Home Alabama	8	–
1974	Freebird	19	21
Albums			
1975	Nuthin' Fancy	9	43
1976	One More For The Road	9	17
1977	Street Survivors	5	13

MADONNA

One of most successful chart artists of the 1980s, Madonna (born Madonna Louise Ciccone, 1959) worked in various dance troupes before joining disco artist Patrick Hernandez's backing singers in 1979. Later that year she joined Breakfast Club as drummer and vocalist, and in 1980 formed Emmenon (AKA Emmy), made solo demos and starred in her first film A Certain Sacrifice.

Two US club successes, 'Everybody' and 'Physical Attraction', followed her signature to a major label in 1982, and preceded her first pop hit 'Holiday' (1983) from her eponymous debut album, which went quadruple platinum in the US and was a transatlantic Top 10 hit. In 1984, she started an unprecedented run of 16 US Top 5 singles with 'Lucky Star'. Her first major film Desperately Seeking Susan, was released that year, as was her first US chart topper, 'Like a Virgin'. The 'Like A Virgin' album, produced by Nile

Rodgers, sold seven million in the US and was a transatlantic No. 1 in 1985 when she scored her first UK No. 1 single with 'Into The Groove'. While it held the UK top spot, 'Holiday' returned to the chart and reached No. 2 – making her the first US act and first female to accomplish this feat.

She appeared in Live Aid and her wedding to actor Sean Penn attracted world-wide media coverage (they were subsequently divorced). By the end of 1985 she had chalked up another record, becoming the first female artist to have eight UK Top 10s in one calendar year. In 1986 her album, 'True Blue', sold over five million in the US and was another transatlantic No. 1. In 1987 she became the first woman to have four UK No. 1 singles when 'La Isla Bonita' hit the top. Although her films Shanghai Surprise and Who's That Girl were not successes, the latter's soundtrack hit the Top 10 in 1987, as did 'You Can Dance'.

In 1989 her album, 'Like A Prayer', topped the US chart for six weeks. She hit the UK Top 5 in 1990 with her 'I'm Breathless' album, inspired by her role in the hit film Dick Tracy, and her 21st consecutive US Top 20 single 'Vogue' (her 23rd consecutive UK Top 10 hit) sold over two million in the US. Also in 1990 she released 'The Immaculate Collection', a double greatest hits package, including two new songs.

Known as much for her outrageous image as her music, Madonna has smashed nearly all the records for female artists, is only beaten by Elvis and The Beatles as the most successful chart artist of all time, and in all has sold over 80 million albums world-wide.

Greatest Hits

Singles	Title	US	UK
1984	Like A Virgin	1	3
1985	Crazy For You	1	2
1985	Into The Groove	–	1
1986	Live To Tell	1	2
1986	Papa Don't Preach	1	1
1986	True Blue	3	1
1987	Open Your Heart	1	4
1987	La Isla Bonita	4	1
1987	Who's That Girl	1	1
1989	Like A Prayer	1	1
1990	Vogue	1	1
Albums			
1984	Like A Virgin	1	1
1986	True Blue	1	1
1989	Like A Prayer	1	1

TAJ MAHAL

Born Henry St Clair Fredericks (1942), Taj Mahal's musical range across country blues, ragtime, jazz, R&B, reggae, calypso and African music marks him out as an exponent of world music well before the one album featuring Jesse Ed Davis, Chuck Blackwell on drums and Gary Gilmore on bass, the other a solo, with Mahal performing a collection of worksongs, blues and rags. Mahal's rampant eclecticism reached its apotheosis between 1971 and 1973 on the live 'Real Thing' (1971), 'Happy To Be Just Like I Am' (1971), 'Recycling The Blues And Other Related Stuff' (1972) and 'Ooh So Good'n Blues' (1973) which collectively featured tubas, a string quartet, an African drummer (Kwasi Dzizorhu), a Caribbean steel drummer (Andy Narell), flamenco guitar and The Pointer Sisters. The last album signalled Mahal's move away from the blues to explore reggae, cajun, calypso and funk on 'Mo Roots' (1974), 'Music Keeps Me Together' (1975) and 'Satisfied 'n' Tickled Too' (1976) after which he changed labels. Mahal also scored for movies; Martin Ritt's excellent evocation of black sharecropper experience in the 1930s *Sounder* (1972) in which Mahal appeared and the less successful *Brothers* (1977), based on the relationship between black militant Angela Davis and literate black convict George Jackson.

Two further albums, 'Music Fuh Ya' (1977), and 'Evolution: The Most Recent' (1978), made extensive use of Trinidadian steel drums to create a carnival atmosphere. In 1979 Taj Mahal decided to release direct cut recordings of his albums of which 'Taj Mahal And The International Rhythm Band' (1979) was the first. He went into semi-retirement during the 1980s, returning again for 'Taj' (1987).

By refusing to follow fashions or submit to easy classification, Taj Mahal has been denied the commercial success he so richly deserves.

Greatest Hits

Albums	Title	US	UK
1969	Giant Step/De Ole		
	Folks At Home	85	–
1971	The Real Thing	84	–

Taj – impossible to pigeonhole

The Madonna mediahype – immaculate conception from Seeking Susan to superstardom

phrase became fashionable.

His mother sang gospel and classical songs, while his father was a jazz arranger, and while at college on an animal husbandry course, Taj Mahal sang blues in his spare time. Later, he abandoned his education to join LA band, the Rising Sons, including Ry Cooder, the late Jesse Ed Davis, Byrd-to-be Kevin Kelley and future Spirit drummer Ed Cassidy. They released a single 'Candy Man' (1966), but the album they recorded was never officially released.

Mahal, Cooder and Davis stayed together for Mahal's eponymous 1967 solo album. Urban electric blues in presentation, the songs also paid homage to Mahal's love of country blues with tracks by Robert Johnson, Sleepy John Estes and Blind Willie McTell.

'Natch'1 Blues' (1968) saw Mahal going over similar ground, but showcasing other influences, covering William Bell's soul ballad 'You Don't Miss Your Water' (a hit for Otis Redding in 1966). His double album 'Giant Steps/De Ole Folks At Home' (1969) placed Goffin and King's 'Take A Giant Step' (recorded by the Monkees) alongside Leadbelly,

TAJ MAHAL ◀ ◀ ◀

The **MAMAS** & The **PAPAS**

Cass Elliott
Michelle Gilliam
John Phillips
Denny Doherty (vocal group)

With their exuberant and irresistible vocal harmonies coupled with a hippy drop-out image, The Mamas & The Papas mined a profitable seam of soft-rock in the mid-1960s before consolidation rather than development caused the loss of direction that led to their demise.

With Scott McKenzie, singer/songwriter/guitarist John Phillips worked in The Journeymen, mainstays of the Greenwich Village folk circuit, circa 1962, when he married Californian model Gilliam (born 1944). Elliott (born 1943) had toured with a satirical revue before 'resting' as a waitress and singing in the Mugwumps, another New York folk act, with Doherty (born 1941) and Zal Yanovsky (later of The Lovin' Spoonful). In 1964 Doherty, Elliott and the Phillipses were holidaying together in the Virgin Isles when their beach party harmonizing encouraged John to propose the formation of The Mamas & The Papas. The quartet moved to Los Angeles where, on the recommendation of songwriter P.F. Sloan, they soon signed a recording contract.

Backed by top session players, their first two singles, 'California Dreamin'' and the Grammy-winning 'Monday Monday' preceded further world-wide smashes and related albums of mainly John Phillips originals. He also penned the UK chart-topping flower-power anthem 'San Francisco (Be Sure To Wear Flowers In Your Hair)' for old colleague McKenzie who emoted it at 1967's celebrated Monterey Pop Festival. As one of the event's organizers, Phillips ensured that his group performed at an optimum moment, and were represented in D.A. Pennebaker's documentary movie, but after a successful cover of The Shirelles' hit, 'Dedicated To The One I Love', and another smash with the autobiographical 'Creeque Alley', personal ructions (exemplified by the Phillips' divorce) and a run of minor hits led to the group disbanding in 1968. While his ex-wife made headway as an actress, Phillips financed Robert Altman's *Brewster McCloud* movie, and in 1970, recorded 'Wolf King of LA', an album in which country-rock accompaniment belied lyrics that hinted at its writer's descent into drug addiction.

Of the other ex-members, only Elliott – overweight but lovable – made a chart come-back, with 1968's 'Dream A Little Dream Of Me'. A year later, 'It's Getting Better' was a small hit, but a hit all the same. An album with Dave Mason (ex-Traffic) fared badly despite (or because of) the duo's promotional spot on the Andy Williams TV series. Cass rejoined the group for the lacklustre 'People Like Us' album, resulting from a brief Mamas & Papas contractual obligation reunion in 1971, but returned to the cabaret circuit until her sudden 1974 death in London.

Phillips's ascent from his drug abyss is detailed in his harrowing autobiography, *Papa John*, and, if not a picture of health, he was fit enough in 1986 to amalgamate with his daughter Mackenzie (Scott's godchild), familiarly portly Elaine 'Spanky' McFarlane (from Spanky & Our Gang) and Doherty as a reformed Mamas & Papas, who headlined a well-received if poorly attended 1960s Revival Tour.

Greatest Hits

Singles	Title	US	UK
1966	*California Dreamin'*	4	23
1966	*Monday Monday*	1	3
1967	*Dedicated To The One I Love*	2	2
1967	*Creeque Alley*	5	9
Albums			
1966	*If You Can Believe Your Eyes And Ears*	1	–
1966	*The Mamas & The Papas*	4	3
1967	*The Mamas & The Papas Deliver*	2	4

MANFRED MANN

Paul Jones (vocals, harp)
Manfred Mann (keyboards)
Mike Vickers (saxophone, guitar)
Dave Richmond (bass)
Mike Hugg (drums)

Formed by Mann (born 1940) and Hugg (born 1942) as jazz/R&B outfit The Mann-Hugg Blues Brothers, in 1962 and fronted by ex-Oxford student Paul Jones (born Paul Pond, 1942), the band became Manfred Mann in 1963 upon signing a major record deal. After two flop singles, Richmond left and was replaced by Tom McGuinness (born 1941) latterly of R&B outfit The Roosters, which featured Eric Clapton. The group provided the theme tune for the new UK pop TV flagship, *Ready Steady Go*, '5, 4, 3, 2, 1' (1964), which made the UK Top 5, followed swiftly by 'Hubble, Bubble, Toil and Trouble', which reached the UK Top 20, and the UK No. 1, 'Do Wah Diddy', a cover of a US R&B hit by The Exciters.

More cover versions appeared on their debut album, 'Five Faces of Manfred Mann', which made the UK Top 5 later that year, while at the same time 'Do Wah Diddy' reached No. 1 in the US. Two further UK Top 5 singles followed, 'Sha La La', which reached the US Top 20, and 'Come Tomorrow' (US Top 50). An EP release made the UK singles Top 10 in mid-1965, including the title track 'The One In the Middle' and the first of several Bob Dylan covers, 'With God On Our Side'; later in 1965, a second Dylan cover, 'If You Gotta Go, Go Now' reached the UK Top 3. At the end of the year, McGuinness switched to guitar as they were joined by Jack Bruce (born 1943), ex-John Mayall's Bluesbreakers, on bass.

A UK No. 1 single came with 'Pretty Flamingo' (1966), which was a US Top 30 hit. Soon after, Bruce left to form Cream and Jones departed to go solo. Klaus Voorman (born 1942) was recruited on bass along with vocalist Mike D'Abo (born 1944), and the new line-up had its first UK Top 10 hit with a cover of Dylan's 'Just Like A Woman' (1966). Later that year, 'Semi-Detached Suburban Mr James' reached the UK Top 3.

Paul Jones' first solo single, 'I've Been A Bad Bad Boy', hit the UK Top 5 in 1967, and that year he also starred in the film *Privilege* with fashion model Jean Shrimpton. The group's own foray into movies came early in 1968 with *Up The Junction*, where their sound track music showcased their jazz roots. Simultaneously, yet another Dylan cover, the then unknown 'The Mighty Quinn', made the UK Top 3 and US Top 10.

In 1969 Jones dropped out of pop music altogether when he decided to pursue an acting career fulltime; meanwhile Manfred Mann had their final two chart entries – 'Fox On The Run' (1968), a UK Top 5 hit, and 'Ragamuffin Man' (1969), a UK Top 10, single – before disbanding. Mann and Hugg went on to form Chapter Three, a jazz-oriented outfit using session players on two albums, neither of which sold significantly. At the same time, McGuinness formed McGuinness Flint with ex-John Mayall drummer Hughie Flint, Benny Gallagher and Graham Lyne on guitars and Dennis Coulson on keyboards. They scored two UK hit singles with the UK Top 3 entry, 'When I'm Dead And Gone' (1970), which also made the US Top 50, and 'Malt And Barley Blues', which made the UK Top 5. Their eponymous debut album reached the Top 10 in the UK.

Early in 1972 Mann put together Manfred Mann's Earthband, a progressive rock group with rather grandiose ambitions, with Mick Rogers on vocals and guitar, Colin Pallenden on bass, and drummer Chris Slade. The single 'Joybringer' (based on 'Jupiter' from Gustav Holst's *Planets Suite*), made the UK Top 10 in 1973, but their biggest hit came three years later, in 1976, after several personnel changes, with a cover of Bruce Springsteen's 'Blinded By The Light'. Sung by their new vocalist/guitarist Chris Thompson, it was a US No. 1 single, reached the UK Top 10 and pushed the album 'The Roaring Silence' into the UK and US Top 10.

Minor successes followed over the next 10 years, including the albums 'Chance' (1981), a US Top 100 entry, and 'Somewhere In Afrika' (1983), a commentary on Mann's South African homeland, which made the UK Top 100 and the US Top 50. 'Criminal Tango' (1986), and 'Masque' (1987), failed to chart, however, and the Earth Band disbanded.

Manfreds mark 2, with (standing l to r) Voorman, McGuiness (seated), Mann, D'Abo and Hugg

Barry **MANILOW**

Manilow (born Barry Alan Pinkus, 1946) has been derided for his bland approach and delivery, yet he remains a total showbiz professional, able to sell records and fill stadia in rock superstar proportions. After a Brooklyn slum childhood, when he learned accordion and piano, Manilow went through the Juillard music school and eventually moved into arranging. He spent two years as musical director on a TV talent show, *Callback*, in the early 1970s, sang jingles for commercials and played in a nightclub duo before taking a job in 1972 as pianist at a gay club below a Manhattan Turkish bath house. There he was joined by a young unknown, Bette Midler, and went on to co-produce and arrange her first two albums. Promoting the first album, he toured with Midler as MD and pianist, opening the shows with his own spot.

Midler's career took off, and Manilow released his own eponymous debut album in 1974, which failed to make any immediate impact. However, the single 'Mandy', topped the US chart in January 1975, just missing the UK Top 10, and was followed by his second album, 'Barry Manilow II', which made the US Top 10. There followed a string of hits, more than a dozen of which made the UK singles chart between the mid 1970s and 1980s, including what have become cabaret standards, 'It Could Be Magic', a US Top 10 single, and the US chart-topper 'I Write The Songs'. Platinum albums and sell-out world tours followed, including a then record-breaking five nights at London's Royal Albert Hall in 1982; the same year 'Barry Live In Britain' topped the UK album chart, while 1983 saw British Manilowmania at its peak, with an outdoor concert drawing 40,000.

His reputation as singer rather than showman was enhanced in 1984 with the album '2.00 AM Paradise Cafe', which went UK and

'Manilow Magic' - says it all

Tom McGuinness, meanwhile, disbanded McGuinness Flint in 1975, rejoining Jones and Flint in 1979 to form The Blues Band, with Dave Kelly (guitar) and Gary Fletcher (bass). Conceived as a part-time 'fun' band playing the London pub-rock circuit, its live debut album, 'The Official Bootleg Album', (1979) eventually made the UK Top 40, as did 'Ready' (1980), while 1981's 'Itchy Feet' also made the UK Top 60 chart. The part-time band, with Flint replaced by ex-Family drummer Rob Townsend, found itself back on the one-nighter trek round the UK, Europe and Canada, and finally called it a day at the end of 1982, Jones once more returning to the stage in West End shows, including *Cats* and *Guys and Dolls*, and the band leaving another live album, 'Bye Bye Blues', as their farewell in 1983.

A TV-advertised compilation of Manfred Mann 1960s hits, 'Semi-Detached Suburban', made the UK Top 10 in 1979, and the original group reunited in 1983 for the 25th Anniversary of London's Marquee Club. A series of reunions of The Blues Band have made them a permanent (if occasional) part of the UK live rock scene, and they released a studio album, 'Back For More', in 1989.

Greatest Hits

MANFRED MANN

Singles	Title	US	UK
1964	Do Wah Diddy Diddy	1	1
1966	Pretty Flamingo	29	1
1968	Mighty Quinn	10	1
Albums			
1964	Five Faces Of Manfred Mann	141	3

MANFRED MANN'S EARTHBAND

Singles			
1977	Blinded By The Light	1	6
Albums			
1977	The Roaring Silence	10	10

PAUL JONES

Singles			
1966	High Time	–	4
1967	I've Been A Bad Bad Boy	–	5

McGUINNESS FLINT

Singles			
1970	When I'm Dead And Gone	47	2
1971	Malt And Barley Blues	–	5
Album			
1971	McGuinness Flint	155	9

US Top 30 and included jazz giants guests Sarah Vaughan, Mel Torme and Gerry Mulligan. However, despite the similarly prestigious 'Big Fun On Swing Street' (1987) he continued to be the darling of the MOR circuit.

Greatest Hits

Singles	Title	US	UK
1975	Mandy	1	11
1976	I Write The Songs	1	–
1977	Looks Like We Made It	1	–
1982	I Wanna Do It With You	–	8
Albums			
1977	Barry Manilow Live	1	–
1978	Even Now	3	12
1979	Manilow Magic	–	3
1982	Barry Live In Britain	–	1

MARILLION

Fish (vocals)
Steve Rothery (guitar)
Mark Kelly (keyboards)
Diz Minitt (bass)
Mick Pointer (drums)

Progressive rockers formed in 1979 as Silmarillion (from J.R.R. Tolkien's novel of the same name), around Kelly (born 1961), replacing Brian Jelliman, and guitarist Rothery (born 1959). They shortened their name during line-up changes that saw Fish (born Derek Dick, 1958) a burly Scottish ex-woodcutter, join as frontman.

A British radio session in 1982, the year Pete Trewavas (born 1959) joined in place of original bassist Diz Minnitt, led to a major label deal and a London headline gig after just one flop single, 'Market Square Heroes'. Derided by the press as Genesis soundalikes, they earned a huge grassroots following among progressive rock fans harking back to 1970s sounds by touring constantly.

1983's debut album, 'Script For A Jester's Tear' made the UK Top 10, on the heels of their first UK Top 40 single, 'He Knows You Know'. Experienced drummer Ian Mosley (born 1953) replaced Mick Pointer for the following year's 'Fugazi', while the live 'Real To Reel' (also 1984) was an attempt to beat bootleggers who'd latched on to their fanatical following.

The concept album, 'Misplaced Childhood', broke the band in 1985 with a series of superbly commercial UK hit singles, 'Kayleigh', 'Lavender' and 'Heart Of Lothian', which took it to No. 1, but lyricist Fish was already at odds with the rest of the band. After a stormy, far rockier (but only slightly less successful) album, 'Clutching At Straws' (1987), he quit with bad feeling on both sides. The live album 'The Thieving Magpie' closed the chapter in 1989, while a rarities compilation

'B-Sides Themselves', satisfied completists.

Fish (who cut a single in 1986 with Tony Banks of Genesis) recorded the UK Top 5 album 'Vigil In A Wilderness Of Mirrors' in 1990, while Marillion continued with ex-Europeans singer Steve Hogarth on the UK Top 10 album 'Season's End' (1989) and hit single 'Hooks In You'. Both parties had sufficient support to stay in contention, but the match of singer and band had made for some of the decade's most powerful rock.

Greatest Hits

Singles	Title	US	UK
1985	Kayleigh	–	2
1985	Lavender	–	5
Albums			
1985	Misplaced Childhood	–	1
1987	Clutching At Straws	–	2

Bob MARLEY

White intelligentsia had tended to ignore ska, bluebeat and other West Indian music included under the umbrella term 'reggae', even if Millie, Desmond Dekker and similar upmarket practitioners had enjoyed isolated hits beyond the Caribbean during the 1960s. Bob Marley was chief among those who cajoled the rock audience to take its reggae medicine neater. Half-caste Marley (born 1945) grew up in Trenchtown, a depressed shanty suburb of Jamaica's Kingston, where entertainment was provided by sound systems whose operators began recording local musicians in the late 1950s, welding American – and, later, British – pop to West Indian patois and rhythms. On the recommendations of Jimmy Cliff (see separate entry), Marley began his recording career with

Rastaman Marley

Leslie Kong, a noted Chinese-Jamaican producer and owner of a Kingston studio, who released Marley's debut single, 'One Cup Of Coffee' in 1962.

By 1964 Marley was leader and main songwriter of The Wailers, then a vocal group, in which the mainstays of a changing personnel were Peter Tosh (see separate entry) and Bunny Livingston. 'Simmer Down' was the first of many Jamaican hits. By 1966's 'Rude Boy' (which romanticized Trenchtown's teenage delinquents), The Wailers (with Marley on electric guitar) were a complete musical group, and after Marley's rise to fame, a selection of these early tracks were included on the album, 'In The Beginning'.

With a huge parochial reputation, Marley's climb to international stardom began when he and The Wailers were commissioned to compose incidental music in Sweden for a film starring US pop-reggae singer Johnny Nash. Among other songs Marley wrote for Nash was the UK Top 20 hit, 'Stir It Up', but he was unable to capitalize on this triumph as he and Livingston had been jailed for possession of ganja (marijuana). Regular smoking of this illegal herb was a religious prequisite of the Rastafarians, the dreadlocked ghetto sect whose practices also embraced Bible readings and back-to-Africa sermons. Hints of Marley and his group's conversion surfaced in two 1969 albums, 'Soul Rebel' and 'Soul Vibration'. Marley's lyrics were more focussed – and his tunes more melodic – on 1970's 'African Herbsman' and 'Rasta Revolution', which appeared domestically on his own Tuff Gong label.

The group cut 1973's 'Catch A Fire' album as its first for Island, and it was a combination of the company's considerable promotional budget and incessant touring (later with female chorale, the I-Threes) that made Marley a cult celebrity in North America and the UK as well as other territories in Africa and Europe. Eric Clapton's 1974 cover of Marley's 'I Shot The Sheriff' (included on 1973's 'Burnin'' album by Marley) topped the US chart, and George Harrison (see separate entry) opined that a Wailers concert was 'the best thing I've seen in ten years'.

'Natty Dread' (the first Marley album without Livingston and Tosh) crept into the UK album chart in 1975, and a 'live' version of a song from the album, 'No Woman No Cry', was a minor hit single. Marley's US breakthrough came the following year with 'Rastaman Vibration', and while 'Exodus' was less successful, the single of its title track took Marley high in the charts elsewhere. With 1977's 'Punky Reggae Party' in the UK Top 10, Marley weathered the punk-rock storm.

In his next hit single, 'Is This Love', and on 'Kaya' and other late 1970s albums, there were inclinations towards more generalized pop but this was no indication of any dilution of Marley's spiritual and political beliefs. His interventions in West Indian politics brought him both an attempted assassination and, in

1978, a Third World Peace Medal. Marley's final studio album, 1980's 'Uprising', showed signs of a return to the scripture-quoting, autobiographical style of yore, but he died of cancer a year later. Marley has never been replaced, and reggae continues to lack the focal point he provided, as was eloquently proved when a 1984 compilation album, 'Legend', topped the UK album charts, giving Marley his greatest success posthumously. His son, Ziggy Marley, has enjoyed limited international success, but as yet has hardly approached the status achieved by his father.

Greatest Hits

Singles	Title	US	UK
1980	Could You Be Loved	–	5
1983	Buffalo Soldier	–	4
1984	One Love	–	5
Albums			
1976	Rastaman Vibration	8	15
1978	Kaya	50	4
1983	Confrontation	55	5
1984	Legend	54	1

The MARVELETTES

Gladys Horton
Wanda Young
Katherine Anderson
Georgeanna Tillman
Juanita Cowart
Anne Bogan (vocal group)

Formed in Detroit's Inkster High School during 1961 as The Casinyets, The Marvelettes became one of the first signings to Berry Gordy's Tamla label after he changed their name. They have the distinction of providing Gordy with the label's first No. 1, 'Please Mr Postman', covered by The Beatles and now a rock standard, and scored several other pop hits in the 'girl group' style before the commonly accepted 'Motown Sound' had taken root, notably 'Playboy' and 'Beechwood 4–5789'. By 1965 they were a trio consisting of Horton (born 1944), Young (born 1944) and Anderson (born 1944), and scored several R&B hits under the production team Holland-Dozier-Holland, including 'I'll Keep On Holding On' and 'Too Many Fish In The Sea'.

Their artistic peak came in 1966 under the guidance of Smokey Robinson who provided them with songs like 'The Hunter Gets Captured By The Game', 'Don't Mess With Bill' and 'My Baby Must Be A Magician'. 'When You're Young And In Love', their only UK Top 30 entry (1967), was later covered by The Flying Pickets. Their album, 'Sophisticated Soul', is one of the finest and most cohesive released by the label during a time when Motown albums were notoriously padded with filler tracks.

As The Supremes garnered world wide fame, The Marvelettes were pushed further into the background. Horton was replaced by Bogan in 1969 and after leaving the label the group toured consistently on the oldies circuit with at times as little as one original member. In 1989 all the surviving members reformed to record for the Motorcity label which is dedicated to re-recording original Motown artists.

Greatest Hits

Singles	Title	US	UK
1961	Please Mr Postman	1	–
1962	Playboy	7	–
1966	Don't Mess With Bill	7	–
1967	The Hunter Gets Captured By The Game	13	–
1967	When You're Young And In Love	23	13
Albums			
1966	Greatest Hits	84	–

John MAYALL

Like Alexis Korner and Graham Bond, John Mayall (born 1933), was destined to be one of those 'catalysts' who encourage young musicians to greater commercial success than they themselves ever achieve.

Brought up on his father's American jazz records, Mayall taught himself guitar, keyboards, harmonica and took on lead vocals for his first band formed at art school, The Powerhouse Four. He also earned himself local notoriety by living in a tree house. Totally committed to the blues and opting for music rather than art, Mayall formed The Blues Syndicate before moving to London in 1963 at the age of 29 to become a professional musician.

Calling his new band The Bluesbreakers, it took Mayall some months to find a stable line-up – John McVie (bass), Bernie Watson (guitar) and Peter Ward (replaced by Martin

Marvelettes – Postman delivers the goods, and a Motor City milestone

Hart) on drums – the third of what was to be fifteen different versions of the band by 1970. This line-up ran until 1964 when Hughie Flint (Mayall's original drummer in The Blues Syndicate) and Roger Dean (guitar) took over. Line-up number four recorded Mayall's first single, 'Crocodile Walk', and a live album recorded at Klooks Kleek Club in Hampstead, 'John Mayall Plays John Mayall'. Mayall was ruthless when it came to dispensing with a musician, either because he had transgressed Mayall's law about drinking or because a better player came along. Roger Dean was always rather too country-oriented for Mayall's liking, so when Eric Clapton became available in 1965, it was goodbye Roger!

With Clapton in the band for the next 15 months, the popularity of The Bluesbreakers soared, culminating in the release of the 'Bluesbreakers' album in 1966, the seminal British blues recording which gave notice that the Brits could play the blues and made Clapton a star (see separate entry). It was Mayall's most successful record, but by the time of its release, Clapton had left.

In the summer of 1965, Clapton had taken leave of absence to travel in Europe. A number of guitarists filled in including Peter Green who stepped into the breech when Clapton left to form Cream. Another new face was drummer Aynsley Dunbar. This line-up cut 'Hard Road', another excellent album on which Green proved that he was the rightful heir to Clapton's guitar spot in the band with tracks like 'Supernatural' and 'The Stumble'. The band also cut three singles, none of which charted, including an instrumental, 'Curly', made without Mayall but with an Aynsley Dunbar drum solo, 'Rubber Duck', on the B-side. In turn, Mayall recorded a solo album, 'The Blues Alone', playing all the instruments except drums.

Dunbar left in 1967 to be replaced briefly by Micky Waller and then by Mick Fleetwood.

British blues breaker Mayall

who was out almost as soon as he was in, fired for over-imbibing. Peter Green resigned to join Mick Fleetwood in a new venture, Fleetwood Mac, and once it took off in September, John McVie (who had also once been fired by Mayall for drinking) left Mayall for the new band and eventual superstardom.

By now, Mayall was experimenting with brass, hiring saxophonists Chris Mercer and Rip Kant, who soon made way for Henry Lowther on trumpet. After McVie left, Mayall had trouble finding a bass player; in 1967/68 he used Paul Williams (ex-Zoot Money), Keith Tillman and Andy Fraser who went on to form Free. On drums was the highly experienced Keef Hartley (ex-Artwoods and Rory Storm's Hurricanes, who had played drums on Mayall's solo album). The 'new Clapton' was the very young Mick Taylor. Collectively, these musicians recorded 'Crusade' (Mayall's attack on British ignorance of US blues) and 'Diary of a Band' (Volumes 1 and 2), a messy mixture of live recordings, interviews and assorted chat.

In 1968 it was all change again – a more jazz-oriented line-up, with saxophonist Dick Heckstall-Smith, bassist Tony Reeves (ex-New Jazz Orchestra) and an explosive young drummer formerly with Heckstall-Smith in the Graham Bond Organisation, Jon Hiseman. This line-up plus Taylor, Mercer and Lowther, cut 'Bare Wires', a faltering experimental fusion of jazz/blues.

By late 1968 Mayall was tiring of the organizational problems in carrying a large band, and some modest success with The Bluesbreakers in America, home of Mayall's heart music, had whetted his appetite both to live and work there. He needed to offload some musicians, so Heckstall-Smith was ditched and he took Hiseman and Reeves with him to form Colosseum. Meanwhile, Mayall decided to work under his own name and formally disbanded The Bluesbreakers. He then spent three weeks in Los Angeles where he wrote his next album, 'Blues From Laurel Canyon'. The album was recorded back in London with Mayall's new four-piece band of Mick Taylor, ex-Zoot Money drummer Colin Allen and the unknown Steve Thompson on bass. The new band lasted until mid-1969 when Mick Taylor ended his two-year association with Mayall after an offer he couldn't refuse from The Rolling Stones, and Colin Allen also accepted a job offer with Stone The Crows.

Mayall had been considering his most radical step yet, a drummerless band, so in came Jon Mark on guitar and Johnny Almond on saxes/flute for Mayall's first album for a new label, the excellent 'Turning Point' recorded live at New York's Fillmore East in 1969. The same line-up recorded 'Empty Rooms' in 1970 before Mark and Almond formed their own band, Mark Almond, and Thompson joined Allen in Stone The Crows to be replaced briefly by ex-Aynsley Dunbar bassist, Alex Dmochowski.

Americans formed Mayall's next band – ex-Canned Heat members Larry Taylor (bass) and Harvey Mandel (guitar) with Don 'Sugarcane' Harris (violin) for 'USA Union' followed by The Bluesbreakers reunion album, 'Back To The Roots' (1971). Mayall's 1970s albums were developments on the fusion style of 'Bare Wires' – 'Jazz-Blues Fusion' (1972), 'Moving On' and 'Ten Years Are Gone' (both 1973), all with trumpeter Blue Mitchell and guitarist Freddie Robinson. 'New Year, New Band, New Company' (1975 on a third label) and the Allen Toussaint-produced 'Notice To Appear' (1975) featured another vocalist for the first time.

After 'Last of the British Blues' (1978), Mayall moved labels again for 'Bottom Line' (1979), 'No More Interviews' (1979) and 'Road Show Blues' (1981). In 1982 he toured in the US and Australia with John McVie, Mick Taylor and Colin Allen to enthusiastic audiences. The latest hot guitar player with Mayall is Coco Montoya, heard on 'Chicago Line' (1988) and 'A Sense of Place' (1990), Mayall's best album since the 1960s.

John Mayall has always ploughed his own furrow, making no concessions to current fashion. Something of a martinet, his bands have turned out some of Britain's finest musicians and everybody got paid on time!

Greatest Hits

Albums	Title	US	UK
1966	Bluesbreakers	–	6
1968	Bare Wires	59	3
1969	Turning Point	32	11
1970	USA Union	22	50

Curtis **MAYFIELD** and The **IMPRESSIONS**

The Impressions were one of the most influential soul groups of the 1960s, not simply because of their unique close harmony style (borrowed liberally from gospel quartets) but also because of lead singer Curtis Mayfield's writing and producing abilities. Chicagoan Mayfield (born 1942), like most of his contemporaries, sang in gospel groups, and in one, The Northern Jubileers, he befriended Jerry Butler (born 1939), and together they formed a juvenile doowop group, The Alphatones, in 1953. In 1956 they merged with The Roosters, a Tennessee group consisting of Richard and Arthur Brooks and Sam Gooden, whom Butler had discovered.

As Jerry Butler & The Impressions, they had a US Top 20 single with 'For Your Precious Love' in 1958. Butler was persuaded to go solo and Fred Cash was recruited. But when Richard and Arthur Brooks departed, The Impressions became a trio and were dropped by their label when Mayfield spent

After Curtis, 'First Impressions' was a hit with the group's fourth lead singer

guidance of Ed Townsend, notably 'Finally Got Myself Together' (1974) and the UK Top 20 single 'First Impressions' (1976, their only UK hit). Subsequently, they enjoyed sporadic success on various labels, but despite the constant presence of Cash and Gooden faded from view. In 1983 Mayfield, Butler, Cash and Gooden reunited for a one-off 25th Anniversary tour which broke box-office records across America.

Mayfield's first solo album, 'Curtis', spawned the UK Top 20 hit, 'Move On Up', but his major success came with 'Superfly' (1972), the movie soundtrack. Although sporadically inventive, Mayfield's career since the 1970s has been one of promise unfulfilled. For each major album such as 'Back To The World' (1973) or 'No Place Like America Today' (1975), full of concise observations on American malaise, there have been several albums of pointless disco workouts and insipid attempts at hit singles. As for so many artists, the disco boom wiped out Mayfield's credentials, and throughout most of the 1980s he has remained an anachronism, performing around the world regularly to a devoted audience. Now based in Atlanta and recording for his own label, Mayfield suffered a tragic accident on stage during 1990 which may leave him permanently paralysed. Despite his inability to remain at the forefront in recent years, his work with The Impressions remains one of the most important pop legacies of the 1960s.

Greatest Hits

IMPRESSIONS

Singles	Title	US	UK
1963	It's All Right	4	–
1964	Keep On Pushing	10	–
1964	Amen	7	
1976	First Impressions	–	16
Album			
1964	Keep On Pushing	8	–

CURTIS MAYFIELD

Singles			
1971	Move On Up	–	12
1972	Freddie's Dead	4	–
1972	Superfly	8	–
Albums			
1972	Superfly	1	26

Paul **McCARTNEY**

A part from tangents like his film score for 1966's *The Family Way*, Paul McCartney only embarked on a tangible solo career during the last weeks of The Beatles when, on his Scottish farm, he began overdubbing all instruments and vocals for his 'McCartney' album. Released only days before the group's 'Let It Be', its sketchy charm embraced a paean to his wife ('The Lovely Linda'), a

more time as guitarist, arranger and writer for Butler. In 1961 the trio signed a new record deal under the guidance of arranger/producer Johnny Pate, a former jazzman who had enjoyed a US Top 50 single with 'Swinging Shepherd Blues' (1958). The combination of Mayfield's writing, guitar playing and lyrics with Cash and Gooden's harmonies and Pate's arrangements formed a unique sound which quickly gained radio acceptance. Their first hit, 'Gypsy Woman' (1961), reached the US Top 20, and was unusual for an R&B record in being almost folksy in both delivery and style. However, similar follow-ups like 'Minstrel and Queen', with equally whimsical lyrics, failed to click.

After a two-year dry spell the group re-entered the charts with the US Top 5 single, 'It's Allright', a return to gospel roots which heralded a run of similar hits for the rest of the decade. Mayfield began taking a more radical stance in his lyrics, with 'Keep On Pushing' (1964), 'Amen' (1964), 'People Get Ready' (1965) and 'Meeting Over Yonder' (1965) eloquently speaking of the black struggle in a manner so subtle that pop audiences in America were entranced. During this period Mayfield produced extensively,

enjoying major pop and R&B hits with Major Lance, Billy Butler, Walter Jackson, Gene Chandler and Jan Bradley, and by 1966 he had formed his own label. A flirtation with Motown sounds proved a minor failure and in 1967 Mayfield took The Impressions in a much heavier black direction.

'We're A Winner', a black pride anthem, reached the US Top 20 and topped the R&B chart, but lost the group their pop base; and its follow-up 'We're Rolling On' continued the theme. After a change to Mayfield's own Curtom label, the next few singles – 'This Is My Country' (1968), 'Choice Of Colours', and 'Check Out Your Mind' – were massive R&B hits but only modest pop successes. Mayfield's writing had become more important to him than the group, and he began to look at the rise of the singer/songwriter in pop and at the increasing importance of the album market as a more suitable vehicle for his artistic aspirations.

In 1970 Mayfield quit the group (though he continued to produce and write for them) and was replaced by Leroy Hutson, who himself left in 1972, replaced in turn by Reggie Torian and Ralph Johnson. This line-up eventually enjoyed major hits under the

McCartney – Mulls over mixed reviews and Michael's publishing coup

Trying harder, Wings were rewarded critically for their James Bond movie theme, 'Live And Let Die' and 'Band On the Run', an album combining force and melody that yielded a cathartic send-up of Lennon in 'Let Me Roll It', and hit singles in 'Helen Wheels', 'Jet', and its complex title track. While some of this album was recorded in Nigeria, McCartney next repaired to Nashville for nepotic projects such as a single (as 'The Country Hams') of one of his father's compositions and Wings assistance on brother Mike McGear's 1974 'McGear' album. From Nashville too came part of 'Venus And Mars', which was pleasant but marked time artistically. Much the same applied to 1976's 'At The Speed Of Sound' in which Paul delegated more creative responsibility to others in the group's changing personnel while still taking lead vocals on its attendant hits, 'Let 'Em In' and the rather self-justifying 'Silly Love Songs'.

Beatles songs and the ancient Moody Blues hit, 'Go Now', were heard on the 'Wings Over America' live album recorded during the group's lengthy and well-received world tour. This album's UK chart placing was modest, but 'Mull Of Kintyre', McCartney's 1977 eulogy (co-written by Laine) to his Scottish abode was a million-seller that meant little in the US. In the UK too, McCartney had become a showbiz evergreen to whom plugging 'Mull Of Kintyre' on TV was all in a day's work. Despite the holding operation that was 'London Town', he was the only ex-Beatle to figure in *Melody Maker's* 1979 popularity poll – the year he disbanded Wings after the lacklustre 'Back To The Egg' and a tour blighted by a custodial drugs bust in Japan.

He bounced back with 'Coming Up' and a promotional video featuring him in various guises as every member of a group. This was an apt taster for 'McCartney II' which returned to his solo debut's one-man-band ethos. At George Martin's Monserrat studios in 1982, he reunited with the former Beatles producer (and Ringo Starr) to cut 'Tug Of War'. Among its highlights was 'Here Today' (for the late Lennon) and 'Ebony And Ivory', a duet with Stevie Wonder. Likewise, he was joined by Michael Jackson for 'Say Say Say' from 1983's 'Pipes of Peace' album and other recordings up to 1986, when Jackson outbid McCartney for Beatles publishing rights. Neither was McCartney pleased by most reviews of his self-financed *Give My Regards To Broad Street* movie. *Citizen Kane* it wasn't, but it spawned intriguing reprises of six Beatles songs as well as another hit in the sentimental 'No More Lonely Nights'.

As the 1980s progressed, McCartney sought songwriting partners, such as Eric Stewart (ex-10cc) for most of the 'Press To Play' album. He also expressed an unreciprocated wish to team up with George Harrison after a bond with Elvis Costello had resulted in 1989's 'Flowers In The Dirt', which tem-

Beatles leftover ('Teddy Boy') and songs like 'Maybe I'm Amazed' (covered by The Faces) that suggested that, having soundtracked the 1960s with John Lennon, McCartney (born 1942) might so minister to the next decade. Events proved this judgement premature. Lennon alluded to McCartney's first solo single, the melancholy 'Another Day', in 'How Do You Sleep', a musical attack in vengeance for what he saw as more subtle digs at him on McCartney's 1971 album, 'Ram'. If this, and that same year's 'Wild Life', were each almost as slap-dash as 'McCartney', their creator's earlier form ensured them a fair hearing even if 'Wild Life' was attributed to Wings, McCartney's new band with Linda on rudimentary keyboards,

former Moody Blue Denny Laine on guitar and Denny Seiwell, a New York session drummer.

The quartet trekked across Britain and Europe for mainly surprise gigs before the release of four contrasting singles in 'Give Ireland Back To The Irish ' – after the 'Bloody Sunday' incident in Londonderry – 'Mary Had A Little Lamb' (the nursery rhyme), 'Hi Hi Hi' (banned for sexual innuendo by the BBC) and the syrupy 'My Love' from 1973's 'Red Rose Speedway'. Weak lyrics, catchy jingles and reflection of the growing McCartney family's rural contentment confirmed that despite his agile bass playing, Paul's wispy capacity for what John had derided as 'granny music' continued.

pered an abrasive edge with attractive tunes. Although it topped the UK album chart, this offering was only moderately successful in comparison with past achievements, despite some of its tracks being featured in McCartney's first major tour since pondering his folly in a Japanese prison. The loudest ovations on the tour greeted the many unrevised Beatles selections and a later insertion of a Lennon medley. Audiences were also treated to Fats Domino's 'Ain't That A Shame', one of the anachronisms recorded for Paul's 'Choba B CCCP', a USSR-only album of favourite non-originals.

Though he acquitted himself admirably on stage, the days of instant No. 1s have long gone. Whether the latest by Paul McCarney makes the charts now depends on its commercial suitability rather than the once irresistible appeal of his name.

Greatest Hits

Singles	Title	US	UK
1971	Uncle Albert/Admiral Halsey	1	–
1973	My Love	1	9
1974	Band On The Run	1	3
1975	Listen To What The Man Said	1	3
1976	Silly Love Songs	1	2
1977	Mull Of Kintyre	–	1
1978	With A Little Luck	1	5
1980	Coming Up (Live At Glasgow)	1	2
1982	Ebony And Ivory		
	(with Stevie Wonder)	1	1
1983	Say Say Say		
	(with Michael Jackson)	1	2
1983	Pipes Of Peace	–	1
Albums			
1970	McCartney	1	2
1971	Ram	2	1
1973	Red Rose Speedway	1	5
1973	Band On The Run	1	1
1975	Venus And Mars	1	1
1976	Wings At The Speed Of Sound	1	2
1976	Wings Over America	1	8
1980	McCartney II	1	1
1982	Tug Of War	1	1
1984	Give My Regards To		
	Broad Street	21	1
1989	Flowers In The Dirt	21	1

Michael McDONALD

Keyboardist/vocalist McDonald (born 1952) cut unreleased solo albums as a young hopeful in the early 1970s before joining The Doobie Brothers in 1976. He had previously sung with Steely Dan in the studio (his high, keening harmonies were – and still are – much sought-after as a backing vocalist), and played keyboards with them on the road.

Finding the spotlight at last as lead vocalist with The Doobies, he pointed them in a 'white soul' direction of which their old-time fans (and several band members) clearly

Big Mac shakes chart after Doobie departure

disapproved. Thousands didn't, however, and massive US hits ensued, notably the 1979 US No. 1, 'What A Fool Believes' co-written with Kenny Loggins. By the time The Doobies reformed in 1988, his solo career was going too well for him to contemplate rejoining them.

His first post-Doobie success came as one half of a duo, with Nicolette Larson on the 1980 US Top 40 hit, 'Let Me Go Love'. His first solo album 'If That's What It Takes', released in 1982, contained the single 'I Keep Forgettin' (Every Time You're Near)', a US Top 5 hit.

Seemingly missing a band atmosphere, he collaborated with other artists, from Elton John to James Ingram. His single with the latter, 'Ya Mo Be There' was a US Top 20 hit in 1984 while another collaboration, with Patti Labelle, produced the 1986 US charttopper (and UK Top 3 hit), 'On My Own'. He released a second solo LP, 'No Lookin' Back', in 1985, and the following year, the UK-only compilation 'Sweet Freedom' was released, titled after the film theme from *Runnin' Scared* (a US Top 10 hit) which also gave him his first UK Top 40 single hit in his own right. 1990 saw the release of his long-awaited third solo album proper, 'Take It To Heart'.

McDonald has co-written songs with Carly Simon, among others, as well as maintaining a career as a session singer. He is married to singer Amy Holland.

Greatest Hits

Singles	Title	US	UK
(solo releases only)			
1982	I Keep Forgettin' (Every Time		
	You're Near)	4	43
1986	Sweet Freedom	–	12
Albums			
1982	If That's What It Takes	6	–
1986	Sweet Freedom:		
	Best Of Michael McDonald	–	6

Barry McGUIRE

Barry McGuire (born 1937) was a solo folkie on the West Coast circa 1960 and briefly formed Barry & Barry, a duo with Barry Kane, before becoming a foundermember/lead singer of Randy Sparks's New Christy Minstrels in 1962. The group scored several US hits, notably 'Green Green' (US Top 20, a gold record co-written by McGuire and Sparks), 'Saturday Night' (US Top 30), children's favourite 'Three Wheels On My Wagon' and the 'Ramblin'' album (US Top 20), another gold record, all in 1963. He also wrote 'Greenback Dollar', a US Top 30 hit for The Kingston Trio, in the same year.

He quit in 1964 for a solo career, basing himself in LA, and was the first act signed to Lou Adler's Dunhill label. McGuire's years on the folk circuit (he was proficient on guitar, banjo and harmonica) and his gravelly vocals made him a natural for the burgeoning folk/rock scene: protest songs were fashionable at the time and Adler knew an opportunity when he saw one. P.F. Sloan & Steve Barri (a pair of young songwriters who had written surf hits) were commissioned to write suitable material. 'Eve Of Destruction' was initially a B-side, but when a radio station got behind an unmixed rough cut, it was rush-released, its powerful anti-war sentiments attracting immediate controversy. Despite being banned by many US radio stations, it topped the US chart in 1965, went gold, and generated an answer-disc, 'Dawn Of Correction', by The Spokesmen. In the UK, McGuire's single achieved limited radio play, but still made the Top 3.

Such an auspicious debut proved hard to follow, although McGuire did manage two more minor US hits, and his 'Eve Of Destruction' album made the US Top 40, while two others were critically well-received: 1966's 'This Precious Time', on which he was backed by The Mamas & The Papas and Barry McGuire & The Doctor; but neither charted. Ironically, The Mamas & The Papas made a far greater impact, name-checking McGuire in their autobiographical 1967 hit, 'Creeque Alley'. By the early 1970s, he had become a born-again Christian, cutting several albums of religious material for specialist labels.

Greatest Hits

Singles	Title	US	UK
1965	Eve Of Destruction	3	1
Albums			
1965	Eve Of Destruction	37	–

Maria **McKEE/LONE JUSTICE**

Maria McKee (vocals, guitar)
Ryan Hedgecock (guitar)
Marvin Etzioni (bass)
Don Heffington (drums)

McKee (born 1964) began her musical career at the age of 16, performing in her native Los Angeles with a band fronted by her half-brother, Bryan Maclean (ex-Love). She formed an acoustic duo with Hedgecock in 1982, which developed into the first Lone Justice line-up, and the band signed a major label deal in 1983. Their critically acclaimed eponymous debut album appeared in 1985, with songs by Tom Petty (whose keyboard player, Benmont Tench, was heavily involved with the album) and Maclean bolstering the band's originals. Two singles, 'Ways To Be Wicked' and 'Sweet Sweet Baby (I'm Falling)', both reached the US Top 75, and the album entered the UK Top 50. McKee wrote Feargal Sharkey's UK No. 1 single 'A Good Heart' (1985), and Lone Justice toured both the US (as support to U2 and The Alarm) and Europe, but a major line-up change had taken place by the time their second album, 'Shelter', was released in 1986, only Hedgecock being retained for

what was in effect a solo McKee project. 'I Found Love' was a UK Top 50 single that year, but failed to make the US Top 40.

McKee's official, eponymous, solo debut album appeared in 1989 and was well received, displaying more of a soulful side to McKee's character than the country-tinged Lone Justice output had suggested, but sales were not encouraging. A move to Dublin in 1989 preceded a number of low-key gigs in Ireland, and in 1990, McKee re-emerged with the UK chart-topping single 'Show Me Heaven', from the *Days Of Thunder* film soundtrack. A 1991 album was eagerly awaited from this highly talented songwriter, who, entering the third phase of her career, was still only 26.

Greatest Hits

Singles	Title	US	UK
LONE JUSTICE			
1986	I Found Love	–	45
MARIA MCKEE			
1990	Show Me Heaven	–	1
Albums			
LONE JUSTICE			
1985	Lone Justice	56	49
MARIA MCKEE			
1989	Maria McKee	123	49

Maria and Justice – 'Sweet Baby' and Sharkey single springboards for solo success

Malcolm **McLAREN**

There remains bitter division about McLaren (born 1946). Was he a cynical, manipulative opportunist or merely a bourgeois shopkeeper sucked into a vortex of circumstances he was unable to resist? His management of The Sex Pistols certainly marked the apogee of punk, and facilitated his own emergence as a recording artist.

During a lengthy sojourn as a London art student, the most profound effects on McLaren's future resulted from an amour with clothes designer Vivienne Westwood and his observations of the chaos that accompanied the anti-establishment demonstrations prevalent in post-flower-power Europe. By 1971 he was proprietor of Let It Rock, a Chelsea boutique which specialized in Teddy Boy garments – tailored by Westwood – and vintage records. Atypical of the shop's clientele in 1973 were The New York Dolls (see separate entry), impressive in their seedy-flash flair, who led McLaren to become their manager, although when he arrived in New York, his new charges were on their last legs as a group.

Nevertheless, the publicity generated by projecting them as communist sympathizers and similar outrageous pranks was a valuable lesson, as was fraternizing with other New York musicians, whose sartorial style underlined McLaren and Westwood's wisdom in re-naming Let It Rock as Sex (later Seditionaries) – with bondage gear, strategically-ripped garb and Westwood's avant-garde creations replacing the drapes and bootlace ties.

Back in London, McLaren noticed that a combo including Sex shop assistant Glen Matlock had improved during his absence. Perceiving potential in them, he suggested they replace members with the wrong 'attitude', move vocalist Steve Jones to guitar, and find a charismatic front man. Many auditions later, McLaren and the group, The Sex Pistols, discovered an ideal chief show-off in John Lydon (aka Johnny Rotten). With a wardrobe from Sex, and under the aegis of McLaren's newly formed Glitterbest management company, the group became notorious as a live act and attracted record company interest.

McLaren's grooming process had not tempered the group's boorish behaviour, which made both EMI and A&M drop the group soon after signing them, while allowing Glitterbest to keep the considerable advances, before The Pistols came to rest on Richard Branson's Virgin label. Sarcastically, one financial journal cited the group as 'Young Businessmen of the Year', though the accolade really belonged to their manager.

At McLaren's insistence, Matlock was replaced by Sid Vicious, a novice as a musician, but whose unstable menace was more compatible with the band's anti-everything stance. Soon afterwards, they peaked commercially when their second single almost topped the charts, which encouraged McLaren to follow it with a feature film. During negotiations for what would become *The Great Rock'n'Roll Swindle* movie – with McLaren cast, not unwillingly, in a starring (and singing) role – a US tour ended with the sacking of Rotten who, with Virgin's help, began High Court action to freeze Glitterbest's finances, but not before McLaren had paid escaped Great Train Robber Ronald Biggs to sing on a new Pistols single.

This desperate strategy, coupled with the 1979 death of Vicious and the Rotten litigation, signalled McLaren's self-imposed exile in Paris where he compiled blue movie soundtracks from public domain archives in which he stumbled upon a spell-binding abundance of Third World music. Returning to London, McLaren played a new client, Adam Ant, tapes of African drumming and suggested a beneficial new look, but Ant was understandably miffed when McLaren persuaded Ant's backing trio to leave him and join forces with Annabella Lwin, a teenager whom McLaren had met in a shop. As Bow-Wow-Wow, the new group made the UK Top 40 with 'C30-C60-C90-Go', a paean to home taping, before fizzling out amid a shower of McLaren's doubtful publicity stunts.

Washing his hands of pop management, McLaren moved to Hollywood where his promotion of himself as an artist produced a

body of work that was more fascinating in its fusions of often jarring ideas than anything by his former signings, although co-producer Trevor Horn was responsible for most of the technological donkey work. Incorporating Zulu rhythms and an attendant hit single in a scratch/hip-hop desecretion of the traditional 'Buffalo Gals' hoe-down, McLaren's 1983 debut album, 'Duck Rock', was mild compared to 'Fans', which took 'Un Bel Di Vedremo' from Puccini's *Madame Butterfly* into the chart – albeit suspended over a disco rhythm and interrupted by a modern interpretation that included McLaren's callous monologue.

In 1989 the disparate sounds – and time signatures – of the likes of Jeff Beck (see separate entry), Bootsy Collins and a 60-piece orchestra effected a marriage of the salient points of Viennese waltzes and James Brown (see separate entry) on 'Waltz Darling', the latest intriguing instance of McLaren's flagrant contempt for musical and historical context.

Greatest Hits

Singles	Title	US	UK
1982	Buffalo Gals	–	9
1983	Double Dutch	–	3
Albums			
1983	Duck Rock	–	18
1989	Waltz Darling	–	30

McLean – American Pieman hots up chart with eight-minute epic

Don McLEAN

Always enigmatic, McLean (born 1945) started singing and playing guitar at 15 in his native New York, and by the time he was at Villanova University in 1964, he was performing professionally in US clubs. Deeply committed to folk and blues, by the late 1960s he was appearing with many of his idols, including Josh White – he wrote the sleeve note on a White album – Brownie McGhee, ex-Weaver Lee Hays, and eventually Pete Seeger, with whom in 1968 he undertook an expedition on the Hudson River abroad the sloop *Clearwater*, alerting river people of the dangers of pollution.

His debut album, 1970's folky 'Tapestry', was almost unanimously rejected before being released by a small label. Despite disappointing sales, it attracted excellent reviews, which led to McLean signing with a major, for which he cut 1971's 'American Pie' album. The eight minute plus title track was edited into two halves and released as a single: nostalgic, haunting, and almost impossibly commercial, this allegorical history of rock'n'roll made a huge impact on the imagination of the US public and, defying all conventional wisdom, picked up massive airplay to become a runaway hit, topping the US chart for seven weeks and making the UK Top 3 – each sold well over a million units in less than three months.

Media attention suddenly focused on McLean. Everyone wanted 'American Pie' explained to them, and even 'Tapestry' crept into the US charts and reached the UK Top 20. The fragile, gentle 'Vincent' (about the painter Van Gogh) was released as the follow-up, but although it topped the UK chart it stalled outside the US Top 10, and the next single, 'Dreidel', just missed the US Top 20 in 1973. However, appalled by the intrusions which his newfound celebrity status was wreaking on his life, McLean eschewed fame and turned out a less commercial eponymous third album, which nevertheless reached the US Top 30; but its follow-up, 'Playin' Favourites', a collection of non-originals, failed to chart. He spent the remainder of the 1970s undertaking fairly low-key tours (regulary visiting the UK, where he remains a great favourite) and recording excellent albums which made few concessions to contemporary commercial tastes.

In 1980 he scored a comeback hit with an update of Roy Orbison's 'Crying', a UK chart-topper, which also restored him to the US Top 5 early in 1981. Its parent album, 'Chain Lightning' made the UK Top 20/US Top 30 and was his biggest seller for many years, while a 1980 compilation album, 'The Very Best Of Don McLean', made the UK Top 5. A revival of the 1950s hit by The Skyliners, 'Since I Don't Have You', was a US Top 30 single in 1981, and in the late 1980s he crossed over to the US country chart with two minor hits. His songwriting talent could enable him to make further mainstream comebacks – if he wants them.

Greatest Hits

Singles	Title	US	UK
1972	*American Pie*	1	2
1972	*Vincent*	12	1
1980	*Crying*	5	1
Albums			
1971	*American Pie*	1	3
1973	*Don McLean*	23	–
1980	*The Very Best Of Don McLean*	–	4

MEAT LOAF / Jim STEINMAN

Meat Loaf (born Marvin Lee Aday, 1947) acquired his nickname at high school, before leaving his hometown of Dallas, Texas, for Los Angeles in 1967 where he formed Popcorn Blizzard, who opened for the likes of The Who, Iggy Pop and Ted Nugent. In 1969 he landed a role in *Hair!*, and it was here that he met Stoney, with whom he made one album, 'Stoney And Meat Loaf', from which a single, 'What You See Is What You Get' made the US Top 100.

Hair! closed in New York, where in 1974, Meat first teamed up with local singer/pianist Jim Steinman (born 1943), who had written the musical *More Than You Deserve*, in which Meat played two roles. The following year, Meat starred as Eddy in the Broadway production of *The Rocky Horror Show* (a role he would recreate for the film version), and both he and Steinman toured with the National Lampoon Road Show.

1977 saw the duo doing the rounds of record companies with the demos they'd been refining for some years of Meat Loaf performing Steinman's material, and after some convoluted dealings involving several labels, an independent company signed the duo, licensing their 'Bat Out Of Hell' album (produced by Todd Rundgren) to a major label. During a US chart residency of 88 weeks, it peaked in the US Top 20, as did an excerpted single 'Two Out Of Three Ain't Bad'. The album was released in the UK in 1978 and, although never reaching the Top 5, eventually sold over two million units and established a chart-longevity record of 395 weeks and was similarly successful in other world markets.

The wait for a follow-up dragged on and on amid spiralling rumours of artistic and personal differences, not to mention Meat's vocal problems. Eventually, in 1981, 'Bad For Good' was released, but as a Jim Steinman solo LP. In the UK, it reached the Top 10, but peaked much lower in the US. Meat Loaf's 'Dead Ringer', released later in the same year, topped the UK charts, and made the US Top 50, but marked the end of the Steinman/Loaf partnership.

Meat decided to concentrate his efforts on the UK and Europe and during the early 1980s continued to have chart successes with 'Midnight At The Lost And Found' (Top 10 in 1983, 'Bad Attitude' (Top 10 in 1984), 'Hits Out Of Hell' (mostly Steinman tracks, Top 3 in 1985) and 'Blind Before I Stop' (Top 30 in 1986). However 1987's 'Live At Wembley' stalled outside the Top 50, marking the end of Meat's chart career to date.

Following the split, Steinman elected to initially work on one-off single productions of his own compositions, giving Air Supply a

Top 3 US hit with 'Making Love Out Of Nothing At All', although his soundtrack offering 'Tonight Is What It Means To Be Young' (from the *Street Of Fire* movie) was a chart miss. However, his collaboration with Bonnie Tyler on her 'Faster Than The Speed Of Night' album was a UK chart-topper and made the US Top 5, while 'Total Eclipse Of The Heart' hit No. 1 in both countries.

1984 was probably more notable for his aborted sessions for a Def Leppard album than his singles productions for Barry Manilow ('Read 'Em And Weep', UK/US Top 20) and Barbra Streisand ('Left In The Dark Again', US Top 50). 1985 saw sessions for a second Bonnie Tyler LP, a track from which – 'Holding Out For A Hero' – hit the UK Top 3, doubtless helped by being featured in the movie *Footloose*. However, the album, 'Secret Dreams And Forbidden Fire', though making the UK Top 30, was not a major seller, nor did it generate a hit single, and there was silence from the Steinman camp until the end of 1989, when his new project, Pandora's Box, released 'Original Sin', a critically acclaimed but slow selling double album.

Ironically, a few months earlier a compilation album, 'Bonnie And Meat', containing mostly Steinman compositions was a considerable chart success.

Greatest Hits

Singles	Title	US	UK
1978	*Two Out Of Three Ain't Bad* (Meat Loaf)	32	11
1981	*Dead Ringer For Love*	–	5
Albums			
1981	*Dead Ringer* (Meat Loaf)	45	1
1981	*Bad For Good* (Jim Steinman)	63	7

Meat Loaf man in MOR sessions shock as Steinman backs Barry, Barbra and Bonnie

Melanie – folky flowerchild who defied the elements at Woodstock

MELANIE

A naïve but sincere child of the Woodstock generation, Melanie Safka (born 1947) started as a folk club singer in her native New York. Her brash vocal style was influenced by jazz as well as folk (her mother had been a jazz singer), but her debut single, 'Beautiful People', created little interest. After meeting producer Peter Schekeryk (who later became her manager and husband), she released two albums in 1969, 'Born To Be' and 'Affectionately Melanie', but her breakthrough came at that year's Woodstock Festival, when she performed during the 'legendary' rainstorm and became a touchstone for searchers for simple spiritual enlightenment.

Her single, 'Lay Down (Candles In The Rain)', featuring the Edwin Hawkins Singers and dedicated to the drenched Woodstock hordes, was a US Top 10 hit in 1970, and the album entitled after it made the US Top 20, but in the UK, her version of The Rolling Stones song, 'Ruby Tuesday', provided her first Top 10 hit and propelled the 'Candles In The Rain' album into the Top 5. Her live album, 'Leftover Wine', made the US Top 40 and UK Top 30, and after a minor UK hit single, 'What Have They Done To My Song, Ma', her 1971 'Good Book' album, with its interpretations of children's poems such as 'Christopher Robin' and 'Alexander Beetle', made the UK Top 30. In late 1971 she topped the US singles chart and made the UK Top 5 with 'Brand New Key' (the lyrics of which were so naïve they got her into trouble with US radio) from the 'Gather Me' album which went Top 20 on both sides of the Atlantic.

That was the peak of her success, although she scored minor US hits with 'The Nickel Song', 'Ring The Living Bell' and 'Bitter Bad' and UK hits with the single, 'Will You Still Love Me Tomorrow', and the albums, 'Four Sides Of Melanie' and 'Garden In The City'. In 1973 she eased up to start a family, and has subsequently released albums intermittently and played only occasional gigs.

Greatest Hits

Singles	Title	US	UK
1970	Lay Down (Candles In The Rain)	6	–
1970	Ruby Tuesday	52	9
1971	Brand New Key	1	4
Albums			
1970	Candles In The Rain	17	5
1971	Gather Me	15	18

John Cougar **MELLENCAMP**

A fter achieving limited success as a glam-rocker in the 1970s, Mellencamp later wrote and sang grittily realistic songs in a similar manner to Bruce Springsteen.

Born in Indiana (1951), he began playing and singing with high-school bands Crepe Soul and Snakepit Banana Barn before forming glitter-rock group Trash with guitarist Larry Crane in 1971. After playing the bar band circuit, Mellencamp recorded a demo disc of the old Paul Revere And The Raiders song 'Kicks'.

As a result, he was signed by David Bowie's manager Tony De Fries, who negotiated a record deal and put him in the studio with ex-Bowie guitarist Mick Ronson. With the release of 'Chestnut Street Incident' (1976) he was renamed Johnny Cougar, and De Fries organised a 'Johnny Cougar Day' in his home town. The album flopped, as did the follow-up, 'The Kid Inside' (1977), and Mellencamp left De Fries to sign with a new label.

Still known as Cougar, he wrote most of the material for 'A Biography' (1978), a minor hit in the US where it was issued as 'John Cougar', and contained his first US Top 30 single, 'I Need A Lover'. With ex-Booker T & The MGs guitarist Steve Cropper producing, 'Nothin' Matters And What If It Did' brought Cougar a US Top 20 hit with 'Ain't Even Done With The Night'. Through frequent touring, his popularity had steadily increased and the breakthrough came with 'American Fool' (1982), which sold over three million copies in the US alone and included four US Top 10 hits.

With his glam-rock period firmly behind him, Mellencamp reverted to his original name for 'Uh-Huh' (1983). The album included 'Pink Houses', one of his first songs of social protest. In 1985 he turned down a chance to play at Live Aid but instead joined Willie Nelson in organizing the Farm Aid concert, aimed at raising money for destitute US farming families. He later performed at further Farm Aid events.

1986 brought hit singles from the 'Scarecrow' album, another 3-million-seller. The following year he changed labels, releasing 'The Lonesome Jubilee'. With accordion and fiddle emphasising his Middle West roots, the record included three more US Top 20 hits. In 1988 Mellencamp paid his dues to Woody Guthrie by singing his 'Do Re Mi' on the tribute album 'A Vision Shared'.

Growing disillusionment with the music business fuelled the 1989 album 'Big Daddy', which featured the Guthrie-style portrait of a down-and-out working man 'Jackie Brown'. By now, however, Mellencamp seemed more involved with his new pastime of painting than with songwriting.

Greatest Hits

Singles	Title	US	UK
1982	Hurts So Good	2	–
1982	Jack And Diane	1	25
1986	R.O.C.K. In The USA	2	67
Albums			
1982	American Fool	1	37
1985	Scarecrow	2	–
1987	The Lonesome Jubilee	6	31
1989	Big Daddy	7	25

Harold **MELVIN** and the **BLUENOTES** / Teddy **PENDERGRASS**

Harold Melvin
Bernard Williams
Jesse Gillis Jr.
Franklin Peaker
Roosevelt Brodie

T his Philadelphia-based vocal group was formed and managed by Melvin (born 1934). Although their first recording, 'If You

Love Me', was released in 1956, their chart debut only came with 'My Hero' in 1966. Their ever-changing line-up included Billy Paul ('Me And Mrs Jones') in 1961, but Melvin got lead billing in 1965 when they charted with 'Get Out' featuring their new lead singer John Atkins.

After years of playing supper clubs and unsuccessful recordings, they joined top producer/writers Kenny Gamble and Leon Huff's Philadelphia International label in 1971 with a line-up of Melvin, Lawrence Brown, ex-Epsilon Lloyd Parkes, singer/choreographer Bernard Wilson and new lead singer Teddy Pendergrass (born 1950), who had played drums in their backing band The Cadillacs. Their first single for the label 'I Miss You' hit the soul Top 10, and the next single from their eponymous album, 'If You Don't Know Me By Now', gave the distinctive group a transatlantic Top 10 hit and a gold record.

They helped to make the 'Philly Sound' a major force in the 1970s with Top 20 hits like 1975's million selling 'The Love I Lost', and 'Bad Luck' and their single and album, 'Wake Up Everybody', in 1975. Their biggest UK hit came in 1977 with an album track, 'Don't Leave Me This Way', which outsold the US hit version by Thelma Houston. Pendergrass left in 1976 and was replaced by David Ebo but the group never regained the same heights.

Pendergrass, with his unmistakable rich soulful voice had become a sex symbol to his many fans, who simply knew him as 'Teddy Bear' and flocked to his many 'women only' shows. His eponymous debut LP released in 1977 sold a million, as did 1978's 'Life Is A Song Worth Singing' album, which included his biggest single, the million-selling No. 1 soul hit, 'Close The Door'. His 1979 LP 'Teddy' and 1980's 'TP' album also went platinum and he picked up gold LPs for 'Teddy Live! Coast To Coast' in 1979 and 'It's Time For Love' in 1981. Although he never scored a US Top 20 pop chart hit, he had big soul hits with 'Turn Off The Lights' in 1979, 'Can't We Try' and 'Love T.K.O.' in 1980 and 'You're My Latest, My Greatest Inspiration' and a duet with Stephanie Mills, 'Two Hearts' in 1981.

In 1982 a disastrous car accident left Pendergrass badly paralysed and halted his recording career for over two years. While he was out of action Philly International released two albums of old recordings 'This One's For You' in 1982 and 'Heaven Only Knows' in 1984.

Pendergrass joined Asylum records in 1984 and his 'Love Language' LP, which he recorded in a wheelchair, hit the US Top 40 and went gold. A duet from the album, 'Hold Me', took him back to the black music Top 10 and introduced the world to his singing partner Whitney Houston. In 1988 he released another US gold album, 'Joy', which also gave him his only UK solo chart album, while the

title track was another No. 1 soul hit. In late 1990 his 'Truly Blessed' LP and a duet with Lisa Fisher 'Glad To Be Alive' kept his name on the US charts.

Greatest Hits

Singles	Title	US	UK
1972	If You Don't Know Me By Now	3	9
1973	The Love I Lost	7	21
Albums			
1975	Wake Up Everybody		
	(Blue Notes)	9	–
1979	Teddy (Pendergrass)	5	–

George **MICHAEL** / **WHAM!**

Londoners George Michael (born Georgios Panayiotou, 1963) and schoolfriend Andrew Ridgeley (born 1963) were in ska group The Executive in 1979 before forming the ultra-successful pop duo, Wham!, in 1981.

They first charted with their second single 'Young Guns (Go For It)' in 1982, which they followed with a re-release of their first single, 'Wham Rap', which along with 'Bad Boys' and 'Club Tropicana' gave them three UK Top 10 hits in 1983, the year their LP, 'Fantastic', topped the UK chart. After contractual problems they changed record labels in 1984, making their US Top 40 debut with 'Wake Me Up Before You Go-Go'. The follow-up, 'Careless Whisper' (credited in the UK only to George Michael) became the Top US single of 1985 and their second successive US and UK No. 1, selling over a million on both sides of the Atlantic. 'Make It Big', their second album, also topped both charts and sold over five million copies in the US. At Christmas 1984 Michael was featured on the Band Aid charity single and the duo had their second UK million-seller with 'Last Christmas/Everything She Wants', the latter song later going to the top in the US.

In 1985 they won a BRITS award as Top Group, Michael was the youngest winner of the Ivor Novello songwriters award and the

Wham! Make It Big, Michael moves to A Different Corner

duo became the first Western pop act to perform in China. They also appeared at Live Aid, had a successful US stadium tour and rounded off the year with another UK No. 1, 'I'm Your Man'. In 1986, after five years together and 38 million sales, the duo announced they were splitting. During that year Michael's solo single, 'A Different Corner', hit the top, their double A-sided single, 'The Edge Of Heaven'/'Where Did Your Heart Go', became their fourth UK chart-topper and 72,000 screaming fans packed Wembley Stadium to say goodbye to them.

Michael's first release after Wham!'s demise, a duet with Aretha Franklin, was a transatlantic No. 1 and later in 1987 he also had Top 3 hits with the controversial 'I Want Your Sex' and 'Faith', the Top US single of 1988. Michael not only wrote and produced his solo album, 'Faith', but also arranged it and played most of the instruments. It went on to sell over 14 million copies world-wide, and became the most successful album ever by a solo British artist in the US, topping the charts for 12 weeks and selling over seven million copies there (including one million CDs). In 1988, he was the top act in the US, scored another three No. 1 singles from the album and had a very successful world tour. Surprisingly both 'Faith' and the single, 'One More Try', also topped the US black music charts and won him awards in that field.

In 1989 Michael received the coveted Silver Clef award for Outstanding Achievements in British Music and his album, 'Listen Without Prejudice Vol 1', took him back near the top of the world's charts as did the first single from it, 'Praying For Time'.

Greatest Hits

Singles	Title	US	UK
Wham!			
1984	Wake Me Up Before You Go-Go	1	1
1984	Freedom	3	1
1985	Everything She Wants	1	2
1985	I'm Your Man	3	1
1986	The Edge Of Heaven/Where Did Your Heart Go	10	1
George Michael			
1984	Careless Whisper	1	1
1986	A Different Corner	7	1
1987	I Knew You Were Waiting (For Me) (with Aretha Franklin)	1	1
1987	Faith	1	2
1988	Father Figure	1	11
1988	One More Try	1	8
1988	Monkey	1	13
1990	Praying For Time	1	6
Albums			
Wham!			
1983	Fantastic	83	1
1984	Make It Big	1	1
George Michael			
1987	Faith	1	1
1990	Listen Without Prejudice Vol. I	2	1

Bette MIDLER

Midler (born 1945) graduated from the chorus to a lead role during a three-year run of the Broadway smash *Fiddler on the Roof*, before leaving the show in 1969 when she launched herself onto New York's 'alternative' club circuit. A celebrated period at the Continental Baths where, accompanied by pianist Barry Manilow, she developed an act combining outrageous humour and musical pastiche, led to TV and stage work, followed by a debut album in 1973, 'The Divine Miss M'. Co-produced and arranged by Manilow, the LP made the US Top 10, went gold and earned her a Grammy Award as Best New Artist of the Year. It also included two US Top 20 singles, revivals of 'Do You Wanna Dance' and the Andrews Sisters oldie, 'Boogie Woogie Bugle Boy'. A second eponymous album also went Top 10 in the US.

Having created a bump-and-grind image as a latter-day burlesque singer, collaborations with Bob Dylan on her 'Songs For The New Depression' album (1976) and Tom Waits (on 1977's 'Foreign Affairs') confirmed Midler as an original talent. Her live act moved increasingly over the top, encapsu-lated in the 1980 movie *Divine Madness*, a live concert film, the soundtrack album of which made the US Top 40. In 1979 she moved into films proper, with the lead part in *The Rose*, as a rags-to-riches rock singer based loosely on Janis Joplin; her performance earned her an Oscar nomination, the soundtrack album went platinum and the title song was a US Top 3 single.

Entries into the lower reaches of the album and singles charts marked a mid-1980s move to films as her main activity, with a series of acclaimed roles, including 1986's *Down and Out in Beverly Hills* and *Ruthless People* and the well-received *Beaches* (1989), the soundtrack album of which went Top 3 in the US and provided her with her first US No. 1 single, 'The Wind Beneath My Wings'.

Greatest Hits

Singles	Title	US	UK
1980	The Rose	3	–
1989	The Wind Beneath My Wings	1	5
Albums			
1973	The Divine Miss M.	9	–
1973	Bette Midler	6	–
1989	Beaches	2	21

Bette Midler – bump and grind from the Bath House to Beverly Hills

Steve Miller – jazz experiments followed by jeans-ad Joker revival

Steve **MILLER**

Now in his fourth decade of chart conten-tion, Texan singer/guitarist Steve Miller (born 1943) has seen and done most things during a career in which he has experienced both troughs and triumphs.

Born into the family of a doctor who was also a jazz fan, Miller was taught his first guitar chords by Les Paul's wife, Mary Ford, a family friend. He formed his first R&B/rock'n'roll band, The Marksmen Combo, in the mid-1950s, with Boz Scaggs (born 1944). Miller and Scaggs attended the same university in Wisconsin, where they formed The Ardells, another member of which was Ben Sidran (keyboards). That band ended when Miller moved to a Danish university in the mid-1960s. On his return, he settled in Chicago, where he was part of the local blues/R&B scene along with latterday stars like

Paul Butterfield, Mike Bloomfield and keyboard player Barry Goldberg, with whom he worked in The Goldberg/Miller Blues Band (known as The World War Three Blues Band prior to Goldberg joining). Although they cut a few singles, this band made little national impact, and in 1966 Miller decided to move to San Francisco, where the psychedelic era was about to start. After forming The Steve Miller Band with Tim Davis (drums) and singer/guitarist James 'Curley' Cooke, both of whom he knew from Wisconsin, and Lonnie Turner, a Bay Area bass player, Miller's first significant album project came in 1966, when the band backed Chuck Berry on 'Live At The Fillmore Auditorium', a somewhat average album in comparison with Miller's later work. The band was also featured, along with Quicksilver Messenger Service and Mother Earth, on the soundtrack to a hippie movie titled *Revolu-*

tion, before Miller's group became the last major band of the early wave of Bay Area acts to acquire a major label deal, in 1967.

Before they recorded 'Children Of The Future', which was released in 1968, the group had expanded with the addition of Jim Peterman (bass), while Cooke had left and been replaced by ex-Ardell, Boz Scaggs, (vocals, guitar). This line-up cut that debut album, which was produced by Glyn Johns in London, and while it was well-regarded at the time, it has not stood the test of time as well as the second album, 'Sailor', again produced by Johns, which was also released in 1968. Its pioneering use of sound effects made this a critical hit which also reached the US Top 30, after which Peterman and Scaggs left, the latter for an eventually successful solo career. 1969's 'Brave New World' album, which again made the US Top 30, was made by Miller, Turner and Davis, with help from another ex-Ardell, Ben Sidran, and from Paul McCartney (credited as Paul Ramon) on one track, 'My Dark Hour'. A final album pro-duced by Johns, 'Your Saving Grace', made the US Top 40 also in 1969, but for 1970's 'Number 5', Miller and Davis, the only two original band members left, recorded in Nashville with that city's hottest pickers, and the album made the US Top 30. 1971's 'Rock Love' and 1972's 'Recall The Beginning – A Journey From Eden' were much less success-ful, although both did make the US chart, while 'Anthology', as its title suggests, was a compilation which remained longer in the US chart than any of its predecessors, but just failed to make the Top 50.

By this time Miller's band had changed personnel almost totally, the group now in-cluding noted black bass player Gerald John-son. By 1973 Miller had been working flat out since 1968, and despite having three substan-tial hit albums under his belt, had failed to get a major hit single, although 'Living In The USA' (from 'Sailor') and 'Going To The Country' (from 'Number 5') had both briefly made the US chart. In 1973 Miller cut his biggest ever hit, 'The Joker', which topped the US chart in 1973 and did the same in Britain in 1990 after it had been used in a TV commercial. The album of the same name was a US Top 3 hit, but the struggle to achieve major success, and the pressures that then attended it, resulted in Miller becoming seriously ill and not releasing a new album for three years.

With Gary Mallaber on drums and Lonnie Turner returning to bass, 'Fly Like An Eagle' (1976) became Miller's first platinum album, reaching the Us Top 3 and becoming his first UK hit of any sort. The album also spawned several hit singles: 'Take The Money And Run', which made the US Top 20, 'Rock'n' Me', a US chart-topper and Miller's first UK hit single, and the title track of the album, a US Top 3 single. Much of 1977's 'Book Of Dreams' album was recorded during the sessions which produced 'Fly Like An Eagle' and the new album was similarly successful, also going platinum in reaching the US Top 3 and including three US hit singles, the biggest of which, 'Jet Airliner', made the US Top 10. 1978's 'Greatest Hits 1974–78' was a predictable platinum US Top 20 album, after which Miller proceeded to take another three-year sabbatical.

He returned in 1981 with another new band, comprising Johnson, Mallaber and keyboard player Byron Allred, but the 'Circle Of Love' album failed to make the US Top 20, despite two medium-sized hit singles. One reason for this comparative failure was the inclusion of 'Macho City', a track lasting nearly 20 minutes, which took up one complete side of the album. Undaunted, Miller expanded the band to include two more guitarists, John Massaro and Kenny Lee Lewis, and blasted back into the US Top 3 and debuted in the UK album chart Top 10 with 'Abracadabra', the title track of which topped the US singles chart and made the UK Top 3. Completing this cycle of Miller's career were 'Steve Miller Band Live!', which didn't make gold status, although it was impressive and featured the 'Abracadabra' line-up augmented by harmonica virtuoso Norton Buffalo (for whom Miller served as executive producer on two albums released in 1977/8), and 1984's 'Italian X-Rays', his least successful original album in 12 years, for which the line-up was Miller, Lewis, Allred and Mallaber.

This band was still together for 1986's under-appreciated 'Living In The 20th Century' album, but for 1988's 'Born 2B Blue', Miller worked with The Ben Sidran Trio (completed by bassman Billy Peterson and drummer Gordy Knudtson) plus jazz stars like Milt Jackson of the Modern Jazz Quartet. This was an unexpected change of musical direction which seemed to alienate many of Miller's established fans, and ultimately resulted in his leaving the label with whom he had remained in the US for over 20 years, and signing with another major in the wake of his unexpected UK No. 1 with the 17-year-old reissue, 'The Joker'.

It remains to be seen whether Miller can resurrect his career for a third time as he nears the age of 50, but many would relish his return.

Greatest Hits

Singles	Title	US	UK
1973	The Joker	1	–
1976	Rock'n'Me	1	11
1976	Fly Like An Eagle	2	–
1977	Jet Airliner	8	–
1982	Abracadabra	1	2
1990	The Joker	–	1
Albums			
1973	The Joker	2	–
1976	Fly Like An Eagle	3	11
1977	Book Of Dreams	2	12
1982	Abracadabra	3	10

MILLI VANILLI

The most successful new duo of 1989 were masterminded by German producer/writer Frank Farian, who had been the man behind the multi-million-selling Boney M in the 1970s. On their records, the vocals were by German-based singers Brad Howell and Johnny Davis plus American-born rapper Charles Shaw. However, photogenic Rob Pilatus (born 1965) from Germany and Fabrice Morvan (born 1963) from Guadeloupe fronted the group. Pilatus had recorded with the group Dupont on MCA before joining Morvan, who like himself was the son of an American serviceman. They sang together in the 1987 Eurovision Song Contest.

The pop/soul act first charted in the UK in 1988 with their version of the song by US group Numarx, 'Girl You Know It's True'. In 1989 it climbed to the US Top 3 where their UK album, 'All Or Nothing', was re-titled 'Girl You Know It's True' and climbed to the No. 1 position. To cash in on their US success, the album was repackaged for the UK with a free re-mix album '2 x 2' and made the Top 10.

1989 saw the act secure three US No. 1 singles – 'Baby Don't Forget My Number', 'Girl I'm Gonna Miss You' and 'Blame It On The Rain' and saw their debut album, which contained four gold singles, soar over the six million sales mark in the US alone. Until then, no other group had ever had three No. 1 singles from their debut album. In mid 1990 'The Re-Mix Album', mainly re-mixes of tracks from their first album, went gold and made the US Top 40.

When Pilatus and Morvan insisted on singing on future recordings Farian decided he would rather scrap the act. His announcement in late 1990 that the duo did not sing on their records created a stir and they had to return awards they had won including the Grammy for Best New Act of 1989.

Greatest Hits

Singles	Title	US	UK
1989	Baby Don't Forget My Number	1	16
1989	Girl I'm Gonna Miss You	1	2
1989	Blame it On The Rain	1	52
Albums			
1989	Girl You Know It's True (UK title: All Or Nothing)	1	6
1990	The Remix Album	32	–

Joni MITCHELL

A pivotal figure on the US West Coast scene since the late 1960s – both musically and socially – Joni Mitchell progressed from her early folk albums to become one of rock music's most significant female singer/songwriters.

Born Roberta Joan Anderson in 1947, Canadian Joni was studying commercial art when she became interested in folk music and started playing clubs. She married folk singer Chuck Mitchell in 1965 (although the marriage didn't last long) and her reputation spread as her songs were recorded by Judy Collins ('Both Sides Now'), Tom Rush ('The Circle Game') and Fairport Convention ('Eastern Rain'). Her own career began when Elliott Roberts started managing her in 1967 and her debut album, 'Song To A Seagull', was produced by David Crosby. It made little impact but after a year touring the US, her second album, 'Clouds', released in 1969 and containing her own versions of 'Both Sides Now' and 'Chelsea Morning', reached the US Top 40.

By then she had moved to California – Crosby, Stills & Nash first got together at her house – and her 'Ladies Of The Canyon' album in 1970 was a major breakthrough, reaching the US Top 30 and UK Top 10, 'Big Yellow Taxi' was a hit single and 'Woodstock' was successfully covered by Crosby, Stills, Nash & Young and Matthews Southern Comfort, who had hits with their versions. Mitchell's 1971 album, 'Blue', was a poetic masterpiece, a suite of songs to a former lover. It featured top US session players and James Taylor and reached the UK Top 3 and US Top 20.

1972s 'For The Roses' found her stretching her song format. It reached the US Top 20 and included a US Top 30 single, 'You Turn Me On, I'm A Radio', but failed to dent the UK chart, although rock band Nazareth had a UK Top 20 hit with a version of 'This Flight Tonight'. 1974's 'Court And Spark', her first 'all-electric' album, moved towards a jazzier style with Tom Scott's LA Express as her backing band and a version of Annie Ross's 'Twisted', the first non-original song recorded by Mitchell. The album reached the US Top 3 and the UK Top 20, producing two more US hit singles with 'Help Me' and 'Free Man In Paris' and earning Mitchell and Scott a Grammy for Best Arrangement for 'Down To You'. The following year, a double album with The LA Express, 'Miles Of Aisles', again reached the US Top 3.

She switched direction again for 'The Hissing Of Summer Lawns', a rhythmic evocation of Middle American life and attitudes which reached the US Top 5 and the UK Top 20, and followed that direction still further on 'Hejira' (1976) and 'Don Juan's Reckless Daughter' (1978), which featured Wayne Shorter and Jaco Pastorius from Weather Report, Chaka Khan, Glenn Frey of The Eagles and J.D. Souther. She reached the end of that particular road with 'Mingus' (1979), a project she started with the legendary jazz bassist and completed after his death. The following year she recorded and filmed a concert at Santa Barbara with Pastorius, guitarist Pat Metheny and saxophonist Michael Brecker which was released as a

'Blue' album follows green anthem 'Yellow Taxi'

double album, 'Shadows And Light', and screened on TV.

Her achievements were recognized in 1981 by Canadian Prime Minister Pierre Trudeau, who inducted her into Canada's Juno Hall Of Fame. During the 1980s Mitchell's career proceeded in a more relaxed style after she married bassist Larry Klein. No longer at the cutting edge but never less than interesting, 'Wild Things Run Fast' (1982) featured duets with Lionel Richie and James Taylor as well as a version of the Presley classic, 'Baby I Don't Care'. 1985's 'Dog Eat Dog' had contributions from Michael McDonald, Thomas Dolby and Rod Steiger (playing an evangelist) while 1988's 'Chalk Mark In A Rainstorm' featured appearances from Peter Gabriel, Don Henley, Tom Petty, Willie Nelson and Billy Idol.

Greatest Hits

Singles	Title	US	UK
1970	Big Yellow Taxi	67	11
1974	Help Me	4	–
Albums			
1971	Blue	15	3
1974	Court And Spark	2	14
1975	Miles Of Aisles	2	34
1976	The Hissing Of Summer Lawns	4	14

204

MOBY GRAPE

Alexander 'Skip' Spence (guitar, lead vocals)
Peter Lewis (guitar, vocals)
Jerry Miller (guitar)
Bob Mosley (bass)
Don Stevenson (drums)

Although one of the more interesting and musically structured bands to emerge from the mid-1960s US West Coast, Moby

Grape were so severely over-hyped by their record label during their formative stages that they never really recovered and remain a classic example of underachievement. Formed as a quartet in San Francisco in 1966 by Lewis (born 1945, ex-Peter & The Wolves) and Mosley (born 1942, ex-Frantics), the original line-up included Joel Scott-Hill (guitar/vocals) and Kent Dunbar (drums), who soon gave way to Spence (born 1946, formerly drummer with Jefferson Airplane) and ex-Frantics Miller (born 1943) and Stevenson (born 1942). Their gigs at San Francisco's Fillmore West and Winterland venues generated a wildly enthusiastic response, their convincing synthesis of R&B, folk/rock and embryonic psychedelia establishing them as a local cult band.

They signed with a major label in 1967, having reportedly been chased by 14 different companies, and their eponymous debut album was supported by one of the more eccentric promotional campaigns of the era: a purple elephant paraded Sunset Strip in Los Angeles; helium filled balloons bearing their unmistakable logo choked San Francisco's Golden Gate Park; Hollywood journalists received bunches of grapes, delivered by horse & cart; and no less than five singles were released simultaneously, featuring 10 of the tracks from the album. The album sleeve sported a photograph in which Stevenson could clearly be seen giving 'the finger', which

'Grape vinyl hype crushed by sober press

resulted in the album being promptly recalled and the offending finger airbrushed out. The press were decidedly underwhelmed by the hype, and the album was trashed, although it was an auspicious debut, showcasing their powerful vocals and distinctive guitars and was retrospectively hailed as a classic in certain quarters. However, the group were obliged to spend the next year touring in order to repair the damage, during the course of which they managed to push the album into the US Top 30.

Their second album, 'Wow' (1968), further compromised their credibility by including a track which could be played only at 78 rpm, although it was salvaged by the inclusion of a 'bonus' live album, 'Grape Jam', on which the group were augmented by Mike Bloomfield & Al Kooper (this was effectively a precursor to the duo's later 'Super Session' albums). Although the album was somewhat inferior to its predecessor, promotional activity managed to hoist it into the US Top 20; but shortly after its release, drug problems caused Spence to quit (he re-emerged briefly with a solo album, 'Oar', in 1969, which became a collector's item). Moby Grape drifted apart for several months, eventually regrouping as a quartet to cut their third album and undertake a European tour, which veered between brilliance and absolute disaster. By the time 1969's 'Moby Grape '69' was released (largely to commercial indifference), Mosley had left

the band, further jeopardising their continuity; he was to release an eponymous solo album in 1972.

The remaining trio cut the contract-fulfilling 'Truly Fine Citizen' in Nashville, using veteran sessionman Bob Moore on bass, but by the time of its release the group had broken up, Miller and Stevenson joining Bill Champlin's Rhythm Dukes. A fake Moby Grape (the name was owned by their manager Matthew Katz) played several West Coast gigs in 1970, prompting a brief reunion in 1971, when the original quintet signed with a new label and made 1972's '20 Granite Creek' album, but split again upon its completion. During the 1970s various permutations of the group would reform, appearing as Maby Grope, Grape, or The (Original) Grape – all to great confusion: a problem further exacerbated when Katz released a compilation, 'Great Grape', in 1974. A late-1970s reunion including Spence, Lewis, Mosley and Miller cut a 1978 live album, 'Grape Live', after which Spence and Lewis left. With an ever-fluctuating personnel, Moby Grape continued into the 1980s via low-key gigs on the Californian live circuit. Their first album, despite the hype, remains one of the best 1960s albums from San Francisco.

Greatest Hits

Singles	Title	US	UK
1967	*Omaha*	88	–
Albums			
1967	*Moby Grape*	24	–
1968	*Wow*	20	–

The **MONKEES**

Mickey Dolenz (vocals, drums)
Davy Jones (vocals, percussion)
Michael Nesmith (guitar, vocals)
Peter Tork (guitar, vocals)

The mid-1960s 'British Invasion' of North America was dealt its hardest blow by a cabal of Californian businessmen who hired four amenable young men to play an Anglo-American pop group, The Monkees, in a nationwide TV sitcom with musical interludes. They also sang on records for which the services of top songwriters, session players and producers had been negotiated.

The project's blueprint was the 1964 Beatles and Herman's Hermits – Jones (born 1946) was not only the Monkee with the best teenybop appeal, he was also from Manchester, like Peter 'Herman' Noone. He and the other three had been selected after a host of individual applicants, including Stephen Stills and, allegedly, Charles Manson, had been considered. Jones had gone to the US to work in a Broadway show, while Dolenz (born 1945), Nesmith and Tork (both born 1942)

Did Monkees thumbs-down drive mass-murderer Manson nuts?

were Americans. Like Jones, Dolenz had been a child actor on television – and multi-instrumentalists Tork and guitarist Nesmith were each folk circuit veterans – Nesmith was also no slouch as a composer. Bar Tork, all The Monkees had recorded earlier flop singles as individuals, and some were later resurrected to cash in on the group's fame.

Coping admirably with simple, self-contained episodes, The Monkees were an immediate success, especially with pre-teens. Even prior to the first screened episode in 1966, their debut single, 'Last Train To Clarksville', had been a big US hit. After an international breakthrough with Neil Diamond's 'I'm A Believer', further attractive if lightweight hits kept the group in the charts beyond the final series in 1968. Their early albums endure as strong evocations of the era with their mixture of ersatz Merseybeat, crafted folk-rock, romantic ballads (emoted

by Jones) and a few Nesmith originals for good measure.

Cracks first appeared when a disgruntled Nesmith revealed to the press that the Monkees did not play on their own sessions (although they were responsible for vocal parts). Soon afterwards, 'The Witchita Train Whistle Sings', an orchestral album of his songs was recorded, and Nesmith's honesty also led to the group writing around half the tracks (including Dolenz's 'Alternate Title' single, released in the US as 'Randy Scouse Git') on the 'Headquarters' album, and 1968's 'Pisces, Aquarius, Capricorn and Jones Ltd.'. They also managed a world tour and were given a bigger (and commercially detrimental) say in their TV output, and in their feature film, *Head*, with its free association scenarios, psychedelic soundtrack and guest stars as diverse as Annette Funicello and Frank Zappa. Million-sellers were no longer automatic by then, and the four sounded tired on 'The Birds, The Bees And The Monkees' (with no Tork lead vocal) and on modest single hits like a revival of The Coasters hit, 'D.W. Washburn', which was preceded by the two-year-old 'Valleri'.

As The Monkees weren't much of a group any more, Tork left followed by Nesmith, who formed his First National Band with pedal steel star Orville 'Red' Rhodes, Texan bass player John London and session drummer John Ware. From 1970's 'Magnetic South', 'Joanne' (covered by Andy Williams) was Nesmith's highest post-Monkees chart entry but he became a respected music and video industry figure as well as a cult celebrity, particularly for mid-1970s albums such as the sardonic and all-acoustic 'And The Hits Just Keep On Comin''', the countrified 'Pretty Much Your Standard Ranch Stash' and 1974's bold 'The Prison', a soundtrack to a book and then a ballet. Though re-issued in 1990, 'The Prison' as yet remains only a critical triumph.

Six years after the posthumous 'Instant Replay' and 'The Monkees Present' albums, Dolenz and Jones teamed up with the group's principal tunesmiths, Tommy Boyce and Bobby Hart, for a tour in which they plugged an eponymous album and the old group's best-remembered hits. Remembering them too were Robert Wyatt (who retrod 'I'm A Believer' in 1974), and, later, The Sex Pistols (with 'I'm Not Your Stepping Stone'). The Monkees also influenced the marketing of the likes of The Archies, Bay City Rollers, Osmonds and, more recently, New Kids On The Block.

With re-screenings of the old shows as well as repackaged albums and rarities com-pilations appealing to 1980s consumers, three Monkees and some backing musicians recon-vened for a global tour and 'Pool It', a new album. From New York, Tork had left his New Monks band in neutral while, over in England, renowned West End and children's TV director Dolenz had conferred with Jones who, since 1969, had served as a radio presenter and in the *Godspell* musical. As it was before 1966, neither he nor Dolenz had made much impact as solo recording artists.

Greatest Hits

Singles	Title	US	UK
1966	Last Train To Clarksville	1	23
1966	I'm A Believer	1	1
Albums			
1966	The Monkees	1	1
1967	More Of The Monkees	1	1
1967	Headquarters	1	2
1967	Pisces, Aquarius, Capricorn And Jones Ltd.	1	5

The **MOODY BLUES**

Denny Laine (guitar, vocals)
Ray Thomas (flute, percussion, vocals)
Mike Pinder (keyboards)
Clint Warwick (bass)
Graeme Edge (drums)

Over a quarter of a century after their first hit, Birmingham (England) group, The Moody Blues, retain two original members and substantial popularity, although the 1990 version is a very different musical prop-osition from the group's early R&B/British Beat style.

Initially described as a 'Birmingham super-group', the five Moody Blues had played in popular local bands, Thomas (born 1942) and Pinder (born 1942) in El Riot & The Rebels, Edge (born 1942) in Gerry Levene & The Avengers (with Roy Wood) and Laine (born Brian Hines, 1944) as leader of Denny Laine & The Diplomats, which also included Bev Bevan, later of ELO. Their second single, 'Go Now' (1964), a cover of a US soul hit by Bessie Banks, was an international smash, topping the UK chart, but proving impossible to follow – the next three hits didn't make the UK Top 20, and their debut album, 'The Magnificent Moodies', was inappropriately titled and died in 1965. Losing the con-fidence of their label, the group spiralled downwards until the end of 1966, when Laine left to launch the first of several short-lived and mainly unsuccessful projects before joining Wings in 1971, where he was Paul McCartney's right hand man for most of the 1970s.

The remaining trio recruited another ex-member of El Riot & The Rebels, John Lodge (born 1945, bass, vocals) and Justin Hayward (born 1946), a singer/guitarist who had worked with UK rock pioneers Marty Wilde and Lonnie Donegan, and soon became vital to the group both as a performer and as a songwriter. The first two singles with the new recruits were flops and their label was about to drop the band, but fate played a card: as well as being a record company, the label manufactured hi-fi equip-ment and, in those early days of stereo, needed a demonstration album to illustrate the equipment's capabilities. The Moody Blues agreed to record a rock version of Dvorak's *New World Symphony* backed by an orchestra, but used the studio time to record an album of original songs, which was re-leased as 'Days Of Future Passed' (1967). This showcased Hayward's songs and voice, and included 'Nights In White Satin', a song that became a hit then and on several occa-sions subsequently. Both the album and single were major successes, and from that point on the group became known for their fusion of rock with light classical music, a sound later achieved onstage by Mike Pinder's pioneering use of the mellotron (a keyboard instrument which can sound like a string section).

The group continued in this vein for the next four years, releasing a string of big-selling albums produced by Tony Clarke (who was regarded as an auxiliary group member): 'In Search Of The Lost Chord' (1968), 'On The Threshold Of A Dream' (1969), 'To Our Children's Children's Children' (also 1969, and the first album on the group's own Threshold label), 'A Ques-tion Of Balance' (1970), 'Every Good Boy Deserves Favour' (1971), and 'Seventh Sojourn' (1972), some of which also included

Yuppy-rock before its time, the Moodies mellow out into middle age

major hit singles, such as 'Question', a 1970 UK Top 3 hit, and 'Isn't Life Strange?', which made the UK Top 20 in 1972. By 1973 the group members were ready for a break from the continual album/tour/album/tour treadmill, and decided to put the group on ice while concentrating on individual projects. A compilation album, 'This Is The Moody Blues', was released in 1974 to remind the world of the group's existence, as it became clear that if any of the solo projects took off, the group might be shelved indefinitely.

First off the mark were Hayward & Lodge, whose 'Blue Jays' album (1975) was a Top 5 UK/Top 20 US hit, and spawned a UK Top 10 single, 'Blue Guitar'; but neither of Thomas's albums, 'From Mighty Oaks' (1975) and 'Hopes, Wishes & Dreams' (1976), nor the two by The Graeme Edge Band (1975's 'Kick Off Your Muddy Boots' and 1977's 'Paradise Ballroom') nor Pinder's 'The Promise' (1976) made the UK album chart, and US results were little better. Lodge's 1977 album, 'Natural Avenue', made the UK Top 40, and Hayward's 'Songwriter' made the UK Top 30/US Top 40 in that year, but it was clear that the appeal of The Moody Blues was much greater than that of its individual members, and in 1977, a double album, 'Caught Live + 5', including both live and previously . unreleased studio tracks, restored the group to the US Top 30, whereupon they reconvened for 1978's 'Octave' album, which made the UK Top 10 and the US Top 20.

However, Pinder was not willing to be part of the obligatory world tour, and left the band as the album was released, retiring to live in California. He was replaced by Swiss keyboard star Patrick Moraz (born 1948, ex-Refugee, Yes, etc.) for the tour and for future records. The group decided on a less prolific approach during the 1980s, when albums were released less frequently: 1981's 'Long Distance Voyager' topped the US album chart, 1983's 'The Present' was somewhat less notable, 1986's 'The Other Side Of Life' proved that the group's 'cosmic hippy' audience would remain interested whenever the band toured, and 1989's 'Sur La Mer' (their second album produced by Tony Visconti) was similarly successful. There seems little to prevent the group continuing ad infinitum, unless Hayward, who remains the only group member to have experienced significant success as an individual (especially with his guest vocal on 'Forever Autumn', a 1978 UK Top 5 hit from producer Jeff Wayne's 'War Of The Worlds' concept album, a huge international seller), decides to work solo – although his later solo albums like 1980's 'Night Flight', 1985's 'Moving Mountains' and 1989's 'Classic Blue', on which he collaborated with Mike Batt, have all made the UK charts without being major commercial successes.

A major international act, The Moodies may be justifiably criticized for rarely venturing beyond a well-trodden path, but have managed to sustain their popularity with a vast audience which now includes two complete generations.

Greatest Hits

Singles	Title	US	UK
1964	Go Now	10	1
1967	Nights In White Satin	2	9
1970	Question	21	2
1975	Blue Guitar		
	(Hayward & Lodge)	94	5
1978	Forever Autumn (Hayward)	47	5
Albums			
1969	On The Threshold Of A Dream	20	1
1970	A Question Of Balance	3	1
1971	Every Good Boy Deserves		
	A Favour	2	1
1972	Seventh Sojourn	1	5
1975	Blue Jays (Hayward & Lodge)	16	4
1981	Long Distance Voyager	1	7

Van MORRISON

One of the most revered singer/ songwriters of the rock era (although his music has by no means always been in the rock genre), Belfast native Van Morrison (born George Ivan Morrison, 1945) has maintained an incredibly high quality in over 25 years of successful recording which happily shows no sign of coming to an end.

Morrison's parents were very interested in music, and their son heard American music on the radio as a child, and learned to play harmonica, guitar and saxophone during his schooldays, when he played in several local bands. While still in his teens, he launched a very popular club in Belfast, from which his first internationally successful group, Them, emerged. The group enjoyed success in the UK during the mid-1960s, notably with two UK hit singles, 'Baby Please Don't Go' (a cover of a US R&B classic) and 'Here Comes The Night', which was written by US producer Bert Berns. Ultimately of equal note was the former hit's B-side, a Morrison original titled 'Gloria', which later became a staple of garage bands like The Shadows Of Knight, whose 1966 cover version made the US Top 10. After a chaotic 1966 US tour, Them fell apart when Morrison left the band to record with Berns in America for the latter's Bang label. The partnership was instantly successful, with a Morrison original, 'Brown Eyed Girl', making the US Top 10 in 1967, but follow-up singles failed to chart, and Morrison was unhappy with the release later that year of 'Blowin' Your Mind', an album which he felt was incomplete, and which Berns released without consulting him. Berns died shortly afterwards and Morrison signed to a major label for whom he cut 1968's 'Astral Weeks', which did not chart but has remained one of the most acclaimed rock albums ever made.

By 1970 Morrison had begun to assemble a superb backing band, The Caledonia Soul Orchestra, which would back him (with inevitable individual personnel changes) until 1974. During this period Morrison released five single albums and one double, which form possibly the most consistently excellent body of work produced by any rock artist during the 1970s. Among the notable musicians involved were David Shaw (drums), David Hayes (bass), John Platania (guitar), Jeff Labes (keyboards), Jack Shroer (saxophone), Colin Tillton (trumpet) and others. Few, if any, of them had significant previous credits, but under Morrison's command (as songwriter, vocalist, arranger, leader and producer) they cut albums like 'Moondance' (1970, US Top 30), 'His Band & The Street Choir' (1970, US Top 40, with a single, 'Domino', which made the US Top 10), 'Tupelo Honey' (1971, US Top 30), 'St. Dominic's Preview' (1972, US Top 20), 'Hard Nose The Highway' (1973, US Top 30) and the staggering double live album recorded on a lengthy world tour, 'It's Too Late To Stop Now' (1974, US Top 100), on which the band was augmented by a string quartet. These albums included numerous songs which have been recorded by others, although in the vast majority of cases Morrison's original versions remain the yardstick by which others are judged.

Also released in 1974 were 'T.B. Sheets', an album of material recorded in the 1960s for Bang, which briefly made the US chart, and 'Veedon Fleece', his least successful new album since 'Moondance', by which time most of The Caledonia Soul Orchestra had departed. Morrison later confirmed that he felt that a change was necessary, and after 'Veedon Fleece' (which many found far less accessible than most of his previous work), he did not release an album for two and a half years. He broke his silence in 1977 with the accurately titled 'A Period Of Transition', on which he worked with Dr John, but the results were somewhat unsatisfactory, although the album made the US Top 50. 1978's 'Wavelength' marked a return to form (and the US Top 30), after which Morrison changed labels in Europe, and began moving his home base back to Britain after living in the US since 1967. This relocation coincided with (and possibly resulted in) 'Wavelength' being Morrison's last US Top 40 album to date.

1979's 'Into The Music' saw another superb band working with Morrison, many of whom would remain with him for much of the 1980s, including Pee Wee Ellis, a remarkable saxophonist, Mark Isham (keyboards), Peter Van Hooke (drums) and the returning David Hayes (bass), while Ry Cooder guested on one track, 'Full Force Gale'. The album, which included Morrison's first (minor) UK hit single, 'Bright Side Of The Road', made the US Top 50 and was his highest charting UK album to date, just missing the Top 20.

Pee Wee Ellis or Jack Schroer. The album also included an unlikely duet between Morrison and Cliff Richard, 'Whenever God Shines His Light', which became easily Morrison's biggest ever UK hit single (although, as he said in one of the few revealing interviews he has granted in recent times, hit singles can create artistically limiting precedents and expectations).

In late 1989, 'The Best Of Van Morrison' was marketed more aggressively than any of his previous albums, and was a carefully chosen package including both rare tracks (eg 'Wonderful Remark', a track he recorded for the Robert De Niro movie *King Of Comedy*), and all the hits plus many other singles which might have received radio play. This was a successful ploy, as the album sold more quickly than any he had made in the previous 25 years, but from an artistic point of view it may not turn out to have been such a good idea, as Morrison is not an artist who makes albums of short songs, and the compilation may be misleading. At least a lot more people than ever before were exposed to one of the finest artists of the 20th century. Although recently artistically inconsistent, as evidenced by 1990's 'Enlightenment' album, Van Morrison is an essential part of any serious CD collection. A measure of the esteem in which he is held by his peers within the music business is that Morrison not only fronted The Band on a track on the latter's 1971 album, 'Cahoots', but also appeared as a featured guest at their remarkable farewell concert, filmed as *The Last Waltz*. Morrison, despite his irascible manner, is an artist who rarely disappoints.

Once one of Them, now all-purpose Van defies categorization

1980's 'Common One' was a continuation of its predecessor's direction and critically regarded as superior, but was less successful in chart terms; while 1982's 'Beautiful Vision' included guest spots from Mark Knopfler and was more successful chart-wise. 1983's 'Inarticulate Speech Of The Heart' was his first UK Top 20 album, but failed to make the US Top 100. By this time, the musical hints in his 1980s albums that Morrison was looking back to his Celtic roots were confirmed with the use of ex-Moving Hearts Uillean piper Davy Spillane and Irish guitarist Arty McGlynn. The sleeve credit to Scientology founder L. Ron Hubbard caused raised eyebrows among those unaware that Morrison reputedly owns a vast library of literature on the subject of comparative religions.

In 1984 'Live At The Grand Opera House, Belfast' was another excellent showcase for the power and subtlety which Morrison can inspire in the musicians in his band, although its UK Top 40 chart position was poor compared to 1985's UK Top 30 peak for 'A Sense Of Wonder', which included the track 'Boffyflow & Spike', the latter apparently

referring to cult British humourist Spike Milligan. 1986's 'No Guru, No Method, No Teacher' also made the UK Top 30, its title suggesting that Morrison was addressing those critics who made incorrect assumptions about him, and included return appearances by Platania and Labes, erstwhile members of The Caledonia Soul Orchestra.

1987's 'Poetic Champions Compose' introduced another new band, mainly consisting of previously little known British musicians, and made the UK Top 30, although possibly due more to the competition than to its own virtues – bearing in mind that only two of the six albums with The Caledonia Soul Orchestra even reached the UK chart. A special project came next – 'Irish Heartbeat', an uneasy collaboration between Morrison and famed Irish folk group The Chieftains which featured mainly traditional Irish material, and made the UK Top 20 in 1988.

Before 1989's 'Avalon Sunset', Morrison had recruited an early contemporary, Georgie Fame, as keyboard player and musical director, possibly recognizing that the band on 'Poetic Champions' lacked a personality like

Greatest Hits

Singles	Title	US	UK
1967	*Brown Eyed Girl*	10	–
1970	*Domino*	9	–
1989	*Whenever God Shines His Light* (with Cliff Richard)	–	20
Albums			
1970	*Moondance*	29	32
1972	*St. Dominic's Preview*	15	–
1978	*Wavelength*	28	27
1983	*Inarticulate Speech Of The Heart*	116	14

MOTLEY CRUE

Nicki Sixx *(bass)*
Vince Neil *(vocals)*
Mick Mars *(guitar)*
Tommy Lee *(drums)*

Bizarre from the beginning, Motley Crue have courted sensation throughout their 10-year history. Nicki Sixx (born Frank Ferrano, 1958) recruited Mars (born Bob Deak, 1955), Lee (born 1962) and Neil (born

Vincent Wharton, 1961) in 1981 from the LA heavy-metal scene. They swiftly attracted attention for their stage act, which included the dismemberment by chainsaw of female mannequins onstage. Following an independent album, 'Too Fast For Love' (1982), they signed to a major for 'Shout At The Devil' (1983), which reached the US Top 20, helped by a support slot on a 1984 Kiss tour. Near-disaster struck the same year when Neil was involved in a drink-driving fatality. He was given 20 days in jail, a huge fine, and committed to 200 days community service, lecturing to schools on the dangers of drugs and alcohol.

A cleaner-than-thou image began to develop with their third album, 'Theatre of Pain' (1985), which carried a sleeve warning against drink-driving. Neil and Mars then took part in an HM charity disc for Ethiopia, 'Stars', while a cover of Brownsville Station's 1973 US hit 'Smokin' In The Boys Room' (1985) made the US Top 20 singles. A six-month world tour confirmed their place in the hard-rock superleague, after which Tommy Lee married Heather Locklear from US TV soap opera *Dynasty*. During the world tour to promote their US Top 5 album, 'Girls Girls Girls' (also a UK Top 5 entry), Sixx,

having overcome a heroin habit, announced his own wedding plans, to Prince's ex-girlfriend Vanity. But no public announcements could compare to the publicity volcano which erupted early in 1988.

US bass-player Matthew Tripp sued Motley Crue's management, claiming he had masqueraded as Sixx for two years after the latter had been injured in a serious car crash in 1983. Tripp claimed unpaid royalties for material he had contributed when with the band and while taking on the role of Sixx, songwriting included. However, the problem did little to affect the performance of the 1989 'Dr. Feelgood' album, which topped the US album chart and reached the UK Top 5, the title track giving them their first US Top 10 single.

Greatest Hits

Singles	Title	US	UK
1985	Smokin' In The Boys Room	16	71
1987	Girls Girls Girls	12	26
1989	Dr. Feelgood	6	50
Albums			
1985	Theatre of Pain	6	36
1987	Girls Girls Girls	2	14
1989	Dr. Feelgood	1	4

Mixed-up Motley – Tripp to court knocks band for Sixx

MOTORHEAD

Lemmy *(bass, vocals)*
Larry Wallis *(guitar)*
Lucas Fox *(drums)*

Ian 'Lemmy' Kilminster (born 1945) began playing in Manchester mid-1960s soul bands before moving to London and the more psychedelic environment of Sam Gopal's Dream and Opal Butterfly, eventually landing a roadie's job with Jimi Hendrix. He joined Hawkwind in 1971, to be sacked in 1975 after being busted for drugs during a Canadian tour. On his return to the UK, he put together a trio with Wallis (ex-Pink Fairies) and Lucas Fox on drums, initially calling the band Bastard.

From the start, the band's sound was as uncompromising as the name, though the latter was soon changed to the slang for 'speed freak', Motorhead, and after a handful of gigs, an album was cut, initially with Dave Edmunds producing, but studio arguments led to its being shelved. Fox and Wallis were replaced by Phil Taylor, a friend of Lemmy's, on drums, and 'Fast' Eddie Clarke, who'd worked with Curtis Knight, on guitar in 1976. A period of record company hassles contrasted with a burgeoning following on the punk circuit, despite their being considered a heavy metal outfit. Eventually, an indie deal paid off, the band's eponymous 1977 debut album making the UK Top 50, leading to a longer major label deal. 'Overkill', produced by ex-Rolling Stones producer Jimmy Miller, and 'Bomber' both hit the UK album chart in 1979, and both title tracks were UK Top 50 singles.

Heavy touring attracted a strong grass-roots following in the UK and a 1980 EP, 'Golden Years', made the UK singles Top 10. 'Ace of Spades' (1980) was a UK Top 20 single, while the album of the same name reached the UK Top 5. A live album in 1981, 'No Sleep Till Hammersmith', went straight into the UK chart at No. 1. Lemmy's liking for 'guest' projects included duet singles with label mates Girlschool ('Please Don't Touch' being a 1981 UK Top 10 hit) and a proposed version of Tammy Wynette's 'Stand By Your Man' with Plasmatics' Wendy O. Williams, which led to Clarke's departure in 1982 in exasperation, just as the 'Iron Fist' album made the UK Top 10. Brian Robertson joined from Thin Lizzy, bringing a touch of relative sophistication to the raw basics that were the Motorhead trademark, resulting in the UK Top 20 album, 'Another Perfect Day' (1983).

The entire band was reorganized in 1984 with Phil Campbell and Wurzell joining to make it a two-guitar quartet, along with drummer Peter Gill from Saxon. A double album of old material, 'No Remorse' (1984), hit the UK Top 20 during a label dispute that prevented the group from recording for over two years. Eventually a new label deal in 1986

Lemmy (second left) and Motorhead, rebel rockers now an institution in the HM Hall of Fame

saw the release of the UK Top 30 album 'Orgasmatron' and the re-release of the band's back catalogue. 1987's 'Rock'n'Roll' and the live 'No Sleep At All' (1988) continued to keep the band on the road with a crowd-pleasing effects-laden live act. Now a heavy-metal institution, at their peak Motorhead were the only band that managed to bridge heavy rock and power punk in the late 1970s.

Greatest Hits

Singles	Title	US	UK
1980	The Golden Years (EP)	–	8
1981	Motorhead Live	–	6
Albums			
1980	Ace Of Spades	–	4
1981	No Sleep Till Hammersmith	–	1
1982	Iron Fist	174	6

MOTT THE HOOPLE / Ian HUNTER

Verden Allen (keyboards)
Dale 'Buffin' Griffin (drums)
Mick Ralphs (guitar, vocals)
Stan Tippins (vocals)
Pete 'Overend' Watts (bass)

Ralphs (born 1944), Watts (born 1949), Allen (born 1944), and Griffin (born 1948) performed as members of The Doc Thomas Group and The Shakedown before recruiting vocalist Tippins and changing their name to Silence in 1968. Vocalist and pianist Ian Hunter (born 1946) joined the band in 1969, replacing Tippins, who became the group's tour manager. Manager and producer Guy Stevens renamed the band Mott The Hoople (after a character in a novel by Willard Manus), and they released their eponymous debut album in 1969, featuring both Hunter's Dylanesque vocal style and Ralphs' plaintive, Neil Young-like whine. The album reached the UK Top 75, but it was as a live act that Mott built up a devoted following. The next two albums, the manic 'Mad Shadows' (1970) and the mellower 'Wildlife' (1971), both reached the UK Top 50, but the raucous 'Brain Capers' (1971) failed to repeat even that modest success, and the band decided to split.

Long-time fan David Bowie stepped in with an offer to produce the band on one of his songs, 'Suffragette City', but they held out for the anthemic 'All The Young Dudes', which gave them a UK Top 3/US Top 40 hit single in 1972. The Bowie-produced album of the same name made the US Top 100 and the UK Top 30, and the revitalized band toured the US, after which Allen quit. 1973's 'Honaloochie Boogie' single hit the UK Top 20, and that year's 'Mott' album, recorded as a quartet, provided their first UK Top 10 placing, also reaching the US Top 40. Erstwhile Love Affair keyboardist Morgan Fisher joined, allowing Hunter to move to rhythm guitar, but Ralphs left to form Bad Company, unhappy at Hunter's dominance of the band.

Two further UK Top 10 singles followed that year, 'All The Way From Memphis' and 'Roll Away The Stone', although neither featured Ralphs' replacement, Luther Grosvenor (ex-Spooky Tooth), re-christened Ariel Bender, who made his first appearance on 'The Golden Age Of Rock'n'Roll', a 1974 UK Top 20 single. 'The Hoople' and 'Live' (both 1974) gave the band two US Top 30 albums, but Bender left before the latter's release, being briefly replaced by ex-David Bowie guitarist Mick Ronson. The band split after one further single and a European tour, Hunter and Ronson forming The Hunter/Ronson Band to promote each other's solo albums. The others, now called simply Mott, recruited Nigel Benjamin (vocals) and Ray Major (guitar) as replacements, releasing two albums, before another name change to The British Lions, with ex-Medicine Head singer John Fiddler replacing Benjamin, and cut two further albums before being submerged by the very New Wave which the Hunter-era Hoople had influenced.

Hunter continued with seven solo albums, his eponymous 1975 debut going Top 30 in the UK and Top 50 in the US, and 1979's 'You're Never Alone With A Schizophrenic' making the Top 40 of the US album chart. Five of his albums featured Ronson, but it was not until 1989's 'Y U I Orta' that they released an album under their joint names. Hunter has produced Generation X, Ellen Foley and David Johansen (the last two with Ronson), and his songs have provided hits for MOR star Barry Manilow and hard-rock band Great White.

Greatest Hits

Singles	Title	US	UK
1972	All The Young Dudes	37	3
1973	Roll Away The Stone	–	8
1975	Once Bitten Twice Shy (Hunter solo)	–	14
Albums			
1973	Mott	35	7
1974	The Hoople	28	11
1974	Live	23	32
1975	Ian Hunter (Hunter solo)	50	21
1979	You're Never Alone With A Schizophrenic (Hunter)	35	49

MOUNTAIN

Leslie West (guitar, vocals)
Steve Knight (keyboards)
Felix Pappalardi (bass)
Norman Smart (drums)

Supervising recording for such as Joan Baez, Tim Hardin and the Lovin' Spoonful (see separate entries), Italian-American Pappalardi (born 1939) had been a familiar face around the Greenwich Village folk scene,

Leslie West at Mountain's peak

and was – with Knight (born 1941) – in a promising group called Devil's Anvil. However, his plum job producing Cream (see separate entry) opened Pappalardi's eyes to possibilities inherent in filling the market void left when the British power trio fragmented in 1968.

Among Pappalardi's lesser production clients were New York's Vagrants who were remarkable only for West (born 1945), a fast instrumentalist in artistic debt to Cream's Eric Clapton (see separate entry). During the recording of West's 1969 solo album, Mountain was born and named after the record's title (a reference to its maker's physique).

As 'the new Cream', the outfit were well-received at Woodstock. Only their fourth engagement, this inspired their single, 'For Yasgur's Farm' (the site of the event), though their set consisted for triple-forte workouts of selections from their forthcoming debut album, 'Mountain Climbing'. Nevertheless, before sessions for 'Nantucket Sleighride', Smart was replaced by Canadian Corky Laing (born 1948). The title track of this second album was later used as the signature tune for a highbrow UK TV series, and also extrapolated Cream-style for over seventy minutes on a 1974 Japan-only 'live' double album, but derivative though they were, Mountain's albums charted in the US and meant little in the UK.

Pappalardi's studio commitments necessitated Mountain's disbandment in 1972 but, for West and Laing, it was business as usual with their opportunist merger with ex-Cream bass player Jack Bruce, who didn't mind shelving more ambitious projects for a year to wring monetary drops from another ersatz Cream and the two dull albums that were West, Bruce and Laing's corporate legacy.

Leslie West's Wild West Show, who did not record commercially, followed before the 1974 reformation of the more bankable Mountain with Pappalardi – now doubling on keyboards – and second guitarist Dave Perry. After the release of 'Avalanche' and the bulky West's second solo album, 'The Great Fatsby' (with star-studded sleeve credits), Pappalardi – soon to die in bizarre circumstances – left with hearing problems at least partially resulting from his proximity and exposure to Mountain's thunderous live sound.

Beginning with an eponymous 1975 album from his Leslie West Band, the guitarist – with the faithful Laing – continues to cast workmanlike records adrift on the vinyl ocean while gigging for good money, even in the UK where he has recently been welcomed with some affection.

Greatest Hits

Singles	Title	US	UK
1970	*Mississippi Queen*	21	–
Albums			
1970	*Mountain Climbing*	17	–
1971	*Nantucket Sleighride*	16	43
1972	*The Road Goes Ever On*	63	21

On the Move towards ELO, Lynne, Wood and (front) Bevan

The MOVE

Carl Wayne (lead vocals)
Roy Wood (guitar, vocals)
Trevor Burton (guitar)
Ace Kefford (bass)
Bec Bevan (drums)

As its personnel had all served in other outfits that were big in Birmingham, UK, but unknown nationally, The Move were well-placed to amass a strong local reputation with a repertoire that developed from soul and classic rock in 1965 to a diverting mixture of mostly Californian acid-rock and Wood's compositions, which provoked enough interest to land them a record deal.

Both creative and remunerative, The Move's five-year chart run began in 1967 with 'Night Of Fear'. Further examples of the quintet's then stoned-hippy image followed with 'I Can Hear The Grass Grow', 'Flowers In The Rain' and tracks from an eponymous album. Their passages into the UK Top 10 were aided by a refinement of The Who's stage act, exemplified by Wayne (born 1944) using an axe to hack up props that included effigies of world figures such as then UK Prime Minister Harold Wilson who, after a more insulting publicity stunt, won a libel suit against The Move.

Among legal penalties was Wood (born 1946) losing his 'Flowers In The Rain' song-writing royalties, although his royalties from all other Move A-sides were substantial, greater than for songs he wrote for rival acts like The Idle Race and Amen Corner. The less prolific Kefford (born Christopher Kefford, 1949) was responsible for writing, and Burton (born 1947) for co-producing, 'William Chalker's Time Machine', the best-remembered single by fellow Midlanders, The Lemon Tree.

Kefford left in 1968 and Burton switched to bass but departed the following year, irked by Wood's increasing control of The Move's destiny. After they tried rock'n'roll revival with 'Fire Brigade', Wood assumed lead vocals on every subsequent single, bar the

flop, 'Wild Tiger Woman'. With pride smarting, Wayne was next to go, but not before advocating the group's unhappy stab at cabaret, at which he worked after leaving the group with qualified success as an 'all-round entertainer'. The short-lived Ace Kefford Stand died hitless, and Burton joined Steve Gibbons and ex-Moody Blue Denny Laine in the similarly brief career of Balls, before travelling a road that led by 1988 to semi-pro status.

With 1970's 'Shazam' album by the old line-up as a holding operation, Bevan (born 1945) and Wood enlisted Jeff Lynne, The Idle Race's leader, to share the central spot-light. Garbed and painted like a psychedelic Wild Man Of Borneo, Wood sand 'Bronto-saurus' and the group's three remaining UK chart entries during his planning of The Electric Light Orchestra with Lynne and

Bevan. However, it was due to the more democratic fourth and final album, 'Message To The Country' and the rise of Lynne's B-side, 'Do Ya' (also later recorded by ELO) to the US Top 100 that The Move surfaced as cult celebrities in the USA.

A few months after The Move disbanded and the Orchestra went public in 1972, Wood quit to re-emerge with Wizzard, a flamboyant group which scored six UK Top 10 hits in two years, including two chart-toppers, 'See My Baby Jive' and 'Angel Fin-gers', and a perennial seasonal favourite, 'I Wish It Could Be Christmas Everyday'. He then formed Roy Wood's Wizzo Band and his parallel solo career also flourished, his biggest hit under his own name being 1973's 'Forever', which reached the UK Top 10. Wood has been largely absent from the UK chart since 1975, although several releases (e.g. leading Roy Wood's Helicopters) have shown promise, and he was credited as a featured guest on a UK Top 50 single by Doctor & The Medics, 'Waterloo', in 1986.

Greatest Hits

Singles	Title	US	UK
1967	Flowers In The Rain	–	2
1968	Blackberry Way	–	1
1973	See My Baby Jive (Wizzard)	–	1
1973	Angel Fingers	–	1
Albums			
1968	Move	–	15
1973	Split Ends	172	–
1973	Boulders (Roy Wood solo)	173	16
1974	Introducing Eddy & The Falcons (Wizzard)	–	19

Alison **MOYET/YAZOO**

Essex-born (1961) Genevieve Alison 'Alf' Moyet, who had previously sung with Southend punk/rock bands like The Vicars, The Vipers and The Screaming Abdabs, advertised in the music press in 1982 for a 'rootsy blues band'. The ad was answered by technical wizard and keyboard player Vince Clarke who had recently left Depeche Mode, after penning three hits for them. He was looking for a vocalist to work with and together this incongruous combination be-came the short-lived and very successful Yazoo (named after an early blues record label).

Their first single, 'Only You', went Top 3 in the UK as did their debut album 'Upstairs At Eric's'. In the UK they quickly followed it with three other Top 20 singles, 'Don't Go' and 'The Other Side of Love' in 1982 and Moyet's song, 'Nobody's Diary' in 1983. In the US, where their name was shortened to Yaz to avoid confusion with another act, the album just made the Top 100 but eventually sold over a million. They also had US Top

Vince'n'Alf, short-lived success as Yazoo before Moyet makes it solo

100 singles with 'Situation' and its British 'A' side, 'Only You'. 'Situation' also made the black music chart and was one of three US Dance Music No. 1s for them, the others being 'Don't Go' and 'State Farm'/'Nobody's Diary'. The duo split up amicably after recording their second LP, 'You And Me Both', which topped the UK chart and was another US Top 100 hit.

Clarke went on to achieve more success in Assembly and then Erasure. After legal battles over her contract, Moyet joined CBS in 1983. Her first single, 'Love Resurrection' in 1984, made the UK Top 10 as did the follow up, 'All Cried Out'. Her debut solo album, 'Alf', topped the UK chart, selling over a million copies and helping to earn her the BRITS award as Top British Female Artist of the year. In 1985 the large framed bluesy vocalist's revival of the Billie Holiday classic, 'That Ole Devil Called Love', produced by Pete Wingfield, became her biggest hit to date. Later that year, her duet with Paul Young at 'Live Aid' was acclaimed but a subsequent tour, accompanied by a jazz band, did not meet with critical approval.

In the US, both Yaz(oo) and Moyet had a cult following which gave them chart success, the biggest single being Moyet's version of Lamont Dozier's composition 'Invisible', a US Top 40 hit in 1985.

Moyer's second album, 'Raindancing', released in 1987, was a UK No. 2 and two tracks from it, 'Is This Love', which she co-wrote with Dave Stewart, and 'Weak in The Presence Of Beauty', made the UK Top 10, as did her revival of Ketty Lester's 1962 hit, 'Love Letters', later that year.

Greatest Hits

Singles	Title	US	UK
1982	Only You (Yazoo)	67	2
1985	That Ole Devil Called Love (Moyet)	–	2
Albums			
1983	You And Me Both (Yazoo)	69	I
1984	Alf (Moyet)	45	I

Johnny **NASH**

Texan Nash (born 1940) began his singing career as a pop/soul singer in the late 1950s with a TV talent spot which led to a major recording contract. He had a US Top 30 hit with 'A Very Special Love' (1957), and began to branch out into a parallel career in films. Two influences came to bear on the otherwise steady MOR direction his music was taking, a visit to the Caribbean in 1958 while filming *Take A Giant Step*, and hearing the music there; and the soul-style of Sam Cooke, at his peak at the beginning of the 1960s.

Nash's singing took on a more soulful aspect, which paid off in 1965 when the 'Let's Move and Groove (Together)' single made the Top 5 in the US soul charts and entered the US Top 100. While producing for his own labels, Nash returned to Jamaica with producer Byron Lee and began a series of reggae-based recordings which were to make him a star name and help popularize the form, at that time, still the preserve of the Caribbean and immigrant communities in the UK. 'Hold Me Tight' went Top 5 in the US and UK in 1968, followed by 'You Got Soul' and a cover of Sam Cooke's 'Cupid' the following year.

He was an early supporter of the still-to-be-discovered Bob Marley, and made the Top 20 in the UK and US with the latter's 'Stir It Up' (1973). His biggest breakthrough had come with his own song 'I Can See Clearly Now', a US No. 1 (UK Top 5) in 1972 that became something of an anthem of populist reggae. An album of the same name followed, and included four Marley titles plus backing by The Wailers. 'Tears On My Pillow' reached No. 1 in the UK singles chart in 1975, and a cover of Sam Cooke's 'Wonderful World', reached the UK Top 30 the following year. Nash, still running a studio in Jamaica and making the occasional movie appearance, was a catalyst in the popularization of reggae, his being among the few genuinely pop records that have survived in the style.

Greatest Hits

Singles	Title	US	UK
1968	Hold Me Tight	5	5
1972	I Can See Clearly Now	I	5
1975	Tears On My Pillow	–	I
Albums			
1972	I Can See Clearly Now	23	39
1977	Johnny Nash Collection	–	I8

Ricky **NELSON**

Ricky Nelson (born Eric Nelson, 1940) was one of the most accomplished young white American pop-rockers to emerge after the first explosion of rock'n'roll and fill the void during 1958–60 when Elvis Presley was in the US Army. Nelson's eminence was helped by consistently strong material and the fact that he always surrounded himself with the best musicians. In post-teen-idol years, when he re-invented himself as a country/rock artist, this edge of quality remained with him, and 50 of his US hit singles were achieved before 1970.

The son of star showbiz couple Ozzie & Harriet Nelson, he was a performer from the age of eight, portraying himself in the family radio sitcom, *The Adventures Of Ozzie & Harriet*. This moved to TV in 1952, just in time for the nation to see young Ricky hit his teens. A good-looker, he gathered a big teenage following, and when in 1957 he sang for the first time on the show, the audience response was ecstatic, so Ozzie Nelson arranged a session at Verve Records (normally a jazz label) in order to make the featured song – a cover of Fats Domino's current hit, 'I'm Walkin'' – commercially available.

The debut single was an immediate smash. Since Nelson was able to plug both sides of it on a rapidly-instituted musical slot on the TV show (which became a permanent fixture – he was the first artist in history to benefit from the equivalent of today's high-rotation promo video play), both 'I'm Walkin'' and its teen ballad coupling, 'A Teenager's Romance', made the US Top 20, the latter entering the Top 3.

Nelson had no longterm contract with Verve, and before the label had issued a US Top 20 follow-up, 'You're My One And Only Love' (the last recording from that debut session), a lengthy deal had been signed with Imperial Records. It served both sides well: Nelson was one of the most consistent hit-makers of the next five years, scoring million-sellers with 'Be-Bop Baby', 'Stood Up', 'Poor Little Fool' (his first US No. 1), 'Lonesome Town', the double A-side 'It's Late'/'Never Be Anyone Else But You', and another double-header, 'Travelin' Man'/'Hello Mary Lou', which was his all-time biggest seller. These were just the cream of the crop; many more singles also hit the US Top 10, while even Nelson's debut album topped the US chart in 1958, an unheard-of feat in the 1950s by any teen-oriented act other than Presley.

This pre-eminence was not only due to TV exposure. Not a songwriter himself, Nelson

Ricky – teen idol with rockabilly roots

picked material from strong sources, including Johnny & Dorsey Burnette, Sharon Sheeley, Baker Knight, and later Jerry Fuller and Gene Pitney. When he assembled a band in 1958 for both stage and recording work, the same care was taken, and paid off equally. James Burton, later one of *the* legendary rock guitarists (working with Elvis Presley and Emmylou Harris' Hot Band), was the lynchpin of the group: his uncluttered accompaniments and riveting breaks were essential to Nelson's sound.

Nelson began a film career in 1959, costarring with John Wayne and Dean Martin in *Rio Bravo*. In 1961, as 'Travelin' Man' topped the US chart and he reached his 21st birthday, he announced that his performing name would now be the more adult-sounding Rick Nelson. In 1963, he married (his wife also joined him on the TV show, in which he still regularly appeared), and as his Imperial deal ended, he signed an almost unheard-of $1 million 20-year contract with US Decca. Unfortunately, his former consistency meant little after the 'British Invasion' a year later; a year's downward spiral of chart placings was followed by five years of complete absence from the US chart. The rug pulled from under his traditional musical approach, Nelson followed his inclinations rather than fashion, and found country music. Early country/folk albums were critically rated but sold poorly, and it was not until 1970, when he formed the country/rock Stone Canyon Band, that he hit a commercial groove again, charting with a cover of Bob Dylan's 'She Belongs To Me' and his own 'Easy To Be Free'.

In 1972, he confounded expectations with another million-seller and a return to the US Top 10 with 'Garden Party', an ironic self-composition which commented upon the blinkered attitudes of those (specifically, at a Madison Square Garden rock revival show the previous year) who ignored his new material alongside the old hits.

The late 1970s brought more mixed fortunes, as the hits stopped once more, The Stone Canyon Band broke up, his record deal was terminated several years early, and, in 1977, his wife divorced him. This period, lasting into the early 1980s, saw him touring widely and taking guest acting roles in several TV movies and series, though recording only sparsely, with an album apiece for Epic and Capitol. In late 1985, he toured the UK in an extremely successful nostalgia package with Bo Diddley and others, but just one month later, on New Year's Eve, was killed along with his band musicians, when the aircraft carrying them between concert dates in Alabama and Texas caught fire and crashed.

Greatest Hits

Singles	Title	US	UK
1957	A Teenager's Romance	2	–
1957	Stood Up	2	27
1958	Poor Little Fool	1	4
1961	Travelin' Man	1	2
Albums			
1957	Ricky	1	–
1958	Ricky Nelson	7	–
1961	Rick Is 21	8	–

Michael **NESMITH**

A former member of The Monkees, Nesmith pursued a personal vision of country-rock in the 1970s before becoming a pioneer of video publishing.

As a former member of the Los Angeles folk scene, Nesmith (born 1942) soon felt frustrated at the lack of opportunity for self-expression in The Monkees. Before leaving the band in 1970, he wrote Linda Ronstadt's 1967 US hit 'Different Drum' and recorded the instrumental album, 'Wichita Train Whistle Sings' (1968).

Nesmith's first solo venture was the First National Band featuring pedal-steel player Red Rhodes. The group made three albums, 'Magnetic South' (1970), 'Loose Salute' (1971) and 'Nevada Fighter' (1972). The plaintive ballad 'Joanne' was a US Top 30 hit in 1970. Guitarist Johnny Meeks (formerly with Gene Vincent) was the mainstay of a shortlived Second National Band which made only one album, 'Tantamount To Reason' (1972), before Nesmith and Rhodes alone cut the ironically-titled but excellent 'And The Hits Just Keep On Comin'' (1972).

As well as 1973's 'Pretty Much Your Standard Ranch Stash', on which he was backed by musicians who worked at his next venture, a studio and label, Countryside, which issued little more than an album by Red Rhodes, Nesmith produced an album by British singer, Ian Matthews, before major label politics closed Countryside. This was followed by the formation of Pacific Arts, a record and video company. Nesmith wrote and recorded the

Ex-Monkee apes actor as DeNiro lookalike

concept piece, 'The Prison' (a book with a soundtrack) in 1975, the year he turned down the chance to join a Monkees reunion project.

Nesmith's later sporadic recordings included 'From A Radio Engine To A Photon Wing' (1976) which included the UK Top 30 hit 'Rio' and 'Infinite Rider On The Big Dogma' (1981). 'The Later Stuff', a selection of songs written after 1976 was released in 1989.

In the 1980s, Nesmith largely concentrated on sound-and-vision projects like *Elephant Parts*, the winner of the first music video Grammy in 1981. Pacific Arts also produced such movies as *Elephant Parts* and *Repo Man*.

Greatest Hits

Singles	Title	US	UK
1970	Joanne	21	–
1977	Rio	–	28
Albums			
1970	Magnetic South	143	–

The **NEVILLE BROTHERS**/ The **METERS**/Aaron **NEVILLE**/ Art **NEVILLE**

The Neville family is a New Orleans institution now entering its fourth decade of musical endeavour. Various permutations of the four brothers, Art (born 1937), Aaron (born 1941), Charles and Cyril (born 1948) have enjoyed hit records since 1954. Art was a member of The Hawketts, who enjoyed local success with 'Mardi Gras Mambo' (1954), still a staple of Mardi Gras in New Orleans over 35 years later. Art joined the band of local star Lee Diamond and also recorded as a solo artist.

By the late 1950s both Aaron and Art were recording, and Aaron enjoyed his first US R&B chart hit with 'Over You' in 1960, while Art's ballad, 'All These Things', was a local hit in 1962. Brother Charles, having worked with various bluesmen, joined Joey Dee & The Starliters in 1962. Younger brother Cyril joined Art and Aaron in The Neville Sounds, who gigged around New Orleans. Aaron scored a US Top 3 single with the haunting ballad, 'Tell It Like It Is' (1966), although subsequent singles flopped. When the independent label which had released 'Tell It Like It Is' folded, The Neville Sounds continued to gig around New Orleans before becoming the nucleus of the band for Seasaint Studios owned by Marshall Sehorn and Allen Toussaint, New Orleans's most prolific and talented writer and producer.

When the band split in 1968, Art formed The Meters with George Porter (bass) Joseph Modeliste (drums) and Leo Nocentelli (guitar). Taking its inspiration from the Booker T & The MGs format, the group enjoyed hits with instrumentals with such titles as 'Sophisticated Cissy' (US Top 40, 1969) 'Cissy Strut' (US Top 30, 1969) and 'Chicken Strut' (US Top 50, 1969). Thanks in the main to the endorsements of artists like The Rolling Stones and Dr John, a major label deal was signed for 'Cabbage Alley' in 1972, which caused much media attention but less than exciting sales. With the addition of Cyril Neville, The Meters continued to work on Allen Toussaint's productions, for artists as diverse as British vocalist Robert Palmer and Labelle.

Despite having worked with Paul McCartney and toured with The Rolling Stones, The Meters were simply not making it. Serious financial disputes with Toussaint and Sehorn which were to take almost 15 years to resolve caused the group to split. The four brothers came together for the 1976 album 'The Wild Tchoupitoulas' with a group of Mardi Gras Red Indians before recording their own eponymous debut in 1978 and, after a label change 'Fiyo On The Bayou' (1981) neither of which were commercial successes. The Nevilles regrouped on their home base and began to build a formidable local following resulting in their becoming a major tourist attraction and a beacon for visiting musicians. Word of mouth was remarkable and the group became very much in demand, recording a live album 'Neville-ization', in 1982.

The turning point came in 1987 when they appeared in the cult movie *The Big Easy*, which resulted in another record deal, but the subsequent album, 'Uptown' (1987) featuring Keith Richards, Carlos Santana and Jerry Garcia (they had supported The Grateful Dead on tour), was a pale imitation of their live shows. A collection of doo-wop classics, interpreted by Aaron appeared as a mini-album, 'Orchid In The Storm'. A further label change saw the band being produced by Daniel Lanois, the resultant album, 'Yellow Moon' (1989), becoming a major domestic and international hit, following which a second volume of 'Neville-ization', titled 'Live At Tipitinas' was released. That year also saw Aaron recruited by Linda Ronstadt to duet with her on several tracks, including 'Don't Know Much', a UK and US Top 3 single.

Subsequent tours of Europe were major triumphs for the group, and the 1990 album, 'Brother's Keeper', despite somewhat pretentious leanings, further consolidated the group's status. Self-produced, with help from Malcolm Burn and Steve Jordan, the album featured a version of Leonard Cohen's 'Bird On A Wire' (produced by The Eurythmics' Dave Stewart), a movie title theme. Guests on the album included Leo Nocentelli, Linda Ronstadt, Buffy St Marie and Aaron's son, Ivan Neville, himself a successful artist, representing yet another generation of New Orleans's first family of music. In 1990, The Meters were re-formed and played in the UK and Europe with a view to recording again eventually, although the original line-up was

The Neville Brothers, pillars of the New Orleans musical establishment

not complete, as drummer Joseph Modeliste was replaced by David Battiste.

Greatest Hits

Singles	Title	US	UK
Aaron Neville			
1966	*Tell It Like It Is*	2	–
1990	*Don't Know Much*		
	(with Linda Ronstadt)	2	2
Albums			
Neville Brothers			
1989	*Yellow Moon*	66	–
1990	*Brother's Keeper*	60	35

NEW KIDS ON THE BLOCK

Jonathan Knight
Jordan Knight
Joe McIntyre
Donnie Wahlberg
Danny Wood *(vocal group)*

The most successful US pop group of the last decade, New Kids On The Block, were put together in 1984 by producer/writer Maurice Starr who had masterminded previous teen stars New Edition which included latter-day US chart star Bobby Brown. Starr selected Wahlberg, who found Wood and the Knight brothers, and McIntyre, then 13, was the last to join the group, initially known as Nynuk. In 1986 their first single, 'Be My Girl', made the Black Music Top 100 and their eponymous debut album, which eventually sold two million, was released.

Their second album 'Hangin' Tough' (1988) featured the single 'Please Don't Go Girl' which reached the US Top 10 and became the first of a record nine consecutive US Top 10 entries for them. In 1989 the well-choreographed pop/dance group were the top recording act in the US and 'New Kids-mania' reached epidemic proportions with even their Christmas album 'Merry Merry Christmas' selling over two million copies. Their video tapes 'Hangin' Tough' and 'Hangin' Tough Live' were the first music videos to sell over a million, and they simultaneously had four tracks on the US singles chart and three charted albums, including both No. 1s – never before accomplished by a teen group.

In the UK they became the top act of 1990, scoring seven Top 10 singles – something no other US group had ever achieved. In the US that year the 'Hangin' Tough' album passed the eight million mark and their fourth album, 'Step By Step', went triple platinum. A remix album entitled 'No More Games'

New Kids up to old tricks, latest in long line of teenyhype groups through Osmonds, Rollers et al

was issued in 1990.

New Kids On The Block have an enormously successful merchandising machine behind them, and sponsorship deals with McDonalds and Pepsi for over $15 million.

Greatest Hits

Singles	Title	US	UK
1989	*You Got It (The Right Stuff)*	3	I
1989	*I'll Be Loving You Forever*	I	5
1989	*Hangin' Tough*	I	I
1990	*Step By Step*	I	2
Albums			
1988	*Hangin' Tough*	I	2
1990	*Step By Step*	I	I

The **NEW YORK DOLLS**

David Johansen (lead vocals)
Rick Rivets (guitar)
Johnny Thunders (guitar)
Arthur Kane (bass)
Billy Murcia (drums)

Though artists as diverse as David Bowie and Motorhead were among some of the few older performers acceptable to punk/rockers, more in keeping with the movement's avowed nihilist stance were The New York Dolls who, on their last legs, had been managed by Malcolm McLaren whose later manipulation of The Sex Pistols marked the zenith of the punk era.

Mick Jagger lookalike Johansen had sung with two Staten Island bands while Murcia and Thunders had played in Actress before The Dolls found each other and fermented in the Bowery, a run-down New York suburb. With a glam/rock look, The Dolls were not influenced by The Dave Clark Five or Herman's Hermits, but by The Rolling Stones, Pretty Things, Kinks and other hairy monsters who played mean R&B. It was as ersatz Stones that The Dolls were portrayed in *Rolling Stone* magazine in 1972, as they were

about to cut their eponymous debut album. With Sylvain Sylvain, another Actress veteran, replacing Rivets, producer Todd Rundgren captured much of the exuberance of their stage act during which they'd hit all their instruments at once and convey the exciting impression that it could all fall to bits at any moment. The Dolls' own compositions, though period rockers in construction, were strengthened by state-of-the-art technology and loaded lyrics. 'Looking For A Kiss', 'Personality Crisis' etc., were reflective of their surroundings and collective attitude. Shortly before they sauntered into Malcolm McLaren's London boutique in 1972, Billy Murcia had died of a drug overdose, and the rest of the group also lived close to the edge – Kane's alcoholism led to road manager Peter Jordan serving as his understudy and then successor.

With Jerry Nolan on drums, The Dolls completed an aptly titled second album, 'Too Much Too Soon', produced by George 'Shadow' Morton (who produced The Shangri-Las). If it brought them to a wider public, their older fans figured that the group had never fulfilled its early promise. Desperate strategies like McLaren's projection of them as communists only delayed their demise until the departure of Thunders and Nolan in 1975. After a Japanese tour with new personnel, Johansen and Sylvain threw in the towel too. Later, individuals racked up heftier achievements – notably Thunders who, as leader of The Heartbreakers (with Nolan), became a cult hero in the UK in 1977, and Johansen with a well-received 1978 solo album. The New York Dolls were pioneers who achieved a wider fame after they had folded. Either of their albums will give first-timers the idea.

The mascara was beginning to run in the Dolls' tacky version of glam rock

Randy NEWMAN

One of the most respected songwriters of the rock era, Newman's early penchant for sad love songs gave way to a wry, sardonic and penetrating viewpoint on the foibles and inequities of American life.

From a show business family with two uncles and a cousin involved in film music, Newman (born 1944), studied composition in Los Angeles and released an unsuccessful single, 'Golden Gridiron Boy' in 1961.

He next became a staff writer at Metric Music, a division of Liberty Records. Some of his earliest songs were recorded by such artists as The Fleetwoods, Gene McDaniels and Jerry Butler but his first success came in the UK, where Cilla Black had a Top 20 hit with the romantic ballad, 'I've Been Wrong Before' (1965), while former Animals organist Alan Price latched onto the quirky side of Newman's talent. Price's version of 'Simon Smith And His Amazing Dancing Bear', a circus portrait, reached the UK Top 10 in 1967.

Newman songs also provided hits for Gene Pitney (the histrionic 'Nobody Needs Your Love') while Judy Collins made a memorable recording of the melancholic 'I Think It's Gonna Rain Today' in 1966. In that year, he made his first album, an instrumental collection of TV themes, before moving to a job as arranger and producer at Warner Bros.

A recording deal followed and 'Randy Newman' (1968) wreathed his compositions in orchestral arrangements. Although 'So Long Dad' had been a small UK hit for Manfred Mann, the album sold poorly but Newman's growing reputation as an original songwriter was enhanced in 1970 when Harry Nilsson released an album of his material 'Nilsson Sings Newman', shortly before Newman's own 'Twelve Songs'. With Ry Cooder and members of The Byrds among the backing musicians, the album included 'Mama Told Me (Not To Come)', which became a US No. 1 hit in Three Dog Night's raucous version.

A 1971 live recording illustrated both the lyrical and the sardonic sides of Newman's early work, but 'Sail Away' (1972) found him decisively involved with broad political and social themes. The challenging title song was typical: in it Newman adopted the persona of a ship's captain giving a lyrical picture of life in America to his cargo of slaves.

As well as including the fervent, bluesy 'Guilty', 'Good Old Boys' (1974) developed this approach in a set of songs concerned with the bigotry but also the musical beauty of the 'Old South'. By now, Newman's audience was growing and his next album, 'Little Criminals' (1977), sold a million copies, partly on the strength of his surprise hit, 'Short People', an attack on prejudice wrapped up in a catchy tune and satirical lyrics.

It was to remain his biggest-selling record and in the 1980s, Newman divided his time

Randy's 'Small People' made him a new man

between live performance and film scores, releasing only two albums of new songs after 1979's 'Born Again', 'Trouble In Paradise' (1983) brought a minor hit with 'The Blues', a duet with Paul Simon, and contained a near-autobiographical statement in 'I'm Different' (And I Don't Care Who Knows It)'. 'Land Of Dreams' (1988) was co-produced with Mark Knopfler of Dire Straits. In the double-edged 'Follow The Flag', it contained the nearest Newman had come to patriotism.

Newman's movie writing career had begun in 1970 with a contribution to the Mick Jagger vehicle, *Performance*, and the Bob Newhart comedy *Cold Turkey*. He later provided full scores for *Ragtime* (1982) *The Natural* (1984) and *Three Amigos* (1986). The vast majority of his work will delight those with discriminating taste in popular music, although he has rarely received his commercial dues as an artist.

Greatest Hits

Singles	Title	US	UK
1978	*Short People*	2	–
Albums			
1978	*Little Criminals*	9	–

Olivia NEWTON-JOHN

By concentrating on the possible, Newton-John (born 1948) has entered middle life as a showbusiness evergreen with every re-cord release an automatic million-seller in North America, where she remains among the continent's most successful female vocalists.

Olivia's family emigrated in the early 1950s from Britain to Australia, where her father became Master of Ormond College. Her first taste of fame came in 1960 when she won a local contest as the girl who looked most like teenage film star Hayley Mills. Later, with three school friends, she formed The Sol Four, and after this vocal group disbanded, the urging of customers who heard her sing solo in a coffee bar led her to enter and win a TV talent show. Her prize was a trip to London where she sang briefly in a duo with Pat Carroll, and released her 1966 debut single, Jackie de Shannon's 'Till You Say You'll Be Mine'.

Staying on in England, Olivia was selected to join Toomorrow, a group manufactured by bubblegum mogul Don Kirshner to plug the hole in the market left by The Monkees (see separate entry). As well as a feature film of outer space persuasion and its soundtrack, Toomorrow was also responsible for an equally inglorious 1970 single, 'I Could Never Live Without Your Love', produced by Bruce Welch of The Shadows, with whom Olivia was romantically involved.

Although Toomorrow floundered, Newton-John's association with Cliff Richard and The Shadows (see separate entries) had a lasting, beneficial effect. Tours as guest star in *The Cliff Richard Show* and regular spots – as a comedienne as well as a singer – on TV's *It's Cliff!*, ensured healthy sales of her eponymous debut album, and the start of an erratic UK chart run with 1971's Top 10 cover of Bob Dylan's 'If Not For You'. That a person-able variety artist such as herself was record-ing songs composed by the likes of Dylan and George Harrison (see separate entries) ren-dered them palatable to an easy-listening audience otherwise turned off by post-Woodstock rock. More typical of her work were singles like 'Banks Of The Ohio', John Denver's 'Take Me Home Country Roads' and from the pen of the late John Rostill of The Shadows, 1973's 'Let Me Be There' which, triggered by a TV performance, won her a controversial Grammy for Best Female Country Vocal, and crossed from the US country charts to the Hot 100.

After an appearance in 1974's Eurovision Song Contest, Newton-John became omni-present in the US, initially as its top-selling country star, though her status as a pop chanteuse improved immensely after a US No. 1 with 'I Honestly Love You', produced by John Farrar, another latter-day Shadow (and husband of Pat Carroll), who had taken over the job after Bruce and Olivia broke off their engagement.

Like Emmylou Harris (see separate entry), Newton-John also became renowned for her duets with other artists. The resumption of her film career, in the *Grease* musical, pro-vided her and co-star John Travolta with 'You're The One That I Want', *the* hit song of 1978.

Less lucrative were a later movie with Travolta, *Two Of A Kind* in 1983, a single, 'After Dark', with the late Andy Gibb in 1980, and 'Now Voyager', a 1984 album with his brother Barry (see Bee Gees) but the title theme to her *Xanadu* movie, with the Electric

Light Orchestra (see separate entry), was another world-wide smash.

However patchy her output as an actress and despite lengthy gaps between her more recent record releases, Olivia Newton-John's US chart strikes continue, even if singles like 1981's 'Physical' and the 1986 album, 'Soul Kiss', portray her with less of her original perky ingenuity.

Greatest Hits

Singles	Title	US	UK
1974	*I Honestly Love You*	1	22
1975	*Have You Never Been Mellow?*	1	–
1978	*You're The One That I Want* (with John Travolta)	1	1
1978	*Summer Nights* (with John Travolta)	5	1
1980	*Xanadu* (with E.L.O.)	8	1
1980	*Magic*	1	32
1981	*Physical*	1	7

Albums			
1974	*If You Love Me, Let Me Know*	1	–
1975	*Have You Never Been Mellow?*	1	37
1978	*Grease* (with John Travolta and others)	1	1
1980	*Xanadu* (with E.L.O and others)	4	2

Harry **NILSSON**

Singer/songwriter Nilsson (born Harry Edward Nelson III, 1941) remains one of rock music's great enigmas, seemingly content to have fulfilled only a fraction of his full potential. Having moved to California with his parents as a child, during the early 1960s he worked as a computer specialist at the Security First National Bank in Van Nuys by night (where he was known as Harry Nelson), whilst by day he was building a parallel career as a budding songwriter using the name Nilsson, hawking his songs to producers, studios, labels etc. He recorded demos for various music publishers, and cut unsuccessful singles as Johnny Niles, some of which were later compiled after he had achieved some success. An early liaison with Phil Spector promised much, but the three songs Spector recorded with him remained unissued for over 10 years. However the Spector connection opened doors, and led to him having songs recorded by The Turtles, Rick Nelson, Lulu, Mary Hopkin, and Blood, Sweat & Tears. He eventually signed with a major label in 1967 after The Monkees had included his song, 'Cuddly Toy', on their 'Pisces, Aquarius, Capricorn And Jones Ltd.' album.

Nilsson's own debut album, 'Pandemonium Shadow Show' (1967) presented an intriguing blend of his idiosyncratic original material and contemporary covers, including a couple of Beatles tracks, 'You Can't Do That' (with new lyrics composed of Beatle song titles) and 'She's Leaving Home', which

Beatle boost hypes Harry's debut disc

prompted John Lennon to nominate Nilsson as his group's 'favourite American singer', thus giving his career a remarkable, unexpected lift. Several of the original songs attracted cover versions, notably '1941' (by Billy J Kramer) and 'Without Her' by both Jack Jones and Blood, Sweat & Tears.

His second album, 'Aerial Ballet' (1968) contained a cover version of Fred Neil's 'Everybody's Talking', which was a big hit single the following year due to its inclusion in the movie, *Midnight Cowboy*: it later won a Grammy. In 1969, Nilsson's career as an artist began to move, as 'I Guess The Lord Must Be In New York City' was a US Top 40 single, Three Dog Night's cover of 'One' (from 'Aerial Ballet') made the US Top 5, selling over a million units, and 'Harry' (which included 'The Puppy Song', later a worldwide hit for David Cassidy), became his US album chart debut.

Although he was predominantly a songwriter, 1970's 'Nilsson Sings Newman' was an album of songs by Randy Newman which, although critically well-received, did not sell. He had written the score for Otto Preminger's movie *Skidoo* (released 1969), and he wrote, narrated, and sang the songs in *The Point*, an animated TV movie, the soundtrack of which gave him his first US Top 30 album in 1971, and also yielded a US hit single, 'Me And My Arrow'. His major commercial breakthrough came in 1972 with the US Top 3/UK Top 5 album, 'Nilsson Schmilsson', his first gold (and ultimately platinum) record, which spawned two US Top 10 hits, 'Without You' (written by Badfinger's Pete Ham & Tom Evans), which topped both the US and UK charts, selling nearly two million copies (and eventually winning him a second Grammy), and 'Coconut', while a third single, 'Jump Into The Fire', reached the US Top 30. 1973's 'Son Of Schmilsson' album followed and rapidly provided him with another gold album and a further US Top 30 single, 'Spaceman'.

While on the verge of establishing himself as a major artist, he somewhat surprisingly emphatically failed to consolidate. 1973's 'A Little Touch Of Schmilsson In The Night' saw him take his alter-ego too far with an album of standards like 'Makin' Whoopee' and 'As Time Goes By' etc., with full orchestral backing, which may or may not have been a satirical exercise (and suggested that his voice had seen better days). It made the US Top 50 and UK Top 20, but seriously dented his rock credentials – in fact, it pioneered what other artists would also do 15 years later, although probably more by chance than design.

He spent much of the mid-1970s hanging out with drinking chums (he was John Lennon's constant companion during the latter's infamous 'lost weekend') as is reflected in his work: having supplied back-up vocals to Ringo Starr's million-selling 'You're Sixteen' in 1973, he appeared alongside Ringo in *Son Of Dracula*, a spoof horror musical from which 'Daybreak' became his last US Top 40 single, and the same year's 'Pussy Cats' (produced by Lennon), was his final US Top 100 album to date, although 1977's 'Knnillssonn' came close. He continued to release an album a year until his recording contract expired in 1978, since when he has released just two albums. Having spent the 1980s in apparent retirement, it will be interesting to see if he can pick up the threads again to a once promising career.

Greatest Hits

Singles	Title	US	UK
1969	*Everybody's Talkin'*	6	23
1972	*Without You*	1	1
1972	*Coconut*	8	42

Albums			
1971	*Nilsson Schmilsson*	3	4
1972	*Son Of Schmilsson*	12	41
1973	*A Little Touch Of Schmilsson In The Night*	46	20

NITTY GRITTY DIRT BAND

Jeff Hanna *(vocals, guitar)*
Jimmie Fadden *(drums, vocals, harmonica)*
John McEuen *(banjo, guitar, vocals)*
Les Thompson *(bass, guitar, vocals)*
Bruce Kunkel *(guitar, bass, vocals)*
Ralph Barr *(guitar, vocals)*

Launched in 1966 The Nitty Gritty Dirt Band has released well over 20 original albums plus almost as many compilations, and while never really achieving superstardom, has enjoyed critical acclaim as a jug band, a folk/rock band, a country/rock band and most recently as country music chart stars in the US.

Formed in LA, the group's initial launch

Gettin' down to the Nitty Gritty, the Dirt Band relax backstage

was as a jug band, when an early member was Jackson Browne, who contributed the song 'Holding' to their 1967 eponymous debut album before leaving soon afterwards, and being replaced by McEuen. A track from that album, 'Buy For Me The Rain', made the US Top 50, and the album briefly charted in the US, but three years elapsed before further US chart activity. During that time, the group released several further albums: 'Ricochet' (1967, including two more Jackson Browne songs), 'Rare Junk' and 'Alive' – a live album (both 1968, by which time Kunkel had been replaced by singer/guitarist Chris Darrow). The band shared a house in Hollywood with Duane & Gregg Allman, comedian Steve Martin and the manager of all of them, William E. McEuen (John McEuen's brother). A substantial live attraction at this time with their music metamorphosing from jug band to folk/rock, the group co-headlined a concert with The Doors and played Carnegie Hall, also making a cameo appearance in the movie, *Paint Your Wagon* (starring Clint Eastwood and Lee Marvin – The Dirt Band backed the latter on 'Hand Me Down That Can O' Beans'.)

In late 1968, Darrow and Barr left the band, which recruited Jimmy Ibbotson (guitar, bass, vocals), and the band moved *en masse* to Colorado, returning to the US chart with 1970's superb 'Uncle Charlie & His Dog Teddy', a classic country/rock album which included 'House At Pooh Corner' (written by

Kenny Loggins), 'Some Of Shelley's Blues' (written by Michael Nesmith) and Jerry Jeff Walker's 'Mr Bojangles', all of which were US hit singles, the last their biggest US single to date, while the album spent over six months in the US chart. 1971's 'All The Good Times' was virtually a second volume of 'Uncle Charlie', but despite a hit single with 'Jambalaya', was a much smaller album commercially.

1972 produced the legendary 'Will The Circle Be Unbroken', a momentous triple album featuring many country music notables, including Earl Scruggs, Doc Watson, Roy Acuff, Merle Travis and Vassar Clements, which deservedly went platinum. By 1972's 'Stars And Stripes Forever' (a double album), Thompson had left the band, but this virtually re-recorded 'Best Of' became the group's first US Top 30 album, while 1975's 'Dream', which included a US hit single, 'All I Have To Do Is Dream', also made the US Top 100. The multi-instrumental talents of each of the group members resulted in them actually playing a bluegrass festival the day before opening for Aerosmith! In 1975, Ibbotson left the band, and another triple album, 'Dirt, Silver And Gold', was released in 1976, making the US Top 100, with Hanna, McEuen and Fadden being joined by singer/guitarist John Cable, bass player Jackie Clark and (briefly) Michael Buono. The group had become known for the unbelievably lavish packaging of their albums, from 'Uncle Charlie' onwards, but despite being

among the most successful ever in artistic terms, the band's albums were not selling as well as they deserved, although their admirable qualities were better recognized outside the US, as evidenced by the fact that they were selected by the Soviet Government as the first US band to tour the USSR, where they played for a month, including a televised concert watched by an estimated 145 million people (almost a decade before Live Aid).

The new recruits left the band soon after, and were replaced by Al Garth (saxophone, violin) and Merel Bregante (drums, vocals), both ex-Loggins & Messina, Richard Hathaway (bass) and Bob Carpenter (keyboards) for 'Wild Nights' (1978, reissued as 'The Dirt Band', after a decision was made to abbreviate the goup name to reflect a change in musical direction) and 1979's 'An American Dream', a considerably superior album which restored them to the US Top 100 and included a US Top 20 single in the Rodney Crowell-penned title track, on which Linda Ronstadt guested. By 1980, Bregante had left the band (although Fadden did not immediately return to the drums, working as a harmonica player), and that year's 'Make A Little Magic' album, which included a US Top 30 single in the title track (with guest vocals from Nicolette Larson), charted higher in the US than any of the group's albums since 'Stars And Stripes Forever', while an excellent compilation album, 'Gold From Dirt', was also released in the UK in 1980.

1981's 'Jealousy' album failed to make the US Top 100, and Garth, Hathaway and two other musicians who briefly joined all departed soon afterwards, upon which Ibbotson rejoined in 1982, virtually coinciding with the group changing management from William McEuen (who had certainly masterminded many of the group's most celebrated projects, including the 'Circle' album) to a company more attuned to the country music market. The group also reverted to its original name for 1983's 'Let's Go' album, which included a US country chart Top 10 single, 'Dance Little Jean'.

The group then entered a period of relative stability, with a line-up of Hanna, McEuen, Fadden, Ibbotson and Carpenter, and changed labels after over 15 years with the same company. 1984's 'Plain Dirt Fashion' album included a US country chart-topper, 'Long Hard Road (Sharecropper's Dream)', which was the group's first No. 1 record, plus two more US country Top 3 singles, and it became clear that they regarded Nashville as the centre of their musical universe, although John McEuen seemed less involved than in earlier albums. 1985's 'Partners, Brothers & Friends' also included three US country Top 10 singles, notably the chart-topping 'Modern Day Romance' while 1986's compilation, 'Twenty Years Of Dirt' actually featured only two tracks recorded before 1979, and largely ignored early glories.

At the end of that year, John McEuen finally left the band – his apparent boredom with the comparatively minor role he had been forced to assume (effectively since his brother had stopped managing the band), together with constant battles with Hanna, who was generally regarded as the group's leader, led him to opt for a solo career which has taken him further from the public eye (and the chart), but has apparently helped him regain his enjoyment at making music. 1987's 'Hold On' album was made by the remaining quartet, and again included three US country chart Top 10 singles, one of which, 'Fishin' In The Dark', topped that chart. In 1987/88, a replacement was recruited in the shape of ex-Flying Burrito Brother/Eagles founder Bernie Leadon, who played on 1988's 'Workin' Band' album, which again spawned three US country chart Top 10 singles, although Leadon had left the band by the time the album was released.

1989 saw another change of label, resulting in another retrospective, 'More Great Dirt', from the old label, while the group were the first act signed to Jimmy Bowen's short-lived Universal label. Their only release on that label was the Grammy Award-winning 'Will The Circle Be Unbroken Volume Two', a mainly successful attempt to repeat the huge success of the 1972 triple album (which had grown considerably in stature in the interim), but this time with more contemporary country artists, including Leadon, McEuen, Chet Atkins, Johnny Cash, John Denver, Emmy-

lou Harris, John Hiatt, Bruce Hornsby, Byrds founders Roger McGuinn and Chris Hillman, New Grass Revival, John Prine and Ricky Skaggs, plus many others. This was a huge success, although it inevitably lacked the spontaneity of what became known as 'Circle Volume One', which by this time had entranced a fresh generation of followers after being reissued on CD. 'Circle Two' was even the subject of a video, *The Making Of The Circle Volume Two*, and restored the band to the US pop chart, from which they had been absent for most of the decade.

In 1990 The Nitty Gritty Dirt Band decided to continue as a quartet of Hanna, Fadden, Ibbotson and Carpenter, using session musicians to enhance recordings. The first album of the new decade was 'The Rest Of The Dream', which was somewhat less successful than any of their albums since 1983's 'Let's Go'. Many will be interested to see which musical direction will next be taken by the band in the wake of their 25th Anniversary in 1991.

Greatest Hits

Singles	Title	US	UK
1970	*Mr Bojangles*	9	–
1979	*An American Dream* (with Linda Ronstadt)	13	
Albums			
1970	*Uncle Charlie And His Dog Teddy*	66	–
1972	*Will The Circle Be Unbroken*	68	–
1974	*Stars And Stripes Forever*	28	–
1989	*Will The Circle Be Unbroken Volume Two*	95	–

Ted **NUGENT** / The **AMBOY DUKES**

Ted Nugent (guitar)
Steve Farmer (guitar)
Bill White (bass)
Rick Lober (keyboards)
David Palmer (drums)
John Drake (vocals)

A pioneer of pre-metal heavy rock, Detroit's Ted Nugent (born 1948) spent his early teens in local band, Lourdes, before moving to Chicago where he formed archetypal garage band The Amboy Dukes in 1965, playing 'heavy psychedelic' rock which garnered a strong local following. A 1967 debut single, a cover of R&B standard 'Baby Please Don't Go', sold well locally, as did an eponymous album the same year. Their second album in 1968, 'Journey To The Centre Of The Mind', was with Andy Solomon and Greg Arama in place of Lober and White; the title-track single made the US Top 20, the album went Top 100, but the follow-up album, 'Migration', was a poor seller.

Increasing emphasis on Nugent's extravagant guitar style marked a label change for the 1969 'Marriage On The Rocks/Rock Bottom' album and more personnel changes produced a quartet billed as Ted Nugent & The Amboy Dukes. A further move towards solo status and another label change came in 1974, as, now named Ted Nugent's Amboy Dukes, they released two albums 'Call Of The Wild' and 'Tooth Fang And Claw'. Neither album charted, but they did succeed in highlighting Nugent's image as an all-American huntin' and shootin' 'New Frontiersman', a strong supporter of the gun lobby and a clean-living family man who was inclined to fire musicians or roadies at the slightest sniff of drug use.

Yet another label shift in 1975 saw the group name disappear altogether, and Nugent embarked on a hefty touring schedule, building a live following which ensured the record success which had previously eluded him. 1976 saw his second US Top 100 single, 'Hey Baby', taken from his eponymous album, which reached the US Top 30 and went gold after over a year in the US chart. It also broke into the UK album chart while 'Free For All' (1976) (with some vocals by Meatloaf) made the US Top 30 and UK Top 40, and gave him his first platinum album.

1977's 'Cat Scratch Fever' reached the US Top 20 and UK Top 30, and by 1978 he was in the front line of mega-grossing metal stars; his 'Double Live Gonzo' was his third platinum album, a quarter of a million fans saw him with Aerosmith, Santana and others at the second California Jam festival, and 'Weekend Warriors' became his fourth platinum album, making the US Top 30.

As punk and metal polarized fans and bands in the early 1980s, Nugent became established in the pantheon of the latter, with the US Top 20 albums 'State of Shock' (1979) and 'Scream Dream' (1980) going gold, before a label change heralded a new touring band including pedigree drummer Carmine Appice. However, the 1982 album 'Nugent' failed to make the US Top 50. Despite similar chart performances for 1984's 'Penetrator', and 'Little Miss Dangerous' (1986), a 1985 part in TV's *Miami Vice*, and participation in the 1986 HM charity project, Hear'n'Aid confirmed that Nugent is still regarded as part of the mainstream establishment of heavy rock, 1988's 'If You Can't Lick 'Em . . . Lick 'Em' confirming that status.

Greatest Hits

Singles	Title	US	UK
1968	*Journey To The Centre Of The Mind* (Amboy Dukes)	16	–
1977	*Cat Scratch Fever*	30	–
Albums			
1977	*Cat Scratch Fever*	17	28
1978	*Double Live Gonzo*	13	47
1980	*Scream Dream*	13	37

Billy OCEAN

Born Leslie Sebastian Charles in Trinidad, West Indies in 1950, Ocean moved to London as a child with his family. In the early 1970s this talented singer/songwriter was in the groups Shades Of Midnight, Dry Ice and The Go before releasing his first record in 1974 under the name Scorched Earth.

In 1975 Ocean's second release as Billy Ocean, 'Love Really Hurts Without You' made the UK No. 3 and US Top 40. UK hits continued with Motown-influenced records like 'L.O.D.', 'Stop Me' and the 1977 UK Top 3 hit, 'Red Light Spells Danger'.

After four quiet years, 'Nights' was a US Top 10 black music hit and he was voted most promising new R&B artist, but it was not until 1984 that the big hits returned the first being the million selling 'Caribbean Queen' (previously released unsuccessfully as 'European Queen') which earned him a Grammy and helped make his fifth album 'Suddenly' a transatlantic Top 10 hit and a two million seller in the US. In 1985 Ocean appeared in Live Aid and his US Top 5 hit singles run continued with 'Loverboy' and 'Suddenly'. A year later he had his first UK No. 1 'When The Going Gets Tough, The Tough Get Going' and his second US chart-topper, 'There'll Be Sad Songs', both from his double platinum album 'Love Zone'.

His 1988 album, 'Tear Down The Walls', made the UK Top 5 and sold a million in the US. It included another US No. 1 single, 'Get Outta My Dreams Get Into My Car'.

Ocean – transatlantic triumph

Ocean, who is the most successful soul singer from the West Indies, also hit gold in 1989 with his 'Greatest Hits' album which was another UK Top 5 item.

Greatest Hits

Singles	Title	US	UK
1984	Caribbean Queen		
	(No More Love On The Run)	1	6
1986	When The Going Gets Tough	2	1
1986	There'll Be Sad Songs		
	(To Make You Cry)	1	12
1988	Get Outta My Dreams		
	Get Into My Car	1	3
Albums			
1986	Love Zone	6	2

Phil OCHS

Beginning in the 1960s with a flood of melodic but passionate protest anthems like 'There But For Fortune' and 'I Ain't Marchin' Anymore', Ochs' career lost direction in the 1970s ending in his suicide.

Born in 1940, Ochs briefly trained at a military academy before becoming a journalism student in Ohio. There he formed a folk duo with Jim Glover (later of Jim & Jean) and wrote his 'Ballad Of The Cuban Invasion', which attacked the attempt to overthrow Fidel Castro by Cuban exiles from Miami.

In 1961, Ochs moved to New York joining Bob Dylan, Tom Paxton and others in the group of topical songwriters associated with *Broadside* magazine. As he made a name for himself singing in Greenwich Village clubs, his first recordings appeared on *Broadside* compilation albums. In 1964, he was signed by Jac Holzman to top folk label Elektra, releasing 'All The News That's Fit To Sing'. Along with songs about the Vietnam war and unemployment was a setting of Edgar Allen Poe's poem, 'The Bells'.

Now a leading figure in the folk revival, Ochs recorded 'I Ain't Marchin' Anymore' (1965), with its bitter attack on racial discrimination 'Here's To The State Of Mississippi'. The next year Elektra issued a live album which included 'There But For Fortune', which was a hit for Joan Baez in the UK.

Dissatisfied with his poor record sales and, like Dylan, keen to expand his musical range, Ochs then moved to a more rock-oriented label. 'Pleasures Of The Harbour' contained longer, lushly poetic numbers with arrangements to match by producer Larry Marks. But it also had the jaunty but sarcastic 'Outside Of A Small Circle Of Friends', a turntable hit in the US.

'Tape From California' (where he now lived) was in a similar vein to 'Pleasures' but the introspective 'Rehearsals For Retirement' introduced a more rock-based sound. This was intensified on the ironically-titled

'Greatest Hits' (1970), featuring the bitter 'Chords Of Fame', and on 'Gunfight At Carnegie Hall' (1971). This live album contained mostly rock'n'roll classics, exemplifying Ochs's new political view that 'what America needs is for Elvis Presley to become Che Guevara'.

During the next five years, Ochs recorded only three singles and toured and performed intermittently. He was increasingly mentally unstable and in 1976 he committed suicide at his sister's house in New York. A memorial double album, 'Chords Of Fame', was released after his death, and is the best place for the inquisitive to begin a study of Ochs, as his commercial success was almost non-existent.

Greatest Hits

Albums	Title	US	UK
1966	Phil Ochs In Concert	149	–

Sinead O'CONNOR

Dublin-born singer whose uncompromising appearance and music brought her to a cult audience before a huge hit single penned by Prince brought a slightly less confrontational O'Connor (born 1966) to world renown. She shaved her head when a record company asked her to be 'more girly'. Early collaborations included work with U2: she sang on the soundtrack of 'The Hostage', scored by U2 guitarist The Edge, and also sang with In Tua Nua, but quit before they recorded, then with Ton Ton Macoute. She wrote her first LP at age 16, at that time likening herself to Kate Bush and Madonna.

Moving to London, her first album 'The Lion And The Cobra' made waves but she dismissed her band (including ex-Stiff Little Finger Ali McMordie). The Smiths rhythm section of Andy Rourke and Mike Joyce played on her first UK tour.

The single, 'Mandinka' (about the Gambian tribe from which *Roots* subject, Kunta Kinte, came) reached the UK Top 20 in 1988 and marked her out as a talent to watch. The album went platinum in Canada and Holland and gold in the UK, Eire and the US, where it was nominated for a Grammy in 1989.

1990's 'I Do Not Want What I Haven't Got' album mixed attacks against politicians and policemen ('Black Boys On Mopeds') with Irish roots – 'I Am Stretched On Your Grace' combined a traditional song with a beatbox to surprising effect. The single, 'Nothing Compares 2 U', a Prince cover, helped by a video in which she cried 'real tears' giving the appealing image of androgyny and vulnerability, reached No. 1 in 19 countries. O'Connor retracted her well-publicized support for the IRA 'once I started to get more involved in my spiritual beliefs', a move that obviously increased her record-selling

Sinead's street cred soars as Sinatra snaps over 'Star Spangled Banner'

potential but dented the hard-nut image. Conversely, in 1990, she refused to play in front of 9,000 at a New Jersey concert hall unless the traditional US national anthem was dropped, a move that still did not prevent her being voted 'Artist of the Year' by readers of *Rolling Stone* in 1991. Frank Sinatra reportedly wanted to 'kick her ass'. She guested on the live version of Roger Waters's 'The Wall' in Berlin in 1990.

A mother, she is married to drummer John Reynolds who plays in her band. Despite a rough ride from the press, O'Connor has achieved far more than her uncompromising early work suggested. (NME called her 'the Johnny Rotten of the Eighties'.) 'I don't really regret anything I've done,' she says. 'I just want to make records . . . and don't want to feel I have to explain myself.'

Greatest Hits

Singles	Title	US	UK
1988	*Mandinka*	–	17
1990	*Nothing Compares 2 U*	1	1
Albums			
1988	*The Lion And The Cobra*	–	27
1990	*I Do Not Want What*		
	I Haven't Got	1	1

Mike **OLDFIELD**

With Pink Floyd's 'Dark Side Of The Moon', Mike Oldfield's 'Tubular Bells' was one of the most ubiquitous albums of the 1970s, introducing a new style of progressive rock and spending five years in the UK charts while selling ten million copies world-wide. It was the album that launched Virgin Records in 1973 and virtually funded the label until the 1980s although Oldfield himself remained a reclusive figure who gave no interviews and performed his *meisterwerk* live just twice. Oldfield (born 1953) formed his first group in 1968 with his sister Sally. Called Sallyangie, they cut an album, 'Children Of The Sun', which received little attention, and they disbanded.

In 1970 Oldfield joined Kevin Ayers & The Whole World as guitarist, playing on the 'Shooting At the Moon' album in 1970. During this period, he conceived the idea for 'Tubular Bells', a collage of rock, folk and classical melodies, encouraged by fellow band member David Bedford who was already establishing a reputation as an avant-garde classical composer. Oldfield made a demo tape during 1971 which impressed Richard Branson, who was keen to start his own label after founding the Virgin record retail chain, but Branson wasn't ready and suggested Oldfield approach other record companies.

A year later, when Branson was preparing to launch Virgin Records, Oldfield still had no deal, and became the first act on the new label. He started recording 'Tubular Bells' in 1972 using Virgin's Manor Studio when it was not booked by paying customers over a six-month period, playing most of the instruments himself, while Vivian Stanshall of The Bonzo Dog Doo Dah Band played the part of Master Of Ceremonies. The 49-minute opus was released in 1973 and received unanimous critical acclaim. After a London concert featuring Oldfield, Bedford, Ayers and Rolling Stone Mick Taylor, sales took off and it eventually topped the UK charts and reached the US Top 3, earning Oldfield a Grammy, and becoming the second-biggest selling album of the decade (after a Simon & Garfunkel epic).

In 1974 an extract was used as the theme for the celebrated movie, *The Exorcist*, which made the US Top 10 as a single. Later in 1974 Oldfield released the similarly constructed but more sophisticated 'Hergest Ridge' album (inspired by a part of Herefordshire), which entered the UK album chart at the top, but only briefly made the US Top 100, although an orchestral version of 'Tubular Bells', conducted by David Bedford, made the UK Top 20 in 1975. Oldfield's 1975 double album, 'Ommadawn', incorporated Celtic and African elements and reached the UK Top 5, while a boxed set of four albums, 'Boxed', narrowly missed the UK Top 20. Oldfield also scored UK Top 5 singles in 1976 with the Christmas carol, 'In Dulce Jubilo', backed by 'On Horseback', and a 1977 version of the traditional hornpipe, 'Portsmouth'. Another double album, Incantations', made the UK Top 20 in 1978 and included a disco single, 'Guilty', which made the UK Top 20 in 1979. Oldfield finally decided to tour (backed by a 50-piece group) and the subsequent live double album, 'Exposed', was another UK Top 20 success in 1979.

His next two albums, 'Platinum' (1979) and 'QE2' (1980, with a guest spot from Phil Collins), were lighter in tone and both made the UK Top 30, but there was no sign of a further US breakthrough – although Hall & Oates had a Top 10 hit in 1983 with Oldfield's 'Family Man'. Oldfield became only the second rock musician to get an entry in the UK's prestigious *Who's Who* in 1981 (following Paul McCartney) and he was given the Freedom of the City of London the same year after composing music to celebrate the wedding of Prince Charles and Lady Diana Spencer. He was also back in the UK Top 10 in 1982 with his 'Five Miles Out' album and in 1983 with 'Crises', featuring vocalist Maggie Reilly on the UK Top 5 single, 'Moonlight Shadow'. 1984's 'Discovery' album kept him in the UK Top 20 and after composing the soundtrack to the movie, *The Killing Fields*, later that year, Oldfield embarked on an expensive and time-consuming 'video album' project, 'Wind Chimes', released in 1986. Later albums have yet to approach the success of 'Tubular Bells'; 'Islands' (1987), with an appearance from Bonnie Tyler, 'Earth Moving' (1989) and 'Amarok' in 1990 while early 1991 saw the release of 'Heavens Open'.

Greatest Hits

Singles	Title	US	UK
1975	*In Dulce Jubilo/On Horseback*	–	4
1976	*Portsmouth*	–	3
Albums			
1973	*Tubular Bells*	3	1
1974	*Hergest Ridge*	87	1

Mike's 'Bells ring in boom for Branson

Alexander O'NEAL

This soulful vocalist (born 1953) became a founder member of Minneapolis group Flyte Time (who later became Time), which also included the future production/writing team of Jimmy Jam and Terry Lewis. The group became Prince's backing band and shortly afterwards O'Neal left to form a less successful rival group.

In 1984 he joined with his old associates Jam and Lewis, and the duo produced, wrote and played on O'Neal's eponymous debut LP. Despite the fact that the album included three US black music Top 20 hits it only just made the US Top 100, but it reached the UK Top 20 in 1985. Later that year, O'Neal had his first UK Top 20 single with 'Saturday Love', a duet with his label-mate Cherrelle.

1986 saw his first solo Top 20 hit with 'If You Were Here Tonight' and a year later, after overcoming a drug problem, his classic 'Hearsay' album was released. A Jam & Lewis production, it made the UK Top 5, selling over half a million and over a million in the US. The album included eight UK chart singles, five of them making the Top 30. The album also contained 'Fake', which charted twice in the UK and topped the US black music and 12-inch singles charts.

At the end of 1988 O'Neal's seasonal album, 'My Gift To You', joined the remixed version of his 'Hearsay' album, titled 'All Mixed Up' in the UK charts.

Greatest Hits

Singles	Title	US	UK
1985	*Saturday Love* (with Cherrelle)	26	6
1987	*Criticize*	74	4
Albums			
1985	*Alexander O'Neal*	91	19
1987	*Hearsay*	29	4

Yoko ONO

With a well-to-do Japanese background, visual artist Ono (born 1933) moved to New York in 1953, working on the fringes of the avant-garde art scene. In the mid-1960s, at a time when New York painters led by Alan Kaprow were experimenting with 'happenings' (a move towards 'performance' works), Ono soon emerged with conceptual pieces in exhibitions around the lofts and galleries of Greenwich Village, involving sculpture, film and poetry. Under the auspices of first husband, art hustler Anthony Cox, she toured the UK with performance pieces and had a daughter Kyoko by Cox – the child was later featured in a Plastic Ono Band songtitle – and in 1966 an exhibition of her artworks opened at London's Indica Gallery, where she met John Lennon. His subsequent involvement with Ono was the catalyst in his

Ono, Yoko sings again

eventual estrangement from both his wife, Cynthia, and The Beatles, though Yoko was clearly not solely instrumental in the latter, which would have happened anyway.

Although her free-form participation in subsequent Lennon projects was musically dubious, Ono was credited with introducing the ex-Beatle, whom she married in 1969, to electronic music, (as on the albums 'Two Virgins' and 'Life With The Lions'), free improvisation and abstract concepts that produced – at its best – songs like 'Imagine'. Alongside her much-publicized activities with Lennon – the Peace Bed-In, New York left-wing protests and so on – she began making records under her own name, starting with the 1970 album, 'Yoko Ono/Plastic Ono Band', of which 'Approximately Infinite Universe' (1973) marked a move to a more disciplined style.

After his years of self-imposed retirement following the birth of their son, Sean, in 1975, Lennon's re-emergence in 1980 with the album, 'Double Fantasy', was a collection of tracks alternating democratically between himself and Yoko as vocalist, an approach originally heard on Lennon's 1972 album, 'Some Time In New York City'. His murder soon after the album's release blurred any objective view for some time, but Ono's efforts sit more comfortably with those of her husband than they usually did in their earlier collaborations. Since Lennon's assassination, she has identified herself with his legacy, legally, artistically and financially. She supervised the release of the follow-up tracks to 'Fantasy', in 1982's 'Milk and Honey' album, and the 1986 album of Lennon out-takes 'Menlove Avenue', and has continued to release her own albums sporadically.

Greatest Hits

Singles	Title	US	UK
1981	*Walking On Thin Ice*	58	35
Albums			
1981	*Season Of Glass*	49	47

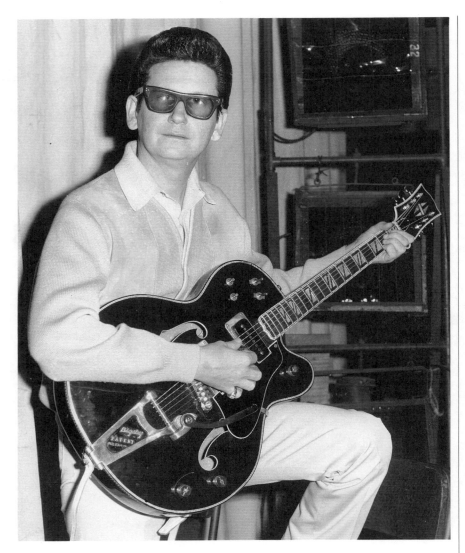

It's over for the O as Roy returns to the chart for the last time

Roy **ORBISON**

uring the last concerts before his sudden death in December 1988, Roy Orbison's latest single, 'You Got It', was received as ecstatically as any of his 1960s hits – familiar though they were through years of airplay and compilation albums. 'The Big O' was back in favour. An unlikely-looking pop star, Orbison's saturnine image, stylistic consistency and almost operatic vocal control were immune to changing musical fashion.

Orbison (born 1936) was taught guitar by his father, from whom he inherited his powerful baritone voice. A 'featured popular vocalist' on regional commercial radio, Roy led his high school band, the Wink Westerners, who changed both their repertoire and name with the advent of rock'n'roll.

As the Teen Kings, the outfit amassed a strong local reputation, and cut a single, 'Ooby Dooby', under the supervision of Buddy Holly producer Norman Petty. When Sam Phillips invited the group to his Sun Studios in Memphis to re-record 'Ooby Dooby', it reached the US Top 100 (1956). Phillips compelled Orbison to record rockabilly material despite the Texan's preference for self-written ballads.

Orbison considered leaving the music business, but in the same month in 1958, both The Everly Brothers and Jerry Lee Lewis notched up Top 10 hits using Orbison compositions as B-sides. Consequently, he was contracted as a house songwriter to Acuff-Rose, the Nashville music publishing and management concern, where he remained for nearly a year, recording a couple of innocuous singles.

On transferring to an independent label in 1959, Orbison's 'Uptown' crept into the US Top 100 but its follow-up, 'Only The Lonely', was a world-wide smash. Many subsequent singles were of the same melancholy persuasion, establishing Orbison's image as a purveyor of woe. This typecasting was fully justified when the rush-released 'Running Scared' topped the US charts in 1961. Almost

as big were the lachrymose 'Cryin'' and 'Dream-Baby', an upbeat non-original.

After parting from co-writer Joe Melson, Orbison's chart career sagged until 1963's 'In Dreams' restored him to the US Top 10 – climbing higher in Britain where he came to command the most devoted following of any American pop star bar Elvis Presley even when the hits petered out after two consecutive No. 1s in 1964 (composed with new collaborator, Bill Dees). Fans also overlooked his starring role in 1967's *The Fastest Guitar Alive*, a vapid musical feature film.

After Orbison's first wife and two sons died in separate accidents in the mid-1960s, he plunged into a relentless round of world-wide touring mostly in venues where it made more sense for him to plug his old hits rather than his latest records, though these continued to sell just enough to make them a worthwhile exercise. He dabbled with various musical forms such as psychedelia in 'Southbound Jericho Parkway', country on a US-only Hank Williams tribute album and, disco on 'Hung Up On You' (1975).

By the mid-70s, he had moved into country-rock, exemplified by 1977's 'Regeneration' album which included songs by Kris Kristofferson and Tony Joe White, which was well received though flawed. A flush of hit covers of earlier Orbison recordings – among them Don McLean's UK No. 1, 'Cryin'', meant that the time was ripe for a possible chart comeback, but the moment was lost following Orbison's heart operation in 1978.

1979's 'Laminar Flow' was characterized by forgettable songs and bland production, but the following year, 'That Lovin' You Feelin' Again', a duet with Emmylou Harris, earned Orbison a Grammy award and a tour of California with The Eagles.

Although he rested on past laurels for most of the 80s, 1985's 'Wild Hearts' was his strongest single in years, taken from the soundtrack of the Nicolas Roeg movie *Insignificance*. At the instigation of another film director, David Lynch, Orbison re-recorded an album's worth of his old hits including a version of 'In Dreams' produced by T-Bone Burnett. In 1987 Bruce Springsteen, Elvis Costello, Jackson Browne and Bonnie Raitt were among the stars gathered by Burnett to accompany Orbison in a filmed concert in Los Angeles. During this spectacular, he unveiled items such as Costello's 'The Comedians' which would appear on 'Mystery Girl', the album that turned out to be Orbison's epitaph.

It was co-produced by Jeff Lynne whose prior commitment to a George Harrison album led Roy to join the two Englishmen's Traveling Wilburys 'supergroup' with Tom Petty and Bob Dylan.

Through this liaison and 'You Got It' from 'Mystery Girl', Orbison returned to the charts and attracted a new audience young enough not to have heard of his past. With Dylan and

Springsteen as certain donors of songs for his next album, it seemed that his best records lay in the future. Indeed, when the post-humous 'Mystery Girl' was issued in 1989, many ranked it with his most enduring work – and everything suggests that, had he lived, the Big O's time would have come yet again.

Greatest Hits

Singles	Title	US	UK
1960	Only The Lonely	2	1
1961	Running Scared	1	9
1964	It's Over	9	1
1964	Oh! Pretty Woman	1	1
Albums			
1975	The Best Of Roy Orbison	–	1
1988	The Legendary Roy Orbison	–	1
1989	Mystery Girl	5	2

Ozzy OSBOURNE

Ozzy (born John Osbourne, 1948) has long held a reputation as the archetypal crazy man of heavy rock – a genre which can lay claim to more than its share of larger-than-life eccentrics. Osbourne's legend is attributable to a few genuinely outrageous incidents and careful image creation, but beneath the hype he is also a model hard rock vocalist with a gift for showmanship.

Having first made his name as vocalist with Black Sabbath during the 1970s, Osbourne left, rejoined and then parted for good from the band in 1978, his departure mainly due to continual arguments with guitarist Tony Iommi. The following year, he recruited three musicians from established heavy metal backgrounds: guitarist Randy Rhoads (ex-Quiet Riot), bassist Bob Daisley (ex-Rainbow), and drummer Lee Kerslake (ex-Uriah Heep), to form Blizzard of Ozz. They recorded an album, and in mid-1980, this got them a deal with Jet Records, owned by Sabbath's former manager, Don Arden. Supported by a UK tour, the album, 'Ozzy Osbourne's Blizzard Of Ozz', made the UK Top 10 and spun off a couple of minor hit singles – Osbourne, like many top heavy metal names, has rarely featured strongly in the singles charts, selling vastly greater quantities of albums.

In 1981, the album also made the US Top 30, and the group toured the US to promote it, with bassist Rudy Sarzo and drummer Tommy Aldridge replacing Daisley and Kerslake, who had both left to join Uriah Heep. In mid-tour, at a record company gathering in Los Angeles, Osbourne caused calculated uproar (and huge publicity) by biting off the head of a supposedly live dove. Back on the road, however, the incident rebounded on him: a fan threw a bat onstage, and Ozzy, believing it to be a rubber model, snatched it to repeat the decapitation trick.

Unfortunately, the bat was real, angry and bit back, and Osbourne had to undergo a series of precautionary anti-rabies injections. His legend, however, was now off and running.

After a second successful album, 'Diary Of A Madman', Blizzard Of Ozz expanded with the addition of Don Airey (ex-Rainbow) on keyboards. Disaster struck, however, soon after the start of a second US tour, when Rhoads was killed in a plane crash witnessed by the rest of the band – the aircraft he was aboard went out of control while 'buzzing' the tour bus.

Osbourne brought in guitarist Brad Gillis for, 'Talk Of The Devil', a double set of old Black Sabbath material issued partly to foil a live Sabbath album of similar repertoire sung by Ronnie Dio. Jake E. Lee then became the band's full-time guitarist.

In mid-1982, Osbourne confounded those who thought him the devil incarnate by marrying his personal manager, Sharon Arden (daughter of Don). They became a formidable partnership, taking Osbourne from Arden senior's control and from his label, to sign a new deal in 1983. This produced the album and hit single, 'Bark At The Moon', for which Osbourne assumed a werewolf image. His wife also persuaded him to enter the Betty Ford Clinic in an attempt to conquer his heavy drinking habit.

Ozzy – bat bites back at Blizzard boss

Osbourne had a one-off reunion with the other original members of Black Sabbath in 1985 for the Philadelphia Live Aid concert, but otherwise continued to tour with Blizzard Of Ozz, now with a largely new line-up including bassist Phil Soussan and drummer Randy Castillo, which recorded the 1986 album, 'The Ultimate Sin', Osbourne's biggest US and UK chart success. However, it was almost equalled by 1987's 'Tribute', a compilation of 1981 live recordings dedicated to, and featuring, Randy Rhoads.

A conservative backlash to his perceived image continued to plague Osbourne, particularly in the US, where a lawsuit (thrown out of California Supreme Court) tried to claim that a teenage boy's suicide was inspired by Osbourne's song, 'Suicide Solution'. Osbourne learned to live with regular fundamentalist denunciations, but he did serve tongue-in-cheek revenge on his detractors via a role in the heavy metal horror movie, *Trick Or Treat*, in which he actually played an over-the-top anti-rock preacher.

As the 1980s closed, Osbourne was maintaining a lower public profile and spending more time off the road in the UK with his wife and small children, but he still came up with hit albums: 'No Rest For The Wicked' (presumably an ironic title), which was a UK Top 30 success in 1989.

Greatest Hits

Singles	Title	US	UK
1986	*Shot In The Dark*	68	20
Albums			
1986	*The Ultimate Sin*	6	8
1987	*Tribute*	6	13

The **OSMONDS**

Alan Osmond
Wayne Osmond
Merrill Osmond
Jay Osmond
Donny Osmond
Jimmy Osmond
Marie Osmond (*Vocal group*)

Singing at the family Mormon Church in Utah, the original quartet of brothers Alan (born 1949), Wayne (born 1951), Merrill (1953) and Jay (1955) formed while still young children as The Osmond Brothers, a barber shop style harmony group. They were discovered during a 1962 visit to Disneyland in Los Angeles, and through a Disney talent show landed a spot on the NBC-TV *Andy Williams Show*. The residency lasted five years; after the first, they were joined by six-year-old Donny (born 1957), and when the show finished, they moved to *The Jerry Lewis Show* for a couple of years during which time they made a recording debut on Andy Williams's label, Barnaby, with no chart success.

With their name shortened to The Osmonds, they signed with a major label in 1971. The company saw them as another Jackson Five, and their first single 'One Bad Apple' topped the US chart, selling over a million. The debut album 'Osmonds' went gold in the US Top 20.

Osmondmania began with a vengeance almost immediately. Seeing 13-year-old Donny as the teenybopper favourite, he was recorded solo on 'Sweet And Innocent' which made the US Top 10. More family hits ensued, while Donny's first solo album, 'The Donny Osmond Album', went gold in the US Top 20. He went on to top the US singles chart with the Goffin and King song, 'Go Away Little Girl', his second million seller, while the group went gold with 'Yo Yo' and a second Donny album, 'To You With Love', also sold gold – all in the latter half of 1971.

Donny's third gold single came early in 1972, while the group's 'Down By The Lazy River' (written by Merrill and Alan) went US Top 5, with an album, 'Phase Three', also charting. 'Lazy River' marked the group's UK chart debut, and Donny's 'Puppy Love' hit the US Top 3 and topped the UK chart as his 'Portrait Of Donny' album made the US and UK Top 10.

As if this was not enough, 1972 saw the debut of Little Jimmy Osmond (born 1963)

A family affair – Marie poses with the Brothers grin

with the US Top 40 novelty hit, 'Long Haired Lover From Liverpool'. Meanwhile, Donny's 'Puppy Love' topped the UK chart for a month, and sparked off teeny Osmond-obsession which was to rival that accorded The Beatles in their heyday.

Donny's solo efforts took off well ahead of his brothers in the UK, unlike in the US, where the group's records vied in million-selling popularity. His revival of the standard, 'Too Young', made the US Top 20 and UK Top 5, an 'Osmonds Live' album hit the UK Top 20 in late 1972, then Little Jimmy's 'Long Haired Lover' topped the UK chart at the end of the year, with The Osmonds single, 'Crazy Horses', at No. 2 and Donny's 'Why' at No. 3! Both the group's album, 'Crazy Horses', and Donny's 'Too Young' also featured in the UK LP Top 10 simultaneously.

1973 represented another catalogue of chart success, particularly in the UK. Donny's

revival of the Johnny Mathis hit, 'The Twelfth Of Never', made the US Top 10, and was a UK chart topper; Jimmy's 'Tweedle Dee' failed to make the US Top 50, but was a UK Top 5 entry; the group's 'Goin' Home' just hit the US Top 50, and again made the UK Top 5. Even their unlikely religious-tract album, 'The Plan', went Top 10 in the UK while missing the US Top 50.

After Donny's 'Young Love' topped the UK chart for four weeks, the close of 1973 saw the debut of sister Marie Osmond (born 1959) with a country oldie, 'Paper Roses', that immediately went gold in the US Top 5.

Christmas in the UK was marked by the group's 'Let Them In' being overtaken by 'Paper Roses', while Donny's 'When I Fall In Love' single and 'A Time For Us' album both went Top 5.

UK dominance continued through 1974 with Jimmy's 'I'm Gonna Knock On Your

Door' nudging the Top 10, the group's 'Our Best To You' album going Top 5, and their single 'Love Me For A Reason' topping the chart and coinciding with a live BBC TV series.

Toothpaste sales rocketed as Donny and Marie embarked on a series of duet records – their debut 'I'm Leaving It (All) Up To You' went Top 5 in the US and UK – that made the sparkling smile a fashion item.

Not surprisingly, after Donny and Marie's 'Morning Side Of The Mountain' smash early in 1975 made the US Top 10 and UK Top 5, things began to pall slightly as the pair matured into their late teens and the geriatric elder brothers hit their twenties. Nevertheless, it didn't stop the album, 'Donny', going Top 20 in the UK, followed by the group's 'I'm Still Gonna Need You' and single 'The Proud One', a Top 5 hit.

A deliberate move into the family living room was instigated in 1976 by a TV series, *Donny and Marie*, featuring the whole Osmond clan, an album from the show, a UK TV series, and the seasonal 'Osmonds Christmas Album'.

The *Donny and Marie* show lasted until early 1979, when chart success was less spectacular than before. The group itself had one more UK TV series before breaking up in mid-1980.

Marie featured on her own TV show from late 1980, while Donny opted out of the pop mainstream. The four elder brothers, meanwhile, reformed in 1982 with the emphasis on country music, and scored a minor country hit, 'Any Time', in 1985.

Donny reappeared in 1987 with an attempt to find credibility in the adult market, with little success; little Jimmy emerged as a pop and property entrepreneur, running the family home-cum-TV studio, while Marie continued to chart as a solo country singer, including the albums 'There's No Stopping Your Heart' (1985) and 'I Only Wanted You' the following year, plus a duet single with Dan Seals in 1985, 'Meet Me In Montana', which was a country chart topper.

Greatest Hits

Singles	Title	US	UK
1971	*One Bad Apple*	1	–
1971	*Yo Yo*	3	–
1972	*Crazy Horses*	14	2
1974	*Love Me For A Reason*	10	1
1971	*Go Away Little Girl* (Donny)	1	–
1972	*Puppy Love* (Donny)	3	1
1972	*Long Haired Lover From Liverpool* (Jimmy)	38	1
1973	*The Twelfth Of Never* (Donny)	8	1
1973	*Young Love* (Donny)	23	1
1973	*Paper Roses* (Marie)	5	2
Albums			
1972	*Crazy Horses*	14	9
1972	*Portrait Of Donny* (Donny)	6	5
1973	*A Time For Us* (Donny)	58	4
1974	*Our Best To You*	–	5

Gilbert O'SULLIVAN

If his laughable public image lessened his impact as a singer-songwriter, it helped Gilbert O'Sullivan (born Raymond O'Sullivan, 1946) to a chart career longer than those of many similar but more conservatively garbed entertainers.

His family crossed from Eire to England in 1960, and at Swindon Art College, he played piano and sang with The Prefects and Rick's Blues before moving to London where he toiled in a chain store's mail office while touting demos round record companies. As Ray O'Sullivan, he cut a few singles, and although 'Disappear' was a favourite of 'hip' radio star John Peel, O'Sullivan made little headway until his deft lyrics and knack for melody caught the ear of Gordon Mills, mentor to Tom Jones. Kept under wraps while he worked on new material, O'Sullivan surfaced in 1970 with 'Nothing Rhymed', a pudding-basin haircut and a stage costume that included a cloth cap, an ill-fitting flannel suit and hobnail boots, but the joke was on his detractors when the song (covered by Jones) and the hits that followed exacted a grudging respect, especially when the resigned 'Alone Again (Naturally)', 'Clair' (about Mills's infant daughter, for whom he babysat) and re-promotions of his first two albums,

Gilbert – 'boots and braces' image boosts ballads

'Himself' and 'Back To Front', established him in the US. He peaked with 'Get Down', before suffering his first serious flop with the sexist 'A Woman's Place'. As 1973's 'I'm A Writer Not A Fighter' and later albums showed, he had lost much of the whimsicality that buyers had found endearing. Apart from a surprise UK Top 20 entry in 1980 with 'What's In A Kiss', the hits ceased after 1975's 'I Don't Love You But I Think I Like You'.

O'Sullivan's vast earnings were made secure through his bitter legal victory against Mills over publishing rights and royalty discrepancies in 1982, a judgement that set precedents for further High Court battles between artists and managers. Sales of O'Sullivan's subsequent sporadic output have been sufficient to make an album like 1990's 'In The Key Of G' a practical proposition and further chart comebacks not improbable.

Greatest Hits

Singles	Title	US	UK
1972	*Alone Again (Naturally)*	1	3
1972	*Clair*	2	1
1973	*Get Down*	7	1
Albums			
1971	*Himself*	9	5
1972	*Back To Front*	48	1

Robert PALMER

A highbrow R&B soul connoisseur, Palmer (born 1949) keeps North American FM radio in tasteful focus, resulting in automatic US chart entries, while being regarded as only as good as his last record in the UK by all but the hardcore fans who always guarantee him a short-lived spell in the album charts.

In 1968 Yorkshireman Palmer moved from a local group, Mandrake Paddle Steamer, to succeed Jess Roden as singer with The Alan Bown Set but transferred to Dada, a 12-piece jazz-rock outfit which metamorphosed into the more streamlined Vinegar Joe in 1972. As joint lead vocalist with Elkie Brooks, he stayed with the group until its dissolution after three albums by 1973. Highly regarded by Island Records founder Chris Blackwell, Palmer cut his first two solo albums, 'Sneakin' Sally Through The Alley' and 1975's 'Pressure Drop', in the US, with supporting players like New Orleans stars The Meters, noted session musicians like drummer Bernard Purdie and Motown bass guitarist James Jamerson, and members of Little Feat. Both albums made the US chart, and Palmer moved his base to the Bahamas, where he lived until 1987.

'Every Kinda People' (penned with Andy Fraser, formerly of Free) from 1978's 'Double Fun' eventually reached the US Top 20, a feat consolidated with a version of Moon Martin's 'Bad Case Of Loving You' from the following

Smooth soul stylist Palmer

year's 'Secrets' album. Though 'Clues' and its minor hits ('Looking For Clues' and the narrative 'Johnny And Mary') marked time commercially while he produced a variety of other artists from Peter Baumann (ex-Tangerine Dream) to Desmond Dekker, 1982's 'Maybe It's Love' included an international hit with 'Some Guys Have All The Luck' (revived with instrumental backing, unlike the original accapella lament by The Persuaders), which elicited a countrified 'answer' disc from Louise Mandrell, and a cover two years later by Rod Stewart.

After 1983's off-beat and commercially disappointing 'Pride', 1985 saw chart excursions by Palmer as an ad hoc member of Power Station (with members of Chic and Duran Duran) with 'Some Like It Hot', an arrangement of T. Rex's 'Get It On' and 'Communication', all from the group's eponymous album. The success of this enjoyable tangent helped his solo return to prominence, although perhaps less than the controversial video which featured an all-female backing band for the million-selling 'Addicted To Love' from 1986's 'Riptide' (his last original Island album), which also contained lesser hits in 'Hyperactive' and 'I Didn't Mean To Turn You On'. In 1987 he worked on music for a movie, *Sweet Lies*, and later was involved in writing a musical, *Don't Explain*.

For a new label, the self-produced 'Heavy Nova' album and 1990's adventurous double, 'Don't Explain', embraced singles like 'Simply Irresistible' and the catchier 'Change His Ways' (featuring yodelling and Zydeco accordion), as well as expected genre re-makes (e.g. The Gap Band's 'Early In The Morning' plus older material by Otis Redding and Marvin Gaye), although his first label deflected the commercial spotlight away from new material by the release of 'Addictions Volume One', presumably the first in a continuing series of repackaged albums. Nevertheless, Palmer was now recording more of his own material than before and extending his style with items like Bob Dylan's 'I'll Be Your Baby Tonight' (with UB40). There are also hints, both on stage and on record, of him maturing into a 'quality' artiste (e.g. the Latin-tinged 'Aeroplane' and attempts at evergreens like 'It Could Happen To You' from the 1930s), but however well he executes numbers like these, his popularity still hinges today on less sophisticated material.

Greatest Hits

Singles	Title	US	UK
1986	Addicted To Love	1	5
1986	I Didn't Mean To Turn You On	2	9
1988	Simply Irresistible	2	44
1988	She Makes My Day	–	6
Albums			
1979	Secrets	19	54
1986	Riptide	8	5
1988	Heavy Nova	13	17
1989	Addictions Volume One	79	7

Mica PARIS

B orn Michelle Warren (1969), daughter of a Jamaican singer/instrumentalist father and Cuban mother, Londoner Paris sang her first sessions at 13, provided backing vocals for Shakatak at the age of 14, and on leaving school was the driving force behind the gospel group Spirit of Watts.

A recording deal followed a stint with Hollywood Beyond as backing singer, and she was carefully promoted via press previews at Ronnie Scott's jazz club in London, building an image that consistently exuded a sophistication rare in a teenager. Her first single, 'My One Temptation' (1988), went Top 10 in the UK, followed by the Top 30 entry, 'Like Dreamers Do', co-credited to jazz saxophonist Courtney Pine, later that year. 'Breathe Life Into Me' equalled its precedessor's position, while her debut album, 'So Good', reached the Top 10 also in that year.

Her soul roots were displayed on the cover of the 1970s soul classic, 'Where Is The Love' (a hit for Roberta Flack and Donny Hathaway) with Will Downing, a Top 20 single. Paris relocated to New York but it was two years before the second album, 'Contribution', was released, late in 1990. Prince had pulled her on stage at a London post-show party in 1988, apparently not knowing who she was, and paid her the compliment of a song 'If I Luv U 2Nite' (included on 'Contribution'); while the title track, a single, included a rap by Rakim. Production was by two unknowns, Camus Celli and Andreas Levin, and elements of rock were also incorporated – the guitar solo in 'Who Can We Blame' indicates a Michael Jackson-like mind at work.

Careful nurturing of her career to date – to say nothing of a fine voice – suggests that Mica Paris will be around for a long time.

Greatest Hits

Singles	Title	US	UK
1988	My One Temptation	–	7
1988	Like Dreamers Do	–	26
1988	Breathe Life Into Me	–	26
Albums			
1988	So Good	–	6
1990	Contribution	–	26

Graham PARKER and The RUMOUR

Graham Parker (vocals)
Brinsley Schwarz (guitar)
Bob Andrews (keyboards)
Martin Belmont (guitar)
Andrew Bodnar (bass)
Stephen Goulding (drums)

D escribed by Rumour guitarist Brinsley Schwarz as a man 'who writes songs that have already been written as if they never

Parker (centre), now solo, began 1991 with Dylan support slot

had', Graham Parker (born 1950) was brought up in London's East End, dropped out of school, had a series of dead-end jobs and travelled in Morocco before sending a demo tape of original R&B-styled songs to manager Dave Robinson, who teamed him up with The Rumour, a group formed by members of pub-rock bands Brinsley Schwarz and Ducks DeLuxe. Robinson also got them a record deal, and Parker & The Rumour's 1976 debut album, 'Howlin' Wind', produced by Nick Lowe, earned critical acclaim which was boosted by an 'official' bootleg, 'Live At Marble Arch', and another studio album, 'Heat Treatment', produced by Robert 'Mutt' Lange. Impassioned live shows (notably when they toured with Southside Johnny & The Asbury Jukes) also enhanced their reputation.

Parker made the UK Top 30 in 1977 with 'The Pink Parker EP' (on pink vinyl) featuring a cover of 'Hold Back The Night' (originally by The Tramps) before achieving a Top 20 album with 'Stick To Me', for which he reverted to Nick Lowe as producer. Meanwhile, The Rumour released their own album, 'Max', whose title was a response to Fleetwood Mac titling their mega-album 'Rumours'. A live double album, 'The Parkerilla', also made the the UK Top 20 in 1978, as did 'Squeezing Out Sparks', produced by Jack Nitzsche in 1979, but success in America, where competition was tougher, eluded the group. Their biggest UK success came in 1980 with 'The Up Escalator', which featured Bruce Springsteen on backing vocals for the jointly written 'Endless Night' – the album all but made the US Top 10.

Parker split from The Rumour (who were themselves splitting, having released three Parker-less albums) soon afterwards, and embarked on a solo career with 'Another Grey Area' (1982) and 'The Real Macaw' (1983). He was reunited with Schwarz (as a member of Graham Parker & The Shot) for 1985's 'Steady Nerves' album, and even squeezed into the US Top 40 with 'Wake Up (Next To You)', but failed to capitalize on it, and it was three years before his next album, 'The Mona Lisa's Sister'. 1989 saw a solo live album, 'Live! Alone In America', following which Parker released another highly regarded studio set, 'Human Soul', in 1990, when he also toured Europe as one of the stars of a package featuring Dion, Dave Edmunds and Steve Cropper. At the end of 1990, he was living in Woodstock and working with neighbours John Sebastian (ex-Lovin' Spoonful) and Garth Hudson (formerly of The Band), who appear on Parker's 1991 album, 'Struck By Lightning'.

Greatest Hits

Albums	Title	US	UK
1979	Squeezing Out Sparks	40	18
1980	The Up Escalator	40	11

Van Dyke PARKS

Van Dyke Parks (born 1941) is best known as a singer/songwriter with a cult following and as a Brian Wilson collaborator during The Beach Boys most enigmatic period in the mid-1960s. Long before that, however, he made his showbiz debut as a child actor in Hollywood, usually in winsome productions he would now care to forget. He studied piano and in the early 1960s was signed as a songwriter for Walt Disney soundtracks. In due course he recorded a couple of forgotten singles and began working as a session musician with The Byrds ('Eight Miles High') and Judy Collins ('Who Knows Where The Time Goes'), as well as appearing in lesser known efforts by the likes of Harper's Bizarre (who also recorded his song 'High Coin').

In 1966/7, he collaborated with Brian Wilson on the ill-fated 'Smile' project, contributing surreal 'American Gothic' lyrics. The project started well; 'Heroes And Villains' becoming a big hit, but for various reasons the project was scrapped, prior to which Parks had quit. Versions of several tracks, notably 'Surf's Up', cropped up on later Beach Boys albums. Concurrently, he was working on his own 'Song Cycle' album (1968), which allegedly took four years to complete. Its strange arrangements and vocal passages led to its labelling as 'Art Rock': for some a masterpiece, for others incomprehensible.

Further sessions were followed by a period as director of Warner Bros Audio/Visual Services (1970-1). After leaving, he pursued his interest in Trinidadian music, producing an album for The Esso Trinidad Steel Band, who also played on his (decidedly Caribbean flavoured) 'Discover America' album (1972). A third album, the more mainstream 'Clang Of The Yankee Reaper' appeared in 1974, but a ten-year gap separated it from his follow-up, 'Jump'. None of the albums were commercially successful. Parks and his music still crop up from time to time (in 1988 he toured with old friend Ry Cooder) but he remains an eccentric figure, musically and personally. He has produced The Mojo Men, Judy Collins, Cooder, Phil Ochs and Arlo Guthrie. Never likely to make a hit album, he is nevertheless regarded as legendary, if often obscure.

Alan PARSONS PROJECT

Formed in 1974 by producer/engineer Parsons (born 1949), who chose the progressive rock 'concept album' format to employ a floating team of musicians/singers. The basis of The Alan Parsons Project was initially Scottish pop group, Pilot. Singers were brought in for individual songs, the most regular of these being Parsons' partner and executive producer Eric Woolfson who claimed to write '90% of the music and 100% of the lyrics', though Parsons was co-credited on all songs.

Parsons had made his name at EMI's Abbey Road studios, where he was assistant engineer on the eponymous Beatles album in 1969, going on to work with The Hollies and Paul McCartney as engineer and earning a Grammy nomination for his work on Pink Floyd's 'Dark Side Of The Moon' (1973). He also mixed Floyd's live sound, but kept his own Project a purely studio exercise.

Producing pop/rock acts such as Cockney Rebel, Al Stewart, John Miles and Pilot, he took his first step as an artist when Woolfson (then his business manager) suggested Edgar Allan Poe's *Tales Of Mystery And Imagination* as a concept to fit music to. Released in 1976, it was the fruit of two years' labour and featured vocalists Arthur Brown and Ambrosia's David Pack (the 1987 CD reissue added an Orson Welles narration). Andrew Powell arranged his early recordings, and later released his own instrumental album of Parsons themes.

The sci-fi 'I Robot', which was his first UK Top 30 album in 1977, sold a million in America, and set the tone for original concepts like 'Pyramid' (history, 1978), 'Eve' (the battle of the sexes, 1979), 'The Turn Of A Friendly Card' (gambling, 1980) and 'Eye In The Sky' (the police state, 1982). Vocalists employed included Lenny Zakatek, Colin Blunstone, Steve Harley, Peter Straker, Elmer Gantry and Chris Rainbow.

Following the 1983 'Best Of' came 'Ammonia Avenue' (1984 – his highest charting UK album), 'Vulture Culture' (1985 – No.1 in several European countries), and 'Stereotomy' (1986), featuring ex-Procol Harum vocalist Gary Brooker and singer/guitarist John Miles. 'Gaudi' (1987) was based on the building of Barcelona Cathedral by the architect of that name in the late 19th century.

Parsons has perfectly packaged progressive rock for the compact disc market. Remarkably successful for a faceless group, he and Woolfson seem likely to continue their success until the themes run out, though he remains relatively unacknowledged in the UK.

Greatest Hits

Singles	Title	US	UK
1981	Time	15	–
1982	Eye In The Sky	3	–
1984	Don't Answer Me	15	58
Albums			
1977	I Robot	9	30
1982	Eye In The Sky	7	28

Gram **PARSONS**

Of the several artists who made contributions to the birth of country-rock, Parsons was perhaps the most important. The mournful intensity of his best work has influenced numerous younger performers.

Parsons (born Cecil Connor, 1946), was the son of Coon Dog Connor, a minor C&W composer and singer. As a teenager, Parsons recorded as The Shilos with Louisiana songwriter Jim Stafford (who sold a million in 1973 with 'Spiders And Snakes'). While at Harvard University, Parsons formed The International Submarine Band with Bob Buchanan in 1966.

Claimed to be the first group to attempt to merge country music with rock, they moved west to Los Angeles and cut 'Safe At Home' for Lee Hazelwood's LHI label with Jay D. Maness on steel guitar and Earl Ball on piano At this time, Parsons met Chris Hillman of The Byrds, who were themselves moving towards a country-rock approach.

Parsons soon joined The Byrds and while he stayed for only a few months, he made a crucial contribution to the heavily country-influenced 'Sweetheart Of The Rodeo' (1968), notably through his compositions 'Hickory Wind' and '100 Years From Now'. But, after refusing to play to segregated audiences in South Africa, he left the group to form a new band, The Flying Burrito Brothers.

With Hillman on bass and Michael Clarke (another ex-Byrd) on drums, The Burritos set the tone for Californian country-rock. The group performed with The Rolling Stones at the ill-fated Altamont concert and in 1969 released 'The Gilded Palace Of Sin' a mixture of country standards such as Dan Penn and Spooner Oldham's guilt-ridden 'At The Dark End Of The Street' and Parsons originals.

Future Eagles' guitarist Bernie Leadon joined for 'Burrito De Luxe' (1970), with its version of the Mick Jagger/Keith Richard song, 'Wild Horses', but soon afterwards Parsons left the group to pursue a solo career whose launch was delayed by a serious motorcycle accident.

He returned to recording with 'G.P.'

Gram's 'Grievous Angel' epitaph

(1972), on which he was accompanied by Emmylou Harris, master guitarist James Burton and ex-Family and Blind Faith bassist Ric Grech. The album included such Parsons compositions as 'She' and 'The New Soft Shoe'.

He performed live with Harris and her Hot Band before returning to the studio to make 'Grievous Angel', whose highlights included the up-tempo 'Ooh Las Vegas' (co-written with Grech) and a poignant duet with Harris on the Felice and Boudleaux Bryant classic, 'Love Hurts'. However, shortly before the album's 1973 release Parsons was found dead of a suspected (but unproven) drug overdose.

The spirit of his music lived on, however, as Emmylou Harris continued to tour with The Hot Band and to record Parsons material on her highly successful solo albums of the late 1970s. Among other Parsons devotees were Elvis Costello, who wrote sleeve notes for the 1982 UK reissue of the solo work, and such younger generation bands as The Long Ryders, whose Sid Griffith wrote a biography of Gram Parsons in 1985. The 1980s saw much of the original Parsons *oeuvre* reissued on CD for a young appreciative audience.

Greatest Hits

Albums	Title	US	UK
1974	Grievous Angel	195	–

Dolly **PARTON**

Despite her showbiz 'glitz & tits' reputation gained in the late 1970s and 1980s, Parton was among the most accomplished country singers of her era. Particularly in the early stages of her career, she was also a notable songwriter, using traditional rural themes.

From a poor Tennessee family, Parton (born 1946) was the fourth of 12 children, and six of her siblings were also musicians, most notably her younger sister Stella, a solo vocalist who enjoyed a brief chart career. At ten, Dolly had a regular spot on a local radio station and three years later appeared on the *Grand Ole Opry* and released a version of 'Puppy Love' on a local label.

In 1964, Parton moved to Nashville to form a songwriting team with her uncle. She recorded for Fred Foster's Monument label and in 1967, her own 'Dumb Blonde', with its typically self-confident lyric, became her first hit. As a result, she was invited to join the highly-rated Porter Wagoner TV and touring troupe.

She was with Wagoner for six years, during which time over a dozen of their duets were country hits. They included Tom Paxton's 'Last Thing On My Mind' (1967), 'Just Someone I Used To Know' (1969) and 'Daddy Was An Old Time Preacher Man' (1970). On

Wagoner's television show, she also appeared as 'Miss Dolly', a comic caricature of a dumb blonde starlet.

From 1970, Parton also began to make solo records of her own songs, topping the US country chart with 'Joshua' and reaching the Top 5 with the autobiographical 'Coat Of Many Colors' (1971), drawing on the hard times of her childhood. The success of 'Jolene' (1974) led Parton to leave the Wagoner organization, though she continued to record with him on such weepies as 'Is Forever Longer Than Always?' (1976).

Throughout the rest of the 1970s, Parton was the outstanding female singer in country music through such hits as 'Bargain Store' (1975), 'All I Can Do' (1976) and 'Light Of A Clear Blue Morning' (1977). Her own songs were also attracting the attention of a newer group of country-rock singers including Maria Muldaur (who recorded 'My Tennessee Mountain Home') and Emmylou Harris ('Coat Of Many Colors').

Her career changed decisively in 1977 when 'Here You Come Again' became her first 'crossover' success in the US ('Jolene' had reached the UK Top 10 the previous year). Composed by New York pop songwriters, Barry Mann & Cynthia Weil, the ballad reached the US pop chart Top 10 and was accompanied by 'New Harvest . . . First Gathering', an album which included such soul songs as 'My Girl' and 'Higher And Higher'. There were further pop successes with 'Two Doors Down' (1978) and the disco-styled 'Baby I'm Burnin' ' (1979).

In 1980, Parton took another step towards mainstream stardom by appearing with Jane Fonda in the film 9 To 5. The Parton-composed theme song topped the US chart and the US Top 20 album '9 To 5 And Odd Jobs' showed her versatility on such songs as 'House Of The Rising Sun', Woody Guthrie's 'Deportee' and Merle Travis's 'Dark As A Dungeon' as well as four of her own compositions. Later film appearances, including The Best Little Whorehouse In Texas (1982, with Burt Reynolds), Rhinestone (1984, with Sylvester Stallone) and Steel Magnolias (1990) were less successful, while a networked variety show hosted by Parton failed to attract large enough audiences in 1987. However by this time, she was established as one of the greatest country music success stories and had invested some of her royalties in Dolly-wood, an entertainment complex in Tennessee.

Meanwhile her greatest pop successes came with collaborations with other singers. In 1983, she and Kenny Rogers recorded the million-selling 'Islands In The Stream', written by The Bee Gees, and four years later 'Trio' reached the Top 10. This album was a long-planned effort by Parton with two newer stars of country-rock, Linda Ronstadt and Emmylou Harris.

It won a Grammy award for best country album and during these years, her appeal to country music audiences was undiminished

Despite Dolly image, Parton's a pedigree performer

as such songs as the keening 'I Will Always Love You' (1981), 'Tennessee Homesick Blues' (1984) and 'Real Love' (with Rogers, 1985) reached No 1.

In 1987 Parton changed labels, releasing 'Rainbow', which was very much a mainstream pop album. In a change of emphasis, 'White Limozeen' (1989) emphasized her credentials as a country songwriter and was produced by Ricky Skaggs.

Greatest Hits

Singles	Title	US	UK
1976	Jolene	–	7
1977	Here You Come Again	3	75
1980	9 To 5	1	47
1983	Islands In The Stream		
	(with Kenny Rogers)	1	7
Albums			
1980	9 To 5 And Odd Jobs	11	–
1987	Trio (with Ronstadt and Harris)	6	60

Les PAUL

Paul (born Lester Polfus, 1915) will be best remembered for the Gibson guitar that carries his name.

As a teenager, he learnt harmonica, guitar and banjo and played with semi-pro country bands in the US Midwest before moving to Chicago and the radio station WLS. Under pseudonyms such as Hot Red and Rhubarb Red, he became a radio star before forming The Les Paul Trio in 1936 and moving to New York the following year where they appeared regularly on Fred Waring's NBC show and for five years in his orchestra.

Aside from playing, Paul pursued his long-time interest in electronics, and by 1941 had built a prototype solid body electric guitar called 'The Log'. He carried on his performing career in the Army, playing behind Bing Crosby, Johnny Mercer, Rudy Vallee and others. Crosby encouraged Paul to build his first recording studio in 1945 where he pioneered many of the studio techniques used today.

In December 1949 he married Mary Ford (born Colleen Summer, 1928, died 1977) and together they had a string of hits throughout the 1950's. In 1952 Paul finally convinced Gibson to manufacture his electric guitar which dominated the market alongside Fender's Stratocaster, numbering Jimmy Page and Jeff Beck among its devotees. Paul went on to revolutionize the electric guitar even further with developments in pick-up technology.

In 1961 the hits stopped and two years later Paul and Ford were divorced, after which Paul concentrated on his studio business. In 1974 he returned to playing, winning a Grammy with a 1977 Chet Atkins collaboration, 'Chester And Lester', and a TV documentary *The Wizard Of Waukesha* was broadcast in 1980. From 1984 to 1987 Paul had a residency at New York's Fat Tuesdays club and in 1988 he was inducted into the Rock'n'Roll Hall Of Fame.

Greatest Hits

Singles	Title	US	UK
1951	Mocking Bird Hill	3	–
1951	How High The Moon	1	–
1951	The World Is Waiting For Sunrise	3	–
1953	Vaya Con Dios	1	7
Albums			
1955	Les and Mary	15	–

Tom **PAXTON**

Part of the Greenwich Village folk scene of the early 1960s, Paxton (born 1937) emerged as one of its more solidly committed voices when all around 'protest music' was giving way to the softer-centred folk/rock. Born in Chicago, he moved with his family to Oklahoma where he took up guitar. Deeply influenced by Woody Guthrie, The Weavers and folk populist Burl Ives, he moved to New York in 1960 as a new folk scene was developing with Phil Ochs, Peter Paul & Mary and the young Bob Dylan.

His first albums appeared in the mid-1960s after the encouragement and patronage of Pete Seeger, the debut album, 'Ramblin' Boy' (1965), revealing a lyrical sophistication not common on the folk scene. His stance as a political commentator was established on tracks like 'The Willing Conscript' from 'Ain't That News' (1965), and confirmed in the 1966 album, 'Outward Bound'. He toured extensively, as important a live performer as a recording artist, and at the time of 1969's 'The Things I Notice Now' album, he was an unexpected sensation at the Bob Dylan Isle of Wight concert.

Politico poet Paxton

His songs have included children's favourites ('Jennifer's Rabbit' and 'Going To The Zoo'), social comment with 'Forest Lawn' (about US funeral parlours) and 'Is This The Way To Run An Airline', and of course hard-core protest, in 'Talking Vietnam Pot Luck Blues', 'White Bone of Allende' (1977) and the 1986 collection 'One Million Lawyers . . . and Other Disasters'. He remains a unique and dynamic concert performer in a genre that has all too often become mannered, jaded or plain tired; but has rarely achieved chart recognition, although his warm performances, both onstage and on record, have entranced millions world-wide.

Greatest Hits

Albums	Title	US	UK
1970	No. 6.	184	23
1971	The Compleat Tom Paxton	–	18

Carl **PERKINS**

Carl Perkins (born 1932) is acknowledged as one of the all-time great rockabilly singer/guitarists, yet for all his influence on later generations of musicians, his own commercial success was surprisingly limited, centring almost entirely around one song, 'Blue Suede Shoes'. From a poor rural Tennessee background, he began to play honky tonks and bars in the early 1950s, in a trio with his brothers, Jay and Clayton. Their material ran the gamut of Southern styles, from hillbilly and C&W to blues and R&B numbers, and it was hearing a similar blend on Elvis Presley's debut single in mid-1954 which inspired Perkins to seek an audition with Presley's mentor, Sam Phillips, at Sun Records in Memphis. Phillips was impressed by the trio's style and its leader's own songs; a

recording deal was struck on the strength of the latter.

By early 1955, Perkins was supporting Presley on a Southern tour, and his first singles were released, initially to little reaction, but by the end of the year, Phillips had sold Presley's contract to RCA, and was grooming Perkins as a replacement, encouraging him to boost the rock'n'roll element in his new songs. 'Blue Suede Shoes', an observation of teenage preoccupations inspired by an incident witnessed on tour, was rush-released at the start of 1956, and by the spring of that year, it was riding the US chart alongside Presley's RCA debut, 'Heartbreak Hotel', and eventually peaked immediately behind the latter chart-topper, selling over a million copies.

Perkins, however, was unable to follow-up his triumph. The band's car crashed on the way to a TV appearance in New York, and he spent three weeks injured in hospital when he could have been capitalizing on the media opportunities. Presley sang 'Blue Suede Shoes', on TV instead, and his version also charted, just beating the Perkins original in the UK Top 10. Only minor hits followed, as rockabilly was commandeered by good-looking teen idols. Perkins switched labels in 1958, and then again in 1963, but with small commercial success. 1964, when Perkins first toured Britain, brought home the legacy of his early work. The Beatles sought him out to express their admiration, and covered three of his oldies, 'Matchbox', 'Honey Don't' and 'Everybody's Trying To Be My Baby' as early album tracks. After problems with alcohol, he joined Johnny Cash's touring group in 1967, and settled in this niche for some years, appearing on Cash's TV show, and undertaking occasional recording projects of his own.

In the late 1970s Perkins launched his own road band again, with his two sons now in the line-up. Regular live work through the 1980s

'Shoes' Carl's sole success

was punctuated by projects such as recording the 'Tug Of War' album with Paul McCartney, and taking an acting role in the Jon Landis film, *Into The Night*. In 1985, he made a TV special in London to celebrate the 30th Anniversary of 'Blue Suede Shoes', which featured him playing with friends and disciples such as George Harrison, Dave Edmunds and Eric Clapton. In 1987 he was inducted into America's Rock'n'Roll Hall Of Fame, and in 1990, he was granted the supreme accolade of having a six-hour boxed CD set of his work – including the out-takes – released by a specialist German label.

Greatest Hits

Singles	Title	US	UK
1956	*Blue Suede Shoes*	2	10

PET SHOP BOYS

Neil Tennant (vocals)
Chris Lowe (keyboards)

This UK synth-pop duo formed in 1981 when Tennant (born 1954), formerly with folk band Dust and at the time assistant editor of *Smash Hits* magazine, joined forces with Lowe (born 1959), ex-One Under The Eight.

Their first single 'West End Girls' produced by Bobby 'O' Orlando, in 1984, failed to chart and, despite a label change, neither did 'Opportunities' the following year. Later in 1985, a re-recording of 'West End Girls' produced by Stephen Hague, became their first hit, reaching No. 1 in the US and UK and winning a BRIT award.

Their first album, 'Please', in 1986 went platinum in both the UK and US and a re-mix of 'Opportunities' made the Top 20 as did 'Disco', an album of 12-inch remixes. In 1987 their video collection, 'Television', topped the UK chart and their second album, 'Actually', went Top 3 in the UK and gold in the US. That year they had two more UK No. 1 singles and wrote and produced Dusty Springfield's 'What Have I Done To Deserve This', which went Top 3 in both the UK and in the US.

The unsmiling duo won the BRIT award for Best British Group in 1988 and the Ivor Novello International Hit of the Year songwriting award for 'It's A Sin'. The same year's 'Heart' was their fourth UK chart-topper – a record for duos that they share with The Everly Brothers and Wham! Their 1988 film, *It Couldn't Happen Here*, was not a success but their album 'Introspective' (1988) which included the hits 'Domino Dancing' and 'Left To My Own Devices' went Top 3 in the UK and earned them another US gold record.

In 1989 they produced Liza Minnelli's UK Top 10 album, 'Results', and hit single 'Losing

'West End Girls' tops with Pet Shop Boys

My Mind', had their 10th UK Top 10 entry with Sterling Void's song, 'It's Alright', and successfully played their first live dates. They produced their 1990 album 'Behaviour' with Harold Faltermeyer which contained UK hit singles 'So Hard' and 'Being Boring'.

Greatest Hits

Singles	Title	US	UK
1985	*West End Girls*	1	1
1987	*It's A Sin*	9	1
1987	*Always On My Mind*	4	1
1988	*Heart*	–	1
Albums			
1986	*Please*	7	3
1987	*Actually*	25	2
1990	*Behaviour*	45	2

PETER and GORDON

Peter Asher (born 1944) and Gordon Waller (born 1945) were a UK harmony duo who, helped by Beatles associations, rode the crest of the 'British Invasion' of the US charts in 1964, and managed consistent success through much of the 1960s, especially in America.

Having met at school, the duo were playing a London club early in 1964 when they were spotted, auditioned and signed by EMI. Asher's actress sister, Jane, was Paul McCartney's girlfriend at the time, and they

used the connection well, persuading him that the just-completed Lennon/McCartney song, 'A World Without Love', was ideal for their style. It was released as their first single, and in 1964 replaced 'Can't Buy Me Love' by The Beatles at No. 1 in the UK, going on to top the US chart a month later. 'Nobody I Know' was a solid Top 20 follow-up in both countries, and the duo followed it to America, touring extensively and playing TV shows, building a bigger profile in the US than they so far had at home.

Lack of UK promotion meant that 'I Don't Want To See You Again' (by McCartney once more) and 'I Go To Pieces' (donated by Del Shannon) were major US hits which meant nothing in the UK, but the home situation was rectified in 1965, when the duo revived two oldies, Buddy Holly's 'True Love Ways' and Phil Spector's 'To Know You Is To Love You'. Both were pushed hard via TV appearances, and both made the UK Top 5, but it was in the US that the duo's following was most consistently strong: several albums were released for US fans which never saw the light of day in the UK, where their soft pop image came sooner under threat from the harder R&B group sound.

1966's Top 30 hit, 'Woman', benefitted from publicity generated by the story that its writer, 'Bernard Webb', was Paul McCartney using a pseudonym, while further publicity accrued later in the year to the music hall-ish novelty, 'Lady Godiva', when it was banned in its subject's home town of Coventry, and branded obscene by the city's Mayor. A UK

Peter (left) and Gordon – softcore pop

Top 20 hit, it was the duo's British chart swansong, but performed far better in the US, where its sales topped a million and paved the way for the similar novelty, 'Knight In Rusty Armour', to reach the US Top 20 in its wake.

In 1967 possibly noting the lack of direction in the duo's recording career, Waller began also to make (unsuccessful) solo records, and in mid-1968, Peter & Gordon split, Asher becoming A&R manager at Apple Records (the label launched by The Beatles), and Waller continuing as a soloist. Starting with James Taylor at Apple, Asher's production and management career was to flourish,

particularly after he went to the US with Taylor, and even more so during his lengthy association with Linda Ronstadt in the 1970s. Waller's career as a solo singer, however, never bloomed commercially, and in the mid-1970s he retired to pursue non-musical business interests.

Greatest Hits

Singles	Title	US	UK
1964	A World Without Love	1	1
1965	True Love Ways	14	2
1965	To Know You Is To Love You	14	5
1966	Lady Godiva	6	16
Albums			
1964	A World Without Love	21	18

PETER, PAUL & MARY

Mary Travers (vocals)
Paul Stookey (guitar, vocals)
Peter Yarrow (guitar, vocals)

This merger of three former solo artists was the first commercially successful 'New Left' act to emerge from Greenwich Village, New York's vibrant beatnik district where the early 1960s civil rights movement had fused with topical folk song to be labelled 'protest'. While their light pop/folk was similar to that of the UK's Springfields, Peter, Paul & Mary helped popularize the songs of performers who might otherwise have remained cults, like Woody Guthrie, Pete Seeger, and Bob Dylan (see separate entry) who first reached the pop charts (albeit by proxy) when the trio recorded his anti-war opus, 'Blowing In The Wind'.

A psychology graduate, Yarrow (born 1938) had achieved qualified fame as an entertainer, epitomized by a well-received spot at 1960's Newport Folk Festival, while Travers (born 1937) was as steeped in folk music, and had appeared (usually as part of a group) at the prestigious Carnegie Hall, and worked in a Broadway musical. By contrast, ex-rock'n'roller Stookey (born 1937) was also a stand-up comedian.

Assembled by Dylan's manager Albert Grossman as an up-dating of the Kingston Trio, an extensive US touring schedule rewarded them with several US hits taken from two million-selling albums of 1963, 'Movin'' and 'In The Wind'. Co-written by Yarrow, children's ditty 'Puff The Magic Dragon' paved the way for the Grammy-winning 'Blowing In The Wind' and other singles that climbed charts beyond the US, though much of their thunder was stolen by Trini Lopez's competing versions of 'Lemon Tree' and Seeger's 'If I Had A Hammer'.

After 1964 hit singles were rare, although odd albums, like 1967's 'Album 1700' (titled after its US catalogue number), sold steadily,

Protest into pop – Peter, Paul and Mary's 'Jet Plane' takes Greenwich Village sound to the global village

and the 1970s began with a world-wide smash in 'Leaving On A Jet Plane' from the pen of John Denver (see separate entry) whose profile, like Dylan's, had been raised by Peter, Paul & Mary's cover versions.

'Jet Plane' was also the trio's Top 40 swansong. Bad publicity when Yarrow was jailed for an offence involving an under-age female contributed to their separation in 1971. A plethora of solo albums followed and the trio periodically re-form for tours and occasional albums.

Greatest Hits

Singles	Title	US	UK
1963	Puff The Magic Dragon	2	–
1963	Blowing In The Wind	2	13
1969	Leaving On A Jet Plane	1	2
Albums			
1962	Peter, Paul & Mary	1	18
1963	Movin'	2	–
1963	In The Wind	1	11

Tom PETTY

A side from the numerous hits in which he has been involved since his emergence in the late 1970s, one measure of the influence wielded by Tom Petty (born 1953), is that such major stars from previous generations as George Harrison, Roy Orbison and Bob Dylan have successfully collaborated with him on equal terms.

The son of an insurance salesman from Florida, singer/guitarist Petty first played in a local band, The Epics, where he learned a repertoire of classic songs from the 1960s. Leaving school in 1970, he joined Mudcrutch, a hotshot band which also included guitarist Mike Campbell and keyboard player Benmont Tench. After the band had been discovered and signed by Shelter Records, the label jointly owned by producer Denny Cordell and Leon Russell, Mudcrutch moved to Los Angeles, but split up soon afterwards. Petty attempted to make a solo album, but after it came to nothing, he teamed up with Campbell, Tench, Ron Blair (bass) and Stan Lynch (drums) to form Tom Petty & The Heartbreakers.

In 1976 the group cut its eponymous debut album, composed of original songs mainly written by Petty, which included three Top 40 singles. In the UK, where the group were hailed as musically superior punk rockers (their attitude seemed classically punkish, yet their musical ability clearly overshadowed most of their peers), 'Anything That's Rock-'n'Roll' made the Top 40, and its follow-up, 'American Girl', a song which sounded like an undiscovered classic by The Byrds (and was covered by head Byrd Roger McGuinn, a major accolade), both charted, as did the album, while in the US, it took a little longer

Petty – prohibits price-rise on 'Promises' platter

before 'Breakdown' made the Top 40 of the singles chart, following the album, which made the Top 100.

At a time when fans of rock music were trying with difficulty to adapt to the challenge of the New Wave, The Heartbreakers seemed to have a foot in both camps, the limited edition release of a single-sided live album with versions of classic oldies like Chuck Berry's 'Jaguar And The Thunderbird' helping their cause further, as did the inclusion on the soundtrack of the movie, *FM*, of 'Breakdown'. However, 1978's 'You're Gonna Get It' album seemed to have less appeal, although it went gold and briefly reached the US Top 30/UK Top 40. After Petty declared bankruptcy in order to achieve a more equitable recording contract successfully, 1979's 'Damn The Torpedoes' made the US Top 3 and went platinum and included the US Top 10 single, 'Don't Do Me Like That', and two more US hit singles, 'Refugee' and 'Here Comes My Girl'.

Petty then refused to allow 1981's 'Hard Promises' album to sell at a higher price than his previous albums, as he had been a major contributor to the label's profits, and surprisingly triumphed. When the album was released, it went platinum and reached the US Top 5 and spawned a US Top 20 single, 'The Waiting', while later that year he and

The Heartbreakers backed Stevie Nicks on a US Top 3 single, 'Stop Draggin' My Heart Around'. Petty had also produced an album, 'Drop Down And Get Me', for 1960s star Del Shannon, and when Ron Blair decided to leave the band, Petty recruited Shannon's bass player, Howie Epstein, who appeared on 1982's 'Long After Dark' album, which made the US Top 10, but only went gold, although it included a US Top 20 single, 'I Got Lucky', and a US Top 30 single, 'Change Of Heart'.

Petty at this point was feeling the pressure of touring for most of the past seven years, and no new album appeared until 1985's 'Southern Accents', with a distinct change of musical direction, which returned the band to platinum status, made the US Top 10/UK Top 30 and included three US hit singles. The group then embarked on more touring, which resulted in an exceptional double live album, 'Pack Up The Plantation', which included creditable cover versions of 'So You Want To Be A Rock & Roll Star' (The Byrds), 'Needles And Pins' (The Searchers – the Petty version was a US Top 40 single) and John Sebastian's 'Stories We Could Tell'. The album made the US Top 30, but Petty severely injured his hand in frustration at finding himself back on the treadmill after 1987's 'Let Me Up (I've Had Enough)' album (clearly a cry from the heart).

1989	I Won't Back Down	12	28
Albums			
1977	Tom Petty And The		
	Heartbreakers	55	24
1979	Damn The Torpedoes	2	57
1981	Hard Promises	5	32
1985	Southern Accents	7	23
1989	Full Moon Fever	3	8

Wilson **PICKETT**

Raised in Detroit, Pickett (born 1941) first recorded with vocal group The Falcons in 1962. Their R&B hit, 'I Found A Love', also made the US Top 100, on which Pickett contributed wild lead vocals. More gospel-tinged wailing characterized his two releases on the Lloyd Price-owned Double L label, 'If You Need Me', and 'It's Too Late', both in 1963.

He signed with a major label in 1964, and after a couple of insignificant releases, was teamed with the top session outfit of Steve Cropper, Duck Dunn, Booker T, etc., at the Stax Studios in Memphis. The first result was musical dynamite, 'In The Midnight Hour', a 1965 hit that made the UK Top 20, and just missed the US Top 20. It became the dance-floor anthem for the Mods in Britain, and an obligatory cover for US and UK rock groups plugging into the soul music that had grown out of black R&B.

'Don't Fight It', which made the US Top 100 and UK Top 30, followed late that year, and in 1966 Pickett moved his recording base to the equally influential Fame Studios in Muscle Shoals, Alabama for '634–5789' – again hitting the charts on both sides of the Atlantic – and a series of soul smashes that established him as a star. With direct, no-nonsense songs like 'Land of 1,000 Dances' (his biggest US Top 10 hit) and 'Mustang Sally', disco club classics such as 'Funky Broadway' (an R&B chart topper) and slower offerings such as a cover of The Beatles hit, 'Hey Jude', he utilized a breadth of repertoire that made the best use of his tough, grainy voice.

As straight soul gave way to more 'produced' disco music, he moved with the times, teaming up with Philadelphia producers Gamble and Huff. 'Engine No. 9' was the first result, in 1970, which reached the US Top 20 just prior to his first million seller, 'Don't Let The Green Grass Fool You', in 1971. His last big hit before another change of label, recorded back in Miami, was 1972's 'Don't Knock My Love', his second gold single.

The move in 1973 was marked by 'Mr Magic Man', a single which just scraped into the US Top 100, presenting a smoother, show-biz manicured Wilson Pickett. The early 1980s saw him releasing the albums, 'I Want You' and 'The Right Track', neither of

Wicked Pickett – musical dynamite In The Midnight Hour

It was at this point that his fortunes began to improve. Bob Dylan headlined a tour in which he was backed by Petty & The Heart-breakers, who also played their own set and additionally worked with opening act Roger McGuinn. As a result, he became friendly with Dylan, through whom he also got to know George Harrison and Roy Orbison, for both of whom Jeff Lynne had produced albums. Thus was born The Traveling Wilburys (in alphabetical order Dylan, Harrison, Lynne, Orbison and Petty), whose debut album, 'Volume 1', was a loose good-time album which proved hugely successful and was a major hit. In 1989 Petty resumed his own career with his finest album to date, 'Full Moon Fever', which became his most successful album in Britain and included a number of hit singles, notably the classic 'I Won't

Back Down'. The group's most acclaimed album thus far, it strongly suggested that Petty and his band were deservedly among the biggest acts in the world at the start of the 1990s, which a second hit album by The Traveling Wilburys, the ironically titled 'Volume 3', seemed to confirm.

Petty has not been the only member of The Heartbreakers to make his mark as an individual, as both Campbell and particularly Tench are regularly in demand to guest on records by others.

Greatest Hits
Singles	Title	US	UK
1979	Don't Do Me Like That	10	–
1981	Stop Draggin' My Heart Around		
	(with Stevie Nicks)	3	50

which captured the raw power of 'The Wicked Pickett' in his 1960s heyday.

PINK FLOYD

Syd Barrett (guitar, vocals)
Roger Waters (bass, vocals)
Rick Wright (keyboards)
Nick Mason (drums)

Formed in the UK as the psychedelic 1960s dawned, Pink Floyd survived the loss of their first mentor, Syd Barrett, to become one of the most successful bands of the 1970s courtesy of their 'Dark Side Of The Moon' album. They even survived the loss of their second mentor, Roger Waters, to make one of the major comebacks of the late 1980s.

Syd Barrett (born Roger Barrett, 1946) and Roger Waters (born 1944) had been at the same Cambridge school before Waters met Rick Wright (born 1945) and Nick Mason (born 1945) in 1965. They quit their bands and formed Pink Floyd, supposedly named after Georgia bluesmen Pink Anderson and Floyd Council. Between Chuck Berry songs, Barrett began to experiment with guitar feedback, and the group became darlings of the London underground scene, especially when they extended songs and incorporated slide projections and lighting effects into live performances. Their first single, 'Arnold Layne', reached the UK Top 20 in 1967, although its curious lyrics caused some radio station bans. The follow-up, 'See Emily Play', reached the UK Top 10, as did their 1967 debut album, 'Piper At The Gates Of Dawn'.

However, Barrett, who had written much of the album, had become increasingly unstable due to his LSD habit. After a nerve-racking US tour and a failed single, 'Apples And Oranges', the band recruited Dave Gilmour (who had taught Barrett to play guitar) in 1968, and for two months played as a five-piece before Barrett bailed out. Subsequent singles bombed, but they successfully re-emerged with a more grandiose second album, 'A Saucerful Of Secrets', which made the UK Top 10 in 1968. They continued to be innovative in concert, experimenting with 360-degree sound, and in 1969, recorded the movie soundtrack, *More*, and released the double album, 'Ummagumma', which fea-

The early flower power Floyd, heroes of the London hippy scene

tured one live album, while the other contained indulgent solo tracks. Antonioni also used their music for *Zabriskie Point*.

1970's 'Atom Heart Mother' album was an ambitious classical/rock fusion complete with choir and horn section that topped the UK charts as the band played a series of spectacular outdoor shows, and came closer to the US Top 50 than any previous album. That same year, Syd Barrett emerged with two idiosyncratic solo albums, 'The Madcap Laughs' (which made the UK chart for one week) and 'Barrett', before retiring for good. 1971's 'Meddle' album made the UK Top 3 and spent over a year in the US chart, featuring the 20-minute opus, 'Echoes'. Another soundtrack album, 'Obscured By Clouds', became their seventh UK Top 10 album and their first to make the US Top 50 in 1972, and the group made their own movie, *Pink Floyd Live At Pompeii* (which wasn't released until 1974), in between lengthy recording sessions for their next album, 'Dark Side Of The Moon', released in 1973.

A meticulously constructed album that explored stress, madness and death, 'Dark Side Of The Moon' was superbly recorded and produced, and its release coincided with the mass availability of stereo. It shot to the top of the US charts (ironically peaking at No. 2 in the UK) and was still in the US chart a decade later, selling over 10 million copies worldwide. They also had a US Top 20 single with 'Money', but following this gigantic

success was a daunting prospect – it was over two years before the release of 'Wish You Were Here' in 1975, which instantly topped the US and UK charts despite critical reservations. In retrospect, it was a worthy successor to 'Moon', featuring a Waters-penned tribute to Syd Barrett, 'Shine On, You Crazy Diamond', and the tense, brittle 'Welcome To The Machine'. By now, live shows had become monumental epics with gigantic screens and crashing aeroplanes, but the band themselves remained anonymous both on and off stage.

1977's 'Animals' was another jaundiced look at the human species by Waters, who had now assumed the main songwriting role within the band. It reached the UK/US Top 3 and the band toured with a huge inflatable pig which hovered menacingly above the audience. (The pig was also on the album sleeve, moored above London's Battersea Power Station, but broke free and floated into the sky causing London air-traffic controllers to alert pilots to a flying pig!). The collapse of an investment company in 1979 cost Pink Floyd much of the fortune which it had earned and the group briefly became tax exiles while recording the next Waters tour-de-force, 'The Wall', a 1979 double album which pursued the themes of alienation and cruelty. It topped the US chart for 15 weeks and was performed in Los Angeles, New York, London and Dusseldorf while the road crew built a 30ft wall across the stage, obscur-

Pitney back in the charts, twenty five years from 'Tulsa'

ing the band until the wall was demolished as the climax. The album included their first UK/US No. 1 single, 'Another Brick In The Wall (Part II)'.

Tensions were starting to surface and Wright quit after the tour. Waters immersed himself in the film of *The Wall*, directed by Alan Parker and starring Bob Geldof as 'Pink', before recording the bleak anti-war album, 'The Final Cut', in 1983. Pink Floyd's third UK chart-topper, its title seemed appropriate as the band fell apart. Gilmour, who had already released an eponymous solo album which reached the UK Top 20 and US Top 30 in 1978, released 'About Face' with similar results in 1984 and Waters released 'The Pros And Cons Of Hitch Hiking' (also UK Top 20 and US Top 30) the same year and toured with Eric Clapton guesting on guitar, while Mason and Wright also made extra-mural albums.

In 1987, Gilmour and Mason decided to revive Pink Floyd. Waters was furious but legally powerless and with Wright returning as a hired hand along with other musicians, 'A Momentary Lapse Of Reason' made the US/UK Top 3 in 1987. A subsequent two-

year record-breaking tour of the world's stadia with state of the art sound and a light show encompassed Floyd's greatest hits, while Waters released his second solo album, 'Radio KAOS', which peaked outside the UK Top 20, suggesting that few of the audience were aware that he had been responsible for many of the group's greatest successes.

However, Waters was in the spotlight in 1990, performing 'The Wall' at the already dismantled Berlin Wall before a live audience of 200,000 and a TV audience of millions in aid of the Disaster Relief Fund, with Van Morrison, Bryan Adams, Cyndi Lauper and Marianne Faithfull among the guest artists.

Greatest Hits

Singles	Title	US	UK
1979	Another Brick In The Wall	1	1
Albums			
1970	Atom Heart Mother	55	1
1973	Dark Side Of The Moon	1	2
1975	Wish You Were Here	1	1
1979	The Wall	1	3
1983	The Final Cut	6	1
1987	A Momentary Lapse Of Reason	3	3

Gene PITNEY

By the time of his first US hit, Pitney (born 1941) had acquired sufficient pop industry experience to sustain a 30-year career, much of it spent touring overseas where he staggered his many chartbusters. As crucial to his longevity (and resulting wealth) as his understated stage persona and distinctive nasal tenor was a business sensibility which maintained an intense interest in every aspect of the promotion of his artistic output.

As half of a duo called Jamie and Jean, Pitney first recorded while at university, but unconvinced about a future as a performer, he first became known (sometimes under a pseudonym) as a jobbing composer, providing hits for Ricky Nelson, Roy Orbison (see separate entries) and others. In 1961 '(I Wanna) Love My Life Away', a demo on which the talented Pitney had multi-tracked most of the instrumental and vocal parts, was considered by his publisher as worthy of release as it stood, and made the US Top 40.

Later that year, Pitney scored again with the title song to *Town Without Pity*, a Kirk Douglas movie, following it with *The Man Who Shot Liberty Valance*, another film theme, which was nominated for an Oscar. Bacharach & David also wrote hits for Pitney, including 1963's 'Twenty-Four Hours From Tulsa', his Top 10 debut in Britain, where he was one of the few US vocalists to usually make the UK charts during the British Beat era. Respected for his stylistic consistency (or 'squareness', some would say), Pitney, despite his short-haired, besuited image, was a friend of The Rolling Stones (see separate entry), playing on their debut album, and cutting 1964's 'That Girl Belongs To Yesterday', the first Jagger-Richards song to make the US charts.

Other ballad hits such as 'I'm Gonna Be Strong', the 1965 million-seller, 'Looking Through The Eyes Of Love' and 1967's 'Something's Gotten Hold Of My Heart', amassed an audience who would support Pitney unswervingly even when, as the decade ended, his records rarely made the Top 20. Though stereotyped as a merchant of melancholy, Pitney could make intriguing musical diversions, like two Country & Western album collaborations with George Jones, and take on quite tough material like 1968's 'Somewhere In The Country', an opus about an unmarried mother. This was his last UK Top 20 hit before 1989, when a re-make of 'Something's Gotten Hold Of My Heart', a duet with Marc Almond, became his first UK chart-topper and ended a long series of chart failures for Pitney, whose past successes guarantee well-paid work until retirement.

Greatest Hits

Singles	Title	US	UK
1962	Only Love Can Break A Heart	2	–
1963	Twenty Four Hours From Tulsa	17	5
1964	I'm Gonna Be Strong	9	2

The PLATTERS

Tony Williams
David Lynch
Paul Robi
Herb Reed
Zola Taylor *(vocal group)*

The most successful black group of the 1950s, The Platters broke down accepted conventions by consistently appealing to a multi-racial audience, via a ballad-based repertoire and a skilled blend of black vocal styling and sophisticated white-orientated arrangements.

Williams, Lynch and Reed originally formed as a doo-wop quartet in Los Angeles in 1953, with Alex Hodge, who was replaced by Robi in 1954 when the group signed a management deal with producer Buck Ram, who also brought in Taylor (ex-Teen Queens) to sweeten their sound with a female voice. 'Only You (And You Alone)' and other early recordings on a small label meant little, but when they moved to a major in 1955 (in a 'package deal' with Ram's already successful group, The Penguins), a new version of 'Only You' shot them into the US Top 5 as the group appeared in the pioneering *Rock Around The Clock* movie, and this hit was followed in 1956 by consecutive million sellers in 'The Great Pretender', '(You've Got) The Magic Touch' and 'My Prayer'. All had Williams as featured soloist, with the others essentially providing harmony back-up. Similar international success soon followed, and The Platters moved into major tours, lucrative cabaret stints and other film cameos, much of this crossover attributable to Ram promoting them as a quality ballad act rather than a black vocal group.

1957 saw a slew of lesser hits, but the group were back among the million-sellers in 1958 with 'Twilight Time' (a song resurrected from Ram's own early 1940s songwriting back-catalogue), and again in 1959 with a revival of the 1930s evergreen, 'Smoke Gets In Your Eyes'. Recorded in Paris during a European tour, this topped both US and UK charts, and was perhaps the finest showcase of the soaring lead tenor voice of Tony Williams. An incident later in 1959 almost finished the group. The male members were arrested in Cincinnati in the extremely close company of four 19-year-olds, three of whom were white, and although they were acquitted

The Platters – doo-wop delivery with barnstorming ballads

of charges of lewdness and abetting prostitution, there was at least temporarily a severe radio backlash against their records. In a sense, The Platters suddenly found that they were a black vocal group after all.

After further hits, notably 'Harbour Lights', which made the US Top 10, Tony Williams left the group in 1961, wanting to study to improve his vocal technique. Frank Sinatra signed him to his Reprise label as a

239

soloist, but Williams surprisingly faded quickly into obscurity. Meanwhile, Ram was fighting Mercury, which objected to Platters records on which Williams did not sing – he had been replaced by Sonny Turner. Early in 1962 the hits ended and the contract expired, and the group's stability was also shaken as Robi and Taylor left for (obscure) solo careers, Nate Nelson and Sandra Dawn replacing them.

While the 1950s R&B genre grew into the 1960s soul movement, The Platters were off in the wings. In 1966, however, they unexpectedly returned, still under Ram's aegis, but with a contemporary soul group sound. 'I Love You 1000 Times' was a US Top 40 hit, and the Detroit-styled 'With This Ring' took them back into the US Top 20 the following year, before they again dipped out of the commercial limelight.

The advent of the rock revival and nostalgia circuits during the 1970s put the group before larger live audiences once again, while the nature of their repertoire has ensured that, regardless of personnel changes, The Platters would always be an in-demand nightclub attraction – which they have remained to this day, still guided by the ubiquitous Buck Ram until he retired in the mid-1980s.

Greatest Hits

Singles	Title	US	UK
1955	The Great Pretender	1	5
1956	My Prayer	1	4
1958	Twilight Time	1	3
1959	Smoke Gets In Your Eyes	1	1
Albums			
1956	The Platters	7	–
1960	Encore Of Golden Hits	6	–

POCO

Richie Furay (guitar, vocals)
Jim Messina (guitar, vocals)
Rusty Young (pedal steel guitar)
George Grantham (drums)
Randy Meisner (bass, vocals)

Part of the California country-rock movement of the 1970s, Poco was one of the most durable groups of its type, making 18 albums over a 20-year period. Its ex-members contributed to numerous other bands including The Eagles and Loggins & Messina.

Furay (born 1944) and Messina (born 1947) were former members of Buffalo Springfield. When that group split up in 1968, the duo joined forces with three musicians from Colorado bands: Meisner (born 1946) from The Poor, and Young (born 1946) and Grantham (born 1947) from Boenzee Cryque. The new band chose the name Pogo, but changed after threats of legal action from the creator of the Pogo comic strip.

Meisner left the group to join Rick Nelson's Stone Canyon Band just before Poco signed to Epic. With Messina playing bass, the remaining quartet cut 'Pickin' Up The Pieces' (1969) which was a minor US hit. With Furay's flawless tenor vocals and Beatles-influenced harmonies allied to country instrumentation, it was an impressive debut. Californian bassist Tim Schmidt (born 1947) joined the band in 1970 and played on the second album, 'Poco'. The group toured frequently and the live album, 'Deliverin'' reached the US Top 30.

At this point Messina left to concentrate on studio work, soon teaming up with Kenny Loggins for a successful recording career. His replacement was Paul Cotton from Illinois Speed Press. Poco released the Steve Cropper-produced 'From The Inside' (1971) and 'Good Feelin' To Know' (1973) before founding member Furay departed to set up the Souther-Hillman-Furay Band, a country-rock 'supergroup' that failed to gel and made two disappointing albums before disbanding in 1975.

Despite the loss of its main songwriter, Poco made five more albums as a four-piece, with both 'Crazy Eyes' (1973), with its Bob Ezrin-orchestrated title track, and 'Head Over Heels' (1975, after a change of label) reaching the US Top 50. Nevertheless, in nearly a decade, the group had failed to produce any big hits and after the excellent, but no more successful 'Rose of Cimarron' and 'Indian Summer' (1976), the group abandoned its country roots for a mainstream rock sound with Donald Fagen of Steely Dan on synthesizers.

When that album sold only moderately, both Grantham and Schmidt decided to leave, the latter to replace Randy Meisner as a member of The Eagles, the band which had found the winning country-rock formula that had eluded Poco. However, Cotton and Young now remodelled Poco once again, recruiting a British-born rhythm section Charlie Harrison (bass) and Steve Chapman (drums), who had previously played with Leo Sayer and Al Stewart. Keyboards player Kim Bullard (formerly with Crosby Stills & Nash) also joined.

Playing R&B-tinged rock, the new line-up brought Poco's long-awaited US Top 20 album triumph with 'Legend' (1979), which went gold, and the singles 'Crazy Love' and 'Heart Of The Night'. However this success was shortlived, and 'Under The Gun' (1980) and 'Blue And Gray' (1981) were only minor hit albums. After the failure of 'Cowboys And Englishmen' (1982), the group changed labels again, reaching the US Top 50 with 'Shoot For The Moon' from 'Ghost Town'.

In 1983, with Rusty Young the only remaining member from the first line-up, Poco disbanded. There were two reunions of those original members to come, however. Furay put together the band in 1984 to make 'Inamorata' and had become a minister of religion before, five years later, Young instigated the sessions that were released by RCA as 'Legacy'.

Greatest Hits

Singles	Title	US	UK
1979	Crazy Love	17	–
1979	Heart Of The Night	20	–
Albums			
1971	Deliverin'	26	–
1978	Legend	14	–

POINTER SISTERS

Sisters Bonnie (born 1951) and June Pointer (born 1954) from Oakland, California, started as a duo, The Pointers, in 1969. Sister Anita (born 1948) joined soon after and they performed backing vocals for acts like Boz Scaggs and Dr Hook. In 1972 sister Ruth (born 1946) completed the versatile vocal quartet.

Their debut single, 'Don't Try To Take The Fifth', on Atlantic in 1972 was unsuccessful and they signed to Blue Thumb Records in 1973 and quickly charted with 'Yes We Can Can' and their eponymous debut album, which went gold and made the US Top 20. Initially sporting a jazzy 1940s image, the quartet released 'Live At The (San Francisco) Opera House' the following year and earned another gold album with 'That's A Plenty'. Also in 1974, they became the first black group to hit the country Top 40 and the first to win a country Grammy Award, which they did with Anita and Bonnie's song 'Fairytale', which was also a US Top 20 pop hit, before topping the black chart with 'How Long' from their 1975 US Top 40 album, 'Steppin'.

Bonnie left to join Motown in 1978, where she had one US Top 20 hit, and the trio signed with Planet Records. Their 1979 LP, 'Energy', went gold, as did their version of Bruce Springsteen's 'Fire', their first US Top 3 single and their first UK Top 40 hit. They hit the US Top 3 singles again with 'He's So Shy' in 1980, from the LP 'Special Things', and also in 1981 with 'Slow Hand' from their gold album, 'Black And White'.

Their 1984 album, 'Break Out', sold three million and included four US Top 10 singles: 'Automatic' and the Grammy-winning 'Jump (For My Love)' which also made the UK Top 10 as well as the US Top 10s and 'Neutron Dance' and 'I'm So Excited'.

The sisters, who took part in the USA for Africa project, changed labels in 1985 and their debut album for RCA, 'Contact', went platinum. Later albums like 'Hot Together', 'Goldmine' and 'Serious Slammin'' failed to equal that success. In 1989 a hits compilation made the UK Top 20 and the sisters joined Motown in 1990.

'Seventies 'Can Can' smash – an early Pointer for the Sisters

Greatest Hits

Singles	Title	US	UK
1978	*Fire*	2	34
1980	*He's So Shy*	3	–
1981	*Slow Hand*	2	10
1984	*Automatic*	5	2
1984	*Jump (For My love)*	3	6
Albums			
1981	*Black And White*	12	21
1983	*Break Out*	8	9

The POLICE

Sting (vocals, bass)
Stewart Copeland (drums)
Andy Summers (guitar)

One of the first mega-bands of the 1980s, The Police paid their dues in the UK punk scene before showing their class with a series of singles that propelled them to major success on both sides of the Atlantic. The group was formed by drummer Stewart Copeland (born 1952), who arrived in the UK from his native US in 1975 and played with progressive rock band Curved Air before they were swept aside by the New Wave. Fired by the energy of punk, Copeland recruited Sting

(born Gordon Sumner, 1951) from Newcastle jazz-rock combo Last Exit and French punk guitarist Henri Padovani in 1977, and set about establishing The Police on the London circuit. They wrote, recorded, packaged and distributed their first single, 'Fall Out', on Illegal Records (run by Copeland's brother, Miles Copeland) which sold 2,000 copies, but their punk credibility was always in doubt. When veteran guitarist Andy Summers (born 1942, ex-1960s bands Zoot Money's Big Roll Band, Soft Machine and The Animals, and a member of 1970s bands led by Kevin Coyne and Kevin Ayers) expressed an interest in joining, main songwriter Sting (an ex-schoolteacher) gave up pretending and Padovani was replaced by Summers.

His arrival prompted Sting to expand his songwriting talent, and the band developed a 'white reggae' style. 'Roxanne' (inspired by the Parisian red light district) secured them a deal with a major label. Released in 1978, the single received little attention in the UK but reached the US Top 40 the following year after the trio played a budget tour of the US East Coast and inadvertently gave themselves a stronger image by dyeing their hair blond for a Wrigleys TV commercial. In the UK, 'Can't Stand Losing You' created more interest, reaching the Top 50, and their debut album, 'Outlandos D'Armour', suddenly took

off, reaching the UK Top 10 and US Top 30 and sending a re-released 'Roxanne' to the UK Top 20 and a re-released 'Can't Stand Losing You' to the UK Top 3.

The band toured the UK through the summer of 1979, headlining the Reading Rock Festival, and were rewarded when their next single, 'Message In A Bottle', stormed to the top of the UK chart and was followed by a UK chart-topping album, 'Regatta De Blanc', which made the US Top 30 with the title track earning them their first Grammy for rock instrumental and another UK chart-topping single, 'Walking On The Moon'. As Sting asserted himself, his photogenic features stared out from newstands across the country and The Police finished the year as the UK's top pop stars. For their next move they bypassed America and opted instead for Hong Kong, Japan, India and Egypt. It was an experience for the band and an exotic media opportunity. America finally fell to the 'Zenyatta Mondatta' album late in 1980 which went Top 5 in the US and topped the UK charts for a month, yielding two perfect pop hits with 'Don't Stand So Close To Me' (a Grammy winner) and 'De Do Do Do De Da Da Da'. They earned another Grammy with the Andy Summers instrumental, 'Behind My Camel', and even made the disco charts with 'Voices Inside My Head'.

Post-punk trio Police copped for superstadium status

Sting added more lyrical substance to the next Police album, 'Ghost In The Machine' in 1981. The title was inspired by philosopher Arthur Koestler and the UK Top 3 single, 'Invisible Sun', by the troubles in Northern Ireland. America preferred the calypso pop of 'Every Little Thing She Does Is Magic', and the album spent six weeks in the US Top 3, while Grace Jones scored a hit with a cover of 'Demolition Man'. Sting had meanwhile been pursuing an acting career with film and TV roles in *Quadrophenia, Radio On, Dune* and *Brimstone and Treacle*, which also brought him a UK Top 20 single with a revival of 'Spread A Little Happiness'. He maintained a thematic approach to the next Police album, 1984's 'Synchronicity', which dabbled in Carl Jung's philosophy and topped the US charts for over four months, winning more Grammies, while 'Every Breath You Take', a song about obsession and jealousy, topped the UK & US singles chart, the latter for eight weeks.

However, egos within the band were becoming fragile and after a stadium tour of the US, the trio concentrated on solo projects: Copeland with film scores and Summers into albums with Robert Fripp. Although they never formally disbanded, Sting made his frustration with the group format plain and

when he embarked on a solo career with a new band, his future clearly lay beyond The Police. He had already branched out, co-writing the Dire Straits hit, 'Money For Nothing', with Mark Knopfler, duetting with Phil Collins on the latter's 'No Jacket Required' album, singing on Band Aid's 'Do They Know It's Christmas' and appearing at Live Aid in 1985, which coincided with Sting's first solo album, 'Dream Of The Blue Turtles', which took him back towards his jazz roots with a band that included sax player Branford Marsalis, keyboard player Kenny Kirkland, drummer Omar Hakim and bass player Daryl Jones, while Sting sang and played guitar. The album reached the US Top 3 and topped the UK chart, featuring two US Top 10 singles in 'If You Love Somebody Set Them Free' and 'Fortress Around Your Heart' and two more US Top 20 hits. The ensuing world tour was documented on the double live album and video, 'Bring On The Night', released in 1986. Sting also took part in a London anti-apartheid festival and the US Conspiracy Of Hope charity tour with Bob Dylan, Peter Gabriel, Tom Petty, Bryan Adams and U2, as well as sundry European jazz festivals.

His 'Nothing Like The Sun' album in 1987

used the same core group but broadened out, with contributions from guitarists Eric Clapton, Mark Knopfler and former Police colleague, Andy Summers. Again it topped the UK charts and went Top 10 in the US and gave him a US Top 10 single with 'We'll Be Together', while 'Be Still My Beating Heart' was a US Top 20 single. The world tour included the Nelson Mandela Birthday Tribute at London's Wembley Arena and the Amnesty International Human Rights Now! tour with Bruce Springsteen, Peter Gabriel and Tracy Chapman, where he performed his 'ode' to murderous Chilean dictator General Pinochet, 'They Dance Alone'. His more affectionate ode to English eccentric Quentin Crisp, 'Englishman In New York', was used as the theme tune to the *Stars And Bars* movie and was a remixed US hit in late 1990. A new album was released early in 1991.

Greatest Hits

Singles	Title	US	UK
1979	*Can't Stand Losing You*	–	2
1979	*Message In A Bottle*	74	1
1979	*Walking On The Moon*	–	1
1980	*Don't Stand So Close To Me*	10	1
1981	*Invisible Sun*	–	2

IGGY POP / The STOOGES

Iggy Pop (born James Osterberg, 1947) joined his first band, the Iguanas, as drummer in 1964, taking the 'Iggy' moniker with him when he joined Detroit blues combo, The Prime Movers in 1965. After a spell in Chicago with ex-Paul Butterfield Band drummer Sam Lay in 1966/67, Pop returned home to form an instrumental band, The Psychedelic Stooges, with high school buddies Ron (bass) and Scott (drums) Asheton, Iggy playing Hawaiian guitar and piano. In 1968 he moved to vocals, Ron Asheton switched to guitar and Dave Alexander joined on bass. Dropping the 'Psychedelic' tag, the band attracted much attention for Pop's on-stage performances.

The Stooges signed a record deal in 1968, their eponymous debut album, produced by ex-Velvet John Cale (see separate entry), emerging in 1969. Via repetitive three-chord rock'n'roll, 'The Stooges' articulated American post-adolescent boredom in a way no rock album had done before. Sax player Steven MacKay joined the band in 1970, and they released 'Funhouse', an accurate studio representation of their on-stage sound. It sold as poorly as their debut despite enthusiastic US press reviews. Amid a welter of personnel changes and a cloud of serious drug abuse, The Stooges ploughed on through 1970, with Iggy's stage act becoming increasingly manic, but were dropped by their label in 1971, when the line-up included the Asheton brothers, bassist Jimmy Recca, guitarist James Williamson and Pop.

Long-time Stooges fan David Bowie and his then manager Tony De Fries convinced Pop to revive The Stooges, bringing Pop and Williamson to London in 1972 to record the 'Raw Power' album, with Ron and Scott Asheton being drafted in as a rhythm section. Despite a curious Bowie mix, 'Raw Power' remains a classic, but sales were again disappointing. Back in the US, the band split from De Fries, added pianist Scott Thurston (later of The Motels), and undertook a

Iggy – ahead of Stooges in Pop stakes

punishing touring schedule. Drink and drug problems again plagued the group, with Pop's increasingly confrontational, self-destructive persona almost out of control. The 'Metallic KO' album perfectly captures the frenzy of the period.

The Stooges finally folded in 1974. Ron Asheton formed The New Order and later Destroy All Monsters, and Pop checked in to a psychiatric institute. In 1975 he re-united with Williamson for the 'Kill City' album, largely recorded during his weekend leaves from the hospital, which remained unreleased until 1977. Bowie kept in touch with Pop during this period, and 1976 saw the duo in Europe recording Iggy's comeback album, 'The Idiot'. Released in 1977, it was a disconcerting slab of gloomy rock, but featured some of Pop's strongest performances, including 'China Girl', a worldwide hit for Bowie in 1983. Pop had by then been adopted as a 'father figure' by the UK punk scene, whose energy was reflected in 1977's 'Lust For Life', possibly his finest album.

After 1978's poor live album, 'TV Eye', Pop moved labels for the excellent 'New Values' album, produced by James Williamson.

The pair were teamed again for 1980's 'Soldier', but after intense disagreement, Williamson was dismissed. Despite the presence of ex-Sex Pistol Glen Matlock and ex-Patti Smith sideman Ivan Kral, 'Soldier' didn't sell too well, and when 'Party', his attempt at a 'commercial' follow-up, flopped in 1981, Pop found himself without a deal, back on the live treadmill and once more heavily into drink and drugs. A one-off deal resulted in 1982's 'Zombie Birdhouse', after which Iggy set off on the road again – then undertook a lengthy detoxification course.

A cleaned-up Pop got married, took acting lessons, and in 1985 began recording with ex-Pistol Steve Jones. Bowie was involved with this project, which spawned 'Blah Blah Blah' (1986) and a spin-off hit single, 'Real Wild Child'. Back on form, Iggy released the hard rock 'Instinct' album (1988), again with Steve Jones, followed in 1990 by 'Brick By Brick', an impressively varied album which brought him to the attention of the MTV generation for the first time. Lately, Pop has also pursued an acting career, appearing in the movies *Sid & Nancy*, *The Colour Of Money*, *Cry Baby* and *Hardware*.

Greatest Hits

Singles	Title	US	UK
1986	Real Wild Child	–	10
Albums			
1977	The Idiot	72	30
1977	Lust For Life	120	28
1986	Blah Blah Blah	75	43

PREFAB SPROUT

Patrick McAloon (guitars, vocals)
Martin McAloon (bass)
Wendy Smith (vocals)

Formed in Newcastle in the middle of the 1978 New Wave, though scarcely related to it, fronted by eclectic songwriter Paddy McAloon (born 1957) who was compared somewhat prematurely to Elvis Costello, Prefab Sprout was completed by his brother, Martin, (born 1962), and Wendy Smith (keyboards, backing vocals) who later attracted criticism for being little more than decorative. Neil Conti (drums) was soon added.

After critical success with the privately pressed 'Lions In My Own Garden', they signed to a small local record label boasting The Kane Gang, Hurrah, etc, and proved to be the best prospect of them all. Licensed to a major, 1984's 'Swoon' was a cult success, while 'Steve McQueen' (1985) became 'Two Wheels Good', in the US, where the late filmstar's family objected to the use of his name. Produced by Thomas Dolby, who also played keyboards, it became their second UK Top 30 album, and 'When Love Breaks Down' gave them their first Top 40 single.

1988's 'From Langley Park To Memphis' confirmed them not only as critical favourites but also finally as a best-selling band, reaching the UK Top 5. With its pastiche of rock'n'roll icons like Elvis and Springsteen both in its title and songs like 'Cars And Girls' and 'The King Of Rock'n'Roll', it exuded a canny commercial sheen – witness the last-named song with its catchy yet inane chorus, which made the UK Top 10.

'Protest Songs' was an album of unreleased material which made the UK Top 20 in 1989 with minimal publicity while McAloon completed 1990's acclaimed 'Jordan: The Comeback', containing a marathon 19 songs which vaulted into the UK Top 10 on release.

A band whose commercial album success has finally coincided with ever-present critical acclaim, their future hit singles will depend on McAloon's whim.

Greatest Hits

Singles	Title	US	UK
1985	When Love Breaks Down	–	25
1988	The King Of Rock'n'Roll	–	7
Albums			
1988	From Langley Park To Memphis	–	5
1990	Jordan: The Comeback	–	7

Elvis PRESLEY

Elvis Presley was the catalyst which lit the rock'n'roll explosion of the 1950s, the most influential musical figure of that decade, and along with The Beatles, the biggest influence on popular culture this century. Virtually every popular male singer who has picked up a microphone or guitar since 1956, has done so either in direct or indirect response to Presley. As well as being musically the natural synthesis of several native American forms – country, R&B, gospel and the popular ballad – he also rolled them into a visual package which yielded exuberance, rebellion, and above all, sex appeal: Presley gave meaning to the concept of a rock teenage idol.

Born in 1935 (with a twin brother who died at birth), Presley came from a poor Southern rural background in Tupelo, Mississippi. His parents moved to Memphis, Tennessee, in search of work when he was 13, and here he completed a basic education before leaving to become a truck driver for an electrical company in 1953. Though he listened avidly to both the local black and white music, and sang gospel regularly with the family in church, Presley was a shy individual who would probably have never considered a singing career, but the hint of natural magic in his style was noted when he went to the Sun studio in July 1953 to cut a $4 private record for his mother Gladys's birthday present. Sun's owner Sam Phillips, a noted recorder of Southern blues talent, listened to him when he returned the following January for a second $4-worth, and offered to try some recordings with him if suitable material came up.

When an opportunity arose in April 1954, Phillips, good to his word, called Presley into Sun to try some songs, but the session was a disaster. Phillips wanted to persevere, however, and put Presley into rehearsals with two members of a local band, The Starlite Wranglers – guitarist Scotty Moore and bass player Bill Black. Early in July, this trio returned to the studio, and after a lacklustre start, spontaneously cooked up an exciting version of bluesman Arthur Crudup's 'That's All Right Mama', followed by an electric jive through Bill Monroe's bluegrass number 'Blue Moon Of Kentucky'. This, finally, was the fire of which Phillips had been sensing the spark. He pressed the two tracks as a single, and got 'That's All Right Mama' an airing on Memphis radio (Dewey Phillips at WHBQ) within days of the session. Audience reaction the first evening was so strong that the DJ had to repeat-spin the track, and have Presley (who was closeted in a cinema, embarrassed to hear himself singing on the radio) brought in for an interview.

Before the end of July, the single was released with 5000 advance orders from the Memphis area, Presley had signed a recording contract with Sun, and Moore and Black had left their band to play live gigs with him.

The rest of the year saw them playing throughout several Southern states, with Presley's animated body movements on the uptempo material whipping youthful audiences into a frenzy. An attempt to play the *Grand Ole Opry* radio show in Nashville proved misjudged, the staid theatre audience remaining unimpressed, but Presley found far greater success on the rival *Louisiana Hayride* from Shreveport, on which he became a weekly regular.

In 1955, Presley's growing popularity across the South came to the attention of C&W entrepreneur/manager Col. Tom Parker, a former travelling showman who was managing Hank Snow. Parker added him to Snow's touring show, and having managed to persuade Presley's father, Vernon, that he needed stronger management and a move away from Sun, he began to publicize him to key DJs and record companies outside the South. The word was spreading anyway, as Presley's fourth and fifth Sun singles, 'Baby Let's Play House' and 'I Forgot To Remember To Forget', both made the Top 10 of *Billboard* magazine's US country music chart.

The autumn of 1955 saw a sudden scramble of large labels, alerted by a Parker suggestion that his contract might be for sale, to buy Presley out from Sun. Phillips turned down early bids in the $5000–$7500 range from Decca and Dot Records, but by November found it impossible to resist an unheard-of (Parker-orchestrated) offer from RCA Records and Aberbach Music Publishing, which would pay $35,000. With just a year of Presley's contract to run, and realizing that this would capitalize Sun for further expansion, Phillips signed the deal.

1956 transformed Presley from a regional phenomenon into an international star. In January he cut his first RCA single, 'Heartbreak Hotel', and launched into a series of weekly national TV slots as a guest on *Tommy and Jimmy Dorsey's Stage Show*, which piled up huge viewer ratings as word of mouth spread about his performance. In April, 'Heartbreak Hotel' reached the top of the US chart, where it stayed for eight weeks, the first of many million-sellers. It was followed to No. 1 in July by 'I Want You, I Need You, I Love You', and in August by the double-sided smash 'Hound Dog'/'Don't Be Cruel', which was Presley's biggest-selling US single (over 5 million copies) and topped the chart for a further two months. His popularity began to spread across the Atlantic, too, with 'Heartbreak Hotel' hitting No. 2 in the UK.

The whole of US TV wanted Presley: after his Dorsey residency, he appeared on the *Milton Berle*, *Steve Allen* and *Ed Sullivan* shows, picking up plenty of criticism from adults over his hip-swivelling performances but galvanizing America's teenage population. Meanwhile, his debut album, 'Elvis Presley', became RCA's biggest-selling album to date purely on its advance orders of 362,000

244

Legs apart, guitar slung low, Elvis towered over any of his contemporaries in terms of sex appeal, solid gold success and sheer rock'n'roll style

and it too topped the chart, for 10 weeks.

Hollywood grabbed Presley quickly, too. After signing a $450,000 three-film deal with Paramount producer Hal Wallis, he was immediately loaned out to 20th Century Fox for a role written into a Civil War period picture called *The Reno Brothers*. Presley was clearly awkward in his debut role, but four songs were added, and the movie retitled *Love Me Tender*; this undistinguished western starring Richard Egan and Debra Paget became a box office smash. Presley sang the ballad title song on the *Ed Sullivan Show* before he had even recorded it, with the result that RCA had to cut and rush-release a single to meet staggering advance orders of over 850,000. It too shot to No. 1, replacing 'Don't Be Cruel', while 'Hound Dog' became

Presley's second major UK hit, reaching No. 2. By the end of the year, his second LP, 'Elvis', was also topping the US charts, while Presley, returning to Memphis for a Christmas rest, dropped into the Sun studio and was taped by Phillips jamming with the label's new stars Carl Perkins and Jerry Lee Lewis – an event finding legendary status as the 'Million Dollar Session'.

In 1957, Presley made two more box office-smash films, both cementing his image rather more securely than *Love Me Tender*: *Loving You* saw him as a country boy who becomes a singing star, and *Jailhouse Rock* as a roughneck who reforms in prison and *also* becomes a singing star. Both had plenty of songs, and benefitted from some of the best being written by Jerry Leiber and Mike Stoller, a talented pair of white tunesmiths who normally specialised in R&B (but had also written Presley's biggest hit 'Hound Dog'). He also topped the US singles chart four more times in 1957, with 'Too Much', 'All Shook Up' (also his first UK No. 1), 'Teddy Bear' (from *Loving You*), and the title song from *Jailhouse Rock*, while the year closed with another chart-topping LP, the seasonal 'Elvis's Christmas Album' – the butt of some radio bans by conservative programmers who disliked Presley's distinctly black approach to Christmas standards.

The end of 1957 also brought Presley the news that the US Army wanted him for two years. Paramount asked for and got a deferment so that he could film the movie *King Creole* – his strongest dramatic role, as a young misfit mixed up with gangsters in New Orleans, but again with a batch of strong songs. However by the end of March 1958, he was sworn in as US Private 53310761, and off the performing scene.

Absence, however, barely affected his commercial success in 1958. In January, the Leiber/Stoller-penned 'Jailhouse Rock' entered the UK chart at No. 1, the first single ever to do so, and became his biggest British seller to date, topping 750,000. 'Don't' and 'Hard Headed Woman' were US chart-toppers and million sellers, while 'Wear My Ring Around Your Neck' reached No. 2 on both sides of the Atlantic.

Presley's personal world was shattered in August, however, when his mother Gladys contracted hepatitis and died. Little over a month later, he was shipped across the Atlantic for a tour of Army duty in West Germany, and eager to be close to his family following their tragic loss, he also moved his father and grandmother to live with him off-base.

1959 saw the release of most of the cream of the remaining material Presley had recorded before enlisting, and it gave him three more million-selling singles: 'One Night'/'I Got Stung', 'A Fool Such As I'/'I Need Your Love Tonight', and 'A Big Hunk O'Love'. Meanwhile, in West Germany, Presley met American teenager Priscilla Beaulieu, whom he started to date regularly.

Presley returned home and was demobbed in March 1960, and almost at once it seemed business as usual: a TV show (with Frank Sinatra), the hastily-recorded 'Stuck On You' atop the charts, and a film in production. However, a change of career emphasis began to become apparent. The movie *G.I. Blues* was a light, song-heavy concoction, more obviously family-aimed rather than pure teenage fare. A trend towards light-heartedness, songs and comedy would become more and more emphasized in the Presley celluloid world through the 1960s – particularly after *Flaming Star* and *Wild In The Country*, the two immediate follow-ups to *G.I. Blues*, and both non-musical dramas – proved to be comparative financial stiffs. At first, the candyfloss approach worked: *Blue Hawaii*, *Follow That Dream* and *Viva Las Vegas* (which co-starred Presley with Ann-Margret) were all entertaining and commercial winners, but thereafter most Presley films were bywords for plot banality, production shoddiness and musical mediocrity. Turned out at a rate of about three a year because Col. Parker saw them as the most cost-and-effort-effective way of performing to Presley's worldwide audience, these movies contributed heavily to a loss of credibility in the mid-60s.

Change also became apparent from 1960 in Presley's choice of recording material. He broadened his horizons to encompass a wider audience, and here, for the first few years, he succeeded admirably. The follow-up to 'Stuck On You' was, incredible as it first seemed, an Americanization of the Neapolitan ballad 'O Sole Mio', rewritten as 'It's Now Or Never'. The public, including people who had never listened to Presley before, fell over themselves for it. Topping the US chart, it became, globally his biggest-selling single; in the UK it entered the chart at No. 1 and stayed at the top for nine weeks, becoming his only single to top a million sales in the UK alone. It also began his strongest run ever on the British charts: from 'It's Now Or Never' at the end of 1960 to 'Return To Sender' at the close of 1962, Presley had nine UK chart-toppers, the others being 'Are You Lonesome Tonight', 'Wooden Heart' (from *G.I. Blues*), 'Surrender' (another Neapolitan ballad), 'His Latest Flame', 'Can't Help Falling In Love' (from *Blue Hawaii*), 'Good Luck Charm' and 'She's Not You'. Only the title song from *Wild In The Country* stalled, comparatively, at No. 2. All these singles were global million sellers, and several of them topped the US chart too.

On the LP front, the soundtrack albums from *G.I. Blues* and *Blue Hawaii* were gigantic sellers, while the mixed rock/ballad sets 'Elvis Is Back', 'Something For Everybody' and 'Pot Luck' also scaled the heights. The 1961 gospel album 'His Hand In Mine', though a labour of love for Presley, and

highly respected in later years, was regarded as rather a damp squib at the time.

Presley's UK sales fell off as soon as The Beatles and Merseybeat appeared in 1963 with America following suit a year later as the 'British Invasion' hit. Presley's singles and albums usually made the Top 20, since he had such a huge fan base which eroded only slowly, but they rarely made the Top 3 any more (1963's 'Devil In Disguise' and 1965's 'Crying In The Chapel' were the exceptions). Moreover, as his film commitments escalated ever higher (they had already stamped out live performances – two charity concerts in 1961 in Memphis and at Pearl Harbor were his only early 60s stage shows), Presley had less and less time to record material not intended for film soundtracks, while the standard of the film songs themselves became ever more mediocre.

In the mid-1960s, he seemed to have lost touch with the musical mainstream, and totally abdicated his role as a high-profile trend-setting artist. A bright exception to this mediocrity was a second gospel album, 1967's 'How Great Thou Art' which won Presley his first coveted Grammy award as the year's best religious recording. A notable personal event also occurred in 1967 – having closely courted Priscilla Beaulieu for more than seven years, Presley suddenly married her.

A career turnaround came in 1968. Though the flood of movies was still slow to dry up, Presley made a TV special with director Steve Binder, who returned him to the roots of his music and image, and made a show full of energy, tough production numbers and sweaty, classic rock'n'roll. It got a ratings bonanza, and simultaneously whetted Presley's appetite for a return both to serious non-movie recording and for live concerts.

In 1969, he did both, first recording in Memphis for the first time since his Sun days, and then re-launching himself as a live performer with a show, mostly based on his classic hit repertoire, at the International Hotel in Las Vegas. Both projects were resounding successes: the sessions produced the album 'From Elvis In Memphis', his most critically-acclaimed for nine years, and also gave him a slew of million-selling singles like 'In The Ghetto', 'Suspicious Minds' (which returned him to No. 1 in the US) and 'Don't Cry Daddy'. The live show also brought critical raves and huge audiences – Presley found himself being re-booked in Vegas because of the demand to see him perform. His return to the stage was the subject of the documentary film *Elvis: That's The Way It Is* – almost the last of the Presley movies, and significantly a box-office success far outstripping his previous 'candyfloss' comedies.

The successes of 1969, because they were such successes, set the pattern for the decade which followed. Presley did not return to Hollywood, he recorded songs for single and album projects instead of movies, and with the buzz of singing to an audience once more motivating him, he began to tour the US again, always to capacity audiences. All was just as frustrated fans back in the 60s had wished it would be: the records sold strongly, with frequent major hit singles like 'The Wonder Of You', 'Burning Love', 'Always On My Mind', 'My Boy' and 'Promised Land'. LP projects like 'Elvis Country' showed Presley's renewed interests in his material, and an imaginative satellite telecast from Hawaii gained a huge worldwide audience.

However, it all went stale and then wildly wrong. Once he started touring again, Presley's relationship with his wife (who had presented him with a daughter, Lisa Marie) started to become difficult; she found his lifestyle, full of hanger-on buddies hired to fill minor administrative roles and provide companionship, hard to relate to. In 1972, they legally separated, and the following year were divorced. The rift hurt Presley deeply, as his recordings showed: he began to concentrate on material dealing with similar situations, and moved excessively into maudlin country ballads.

More seriously, his health problems, to a large degree psychologically-based and partly self-inflicted, began to manifest themselves. During the movie and early 70s concert years he had disciplined himself to maintain a peak of physical fitness, but after the separation, an unwillingness to control is diet properly (reference to his cheeseburger binges became common stand-up comic fare), allied to a blind faith in the ability of prescription drugs to conquer any problem, conspired to begin to destroy him. Abetted by the hangers-on, he over-indulged pills and medicines almost pathologically, using one to counteract another in an endless cycle.

Problems began to become noticeable in his stage shows: periods of ballooning weight, incomprehensible monologues, frequent incoherence, and eventually, cancelled shows due to illness. Little could keep him from touring, which seemed to have developed into another pathological need, but RCA found it ever more difficult to get him into a studio, and by 1976 he would record only in Memphis at his Graceland mansion. In the UK, the problem of a lack of new product was solved by using past LP tracks as new singles, and the well-chosen 'Suspicion' and 'The Girl Of My Best Friend', followed by the newly-recorded 'Moody Blue', brought back his Top 10 consistency.

Then, on August 16, 1977, on a vacation between tours, Presley was found dead, from heart failure directly attributable to his prescription abuse, on a Graceland bathroom floor. Millions mourned worldwide, several thousand around the gates of Graceland itself. Presley's death brought a public eulogy from US President Jimmy Carter, media tributes of every kind, and sent his record sales into the stratosphere: RCA's normal production could not keep pace with the huge demand for his entire catalogue. A month

after his burial in Memphis's Forest Hills Cemetery (his body was later moved into the garden of Graceland, beside that of his mother and father when Vernon Presley died, in turn, two years later), his single 'Way Down' was topping the UK chart, and both single and the LP 'Moody Blue' had sold a million in America.

In the years after his death, Presley continued to be a huge record seller. Compilations, archive releases and reissues all found a market, and his singles were charting in the UK until 1988. The artist may have passed on, but the Presley musical legacy – and a gigantic memorabilia industry – continue to make their mark. More than a charistmatic singer or a passion-arousing performer, Elvis Presley was – and is – a cultural phenomenon.

Greatest Hits

Singles	Title	US	UK
1956	Heartbreak Hotel	I	2
1956	I Want You, I Need You, I Love You	I	14
1956	Houng Dog/Don't Be Cruel	I	2
1956	Love Me Tender	I	11
1957	Too Much	I	6
1957	All Shook Up	I	I
1957	Teddy Bear	I	3
1957	Jailhouse Rock	I	I
1958	Don't	I	2
1958	Hard Headed Woman	I	2
1959	One Night/I Got Stung	4	I
1959	A Fool Such As I	2	I
1959	A Big Hunk O'Love	I	4
1960	Stuck On You	I	2
1960	It's Now Or Never	I	I
1960	Are You Lonesome Tonight	I	I
1961	Wooden Heart	–	I
1961	Surrender	I	I
1961	His Latest Flame	4	I
1962	Can't Help Falling In Love	2	I
1962	Good Luck Charm	I	I
1962	She's Not You	5	I
1962	Return To Sender	2	I
1963	(You're The) Devil In Disguise	3	I
1965	Crying In the Chapel	3	I
1969	In The Ghetto	3	I
1969	Suspicious Minds	I	2
1970	The Wonder Of You	9	I
1977	Way Down	18	I

Albums			
1956	Elvis Presley	I	–
1956	Elvis	I	3
1957	Elvis's Christmas Album	I	7
1960	Elvis Is Back	2	I
1960	G.I. Blues	I	I
1961	Something For Everybody	I	2
1961	Blue Hawaii	I	I
1962	Pot Luck	4	I
1964	Roustabout	I	12
1969	From Elvis In Memphis	13	I
1973	Aloha From Hawaii Via Satellite	I	11
1975	40 Greatest Hits	–	I

The PRETENDERS

Chrissie Hynde (vocals, guitar)
James Honeyman-Scott (guitar)
Pete Farndon (bass)
Martin Chambers (drums)

Recording only five original albums in twelve years, Hynde (born 1952) is to The Pretenders much as Ray Davies is to The Kinks, who were among the 'British Invasion' acts she admired during a childhood in Ohio.

Later, she was attending Kent State University at the time when anti-Vietnam war protesters were fired upon by the National Guard in 1970 (a confrontation detailed in the songs 'Student Demonstration Time' by The Beach Boys and 'Ohio' by Crosby, Stills, Nash & Young), and briefly worked with

Kinks connection proved productive for Pretenders

future Devo keyboard player Mark Mothersbaugh before moving to the UK in 1973. She worked at Malcolm McLaren's Chelsea shop and wrote for *New Musical Express* before forming The Pretenders in 1978 with Honeyman-Scott (born 1956) and Farndon (born 1953). They recorded a cover version of 'Stop Your Sobbing' by The Kinks, produced by Nick Lowe, which made the UK Top 40 early in 1979 thanks to Hynde's distinctive warble, national airplay and the group's on-stage popularity.

With Chambers (born 1952) added to the line-up, the band's second UK Top 40 single, 'Kid', preceded their breakthrough, 'Brass In Pocket', written by Hynde and Honeyman-Scott, which topped the UK chart and also made the US Top 20. Like its predecessors, it was included on their eponymous debut album, which also topped the UK chart and made the US Top 10, and was characterized by Hynde's brash style. The hits began to pile up on both sides of the Atlantic with 'Talk Of The Town', 'Message Of Love' and 'I Go To Sleep', but their second album, 'Pretenders II' (1981), displayed little progress although it still made the UK Top 10. Hynde's love affair with Ray Davies seemed to pervade several songs from the album, such as its principal single, the haunting 'I Go To Sleep', a Davies song which The Kinks had never released but had been covered during the 1960s by artists as diverse as The Applejacks and Peggy Lee. The run of hits by The Pretenders continues today, most of them being included on 1987's 'The Singles' compilation.

The group's touring schedule was disrupted when Martin Chambers injured first one hand then the other, as the band became over-addicted to the rock'n'roll lifestyle. But his was a minor problem compared to occurrences in 1982, when Farndon was fired and two days later, Honeyman-Scott died of a drug overdose, while Farndon met the same fate in 1983. Chrissie Hynde then bounced back with a US Top 5/UK Top 20 single, 'Back On The Chain Gang'. Her pregnancy and estrangement from Davies made the mere completion of 1984's US Top 5 album, 'Learning To Crawl', with its attendant US hit singles, 'Show Me' and 'Middle Of The Road', no mean feat; plus her fine cover of 'Thin Line Between Love & Hate' which made the US Top 50, and world tour. Chambers and Hynde had rallied by recruiting players similar in style to their departed colleagues, including Robbie McIntosh on guitar, and had more hits with a Christmas single, '2000 Miles, And Middle Of The Road'. The following year she performed at Live Aid in Philadelphia and teamed up with UB40 for a revival of Sonny & Cher's 'I Got You Babe', which topped the UK chart and made the US Top 30.

The most famous of her accompanists was guitarist Johnny Marr (ex-Smiths) for a US tour after his predecessor, Robbie McIntosh, had left during sessions for 1986's 'Get Close'

album, which made the UK Top 10 and US Top 30, and included a US/UK Top 10 single, 'Don't Get Me Wrong'. Hynde toured the US through much of 1987, when 'The Singles' made the UK Top 10. In 1988, she teamed up with UB40 again for the Nelson Mandela Birthday Tribute in London, and another joint single, Lorna Bennett's 'Breakfast In Bed', a Dusty Springfield album track from 'Dusty In Memphis', was a UK Top 10 hit. A new Pretenders album, 'Packed', was released in 1990.

Greatest Hits

Singles	Title	US	UK
1979	*Brass In Pocket*	14	1
1981	*I Go To Sleep*	–	7
1983	*Back On The Chain Gang*	5	17
1985	*I Got You Babe (with UB40)*	28	1
1986	*Don't Get Me Wrong*	10	10
Albums			
1980	*Pretenders*	9	1
1984	*Learning To Crawl*	5	11
1986	*Get Close*	25	6

Lloyd **PRICE**

A seminal figure in the early history of rock'n'roll, New Orleans-based Price (born 1933) was originally turned down by the biggest local label, Imperial Records, who preferred to sign Fats Domino.

With 'Lawdy Miss Clawdy', originally written as a local radio commercial jingle, he was signed to Art Rupe's Specialty label in 1952, and the single – with the house band led by Dave Bartholomew and with Domino on piano – topped the R&B charts, and going gold on one of the first cross-overs to white audiences heralded the rock'n'roll revolution to come.

A stint in the US Army halted his career until 1957, when a new recording contract produced a US Top 30 ballad hit, 'Just Because'. After a brief spell with his own label, KRC, he re-signed with the previous company for a chart-topping version of 'Stagger Lee', a reworking of the old southern folk song 'Stack O'Lee Blues', that also made the UK Top 10.

Further US Top 3 entries followed in 1959 with 'Personality' (which made the UK Top 10) and 'I'm Gonna Get Married', before a move away from New Orleans style numbers proved less productive sales-wise.

With his own labels, Double L and Turntable, plus his ownership of the Turntable club in New Orleans, Price moved into the entrepreneurial end of the local music scene with some success, but his contribution to early rock, acknowledged by cover versions from Elvis Presley to John Lennon, remains far more important than his modest string of hits would suggest.

Greatest Hits

Singles	Title	US	UK
1959	*Stagger Lee*	1	7
1959	*Personality*	2	9
1959	*I'm Gonna Get Married*	3	23

PRINCE

The flamboyant and controversial multi-talented pop/funk/rock superstar Prince (born Prince Rogers Nelson, 1958) joined Minneapolis high-school band Grand Central (later called Champagne) in 1972 and formed Flyte Tyme, which briefly included Alexander O'Neal, in 1974. He recorded with 94 East (with Colonel Abrams) in 1976 and signed a lucrative deal as a solo artist in 1977.

His self-produced debut album, 'For You' and single, 'Soft And Wet', were US soul hits in 1979 and that year's eponymous album went platinum as 'I Wanna Be Your Lover' became his first US Top 20 single. His controversial third album, 'Dirty Mind', went gold in 1980 and 1981's 'Controversy' went platinum. Prince & The Revolution's 1982 double album, '1999', broke his keyboard dominated 'Minneapolis Sound' wide open in 1983 thanks to the MTV-promoted hit singles, '1999' and 'Little Red Corvette'. His semi-autobiographical first movie, *Purple Rain*, was released in 1984 – its soundtrack album sold a million copies on the day of release, and over 10 million altogether in the US, where it topped the chart for 24 weeks! The excerpted singles, 'When Doves Cry' (which sold over two million in the US), and 'Let's Go Crazy', both topped the US chart.

In 1985 the man with a flair for blatantly sexual lyrics and music won a BRITS award for Best International Artist and 'Purple Rain' earned him a Grammy For Best Rock Vocal

Price – influence outweighed affluence

Performance and also won the Academy Award for Best Original Score. His next album, the psychedelic 'Around The World In A Day', was cut at his new Paisley Park studios in 1984 and released on his Paisley Park label in 1985. It went double platinum and topped the US chart, and tracks from it kept him in the Top 10.

The soundtrack from his 1986 film, *Under A Cherry Moon*, titled 'Parade', kept him in the US Top 5 and included 'Kiss', which topped the US chart and went gold. Shortly after treating the SRO crowds in Britain to his amazing stage show, he announced the end of his group, The Revolution, and with a new group he recorded the 'Sign 'O' The Times' album and film in 1987. The album became another transatlantic Top 10 item and its title track and a duet with Sheena Easton, 'U Got The Look', were the most successful singles from it.

He suppressed his 'Black Album' (which became a huge selling bootleg) and his next official LP was 'Lovesexy', which included the transatlantic Top 10 single 'Alphabet Street'. Released in 1988, this became his first UK No. 1.

After five relatively quiet years Prince shot back to the top in 1989 with his 'Batman' soundtrack album, which went double platinum in the US and topped the charts on both sides of the Atlantic, with the million-selling single, 'Batdance'. His *Graffiti Bridge* movie was released in 1990 and its soundtrack double album topped the UK chart.

Apart from writing and producing all his own hits, this very influential and prolific multi-instrumentalist has written big hits for acts like Chaka Khan, Sheena Easton, The Bangles and Sinead O'Connor, and produced and written many albums for other artists. He is undoubtedly one of the most outstanding performers and truly one of the great figures of modern music.

Sonic stylist Prince, platinum superpop for the 'Eighties

Greatest Hits

Singles	Title	US	UK
1984	*When Doves Cry*	1	4
1984	*Let's Go Crazy*	1	7
1986	*Kiss*	1	6
1989	*Batdance*	1	2
Albums			
1984	*Purple Rain*	1	7
1985	*Around The World In A Day*	1	5
1988	*Lovesexy*	11	1
1989	*Batman*	1	1
1990	*Graffiti Bridge*	6	1

John PRINE

One of several 1970s artists to have the 'New Dylan' label thrust upon him, Prine, like such writers as Kris Kristofferson and Mickey Newbury, created country songs which had the toughness and fervour of the best of the Greenwich Village folk songwriters.

Prine (born 1940) came from Chicago, the son of poor white immigrants from the Kentucky coalfields, the subject of one of his best songs, 'Paradise'. Prine did army service and worked as a mailman before he began performing in Chicago clubs in 1970. Fellow Chicagoan Steve Goodman included Prine songs in his stage act and as a result, Prine was discovered by Kristofferson and Paul Anka.

He was signed to Atlantic by producer Jerry Wexler and released an eponymous album in 1971 which featured 'Sam Stone', about a drug-addicted Vietnam veteran. While neither that, nor 'Diamonds In The Rough' (1972) and 'Sweet Revenge' (1973) sold well, other artists began to cover Prine's compositions, including Bette Midler ('Hello In There', about the plight of lonely old people), the Everly Brothers ('Paradise') and Bonnie Raitt ('Angel From Montgomery').

By 1975, Prine was attempting a new direction, forsaking his acoustic/country approach for hard rock on 'Common Sense', with its version of Chuck Berry's 'You Never Can Tell'. After two years without a record deal, Prine signed to another artist-based label, releasing the Goodman-produced 'Bruised Orange' in 1978. It included a song co-written with Phil Spector ('If You Don't Want My Love') as well as an attack on record business hype, 'Sabu Visits The Twin Cities Alone'.

After recording the rock-inspired 'Pink Cadillac' (1979) and 'Storm Windows' (1980), Prine concentrated on songwriting, composing the controversial 'Unwed Fathers' which was covered by several top country singers. He returned to recording in 1985 by setting up his own label, Oh Boy!, to release 'Aimless Love', 'German Afternoons' (1986) and a live double-album.

Greatest Hits

Albums	Title	US	UK
1975	*Common Sense*	66	–
1978	*Bruised Orange*	116	–

Two heads are better than one

The **PROCLAIMERS**

Craig Reid (vocals, percussion)
Charlie Reid (guitar, vocals)

Béspectacled, short-haired Scottish twins, the Reids' musical approach harks back to basics in a highly technological age. The duo's original appeal was that their folky, lyrically direct music could be reproduced on stage with no added personnel or instruments and indeed, they signed their record deal after an acoustic audition in the record company's boardroom.

Released in 1987, their first album, 'This Is The Story', consisted solely of acoustic guitar, percussion and vocals and was initially considered too uncompromising by many critics, highlighting the problem of the Reids making themselves understood outside of their Scottish homeland.

A re-recorded version of the album track 'Letter from America', produced by Gerry Rafferty, provided a UK Top 3 hit single and propelled the album to gold status, setting the tone for 1988's 'Sunshine On Leith', a more upbeat album that augmented the brothers with a full band. Produced by Pete Wingfield, who had performed the same role for the Reids' idols, Dexys Midnight Runners, it diluted their abrasive original sound, though the commercial results were clear when the album went Top 10. The UK Top 20 hit 'I'm Gonna Be (500 Miles)' and a cover version of Steve Earle's 'My Old Friend The Blues' were the standout tracks, but no further hit singles resulted.

The twins then took a two-year break to rethink and solve the dilemma of making commercially acceptable music without losing their individuality, returning in 1990 with an international hit single in a cover of Roger Miller's 1965 hit, 'King Of The Road', which went Top 20 in the UK.

Greatest Hits

Singles	Title	US	UK
1987	Letter From America	–	3
1988	I'm Gonna Be (500 Miles)	–	11
1990	King Of The Road	–	9
Albums			
1987	This Is The Story	–	23
1988	Sunshine On Leith	125	6

PROCOL HARUM / Gary **BROOKER** / Robin **TROWER**

Gary Brooker (piano, vocals)
Matthew Fisher (organ)
Ray Royer (guitar)
Dave Knights (bass)
Bobby Harrison (drums)

Procol Harum scored a No. 1 with their first single . . . then failed to repeat the feat over the next nine years despite producing solidly English music and regulary touring in the UK and US. That hit was 'Whiter Shade Of Pale', released at the height of the Summer of Love in 1967, and musically reminiscent of a Bach cantata.

Their first eponymous album appeared a full year later due to personnel changes – session drummer Bill Eyden and guitarist Ray Royer (born 1945), both on the single, were replaced by BJ Wilson (born 1947) and Robin Trower (born 1945), both from R&B band The Paramounts, whence Brooker (born 1945) had come. A UK record company problem meant that the album, recorded in haste with producer Denny Cordell, not surprisingly failed to chart in the UK until re-released in 1972 as a doubleback with their second album 'A Salty Dog'. In the US, it had been titled after the hit, a shrewd move given the single's Top 5 chart placing, and made the Top 50.

Some critics compared the piano and organ line-up to The Band, whose 'Music From Big Pink' was breaking new ground in the US, but Gary Brooker's vocals and the lyrics of non-playing member Keith Reid made Procol unique. Trower left after 'Broken Barricades' to pursue his Hendrix fixation. His career was haunted by the comparison, but in harness with ex-Stone The Crows bassist/vocalist Jimmy Dewar and a succession of drummers, he found success in the UK and, more consistently, the US, where 'Bridge Of Sighs', 'For Earth Below' and 'Live!' all went Top 10 between 1974 and 76. Trower subsequently teamed up with Jack Bruce (ex-Cream) in 1981. Procol's 'Shine On Brightly' (1968) 'A Salty Dog' (1969), and 'Home' (1970) were all solid releases, but only the second-named made it into the UK Top 30, though 'Homburg', the follow-up single to 'Whiter Shade . . . ' reached the UK Top 10. Like many distinctively British groups (Jethro Tull, The Kinks etc.) Procol Harum prospered in the US when UK success was hard to come by, producing albums that were instrumentally

'Whiter' winners Procul Harum with Gary Brooker (far right)

almost flawless but sometimes unexciting.

Just as the first album was re-released to become their second UK Top 30 chart item in 1972, the band added that much-needed element to their music via a live album with Canada's Edmonton Symphony Orchestra. Ironically, it was a remake of a track from that first album, 'Conquistador', which yielded a rare transatlantic hit single. At the same time a re-issued 'Pale' reached the UK Top 20.

Personnel changes centred around the organ, guitar and bass slots: Fisher (who opted for production) and Knights were replaced by Chris Copping (born 1945) doubling on bass and keyboards before bassist Alan Cartwright joined in 1971. Guitarist Mick Grabham replaced Trower's stand-in, Dave Ball (born 1950), and Pete Solley was a late addition on organ in 1976 when Copping returned to bass. None of this made much difference to the band's distinctive sound, and they carried on for four more albums, including 1975's 'Procols Ninth', produced by Lieber and Stoller, which yielded a UK Top 20 single, 'Pandora's Box'.

On Procol's 1976 demise, Brooker commenced an unsuccessful solo career, interspersing his own unexceptional albums with a stint in Eric Clapton's band and a guest appearance with The Alan Parsons Project on 'Stereotomy' (1986).

Greatest Hits

Singles	Title	US	UK
1967	A Whiter Shade Of Pale	5	1
1967	Homburg	34	6
Albums			
1972	Live In Concert With The Edmonton Symphony Orchestra	5	48
1973	Grand Hotel	21	–

PUBLIC IMAGE LTD

John Lydon (vocals)
Keith Levene (guitar)
Jah Wobble (bass)
Jim Walker (drums)

Also known as PiL, Public Image Ltd achieved UK chart success with 'Public Image' in a blaze of post-Sex Pistols publicity in late 1978, since when PiL has become an ever-changing backing band for Lydon (born 1956), whose subsequent minor triumphs have relied on his cult status as much as actual output.

The original line-up featured the crazed guitar of Keith Levene and Wobble's reggae-inspired bass – evident on the 'Metal Box' compilation of the first three 12″ singles, which also featured a change of drummer to Martin Atkins (born 1959).

Before long, Wobble and Atkins departed, but were featured on the live 'Paris Au Printemps', recorded in the spring of 1980. It was released in late 1980, as they were joined by Jeanette Lee as 'visual assistant' handling 1960s-style light projections during their act.

An album, 'Flowers of Romance', followed in 1981, taking its title from that of an early group which included Sid Vicious, and making the UK Top 20. Although the band consistently failed, despite various attempts at McLarenesque media-hype, to make an impact in the US, Lydon settled there in 1982. From this vantage point, he became the only regular member of the outfit as Levene left in 1983, while the single, 'This Is Not A Love Song', made the UK Top 5.

After 1984's 'That Is What You Want, This Is What You Get' album, Lydon collaborated with New York hip-hop artist, Afrika Bambaata, on 'World Destruction' under the name Time Zone; further collaborations included the use of Ginger Baker on drums on 'Album', from which was taken the single 'Rise' which made the UK top 20.

After a long dormant period, Lydon assembled a live PiL comprising himself, John McGeogh (guitar), Lu Edmonds (keyboards and guitar), Alan Diass (bass) and Bruce Smith on drums. They supported Big Country on tour, before a full-scale riot at an Athens concert caused a reported million pounds-worth of damage.

Since 1988 Lydon has had cameo roles in films while working on minor PiL projects employing, ironically, self-promotion techniques reminiscent of his one-time mentor, Malcolm McLaren. After the 1989 album, '9', 1990 saw a 'Greatest Hits' compilation make the Top 20 of the UK album chart, while a new single, 'Don't Ask Me', charted towards the end of the year.

Greatest Hits

Singles	Title	US	UK
1978	Public Image	–	9
1983	This Is Not A Love Song	–	5
1986	Rise	–	11
1990	Don't Ask Me	–	15
Albums			
1979	Metal Box	–	18
1981	Flowers Of Romance	114	11
1986	Album	–	14

Gary PUCKETT & The UNION GAP

Gary Puckett (vocals)
Dwight Bement (sax)
Kerry Chater (bass)
Mutha Withem (piano)
Paul Wheatbread (drums)

Best remembered for the durable 'golden oldie' 'Young Girl', Puckett and his group created a vibrant version of blue-eyed soul in the mid 1960s.

Former college students in San Diego, California, the quintet played the local bars as The Outcasts, becoming noted for their ability to reproduce current Top 40 hits. In 1967,

Gary and The 'Gap: Beads'n'barrackroom – who said 'Sixties style was tasteless?

they changed their name, choosing Union Gap because it was the small town in Washington State where Puckett (born 1942) had grown up.

The group recorded with producer Jerry Fuller – after a brief career as a teen balladeer, Fuller had written several of Rick Nelson's hits (including 'Young World' and 'It's Up To You') before finding success as a producer with Beatles imitators, The Knickerbockers.

Fuller featured Puckett's big and clear, if characterless, voice on a cover of Jimmy Payne's 'Woman Woman'. With the group appearing on television in Civil War style uniforms, it was the first of four US Top 10 hits in 1968. Fuller himself wrote 'Young Girl', a yearning beat ballad that was a worldwide hit in 1968, when it topped the UK chart, and made the UK Top 10 on its re-release six years later.

Eager to capitalize on the band's success, their label kept the group in the studio, cutting three albums in 1968 alone. Not unexpectedly, these were of a poor standard, with Outcasts-style versions of songs by Bob Dylan, The Beatles and Bobby Goldsboro alongside a few originals by Chater (born 1945), the group's main songwriter.

Maybe it was overkill, but after the 1969 hit 'This Girl Is A Woman Now', the hits stopped coming for The Union Gap. They carried on for two more years and then disbanded. Chater attempted a solo career with Warners, releasing 'Part Time Love' and 'Love On A Shoestring' (1978). The others disappeared from sight, while Puckett himself went solo, ending up on the rock revival circuit. He appeared in a 1989 TV movie, *My Boyfriend's Back*.

Greatest Hits

Singles	Title	US	UK
1968	*Woman Woman*	4	48
1968	*Young Girl*	2	1
1968	*Lady Willpower*	2	5
1968	*Over You*	7	–
1974	*Young Girl (re-issue)*	–	6
Albums			
1968	*Incredible*	20	–
1968	*Union Gap*	–	24

Suzi **QUATRO**

Leather-clad Suzi Quatro (born 1950) was a bass-playing rocker from Detroit who paradoxically found success in Britain singing the bubblegum of songwriters/producers Nicky Chinn and Mike Chapman.

The daughter of a semi-pro jazzband leader, she formed all girl garage band, The Pleasure Seekers at age 17 with her sister Patti (later a member of Fanny). They played for the troops in Vietnam in 1968 and cut a flop single, but on returning to the US, adopted the then-fashionable progressive rock, added sister Nancy and became Cradle. Producer Mickie Most, Jeff Beck's mentor, saw the group and invited Quatro to the UK. Here she recruited a band – future husband Len Tuckey on guitar, Alastair McKenzie on keyboards and Keith Hodge on drums – and was introduced to the Chinn/Chapman team. After an initial flop, she topped the UK singles chart with Chinnichap's infectiously raucous 'Can The Can'.

Her soundalike follow-ups inevitably dented the UK Top 20 – '48 Crash', 'Daytona Demon', 'Devil Gate Drive' (her second chart-topper), 'Too Big' and 'The Wild One'. The androgynous charm of a diminutive girl in leather combined with a rasping vocal delivery and ultra-commercial material made her stand out from the crowd. Her latter-day hits were mellower: 1978's 'If You Can't Give Me Love' and 1979's 'She's In Love With You'.

As glam-rock and bubblegum faded, she moved into acting as herself, alias Leather Tuscadero in *Happy Days* and a British TV cameo in *Minder*. Among her last recordings for Most's label was 'Stumblin' In', a duet with Smokie's Chris Norman, her sole US Top 40 hit.

A comeback in 1980 proved short-lived (one album, 'Rock Hard'), though the same year's TV-advertised 'Greatest Hits' made the UK Top 5. Her original recordings thereafter were few, but in the 1980s, she broadened her appeal by hosting chat shows and starring as Annie Oakley in the 1986 production of Irving Berlin's musical *Annie Get Your Gun*, while enjoying a country lifestyle with Tuckey.

Greatest Hits

Singles	Title		US	UK
1973	*Can The Can*		56	1
1974	*Devil Gate Drive*		–	1
1979	*Stumblin' In*			
	(with Chris Norman)		8	41
Albums				
1973	*Suzi Quatro*		142	32
1980	*Suzi Quatro's Greatest Hits*		–	4

QUEEN

Freddie Mercury *(vocals, keyboards)*
Brian May *(guitar, vocals)*
John Deacon *(bass)*
Roger Taylor *(drums, vocals)*

Initially – and inaccurately – regarded as a part of the Glam Rock movement (largely due to their name), Queen have retained substantial popularity as an innovative and often brilliant rock band, not only in their native UK, for over 15 years without a personnel change, a major achievement in itself. May (born 1947) played in a school group named 1984 with Tim Staffell, and the two went on to the short-lived Smile, a group which released one unsuccessful single in the US only during 1969, and included Taylor (born Roger Meddows-Taylor, 1949). In 1970, after the group broke up, Staffell left to join an equally unsuccessful combo, but persuaded his flatmate, Mercury (born Frederick Bulsara in Zanzibar, 1946), to leave the group for which he was singing, Wreckage, and join May and Taylor in a new venture, Queen, later completed by the recruitment of Deacon. During the group's early months, each of its members was also involved in work and/or study, Deacon as a teacher, Taylor and May doing degree courses and Mercury studying design and running a market stall.

In 1982 the group were given the chance to use the facilities of a new recording studio as 'guinea pigs' to ensure that it functioned correctly, and this also served as an audition, as two engineers who were present recommended the group to the production company which employed them, who also signed the group in 1972. In 1973 their first album was leased to a major label, but before it was released, a single by an artist credited as Larry Lurex (in fact, most of Queen) coupling cover versions of two 1960s oldies, 'I Can Hear Music' (Phil Spector, The Beach Boys) and 'Going' Back' (Carole King, The Byrds, etc.) was released to zero impact. A few weeks later, Queen's eponymous debut album and a single, 'Keep Yourself Alive', were released, but failed to reach the UK chart, although the album eventually went gold and made the US Top 100.

1974's 'Queen II' album was considerably more successful, reaching the UK Top 5 and the US Top 50, while an excerpted single, 'Seven Seas Of Rhye', became the group's UK singles chart debut, peaking in the Top 10, while the first album belatedly made the UK Top 30 in the wake of its successor's success. Later that year, their third album, 'Sheer Heart Attack', made the UK Top 3/US Top 20, fuelled by a transatlantic hit single, 'Killer Queen' (UK Top 3/US Top 20), and was followed in 1975 by a second UK Top 20 single, 'Now I'm Here'. At the end of that year, the group and producer Roy Baker (with whom they had also worked on the three previous albums) cut 'A Night At The Opera', which topped the UK album chart and reached the US Top 5 with the help of an epic single, 'Bohemian Rhapsody', which topped the UK chart for nine weeks at the end of 1975 and made the US Top 5. With innovative neo-operatic vocal arrangements and arguably the first rock video (it would have been impossible for the quartet to recreate

Freddie – and flairs – in full flight with quintessentially camp Queen

the music live without the use of multiple overdubs), this was Queen's first commercial peak.

1976's 'A Day At The Races' album (continuing the tradition of borrowing titles from well-loved Marx Brothers movies) also topped the UK album chart and made the US Top 5, assisted by the UK Top 3/US Top 20 single, 'Somebody To Love', while Mercury, May and Taylor also guested on Ian Hunter's 'All American Alien Boy' album. After minor UK hit singles, late 1977's 'News Of The World' album was a comparative flop in the UK, peaking in the Top 5, but making the US Top 3 and including four UK hit singles, notably 'We Are The Champions', which made the UK Top 3.

1978's 'Jazz' album made the UK Top 3/ US Top 10, and six months later came the double album, 'Queen Live Killers', which made the UK Top 3 but was a far smaller US success in 1979, but the group returned in strength in 1980 with 'The Game', which became their first UK/US chart-topping album, and was produced in Germany by Reinholdt Mack. The album included two singles which topped the US chart, 'Crazy Little Thing Called Love' and 'Another One Bites The Dust' and was their biggest international album thus far. Later that year, the group wrote the music for the movie, *Flash*

Gordon, the soundtrack album of which made the UK Top 10/US Top 30, and included the UK Top 10 single, 'Flash'. 1982's 'Greatest Hits' album topped the UK chart (where it remained for around six years) and became the group's fourth platinum album in making the US Top 20, where it was listed for a mere six months. A video clip compilation, 'Greatest Flix', also sold prodigiously.

By this time, Taylor had also released his first solo album, 'Fun In Space' (1981), which made the UK Top 20, but the end of 1981 saw a summit meeting between the group and David Bowie, one of their neighbours in the tax haven of Switzerland. The result was a huge UK chart-topping single, 'Under Pressure', which strangely peaked well outside the US Top 20.

1982's 'Hot Space' album was disappointing aesthetically and commercially, although it made the UK Top 5, which by this time was virtually guaranteed for every new Queen album. The group did little in 1983, over ten years of togetherness apparently becoming a surfeit, although May worked on a solo project titled 'Star Fleet' with guitar hero Eddie Van Halen. The resulting mini-album made the UK Top 40, but was a one-off project, as the group's 1984 album, 'The Works', made the UK Top 3, remaining in the UK album chart for nearly two years and

including four UK Top 20 singles, two of which, 'Radio GaGa' and 'I Want To Break Free', made the UK Top 3. At the end of that year, Mercury contributed to the updated Giorgio Moroder soundtrack for the celebrated 1920s Fritz Lang film, *Metropolis*, but the group reunited for a Christmas single with the possibly offensive title, 'Thank God It's Christmas', which almost made the UK Top 20. In 1985 a Mercury solo· single, 'I Was Born To Love You', reached the UK Top 20, and was included on his first solo album, 'Mr Bad Guy', which made the UK Top 10, while the end of the year saw a 14 album boxed set of most of the group's earlier work. Despite the group members being reportedly less than devoted to each other, 1986's 'A Kind Of Magic' album topped the UK chart, and included two UK Top 10 hits, while Mercury contributed three tracks to Dave Clark's *Time* musical and Deacon formed an ad hoc group, The Immortals, to provide a song for the *Biggles* movie. The band embarked on a huge tour which was filmed and recorded and remarkably, an album, 'Live Magic', featuring many of the songs on 'A Kind Of Magic', made the UK Top 3.

1987 was another solo year, with Mercury and Taylor moving in increasingly bizarre directions. Taylor formed a group, The

Cross, for which he was singer/rhythm guitarist rather than drummer/vocalist, and Mercury cut a duet album with opera diva Montserrat Caballe which produced a UK Top 10 single, 'Barcelona', while the 1988 album of the same title made the UK Top 30. May produced a cover version of 'Bohemian Rhapsody' by the fictional TV group, Bad News, and also supervised singles by *East-Enders* actress, Anita Dobson, with whom he was sharing a romance.

1989 saw a long-awaited reunion by the group, whose new album, 'The Miracle', was clearly accurately titled as it entered the UK chart at No. 1. At the end of that year, an album of early sessions which the group had recorded for the BBC reached the UK chart. It seems unlikely that Queen will need to break up due to lack of success, particularly in the UK, but whether the group members will ever again be sufficiently enthusiastic to record together is a more debatable point. Whether they decide to reunite or not, Queen has made a substantial mark on rock history with virtually every one of the group's fifteen albums going gold or better. As yet, solo success has been both inconspicuous and inconsistent, so there seems every chance of the group at least continuing until its 20th Anniversary.

Greatest Hits

Singles	Title	US	UK
1975	Bohemian Rhapsody	9	1
1980	Crazy Little Thing Called Love	1	2
1980	Another One Bites The Dust	1	7
1981	Under Pressure (with David Bowie)	29	1
Albums			
1975	A Night At The Opera	4	1
1976	A Day At The Races	5	1
1980	The Game	1	1
1981	Greatest Hits	14	1
1986	A Kind Of Magic	46	1
1989	The Miracle	24	1

QUICKSILVER MESSENGER SERVICE

John Cipollina (guitar)
Gary Duncan (guitar)
Greg Elmore (drums)
David Freiberg (bass)
Jim Murray (vocals, harmonica)

In many ways the quintessential San Francisco rock band, Quicksilver Messenger Service nevertheless failed to achieve the wider acclaim enjoyed by their contemporaries, Jefferson Airplane and Grateful Dead.

Cipollina (born 1943) was the godson of light classical pianist Jose Iturbi, while Duncan (born Gary Grubb, 1946) and Elmore (born 1946) had been members of

California couriers – Quicksilver Messenger Service

local band, The Brogues. With Freiberg (born 1938) and Murray they developed a blues-based sound using long guitar improvisations in 1966/67, playing at such seminal events as San Francisco's Human Be-In and 1966's Monterey Pop Festival.

After performing two songs in the hippie movie, *Revolution*, Quicksilver Messenger Service signed a major label deal, releasing a debut album in 1968. By this time Murray had left (to study the sitar) and Duncan also quit before the release of 'Happy Trails' (1969), with its double lead-guitar solos on the Bo Diddley numbers 'Who Do You Love' and 'Mona'. Sporting cover art by top psychedelic poster designer George Hunter, the album reached the US Top 30, as did 'Shady Grove', on which the group was joined on piano by noted UK session piano player, Nicky Hopkins.

1970 saw a decisive change of emphasis as Duncan returned and vocalist and songwriter Dino Valenti (born 1943) joined. It had been planned he should be a member of the band in 1965 but a prison sentence on drugs charges intervened. The composer of 'Hey Joe' (made famous by Jimi Hendrix), Valenti dominated 'Just For Love' to the extent that Cipollina left to work with Murray in a new band, Copperhead.

The Valenti-Duncan-led band continued to record prolifically, releasing 'What About Me', 'Quicksilver' and 'Comin' Thru' in 1971/ 72 despite a series of personnel changes. Hopkins had been replaced first by ex-Butterfield Blues Band player Mark Nataflin, then by Chuck Steales. The long-serving David Freiberg was recruited by Jefferson Starship, and his replacement, Mark Ryan, in turn gave way to John Nicholas (from It's A Beautiful Day) in 1973.

By now, Quicksilver Messenger Service had returned to its Bay Area roots, playing only occasional gigs with a variety of musi-

cians supporting Valenti, Elmore and Duncan. In 1975 they returned to the studio for the poor-selling 'Solid Silver', after which the group formally disbanded.

While Gary Duncan formed a new Quicksilver Messenger Service for 'Peace By Piece' (1987), only Cipollina strongly surfaced musically throughout the 1980s. He played on over 30 albums with such artists as the Welsh group, Man, Nick Gravenites and Barry Melton. He was lead guitarist for The Dinosaurs, a line-up of 1960s San Francisco survivors, shortly before his death in 1989 from emphysema.

Greatest Hits

Singles	Title	US	UK
1970	Fresh Air	49	–
Albums			
1969	Happy Trails	27	–
1970	Shady Grove	25	–
1970	Just for Love	27	–
1971	What About Me	26	–

RAINBOW

Ronnie Dio (vocals)
Ritchie Blackmore (guitar)
Mickey Lee Soule (keyboards)
Craig Gruber (bass)
Gary Driscoll (drums)

Among the most omnipotent of British lead guitarists, Blackmore (born 1945) led Rainbow, a Deep Purple spin-off, for almost a decade before re-uniting with his old colleagues in 1984.

Disgruntled with other personnel's indifference towards material he'd submitted for Purple's 'Stormbringer' album, Blackmore intended to cut a solo album before electing to form a new band with members of Purple protégés, Elf. Recorded in Munich, 1975's 'Ritchie Blackmore's Rainbow' disappointed bigoted fans because its guitar solos and riffs were unobtrusive when set against the flash on Blackmore's Purple work. Shortly after Rainbow's stage debut in Bristol, Blackmore dismissed all but songwriting partner Dio to recruit more experienced musicians. Drummer Cozy Powell (ex-Jeff Beck Group and perpetrator of three solo UK Top 20 singles), session player Tony Carey (keyboards) and bass player Jimmy Bain from Harlot played on 1976's 'Rainbow Rising', which contained 'Stargazer', a long-term stage favourite.

Bain was replaced by Mark Clarke (ex-Uriah Heep) for 'On Stage', a double live album issued partly to thwart bootleggers. The group had also adopted more hard-sell approach, as shown by the title track of 1978's 'Long Live Rock'n'Roll' album becoming a UK Top 40 hit. 'LA Connection' from the smoother 'Down To Earth' did likewise, despite the exit of three-fifths of the band – including Dio (to Black Sabbath) – who disagreed with Blackmore's concessions to American FM radio. This was particularly evident on the major hit singles, 'Since You've Been Gone' and 'All Night Long', which involved ex-Purple bass guitarist Roger Glover's playing and production and the singing of Graham Bonnet (half of one hit wonders, Marbles, in 1968).

The departure of Powell and Bonnet (replaced by Americans Bob Rondinelli and Joe Lynn Turner) was not disastrous, as a cover of Russ Ballard's 'I Surrender' became a UK Top 3 hit and 1982's 'Straight Between The Eyes' became Blackmore's biggest post-Purple UK album and re-established him in the US where previously only the debut album had made much headway.

Greatest Hits

Singles	Title	US	UK
1979	Since You've Been Gone	57	6
1980	All Night Long	–	5
1981	I Surrender	–	3
Albums			
1977	On Stage	65	7
1978	Long Live Rock'n'Roll	89	7
1979	Down To Earth	66	6
1981	Difficult to Cure	50	3
1982	Straight Between The Eyes	30	5

Bonnie RAITT

One of the most critically admired yet commercially ignored white R&B singers in the history of popular music, Bonnie Raitt only achieved the success and respect she had so obviously deserved with her tenth album, almost 20 years after her recording debut.

The daughter of Broadway star John Raitt (of *Carousel* and *The Pajama Game* fame), Bonnie Raitt (born 1949) was first captivated by the blues and began learning guitar at the age of 12. After dropping out of college in 1969, she began playing on the US folk and blues circuit, turning heads due to her ability – almost unique in a white female – to play credible bottleneck guitar. She became friendly with many of the surviving blues legends, including Howlin' Wolf, Mississippi Fred McDowell and particularly Sippie Wallace, with whom she later recorded. After paying her dues in clubs, she signed with a major label in 1971, when she released her eponymous debut album, which featured a disastrous sleeve photo which made her look twice her age, and included both contemporary songs by Stephen Stills and Paul Siebel and a number of blues covers, plus two self-penned originals. Backed largely by R&B musicians who normally worked with producer Willie Murphy, Raitt was somewhat sold short by the album, as became clear with the release of 1972's greatly improved 'Give It

Up' album, which made the US chart and featured mainly white rock players and superb songs written by under-appreciated songwriters like Eric Kaz and Jackson Browne, plus three originals and several R&B covers.

The improvement was maintained on 1973's 'Takin' My Time' album, which was her first to make the US Top 100. Backed by most of Little Feat plus Taj Mahal, Van Dyke Parks and the only musician who had played on each of her albums thus far, bass player Freebo (real name Daniel Freenberg), the album included more songs by Kaz and Browne, as well as a breathtaking version of Randy Newman's 'Guilty'. 1974's 'Streetlights' album seemed to mark time as Raitt tried recording in New York with session musicians, although it did include a superb version of John Prine's 'Angel From Montgomery' and songs by Joni Mitchell, James Taylor and Allen Toussaint. 1975's much improved 'Home Plate' album was recorded in her native Los Angeles and was a welcome return to form which was her US Top 50 debut, and included songs by Toussaint, J.D. Souther and Kaz's heartbreaking 'I'm Blowin' Away', with backing help from a galaxy of stars, including Souther, Browne, Emmylou Harris, John Sebastian, Tom Waits and many more, but even such a clearly superior piece of work failed to convince the majority of punters that hers was a rare and precious talent.

A two-year gap ensued before her sixth album, 'Sweet Forgiveness', which included material by all the right songwriters (Browne, Kaz, Siebel, etc.), although her minor commercial breakthrough came with a revival of Del Shannon's hit from the early 1960s, 'Runaway', which made the Top 40 of the US singles chart, while the album went gold in reaching the US Top 30. It seemed that perhaps she had finally reached the commercial first division, but another two-year hiatus preceded 1979's rather disappointing album, 'The Glow', produced by Peter Asher and with backing from many noted LA musicians, which made the US Top 30. Longtime admirers wondered what was wrong, and it wasn't until 1982's 'Green Light' that it became clear that Raitt was being badly advised and was not following the route which had first brought her acclaim, although the album did make the US Top 40. A four-year gap then occurred before her ninth album, 'Nine Lives', escaped in 1986, by which time it was clear that a major reappraisal was urgently required.

1989's 'Nick Of Time' found Raitt on a different record label after 18 years with one company, and with production by Don Was, Raitt finally found herself receiving the commercial rewards (and Grammy Awards) her mainly excellent body of work had always deserved. With guest helpers from such different musical areas as R&B combo The Fabulous Thunderbirds, country group The

After a decade of looking for the pot of gold, Richie eventually got over the Rainbow

Fans and fellow musicians all rate Bonnie

The **RAMONES**

Joey Hyman (vocals, drums)
Johnny Cummings (guitar)
Douglas 'Dee Dee' Colvin (bass)

A 1976 gig in London by New York quartet The Ramones was one of the more important pointers to the cohesion of the punk movement, showcasing these early perpetrators of speedy bursts of thrashed three-chord guitars, machine gun drumming and ranted two-line lyrics. However, unlike many of their admirers in UK bands, The Ramones maintained public respect for pop history with regular revivals of 1960s material.

They were formed in 1974. Manager Tommy Erdelyi took over on drums to allow Hyman to concentrate on singing, and all four had adopted the stage surname 'Ramone' by the start of a virtual residency at CBGB's, the Bowery club that they ruled as The Beatles had ruled The Cavern. Rivalry with other acts dissolved into a camaraderie exemplified by the composition of New Wave standard 'Chinese Rocks' by Colvin and three members of competing New York band The Heartbreakers, including bass player Richard Hell.

Signed to a discriminating New York independent label, The Ramones delivered an eponymous debut album that caught the essence of their driving performances. Although its singles, 'Blitzkrieg Bop' and the token 'slow' number, 'I Wanna Be Your Boyfriend', were chart failures, 'Now I Wanna Sniff Some Glue' inspired the title of a high profile British punk fanzine and raised questions in the House of Commons. 'Leave Home' and 'Rocket To Russia' (both 1977 albums) were technical advances on the first album while retaining its lyrical direction with the likes of 'Gimme Gimme Shock Treatment', 'Suzie Is A Headbanger', the cover of The Trashman's 'Surfin' Bird' and the UK hit 'Sheena Is A Punk Rocker'.

After their UK tour with label-mates The Rezillos, Marc Bell (of Richard Hell & The Voidoids) replaced Erdelyi, who became a full-time producer. His absence may account for the comparative listlessness of 1978's 'Road To Ruin', but commercial momentum was sustained with 'It's Alive', a double concert album, and the group's dramatic and musical involvement in 1979's *Rock'n'Roll High School* movie. Its soundtrack was mixed by Phil Spector who, as well as the group's contributions to the 1980 film *Times Square*,

Pre-punk pimplies The Ramones, promoting themselves as teenage rock'n'role models

Desert Rose Band and notables like David Crosby, Graham Nash and Herbie Hancock, and including a great John Hiatt song, 'Thing Called Love', the album was perhaps not quite up to the standard of 'Takin' My Time' or 'Home Plate', but few of her discriminating fans could object in view of the fact that she was finally a star.

1990 saw her winning another Grammy Award for her work on John Lee Hooker's 'The Healer' album, which was to some extent a return to the roots for two truly great artists from different generations. Raitt can also be heard on such albums as 'Ann Arbor Blues' and 'Jazz Festival 1970', on which she duets with Sippie Wallace on the latter's 'Woman Be Wise', and on 1985's 'Tribute To Steve Goodman' album, on which she duets with Goodman's best friend, John Prine, on the latter's 'Angel From Montgomery'. Both these duets were included on the excellent 'Bonnie Raitt Collection' album, released in 1990 by her first label in the wake of the success of 'Nick Of Time'.

Raitt is much admired by other notable contemporary musicians such as Prince, who was eager to produce her in the 1980s, when she was obviously out of commercial favour, and (although the album they started was never completed), Little Feat, with whom she guested on their reunion tour. Wynonna Judd (of The Judds), has frequently cited Raitt as her role model. Chart positions are largely irrelevant in Bonnie Raitt's case, but anyone who enjoys great music is missing something should they decide to ignore this supremely tasteful and utterly sincere artist.

produced their next album, 'End Of The Century', on which each faction delved into respective back catalogues for 'Baby I Love You' and 'Chinese Rocks'.

With noted songwriter Graham Gouldman (ex-10cc) producing, 1981's 'Pleasant Dreams' was a fresher collection but it signalled a two-year vinyl silence from the quartet broken only by a duet of 'I Got You Babe' by Hyman and Holly Vincent, leader of New York's Holly and the Italians. 'Subterranean Jungle' featured a minor UK hit in 'Time Has Come Today' and a lead vocal on 'Time Bomb' by Colvin. The following year's 'Too Tough To Die' featured new drummer Richard Beau and used three producers: Eurythmics' Dave Stewart supervised its main single, 'Howling At The Moon'. A comment on President Reagan's 1985 visit to Germany, 'Bonzo Goes To Bitburg' was included on the patchy 'Animal Boy' album. Bell rejoined the band, but 1988's 'Halfway To Sanity' and 1989's 'Brain Drain' seemed rather predictable and lacking in progression. Colvin left the band shortly after, and although The Ramones performed the title theme to the 1990 horror movie *Pet Semetary*, their US tour with Deborah Harry and the Tom Tom Club that year was regarded by many as almost nostalgia.

Greatest Hits

Singles	Title	US	UK
1977	*Sheena Is A Punk Rocker*	81	22
1980	*Baby I Love You*	–	8
Albums			
1977	*Rocket To Russia*	49	60
1980	*End Of The Century*	44	14

RASPBERRIES / Eric CARMEN

Eric Carmen (vocals, keyboards, guitar)
Wally Bryson (guitar)
Jim Bonfanti (drums)
Dave Smalley (bass, guitar)

US band the Raspberries were formed in 1970 by Carmen (born 1949), a former classical music student. Lead guitarist Bryson (born 1949) and drummer Bonfanti (born 1948) met up with bassist Smalley (born 1949) in The Choir, a group that had a small US hit, 'It's Cold Outside', in 1967.

Carmen joined Cyrus Erie an English beat-style outfit, switched to a frontman role on guitar and keyboards and brought in Bryson and drummer Mike McBride. Dave Smalley returned from Vietnam in 1970 to pick up bass duties in the newly formed Raspberries, with Jim Bonfanti on drums, following which they signed to a major label. 'Don't Want To Say Goodbye' and 'Go All The Way' (a US Top 5 single) from 1972's 'Raspberries' proved they could mix ballads with rockers,

though it was the former that gave smooth-voiced Carmen his chance to shine. 'Fresh' was released later in 1972, but the following year's 'Side 3' saw a split as the rhythm section quit, claiming Bryson and Carmen were selling out to the teenybop market. The dissenting duo were replaced by ex-Cyrus Erie drummer McBride and unknown bassist Scott McCarl.

Released in 1974, 'Starting Over' (one of *Rolling Stone's* albums of the year) signalled a new beginning in its title and boasted a US Top 20 hit in 'Overnite Sensation (Hit Record)' showcasing harmonies that would put The Beach Boys to shame. But sales disappointed and the band split in March 1975.

Solo, Carmen found a more consistent vein of success with eight US hit singles in 12 years. First and biggest was a 1976 US Top 3 hit in 'All By Myself'. He became involved in teen film music through *Footloose* in 1984, while 'Hungry Eyes' from *Dirty Dancing* was a US Top 5 hit for him in 1987, and Carmen has also written for others, notably Shaun Cassidy, Olivia Newton-John and Frankie Valli.

Greatest Hits

Singles	Title	US	UK
Raspberries			
1972	*Go All The Way*	5	–
1972	*I Wanna Be With You*	16	–
Eric Carmen			
1976	*All By Myself*	2	12
1988	*Make Me Lose Control*	3	–
Albums			
Raspberries			
1973	*Fresh*	36	–
Eric Carmen			
Albums			
1976	*Eric Carmen*	21	58

Chris REA

An object lesson in self-belief, singer/songwriter/guitarist Chris Rea spent most of the 1970s quietly building a substantial audience without ever being regarded as fashionable, but by the end of the 1980s, had emerged to become a significant international star.

Rea (born 1951, Middlesborough, UK of Irish/Italian descent – his family own the local ice-cream parlour) was first moved to play guitar after hearing albums by Joe Walsh and Ry Cooder. He joined local band Magdalene (whose vocalist, David Coverdale, had recently defected to Deep Purple) where he began writing original material and polishing his slide guitar technique. After a change of name, to The Beautiful Losers, the group won the *Melody Maker*, 'Best Newcomers of 1975' award, but were unable to capitalize on

A fullsome frontview of Chris Rea

it, and Rea eventually left.

Signing a solo deal in 1977, his debut album, 'Whatever Happened To Benny Santini?', appeared in 1978. Released at the height of Punk/New Wave, Rea's haunting tunes, tasteful guitar, and throaty vocals were deemed old hat, and the album stiffed – but astonishingly reached the US Top 50, going gold and spinning off a US Top 20 single, 'Fool (If You Think It's Over)'. Repromoted in the UK, the single reached the Top 30.

By the mid-1980s, Rea had been quietly releasing an album per year, each one steadily outselling its precedessor, and promoting them via an endless touring schedule and occasional spinoff singles, all of which gradually expanded his audience. Ironically, he was unable to build on his initial US success, but nevertheless became a major star in Europe, especially in Ireland, where he was regarded as a superstar. 1983's 'Water Sign', although only a modest UK success, sold over half a million copies in Europe, and a year later, 'Wired To The Moon' was his first UK Top 40 album.

'Shamrock Diaries' (1985) and 'On The Beach' (1986) were both steady sellers, both making the UK Top 20 and finally establishing Rea as a major artist in the UK and preparing the ground for 1987's 'Let's Dance', his first UK Top 20 single. Its parent album, 'Dancing With Strangers', went gold in the week of release and was only prevented from topping the UK chart by Michael Jackson's 'Bad'. His new-found status was further consolidated when 'On The Beach Summer '88', a remixed version of an earlier single, reached the UK Top 10, and was followed closely by

'New Light Through Old Windows', a 'Best Of' album with re-recordings of several other earlier tracks, which made the UK Top 5.

In 1989, 'The Road To Hell' became Rea's first UK No. 1 album, and an edit of the title track provided his first UK Top 10 single. Rea remains one of the UK's most enduring talents and should thrive during the 1990s.

Greatest Hits

Singles	Title	US	UK
1978	Fool (If You Think It's Over)	12	30
1987	Let's Dance	–	12
1987	On the Beach Summer '88	–	12
1989	The Road To Hell	–	10
Albums			
1978	Whatever Happened To Benny Santini?	49	–
1985	Shamrock Diaries	–	15
1987	Dancing With Strangers	–	2
1989	The Road To Hell	107	1

Otis **REDDING**

With his pleasing, intense ballad style and funky revivalist uptempo delivery, Redding (born 1941) virtually defined the 1960s development of southern soul music. Despite a relatively short recording career, ended by a tragic early death, his influence as a stylist was extensive. He first performed in his teens in his native Macon, Georgia, as a 'Little Richard imitator', cutting unsuccessful one-off small-label singles in this style between 1959 and 1961. By 1962, he was singing regularly with touring R&B band Johnny Jenkins & The Pinetoppers (for whom he also chauffeured) and sang on their regional hit single, 'Love Twist!' When the band recorded at Stax studio in Memphis, Redding persuaded Stax co-founder Jim Stewart to let him use spare studio time to cut two songs himself. Impressed by the ballad, 'These Arms Of Mine', Stewart released it as a single, which made the Top 20 of the US R&B chart, and eventually the US Pop chart.

The Jenkins band failed to achieve anything further, but on the strength of his debut, Redding was signed by Atlantic and, via a special arrangement, continued to record at Stax and have his records issued by Stewart. He recorded with Stax house band Booker T & The MGs, and had further R&B and minor pop hits with 'Pain In My Heart' in 1964 and 'Mr Pitiful' early in 1965, before scoring major crossovers later that year with another classic soul ballad, 'I've Been Loving You Too Long', and the funky, uptempo 'Respect' (later covered by Aretha Franklin).

In the UK, Redding was initially a cult favourite who sold to Mod R&B fans, but his first pop Top 20 hit came in Britain, when his subtly cooking cover of The Temptations hit, 'My Girl', was selected from the 'Otis Blue'

Otis – the consummate 1960s soulman

album as a UK single in early 1966, while the album made the UK Top 10. The cult figure became a pop sensation: TV's *Ready Steady Go!* devoted an edition to his live performance, and more UK Top 30 singles followed with 'I Can't Turn You Loose' and 'Fa-Fa-Fa-Fa-Fa (Sad Song)'.

Early in 1967, Redding stormed Europe again as the headliner on the Stax/Volt package tour, and in mid-year he also made his breakthrough to the comparable young, white US audience, via a well-timed appearance at the hip, largely white and rock-orientated Monterey Pop Festival, where his passionate stage act went down a storm.

Redding widened his activities to launch his own Jotis label, and write and produce the million-selling 'Sweet Soul Music' for his protégé Arthur Conley. He also recorded an album with Stax songstress Carla Thomas, from which a cover of Lowell Fulson's 'Tramp' was another international hit. But disaster struck on December 10, 1967, when the plane carrying him and his road band, The Bar-Kays, crashed into Lake Monoma, Wisconsin, killing all but one passenger.

The posthumous single, '(Sittin' On) The Dock Of The Bay', recorded only three days before his death, ironically became Redding's biggest hit, topping the US chart and selling over a million. A wistful, philosophical ballad, it could have presaged a new direction for the singer, and won two Grammy awards as the best R&B record of 1968.

Redding's stature ensured that his releases continued to chart years after his death, and his work was still being anthologized over 20 years later. His three sons also took up their heritage during the 1980s, successfully recording as a soul trio, The Reddings.

Greatest Hits

Singles	Title	US	UK
1968	The Dock Of The Bay	1	3
Albums			
1967	History Of Otis Redding	9	2
1968	The Dock Of The Bay	4	1

Helen **REDDY**

Sometimes unjustly stuck with an MOR label that belies an original voice, albeit often handling bland material, Helen Reddy (born 1942) had a solid show business background in her native Australia.

From a stage family, she debuted on the boards at four; by her teens, she was on the road in a variety show, which led to regular Australian TV work. A talent contest win in 1966 awarded her a US trip, where she met her future manager and husband, theatrical agent Jerry Wald.

Considerable US TV work helped her 1971 debut single, 'I Don't Know How To Love Him' from the Andrew Lloyd-Webber/Tim Rice musical, *Jesus Christ Superstar*, into the US Top 20; it was followed by a chart-topper in 1972, her own 'I Am Woman', that became something of a feminist anthem of the time.

Her UK breakthrough also came largely through guest spots on TV shows in 1973/74, when two more singles topped the American chart – Alex Harvey's 'Delta Dawn' and 'Angie Baby'.

The latter song established Reddy as an interesting off-centre vocalist, with an individual style suited to unusual material. Her huge success, however, particularly in the album market, tended to draw her more directly into the mainstream of FM-style adult-pop.

Most of her early 1970s albums made the US Top 20, from 1972's 'I Am Woman', through 'Love Song For Jeffrey' (1974) to 'No Way To Treat A Lady' (1975) . Her material ranged from the strident 'I Am Woman', 'Angie' and 'Leave Me Alone' to the cloyingly sentimental 'You And Me Against The World' which, combined with an increasingly 'glamorous' image, smoothed the edges of an interesting talent.

Helen ready for action

Jimmy REED

For a good ten years, Jimmy Reed was by far the most commercially successful unadulterated bluesman of his generation. While his contemporaries were building reputations that would eventually bring them international acclaim, laconic, simplistic Reed was selling records.

Born Mathis James Reed (1925) in the town of Dunleith, Mississippi, he learned to play guitar from bluesman Eddie Taylor, who filled in the important counterpoint on the majority of Reed's subsequent recordings. Reed also learned to play rudimentary harmonica, and armed with these two musical basics, a supportive wife, and an ever-present bottle of something alcoholic, he relocated to Chicago. There, signed to the Vee–Jay label, he outsold Muddy Waters, Howlin Wolf, B.B. King and the rest of the panoply of blues 'giants'. Simply by being himself, Reed was able to connect with the average man or woman in the street.

He first recorded in 1953 and hit the US R&B Top 10 in 1955 with the deliciously slurred plea, 'You Don't Have To Go', followed over the next decade by a further 16 R&B chart hits and a number of albums of similar take-it-as-it-comes spontaneity. Recordings such as 'Ain't That Loving You Baby', 'You Got Me Dizzy' (1956), 'Honest I Do' (1957), 'Down In Virginia' (1958), 'Take Out Some Insurance', 'Going To New York' (1959), 'Baby What You Want Me To Do' (1960), 'Big Boss Man', 'Bright Lights, Big City' (1961), 'Good Lover' (1962) and 'Shame, Shame, Shame' (1963) were covered by the likes of The Beatles, Rolling Stones, Elvis Presley and Ike & Tina Turner all of whom recognized Reed's talents.

In the mid 1960s Reed continued to record strong sides for various labels while touring with admirable aplomb considering his state of health. Eventually, after several years of alcohol-induced epilepsy he died of a seizure on August 29, 1976.

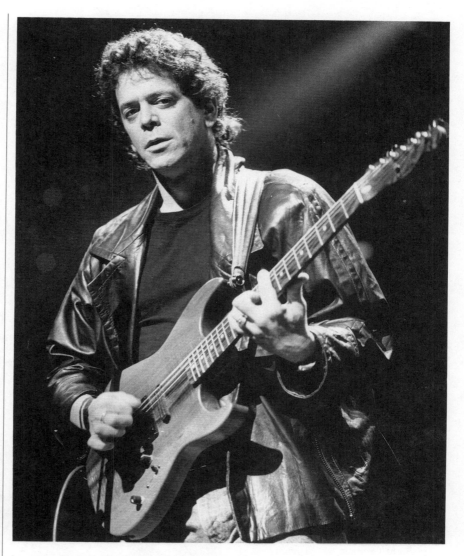

Lou takes a Walk On The Wild Side from Berlin to New York

Lou REED

Lou Reed remains one of rock's most enigmatic and significant performers, but he has enjoyed limited success with his solo career over the last 20 years. Reed (born Louis Firbank, 1942) came from a middle class Long Island family and released his first single, as a member of the Shades in 1957. His family's disapproval of his behaviour and early rock'n'roll ventures allegedly led to his admission to hospital for electro-shock treatment at the age of 18. Reed later attended university, where he came under the influence of poet Delmore Schwarz and met fellow student Sterling Morrison, who would later join him in The Velvet Underground (see separate entry). Reed played in various college bands before finding a job as a songwriter, producing 'soundalike' material, which led to his forming a band to promote a single by The Primitives 'The Ostrich' with John Cale, with whom he founded The Velvet Underground in 1965.

When he left the group in 1970, Reed took a sabbatical from music, returning in 1972 as a solo artist and recording his eponymous debut album in London with rock critic/producer, Richard Robinson. The material on the album was excellent, including a number of unreleased VU songs, but the backing (largely provided by members of Yes) was unsympathetic, and the album flopped. Following a series of gigs backed by New York band The Tots, Reed returned to the UK to record 'Transformer' (1972), produced by fan David Bowie and his guitarist Mick Ronson. Although in many ways a parody of Reed's past work, the album reached the UK Top 20 and spawned a UK Top 10/US Top 20 single, 'Walk On The Wild Side', a roll-call of Warhol 'superstars'.

For the follow-up album, 1973's 'Berlin', Reed employed Alice Cooper producer Bob Ezrin and an all-star cast including Steve Winwood, Jack Bruce and Aynsley Dunbar on a powerful set of songs detailing a doomed, drug-laden relationship ending in

259

suicide . . . which commercially it was for Reed in the US, although it reached the UK Top 10. A planned double live album, 'Rock-'n'Roll Animal' appeared the following year as a single album on which Reed was backed by a slick hard rock band containing veterans of previous Bob Ezrin productions. Reed toured extensively, and amid reports of serious drug abuse, released 'Sally Can't Dance', a return to the camp posturing of 'Transformer'. Despite the poverty of its material, the album reached the US Top 10, but Reed's next venture, 'Metal Machine Music' (1975), baffled fans and critics alike. It was a double album of feedback, machine noise and distortion, variously described as an attempt at modern electronic music or as a contract fulfiller of the most cynical kind, and was swiftly deleted. Reed's record company rushed out the second part of the 'Rock'n'Roll Animal' concert as 'Lou Reed Live' (1975) in an attempt at damage limitation, but it was not until the melodic 'Coney Island Baby' (1976) appeared that Reed's stock rose.

A label change preceded 'Rock & Roll Heart' (1976), which, like its predecessor, reflected Reed's affection for both early rock-'n'roll and his VU past (they each featured unreleased Velvets songs). The title track of 1978's 'Street Hassle' ranked with the best of Reed's work (although the album was patchy) and re-awakened critical interest in his career. A fine live double album, 'Take No Prisoners' (1978) followed, on which Reed talked his way through some of his best known material, sounding closer to Lenny Bruce than a rock singer . . . 1979's 'The Bells' featured songs co-written with Nils Lofgren and contributions from jazz trumpeter Don Cherry, but was disappointing, although Reed retained his basic band for 1980's heavily autobiographical 'Growing Up In Public'.

Another label change heralded a return to form with the albums 1982's 'The Blue Mask' and 1983's 'Legendary Hearts', for which Reed assembled a band including ex-Richard Hell guitarist Robert Quine, ex-Jeff Beck bassist Fernando Saunders and (on 'Hearts') former Material drummer Fred Maher. As a four-piece, they recorded the 1984 double album 'Live In Italy', but Quine was absent for 1984's 'New Sensations', which contained some of Reed's best material since 'Berlin'. Quine toured with Reed in 1984/85, but by the time of 1986's poor 'Mistrial' album, Reed was working with just Saunders and various session men, and the cohesive feel of the previous four albums had been lost.

A one-off remake of 'Soul Man' from the movie of the same name with Sam Moore (who had recorded the original song as half of Sam & Dave) gave Reed a UK Top 50 single in 1987, but a lengthy gap preceded 1989's 'New York', a return to the two guitars, bass and drums format of Reed's finest work, which was hailed as his best solo album to date. In 1990, Reed was re-united with Cale for the 'Songs For Drella' album, a suite of

songs in memory of Velvets mentor Andy Warhol, which drew extensive critical acclaim. Reed has also appeared on albums by Genya Ravan (1978), Rob Wasserman (1988), Tom Tom Club (1988), Maureen Tucker (1989) and Simple Minds (1990), and has taken part in various Amnesty International related live events in recent years.

Greatest Hits

Singles	Title	US	UK
1973	Walk On The Wild Side	16	10
Albums			
1973	Transformer	29	13
1973	Berlin	98	7
1974	Sally Can't Dance	10	–
1989	New York	40	14

Martha **REEVES** & The **VANDELLAS**

Martha Reeves
Rosalind Ashford
Anette Sterling (vocal group)

Perhaps the most exciting of all Motown's girl groups, Martha Reeves (born 1941) & The Vandellas were far more gospel-rooted than their label-mates and Martha's forceful, almost bluesy vocals transcended the pop arrangements that were often provided for them.

Reeves worked initially as A&R head Micky Stevenson's secretary, in order to gain a foothold at the label. She was given demos to record and along with the other Vandellas provided back-up vocals for many of the label's early releases. After a slow start, the group broke through in a big way with Holland-Dozier-Holland's 'Heatwave' in 1964 and enjoyed an almost unbroken string of classic singles until 1967, although their UK success came later.

Their peak was probably the anthemic 'Dancing In The Street', a hit at the height of racial unrest in the USA during 1964. Martha's relationship with Motown boss Berry Gordy, always volatile, came to a head with the push to establish Diana Ross as a world-wide star, a programme which Reeves felt she deserved, and a bitter Reeves folded the group in 1971.

In 1974 she signed a solo deal and released 'Power Of Love', produced by Richard Perry. A commercial failure, the album has the dubious honour of being one of the most expensive recorded at the time. She moved labels in 1977 and again in 1978, working under the guidance of ex-Motowner Henry Cosby. Since then, she has toured the world extensively with pick-up Vandellas and is still very popular. In 1989 she recorded for a label dedicated to the re-recording of former Motown artists.

Martha and The Vandellas – after the Heat Wave, Dancing In The Streets

REM / Michael **STIPE**

Michael Stipe (vocals)
Peter Buck (guitar)
Michael Mills (bass)
Bill Berry (drums)

Formed in Athens, Georgia, REM – which stands for Rapid Eye Movement – came together in a community of students, musicians and artists. Stipe (born 1960) and Buck (born 1956) met at the record store the latter worked at: Berry (born 1958) and Mills (born 1958) had been schoolmates.

REM played their first live gig in 1980 at the city's Koffee Club. A year later, they recorded the limited-circulation 'Radio Free Europe' with producer Mitch Easter: like all their early material, it was notable for indecipherable lyrics which added to the band's mystique plus melodic, McCartneyesque bass runs from Mills and jangly Byrds-like guitar from Buck. Released on a small Atlanta label, it was voted *Village Voice's* 1981 Single of the Year, which helped bookings to fund another record, the five-track 'Chronic Town' EP, which got the band a deal with Miles Copeland's IRS. REM opted for a low advance, high royalties, and artistic freedom.

Their blurred, soft sound was regarded as a problem, so they worked with engineer Don Dixon (also a musician with Easter's group, Let's Active), but 'Murmur' was little more distinct than its predecessor and thus aroused polarized opinion. Nevertheless it reached the US Top 50 after winning the influential *Rolling Stone* magazine's 1983 poll.

Buck and Mills took advantage of a break to record a single, 'Gonna Have A Good Time Tonight', with the equally non-conformist Warren Zevon. Billed as the Hindu Love Gods, this aggregation (with Buck) would release an album of covers on Reprise in 1990.

REM had created a cult following in Europe which 'Reckoning' consolidated in 1984. In the UK, they led the so called 'Paisley Underground' movement of US guitar groups like Green On Red, The Long Ryders and Jason & The Scorchers, and cut their third album, 'Fables Of The Reconstruction', in London with Joe Boyd, whose crystalline production of folkrockers like Fairport Convention was at odds with their muse.

Regrouping in the US, Buck returned to his record shop, while Stipe produced a Hugo Largo LP and joined the Golden Palominos, Anton Fier's band with ever-shifting-personnel, (including Jack Bruce and Richard Thompson, among others). 'Life's Rich Pageant' (1986) was recorded with John Cougar Mellencamp's producer, Don Gehman and became their first gold album – the sound was fortunately more acceptable to US ears, in view of the increasing topicality of Stipe's lyrics for 'Fall On Me' (about the oil pollution of Alaska) and the American Indian saga, 'Cuyahoga'.

'Document' took Stipe's newfound social conscience a stage further while reverting to guitars after a flirtation with keyboard sounds to flesh out the sound. This resulted in their first US Top 10 single, 'The One I Love', and *Rolling Stone* proclaimed them 'America's Best Rock'n'Roll band', after which they signed with Warner Brothers for a reported $10 million plus total artistic freedom.

Mills produced Billy James, Berry worked with songwriter Mitchell Malone, and cut a solo single for a local label. Stipe joined 10,000 Maniacs singer Natalie Merchant on a track on the Walt Disney tribute album, 'Stay Awake', produced his sister's band, Hetch Hetchy, and embarked on a solo album, provisionally titled 'Field Recordings'. Peter Buck guested on a Robyn Hitchcock album, playing with a number of other bands.

1988's 'Green', their most optimistic, lyrically audible and commercially successful album yet, was backed by their first world tour in five years, ex-dB Peter Holsapple adding second guitar on stage. A 'Hits' album, 'Eponymous', joined the previous year's outtakes collection, 'Dead Letter Office', while the singles success of 'Stand' backed up their new-found status. Time will tell how much of their early vague charm they can afford to lose without alienating their early loyal fans, which may bother them more than most groups in their happy position.

REO SPEEDWAGON

Gary Richrath (guitar)
Terry Luttrell (vocals)
Neal Doughty (keyboards)
Greg Philbin (bass)
Alan Gratzer (drums)

Formed by Gratzer (born 1948) and Doughty (born 1946) in 1968 while both were students, REO Speedwagon became a popular live band around Illinois. An eponymous debut album (their name referred to a vintage make of fire engine), largely written by guitarist Richrath (born 1949) in 1972 had Luttrell replaced by Kevin Cronin (born 1951), and although it failed to chart, it put the band on the long-haul touring circuit as support to the likes of Ted Nugent and Kansas.

On 'R.E.O.T.W.O.', the follow-up album, Mike Murphy had replaced Cronin, but this too only sold modestly. Gradually improving

REO – reach Top Twenty after ten years on the turnpike

album sales for 'Ridin' The Storm Out' and 'Lost In A Dream' (both 1974) and 'This Time We Mean It' (1975) saw the latter creep into the US Top 75, after which Cronin returned. The 'R.E.O.' album in 1976 was followed by a live double, 'You Get What You Play For', which made the US Top 75 and went platinum, for which Philbin had been replaced by Bruce Hall (born 1953).

Sales, supported by incessant touring, remained steady but unspectacular, although the albums 'You Can Tune A Piano But You Can't Tuna Fish' (1978) and 'Nine Lives' (1979), both made the US Top 40. In 1981, 'Hi Infidelity' achieved the breakthrough after nearly a decade of hard slog on the road, reaching No. 1 in the US and eventually selling over six million copies. The single, 'Keep On Loving You', from the album was a US No. 1 single, and went on to make the UK Top 10 while 'Take It On The Run' hit the US Top 5. By the end of 1981, the album was in the UK Top 10, and subsequent albums and singles became regular Top 30 entries in the US, and occasionally in Britain.

1985 marked another peak in their fortunes when the platinum 'Wheels Are Turnin'' album made the US Top 10 and 'Can't Fight This Feeling' reached No. 1 in the US singles chart, also making the UK Top 20. The late 1980s saw 'Life As We Know It' (1987), a US Top 30 album, produce two hit singles, 'That Ain't Love' and 'In My Dreams', and a 1985 compilation 'The Hits', placed them firmly in the stadium-rock mainstream.

Greatest Hits

Singles	Title	US	UK
1981	Keep On Loving You	1	7
1985	Can't Fight This Feeling	1	16
Albums			
1981	Hi Infidelity	1	6
1982	Good Trouble	7	29
1985	Wheels Are Turnin'	7	–

Cliff **RICHARD**

Cliff Richard is Britain's all-time most consistent pop artist. His career spans virtually the entire history of British rock, and although his years as a major influence were his own formative ones, 1958–62, he has adapted to every change and development in the musical scene, to emerge in the 1990s with success undimmed. He is the only artist to have scored a UK No. 1 single in five successive decades, from the 1950s to the 1990s, and will probably be the only one ever to achieve such a feat.

Born Harry Webb in India in 1940, of English parents, he moved to the UK with his family after World War II. Leaving school in 1956, he played with a skiffle group in his spare time, then formed a rock'n'roll trio, The

Drifters, in 1958. Augmented by guitarist Ian Samwell, they got a week's booking at London's 2 I's coffee bar, and asked to audition for EMI producer Norrie Paramor.

Richard (he adopted the new name because the group were told the featured lead singer needed a more charismatic name than Harry Webb) signed to EMI and left his day job during the same week in August, 1958. His first single was a Paramor-chosen cover of an American song, 'Schoolboy Crush', with Ian Samwell's hastily-written rocker, 'Move It', on the B-side. However, it was the latter which impressed not only radio DJs but also Jack Good, producer of *Oh Boy*, who gave Richard a residency on the weekly TV show, encouraging him to do a Presleyesque vocal act without playing rhythm guitar.

By November 1958, 'Move It' made the UK Top 3, and Richard was on a national tour headed by The Kalin Twins, backed by a largely new Drifters line-up. Guitarists Hank B. Marvin and Bruce Welch were recruited at the start of the tour, and by its end, Richard also had a new bassist, Jet Harris, and drummer, Tony Meehan.

'High Class Baby' and 'Mean Streak' were further UK Top 10 hits, and early in 1959, Richard also gained his first film role, playing a delinquent would-be rock singer in the Anthony Quayle-starring *Serious Charge*. While not an auspicious start to a movie career, it provided his first UK chart-topping song, the Lionel Bart-penned 'Living Doll', a beat ballad. It was the first signal that Richard's music was more than purely rock-'n'roll, and also made the US Top 30 later in the year to become his first million seller. The similarly-styled follow-up, 'Travellin' Light', also hit No. 1, and his first and second albums both made the UK Top 5.

In 1960, a five-week US package tour with Frankie Avalon, Bobby Rydell and others did not provide sufficient exposure to push other records into the US charts in 'Living Doll's wake, but by contrast, at home everything was turning to gold. A second, and bigger, movie appearance with Lawrence Harvey in *Expresso Bongo* yielded the UK Top 3 ballad, 'A Voice In The Wilderness', and Richard and the group (now renamed The Shadows to prevent confusion with the black US R&B group) followed it with a string of equally big successes, honing an easy-on-the-ear teenbeat sound which became the model for innumerable other pop acts in the UK and most of Europe, until the arrival of The Beatles. 'Please Don't Tease', 'I Love You' and the album, '21 Today', were UK No. 1 hits in 1960/61, while 'Fall In Love With You', 'Nine Times Out Of Ten', 'Theme For A Dream', 'When The Girl In Your Arms Is The Girl In Your Heart', and the albums 'Me And My Shadows' and 'Listen To Cliff' all made the UK Top 3.

Richard's first starring movie role, in the musical *The Young Ones*, was a huge success in 1962, being the second biggest box office

hit of the year. The soundtrack album was a chart-topper, as was the title song – his first single to sell a million in the UK alone. Further hits, 'It'll Be Me', 'I'm Looking Out The Window', and the album, '32 Minutes And 17 Seconds', all made the UK Top 3, and 1963's triumphs were almost a re-run of the previous year. A second movie musical, *Summer Holiday*, spun off two more million-selling hits in the title track and a double-A-side coupling 'The Next Time' and 'Bachelor Boy', plus a chart-topping soundtrack album, while 'It's All In The Game', 'Don't Talk To Him' and the compilation album, 'Cliff's Hit Album', all reached the UK Top 3. This was the year when The Beatles and the groups in their wake overran the UK charts, yet their impact hardly jostled Cliff & The Shadows at all. Moreover, Richard also had another US success when 'Lucky Lips', a UK Top 5 hit, made the US chart, while 'It's All In The Game' reached the US Top 30 in early 1964 – his biggest US hit to date.

Though the 1960s' musical climate changed and re-changed in the wake of The Beatles, the group boom, the R&B/mod scene, the folk/rock boom, the Summer Of Love and every other movement which shook pop during the decade, Richard weathered it all with very little suffering. Some of his material became a straighter alternative to whatever newer excesses prevailed, but vast numbers of people still wanted to hear and buy it. So, he had further UK No. 1 hits in 1965 with the Nashville-recorded 'The Minute You're Gone', and in 1968 with 'Congratulations', also that year's runner-up in the Eurovision Song Contest. Other Top 10 hits during the second half of the 1960s included 'Constantly', 'On The Beach' (from another hit movie, *Wonderful Life*), 'The Twelfth Of Never', 'I Could Easily Fall' (from his London Palladium pantomime, *Alladin*), 'Wind Me Up (Let Me Go)', 'Visions', 'In the Country' (from another pantomime, *Cinderella*), the Hank Marvin-penned 'The Day I Met Marie', 'All My Love', and 'Throw Down A Line' (a duet with Marvin).

Richard's major personal change during the 1960s concerned his adoption of the Christian faith, first announced at a London Billy Graham rally in 1966. For a while, he actively planned to give up his singing career and teach religious instruction, but eventually decided to continue it in parallel with another, unpaid career which included gospel music tours and contributions to various Christian initiatives, notably projects like TEAR Fund, which helped alleviate third world suffering. He has continued this commitment for the last 25 years. At the end of the 1960s, Richard also parted from The Shadows and the group broke up for a while, though various members, notably Hank Marvin, continued to work with him frequently in songwriting, accompanying, producing and other roles.

The early 1970s were the closest that

Into his fourth decade as pro popster, Cliff contemplates the ever-distant prospect of middle age

Richard ever had to 'wilderness years'. Although he continued to score major hits, like the UK Top 10 hits 'Goodbye Sam, Hello Samantha' (his 50th single) and 'Power To All Our Friends', he began to have flops too. 1971's 'Flying Machine' was his first single ever to miss the UK Top 30, while the following year's 'A Brand New Song' was his first not to chart at all. In a growing album market, his releases were generally not big sellers, while his last film musical, 1973's *Take Me High*, proved out of tune with the times, and his uptempo material, in particular, moved out of the pop mainstream into the bouncy showbiz field. The turnaround came in 1976 when Bruce Welch of The Shadows became his producer. Material and arrangements immediately took a more contemporary turn, and the single, 'Miss You Nights', ended a 20-month absence from the

UK charts, to be followed by 'I'm Nearly Famous' (his first UK Top 10 album for seven years), and 'Devil Woman', which not only made the UK but also the US Top 10 to become his all-time biggest US seller.

The 1970s ended on a high note as this comeback momentum continued. A reunion season with The Shadows at the London Palladium was a huge success (and spawned a UK Top 5 live album), he played a historic tour in the USSR, and the British Record Industry gave him a Silver Clef Award as Best UK Male Solo Artist of the last 25 years. Cliff had further UK Top 10 albums with 'Every Face Tells A Story' and 'Rock'n'Roll Juvenile', and in 1979 topped the UK singles chart after an 11 year gap with 'We Don't Talk Anymore', which put him back in the US Top 10, and globally is his biggest seller ever.

The 1980s opened with the award of an

OBE from the Queen, a gratifying start to a decade which saw Richard consolidate his position as a major contemporary artist – a quite different situation from that which prevailed 10 years earlier, and all the more extraordinary when it is recalled that 1980 also marked his 40th birthday. Alan Tarney, the writer of 'We Don't Talk Anymore', became his producer, and well-chosen material provided a string of hits on both sides of the Atlantic with the likes of 'Carrie', 'Dreamin' ', 'A Little In Love', a duet with Olivia Newton-John on 'Suddenly' from her film, *Xanadu*), 'Wired For Sound', and a revival of the doo-wop classic, 'Daddy's Home', which hit the UK Top 3.

Richard also began exercising his pre-eminent musical status by recording with others outside the normal run of his own work. The collaborations were varied, and mostly very successful: he duetted with Phil Everly of The Everly Brothers on the UK Top 10 single, 'She Means Nothing To Me', performed a concert with the London Philharmonic Orchestra, which produced the hit album, 'Dressed For The Occasion', and single, 'True Love Ways', cut singles with Elton John (which charted) and Janet Jackson (which didn't), duetted with Andrew Lloyd-Webber's then wife, Sarah Brightman, on 'All I Ask Of You' from *The Phantom Of The Opera* (which made the UK Top 3), and most offbeat of all, re-cut 'Living Doll' in parody fashion with British alternative comedians The Young Ones. This single topped the UK chart in 1986, nearly 27 years after the original, raising a sizeable sum for the *Comic Relief* charity.

In the early 1970s, Richard had dabbled in stage acting, in repertory productions of *Five-Finger Exercise* and *The Potting Shed*. In 1986, he committed himself to a whole year on stage when he took the lead role in Dave Clark's futuristic musical, *Time*, a major West End success. A Stevie Wonder-produced song from the show, 'She's So Beautiful', was another UK hit. The late 1980s were notable for some of the biggest-selling albums of his career: 1987's 'Always Guaranteed', the 1988 compilation 'Private Collection', and 1989's 'Stronger'. UK Top 5 singles emerged from each: 'Some People' from the first, 'The Best Of Me' (his 100th single, and a Top 3 hit) and the Stock/Aitken/Waterman-produced 'I Just Don't Have The Heart' from the last, and from the compilation, the Christmas anthem, 'Mistletoe And Wine'. The latter was 1988's biggest-selling UK single, and gave him the Christmas chart-topper. He was also to top the 1989 Christmas chart as a part of Band Aid II on 'Do They Know It's Christmas', and completed a remarkable Yule hat-trick when 'Saviour's Day' became the 1990 Christmas No. 1.

1988 marked the 30th anniversary of Richard's professional career. He celebrated it with a massive sell-out UK tour, plus a special live event the following summer: two nights at Wembley stadium before audiences of 72,000 – the biggest ever live audiences of his entire career. *The Event* reunited him not only with The Shadows, but also with his co-stars of the 1958 *Oh Boy* TV show, and The Kalin Twins, bill-toppers on his first tour. Excerpts from it were issued on a double live album at the end of 1990 – a further huge seller. This too spun off hit singles: a revival of the 1950s song, 'Silhouettes', the inspirational 'From A Distance', and the previously mentioned 'Saviour's Day', which marked his fifth chart-topping decade. 1990 had some nostalgia, as Richard reunited with The Shadows at the Knebworth superstar gathering in aid of Music Therapy. It also gave notice, as he sold out the longest season of dates ever scheduled at Birmingham's NEC and London's Wembley Arena, that the longest and most consistent career in British rock still had plenty more to deliver yet.

Greatest Hits

Singles	Title	US	UK
1959	*Living Doll*	30	1
1959	*Travellin' Light*	–	1
1960	*Please Don't Tease*	–	1
1960	*I Love You*	–	1
1962	*The Young Ones*	–	1
1962	*The Next Time/Bachelor Boy*	99	1
1963	*Summer Holiday*	–	1
1965	*The Minute You're Gone*	–	1
1968	*Congratulations*	99	1
1979	*We Don't Talk Anymore*	7	1
1986	*Living Doll*		
	(with The Young Ones)	–	1
1988	*Mistletoe And Wine*	–	1
1990	*Saviour's Day*	–	1
Albums			
1961	*21 Today*	–	1
1961	*The Young Ones*	–	1
1963	*Summer Holiday*	–	1
1977	*40 Golden Greats*	–	1
1981	*Love Songs*	–	1
1988	*Private Collection*	–	1

Jonathan **RICHMAN** / The **MODERN LOVERS**

Jonathan Richman *(vocals, guitar)*
John Felice *(guitar)*
Rolfe Andersen *(bass)*
David Robinson *(drums)*

One of the least likely punk/New Wave bands of the 1970s, The Modern Lovers adopted a totally opposite stance to virtually all their peers and rivals, and leader Jonathan Richman (later a solo performer) remains active and uniquely different 15 years later.

Richman (born 1951) came from Boston (an area which would be glorified in songs like 'New England'), and was captivated in the late 1960s by The Velvet Underground. He wrote strange songs, and after moving back to Boston in 1970, assembled the group line-up as above – Felice had lived next door to him, Robinson answered an advertisement in a music shop, and introduced his cousin, Andersen. This line-up lasted six months before Ernie Brooks and Jerry Harrison (born 1949, keyboards) replaced Andersen and Felice respectively.

In 1972/3, the group recorded demos produced by John Cale (of The Velvet Underground) and others, but a projected record deal fell through, and these tracks only emerged in 1976, when the group signed with the San Francisco independent label, Beserkley, as an album titled 'The Modern Lovers'. Further 1973 demos made with Kim Fowley as producer surfaced in 1981 as 'The Original Modern Lovers', with a sleeve note by Richman saying that the title was inaccurate! In late 1973, Richman moved to Berkeley, California, and signed to the local Beserkley label, and was backed by label-mates The Rubinoos on four tracks released as part of a 1974 album, 'Beserkley Chartbusters Volume 1' (no second volume had surfaced 15 years later), which included the first released version of Richman's masterpiece, 'Road Runner'. 1975 saw Richman's first released album, 'Jonathan Richman & The Modern Lovers', the group by this time including Leroy Radcliffe (guitar, vocals) replacing Harrison (who went on to fame as a member of Talking Heads) and Greg 'Curly' Keranen (bass) instead of Brooks, while in 1976, the original eponymous Modern Lovers album was finally released four years late. None of these records made the US chart, but in 1977/8, Richman reached a UK commercial peak, charting with three singles and an album.

A UK Top 20 single coupling two versions of 'Roadrunner' (from the earliest album and from 'Chartbusters') was followed by the release of a third album, 'Rock'n'Roll With The Modern Lovers', which made the UK Top 50 and included a UK Top 5 single, a bizarre instrumental titled 'Egyptian Reggae'. By this time, Robinson had left to join The Cars, and was replaced by D. Sharpe. A riotously successful UK tour featuring Richman, Radcliffe, Sharpe and bass player Asa Brebner climaxed with a London concert being recorded and also released in 1977 as 'Modern Lovers Live', while a single from it, 'Morning Of Our Lives', made the UK Top 30 in early 1978. This line-up also recorded half 1979's 'Back In Your Life' album, which Richman completed solo.

After a three-year recording silence, Richman re-emerged on a new independent label with five backing musicians including Keranen and two female vocalists. An even bigger group with eight other vocalists including drummer Michael Guardabascio made 1985's 'Rockin' & Romance', after which Richman signed with a bigger label for 1986's 'It's Time For Jonathan Richman &

The Modern Lovers', on which his backing musicians included Brebner, Guardabascio and producer Andy Paley. It was a sadly inaccurate title, and Richman gave up recording for mainstream labels and signed with the ethnic specialist Rounder Records. 'Modern Lovers '88', with Brennan Totten (guitar) and Johnny Avila (drums) was followed by the virtually solo 'Jonathan Richman' in 1989, while 1990's bizarre 'Jonathan Goes Country' found him backed by country pickers and covering a song by Marty Robbins.

The essence of Richman is his unique ability to move in unexpected directions. Many of his songs (e.g. 'Abominable Snowman In The Market', 'Dodge Veg-O-Matic' – about a car that reminds him of a potato peeler!) are so unlikely as to be futuristic in their simplicity, while his insistence at one point on playing so quietly that the audience struggled to get nearer the stage merely to hear his performance verged on the insensitive. Even so, Richman's very weirdness will ensure that his albums will always interest at least a cult following and occasionally even more.

Greatest Hits

Singles	Title	US	UK
1977	*Roadrunner*	–	11
1977	*Egyptian Reggae*	–	5
Albums			
1977	*Rock'n'Roll With The Modern Lovers*	–	50

The **RIGHTEOUS BROTHERS**

Vocalists Bill Medley (born 1940) and Bobby Hatfield (born 1940) were brothers in the exclusive fraternity of great blue-eyed soul voices rather than by any blood link, but their musical kinship produced at least one of pop music's all-time classic singles.

Medley (ex-Paramours) and Hatfield (ex-Variations) became a duo in 1962, and first charted a year later with the R&B dance hit, 'Little Latin Lupe Lu', cut for Moonglow Records. In 1964, when they were performing on the support bill of a Beatles US tour, producer Phil Spector became interested in their potential, and made a deal with Moonglow which would allow them to also record for his Philles label, then cooling from its big hit period with The Crystals, Ronettes, etc.

'You've Lost That Lovin' Feelin' ' was their Philles debut, a song specially commissioned by Spector from hit songwriters Barry Mann and Cynthia Weil, and tailored both to the duo's style and the Spector 'Wall Of Sound'. Early in 1965, it topped both US and UK charts, in Britain outselling a cover by Beatles chum Cilla Black, which was expected to bury the original.

Pre-Spector Righteous Bros, doin' the Lupe Lu

Selling over a million, 'Lovin' Feelin'' was followed into the US Top 10 by the similar (Goffin/King-penned) 'Just Once In My Life' (though not in the UK, where Spector withdrew it from release for never-explained reasons, and thus lost the duo's sales momentum), plus albums both of Spector-produced material on Philles and of earlier tracks on Moonglow.

In mid-1965, the duo's third Philles single, 'Hung On You', was superseded (as a result of radio DJs flipping it) by its B-side, a soaring revival of the 1950s ballad, 'Unchained Melody', on which Hatfield's tenor voice was heard solo. This made the US Top 5 and returned the duo to the UK Top 20, and its success also instigated its successful followup, a similar Hatfield solo on another vintage ballad, 'Ebb Tide'.

In January, 1966, The Righteous Brothers were sold to the MGM label's Verve subsidiary for an irresistible $1 million. This lost the duo the use of Spector's production, but Medley produced a fair approximation of the style and sound on '(You're My) Soul & Inspiration', another Mann/Weil song which took them back to the top of the US chart, but follow-ups were progressively less successful, and by the end of 1967, Medley had decided to strike out as a soloist. Both he and Hatfield made solo records for Verve, but only Medley managed some moderate chart entries. Hatfield continued live work as The Righteous Brothers with new partner Jimmy Walker (formerly of The Knickerbockers), but this duo were contractually prevented from recording, and eventually they split apart in 1970.

Medley and Hatfield teamed up again in 1974, when they took 'Rock And Roll Heaven', Alan O'Day's rocking tribute to deceased rock stars, to the US Top 3. A couple of smaller hits followed, but the duo

then parted again (Medley having a lengthy period of non-performance, due both to family tragedy and severe problems with his voice), to reunite only on specific occasions, like the *American Bandstand* 30th Anniversary and their own 20th anniversary celebrations in 1982/3.

'You've Lost That Lovin' Feelin'' returned again in 1986 when the duo's original version was used in the hit movie, *Top Gun*. The song habitually came back: UK reissues in 1969 and 1977 had seen it become a hit again, making the Top 10 on the first occasion. In 1987, Medley scored a major film-related hit in his own right, this time with a new song, '(I've Had) The Time Of My Life', written for *Dirty Dancing* and recorded as a duet with songstress Jennifer Warnes, which put him back at the top of the US chart for the first time since 1966.

In 1988, Medley had another solo success with a further film-related song, as he revived 'He Ain't Heavy, He's My Brother' for Sylvester Stallone's *Rambo III*, and in 1990, the saga of The Righteous Brothers finally came full circle as, yet again, a movie took a hand. Their 'Unchained Melody' was prominently featured in the year's biggest cinema success, *Ghost*, and this exposure took both the 1965 original and a competing newly-recorded version by the duo into the US Top 20. In the UK, success was even more startling, as the original version topped the chart for a month, becoming the UK's biggest-selling single of the year. Moreover, the UK follow-up was the evergreen 'You've Lost That Lovin' Feelin'', which, as the year closed, bounded into the Top 10 again, becoming the only single in history ever to be a Top 10 hit on three separate occasions. The profile of The Righteous Brothers at the start of the 1990s was the highest it had been since 1965.

Greatest Hits

Singles	Title	US	UK
1965	*You've Lost That Lovin' Feelin'*	1	1
1966	*Unchained Melody*	4	14
1966	*(You're My) Soul And Inspiration*	1	15
1974	*Rock And Roll Heaven*	3	–
Albums			
1965	*You've Lost That Lovin' Feelin'*	4	–
1966	*Soul And Inspiration*	7	–

Johnny RIVERS

Rivers (born John Ramistella, 1942), a singer/guitarist with his original roots firmly in 1950s rock and R&B, found his first commercial success from an unusual direction as a purveyor of danceable live-recorded revivals of old hits. A New Yorker raised in Louisiana, he had already been recording sporadically when, settled in Los Angeles, he became a regular live disco entertainer, play-

ing rock oldies for dancers, in 1963. A major Los Angeles based record label taped his Whisky-A-Go-Go Club act early in 1964 for his debut album, which went into the Top 20 and spun off a US Top 3 single, a revival of Chuck Berry's 'Memphis'. A cover of another Chuck Berry oldie, 'Maybelline', was also a Top 20 hit, and similar singles and live albums followed, all charting consistently in the US.

Rivers widened his covers brief to encompass the folk-rock boom during 1965, and in 1966, began to succeed with original material, notably 'Secret Agent Man', the rocking theme to the US version of Patrick McGoohan's *Danger Man* TV series, and the self-penned (with producer Lou Adler) ballad, 'Poor Side Of Town', which gave him his biggest-selling single and a US No. 1 hit.

'Poor Side Of Town' ushered in a notably more contemporary, melodic, Rivers sound. It also coincided with the launch of his own music publishing company (which signed songwriter Jim Webb) and Soul City Records, an outlet for new Rivers-discovered talent. This hit quick paydirt in 1967 with the beginning of a string of Rivers-produced successes for The Fifth Dimension: their third hit, the Webb-penned 'Up Up And Away', earned a Grammy as 1967's Record Of The Year. His own cover versions now scouted similar contemporary soul territory, with the Motown songs, 'Baby I Need Your Lovin'' and 'The Tracks Of My Tears', providing US Top 10 hits.

In the late 1960s, after helping organize the Monterey Pop Festival, Rivers retired almost completely from the live performances that first made his name. He sold his label and publishing house, and spent considerable time in the Far East, studying various spiritual disciplines.

The 1970s saw a recording return to rock basics, with a revival of 'Rockin' Pneumonia & The Boogie Woogie Flu' selling a million in 1973, and Rivers touring with an all-star band of noted session musicians. Two years later, he changed labels and returned with a revived Beach Boys oldie, 'Help Me Rhonda', and in 1977, he cut 'Swayin' To The Music (Slow Dancin')', which became his ninth US Top 10 single and a million-seller. Not long after this, he virtually retired from recording as well as live work, his only 1980s venture being a religious album made more for his own satisfaction than any commercial reason. He remains a rare commodity: a successful long-term star now content in retirement.

Greatest Hits

Singles	Title	US	UK
1964	*Memphis*	2	–
1966	*Poor Side Of Town*	1	–
Albums			
1964	*Johnny Rivers At The Whisky A-Go-Go*	12	–
1968	*Realization*	5	–

Smokey (centre, back) – 'America's greatest poet' according to the Big Zimm

Smokey **ROBINSON** and The **MIRACLES**

Legend has it that Bob Dylan once descri-bed William 'Smokey' Robinson (born 1940) as America's greatest living poet. True or false, there is no denying that Robinson has a unique way with lyrics and that many of his most famous songs stand up without musical arrangements.

Robinson attended high school with all the future Miracles: Claudette Rogers (later to become his wife), her brother Bobby, Pete Moore and Ron White, and it was at school in 1955 that the group, initially named The Matadors, was formed. A popular live act but frustrated by their lack of a recording deal, Robinson and The Miracles contacted song-writer Berry Gordy who had enjoyed a string of hits with Jackie Wilson. Helping Robinson to hone his songwriting skills, Gordy pro-duced several records by the group which were leased to various record companies, before forming, at Robinson's suggestion, his own label, Tamla Motown.

The Miracles provided Tamla with its first US pop hit, 'Shop Around' (1960), which reached the Top 3. While leading the group through a string of pop hits during the next decade, Robinson ran a dual career as writer and producer for other Motown artists in his capacity as vice-president of the company. 'You Really Got A Hold On Me' (1963) was a US Top 10 single, while Robinson's produc-tion of Mary Wells' 'My Guy' gave Motown its first international hit, consolidating Motown's stature. Throughout the 1960s Robinson was responsible for major hits by The Temptations, Marvin Gaye, The Mar-vellettes, The Supremes and The Four Tops.

During the latter part of the 1960s, the group became known as Smokey Robinson & The Miracles, and in 1971, Robinson left them for a solo career. His replacement, Billy Griffin, sang lead on a number of hits includ-ing 'Do It Baby' (1974) and the international No. 1, 'Love Machine' (1975). In 1976 The Miracles left Motown after a dispute regard-ing the follow-up to 'Love Machine', but failed to make any subsequent impression

and in 1977 the group folded. A new Mira-cles was formed by Bobby Rogers and this group has recently recorded. Griffin enjoyed a UK Top 20 solo hit in 1983 with 'Hold Me Tighter In The Rain'.

Robinson's initial solo projects were mod-est hits but 'A Quiet Storm' (1975) contained the major hit 'Baby That's Backatcha'. Most of the albums that followed have been lack-lustre affairs, notable exceptions being 'Where There's Smoke' featuring 'Cruisin' (1979) and 'Being With You' (1981), the title track of which gave him a UK No. 1 single. During the 1980s, Robinson suffered from serious cocaine addiction, graphically descri-bed in his biography, Smokey, in 1989. He continues to release an album a year and is one of the handful of original artists to remain with Motown after its purchase by MCA. It is a tribute to his talent that in 1990 UB40 were in the US Top 10 with a cover of his 'The Way You Do The Things You Do', while over 25 years earlier, The Beatles covered his song, 'You Really Got A Hold On Me', on their second album.

Greatest Hits

The Miracles

Singles	Title	US	UK
1960	Shop Around	2	–
1963	You Really Got A Hold On Me	8	–
1963	Mickey's Monkey	8	–
1965	Tracks Of My Tears	16	9
1967	I Second That Emotion	4	27
1969	Baby Baby Don't Cry	8	–
1970	The Tears Of A Clown	1	1
1975	Love Machine (without Robinson)	1	2
Albums			
1965	Going To A Go-Go	8	–
1968	Greatest Hits Vol. 2	7	–

Smokey Robinson

Singles			
1979	Cruisin'	4	–
1981	Being With You	2	1
Albums			
1981	Being With You	10	17

Kenny **ROGERS**

For 20 years, Rogers has been one of the biggest crossover stars of country music, specializing in duets with a range of female soul and pop performers.

Rogers (born 1938) came from Houston, Texas, and first recorded at age 17 with high school friends as The Scholars for the local Cue label. His first solo success came as Kenneth Rogers the First when he sang 'That Crazy Feeling' on The Dick Clark Show in 1958. After further singles in a pop vein, Rogers joined the jazzy Bobby Doyle Trio as bassist and singer, recording a CBS album with them in 1962.

After a lengthy residency with Doyle at a Houston night club, Rogers switched styles to pop-folk when he became a member of The New Christy Minstrels in 1966. Although the group had been hitmakers in 1963–4, their popularity was dwindling and Rogers sang on only one album ('New Kick!') before leaving with three colleagues.

The quartet (which included Mike Settle, Thelma Comacho and Terry Williams) called themselves The New Edition and were signed to Frank Sinatra's Reprise label. In 1968, they had a novelty hit with 'Just Dropped In (To See What Condition My Condition Was In)', written by 'New Nashville' songwriter Mickey Newbury. Settle's more conventional country piece 'But You Know I Love You' reached the US Top 20 before the group recorded the Mel Tillis song, 'Ruby Don't Take Your Love To Town' in 1969.

Featuring his warm baritone, it was credited to Kenny Rogers & The First Edition and the histrionic tale of a paralysed Vietnam veteran was a massive international success. It inspired an answer record, 'Billy I've Got To Get To Town' by Geraldine Stevens. The follow-up, the Woody Guthrie folk ballad, 'Ruben James' was a lesser hit, though Rogers' rendering of Mac Davis's passionate 'Something's Burning' emulated the success of 'Ruby' in 1971.

Although The First Edition continued until 1974, its later records sold disappointingly. They included 'Someone Who Cares', from the 1971 movie, *Fools*, Rogers' gospel-flavoured composition 'Take My Hand' and 'The Ballad Of Calico' (1972), an ambitious double concept album about a 19th-century gold rush.

When the group dissolved, Rogers was left $65,000 in debt but his second single under a solo contract with United Artists made him solvent again. Following the 'Ruby' formula, 'Lucille' was a countryfied ballad which the gruff-voiced Rogers made into a million-seller and a UK chart-topper.

'The Gambler' and Don Schlitz's 'Coward Of The County' were other story-songs which brought further big hits in the late 1970s. Both were later turned into TV films, starring Rogers himself.

The early 1980s was the period of his greatest success, principally because he aimed directly for the widest audience, spanning pop, country and even soul music. The starting-point was 'Lady', a soft ballad composed by Lionel Richie, which topped the singles charts of all three genres. At the same time, Rogers was developing as a duettist, having hits in partnership with ex-Christy Minstrel Kim Carnes and with mainstream country singer Dottie West ('What Are We Doin' In Love', 1981).

These were followed in 1983 by contrasting duets. With Sheena Easton, Rogers revived Bob Seger's rock ballad 'We've Got Tonight', while 'Islands In The Stream', with Dolly Parton, was composed by The Bee

Kenny Rogers (left) with the First Edition – baritone ballads strong on storyline

Gees. Rogers and Parton went on to record a set of Christmas songs which sold a million, while his solo album, 'Eyes That See In The Dark', was produced by Bee Gee Barry Gibb.

His 1985 participation in the USA For Africa charity single, 'We Are The World', (a project organized by his and Richie's manager, Ken Kragen) marked the high point of his crossover success. For the remainder of the decade, Rogers had regular country hits, none of which sold in large numbers to the pop audience. Among the C&W releases were singles like 'Make No Mistake, She's Mine' (1985, with Ronnie Milsap) and 'I Prefer The Moonlight' and the 1990 album, 'Something Inside So Strong'. With at least a dozen platinum albums to his credit, Rogers has proved that his targetting of a large audience is impeccable.

Greatest Hits

Singles	Title	US	UK
(with First Edition)			
1968	Just Dropped In (To See What Condition My Condition Was In)	5	–
1969	Ruby, Don't Take Your Love To Town	6	2
1970	Something's Burning	11	8
(Solo)			
1977	Lucille	5	1
1979	She Believes In Me	5	42
1980	Coward Of The County	3	1
1980	Don't Fall In Love With A Dreamer (with Kim Carnes)	4	–
1980	Lady	1	12
1981	I Don't Need You	3	–
1983	We've Got Tonight (with Sheena Easton)	6	28
1983	Islands In The Stream (with Dolly Parton)	1	7

Albums			
1979	Kenny	3	7
1980	Greatest Hits	1	–
1981	Share Your Love	3	–
1983	Eyes That See In The Dark	6	53
1985	The Kenny Rogers Story	–	4

The ROLLING STONES

Mick Jagger (vocals)
Keith Richards (guitar)
Brian Jones (guitar)
Bill Wyman (bass)
Charlie Watts (drums)

Between 1964 and 1972, the Stones produced a body of work which established them as one of popular music's most important bands, kept them astride the pop charts while retaining rock credibility and paid the bills in the subsequent 20 years.

Having attended the same primary school in Kent, Jagger (born 1943) and Richards (born 1943) met again as teenagers in 1960 and discovered they were both R&B fans. Later, while at the London School of Economics, Jagger had a band with guitarist Dick Taylor who was at art school with Richards. Meanwhile, Jones (born 1942), a blues fanatic from Cheltenham, met Jagger, Watts (born 1941) and pianist Ian Stewart (often regarded as the 'sixth Stone', who died in 1985) at Alexis Korner's London blues club, where Jagger occasionally sang in Korner's Blues Incorporated. They began to rehearse and then deputize for Blues Incorporated at London's Marquee Club, taking their name from a Muddy Waters song.

In 1962 Bill Wyman (born 1936) replaced

Taylor, who went on to form The Pretty Things. In 1963 Watts quit his advertising job to join the Stones full time, and they were spotted by Andrew Oldham at the Crawdaddy Club in Richmond and signed to a management contract. By the end of the year, they had released their first two singles, Chuck Berry's 'Come On' and Lennon & McCartney's 'I Wanna Be Your Man', their first Top 20 entry, and completed their first tour of the UK opening a show starring Bo Diddley and The Everly Brothers.

In keeping with the fashion of the day, the Stones released an eponymous EP in January 1964 coinciding with their first headlining tour of the UK, followed in February by another single, Buddy Holly's 'Not Fade Away' which went Top 3 in the UK.

Although Jagger and Richards, had been experimenting with their own songs, their eponymous debut album contained largely R&B covers. June 1964 saw their US debut and a pilgrimage to Chess Records where they recorded Bobby Womack's 'It's All Over Now', their first UK No. 1 single and tracks for the 'Five By Five' EP.

By now, the Stones' public image was well-established; the impassive rhythm section, Richards' moodiness, Jones' preening and Jagger's mocking arrogance. Willie Dixon's 'Little Red Rooster', recorded at Chess and released in November 1964, was the second of five consecutive UK No. 1 singles.

The second UK album, 'Rolling Stones No 2' appeared in January 1965; the next month 'The Last Time' rocketed to No. 1. Offstage, The Stones' loutish image was perpetuated – in July, Jagger, Jones and the usually low-key Wyman were fined for urinating against a wall at a petrol station. 'Satisfaction' (1965), a song which best captured the rebellious nature of the band to the delight of fans and the disgust of everyone else, was perhaps the first major statement of the 'Permissive 60s'.

The voracious Allen Klein took over their management in 1965 just prior to the release of the third UK album 'Out Of Our Heads', and the run of UK chart-topping singles continued with 'Get Off My Cloud' and ended when '19th Nervous Breakdown' only reached No. 2 in early 1966.

The Stones early albums were issued in the US in different forms, with singles, B-sides and EP tracks added. The entirely self-penned 'Aftermath' (1966) was the first to be issued on both sides of the Atlantic in the same configuration, and included 'Under My Thumb', and 'Out Of Time', a UK No. 1 for Chris Farlowe. 'Paint It Black' put the band back at No. 1, while controversy attended the US release of 'Have You Seen Your Mother Baby Standing In The Shadows' – the band being photographed as transvestites for the picture sleeve.

1967 saw the arrest of Jagger and Richards and (in a separate incident) Brian Jones on drug offences. Jagger and Richards were convicted, although eventually Jagger was conditionally discharged, while Richards' sentence was quashed. For Richards, it was the first in a number of arrests as he embarked on a decade of unremitting heavy drug use.

The 1967 album 'Between The Buttons' was unexceptional, and their reply to The Beatles' 'Sgt Pepper', 'Their Satanic Majesties Request' (1967), was a relative failure, straying too far from their natural territory.

Back on familiar ground, 'Jumpin' Jack Flash' was a UK No. 1 in 1968, but they ran into trouble with radio bans in the US with 'Street Fighting Man', during a year which saw massive civil disorder in the UK, Europe and the US. The album 'Beggars Banquet' that year also marked a dramatic return to form, including 'Sympathy For The Devil', 'Stray Cat Blues' and 'Parachute Woman'.

Meanwhile, Brian Jones's drug use too was becoming an increasing liability; his 1967 arrest put US touring in jeopardy and over-indulgence reduced his musical contribution to almost nothing. In June 1969, it was announced he was leaving the band; on July 3 he was found dead in his swimming pool.

Jagger had asked Eric Clapton to consider taking over, but on July 5 Mick Taylor (born 1948) from John Mayall's Bluesbreakers made his debut with the band at a free concert in Hyde Park. 'Honky Tonk Women'

Vocalist and marracas maestro Mick (centre) fronts latest Hit Parade property, The Rolling Stones

topped both UK and US singles charts while 'Let It Bleed' was one of their finest albums. However in December, their ill-starred concert at Altamont ended in the murder of a black fan at the hands of Hell's Angels.

Shaken by the event, the new decade started quietly for the band; the live album 'Get Your Ya Ya's Out' (1970) aside, there were no releases until 'Brown Sugar' in April 1971 on their own label. 'Sticky Fingers' (1971) another strong album, was a glorious brew of ballad and bravado, and 1972's ambitious double 'Exile On Main Street' contained the transatlantic hit, 'Tumbling Dice'.

It would be several years before they came close to matching the quality of his period. 'Goats Head Soup' (1973) and 'It's Only Rock'n'Roll' (1974) broke no new ground; Mick Taylor left at the end of 1974 to be replaced by (ex-Faces) Ron Wood (born 1947), one of a number of guitarists on 'Black And Blue' (1976). A double live album followed in 1977, entitled 'Love You Live', but there were no more studio albums until 'Some Girls' (1978), their best album in years.

The quality of the next four albums was variable, from 1980's 'Emotional Rescue', 'Tattoo You' (1981), 'Stiff Life' (1982) and 'Undercover' (1983) to 'Dirty Work' (1986). However 'Steel Wheels' (1989) was hailed as their best album for a decade, and heralded a huge world tour and subsequent live album.

Collectively, their solo work has been mediocre. Bill Wyman released 'Monkey Grip' (1974), 'Stone Alone' (1976), 'Bill Wyman' (1981), a film soundtrack 'Green Ice' (1982) and scored a surprise 1983 hit single with 'Si Si Je Suis Un Rock Star'. He also recorded an 'all-star' album 'Willie And The Poor Boys' (1985) in aid of Ronnie Lane's multiple sclerosis appeal. Charlie Watts played with Ian Stewart in the ad hoc Rocket 88 and his juggernaut jazz big band released one album, 'The Charlie Watts Orchestra Live At Fulham Town Hall'.

Wood released 'I've Got My Own Album To Do (1974), 'Now Look' (1975), 'Gimme Some Neck' (1979) and '1,2,3,4' (1981) plus the 'Mahoney's Last Stand' soundtrack album (1976) with Ronnie Lane, and toured with the short-lived New Barbarians with Richards in 1979. Richards directed the music for the Chuck Berry biopic *Hail, Hail Rock'n'Roll* (1987) and released a solo album, 'Talk Is Cheap' (1988). Early on, Jagger looked towards film with the interesting *Performance* and the dire *Ned Kelly*, but waited until 1985 for his first solo album, 'She's The Boss', featuring Pete Townshend and Jeff Beck and the single 'Just Another Night'. In the same year, he had a hit duetting with David Bowie on 'Dancing In The Streets', but the 'Primitive Cool' album (1987) was a let-down.

Despite the patchy quality of their post 'Exile' albums, the Stones have continued to tour, with their periodic outings demonstrating that they still possess one of the best live acts in rock'n'roll.

Greatest Hits

Singles	Title	US	UK
1964	Not Fade Away	–	3
1964	It's All Over Now	26	1
1964	Little Red Rooster	–	1
1965	The Last Time	9	1
1965	Satisfaction	1	1
1965	Get Off My Cloud	1	1
1966	As Tears Go By	6	–
1966	Paint It Black	1	1
1967	Ruby Tuesday	1	–
1968	Jumping Jack Flash	3	1
1969	Honky Tonk Women	1	1
1973	Angie	1	5
1978	Miss You	1	3
1985	Dancing In The Street (Jagger/Bowie)	7	1

Albums		US	UK
1964	Rolling Stones	–	1
1965	Rolling Stones 2	–	1
1965	Out Of Our Heads	1	2
1966	Aftermath	2	1
1969	Let It Bleed	3	1
1971	Sticky Fingers	1	1
1972	Exile On Main Street	1	1
1973	Goat's Head Soup	1	1
1974	It's Only Rock'n'Roll	1	2
1976	Black And Blue	1	2
1978	Some Girls	1	2
1980	Emotional Rescue	1	1
1981	Tattoo You	1	2
1989	Steel Wheels	3	2

Solo albums		US	UK
1985	She's The Boss (Jagger)	13	6
1987	Primitive Cool (Jagger)	41	26
1988	Talk Is Cheap (Richards)	24	37

The RONETTES / Ronnie SPECTOR

Veronica 'Ronnie' Bennett
Estelle Bennett
Nedra Talley (vocal group)

The Ronettes were three glamorous New York Puerto Rican girls – Ronnie Bennett (born 1943), her sister Estelle and their cousin – who originally sang together in 1959 in high school. They had been together for four years and were resident singers/dancers at the legendary Peppermint Lounge (and as The Dolly Sisters, appeared in the 1961 movie, *Twist Around The Clock*), and had recorded several unsuccessful singles long before Phil Spector's intervention into their lives. Yet they remain among Spector's most enduring and finest acts, and while they only ever scored one genuinely massive hit, all their Philles singles (produced by Spector) were magnificently crafted classics, featuring Ronnie's fragile, sexy, pleading vocals, the cascading Wall Of Sound, and swirling back-up harmonies.

After signing them in 1963, Spector spent a month working on their first single. With its magnificent arrangement, powerful hook, archetypal Wall Of Sound backing, and the trio's striking looks, 'Be My Baby' was destined to be a smash hit, and it made the US Top 3 and UK Top 5, selling over a million copies, but sadly, follow-ups fared less well: 1964's 'Baby I Love You' made the UK Top 20/US Top 30, but deserved far greater success, as did '(The Best Part Of) Breakin' Up' and the

Ronnie Spector (centre) back in Britain in 1991 plugging her autobiography

sublime 'Do I Love You' (also both 1964), 'Walking In The Rain' (US Top 30, 1965 – this won a Grammy for its sound effects), 'Born To Be Together' (1965), 'Is This What I Get For Loving You' (1965) and 'I Can Hear Music' (1966).

In 1965, they toured the US supporting The Beatles, but without Ronnie, who was by now living with Spector (they would marry in 1968); her deputy was another cousin, Elaine. By 1966, they had finally split, largely due to Spector's objections to Ronnie undertaking live appearances. Following a period of inactivity, Spector started producing again in 1969, and among his early releases was 'You Came, You Saw, You Conquered' credited to 'The Ronettes featuring Veronica' – in reality, Ronnie solo. Two years later, 'Try Some, Buy Some' (released on Apple Records, the label launched by The Beatles) just dented the US Top 100. Credited to Ronnie Spector, it was ostensibly a trailer for an album which never materialized.

By the early 1970s, she had split with Spector and was working the oldies circuit with two new partners, billed as Ronnie & The Ronettes. After a couple of unsuccessful singles, she abandoned her new colleagues and started hanging out with American rock musicians, lending back-up vocals to Bruce Springsteen, recording with Southside Johnny and Eddie Money and finally releasing her first solo album, 'Siren' in 1981, which was followed somewhat belatedly by 'Unfinished Business' in 1987.

While her post-1960s work has mainly left something to be desired, Ronnie Spector will remain an ultimate girl group icon for lovers of 1960s music.

Greatest Hits

Singles	Title	US	UK
1963	Be My Baby	2	4
1964	Baby I Love You	24	11
1964	Walking In The Rain	23	–
Albums			
1964	Presenting The Fabulous Ronettes Featuring Veronica	96	–

Linda **RONSTADT**

One of the most popular and successful female vocalists of the past 20 years, Linda Ronstadt took several years to discover a formula for success, but she was not content to repeat herself and ultimtely retained her audience despite taking several surprising detours during the 1980s.

Linda Marie Ronstadt (born 1946 in Arizona to German/Mexican parents) was encouraged musically as a child by her father, who taught her Mexican folk songs. At high school, she began singing locally with her brother and sister and guitarist Bob Kimmel,

Lovely Linda in 'Seventies spotlight

and in 1964 she dropped out of the University of Arizona after just one semester, moving to Los Angeles, where she formed The Stone Poneys with Kimmel and another guitarist, Kenny Edwards, as a Peter, Paul & Mary-styled folk/country trio.

Promoter Herb Cohen took over as their manager and organized a record deal. Their eponymous debut album (1966) did little, but the follow-up, 1967's 'Evergreen Vol. 2', crept into the US Top 100 and included a US Top 20 single, Michael Nesmith's 'Different Drum'. However, the trio split up soon afterwards, and Ronstadt finished the third album, 'Stone Poneys & Friends Vol. 3', using session musicians.

Due to managerial hassles, her solo career got off to a shaky, uncertain start, and although she was an excellent, highly-regarded live performer (in spite of her natural shyness), her early solo albums always seemed to leave something to be desired. 'Hand Sown . . . Hand Grown' (1969), 1970's 'Silk Purse' (which peaked just outside the US Top 100, and included a US Top 30 single, 'Long, Long Time'), and 1972's 'Linda Ronstadt' (on which she was backed by her regular road band, who later became The Eagles) are all at least adequate, but could have been better. It wasn't until Peter Asher (formerly half of 1960s UK pop duo, Peter & Gordon, and latterly James Taylor's producer) took over Ronstadt's production that she found a cohesive musical direction and recorded with confidence.

Asher was the third (and last) producer to work on her first album for Elektra/Asylum (a company to which she has been signed ever

since), 'Don't Cry Now', which fortunately went gold and made the US Top 50 (as it had cost a small fortune to complete). It included 'Love Has No Pride', a single which just failed to reach the US Top 50. At this point, her previous label demanded a contractual obligation album, and 1974's 'Heart Like A Wheel' topped the US chart, establishing a recipe which would make her a major star – a blend of carefully chosen oldies and contemporary material performed to perfection in a country/rock vein, which ensured that every subsequent original album went at least gold. 'Wheel' included two US Top 3 singles, covers of Betty Everett's 'You're No Good' (a gold chart-topper, whose flip side, a cover of 'I Can't Help It' by Hank Williams, won her a Grammy Award for Best Female Vocal) and Phil Everly's 'When Will I Be Loved', which also topped the US country chart.

1975's 'Prisoner In Disguise' album made the US Top 5 and included a US Top 5 single, a cover of 'Heat Wave' (Martha & The Vandellas), plus a similar cover of Smokey Robinson's 'Tracks Of My Tears', which made the US Top 30. 1977's 'Hasten Down The Wind' album was her first to go platinum, making the US Top 3 and including a US Top 20 revival of Buddy Holly's 'That'll Be The Day', while a rare example of label co-operation saw the same year's 'Greatest Hits' album also sell platinum. 1977's double album, 'A Retrospective', made the US Top 50 and went gold. Also that year, 'Simple Dreams' exercised the formula again to become her second US chart-topping album, and included a US Top 3 cover of Roy Orbison's 'Blue Bayou' and a US Top 5 cover of another Holly classic, 'It's So Easy', while 1978's 'Living In The USA' also topped the US album chart and featured another Smokey Robinson cover, 'Ooh Baby Baby', which made the US Top 10. The album also included a cover of Elvis Costello's 'Alison' (of which its composer reportedly disapproved).

At this point, she was also involved in a personal relationship with Jerry Brown, the Governor of California, and the couple appeared on the cover of *Time* magazine. 1980's 'Mad Love' reached the US Top 3 and included two US Top 10 hits, as well as three more songs by Costello and three by Mark Goldenberg (of US New Wave act, The Cretones), who played guitar on the album, which went platinum, but was regarded with suspicion by her established fans. Later that year came 'Greatest Hits Volume 2', which inevitably went gold. Another recording hiatus followed, as Ronstadt proved her adaptability by appearing in both stage and film versions of Gilbert & Sullivan's 'Pirates of Penzance', to critical and public acclaim. When she resumed her recording career in 1982, it was with her least successful original album for 10 years, 'Get Closer', her first non-platinum original work since 1975, and one without significant hit singles.

A change was obviously necessary, and it came with a trilogy of albums on which Ronstadt was backed by an orchestra conducted by Nelson Riddle, who had performed a similar function on classic albums of the 1950s such as Frank Sinatra's 'Songs For Swinging Lovers'. The major failing of these albums, 'What's New' (1983), 'Lush Life' (1984) and 'For Sentimental Reasons' (1986, released after Riddle's death), was that the material (mainly standards by Gershwin, Berlin, Rodgers & Hart, etc.) seemed either too hackneyed or too obscure – when the choice was right (e.g. 'What's News' excellent 'Someone To Watch Over Me'), it was close to perfection, and the first of the three albums made the US Top 3 and went platinum. But Ronstadt aficionados suspected that her heart was not totally in the complete trilogy. In an even less likely move she contributed vocals to minimalist composer Philip Glass's 'Songs From Liquid Days' in 1985, and in 1986 'Somewhere Out There', a duet with James Ingram featured on the soundtrack of Steven Spielberg's cartoon feature *An American Tail*, was a US Top 3 hit. In 1987, she returned to her country music roots, collaborating with Dolly Parton and Emmylou Harris on 'Trio', a project they had been trying to arrange for several years: the album went platinum, earning her another Grammy, and their revival of the Phil Spector/Teddy Bears oldie, 'To Know Him Is To Love Him', topped the US country chart.

She reached even further back into her roots for her 1988 album, *'Canciones De Mi Padre'* (My Father's Songs), a collection of Mexican folk songs that she remembered from her childhood, which she performed in Spanish, and which she followed with a major international tour on which she sang only Spanish material. 1989's 'Cry Like A Rainstorm – Howl Like The Wind' album was more of a mainstream success, and included four tracks on which she duetted with Aaron Neville of The Neville Brothers, one of them, 'Don't Know Much', becoming a major hit single on both sides of the Atlantic. Between 1975 and 1990 most of her 15 albums went platinum and few other performers would have risked tackling the wide variety of material which Ronstadt seems to have taken in her stride. Her output has been eclectic (to say the least) and generally highly successful in the US, if less so in the UK. Her numerous fans will be fascinated to discover in which direction she will proceed next.

Greatest Hits

Singles	Title	US	UK
1975	*You're No Good*	I	–
1975	*When Will I Be Loved*	2	–
1975	*Heat Wave/Love Is A Rose*	5	–
1977	*Blue Bayou*	3	35
1977	*It's So Easy*	5	–
1978	*Ooh Baby Baby*	7	–
1986	*Somewhere Out There* (with		
	Luther Ingram)	2	8
1989	*Don't Know Much*		
	(with Aaron Neville)	2	2

Albums			
1975	*Heart Like A Wheel*	I	–
1975	*Prisoner In Disguise*	4	–
1976	*Hasten Down The Wind*	3	32
1977	*Greatest Hits*	6	37
1977	*Simple Dreams*	I	15
1978	*Living In The USA*	I	39
1980	*Mad Love*	3	65
1983	*What's New*	6	31
1987	*Trio* (with Dolly Parton		
	& Emmylou Harris)	6	60
1989	*Cry Like A Rainstorm –*		
	Howl Like The Wind	9	43

Diana **ROSS**

Since quitting the group she fronted to superstardom, The Supremes, in 1970, Ross (born Diane Earle, 1944) has emerged as a *grande dame* of pop via major film roles and, taken from over thirty albums, a continuing run of hit singles, even if several US smashes failed in the UK and vice versa (e.g. 'I'm Still Waiting' and 'Chain Reaction' respectively). She is also renowned for duets with Marvin Gaye (on 1973's 'Diana & Marvin' album), Michael Jackson and Lionel Richie, composer of her 1980 tribute to the late Gaye, 'Missing You'.

After a false start with the preachy 'Reach Out And Touch', her revival of Gaye and Tammi Terrell's 'Ain't No Mountain High Enough' (also from 1970's 'Diana Ross' album) was followed by smaller chart successes as she concentrated on establishing herself as a movie actress. This ambition was fully realized with starring roles in the Billie Holiday biopic *Lady Sings The Blues*, which won her an Oscar nomination, and *Mahogany* (financed by Tamla-Motown supremo Berry Gordy). More light-hearted was her role of 'Dorothy' in *The Wiz*, a 1978 re-make of *The Wizard Of Oz*. Among its spin-offs was 'Ease On Down The Road', a single by Ross and 'Scarecrow' Michael Jackson.

While her cinematic activities were at their most intense, Ross's recording career peaked again with 1973's 'Touch Me In The Morning' with its hit title track. As lucrative was a second eponymous album and its principal single, 'Love Hangover'. 1977 saw both a studio offering ('Baby It's Me') and a l album, 'An Evening With . . . '

The decade ended with a crack at disco with 'The Boss'. 1980's 'Diana' (produced by hitmakers Chic, but apparently and controversially remixed by Ross) with its attendant US million-seller, 'Upside Down', 'To Love Again' (her last Motown album), and 1981's 'Why Do Fools Fall In Love', were more typical fare. Throughout the 1980s, Ross was able to absorb just enough of prevailing

Motown's Supreme songstress, Diana Ross

trends to not alienate older consumers. With an Andy Warhol cover design, 'Silk Electric' contained more credible stabs at disco while 'Work · That Body' (from 1984's 'Swept Away') related to a physical fitness craze. Less well-received was 'Red Hot' which, in retrospect, is a fair modern R&B album.

Backed by an orchestra that included the formidable horn section of Southside Johnny's Asbury Jukes, she had seemed more out of her depth in the civic uproar that had accompanied her 1983 televised free concert before an audience approaching a quarter of a million in New York's Central Park. That same year, she had reunited with The Supremes for the finale of Motown's 25th Anniversary TV spectacular. Seven years later, a medley of Supremes showstoppers was also a highlight of her strained 'Greatest Hits Live', recorded in London. However, the mere familiarity of later selections on this double album was adequate evidence why Diana Ross will be remembered as the only female performer on Motown to sustain success after leaving the label.

Greatest Hits

Singles	Title	US	UK
1970	*Ain't No Mountain High Enough*	I	5
1971	*I'm Still Waiting*	63	I
1973	*Touch Me In The Morning*	I	9
1976	*Theme From 'Mahogany'*	I	5
1976	*Love Hangover*	I	10
1980	*Upside Down*	I	2
1981	*Endless Love*		
	(with Lionel Richie)	I	7
1981	*Why Do Fools Fall In Love*	7	4
1982	*Mirror, Mirror*	8	36
1986	*Chain Reaction*	66	I

Albums			
1973	*Lady Sings The Blues*	I	50
1979	*20 Golden Greats*	–	2
1980	*Diana*	2	12

Todd **RUNDGREN**

Often too clever for his own commercial good, singer/songwriter/multi-instrumentalist Rundgren (born 1949) is nonetheless guaranteed a cult following and well-paid work as a producer, engineer, session musician and composer until he chooses to retire.

Servitude with Woody's Truckstop at his Philadelphia high school preceded Rundgren's formation of The Nazz in 1968 with Stewkey (aka Robert Antoni, keyboards), Carson Van Osten (bass) and Tom Mooney (drums). Of the outfit's three psychedelic US-only albums, only the eponymous first was even a moderate seller, although the singles, 'Hello It's Me' and 'Open My Eyes' were turntable hits. However, Rundgren's songwriting monopoly and studio skills on 'Nazz Nazz' and 1969's 'Nazz III' (which Rundgren tried to disown after an outside remix), as well as his pop star potential, were noticed by Bob Dylan's erstwhile manager, Albert Grossman, who signed the lanky *wunderkind* with dyed multi-coloured long hair to his label.

As a producer/engineer, Rundgren worked with the likes of The Band, Paul Butterfield, Janis Joplin and UK group Badfinger, before taking on such clients as US female quartet Fanny, Grand Funk Railroad, The New York Dolls, Patti Smith and Tom Robinson. On Rundgren's recommendation Grossman in 1971 signed Halfnelson, who later became Sparks. Meatloaf's 1978 'Bat Out Of Hell' album was Rundgren's greatest production success in Britain.

His parallel career as a recording artist began with 1970's 'Runt', on which he played and sang every note via overdubs. Disc jockeys who recalled its 'We Gotta Get You A Woman' single were reminded of it by the arrival of 'The Ballad Of Todd Rundgren',

for which he hired other players (including brothers Hunt and Tony Sales, once of Sparks and later to join David Bowie's Tin Machine in 1989). These products paved the way for 1972's 'Something/Anything', which established Rundgren if not as a superstar, then at least as an enigma. On his next album, 'A Wizard A True Star', and 1974's more experimental 'Todd', Rundgren embraced both a diversity of cover versions and his own songs, such as the singles, 'I Saw The Light' and his biggest hit, a revival of 'Hello It's Me'. Not one to ignore his past, 'Open My Eyes' also remained in Rundgren's live set, of which extracts were heard on 'Utopia' with his new band of the same name. Its studio tracks – mostly space-rock styled – were less impressive; nor was 1975's lengthy 'Initiation', with its Zen Buddhist buzz-words, saved from open pretentiousness by his grace-saving humour.

The self-explanatory 'Another Live' was divided equally between covers (eg The Move's 'Do Ya') and remarkable new songs like 'Just One Victory'. A similar repertoire applied to 1976's 'Faithfull', which was notable for the flowering of its creator's idiosyncratic fretboard style and for showy interpretations of 'Strawberry Fields Forever', 'Good Vibrations' and Jimi Hendrix's 'If Six Was Nine'.

While 'Oops Wrong Planet' and 1980's 'Adventures In Utopia' were attributed to his Utopia group, Rundgren's own 'Ra' and the critically-acclaimed 'Hermit Of Mink Hollow' – his was the only house in an upstate New York road named Mink Hollow – generated more income. This statistic may have led to Rundgren's name alone being the principal selling point on his sporadic subsequent output. He last broke cover in 1989 with 'Nearly Human', as consistently strong a collection as any he'd cut in his youthful prime.

Todd Rundgren (second left) with the optimistically-named Utopia

Greatest Hits

Singles	Title	US	UK
1970	*We Gotta Get You A Woman*	20	—
1972	*I Saw The Light*	16	36
1973	*Hello It's Me*	5	—
Albums			
1973	*Something/Anything*	29	—
1977	*Ra*	—	27
1978	*Hermit Of Mink Hollow*	36	42
1980	*Adventures In Utopia* (Utopia)	32	57

RUSH

Alex Lifeson *(guitar)*
Geddy Lee *(bass, vocals)*
John Rutsey *(drums)*

Despite the lukewarm attitudes of radio programmers and critics, Rush have been one of the most durable heavy metal bands of the last 20 years.

Inspired by Cream and Led Zeppelin, Toronto high school students Lifeson (born 1953) and Lee (born 1953) formed Rush with Rutsey in 1969. When the Canadian government dropped the legal drinking age to 18, they gained access to the local bar band circuit. The trio's first recording was a version of Buddy Holly's 'Not Fade Away', released on their own Moon label in 1973.

Next they brought in producer Terry Brown to supervize a debut album which was released by Mercury in the US (a significant achievement for a Canadian bar band). With Rutsey replaced by Neil Peart (born 1952), Rush made its first US tour supporting Kiss and Aerosmith. In 1975, Rush were recognized as most promising new band in Canada and released 'Fly By Night' and 'Caress Of Steel'. The latter featured newcomer Peart's lyrics on the 'Fountains Of Lamneth' suite, its themes taken from sword and sorcery literature.

For the next five years, Rush followed a gruelling routine of touring and recording which was rewarded by a Top 10 album on both sides of the Atlantic. Among their album releases were the science-fiction song-cycle '2112' (1976), the live double, 'All The World's A Stage' (1977), and 'A Farewell To Kings', which was recorded at Rockfield Studios in Wales and told part of the adventure saga which was completed on 'Hemispheres' (1978).

The big breakthrough came in 1980 with 'Permanent Waves', which was supported by a five month US tour and provided a UK Top 20 single, 'Spirit Of The Radio'. 'Moving Pictures' was equally successful while 'Signals' saw a shift in style with a greater use of keyboards. With Rush having become the most successful Canadian rock export, Geddy Lee's guest vocals on 1982's 'Great White North', a comedy album by TV performers Dave Thomas and Rick Moranis masquerading as Bob & Doug McKenzie, helped it to reach the US Top 10.

'Signals' was also the last Rush album to involve Terry Brown. Former Supertramp producer Peter Henderson was brought in for the 1984 album, 'Grace Under Pressure'. Showing Peart's literary leanings, the title was novelist Ernest Hemingway's definition of 'guts'. Though touring less frequently now, live shows remained vital to Rush's continuing success and in 1984 the trio made their first tour of Japan.

Henderson was replaced by UK producer Peter Collins for 'Power Windows', the group's sixth successive US Top 10 album, and 'Hold Your Fire' (1987). Recorded in Europe, Canada and the Caribbean, the album's single release, 'Time Stand Still', had guest vocals by Aimee Mann of Til Tuesday.

'A Show Of Hands' (1989), Rush's 15th album for the same label, was also their last for the company. In 1990 the group signed new deals, and the first release under the new arrangement was 'Presto'. Produced by Rupert Hine, it showed a move back from synthesizers to a more streamlined rock trio sound.

Greatest Hits

Singles	Title	US	UK
1980	*Spirit Of Radio*	51	13
1982	*New World Man*	21	42
Albums			
1980	*Permanent Waves*	4	3
1981	*Moving Pictures*	3	3
1981	*Exit . . . Stage Left*	10	6
1982	*Signals*	10	3
1984	*Grace Under Pressure*	10	5
1985	*Power Windows*	10	9

Leon RUSSELL

Leon Russell (born 1941) is an undoubtedly talented singer, songwriter, pianist, guitarist, bandleader and producer, yet despite bursts of personal success at various stages of his career, his contributions to rock remain somewhat unrecognized.

Russell formed his first band as a teenager in the late 1950s, playing behind Jerry Lee Lewis among others. In 1959 he moved to Los Angeles and in the early 1960s, played

Shelter showman eclipsed multi-talented musician

on hundreds of sessions (e.g. most of the Phil Spector hits as well as several by Frank Sinatra, Paul Revere, The Byrds etc.). After work with Delaney & Bonnie he formed The Asylum Choir with Marc Benno in 1968. Their first album, 'Look Inside The Asylum Choir' failed, despite critical acclaim, and a second album, 'Asylum Choir II' (recorded in 1969 but not released until 1971) shared the same fate. In the meantime he had become part of Delaney & Bonnie & Friends, the road band they had finally put together. Russell had also written 'Delta Lady' (supposedly about Rita Coolidge) and produced Joe Cocker's hit version of it.

At the end of 1969, Russell and producer Denny Cordell came to London and, working with engineer Glyn Johns, recorded the backing tracks for Russell's first solo album. The album, 'Leon Russell' (1970) was a minor US hit and featured several notable sidemen including Eric Clapton, Steve Winwood, Ringo Starr and George Harrison. In 1970 Russell masterminded the musical end of Joe Cocker's mammoth Mad Dogs And Englishmen US tour. The resulting double album was a huge success and the film of the tour showed how much of a star Russell was becoming (largely at Cocker's expense).

The early 1970s saw Russell at the height of his commercial success. His music was essentially gritty white R&B, but his use of horns and gospel-flavoured singing coincided with a general return to more roots-orientated music after the excesses of the late 1960s. Between 1971 and 1976, each of Russell's albums was a US Top 40 hit. 'Leon Russell And The Shelter People' (1971) used four separate backing groups and made the US Top 20, but failed to produce a hit single. By contrast 1972's US Top 3 album, 'Carney', produced Russell's biggest hit single, 'Tight Rope', which made the US Top 20.

The triple live album, 'Leon Live' (1973), which reached the US Top 10 demonstrated

Musicians join Rush as teenage booze ban is lifted

what a fine performer Russell was – not to mention showman; his long hair, wispy beard and ubiquitous stove-pipe hat had become as well-known as his music. 'Leon Live' was Russell's last Top 10 entry, although the Top 30 album 'Hank Wilson's Back' (1973) was a notable Country & Western collection. In 1975 he formed a new label, his first album for which, 'Wedding Album', was recorded with his new wife Mary (née McCreary). A further duet album with Willie Nelson, 'One For The Road' (1979) made the US Top 30, but since then his profile has dropped considerably with only two albums released in the 1980s ('The Live Album' with New Grass Revival, 1981, and 'Hank Wilson Volume II', 1984).

Greatest Hits

Singles	Title	US	UK
1972	*Tight Rope*	11	–
1975	*Lady Blue*	14	–
Albums			
1971	*Leon Russell And The Shelter People*	17	29
1972	*Carney*	2	–
1973	*Leon Live*	9	–

Mitch **RYDER**

R yder (born William Levise Jr, 1945), along with his group, The Detroit Wheels, found much US chart success in the latter 1960s as a white act working in a style which its major black originators had all but left behind – booting, raucous R&B of the kind epitomized by Little Richard in the 1950s and James Brown's Famous Flames in the early 1960s.

Ryder was from Detroit, and absorbed that city's black music traditions, singing with R&B outfits from his mid-teens. In 1963, he formed Billy Lee & The Rivieras, rapidly building a red-hot club reputation which led within a year to a residency which drew 3,000 punters to each show. Here, the group came to the attention of The Four Seasons' producer Bob Crewe, who signed them to his New Voice label and moved them to New York, changing their name to Mitch Ryder (found in a phone book) and The Detroit Wheels. The hits began in 1966, when a medley of Little Richard's 'Jenny Jenny' and the R&B standard, 'See See Rider', rocked into the US Top 10, setting a pattern for follow-up singles, many of which were similar medleys, and most of which translated on to vinyl the R&B dance sound which was the group's hugely popular live act.

A revival of The Righteous Brothers' hit, 'Little Latin Lupe Lu', was another 1966 hit, while the year closed with the group's biggest hit, the million-selling medley of 'Devil With A Blue Dress On'/'Good Golly Miss Molly',

which made the US Top 5. By the time 1967 had kicked off with 'Sock It To Me Baby' in the US Top 10, Crewe had decided that Ryder's future lay as a soloist, and he split singer and group to record them separately. The Detroit Wheels without their vocalist quickly split, but Ryder went on (with notably less wild soul-based material) to solo chart success, albeit on a smaller scale – his biggest solo single, a revival of 'What Now My Love', just made the US Top 30. On the road, the act was also less dance and more showbiz-orientated, the inevitable consequence of replacing an R&B combo with a 40-piece orchestra.

After splitting from Crewe, Ryder turned the clock back again in 1970 when he formed Detroit, a septet playing R&B and hard rock, but the commercial success of The Detroit Wheels eluded them. After several further years in comparative wilderness, he found an unlikely spiritual home in Germany, where he became a cult figure in the late 1970s and began to record again. Eventually, US recognition returned when his 1983 album, 'Never Kick A Sleeping Dog', produced by John Cougar Mellencamp, made the charts alongside the single, 'When You Were Mine', written by Prince. Despite a lack of successful follow-ups, this revitalized his live performance career at home – as did the tribute paid by Bruce Springsteen via the 'Devil With A Blue Dress Medley' of Ryder's 1960s hits, included on the 'No Nukes' compilation album and regularly a part of Springsteen's stage act.

Greatest Hits

Singles	Title	US	UK
1966	*Devil With A Blue Dress On*	4	–
1967	*Sock It To Me Baby*	6	–
Albums			
1966	*Breakout . . . !!!*	23	

Buffy **SAINTE-MARIE**

B uffy Sainte-Marie (born 1941) was part of the early 1960s generation of US folk singers. Originally she intended to be a teacher, but a weekend in Greenwich Village convinced her otherwise. An early encounter (c. 1963) with the drug codeine led to her temporary withdrawal from the scene, but she recovered and wrote one of her most famous songs, the much-covered 'Cod'ine', about it. It appeared on her first album, 'It's My Way' (1964) which also contained her classic protest song, 'Universal Soldier' (best known in versions by Donovan and Glen

Buffy Sainte-Marie, true American

Campbell). Through her friend and fellow singer, Patrick Sky, she rediscovered her Native American (i.e. Red Indian) roots, celebrated in such songs as 'My Country 'Tis Of Thy People You're Dying' (from 'Little Wheel Spin And Spin' a US Top 100 album in 1966) and 'Now That The Buffalo's Gone' (from 'I'm Gonna Be A Country Girl Again', 1968). Like most of her contemporaries, her early albums mixed traditional folk songs with her own material, played in a simple acoustic style but emphasizing the unique quality of her voice. 'Country Girl' was her first real departure, being all-country and recorded in Nashville. The title song was one of her best, but despite being pushed by her record company several times it was never a major hit, although it did reach the UK Top 40 in 1972.

'Illuminations' (1970) was even more experimental, containing electronic material as well as electric instrumentation. 'She Used To Wanna Be A Ballerina' (1971) featured Neil Young, Crazy Horse and Ry Cooder and contained the UK Top 10 single 'Soldier Blue', the title song of the movie which culminated in a bloody and realistic Indian massacre. Elvis Presley had a UK Top 5 single in 1972 with her 'Until It's Time For You To Go'. Examples of her 'Indian' material were gathered together on the 1974 compilation, 'Native North American Indian Child: An Odyssey', and on 'Sweet America' (1976) she incorporated Indian music for the first time. Although none of her albums have sold in large quantities, much of her work is of a very high standard and warrants further investigation.

Her support for Indian causes has continued and included the setting up of Native Creative, which helps provide education and cultural awareness for American children. This work had largely kept her out of the public eye since the mid-1970s, although she has remained active as a songwriter, co-writing the 1982 US No. 1, 'Up Where We Belong' for Joe Cocker and Jennifer Warnes, she also appeared on The Neville Brothers' 'Brother's Keeper' album in 1990.

SAM and DAVE

Probably black music's all-time most successful vocal duo, Sam Moore (born 1935) and Dave Prater (born 1937) were also among the biggest acts to emerge from the Stax studio in Memphis during its mid-1960s heyday. The duo met in Miami in 1961, when gospel-turned-R&B singer Moore invited club chef/part-time vocalist Prater to partner him after impromptu stage duets proved popular. They recorded for three years without any success, and eventually switched labels in late 1965.

Wanting them to record in the South, Atlantic's Jerry Wexler arranged a deal with Jim Stewart of Stax, whereby the duo's recordings cut in Memphis would be released by Stax (then tied to Atlantic). Sessions followed with writer/producers Isaac Hayes and David Porter, and a string of successful singles began early in 1966, varying from the powerhouse gospely funk of 'You Don't Know Like I Know' and 'Hold On I'm A-Comin' ' (their first US Top 30 hit) to intense ballads like 'When Something Is Wrong With My Baby'. International success followed in 1967 after the duo triumphed on the Stax/Volt European Tour with Otis Redding. Later that year came their biggest-selling and most enduring song, 'Soul Man', which reached the US Top 3 and UK Top 30, and sold over a million. It won a Grammy as 1967's Best Group R&B Performance, and was followed by the US Top 10 hit, 'I Thank You'. When Atlantic and Stax parted in 1968, the duo lost access to their writers, producers and the Memphis studio, and Prater's career was almost summarily halted when he shot his wife during a domestic incident; he escaped prosecution because of circumstances surrounding the event.

It was by now widely known that the relationship between Moore and Prater was less harmonic than their records, but they stayed together until 1970, by which time their hits had become infrequent, the one notable later seller being 1969's 'Soul Sister, Brown Sugar', a UK Top 20 hit. The 1970s saw periods of solo work and recording by the two men, along with a mid-decade reunion, but all to little commercial avail. However, in

1979 The Blues Brothers successfully revived 'Soul Man', and Sam & Dave teamed up again to take advantage of renewed interest in their music, further boosted by its wide use in *The Blues Brothers* movie. The duo toured the US as unlikely (though specially requested) support to The Clash, and appeared with Paul Simon in his movie, *One Trick Pony*. However, it was not to last. Personal animosity split them again, though Prater attempted to continue the act in surrogate form with new partner Sam Daniels.

In 1987 'Soul Man' was revived again as the theme for the film of the same name; this time, it was recorded by Moore in unlikely but effective parternship with Lou Reed, and was a UK Top 30 hit. Since then, Moore has pursued an active solo career, including dueting on his old hits with ex-Blues Brother Dan Aykroyd at Atlantic's 40th Birthday concert in 1988. Prater, however, was not so lucky. Arrested on drug trafficking charges, he died at the wheel of his car in 1988, just a month before that same anniversary concert.

SANTANA

Carlos Santana (guitar, vocals)
Mike Carrabello (congas, percussion)
Dave Brown (bass)
Jose 'Chepito' Areas (timbales, percussion)
Mike Shrieve (drums)
Gregg Rolie (keyboards)

Raised in Tijuana and San Francisco, Carlos Santana (born 1947) started fusing Latin music with the blues when he formed The Santana Blues Band in 1968 with high school friend Gregg Rolie. Carlos Santana's solo recording debut was on 1968's 'Live Adventures Of Mike Bloomfield & Al Kooper', after which the Santana band acquired its own record deal in 1969. During that year, the band played several open-air festivals, including Woodstock, which boosted their reputation in quantum leaps. Their eponymous debut album made the US Top 5 later that year, spending two years in the charts and producing a Top 10 single, 'Evil Ways'. 1970's 'Abraxas' did even better, topping the US charts for six weeks, and including a US Top 5 single, a cover of Fleetwood Mac's 'Black Magic Woman', plus a US Top 20 hit with Tito Puente's 'Oye Como Va'.

The band's line-up was fluid but Carlos Santana's melodic style provided a clear direction. Guitarist Neil Schon and percussionist Coke Escovedo joined for 1971's 'Santana III', which spent five weeks at the top of the US album chart, before Rolie and Schon quit to form Journey. From 1972, Santana expanded his output, cutting a duet album, 'Carlos Santana & Buddy Miles! Live!' (US Top 10), a new Santana group album, 'Caravanserai' (US Top 10), a US Top 20 album with fellow Sri Chinmoy devotee, Mahavishnu John McLaughlin, titled 'Love Devotion Surrender', an excellent fifth group album, 'Welcome' (US Top 30), another duet album, 'Illuminations', with Turiya Alice Coltrane (US Top 100), a US Top 20 'Greatest Hits' album and another group album, 'Borboletta' (US Top 30), all before the end of 1974 – seven albums in under three years, five of which went gold and made the UK Top 10. 1975 saw the release of a lavishly packaged triple live album, 'Lotus', recorded in Japan and only available there

Walking rhythm section Carlos Santana (far left) with his eponymous powerhouse of percussion

until some years later, capturing what was arguably the finest Santana line-up, including Areas, Shrieve, Tom Coster (vocals, keyboards), Armando Peraza (guitar, vocals) and Doug Rauch (bass) behind Santana himself.

The chart albums continued in 1976 with 'Amigos', which made the US Top 10, although the follow-up, 'Festival' only reached the US Top 30. However, the second 1977 album, the mostly live 'Moonflower', became Santana's final US Top 10 album for three years, suggesting that ten albums in five years had made what was certainly innovative, exciting and well-planned music in 1973 rather too easy to acquire by then.

Not that the hit albums stopped: 1978's 'Inner Secrets' and 1979's 'Marathon' both made the US Top 30, although a half live solo album by the group leader, 'Oneness/Silver Dreams – Golden Reality', possibly deserved little more than it achieved (US Top 100). 1980 was also a solo album year, but 'The Swing Of Delight', which featured Herbie Hancock, Wayne Shorter and Ron Carter, was little more successful than 'Oneness', after which the band returned in 1981 with what may turn out to be Carlos Santana's farewell to the Top 10 of the US album chart, 'Zebop!'. Occasional hit singles like 'Winning', a cover of The Zombies hit, 'She's Not There', and 'Hold On' in 1982 have kept him in contention, while another solo album in 1983, 'Havana Moon', made the US Top 40 and pitted him against the diversity of Willie Nelson, Booker T Jones (of the MGs) and The Fabulous Thunderbirds. 1985's band album, 'Beyond Appearances', proved that there was still interest in the Santana band, which has continued to sell out international tours, although Journey seemed of more interest to US fans than the man from whose band Journey was a spin-off.

A longtime band member during the 1980s was Scottish vocalist Alex Ligertwood,

Leo Sayer: The Show Must Go On

who atoned for his 1970s disappointment at leaving The Jeff Beck Group by recording with a guitarist who has made twice as many albums as Beck, while other notable album guests over the years have included Jan Hammer, Billy Cobham, Stanley Clarke, Herbie Hancock, Narada Michael Walden, etc.

Greatest Hits

Singles	Title	US	UK
1970	Evil Ways	9	–
1970	Black Magic Woman	4	–
1977	She's Not There	27	11
Albums			
1969	Santana	4	26
1970	Abraxas	1	7
1971	Santana III	1	6
1972	Caravanserai	8	6
1981	Zebop!	9	33

Leo **SAYER**

Launched in the guise of a pierrot during the heyday of early 1970s glam-rock, Sayer (born 1948) actually emerged from the busking/folk field in the singer-songwriter tradition.

After leaving Worthing College of Art in 1968, where he had formed the Terraplane Blues Band, Sayer moved to London, working as an illustrator and busking on the streets and around the folk clubs. In 1972, he formed a rock group, Patches, with fellow songwriter David Courtney, who had previously played drums with Adam Faith. Faith, along with The Who's Keith Moon, took an interest in the group and secured a record deal, but the group failed to make any impact, and when they split up, Faith signed Sayer to a solo management contract.

Courtney and Faith began recording Sayer's first album at studios belonging to Who vocalist Roger Daltrey, the latter being so impressed that he used Sayer/Courtney songs for most of his own debut solo album. When it appeared as 'Daltrey', it gave The Who's vocalist his biggest solo hit with the Sayer/Courtney song, 'Giving It All Away', a UK Top 5 hit.

Faith secured Sayer a recording contract, and after a failed single 'Why Is Everybody Going Home' he hit the UK Top 3 in 1974 with 'The Show Must Go On'. His debut album, 'Silverbird', also made the UK Top 3, and Sayer adopted the pierrot costume that had featured on the album cover. A promotional tour with Roxy Music was followed by a trip to the US, where he failed to make the right impression, although Three Dog Night charted with a cover of 'The Show Must Go On' a couple of months later.

More UK Top 10 hits, 'One Man Band' and 'Long Tall Glasses', were followed by the

UK Top 5 album, 'Just A Boy', in late 1974. Six months later, after a second tour, it broke into the Top 10 of the US album chart, while 'Long Tall Glasses' was a US Top 10 single.

Sayer's lyrical talents were often sublimated to dance-oriented offerings; his 1975 UK Top 3 hit was the narrative gem, 'Moonlighting', but a year later the same heights were reached by the disco blandness of 'You Make Me Feel Like Dancing', which nevertheless went gold as a US chart-topper.

The biggest Sayer smash of 1977 was 'When I Need You', a No. 1 single on both sides of the Atlantic. Written by Albert Hammond and Carol Bayer Sager, it marked a move away from predominantly self-penned hits. Its platinum parent album, 'Endless Flight', went Top 5 in the UK, and Top 10 in the US.

Subsequent releases included a 1978 cover of Buddy Holly's 'Raining In My Heart', which made the UK Top 30, followed two years later by the hugely successful Bobby Vee cover, 'More Than I Can Say', a transatlantic Top 3 hit.

1982 saw another UK Top 10 hit, 'Have You Ever Been In Love?', but the chart entries were beginning to wane. Much of Sayer's UK impact lay in television – he fronted two BBC series of his own during his peak years, and by 1988 he found himself without a record contract, deciding to release further material independently.

Greatest Hits

Singles	Title	US	UK
1973	The Show Must Go On	–	2
1975	Moonlighting	–	2
1976	You Make Me Feel Like Dancing	1	2
1977	When I Need You	1	1
1980	More Than I Can Say	2	2
Albums			
1974	Silverbird	–	2
1974	Just A Boy	16	4
1976	Endless Flight	10	4
1979	The Very Best of Leo Sayer	–	1

Boz **SCAGGS**

One of the most stylish white US soul singers of the 1970s, Scaggs made a surprise comeback in the late 1980s.

William Royce Scaggs (born 1944) formed his first group in high school in Texas with fellow singer/guitarist Steve Miller. The duo went on to the University of Wisconsin where they played R&B in The Ardells. Scaggs next joined The Wigs, a group which travelled to Europe in 1964, where Scaggs made an obscure solo album in Sweden.

He continued to travel round the world, reaching California in 1967 where he was reunited with Miller. Scaggs worked on the Steve Miller Band's 1968 albums, 'Children

Of The Future' and 'Sailor', before leaving to start a solo career. Championed by Jann Wenner, editor of *Rolling Stone* magazine, Scaggs was signed by Atlantic.

With Scaggs, Wenner and Marlin Greene co-producing, 'Boz Scaggs' was recorded in 1969 at Muscle Shoals, Alabama. The album was a critical success but sold poorly and was also notable for the guitar solos of Duane Allman, especially on 'Loan Me A Dime'. Scaggs himself returned to San Francisco, formed a band and signed a new record deal.

Over the next five years, he toured regularly and made a series of modest-selling but well-reviewed albums. Top British producer Glyn Johns supervised 'Moments' and 'Boz Scaggs & Band' (both 1971), while Roy Halee produced 'My Time' (1972), with the hard rocking 'Dinah Flo' and 'Slow Dancer' (1974) being produced by soul veteran Johnny Bristol. The breakthrough came in 1976 with 'Silk Degrees' and its hit singles 'Lowdown', 'Lido Shuffle' and 'What Can I Say?'. Produced by Joe Wissert with arrangements by Toto's David Paich, the album emphasized the softer crooning side of Scaggs's bluesy voice. 'We're All Alone', a Scaggs composition from 'Silk Degrees', was also a US Top 10 hit for Rita Coolidge.

'Down Two Then Left' (1977) and 'Middle Man' (1980) continued the success story along with Top 20 singles like 'Breakdown Dead Ahead' and 'Miss Sun', a 1981 duet with Lisa Dal Bello. However, in 1983 Scaggs left music to open a restaurant in San Francisco. Apparently now semi-retired, Scaggs returned to the studio in 1988, releasing 'Other Roads', which scraped into the US Top 50.

Greatest Hits

Singles	Title	US	UK
1976	*Lowdown*	3	28
1977	*What Can I Say*	42	10
1977	*Lido Shuffle*	11	13
Albums			
1976	*Silk Degrees*	2	37
1980	*Middle Man*	8	52

Brinsley SCHWARZ / Nick LOWE

Brinsley Schwarz (guitar, sax)
Nick Lowe (bass, vocals)
Bob Andrews (keyboards)
Billy Rank (drums)

Brinsley Schwarz grew out of the remnants of Kippington Lodge, an unsuccessful English harmony pop group who released five singles during the period 1966–69. Prime movers in Kippington Lodge were Brinsley Schwarz himself (guitar, later sax as well) and Nick Lowe (bass and vocals), both of whom had also been in bands together back in their school days some five years previously. Despite the failure of Kippington Lodge, the two resolved to continue and, with Bob Andrews on keyboards plus new recruit Billy Rankin on drums, hit the road as Brinsley Schwarz. By the beginning of 1970 they were going nowhere and on the verge of disintegration when they were 'selected' by an agency, Famepushers, whose idea was to take an unknown group and propel them to fame and fortune. The agency's major scam was to get them on a bill at the prestigious Fillmore East in New York (with the likes of Van Morrison and Quicksilver Messenger Service) and fly a batch of 'influential' journalists out to see them. It was hype of the worst kind and when the idea backfired, the band never really recovered from it.

At the time, their music varied between CSN&Y harmonies and heavy blues, as exemplified by their first album 'Brinsley Schwarz' (1970), which received poor reviews. Critical reassessment started with their second album 'Despite It All' (1971) a much improved offering. Keeping a low profile, the band started to build up a loyal, if small following via pub and club gigs, and over the next 18 months improved dramatically, absorbing new, frequently country, influences. The changes are noticeable on their excellent third album, 'Silver Pistol', the first to feature additional guitarist/vocalist Ian Gomm. Further albums 'Nervous On The Road' (1972), 'Please Don't Ever Change' (1973) and 1975's 'New Favourites' (produced by Dave Edmunds) were uniformly excellent, but by restricting their gigs almost exclusively to the emerging London pub/rock circuit, lack of commercial success was almost inevitable. By opening up that circuit though, they did act as catalysts for a new generation, who included Kilburn & The High Roads (with Ian Dury), Elvis Costello and Graham Parker. Seemingly unable or unwilling to broaden their horizons, the band broke up in early 1975.

Most of the band went on to varying degrees of fame and fortune. Schwarz and Andrews spent several years in The Rumour, Graham Parker's backing band, and Ian Gomm made several pleasant, if not outstanding solo albums. The most visible by far, however, was Nick Lowe. When Stiff Records was launched in the UK by Jake Riviera (Lowe's manager) and Dave Robinson, in 1976, Lowe released the first single on the label and became virtually their staff producer, working with The Damned, Wreckless Eric and most notably Elvis Costello (whose first five albums he produced). Parting company with Stiff along with Riviera and Costello in 1977, Lowe scored a UK Top 10 single with 'I Love The Sound Of Breaking Glass' (1978), while 'Cruel To Be Kind' (1979) was a Top 20 single in the UK and US.

In 1978 he formed Rockpile with Dave Edmunds, Billy Bremner (guitar) and Terry Williams (drums), mixing Edmunds's rock 'n'roll material with his own quirky but memorable pop extravaganzas. Unfortunately, due to contractual difficulties, they were not allowed to release albums as Rockpile during their heyday, but since they appeared briefly on Lowe's solo debut album, 'Jesus Of Cool' (1978), retitled 'Pure Pop For Now People' in the US, and were the backing musicians on 1979's 'Labour Of Lust', it made little difference (especially as they all played on Edmunds's albums as well). Rockpile also backed Carlene Carter and Mickey Jupp on record, but ironically, the one album that they did finally record under the group name, 'Seconds Of Pleasure', (1980) was a poor reflection of the group's abilities and they broke up shortly afterwards.

Having achieved real fame in the late 1970s, Lowe's subsequent career has meandered to say the least. Good, well produced albums like 'Nick The Knife' (1982), 'Abominable, Showman' (1983), 'Nick Lowe And His Cowboy Outfit' (1984) and 'Rose Of England' (1985) lacked the sparkle of his best work, although he returned to form with 'Pinker And Prouder Than Previously' (1988) and the Edmunds-produced 'Party Of One' (1990). As a producer, Lowe has worked with his (now ex-) wife Carlene Carter, The Pretenders, John Hiatt, The Fabulous Thunderbirds and The Katydids.

Greatest Hits

Singles	Title	US	UK
1978	*I Love The Sound Of Breaking Glass*	–	7
1979	*Cruel To Be Kind*	12	12
Albums			
1978	*Jesus Of Cool*	–	22
1979	*Labour Of Lust*	31	43

The SEARCHERS

John McNally (guitar)
Mike Pender (guitar)
Tony Jackson (bass)
Chris Curtis (drums)

The Searchers were formed initially by McNally (born 1941) to back fellow Merseysider Johnny Sandon, but when Sandon left to front another outfit in 1962, Jackson (born 1940), Pender (born 1942) and, to a lesser degree, Curtis (born 1941) elected to share the lead singing henceforth.

In the clubs of Liverpool and Hamburg, the group became noted for their tidy vocal harmonies and a distinctive two-guitar sound, which would be adapted by later acts, most notably The Byrds when The Searchers became one of the most successful Merseybeat groups. The initial line-up scored a UK No. 1 single with its debut, 'Sweets For My Sweet' (1963), followed by the Top 3 'Sugar and

The Searchers mark 2, with Frank Allen (second right) replacing Tony Jackson on bass

Spice' and the two Top 5 albums, 'Meet The Searchers' and 'Sugar and Spice' that same year. 1964 saw two further No. 1 singles in the UK, 'Needles And Pins' and 'Don't Throw Your Love Away', but also saw the departure of Jackson, replaced by Frank Allen (born 1943) from Cliff Bennett's Rebel Rousers.

Their decline had become perceptible by mid-1964 when 'Someday We're Gonna Love Again' stalled outside the UK Top 10 – a real comedown by earlier standards. Because they'd stuck to much the same formula for most of their singles, they were beginning to sound dated, although 1965's 'He's Got No Love' was a triumph for them, being the only group original to grace a UK Top 20 A-side in those days.

Progress in the US was sluggish although they managed a modest Top 40 run there in the wake of the 'British Invasion', and 'Love Potion Number Nine' went Top 3. However, they went off the boil there as suddenly as they had at home. Having lost the knack of making hits, The Searchers also lost Curtis in 1966, and, with a new drummer, John Blunt, stayed on the road in Britain and Europe well into the 1970s, Blunt being replaced by Billy Adamson in 1969. In 1973 they joined a 'British Invasion Revival' tour of the US where audiences were confused by a mixture of oldies and more contemporary items.

Six years later, the group recorded two well-received albums of new material and an attendant single was a near hit. This episode may have had a bearing on the quartet's split into two separate factions in 1986 but, whatever artistic disagreements caused this, both Mike Pender's Searchers and an 'official' Searchers (led by McNally and Allen) are still playing on the nostalgia circuit.

Greatest Hits

Singles	Title	US	UK
1963	Sweets For My Sweet	–	1
1964	Needles And Pins	13	1
1964	Don't Throw Your Love Away	16	1
Albums			
1963	Meet The Searchers	22	2

Neil **SEDAKA**

One of the first successful teen-oriented singer/songwriters in the late 1950s and early 1960s, Neil Sedaka (born 1939) was almost unique among his contemporaries in renewing his hitmaking career in more mature mode as part of the singer/songwriter movement of the 1970s. Along the way, he wrote or co-wrote a considerable number of classic pop songs.

A piano graduate of New York's Juilliard School of Music, Sedaka had already been writing pop songs in partnership with high school friend Howard Greenfield for over five years when the duo were contracted in 1958 to Don Kirschner's Brill Building-based Aldon Music hit-writing 'factory'. By the end of the year, Connie Francis had scored a major hit with the Sedaka/Greenfield song, 'Stupid Cupid', and Sedaka was signed to RCA as a singer on the strength of his demo of 'The Diary', which became his first US Top 20 hit early in 1959. The follow-up, 'I Go Ape', meant less in the US, but gave him his UK Top 20 debut and led to his first UK tour.

Sedaka's major hit run began at the end of 1959 with the million-selling 'Oh Carol'

(dedicated to Carole Klein, later King, another high school friend), and continued through transatlantic Top 20 hits like 'Stairway To Heaven', 'Calendar Girl', 'Little Devil' and 'Happy Birthday Sweet Sixteen', peaking in 1962 with the US chart-topper, 'Breaking Up Is Hard To Do', another million seller. However, the hits dried up in the UK in 1963 when the Merseybeat boom took hold, and during 1964's 'British Invasion' of the US charts, Sedaka's US sales, like those of his contemporaries, also plummeted. In 1966, Sedaka retired from recording and live performances, and he and Greenfield concentrated on writing songs, providing hits for (among others) The Fifth Dimension ('Workin' On A Groovy Thing'), Tom Jones ('Puppet Man') and Tony Christie ('Is This The Way To Amarillo') over the next five years.

In 1972, Sedaka returned to recording, inspired by Carole King's success with 'Tapestry', and also fired by the enthusiasm generated by two lengthy UK tours. The albums 'Emergence' and 'Solitaire', recorded for Don Kirshner's label, highlighted a more mature pop ballad style, and the title song from the latter became a major hit for Andy Williams. The 'Solitaire' album was recorded in the UK (with the musicians who soon afterwards became 10cc), Sedaka having moved his base and family to London – where, being geographically distant from Greenfield, he struck up a new songwriting partnership, with British lyricist Phil Cody. A new UK recording deal also followed, and he returned to the UK chart with singles like 'That's When The Music Takes Me', 'Standing On The Inside' and 'Laughter In The Rain' (also the title song of an album), as well as a live album, 'At The Royal Festival Hall', which teamed him with The Royal Philharmonic Orchestra.

Sedaka – songwriter supreme

This British renaissance then rubbed off in the US, partly thanks to fan and friend Elton John, who released the UK recordings in the US on his own Rocket label. 'Laughter In The Rain' topped the US singles chart early in 1975, as did 'Bad Blood' (with Elton on backup vocals) later in the year, both selling over a million. In the same year, The Captain & Tennille also had a chart-topping million-seller with a cover of Sedaka's 'Love Will Keep Us Together', and Sedaka himself re-vived 'Breaking Up Is Hard To Do', slowing it down into a smokey nightclub ballad and returning it to the US Top 10. The hits continued through the next five years, includ-ing a UK Top 3 album in 1976 with 'Laugh-ter And Tears', and a US Top 20 single, a duet with his daughter Dara, 'Should've Nev-er Let You Go', in 1980. After this, releases became sparser again and he vanished from the charts once more, but his 1970s record revival had brought Sedaka a renewed career worldwide as an in-demand concert artist, a position he maintained throughout the 1980s, drawing on two generations of familiar reper-toire to attract his audiences. In 1987, he published his autobiography, also titled *Laughter In The Rain*.

Greatest Hits

Singles	Title	US	UK
1962	*Breaking Up Is Hard To Do*	1	7
1974	*Laughter In The Rain*	1	15
1975	*Bad Blood*	1	–
Albums			
1963	*Greatest Hits*	55	–
1976	*Laughter and Tears: Best Of Neil Sedaka Today*	–	2

Bob SEGER

Detroit's best kept secret for more than a decade, Bob Seger paid his dues with a string of local hits that failed to break nationally before becoming recognized as one of America's great rock singers at the end of the 1970s. Seger (born 1945) put his first band together in high school and recorded demos paid for by local hero Del Shannon, who later became his music publisher. After a parody of Barry Sadler's 'Ballad Of The Green Berets' (withdrawn after Sadler found out), Seger released his first single in 1966, 'East Side Story', which sold 50,000 copies in Detroit before being picked up by a bigger label, which fell apart in 1968 after more Seger singles, including 'Heavy Music', another major hit in Detroit.

In 1968, Seger formed The Bob Seger System and signed to a major label. He finally broke into the US Top 20 with 'Ramblin' Gamblin' Man' in 1969, but the album of the same name peaked outside the US Top 50, and neither 'Noah' (1970), 'Mongrel' (1970)

Silver Bullet superstar Seger

nor the solo acoustic 'Brand New Morning' (1971) made commercial waves. A new label in 1972 and the 'Smokin' OPs' album (which included a remake of 'Heavy Music') did not improve his chart rating, nor did 'Back In '72' (1973) or 'Seven' (1974), but then the tide began to change. His next album, 'Beautiful Losers', was rejected by his then current label, but surprisingly picked up by his pre-vious label in 1975. While it peaked well outside the US Top 100, a single, 'Katmandu', almost made the US Top 40.

All this time Seger had been touring relentlessly and his Silver Bullet Band had settled on a core of guitarist Drew Abbott, keyboard player Robin Robbins, saxophonist Alto Reed, bassist Chris Campbell and drum-mer Charlie Martin, and it was 1976's 'Live Bullet' double album (recorded at Detroit's Cobo Hall) which finally broke through, staying nearly three years in the US chart (but peaking only just inside the US Top 40) and selling a million copies. It laid out all Seger's credentials in one swoop from rockers like 'Nutbush City Limits' and 'Get Out Of Denver' to ballads such as 'Turn The Page'.

The word was out and 'Night Moves' (recorded with the Silver Bullet Band and the Muscle Shoals Rhythm Section) went US Top 10 in 1977. The title track hit the US Top 5, while 'Mainstreet' and 'Rock And Roll Never Forgets' were also US hit singles. 1978's 'Stranger In Town' album did even better, making the US Top 5 during a two year chart stay as 'Still The Same' also made the US Top 5 and 'Hollywood Nights' (his first UK chart success) and 'We've Got Tonight' went Top 20. He took a break before releasing 1980's

'Against The Wind', which was produced by Eagles producer Bill Szymczyk. It was the peak of his success, topping the charts for six weeks during a 110-week stay and making the US Top 30. He also had US Top 10 singles with 'Fire Lake' and the title track.

It was time for another live album and 1981's 'Nine Tonight' was more polished but less dynamic than its predecessor, although it was far more successful, reaching the US Top 3/UK Top 30 and providing a Top 5 single with 'Tryin' To Live My Life Without You'. It was another two years before his next single, a version of Rodney Crowell's 'Shame On The Moon' which made the US Top 3, setting up the US Top 5 album, 'The Distance', on which he was backed by new musicians. Another US Top 20 came with 'Under-standing' from the film, *Teacher*, in 1984, and his 'Like A Rock' album made the US Top 3 in 1986. The following year he finally achieved a Number One hit with 'Shakedown' from the feature movie, *Beverly Hills Cop II* – it was a song he only recorded after former Michigan buddy and Eagle Glenn Frey (who had played on 'Ramblin' Gamblin' Man' many years earlier) caught laryngitis. Since then, Seger has maintained a low profile, apart from a guest appearance on Little Feat's come-back album, 'Let It Roll'. A new album was expected in 1991.

Greatest Hits

Singles	Title	US	UK
1977	*Night Moves*	4	–
1978	*Still The Same*	4	–
1978	*Hollywood Nights*	12	42
1978	*We've Got Tonite*	13	41
1983	*Shame On the Moon*	2	–
1987	*Shakedown*	1	–
Albums			
1978	*Stranger In Town*	4	31
1980	*Against The Wind*	1	26
1981	*Nine Tonight*	3	24
1986	*Like A Rock*	3	35

The SEX PISTOLS

Johnny Rotten (vocals)
Steve Jones (guitar)
Glen Matlock (bass)
Paul Cook (drums)

1970s popular music tends to be dated either pre- or post-Sex Pistols. Festering initially beneath the 'street level' popularity of pub-rock, the group was also a reaction against the distancing of the humble pop combo from its essentially teenage audience. Older consumers searched out overlooked artefacts from earlier pop eras – anything to hold the ghastly present, with its stadium 'superstars', at arm's length. One of the few vintage record shops in mid-1970s London

Retarded rock as hyped happening, the Pistols pull the plug on pop pretensions

was Chelsea's Let It Rock. Its proprietor, Malcolm McLaren, was mentor of The Swankers, a group which contained his counter assistant, Matlock and three ex-pupils of a West London school – Cook (born 1956), Jones (born 1955, then the group's vocalist) and guitarist Wally Nightingale. As well as a handful of originals, their exploratory rehearsals hinged on erudite 1960s oldies by the likes of The Small Faces, The Monkees and The Love Affair. Also much admired were Iggy Pop's Stooges and The New York Dolls, once managed by McLaren.

The act became more cohesive when McLaren fired the uncharismatic Wally and transferred Jones to guitar. After approaching future Pretenders leader Chrissie Hynde, Midge Ure (ex-Slik) and Television's Richard Hell, as well as considering many less likely chief show-offs (even himself), McLaren and the group (re-named Sex Pistols) settled for Rotten (born John Lydon, 1956) who had auditioned before the shop juke box by snarling along to an Alice Cooper disc. The main point in his favour was his anti-hippy attitude which was expressed externally in a short, spiky haircut (like Hell's) and ripped apparel held together with safety-pins that included a self-customised T-shirt proclaiming 'I Hate Pink Floyd'.

From their first gig at an art college in 1975, the group's excitingly splishod recitals, frequently accompanied by violence, drew gobbets of appreciative spit from a growing body of 'punks'. Among the most rapt fans was one Sid Vicious (born John Beverley) of the group's fan club, known as The Bromley Contingent. Vicious invented the Pogo, a dance appropriate to the music, which, like skiffle before it, anyone could try. As punk fanzine *Sniffin' Glue* said, 'all you needed was three chords'. By 1976, every week found another hot 'New Wave' band trying their luck, and most looked and sounded just like the Sex Pistols.

Of unsolicited offers from record companies, EMI's £40,000 advance was accepted, and The Pistols dutifully cut their debut single, 'Anarchy In The UK'. During the attendant promotional campaign, the quartet gained national notoriety by cursing on an early evening TV show, and for a public instance of beer-induced vomiting. With most dates of their *Anarchy* tour of Britain cancelled, they were dropped by EMI and then, after a drunken invasion of its offices, A&M Records.

The Pistols come home to roost in 1977 on the fledgling Virgin label, which issued their 'God Save The Queen' (insulting reflections on Queen Elizabeth II's Silver Jubilee), which sparked off airplay bans, assaults on Pistols associates and five necessarily 'secret' UK gigs by the group. This episode was preceded by the replacement of Matlock with the unstable Vicious. A stronger qualification than his dubious musicianship had been the new recruit's hand in beating up a journalist during one of the outfit's many performances at London's 100 Club. Ousted for his advocacy of melody and technical precision, Matlock formed Rich Kids (with Midge Ure) before backing old idol Iggy Pop. In 1989, he was heard on an album by former 1960s wild

men, The Pretty Things.

1977's 'Pretty Vacant' (penned largely by Matlock) and 'Holidays In The Sun' were thought mild enough for radio play, although each was selected (with previous singles) for inclusion on the X-rated 'Never Mind The Bollocks, Here's The Sex Pistols', an album that indicated a dearth of fresh angles. A lack of new ideas also pervaded *The Great Rock-'n'Roll Swindle*, a feature film mixing archive footage, cartoons, musical excerpts and drama, which was director Julian Temple's idiosyncratic account of the Pistols' rise – and disintegration, after a harrowing US visit ended with Rotten's sacking and the elevation of the bloodily exhibitionist Vicious to centre stage.

Rotten had refused to co-operate with McLaren's plan for the group to record with Great Train Robber Ronnie Biggs – featured in both the film and on the group's next single, 'No-one Is Innocent'. Vicious had been absent from the sessions, incapacitated by heroin addiction. By moving to the US, he had effectively left the group. They continued to make money with more singles from the movie soundtrack, such as 'My Way', 'Silly Thing' and 'Who Killed Bambi?' (sung respectively by Vicious, Cook and Ten Pole Tudor). They covered versions of two Eddie Cochran oldies ('sung' by Vicious) and even Bill Haley's 'Rock Around The Clock' (sung by Tudor, better known as an actor than a vocalist) as well as posthumous barrel-scraping albums like 1979's spoken-word 'Some Product – Carri On Sex Pistols'. Even more posthumous was 'Sid Sings', a live album recorded in New York, which was released after Vicious's drug-related death while awaiting trial for the murder of his girl friend, Nancy Spungen.

After a Pistols relaunch with members of Sham 69 failed, Cook and Jones dabbled in myriad ineffectual projects exemplified by their output as The Professionals and Jones's limp 1989 solo album, 'Fire And Gasoline'. With a constantly changing line-up for his Public Image Ltd. group, Rotten (now known as John Lydon) enjoyed occasional chart success as the grubbing music industry stole punk's more viable ideas, got the more palatable acts to de-brutalise themselves, and prepared to rake in the money.

Greatest Hits

Singles	Title	US	UK
1977	God Save The Queen	–	2
1977	Pretty Vacant	–	6
1979	Something Else/Friggin' In The Riggin'	–	3
1979	C'mon Everybody	–	3
Albums			
1977	Never Mind The Bollocks, Here's The Sex Pistols	106	1
1979	The Great Rock'n'Roll Swindle	–	7
1979	Some Product – Carri on Sex Pistols	–	6

The SHADOWS

Hank B Marvin (lead guitar)
Bruce Welch (rhythm guitar)
Brian Bennett (drums)

Despite a career-long lack of success in America, The Shadows are probably the most influential rock instrumentalists of all time, with Hank Marvin having inspired a whole early 60s generation in the UK, across Europe, Japan and Australasia (and even Neil Young in Canada), to pick up an electric guitar. Their distinctive image (Marvin's horn-rim spectacles and red guitar, the group's unison high-kick stage act) was also pervasive before The Beatles arrived.

Marvin (born Brian Rankin, 1941) and Welch (born Bruce Cripps, 1941), both formerly of The Railroaders Skiffle Group and The Chesternuts, were operating as guitar duo The Geordie Boys at London's 2 I's coffee bar when they were recruited to accompany Cliff Richard on his first UK tour dates in October 1958 – Cliff's existing musicians, known as The Drifters, consisted only of guitarist Ian Samwell and drummer Terry Smart at the time. By the end of the year, bassist Jet Harris (born Terence Harris, 1939) and drummer Tony Meehan (born Daniel Meehan, 1943) had replaced Samwell and Smart, and this quartet became Cliff's regular backing group both on stage and record.

EMI gave the group a recording deal in their own right early in 1959, but singles (two vocal, one instrumental) released during the year meant little. The first two were issued as by The Drifters, but by July the group had been made aware of the US vocal outfit of the same name, and renamed themselves, at Harris' suggestion, The Shadows.

'Apache', a dramatic guitar-led instrumental penned by singer/songwriter Jerry Lordan, was their breakthrough, topping the British chart for six weeks, and selling a million in the UK and Europe. Lack of promotion in the US, however, left the field there to another version of the tune by Danish guitarist Jorgen Ingmann, and the group were never thereafter able to crack the US charts.

However, they found consistent success virtually everywhere else. While the majority of Cliff's fans at the time were adoring girls, The Shadows had legions of young male followers, many of them the aspiring copyists already mentioned above. A stream of rock instrumentals, including 'FBI', 'Kon-Tiki' (another No. 1) and the movie theme 'The Frightened City', hit the UK Top 5 in 1961. 'Wonderful Land' (a slower, melodic number and their first with orchestral accompaniment) topped the chart for two months in 1962, and the following year the group had two more UK No. 1's with 'Dance On' and 'Foot Tapper'. The first two Shadows albums were also chart-toppers, and the group were the UK's biggest EP sellers of the early 60s.

'Apache', 'Frightened City' – tough titles for the polite pop of the Foot Tappin' Shadows

Such successes made The Shadows a star live attraction in their own right, but the pressures of success also highlighted instabilities within the group. Meehan left to go into A&R work in late 1961, and six months later Harris, who rarely saw eye-to-eye with Welch, also departed, for a career as a solo guitarist. They were replaced by acquaintances from the UK touring circuit: former Marty Wilde group drummer Brian Bennett (born 1940) and bassist Brian 'Liquorice' Locking – the latter for only 18 months before being replaced in turn by ex-Intern John Rostill.

The group hit their own commercial peak while continuing to back Cliff Richard on record and stage. They also appeared in Cliff's successful movie musicals, wrote music for these and his London pantomimes, and co-wrote hit singles for him, including the chart-topping 'Please Don't Tease', 'Bachelor Boy' and 'Summer Holiday'.

The group's early hip image rapidly evaporated as the Beat Boom arrived, though their chart success declined gradually but steadily through the mid-60s. They made comparatively little style adjustments to the new musical climate, however, apart from moving back to occasional vocal singles (they had two Top 20 vocal hits in 1965 with 'Mary Anne' and 'Don't Make My Baby Blue'.)

In 1968, after celebrating 10 years with Cliff with the 'Established 1958' album, the group, suffering more internal wrangles, feeling stale and at a creative low ebb, split.

While Welch, in poor health, took an extended break, Marvin retained a high profile through solo records, two Cliff And Hank duet hits with Cliff Richard, and residencies on the latter's TV series. In 1971, Marvin and Welch teamed with Australian singer/guitarist John Farrar as the Crosby, Stills & Nash-styled vocal harmony group Marvin, Welch & Farrar. (Brian Bennett, though uncredited, was their drummer). Their records were highly critically-rated, but poor sellers, and live show audiences kept requesting Shadows material in the act. Slowly, they began to metamorphose back into The Shadows again, releasing vocal discs under one name and instrumentals under the other.

Bruce Welch attempted suicide in 1972 following a broken romance with singer Olivia Newton-John, but recovered, though tragedy did strike the following year when Rostill, who had been working with Tom Jones, died in a home studio accident.

Though they still had a nebulous existence, with no full-time bassist, the group were invited to represent the UK in the 1975 Eurovision Song Contest, in which they were runners-up with 'Let Me Be The One' – which also returned them to the UK singles chart.

In 1977, following Farrar's departure to work in the US with Olivia Newton-John, EMI released the album '20 Golden Greats', a compilation of classic Shadows hits. Aided by an arresting TV ad, it topped the UK chart and became the group's biggest-ever seller, topping the million in the UK alone. It also finally brought The Shadows back into full-time action, as they toured, reunited with Cliff for a London Palladium season, and even started to rack hit singles again, as 'Don't Cry For Me Argentina', 'Theme From *The Deer Hunter*' and 'Riders In The Sky' all made the UK Top 20 consecutively.

In 1980, the group left EMI, and recorded for Polydor through the next decade. Although they drifted from the singles charts again, a regular flow of albums made the UK charts, with sales actually rising in the later years via major hit albums like 1986's 'Moonlight Shadows' and 1990's 'Reflection'. The group's long-term achievements were recognised in 1983, via an Ivor Novello Award to mark 25 years of outstanding contribution to British music.

Out of respect to Rostill's memory, no bass player has subsequently been made a full member of the group, which latterly consists of a pool of musicians on keyboards, bass, etc, around the nucleus of Marvin, Welch and Bennett. Though each of this triumvirate pursues private projects for much of the time (and Marvin now lives in Australia), they regularly regroup for Shadows tours, and have even reunited with Cliff Richard on major occasions, most recently Cliff's Wembley Stadium 'Event' in 1989, and the 1990 Knebworth Festival.

Greatest Hits

Singles	Title	US	UK
1960	Apache	–	1
1961	Kon-Tiki	–	1
1962	Wonderful Land	–	1
1962	Dance On	–	1
1963	Foot Tapper	–	1
Albums			
1961	The Shadows	–	1
1962	Out Of The Shadows	–	1
1977	20 Golden Greats	–	1
1979	String Of Hits	–	1

The **SHANGRI-LAS**

Mary Weiss
Marge Ganser
Mary Ann Ganser
Betty Weiss (vocal group)

The Shangri-Las were the most successful white exponents of the girl group sound which carved an important niche in US pop during the first half of the 1960s. Most of their records were theatrical three-minute melodramas, heavy with emotional anguish and atmospheric sound effects, and with lyrics frequently involving loss and death.

If this seemed heavy stuff from two sets of teenage sisters who first sang in high school in Queens, New York, it was because the group were, Phil Spector-like, merely the vocal dressing on these records; the architect of each Shangri-Las hit was writer/producer George 'Shadow' Morton, who brought them to Red Bird Records in New York in the summer of 1964. Previously, the Weiss sisters and the Ganser twins had made a one-off single, 'Wishing Well', for a tiny label, but they were barely semi-professional when Morton heard of them via a friend and hired them to sing on his own composition, 'Remember (Walkin' In The Sand)'. Morton then took his demo production to Jeff Barry and Ellis Greenwich, writer/producers at Red Bird, and both he and the group were signed, after which it became the first hit by The Shangri-Las and a million-seller in late 1964.

The follow-up, 'Leader Of The Pack' exchanged 'Remember's' seagull sound effects for those of a revving motorbike. The rebel/death lyric earned the single radio bans, but it was an even bigger hit, topping the US chart. The group became a touring attraction around America during 1965, its personnel shunting between three and four girls as the Weiss sisters also tried to complete their education. Follow-up records did less well, however, partly due to odd release scheduling by Red Bird (like two singles on the same day), and contractual discord between the label and their management. Nevertheless, they made the US Top 10 again at the end of the year with 'I Can Never Go Home Anymore', their most melodramatic effort yet.

The group's chart run continued until their mid-1966 Red Bird swan-song 'Past, Present And Future', a tearful spoken Mary Weiss monologue over the melody of Beethoven's 'Moonlight Sonata'. After this came two unsuccessful singles for a different label, and the group split up in 1969. However, their singles kept coming back – 'Leader Of The Pack' was twice a UK Top 10 hit upon reissue in 1972 and 1977 – and three of the girls (Marge Ganser died in 1971) eventually reformed as an oldies circuit act from the mid-1970s onwards, the appeal of their unique hits proving timeless.

Greatest Hits

Singles	Title	US	UK
1964	Remember (Walkin' In The Sand)	5	14
1964	Leader Of The Pack	1	3

Del **SHANNON**

Shannon (born Charles Westover, 1939) was one of the most notable white pop music talents to appear in the early 1960s prior to the arrival of The Beatles: a singer/guitarist with a distinctive vocal style who also, unusually for the period, wrote most of his own material.

He first performed in high school and then with Special Services in the US armed forces, but his commercial break came in 1960 when he and his co-writer, keyboard player Max Crook, were playing in a Michigan club band. Ann Arbor DJ Ollie McLaughlin recommended him to manager/producers Harry Balk and Irving Micahnik, and a recording deal followed.

The first single, 'Runaway', was an instant classic. An urgent, anguished rocker, with Shannon soaring into falsetto on the chorus and Crook taking an ear-bending instrumental break on a high-pitched patent electronic keyboard dubbed The Musitron, it topped the charts in the US, UK and around the world in 1961, becoming one of the year's top sellers. It was unusual enough to have all the hallmarks of a gimmicky one-off hit, but Shannon proved otherwise by taking the similar 'Hats Off To Larry' into the US Top 10. Strong follow-ups continued into 1962, notably 'Hey Little Girl' and 'The Swiss Maid', both Top 3 hits in the UK, where Shannon became a regular visitor and a particularly consistent chartmaker, and on a UK tour in 1963, he met The Beatles, returning to America not only singing their praises but also with a cover of 'From Me To You', which became a moderate US hit and the first Lennon/McCartney composition to achieve this feat.

Shannon lost commercial ground like most of his contemporaries when The Beatles themselves blitzed the US market early in 1964, but regained his chart niche through more astute covers (of Jimmy Jones's 'Handy Man' and Bobby Freeman's 'Do You Want To Dance') before having a last transatlantic Top 10 hit in 1965 with 'Keep Searchin'', which reiterated many of the classic ingredients of 'Runaway'. Simultaneously, his composition, 'I Go To Pieces', also hit the US Top 10, as recorded by UK duo Peter & Gordon, after which Shannon went into commercial decline as an artist, though widened his musical parameters during spells with other labels, including an album with Rolling Stones producer Andrew Oldham.

Shannon found the big time again at the end of the 1960s as a producer, having huge sellers with Brian Hyland's 'Gypsy Woman' and Smith's 'Baby It's You', but although he remained an exciting live performer, and was still particularly well received in the UK, Shannon had problems with alcohol during the 1970s, which often blunted his creativity. His own recordings became more sporadic, though he recorded a strong live album in Britain, and made worthy singles with UK producers Dave Edmunds and Jeff Lynne, both of whom admitted his own influence on them a decade earlier.

Another liaison with a star producer, Tom Petty, made for a US chart coda in 1981, when a revival of Phil Phillips's 'Sea Of Love' returned him to the US Top 40 after a 16-year absence, while an album produced by

Hats off to Del, unique in his time

Petty, 'Drop Down & Get Me', was a minor US hit.

In 1988, he recorded again with both Petty and Jeff Lynne (and another old acquaintance, George Harrison), but the results of the sessions were still unreleased when Shannon shot himself dead at his California home while ill and in a fit of deep depression in February 1990. A rumour circulating before this tragedy suggested that Petty, Lynne and Harrison might offer him the late Roy Orbison's place in The Traveling Wilburys, but with his death, this possibility became purely academic.

Greatest Hits

Singles	Title	US	UK
1961	Runaway	1	1
1964	Keep Searchin' (We'll Follow The Sun)	9	3
Albums			
1963	Little Town Flirt	12	15

The SHIRELLES

Addie Harris
Shirley Owens Alston
Beverly Lee
Doris Kenner (vocal group)

One of the earliest of the 1960s girl groups, predating both Motown and Phil Spector, New Jersey schoolfriends Harris (born 1940), Owens (born 1941), Lee (born 1941) and Kenner (born 1941) were taken up by local Tiara label owner Florence Greenberg who recorded their self-penned 'I Met Him On A Sunday'. The single did so well locally that the company leased it out for national distribution, and it made the US Top 50 in May 1958.

A couple more unsuccessful releases followed, before Greenberg formed Scepter Records in 1959. A debut cover of the hit by The Five Royales, 'Dedicated To The One I Love', reached the US Top 100, followed by the haunting ballad, 'Tonight's The Night' (written by Owens and producer Luther Dixon), which made the US Top 40 in 1960. Early in 1961, a classic recording of Gerry Goffin & Carole King's 'Will You Still Love Me Tomorrow' topped the US chart, also reaching the UK Top 5; 'Dedicated' was reissued, this time going gold, with 'Mama Said' becoming a third US Top 5 hit in six months.

Early 1962 saw the Bacharach song, 'Baby It's You', in the US Top 10, before the slightly mawkish 'Soldier Boy' became another US No. 1, just missing the UK Top 20.

In mid-1962, Greenberg turned down a Gene Pitney song, 'He's A Rebel', only to see it top the chart when Phil Spector recorded it with The Crystals. In many ways this signalled the decline of The Shirelles in the genre they had pioneered – by the mid-1960s, it had become the province of The Crystals, The Ronettes, The Supremes, The Vandellas, etc.

They had two more US Top 20 hits in 1963, 'Everybody Loves A Lover' and 'Foolish Little Girl', which made the US Top 5 the year when their work was acknowledged by The Beatles in covers of 'Baby It's You' and the 'Will You Love Me Tomorrow' flipside, 'Boys'.

'Rebel' rejection signals Shirelles singles slide

The group continued through the 1960s, then when Kenner left in 1968 they signed a new deal as Shirley & The Shirelles. Little disc success didn't prevent various 'rock revival' appearances, including the first of the Richard Nader Rock'n'Roll Revival Concerts in 1969 and the 1973 movie documentary, Let The Good Times Roll.

Kenner reappeared when Owens (now using her married name, Alston) left to go solo in 1975, making the 'With A Little Help From My Friends' album featuring songs made famous by other vocal groups. The Shirelles continued, before Harris collapsed and died at a concert in Atlanta, Georgia, in 1982. She was replaced by Louie Bethune, but the group soon disbanded, although re-forming briefly the following year to sing back-up on Dionne Warwick's 'Can We Say Goodbye' album, including a new version of the now classic 'Will You Love Me Tomorrow'.

Greatest Hits

Singles	Title	US	UK
1960	Will You Love Me Tomorrow	1	4
1961	Dedicated To The One I Love	3	–
1961	Mama Said	4	–
1962	Soldier Boy	1	23
Albums			
1963	Greatest Hits	19	–

Carly – chart singles to screen themes

Carly **SIMON**

Best known in her early career for her marriage to James Taylor and for 'You're So Vain', Simon developed into an accomplished songwriter, composing several film themes in the 1980s.

Born in 1945 into a New York publishing family, she first recorded in 1964 as The Simon Sisters with her elder sister, Lucy. 'Winkin', Blinkin' and Nod' was a minor hit in the US and the duo later released an album of children's songs. After an abortive attempt to start a solo career through Bob Dylan's manager Albert Grossman, Simon began writing with film critic Jacob Brackman.

Their 'That's The Way I Always Heard It Should Be' was a hit when released on Elektra in 1971, while the title track from Simon's second album, 'Anticipation', made the US Top 30 the same year. With a chart-topping single ('You're So Vain') and album ('No Secrets'), 1972 was Carly Simon's most successful year in commercial terms.

She married Taylor in the same year and he provided backing vocals on the 'Hotcakes' album as well as duetting on the revival of Charlie and Inez Foxx's 1963 R&B track, 'Mockingbird'. 'Playing Possum' was the third Simon album to be produced by Richard Perry, but it marked the end of Simon's first phase of chart success.

Between 1974 and 1986, her only major hits came from the James Bond movie theme, 'Nobody Does It Better', composed by Marvin Hamlisch and Carole Bayer Sager, and 'You Belong To Me', from the 1978 album, 'Boys In The Trees', co-written with Michael McDonald.

Those years saw her changing labels in 1980, when 'Jesse' reached the US Top 20 and dabbling in pre-Second World War oldies on 'Torch' (1981). Another film song, 'Why' was produced by Chic and sold well in Britain in 1982. The low point in Simon's career was reached in 1985 when the 'Spoiled Girl' album failed even to reach the US Top 200.

However, a move to a fourth major label in 1986 heralded a new era for Carly Simon. She had Top 20 hits with 'Comin' Round Again', from the film *Heartburn*, and with the Oscar-winning 'Let The River Run', featured in the 1988 movie, *Working Girl*. In that year she also recorded 'Greatest Hits Live' at an outdoor concert in Martha's Vineyard, Massachusetts, which also became a TV show. In 1990, she released 'My Romance', a selection of standard love songs and an album of her own compositions, 'Have You Seen Me Lately?'

Greatest Hits

Singles	Title	US	UK
1971	That's The Way I've Always Heard It Should Be	10	–
1973	You're So Vain	1	4
1974	Mockingbird (with James Taylor)	5	34
1977	Nobody Does It Better	2	7
1978	You Belong To Me	6	–
1982	Why	74	10
1987	Coming Round Again	18	10
Albums			
1972	No Secrets	1	3
1974	Hotcakes	3	19
1974	Playing Possum	10	–
1978	Boys In The Trees	10	–

SIMON and **GARFUNKEL** / Paul **SIMON**

New York schoolfriends Paul Simon (born 1941) and Art Garfunkel (born 1942) began singing at parties, bar mitzvahs and high school assemblies in the 1950s, heavily influenced by The Everly Brothers. In 1957, they made a single, 'Hey Schoolgirl' (written by Simon), as Tom and Jerry, which reached the US Top 50, giving the two 15-year-olds a taste of fame. When the follow-up failed, the two simply went back to school. Material from this era was excavated in 1967, when it was presented as being a new album by Simon & Garfunkel (the album's title in fact). The duo were not amused.

By 1958, both had gone on to university, where Simon met Carole Klein, with whom he wrote and occasionally performed. Klein dropped out, changed her surname to King, and became a full-time songwriter, later enjoying substantial success in her own right. Simon stayed on, but occasionally dabbled with pop (e.g. recording a single in 1962 with

an ad hoc group, Tico And The Triumphs) and Garfunkel released two unsuccessful singles. Simon's interest began moving away from pop towards the emerging folk and protest movement and he began writing socially conscious songs such as 'He Was My Brother' (1964).

In 1964, he moved to England, where he roamed the length and breadth of the country, playing in clubs and becoming as well known as the scene allowed. He also linked up with Garfunkel (holidaying in Europe) and the two resolved to play together again back in the US. On their return, the duo (now officially Simon & Garfunkel) cut their first album 'Wednesday Morning 3am' (1964). By contemporary standards it was nothing special, a mixture of folk standards and a few Simon originals, of which only 'Sounds Of Silence' stood out.

Simon returned to the UK in 1965, and recorded a solo album, 'Paul Simon Songbook' (1965) which, though rushed, was nevertheless an excellent record, versions of several songs like 'I Am A Rock', 'Kathy's Song' and 'Flowers Never Bend In the Rainfall' being superior to later re-recordings with Garfunkel.

Simon was still in Europe in the autumn of 1965, when he was informed that a folk-rock backing had been grafted on to 'Sounds Of Silence' and it was heading up the US charts. Returning to the US, the duo hurriedly put together a new album, utilizing the re-vamped 'Sounds Of Silence', which reached No. 1 in the US, as its title track. The majority of the tracks were new versions of songs from 'Songbook' with unsympathetic folk-rock backings, the one exception being 'Homeward Bound', written on the platform of Widnes station, during the recent English visit. Despite the clumsy arrangements, the album reached the US Top 30 and the UK Top 20 and the single 'Homeward Bound' (1966) made the UK and US Top 10.

Simon's other classic alienation song of the era, 'I Am A Rock', reached the US Top 5 and the UK Top 20, but 'Dangling Conversation' (1966), the duo's most ambitious and complex work up to that time, only reached the US Top 30 and failed to reach the UK chart.

The duo's third album, 'Parsley, Sage, Rosemary & Thyme' (1966), was less rushed than its predecessors and remains their most cohesive work, chiefly remembered for 'Scarborough Fair', a traditional English folk song given an extraordinary vocal arrangement, which reached the US Top 20 when released as a single in 1968.

Simon had become a real perfectionist and his output slowed; over the next eighteen months only four new singles appeared. The first three 'A Hazy Shade Of Winter', 'At The Zoo' and 'Fakin' It' were amongst his best, but none breached the US Top 10.

All that changed in early 1968 when the duo wrote songs for the successful Dustin

Hoffman movie, *The Graduate*. The sound-track album reached No. 1 in the US and went Top 5 in the UK and the single nominally taken from it (in fact it was a different version) 'Mrs Robinson', was a US No. 1 and a UK Top 5 hit. Shortly after the release of the soundtrack album, the duo released their official new album, the critically acclaimed 'Bookends'. Despite the presence of four previously released cuts and one track that contained only taped voices, it was a fine collection and gave Simon & Garfunkel a No. 1 album in the UK and US.

Another gap followed before the release of 'The Boxer' (1969), which was a Top 10 single in the US and UK. The 'Bridge Over Troubled Water', single and album from 1970 were both hugely successful, although the album was a very mixed affair, several of the tracks being either second rate and/or lacking in substance, but despite that fact, it remains one of the biggest selling albums in history. Simon's annoyance at Garfunkel getting all the applause when he sang 'Bridge', has been cited as a factor in the duo's break-up, and apart from his harmony singing, Garfunkel did not contribute a great deal to their output. Simon obviously had enough ego to want the recognition that it was his music – so he went solo.

It was nearly two years before 'Paul Simon' (1972) appeared and it proved to be a much more solid and cohesive collection than 'Bridge Over Troubled Water'. His excursions into different areas of music such as reggae, jazz and latin were much more effective than S&G's attempts in similar directions. The album was a UK No. 1 and reached the US Top 5, and produced the UK and US Top 5 single 'Mother And Child Reunion'.

The follow-up album 'There Goes Rhymin' Simon' (1973), a UK and US Top 5 album, was a less eclectic affair, but still produced a UK Top 10 single in 'Take Me To The Mardi Gras' and two US Top 5 hits, 'Kodachrome' and 'Loves Me Like A Rock'. 'Live Rhymin'' (1974) mixed new songs with inevitable S&G favourites and reached the US Top 40, but was essentially a holding job until 'Still Crazy After All These Years' (1975) Simon's first solo US No. 1 album. The album's major song, 'Fifty Ways To Leave Your Lover' went to No. 1 in the US, but the laid back title track barely reached the UK Top 40. It was Simon's last new album for five years during which time he contributed to the soundtrack of *Shampoo* and made a cameo appearance in *Annie Hall*, scoring a US Top 10 hit with 'Slip Sliding Away' (1977) from the compilation album 'Greatest Hits Etc' (1977).

His major project was the film *One Trick Pony* (1980), in which he starred and he wrote the soundtrack. Despite a good performance, unfavourable critical response has led to the film's virtual disappearance.

The next three years were spent working on 'Hearts And Bones' (1983), which had

Simon – life after Art

been intended as a studio reunion with Garfunkel, it failed to work out and all of his ex-partner's contributions were scrapped and it finally appeared as another solo album. It was supposed to be a follow-up to the duo's UK and US Top 10 'Reunion In Central Park' live double album and film (1981).

Another limbo period followed until 1986's 'Graceland', which reached No. 1 in the UK and was a US Top 5 album, and is regarded as one of the albums of the decade. One track each features Rockin Dopsie (cajun) and Los Lobos (Tex-Mex) but all the others feature various African musicians and groups. Simon was criticized for possible exploitation of the black South Africans involved, but as an example of the possibilities of marrying music from different cultures it is unsurpassed. The album produced a UK Top 5 single, 'You Can Call Me Al', which reached the US Top 30 in 1987, supported by a notable video starring Chevy Chase.

The follow-up album, 'Rhythm Of The Saints' (1990), could hardly hope to equal the success of 'Gracelands', but was well received, and reached the UK and US Top 10.

Greatest Hits
SIMON AND GARFUNKEL

Singles	Title	US	UK
1965	*Sounds Of Silence*	1	–
1966	*Homeward Bound*	5	9
1968	*Mrs Robinson*	1	4
1969	*The Boxer*	7	6
1970	*Bridge Over Troubled Water*	1	1
Albums			
1968	*The Graduate*	1	3
1968	*Bookends*	1	1
1970	*Bridge Over Troubled Water*	1	1
1972	*Greatest Hits*	5	2
1982	*The Concert In Central Park*	6	6

PAUL SIMON

Singles	Title	US	UK
1972	*Mother & Child Reunion*	4	5
1973	*Kodachrome*	2	–
1976	*50 Ways To Leave Your Lover*	1	23
1986	*You Can Call Me Al*	23	4
1990	*The Obvious Child*	92	15
Albums			
1972	*Paul Simon*	4	1
1975	*Still Crazy After All These Years*	1	6
1986	*Graceland*	3	1
1990	*Rhythm Of The Saints*	4	1

SIMPLE MINDS

Jim Kerr (vocals)
Charlie Burchill (guitar)
Duncan Barnwell (guitar)
Tony Donald (bass)
Mike MacNeil (keyboards)
Brian McGee (drums)

Scottish band Simple Minds began life as Johnny & The Self Abusers, a punk septet who released one independent single, 'Saints and Sinners' in 1977, before dividing to form The Cuban Heels and Simple Minds, led by Kerr (born 1959) and Burchill (born 1959), with McGee and Barnwell and Donald completing the line-up alongside Mike Mac-Neil (born 1958). In 1978 Derek Forbes joined on bass but Barnwell left before the recording of their debut album 'Life In A Day' (1979). Simple Minds gigged heavily throughout the UK, and the album reached the UK Top 30. They then entered an experimental phase with the awkward 'Real To Real Cacophony' album and single, 'Changeling', both of which failed to chart.

Their next album, 'Empires and Dance' (1980), fared better reaching the UK Top 50 but two subsequent flop singles, 'I Travel' and 'Celebrate' in early 1981, preceded a label change. After one single for the new label, McGee left to be replaced by ex-Slik drummer Kenny Hyslop for the twin album release 'Sons and Fascinations' and 'Sister Feelings Call' (1981), produced by former Gong guitarist Steve Hillage, which reached the UK Top 20. Hyslop left before the release of the 'New Gold Dream' album (1982), eventually being replaced by session drummer Mel Gaynor. The album went Top 3 in the UK and Top 100 in the US, and provided the band with their first UK Top 20 hit singles, 'Promised You A Miracle' and 'Glittering Prize'. The Top 20 'Waterfront' (1983) single introduced a new, more 'stadium rock' sound, and preceded the similarly bombastic 'Sparkle In The Rain' (1984), which went to No. 1 in the UK album chart, spinning off two further UK Top 30 singles.

Kerr married Pretenders' vocalist Chrissie Hynde in 1984, and the following year Simple Minds finally achieved their US breakthrough with the 'Don't You (Forget About Me)' single, which reached No. 1 in the US, taken from the teen movie soundtrack, 'The Breakfast Club'. Forbes left shortly before the track was

released, being replaced by John Giblin, and subsequently joined McGee in Propaganda. In 1985 the UK No. 1 album 'Once Upon A Time' went Top 10 in the US, and the single, 'Alive And Kicking', reached the Top 10 in the UK and US charts. A double live album, 'Live In The City Of Light' (1987), gave the band a third No. 1, but it performed poorly in the US. The 1989 'Street Fighting Years' album and 'Belfast Child' single both topped their respective UK charts, but subsequent departures have left the future of the band uncertain.

Greatest Hits

Singles	Title	US	UK
1985	*Don't You (Forget About Me)*	1	7
1985	*Alive And Kicking*	3	7
1986	*Sanctify Yourself*	14	10
1989	*Belfast Child*	–	1
Albums			
1984	*Sparkle In The Rain*	64	1
1985	*Once Upon A Time*	10	1
1987	*Live In The City Of Light*	96	1
1989	*Street Fighting Years*	70	1

SIMPLY RED

Mick Hucknall (vocals)
David Fryman (guitar)
Fritz McIntyre (keyboards)
Tony Bowers (bass)
Tim Kellett (keyboards, trumpet)
Sylvan Richardson (guitars)
Chris Joyce (drums)

Simple Minds – Scots punksters move to stadium power pop

North West new wavers Simply Red, named no doubt after Hucknall's hair

Manchester born (1960) singer/songwriter and ex-club DJ Hucknall led the Frantic Elevators who, between 1979 and 1983 recorded on indie labels Crackin' Up, Erics, No Waiting (where they first recorded Hucknall's song 'Holding Back The Years') and TJM. In 1984 this soulful white singer with the unmistakable mop of red hair formed Simply Red, which included Bowers, Kellett and Joyce from Durutti Column, and signed to Elektra records in 1985.

The group's debut, a revival of the Valentine Brothers's 'Money's Too Tight (To Mention)' was a big US dance hit and made the UK Top 20 in 1985. After limited success in 1985 their debut album 'Picture Book' and the single 'Holding Back The Years' both became Top 3 UK hits in 1986. In the US the single topped the chart and the album went platinum.

Guitarist Aziz Ibrahim, sax player Ian Kirkham and singer Janette Sewell joined the group in 1987 and their album, 'Men And Women', made the UK Top 3 and singles from it 'The Right Thing' and a revival of Cole Porter's 'Ev'rytime We Say Goodbye' gave them two more UK Top 20 singles.

They had the second biggest selling album

in Britain in 1989 with the chart-topping 'A New Flame' which sold over a million in the UK, went gold in the US and sold over five million world-wide. This album included the UK Top 20 hits 'It's Only Love', which had previously been recorded by Barry White, and 'A New Flame'. It also contained their soulful rendition of Harold Melvin & The Blue Notes' 1972 hit 'If You Don't Know Me By Now' which earned them an American gold disc and their second US No. 1 and narrowly missed the top in the UK.

Greatest Hits

Singles	Title	US	UK
1986	Holding Back The Years	1	2
1989	If You Don't Know Me By Now	1	2
Albums			
1985	Picture Book	16	2
1989	A New Flame	22	1

SLADE

Noddy Holder (vocals, guitar)
Dave Hill (guitar)
Jim Lea (bass, violin, keyboards)
Don Powell (drums)

England's Black Country finally produced a world class beat combo in 1973 when Slade's 'Cum On Feel The Noize' crashed straight in to the UK chart at No. 1. If their career has had its ups and downs since, the group still racked up more chart entries than The Beatles – even if the number of weeks spent there was rather less impressive.

To Wolverhampton as The Beatles are to Liverpool, Slade's longevity and unself-conscious stage craft owed much to years spent by its members in the ranks of locally renowned outfits such as The Vendors and Steve Brett's Mavericks, with whom Holder (born Neville Holder, 1950) had a near-hit with 'Sugar Shack'. By 1966, he had joined Powell (born 1950), Hill and Lea (both born 1952) in The 'N Betweens, who evolved from a Mod act to cover versions from the likes of Traffic, Procol Harum, Frank Zappa and The Young Rascals, whose 'You Better Run' they recorded under the supervision of Hollywood jack-of-all-trades Kim Fowley. When this single failed, The 'N Betweens became Ambrose Slade for 1969's 'Genesis'. Promoting it in a London club, the group was spotted by ex-Animal Chas Chandler who had moved into management. On his advice, they cut 'Wild Winds Are Blowing' as just Slade, and adopted a skinhead image for which their next single, 'Shape Of Things To Come', was even less suited – though it gained them a TV slot on *Top Of The Pops*. The self-penned 'Dapple Rose' and a better received album, 'Play It Loud' preceded their first UK Top 20 strike with Little Richard's

(l to r) Lea, Powell, Holder and Hill – early 1970s British chart superstars

'Get Down And Get With It'. With 1971's 'Coz I Luv You', Slade had arrived.

As glam-rockers now, Slade enjoyed three fat years as hit chased misspelt, stomping smash: 'Take Me Bak 'Ome, Mama Weer All Crazee Now', the inspired 'Merry Xmas Everybody' and the rest of them – all composed by Lea and Holder. Doing briskest business was the 'Sladest' hits collection, but other hit albums included 1972's 'Slade Alive' concert set that was mild compared to later scream-rent bashes which were only kept from rampant chaos by Holder's instinctive if indelicate crowd control.

Though the four coped well as film actors in 1974's almost cameo *Flame*, its soundtrack and spin-off singles signalled a chart decline. Powered by Holder's raw vocal exuberance, Slade's releases still sounded like hits but were becoming too similar in style. After the title track of 1976's 'Nobody's Fool' failed completely, Slade moved to Chandler's own label for minor sellers like 'Gypsy Road Hog' and a 1977 Elvis Presley medley as well as desperate strategies such as the 'Give Us A Goal' football anthem. Too apt was the title of one of their two albums during this nadir, 'Whatever Happened To Slade'.

The tide turned when the quartet earned unexpected acclaim at the 1980 Reading Festival. An EP recorded at the event sparked off a second chart run with 'We'll Bring The House Down' and more items from both the album of the same name and 1981's 'Till Deaf Us Do Part', but when neither of their 1982 singles made the UK Top 50, disbandment was considered.

Although none of their 1970s UK walk-overs could be re-run in the US (despite several attempts), Quiet Riot's US Top 5 revival of 'Cum On Feel The Noize' in 1983 (and the same group's 1984 US revival of 'Mama Weer All Crazee Now') ensured a fairer hearing there for Slade's future output. This red-letter year also saw the group in the UK chart for the fifth time in ten years with 'Merry Xmas Everybody', and their latest

single, 'My Oh My', in the UK Top 3. 1984 brought their first US Top 20 single, 'Run Runaway' and even a US Top 40 album, 'Keep Your Hands Off My Power Supply'.

Despite a further quiet period, Slade's sell-out concerts and Holder's new-found popularity as a radio presenter means that yet more major chart comebacks can never be ruled out.

Greatest Hits

Singles	Title	US	UK
1971	Coz I Luv You	–	1
1972	Take Me Bak 'Ome	97	1
1972	Mama Weer All Crazee Now	76	1
1972	Gudbuy T'Jane	68	2
1973	Cum On Feel The Noize	98	1
1973	Skweeze Me Pleeze Me	–	1
1973	Merry Xmas Everybody	–	1
1983	My Oh My	37	2
1984	Run Runaway	20	7
Albums			
1972	Slayed	69	1
1973	Sladest	129	1
1974	Old New Borrowed And Blue	–	1
1984	Keep Your Hands Off My Power Supply	33	–

Percy SLEDGE

While a teenager, Sledge (born 1941) sang with his cousin Jimmy Hughes's gospel group, The Singing Clouds, and later a local Alabama band called The Esquires Combo. The quartet played covers of Beatles, Bobby Bland, Miracles and other familiar material, and Sledge was only brought in when a previous singer fell ill. In 1965, they were heard by producer Quin Ivy, who was impressed by Sledge's delivery of a song titled 'Why Did You Leave Me Baby', although he was less convinced about the number itself.

Ivy invited Sledge, who was working as a

hospital orderly at the time, to his Quinivy Studios in Oxford, Mississippi. They played around with 'Why Did You Leave Me Baby', changed the lyrics, altered the melody, until the song had evolved into 'When A Man Loves A Woman'.

The raw cut, with out-of-tune overlayed horns, was presented to Jerry Wexler at Atlantic Records, who was impressed by the vocals but wanted to re-record the track. Eventually, Wexler gave way to Ivy's instinct that the rough version had a charm that might catch on in a big way, and the original went out, becoming one of the biggest southern soul records to cross over into mainstream pop.

The record topped the US pop and soul charts, made the Top 5 in Britain, and became an archetype for many southern productions of the period, setting a pattern for most of Sledge's subsequent releases.

These included 10 more soul chart entries between 1966 and 1969, several of which crossed over into the main chart, including the Top 20 'Warm And Tender Love' and 'It Tears Me Up' (both 1966) and 'Take Time To Know Her' (US Top 20, 1968). Some fine album tracks also distinguished his work, like 1967's 'Dark End Of The Street', and later singles such as 'Any Day Now' (1969), and his minor 1974 comeback 'I'll Be Your Everything'.

His original hit continues to resurface. When it was used in a UK TV commercial in 1987, Atlantic repackaged the best of the limited but powerful Sledge output, and the single graced the upper echelons of the UK chart once again after twenty-one years.

Greatest Hits

Singles	Title	US	UK
1966	*When A Man Loves A Woman*	1	4
1966	*Warm And Tender Love*	17	34
1968	*Take Time To Know Her*	11	–
1987	*When A Man Loves A Woman (reissue)*	–	2
Albums			
1966	*When A Man Loves A Woman*	37	–
1987	*When A Man Loves A Woman (The Ultimate Collection)*	–	36

SLY and the FAMILY STONE

Sly Stone (vocals, keyboards, guitar)
Freddie Stone (guitar)
Cynthia Robinson (trumpet)
Larry Graham (bass guitar)
Rosemary Stone (vocals, piano)
Jerry Martini (saxophone)
Greg Errico (drums)

Sly Stone (born Sylvester Stewart, 1944) formed the band with brother Freddie (born 1946), sister Rosemary (born 1945) and

cousin Graham (born 1946) having already worked with Robinson (born 1946) in an earlier group, The Stoners.

Fusing jazz, soul and dance with rock rhythms and psychedelic guitars, the band appealed immediately to the open-minded San Francisco music fans when they first appeared in 1966. In 1967 they released a major label debut album, 'A Whole New Thing'.

The 1968 smash 'Dance To The Music' was a hit for them on both sides of the Atlantic, but a UK tour was aborted after Graham was arrested on drugs charges.

'Everyday People' was also a hit in the US and UK in 1969, and the album, 'Stand', made the US Top 20. The band appeared at the Newport Jazz Festival and Woodstock – such was their broad appeal and cross reference of influence and style. 'I Want To Take You Higher' and 'Hot Fun In The Summertime' were both hits, soon after which in 1970 the group released the 'Greatest Hits' album which earned them their second gold disc.

In 1971 'Family Affair' – the multi-layered soul/funk classic – and the album, 'There's A Riot Goin' On', topped the US charts. In 1972, Graham left to form Graham Central Station to be replaced by Rusty Allen. Sax player Rat Ricco joined the line-up, and Errico was replaced by Andy Newmark. The personnel changes did not stop the run of

hits, and both 'Runnin' Away' and 'Smilin'' made the US Top 30 that year.

Sly Stone married Kathy Silva on stage at New York's Madison Square Garden in June 1974; four months later she divorced him. Throughout the rest of the decade, Graham's group experienced more success than the flailing Family Stone. The LP 'High On You' (1975) was credited to Sly as a solo venture, and only just broke into the US Top 50.

1981 saw Sly feature on Funkadelic's album, 'The Electric Spanking Of War Babies'. He helped launch 1987's Fight For Literacy Day, while in 1988, 'Family Affair' was reissued to a new generation of dance fans, establishing it as a classic among funk singles.

Greatest Hits

Singles	Title	US	UK
1968	*Dance To The Music*	8	7
1969	*Everyday People*	1	36
1969	*Hot Fun In The Summertime*	2	–
1970	*Thank You (Falettinme Be Mice Elf Agin)*	1	–
1971	*Family Affair*	1	15
1973	*If You Want Me To Stay*	3	–
Albums			
1970	*Greatest Hits*	2	–
1971	*There's A Riot Goin' On*	1	31
1973	*Fresh*	7	–

Hip soulster for the late 'Sixties, Sly Stone fused rock rhythms with Family funk

The SMALL FACES

Steve Marriott (vocals, guitar)
Ronnie 'Plonk' Lane (bass)
Jimmy Winston (organ)
Kenny Jones (drums)

Originally the epitome of the mid-1960s R&B-obsessed British Mod scene, The Small Faces quickly outgrew the straitjacket of their origins to forge an original and distinctly British sound of their own. The group formed in mid-1965, when Marriott (born 1947), already a stage veteran (of *Oliver* and other musical productions) since the age of 12, was recruited by pub circuit trio Lane (born 1946), Jones (born 1948) and Winston (born 1945) as their singer/guitarist. Rapidly signed by a major label, they debuted with the UK Top 20 hit, 'Whatcha Gonna Do About It', a typical mod band dancer owing its rhythmic structure to Solomon Burke's R&B hit, 'Everybody Needs Somebody To Love'.

With the single still in the chart, Winston left, and was replaced by Ian McLagan (born 1945), who settled quickly into the group's concentrated round of live work: gigs which revealed a raucous rock spirit never fully incorporated into the more controlled world of their recordings. 1966 was the group's biggest year, with 'Sha La La La Lee', 'Hey Girl' (their first self-penned hit, written by Marriott and Lane) and 'My Mind's Eye' all reaching the UK Top 10, and 'All Or Nothing' topping the UK chart. Their relationship with their label was uneasy, however, and when early 1967 saw a couple of singles perform considerably less well, they left for the potentially more creative environs of Andrew Oldham's independent label, Immediate. The looser, vaguely drug-oriented 'Here Comes The Nice' put them back in the UK Top 20, while the spacey 'Itchycoo Park' (a gentle mocking of portentous psychedelia which was ironically viewed as a British classic of the genre) made the UK Top 3, and also provided a US Top 20 breakthrough. 'Tin Soldier', another complex production and UK Top 10 hit, opened 1968. The group's debunking tendencies then surfaced solidly again in the follow-up, the Cockney-tinged 'Lazy Sunday', which made the UK Top 3, and was followed by their most successful album, the circular-sleeved 'Ogden's Nut Gone Flake', which topped the UK chart for six weeks.

By the end of 1968 Marriott had forged strong links with The Herd's singer/guitarist Peter Frampton. They made plans for a new, less teen-orientated group, and in early 1969, Marriott left to pursue this project, which became Humble Pie. The other three Faces initially disbanded, but within six months were together again, with ex-Jeff Beck Group members Rod Stewart and Ron Wood, as The Faces (see separate entry).

There was an unexpected coda to The

Most 'Sixties stars dressed like fruitcakes from time to time, and Small Face Stevie was no exception

Small Faces story, 'Itchycoo Park' was reissued in Britain at the end of 1975, and became a Top 10 hit again – ironically, just as The Faces were breaking up. When 'Lazy Sunday' also re-charted in its wake, Jones and McLagan teamed again with Marriott and new bassist Rick Wills to recreate The Small Faces. Over 18 months, they toured twice and cut two albums, but there was no chart success for the new material, and this second incarnation fell apart in mid-1978.

Greatest Hits

Singles	Title	US	UK
1966	*All Or Nothing*	–	1
1967	*Itchycoo Park*	16	3
Albums			
1966	*Small Faces*	–	3
1968	*Ogden's Nut Gone Flake*	159	1

Patti SMITH

Punk's prime poetess, Patti Smith (born 1946) was brought up in New Jersey, Paris and London before settling in New York and hanging out in Greenwich Village at the end of the 1960s. She soon became part of the avant garde rock set and during the early 1970s, wrote two published volumes of poetry, collaborated with playwright Sam Shepherd, wrote lyrics for Blue Oyster Cult and poems for Todd Rundgren before recording a single, 'Hey Joe/Piss Factory' for photographer Robert Mapplethorpe's Mer label in 1974. She formed a band with guitarist/rock journalist Lenny Kaye, guitarist/

keyboard player Ivan Kral, keyboard player Richard Sohl and drummer Jay Dee Daugherty, who at that time played at the celebrated New York club, CBGB.

Smith signed a major label deal in 1975 and her debut album, 'Horses', was produced by John Cale. It featured untamed versions of 'Land Of A Thousand Dances' and 'Gloria' and reached the US Top 50. Her live performances were even more intense and a version of The Who's 'My Generation' had to be edited for airplay.

The band toured internationally in support of 1976's 'Radio Ethiopia' album, produced by Jack Douglas, which was more rock influenced, but less successful, and early 1977, she broke her neck falling offstage in Tampa, Florida, putting her career on hold until 1978, when she returned with 'Easter'. Produced by Jimmy Iovine, this album refined her sound and made the US and UK Top 20, thanks largely to her superb version of a song she co-wrote with Bruce Springsteen, 'Because The Night', which hit the UK Top 5 and the US Top 20. Neither was her poetry neglected, as her fifth volume, *Babel* was published in 1979.

Her fourth album, 'Wave' (also 1979), was produced by Todd Rundgren and lacked the discipline of 'Easter', although it featured two more memorable songs, 'Dancing Barefoot' and 'Frederick', a minor US and UK chart single. The album made the US Top 20 but soon afterwards, she married Fred 'Sonic' Smith, ex-MC5, and retired to raise a family back in Detroit. Apart from occasional poetry readings little was heard from her until she reunited with Sohl and Daugherty in 1988 for 'Dream Of Life', which briefly made the UK album chart.

Greatest Hits

Singles	Title	US	UK
1978	*Because The Night*	13	5
Albums			
1978	*Easter*	20	16
1979	*Wave*	18	41

The **SMITHS/MORRISSEY**

Stephen Morrissey (*vocals*)
Johnny Marr (*guitar*)
Andy Rourke (*bass*)
Mike Joyce (*drums*)

Manchester-based glam rock fan Morrissey (born 1959) had auditioned unsuccessfully for local punk heroes Slaughter & The Dogs but had absorbed the sexless pop of The Buzzcocks when he met guitarist Johnny Marr (born John Maher, 1963) in 1982. The unlikely duo hit it off as lyricist and musician: Marr's schoolfriend Andy Rourke was brought in on bass and Mike Joyce (born 1963), formerly of Belfast punks, Victim, took the drum stool to form The Smiths.

Playing their first gig in late 1982, the band went on to entrance disc jockey John Peel, and via his radio show, the nation. Marr, a Byrd-fixated guitarist, contrasted vividly with the androgynous, often bespectacled Morrissey whose stage moves were unconventional with greenery hanging out of his jeans back pocket. The rhythm section provided tight back-up. Morrissey's monotone contrasted with Marr's florid guitarwork, and the lyrics of the first singles, 'Hand In Glove' and 'This Charming Man', were defiantly unrock'n'roll.

'What Difference Does It Make' gave them their first UK Top 20 hit and continued Morrissey's quirky habit of putting his childhood heroes (in this case, actor Terence Stamp) on the single sleeve. The eponymous debut album (1984) caused controversy with 'Suffer Little Children' (about the Moors Murders), and that same year, 1960s chanteuse Sandie Shaw came out of retirement to cut 'Hand In Glove' (the band backing her), while 'Heaven Knows I'm Miserable Now', the quintessential Morrissey lyric, gave them their first UK Top 10 hit. 'Hatful Of Hollow', followed, a compilation of singles, B-sides and radio sessions, and duly reached the UK Top 10 in late 1984.

The UK chart-topping album 'Meat Is Murder' (1985) re-established momentum, but that year's singles, 'How Soon Is Now', 'Shakespeare's Sister' and 'That Joke Isn't Funny Anymore' failed to crack the UK Top 20 and Morrissey's publicity verged on overkill. 'The Queen Is Dead' (1986) came out six months later than scheduled due to arguments with their label compounded by Rourke's sacking due to drug problems (he was replaced by Craig Gannon, but returned shortly after to expand the group briefly to a five-piece with Gannon on second guitar). After 'Panic' had given them their first UK Top 10 single in two years, another compilation 'The World Won't Listen', appeared, fuelling speculation that the band was in difficulty.

Morrissey's decision to follow a solo career and Marr's departure (he had played sessions for Talking Head, Bryan Ferry and others) in 1987 made the 'Strangeways Here We Come' album an epilogue and 1988's live 'Rank' (the last album before a planned move to a major label) an obituary.

Since then, Marr has juggled careers in The Pretenders, The The and New Order spin-off Electronic; Morrissey has released several singles, one chart-topping album, 'Viva Hate' (1988), and yet another singles compilation, 'Bona Drag' (1990), without establishing consistency. Rourke and Joyce have sessioned for Sinead O'Connor, Brix Smith and others. The Smiths spawned a myriad of other guitar groups, but there was and is only one Morrissey.

Greatest Hits

Singles	Title	US	UK
1984	*Heaven Knows I'm Miserable Now*	–	10
1986	*Panic*	–	11
1987	*Sheila Take A Bow*	–	10
Albums			
1984	*The Smiths*	–	2
1985	*Meat Is Murder*	–	1
1986	*The Queen Is Dead*	–	2
1987	*The World Won't Listen*	–	2
1987	*Strangeways Here We Come*	–	2
1988	*Rank*	–	2
Morrisey			
Albums			
1988	*Viva Hate*	–	1
1990	*Bona Drag*	–	9

SOFT CELL/Marc **ALMOND**

Soft Cell were formed in 1979 by singer/songwriter (Peter) Marc Almond (born 1959) from Southport and keyboard player David Ball (born 1959) from Blackpool. They released a 4-track EP 'Mutant Moments' on their own Big Frock label in 1980 and later that year had a track on the futurist compilation LP 'Some Bizzare Album'.

Their first single on Some Bizzare records, 'Memorabilia', did little but their re-issued version of Gloria Jones's Northern Soul favourite, 'Tainted Love', became the biggest UK hit of 1981 and in 1982 made the US Top 10, spending a record 43 weeks on the US chart. Over the next year the unique electro-rock duo, who were noted for their clever videos, scored UK Top 10 singles with 'Bedsitter', 'Say Hello Wave Goodbye', 'Torch' and another Northern Soul song, 'What', which made them the Top UK Act of 1982. Their debut album, 'Non-Stop Erotic Cabaret' (1981) and its dance remix version, 'Non-Stop Ecstatic Dancing' (1982), hit the UK Top 10 and also made the US charts.

In 1982 Almond formed Marc & The Mambas whose debut album, 'Untitled', also charted. In 1983 Soft Cell's 'Art of Falling Apart' was a UK Top 5 album, Marc & The Mambas charted with their LP, 'Torment And Toreros', but Ball's solo album, 'In Strict Tempo', was unsuccessful. The duo split in 1984 as 'This Last Night in Sodom' gave them their fourth Top 20 LP.

Almond's first solo single, 'The Boy Who Came Back', missed the Top 40 in 1984,

Smiths' crisp rhythm section at odds with vacuous vocals and Marr's galactic guitar licks

while his album, 'Vermin In Ermine', just scraped in. He returned to the UK Top 10 in 1985 as guest vocalist with Bronski Beat on their 'I Feel Love' medley. His solo albums (backed by The Willing Sinners), 'Stories Of Johnny', (1985) and 'Mother Fist And Her Five Daughters' (1987), were fairly successful.

After a change of label, his 1988 album, 'The Stars We Are', contained the US dance hit 'Tears Run Rings' and 'Something's Gotten Hold of My Heart' which, with the addition of Gene Pitney's voice, returned to the top of the UK charts and sold over a million in Europe. In 1990 his more experimental album, 'Enchanted', was critically acclaimed but missed the Top 40 and his old partner David Ball, then with The Grid, helped remix some tracks for him.

Greatest Hits

Singles	Title	US	UK
1981	Tainted Love	8	1
1989	Something's Gotten Hold Of My Heart (Almond/Gene Pitney)	–	1
Albums			
1981	Non-Stop Erotic Cabaret	22	1
1982	Non-Stop Ecstatic Dancing	57	6

SONNY & CHER / Sonny BONO/CHER

Salvatore Philip Bono (born 1935, Detroit) worked as A&R man for Specialty Records during the late 1950s, when he wrote 'She Said Yeah' (later covered by The Rolling Stones) and 'High School Dance' for Larry Williams. Bono duly graduated to production, and in 1962 co-wrote 'Needles & Pins' with Jack Nitszche (a minor hit for Jackie DeShannon, later a worldwide smash for The Searchers), and Nitzsche introduced him to Phil Spector at the outset of the latter's Wall Of Sound phase. Bono completed his apprenticeship as Spector's assistant, working variously as percussionist, arranger, promo man, A&R, etc., eventually meeting 17-year old back-up vocalist Cher (born Cherilyn Sarkasian La Pier, 1946) at one of Spector's sessions. Cher sang on several of Spector's classic recordings, including hits by The Crystals and The Ronettes.

Bono appointed himself as Cher's mentor, married her, and began directing her career. He persuaded Spector to release a 1964 Beatles cash-in single, 'I Love You Ringo' by Cher (as Bonnie Jo Mason) on Spector's Annette subsidiary label. Cher's lack of self-confidence led to Sonny & Cher developing as a duo: they cut 'The Letter', then 'Love Is Strange' and 'Baby Don't Go' (1964), which Bono leased to Reprise, on which they were billed as Caesar & Cleo. In 1965, 'Just You' flopped but the magnificent 'I Got You Babe' was a smash, topping both the US and UK charts and selling well over a million copies.

Written, arranged, and produced by Bono, with its strong melody, memorable hook, it straddled folk/rock and mainstream pop. Visually, the duo's long hair, colourful threads and gypsyish appearance presented the acceptable face of hippiedom.

Overnight, they were big stars, and the market was immediately flooded with product: 'The Letter' (US Top 100), 'Baby Don't Go' (US Top 10, UK Top 20), and 'Just You' (US Top 20) were all successfully reissued, and solo releases were rushed out. Bono's semi-autobiographical 'Laugh At Me' (US and UK Top 10), and Cher's cover of Bob Dylan's 'All I Really Want To Do' (US Top 20, UK Top 10), which beat a version by The Byrds, while their joint album, 'Look At Us' (US Top 3, UK Top 10), went gold.

Follow-up singles 'But You're Mine' (1965), 'What Now My Love' and 'Little Man' (both 1966) charted, but they lost impetus: 1967's 'The Beat Goes On' was their last major hit in the 1960s. Cher's solo career also stuttered, only 'Bang Bang' (1966, US and UK Top 3) and 'You Better Sit Down Kids' (1967, US Top 10) making an impact. The films *Good Times* (1966) and *Chastity* (1968, also the name of their daughter) were disastrous, and they finally destroyed their hard-won credibility by appearing in a government-sponsored anti-drug film, and by the end of the decade, were viewed as an anachronism.

With a restructured repertoire built around self-effacing humour, the duo moved to the Los Angeles cabaret circuit and revitalized their careers via a hit US TV series, returning to the charts in 1971 with 'All I Ever Need Is You' (US and UK Top 10 – the album of the same title also made the US Top 20, going gold), 'Sonny & Cher Live' (US Top 40, another gold album), and 'A Cowboy's Work Is Never Done' (US Top 10, 1972). Cher's comeback was even more spectacular: 'Gypsies, Tramps & Thieves' topped the US singles chart and made the UK Top 5, 'The Way Of Love' made the US Top 10 in 1972, and two further US No. 1 singles followed: 'Half Breed' in 1973 and 'Dark Lady' in 1974, a fourth solo million-seller. The duo divorced in 1974 and despite another TV series together in 1976, their joint recording career was over.

By the late 1970s, Bono had moved into acting in TV crime dramas, and later graduating to movies, like *Airplane II*, *Hairspray*, etc. Meanwhile Cher had lost direction: unsuccessful flirtations with rock, 1977's 'Allman & Woman' (with second husband Gregg Allman – see separate entry), and liaisons with hard rock bands Kiss and Black Rose (on whose 1980 eponymous album she contributed lead vocals) achieved little. She appeared on Meat Loaf's 'Dead Ringer' (1981) plus the memorable promo video, which did nothing in the US, but was a UK Top 5 hit. Her only significant US hit during this period was the 1979 Top 10 disco single, 'Take Me Home', while the album of which it was the title track made the US Top 30, and both went gold. Cher concentrated on acting in the 1980s. After her Broadway debut in *Come Back To The Five And Dime, Jimmy Dean, Jimmy Dean* in 1982, she appeared in

Music biz boss Bono marries chanteuse Cher in perfect pop partnership

the subsequent movie, and has also starred in *Silkwood* (1984), *Mask* (1985), *Witches Of Eastwick* (1987), *Moonstruck* (1988, winning an Academy Award), and *Suspect* (1988). Perversely, her recording career picked up again in the late 1980s with 'I Found Someone' (US Top 10, UK Top 5, 1987) and 'You Wouldn't Know Love' (1990), plus two gold albums, 1987's 'Cher' and 1990's 'Heart Of Stone', and to complete a remarkable double, Bono was elected Mayor of Palm Springs in April 1988, in the same week that Cher won her Oscar.

Greatest Hits

Singles	Title	US	UK
1965	*I Got You Babe* (Sonny & Cher)	1	1
1965	*All I Really Want To Do* (Cher)	15	9
1965	*Laugh At Me* (Sonny)	10	9
1966	*Bang Bang* (Cher)	2	3
1966	*Little Man* (Sonny & Cher)	21	4
1967	*The Beat Goes On* (Sonny & Cher)	6	29
1971	*All I Ever Need Is You* (Sonny & Cher)	7	8
1971	*Gypsies, Tramps & Thieves* (Cher)	1	4
1973	*Half-Breed* (Cher)	1	–
1974	*Dark Lady* (Cher)	1	36
1987	*I Found Someone* (Cher)	10	5

Albums			
1965	*Look At Us* (Sonny & Cher)	2	7
1965	*All I Really Want To Do* (Cher)	16	7
1971	*Gypsies, Tramps & Thieves* (Cher)	16	–
1972	*All I Ever Need Is You* (Sonny & Cher)	14	–
1979	*Take Me Home* (Cher)	25	–
1988	*Cher* (Cher)	32	26

SPANDAU BALLET

Tony Hadley (vocals)
Gary Kemp (guitar)
Steve Norman (rhythm guitar, saxophone)
Martin Kemp (bass)
John Keeble (drums)

Style leaders of the UK New Romantic rock movement which backlashed against punk in the early 1980s, Spandau Ballet managed to assert a musical authority beyond the confines of this image-obsessed genre. Allying the synthesisers and smooth vocals of New Romanticism to their ingrained soul-boy inclinations, they created a distinctive white soul-dance style which gave them a string of hits.

The group was formed in London in 1979 by Gary Kemp (born 1960) and his erstwhile school friend, Steve Dagger, who became their manager. Kemp recruited his brother Martin (born 1961), Hadley (born 1959), Keeble (born 1959) and Norman (born 1960),

New Romantics, Spandau Ballet, proved that stylistic silliness didn't cease with the 'Seventies

most of whom had been members of his Islington school sixth form group, The Makers, in 1976. All doyens of London's hip West End night club scene, they honed a sophisticated club-funk style, took their visual cues from the cutting edge of club fashion, and began a round of highly selective London gigs aimed (successfully) at teasing the music press and style hounds.

Dagger set up the group's own Reformation label before they had even recorded; as soon as the media buzz started, he quickly got a deal licensing both it and them to Chrysalis – which also got behind the style concept via arty record sleeves and advertising. The sheer weight of hype could well have sunk the band, but the commerciality of their releases cut through it: both the debut single, 'To Cut A Long Story Short', and album, 'Journey To Glory', hit the UK Top 5, and as they became established as a musical and chart force, Spandau were able to shrug off and leave behind the style excesses, although they always maintained an impeccably urbane stage image which mirrored their material.

The group first played the US in 1981, but their record success was mostly confined to the UK (via more Top 10 hits like 'Chant No. 1', 'Instinction' and 'Lifeline') until 1983, when Gary Kemp's ballad, 'True', topped the UK chart, along with the album of the same title, and the follow-up, 'Gold', made the Top 3. All these records also charted in the US, with 'True' going Top 5. 1984's 'Parade' album was similarly big, with a further com-

plement of hit singles which included the UK Top 3 single, 'Only When You Leave'. At the end of 1984, the group also became part of Band Aid's 'Do They Know It's Christmas', with Hadley singing one of the lead lines.

In mid-1985, Spandau Ballet featured in the Live Aid concert, but they fell out with Chrysalis over alleged poor promotion in the US, and the resulting legal dispute prevented the release of new material. The label countered with a Christmas TV-promoted singles compilation album, which was a major success but angered the group.

It was mid-1986 before Reformation and Spandau Ballet were legally free of Chrysalis, and a new deal was soon struck, its first fruit being 'Through The Barricades', another UK Top 10 album, which was lyrically more overtly political than previous material. A considerable gap ensued before 1989's 'Heart Like A Sky' album, and the group's chart profile suffered as they spent ever more time out of the current release limelight.

The group's thoughts, however, were not wholly on music at this time. The Kemp brothers were chosen in 1988 to play the Kray twins in a UK movie based on the lives of the celebrated London East End gangsters of the 1960s. By 1990, *The Krays* had been a success both at the box office and on video, and the brothers emerged with general critical approval of their performances. A sequel was mooted, while Spandau Ballet, on the 10th anniversary of the group's initial success, appeared to be waiting on hold.

Greatest Hits

Singles	Title	US	UK
1983	*True*	4	1
1983	*Gold*	29	2
Albums			
1983	*True*	19	1
1984	*Parade*	50	2

SPARKS

Russell Mael (vocals)
Ron Mael (keyboards)
Earle Mankey (guitar)
Jim Mankey (bass)
Harley Fernstein (drums)

From the indignity of being booed off UK stages in 1973, Sparks enjoyed nine UK hit singles, beginning with 1974's remarkable 'This Town Ain't Big Enough For Both Of Us'.

Former child actors and members of a Los Angeles group, Urban Renewal Project, the Mael brothers formed Halfnelson in 1968 with rock critic John Mendelssohn on drums. By 1971 the group's personnel was as above, they were known as Sparks, and on the recommendation of their eventual producer Todd Rundgren (see separate entry), had a recording contract. Though it spawned a regional US hit in 'Wonder Girl', the group's eponymous debut album sold poorly, as did 1972's 'A Woofer In Tweeter's Clothing'. A tour of Europe, when they often got the bird, gained them a cult following in glam-rock London where the Maels migrated in 1973 to sign a new deal, and recruit a new Sparks from local musicians. Bass player Martin Gordon and ex-Sound Of Time drummer, Norman 'Dinky' Diamond, were among the mainstays of this UK episode of the group's career but the many others passing through included ex-Jook bass player Ian Hampton and guitarist Adrian Fisher from Toby.

Produced by Muff Winwood (formerly of The Spencer Davis Group), chart success was immediate with the 'Kimono My House', album and its singles, 'This Town Ain't Big Enough For Both Of Us' and 'Amateur Hour', which were conspicuous for manic arrangements in the Roxy Music vein, Ron's rapid-fire lyrics and wide stereo separation between the bass and Russell's twittering falsetto. Visually, their appeal lay in the amusing disparity between Russell's normality and spooky Ron's toothbrush moustache and conservative attire.

Released later in 1974, 'Propaganda' was a stylistic departure but the essential gimmicks remained intact, although over-reliance on them plus a rather creaky stage act led to decreasing sales. Despite strategies such as replacing Winwood with Tony Visconti for 1975's 'Indiscreet', the Mael brothers returned to California to make 1976's 'Big Beat'

album with top session players. 1978's incongruously titled 'Introducing Sparks' album included the under-rated 'Forever Young' showing that all was certainly not yet lost, and the duo managed a short-lived comeback to the UK Top 20 in 1980 with two singles from 'Number One In Heaven', an album produced by German disco paladin Giorgio Moroder, while 'When I'm With You' from 1981's 'Terminal Jive' album was a huge hit in France. The Maels (as Sparks) scored their first US Top 50 single in 1983 with 'Cool Places', a 1983 duet with Jane Weidlin of The Go-Gos, continuing a career in which brief periods of success are punctuated by longer years of silence.

Greatest Hits

Singles	Title	US	UK
1974	*This Town Ain't Big Enough For Both Of Us*	–	2
1974	*Amateur Hour*	–	7
1979	*Beat The Clock*	–	10
Albums			
1974	*Kimono My House*	–	4
1974	*Propaganda*	63	9

The SPECIALS / FUN BOY THREE

Jerry Dammers (keyboards)
Terry Hall (vocals)
Neville Staples (vocals, percussion)
Lynval Golding (guitar)
Roddy Radiation (guitar)
Horace Gentleman (bass)
John Bradbury (drums)

Pioneers of the 2-Tone sound, The Specials were formed in 1977 around Jerry Dammers (born Gerald Dankin, 1954) who was looking for a punk/reggae fusion and found it in ska. They supported The Clash on tour in 1978 and were briefly lured to London but they soon returned home to the Midlands to follow their own instincts. In 1979, they recorded 'Gangsters', a single they shared with The Selecter (because neither group could afford to record a B-side) and launched their own 2-Tone label with it. When Chrysalis purchased the label, the single went Top 10 and after a UK tour, the band released its eponymous debut album, produced by Elvis Costello, which reached the UK Top 5 and included another UK Top 10 hit, 'A Message To You Rudy'.

Adding a brass section of Rico Rodriguez and Dick Cuthell, they released a live EP, 'The Special AKA Live', featuring 'Too Much Too Young', which topped the UK charts. They created interest but no chart success on a US tour, but made the UK Top 5 with 'Rat Race' and their second album, 'More Specials'. More rumbustious touring and UK hits with 'Stereotype' (Top 10) and 'Do Nothing' (Top 5) left Dammers suffering from nervous exhaustion at the start of 1981 and a US tour was abandoned, but the band remained in the limelight with the *Dance Craze* movie based around 2-Tone music (also played by Madness, The Beat, The Selecter, etc.) and the soundtrack album made the UK Top 5. Also that year saw the group topping the UK chart for three weeks with 'Ghost Town', which vividly portrayed inner city desolation.

Group tensions led to Hall, Golding and Staples leaving in 1981 to form Fun Boy

Coventry cool cats The Specials, a ska-boy seven before Fun Boy Three

Three, who had a bunch of hits over the next couple of years including 'The Lunatics (Have Taken Over The Asylum)', 'The Telephone Always Rings', 'It Ain't What You Do It's The Way That You Do It' and 'Really Saying Something' (duets with Bananarama), 'Our Lips Are Sealed' and 'Tunnel Of Love'. They broke up in 1984 and Hall formed Colourfield for a couple of albums before going solo in 1989 with 'Ultra Modern Nursery Rhymes'.

Dammers meanwhile re-formed the band with Bradbury as the only surviving member and slowly began to assemble his next album, one single at a time. 'Racist Friend', 'The Boiler' and 'Nelson Mandela' (which made the UK Top 10 and later became an anthem for the cause to free the African leader) were all released as singles before 'In The Studio' finally came out in 1984 sounding very familiar. By now Dammers was becoming increasingly politically involved and after recording the Pioneers song, 'Starvation', in aid of Ethiopia with Madness, General Public and UB40 in 1985, he formed Artists Against Apartheid in 1985, organized a free concert in London featuring Elvis Costello, Peter Gabriel, Sting, Sade, Boy George, Billy Bragg and Hugh Masekela in front of over 200,000 people, and in 1988 was the prime mover behind the Nelson Mandela Birthday Tribute headed by Dire Straits and Whitney Houston, which was televised live around the world and was a turning point in mobilizing opinion against apartheid. Dammers diffidently performed the anthem that had made it all possible. Since then, compassion fatigue appears to have set in.

Greatest Hits

Singles	Title	US	UK
1980	Too Much Too Young (EP)	–	1
1980	Do Nothing	–	4
1981	Ghost Town	–	1
1982	It Ain't What You Do It's The Way That You Do It (Fun Boy Three with Bananarama)	–	4
Albums			
1979	Specials	84	4
1980	More Specials	98	5
1982	Fun Boy Three (Fun Boy Three)	–	7

Phil SPECTOR

Through the creation of his 'Wall Of Sound' in the mid-1960s, songwriter and producer Phil Spector was acclaimed as a pop revolutionary. Though he worked closely with members of The Beatles, his later productions never matched the grandeur of his early recordings.

He was born in New York in 1940 but moved to Southern California as a child. Spector took up guitar and in 1957 won a local TV talent contest. Forming a vocal trio, The Teddy Bears, with schoolmate Marshall Lieb and Annette Kleinbard, he recorded his own song 'To Know Him Is To Love Him' for a local label. The song was supposedly inspired by the memory of his father, who had died when Spector was 12.

The lilting, lullaby-like ballad was a huge US hit and the group moved to a bigger label, but neither later singles nor an album, 'The Teddy Bears Sing', could repeat its success. After Spector disbanded the trio, both Lieb (as an arranger) and Kleinbard (writing film and TV themes as Carol Connors) had music business careers.

Spector now formed a partnership with publisher/label owner Lester Sill, recording as Spector's Three before moving to New York in 1960. There he soon began a hectic apprenticeship as a writer and producer. He co-wrote a hit for The Drifters, 'Spanish Harlem' and produced successful tracks by Ray Peterson ('Corrine Corrine'), Johnny Nash and Curtis Lee. On a return trip to Los Angeles, Spector created a US Top 10 hit for The Paris Sisters, 'I Love How You Love Me', very much in The Teddy Bears vein.

After briefly working as A&R man for Atlantic and Liberty, Spector finally launched his own label, Philles, with Sill in 1962. There followed a four-year period when it seemed he could do no wrong, with over 20 hit singles.

The first Philles act was The Crystals, a black female vocal group from New York. Written by Barry Mann and Cynthia Weil, 'Uptown' reached the US Top 20 and though 'He Hit Me (And It Felt Like A Kiss)' was banned by radio stations, the Gene Pitney song, 'He's A Rebel', topped the US chart in 1963.

This was Spector's first great production. Recorded at Gold Star Studio in Los Angeles, it was performed by a massive orchestra including five guitars, three pianos and numerous percussion instruments. It was also a prime example of Spector's dismissive attitude towards his artists. Unlike earlier Crystals records, the lead singer was not New Yorker La La Brooks but Darlene Love from West Coast vocal group, The Blossoms. However, Brooks returned for the group's later successes, 'Da Doo Ron Ron' and 'Then He Kissed Me'.

Love also sang on another of Spector's early successes, a bizarre revival of the Walt Disney film song, 'Zip-A-Dee-Doo-Dah', by Bob B. Soxx & The Blue Jeans : the male lead was Bobby Sheen. Under her own name, Darlene Love sang the more conventional 'Today I Met The Boy I'm Gonna Marry' and 'Wait 'Til My Bobby Gets Home'.

The second of Spector's great female vocal groups was The Ronettes, another New York group that had been performing since 1959. Spector placed them in front of a churning mass of instrumental sound to wail 'Be My Baby', a song he composed with Ellie Greenwich and Jeff Barry. None of their later singles was as successful, though 'Baby I Love You' (1964) and 'Walking In The Rain' were US Top 30 hits.

Spector ended 1963 with the remarkable album, 'A Christmas Gift For You'. This featured The Crystals ('Rudolph The Red-nosed Reindeer'), The Ronettes ('I Saw Mommy Kissing Santa Claus'), Love and his other artists singing distinctive 'Wall Of Sound' arrangements of traditional seasonal songs. It has since been successfully re-released on several occasions, but was a flop when first released. The assassination of President Kennedy has been blamed for diverting the attention of the US public from the just released album.

In 1964, Spector discovered his third major act in a white male duo who had been recording unsuccessfully for a small West Coast label. He signed The Righteous Brothers and with arranger Jack Nitzsche, created his most imaginative production yet in 'You've Lost That Lovin' Feelin''. Using a dramatic build-up to a deafening crescendo he created an immediate pop classic which has returned to the charts on both sides of the Atlantic ever since, most recently after its use in the 1990 hit movie, *Ghost*.

Other Righteous Brothers hits followed, but Spector became involved in lawsuits over the duo's contract and in 1965, they signed to another label, while he left New York for California. There he went into semi-retirement, until in 1966 he decided to return to the studio with a black R&B singer, Tina Turner.

'River Deep, Mountain High' took the operatic approach of his work with The Righteous Brothers a stage further as Turner soared above massive string arrangements. The result proved too avant-garde for US audiences, although the record was a major hit in Europe. Its failure in America caused Spector to withdraw altogether from the music business.

In 1968, he married Veronica Bennett, lead singer of The Ronettes, and the next year he had a cameo role in the noted film, *Easy Rider*, as a drug dealer. He returned to the recording studio after signing an ill-fated production deal with A&M which resulted in only a few tracks by The Checkmates Ltd and Ronnie Spector.

The next phase of Spector's career was about to begin – in England. With the group in its death throes, the four members could not agree on how to remix the tapes of the final Beatles album, 'Let It Be'. Eventually, Spector was called in and prepared the songs for their 1969 release, giving McCartney's 'Long And Winding Road' its now familiar string backing, a kind of modified wall of sound.

As a result, Spector formed a close relationship with John Lennon and George Harrison, working with both over the next five years. He adapted to the intimate mood

Freaky Phil – genius, joker, rock revolutionary and recluse

of Lennon's 'Imagine' and was able to call on his more grandiose techniques for Harrison's 'All Things Must Pass'. He was also responsible for the recording of the 'Concert For Bangladesh' in 1971 and later produced Lennon and Yoko Ono's 'Some Time In New York City' as well as the sessions eventually released by Lennon as 'Rock'n'Roll'. In between times, Ronnie Spector cut a single ('Try Some Buy Some') for The Beatles-owned Apple label.

Spector's last attempt to run his own label was Warner-Spector, set up in 1973. Although he worked with Cher, Nilsson, Dion and Darlene Love, it was a failure. His only other album productions in the late 1970s were with Leonard Cohen ('Death Of A Ladies' Man') and The Ramones ('End Of The Century'). The punky Ramones version of 'Baby I Love You' was a UK Top 10 hit.

During the 1980s, Spector became an almost total recluse. He occasionally co-wrote songs (among others with John Prine) and was approached to do production work, but his only significant move was to appoint lawyer Allen Klein to organize reissues of the Philles classics. He also took out a writ against a 1989 biography of him by Mark Ribowsky, causing the book to be withdrawn from circulation.

Spector's work with The Beatles (individually and collectively), The Righteous Brothers, The Ramones, Cohen and Ike & Tina Turner can be found on albums by those artists, while compilation albums should be readily available featuring his productions for The Crystals, The Ronettes, Bob B. Soxx, etc. Should he ever decide to return to production, many will be interested – and hopefully delighted.

SPIRIT

Randy California (guitar, vocals)
Jay Ferguson (vocals)
John Locke (keyboards)
Mark Andes (bass)
Ed Cassidy (drums)

Formed in Los Angeles in 1967, Spirit (originally Spirits Rebellious) grew out of an earlier band, The Red Roosters. Founder members were California (born Randle Craig Wolfe III, 1951) and his stepfather, shaven-headed ex-jazz drummer Cassidy (born 1931), who recruited Ferguson (born 1947), Andes (born 1948) and Locke (born 1943).

California, something of a teenage prodigy, had already played with a pre-fame Jimi Hendrix in New York and the latter's musical influence on California remains undiminished to this day. Locke (like Cassidy) came from a modern jazz background and whilst Spirit undoubtedly played acid-rock, the jazz influence singled them out from their competition. Their eponymous debut album (1968) was full of good songs and playing (notably the classic 'Fresh Garbage', which was often played for up to twenty minutes live) but at times seemed a trifle overproduced.

Its follow-up, 'The Family That Plays Together' (1969) had a tougher sound, without loss of subtlety and was their highest-charting album, and included their only US Top 30 single, 'I Got A Line On You'. The third album, 'Clear Spirit' (1969), included parts of a soundtrack they had written for a movie, *The Model Shop*, in which they also appeared – unfortunately not playing. While underrated, the album contained their best jazz-tinged offerings, the title track and 'Ice'.

Lack of commercial success led to in-fighting and the original band's last album, 'The 12 Dreams Of Dr Sardonicus', suffers as a result. Some regard it as one of the great 1960s albums, others as rather mainstream in comparison with earlier efforts, but it went gold.

The band split shortly afterwards. Ferguson and Andes formed Jo Jo Gunne, who were quite successful in the early 1970s, while Ferguson subsequently went solo. California also made a solo album, the bizarre 'Kaptain Kopter & The Fabulous Twirlybirds' (1972), but Spirit's name lived on, as Locke and Cassidy cut the decidedly lacklustre 'Feedback' (1972) with other musicians. When the last two original members then quit, a totally bogus Spirit existed for over a year, until California retrieved the group name.

Meanwhile, Cassidy and California recorded the legendary 'Potatoland' album, which for various reasons didn't surface until 1981 (in a decidedly revamped form) and again in 1988 (closer to the original).

California's period of frustration ended in 1975 with a new deal and a new Spirit (California, Cassidy and bass player Barry Keene). This line-up cut the interesting, if

self-indulgent 'Spirit Of '76', in (1975). The following year saw the return of John Locke in time for 'Son Of Spirit' which was an improvement and 'Farther Along', their best album since the 1960s.

All but ignored in the States, the band remained a huge cult in Europe and various line-ups (without Locke) toured in the late 1970s. 1977's 'Future Games' was consequently lapped up in Europe, but probably deserved less acclaim. The London gig of the 1978 tour was recorded and released as 'Spirit Live' (1979), a poor recording if only on technical grounds.

Even devoted fans wondered at California's subsequent direction. Always under Hendrix's spell, he began to take the overtly heavy side of Hendrix's music to its logical conclusion especially in the periods when Spirit were down to a trio. The 1982 album 'Euro-American' (credited as a California solo album, though in terms of personnel, it was actually Spirit) provided altogether too much evidence of a fondness for heavy metal. Yet another reunion took place in 1983 (this time with Ferguson as well) but the resulting album, 'The Thirteenth Dream' was little more than AOR.

Another poor California solo album, 'Restless', appeared in 1985, since when two further Spirit albums have been released 'Rapture In Chambers' and 'Tents Of Desire' (1990) the latter being the group's best for several years.

There is no denying California's (and Spirit's) legendary status, but one is left to wonder whether he understands what he does best.

Greatest Hits

Singles	Title	US	UK
1969	I Got A Line On You	25	–
Albums			
1968	Spirit	31	–
1969	The Family That Plays Together	22	–
1981	Journey To Potatoland	–	40

Dusty SPRINGFIELD

Regarded in the 1960s as Britain's most authentically American-sounding female singer, Dusty Springfield's success rating dropped dramatically in the 1970s, although a chart return in the late 1980s augured fairly well for a return to former greatness.

After seven unsuccessful singles in 1959/60 as one of The Lana Sisters, Dusty Springfield (born Mary O'Brien, 1939) and her brother, Tom, formed The Springfields, a commercial folk trio, initially with Tim Field, and later with Mike Hurst. The trio scored five UK hit singles in two years, including two which made the Top 5, 'Island Of Dreams' and 'Say I Won't Be There', plus (remarkably for a

Soul-searching Dusty dumps Springfields

pre-Beatles UK act), two US hit singles, including 'Silver Threads & Golden Needles', which made the Top 20. A UK equivalent of Peter, Paul & Mary, the group split as Hurst moved into record production and Dusty went solo, having publicly expressed her greater love for American R&B and soul music than for cheerful folk songs.

Her much-awaited debut single, 'I Only Want To Be With You', was a smash hit, making the UK Top 5 and US Top 20, although its early 1964 follow-up, 'Stay Awhile', only made the UK Top 20/US Top 40. A swift US follow up, 'Wishin' & Hopin'', was a US Top 10 hit at the same time as 'I Just Don't Know What To Do With Myself' was making the UK Top 3, but thereafter big US hits were rare, although a dozen UK hit singles before 1969, including her only chart-topper, 1966's 'You Don't Have To Say You Love Me', ensured that she was a notable international star.

A 1967 US Top 30 single, 'The Look Of Love', which featured in the parody James Bond movie, *Casino Royale*, became a UK B-side, and unfortunately, her UK record label allowed the release of almost as many compilations as original albums in that same period. While her first two albums, the timelessly impressive 'A Girl Called Dusty' (1964) and 'Everything's Coming Up Dusty' (1965), both made the UK Top 10, they were overshadowed in chart terms by 1966's 'Golden Hits', which made the UK Top 3, although this compilation was virtually a disaster in the US, where less singles had been big hits, and her albums were never big US sellers.

After 1967's 'Where Am I Going?' album (regarded by some fans as a question she was addressing to her label) also disappointed, 1968's 'Dusty . . . Definitely' seemed a partial return to form, clipping the Top 30 of the UK album chart, but Springfield was begin-

ning to despair at the quality of her records. They were largely made in Britain with session musicians she felt lacked the soul found in Motown or Atlantic records, while much of her material consisted of cover versions of originals by US R&B artists, including The Supremes, Dionne Warwick, Inex Foxx and others.

In 1969, she released 'Dusty In Memphis', a stunning album produced by the Atlantic Records triumvirate of Jerry Wexler, Tom Dowd and Arif Mardin (and the first of two albums released by Atlantic in the US). Including a US and UK Top 10 single, 'Son Of A Preacher Man', the album made the US Top 100, but was commercially ignored in the UK, whereupon she began an eventual move to the US during the early 1970s as her record sales decreased around the world. 1970's 'From Dusty . . . With Love' album, 1972's 'See All Her Faces' and 1973's 'Cameo' seemed increasingly patchy albums, as Springfield grappled with personal problems, and the next five years saw only continual repackaging of her back catalogue breaking a recording silence.

In 1978, she re-emerged with 'It Begins Again', which briefly returned her to the UK album chart after an eight-year absence and in 1979 made the UK singles chart after a nine-year gap with 'Baby Blue', although her 1982 album, 'White Heat', was not released in the UK, and the revival was short-lived. In 1987, she duetted with the fashionable Pet Shop Boys (who were long-time fans) on a UK Top 3 hit, 'What Have I Done To Deserve This', and after a duet with Richard Carpenter on 'Something In Your Eyes', her biggest hit in over 20 years was followed only weeks later in 1988 by a superb compilation album, 'The Silver Collection', which made the UK Top 20 in celebration of the 25th Anniversary of her first successful solo year.

Clearly, the CD generation was interested, and she was appropriately invited to appear as a vocalist on the soundtrack of the *Scandal* movie, which was based on events which occurred during the early 1960s concerning the celebrated Christine Keeler. While most of the film's music featured hits from the relevant era, 'Nothing Has Been Proved' was specially written and produced by The Pet Shop Boys for Springfield, and became a UK hit. In 1990, her first new album in eight years, 'Reputation', became her first original UK chart album in twelve years, with help from The Pet Shop Boys and several other producers. This comeback, coinciding with her return to live in Britain, gives her many fans — young and now middle-aged — cause for much more optimism than the inaccurately-titled 'It Begins Again'.

Greatest Hits

Singles	Title	US	UK
1962	Silver Threads & Golden Needles (Springfields)	20	–
1962	Island Of Dreams (Springfields)	–	5
1963	Say I Won't Be There (Springfields)	–	5
1963	I Only Want To Be With You	12	4
1964	I Just Don't Know What To Do With Myself	–	3
1964	Wishin' & Hopin'	6	–
1966	You Don't Have To Say You Love Me	4	1
1968	I Close My Eyes And Count To Ten	–	4
1987	What Have I Done To Deserve This (with Pet Shop Boys)	2	2
1989	Nothing Has Been Proved	–	16
Albums			
1964	A Girl Called Dusty	–	6
1965	Everything's Coming Up Dusty	–	6
1966	Golden Hits	137	2
1990	Reputation	–	18

Rick **SPRINGFIELD**

An Australian singer and actor, Springfield (born 1949) was the son of an army officer. With the itinerant lifestyle that this career involved, the family's many addresses included the UK during his formative years.

He left school in the mid 1960s and formed a Rolling Stones style group, Jordy Boys, followed by Rock House who made a troop-entertainment trip to Vietnam.

His major Australian success was with the group Zoot who were the major Australian teenybop idols in the early 1970s with a chart-topping single, 'Speak To The Sky'.

Dissatisfied with Zoot, he moved to London and recorded his first solo album, 'Beginnings', in 1972, which included a new recording of 'Speak To The Sky' which became a US Top 20 hit.

This precipitated a move to the US, where the album went Top 40 as Springfield was promoted as another David Cassidy or Donny Osmond. A label change in 1974 did nothing for his chart career – an album, 'Comic Book Heroes', failed to score and a single, 'American Girls', just scraped into the US Top 100. Added to this were additional problems over work permits and management contracts, so, biding his time, he stayed in the US by enrolling in drama school.

Another album on the short-lived Chelsea label followed in 1976, 'Wait For The Night'. It did no better than the previous one, but a single did make the US Top 50. Springfield meanwhile was becoming better known for his TV work, and spots on youth-oriented adventure series such as *Six Million Dollar Man* and *Wonder Woman* gave him the image boost that had so far eluded him in the pop field.

This was cemented in 1981 with a regular role in the major US soap *General Hospital*, and a new recording contract at the same

Rick – London move after Zoot didn't suit

time produced a US chart-topping single, 'Jessie's Girl' and the US Top 10 album, 'Working Class Dog'.

This started a series of early 1980s hits including 'I've Done Everything For You' (US Top 10, 1981), and 'Don't Talk To Strangers' (US Top 3, 1982). A second hit album, 'Success Hasn't Spoiled Me Yet', made the US Top 5 and went platinum.

Subsequent releases have been less successful, after the 1983 US Top 5 single, 'Affair Of The Heart', his biggest successes came with spin-offs to the movie, *Hard To Hold*, which included a US Top 20 soundtrack album and a US Top 5 single, 'Love Somebody'. 1983's intervening 'Living In Oz' album also made the US Top 20, and like 'Hard To Hold', went platinum, but 1985's 'Tao' album only went gold, before a very quiet period. In 1988, he returned with a US Top 30 single, 'Rock Of Life', the title track of a new album.

A 'face' on the US youth market, Springfield in the 1990s may return to a more lucrative concentration on his cinematic career.

Greatest Hits

Singles	Title	US	UK
1981	*Jessie's Girl*	1	23
1982	*Don't Talk To Strangers*	2	–
1984	*Love Somebody*	5	–
Albums			
1981	*Working Class Dog*	7	–
1982	*Success Hasn't Spoiled Me Yet*	2	–
1983	*Living In Oz*	12	41
1984	*Hard To Hold*	16	–

Bruce SPRINGSTEEN

Perhaps the last of the great rock'n'roll romantic heroes, Bruce Springsteen dominated 1980s rock culture and embodied his generation's search for the American Dream with the 'Born To Run' album.

Springsteen (born 1949) had a working-class upbringing which greatly influenced his lyrics. As a child, he saw Elvis Presley on TV on *The Ed Sullivan Show*, at age 13 he bought a second-hand guitar for $18 and learned how to play, and at 16 he hustled himself into his sister's boyfriend's band, The Castiles. He then formed Steel Mill with drummer Vini Lopez and organist Danny Federici and gained a strong local reputation in his native New Jersey. Springsteen also played solo acoustic shows and worked in Asbury Park with the nucleus of his next band, black sax player Clarence Clemons, guitarist 'Miami' Steve Van Zandt, bassist Garry Tallent and piano player David Sancious.

In 1972, Springsteen was signed by manager Mike Appel (on a car bonnet in a parking lot). An audition was arranged with legendary CBS talent spotter John Hammond, who had signed Bessie Smith, Billie Holiday, Aretha Franklin, Bob Dylan, etc. He also signed Springsteen, who cut his first album with Clemons, Tallent, Sancious and Lopez. The album, 'Greetings From Asbury Park, N. J.' (1973), focused on Springsteen the singer/songwriter and he was called 'The New Dylan' on the strength of songs like 'Blinded By The Light' and 'Spirit In The Night'. His 1974 album, 'The Wild, The Innocent And The E Street Shuffle', put Springsteen in a band context with Federici joining the previous album's line-up, and added to Springsteen's reputation with songs like '4th Of July', 'Asbury Park (Sandy)' and 'Rosalita (Come Out Tonight)', but neither album charted.

The breakthrough came with 1975's 'Born To Run', which pitched him with producer Jon Landau, who added layers of sound to the E Street Band (as Springsteen's group were now known), which included Tallent, Clemons, Federici, and new recruits Roy Bittan (keyboards) and Max Weinberg (drums). The title track made the US Top 30 and the album went gold, reaching the US Top 3, as songs like 'Jungleland', 'Thunder Road', 'Tenth Avenue Freeze Out', and 'Backstreets' cemented Springsteen's status, although the growing excitement over his dynamic live shows had belatedly dragged the earlier two albums into the US Top 100 six weeks before 'Born To Run' was released. In the ensuing hype, he became the first entertainer to appear simultaneously on the cover of *Time* and *Newsweek* magazines. Unfortunately, he had fallen out with Appel, who took out an injunction against Springsteen recording. Frustrated, he hit the road with Van Zandt added to the line-up and developed an epic 3-hour show, that seldom stayed the same two nights running, and was bursting with new songs plus his rock'n'roll favourites. In the absence of new records, the bootleggers flourished, while Manfred Mann topped the US chart with 'Blinded By The Light', The Pointer Sisters hit the US Top 3 with 'Fire', Patti Smith scored an international hit with 'Because The Night', and Springsteen became known as 'The Boss'.

Finally free of his management problems in 1977, he released 'Darkness On The Edge Of Town' a year later, again with Landau producing. Unsurprisingly, it had a pensive quality on tracks like 'Racing In The Street', 'The Promised Land' and 'Prove It All Night' (which made the US Top 30), but still went platinum. After another bout of touring, Springsteen went back into the studio again early in 1979, but a motorcycle accident interrupted his schedule although he was still able to celebrate his 30th birthday by playing the No Nukes benefit concert in New York's Central Park, and appearing on the subsequent triple album performing his much-bootlegged 'Devil With A Blue Dress' medley (of Mitch Ryder oldies).

It was another year before 'The River' emerged in November 1980. A double album trimmed from 60 to 20 songs that topped the US charts for a month and reached the UK Top 3, its strength was in its diversity, from the stark 'Point Blank' to rockers like 'Cadillac Ranch' and 'You Can Look (But You Better Not Touch)', as well as a US Top 5 single, 'Hungry Heart'. For the next year, he toured a four-hour show around the US and Europe to ecstatic acclaim, but still found time to produce and write songs for two albums by Gary 'US' Bonds, whose 1961 hit, 'Quarter To Three', was a cornerstone of the Springsteen show, and to help an old friend, 'Southside' Johnny Lyon and his band, The Asbury Jukes, with several excellent unrecorded original songs such as 'The Fever'.

Springsteen's next album was a deliberate contrast. 'Nebraska' (1982), was a solo acoustic set, recorded on a four-track recorder (as opposed to the then industry standard 24 tracks or more), that delved back beyond Dylan for inspiration to Woody Guthrie and Hank Williams. It was released with little fanfare and reached the US and UK Top 3, but charted for a mere six months. Springsteen meanwhile carried on working on his next album which was released in 1984. 'Born In The USA' sealed Springsteen's superstar status, spending seven weeks at the top of the US chart, where it was resident for over two years. The album was a double-edged patriotic sword as Springsteen laid his integrity on the line, and seven of its 12 tracks were big US hit singles, including 'Dancing In The Dark' (also a UK Top 30 hit as covered by US rock revivalists Big Daddy in the style of Pat Boone's 'Moody River'!) and 'Glory Days' (both Top 5), and 'Cover Me', 'I'm On Fire', 'I'm Goin' Down', 'My Hometown' and the title track (all Top 10).

Springsteen celebrated by marrying model/actress Julianne Phillips and undertaking a memorable world tour with Nils Lofgren replacing Van Zandt – Springsteen appeared on Van Zandt's 'Sun City' anti-apartheid single as well as singing on USA For Africa's 'We Are The World' charity single. After that, Springsteen listened to a decade's worth of live tapes and tried to come up with a

Born In The USA, 'The Boss' epitomizes the essentially American heart of rock'n'roll

better live album than the bootleggers. The 40-track multi-album 'Live: 1975–85', released in late 1986, succeeded by including material the bootleggers had missed as well as making Springsteen's own versions of 'Because The Night' and 'Fire' legally available, and topped the world's charts as an excerpted single, a cover of Edwin Starr's 'War', made the US Top 10 and UK Top 20.

After a brief – by Springsteen's standards – lull, he released 'Tunnel Of Love' in late 1987, a brooding, restless album that topped the charts on both sides of the Atlantic again and included US Top 10 hits with the title track and 'Brilliant Disguise', as well as 'One Step Up', which made the US Top 20. The reason for the restlessness became evident during the next world tour when his wife filed for divorce and Springsteen started escorting his back-up singer, Patti Scialfa. Soon after the tour finished in 1988 he took part in the Amnesty International Human Rights Now! world tour with Peter Gabriel, Sting and others. He also contributed two tracks to 'A Vision Shared', a tribute album to Woody Guthrie and Leadbelly.

Since then he has maintained a low profile, occasionally jamming with a bar band in Texas or at a benefit for an old Asbury Park buddy. After Scialfa bore his child in 1990, he made his first 'official' live appearance in two years at a Los Angeles benefit show, Bruce Springsteen underlined his superstar status in the 1980s, and many will be waiting for a new album, perhaps with his first chart-topping single . . .

Greatest Hits

Singles	Title	US	UK
1980	*Hungry Heart*	5	44
1984	*Dancing In The Dark*	2	4
1985	*I'm On Fire*	6	5
1985	*Glory Days*	5	17
1987	*Brilliant Disguise*	5	20
Albums			
1975	*Born To Run*	3	17
1980	*The River*	1	2
1982	*Nebraska*	3	3
1984	*Born In The USA*	1	1
1986	*Live: 1975–1985*	1	4
1987	*Tunnel Of Love*	1	1

SQUEEZE

Chris Difford (guitar, vocals)
Glenn Tilbrook (guitar, vocals)
Julian 'Jools' Holland (keyboards)
Harry Kakoulli (bass)
Gilson Lavis (drums)

Created in South-East London in 1974 as a result of Tilbrook's response to Difford's ad in a music paper, the embryonic Squeeze formed as a quartet, supposedly taking their name from a Velvet Underground album. Following a couple of personnel adjustments, they realigned as a quintet and quickly carved out a local reputation, releasing an independent label EP, 'Packet Of Three', (produced by John Cale) before signing with a major label in 1977. Although their first single, 'Take Me I'm Yours', made the UK Top 20 in 1978, their eponymous debut album failed to chart. They had to tour the US using the name UK Squeeze (to avoid legal hassles with US band Tight Squeeze), but made little impact. After a couple of minor chart entries, they broke through in the UK in 1979 with 'Cool For Cats' and 'Up The Junction', both of which made the UK Top 3, plus 'Slap & Tickle', a UK Top 30 hit, while their 'Cool For Cats' album reached the UK Top 50.

1980's 'Argybargy' album (with new bass player John Bentley replacing Kakoulli) made the UK Top 40, while an excerpted single, 'Another Nail In My Heart', reached the UK Top 20, but Holland then left the band for a dual career as a TV presenter and to front his own band, The Millionaires. His replacement, Paul Carrack (ex-Ace), played on 1981's classic 'East Side Story' album, which made the UK Top 20, and which many regard as Squeeze's finest recorded work. Carrack took lead vocals on the soulful 'Tempted' which became the group's first US hit single after considerable US FM airplay, while the album received sensational reviews in the US and was their first to make the US Top 50. After a Top 5 UK single, 'Labelled With Love', Carrack left the band and was replaced by Don Snow (ex-Sinceros).

1982's 'Sweets From A Stranger' album made the UK Top 20 and US Top 40 after the band sold out New York's Madison Square Garden, but because Difford (born 1954) and Tilbrook (born 1957) were being hailed as the second coming of Lennon & McCartney by certain rock writers, they were put under intense pressure, and by the end of the year, the group had split. A posthumous compilation album, 'Singles – 45s And Under', then became their biggest UK album, reaching the Top 3.

Difford and Tilbrook continued to work together, and released an eponymous album which made the UK Top 50 in 1984. However a one-off reunion at a charity gig early in 1985 became a permanent revival, with a revised line-up of Tilbrook, Difford, Lavis, and bassist Keith Wilkinson, plus the return of Holland, whose own group had disbanded some time before.

By this time, the group had attained cult status in the US, and their comeback seemed chiefly geared towards the US market, but 1985's 'Cosi Fan Tutti Frutti' album failed to reach the US Top 50 although it almost made the UK Top 30. Boosted by further US tours, 1987's 'Babylon And On' album, featuring an additional keyboard player, Andy Metcalfe, was a commercial success, but 1989's 'Frank' album was a disappointment, only charting for a single week in Britain.

In 1990, after a live album, 'Around & About', on a new label, with a line-up of Difford, Tilbrook, Holland, Lavis, Wilkinson and yet another keyboard player, Matt Irving, Squeeze seemed to be uncertain of what to do next, and rumours of Holland departing again suggested that another hiatus might follow, although many will be interested in what the group, and particularly Difford, Tilbrook and Holland, will do in the future.

Greatest Hits

Singles	Title	US	UK
1979	Cool For Cats	–	2
1979	Up The Junction	–	2
1981	Tempted	49	41
1981	Labelled With Love	–	4
1987	Hourglass	15	16
Albums			
1981	East Side Story	44	19
1982	Sweets From A Stranger	32	20
1982	Singles – 45s And Under	47	3
1987	Babylon And On	36	14

Edwin STARR

Starr (born Charles Hatcher, 1942) hailed from Nashville and was educated in Cleveland, Ohio. The brother of singers Roger and Willie Hatcher, he was in a teenage vocal group, The Futuretones, who recorded for a tiny label in 1957. After graduating, he joined the forces where he was posted to Europe, during which time he began singing at servicemen's clubs when off duty.

His first band back in civilian life was with Bill Doggett's Philadelphia-based R&B outfit in the early 1960s, before he formed his own group and signed with a Detroit label. His solo debut was a US Top 30 hit in 1965; cashing in on the spy movie craze, it was titled 'Agent Double O Soul'. Smaller hits, including 'S.O.S.' and 'Headline News', which both made the UK Top 40, followed, before the label was taken over by Motown. In 1968, the latter two hits were reissued back to back in the UK, where they almost made the Top 10 of the singles chart.

A couple of lean years transpired before

Edwin, a Starr on the UK disco scene

two big smashes on a Motown subsidiary label; 1969's '25 Miles' went US Top 10, followed by the US chart-topping 'War' the following year (which was covered very successfully by Bruce Springsteen in 1986). Starr's 1970 version also made the Top 3 in Britain, where his later output fared better than in the US. In 1979, he made the UK Top 10 twice, with 'Contact' and 'H.A.P.P.Y. Radio', both breaking via the thriving disco club scene.

Greatest Hits

Singles	Title	US	UK
1969	25 Miles	6	36
1970	War	1	3
1979	Contact	65	6
1979	H.A.P.P.Y. Radio	79	9
Albums			
1970	War And Peace	52	–

Ringo STARR

The 'straightest' Beatle, Starr (born Richard Starkey, 1940) might have returned to comparative anonymity when the group disbanded in 1970. Instead, his records often outsold concurrent offerings by his former colleagues, and he was the only ex-Beatle to make real headway in films.

During the hiatus before The Beatles dissolved, Starr cut his first solo album, 'Sentimental Journey', consisting of pre-rock'n'roll favourites. At a loss afterwards, he accepted an invitation from pedal steel guitarist Pete Drake to cut a second album, 'Beaucoups Of Blues', in Nashville. The completion of this quota of new Country & Western songs renewed Ringo's confidence as a composer himself. However, after he wrote his first solo

single, 'It Don't Come Easy', some alleged that its follow-up, the repetitive 'Back Off Boogaloo', was ghosted by T. Rex's Marc Bolan, subject of Born To Boogie, Starr's debut as a film director.

Affirming respect still held for him as a drummer, he joined the likes of Bill Wyman, Steve Marriott and Steve Winwood on albums by venerable bluesmen Howlin' Wolf and B.B. King. As a singer, Ringo's distracted clumsiness was endearing during his main spot in George Harrison's Bangladesh show in 1971. More than this spectacular, 1973's 'Ringo' album was the closest The Beatles ever came to a musical reunion, embracing as it did contributions from all four, including the Harrison/Starr hit single, 'Photograph'.

The 'Ringo' sleeve featured a still from Son Of Dracula, a film in which he starred with Nilsson. Another major part for Starr was in the spaghetti Western movie, Blindman, for which he also penned incidental music. Arguably, his finest thespian role was as Teddy Boy, confidant to the hero (David Essex) of 1973's That'll Be The Day. He also appeared in Frank Zappa's 200 Motels (playing one of several Zappas in the film) and Ken Russell's Lisztomania during this period.

1974 began well with hit revivals of Johnny Burnette's 'You're Sixteen' and the 1950s Platters classic, 'Only You', as well as another big-selling album in 'Goodnight Vienna'. With Graham Bonnet and Rab Noakes among its signings, he also formed the short-lived Ring O' Records but a boozy period in California with John Lennon (during Lennon's lengthy 'lost weekend') was co-related with Ringo's commercial decline, as 'Ringo's Rotogravure' (an album produced by Arif Mardin) was not a success, and its single, 'A Dose Of Rock'n'Roll', his final US Top 40 single.

Ringo stayed in the limelight, guesting on stage with Bob Dylan, Wings and The Band (in their Last Waltz farewell), but both his 'Ringo The Fourth' (which included duets with Bette Midler and Lionel Richie) and 'Bad Boy' albums were swiftly deleted, and 'Stop And Smell The Roses' was deemed 'Worst Record Of 1981' by one noted journal. Finally, no US or UK company would release 'Old Wave' with its large helping of non-originals like 'Be My Baby' and 'She's About A Mover'.

This humiliating episode had been compounded by a perceptible falling off of interest in Starr's screen ventures – among them Sextette, with Mae West and Tony Curtis, and an eponymous TV special based loosely on The Prince And The Pauper. Though Caveman, his last major movie, was a flop too, romance had blossomed between Ringo and leading lady Barbara Bach, whom he married in 1981. Gladly, he narrated the story of The Beatles for a US radio network and, later, the Thomas The Tank Engine children's series for British television. He also read the title role of Scouse The Mouse, a

It Don't Come Easy, having been a Beatle

concept album created by Donald Pleasance.

Starr's vocational disappointments contributed to a bout of alcoholism but his recovery became tangible by the late 1980s when he recorded a new version of his Beatles showcase, 'Act Naturally', with its composer, Buck Owens, and was spotted as a supporting actor in Paul McCartney's *Give My Regards To Broad Street* film. Heading an all-star line-up for a US tour in 1989 (which produced concert album/video spin-offs), Ringo was received as a loveable curio – but, with and without The Beatles, past achievements had already guaranteed him a certain place in pop history.

Greatest Hits

Singles	Title	US	UK
1971	*It Don't Come Easy*	4	4
1972	*Back Off Boogaloo*	9	2
1974	*Photograph*	1	8
1974	*You're Sixteen*	1	4
Albums			
1973	*Ringo*	2	7
1974	*Goodnight Vienna*	8	30

300

STATUS QUO

Mike Rossi (vocals, guitar)
Rick Parfitt (guitar, vocals)
Roy Lynes (keyboards)
Alan Lancaster (bass)
John Coghlan (drums)

Respected by fans (if not critics) for their predictable presentation and artistic consistency, Status Quo exude a strong camaraderie acquired since 1962 when Lancaster (born 1949) and Rossi (born 1949) formed South London's Spectres.

After three flop singles, The Spectres became Traffic Jam for 1967's aptly-titled single, 'Almost But Not Quite There' before

releasing 'Pictures Of Matchstick Men' as Status Quo in 1968, by which time Coghlan (born 1946), Parfitt (born Rick Harrison, 1948) and Lynes had been recruited. Riven with trendy wah-wah guitar, this excellent sample of psychedelic pop was followed by the soundalike 'Black Veils Of Melancholy', before a non-original, Marty Wilde's 'Ice In The Sun', restored the group to the UK Top 10. All three 1968 singles appeared on 'Picturesque Matchstickable Messages' which, like the more formulated second album, 'Spare Parts', leaned uneasily upon post-flower power whimsy and string-laden ballads – neither element reconciling with the outfit's hard rock stage act, epitomized by a grinding revival of The Everly Brothers hit, 'The Price Of Love', a concert favourite and 1969 single. Its chart failure and the chart climbs of two harder R&B singles, 'Down The Dustpipe' (UK Top 20) and 1970's 'In My Chair' (UK Top 30, and their last chart entry until 1973), justified the budget repackaging of Quo's output that continued long after the group completed its commitments to the label with two more original albums, 'Ma Kelly's Greasy Spoon' and 1971's 'Dog Of Two Head', which each gave strong clues of what they were to become.

When Lynes left, the band soldiered on as a quartet with Rossi reverting to his baptismal forename (Francis). Quo's decision to build a new audience from scratch became more tangible when countless one-nighters

wrought a hirsute, bedenimmed image and a blues-boogie style that would recur on all albums from their 1973 debut album for a different label, 'Piledriver' to 1989's 'Perfect Remedy'.

Commercially, Quo (augmented from 1976 by ex-Herd hitmaker Andy Bown on keyboards) peaked in the mid-1970s with 'Hello', 'Quo', 'On The Level', 'Blue For You' and their retinue of hit singles – 'Caroline', 'Break The Rules', 'Down Down' and others. There were occasional changes of pace such as the slow 'Most Of The Time' from 1975's 'On The Level' album, and a revival of country singer Hank Thompson's 'Wild Side Of Life' (produced by Deep Purple's Roger Glover), but fans preferred the churning 12-bars that Quo delivered on the boards, as on 1977's 'Live', recorded in Glasgow.

John Fogerty's 'Rockin' All Over The World' lent its name to the group's next single, album and global tour concept. The proceeds forced Quo into tax exile in Holland where they cut 1978's 'Can't Stand The Heat'. After 1979's 'Whatever You Want' (whose title track lived on in a TV commercial), fan acceptance of a softer approach on the 'Living On An Island' single facilitated repetition of this tangent since – notably on 'Rock'n'Roll' (from 1980's 'Just Supposin' ' album), 'In The Army Now' and the ballad, 'I Know You're Leaving', on 1988's 'Ain't Complaining' album.

Though huge sales for 'Never Too Late',

Quo – Status undiminished after thirty years of Rockin' All Over The World

'1982', 'From The Makers Of . . .' (a triple album compilation that included a concert bash in Birmingham) and singles like 'Dear John' – co-written by Johnny Gustafson (ex-Big Three) – indicated continuing popularity, the early 1980s was a difficult period for Quo, as Coghlan had departed during the '1982' sessions, and domestic problems beset Parfitt and Rossi. Furthermore, Lancaster – now resident in Australia – was airing grievances against the rest of the group in the High Court. Nevertheless, with Pete Kircher on drums, the group found its feet again with 1983's 'Back To Back' (and its four hit singles) and another 'Live' offering.

A re-make of Dion's 'The Wanderer' heralded a temporary disbandment for profitless solo projects before Quo were chosen to open Live Aid at Wembley. However, the subsequent 'Rollin' Home' (produced by Dave Edmunds) and 'In The Army Now' albums were made without Lancaster, and he was also absent for 'Perfect Remedy' and 1990's 'Anniversary Waltz', a medley single celebrating a quarter of a century as professionals. Regarded by critics very much as the ultimate non-progressive rock act, Status Quo have continued to delight European fans for many years, although their almost total absence from the US charts since the 1960s is indicative of their somewhat one-dimensional approach.

Greatest Hits

Singles	Title	US	UK
1968	Pictures Of Matchstick Men	12	7
1974	Down Down	–	1
1977	Rockin' All Over The World	–	3
1980	What You're Proposin'	–	2
1983	Marguerita Time	–	3
1983	In The Army Now	–	2
Albums			
1973	Hello	–	1
1974	Quo	–	2
1975	On The Level	–	1
1976	Status Quo	148	–
1976	Blue For You	–	1
1981	Never Too Late	–	2
1982	1982	–	1

STEELEYE SPAN

Maddy Prior (vocals)
Gay Woods (vocals, concertina)
Terry Woods (guitar, vocals)
Tim Hart (vocals, guitar, dulcimer)
Ashley Hutchings (bass)

While the group unsettled purists, Steeleye Span earned two UK Top 20 hits as they broadened the scope of folk music via a tasteful welding of rock instrumentation to rustic airs and country dance.

The group was launched in 1970 by

Maddy (centre) – disc debut Prior to success with Steeleye

Hutchings (ex-Fairport Convention) and two folk club duos – Hart & Prior had already cut two volumes of 'Folk Songs Of Old England', and Terry Woods (ex-Sweeney's Men) and his wife, Gay, were highly regarded in Ireland. However, during sessions for their debut album, 'Hark! The Village Wait', it transpired that Mr & Mrs Woods were not in artistic accord with the others. They were replaced by renowned folk revivalist singer Martin Carthy and Peter Knight (violin, mandolin) for projects that included Keith Dewhurst's *Corunna* play at London's Royal Court Theatre, and 1971 albums 'Please To See The King' and 'Ten Man Mop Or Mr Reservoir Butler Rides Again'.

After Hutchings left to form The Albion Country Band and Carthy to resume a solo career, the group enlisted Rick Kemp (ex-bass player for Michael Chapman) and guitarist Bob Johnson who, prior to becoming an accountant, had served P.J. Proby and Gary Glitter. After 1972's 'Below The Salt' spawned a late 1973 hit in the accapella Latin ditty, 'Gaudete', the next album ('Parcel Of Rogues'), was their first to make the UK Top 30, while the group also took on a television series they compounded their 'selling out' to pop by augmenting with drummer (and flautist) Niegel Pegrum (ex-Gnidrolog) and attempting decidedly unethnic material for 1974's 'Now We Are Six', an album produced by Jethro Tull's Ian Anderson, which contained an arrangement of the 1950s Teddy Bears hit, 'To Know You Is To Love You' (with guest saxophonist David Bowie) while Peter Sellers was heard on ukelele for 'New York Girls' from 1975's 'Commoner's Crown'. Concerts embraced back-projected films to enhance narrative songs, a Mummers

Play and a version of 'John Barleycorn' thought less 'pure' than one by Traffic, less recognized as folkies.

1975's 'All Around My Hat' and its title track single marked the zenith of Steeleye Span's commercial success but they had gone off the boil by the release of the following year's 'Rocket Cottage'. Though some found Hart's developing 'mediaeval peasant' vocals too grating by then, individual members were less committed to the group, as demonstrated by Prior's recording and touring with June Tabor as The Silly Sisters – they made a second album in 1988 – and the departures of Knight and Johnson before 1978's 'Storm Force Ten'. Though the survivors had rallied by calling on Carthy and accordionist John Kirkpatrick, 1980's 'Sails Of Silver' (for which the 'All Around My Hat' line-up reunited) was also Steeleye Span's valediction until a cautious late 1980s re-formation without Hart, who had given up music, for 1986's 'Back In Line' album, and 1989's consequent 'Tempted And Tried' album, for which Kemp was absent, but which sounded much the same as the group's biggest selling 1970s albums.

Prior and Kemp now lead an eponymous recording band, and it seems likely that Steeleye Span may re-form and record periodically in the future.

Greatest Hits

Singles	Title	US	UK
1973	Gaudete	–	14
1975	All Around My Hat	–	5
Albums			
1974	Now We Are Six	–	13
1975	All Around My Hat	–	7

Dan's Fagen and Becker switch to guitar and sax

STEELY DAN

Donald Fagen (vocals, keyboards)
Walter Becker (bass, vocals)
Jeff 'Skunk' Baxter (guitar)
Denny Dias (guitar)
Jim Hodder (drums, vocals)
David Palmer (vocals)

An ambitious but successful band who set themselves high lyrical and musical standards, Steely Dan was formed by Fagen (born 1948) and Becker (born 1950) who met as college students in upstate New York, and spent five years trying to peddle their songs, recording demos, writing soundtracks and playing in Jay & The Americans and in a jazz-influenced band with Denny Dias.

Fagen and Becker chose the name Steely Dan (after a steam-powered dildo in William Burroughs's novel, *The Naked Lunch*) when producer Gary Katz signed them to a Los Angeles label in 1971. Their 1972 debut album, 'Can't Buy A Thrill', made the US Top 20 on the strength of two hit singles: 'Do It Again' (US Top 10) and 'Reelin' In The Years' (US Top 20). Palmer, who had not sung lead on either of the singles, quit soon after. 1973's 'Countdown To Ecstasy' album included no major singles, but made the US Top 40, while 1974's 'Pretzel Logic' shifted towards jazz and made the US 10 with a boost from its included US Top 5 single, 'Rikki Don't Lose That Number'.

By this time it was clear that Fagen and Becker, plus producer Katz, were the nucleus of Steely Dan, but the duo recruited new musicians including ex-Doobie Brother Michael McDonald and session drummer Jeff Porcaro plus numerous other session musicians for 1975's 'Katy Lied' album, which was

nearly destroyed by faulty recording equipment. However, it made the US and UK Top 20 as did 1976's 'The Royal Scam' (which featured their only UK Top 20 single, 'Haitian Divorce'), by which time Porcaro had left (eventually to launch Toto). 'Aja' in 1977 made the US Top 3 (and won them a Grammy for best-engineered album) and included two US Top 20 singles, 'Peg' and 'Deacon Blues', while they also made the US Top 30 in 1978 with the title song from the movie, *FM*. A three-year silence before late 1980's 'Gaucho' album was only interrupted by a platinum 'Greatest Hits' album, while 'Gaucho' itself made the US Top 10 and brought a US Top 10 single, 'Hey Nineteen', but Fagen and Becker had split by the end of the year.

Becker went into production while Fagen released a critically acclaimed US Top 20 solo album, 'The Nightfly', in 1982 and worked on various soundtrack projects, including Martin Scorsese's *King Of Comedy* and *Bright Lights, Big City*. The duo collaborated on the Gary Katz-produced eponymous album by Rosie Vela in 1987 and Fagen's next album is likely to feature Becker.

Greatest Hits

Singles	Title	US	UK
1973	Do It Again	6	39
1974	Rikki Don't Lose That Number	4	58
Albums			
1974	Pretzel Logic	8	37
1977	Aja	3	5
1980	Gaucho	9	27
1982	The Nightfly		
	(Donald Fagen solo)	11	44

STEPPENWOLF

John Kay (vocals)
Michael Monarch (guitar)
Goldy McJohn (organ)
Rushton Morave (bass)
Jerry Edmonton (drums)

Traffickers of a potent brew of psychedelia and hard rock, Steppenwolf began in Toronto as Sparrow. 'Hoochie Coochie Man', 'Corrina Corrina' and other mainstays of their blues repertoire remained in the set when the group broke loose from its local orbit to seek work – and a record contract – in New York and then California.

Some Sparrow tracks were issued eventually on 'Early Steppenwolf' but, with both a new bass guitarist (John Russell Morgan) and fashionable new name (from the Hermann Hesse novel), the Canadians cut 'Steppenwolf', a 1968 album remarkable for its arrangement of Hoyt Axton's 'The Pusher' and the hit single, 'Born To Be Wild' – covered by such diverse artists as The Nashville Teens and Wilson Pickett. After its inclusion (with 'The Pusher') on 1969's *Easy Rider* film soundtrack, 'Born To Be Wild' emerged as a biker's anthem – and, via stunning performances at optimum moments during outdoor festivals, Steppenwolf as a biker's band.

'The Second' album spawned another smash single in 'Magic Carpet Ride' while Kay's solo performance of 'Rock Me Baby' turned up in *Candy*, a movie with Ringo Starr and Charles Aznavour among its stars. However, after the album 'At Your Birthday Party', internal turmoil led to the replacement of Monarch and Morgan with, respectively,

Steppenwolf – hippy head band's 'Born To Be Wild' anthem for the Angels

Larry Byrom and Nick St. Nicholas. Though this pair were themselves supplanted by George Biondi and Kent Henry, they were heard on 'Monster', which was less successful than its predecessor. Nonetheless, its overtly political title song became an eternal stage favourite after Steppenwolf included it during a benefit concert for the Vietnam Moratorium Day Committee.

That 'Live' was their highest UK album entry affirmed the group's might on the boards but lesser global sales for studio efforts 'Seven', 'For Ladies Only' and even 1971's 'Gold' 'best of' compilation precipitated the announcement of Steppenwolf's disbandment in 1972.

Comparative public indifference towards Edmonton and McJohn's Manbeast combo, and Kay's solo albums, 'Forgotten Songs And Unsung Heroes' and 'My Sporting Life', contributed to Steppenwolf's re-forming two years later with its 1972 personnel, though McJohn left to start his own eponymous outfit during rehearsals for the 'Slow Flux' album. Wayne Cook played keyboards on 'Hour Of The Wolf' and 1976's 'Skullduggery', but as neither restored the band's fortunes, an even lengthier lay-off ensued. After Steppenwolf – with Kay the only original member – hit the road again in the mid-1980s, a new album, 'Rise And Shine', was released to tie-in with a 1990 transatlantic tour.

Greatest Hits

Singles	Title	US	UK
1968	Born To Be Wild	2	30
1968	Magic Carpet Ride	3	–
Albums			
1968	The Second	3	–
1970	Live	7	16

Cat STEVENS

A capable singer-songwriter, Stevens (born Steven Georgiou, 1947) is the son of a Greek restaurateur in London. While a student in 1966, Stevens was discovered by producer Mike Hurst, formerly of The Springfields, and signed to a major company's 'new talent' label as its first act.

His first single, 'I Love My Dog', made the UK Top 20, to be eclipsed by the UK Top 3 success of 'Matthew And Son' early in 1967. 'I'm Gonna Get Me A Gun' followed it into the chart, with a debut self-penned album, 'Matthew and Son', also going into the UK Top 10, also writing 'The First Cut Is The Deepest', a 1967 hit for P.P. Arnold and a 1977 UK chart-topper for Rod Stewart.

His career was interrupted by illness for two years, after which he made a 1970 comeback on Island Records, now as a serious singer/songwriter rather than a pop star, with 'Mona Bona Jakon', which included the UK

Cats' 'Catch' hits bullseye in 'States

Top 10 single 'Lady D'Arbanville'. At the end of that year, 'Tea For The Tillerman' made the UK album Top 20, and became his US chart debut inside the Top 10. A single taken from the album, 'Wild World', also made the US Top 20, while in the UK it was covered successfully by Jimmy Cliff.

Garnering much respect as a serious songwriter, Stevens followed 'Tillerman' in 1971 with 'Teaser And The Firecat', making the Top 5 on both sides of the Atlantic, and including one of his most durable songs, 'Moon Shadow', as well as the US hit, 'Peace Train'. A third single from the album, 'Morning Has Broken', again made both the US and UK Top 10 in 1972.

An increasing sophistication, both musically and lyrically, did not prevent continued commercial success; 'Catch Bull At Four' topped the US chart at the end of 1972, and the extended song-suite 'Foreigner' also went Top 3 in both the US and UK in 1973.

Stevens, however, had become increasingly disenchanted with the music business, and a growing interest in spiritual affairs distanced him further from his audience as his live performances became less frequent. He still had hits – 1974's 'Buddah And The Chocolate Box' was a US/UK Top 3 album, with two US Top 10 singles, 'Oh Very Young', a revival of Sam Cooke's 'Another Saturday Night', 'Numbers' in 1976 and 'Izitso' (1977) both charted, but interest could not be sustained for ever in an artist living as a virtual recluse. After the disappointing showing of 'Back To Earth' in 1979, a US Top 40 hit which failed to reach the UK chart, he opted out of music altogether, taking up the Muslim faith and changing his name to Yusef Islam.

Hit compilation albums have appeared in the 1980s and his legacy as a songwriter is acknowledged by being regularly trawled by other artists.

Greatest Hits

Singles	Title	US	UK
1967	Matthew And Son	–	2
1967	I'm Gonna Get Me A Gun	–	6
1970	Lady D'Arbanville	–	8
1971	Peace Train	7	–
1972	Morning Has Broken	6	9
1974	Another Saturday Night	6	19
Albums			
1971	Teaser And The Firecat	2	3
1972	Catch Bull At Four	1	2
1973	Foreigner	3	3
1974	Buddah And The Chocolate Box	2	3
1975	Greatest Hits	6	2

Rod STEWART

With his inimitable gravelly voice and his flamboyant lifestyle, Rod Stewart (born 1945) successfully made the transition from British R&B singer to international rock performer.

Briefly becoming a professional soccer player before joining the beatnik trail round Europe, Stewart, a blues enthusiast, then played harmonica with Jimmy Powell and The 5 Dimensions and Long John Baldry's Hoochie Coochie Men before cutting a version of the R&B standard, 'Good Morning Little Schoolgirl' in 1964.

In 1965/66 he sang and played with Steampacket and Shotgun Express, two of the most admired groups on the burgeoning R&B club circuit in England. He gained greater prominence the following year as vocalist with the Jeff Beck Group, led by the former Yardbirds guitarist. The band toured Europe and the US and made 'Truth' (1968) and 'Cosa Nostra – Beck Ola' (1969). Stewart provided the impassioned vocals for 'In A Broken Dream', which was issued under the name Python Lee Jackson and became a UK hit.

When Beck broke up the band, Stewart accepted an offer to front The Faces, the new name adopted by the remnants of The Small Faces. However, he also signed a solo recording deal, which began with 'An Old Raincoat Never Lets You Down' (1970) and 'Gasoline Alley'. Both showed Stewart's hitherto unknown talents as a songwriter. His dual role as soloist and band member continued until 1975 with live performances by The Faces gaining them the reputation as the biggest 'ravers' on the circuit.

Stewart's writing reached a peak on 'Every Picture Tells A Story' (1971) which contained the classic 'Maggie May' with its evocative tale of love with an older woman. The song's impact was matched the next year by 'You Wear It Well' from 'Never A Dull Moment', when he was matching Elton John as the UK's leading rock superstar. In 1974, he combined his continuing fascination with soccer and his patriotism by singing on an album made by the Scottish World Cup squad.

The tension between Stewart's solo career and his membership of The Faces had reached breaking point and after a 1974 world tour, he left the group. In 1975, he also left Britain to take up permanent residence in Los Angeles. This move coincided with the release of Stewart's first album to be made in the US, 'Atlantic Crossing', produced by Tom Dowd in Muscle Shoals, Alabama. His popularity in Britain was not affected, however, as both the album and 'Sailing', written by Gavin and Iain Sutherland, topped the UK charts. He also demonstrated his continuing debt to soul by covering the hit by The Isley Brothers, 'This Old Heart Of Mine', which he remade in 1989 with Ronald Isley.

During the late 1970s, Rod Stewart made the transition from simple rock star to major showbiz personality. This was partly due to his well-publicized romances with a series of film stars and models, but also because of the increasingly slick and glitzy nature of his shows and records. The title track of 'Tonight's The Night' (1976) was typical. A lurid tale of loss of virginity delivered with all his considerable elan, it spent seven weeks at the top of the US charts.

More impressive were the dramatic 'The Killing Of Georgie', dealing with the murder of a homosexual in New York and Stewart's version of Danny Whitten's 'I Don't Want To Talk About It' (1977) which prevented 'God Save The Queen' by The Sex Pistols from topping the UK chart.

In 1978, Stewart once more showed his support for Scottish soccer by making 'Ole Ola' with the World Cup team, and he also cut perhaps his most famous song, 'Da Ya Think I'm Sexy'. Written with his tour drummer Carmen Appice, it seemed a brazen endorsement of the lecherous image given him by the gossip columnists as did the title of the accompanying album, 'Blondes Have More Fun'.

Although he toured less frequently, Stewart's work in the 1980s tended to reinforce his playboy image and also to sell well. In addition to recording his own compositions, he continued his tradition of paying homage to great songs of the past. The Temptations classic, 'My Girl', Ace's 'How Long' and in 1990, Tom Waits' 'Downtown Train' were all issued as singles.

He also participated in the new trend towards providing music for Hollywood films. Among his movie themes were 'That's What Friends Are For' (later Dionne Warwick's charity single) in *Night Shift* (1982), 'Love Touch' from *Legal Eagles* (1986) and 'Twistin' The Night Away' for *Innerspace* (1986).

Although his constant cockatoo hairstyle showed him to be apparently unconcerned with changes in the marketplace, Stewart also found new collaborators during the 1980s. His 1986 single, 'Another Heartache', was co-written with Bryan Adams and 'Out Of Order' (1988) found him writing with Simon Climie of UK hitmakers Climie Fisher. That album was produced by Chic's Bernard Edwards and Andy Taylor of Duran Duran and included the hit, 'My Heart Can't Tell You No'. By the start of the 1990s, he seemed well set to spend another decade at the top of the AOR ladder.

Ex-Mod Rod Faces the future with haircut that harks back to the past

Greatest Hits

Singles	Title	US	UK
1971	Maggie May	1	1
1972	You Wear It Well	13	1
1972	Angel	40	4
1975	Sailing	58	1
1975	This Old Heart Of Mine	83	4
1976	Tonight's The Night (Gonna Be Alright)	1	5
1977	The Killing Of Georgie	30	2
1977	I Don't Wanna Talk About It	46	1
1977	You're In My Heart (The Final Acclaim)	4	3
1978	Hotlegs/I Was Only Joking	22	5
1978	Ole Ola (Muhler Brasiliera)	–	4
1979	Da Ya Think I'm Sexy?	1	1
1981	Passion	5	17
1983	Baby Jane	14	1
1983	What Am I Gonna Do (I'm So In Love With You)	35	3
1986	Every Beat Of My Heart	83	2
1989	My Heart Can't Tell You No	4	49
1990	Downtown Train	3	10
Albums			
1971	Every Picture Tells A Story	1	1
1972	Never A Dull Moment	2	1
1974	Smiler	14	1

STONE ROSES

Ian Brown (vocals)
John Squire (guitar)
Gary 'Mani' Mountfield (bass)
Alan 'Reni' Wren (drums)

Described as 'The Sex Pistols of the 1990s' and the leading band in the UK's Manchester 'musical revolution' of 1990, Stone Roses formed in 1985 playing their first gigs in Sweden and returning to play Manchester warehouse parties. Squire (born 1962), Brown (born 1963), Wren (born 1964) and Mountfield (born 1962) drew up the blueprint for a new indie/dance sound, which crossed dance rhythms with rock guitars in an updated psychedelic version of 'The Smiths' style.

After three singles including 'Elephant Stone', produced by New Order's Peter Hook on independent labels, the band signed to a long-term indie deal in the UK, and produced a string of hit singles: 'Made Of Stone', 'She Bangs The Drums' (their first UK Top 40 hit) and 'Fool's Gold' (UK Top 10), all sleeved in John Squire's Jackson Pollock-style art. The eponymous album released in the spring of 1989 was in one critic's words 'the worst elements of 1980s independent rock rolled into a shapely ball'.

A 7,000-capacity secret gig in Glasgow sold out by word of mouth and their show at Spike Island on Merseyside sold 28,000 tickets, confirming the Roses as a major live attraction. The only market left to conquer is the US, where the album stalled, despite 17-weeks in the US Top 200 and sales figures of 90,000. They now refuse to support anyone, having apparently turned down offers as disparate as The Rolling Stones and Bros.

Courting publicity with anti-monarchy sentiments, bizarre interviews, riotous press conferences and tales of gigs in Beirut, the band were fined £3000 ($5500) each for overstepping the mark by causing criminal damage to the office of one of their previous record companies, after the re-issue of their early 'Sally Cinammon' single with a new, apparently unacceptable, video: nevertheless, it reached the UK Top 40 on re-release. The 'One Love' single (1990) went Top 5, but a period of unrest followed with the band allegedly trying to change to a major label. If true, the advance could be truly staggering for a group which is dragging pop music kicking and screaming into the next century.

Greatest Hits

Singles	Title	US	UK
1990	Fool's Gold	–	8
1990	One Love	–	4
Albums			
1989	Stone Roses	–	19

Psychopunks Stone Roses mark Manchester's move to orchestrated anarchy

The STRANGLERS

Hugh Cornwell (vocals, guitar)
Jean-Jacques Burnel (vocals, bass)
Dave Greenfield (keyboards)
Jet Black (drums)

Once cited as a punk-heavy metal crossover band, the brash outer shell of The Stranglers was found to contain a surprising sensitivity that kept them in the UK chart throughout the 1980s.

All had had previous experience in pop groups when they began in 1974 as The Guildford Stranglers – a fusion of University graduates and the more artisan Black and Greenfield. Developing a seedy, monochrome image, a suspiciously sexist, if political, lyrical style, and a punchy but almost Gothic sound that owed much to The Doors, the quartet's work schedule extended nationally with the advent of punk. 1977's '(Get A) Grip (On Yourself)' made the UK Top 50, and heralded a UK Top 10 hit, the leering 'Peaches' (also the first New Wave disc to crack the Australasian charts). Both singles were included on their debut album, 'IV/Rattus Norvegicus', along with other stage mainstays such as 'Hanging Around' (revived in 1981 by Hazel O'Connor). Equally well received were 'Something Better Change' and 'No More Heroes', the title track of their second 1977 album, which were both UK Top 10 singles.

Another song, 'Dagenham Dave', was a requiem to one of their rabid army of devotees, who enacted bloody reprisals against anyone who slighted their favourite group. The Stranglers welcomed disturbance at their bookings, even provoking it themselves by hiring strippers, engaging in incendiary dialogue with audiences and other crass but effective publicity stunts – as proved by continued chart success in 1978 with their third album, 'Black And White'.

Fan acceptance of a version of Dionne Warwick's 'Walk On By' facilitated regular recordings of similarly gentle and melodic originals such as 1982's 'Golden Brown' (their first UK Top 3 hit, despite controversy over whether the song was hard drug-related), 'Strange Little Girl', 'European Female' and, from 1986's 'Dreamtime' album, 'Always The Sun'. In like vein, 'Duchess' was the main single from the 1979 album, 'The Raven'. That year also saw the release of 'Euroman Cometh', the first of two Burnel solo albums, and 'Nosferatu' (with a single of 'White Room' – the Cream hit) by Cornwell with Captain Beefheart's drummer, Robert Williams. Later extra-mural projects included a slim volume by Cornwell describing his 1980 sojourn in prison for drug offences, his second solo album, 1988's 'Wolf', which briefly charted, and Burnel's formation of The Purple Helmets to perform 1960s classics.

1981's 'Themeninblack' (sic) album spawned no hits, and quickly left the UK

(l to r) Burnel, Black, Greenfield, Cornwell – Stranglehold on post-punk pop charts

album chart, but the same year's 'La Folie' (with 'Golden Brown'), 1983's 'Feline' and, embracing the catchy UK Top 20 single, 'Skin Deep', 1984's 'Aural Sculpture', restored and retained much lost popularity. From a 1988 album came their title re-arrangement of The Kinks hit, 'All Live And All Of The Night', and also reaching the UK Top 20 was a version of the ? and The Mysterians hit, '96 Tears', from 1990's 'Ten' – Cornwell's final album with the group. His departure to pursue an acting career was thought regrettable but not disastrous by The Stranglers, who plan to continue after auditions for a suitable replacement. Whether they will ever be able to equal their enduring major UK success in the US music market seems less likely as time progresses.

Greatest Hits

Singles	Title	US	UK
1977	Peaches	–	8
1977	No More Heroes	–	8
1982	Golden Brown	–	2
1982	Strange Little Girl	–	7
1988	All Day And All Of The Night	–	7
Albums			
1977	Stranglers IV/Rattus Norvegicus	–	4
1977	No More Heroes	–	2
1978	Black And White	–	2
1979	The Raven	–	4
1983	Feline	–	4

The **STRAWBS**

Dave Cousins (vocals, guitar, banjo, dulcimer)
Tony Hooper (guitar, vocals)
Arthur Philips (mandolin)

As The Strawberry Hill Boys, they were Britain's first bluegrass outfit but after truncating their name to The Strawbs and going electric with a rock rhythm section,

they were prevented from topping the UK charts in 1973 only by The Sweet's 'Blockbuster'.

Ex-University student Cousins ran the Hounslow Arts Centre where the trio found each other in 1967. When Philips left the following year, Rod Chesterman (double bass) and singer Sandy Denny (awaiting her destiny with Fairport Convention) were enlisted for a residency in a Copenhagen club. Some tracks recorded there were eventually issued on a budget label as 'All Our Own Work', but Denny was not on 1969's 'The Strawbs' and its 'The Man Who Called Himself Jesus' single. With cellist Claire Deniz, producer Tony Visconti and Rick Wakeman (keyboards), The Strawbs completed 'Dragonfly' before Wakeman joined full-time, along with drummer Richard Hudson and guitarist bass player John Ford (ex-Velvet Opera).

Though Cousins sang distinctively, his style was an acquired taste. The group cut a 1970 concert album, 'Just A Collection Of Antiques And Curios', from London's prestigious Queen Elizabeth Hall, but 1971's studio offering, 'From The Witchwood', suffered from dissent over composing credits, musical differences and individual critical attention paid to Wakeman, who was head-hunted by Yes and replaced in The Strawbs by Blue Weaver from Amen Corner for 'Grave New World' and its resulting singles chart action with 'Lay Down'.

Unhappy about this mutation into a pop group, Hooper quit just before the group's commercial peak with the 'Bursting At The Seams' album and the smash single, 'Part Of The Union'. A Ford-Hudson opus, this sardonic singalong was a highlight of the subsequent tour (with new member Dave Lambert) during which many older devotees were irked by a pronounced comedy element that had crept into the act. With the follow-up, 'Shine On Silver Sun', only a minor hit, Cousins cut a solo album, 'Two Weeks Last Summer', while Ford and Hudson struck out

on their own as Hudson-Ford. Three hit singles later, including 1973's UK Top 10 item, 'Pick Up The Pieces', lack of fan commitment led to the duo's belated and cynical crack at punk as The Monks with 'Nice Legs, Shame About The Face'.

Cousins had re-launched The Strawbs with Lambert, Chas Cronk (bass), drummer Rod Coombes (ex-Stealers Wheel) and ex-Nashville Teen/Renaissance pianist John Hawken. A misjudged concentration on the US market and lukewarm reviews for 1974's 'Hero And Heroine' led to a growing indifference towards the band, who managed several more albums: 'Ghosts', 'Deep Cuts', 'Nomadness', 'Burning For You' and 'Deadlines' before the last rites. Cousins also made an independent album, 'Old School Songs', with final Strawb guitarist Brian Willoughby (another ex-Monk) in 1979. Now head of a Devon radio station, Cousins re-formed The Strawbs in the early 1980s with Hooper, Willoughby and Hudson for a 1989 album, 'Don't Say Goodbye', but a return to former prominence seems unlikely.

Greatest Hits

Singles	Title	US	UK
1972	Lay Down	–	12
1973	Part Of The Union	–	2
Albums			
1973	Bursting At The Seams	121	2
1975	Ghosts	47	–

The **STYLISTICS**

Russell Thompkins Jr
Herb Murrell
Airrion Love
James Dunn
James Smith (vocal group)

The Stylistics were the epitome of the 'sweet soul' genre which appeared in the US in the early 1970s, standing out thanks to the signature high tenor voice of Thompkins and the silk-smooth arrangements of producer Thom Bell. Formed in Philadephia in 1968 from the remnants of two earlier groups, The Percussions and The Monarchs, The Stylistics recorded their 1969 debut single, 'You're A Big Girl Now', for a small local indie label. Consistent sales in areas where the group performed kept the record bubbling, eventually attracting the attention of the New York-based Avco Embassy label, which signed them in 1971 and reissued 'You're A Big Girl Now' nationally, to be rewarded with a US Top 100 entry.

The group were then teamed at Philadelphia's Sigma Sound studios with producer Thom Bell and songwriting partner Linda Creed, and here a string of melodic ballads, lush production dovetailing into the group's

Disco dominance meant Stylistic stagnation – in their outfits as well as output

harmonic blend to highlight Thompkins's sparkling tenor, was produced. The first release, 'Stop, Look, Listen (To Your Heart)', made the US Top 40, and the next two singles, 'You Are Everything' and 'Betcha By Golly Wow', were both million sellers, the latter also providing their first UK hit.

The group worked with Bell & Creed until the end of 1973, through three big-selling albums and a flurry of further hit singles, including three more million sellers in 'I'm Stone In Love With You', 'Make Up To Break Up' and 'You Make Me Feel Brand New', the latter being their biggest seller, and notable because deeper-voiced Airrion Love took most of the lead, rather than Thompkins.

Mid-1974 saw a move to New York, and a new production tie-up at Media Sound studios with veterans Hugo (Peretti) & Luigi (Creatore) and arranger Van McCoy. Although the group's vocal sound was essentially unchanged, the subtle sweetness of the Thom Bell recordings began to be supplanted by brasher yet blander production, and US sales began to wane after a promising start with the album and single, 'Let's Put It All Together'. Perversely, Britain warmed to this less soulful, more MOR, version of the group, and during 1975–6 they topped the UK chart with 'I Can't Give You Anything (But My Love)', and Top 10 hits with 'Sing Baby Sing', 'Na Na Is The Saddest Word', 'Funky Weekend', 'Can't Help Falling In Love' and '16 Bars', all of which meant little or nothing in America. 1975's compilation album, 'Best Of The Stylistics', was also the UK's biggest-selling album of the year, and the best UK seller ever by a black group.

When disco hijacked much of the black music scene in the late 1970s, The Stylistics did not board the bandwagon, and their hits ceased. They moved back to Philadelphia in 1980 and signed to Gamble & Huff's TSOP

label, but no chart revival resulted. The group spent the rest of the 1980s as a popular cabaret act (especially in the UK), leaning upon their considerable hit repertoire and undiminished vocal talents.

Greatest Hits

Singles	Title	US	UK
1974	You Make Me Feel Brand New	2	2
1975	Can't Give You Anything (But My Love)	51	1
Albums			
1975	The Best Of The Stylistics	41	1
1976	Best Of The Stylistics, Vol. 2	–	1

Donna SUMMER

The most successful artist to emerge from the Disco boom of the 1970s was Donna Summer (born Donna Gaines, 1948). Under the initial guidance of Giorgio Moroder she charted the course of what was to become known as Euro-Disco with 1975's 16-minute erotic extravaganza, 'Love To Love You Baby', recorded and initially released in Germany, where she was living.

After beginning her career in gospel music in her native USA and in the short-lived group Crow, she joined the German cast of *Hair* and lived in Munich from 1970. 'Love To Love You Baby' was a UK hit, and was then acquired by a new label in the US, where it sold a million in 1976.

Summer moved into a career as an album artist while retaining her fame as a Disco Diva, and enjoyed an enviable string of hit singles and albums, garnering 17 gold and platinum awards during the 1970s, topping the US singles chart with a disco version of

'MacArthur Park', 'Bad Girls', 'Hot Stuff' and a duet with Barbra Streisand, 'Enough Is Enough'.

At the end of the decade after an acrimonious lawsuit with her US label, she moved to a rival and continued to produce gold and platinum. As a born-again Christian, she rejected her former lifestyle and began to produce music that reflected her new state of mind. Her relationship with her new label was erratic – her 1989 album, 'Another Place And Time', produced by UK hitmakers Stock Aitken and Waterman, was rejected by her US label but picked up by major companies in both the US and UK, providing her with more hits.

With 24 gold and platinum certifications and 4 Grammy awards, Summer is the single most successful artist to emerge from the Disco era.

Greatest Hits

Singles	Title	US	UK
1976	Love To Love You Baby	2	4
1977	I Feel Love	6	1
1978	MacArthur Park	1	5
1979	Hot Stuff	1	11
1979	Bad Girls	1	14
1979	Dim All The Lights	2	29
1979	Enough Is Enough (with Barbra Streisand)	1	3
1983	She Works Hard For The Money	3	25
Albums			
1978	Live And More	1	16
1979	Bad Girls	1	23
1979	On The Radio/Greatest Hits Vols 1 and 2	1	24
1989	Another Place And Time	53	17

1976 – Summer of 'Love To Love You'

SUPERTRAMP

Richard Davies (vocals, keyboards)
Roger Hodgson (guitar)
John Helliwell (sax)
Dougie Thomson (bass)
Rob C Benberg (drums)

Formed in the UK's progressive rock heyday of the late 1960s, Supertramp found their greatest success a decade later, having followed a musical course diametrically opposite to most UK rock in the 1970s.

The band was formed in 1969 by Davies (born 1944) with financial backing from a Dutch millionaire, known colloquially as Sam, whom he had met in Germany. Hodgson (born 1950) was one of four players recruited, and (with Davies) the only original member who would have an extended stay in the band. Davies and Hodgson would also henceforth be the band's songwriting mainstays. Other early group members who played on the group's first two unsuccessful albums, 'Supertramp' (1970) and 'Indelibly Stamped' (1971), included drummers Bob Miller and Kevin Currie, bass player Frank Farrell and Richard Palmer (guitar). Named Supertramp (from the novel *Autobiography Of A Supertramp*) at the suggestion of their first sax player, Dave Winthrop, they signed to A&M in mid-1970, but less than two years later, with two unsuccessful albums behind them, the band broke apart and split from Sam, who wrote off money they still owed him. Davies and Hodgson were left with the name, and put together the stable line-up which would see the group through their successful years. Benberg (ex Bees Make Honey) was related to Thin Lizzy guitarist Scott Gorham, while Thompson (born 1951) and Helliwell joined from The Alan Bown Set.

The 1974 album 'Crime Of The Century', proved a turning point, hitting the UK Top five and making the US Top 40 in early 1975. It also brought the band to an audience outside the progressive LP market by spinning off two hit singles – 'Dreamer' in the UK and 'Bloody Well Right' in the US. A US tour at this time also initiated a huge live following for Supertramp in the US.

Two further albums in 'Crisis? What Crisis?' (1976) and 'Even in the Quietest Moments' (1977) found similar transatlantic success, but the real blockbuster came along – ironically, at the height of the disco and New Wave explosions – with 1979's album 'Breakfast In America', a multi-million seller worldwide, and a chart-topper in the US. A collection of extremely commercial songs, it duly spun off several major hit singles, including the title track, 'Take The Long Way Home', and 'The Logical Song' – the latter becoming Supertramp's best-known number.

A double live LP, 'Paris' (which is where it was recorded), was big in 1980, and was followed two years later by 'Famous Last Words', appropriately titled as it was Hodg-

son's last work with the band before leaving for a solo career. They did not replace him, but continued as a quartet, re-emerging in 1985 in slightly funkier guise with the album 'Brother Where You Bound' – a Top 30 hit both sides of the Atlantic, but with only a fraction of the sales of 'Breakfast In America'.

Both Supertramp and Hodgson continued to work and record throughout the 1980s briefly reuniting in 1986 to promote the Top 10 compilation 'The Autobiography Of Supertramp'. Another live album, 'Supertramp Live 88', showed the group's traditional style still intact and pulling an audience, but they also still carried an edge of experimentation, making it big on the US dance chart in 1987 with 'I'm Begging You'.

Greatest Hits

Singles	Title	US	UK
1979	*The Logical Song*	6	7
1979	*Take The Long Way Home*	10	–
1979	*Breakfast In America*	62	9
Albums			
1974	*Crime of The Century*	38	4
1979	*Breakfast In America*	1	3
1982	*Famous Last Words*	5	5

The **SUPREMES**

Mary Wilson
Cindy Birdsong
Jean Terrell
Linda Lawrence
Scherrie Payne
Susaye Greene (vocal group)

After the departure of Diana Ross as lead singer in 1969, popular mythology would have it that The Supremes were a spent force, neutered without the sparkling glamour and worldwide popularity of Ms Ross. The truth is somewhat different.

Because of Motown boss Berry Gordy's infatuation with Ross, both in a business and personal sense, he threw the weight of his company behind her launch as a world-class MOR singer and serious actress. Despite the resultant loss of the songs and production input of Motown's first division talent, The Supremes initially continued as though Ms Ross had never existed, most notably in the UK. Ross was replaced by Jean Terrell, although Gordy had proposed Syreeta Wright, who later married Stevie Wonder.

The majority of post-Ross recordings were produced by Frank Wilson, including three collaborations with The Four Tops beginning with the 1970 album 'The Magnificent Seven', the most successful of all Supremes albums in the UK excepting hits collections.

The hits continued for three straight years with the band using other producers such as Smokey Robinson and Stevie Wonder. When Cindy Birdsong left in 1972 she was replaced by Linda Lawrence, a singer with Stevie Wonder's touring group. The following year Terrell departed, replaced by Scherrie Payne, sister of Freda, of 'Band Of Gold' fame. Birdsong returned briefly, to be replaced by Susaye Greene, also from the Wonder entourage. Wilson, Payne and Greene became the longest-lived line up since 1970 although major hits eluded them.

The swansong of The Supremes came with the 1976 return to form, 'High Energy', a commercial album in the then-obligatory disco style. A second album from the same sessions, 'Mary, Scherrie and Susaye' was their final album and they folded in 1977.

Wilson stayed with Motown for one solo project, 'Red Hot', before departing acrimo-

Regardless of Ross (right), The Supremes stayed with it through the 'Seventies

niously, in the 1980s touring throughout the world often billed as 'The Supremes featuring Mary Wilson', using various pick-up singers amidst a flurry of lawsuits. In 1989 Terrell, Payne and Lawrence regrouped as The Supremes for recording and touring, but injunctions, this time from Wilson, followed. A sad end for a group so popular that they inspired a Broadway show, *Dreamgirls*.

Greatest Hits

Singles	Title	US	UK
1970	Up The Ladder To The Roof	10	6
1971	Stoned Love	7	3
1971	Nathan Jones	–	5
1972	Floy Joy	–	9
1972	Automatically Sunshine	–	10
Albums			
1970	Right On	25	–
1970	The Magnificent Seven (with The Four Tops)	113	6
1976	High Energy	42	–

T'PAU

Carol Decker (vocals)
Paul Jackson (bass)
Tim Burgess (drums)
Michael Chetwood (keyboards)
Taj Wyzgowski (guitar)
Ronnie Rogers (guitar)

The boyfriend/girlfriend team of Decker (born 1957) and Rogers (born 1959) had been in various bands in the Shrewsbury (English Midlands) area (The Lazers being the first) for the first half of the 1980s before signing a major recording contract 1986. The group took its name from a character in the *Star Trek* television series.

The ballsy 'Heart And Soul' single was a surprise hit in the US where it reached the Top 5 in mid-1987, assisted in no small way by flame-haired Decker's MTV-friendly looks. Success soon filtered back to the UK, where their first album, 'Bridge Of Spies', shot up the charts in its wake. Tracks on the album varied from raunchy rock to the creamy balladry of 'China In Your Hand', which was a UK chart-topper, (doing nothing in the US), but the band failed to build on these foundations, despite 18 months' solid roadwork. They replaced lead guitarist Wyzgowski, who had appeared on the record, with Dean Howard (ex-Ore).

The altogether tougher second album, 'Rage', released in 1988, reflected the influence of Bryan Adams with whom they had

toured, but their sound's harder edge didn't help record sales, 'China' having perhaps pigeonholed them as Berlin/Heart AORockers, and 'I Will Be With You' and 'Secret Garden' both failed to make the UK Top 10. T'Pau changed record labels in 1990, looking perhaps to rekindle the short-lived American success that first sent them to stardom.

Greatest Hits

Singles	Title	US	UK
1987	Heart And Soul	4	4
1987	China In Your Hand	–	1
Albums			
1987	Bridge Of Spies	33	1
1988	Rage	–	4

TALKING HEADS

David Byrne (vocals, guitar)
Jerry Harrison (keyboards, guitar)
Tina Weynouth (bass)
Chris Frantz (drums)

Daring to mix intellect with a rock'n'roll beat, Talking Heads were among the most fascinating groups of the 1980s – creative, artistic, challenging and successful.

Byrne (born 1952), Weymouth (born Martina Weymouth, 1950) and Frantz (born 1951) met at Rhode Island School of Design. They formed a trio in 1974 and moved to New York, creating a buzz at CBGBs and other clubs with their sparse, arty punk and 1960s cover versions. At a Boston show they intrigued ex-Modern Lovers keyboard player Jerry Harrison, who joined in 1976, just as the band signed to a top New York independent label. Their first single, 'Love Goes To A Building On Fire', failed to chart but gained critical attention, as did their debut album,

'Talking Heads '77', which featured the punk classic, 'Psycho Killer', and stayed six months in the US chart, but only just made the Top 100. They also found an enthusiastic response in the UK and Europe, where they toured twice in 1977.

For their second album, they began an association with ex-Roxy Music keyboard player/producer Brian Eno,who produced 1978's 'More Songs About Buildings And Food', adding more percussion to the sound. The album went Top 30 in the US and UK and their version of Al Green's 'Take Me To The River' was a US Top 30 hit. For 1979's 'Fear Of Music' album, Eno moved the rhythms to the fore, notably on 'I Zimbra', and the album made the US Top 30 despite the lack of singles. The Eno collaboration climaxed with 'Remain In Light', which made the US Top 20 in 1980 and featured guest guitarist Adrian Belew, singer Nona Hendryx and a brass section to augment the Afro-funky rhythms as Byrne's songwriting reached new heights on 'Once In A Lifetime' and 'Houses In Motion'.

The band dispersed for solo projects in 1981. Byrne linked up with Eno again for his first solo album, 'My Life In The Bush Of Ghosts', wrote the score for a ballet, *The Catherine Wheel*, choreographed by Twyla Tharp, the album of which almost made the US Top 100, and produced the 'Mesopotamia' album for the B-52s. Harrison also recorded a solo album, 'The Red & The Black', while Weymouth and Frantz formed The Tom Tom Club with three more Weymouth sisters. Their debut album went US Top 30 and they had a UK Top 10 single with 'Wordy Rappinghood'. In 1982, a double live album, 'The Name Of This Band Is Talking Heads', documented the parent group's career and made the US Top 40 as an expanded band line-up toured the US and Europe once more. 'Speaking In Tongues', produced by the band in 1983, returned them

Byrne brainchild the Talking Heads, took bizarre rock into bestsellers

to the US Top 20 and gave them their first US Top 10 single with 'Burning Down The House'. Later that year, director Jonathan Demme filmed the band in concert for the critically acclaimed *Stop Making Sense* movie/live album released in 1984. The following years, the group's 'Little Creatures' album made the UK Top 10 and US Top 20 and included a UK Top 10 single, 'Road To Nowhere'. Byrne then took time off to work on a theatre project, *Music From The Knee Plays*, and a bizarre movie, *True Stories*, but Talking Heads albums became increasingly successful, especially in the UK, where 'True Stories' went Top 10 and 'Naked', recorded in Paris with producer Steve Lillywhite, made the Top 3 in 1988.

However, Byrne was tired of touring, preferring to write music for Bertolucci's *The Last Emperor*, direct documentaries and make albums of Latin-American music: 'Beliza Tropical' in 1989 and 'Rei Momo' in 1990. Frantz and Weymouth revived The Tom Tom Club and Harrison formed The Casual Gods. In 1990, Harrison, Frantz and Weymouth played as Talking Heads without Byrne on a CBGBs revival package tour with Blondie and The Ramones. Byrne was still not committed to another Talking Heads project at the end of 1990.

Greatest Hits

Singles	Title	US	UK
1981	Wordy Rappinghood (Tom Tom Club)	–	7
1983	Burning Down The House	9	–
1985	Road To Nowhere	–	6
Albums			
1978	More Songs About Buildings & Food	29	21
1980	Remain In Light	19	21
1983	Speaking In Tongues	15	21
1985	Little Creatures	20	10
1986	True Stories	17	10
1988	Naked	19	3

James **TAYLOR**

James Taylor's career has had three distinct phases. Beginning in the 1970s as the epitome of the 'sensitive singer-songwriter', Taylor had later hits with gentle revivals of rock oldies and in the late 1980s, joined Jackson Browne and others as a socially conscious songwriter.

Taylor (born 1948) grew up in Massachusetts before moving to New York and joining his childhood friend, Danny Korchmar, in folk-rock band The Flying Machine. Their early recordings were issued in 1971. In 1968, he moved to London and was signed by Peter Asher to Apple Records, the label launched by The Beatles, and the acoustic 'James Taylor' album was released.

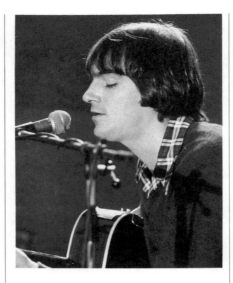

Sweet Baby James minus mustache

Returning to New England, Taylor was hospitalized to help him overcome drug addiction. His experiences there coloured many of the songs on the highly praised 'Sweet Baby James' album, produced by Asher and released in 1970. Both the album and the elegiac 'Fire And Rain' single were big hits.

His popularity reached new heights in 1971, when he starred in the film *Two Lane Blacktop* as well as heading the charts with the charming Carole King lullaby, 'You've Got A Friend', from his third album, 'Mud Slide Slim And The Blue Horizon'. However, Taylor's own slim vein of lyricism seemed to have run out and 'One Man Dog' (1972) offered no songs to match his earlier successes, though the romantic 'Don't Let Me Be Lonely Tonight' was a US Top 20 hit.

While his biggest hits of the mid-1970s were rather pale revivals of boisterous oldies – notably 'Mockingbird', a duet with his then wife, Carly Simon – Taylor's albums continued to sell well. Among them were 'Walking Man' (1974) produced by David Spinozza, 'In The Pocket' (1976) produced by Russ Titelman and Lenny Waronker and 'JT', his debut album for his third label in 1977.

From 1978, Taylor began to take an anti-nuclear stance, appearing at benefit concerts and contributing two tracks to the 'No Nukes' album (1979). He made only three solo albums during the 1980s, but the self-produced 'That's Why I'm Here' (1985) included guest appearances from Graham Nash and Joni Mitchell, while 'Never Die Young' (1988) was a minor US hit.

Greatest Hits

Singles	Title	US	UK
1970	Fire And Rain	3	42
1971	You've Got A Friend	1	4
1974	Mockingbird (with Carly Simon)	5	34
1975	How Sweet It Is (To Be Loved By You)	5	–
1977	Handy Man	4	–
Albums			
1970	Sweet Baby James	3	7
1971	Mud Slide Slim And The Blue Horizon	2	4
1972	One Man Dog	4	27
1975	Gorilla	6	–
1979	Flag	10	–
1981	Dad Loves His Work	10	–

TEARS FOR FEARS

Curt Smith (vocals, bass)
Roland Orzabal (guitar, keyboards)

Smith (born 1961) and Orzabal (born Orzabal de la Quintana in 1961) first recorded together in the five piece ska group, Graduate, whose album, 'Acting My Age', was produced by Tony Hatch in 1980. After that group split in 1981, they formed the short-lived Neon with Rob Fisher (of Climie Fisher) and then this self-contained UK synth-pop duo, whose name was inspired by a book on primal therapy, signed to a major label. Their first two singles 'Suffer Little Children' and 'Pale Shelter' failed to chart but their third, 1982's 'Mad World', gave them their first UK Top 10 hit.

In 1983 the duo returned to the Top 10 with 'Change', and a remixed version of 'Pale Shelter'. Their debut album, 'The Hurting', topped the UK chart and made the US Top 100, but was overshadowed by 'Songs From The Big Chair' their 1985 album, which topped the US chart selling eight million copies world-wide. Singles taken from the album included 'Everybody Wants To Rule The World', which won an award as 1985's Top Single, 'Shout', which topped the US charts, and 'Head Over Heels', a big trans-atlantic hit.

With the amended title 'Everybody Wants To Run The World', their hit from 1985 returned to the UK Top 10 in 1986 when it was used as the theme for Sport Aid's 'Race Against Time'. The successful duo then took an extended break, emerging in 1989 with a new album, 'The Seeds Of Love', while the Beatlesque single, 'Sowing The Seeds Of Love', with its award-winning video, restored them to the UK and US Top 10s.

Greatest Hits

Singles	Title	US	UK
1985	Shout	1	4
1985	Everybody Wants To Rule The World	1	2
Albums			
1983	The Hurting	73	1
1985	Songs From The Big Chair	1	2
1989	Seeds Of Love	8	1

TELEVISION

Tom Verlaine (guitar, vocals)
Richard Hell (bass, vocals)
Richard Lloyd (guitar)
Billy Ficca (drums)

One of the most talented and innovative bands to emerge from the US New Wave scene of the mid-1970s, New York outfit Television had their roots in The Neon Boys, a band formed by high school drop-out Verlaine (born Tom Miller, 1949), former school-mate Hell (born Richard Meyers, 1949) and Ficca in 1973. The band recorded demos (which remained unreleased for several years) and added Lloyd later that year before renaming themselves Television, gigging regularly and attracting the attention of luminaries such as David Bowie, then resident in New York. Verlaine played guitar on the debut single by Patti Smith, a version of 'Hey Joe' (1974), but by the time of Television's own vinyl debut, the independent 'Little Johnny Jewel' single, Hell had left to form The Heartbreakers with ex-New York Doll Johnny Thunders, being replaced by Fred Smith (born 1950). Hell in turn left The Heartbreakers for a solo career backed by his own band, The Voidoids, and released two albums, 'Blank Generation' (1977), and 'Destiny Street' (1983), plus a compilation of unreleased tracks, 'R.I.P.' (1984) before concentrating on an acting and writing career. Hell's image (short, spiky hair, torn jeans, safety pins and ripped T-shirts) was to have a significant impact on late 1970s punk fashion, but after his departure, Television took on a more sober look.

Verlaine now became the focal point of the band, and after an abortive attempt at recording an album with producer Brian Eno, they signed a major label deal. 'Marquee Moon', a UK Top 30 album, appeared in 1977 to rapturous critical acclaim, and provided two UK Top 10 singles, 'Prove It' and the lengthy title track. One of rock's most impressive debuts, the album featured Verlaine's Reed/Dylan-like lyrics and distinctive guitar style (heavily influenced by Barry Melton of Country Joe & The Fish), complemented by Lloyd's more orthodox rock playing and Ficca's jazzy drumming. It proved a hard act to follow, however, and 1978's album 'Adventure' showed very little progression, although it reached the UK Top 10, and the 'Foxhole' single reached the UK Top 40. The band split in 1978, leaving a posthumous live collection, 'The Blow Up' (1982) as their epitaph.

Lloyd was first to re-surface, co-producing and writing a 1978 single for fellow New Yorkers Chris Stamey & The Dbs, while Verlaine released his eponymous solo debut in 1979. From the album, which closely followed the Television blueprint, David Bowie covered 'Kingdom Come' on his 1980 'Scary Monsters' album. Verlaine followed up with two excellent albums, 'Dreamtime' (1981) and 'Words from The Front' (1982), but hit a low point with 1984's ponderous 'Cover'. However 'Flash Light' (1987) and 'The Wonder' (1990) saw him back on form. Smith has played on all of Verlaine's albums (also co-producing 'The Wonder'), as well as with a number of other US acts, including The Roches and singer-songwriter Willie Nile, and appeared on Lloyd's first solo set, 'Alchemy' (1979). Unfortunately, Lloyd had become heavily involved with drugs, and it was 1985 before the cleaned-up guitarist released a second album, 'Field Of Fire', recorded in Sweden. A live album, 'Real Time', followed in 1987, and in 1990, he joined former X vocalist John Doe's band for his 'Meet John Doe' album. Ficca has played with several US bands, most notably The Waitresses, who scored a UK Top 40 hit with 'Christmas Wrapping' and a US Top 75 single with 'I Know What Boys Like' in 1982.

Although large-scale commercial success eluded Television and Verlaine, their influence can be seen in a number of late 1970s/early 1980s bands, most notably REM, Echo & The Bunnymen and early U2.

Greatest Hits

Singles	Title	US	UK
1977	Marquee Moon	–	30
1977	Prove It	–	28
Albums			
1977	Marquee Moon	–	28
1978	Adventure	–	7

The **TEMPTATIONS**

Only perhaps The Dells and The Four Tops, both formed in 1952, can match the longevity of The Temptations in the pantheon of black vocal groups. Due to a diversity of style and an ability to adapt to all the changes in soul music, they are now entering their fourth decade.

Part of their enduring popularity has to be the high calibre of lead singers utilized and the versatility that enabled them to have hits using both tenor and falsetto leads. These singers included David Ruffin (born 1941), Eddie Kendricks (born 1939) and Dennis Edwards (born 1943), all of whom enjoyed solo hits after leaving the group. This advantage, coupled with producers as talented as Smokey Robinson and Norman Whitfield, became an unbeatable formula.

Formed in Detroit around 1959 with Eldridge Bryant, Melvin Franklyn (born 1942), Otis Williams (born 1941), Paul Williams (born 1939) and Kendricks, from the ashes of various high school groups they were initially known as The Primes until signed by Berry Gordy who renamed them The Temptations in 1960. Bryant left in 1961 to be replaced by Ruffin and their most famous line-up was intact.

Their earliest releases were true to the spirit of doo wop and it was not until placed under the production supervision of Robinson that the hits began with 'The Way You Do The Things You Do' a US Top 20 single in 1964. They followed this with an almost unbroken string of pop hits. The change of producer to Whitfield in 1966 had no adverse effect and in fact readied the group for even greater popularity in the 1970s.

Acutely aware of the major changes being spearheaded in black music by artists like Curtis Mayfield and Sly Stone, Whitfield steered the group on a course of progressive soul beginning with the long social commentary workouts of 'Cloud Nine' and 'Runaway Child, Running Wild', in 1968.

Under Whitfield's control, the group seemed to become merely an extension of his studio prowess. In such epic album productions as 'Papa Was A Rolling Stone' (1972) and 'Masterpiece' (1973), The Temptations were just one element in his complex, almost symphonic, arrangements.

Ruffin had departed in 1968, to be replaced by Edwards, when the former embarked on an erratic solo career. One of the greatest voices in soul, he has never achieved his due recognition and remains a cult favourite only. Edwards was a former member of The Contours, another Motown group. In 1971, after the US chart-topping single, 'Just My Imagination (Running Away With Me)', Kendricks also left and enjoyed an equally erratic solo career. Ruffin and Kendricks had a brief revival in the 1980s after appearing on Live Aid with Hall & Oates. Kendricks was replaced by Damon Harris (born 1950), who sang lead on most of the later Whitfield productions. Paul Williams also left in 1971 after becoming increasingly dependent on drink and drugs, and eventually committed suicide in 1973.

Tired of being Whitfield's puppets, the group demanded a change of producer and got Jeffrey Bowen, whose work on 1975's 'A Song For You' album maintained the hit streak. However, in 1977, though the Disco boom had all but wiped out the group's popularity, they signed with Atlantic, producing two mediocre albums before rejoining Motown in 1980.

Their career throughout the 1980s has been erratic, with members changing rapidly, especially Edwards who left and returned twice during the decade. There were many soul hits, notably 'Standing On The Top' (1982) from the album, 'Reunion', which featured Ruffin and Kendricks and was produced by Motown's then hottest star, Rick James. 1984's 'Treat Her Like A Lady' was their only substantial UK hit during this period.

With Franklyn, Williams and Richard Street (who replaced Paul Williams in 1973) being the only originals, The Temptations,

The Temptations – resisted pressure to part through ups and downs of thirty-year career

with over 80 hit singles since 1962, look likely to match the longevity of their pre-war inspirations, The Inkspots and The Mills Brothers.

Greatest Hits

Singles	Title	US	UK
1965	*My Girl*	I	43
1966	*Beauty Is Only Skin Deep*	3	21
1968	*I Wish It Would Rain*	4	45
1968	*I'm Gonna Make You Love Me* (with Diana Ross & The Supremes)	2	3
1969	*I Can't Get Next To You*	I	13
1970	*Ball Of Confusion*	3	7
1971	*Just My Imagination* (Running Away With Me)	I	8
1972	*Papa Was A Rolling Stone*	I	14
Albums			
1966	*Greatest Hits*	5	26
1968	*Diana Ross & The Supremes Join The Temptations* (with Diana Ross & The Supremes)	2	I
1969	*TCB* (with Diana Ross & The Supremes)	I	11
1968	*Cloud Nine*	4	32
1969	*Puzzle People*	5	20
1972	*All Directions*	2	19

10CC/WAX/GODLEY and CREME

Lol Creme (vocals, guitar)
Eric Stewart (vocals, guitar)
Graham Gouldman (vocals, bass)
Kevin Godley (vocals, drums)

Formed in 1972 from the ashes of Hotlegs, a one-hit wonder outfit featuring Creme (born 1947), Godley (born 1945) and Stewart (born 1945), who scored a UK Top 3 hit in 1970 with the stomping 'Neanderthal Man'. Stewart had considerable experience with Wayne Fontana & The Mindbenders (which he disbanded at the end of 1968 as the only surviving original member), while Godley and Creme had played with the lesser-known Mockingbirds and Sabres respectively.

Stewart ran Strawberry Studios in Manchester with another former Mockingbird Graham Gouldman (born 1946), a Tin Pan Alley songwriter of hits for The Yardbirds ('For Your Love'), The Hollies ('Bus Stop') and Herman's Hermits ('No Milk Today'), as well as working with top New York bubblegum producers Kasenetz & Katz. He joined the Mancunian trio for sessions backing Neil Sedaka, and their evident rapport and mutual respect led to a single being cut. 'Donna' reflected the quartet's grounding in 1960's

music, being a respectful pastiche of The Beach Boys. It was a surprizing hit, while the follow-up, 'Rubber Bullets', reached No. 1 in the UK.

The first album, '10cc', also included 'The Dean And I', a hit, which, like the others, showed off their four-part vocal talents: all four also wrote, in varying combinations. 1974's 'Sheet Music' showed the first signs of excessive cleverness despite two UK Top 30 hits, 'Wall Street Shuffle' and 'Silly Love'. After two more albums, 'The Original Soundtrack' (including the lush, highly produced UK No. 1/US Top 3 hit, 'I'm Not In Love') and 'How Dare You', the partnership fragmented with Godley and Creme going their own way to develop a gadget called the Gizmo, the other two retaining the name.

10cc continued with two more UK Top 5 albums 'Deceptive Bends' (1977) and 'Bloody Tourists' (1978), with a line-up now including guitarist Rick Fenn, ex-Pilot drummer Stuart Tosh and Kokomo keyboardist Tony O'Malley. Their finest hour was 'Dreadlock Holiday', a reggae pastiche UK No. 1 from 'Tourists'. Two more US hit singles were also obtained in 'The Things We Do For Love' (Top 5) and 'People In Love' (Top 40). US songwriter Andrew Gold's guesting on 1981's flop album 'Ten Out Of Ten' presaged Wax, by his duo with Gouldman, but they were commercially unsuccessful apart from the single 'Bridge To Your Heart'. After the final split, Stewart played guitar with Paul McCartney on 1982's 'Tug Of War' album and the film *Give My Regards To Broad Street* and like Gouldman (who recorded the solo soundtrack 'Animalympics' and produced the Ramones' 1981 effort 'Pleasant Dreams') went into production, with local group Sad Cafe.

Godley and Creme abandoned the Gizmo (a device to expand the capabilities of the electric guitar) and after a false start with the

Sophisticated studiorock for the 'Seventies, 10cc managed to make it work onstage as well

overblown box set, 'Consequences' became successful pop video directors, masterminding the award-winning clip for Herbie Hancock, 'Rockit', with animated dummies and the Frankie Goes To Hollywood epic that helped propel 'Two Tribes' to the UK No. 1 slot. Applying their experience to their own songs, they charted with 'Cry', a Top 20 hit propelled by a clever changing-face video, following a pair of bigger hits, 'Wedding Bells' and 'Under Your Thumb'. In 1989 Godley was the motivating force behind the 'One World' video/musical project, with Creme less visible. As the first 10cc albums emerged on CD, however, it was tempting to note that the original quartet never bettered their mixture of musical pastiche and witty wordplay. The origin of the group name 10cc is reputedly the quantity of semen produced by the average male ejaculation.

Greatest Hits

10cc

Singles	Title	US	UK
1972	Rubber Bullets	–	1
1975	I'm Not In Love	2	1
1978	Dreadlock Holiday	–	1
Albums			
1977	Deceptive Bends	31	3
1978	Bloody Tourists	69	3

Wax

Singles			
1987	Bridge To Your Heart	–	12

Godley & Creme

Singles			
1981	Under Your Thumb	–	3
1981	Wedding Bells	–	7
Albums			
1981	Ismism	–	29
1985	The History Mix Volume I	37	–

Joe **TEX**

During his late 1960s heyday, Joe Tex was touted as 'The New Boss' (updating the Atlantic Records 1950s claim for Joe Turner as 'The Boss Of The Blues') and as the alternative 'Soul Brother No. 1' (contesting James Brown's title). In truth he was neither, but he was certainly one of the most individually creative, successful and best-loved country soul men of the era.

Born Joseph Arrington Jr in Rogers, Texas in 1933, he won a local talent contest that took him to New York in 1954. He claimed that he wrote the lyrics to 'Fever' as this time, selling his rights to the song to pay a hotel bill. He first recorded in 1955 and, for the next decade he remained a well kept secret, popular on the 'chitlin' circuit because of his good looks and athletic stage act, but absent from all charts. Most of his records at this time were journeyman R&B and rock'n'roll, his first minor success coming in 1960 when

Rural rapman Tex, talked his way to 'Sixties soul success

his spontaneously extended 'rap' rendition of the Etta James' hit, 'All I Could Do Was Cry', was a southern regional breakout, and became the precursor to his eventually renowned, storybook style.

In 1961 while James Brown was hitting with Tex's composition, 'Baby You're Right', the originator was signed by Nashville song publisher and producer, Buddy Killen, whose faith in the singer developed into a tight working friendship that endured until Tex's unexpected death from a heart attack on August 13, 1982.

To showcase his signing, Killen founded Dial Records in 1961. Ten releases and three years later, Atlantic assumed distribution of Dial. Tex's first Atlantic-distributed release, 'Hold What You've Got', was major news at the beginning of 1965, and was followed by a solid run of 20 self-composed hits. During this period Tex occasionally, and without much personal enthusiasm, knocked out a dance track. He was most comfortable and at his best, however, when spinning a yarn, preaching a homily, relating to his southern audience, and making records that were too downhome for international pop success, but made him a major soul star.

Becoming disillusioned with life on the road, in 1972 he adopted the Muslim religion

and the name Joseph Hazziez, and for much of his final decade was content to farm back home in Texas. When motivated to tackle showbiz, though, he remained a strong contender. Indeed, after his 'semi-retirement' he scored his biggest selling hit with the lecherous funk of 'I Gotcha' (1972) and an international success with 'Ain't Gonna Bump No More (With No Big Fat Woman)' (1977). As disco records went, this was one of the better examples of the genre.

A posthumous compilation of mainly previously unissued 1970s recordings (in 1989) proved that Joe Tex was still writing and singing with wit and vigour during his latter years. But would he have continued to be successful? Unlikely. His style of rapping was country miles away from the urban electro-rap of today.

Greatest Hits

Singles	Title	US	UK
1965	Hold What You've Got	5	–
1967	Skinny Legs And All	10	–
1972	I Gotcha	2	–
1977	Ain't Gonna Bump No More (With No Big Fat Woman)	12	2
Albums			
1972	I Gotcha	17	–

Thompson – ex-Convention cult fugure

Richard **THOMPSON**

Richard Thompson (born 1949) was Fairport Convention's lead guitar player and occasional composer/vocalist, from their inception in early 1967 until 1971. With them, he developed into one of the finest guitarists in Britain. Always self-effacing, he spent a year after leaving Fairport as back-up guitarist on tours by Ian Matthews and Sandy Denny (both also ex-Fairport) and undertook numerous sessions for the likes of John Martyn and Nick Drake, as well as Matthews and Denny. His first solo album, 'Henry The Human Fly' appeared in 1972 and despite being ignored at the time, is now viewed as an important work, even if overshadowed by later releases. Songs like 'The New St. George' showed that he was adept at utilizing images that suggested an empathy with the British folk tradition, whilst placing them in a modern context.

His next album was the first to also credit his first wife, Linda (née Peters). 'I Want To See The Bright Lights Tonight' (1973) was a quantum leap forward, quintessentially English, with his highly evocative lyrics, and further enhanced Thompson's reputation as the poet of gloom – like a medieval troubadour laughing at the folly of humanity. Throughout this period, the couple played occasional gigs as an acoustic duo, but in early 1974, assembled a band, Sour Grapes, to promote their new album 'Hokey Pokey', although only ex-Fairporter Simon Nichol remained from the album sessions. 'Hokey Pokey' (despite a couple of excellent ballads including the wonderful 'A Heart Needs A Home') is more upbeat than its predecessor and shows a slow move towards the gutsy kind of rock orientated folk of the early Fairport Convention. 'Pour Down Like Silver' (1975) continued the movement toward rock, but was just as bleak and demanding as

'Bright Lights'. Never more than a cult, their public profile dropped even lower when they 'retired' in 1976 for nearly two years. In that time, a double album, 'Guitar And Vocal', containing out-takes, rare tracks and live material, showcased Thompson's stunning guitar work (e.g. 'Calvary Cross') that was all but missing from the studio albums.

By this time, the Thompsons had been practising the Sufi faith for several years and their 1977 comeback tour was the most public manifestation of their faith – they performed several Islam inspired numbers (some of which were never recorded) and even the band members, though British, used their Islamic names. The album from the period, 'First Light' (1978), although brilliant, was a disappointment after the tour, as though they had pulled back from total commitment. 1979's 'Sunnyvista' ushered in a new era, at least in terms of live performance, as they were now very much a rock band with folk roots, rather than the other way around. Unfortunately, the album was disappointing, partly due to its (again) being recorded with session musicians rather than the road band.

'Strict Tempo' (1981) was a quirky (even self-indulgent) solo album on which Thompson demonstrated his ability to play almost any stringed instrument in any given style.

The next genuine album, 'Shoot Out The Lights', was probably their best ever, if only because it was a genuine band recording (the Thompsons, plus Nicol, Dave Mattacks on drums and either Dave Pegg or Pete Zorn on bass) and because Thompson, at last, decided to play guitar solos on record, notably on the title track.

Following the album's release, Richard and Linda separated, and Richard Thompson carried on as before – he simply sang all his own songs. The first post-Linda album, 'Hand Of Kindness' (1983), is regarded by many as one of his best (his break-up if nothing else, gave him subject matter for song). 'Small Town Romance' (1984) was a live acoustic album recorded in New York, a measure of his rapidly growing popularity in the US, and was well received, but the next band album, 'Across A Crowded Room' (1985), was disappointing. In fact both subsequent albums, 'Daring Adventures' (1986) and 'Amnesia' (1988) have been patchy. Some feel that his best work in recent years has been as part of the French/Frith/Kaiser/ Thompson band, an 'occasional' outfit who have so far produced two albums, 'Live, Love, Larf & Loaf' (1987) and 'Invisible Means' (1990). Ironically, he is more popular now (especially in the US) than ever, although he is still only a cult figure – and it's doubtful if he will ever be anything else.

A listing of Richard Thompson's chart statistics would be misleading, but like a few other artists in this volume, much of his work will be of great interest to discriminating listeners.

George **THOROGOOD** and The **DESTROYERS**

George Thorogood (guitar, vocals)
Ron Smith (guitar)
Billy Blough (bass)
Jeff Simon (drums)

Highly respected high-energy blues guitarist Thorogood and his band The Destroyers have kept alive the spirit of Elmore James in concert halls and colleges around the world since the late 1970s. Committed to good-time boogie and no-holds-barred live shows, Thorogood has seen his faith in the blues result in ever-increasing album sales. He was inspired to pick up the guitar through reissues of old Chuck Berry records, and from this progressed to such bluesmen as Elmore James, Hound Dog Taylor and John Lee Hooker.

He formed The Destroyers in Delaware in 1973 after a period of solo work and street busking, and in 1974 they moved to the Boston area, working regularly supporting visiting bluesmen. They released their debut album in 1976 on an independent label, and their reputation spread swiftly. Their version of Amos Milburn's 'One Scotch, One Bourbon, One Beer' became a West Coast radio hit and the second album, 'Move It On Over', went gold in the US as did all their subsequent albums. In 1980 Smith left, replaced by sax player Hank Carter.

In 1981 a deal with a major label which allowed Thorogood to retain creative control over his output led to a support tour with The Rolling Stones in the US and in 1985, the band made a spectacular appearance on Live Aid where Thorogood shared the spotlight with blues great Albert Collins.

Greatest Hits

Albums	Title	US	UK
1985	*Maverick*	32	–
1988	*Born To Be Bad*	32	–

THREE DOG NIGHT

Danny Hutton (vocals)
Cory Wells (vocals)
Chuck Negron (vocals)
Mike Allsup (guitar)
Jimmy Greenspoon (organ)
Joe Schermie (bass)
Floyd Sneed (drums)

Three Dog Night, one of America's most commercially successful acts of the early 1970s, were in several ways unusual. Built around a core of three lead vocalists, they were mostly (including the singers) white, but their basic live style was that of a funky R&B revue. They wrote little of their own material,

'Black and White' Greyhound hit is third thoroughbred smash for Three Dog Night

but had a rare instinct for a likely cover version which helped them chalk up nine million-selling singles in five years.

The group was formed in Los Angeles in 1968 by Hutton (born 1946), who had previously had minor chart success as a soloist. He conceived the idea of the triple-vocal front line, and enlisted complementary voices Wells (born 1944) and Negron (born 1942), while assembling a backing group from LA session musicians. They recorded a 1969 debut album of material by their favourite songwriters, which included both their debut US chart hit ('Try A Little Tenderness') and first million seller (Nilsson's song, 'One'). Once established, the group's formula of carefully selected covers was to become consistently successful. Their second album yielded the million-selling 'Easy To Be Hard' (from the musical *Hair*) later in 1969, and their third (a live set) was the first of several US Top 10 albums.

1970 saw the group's first US chart-topping single, Randy Newman's 'Mama Told Me (Not To Come)', their first major international hit, which made the UK Top 3. The following year, a version of Hoyt Axton's 'Joy To The World' (given to them by the composer) was the biggest selling single of the year in the US, where it was No. 1 for six weeks, and also an international hit. On a 1971 European tour, the group heard Greyhound's hit reggae version of the 1950s racial harmony song, 'Black And White', which they duly covered, and it became their

third US chart-topper during 1972, with two more million sellers, 'An Old Fashioned Love Song' and 'Never Been To Spain', preceding it. Some changes in instrumental personnel during 1973 made little difference to the group's sound, and their US – if not international – success run continued: 'Shambala' was a million-selling US Top 5 hit in 1973, as was a cover of Leo Sayer's 'The Show Must Go On' in 1974.

The bubble burst in 1975, when personal problems and the absorption of the label to which they were signed coincided with the group's string of commercial singles – and hits – drying up. Hutton left in 1976 after the release of their worst-selling album, and there were wholesale changes among the instrumentalists. This new line-up did not record, but soldiered on as a live act before eventually disbanding.

In 1981 the original three vocalists regrouped again as Three Dog Night, but some live success did not translate into a new recording career, and little more was heard of the group during the remainder of the 1980s.

Greatest Hits

Singles	Title	US	UK
1970	Mama Told Me Not To Come	1	3
1971	Joy To The World	1	24
1972	Black And White	1	–
Albums			
1969	Captured Live At The Forum	6	–
1971	Golden Bisquits	5	–

TOTO

Bobby Kimball *(vocals)*
David Paich *(keyboards and vocals)*
Steve Lukather *(guitar)*
Steve Porcaro *(keyboards and vocals)*
David Hungate *(bass)*
Jeff Porcaro *(drums)*

Originally a team of Los Angeles session musicians, Toto's brand of melodic rock brought a string of successes in the 1980s.

By 1978, the sextet were among the most respected backing groups on the West Coast, having toured with Aretha Franklin and Jackson Browne and played on hit albums by Boz Scaggs. The Porcaros (Jeff born 1954, Steve born 1957) were sons of a noted jazz percussionist while famous arranger Marty Paich was father of David (born 1954). When the team decided to form a band, the name Toto came from the dog in *The Wizard Of Oz* as well as Robert Toteaux, reputedly the real name of Kimball (born 1947).

With Paich as principal songwriter, they signed to a major label and both the eponymous debut album and their debut single, 'Hold The Line', sold a million. Toto followed up with the more rock-sounding albums 'Hydra' (1979) and 'Turn Back' (1981), but their most successful release was 'Toto IV'.

It contained the hits 'Rosanna' (dedicated to the actress Rosanna Arquette), 'Make Believe' and 'Africa'. Written by Paich and Jeff Porcaro, this was the band's first major

UK success. Between them, 'Rosanna' and 'Africa' won Toto six 1983 Grammy Awards.

1984 brought upheavals in the band as both Hungate and Kimball departed. Their replacements were Mike Porcaro (born 1955) and Dennis Frederikson (born 1951). The next album 'Isolation', struggled to reach the US Top 50 and in 1985, Toto's soundtrack album from the science fiction movie, *Dune*, sold poorly. In that year, members of the group also worked on the backing tracks for the charity single, 'We Are The World'.

With new lead vocalist Joseph Williams, Toto returned to the chart in 1986 with 'I'll Be Over You', written by Lukather (born 1957) and Randy Goodrum. It came from 'Fahrenheit', the last album to feature Steve Porcaro, who returned to full-time session work.

Toto's seventh LP, logically titled 'The Seventh One', was produced by Little Feat's Bill Payne and Earth Wind & Fire producer George Massenburg. It provided a Top 30 hit with 'Pamela' in 1988.

Greatest Hits

Singles	Title	US	UK
1978	*Hold The Line*	5	14
1982	*Rosanna*	2	12
1983	*Africa*	1	3
Albums			
1978	*Toto*	9	37
1982	*Toto IV*	4	4

Pete Townshend – one of rock's good guys

Pete **TOWNSHEND**

An enigmatic and troubled spirit, Townshend was the creative force behind The Who, fashioning music with which fans could readily identify. As a solo artist on record, his work has tended towards the introspective while in public life he has always given freely of his time for charitable causes. In 1972 he released 'Who Came First' an album tribute to his then-guru Meher Baba which contained versions of songs from The Who's aborted 'Lifehouse' project. In 1973 he organized a comeback concert in London for Eric Clapton, then recovering from heroin addiction, which resulted in a live album. During 1977 with The Who dormant, he recorded an album with Ronnie Lane, 'Rough Mix', and in 1979 made charity appearances for Rock Against Racism. However, with the deaths of Who drummer Keith Moon (1978) and ex-manager Kit Lambert (1981), Townshend entered a drink-and-drugs-fuelled downward spiral. In the middle of this period he released the intensely personal 'Empty Glass' (1980), an excellent set of songs dedicated to his wife and daughters. During 1981/82, he underwent treatment, first for alcoholism, and then heroin addiction.

After his recovery, he devoted himself to campaigning against drug abuse, utilizing the already established Who charity the Double-O (as in the 'OO) to raise funds for drug projects and playing charity gigs with Deep End (including Pink Floyd's Dave Gilmour). Backed by Big Country's rhythm section, he released 'All The Best Cowboys Have Chinese Eyes' (1982) and appeared for Amnesty International. In 1983, he became an editorial consultant with the publishers Faber, who published his own book of poetry *Horse's Neck* (1985), and released an album of demos stretching back twenty years 'Scoop'. The ambitious album and video project 'White City' (1986), referring to a West London housing estate and intended as a reflection on personal roots, tended to self-indulgence and sold poorly. This was followed by more demo recordings on 'Another Scoop' (1987). Townshend released an adaptation of poet Ted Hughes' modern fairytale, *Iron Man*, using the voices of Nina Simone, John Lee Hooker and Roger Daltrey among others, in 1989, following which the reformed Who toured the US and Europe, with an army of supporting musicians.

Greatest Hits

Singles	Title	US	UK
1980	*Rough Boys*	–	39
1980	*Let My Love Open Your Door*	9	46
1985	*Face The Face*	26	–
Albums			
1980	*Empty Glass*	5	11
1982	*All The Best Cowboys Have Chinese Eyes*	26	32

TRAFFIC

Steve Winwood (*guitar, keyboards, bass, vocals*)
Dave Mason (*guitar, bass, vocals*)
Chris Wood (*woodwinds*)
Jim Capaldi (*drums, vocals*)

Just after breaking into the US Top 40, it was the misfortune of The Spencer Davis Group to lose the talented Winwood (born 1948) who had been performing and even recording with the other members-to-be of Traffic, Capaldi, Mason and Wood (all born in 1944), long before the band's official inception in 1967.

Traffic's initial image was of stoned hippies united in an isolated English cottage by a collaborative artistic ethos; taking their cue from Winwood *et al*, many other bands would also try 'getting it together in the country' in the late 1960s. With a sophistication which labelled it 'progressive' yet keeping a weather eye on the charts, Traffic's debut single, 'Paper Sun', rose to the UK Top 5. Before a calculated retreat from mainstream pop, the band had a Top 3 UK single with 'Hole In My Shoe'. This 'flower-power' anthem was composed and sung by Mason (like Capaldi and Wood, a veteran of various failed UK pop bands) whose disagreements with Winwood – who preferred creating musical moods through improvisation – caused his seemingly amicable resignation shortly after the release of the group's 'Mr. Fantasy' album later that year.

When the remaining three toured the US in 1968, the homespun spontaneity of 'Mr. Fantasy' degenerated into lengthy improvisations – albeit to thunderous ovations. Finding themselves short of new material for their eponymous second album (1968), Mason was invited to rejoin, only to leave them again after further ructions with Winwood, the related tension leading to Traffic's disbandment the following winter. While Wood and Capaldi drifted from project to unsatisfactory project – including a link-up with Mason – Winwood joined ex-Cream and Family members in Blind Faith but, after this 'supergroup' broke up in 1969, Capaldi and Wood were drawn into sessions for an intended Winwood solo effort. Instead, the resulting excellent 'John Barleycorn Must Die' was issued as a Traffic album (1970).

Bass player Rick Grech (ex-Family/Blind Faith), percussionist Reebop and drummer Jim Gordon (ex-Derek & The Dominoes) were recruited – initially to ease technical problems onstage and allow the extrovert Capaldi to leave his kit for duties nearer the footlights. The presence of Mason on 'Welcome To The Canteen', a 'live' album in 1971 did not indicate his permanent reinstatement or any hand later that year in Traffic's only million-seller, 'Low Spark of High-heeled Boys', following which Grech and Gordon were replaced by US sessionmen David Hood and Roger Hawk. The new members

Traffic jam sessions in country cottage set style for rural rehearsals

appeared on the follow-up, 'Shoot Out At The Fantasy Factory' (1973) which suffered from clumsy lyrics, long-winded soloing and dull melodies.

Extrapolations of this offering's five tracks were the core of the material on Traffic's subsequent world tour (with Barry Beckett on keyboards) and in-concert album 'On The Road'. By 1974, the band had shrunk to a more controllable four-piece of Winwood, Capaldi, Wood and bassist Rosko and the album, 'When The Eagle Flies', had many critics agreeing that Traffic had finally 'got it together'. Owing mainly to Winwood's disenchantment with life on the road, however, 'finally' was too real a word – because 'When The Eagle Flies' was Traffic's epitaph.

Until his death in 1983 Wood found sporadic employment as a session player while Mason and Capaldi enjoyed modestly successful solo careers. An established pop star before Traffic's formation, Winwood enjoyed infinitely more success but, as a well-received Traffic medley during his last tour demonstrated, his old band will always be part of him.

The TRAVELING WILBURYS

Bob Dylan
George Harrison
Jeff Lynne
Roy Orbison
Tom Petty (all vocals, guitars)

A bonus B-side for a 1988 European single from Harrison's 'Cloud 9' album led to the formation of The Traveling Wilburys after he and co-producer Lynne met to discuss it in a Los Angeles restaurant. After Orbison, another Lynne client, volunteered to sing on this extra track, Harrison called Dylan whose unsophisticated home studio in Santa Monica was available the next day.

From merely providing refreshments, Dylan lent a hand to what became 'Handle With Care'. With Petty pitching in too, the gathering was not intended as any permanent 'supergroup'. However, when Harrison presented the song to his record company, it was deemed too potentially commercial to be buried on a flip-side, and the notion of an entire album by the 'Handle With Care' quintet surfaced.

Most of the songwriting took place at the house of Eurythmic Dave Stewart, where the word 'wilbury' (referring to studio gremlins) entered the quintet's vocabulary. Masquerading as half-brothers all sired by a Charles Truscott Wilbury, each Traveling Wilbury was listed pseudonymously on the cover of 'Volume One'. Only ten days had been set aside for its taping owing to 'Lucky Wilbury' Dylan's forthcoming tour, but any lifting of this restriction might have detracted from the rough-and-ready spontaneity and endearing imperfections of the proceedings, which were close in execution to skiffle or rockabilly. Vocally, other than specific lead vocals by Orbison on 'Not Alone Any More' or Dylan for 'Tweeter And The Monkey Man', verses, harmonies *et al* were more or less doled out equally.

When 'Volume One' was completed, the personnel returned to individual projects, but, bound by the Wilbury 'brotherhood', each performed services for the others. Dylan, for example, wrote a contribution for the follow-up to Orbison's 'Mystery Girl' album, although it was never recorded owing to the ill-starred Orbison's death in December 1988.

Certain media folk speculated on who would be the new Wilbury but Orbison had not been replaced when the surviving members began rehearsing again in April 1990.

The Traveling Wilburys – middle-aged megastars form skiffle supergroup

The first public manifestation of these sessions was the 'Nobody's Child' charity single for Harrison's wife's Romanian Angel Appeal. Though more contrived than its predecessor, the misleadingly-titled second album, 'Volume Three' still sounded as if its creators (now using different names) had knockabout fun via 'She's My Baby, Inside Out' and all the rest on this escape valve from the straightforward expectations of fans of their respective solo records. Though the 'group' going on the road seems improbable, there have been plausible reports of 'The Traveling Ovaries' playing unannounced acoustic floor spots in and around Los Angeles.

Greatest Hits

Singles	Title	US	UK
1988	Handle With Care	45	21
1990	Nobody's Child	–	44
Albums			
1988	Volume One	3	16
1990	Volume Three	11	14

Troggs – Wild Things that never grow old

The **TROGGS**

Reg Presley (vocals)
Chris Britton (guitar)
Pete Staples (bass)
Ronnie Bond (drums)

Best remembered internationally as the popularizers of one of the all-time garage/punk band staples, 'Wild Thing', The Troggs were regular chartmakers for some three years in the 1960s, yet always seemed a somewhat schizophrenic proposition, combining a country bumpkin image with several hit songs open to salacious interpretation, which got them banned in some parts of the world.

Presley (born Reg Ball, 1943) and Bond (born 1943) were in the group's original 1964 incarnation as The Troglodytes, based in Andover, UK. Staples (born 1944) and Britton (born 1945) both replaced earlier members in 1965, when the group were signed by Kinks manager Larry Page, who saw potential in their very rawness. After a failed one-off single, they cut 'Wild Thing', a song by US writer Chip Taylor. Page had the group outrageously exaggerate the rhythm track, inserted an ear-catching ocarina solo, and told Ball to snarl the lyrics with maximum innuendo. The single was leased to a major UK label, and Ball's named was changed to Presley so that the music press would have something offbeat to hook into. All this, allied to quick TV exposure, paid off, as the single shot into the UK Top 3, and did even better in the US by topping the chart, despite a licensing rights dispute which saw it simultaneously released on two US labels.

The Presley-composed 'With A Girl Like You' followed, topping the UK chart, while the group's debut album, 'From Nowhere ... The Troggs', made the UK Top 10, and another Presley-penned single, 'I Can't Control Myself', reached the UK Top 3. This lyric, grunted lasciviously by the homely-faced Presley as usual, rather spoke for itself, and drew widespread radio bans in the US and Australia. The group continued strongly through 1968 with another Chip Taylor song, 'Any Way That You Want Me', the moronic chant, 'Give It To Me' (another radio no-no), and the gentle 'Love Is All Around'. The latter might have presaged a new musical direction, but the group missed the chance, fell from chart grace, and split in 1969.

Presley and Bond put a new Troggs together in the early 1970s to work the lucrative European club circuit, and got a lot of publicity over a bootleg studio tape which featured bumbled efforts to record a song, and increasing bad language as the session deteriorated. New singles and an album for Page's Penny Farthing label found few buyers, however.

More significant at this time was the group's apparent influence on newly-emerging punk bands, many of whom tackled

'Wild Thing', and cited the fragile musical abilities of The Troggs as a role model. Of such are cult bands made, and indeed The Troggs have always found live work (and occasional recordings, like their 1980 US deal to cut a live album at New York's Max's Kansas City club) on such cult appeal. The latter, plus nostalgia, has kept them active for club work and 1960s revival tours throughout the 1980s. Ronnie Bond scored an unlikely minor UK hit single in 1982 with 'It's Written On Your Body', but this like most latterday group activities, was a one-off occurrence.

Greatest Hits

Singles	Title	US	UK
1966	Wild Thing	1	2
1966	With A Girl Like You	29	1
1966	I Can't Control Myself	43	2
1968	Love Is All Around	7	5
Albums			
1966	From Nowhere ... The Troggs	–	6
1966	Wild Thing	52	–

IKE & TINA TURNER

For today's audiences the longtime title of one of R&B's most enduring duos may seem a real misnomer. In the 1980s, Tina Turner developed into one of the world's top performers, while her former Svengali and husband languished in jail.

It is a shame that Tina's spectacular career has now so overshadowed Ike's dramatically important pivotal role in the development of black music.

Ike Turner was born in Mississippi in 1931 and by the mid 1940s was working as a DJ while already proficient on piano and guitar, actually playing in the band of Sonny Boy Williamson in Arkansas. Around 1950 he formed The Kings Of Rhythm, primarily a dance band with featured vocalists, and the group travelled to Memphis, the nearest recording centre, to make a record at the famous Sun studios. 'Rocket 88', featuring singer Jackie Brenston, was leased to Chicago's Chess records, and became the biggest R&B hit of 1951 and is generally considered to be one of the first rock'n'roll records.

Sam Phillips, the owner of Sun, was impressed enough with the youthful Turner to offer him a position as talent scout and producer. Turner's later reputation as a hard nosed businessman began at this time, as he simultaneously provided the same services to other independent labels. Among the major blues talents that Ike either discovered or nurtured were Howlin' Wolf, Elmore James and B.B. King.

In the mid-1950s Turner was based in St Louis, where his Kings Of Rhythm were an established night club attraction. By this time, he was also a remarkable blues guitarist in the B.B. King mould, a talent sadly overlooked during the ensuing years both by himself and the new found audience for the blues genre.

In 1957, he was introduced to a would-be singer, Annie Mae Bullock (born 1938), during a performance, eventually marrying her and christening her Tina Turner when she fronted his band. Contrarily, her first recordings were billed as 'Little Ann'!

1960 saw the Turners signed to the New York based Sue Records, where they finally hit nationally with the gospel-based 'A Fool In Love' (1960) and 'It's Gonna Work Out Fine' (1961). With Tina's dynamic stage presence and stunning looks, Ike built a stage show around her that put them at the forefront of the emerging 'soul' boom. With comedians, support singers, dancers and The Ikettes (the review's back up singers), The Ike & Tina Turner Review, along with the similar shows of James Brown and Bobby Bland, were the hottest ticket on the black circuit in the early 1960s.

By now based in Los Angeles, the duo became idolized by influential voices amongst the British beat groups, notably The Animals and The Rolling Stones. After recording for numerous labels, these accolades resulted in their signing to Phil Spector's Philles label in 1966.

Spector only wanted Tina and although annoyed, Ike, seeing the commercial potential, accepted the situation. The resultant debut single, 'River Deep Mountain High', one of the greatest pop records ever made, was a commercial failure in America but did achieve Top 3 status in the UK, opening up a new market for the Turners.

They toured with The Rolling Stones in 1969 and finally ended their incessant label hopping by signing with Minit Records, a label soon to be swallowed by United Artists, where they remained for some years. Exposure to the rock market inspired Ike into covering rock hits, resulting in their biggest pop single, a cover of Creedence Clearwater's 'Proud Mary' (1974).

Throughout the marriage their relationship had been turbulent and Tina's 1980s biography *I, Tina*, graphically illustrates the abuse heaped upon her by Ike, who by 1973 was a serious cocaine addict.

In 1975, she left him and slowly began to assemble a solo career. Ken Russell cast her as 'The Acid Queen' in his movie of The Who's *Tommy*, which brought her international acclaim, but little in the way of record sales. By 1982, she was reduced to playing small clubs and the business convention market, until approached by British group, Heaven 17, to record a version of The Temptations hit 'Ball Of Confusion', with them.

In 1983, Heaven 17 members Martin Ware and Ian Craig Marsh produced her on a version of Al Green's 'Let's Stay Together' which became a major international hit. Her

Tina checks out Ike during 'Sixties TV soul spectacular

subsequent solo album, 'Private Dancer' (1984), became one of the biggest albums of the year thanks to the involvement of Mark Knopfler and David Bowie. The album has subsequently sold some 12 million copies around the world.

Major tours consolidated her stardom, and in 1986 she starred with Mel Gibson in the third *Mad Max* movie, *Beyond Thunderdome*. Her album of the same year. 'Break Every Rule', was another multi-million seller featuring guest artists Phil Collins and Steve Winwood.

'Foreign Affair' (1989) showed no sign of slowing the momentum. Ike Turner was imprisoned in 1988 for cocaine trafficking, but he continues to monitor the career of the star who, in most senses of the word, he created. In 1990, he announced that he was to sue Tina for the illegal use of a trademark he owned – Tina Turner. No one seemed particularly worried.

Greatest Hits

IKE & TINA TURNER

Singles	Title	US	UK
1966	River Deep Mountain High	88	3
1971	Proud Mary	4	–
1973	Nutbush City Limits	22	4
Albums			
1966	River Deep Mountain High	102	27
1971	What You Hear Is What You Get	25	–

TINA TURNER

Singles		US	UK
1983	Let's Stay Together	26	6
1984	What's Love Got To Do With It	1	3
1984	Better Be Good To Me	5	45
1985	We Don't Need Another Hero (Thunderdome)	2	3
1986	Typical Male	2	33
Albums			
1984	Private Dancer	3	2
1986	Break Every Rule	4	2
1989	Foreign Affair	31	1

Bogus Brits, the Crossfires, enter charts as retitled Turtles

The **TURTLES / FLO & EDDIE**

Howard Kaylan (vocals)
Mark Volman (vocals)
Al Nichol (guitar)
Jim Tucker (guitar)
Chuck Portz (bass)
Dale Walton (rhythm)
Don Murray (drums)

The Turtles had their origins in a Westchester (a Los Angeles suburb) surf band, The Crossfires. Prime movers were Howard Kaylan (née Kaplan) and Mark Volman (both born 1947). By late 1964, The Beatles had arrived and The Crossfires responded by growing their hair, ditching the saxes and pretending to be English. With no commercial success, the band nearly broke up until they were saved by the unknown White Whale record label. The group instantly decided on a name change to The Turtles and declared they were a folk-rock band (à la The Byrds). Their version of Bob Dylan's 'It Ain't Me Babe' became a US Top 10 hit within weeks of the name change, and they assumed they had cracked it. Unfortunately, the follow-up 'Let Me Be' (written by P.F. Sloan), only reached the US Top 30, at which point they ditched folk/protest for harmony-pop and recorded the excellent 'You Baby', which fared better, but only reached the US Top 20. They were going nowhere fast, until they hit on 'Happy Together' which topped the US chart and gave them their first UK Top 20 hit.

It also became the title track of their only hit album, the previous two, 'It Ain't Me Babe' (1965) and 'You Baby' (1966), had missed completely. A quick follow-up to 'Happy Together' in the same vein, 'She'd Rather Be With Me' went Top 10 on both sides of the Atlantic, but it was followed by another dry spell (although the excellent 'She's My Girl' reached the US Top 20 in 1967). Ironically, The Turtles were at their best – on stage at least. Johnny Barbata (later with CS&N and Jefferson Starship) came in

on drums and Jim Pons (ex-Leaves) was now playing bass. Nor were the band that bothered about singles, however under pressure from their label to come up with another 'Happy Together', they produced 'Elenore' in late 1968. It was another Top 10 hit, but a cursory examination reveals it as a joke.

Several more (excellent) singles followed, but were failures. In late 1968, however, they produced their best album - 'Battle Of The Bands', a marvelous parody in which all the tracks were in different styles and supposedly by different bands. The cover showed The Turtles posing as the different groups.

Ray Davies of The Kinks produced their last (released) album, 'Turtle Soup' (1969), but despite some good songs, it was rather messy. The group, by then, were going through legal traumas with their record company and manager and finally fell apart in mid-1970. Robbed not only of the group name, Volman and Kaylan were also, temporarily, forbidden to record under their own names and so they became 'The Phlorescent Leech & Eddie', in due course shortened to Flo & Eddie.

They initially found a home with The Mothers Of Invention (Frank Zappa's satire was not much more extreme than that of Volman and Kaylan) and between 1970 and 1972 appeared on the albums, 'Chunga's Revenge', 'Live At The Fillmore East' and 'Just Another Band From LA', as well as appearing in Zappa's *200 Motels* movie. After The Mothers broke up, Flo & Eddie went solo and over the next four years produced four remarkable albums 'The Phlorescent Leech & Eddie' (1972), 'Flo & Eddie' (1973), 'Illegal, Immoral And Fattening' (1975) and 'Moving Targets' (1976). Despite a big following, their bizarre mixture of satire, humour, parodies and straight Turtles-style pop was too much for most people. After 1976, Flo & Eddie kept a lower profile; they have had their own radio show, produced an X-rated cartoon ('Dirty Duck'), sung back-up and produced countless records. They did record one further album (bizarre even for

them) – a reggae album, recorded in Jamaica, entitled 'Rock Steady With Flo & Eddie' (1981). They seem to have spent a great deal of time since then working on reissues of their old material.

Greatest Hits

Singles	Title	US	UK
1965	It Ain't Me Babe	8	–
1967	Happy Together	1	12
1967	She'd Rather Be With Me	3	4
1968	Elenore	6	7
1969	You Showed Me	6	–
Albums			
1967	Happy Together	25	18
1967	Golden Hits	7	–

U2

Bono (vocals)
The Edge (guitar)
Adam Clayton (bass)
Larry Mullen (drums)

The last great stadium rock band of the 1980s, U2 rose inexorably through the decade, crusading on a self-generated tide of passion that was impossible to deny.

Bono (born Paul Hewson, 1960), The Edge (born David Evans, 1961), Clayton (born 1960) and Mullen (born 1961) came together as Dublin schoolboys in 1976, first as Feedback, playing Rolling Stones and Beach Boys covers, then as The Hype after they saw The Clash, and then as U2.

Winning a talent contest brought them an audition for Irish CBS, who signed them, and their first EP, 'U2:3', topped the Irish charts in 1979, but CBS in the UK passed on that and its follow-up, 'As Another Day', in 1980. The band signed with Island but three further singles, including 'I Will Follow', failed to chart in the UK. However, the band had amassed a live following, and the adolescent angst of their debut album, 'Boy', produced by Steve Lillywhite at the end of 1980, brought critical acclaim and steadily growing sales through 1981 as they kept up the touring pressure. 1981's 'Fire' single made the UK Top 40, and although 'Gloria' stalled outside the UK Top 50, their second album, 'October' (1981), again produced by Lillywhite, almost reached the UK Top 10.

After another tour and a UK Top 50 single with 'A Celebration', the band spent the rest of 1982 in the studio, emerging in 1983 with a UK Top 10 single, 'New Year's Day', followed by the third Lillywhite-produced album, 'War', which immediately entered the

UK chart at No. 1, and also went platinum to become their first US Top 20 album, as the band toured. By this time, Bono's lyrics had taken on a new zeal and passion with songs like 'Sunday Bloody Sunday' and 'New Year's Day', their first UK Top 10 single. A live album, 'Under A Blood Red Sky', reached the UK Top 3 and US Top 30 at the end of 1983, and the spin-off concert video gave the band a breathing space to prepare their next move in Dublin.

In late 1984, they returned from this lay-off with 'The Unforgettable Fire', an album produced by Brian Eno & Daniel Lanois, who brought a more grandiose resonance to their sound. The album stormed to the top of the UK charts and made the US Top 20. More arena tours of the US followed and U2 were in fine fettle for their appearance at Live Aid in London in 1985, after which their world-wide album sales rocketed. In the US, they even made the Top 40 of the US album chart with a four-track EP, 'Wide Awake In America', for one week before the mistake was realized. Bono also participated in Miami Steve Van Zandt's anti-apartheid project, Sun City, and in 1986, the band played the US leg of the Amnesty International Conspiracy Of Hope tour with Peter Gabriel, Lou Reed, Sting, etc., and also the Dublin Self Aid benefit for the Irish unemployed, before recording their next album. The Edge also cut a soundtrack album, 'The Captive', with Sinead O'Connor.

'The Joshua Tree', released in 1987 and again produced by Eno & Lanois, spent nine weeks at the top of the US album chart and sold 250,000 copies in two days in the UK, where it also topped the chart. U2 then embarked on a 110-date world arena tour, during which they also organized ad hoc events like playing live on the streets of San Francisco and recording at Memphis's Sun Studios to maintain interest and momentum, and to provide footage for the movie, *U2 Rattle & Hum*. Meanwhile, 'Within Or Without You' was their first US chart-topping single, and its position was equalled only weeks later by 'I Still Haven't Found What I'm Looking For'.

In 1988, the band's achievements were recognized when they won Grammy Awards for Best Album and Best Rock Vocal Group, while Bono and The Edge contributed to Roy Orbison's comeback album, 'Mystery Girl', before U2's 'Rattle & Hum' soundtrack album put them instantly back on top of the US and UK album charts. They also topped the UK singles chart with 'Desire', and scored hits with 'Angel Of Harlem' and 'When Love Comes To Town', with B.B. King. Most of 1989 was spent resting, but they saw in the 1990s with a hometown concert broadcast live across Western and newly-liberated Eastern Europe. Their only 1990 release was a version of Cole Porter's 'Night And Day', on the AIDS benefit album, 'Red Hot & Blue'. A new album is eagerly awaited in late 1991.

Stadium superstars in the US, U2's success sparked off a rock renaissance in their native Dublin

Greatest Hits

Singles	Title	US	UK
1987	With Or Without You	1	4
1987	I Still Haven't Found What I'm Looking For	1	6
1988	Desire	3	1
Albums			
1983	War	12	1
1984	The Unforgettable Fire	12	1
1987	The Joshua Tree	1	1
1988	Rattle & Hum	1	1

UB40

Ali Campbell (vocals, guitar)
Rob Campbell (guitar, vocals)
Earl Falconer (bass)
Brian Travers (saxophone)
Mickey Virtue (keyboards)
Astro (Terence Wilson) (vocals, toaster)
Norman Hassan (percussion)
Jim Brown (drums)

A Birmingham (UK) based multi-racial reggae group which includes Ali (born 1959) and Rob Campbell (born 1954), sons of folk star Ian Campbell, UB40 were named after the number on the British unemployment benefit form. They signed to a local label in 1979 and their first release 'King'/ 'Food For Thought' hit the UK Top 10 in 1980 as did two other double-sided hits and their debut album 'Signing Off'.

They formed their own label in 1982 and made the UK Top 3 with the album 'Present Arms' (a dub version of which made the UK

Top 40 later that year) while the single 'One In Ten' reached the UK Top 10. Their album 'UB44' gave them another Top 3 UK hit in 1982 and a year later they reached No. 1 in the UK with Neil Diamond's 'Red Red Wine' (Top 40 US) and the album on which it was included, 'Labour Of Love'. They had four more UK Top 20 singles and a UK Top 3 album, 'Geffrey Morgan', before their 1985 revival of 'I Got You Babe', featuring Chrissie Hynde, made No. 1 in the UK and gave them their second US Top 40 entry.

Their string of UK hit singles continued and 'Baggaraddim' (1985) 'Rat In The Kitchen', (1986) their 'Best Of' album (1987) and 'UB40' (1988) kept their name in the Top 20 albums chart. Extraordinarily in 1988 their old UK No. 1, 'Red Red Wine', shot to the top in the US and the album, 'Labour of Love', also made the US Top 20. In 1989 the group, who are not afraid of putting across political messages through their music, had their second US gold and 11th UK Top 20 album with a second volume of reggae covers, 'Labour of Love II'. In 1990 a single with Robert Palmer, a cover of Bob Dylan's 'I'll Be Your Baby Tonight', gave them their 19th UK Top 20 single and they returned to the US Top 20 with 'The Way You Do The Things You Do'.

Greatest Hits

Singles	Title	US	UK
1983	Red Red Wine	34	1
1985	I Got You Babe	28	1
Albums			
1983	Labour of Love	14	1
1989	Labour of Love II	49	1

UB 40 – doling out the hits on both sides of the Atlantic

ULTRAVOX

John Foxx (vocals, guitar)
Billy Currie (violin, keyboards)
Chris Cross (bass)
Warren Cann (drums)

The career of Ultravox can be separated into two distinct parts: before 1980 (with John Foxx as frontman) commercially barren, but artistically challenging, and from 1980 (with Midge Ure) infinitely more successful, but rather unexciting.

Inspired by Roxy Music, John Foxx (born Dennis Leigh) formed Tiger Lily with Cross (born Chris St. John, 1952), Cann (born 1952 in Canada) and Currie (born 1952) in 1973. After cutting a version of Fats Waller's 'Ain't Misbehavin'' for the soundtrack of an art movie, the band underwent several name changes, finally settling on Ultravox. After signing to Island in 1976, their eponymous debut album, with the group augmented by Steve Shears (guitar), was produced by Brian Eno in 1975. It was well received without charting and Shears also played on a second 1977 album, 'Ha! Ha! Ha!', which was no more successful. By 1978's 'Systems of Romance', produced by Conny Plank at his German studio, Shears had been replaced by Robin Simon (guitar), but the album provoked a similar lack of chart success. Ultravox were undoubtedly an influence on both the electro-pop and New Romantic movements, but after it became clear that conflict with their label was imminent in 1979, Foxx left for a solo career, releasing such albums as

'Metamantic' (1980), 'The Garden' (1981), 'The Golden Section' (1983) and 'In Mysterious Ways' (1985), while Simon also departed.

Curiously, both the group and their ex-vocalist became heavily involved with synthesizers, ultimately sometimes to the exclusion of all other instruments – later group albums featured everyone playing synthesizers. The remaining trio recruited singer/ guitarist Midge Ure (born James Ure, 1954), who had previously played in chart-topping Glaswegian teenybop band Slik, and then The Rich Kids with ex-Sex Pistol Glen Matlock. It seemed an unlikely marriage, but with Plank again at the controls, they developed a more symphonic sound with the electronic instruments which was precisely right for the UK market, and quickly signed a new record deal. Their 1980 album, 'Vienna', made the UK Top 3, as did the brooding, dramatic title track as a single, and 'All Stood Still' made the UK Top 10. 1981's 'Rage In Eden' album made the UK Top 5 and included a couple of UK Top 20 hits, after which George Martin produced 'Quartet', which made the UK Top 10 and included two more hit singles. But it seemed that there was little progression with each new release, and this may have been one reason why the US resolutely refused to respond to Ultravox's releases, despite several tours.

Ure's 1982 solo single 'No Regrets' made the UK Top 10 before Ultravox returned with a live album, 'Monument', in 1983 and 1984's 'Lament', while later that year, a retrospective singles album, 'The Collection', which included their final UK Top 3 single, 'Dancing With Tears In My Eyes', made the UK Top 3; but US approval was no nearer. Not even Ure's major involvement in the Band Aid single, 'Do They Know It's Christmas?' (which he co-wrote), and 1985's Live Aid concert (which he helped to organize) could provoke interest in the US. By the time the 'U-Vox' album was released in 1986 and made the UK Top 10, Ure had already topped the UK chart with a solo single, 'If I Was', from his album 'The Gift', which reached the UK Top 2. The other members

Ultravox – synthesised stylists with electronic pop for the 'Eighties

of the band had each worked on other projects to little commercial avail (apart from Currie, who participated with Ure in the brief success of Visage), and Ultravox broke up soon afterwards with little ceremony, and Ure continued his solo career in 1988 with the 'Answers To Nothing' album.

Greatest Hits

Singles	Title	US	UK
1980	*Vienna*	–	2
1984	*Dancing With Tears In My Eyes*	–	3
1985	*If I Was* (Midge Ure solo)	–	1
Albums			
1980	*Vienna*	164	3
1981	*Rage In Eden*	144	4
1984	*The Collection*	–	2
1985	*The Gift* (Midge Ure solo)	–	2

Ritchie **VALENS**

Until 1987's *La Bamba* bio-pic and the million-selling version of its title song by Los Lobos, Valens (born Richard Stephen Valenzuela, 1941) was remembered by the general public only as dying in the same air crash as Buddy Holly. However, prior to that fatal journey in 1959, Holly was seen in the US as rather a has-been, and Valens the up-and-coming star. He tested the path for later Mexican/Californian (or 'Chicano') stars like Chan Romero, Trini Lopez, Chris Montez and Cannibal & The Headhunters. Of Mexican/Red Indian stock, Valens played guitar from an early age. Though influenced by black vocal groups, he was a greater admirer of the more clamorous Little Richard, which was evident when he sang with The Silhouettes (not the 'Get A Job' hitmakers) at Pacoima High School, Los Angeles. As the outfit's main 'personality', Valenzuela was noticed by a local talent scout for whom he shortened his surname and cut a debut single, the self-penned 'Come On Let's Go', in 1958.

It was covered by Tommy Steele in the UK, but the original hovered around the middle of the US Hot 100, thanks largely to handsome Valens plugging it on TV. Even more successful was the follow-up, 'Donna', which, as well as the expected UK heist (by Marty Wilde), elicited an obscure 'answer' disc in The Kittens' 'A Letter To Donna', but its throwaway B-side – an updated Spanish wedding song – gave Valens pop immortality. A hit in its own right, 'La Bamba' with its three-chord arrangement was deified later as nascent punk.

Shortly after he had cajoled guitarist

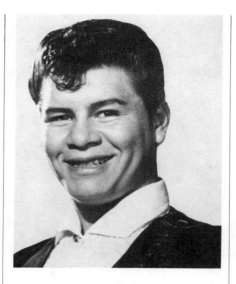

Ritchie Valens, revived via La Bamba

Tommy Allsup into giving up his seat on that wintry flight from Iowa, he was billed as 'the late Ritchie Valens' for his only film appearance (miming 'Ooh My Head', derived from Little Richard's 'Ooh! My Soul', in the Jimmy Clanton movie, *Go Johnny Go*. Before they had even wiped away the tears, Valens's record company had released 'That's My Little Suzie', and were sifting through a mastered output of 30 tracks (including 'Fast Freight', a Valens instrumental issued in 1958 under the pseudonym 'Arvee Allen'). Permutations of his few hits and tracks from 1960's posthumous 'Ritchie' album are still repackaged but more reverential were the host of continuing revivals of Valens numbers by acts as diverse as The McCoys, Neil Diamond, Cliff Richard, Gary Glitter, Shirley Bassey and, with 'Come On Let's Go' in 1979's *Rock'n'Roll High School* flick, The Paley Brothers & The Ramones.

Greatest Hits

Singles	Title	US	UK
1958	*Come On Let's Go*	42	–
1959	*Donna/La Bamba*	2	29
Albums			
1959	*Ritchie Valens*	23	–

VAN HALEN

David Lee Roth (*vocals*)
Eddie Van Halen (*guitar*)
Michael Anthony (*bass*)
Alex Van Halen (*drums*)

The dominant US heavy metal band of the first half of the 1980s, Van Halen reigned with a flamboyant sense of outrage and excess, managing to survive frontman Roth's departure with a more tempered style.

The nucleus of the band formed in Pasadena, California, in 1973 when the medically diagnosed hyperactive David Lee Roth (born 1955) linked up with the Van Halen brothers, Alex (born 1955) and Eddie (born 1957), to form Mammoth. They became Van Halen after linking up with Michael Anthony (born 1955) a year later and soon gained a reputation as the loudest band in Los Angeles where they became favourites at the Starwood Club. A 1976 demo produced by Gene Simmons of Kiss was rejected by every label they approached but they carried on undaunted, writing more songs while Roth developed his energetic stage act to new extremes. In 1977, they were seen by noted producer Ted Templeman, who got them a record deal and produced their eponymous first album. Released in 1978, it was a remarkably assured debut that amassed two million sales in a year while peaking only just inside the US Top 20. They also had a US Top 40 single with a cover of The Kinks hit, 'You Really Got Me', as they toured the US and Roth's antics received growing media attention. A tour of Britain also pushed their album into the UK Top 40.

Still undaunted they recorded the follow-up album, 'Van Halen II', in a week. It sold five million in 1979, reaching the US Top 10 and included a US Top 20 single, 'Dance The Night Away'. They took their increasingly wild on- and off-stage behaviour on a ten-month world tour and repeated the whole process in 1980 after their next platinum album, 'Women & Children'. The roll continued through 1981 and 1982 as 'Fair Warning' became their third US Top 10 album, and 'Diver Down' did even better, reaching the US Top 3. The band's horizons expanded further in 1983 with a South American tour and Eddie Van Halen set new standards in rock guitar solos on Michael Jackson's 'Beat It'. Ironically, Van Halen's next album, '1984', was kept from the top of the US album chart by Jackson's 'Thriller', but the quartet had the consolation of a US chart-topping single for five weeks running with 'Jump' (which was "hyped" into the UK Top 10, and their label fined as a result).

By now, Roth was growing apart from the rest of the band and after a US Top 3 solo single with a cover of The Beach Boys oldie, 'California Girls', another US Top 20 single with 'Just A Gigolo'/'I Ain't Got Nobody' and a US Top 20 album, 'Crazy From The Heat', he confirmed his departure from Van Halen. Ignoring record company advice to change their name, the others carried on, surprising everyone by recruiting Sammy Hagar, who had first come to prominence back in 1973 with Montrose, before pursuing a solo career that included US hit singles in the early 1980s with 'Your Love Is Driving Me Crazy' and 'I Can't Drive 55'. Van Halen returned with a vengeance, topping the US chart and reaching the UK Top 20 with 1986's '5150' album and making the US Top 3 and UK

Top 10 with a single, 'Why Can't This Be Love'.

Meanwhile, Roth continued with more cover versions for his 'Eat 'Em & Smile' album, which made the US Top 5 in 1986 and yielded a US Top 20 single, 'Yankee Rose', and he released a third album, the US Top 10 and UK Top 20 hit 'Skyscraper', before Van Halen returned from a two-year lay-off in 1988 with 'OU812', which restored them to the top of the US album chart. Hagar had also maintained his solo career with an eponymous US Top 20 album in 1987, and Roth was back again early in 1991 with his fourth solo album, 'A Little Ain't Enough', which even featured the occasional metal track.

Greatest Hits

Singles	Title	US	UK
1984	Jump	1	7
1985	California Girls		
	(David Lee Roth)	3	68
1986	Why Can't This Be Love	3	8
1988	When It's Love	5	28
Albums			
1981	Fair Warning	5	49
1982	Diver Down	3	36
1984	1984	2	15
1986	5150	1	16
1986	Eat 'Em And Smile		
	(David Lee Roth)	4	28
1988	OU812	1	16

Luther VANDROSS

US soul superstar Vandross (born 1951) formed his first group, Listen My Brother in the early 1970s with guitarist Carlos Alomar and singer Robin Clark. The group split up, but when Alomar began working with David Bowie on his highly successful 'Young Americans' album (1975) he brought Vandross and Clark in on the sessions, Luther working on vocal arrangements as well as singing. Subsequently Vandross toured with Bowie on his 1975 US dates, also opening the show with his own act. The singer/writer/producer debuted on the R&B singles chart as leader of short-lived vocal group Luther in 1976, following which he earned a living singing jingles for commercials, before returning to work as a backing vocalist in 1978/9 with Quincy Jones, Chic, Sister Sledge and Donna Summer. He earned his first US gold disc in 1980 as lead vocalist of Change on their 'The Glow Of Love' album which included the UK Top 20 hits 'A Lover's Holiday' and 'Searching'.

Vandross's first solo album, 'Never Too Much', in 1981 hit the US Top 20, and its title track became a No. 1 R&B hit. In 1982 he produced Aretha Franklin's successful 'Jump To It' album and his own album

'Forever, For Always, For Love' went platinum. 'Busy Body', his 1984 album, gave him his UK album chart debut. He had UK and US Top 20 albums in 1985 with the Grammy-nominated 'The Night I Fell In Love' and in 1986 with 'Give Me The Reason', the latter selling nearly a million copies in the UK. An in-demand session vocalist and producer, Vandross worked with Chaka Khan, Dionne Warwick, Carly Simon and The Average White Band during this period. 'I Really Didn't Mean It' and 'Stop To Love' were Top 30 singles for him in 1987, and in 1988 his sixth No. 1 R&B album, 'Any Love', became his first Top 10 album in the UK and US. A re-mix of 'Never Too Much' gave him his biggest UK hit in 1989 and his 'Best Of' album returned him to the UK Top 20 and became his seventh successive platinum album in the US. Despite huge album sales over the years on both sides of the Atlantic it took Vandross until 1990 to have a US Top 10 single, which he did with 'Here And Now'.

Greatest Hits

Singles	Title	US	UK
1981	Never Too Much	33	13
1990	Here And Now	6	43
Albums			
1986	Give Me The Reason	14	3
1988	Any Love	9	3

Luther Vandross – hits from the early 'Eighties to Here And Now

VANILLA FUDGE

Mark Stein (vocals, organ)
Vinnie Martell (guitar)
Tim Bogert (bass)
Carmine Appice (drums)

Vanilla Fudge was a New York group who rode the mid-1960s US wave of psychedelic progressive rock dominated by West Coast bands. Their speciality – a familiar cover version as a slowed-down, stretched-out, hard rock melodrama – ensured them a key niche in a scene generally dominated by a more frenzied instrumental approach.

The group was formed in 1966 by Stein (born 1947) and Bogert (born 1944), originally as The Pigeons. When Martell (born 1945) and Appice (born 1946) replaced earlier members, the group name was changed to Vanilla Fudge. Their mid-1967 debut album teamed them with producer George 'Shadow' Morton, best known for his 1964 work with the Shangri-Las. A revival of 'You Keep Me Hangin' On' (previously a Supremes hit), which widely established the key elements of their style, was a hit single on both sides of the Atlantic, and the group's eponymous debut album charted equally strongly in its wake. It included two covers of Beatles songs, and a revamp of the R&B number, 'Take Me For A Little While', which was another US Top 40 hit when issued as a single.

324

Seminal psycho-heavies Vanilla Fudge, masterminded by Shangri-Las' Shadow Morton

1968 saw two more Vanilla Fudge albums, 'The Beat Goes On' and 'Renaissance'. Both were US Top 20 hits, but by the end of the year, the group's essentially unchanged formula was sounding tired, and they were being accused of pretentiousness, largely on account of 'The Beat Goes On', which offered a summary of world and musical history in rock suite form.

1969 delivered another pair of albums, the half-live, half-studio 'Near The Beginning' and 'Rock & Roll', but it was also a year during which internal disagreements began to pull the band apart, and they eventually split in 1970. Bogert and Appice stayed together to form Cactus, and then linked with UK guitarist Jeff Beck as BB&A ('Beck, Bogert & Appice'). Stein and Martell kept a lower profile until the early 1980s, when the original Vanilla Fudge regrouped to cut the unsuccessful 'Mystery' album before disbanding again.

A more recent one-off reunion saw them play at the Atlantic Records Madison Square Garden 40th Anniversary concert in 1988.

Greatest Hits

Singles	Title	US	UK
1967	*You Keep Me Hangin' On*	6	18
Albums			
1967	*Vanilla Fudge*	6	31

Stevie Ray **VAUGHAN**

Tragically killed in a helicopter accident on his way between concerts with Eric Clapton in 1990, Stevie Ray Vaughan (born 1956) was a much-respected blues session player carving a name for himself in his own right.

The brother of Jimmy Vaughan (lead guitarist with The Fabulous Thunderbirds), Texan Stevie was a precocious child musician, playing with a group called the Chantones at the age of eight! After having performed with various high-school and teen groups, he formed the trio Triple Threat Revue in the late 1970s. They were followed by Double Trouble, a guitar, bass and drums band which reflected Vaughan's musical influences, through B.B. King to Cream, and included Johnny Winter's former bass player,

Tommy Shannon.

Vaughan came to the attention of Jackson Browne, who arranged studio time for him; a burgeoning reputation led to an appearance at the prestigious Montreux Jazz Festival in Switzerland in 1982, where he was discovered by seminal CBS talent-spotter and producer John Hammond (whose track record stretched from Bessie Smith through Billie Holiday to Bob Dylan).

Hammond produced Vaughan's 'Texas Flood' album in 1983, and as a result big name sessions began to follow, including work on David Bowie's 'Let's Dance'. A second Hammond-produced album, 'Couldn't Stand The Weather', in 1984 set the stamp on an eclectic blues repertoire that included Hendrix, Willie Dixon and Vaughan's own originals. The album went gold, as did the 1987 Double Trouble offering 'Soul To Soul'.

His most applauded work appeared in 1986 on the live double album, 'Live Alive', which triggered more big-name collaborations with blues legends Johnny Copeland, Lonnie Mack (whom he produced) and Albert King.

His 1989 album, 'In Step', marked a widening recognition, going into the UK Top 100, and his inclusion in the 1990 Clapton shows was confirmation of his status as a 'musician's musician'. His most tragic and untimely death has left a large gap in contemporary blues which will not be easy to fill.

Greatest Hits

Albums	Title	US	UK
1984	*Couldn't Stand The Weather*	31	—
1985	*Soul To Soul*	34	—
1989	*In Step*	33	63

Stevie Ray – will be much missed as a 'musicians musician'

Bobby **VEE**

In many ways the epitome of the good-looking teenbeat singer whose genre dominated US pop between 1959 and the advent of The Beatles, Bobby Vee (born Robert Velline, 1943) had the twin advantages of firm rock'n'roll roots, and access to material from the best teen-oriented songwriters of the day. These assets helped him maintain a commercially successful career for far longer than most of his contemporaries.

Vee and his group, The Shadows, formed in high school in Fargo, North Dakota. Strongly influenced by Buddy Holly & The Crickets, they ironically got their first break when they appeared as local stand-ins on the 1959 Winter Dance Party package tour's Fargo date – the bill was light following the plane crash deaths of Holly, Ritchie Valens and the Big Bopper the night before. That summer, the group made a self-financed single of Vee's song, 'Suzie Baby'. Released regionally, it attracted the attention of LA-based Liberty Records, who reissued it and it made the US Top 100.

Liberty signed the group (which had just dumped temporary pianist 'Elston Gunn' – later Bob Dylan), but producer Snuff Garrett concentrated on Vee as a soloist, and by the end of 1960, he had a US Top 10 hit with a revival of a hit by The Clovers, 'Devil Or Angel'. With this success, when Vee's face began to adorn the teen mags, a commercial ball began to roll, and Garrett could cherry-pick songs from New York's Brill Building songwriters and others. 1961 saw Vee score major international hits with Gene Pitney's 'Rubber Ball', 'More Than I Can Say' (by Sonny Curtis of The Crickets), and two Goffin/King songs, 'How Many Tears' and 'Take Good Care Of My Baby'. The first and last of these were million sellers, and the latter was his most successful record, a chart-topper on both sides of the Atlantic.

Further hits followed in 1962/63, including two more million sellers in 'Run To Him' and 'The Night Has A Thousand Eyes', while Vee also made his most successful album, a collaboration with The Crickets, whose presence dovetailed well with Vee's always Holly-influenced vocals. Vee's chart successes wilted under the 'British Invasion', although he eagerly embraced the UK beat sound on his own records for a while. He then made an impressive comeback in 1967, in a folkier style, with 'Come Back When You Grow Up', another million seller. A two-year run of similarly more mature hits followed, and in 1972, Vee made a real attempt to ditch his teenybop past with an introspective country/rock album, 'Nothing Like A Sunny Day', billed under his real name of Robert Thomas Velline.

The 1970s singer-songwriter path was not to be Vee's, however, and with chart success a thing of the past, he found a busy career on the oldies/nostalgia circuit, touring both the

US and overseas with many of his early 1960s contemporaries. He made several well-received UK visits during the 1980s, and the durability of his old hits was shown in 1980 by 'The Bobby Vee Singles Album', a compilation which reached the UK Top 5.

Greatest Hits

Singles	Title	US	UK
1961	*Take Good Care Of My Baby*	1	1
1963	*The Night Has A Thousand Eyes*	3	3
Albums			
1962	*Bobby Vee Meets The Crickets*	42	2
1980	*The Bobby Vee Singles Album*	–	5

Suzanne **VEGA**

Part of the US folk revival in the late 1980s, the shy, introverted Suzanne Vega grew up in Manhattan and attended the High School of Performing Arts (later immortalized in *Fame*) in 1975, studying dance and songwriting. She started playing in folk clubs in 1977 and an accidental attendance at a Lou Reed concert had an invigorating effect on her style, but she remained unfashionable until 1984, when a glowing *New York Times* review encouraged record companies to visit Folk City for the first time in years.

After signing to A&M, her eponymous debut album was released in 1985, produced by former Patti Smith guitarist Lenny Kaye. It reached the US Top 100, but her lyrical imagery and gently amplified folk style found a more enthusiastic response in the UK,

Vega – lyrical vocals

where the album reached the Top 20 and 'Marlene On The Wall' was a Top 30 single, and she was able to sell out London's Royal Albert Hall twice at the end of 1986. She had more UK success that year with the Top 40 single, 'Left Of Center', which was used in the film, *Pretty In Pink*, and she wrote two songs for the Philip Glass album, 'Songs From Liquid Days'.

Her next single, 'Luka', made the UK Top 30 early in 1987 and suddenly took off in America, eventually peaking in the Top 3. Her second album, 'Solitude Standing', was an international hit, reaching the UK Top 3 and US Top 20, as she toured the world for a year, including a prestigious stint at New York's Carnegie Hall. Later in 1988 she contributed the title track to the Disney compilation, 'Stay Awake', and returned with her third album, 'Days Of Open Hand', in 1990, which broadened her style and reached the UK Top 10. She undertook another world tour, but the lack of a hit single hampered her profile, until she scored an unlikely hit at the end of 1990 when mysterious UK dance remix team, DNA, put a heavy beat behind her acapella 'Tom's Diner' from the 'Solitude Standing' album. Originally unauthorized, the single was legitimized by A&M and made the UK Top 3 and US Top 10. Ms Vega was reportedly nonplussed by her sudden crossover appeal.

Greatest Hits

Singles	Title	US	UK
1987	*Luka*	3	23
1990	*Tom's Diner* (DNA remix)	7	2
Albums			
1987	*Solitude Standing*	11	2

The **VELVET UNDERGROUND**

Lou Reed (guitar, vocals)
John Cale (bass, keyboards, viola)
Sterling Morrison (guitar)
Angus MacLise (drums)

Despite the brevity of their career, The Velvet Underground remain a major influence on rock music some 20 years after their demise. Formed in 1965 by New Yorker Reed and Welsh exile Cale (see separate entries), the band was completed by Reed's former university friend Morrison (born 1942) and former La Monte Young sideman MacLise. Initially known as The Warlocks (a name also used by the early Grateful Dead), they became The Falling Spikes before renaming themselves The Velvet Underground, after a novel by Michael Leigh.

Reed was the main songwriter, and his themes were unique for 'pop' music at the time, covering such taboo subjects as sado-masochism, paranoia and heroin addiction.

After recording basic demos and playing gigs around New York, MacLise (who died in 1979) left, being replaced by Maureen 'Mo' Tucker, sister of a friend of Reed. The band came to the attention of pop artist Andy Warhol, then at the height of his notoriety, who introduced them to German chanteuse Nico (born Christa Paffgen c 1940). Nico had appeared in the Fellini film *La Dolce Vita* (1961) and released one single in the UK, becoming involved with Rolling Stone Brian Jones, Bob Dylan and eventually Warhol's 'Factory' group of actors/performers/filmmakers in 1965/66. At Warhol's instigation, the band teamed up with Nico in 1966, when they toured as part of Warhol's *Exploding Plastic Inevitable* multi-media event, and released their first album, 'The Velvet Underground & Nico Produced By Andy Warhol' in 1967. Despite intense critical interest and subsequent much-covered songs such as 'I'm Waiting For The Man' and 'Femme Fatale', the album only reached the lower reaches of the US Top 200, and Nico left before the year was out.

A second album, 'White Light/White Heat' appeared in 1968, with a markedly more extreme sound than the debut, particularly on 'I Heard Her Call My Name' and the 17-minute epic 'Sister Ray', reflecting both Cale's interest in noise as music and the fact that the band's hectic touring schedule left little time for the niceties of recording. Disagreements between Reed and Cale led to the latter's departure in 1968, swiftly replaced by bassist Doug Yule from Boston band Glass Menagerie. The new line-up recorded the mysterious, low-key eponymous third album (1969), which contained some of Reed's finest songs. Commercial success still proved elusive, however, and the band were forced to tour constantly to stay solvent. The fourth album, 'Loaded' (1970), recorded for a new label, contained many more melodic, up-tempo numbers, including Reed anthems 'Rock'n'Roll' and 'Sweet Jane', and featured Yule on several lead vocals, Reed's voice having been strained during a lengthy series of gigs. Yule's brother, Billy, also played drums on the album, Tucker being absent due to pregnancy. Before 'Loaded' was released, however, Reed had quit the band, and he would later claim that the album was edited and mixed without his participation or approval.

Tucker re-joined the band, who recruited, vocalist Walter Powers and, after Morrison's departure in 1971, Bostonian guitarist/keyboard player Willie Alexander. This line-up toured Europe before Tucker departed, leaving Yule to release an album of his own songs, 'Squeeze' (1972), credited to The Velvet Underground. Yule later toured with Reed in 1975, and played on his 'Sally Can't Dance' album before joining US country-rock band American Flyer. Reed's solo success sparked the release of two live Velvets albums, the bootleg quality 'Live At Max's Kansas City' (1972), recorded at his last gig with the band in 1970, and the excellent double album 'Live 1969' (1974). In 1985, an album of previously unreleased material, 'VU', was released, and proved to be of a very high standard, although a second volume, 'Another View' (1986) was scrappier.

Nico had pursued her own solo career, and released her debut album, 'Chelsea Girls' (1967), featuring songs by Reed and Cale, Bob Dylan and the young Jackson Browne, who had become infatuated with her, as would many other rock artists, including Jim Morrison and Iggy Pop. Subsequent albums 'The Marble Index' (1969), 'Desertshore' (1971) and 'The End' were recorded with Cale, while 1981's 'Drama Of Exile' included a new version of Reed's 'Waiting For The Man'. Cale and Nico were re-united for 'Camera Obscura' (1985), which was to be her final original album, as she died of a heart attack in 1988. Morrison became a university lecturer in Texas, and Tucker also retired from music for several years before releasing the 'Playin' Possum' album (1981) and 'Life In Exile After Abdication' (1989), which included appearances from Reed and members of New York cult band Sonic Youth. Tucker also appeared on Reed's 1989 'New York' album. Like Reed, Nico, and Cale, her live appearances featured a number of Velvet Underground songs.

In 1990, Reed, Cale, Morrison and Tucker were re-united for a brief on-stage performance at a French festival in memory of Warhol, sparking as yet unfulfilled rumours of a new joint project.

Warhol wunderkind The Velvet Underground, with Lou Reed (left)

Greatest Hits

Albums	Title		US	UK
1967	Velvet Underground & Nico			
		Produced By Andy Warhol	171	–
1968	White Light/White Heat		199	–
1985	VU		87	47

VILLAGE PEOPLE

Victor Willis
Alex Briley
David Hodo
Glenn Hughes
Randy Jones
Felipe Rose *(vocal group)*

The successful disco group was formed in 1977 by the US-based French producer/writer Jacques Morali. Morali's idea was to assemble a visual group representing six male stereotypes – the motor-cycle cop, the cowboy, the Indian chief, the construction worker, the solider, and the biker. He built the group around lead singer Willis and named them after New York's Greenwich Village.

Their eponymous album went gold in the US and their debut single, 'San Francisco (You've Got Me)', topped the US dance chart and was a transatlantic chart entry in 1977. The 'camp' sextet were heard in the disco film, *Thank God It's Friday*, in 1978, earning a platinum album for 'Macho Man' and a gold single for the title track.

The group peaked in 1979 when their tongue in cheek single, 'YMCA', sold over a million in the UK and two million in the US, and the follow-up, 'In The Navy', was another US gold record, while their album, 'Cruisin'', which contained both singles, made the US Top 10 and went platinum as did its successor, 'Go West'.

Their 1979 double album, 'Live And Sleazy', was their final gold record and at the height of their fame, Willis was replaced by Ray Simpson (whose sister, Valerie, was half of Ashford & Simpson) and Jones was replaced by Jeff Olson. The group played themselves in the 1980 film, *Can't Stop The Music*, and the soundtrack album gave them their last US Top 100 entry, while the title track was their last UK Top 20 hit.

A 'New Romantic' image was introduced when they changed labels in 1981, but as this was unsuccesful, Simpson left to be replaced by Miles Jay. In 1985, they briefly returned to the UK chart, but the good times are unlikely to return for an act which reportedly sold 20 million singles and 18 million albums worldwide.

Greatest Hits

Singles	Title	US	UK
1979	Y.M.C.A.	2	1
1979	In The Navy	3	2
Albums			
1978	Cruisin'	3	24
1979	Go West	8	14

Gene **VINCENT**

Vincent (born Eugene Vincent Craddock, 1935) is one of the small pantheon of first generation rock'n'rollers whose name and music have assumed legendary status, despite fairly short-lived success in his native USA. The latter years of his career were

Dogged by disaster, Gene Vincent

characterized by a misfortune-puncutated steady decline in status and health, ending in an early death, yet his influence was such on a succeeding generation of rockers – particularly in Europe – that his importance outweighs his commercial achievements. Partly disabled with a leg injury after US Navy service, Vincent was, early in 1956, an occasional singer/guitarist with the house band at a radio station in his home town of Norfolk, Virginia, where DJ 'Sheriff' Tex Davis recorded him and a four-man backing group performing Vincent's own songs, and sent the demo to a major label.

With the label scouting for an Elvis Presley of its own, the timing was perfect. Vincent and the group (who became The Blue Caps) were signed, sent to Nashville to record, and debuted on record with 'Be-Bop-A-Lula', which made the US Top 10 and UK Top 20. Extensive live and TV work followed, and their first album, 'Blue Jean Bop', also reached the US Top 20, a rare feat for a 1950s rock act. They also filmed a cameo slot for the hit movie, *The Girl Can't Help It*, in which they performed 'Be-Bop-A-Lula', but problems followed. Vincent's leg injury refused to heal, and constant travelling and stage work did little to help it. The line-up of The Blue Caps also proved unstable, with numerous personnel changes in their first two years, while Vincent's hit singles did not flow with Presley-like consistency: 1956 brought no more US Top 40 hits, though 'Blue Jean Bop' was a UK Top 20 hit.

Hospitalization and the fitting of a leg brace forcibly lowered Vincent's profile during 1957, but he recovered in time of a triumphant Australian tour with Little Richard and Eddie Cochran; he appeared in another teen movie, *Hot Rod Gang*, and had his final US Top 20 hit with 'Lotta Lovin''. In 1958 the hits and tours dried up, and Vincent parted from The Blue Caps. A visit to Britain at the end of 1959 was the unexpected catalyst of a revived live career in Europe. In a country starved of US rock visitors, Vincent was hugely successful on tour and TV in the UK. He moved on to France and Germany with equal success, then returned to Britain for a longer tour in 1960 with his friend Eddie Cochran, which ended in tragedy when a car crash killed Cochran and left Vincent badly injured.

Vincent recovered and spent much of the 1960s pursuing a live performing career in Europe and the UK, where his black leather rebel image (fostered for UK TV by producer Jack Good) was always a powerful rallying image for followers of traditional rock'n'roll. However, his last British hit single was in 1961, and his recording contract expired in 1962, after which he tended to record piecemeal, flitting between rock and country material. Health, management, domestic, and eventually alcohol problems gradually wore him down during the decade, and eventually affected the previously undimmed consisten-

cy of his live performances. He was a figure in sad decline when he died of a bleeding ulcer in 1971, aged 36 – but his music is still being played, sold (on CD!) and imitated 20 years later.

Greatest Hits

Singles	Title	US	UK
1956	Be-Bop-A-Lula	7	16
Albums			
1956	Blue Jean Bop	16	–
1960	Crazy Times	–	12

Loudon **WAINWRIGHT** III

Cult US singer/songwriter and son of a respected journalist on *Life* magazine, Loudon Wainwright III (born 1946) came to prominence as a Dylan-esque balladeer after serving a Greenwich Village coffee-house apprenticeship *à la* Joan Baez, etc. Entering the music world after studying to be an actor, his sardonic wit marked him as a different talent.

Two albums imaginatively titled 'Album I' (1970) and 'Album II' (1971) were followed after a label change by 1972's 'Album III' which distinguished itself from its similarly titled predecessors by including an unlikely US Top 20 single in the novelty song 'Dead Skunk' (which he has since disowned). His musical career foundered slightly in the mid-1970s as his marriage to singer Kate McGarrigle hit difficulties, although this later provided fodder for his songs. Two more albums, the country-flavoured 'Attempted Mustache' (1973) produced in Nashville by Dylan producer Bob Johnston and 'Unrequited' (1975) predeced a switch to a new label, where commercial pressures persuaded him to pick up a backing band for 'T-Shirt' (1976) and 'Final Exam' (1978), albums which included a good deal of political comment.

Wainwright's remarkably good 1980s output appeared on independent labels, starting with 'A Live One', an in-concert acoustic record followed by 'Fame And Wealth', 'I'm Alright' and 'More Love Songs', the last three collaborations with ex-Fairport Convention guitarist Richard Thompson. 'Therapy' followed in 1989. Wainwright and his partner Suzzy Roche (of singing trio The Roches) had a daughter, Lucy in 1982.

Falsely accused of being 'the new Dylan', 'the Woody Allen of folk', the 'Charlie Chaplin of rock' and 'the male Melanie', Wainwright has also appeared on TV in the successful Korean War comedy series

M*A*S*H (1975), picking up the threads of his intended acting career by appearing in stage productions *Pump Boys And Dinettes* and *Owners* (in the latter playing a suicidal, gun-toting character – 'Typecasting', he claimed) and the 1988 film *Jacknife*.

Greatest Hits

Singles	Title	US	UK
1973	*Dead Skunk*	16	–
Albums			
1973	*Album III*	102	–

Tom **WAITS**

At the start of his career in the early 1970s, Tom Waits (born 1949) seemed like an anachronism possessed solely of novelty value. His now famous quote, 'I slept through the 1960s' spoke volumes for a man whose world seemed to have stopped sometime in the late 1950s.

Waits began performing in his native Los Angeles in 1969 and cut his first album, 'Closing Time', in 1972. It was a partial compromise: 'I wanted to hear upright bass and muted trumpet,' he stated. He got a slightly more mainstream early 1970s singer/ songwriter sound, though his unusual voice, (gruff but not yet the infamous gravel tone) and good songs like 'Ol '55' (covered by The Eagles) and 'Martha' (covered by Tim Buckley) marked him as an interesting prospect.

Successive albums saw him get more of what he wanted. 1974's 'Heart Of Saturday Night' was vastly superior, full of excellent songs like the title track and the first of his semi-spoken monologues, 'Diamonds On My Windshield'. We were gradually being introduced to his dime-novel world of dead-beats, losers, hookers and other barroom and flop house characters.

'Nighthawks At The Diner' (1976) was his first US chart album, a fine live record full of new songs and monologues, and 'Small Change' (also 1976) featured possibly his finest work 'Tom Traubert's Blues', a majestic song about being drunk and broke in a foreign country.

This was his only US Top 100 album of the decade. Successive albums in the late 1970s 'Foreign Affairs' (1977), 'Blue Valentine' (1978) and 'Heart Attack And Vine' (1980) drew us further into his world and his live performances became increasingly theatrical. It was no surprise, therefore, that he should drift into film. Small parts in *Paradise Alley* (1978) and *One From The Heart* (1982) led to bigger roles e.g. *Down By Law* (1986). His first 'proper' album for three years 'Swordfishtrombones' (1983) saw a move away from the standard jazz settings to a more experimental approach. The album included 'In The Neighbourhood' (one of his

Wainwright – Loudon clear

best) and used a strange brass band backing.

'Rain Dogs' (1985) was his first Top 40 album, the tour for which featured his most impressive stage set to date. It was topped, however, by 'Frank's Wild Years' (1987) a musical play that had grown out of a track on 'Swordfishtrombones' and was used as the basis for *Big Time* (1988) which was somewhere between a feature film and an extended promo video.

Waits is now a major figure in the music world considerably further up the ladder than even his most fervent admirers assumed he would attain.

Greatest Hits

Albums	Title	US	UK
1985	*Rain Dogs*	–	29
1987	*Frank's Wild Years*	115	20

The **WALKER BROTHERS**

John Maus (vocals, guitar)
Scott Engel (vocals, bass)
Gary Leeds (drums)

Current interest in The Walker Brothers was triggered partly by their unexpected re-formation in the mid-1970s but principally through the hero-worship that has developed for Engel (born 1944) after his solo offerings were subject to favourable reassessment.

The Brothers had been in showbusiness for years before making their chart debut. Leeds (born 1944) had left The Standells to back P.J. Proby for a UK tour. On his return to Los Angeles, he joined forces with Maus (born 1943) and Engel who, as The Dalton

Brothers, had recorded a Proby number, 'I Only Came To Dance With You', which was reissued at the height of their fame as The Walker Brothers, all three adopting the surname for professional purposes. After a session that yielded a version of a latterday Everly Brothers single, 'Love Her', Leeds suggested that there might be greater rewards in Britain than the US.

On arrival in London, their first single, 'Pretty Girls Everywhere' (with Maus on lead vocal) was a flop, but after a TV spot on *Thank Your Lucky Stars*, 'Love Her' made the UK Top 20 in 1965. It also set a precedent for all the trio's A-sides until disbandment two years later: Engel would emote what were invariably slow ballads, while Maus waded in with supporting harmonies. Omnipresent in Britain, the trio emerged as top pin-ups in teenage magazines. On tour, they were augmented initially by Jimmy O'Neill (keyboards) from Birmingham's Ugly's but, as manhandling by hysterical females became more frequent, Engel and Maus shelved their instruments to concentrate on singing, accompanied by Leeds plus Coventry combo, Johnny B. Great & The Quotations.

Following 'Make It Easy On Yourself', 'My Ship Is Coming In' and 'The Sun Ain't Gonna Shine Any More' were also massive sellers, as were their albums, 'Portrait' (1966) and 'Images' (1967). These collections relied mainly on ravers from the Dalton days ('Dancing In The Street,' 'Land Of 1000 Dances', etc.), soul/gospel favourites such as Curtis Mayfield's 'People Get Ready', plus standards by the likes of Gershwin and Louis Armstrong. Engel also made headway as a composer with tracks like 'Experience' and (with producer Johnny Franz) the title theme to 1966's *Deadlier Than The Male* movie.

Leeds's drum solos were habitual crowd-pleasers but contractual problems prevented his participation in the group's studio output. To offset his chagrin, he cut two 1966 solo singles, 'You Don't Love Me' and 'Twinkie Lee', which both made the UK Top 30, but the trio found the going harder when all singles after 'The Sun Ain't Gonna Shine Any More' failed to dent the UK Top 10 – largely because they all sounded similar – though they were still startling moments such as Engel's 'Archangel', a B-side hinged on a Bach fugue. The advent of psychedelia made the group seem archaic, yet too youthful and long-haired to cut much ice with maturing fans.

By 1967, Maus had to resign himself to the fact that Engel was the proverbial 'pop singer who can really sing', while the latter's growing disenchantment with being a star caused him to refuse all interviews and leave onstage continuity to Maus. A 1967 EP, 'Solo Scott Solo John', was symptomatic of the schism, which ended the partnership in 1967.

After the split, Maus made the first move with a fast UK hit single, 'Annabella', before

Witty Walkers pose under 'pedestrians only' plaque

drifting back to the US. Rumour said that Leeds took a run-of-the-mill job in London. By the end of 1967, Engel was back with a UK Top 30 single, 'Jackie', written by the fiercely emotional Belgian, Jacques Brel, whose uncompromising lyrics restricted airplay. With two more hits and a chart-topping second album, 'Scott 2', Engel surfaced as Brel's foremost interpreter as well as advancing his own writing skills, most markedly on 1969's 'Scott 4'. Unhappily, his talent was not fully appreciated until acts such as Ultravox, A Teardrop Explodes, David Bowie and Marc Almond acknowledged Engel's influence. Meanwhile, disgusted with critical indifference to his new music, Engel lapsed into easy-listening efforts like 'Songs From His TV Series' (also 1969) and budget albums like 'The Moviegoer'.

1975 saw The Walker Brothers warily regrouping for three albums and attendant singles. The most immediate outcome was a 1976 UK Top 10 hit with the title track of 'No Regrets' – which, like 1976's 'Lines', contained all non-originals and was aimed at the MOR market that Engel had been cultivating. However, the next project, 'Nite Flights', flirted with the avant-garde and the morbid surreal lyricism that Engel would continue on 1984's 'Climate Of Hunter', the only album thus far from his resumed solo career. 'Nite Flights' was a courageous step that sold only moderately. Nevertheless, it was a worthy if strange epitaph.

Greatest Hits

Singles	Title	US	UK
1965	Make It Easy on Yourself	16	1
1965	My Ship Is Coming In	63	3
1966	The Sun Ain't Gonna Shine Anymore	13	1
1968	Joanna (Scott Walker solo)	–	7
1976	No Regrets	–	7
Albums			
1966	Take It Easy	–	3
1966	Portrait	–	3
1967	Scott (Scott Walker solo)	–	3
1968	Scott 2 (Scott Walker solo)	–	1
1969	Scott 3 (Scott Walker solo)	–	3

Junior **WALKER** and The **ALL-STARS**

Junior Walker (saxophone, vocals)
Willie Woods (guitar)
Vic Thomas (organ)
Jimmy Graves (drums)

An instrumental voice in the vocal-dominated Motown hit factory, Junior Walker (born Autrey DeWalt, 1942) had a string of hits with his group, The All-Stars, in the mid 1960s.

The band had played from the mid-1950s on the Midwest circuit of clubs and bars, playing gutsy R&B with Walker's alto sax and occasional gravelly vocals taking the lead.

In 1962, they were discovered by singer Johnny Bristol while playing a gig at Battle Creek; Bristol at the time was signed to Harvey Fuqua's Harvey Records in Detroit, one of the early competitors to Berry Gordy's Motown. He suggested to Walker that they should look up Fuqua when next in Detroit, which they did, and three singles appeared on Harvey: 'Twistlackawanna', 'Brainwash Pt.1' and 'Good Rockin' Tonight'. None of them sold particularly well, but set the style for the Junior Walker sound which, after Harvey Records folded, became part of the Motown stable in 1964.

His debut on Motown's Soul subsidiary, 'Monkey Jim', again failed to score, but his second 'Shotgun' – a raunchy 1950s-style honking sax and nonsense-vocals – shot to the top of the US R&B chart and made the Top 5 of the US pop chart.

It was the first hit for the Soul label, and Walker followed it with 'Do The Boomerang' which made the Top 10 of the US R&B chart, and then 'Shake And Fingerpop', another US R&B Top 10 hit that made the Top 30 of the US pop chart. 'Cleo's Mood', which had originally been the B-side of 'Fingerpop', was re-released as a topside and made the US R&B Top 20 in 1966.

The same year, the group attracted the unlikely attention of Motown songwriters Holland-Dozier-Holland, more used to writing sophisticated songs and arrangements for The Supremes and The Four Tops. The team came up with '(I'm A) Roadrunner' and it was another surefire smash, reaching the US Top 20 and becoming a great dancefloor hit on the Mod club circuit in the UK, where it also went Top 20.

A cover of the Holland-Dozier-Holland penned Marvin Gaye hit, 'How Sweet It Is (To Be Loved By You)', came next, a US Top 20 entry, followed by the Harvey Fuqua/Johnny Bristol song, 'Pucker Up Buttercup'.

The hits ran into the 1970s, including 1969's 'What Does It Take (To Win Your Love)' (US Top 5/UK Top 20) and 'These Eyes' (US Top 20) the same year. Walker continues to tour, on Motown revival packages and in his own right, sometimes with son Autrey DeWalt III on drums. His classic records, meanwhile, remain a time capsule evocation of a slice of the soundtrack of the 1960s.

Greatest Hits

Singles	Title	US	UK
1965	Shotgun	4	–
1966	(I'm A) Roadrunner	20	12
1966	How Sweet It Is (To Be Loved By You)	18	22
1969	What Does It Take (To Win Your Love)	4	13
1969	These Eyes	16	–
Albums			
1966	Road Runner	64	–
1969	Greatest Hits	43	–

Joe WALSH and The JAMES GANG

Joe Walsh (born 1947) played rhythm guitar in various school bands, before dropping out of Kent State University and joining The Measles in December 1965. They became local heroes with Walsh (now playing lead) as the star, but in 1968, the band split and Walsh joined The James Gang with Tom Kriss (bass/vocals) and Jim Fox (drums/vocals). They recorded 'Yer Album' (1969) produced by Bill Szymczyk and garnered a large following through extensive touring, but it was Pete Townshend, who admired Walsh's playing, who boosted their fortunes when he invited them to tour Europe with The Who. Dale Peters replaced Kriss and the new line-up released three albums; 'James Gang Rides Again' (1970), 'Thirds' (1971) and 'Live In Concert' (1971), all gold in the US.

The band were huge, but Walsh became dissatisfied, and declining Steve Marriott's offer to join Humble Pie, formed his own band Barnstorm with Kenny Passarelli (bass)

and Joe Vitale (drums). Two Candians – guitarist Dom Troiano and singer Roy Kenner replaced Walsh in the James Gang, and this line-up recorded the undistinguished 'Straight Shooter' (1972) and 'Passin Thru' (1972). Troiano was replaced by Tommy Bolin for the next two albums 'Bang' (1973) and 'Miami' (1974), but both flopped. Bolin left for Deep Purple, but died tragically of a drug overdose in December 1976. The James Gang struggled on with a succession of new guitarists, releasing 'Newborn' (1975) and 'Jesse Come Home' (1976), but they never recovered from the loss of Walsh and finally called it a day in 1976.

The restrained playing on Walsh's solo debut album, 'Barnstorm', (1972), and his initial reluctance to tour were indicative of his desire to move away from arena-based rock lead guitar playing. Instead, he added Rocke Grace on keyboards and released the enigmatically titled US Top 10 album, 'The Smoker You Drink, The Player You Get' (1973). Refreshed, Walsh went out on the road, but Barnstorm split at the end of 1973.

During 1974 Walsh released 'So What', demonstrating his melodic approach with guests including Dan Fogelberg, J.D. Souther and most of The Eagles. Walsh reciprocated by producing Fogelberg's second album 'Souvenirs' and sessioning for The Eagles, as well as Stephen Stills, Rod Stewart and B.B. King. Walsh's live album, 'You Can't Argue With A Sick Mind' (1975), contained all his self-penned party pieces; 'Rocky Mountain Way', 'Help Me Thru The Night', 'Walk Away' and 'Turn To Stone'. He came to Britain in 1975 to join Elton John's Wembley Stadium bill; also playing were The Eagles and by the end of that year, they had recruited Walsh to replace Bernie Leadon. Walsh was with The Eagles for three albums, 'Hotel California' (1977), 'The Long Run' (1979) and 'Live' (1980), before the band split in 1981.

During this period, Walsh released 'But Seriously Folks' (1978), which included the hit single 'Life's Been Good'. Post-Eagles, he picked up his solo career with 'There Goes The Neighbourhood' (1981) and the US Top 40 single 'A Life of Illusion', followed by the albums 'You Bought It – You Name It' (1983), 'The Confessor' (1985) and 'Got Any Gum?' (1987).

The James Gang – their early 'Seventies following the springboard for Walsh's solo success

Greatest Hits

Singles	Title	US	UK
Joe Walsh			
1977	Rocky Mountain Way	23	39
1978	Life's Been Good	12	14
1980	All Night Long	19	–
Albums			
The James Gang			
1970	James Gang Rides Again	20	–
1971	Thirds	27	–
1971	James Gang Live In Concert	24	–
Joe Walsh			
1973	The Smoker You Drink, The Player You Get	6	–
1976	You Can't Argue With A Sick Mind	20	28
1978	But Seriously Folks	8	16

Dionne WARWICK

Like many black performers of her generation Dionne Warwick (born 1941) started in gospel music as a member of The Drinkard Sisters, a family aggregation which also featured her sister Dee Dee, their aunt Cissy Houston and Judy Clay. The Drinkards provided backing vocals for New York's active pop/R&B labels and, while working on a Drifters session that resulted in 'Mexican Divorce' she was spotted by songwriters Burt Bacharach and Hal David.

They saw in her the perfect vehicle for the songs they were touting to Broadway's song publishers. With a recording deal for Dionne,

Bacharach and David discovery Dionne Warwick continues to billtop worldwide

Greatest Hits

Singles	Title	US	UK
1964	Anyone Who Had A Heart	8	42
1964	Walk On By	6	9
1966	Message To Michael	8	–
1967	I Say A Little Prayer	4	–
1968	Do You Know The Way To San Jose	10	8
1969	This Girl's In Love With You	7	–
1970	I'll Never Fall In Love Again	6	–
1974	Then Came You (with the Detroit Spinners)	1	29
1982	Heartbreaker	10	2
1982	All The Love In The World	–	10
1985	That's What Friends Are For (with Elton John, Stevie Wonder & Gladys Knight)	1	16

Albums		US	UK
1964	Presenting . . .	–	14
1964	Make Way For . . .	20	–
1966	Best Of . . .	–	8
1967	Golden Hits Part One	10	–
1968	Valley Of The Dolls	6	10
1969	Soulful	11	–
1979	Dionne	12	–
1980	Night So Long	23	–
1982	Heartbreaker	25	3
1983	The Collection	–	11

The **WATERBOYS**

Mike Scott (vocals, guitar, piano)
Anthony Thistlethwaite (saxophone, mandolin, harmonica)
Kevin Wilkinson (drums)

As much at home with the subtleties of a traditional folk sound as with stadium rock, The Waterboys have always been the vision of Mike Scott (born 1958). Raised on Bob Dylan but a solid supporter of Clash-era punk rock, this Scottish guitarist and song-writer founded his first band, Another Pretty Face, while a student in 1977/78. After a number of singles and a name change to The Red And The Black, Scott floated a new project, Funhouse, which after one single, 'Out Of Control', became The Waterboys. In 1982 Anthony Thistlethwaite and Kevin Wilkinson formed the core of the first Water-boys unit.

After releasing the 'A Girl Called Johnny' indie single (a tribute to Patti Smith), the band were signed in 1983, and delivered their first, eponymous album, which Scott pro-duced, a mooted link-up with Patti Smith guitarist, Lenny Kaye, proving abortive. Welsh keyboardist/bassist Karl Wallinger joined for the second album, 'A Pagan Place' (1984) which made a big splash with the rock cognoscenti, notably U2, but it was 1985's album, 'This Is The Sea', which gave then their first UK Top 40 entry and provided a UK Top 30 single, the anthemic 'The Whole Of The Moon'.

the trio began a relationship that has lasted until the present. Warwick is one of a handful of 1960s artists to own her own recordings.

The team scored an immediate hit with 1963's soulful 'Don't Make Me Over', and began an almost unbroken string of hits throughout the decade. Warwick was keen to move out of the strictly Black market to the relative security of the MOR market, and with the songs of Bacharach and David, soon achieved this goal.

By the end of the 1960s, the songwriters also moved into more sophisticated markets with movie scores and Broadway shows. Eventually there came a parting of the ways which had little effect on her concerts, but plunged her into erratic record sales.

Her soft breathy vocals so unique in the 1960s were out of fashion for the 1970s. A fruitless period produced by Holland-Dozier-Holland bore little fruit, as did duets with Isaac Hayes, and while her concert and TV appearances consolidated her superstar status, her record sales were mediocre. In 1974 producer Thom Bell teamed her with The Detroit Spinners, resulting in her first US chart-topper 'Then Came You', but it was an isolated hit. In 1979 she signed to Arista, whose Clive Davis was a Svengali for fading divas. Davis placed her under the production of Barry Manilow, Luther Vandross and The Bee-Gees, all of which provided much needed hits and re-established her recording creden-tials.

She entered the 1990s with an album of Cole Porter songs and a world tour and shows little sign of losing her stature as one of the world's most popular entertainers.

Karl Wallinger left to form World Party prior to a support slot on a Simple Minds tour, and in early 1986, Scott stayed with Irish fiddle player Steve Wick in Dublin in an attempt to sort out his growing alienation from the London music business.

A new Waterboys of Wickham, Thistlethwaite, Scott and Irish bassist Trevor Hutchinson began working on a brand of Celtic folk-rock which eventually emerged on the 1988 album 'Fisherman's Blues'. The Waterboys toured with a line-up including ex-Patti Smith Group drummer Jay Dee Daugherty before returning to Spiddal on the West Coast of Ireland. An expanded lineup including Sharron Shannon (accordion/fiddle), Colin Blakey (whistle/flute/keyboards) and Skid Row's Noel Bridgeman (drums) produced the disappointing 'Room To Roam' in 1990, after which Wickham left the band. A new line-up of Scott/Thistlethwaite/Hutchinson and new American drummer Kevin Blevins showed The Waterboys returning to electric rock roots.

Greatest Hits

Singles	Title	US	UK
1985	The Whole Of The Moon	–	26
1989	Fisherman's Blues	–	32
Albums			
1985	This Is The Sea	–	37
1988	Fisherman's Blues	76	13
1990	Room To Roam	–	5

Muddy WATERS

Born McKinley Morganfield (1915) in Mississippi, Waters was raised by his grandmother following his mother's death in 1918. Playing in a muddy creek earned him his nickname. He started out on harmonica, switched to guitar at 17 and developed his style under the influence of Son House and Robert Johnson while playing around the Mississippi Delta. In 1943 he moved to Chicago and worked in a paper mill. Back home in 1941/2, Alan Lomax had recorded him playing acoustically for the Library of Congress; in 1944, he went electric and began recording in 1946 as a sideman and later in his own right.

Following early 'race'/R&B hits with 'Rollin' Stone', 'I Can't Be Satisfied' and 'Rollin' and Tumblin'', Waters assembled what, during the early 1950s, was one of the best ever Chicago blues bands – Willie Dixon (bass), Little Walter Jacob (harmonica), Otis Spann (piano), Jimmy Rodgers (guitar) and Elgin Evans (drums). Waters had nine records in the US R&B Top 10 before 1955, including 'She Moves Me', 'Hoochie Coochie Man', 'I Just Wanna Make Love To You', 'I'm Ready', 'Still A Fool' and 'Mad Love', many now recognized as blues classics and a

Muddy – major single influence on Brit blues

major influence on the development of rock in the 1960s.

From 1956 on, rock'n'roll (and later, soul) pushed Waters and most other bluesmen aside, although he continued to have R&B hits until 1958. In the wake of white interest in the blues, his career revived and throughout the 1960s and 70s, he was a regular at festivals and recorded frequently with rock musicians, particularly on 'Fathers and Sons' (1969) and 'London Sessions' (1972). 'They Call Me Muddy Waters' (1971) won him the first of many Grammy awards. In 1976, with albino blues/rock guitarist Johnny Winter, he released two of his best-selling albums, 'Hard Again' (1977) and 'I'm Ready' (1978), plus 'Muddy 'Mississippi' Waters Live' (1979) and 'King Bee' (1981). Although never as popular as B.B. King, he ended his days in 1983 as one of the most venerated bluesmen of modern times.

Greatest Hits

Singles	Title	US	UK
1988	Mannish Boy	–	51
Albums			
1969	Fathers And Sons	70	–

Jimmy WEBB

Webb (born 1946), the son of a Baptist minister, shot to fame in the late 1960s after being discovered as a talented songwriter and arranger by Johnny Rivers. His first major success was with The Fifth Dimension, who had an enormous hit with 'Up, Up, And Away' (a hit in the UK by The Johnny Mann Singers), and this was soon followed by Glen Campbell's 'By The Time I Get To Phoenix', 'Wichita Lineman' and 'Galveston', all of which charted on both sides of the Atlantic.

Actor Richard Harris was next to benefit from Webb's talent, primarily with the epic 'MacArthur Park' (a song, in 1978's Donna Summer version, that gave Webb his only No. 1), but also with two albums, 'A Tramp Shining', a US Top 5 item written entirely by Webb, and 'The Yard Went On Forever'. His own solo career has coughed and spluttered since 1970 when his debut official solo album, 'Words And Music', was released. Five subsequent albums, culminating with 1982's 'Angel Heart', have had little commercial success despite receiving critical acclaim and being packed with all-star backing musicians (Joni Mitchell, Graham Nash, Michael McDonald, Ringo Starr, Lowell George, etc).

However, Webb has been far from idle, having collaborated with numerous artists, including The Supremes (an eponymous post-Ross album), Cher (on 'Stars'), Thelma Houston (on 'Sunshower' and 'Breakwater Cat') and Art Garfunkel (on 'Watermark'). In addition to these collaborations his songs have continued to be recorded through the 1970s and 1980s by Joan Baez, Judy Collins, Joe Cocker, Linda Ronstadt, Barry Manilow and Glen Campbell to name but a few, while his song, 'The Highwayman', gave its name to the Nelson-Cash-Jennings-Kristofferson, country supergroup.

It would be unwise to think of Jimmy Webb now as simply a songwriter, producer or arranger. 1986 saw the release of 'The Animals' Christmas', a cantata for orchestra, choir and soloists (Art Garfunkel and Amy Grant) performed in the cathedral of St John The Divine, New York City. Webb's interest in film work has continued from the 1960s, and credits in this field include *Doc*, *The Hanoi Hilton* and *The Last Unicorn*, the soundtrack of the latter achieving some success in Europe. Othe works in progress include a musical adaptation of Ray Bradbury's science-fiction classic *Dandelion Wine*. Forget 'Greatest Hits' – there haven't been any. A vital singer/songwriter, as all his albums prove.

Mary WELLS

Along with The Miracles and The Marvellettes, Wells (born 1943) was one of Motown's pioneering hitmakers. She had met Motown founder Berry Gordy initially with the intent of selling him songs but was enticed into singing them herself, scoring a US Top 50 entry with her first release, 'Bye Bye Baby', in 1960. In 1962 she began working with Smokey Robinson, whose vocal

Mary Wells, a Motown original

style she imitated uncannily on many of her early recordings.

Scoring three US Top 10 hits with 'Two Lovers', 'You Beat Me To The Punch' and 'The One Who Really Loves You' in 1962, Wells had a quieter year in 1963 before her US No. 1, 'My Guy' (1964) which became Motown's first major UK hit. She duetted with Marvin Gaye on the US Top 20 single 'Once Upon A Time', which also reached the UK Top 50 (1964). She toured with The Beatles and by virtue of their endorsement was offered and accepted a lucrative recording and acting contract and left Motown, much to Gordy's shock, in 1965. However, her success, post Motown, was never consolidated, and several label changes followed. Despite scoring minor chart hits, by the early 1970s she had been relegated to the 'Oldies' shows which have provided her with the bulk of her living to the present day. She married into the Womack family, first to Cecil and then to Curtis.

In 1990 she was diagnosed as suffering from throat cancer and was unable to continue singing. A series of benefit concerts and financial support from her ex-label mates from Motown, as well as large donations from Bruce Springsteen and Berry Gordy, with whom she was finally reconciled, have helped defray her huge medical bills.

Greatest Hits

Singles	Title	US	UK
1962	*The One Who Really Loves You*	8	–
1962	*You Beat Me To The Punch*	9	–
1962	*Two Lovers*	7	–
1964	*My Guy*	1	5
Albums			
1964	*Greatest Hits*	18	–

WET WET WET

Marti Pellow (*vocals*)
Graeme Clark (*bass*)
Neil Mitchell (*keyboards*)
Tommy Cunningham (*drums*)

This group of Glasgow school friends led by photogenic Pellow (born Mark McLoughlin, 1966) formed Vortex Motion in the early 1980s and renamed themselves, after a line in Scritti Politti's 'Getting, Having and Holding'.

After forming their own label, The Precious Organisation, in 1984, they assigned it to a major label in 1985. The soul-orientated pop group first recorded with Al Green's producer Willie Mitchell in Memphis, but their debut single was a remix of their original demo of 'Wishing I Was Lucky', which hit the UK Top 10 in 1987, and was quickly followed by two more UK Top 10 hits 'Sweet Little Mystery' and 'Angel Eyes (Home And Away)', both from their chart-topping debut album, 'Popped In Souled Out', which sold over 1.5 million in the UK.

The group often featured in UK teen magazines and started 1988 by winning the BRITS (the UK version of the Grammys) award for Best Newcomer. They topped the UK chart with the charity record 'With A Little Help From My Friends', played to packed houses around Europe, supported Elton John in the US, appeared on the Nelson Mandela Birthday show and starred in a Prince of Wales Trust concert.

Their Willie Mitchell-produced album, 'The Memphis Sessions', which included alternate versions of 'Sweet Little Mystery' and 'Temptation', finally emerged in late 1988 and made the UK Top 3, and their follow-up 1989 album 'Holding Back The River', instantly went platinum and included the Top 20 hits, 'Sweet Surrender' and 'Broke Away'. In order to promote it, they played to 75,000 people in Glasgow and this show became their hit video, Wet Wet Wet In The Park.

They participated in Band Aid II's 'Do They Know It's Christmas' and in 1990, were among the stars of the John Lennon tribute show in Liverpool.

Greatest Hits

Singles	Title	US	UK
1987	*Wishing I Was Lucky*	58	6
1988	*With A Little Help From My Friends*	–	1
Albums			
1987	*Popped In Souled Out*	123	1
1989	*Holding Back The River*	–	2

Wet Wet Wet – minor US success despite Memphis record sessions

Barry – heavy breathing brother

Barry WHITE / LOVE UNLIMITED

White (born 1944), a large deep-voiced Texan who became a sensual disco superstar, allegedly played piano on Jesse Belvin's 1956 R&B hit, 'Goodnight My Love', and was a member of The Upfronts, who cut five R&B singles between 1960 and 1962. In 1964 he arranged 'Harlem Shuffle', a classic R&B hit by Bob & Earl, and as Barry Lee, recorded two singles in the mid-1960s, when he was also a member of the Five Du-Tones. In 1967 he worked in A&R making unsuccessful solo records, but producing and writing Felice Taylor's hits, 'It May Be Winter Outside' and 'I Feel Love Comin' On'.

This multi-faceted artist also managed female trio Love Unlimited, who earned a 1972 gold record with his song, 'Walkin' In The Rain With The One I Love'. His 1973 debut album, 'I've Got So Much To Give', went gold, as did an excerpted single, 'I'm Gonna Love You Just A Little Bit More Baby', and he had transatlantic Top 20 albums in 1974 with 'Stone Gon'' and 'Can't Get Enough', plus chart-topping singles 'Can't Get Enough Of Your Love Babe' and 'You're The First, The Last, My Everything'. Love Unlimited's debut album went gold as did an instrumental single, 'Love's Theme', and the albums 'Rhapsody in White' and 'White Gold', all released as The Love Unlimited Orchestra.

His string of romance-orientated hit singles continued through the 1970s, with gold albums for 'Just Another Way To Say I Love You' and 'Greatest Hits' in 1975, and sold a million of both 'Barry White Sings For Someone You Love' in 1977 and his sixth black music chart-topper, 'The Man' in 1978.

This charismatic performer, who has apparently sold nearly 100 million records worldwide, formed his own label in 1979, when he earned his last gold album, 'The Message Is Love'. In 1987 he again had chart success albeit on a smaller scale.

Greatest Hits

Singles	Title	US	UK
1974	Can't Get Enough Of Your Love, Babe	1	8
1974	You're The First, The Last, My Everything	2	1
Albums			
1974	Can't Get Enough	1	4
1975	Just Another Way To Say I Love You	17	12

WHITESNAKE

David Coverdale (vocals)
Mick Moody (guitar)
Bernie Marsden (guitar)
David Dowell (drums)
Neil Murray (bass)
Brian Johnston (keyboards)

Of splinter groups formed after its 1976 disbandment, Deep Purple's stylistic determination was in strongest evidence in Whitesnake – especially *circa* 1980 when half its personnel were ex-Purple veterans.

Contractual problems traceable to Deep Purple forced Coverdale to maintain vinyl silence until 1977's introspective 'David Coverdale's Whitesnake' (produced by Roger Glover) and its single, 'Breakdown', concerned with the last rancorous weeks of Deep Purple. The following year's 'Northwinds' was categorized as an outmoded and sexist 'heavy' album in punk circles. However, drawn from 'Northwinds' session players, Whitesnake started with UK club dates rather than risk a less modest milking of hirsute, bedenimmed fans from Coverdale's previous association.

After Johnston and his successor, Pete Solley, departed, Purple's Jon Lord was hired for 1978's 'Trouble' and a headlining UK tour, culminating with a performance taped at Hammersmith Odeon. Then came 'Lovehunter' and the replacement of Dowell with Ian Paice in 1980. The presence of another ex-Purple stalwart in the ranks boosted both Whitesnake's impact at major festivals, and sales of the next album, 'Ready And Willing', which spawned a UK Top 20 entry for its single, 'Fool For Your Loving'. A lesser hit – but a hit nonetheless – was 'Don't Break My Heart Again' from 1981's 'Come And Get It', released on the heels of 'Live In The Heart Of The City' – culled from the Hammersmith show and global treks that included a crack at the US market for which 'Snakebite', a compilation of pre-1979 recordings, had been directed.

Whitesnake's commercial apogee ended with Paice and Lord's defection to a reformed Deep Purple and Murray's to Gary Moore's band as well as the comparative failure of 1982's 'Saints And Sinners' with new recruits Cozy Powell (drums), guitarist Mel Galley and, on bass, Colin Hodgkinson (ex-Back

A Purple shade of Whitesnake as Coverdale regroups his stormtroops

Door). In 1983, John Sykes (ex-Thin Lizzy) stepped into Moody's shoes for 'Slide It In', notable for its single's B-side, a restrained cover of Fleetwood Mac's 'Need Your Love So Bad'. Containing a re-make of a track from 'Saints And Sinners', an eponymous album of 1987, however, was a disappointing reversion to formula.

Greatest Hits

Albums	Title	US	UK
1980	*Live In The Heart Of The City*	–	5
1981	*Come And Get It*	–	2

The **WHO**

Roger Daltrey *(vocals)*
Pete Townshend *(guitar)*
Keith Moon *(drums)*
John Entwistle *(bass)*

The Who started as The Detours in 1962, a skiffle group formed by Daltrey (born 1945) and Entwistle (born 1944), who brought in old schoolfriend Townshend (born 1945). Original drummer Doug Sandom was ousted in 1964 by Keith Moon (born 1947). The Detours became The Who, then The High Numbers, a name chosen by their manager Peter Meaden, who introduced them to London's burgeoning 'Mod' scene. Meaden (who died in 1978) largely fashioned The Who's 'Mod' image and the audience for their brash R&B grew, although the first single 'I'm The Face' (1964), written by Meaden, bombed. Two assistant film directors, Chris Stamp and Kit Lambert, were looking to cast a group in a documentary – they saw The High Numbers, ditched the film and went into the music business, buying out Meaden.

Only Townshend cared much for the 'psychology' of Mod – an alienation and confusion caused in part by the amphetamines the band and their audience frequently used. Townshend began writing songs to express this tension and the live act grew wilder, with Moon and Townshend smashing their instruments on stage, both as a visual manifestation of the lyrics and an influence derived from the 'violence in art' movement abroad during Townshend's art school days.

After a name change back to The Who, the single, 'I Can't Explain' (UK Top 10), was released in 1965 and a residency established at London's Marquee Club. Frequent appearances on UK TV show *Ready, Steady Go* established The Who as major pop artists, and 'Anyway, Anyhow, Anywhere' (1965) gave them their second Top 10 single. Although Mod was waning, Townshend was still wedded to its rebellious attitude, resulting in the climactic 'My Generation' (1965), a Top 3 single in the UK. Behind the scenes,

however, all was not well, with Daltrey and Townshend constantly arguing as Townshend began to dominate what had been Daltrey's band. The first album, 'My Generation' appeared in 1965, reaching the UK Top 5. With the 'Substitute' single (1966), Townshend began to move away from standard pop subject matter, although the single still went Top 5, as did 'I'm A Boy' (1966), 'Happy Jack' (1966) and 'Pictures Of Lily' (1967), which respectively took in ambivalent sexuality, an Isle of Man hermit and masturbation, a subject which saw 'Lily' banned in the US, where success had been slow in coming.

The second album, 'A Quick One' (1966) reached the UK Top 5 and included Entwistle's jokey 'Boris The Spider' and Townshend's 'mini-opera', the nine-minute 'A Quick One While He's Away'. The band's assault on the US began with a show-stopping performance at Monterey in 1967, culminating in their first US Top 10 single, 'I Can See For Miles',

which also reached the UK Top 10. The third album, 'Who Sell Out' (1967), a tribute to pirate radio stations, went Top 20 in the UK and crept into the US Top 50. The single, 'Magic Bus' (1968), made the Top 30 in the UK and US, but Townshend was by now engrossed in a 'rock opera' project, which finally appeared in 1969 as the magnum opus, 'Tommy' a Top 3 UK album, Top 5 in the US, previewed by the single 'Pinball Wizard' (Top 5 UK, Top 20 Us). 'Tommy' finally established The Who in the US as a major albums act. 'Live at Leeds' (1970) was basic rock rock'n'roll, but Townshend was still thinking big; one project, 'Lifehouse', never materialized, although some tracks appeared on 'Who's Next' (1971), the band's only UK No. 1 album, and on Townshend's solo debut. However, 'Quadrophenia' (1973), another concept album and a homage to 'Mod', was more successful even if it was constructed against a background of increasing conflict within the band.

The Who – in Mod they identified an attitude that has fuelled rock, before and since

A film version of *Tommy* appeared in 1975, and the accompanying soundtrack album reached the US Top 3 and the UK Top 30, while a collection of band out-takes, 'Odds And Sods' (1974) filled the gap before 'The Who By Numbers' (1975). Although a Top 10 album in the UK and US, it reflected a band at odds with itself. Inactive during 1977, the 1978 'Who Are You' album and single enjoyed chart success in both the UK and US, but tragedy struck later that year when Keith Moon ovedosed on drugs prescribed to help fight his alcoholism. They decided to carry on, recruiting ex-Faces drummer Kenney Jones, and released a live retrospective double, 'The Kids Are Alright' (1979), but ill-luck dogged them when, in 1979, 11 fans died at a US concert. The band were simply going through the motions on the 'Face Dances' album (1981). Their last studio album was aptly named 'It's Hard' (1982) and the group didn't so much split as peter out, a 'final' live album, 'Who's Last' appearing in 1984. They reformed for Live Aid in 1985, and in 1989 came back for a lucrative tour, which yielded another live album, 'John Together'.

During the 1970s, each member embarked on solo projects (see separate entry for Pete Townshend). Daltrey was the most visible, with film appearances in *Tommy*, *Lisztomania* and *McVicar* among his credits. His first solo album 'Daltrey' (1973) yielded the UK Top 5 single 'Giving It All Away'. Subsequent albums comprised 'Ride A Rock Horse' (1975); 'One of The Boys' (1977); the soundtrack to *McVicar* (1980) and *Under A Raging Moon* (1985), More recently he has graced TV adverts for a major credit card and invested in fish farming.

Moon appeared in the movies *Tommy* (1975), *That'll Be The Day* (1972), and *Stardust* (1974), but his solo album 'Two Sides Of The Moon' (1975) was poor. Entwistle, who had always contributed to The Who's albums released 'Smash Your Head Against The Wall' (1971), 'Whistle Rhymes' (1972), 'Rigor Mortis Sets In' (1973) 'Mad Dog' (1975) and 'Too Late The Hero' (1981) as solo albums.

Greatest Hits (excluding compilations)

Singles	Title	US	UK
1965	*My Generation*	–	2
1966	*Substitute*	–	5
1966	*I'm A Boy*	–	2
1966	*Happy Jack*	24	3
1967	*Pictures of Lily*	–	4
1967	*I Can See for Miles*	9	10
Albums			
1965	*My Generation*	–	5
1966	*A Quick One*	–	4
1969	*Tommy*	4	2
1970	*Live At Leeds*	4	3
1971	*Who's Next*	4	1
1973	*Quadrophenia*	2	2
1978	*Who Are You*	2	6
1981	*Face Dances*	4	2

Kim Smith – born to be Wilde

Kim **WILDE**

Kim Wilde (born Kim Smith, 1960) was the daughter of British rock'n'roll star Marty Wilde, who celebrated her birth by releasing his aptly titled sixth UK Top 20 hit, 'Little Girl'.

After a spell as backing singer on her father's tours in the late 1970s, she signed to Mickie Most's Rak label in 1980. The photogenic pop singer's first single, 'Kids In America', was produced by her brother Ricky and written by him and Marty, and, despite being involved in a hyping scandal, it made the UK Top 3 in 1981, and hit the US Top 40 18 months later. She followed it with three other family-produced UK Top 20 hits in 1981, 'Chequered Love', 'Water On Glass'/'Boys' and 'Cambodia', and her eponymous debut album reached the UK Top 3.

In her first 18 months as a recording artist, Kim sold over six million records worldwide, thanks partly to a 1982 European tour where she promoted her fifth single, 'View From a Bridge', and second album, 'Select'. She won the BRITS award as Top Female Vocalist of 1982 and, after a year concentrating on songwriting, she changed labels in 1984. Her first album for her new company, 'Teases And Dares', was a small transatlantic hit.

'Rage To Love' returned her to the UK Top 20 in 1985 and a year later a revival of the 1966 hit by The Supremes, 'You Keep Me Hangin' On', made the UK Top 3 and in 1987 topped the US chart. In 1987 Wilde performed on two big charity hits, 'Let It Be' by Ferry Aid and 'Rockin' Around The Christmas Tree', with comedian Mel Smith. Also that year a duet with Junior Giscombe, 'Another Step', made the UK Top 10.

She supported Michael Jackson on his record breaking 1988 European tour and her 'Close' album hit the UK Top 10 that year, as did the singles from it, 'You Came', 'Never

Trust A Stranger' and 'Four Letter Word'. Her 1990 album 'Love Moves' and its singles met with success, albeit on a smaller scale.

Greatest Hits

Singles	Title	US	UK
1981	*Kids In America*	25	2
1986	*You Keep Me Hangin' On*	1	2
Albums			
1981	*Kim Wilde*	86	3
1988	*Close*	114	8

Larry **WILLIAMS**

Although not one of the great innovators, Williams (born 1935) left an indelible mark on 1950s rock'n'roll with a handful of memorable records.

Born in New Orleans, he worked on the West Coast where he was the pianist in a number of bands, including those of Roy Brown, Percy Mayfield and Lloyd Price. It was while he was with Price – some say as valet, others as musician – that he was discovered by Art Rupe, boss of Specialty Records. A debut cover of Price's 'Just Because' made little impression commercially but 'Short Fat Fannie' swept to the top of the US R&B charts also making the Top 5 of the US pop chart, in 1957; 'Fannie' was a wild rocker in the classic Specialty style of Little Richard, using the same (mainly New Orleans) nucleus of musicians, but adding a Williams gimmick – he whistled through the instrumental break.

An even bigger hit in the UK, where 'Fannie' just missed the Top 20, was 'Bony Moronie', another frenetic single that has become a rock'n'roll standard, backed with the juke box favourite, 'You Bug Me Baby'. 'Dizzy Miss Lizzy' completed a hat trick of up-tempo classics, alongside which Williams laid down other three-minute masterpieces which included 'Peaches And Cream', 'Bad Boy' and the epitome of the Specialty sound, 'Slow Down'.

Drug problems plagued Williams, who was jailed in 1960, but a 1962 comeback tour was highly successful (with a band that included Johnny 'Guitar' Watson), and was recorded live in the UK as 'The Larry Williams Show' album.

Minor hits in the late 1960s including a creditable 'Mercy, Mercy, Mercy' with Watson, did nothing to alleviate Williams's personal problems, and after an abortive 'comeback' in 1978, the singer committed suicide in January, 1980.

As songwriter as well as performer, Larry Williams contributed hugely to the basic repertoire of rock'n'roll. Many of his songs have been covered – the Beatles alone have recorded three of them. Later, John Lennon recorded 'Bony Moronie'. Williams, with his few classic recordings, complete with

Chuck Berry-like 'high school' lyrics, epitomizes the genre of which he was a significant part.

Greatest Hits

Singles	Title	US	UK
1957	*Short Fat Fannie*	5	21
1957	*Bony Moronie*	14	11

Jackie **WILSON**

Originally set for a boxing career, Wilson (born 1934) joined Detroit R&B outfit The Thrillers (who also included Hank Ballard) in 1950 and a year later recorded a single, 'Danny Boy', on an independent label. He replaced Clyde McPhatter in doo-wop band Billy Ward & The Dominoes in 1953 singing lead on several singles including their first US Top 20 hit, 'St. Therese Of The Roses' in 1956.

His first solo single, 'Reet Petite', (1957) made the UK Top 10, but only reached the US Top 75. His debut US Top 20 single was the million-selling 'Lonely Teardrops' in 1958, and over the next three years the distinctive and influential vocalist was America's most popular black artist scoring a further 10 Top 20 entries, including his second gold record 'Night' (not released in the UK), 'Alone At Last' and 'My Empty Arms', all US Top 10 singles.

His unmistakable tenor returned to the top end of the US singles charts in 1963 with his own song, 'Baby Workout'. Other US Top 20 hits followed, with 'Whispers (Gettin' Louder)' (1966) and '(Your Love Keeps Lifting Me) Higher and Higher' (1967). The latter his sixth and last R&B No. 1 and his first UK Top 20 hit since 1957, when it charted in

Wilson – recent revival of 'Reet Petite'

1969. A re-issue of his 1968 recording, 'I Get The Sweetest Feeling', hit the UK Top 10 in 1972, the year he had the last of his 54 US pop hits. He collapsed on stage in 1975 which led to his being immobile and hospitalized until his death in 1984. A tribute record to him and Marvin Gaye, 'Nightshift' by The Commodores, was a Top 5 single in 1985 both in the US and UK.

In 1986, his first single 'Reet Petite' shot to the top of the UK charts and re-issues of 'I Get The Sweetest Feeling' and 'Higher And Higher' gave him more posthumous UK Top 20 hits – a fitting tribute to a great and original performer.

Greatest Hits

Singles	Title	US	UK
1960	*Night*	4	–
1986	*Reet Petite*	62	1
Albums			
1963	*Baby Workout*	36	–

Johnny and Edgar **WINTER**

Though much of their output has been merely workmanlike since, the Winter siblings left their mark on the early 1970s hard rock circuit.

Boss-eyed and albino, the Winters ignored Mother Nature's cruelty and, together, became prominent in Texan R&B outfits – notably Black Plague – until the younger Edgar's jazzier leanings dictated a parting of the ways. Johnny (born 1944) continued to build a strong local reputation as a guitarist, accompanying visiting blues legends and recording for diverse regional labels. While hawking one such album round major companies, he caught the imagination of a *Rolling Stone* journalist. The resulting eulogy in 1968 catapulted Johnny from obscurity to headlining at New York's Scene club and the prestigious Fillmore East.

Johnny and his new manager, Scene owner Steve Paul, were embarrassed when a collection of old recordings – as 'The Progressive Blues Experiment' – was issued in the same month as the 'official' 'Johnny Winter' album. Nevertheless, Johnny was regarded as a hot act to see by almost every caste of rock fan. Among famous admirers were The Rolling Stones and John Lennon who each proffered songs – respectively, 'Silver Train' and 'Rock 'n' Roll People' – for his consideration. After dismissing his Texan band, Johnny hit the road with Rick Derringer and other ex-members of The McCoys – plus, on keyboards and alto sax, brother Edgar, fresh from singing and playing nearly all instruments on his own album, 1970's 'Entrance'. He stayed for Johnny's 'Second Winter' when Paul suggested that he form White Trash for a 1971 album, produced by Derringer.

That same year saw both 'Johnny Winter And' and the first of several Winter concert albums in international charts, thanks in no small part to the sweaty intensity of Johnny and Rick's duelling guitar work on showstoppers such as 'Stormy Monday', 'Rock 'n' Roll Hoochie Coo' and Eddie Boyd's, 'Five Long Years' – drawn mostly from Black Plague's repertoire and the blues end of The McCoys. However, in ratio to Johnny's increasing drug dependency was a deterioration in quality of successive albums from 'Still Alive And Well' to 1974's 'John Dawson Winter III', causing the pragmatic Derringer *et al* to offer their services to the more stable Edgar.

Boosted by the critical triumph of White Trash's double 'Road Work' 'live' set, Winter Minor was now leading his own Edgar Winter Group – whose personnel included guitarist Ronnie Montrose and, on bass, Dan Hartman – co-writer of all selections on 1972's 'They Only Come Out At Night', with its sleeve send-up of glam-rock. Originally a B-side, the album's 'Frankenstein' synthesizer instrumental sold a million. Hartman was, thereby, well-placed to strike out on his own while Montrose improved his own financial prospects by starting an eponymous band.

With Derringer's boys, Edgar cut three albums but, by the second of these ('Jasmine Nightdress'), Derringer so rivalled his boss as the group's principal asset that it became customary for billing to read 'The Edgar Winter Group Featuring Rick Derringer' – also the title of the third effort. After Derringer departed for solo glory, Edgar's merger with Johnny for 1976's 'Together' album (mostly rock'n'roll and soul favourites) made commercial sense but, by then, the Winters' time in the sun was past.

Short of ideas, Edgar fell back on production and session work, and Johnny returned to backing his blues heroes. If unadventurous, the steady flow of Johnny's albums – particularly on 1987's Grammy-winning 'Third Degree' (with Dr John) – showed a regaining of his former fretboard dexterity.

Greatest Hits

Singles	Title	US	UK
1973	*Frankenstein (Edgar)*	1	18
1973	*Free Ride (Edgar)*	13	–
Albums			
1969	*Johnny Winter*	24	–
1971	*Johnny Winter And Live*	40	20
1972	*They Only Come Out At Night (Edgar)*	3	–

Steve **WINWOOD**

Over three decades, Winwood's exuberant, elastic voice was the common denominator between The Spencer Davis Group, Traffic and Blind Faith (see separate

Stevie – child prodigy in Charles mould

entries), his subsequent solo ventures and a bewildering number of more casual projects.

Younger son of a Birmingham, UK, musical family, Winwood (born 1948) was performing regularly on keyboards and guitar with his father's dance combo while still at primary school. Later, he enlisted in his brother's skiffle group, which evolved into The Muff Woody Jazz Band, initially adopting a vocal style based on that of Ray Charles. In 1963 the Winwood brothers joined The Rhythm & Blues Quartet, later renamed The Spencer Davis Group. When Steve Winwood left Davis in 1967, he formed Traffic, and was a member of the short-lived Blind Faith (1969), before rejoining Traffic, who finally disbanded in 1975.

Before releasing his eponymous debut album in 1977, Winwood earned numerous credits on records ranging from reggae to salsa to folk to avant-garde and less specific categories. These experiences, however, did not noticeably enrich 'Steve Winwood', on which he demonstrated that he hadn't yet extricated himself from many of Traffic's excesses. Musically, it sounded dated – especially in Britain, where punk was in the ascendant. After this false dawn, 1980s million-selling 'Arc of a Diver' was a vast improvement, partly because of a new songwriting collaboration with US wordsmith Will Jennings, and the perpetuation of an old one with former Bonzo Dog Band mainstay Vivian Stanshall. Winwood's own multi-tracking and engineering of all instruments also made for a more disciplined approach than before.

The UK Top 10 and US Top 30 album, 'Talking Back To The Night', two years later was also a consistently strong collection, and included 'Valerie', a single that, remixed in 1987, was a UK Top 20 hit – Winwood's first such entry since the earliest days of Traffic. A certain edge was lost on 'Talking Back To The Night' as Winwood's vocals floated effortlessly over layers of treated, superimposed sound – but this was not the case on 1986's US No. 1, 'Back In The High Life', taped in New York with top session players and guest stars such as Chaka Khan and Joe Walsh.

Winning two Grammy awards, the album was Winwood's (and co-producer Russ Titelman's) commercial peak with its breezy musical force and confident breadth of expression. As nearly always, Winwood's music was better than his songs – though the attendant US No. 1 single 'Higher Love' (UK Top 20), US Top 20 entry 'Freedom Overspill' and Stanshall's 'My Love's Leavin'' were among highlights of his second world tour as a solo artist. Wisely, this trek concentrated on the US, where 'Roll With It', the mellower but less immediately attractive follow-up to 'Back In The High Life', would top the album charts in 1988, reaching the UK Top 5. 1990's 'Refugees Of The Heart' was greeted with mixed reviews, but enjoyed healthy sales figures both in the US and UK.

Greatest Hits

Singles	Title	US	UK
1986	*Higher Love*	1	3
1988	*Roll With It*	1	53
Albums			
1986	*Back in the High Life*	1	8
1988	*Roll With It*	1	4
1990	*Refugees Of The Heart*	27	26

Bill WITHERS

Distinctive US folk-styled soul singer/songwriter Withers (born 1938) was discovered at age 31 by Booker T. (& The MG's) Jones in 1970, having recorded demos in his spare time from his job in an aircraft factory in California. His debut album, 'Just As I Am' (1971), hit the US Top 40 and his first single 'Ain't No Sunshine' (1971) made the US Top 5, sold a million and later won a Grammy award (it was a 1972 UK Top 10 hit for Michael Jackson). His most successful album was his self-produced second album, 'Still Bill', which reached the US Top 5 in 1972, and contained both his US No. 1, 'Lean On Me', which became his first UK chart entry, and the US Top 3 single, 'Use Me', each of which sold over a million.

Neither the double live album, 'Bill Withers Live At Carnegie Hall' (1973), nor studio album ' + Justments' (1974) reached the US Top 40, and following an unsuccessful 'Best Of . . . ' album in 1975, he changed labels. After two minor albums, 'Making Music' (1975) and 'Naked And Warm' (1976), he had a Top 40 album in both the US and UK with 'Menagerie', which went gold in the US. 'Lovely Day', taken from it, gave him his UK Top 10 debut in 1978. His album, 'Bout Love', (1979) performed poorly, although 'Just The Two Of Us', a single he co-wrote and performed with Grover Washington Jr. in 1981, went Top 3 in the US and Top 40 in the UK, winning a Grammy award. His 1985 album 'Watching You, Watching Me' made the UK chart, and in 1987 Club Nouveau had a US No. 1 and UK Top 3 single with a cover of 'Lean On Me', earning him a third Grammy. In 1988 a remixed version of 'Lovely Day' gave him his biggest UK hit to date.

Greatest Hits

Singles	Title	US	UK
1972	*Lean On Me*	1	18
1977	*Lovely Day*	30	4
Albums			
1972	*Still Bill*	4	–
1977	*Menagerie*	39	27

The WOMACK FAMILY

Formed in the late 1950s, Cleveland gospel group The Womack Brothers, consisted of Bobby (born 1944), Cecil, Curtis, Harris and Friendly Jr. After Sam Cooke signed Bobby Womack up as guitarist in his band in 1960, he offered the Womacks a record deal, and in 1961 they released their debut single 'Somebody's Wrong'. After a name change to The Valentinos, they had a Top 10 US R&B hit with 'Lookin' For A Love' (1962), later a US hit for The J. Geils Band (1971), which reached the US Top 75. Their fifth single 'It's All Over Now', which Bobby co-wrote was a US Top 100 entry in 1964, and later a success for The Rolling Stones.

After Cooke's unfortunate death in 1964, Bobby married his widow and began a solo recording career. One of the most soulful singers of the 1960s, he recorded on various labels between 1965 and 1969, notching up a string of small hits including covers of 'Fly Me To The Moon' and 'California Dreamin'' in 1968. During this period he worked as a session guitarist with artists including The Box Tops, Janis Joplin, Ray Charles and Wilson Pickett. He signed a major label deal in 1970 and had his first US Top 100 album the following year with 'Communication' and his first gold record in 1972 for 'Harry Hippie'/'Sweet Caroline'. He recorded the soundtrack to the film, *Across 110th Street*, in 1973 and also that year had his first US Top 40 album success with 'Facts Of Life'. His only Top 20 single came in 1974 with a revival of The Valentinos, 'Lookin' For A Love', from his album 'Lookin' For A Love Again'.

In 1975 Womack released his own album, 'I Don't Know What The World Is Coming To' and produced and played on Ron Wood's 'Now Look', neither commercially successful.

Womack and Womack – US sleepers break big in Britain

in 1984 with the title track of their UK Top 50 album 'Love Wars' and charted again in 1985 with their 'Radio M.U.S.I.C Man' album. They had their biggest UK hits in 1988 with Top 5 single 'Teardrops' and album 'Conscience'. Their records mean little in their homeland but they continue to sell records and attract big crowds in the UK.

Greatest Hits

Singles	Title	US	UK
1974	*Lookin' For A Love*		
	(Bobby Womack)	10	–
1988	*Teardrops*		
	(Womack & Womack)	–	4
Albums			
1973	*Facts of Life* (Bobby Womack)	37	–
1988	*Conscience*		
	(Womack & Womack)	–	4

Stevie **WONDER**

Perhaps the most respected performer in black music, Stevie Wonder was one of the first R&B artists to exploit the potential of electronic instruments and to make use of new trends in rock music.

He was born blind in 1950 and took up harmonica, piano and drums as a child. Signed to Motown, he made his first records at 12 and had a surprise US chart-topper with the gospel-tinged 'Fingertips', and with the appropriately-titled album 'The 12 Year Old Genius'. His next few singles were less successful but in 1964/5, Wonder toured the US and the UK and had cameo roles in the teen movies, *Bikini Beach* and *Muscle Beach Party*.

He now changed style to the more mainstream Tamla soul sound and the million-selling 'Uptight' (1966) was the first of a dozen big hits over the next five years. Although he covered Bob Dylan's 'Blowin' In The Wind' and the Tony Bennett ballad, 'For Once In My Life', most were written by Sylvia Moy and Henry Cosby, members of the Motown in-house team, while 'Signed Sealed Delivered I'm Yours' and 'If You Really Love Me' were co-written with singer Syreeta Wright, who became Wonder's first wife. She and Wonder also recorded 'Where I'm Coming From' (1971) together.

A keen student of musical trends, by 1970 Wonder was keen to take more control of his career and to conceive his work in terms of albums rather than a string of singles. He set up his own Taurus Productions to lease the 'Music Of My Mind' album to Motown. The result of his experiments with synthesizers, the album reached the US Top 30 but also included the million-selling 'Superstition', originally written for British guitarist Jeff Beck.

With 'Talking Book' and 'Innervisions' (1973), Wonder had perfected his new style and had become one of the elite of the rock

After two albums in 1976, 'Safety Zone', and the country album 'BW Goes C&W', Womack changed labels, but neither 'Home Is Where The Hurt Is', still in 1976, nor 'Pieces', in 1978, charted. Without a recording contract, he was recruited by Crusader Wilton Felder to sing on his 1980 album 'Inherit The Wind', which generated a UK Top 40 single with the title track.

Brother Harry died in 1978, and Womack, in a depressed state, became heavily involved in drugs, finally emerging on a US independent label in 1981. The highly acclaimed 'The Poet', a US Top 30 album, gave his career a much needed boost and 'The Poet 2' (1984) his first UK chart entry. This album also contained the US R&B Top 5 hit, 'Love Has Finally Come At Last', a duet with Patti Labelle. In 1985 he re-united with Wilton

Felder and their album 'Secrets' reached the US and UK Top 100.

A new major label deal resulted in the 'So Many Rivers' album (1985), a UK Top 30 entry. His 1986 album 'Womagic' (later re-compiled as 'The Last Soul Man') failed to chart but he was heard that year singing and playing on The Rolling Stones album, 'Dirty Work', and in 1987 reached the UK Top 75 with his 'Living In A Box' single. Recently, Womack has enjoyed R&B chart success with singles in the US.

Another former Valentino, Cecil (born 1947 – once married to Motown star Mary Wells), together with his wife Linda (born 1952 – the daughter of Sam Cooke and one-time step-daughter of Cecil's brother Bobby), returned as Womack & Womack in 1984. This soulful duo made the UK singles Top 20

world, jamming on stage with Elton John only weeks after suffering severe injuries in a road accident. From the mid-1970s, he also became identified with many charitable and political causes, notably the campaign for a Martin Luther King Day – the song 'Happy Birthday' was dedicated to the civil rights leader.

After renegotiating his Motown contract for a reputed $13 million advance, Wonder reached the peak of his commercial success with his 'Songs In The Key Of Life' album, which topped the US chart for 14 weeks in 1977.

The following album, 'Journey Through The Secret Life Of Plants' was primarily instrumental but 1980's, 'Hotter Than July' album provided more rootsy music, notably 'Master Blaster' and 'Happy Birthday'.

During the 1980s, Wonder released only two albums of new material, 'In Square Circle' (1985) and 'Characters' (1988), but he was increasingly active as a collaborator with other musicians. There were duets with Paul McCartney ('Ebony And Ivory' – his first UK No. 1), Michael Jackson ('Get It', in 1988) and Julio Iglesias ('My Love'), and he made guest appearances on records by Elton John, Eurythmics, Chaka Khan and others, as well as contributing much of the soundtrack music to the movie, *Woman In Red*.

His social and political commitments remained prominent as he took part in the charity records 'We Are The World' and 'That's What Friends Are For', as well as performing at 1988's *Nelson Mandela 70th Birthday Concert* in London.

Stevie Wonder – eclectic, experimental, but ultimately commercial, the essence of creative pop

Greatest Hits

Singles	Title	US	UK
1963	Fingertips (Pt 2)	I	–
1966	Uptight (Everything's Alright)	3	14
1967	I Was Made To Love Her	2	5
1968	For Once In My Life	2	3
1969	My Cherie Amour	4	4
1969	Yester-Me, Yester-You, Yesterday	7	2
1970	Signed Sealed Delivered I'm Yours	3	15
1973	Superstition	I	11
1973	You Are The Sunshine Of My Life	I	7
1973	Higher Ground	4	29
1974	You Haven't Done Nothin'	I	30
1975	Boogie On Reggae Woman	3	12
1977	I Wish	I	5
1977	Sir Duke	I	2
1980	Master Blaster (Jammin')	5	2
1981	Lately	64	3
1981	Happy Birthday	–	2
1982	That Girl	4	39
1982	Ebony And Ivory (with Paul McCartney)	I	I
1984	I Just Called To Say I Love You	I	I
1985	Part Time Lover	I	3
Albums			
1963	Recorded Live – The 12 Year Old Genius	I	–
1972	Talking Book	3	16
1973	Innervisions	4	8
1974	Fulfillingness' First Finale	I	5
1976	Songs In The Key Of Life	I	2
1979	Journey Through The Secret Life Of Plants	4	8
1980	Hotter Than July	3	2
1982	Original Musiquarium 1	4	8
1984	Woman In Red (soundtrack)	4	2
1985	In Square Circle	5	5

Roy **WOOD/WIZZARD**

Roy Wood (vocals, guitar, saxophone, etc.)
Rick Price (bass)
Hugh McDowell (cello)
Nick Pentelow (saxophone)
Mike Burney (saxophone)
Bill Hunt (keyboards/French horn)
Keith Smart (drums)
Charlie Grima (drums)

Roy Wood may indeed have cut a bizarre figure with his long, flowing, multicoloured mane and robes, his hirsute face daubed with greasepaint, but this hugely-talented musician was almost single-handedly responsible for no less than 15 UK Top 10 hits between 1967 and 1975, and possesses one of the most fascinating CVs in British rock'n'roll. Born Ulysses Adrian Wood in 1946, his roots go back to the birth of the UK Beat Boom, taking in legendary Midlands groups Gerry Levene & The Avengers and Mike Sheridan & The Nightriders. A founder member of The Move in 1966, Wood ultimately proved to be their most durable and influential member, writing all their 10 UK hits (five of which made the UK Top 5 – see separate entry), an eclectic assortment of vintage rock'n'roll, psychedelia, ballads, Beatles pastiches and hard rock.

By the end of 1971, The Move were a trio of Wood, drummer Bev Bevan and ex-Idle Race frontman Jeff Lynne, who duly formed Electric Light Orchestra (see separate entry) once contractual obligations had been finalized. Although the cumbersome eight-piece ELO had initially been Wood's concept (to expand rock music from the point The Beatles reached with 'I Am The Walrus', mixing guitars, cellos, and violins), there was clearly a clash of interests with Lynne – presumably both wanted to front the new band. Subsequently, Wood left after a dis-

Roy Wood (centre) uses chopper after Wizzard's prang

The group promptly split and Wood issued a second solo album, 'Mustard', which flopped and within a few months he had signed to another label and found himself in breach of contract, thus the album he had recorded with his new band, Wizzo, never appeared. He re-emerged in 1977 as leader of The Wizzo Band, but despite contributions from various rock luminaries, the album stiffed and the band dissolved. He tried again in 1979 with Roy Wood's Helicopters, but there was little interest – by then, Wood had settled into more of a production role, having worked successfully with The Darts and Annie Haslam.

Wood has continued to maintain a low profile during the 1980s, although a compilation of his earlier work charted briefly in 1982, and in 1986, he guested on the Dr & The Medics hit revival of Abba's 'Waterloo', looking on TV exactly the same as he had nearly 15 years earlier. As a genuine hero of UK popular music, Wood must never be written off, although he has surprisingly never risen above cult status in the US.

Greatest Hits

Singles	Title	US	UK
1972	Ball Park Incident	–	6
1973	See My Baby Jive	–	1
1973	Angel Fingers	–	1
1973	I Wish It Could Be Christmas Every Day	–	4
1974	Forever (Roy Wood solo)	–	8
1974	Rock & Roll Winter	–	6
1975	Are You Ready To Rock	–	8
Albums			
1973	Wizzard Brew	–	29
1973	Boulders (Roy Wood solo)	173	15
1974	Introducing Eddy & The Falcons	–	19

The **YARDBIRDS**

Keith Relf (vocals, harmonica)
Tony 'Top' Topham (lead guitar)
Chris Dreja (rhythm guitar)
Paul Samwell-Smith (bass)
Jim McCarty (drums)

astrous debut gig during which more time was spent changing instruments and tuning them than actually playing. However, he had contributed heavily to their eponymous debut album, which made the UK Top 40, and their first UK Top 10 single, '10538 Overture'. With a nucleus comprising Wood, McDowell and Hunt from ELO, and Price (a later member of The Move), Grima and Smart (ex-Mongrel), Wizzard emerged in mid-1972 as the absolute antithesis of ELO: loosely structured, intent on having a good time, a unique hybrid of drunken lunacy and Wood's highly commercial songs aimed directly and unashamedly at the teenage/singles-buying market. They debuted (rather bravely) at London's Rock'n'Roll Festival that summer and immediately found an eager audience.

They struck paydirt with their first single, 'Ball Park Incident', and for two years barely put a foot wrong – between 1972 and 1975, Wizzard registered seven major UK hits (including two No. 1s), alongside which Wood ran a parallel solo career yielding three

further hits. They also charted with two albums, 'Wizzard Brew' (1973) and 'Introducing Eddie & The Falcons' (UK Top 20, 1974), on which each track was presented in the style of one of Wood's 1950s rock'n'roll heroes (Gene Vincent, Duane Eddy, etc.) while he also released a solo album, 'Boulders' (1973, UK Top 20) which he wrote, produced, engineered, performed and for which he even painted the sleeve!

Ever rock's chameleon, this impressive array encompassed Wood's wide range of musical styles and utilized innumerable instruments, even including bagpipes. Several of Wizzard's hits borrowed heavily from Phil Spector's Wall Of Sound production techniques (notably 'I Wish It Could Be Christmas Every Day'), while his solo hit single, 'Forever', was an unlikely fusion of Neil Sedaka and The Beach Boys (on whose '15 Big Ones' album he guested). In 1975, his winning streak ran out – Wizzard had toured the US in 1974 (without much success), and their label refused to subsidize another tour.

Although they may have lacked the cohesive image cultivated by many of their peers, The Yardbirds left a lasting impression on pop. As an R&B band, they pioneered extended improvisation. Later integrating Gregorian chant and other eruditions into their records, they were also (with The Kinks) the first explorers of Indian sounds in rock.

The group began as the Metropolitan Blues Quartet in West London clubs. Deputizing for The Rolling Stones at Richmond's Crawdaddy, they turned professional when Topham (born 1947) was replaced by Eric Clapton (born 1945) in 1962. As The Stones had taken R&B into the charts, The Yardbirds were well placed to do the same, and their second single, 'Good Morning Little Schoolgirl' might have risen higher than the UK Top 50 had not Relf (born 1943) been laid low for several weeks with a collapsed lung, although he was fit enough for the atmospheric 'Five Live Yardbirds' album.

Uneasy about the group's increasingly commercial outlook, Clapton quit in 1965 when 'For Your Love' precipitated two years of hit singles – 'Heart Full Of Soul', 'Evil-Hearted You'/'Still I'm Sad' (their first original A-side), 'Shapes Of Things' and 'Over Under Sideways Down'. Even Relf's solo 'Mr Zero' made the UK Top 50. During this golden age, when several of the group's hits were written by Graham Gouldman (later of 10cc), the group was joined by Jeff Beck (born 1944), a sensational lead guitarist who displayed eclecticism and unpredictability in compatible amounts.

The most ubiquitous Yardbird in the studio, Samwell-Smith (born 1943) left a month before the release of 1966's outstanding 'Yardbirds' album (perhaps better known as 'Roger The Engineer' after McCarty's sleeve cartoon). While their ex-bass player became a full-time record producer with such diverse future clients as Jethro Tull, Carly Simon and especially Cat Stevens, the others soldiered on for another year after persuading Jimmy Page to step in and revert to a more appropriate role as co-lead guitarist with Beck as soon as Dreja (born 1946) was proficient enough on bass. Apart from a cameo appearance in Antonioni's *Blow Up* movie, the only recordings credited to this edition were the psychedelic 'Happenings Ten Years Time Ago' and Beck's rare vocal on its flip-side, 'Psycho Daisies'.

During a 1966 US tour, the erratic Beck departed and was not replaced. The stage set deteriorated further (as evidenced on the doctored – and withdrawn – 'Live Yardbirds' album). On disc, The Yardbirds were driven to outside composers again for hits, and enlisted the services of Mickie Most, renowned manufacturer of chart hits. Forbidding much elaboration, Most's efforts included 'Little Games', and a US-only cover of Manfred Mann's 'Ha! Ha! Said The Clown'. Other than a few half-hearted rehearsals by Dreja, Page and Terry Reid, the group folded in 1968, after which Page launched Led Zeppelin, of which Dreja was at one time expected to become a member, although he ultimately declined to join.

Pooling their resources, McCarty (born 1943) and Relf reunited as Together for a single, 'Henry's Coming Home', which, in its pastoral lyricism and acoustic emphasis, anticipated a longer-term project in Renaissance's eponymous debut album in 1969 with Relf's

The blueswailin' Yardbirds, with a short-cropped Clapton (second right) the emergent Mod

singing sister Jane, ex-Nashville Teen John Hawken (keyboards) and bass player Louis Cennamo (ex-The Herd). Though McCarty co-wrote much of 1972's 'Prologue', he (like the Relfs) had moved on by then. On vocals and keyboards, he led Shoot through the promising 'On The Frontier' album, while Relf re-emerged with Medicine Head, returning to live performance as the duo's bass guitarist. He stepped further into the limelight with Armageddon, an enduring heavy metal outfit of mystical bent.

A group called The Yardbirds played London's Marquee Club in 1983 during its anniversary celebrations. Dreja (now a photographer), McCarty and Samwell-Smith with help from John Knightsbridge (guitarist with McCarty's Ruthless Blues) backed Medicine Head's John Fiddler, whose presence was a poignant touch as Relf has been killed by electrocution in 1978 when the first Renaissance line-up was planning to re-form as Illusion. The latter-day Yardbirds then cut an album under the guise of Box Of Frogs, with guest spots by Beck and Rory Gallagher, which hopped into the US Top 50.

Since Box Of Frogs (which disbanded after a second album), McCarty has drummed in a few blues bands (including one with Topham) and worked on a 1991 reunion album by The Pretty Things, as well as the artistic faux pas that was the British Invasion All-Stars, a merger with members of The Nashville Teens, Downliners Sect and The Creation. However, he keeps the faith for those wondering what became of the creative vision which characterized The Yardbirds as part of Stairway (with Cennamo) who have recorded several albums for the New Age label. This style's reference points are similar to those attempted by his previous groups,

with 'Turn Into Earth' from 'Yardbirds' in Stairway's live repertoire. Though mainly instrumental, Stairway songs such as 'Lavender Down', Bird Of Paradise' and 'Aquamarine' are as strong in their way as any in the Yardbirds/Renaissance canon.

Greatest Hits

Singles	Title	US	UK
1965	*For Your Love*	6	3
1965	*Heart Full Of Soul*	9	2
1965	*Evil Hearted You/Still I'm Sad*	–	3
1966	*Shapes Of Things*	11	3
Albums			
1966	*Yardbirds*	–	20
1967	*Greatest Hits*	28	–

YES

Jon Anderson (*vocals*)
Chris Squire (*bass*)
Bill Bruford (*drums*)
Tony Kaye (*keyboards*)
Peter Banks (*guitar*)

One of the most successful progressive rock bands of the 1970s, Yes were styled around Jon Anderson's high, fluid vocals and the band's flamboyant classical rock style. They survived numerous line-up changes but by the end of the 1980s there were enough one-time Yes members for two groups to be battling in court over the name.

Anderson (born 1944) had played in several Lancashire bands including The Warriors before meeting up with Chris Squire (born 1948) in the London musicians' club La

Chasse in 1968. He was playing in similar no-hopers, The Syn, and together they hatched Yes, recruiting Syn guitarist Peter Banks along with Bill Bruford (born 1948) from Savoy Brown and Tony Kaye. Influenced by bands like The Nice but with their own identity Yes supported Cream at their fare-well London concerts before signing to Atlantic in 1969. Their debut album, 'Yes', included covers of obscure Beatles and Byrds songs but was too self-conscious to make much impact.

Banks quit soon after and was replaced by Steve Howe (born 1947) who had played in The In Crowd and Tomorrow. He added a more forceful guitar sound to their second album 'Time And A Word' in 1970, the first of five albums produced by Eddie Offord, which featured covers of Stephen Stills and Richie Havens songs and created more interest, reaching the UK Top 50.

'The Yes Album' in 1971 was a break-through, making the UK Top 10 and sneak-ing into the US Top 40 as the band's style developed. But Kaye was not happy and left later that year. His replacement, Rick Wake-man, ex-Strawbs (born 1949), added another dimension to the band and the 'Fragile' album at the end of 1971 made the US Top 5 as the band toured heavily to promote it. It also marked the beginning of a long associa-

tion with artist Roger Dean whose sleeve designs became another band trademark. A Top 20 single with 'Roundabout' was the icing on the cake. Bruford stayed just long enough to record their next, 'Close To The Edge' album in 1972 before leaving to join King Crimson. He missed their biggest suc-cess as the album reached the US Top 3 and UK Top 5. But the rest of the band, with ex-Plastic Ono Band drummer Alan White, toured triumphantly across the US and Europe. Where most bands would have been happy with a double live album, Yes went for a triple with 'Yessongs' in 1973 which gave everyone in the band ample opportunity to expound their talents and their egos and still made the UK Top 10 and the US Top 20.

But it wasn't enough for Rick Wakeman who recorded his own concept album, 1973's 'The Six Wives of Henry VIII' which reached the UK Top 10 and the US Top 30. He contributed to the next Yes album, 1974's 'Tales From Topographic Oceans' which top-ped the UK charts for two weeks and hit No. 6 in the US in 1974. But he had become increasingly estranged from the band and quit soon after his second solo album, 'Jour-ney To The Centre Of The Earth' topped the UK charts and made the US Top 3. Yes recruited Swiss-born Patrick Moraz (born 1948) and proved that they too had been

reading the classics by drawing on Leo Tol-stoy's *War And Peace* for the first side of their 'Relayer' album in 1974. But the new line-up had not gelled and the band took a year off to pursue solo projects. Not surpris-ingly, Anderson did best with 'Olias Of Sunhillow', which made the UK Top 10 but Squire, Howe and Moraz all made the UK Top 30 with their solo albums and even White made the Top 50. Wakeman mean-while hit No. 2 in the UK with 'The Myths And Legends Of King Arthur And The Knights Of The Round Table' album, and his soundtrack to the 1976 Winter Olympics movie *White Rock* also went Top 20 in the UK.

So it was a surprise when Wakeman rejoined Yes in 1976 but the move made musical and commercial sense as 'Going For The One' topped the UK charts for two weeks in 1977 (yielding a Top 10 single with 'Wondrous Stories') and made the US Top 10. But the New Wave was coming in and Yes experienced the undertow over the next few years. The 'Tormato' album in 1978 made the US and UK Top 10, but another bout of solo albums only indicated that all was not well within the band. After Anderson had teamed up with Greek keyboard player Vangelis (ex-Aphrodite's child) for the UK Top 5 album 'Short Stories' and the Top 10 single 'I Hear You Now' both he and Wake-

Yes – prototype and prime example of post-pop, pre-punk 'progressive' rock

man left Yes. Squire, Howe and White carried on, recruiting 'Video Killed The Radio Star' duo Buggles – aka keyboard player Geoff Downes and singer/guitarist Trevor Horn. This unlikely combination struck back with a UK Top 3 album 'Drama' in 1980 which also made the US Top 20. They also played a sell-out US tour but it wasn't enough to hold the band together. Howe and Downes went off to form Asia with Carl Palmer and John Wetton while Squire and White played abortive sessions with Led Zeppelin's Jimmy Page and Robert Plant. For the next two years, Yes only existed on record as 'Yesshows', live tracks from recorded 1976 to 1978, made the UK Top 30.

In late 1982 Squire and White got together with South African singer/guitarist Trevor Rabin and original Yes keyboard player Tony Kaye for a band called Cinema. While recording an album produced by their former vocalist Trevor Horn, Jon Anderson, who had had more hit albums both with Vangelis and on his own, was induced to add some vocals and the project soon turned into Yes. 1983's '90215' album put Yes firmly on the contemporary rock market and back in the US Top 5, and 'Owner Of A Lonely Heart' topped the US singles charts early in 1984. They toured and took their time before 'Big Generator' in 1987 which was as laboured as '90215' was fresh. Yet it still made the US and UK Top 20. Anderson bailed out again in 1988 but the experience had given him another idea and he sounded out Wakeman, Howe and Bruford about a reunion. They agreed only to discover that Anderson had left the name behind with Squire, White, Kaye and Rabin. Undaunted they called themselves Anderson Bruford Wakeman Howe – ABWH for short – and released their self titled album – complete with Roger Dean cover just in case anybody missed the point, and set off on a world tour titled *An Evening Of Yes Music*, for which they were unsuccessfuly sued by Squire & Co. However, all eight musicians reunited for a mammoth Yes tour and album in mid 1991.

Greatest Hits

Singles	Title	US	UK
1972	Roundabout	13	–
1977	Wondrous Stories	–	7
1983	Owner Of A Lonely Heart	1	28
Albums			
1971	Fragile	4	7
1972	Close To The Edge	3	4
1974	Tales From		
	Topographical Oceans	6	1
1977	Going For The One	8	1
1980	Drama	18	2
1983	90215	5	16
Rick Wakeman			
1974	Journey To The Centre Of		
	The Earth	3	1
1975	The Myths And Legends Of		
	King Arthur . . .	21	2

Neil YOUNG

In his 25-year career, Neil Young (born 1945, Toronto) has tackled so many different musical formats, it is impossible to guess which musical style he will next adopt. Enigmatic, eccentric, frequently uncommercial, occasionally downright tedious, but rarely predictable, Young has built on his folk roots to carve out one of the more fascinating careers in rock music, amassing as his legacy an extraordinarily rich body of work. Having played in high school rock'n'roll bands, he worked the Toronto folk circuit as Neil Young & The Squires (where he first met Stephen Stills) before briefly joining The Mynah Birds, a group which included US singer Rick James (later a Motown soul star). He moved to Los Angeles in 1965 with bass player Bruce Palmer and linked up with Stills, Richie Furay, and Dewey Martin to form Buffalo Springfield (see separate entry).

Young signed to a solo record deal in 1969 and released a commercially unsuccessful eponymous debut album containing plaintive folk material, including 'The Loner' and the lengthy 'The Last Trip To Tulsa', with Ry Cooder (see separate entry) appearing as a sessionman. He then worked with the nucleus of West Coast band The Rockets – Ralph Molina (drums), Billy Talbot (bass) and Danny Whitten (guitar) – as Crazy Horse, who backed him on several subsequent albums. 1969's 'Everybody Knows This Is Nowhere', which included several of his best known songs, such as 'Cinammon Girl', 'Cowgirl In The Sand' and 'Down By The River' received ecstatic reviews, reached the US Top 40 (eventually going platinum), and established Young as a major new artist.

In 1970, he joined Crosby, Stills & Nash (see separate entry), dividing his time between his career with Crazy Horse and CSN&Y. The success of the latter's 'Deja Vu' album propelled all four members to megastar status, while his own 'After The Goldrush' album (with contributions from Stills and a teenage Nils Lofgren) subsequently made the US and UK Top 10 in 1970 including a US Top 40 single, 'Only Love Can Break Your Heart' and the controversial 'Southern Man'. 1972's 'Harvest', his third consecutive platinum album, remains his most commercial work – it topped both US and UK album charts and included the US chart-topping single, 'Heart Of Gold', with backing musicians including James Taylor and Linda Ronstadt.

Instead of consolidating, Young eschewed commercial success in the early 1970s to pursue low-key, melancholy themes, and made an autobiographical documentary film, *Journey Through The Past* in 1972, a career retrospective drawn from live recordings, but the soundtrack double album only just made the US Top 50, while his next project, the harrowing 'Tonight's The Night' album remained unissued for 18 months. 1973's 'Time

Neil Never Sleeps – forever Young?

Fades Away' (US Top 30, UK Top 20) was a patchy live set, backed by The Stray Gators plus Crosby & Nash, 1974's 'On The Beach' (US Top 20) seemed introspective, and finally, the bleak album which had been delayed, 'Tonight's The Night' (US Top 30) found him wallowing in misery, having been written and recorded following the drug-related deaths of Crazy Horse's Whitten and roadie Bruce Berry.

1976's 'Zuma' (US Top 30) reunited CSN&Y on one track, 'Through My Sails', and signalled a return to form – it was more optimistic, a fine rock album, while 1976's 'Long May You Run' album, credited to The Stills-Young Band, made the US Top 30 and UK Top 20 and was a highly successful collaboration with his sparring partner. 1977's album, 'American Stars & Bars' (US Top 30, UK Top 20), included vocal contributions from Emmylou Harris and Linda Ronstadt (see separate entries). 'Decade' (US Top 50, 1977) was a carefully compiled three-album retrospective, 1978's 'Comes A Time' made the US Top 10 and was a big-selling acoustic folk album, and 'Rust Never Sleeps', which made the US Top 10 and UK Top 20 found Crazy Horse back in tow (with Frank Sampedro instead of the late Whitten) and gave Young his first platinum album for seven years. 1979's 'Live Rust', a live double-album, presented more of the same and made the US Top 20, and the 'Rust' project, built around major tours, also yielded a film directed by Young under the alias of Bernard Shakey.

Neil Young became considerably more experimental/eccentric during the 1980s, if not always successfully: 1980's country-ish US Top 30, UK Top 40 album, 'Hawks & Doves' was recorded using sessionmen; 1981's US Top 30 album, 'Re-ac-tor' fused hard rock with R&B; 1983's US Top 20, UK Top 30 album, 'Trans' saw him working with synthesizers, treating his voice through a vocoder – a concept he took on tour with mixed results; 1984's even more disappointing US Top 50 album, 'Everybody's Rockin', credited to Neil Young & The Shocking Pinks, which may have been intended as ironic.

By the late 1980s, he was making increasingly less chart headway: 1985's excellent hard country album, 'Old Ways', peaked well outside the US Top 50, although 1986's rock-oriented 'Landing On Water' restored him to those chart heights. 1987's 'Life' made little impression, while 1988's bluesy 'This Note's For You' presented him in a new format and generated media attention. 1989's 'Freedom' and 1990's acclaimed 'Ragged Glory' (with Crazy Horse) were both more mainstream albums, and somewhat of a return to form, although CSN&Y's 1988 reunion predictably produced far greater commercial success.

Neil Young has consistently tried to broaden his own musical expertise, sometimes – with 'Rust Never Sleeps' and 'Old Ways' – very successfully, and at others – 'Re-ac-tor' and 'Everybody's Rockin'' – with less spectacular results. Surely even his greatest fan could not accuse him of consistency, yet the chance that each album may turn out to be another 'Zuma' or 'Harvest' will ensure that Young can continue experimenting for as long as he wants.

Greatest Hits

Singles	Title	US	UK
1972	Heart Of Gold	1	10
Albums			
1970	After The Goldrush	8	7
1972	Harvest	1	1
1978	Comes A Time	7	42
1979	Rust Never Sleeps	8	13

Paul **YOUNG**

Paul Young (born 1956) worked with a smalltime group, Kat Kool & The Kool Kats, in the 1970s, before forming a rock group, Streetband, in 1977. After making the UK Top 20 in 1978 with the novelty single, 'Toast'/Hold On', and two unsuccessful albums, 'London', and 'Dilemma', they split in 1979, and Young, with members Ian Kewley and Mick Pearl, formed blue-eyed soulsters Q-Tips. They became a popular live act but failed to sell records and folded after their 'Live At Last' album in 1982.

Young signed a solo deal in 1982, but failed to chart with his first two singles. Then a version of Marvin Gaye's 'Wherever I Lay My Hat (That's My Home)' in 1983 topped the UK single chart, as did his six million selling album, 'No Parlez' and a follow-up single, 'Come Back And Stay' made the UK Top 5, while a re-release of his second single, a cover version of Waylon Jennings's 'Love Of The Common People' hit the UK Top 3 that year. Together with backing group The Royal Family, which included Kewley, he toured heavily in 1984 and continued his string of UK Top 10 hits with his own song, 'Everything Must Change', and a cover of the Ann Peebles classic, 'I'm Gonna Tear Your Playhouse Down', which was a US Top 20 hit the following year.

He appeared at Live Aid and also in 1985 had his biggest US successes when his chart-topping UK album, 'The Secret Of Association', went gold and made the US Top 20, and his version of the Hall & Oates song, 'Every Time You Go Away', topped the US singles chart. An album of original material, 'Between Two Fires', in 1986 made the UK Top 5 but did not contain any big hit singles.

Young spent 1987 with his family and the following year appeared at Nelson Mandela's 70th Birthday Party Concert. His fourth album, 'Other Voices', with Stevie Wonder and Chaka Khan guesting, was released in 1990 and reached the UK Top 5 and his version of The Chi-Lites hit, 'Oh Girl', taken from it, gave him another US Top 10 single.

Greatest Hits

Singles	Title	US	UK
1984	I'm Gonna Tear Your Playhouse Down	13	9
1985	Everytime You Go Away	1	4
Albums			
1983	No Parlez	79	1
1985	The Secret Of Association	19	1

The **YOUNG RASCALS**/ The **RASCALS**

Felix Cavaliere (vocals, keyboards)
Eddie Brigati (vocals, percussion)
Gene Cornish (guitar)
Dino Danelli (drums)

The Young Rascals took a key role in the mid-1960s by eschewing the general garage blues-to-psychedelic rock route of white US groups of the period, instead moulding a style around a blue-eyed variant of soul music. Former Joey Dee & The Starliters (of 'Peppermint Twist' fame) members Cavaliere (born 1944), Brigati (born 1946) and Cornish (born 1945) formed as a trio in New York in 1964, recruiting Cavaliere's friend, Danelli, an experienced jazz and rock player, as their

regular drummer. A lengthy Long Island live residency honed their act, combining oldies, contemporary soul covers and self-penned material for the delight of clubbing dancers.

Their strong live reputation got the group signed to Atlantic in 1965, and in April, 1966, their second single, 'Good Lovin', (a revival of an R&B success by black group, The Olympics) topped the US chart and sold a million copies. Follow-ups 'You Better Run' and 'I've Been Lonely Too Long' were written, like most of the group's subsequent repertoire, by Cavaliere and Brigati, and were further soul-dance variations. Both their songwriting and the group's style fully matured, however, on 1967's 'Groovin', another chart-topping million seller, and the archetypal cool blue-eyed summer soul ballad. This was also the group's only UK Top 10 success, but the similarly cool and euphoric 'A Girl Like You' and 'How Can I Be Sure' were major US hits. In late 1967, the group became heavily involved with Indian philosophy and yoga, though the only overt musical effect of the 'Summer of Love' was the freak-out single, 'It's Wonderful'. In 1968, they returned to overtly soul-styled music, emphasizing new maturity with the removal of the 'Young' prefix from their name. As The Rascals, they then had two further million-sellers in the same year, 'A Beautiful Morning' and the gospelly 'People Got To Be Free' (their reaction to the Robert Kennedy and Martin Luther King assassinations).

The group's alliance with liberal politics was henceforth a continuing lyrical influence, but as their hits began to miss the Top 10, internal politics became even more pertinent. After lengthy dissent, Brigati left early in 1970, and Cornish a year later. Both were replaced, but the sparkle of the original quartet was lost, and a million-dollar lure to CBS when the Atlantic contract expired proved disastrous in terms of creativity and sales, precipitating a break-up in mid-1972.

Individually, the former Rascals quickly involved themselves in other projects. Cavaliere moved into production, as well as a solo career which cruised in low gear before giving him a US Top 40 single in 1980. Cornish and Danelli formed the mildly successful Bulldog, then had similarly mild success in the late 1970s in Fotomaker. Brigati concentrated mainly on session work, making just one album in the mid-1970s, while Danelli worked with 'Miami' Steve Van Zandt in the early 1980s. Much later, in 1988, Cavalieri, Danelli and Cornish reunited as The Rascals for a nostalgic US tour.

Greatest Hits

Singles	Title	US	UK
1966	Good Lovin'	1	–
1967	Groovin'	1	8
1967	How Can I Be Sure	4	–
1968	A Beautiful Morning	3	–
1968	People Got To Be Free	1	

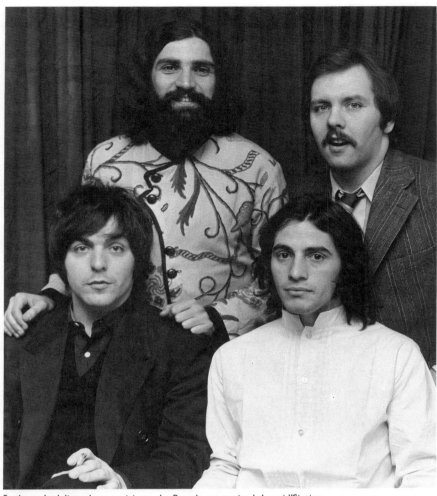

Soul, psychedelia and sermonizing – the Rascals summarized the mid'Sixties

Albums
1967   *Groovin'*   5   –
1968   *Time Peace: The Rascals'*
         Greatest Hits   1   –

Frank **ZAPPA** and the **MOTHERS OF INVENTION**

One of rock's great iconoclasts, Zappa's work with The Mothers Of Invention inspired much progressive rock and jazz-rock of the 1970s. In the 1980s, he became an outspoken opponent of attempts to censor popular music.

Born in 1940, he grew up in California where his earliest musical influences included black vocal groups of the 1950s and European avant-garde classical music. As a teenager,

Zappa made numerous singles under such names as Ned & Nelda and Brian Lord & The Midnighters before forming The Soul Giants in 1964.

Featuring vocalist Ray Collins, Elliott Ingber (guitar), Roy Estrada (bass) and Jimmy Carl Black, 'the Indian of the group' on drums, this group soon mutated into The Muthers and then The Mothers Of Invention. Signing to the Verve label, they made 'Freak Out!' (1966), a double-album that was genuinely experimental in comparison with mid-1960s rock. The wide range of musical styles and lyrical themes covered jazz, avant-garde serious music, R&B and sentimental pop as well as social protest and satire. Zappa and producer Tom Wilson also added sound effects to link the tracks.

1967 was the age of flower-power but Zappa's next album, 'We're Only In It For The Money', was an unrelenting attack on the hippie dream using song titles like 'Flower Punk'. The sleeve was a parody of the 'Sgt Pepper' sleeve collage by The Beatles, and the album entered the US Top 30.

Having established the group identity, Zappa typically made a sideways move in 1968 by issuing a solo instrumental album

inspired by 'musique concrete' ('Lumpy Gravy') and 'Cruisin' With Ruben & The Jets' on which the band adopted the identities of one of his beloved 1950s vocal groups.

Zappa next released the double album, 'Uncle Meat'. Billed as 'the soundtrack of a movie you'll probably never get to see' it was the first release on Bizarre, a label owned by his manager, Herb Cohen. 1970 marked the end of the first phase of The Mothers, when Zappa came off the road because of the costs of running what was now a 10-piece unit. Remaining material by the group was issued on 'Burnt Weeny Sandwich' and 'Weasels Ripped My Flesh'. Estrada left to found Little Feat with Lowell George.

Zappa now recorded what became his most commercially successful album, especially in the UK, where The Mothers had toured. 'Hot Rats' put the spotlight on Zappa's own prowess as a guitarist and also featured violinist Jean-Luc Ponty and vocalist Captain Beefheart (Don Van Vliet). Meanwhile he had organized the first of several line-ups of The Mothers to accompany him throughout the 1970s. This group included vocalists Howard Kaylan and Mark Volman (Flo & Eddie) from 1960s pop group, The Turtles. They appeared in the 1971 film *200 Motels*, a surreal view of life on the road in the US and a 1971 live album, which was a US Top 40 hit.

Zappa's most successful album in America was 'Apostrophe', which included former Cream bassist Jack Bruce, but his albums of the late 1970s lacked the sharpness of his earlier work, although 'Sheik Yerbouti' (1979, a satirical view of the Middle East) featured guitarist Adian Belew, who would become a top session player in the 1980s. Zappa would later discover the talents of Steve Vai, one of the most admired heavy rock guitarists of the late 1980s.

A compulsive archivist, Zappa seemed to spend much of the 1980s ensuring that all of his recorded work was released. He was among the pioneers of digital re-mixing, re-issuing numerous albums through US CD only label, Rykodisc, from 1986 onwards. In 1987, he inaugurated an audio-visual programme on the Honker Home Video label and set up the Barking Pumpkin label for his own records.

Among his new recordings, there were three volumes of 'Joe's Garage' (1980) and of 'Shut Up And Play Your Guitar' (1981). He continued his interest in classical/rock fusions, begun when Zubin Mehta had conducted an orchestral version of '200 Motels', with a collaboration with the London Symphony Orchestra on a 1983 album, while his own instrumental skills were displayed on 'Jazz From Hell' (1986). His only hit of the decade was the satirical single, 'Valley Girl', which included his teenage daughter Moon Unit.

In 1985, the so-called Parents Music Resource Center began its propaganda

Musical anarchist on the apocalyptic rim of radical rock, it's apt that Zappa appears almost at the end of any A–Z account of the music

assault on rock lyrics and Zappa became the most outspoken spokesman for freedom of expression. The battle rekindled the radical-ism of his early records and he included his testimony before a committee of the US Congress on 'Frank Zappa Meets The Mothers Of Prevention' (1986).

After numerous journalists had published biographies of Zappa throughout his career, Zappa himself wrote *The Real Frank Zappa Book* in 1989. Much of it was devoted to his personal philosophy and to his views on such topics as censorship, income taxes and *Star Wars*.

Greatest Hits

Singles	Title	US	UK
1979	*Dancin' Fool*	45	–
1982	*Valley Girl*	32	–
Albums			
1970	*Hot Rats*	173	9
1974	*Apostrophe*	10	–
1979	*Sheik Yerbouti*	21	32
1982	*Ship Arriving Too Late To Save*		
	A Drowning Witch	23	61

The **ZOMBIES**

Colin Blunstone *(vocals)*
Paul Atkinson *(guitar)*
Rod Argent *(keyboards)*
Paul Arnold *(bass)*
Hugh Grundy *(drums)*

Appreciated only in retrospect, the pre-dominantly introspective approach of The Zombies was the antithesis of the blues-wailing aggression of many of their British beat peers. As UK audiences dwindled after a sole Top 20 single, an undignified demise was delayed by success abroad.

Formed in 1962, the group's early musical wares included numbers common to beat groups everywhere. What distinguished them was Blunstone's exquisite tenor and the song-writing talents of Argent (born 1945) and Chris White (born 1943), who replaced Arnold in 1963. Nevertheless, a breathtaking arrangement of Gershwin's 'Summertime' was the clincher that, via a talent contest, won the quintet a recording contract.

Their debut single, Argent's 'She's Not

There' had no obvious precedent. Its drama-tic restraint amid more extrovert efforts of the day guaranteed exposure but the follow-up, White's 'Leave Me Be', was thought too wantonly melancholy for much airplay. A suspected one-hit wonder, the Zombies were hurried through 'Begin Here', a 1965 album containing The Hit – one-take stage favourites – and some originals hinting at what might have been had not the third single, 'Tell Her No', been their UK chart farewell.

Buoyed by much hard graft on the road, the group did not vanish from the US scene with the same haste. A flash of film stardom came with a brief spot (performing 'Remem-ber You') in 1965's *Bunny Lake Is Missing*. One rare flying visit home was to plug 'Whenever You're Ready', but when three successive singles flopped, The Zombies re-sorted to covers. The last of these, Little Anthony's 'Goin' Out Of My Head', arrived to late to prevent another version snatching the slight chart honours.

Unhip but still adventurous, the group went out with a bang with 1969's million-selling 'Time Of The Season' from 'Odessey

And Oracle'. Not even big money for a single concert could bring them together again – though a rash of other outfits began accepting illicit bookings using The Zombies' name.

No-one was fooled when Blunstone (born 1945) resurfaced in the UK Top 30 as 'Neil McArthur', although Argent's eponymous new band falsely attributed its first two US singles to its leader's old group. With items of 'progressive' bent from White, guitarist Russ Ballard (ex-Roulettes) and Argent himself, the new group's albums sold steadily, peaking with 1972's 'All Together Now' which spawned a global smash single, 'Hold Your Head Up'. That same year, Blunstone enjoyed his biggest solo hit with a revival of Denny Laine's 'Say You Don't Mind'.

Blunstone and Argent (most recently as Tanita Tikaram's producer) each racked up more chart strikes than The Zombies, but neither left as insidious a legacy to pop. Apart from remakes of 'She's Not There' by such as Vanilla Fudge and Santana, People earned a US hit in 1974 with 'I Love You', an obscure B-side. The pleasant depression that was the frequent aftertaste of Zombies music infiltrated the vision of later acts like Traffic, Procol Harum and the latter-day Kinks (who recruited Argent's bass player, Jim Rodford, in 1978).

Greatest Hits

Singles	Title	US	UK
1964	She's Not There	2	12
1965	Tell Her No	6	42
1969	Time Of The Season	3	–
Albums			
1965	The Zombies	39	–

ZZ TOP

Frank Beard (drums)
Billy Gibbons (guitar, vocals)
Dusty Hill (bass, vocals)

Gibbons (born 1949) previously played in Texas bands The Saints, The Coachmen and Ten Blue Flames before forming the psychedelic Moving Sidewalks who had a local hit with '99th Floor' (1967). Dusty Hill backed Freddie King and played with Beard in American Blues, who released two albums 'American Blues Is Here' (1967) and 'American Blues Do Their Thing' (1969).

In 1970 as ZZ Top, they released a single 'Salt Lick' on manager/producer Bill Ham's own label before Ham (still in the driving seat after twenty years) concluded a major label deal. 'The First Album' (1970) was derivative of Hendrix/Cream and the English progressive scene, but the hard driving blues of 'Rio Grande Mud' (1972) was more indicative of their natural sound and style which peaked on 'Tres Hombres' (1973), a US Top 10 album. 'Fandango' featuring the US Top 20 single, 'Tush' (1975), was half live and half studio and gave them their first UK album, going Top 10 in the US. With almost no media coverage, the band relied on constant touring to spread the word; in 1976 they staged the year-long Worldwide Texas Tour, corralling a menagerie of live animals on stage, allegedly outgrossing Led Zeppelin and Elvis Presley. The 'Tejas' album (1976) reached the US Top 20, but the band took a three-year sabbatical, before 'Deguello' (1979) followed by 'El Loco' (1981), reaching the US Top 30 and 20 respectively.

By now, the band had established both their two-year pattern of albums and tours and a highly marketable 'beard and boilersuit' image. 'Eliminator' (1983) was their commercial breakthrough, deftly combining metal and electronic pop, promoted by videos and incorporating the American Dream's Holy Trinity – the road, the car and women – heavily laced with humour. Arguably, it was the advent of the rock video that established ZZ Top as one of the major rock acts of the 1980s. 'Afterburn' (1985) repeated the pattern, but after an even longer absence, 'Recycler' (1990), devoid of synthesizers, marked a return to roots.

Greatest Hits

Singles	Title	US	UK
1984	Gimme All Your Lovin'	37	10
1984	Legs	8	16
1985	Sleeping Bag	8	27
Albums			
1973	Tres Hombres	8	–
1975	Fandango!	10	60
1983	Eliminator	9	3
1985	Afterburner	4	2

Gibbons with beard with Beard without beard with Hill with beard

▶ ▶ ▶ ▶

PICTURE ACKNOWLEDGEMENTS

London Features International 1, 6-7, 13 bottom, 14, 16, 20, 22, 24, 26, 29, 30, 33 top, 33 bottom, 35 left, 35 right, 36, 41 top, 43, 44, 49, 51, 53 top, 55 top, 58 bottom, 59, 60, 62, 63 top, 65, 66, 71 top, 72, 74 bottom, 75, 76, 77, 78, 79, 80, 83, 86 bottom, 89, 90, 91, 95, 96, 97, 100, 104, 106, 108, 112, 114, 117, 118, 120 bottom, 122, 124, 125, 126, 127, 128 bottom, 129, 132, 135, 138, 140, 141, 142, 146, 147, 148, 149, 153, 154, 155, 159, 161, 167, 169, 170, 171, 175, 176, 178, 180, 183, 184, 185, 186, 189 top, 192, 193, 197, 200, 204 bottom, 206, 208, 211 top, 211 bottom, 215, 216 bottom, 221, 223 left, 223 right, 224, 227, 229, 232 top, 232 bottom, 234 bottom, 236, 237, 249, 250 bottom, 256 bottom, 257, 258 top, 260, 265, 266, 268, 269, 271, 272, 273 top, 273 bottom, 274, 275, 278 top, 280, 281, 283 top, 284, 289, 291, 296, 297, 298, 299, 300 top, 312 top, 313, 315, 317 top, 318, 319, 320, 325 top, 328, 330, 332, 334 top, 336, 343, 347, 348; London Features International /Julian Barton 238; /Adrian Boot 156 bottom, 301; /Elaine Bryant 303; /Paul Canty 17 right, 19 top, 19 bottom, 27, 41 bottom, 50 bottom, 115, 130, 131, 198, 253, 278 bottom, 333; /R J Capak 151 top; /Andrew Catlin 71 bottom, 139; /Clouds Studios 70 top, 276; /Paul Cox 32, 70 bottom, 84, 85 top, 109, 116, 136, 158, 181, 202, 210, 225, 258 bottom, 286 top, 287, 290, 300 bottom, 306, 312 bottom, 322 top, 334 bottom; /CPS 189 bottom, 204 top, 214, 231; /Kevin Cummins 305; /Nick Elgar 73, 105, 150, 222, 314, 329; /Simon Fowler 8, 38, 52, 128 top, 247, 255, 263; /Andy Freeberg 293; /Frontline Pictures 234 top; /Jill Furmanowsky 45 bottom, 93; /J Goedfroit 340; /Frank Griffin 87, 145, 292; /Harry Hammond 86 top; /Robin Kaplan 10, 285, 335 top, 335 bottom; /Bob King 242; /Lawrence Lawry 337; /Phil Loftus 57, 63 bottom, 233; /Janet Macoska 143, 165, 261, 270, 279 ; /Ross Marino 34 ; /Kevin Mazur 157 ; /Motion Picture and Television Photo Archive 245; /Neil Murray right;/Michael Ochs Archive 13 top, 17 bottom left, 28, 31 bottom, 40, 45 top, 47, 68 top, 68 bottom, 74 top, 82, 94, 99, 101, 113 top, 164, 177, 179, 191, 205, 213, 230, 239, 243, 248, 251, 254, 267, 283 bottom, 295, 302 bottom, 308, 323, 327, 338; /Anastasia Pantsios 151 bottom; /Neal Preston 9 left, 11 left, 31 top, 156 top, 217, 288, 302 top, 307 bottom, 317 bottom; /Michael Putland 18, 54, 69, 103, 123, 134, 162, 163, 199, 226, 304, 307 top, 316, 342, 345; /Steve Rapport 50 top, 85 bottom, 120 top, 168; /Ken Regan 58 top, 187 top; /Derek Ridges 250 top; /Ebet Roberts 11 right, 25, 55 bottom, 81, 110, 113 bottom, 187 bottom, 190, 196, 209, 212, 216 top, 235, 259, 321, 324, 325 bottom, 339, 341, 349; /Govert de Roos 46; /Ann Summa 67, 137, 182; /Geoff Swaine 15, 326; /Topline 172; /Chris Walter 39, 56, 88, 218, 219, 310, 331 ; /Scott Weiner 2-3, 309, 322 bottom, 344; /Barry Wentzell 194; /Ron Wolfson 42, 195, 201, 228, 241, 256 top, 286 bottom; /Charlyn Zlotnik 53 bottom.